TABLE OF CONTENTS

CALIFORNIA ROAD ATLAS & DRIVER'S GUIDE

http://www.thomas.com

Thomas Bros. Maps®
1-800-899-6277

B

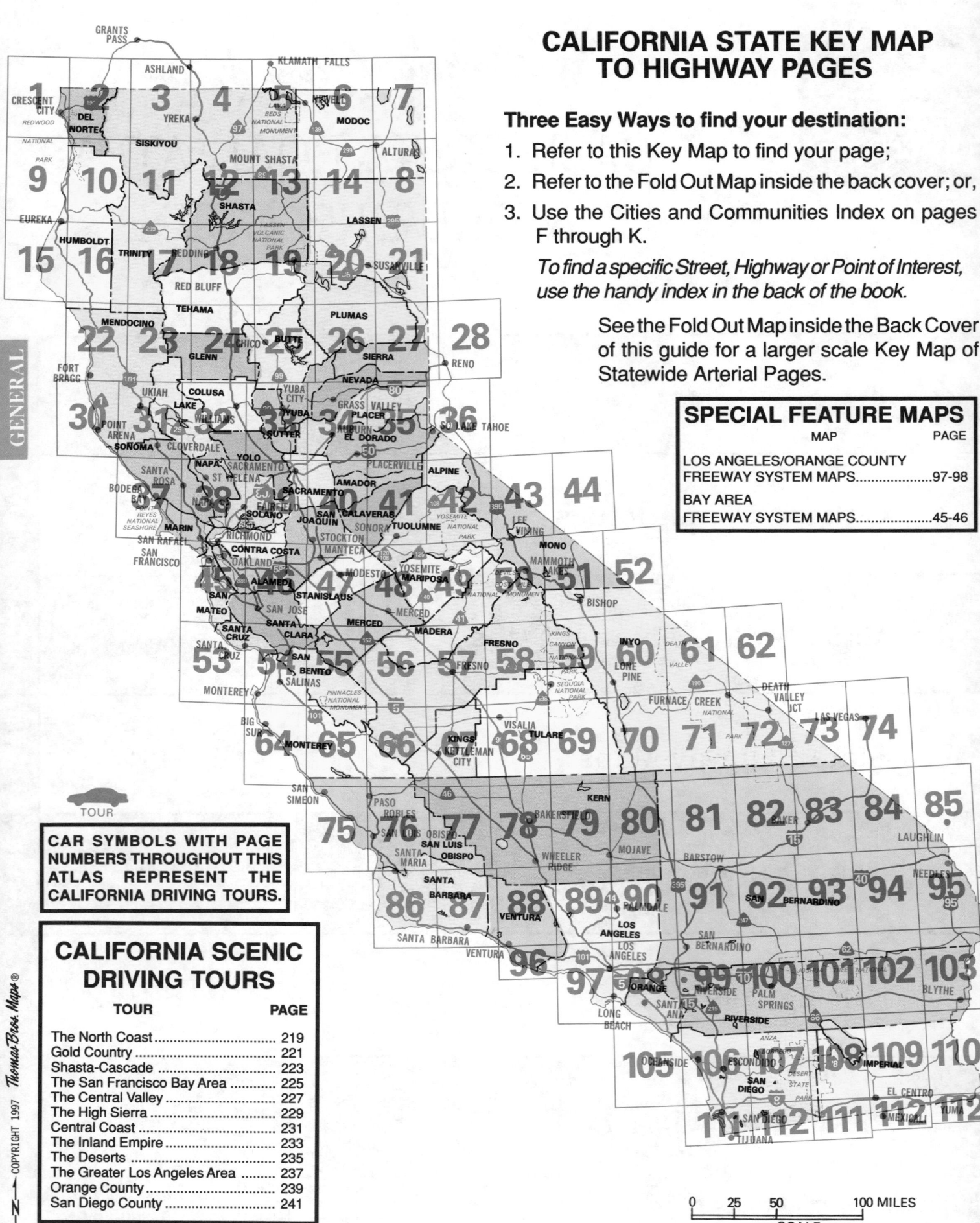

CALIFORNIA STATE KEY MAP TO HIGHWAY PAGES

Three Easy Ways to find your destination:

1. Refer to this Key Map to find your page;
2. Refer to the Fold Out Map inside the back cover; or,
3. Use the Cities and Communities Index on pages F through K.

To find a specific Street, Highway or Point of Interest, use the handy index in the back of the book.

See the Fold Out Map inside the Back Cover of this guide for a larger scale Key Map of Statewide Arterial Pages.

CAR SYMBOLS WITH PAGE NUMBERS THROUGHOUT THIS ATLAS REPRESENT THE CALIFORNIA DRIVING TOURS.

COPYRIGHT 1997 *Thomas Bros. Maps*®

GENERAL

0 25 50 100 MILES
SCALE

LEGEND

EXPLANATION OF MAP SYMBOLS

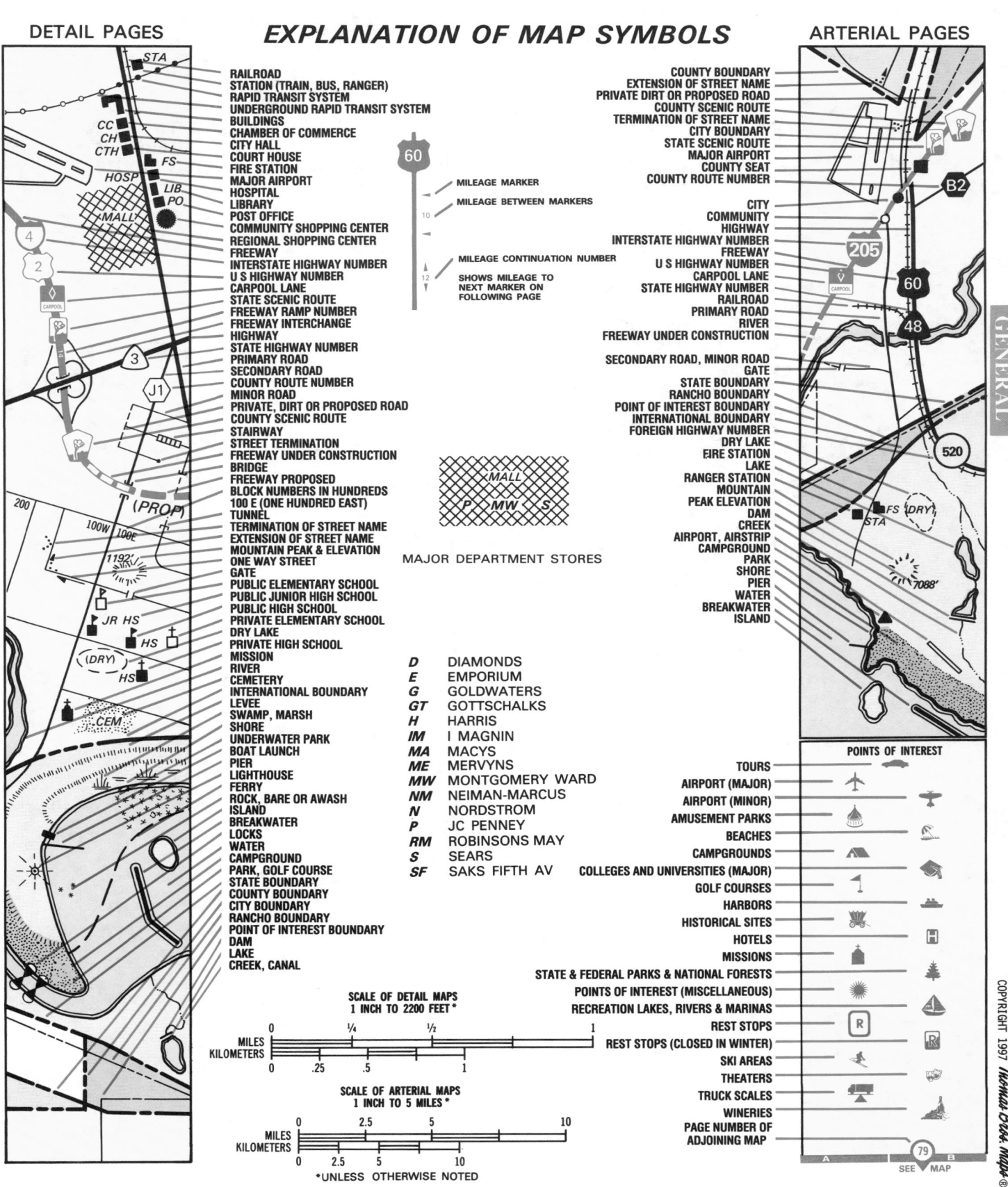

DETAIL PAGES

- RAILROAD
- STATION (TRAIN, BUS, RANGER)
- RAPID TRANSIT SYSTEM
- UNDERGROUND RAPID TRANSIT SYSTEM
- BUILDINGS
- CHAMBER OF COMMERCE
- CITY HALL
- COURT HOUSE
- FIRE STATION
- MAJOR AIRPORT
- HOSPITAL
- LIBRARY
- POST OFFICE
- COMMUNITY SHOPPING CENTER
- REGIONAL SHOPPING CENTER
- FREEWAY
- INTERSTATE HIGHWAY NUMBER
- U S HIGHWAY NUMBER
- CARPOOL LANE
- STATE SCENIC ROUTE
- FREEWAY RAMP NUMBER
- FREEWAY INTERCHANGE
- HIGHWAY
- STATE HIGHWAY NUMBER
- PRIMARY ROAD
- SECONDARY ROAD
- COUNTY ROUTE NUMBER
- MINOR ROAD
- PRIVATE, DIRT OR PROPOSED ROAD
- COUNTY SCENIC ROUTE
- STAIRWAY
- STREET TERMINATION
- FREEWAY UNDER CONSTRUCTION
- BRIDGE
- FREEWAY PROPOSED
- BLOCK NUMBERS IN HUNDREDS
- 100 E (ONE HUNDRED EAST)
- TUNNEL
- TERMINATION OF STREET NAME
- EXTENSION OF STREET NAME
- MOUNTAIN PEAK & ELEVATION
- ONE WAY STREET
- GATE
- PUBLIC ELEMENTARY SCHOOL
- PUBLIC JUNIOR HIGH SCHOOL
- PUBLIC HIGH SCHOOL
- PRIVATE ELEMENTARY SCHOOL
- DRY LAKE
- PRIVATE HIGH SCHOOL
- MISSION
- RIVER
- CEMETERY
- INTERNATIONAL BOUNDARY
- LEVEE
- SWAMP, MARSH
- SHORE
- UNDERWATER PARK
- BOAT LAUNCH
- PIER
- LIGHTHOUSE
- FERRY
- ROCK, BARE OR AWASH
- ISLAND
- BREAKWATER
- LOCKS
- WATER
- CAMPGROUND
- PARK, GOLF COURSE
- STATE BOUNDARY
- COUNTY BOUNDARY
- CITY BOUNDARY
- RANCHO BOUNDARY
- POINT OF INTEREST BOUNDARY
- DAM
- LAKE
- CREEK, CANAL

- MILEAGE MARKER
- MILEAGE BETWEEN MARKERS
- MILEAGE CONTINUATION NUMBER
- SHOWS MILEAGE TO NEXT MARKER ON FOLLOWING PAGE

MAJOR DEPARTMENT STORES

D	DIAMONDS
E	EMPORIUM
G	GOLDWATERS
GT	GOTTSCHALKS
H	HARRIS
IM	I MAGNIN
MA	MACYS
ME	MERVYNS
MW	MONTGOMERY WARD
NM	NEIMAN-MARCUS
N	NORDSTROM
P	JC PENNEY
RM	ROBINSONS MAY
S	SEARS
SF	SAKS FIFTH AV

ARTERIAL PAGES

- COUNTY BOUNDARY
- EXTENSION OF STREET NAME
- PRIVATE DIRT OR PROPOSED ROAD
- COUNTY SCENIC ROUTE
- TERMINATION OF STREET NAME
- CITY BOUNDARY
- STATE SCENIC ROUTE
- MAJOR AIRPORT
- COUNTY SEAT
- COUNTY ROUTE NUMBER
- CITY
- COMMUNITY
- HIGHWAY
- INTERSTATE HIGHWAY NUMBER
- FREEWAY
- U S HIGHWAY NUMBER
- CARPOOL LANE
- STATE HIGHWAY NUMBER
- RAILROAD
- PRIMARY ROAD
- RIVER
- FREEWAY UNDER CONSTRUCTION
- SECONDARY ROAD, MINOR ROAD
- GATE
- STATE BOUNDARY
- RANCHO BOUNDARY
- POINT OF INTEREST BOUNDARY
- INTERNATIONAL BOUNDARY
- FOREIGN HIGHWAY NUMBER
- DRY LAKE
- FIRE STATION
- LAKE
- RANGER STATION
- MOUNTAIN
- PEAK ELEVATION
- DAM
- CREEK
- AIRPORT, AIRSTRIP
- CAMPGROUND
- PARK
- SHORE
- PIER
- WATER
- BREAKWATER
- ISLAND

POINTS OF INTEREST

TOURS	
AIRPORT (MAJOR)	
AIRPORT (MINOR)	
AMUSEMENT PARKS	
BEACHES	
CAMPGROUNDS	
COLLEGES AND UNIVERSITIES (MAJOR)	
GOLF COURSES	
HARBORS	
HISTORICAL SITES	
HOTELS	
MISSIONS	
STATE & FEDERAL PARKS & NATIONAL FORESTS	
POINTS OF INTEREST (MISCELLANEOUS)	
RECREATION LAKES, RIVERS & MARINAS	
REST STOPS	
REST STOPS (CLOSED IN WINTER)	
SKI AREAS	
THEATERS	
TRUCK SCALES	
WINERIES	
PAGE NUMBER OF ADJOINING MAP	

SEE MAP

SCALE OF DETAIL MAPS
1 INCH TO 2200 FEET *

| MILES | 0 | ¼ | ½ | 1 |
| KILOMETERS | 0 | .25 | .5 | 1 |

SCALE OF ARTERIAL MAPS
1 INCH TO 5 MILES *

| MILES | 0 | 2.5 | 5 | 10 |
| KILOMETERS | 0 | 2.5 | 5 | 10 |

*UNLESS OTHERWISE NOTED

DISTANCE MAP

D

DISTANCE BETWEEN POINTS GIVEN IN MILES. MILEAGE DETERMINED BY MOST DIRECT DRIVING ROUTE.

SCALE: 0 — 25 — 50 — 100 MILES

IN ADDITION TO THIS DISTANCE MAP, MILEAGE NUMBERS ARE INCLUDED AS A SPECIAL FEATURE FOR INTERSTATE HIGHWAYS ON HIGHWAY PAGES.

MILEAGE CHART

MILEAGE DETERMINED BY MOST DIRECT DRIVING ROUTE

	BAKERSFIELD	CHICO	EUREKA	FRESNO	LAS VEGAS	LONG BEACH	LOS ANGELES	MERCED	MODESTO	OAKLAND	PALM SPRINGS	REDDING	RIVERSIDE	SACRAMENTO	SALINAS	SAN DIEGO	SAN FRANCISCO	SAN JOSE	SAN LUIS OBISPO	SANTA ANA	SANTA BARBARA	SANTA ROSA	SOUTH LAKE TAHOE	STOCKTON	VENTURA
ALTURAS	577	207	292	470	624	705	650	415	374	379	720	142	645	297	471	741	360	392	577	683	737	367	241	342	692
ANAHEIM	138	505	718	245	274	24	30	302	341	443	100	577	42	415	346	86	449	403	235	4	128	485	490	370	102
AUBURN	306	90	321	199	601	441	420	143	106	115	518	175	473	34	207	539	121	151	339	452	444	131	86	70	421
BAKERSFIELD		362	555	109	284	132	113	163	200	285	209	433	177	272	206	232	283	241	114	143	146	340	360	227	115
BARSTOW	129	491	684	236	155	123	131	292	330	414	123	559	78	401	335	180	412	385	264	116	205	469	395	356	174
BENICIA	292	144	287	177	578	429	396	123	84	37	510	187	466	58	106	513	43	49	236	456	341	61	164	74	374
BISHOP	222	360	553	235	284	308	277	223	252	314	308	396	264	265	347	360	335	321	357	301	327	382	176	240	296
BLYTHE	339	705	918	446	208	228	230	501	521	622	129	775	171	616	530	222	619	575	433	202	314	676	686	568	287
BODEGA BAY	404	189	266	249	632	491	451	194	156	74	568	246	527	141	165	594	64	109	294	516	400	23	256	152	431
BURBANK	104	465	659	210	294	31	9	266	304	383	111	536	67	376	304	127	377	334	200	45	93	421	446	330	64
CHICO	362		218	254	620	498	475	198	160	172	575	73	543	89	264	638	180	212	389	509	490	166	170	134	477
CLAREMONT	135	497	691	308	246	47	26	298	336	415	79	568	23	408	336	107	409	366	226	23	118	453	469	360	88
DAVIS	287	83	282	180	582	422	399	134	87	66	499	155	454	15	158	520	74	102	320	433	425	83	127	60	402
DEATH VALLEY	238	530	703	395	182	229	288	393	422	484	241	566	262	435	475	407	505	491	352	324	366	552	346	410	336
EL CENTRO	322	706	872	427	303	219	213	482	520	615	110	775	154	618	536	110	601	561	413	201	308	660	596	554	279
EUREKA	555	218		446	797	683	669	390	353	288	788	149	743	287	381	776	269	323	508	722	614	219	388	332	643
FAIRFIELD	278	132	276	171	561	412	391	118	79	45	489	173	457	43	132	554	55	78	260	423	362	57	150	51	389
FORT BRAGG	460	199	156	353	730	597	551	292	255	180	674	288	629	217	280	669	176	216	401	608	507	119	319	233	534
FRESNO	109	254	446		416	239	220	56	93	178	316	325	272	165	134	339	185	151	140	250	245	233	251	120	222
GRASS VALLEY	329	78	320	222	624	464	443	166	129	138	541	163	496	57	230	562	144	174	362	475	467	154	115	93	444
LAGUNA BEACH	162	528	741	269	288	34	55	324	363	465	115	598	62	437	368	75	471	425	257	19	150	507	511	391	123
LA JOLLA	219	625	763	326	319	90	103	382	419	507	122	667	79	492	428	13	517	449	309	79	203	536	529	450	172
LASSEN NATIONAL PK	437	102	202	329	695	573	550	273	235	247	650	45	618	164	339	713	255	287	459	584	562	241	199	209	552
LAS VEGAS	284	620	797	408		314	302	446	484	567	276	640	231	567	488	332	568	524	414	269	354	610	466	510	323
LONE PINE	159	420	593	285	224	232	209	283	312	374	277	456	204	325	365	307	395	381	273	245	285	442	236	300	254
LONG BEACH	132	498	683	239	314		24	294	333	417	118	568	60	407	338	103	427	383	218	25	120	477	479	361	93
LOS ANGELES	113	475	669	220	302	24		276	314	393	103	546	56	386	314	119	387	344	204	35	96	431	456	340	66
MAMMOTH LAKES	262	320	513	195	324	348	317	283	212	274	348	356	305	225	307	400	295	281	397	341	367	342	130	200	336
MANTECA	215	147	345	108	499	348	329	54	15	63	425	219	380	44	99	447	73	65	248	382	354	123	144	13	330
MARTINEZ	288	146	290	172	571	424	391	118	79	28	507	191	460	61	101	509	38	47	233	453	338	64	168	70	369
MERCED	163	198	390	56	446	294	276		37	123	368	269	326	109	105	395	130	115	195	305	300	172	194	64	278
MODESTO	200	160	353	93	484	333	314	37		84	410	232	365	72	104	432	92	77	233	344	339	135	156	27	315
MOJAVE	62	424	617	169	229	117	94	225	262	347	162	495	118	334	268	213	345	303	190	130	116	402	351	289	123
MONTEREY	216	278	399	149	504	356	334	115	138	111	433	350	388	190	18	442	122	75	145	367	250	170	272	141	273
NAPA	331	150	255	224	613	463	439	169	130	46	540	191	495	61	145	566	56	88	270	492	363	36	168	69	390
NEEDLES	281	638	821	383	108	269	279	439	476	560	190	729	224	548	481	311	561	517	416	262	352	603	552	508	316
NEVADA CITY	334	83	325	227	629	469	448	171	134	143	546	168	501	62	235	567	149	179	367	480	472	159	110	98	449
NEWPORT BEACH	155	519	735	262	279	21	43	317	366	458	108	592	55	430	361	81	465	418	230	12	141	498	502	382	114
OAKLAND	285	172	288	178	567	417	393	123	84		494	218	449	81	99	520	10	42	224	446	317	60	195	73	344
ONTARIO	141	493	696	247	222	44	37	303	341	420	77	573	21	413	341	125	414	371	232	33	123	458	483	367	103
OXNARD	122	485	650	229	316	85	59	271	322	351	165	555	117	395	252	178	379	329	142	97	38	421	478	349	7
PALMDALE	98	460	653	205	244	81	58	261	298	383	126	531	82	370	304	182	381	339	221	94	116	438	387	325	87
PALM SPRINGS	209	575	788	316	276	118	103	368	410	494		658	56	484	415	135	504	460	306	96	199	554	435	438	172
PALO ALTO	261	213	302	171	544	403	364	135	97	43	480	251	433	120	74	482	33	20	205	426	311	89	223	92	342
PASADENA	109	475	688	216	259	31	7	271	310	394	104	554	52	384	315	134	404	360	210	42	95	454	463	338	68
PLACERVILLE	282	133	331	175	525	416	395	122	83	125	493	205	461	44	177	548	131	127	309	427	429	141	59	55	397
REDDING	433	73	149	325	640	568	546	269	232	218	658		600	161	334	680	218	246	431	579	537	223	249	206	548
RENO	432	172	342	297	444	510	504	241	209	216	510	196	465	132	308	561	223	249	434	503	507	229	61	177	496
RICHMOND	299	163	276	192	581	431	407	137	98	14	508	204	462	74	113	534	24	56	238	460	331	50	181	82	358
RIVERSIDE	177	543	743	272	231	60	56	326	365	449	56	600		439	367	92	463	413	259	43	147	509	379	406	125
SACRAMENTO	272	89	287	165	567	407	386	109	72	81	484	161	439		173	505	87	117	305	418	410	97	107	45	387
SALINAS	206	264	381	134	488	338	314	105	104	99	415	334	367	173		441	101	57	125	349	218	160	251	122	245
SAN BERNARDINO	167	534	714	269	228	63	59	325	362	439	57	595	13	436	360	104	444	401	260	48	154	486	436	389	123
SAN DIEGO	232	638	776	339	332	103	119	395	432	520	135	680	92	505	441		530	462	322	84	216	549	542	493	185
SAN FRANCISCO	283	180	269	185	568	427	387	130	92	10	504	218	463	87	101	530		45	230	452	336	56	192	88	367
SAN JOSE	241	212	323	151	524	383	344	115	77	42	460	246	413	117	57	462	45		185	406	291	96	197	72	322
SAN JUAN CAPISTRANO	163	529	742	270	289	40	55	325	364	466	116	599	63	438	369	66	472	426	258	20	151	508	512	395	124
SAN LUIS OBISPO	114	384	508	140	414	218	204	195	233	224	306	431	259	305	125	322	230	185		238	106	281	382	254	137
SAN MATEO	313	199	288	181	554	413	374	125	86	29	490	237	443	106	84	492	19	30	215	436	321	75	209	78	352
SAN PEDRO	134	496	690	242	285	9	22	298	336	415	126	568	68	408	336	118	409	366	213	37	108	454	478	362	75
SAN RAFAEL	306	167	260	199	588	438	414	144	105	21	515	243	470	83	121	559	18	64	246	470	339	39	181	94	366
SANTA ANA	143	509	722	250	269	25	35	305	344	446	96	579	43	418	349	84	452	406	238		131	488	492	372	104
SANTA BARBARA	146	490	614	245	354	120	96	300	339	317	199	537	147	410	218	216	336	291	106	131		387	490	374	31
SANTA CRUZ	239	230	354	150	524	379	344	116	109	75	456	275	411	146	33	462	74	29	162	390	268	129	229	101	300
SANTA MARIA	145	415	539	171	428	194	170	226	264	255	273	462	221	336	156	290	261	216	31	205	74	312	413	285	103
SANTA ROSA	340	166	219	233	610	477	431	172	135	60	554	223	509	97	160	549	56	96	281	488	387		199	113	414
SAUSALITO	298	183	276	200	583	442	402	145	107	25	519	259	478	99	116	545	15	60	245	467	351	55	207	103	382
SEQUOIA NATIONAL PK	129	343	556	84	408	258	234	139	178	335	235	385	303	252	209	361	272	228	178	269	276	329	335	206	262
SONOMA	331	163	239	224	613	468	439	170	130	46	540	204	495	75	146	584	43	89	271	495	364	20	181	82	391
SONORA	215	189	387	108	498	380	366	52	42	105	420	261	391	86	157	447	115	107	247	357	352	165	139	55	330
SOUTH LAKE TAHOE	360	170	388	251	466	479	456	194	156	195	435	249	379	107	251	542	192	197	382	492	490	199		131	471
STOCKTON	227	134	332	120	510	361	340	64	27	73	438	206	406	45	122	493	88	72	254	372	374	113	131		342
SUSANVILLE	465	105	257	356	599	600	577	299	262	275	677	110	645	191	369	714	252	280	465	613	571	257	133	240	582
UKIAH	402	147	179	295	672	539	493	234	197	135	616	184	571	159	222	611	118	158	343	550	449	62	253	175	476
VALLEJO	310	147	265	203	592	442	418	131	92	25	519	186	474	57	124	545	35	67	249	471	342	46	266	65	370
VENTURA	115	477	643	222	323	93	66	278	315	344	172	548	125	387	245	185	367	322	137	104	31	414	471	342	
YOSEMITE NATIONAL PK	199	263	476	92	435	331	307	83	122	174	408	333	364	172	188	434	184	178	236	342	329	234	133	129	330
YREKA	531	171	205	427	698	657	638	372	335	307	747	98	689	263	423	756	317	346	534	668	630	325	315	297	645
YUBA CITY	313	48	290	206	608	448	427	150	113	122	525	133	480	41	214	546	128	158	346	459	451	201	145	86	428
YUMA	379	742	922	491	299	278	271	545	584	674	169	816	221	655	595	173	655	614	473	260	368	702	646	603	337

COPYRIGHT 1997 Thomas Bros. Maps ®

CITIES AND COMMUNITIES

A

COMMUNITY NAME	CO.	ZIP CODE	POP.	PG.	GD.
ACADEMY	FRCO	93612		57	E2
ACAMPO	SJCO	95220		40	A4
ACTON	LACO	93510		89	E4
ADAMS	LAK	95496		31	E4
ADELAIDA	SLO	93446		75	E1
* ADELANTO	SBD	92301	13,350	91	A3
ADIN	MOD	96006		14	D3
AERIAL ACRES	KER	93523		80	D5
AETNA SPRINGS	NAPA	94567		32	B5
AFTON	GLE	95920		25	A5
AGATE BAY	PLA	95711		35	E1
AGOURA	LACO	91301		97	A1
* AGOURA HILLS	LACO	91301	21,150	97	A1
AGUA CALIENTE	SDCO	92086		107	C2
AGUA CALIENTE	SON	95476		38	B3
AGUA CALIENTE HOT SPGS	SDCO	92036		107	E4
AGUA DULCE	LACO	91350		89	D4
AGUANGA	RCO	92302		107	A1
AGUEREBERRY POINT	INY	92328		71	D1
AHWAHNEE	MAD	93601		49	C4
AINSWORTH CORNER	SIS			5	C2
* ALAMEDA	ALA	94501	78,300	L	D5
-- ALAMEDA COUNTY	ALA		1,356,100		
ALAMO	CC	94507		M	A4
ALAMORIO	IMP	92227		109	B4
ALAMO SQUARE	SFCO	94115		142	B3
* ALBANY	ALA	94706	17,100	L	D4
ALBERHILL	RCO	92303		99	A4
ALBION	MEN	95410		30	B1
ALDER CREEK	SAC	95670		40	B1
ALDERCROFT HEIGHTS	SC	95030		46	A5
ALDERPOINT	HUM	95411		16	D5
ALDER SPRINGS	FRCO	93602		58	A1
ALDER SPRINGS	GLE	95939		23	E3
ALGODONES	BAJA			112	C5
* ALHAMBRA	LACO	91801	88,500	R	C3
ALISO VIEJO	ORCO	92656		98	D5
ALLEGHANY	SIE	95910		26	D4
ALLENDALE	SOL	95688		39	A2
ALLENSWORTH	TUL	93219		68	A4
ALMANOR	PLU	95911		20	B4
ALPAUGH	TUL	93201		67	E4
ALPINE	SDCO	92001		107	B5
-- ALPINE COUNTY	ALP		1,180		
ALPINE HEIGHTS	SDCO	92001		107	B5
ALPINE HIGHLANDS	SDCO	92001		107	B5
ALPINE HILLS	SDCO	92001		107	B5
ALPINE HILLS	SMCO	94025		N	D3
ALPINE MEADOWS	PLA	95730		35	D2
ALPINE PEAKS	PLA	95730		35	D2
ALTA	PLA	95701		34	E1
ALTADENA	LACO	91001		R	C2
ALTA LOMA	SBD	91701		U	D2
ALTAMONT	ALA	94550		M	D5
ALTAMONT	KLAM			5	C1
ALTA SIERRA	KER	93285		69	C5
ALTAVILLE	CAL	95221		41	B4
ALTA VISTA	INY	93514		51	C3
ALTON	HUM	95540		15	D2
* ALTURAS	MOD	96101	3,160	8	A1
ALUM ROCK	SCL	95127		P	C3
ALVISO	SCL	95002		P	B2
* AMADOR CITY	AMA	95601	210	40	D2
-- AMADOR COUNTY	AMA		34,000		
AMARGOSA VALLEY	NYE			62	E4
AMBLER	TUL	93277		68	B1
AMBOY	SBD	92304		93	E3
* AMERICAN CANYON	NAPA	94590	8,900	L	D1
AMERICAN HOUSE	PLU	95981		26	C3
* ANAHEIM	ORCO	92801	293,200	T	D2
ANAHEIM HILLS	ORCO	92807		U	C5
* ANDERSON	SHA	96007	8,650	18	C3
ANDERSON SPRINGS	LAK	95461		31	E4
ANDRADE	IMP	92283		112	C5
ANGEL ISLAND	MAR	94920		45	B1
* ANGELS CAMP	CAL	95222	2,840	41	B4
ANGELUS OAKS	SBD	92305		99	E1
ANGWIN	NAPA	94508		38	C1
ANNAPOLIS	SON	95412		30	E5
ANTELOPE	SAC	95621		34	A5
ANTELOPE ACRES	LACO	93534		89	D2
* ANTIOCH	CC	94509	74,800	M	C3
ANZA	RCO	92306		100	C5
APPLEGATE	PLA	95703		34	D3
* APPLE VALLEY	SBD	92307	52,800	91	C4
APTOS	SCR	95003		54	B2
ARABIA	RCO	92274		101	B5
ARBUCKLE	COL	95912		32	E3
* ARCADIA	LACO	91006	52,100	R	C3
* ARCATA	HUM	95521	16,300	9	E5
ARDEN	CLK			74	D3
ARDEN	SAC	95864		40	A1
ARGUS	SBD	93562		71	B5
ARLINGTON	RCO	92503		99	A3
ARMONA	KIN	93202		67	D1
ARNOLD	CAL	95223		41	C3
ARNOLD HEIGHTS	RCO	92508		99	B3
AROMAS	MON	95004		54	C2
ARROWBEAR LAKE	SBD	92308		99	D1
ARROWHEAD SPRINGS	SBD	92404		99	C1
* ARROYO GRANDE	SLO	93420	15,150	76	B4
* ARTESIA	LACO	90701	16,400	T	A1
ARTOIS	GLE	95913		24	D4
* ARVIN	KER	93203	10,700	78	E4
ASHFORD JUNCTION	INY	92328		72	C4
* ASHLAND	JKSN		16,200	3	E1
ASPENDELL	INY	93514		51	B5
ASTI	SON	95425		31	C5
* ATASCADERO	SLO	93422	24,750	76	A2
* ATHERTON	SMCO	94025	7,300	N	D2
ATOLIA	SBD	93558		80	E3
* ATWATER	MCO	95301	20,900	48	B4
ATWOOD	ORCO	92601		T	E1
* AUBURN	PLA	95603	11,450	34	C3
* AVALON	LACO	90704	3,400	97	E5
* AVENAL	KIN	93204	12,350	66	E3
AVERY	CAL	95224		41	C3
AVILA BEACH	SLO	93424		76	A4
AVON	CC	94553		L	E3
* AZUSA	LACO	91702	43,950	U	A1

B

COMMUNITY NAME	CO.	ZIP CODE	POP.	PG.	GD.
BABBITT	MIN			44	B1
BACHELOR VALLEY	LAK	95493		31	D2
BADGER	TUL	93603		58	D4
BADWATER	INY	92328		72	A2
BAKER	SBD	92309		83	B3
* BAKERSFIELD	KER	93301	212,700	78	D3
BALBOA	ORCO	92661		T	C4
BALBOA ISLAND	ORCO	92662		T	C4
BALCH CAMP	FRCO	93657		58	C2
* BALDWIN PARK	LACO	91706	73,500	R	D3
BALLARAT	INY	93562		71	C3
BALLARD	SB	93463		86	E3
BALLENA	SDCO	92065		107	B4
BALLICO	MCO	95303		48	A3
BANGOR	BUT	95914		25	E5
BANKHEAD SPRINGS	SDCO	92034		111	A4
BANNER	SDCO	92036		107	D4
* BANNING	RCO	92220	23,850	100	A3
BARD	IMP	92222		112	D5
BARDSDALE	VEN	93015		88	D4
BARRETT JUNCTION	SDCO	92017		112	B2
BARRIO LOGAN	SDCO	92113		216	A5
BARSTOW	FRCO	93702		57	B3
* BARSTOW	SBD	92311	22,300	91	E1
BARTLE	SIS	96057		13	B2
BARTLETT	INY	93545		60	B5
BARTLETT SPRINGS	LAK	95443		32	A2
BARTON	AMA	92309		41	B2
BARTON FLATS	SBD			100	A1
BASS LAKE	MAD	93604		49	E4
BASSETT	LACO	91746		R	D4
BASSETTS	SIE	96125		27	A4
BAXTER	PLA	95704		34	E1
BAY FARM ISLAND	ALA			L	D5
BAY POINT	CC	94565		M	B3
BAYSHORE	SMCO	94005		L	C5
BAYSIDE	HUM	95524		9	E5
BAYWOOD PARK	SLO	93402		75	E3
BEAR HARBOR	MEN	95489		22	B2
BEAR VALLEY	ALP	95223		41	E2
BEAR VALLEY	MPA	95338		48	E3
BEAR VALLEY	SDCO	92082		106	E3
BEAR VALLEY SPRINGS	KER	93561		79	B4
BEATTY	NYE			62	B2
BEATTY JUNCTION	INYO	92328		61	E4
* BEAUMONT	RCO	92223	10,450	99	E3
BECKWOURTH	PLU	96129		27	C2
BEE ROCK	SLO	93426		65	D5
BEL AIRE	MAR	94920		L	B4
BEL AIR ESTATES	LACO	90077		Q	B4
BEL MARIN KEYS	MAR	94949		L	B2
BELDEN	PLU	95915		26	A1
* BELL	LACO	90201	36,400	R	B5
BELLA VISTA	KER	93283		79	E1
BELLA VISTA	SHA	96008		18	D2
* BELLFLOWER	LACO	90706	65,300	S	E1
* BELL GARDENS	LACO	90201	43,750	R	B5
BELLOTA	SJCO	95236		40	C4
BELL SPRINGS	MEN	95440		22	D1
BELL STATION	SC	95020		55	A2
* BELMONT	SMCO	94002	24,950	N	C2
* BELVEDERE	MAR	94920	2,250	L	B4
BELVEDERE GARDENS	MAR	94920		L	B4
BENBOW	HUM	95440		22	C1
BEND	TEH	96008		18	D4
* BENICIA	SOL	94510	27,200	L	E2
BEN LOMOND	SCR	95005		N	E5
BENTON	MNO	93512		51	C1
BERENDA	MAD	93637		56	E1
* BERKELEY	ALA	94710	104,700	L	D4
BERKELEY CAMP	SON	95421		37	C1
BERMUDA DUNES	RCO	92201		101	A4
BERRY CREEK	BUT	95916		25	E3
BERRYESSA HIGHLANDS	NAPA	94558		38	D1
BERRYESSA PINES	NAPA	94567		38	C1
BERTELEDA	DN	95531		2	A4
BERTSCH TERRACE	DN	95531		1	E4
BETHANY	SJCO	95376		M	E5
BETHEL ISLAND	CC	94511		M	D3
BETTERAVIA	SB	93455		86	B1
* BEVERLY HILLS	LACO	90210	33,300	Q	C3
BIEBER	LAS	96009		14	B3
BIG BAR	AMA	95704		41	A2
BIG BEAR CITY	SBD	92314		92	A5
* BIG BEAR LAKE	SBD	92315	5,950	92	A5
BIG BEND	SHA	96011		13	A4
BIG BEND	SON	95476		38	B3
BIG CREEK	FRCO	93605		50	B5
* BIGGS	BUT	95917	1,640	25	B5
BIG MEADOW	CAL	95223		41	E2
BIG OAK FLAT	TUO	95305		48	D1
BIG PINE	INY	93513		51	E5
BIG RIVER	SBD	92242		104	A1
BIG SPRINGS	SIS			4	C5
BIG SUR	MON	93920		64	B2
BINGHAMTON	SOL	95625		39	B2
BIOLA	FRCO	93606		57	B3
BIRCH HILL	SDCO	92060		107	A2
BIRCHVILLE	NEV			34	C1
BIRDS LANDING	SOL	94512		39	B4
* BISHOP	INY	93514	3,520	51	D4
BITTERWATER	SBT	93930		65	C1
BLACKHAWK	CC	94526		M	B4
BLACK POINT	MAR	94945		L	B2
BLACKWELLS CORNER	KER	93249		77	C1
BLAIRSDEN	PLU	96103		27	A2
BLOCKSBURG	HUM	95414		16	D4
BLOOMFIELD	SON	94952		37	D3
BLOOMINGTON	SBD	92316		99	A2
BLOSSOM	TEH	96080		18	B5
BLOSSOM VALLEY	SDCO	92021		107	A5
BLUE DIAMOND	CLK			74	B3
BLUE JAY	SBD	92317		91	C5
* BLUE LAKE	HUM	95525	1,240	10	A5
BLUE LAKES	LAK	95493		31	C2
* BLYTHE	RCO	92225	18,350	103	D5
BOCA	NEV	95737		27	E5
BODEGA	SON	94922		37	C3
BODEGA BAY	SON	94923		37	C3
BODFISH	KER	93205		79	C1
BODIE	MNO	93517		43	D3
BOLINAS	MAR	94924		37	E5
BOLSA KNOLLS	MON	93906		54	C3
BOMBAY BEACH	IMP	92257		108	E2
* BONANZA	KLAM		340	5	E1
BONDS CORNER	IMP	92250		112	C4
BONITA	SDCO	92002		V	D4
BONNEFOY	AMA	95642		41	A2
BONSALL	SDCO	92003		106	C2
BOONVILLE	MEN	95415		30	E3
BOOTJACK	MPA	95338		49	B3
BORON	KER	93516		80	E5
BORREGO SPRINGS	SDCO	92004		107	E2
BOSTONIA	SDCO	92021		V	E2
BOULDER CREEK	SCR	95006		N	E5
BOULDER OAKS	SDCO	92062		112	D1
BOULEVARD	SDCO	92005		111	A4
BOUQUET CANYON	LA	91355		89	C4
BOUSE	LPAZ	92363		104	D3
BOWLES	FRCO	93725		57	C4
BOWMAN	PLA	95603		34	C3
BOYES HOT SPRINGS	SON	95416		38	B3
BOYLE HEIGHTS	LACO	90033		R	A4
* BRADBURY	LACO	91010	890	R	E3
BRADLEY	MON	93426		65	E4
BRANSCOMB	MEN	95417		22	D3
* BRAWLEY	IMP	92227	21,550	109	A4
* BREA	ORCO	92621	34,800	T	D1
BRENDA	LPAZ			104	D4
* BRENTWOOD	CC	94513	13,200	M	D3
BRENTWOOD	LACO	90049		Q	B4
BRICEBURG	MPA	95345		49	B2
BRICELAND	HUM	95440		16	B5
BRIDGE HAVEN	SON	95450		37	C2
BRIDGE HOUSE	SAC	95683		40	C2
BRIDGEPORT	MPA	95306		49	A4
BRIDGEPORT	MNO	93517		43	B3
BRIDGEPORT	NEV	95975		34	B1
BRIDGEVIEW	JOS			2	D1
BRIDGEVILLE	HUM	95526		16	C3
* BRISBANE	SMCO	94005	3,120	L	C5
BRITE VALLEY	KER	93561		79	C4
BROOKDALE	SCR	95007		N	E5
* BROOKINGS	CUR		4,450	1	D2
BROOKS	YOL	95606		32	D5
BROWNS VALLEY	YUB	95918		33	E1
BROWNSVILLE	YUB	95919		26	A4
BRUCEVILLE	SAC	95758		39	E3
BRUSH CREEK	BUT	95916		25	E3
BRYN MAWR	SBD	92318		99	C2
BUCKEYE	ED	95634		34	E3
BUCKEYE	SHA	96003		18	B2
BUCKHORN	AMA	95666		41	B2
BUCKHORN SPRINGS	JKSN			4	B2
BUCKMAN SPRINGS	SDCO	92062		112	D1
BUCK MEADOWS	MPA	95321		49	A1
BUCKS BAR	ED	95684		35	A5
BUCKS LAKE	PLU	95971		26	B2
* BUELLTON	SB	93427	3,510	86	D3
BUENA	SDCO	92083		106	C3
* BUENA PARK	ORCO	90620	72,700	T	B1
BUENA VISTA	AMA	95640		40	D3
BUHACH	MCO	95340		48	B4
* BULLHEAD CITY	MOH		26,940	85	D4
BUMMERVILLE	CAL	95257		41	B2
BUNTINGVILLE	LAS	96114		21	B4
* BURBANK	LACO	91501	101,400	Q	E2
BURDELL	MAR	94945		L	A2
* BURLINGAME	SMCO	94010	28,100	N	C1
BURNEY	SHA	96013		13	C5
BURNT RANCH	TRI	95527		10	D5
BURREL	FRCO	93607		57	B5
BURSON	CAL	95225		40	D4
BUTTE CITY	GLE	95920		25	A5
-- BUTTE COUNTY	BUT		197,000		
BUTTE MEADOWS	BUT	95921		25	D1
BUTTONWILLOW	KER	93206		78	A3
BYRON	CC	94514		M	D4

C

COMMUNITY NAME	CO.	ZIP CODE	POP.	PG.	GD.
CABAZON	RCO	92230		100	B3
CABBAGE PATCH	CAL	95223		41	E2
CADENASSO	YOL	95607		32	E5
CADIZ	SBD	92319		94	B4
CADWELL	SON	95472		37	E2
CAIRNS CORNER	TUL	93247		68	C2
CAJON JUNCTION	SBD	92358		91	A5
* CALABASAS	LACO	91302	18,800	97	B1
-- CALAVERAS COUNTY	CAL		36,950		
CALAVERITAS	CAL	95249		41	A3
* CALEXICO	IMP	92231	24,700	112	B4
CALICO GHOST TOWN	SBD	92398		82	A5
CALIENTE	KER	93518		79	B3
* CALIFORNIA CITY	KER	93505	8,825	80	B4
CALIFORNIA HOT SPRINGS	TUL	93207		69	B4
CALIFORNIA VALLEY	SLO	93453		77	B3
* CALIMESA	RCO	92320	7,300	99	D2
* CALIPATRIA	IMP	92233	7,275	109	B3
* CALISTOGA	NAPA	94515	4,710	38	A1
CALLAHAN	SIS	96014		11	D2
CALNEVA	LAS	96113		21	E5
CALPELLA	MEN	95418		31	B1
CALPINE	SIE	96124		27	B3
CALWA	FRCO	93725		57	C3
* CAMARILLO	VEN	93010	58,200	96	C1
CAMBRIA	SLO	93428		75	C2
CAMDEN	FRCO	93656		57	C5
CAMERON CORNERS	SDCO	92006		112	D2
CAMERON PARK	ED	95682		34	C5
CAMINO	ED	95709		35	A4
* CAMPBELL	SCL	95008	38,250	P	B4
CAMP CONIFER	TUL	93271		59	A5
CAMP CONNELL	CAL	95223		41	D3
CAMP KLAMATH	DN	95548		2	A5
CAMP MEEKER	SON	95419		37	D2
CAMPO	SDCO	92006		112	D2
CAMPO SECO	CAL	95226		40	E3
CAMP SIERRA	FRCO	93634		50	B5
CAMPTONVILLE	YUB	95922		26	B5
CANBY	MOD	96015		14	D1
CANE BRAKE	KER	93255		70	B5
CANOGA PARK	LACO	91303		Q	A2
CANTIL	KER	93519		80	C3
CANTUA CREEK	FRCO	93608		56	D5
CANYON	CC			L	E4
CANYON CITY	SDCO	92006		112	D2
CANYON COUNTRY	LACO	91351		89	C4
CANYON CREST HEIGHTS	RCO	92507		99	B2
CANYON DAM	PLU	95923		20	C5
* CANYON LAKE	RCO	92380	11,300	99	C4
CAPAY	YOL	95607		32	E5
CAPETOWN	HUM	95536		15	C3
CAPISTRANO BEACH	ORCO	92624		105	D1
* CAPITOLA	SCR	95010	10,800	54	A2
CARBONDALE	AMA	95640		40	C2
CARDIFF-BY-THE-SEA	SDCO	92007		106	B4
CARL INN	TUO	95321		49	C1
CARLOTTA	HUM	95528		16	A2
* CARLSBAD	SDCO	92008	68,200	106	B3
* CARMEL-BY-THE-SEA	MON	93921	4,460	54	A5
CARMEL HIGHLANDS	MON	93923		54	A5
CARMEL VALLEY VILLAGE	MON	93924		54	C5
CARMET	SON	94923		37	C2
CARMICHAEL	SAC	95608		34	A5
CARNELIAN BAY	PLA	95711		36	A1
CARPENTERVILLE	CUR			1	C1
* CARPINTERIA	SB	93013	14,500	87	E4
CARQUINEZ HEIGHTS	SOL	94590		38	C4
* CARSON	LACO	90745	88,100	S	C2
* CARSON CITY	CRSN		40,443	36	C2
-- CARSON CITY COUNTY	CRSN		40,443		
CARSON HILL	CAL	95222		41	B4
CARTAGO	INY	93549		70	B1
CARUTHERS	FRCO	93609		57	C5
CASA BLANCA	RCO	92504		99	B3
CASA DE ORO	SDCO	92077		V	E3
CASA DIABLO HOT SPGS	MNO	93546		50	E2
CASITAS SPRINGS	VEN	93001		88	A4
CASMALIA	SB	93429		86	B1
CASPER	MEN	95420		22	B5
CASSEL	SHA	96016		13	D5
CASTAIC	LACO	91310		89	B4
CASTELLA	SHA	96017		12	C3
CASTELLAMMARE	LACO	90290		Q	A4
CASTLE CRAG	SHA	96013		12	C3
CASTLE PARK	SDCO	92011		V	D5
CASTRO VALLEY	ALA	94546		L	E5
CASTROVILLE	MON	95012		54	B3
* CATHEDRAL CITY	RCO	92234	35,400	100	D4
CATHEYS VALLEY	MPA	95306		49	A3
CAVE JUNCTION	JOS			2	D1
CAYTON	SHA	96013		13	C4
CAYUCOS	SLO	93430		75	D2
CAZADERO	SON	95421		37	C1
CECILVILLE	SIS	96018		11	B3
CEDAR BROOK	FRCO	93641		58	D3
CEDAR CREST	FRCO	93605		50	C5
CEDAR FLAT	PLA	95711		35	E1
CEDAR GLEN	SBD	92321		91	D5
CEDAR GROVE	ED	95709		35	A4
CEDAR GROVE	FRCO	93641		59	B3
CEDAR RIDGE	NEV	95924		34	C2
CEDARPINES PARK	SBD	92322		91	B5
CEDAR VALLEY	MAD	93644		49	D4
CEDARVILLE	MOD	96104		7	D5
CENTERVILLE	ALA	94536		P	A2
CENTERVILLE	DGL			36	C3
CENTERVILLE	FRCO	93654		57	E3
CENTERVILLE	SHA	96001		18	B2
CENTRAL VALLEY	SHA	96019		18	C1
CENTRE CITY	SDCO	92101		215	D3
CENTURY CITY	LACO	90067		Q	D4
* CERES	STA	95307	31,100	47	D3
* CERRITOS	LACO	90701	55,300	T	B1
CHALFANT	MNO	93514		51	D3
CHALK HILL VALLEY	SON	95448		37	E1
CHALLENGE	YUB	95925		26	B4
CHAMBERS LODGE	PLA	95718		35	E2
CHATSWORTH	LACO	91311		Q	A1
CHAWANAKEE	FRCO	93602		50	A5
CHEMEKETA PARK	SCL	95030		P	A4
CHEROKEE	BUT	95965		25	D3
CHEROKEE	NEV	93602		26	C5
CHERRY VALLEY	RCO	92223		99	E2
CHESTER	PLU	96020		20	A4
CHICAGO PARK	NEV	95712		34	C2
* CHICO	BUT	95926	47,200	25	B3
CHILCOOT	PLU	96105		27	D2
CHINATOWN	SFCO	94108		142	D2
CHINESE CAMP	TUO	95309		41	B5
* CHINO	SBD	91710	63,400	U	D3
* CHINO HILLS	SBD	91709	49,750	98	D2
CHINQUAPIN	MPA	95389		49	D2
CHIQUITA LAKE	ED	95634		35	A3
CHIRIACO SUMMIT	RCO			101	E4

* INDICATES INCORPORATED CITY

CITIES AND COMMUNITIES

G

COMMUNITY NAME	CO.	ZIP CODE	POP.	PG.	GD.
CHLORIDE CITY	INY	92328		62	A4
CHOCTAW VALLEY	KER	93306		78	E2
CHOLAME	SLO	93431		66	D5
CHOWCHILLA	MAD	93610	6,600	48	D5
CHROME	GLE	95963		24	A3
CHUALAR	MON	93925		54	D4
CHULA VISTA	SDCO	92010	153,200	V	D4
CIBOLA	LPAZ			110	D2
CIENEGA SPRINGS	LPAZ			104	C1
CIMA	SBD	92323		84	B4
CIRCLE OAKS	NAPA	94599		38	D2
CISCO	PLA	95728		35	B1
CITRUS HEIGHTS	SAC	95610		34	A5
CITY HEIGHTS	SDCO	92105		V	C3
CITY OF COMMERCE	LACO	90040	12,700	R	B4
CITY OF INDUSTRY	LACO	91744	690	R	E4
CLAIREMONT MESA	SDCO	92117		V	B2
CLAREMONT	LACO	91711	34,050	U	C2
CLARENDON HEIGHTS	SFCO	94114		141	E5
CLARK	STOR			28	E4
-- CLARK COUNTY	CLK		741,459		
CLARKSBURG	YOL	95612		39	D2
CLARKSVILLE	ED	95682		34	C5
CLAY	SAC	95638		40	B3
CLAYTON	CC	94517	9,400	M	B3
CLEAR CREEK	SIS	96039		2	E4
CLEARLAKE	LAK	95422	12,050	32	A3
CLEARLAKE KEYS	LAK	95423		32	A3
CLEARLAKE OAKS	LAK	95423		32	A3
CLEMENTS	SJCO	95227		40	C3
CLEONE	MEN	95437		22	C4
CLIFF HOUSE	TUO	95321		49	B1
CLINTON	AMA	95232		41	A2
CLIO	PLU	96106		27	A3
CLIPPER GAP	PLA	95703		34	C3
CLIPPER MILLS	BUT	95930		26	A4
CLOVERDALE	SHA	96007		18	B3
CLOVERDALE	SON	95425	5,475	31	C4
CLOVIS	FRCO	93612	65,000	57	D3
CLYDE	CC	94520		M	A3
COACHELLA	RCO	92236	21,050	101	B4
COALINGA	FRCO	93210	9,925	66	D3
COALINGA MINERAL SPGS	FRCO	93210		66	B2
COARSEGOLD	MAD	93614		49	C4
COBB	LAK	95426		31	E4
CODORA	GLE	95970		25	A5
COFFEE CREEK	TRI	96091		11	E3
COHASSET	BUT	95926		25	C1
COLD SPRINGS	TUO	95370		42	A3
COLES STATION	ED	95684		35	B5
COLEVILLE	MNO	96107		42	D1
COLFAX	PLA	95713	1,450	34	D2
COLLEGE CITY	COL	95931		33	A3
COLLEGEVILLE	SJCO	95206		40	B5
COLLIERVILLE	SJCO	95220		40	B3
COLLINSVILLE	SOL	94585		39	B4
COLMA	SMCO	94014	1,230	L	B5
COLOMA	ED	95613		34	D4
COLONIA	VEN	93030		176	C3
COLTON	SBD	92324	44,500	99	B2
COLUMBIA	TUO	95310		41	C4
COLUSA	COL	95932	5,275	32	E2
-- COLUSA COUNTY	COL		17,950		
COMPTCHE	MEN	95427		30	C1
COMPTON	LACO	90220	93,300	S	C1
CONCORD	CC	94520	111,800	M	A3
CONFIDENCE	TUO	95370		41	D4
CONSTANTIA	LAS	96019		27	E1
-- CONTRA COSTA COUNTY	CC		870,700		
COOKS STATION	AMA	95666		41	C1
COOL	ED	95614		34	C4
COOLIDGE SPRING	IMP	92274		108	C1
COPCO	SIS	96044		4	C2
COPPEROPOLIS	CAL	95228		41	A5
CORCORAN	KIN	93212	14,600	67	E3
CORDELIA	SOL	93063		L	E1
CORNING	TEH	96021	6,150	24	D2
CORONA	RCO	91720	99,500	U	E4
CORONA DEL MAR	ORCO	92625		T	C5
CORONADO	SDCO	92118	28,500	V	B4
CORONA HEIGHTS	SFCO	94114		142	A5
CORONITA	RCO	91720		98	E3
CORTE MADERA	MAR	94925	8,600	L	A3
COSO JUNCTION	INY	93542		70	C3
COSTA MESA	ORCO	92626	102,100	T	C4
COSUMNES	SAC	95683		40	B2
COTATI	SON	94931	6,500	37	E3
COTO DE CAZA	ORCO	92679		98	E4
COTTAGE SPRINGS	CAL	95223		41	D2
COTTON CENTER	TUL	93257		68	C3
COTTONWOOD	SHA	96022		18	C3
COULTERVILLE	MPA	95311		48	D2
COURTLAND	SAC	95615		39	D3
COVELO	MEN	95428		23	A3
COVINA	LACO	91722	45,950	U	A2
COVINGTON MILL	TRI	96052		11	E5
COWAN HEIGHTS	ORCO	92705		98	C4
COW HOLLOW	SFCO	94123		142	A2
COYOTE	SCL	95013		P	D4
COYOTE WELLS	IMP	92259		111	C3
COZZENS CORNERS	SON	95441		31	D5
CRAFTON	SBD	92374		99	D2
CRANMORE	SUT	95645		33	B3
CRANNELL	HUM	95530		9	E4
CRESCENT CITY	DN	95531	8,800	1	D4
CRESCENT MILLS	PLU	95934		20	C5
CRESSEY	MCO	95312		48	A4
CREST	SDCO	92021		112	A1
CRESTLINE	SBD	92325		91	C5
CRESTMORE	SBD	92316		99	B2
CRESTON	SLO	93432		76	B2
CRESTVIEW	MNO	93514		50	D1
CROCKETT	CC	94525		L	D2
CROMBERG	PLU	96103		27	A2
CROWN POINT	SDCO	92109		V	A3
CROWS LANDING	STA	95313		47	C4

COMMUNITY NAME	CO.	ZIP CODE	POP.	PG.	GD.
* CRYSTAL BAY	WSH		1,200	36	A1
* CUDAHY	LACO	90201	24,400	R	B5
CUESTA BY THE SEA	SLO	93402		75	D3
* CULVER CITY	LACO	90230	40,500	Q	D4
CUMMINGS	MEN	95477		22	D2
CUMMINGS VALLEY	KER	93561		79	B4
CUNNINGHAM	SON	95472		37	E2
* CUPERTINO	SCL	95014	43,650	P	A3
-- CURRY COUNTY	CUR		21,300		
CURRY VILLAGE	MPA	95389		49	D2
CUTLER	TUL	93615		58	B5
CUTTEN	HUM	95534		15	E1
CUYAMA	SB	93214		87	D1
CUYAMACA	SDCO	92335		107	C4
* CYPRESS	ORCO	90630	46,400	T	B2

D

COMMUNITY NAME	CO.	ZIP CODE	POP.	PG.	GD.
DAGGETT	SBD	92327		92	A1
DAIRY	KLAM			5	D1
DAIRYVILLE	TEH	96080		18	D5
DALES	TEH	96080		18	E4
* DALY CITY	SMCO	94014	99,500	L	B5
DANA	SHA	96036		13	D3
* DANA POINT	ORCO	92629	36,000	105	D1
* DANVILLE	CC	94526	37,050	M	A4
DARDANELLE	TUO	95314		42	B2
DARLINGTONIA	DN	95543		2	B3
DARRAH	MPA	95338		49	C3
DARWIN	INY	93522		70	E2
DATE CITY	IMP	92250		112	C3
DAULTON	MAD	93653		57	B1
DAVENPORT	SCR			53	D2
* DAVIS	YOL	95616	52,600	39	C1
DAVIS CREEK	MOD	96108		7	C4
DAVIS DAM	MOH			85	D4
DAY	MOD	96056		13	E3
DAYTON	BUT	95926		25	B3
DAYTON	LYON			36	D1
DEER PARK	NAPA	94576		38	B1
DEHESA	SDCO	92021		112	A1
* DELANO	KER	93215	31,450	68	B5
DEL CERRO	SDCO	92120		V	D3
DEL DIOS	SDCO	92025		106	D3
DELEVAN	COL	95988		24	D5
DELFT COLONY	TUL	93619		58	A5
DELHI	MCO	95315		47	E4
DEL LOMA	TRI	96010		17	A1
* DEL MAR	SDCO	92014	5,125	V	A1
-- DEL NORTE COUNTY	DN		28,650		
DEL PASO HEIGHTS	SAC	95838		33	E5
DEL REY	FRCO	93616		57	E4
* DEL REY OAKS	MON	93940	1,670	54	B4
DEL RIO WOODS	SON	95448		37	E1
DEL ROSA	SBD	92404		99	C1
DELTA	SHA	96051		12	B4
DE LUZ	SDCO	92055		106	B1
DEMOCRAT HOT SPRINGS	KER	93301		79	B2
DENAIR	STA	95316		47	E3
DENNY	TRI	95538		10	E5
DENVERTON	SOL	94585		39	A3
DERBY ACRES	KER	93268		77	E3
DE SABLA	BUT	95978		25	C2
DESCANSO	SDCO	92016		107	C5
DESCANSO JUNCTION	SDCO	92016		107	C5
DESERT BEACH	RCO	92254		101	D5
DESERT CENTER	RCO	92239		102	C4
DESERT HAVEN	RCO	92240		100	D3
* DESERT HOT SPRINGS	RCO	92240	14,850	100	D2
DESERT LAKE	KER	93516		80	D5
DESERT SHORES	IMP	92274		108	C1
DEVILS DEN	KER	93204		67	B5
DEVORE	SBD	92405		99	B1
DIABLO	CC	94528		M	B4
* DIAMOND BAR	LACO	91765	56,000	U	B3
DIAMOND SPRINGS	ED	95619		34	E5
DI GIORGIO	KER	93217		79	A3
DILLON BEACH	MAR	94929		37	D3
DINKEY CREEK	FRCO	93617		58	C1
* DINUBA	TUL	93618	14,650	58	A5
DISCOVERY BAY	CC	94514		39	D5
DIXIELAND	IMP	92251		108	D5
* DIXON	SOL	95620	13,100	39	B2
DOBBINS	YUB	95935		26	B5
DOG TOWN	CAL	95249		41	B4
DOGTOWN	MPA	95311		48	E2
DOGTOWN	SJCO	95220		40	C3
DORRINGTON	CAL	95223		41	D3
* DORRIS	SIS	96023	890	5	A2
* DOS PALOS	MCO	93620	4,360	56	B2
DOS PALOS Y	MCO	93620		56	A1
DOS RIOS	MEN	95429		23	A3
DOUGHERTY	ALA	94566		46	B2
DOUGLAS CITY	TRI	96024		17	D2
-- DOUGLAS COUNTY	DGL		27,637		
DOVE CANYON	ORCO	92679		98	E4
* DOWNEY	LACO	90241	97,600	R	B5
DOWNIEVILLE	SIE	95936		26	D4
DOYLE	LAS	96019		27	E1
DOYLES CORNER	SHA	96040		13	D5
DOZIER	SOL	94535		39	B3
DRAKES BEACH	MAR	94956		37	D5
DRYTOWN	AMA	95699		40	E2
* DUARTE	LACO	91010	21,900	R	D3
* DUBLIN	ALA	94566	26,250	M	B5
DUBOCE TRIANGLE	SFCO	94114		142	B4
DUCOR	TUL	93218		68	D4
DULZURA	SDCO	92017		112	B2
DUNCANS MILLS	SON	95430		37	C2
DUNLAP	FRCO	93621		58	C3
DUNLAP	MEN	95490		30	D1
DUNMOVIN	INY	93542		70	C3
DUNNEVILLE	SBT			54	E2
DUNNIGAN	YOL	95937		33	A4
* DUNSMUIR	SIS	96025	2,020	12	D3
DURHAM	BUT	95938		25	B3
DUSTIN ACRES	KER	93268		78	A4
DUTCH FLAT	PLA	95714		34	D1
DYER	ESM			52	B2

E

COMMUNITY NAME	CO.	ZIP CODE	POP.	PG.	GD.
EAGLE LAKE RESORT	LAS	96130		20	D2
EAGLE MOUNTAIN	RCO	92241		102	B3
EAGLE ROCK	LACO	90041		R	A3
EAGLES NEST	SDCO	92086		107	C2
EAGLEVILLE	MOD	96110		8	D2
EARLIMART	TUL	93219		68	B4
EARP	SBD	92242		104	B1
EAST BAKERSFIELD	KER	93307		78	D3
EAST GUERNEWOOD	SON	95446		37	C1
EAST HIGHLANDS	SBD	92346		99	C1
EAST IRVINE	ORCO	92650		T	E4
EAST LAKE	ORCO	92686		T	E1
EASTLAKE	SDCO	91913		V	D4
EAST NICOLAUS	SUT	95622		33	D3
EASTON	FRCO	93706		57	C4
EAST OROSI	TUL	93647		58	B5
* EAST PALO ALTO	SMCO	94303	24,800	N	E2
EAST QUINCY	PLU	95971		26	D1
EAST SAN DIEGO	SDCO	92105		V	C3
EAST SAN JOSE	SC	95127		46	B4
EASTSIDE ACRES	MAD	93622		56	C3
EASTSIDE RANCH	MAD	93622		56	C3
ECHO DELL	SDCO	92016		107	C5
ECHO LAKE	ED	95721		35	E4
EDEN GARDENS	SDCO	92075		106	B4
EDEN HOT SPRINGS	RCO	92353		99	D3
EDGEWOOD	SIS	96094		12	C1
EDISON	KER	93220		78	E3
EDNA	SLO	93401		76	B4
EDWARDS AIR FORCE BASE	KER	93523		90	C1
EEL ROCK	HUM	95554		16	C4
EHRENBERG	LPAZ			103	E5
EL BONITA	SON	95446		37	C1
* EL CAJON	SDCO	92020	93,400	V	E3
EL CARISO	RCO	92530		99	A4
* EL CENTRO	IMP	92243	37,800	109	A5
* EL CERRITO	CC	94530	23,250	L	C3
ELDERS CORNERS	PLA	95603		34	C3
ELDERWOOD	TUL	93286		58	C5
EL DORADO	ED	95623		34	D5
-- EL DORADO COUNTY	ED		144,900		
EL DORADO HILLS	ED	95630		34	C5
ELDRIDGE	SON	95431		38	B3
ELECTRA	AMA	95642		41	A2
EL GRANADA	SMCO	94018		N	B2
ELIZABETH LAKE	LACO	93550		89	D3
ELK	MEN	95432		30	C2
ELK CREEK	GLE	95939		24	A4
ELK GROVE	SAC	95624		39	E2
ELK VALLEY	DN	95543		2	C2
ELLWOOD	SB	93117		87	B4
EL MACERO	YOL	95618		39	C1
ELMIRA	SOL	95625		39	B2
EL MODENA	ORCO	92669		T	E2
* EL MONTE	LACO	91731	113,300	R	D3
ELMORE	IMP	92227		108	D3
ELM VIEW	FRCO	93725		57	C4
EL NIDO	MCO	95317		56	C1
* EL PASO DE ROBLES	SLO	93446	21,450	76	A1
EL PORTAL	MPA	95318		49	C2
EL PORVENIR	FRE	93608		56	C5
EL RIO	VEN	93030		176	D1
* EL SEGUNDO	LACO	90245	16,050	Q	C5
EL SERENO	LACO	90031		R	A3
EL SOBRANTE	CC	94803		L	D3
EL TORO	ORCO	92630		98	D4
EL TORO MARINE BASE	ORCO	92709		98	D4
EL VERANO	SON	95433		L	B1
ELVERTA	SAC	95626		33	E5
EMERALD BAY	ED	95733		35	E3
EMERALD BAY	ORCO	92651		T	D5
* EMERYVILLE	ALA	94608	6,450	L	C4
EMIGRANT GAP	PLA	95715		35	A1
EMMATON	SAC			M	D2
EMPIRE	STA	95319		47	D2
ENCANTO	SDCO	92114		V	D4
* ENCINITAS	SDCO	92024	57,100	106	B4
ENCINO	LACO	91316		Q	B3
ENGINEER SPRINGS	SDCO	92017		112	B2
ENTERPRISE	SHA	96001		18	C2
* ESCALON	SJCO	95320	5,275	47	C1
* ESCONDIDO	SDCO	92025	118,300	106	D3
-- ESMERALDA COUNTY	ESM		1,344		
ESPARTO	YOL	95627		33	A5
ESSEX	SBD	92332		94	D2
ESTRELLA	SLO	93451		76	B1
ETHEDA SPRINGS	FRCO	93633		58	D4
* ETNA	SIS	96027	780	11	D1
ETTERSBURG	HUM	95440		16	A5
EUCALYPTUS HILLS	SDCO	92040		V	E2
* EUREKA	HUM	95501	27,500	15	E1
EUREKA VLY/DOLORES HTS	SFCO	94114		45	B2
EVELYN	INY	92384		72	E2
EVERGREEN	SC	95121		46	C4
* EXETER	TUL	93221	8,275	68	C1

F

COMMUNITY NAME	CO.	ZIP CODE	POP.	PG.	GD.
* FAIRFAX	MAR	94930	7,025	L	A3
* FAIRFIELD	SOL	94533	86,900	M	A1
FAIRHAVEN	HUM	95564		15	D1
FAIRMEAD	MAD	93610		56	D1
FAIRMONT	LACO	93534		89	C2
FAIR OAKS	SAC	95628		34	A5
FAIR PLAY	ED	95684		41	A1
FAIRVIEW	TUL	93238		69	C4
FALES HOT SPRINGS	MNO	93517		43	A2
FALLBROOK	SDCO	92028		106	C2
FALLEN LEAF	ED	95716		35	E4
FALLON	MAR	94952		37	D3
FALL RIVER MILLS	SHA	96028		13	E4
FAMOSO	KER	93250		78	C1
* FARMERSVILLE	TUL	93223	7,125	68	C1
FARMINGTON	SJCO	95230		40	C5
FAWNSKIN	SBD	92333		91	E5
FEATHER FALLS	BUT	95940		26	A4
FELICITY	IMP			112	C5
FELIX	CAL	95228		41	A4
FELLOWS	KER	93224		77	E4
FELTON	SCR	95018		N	E5
FERN	SHA	96096		19	A1
FERNBROOK	SDCO	92065		107	A4
* FERNDALE	HUM	95536	1,240	15	D2
FETTERS HOT SPRINGS	SON	95416		38	B3
FIDDLETOWN	AMA	95629		40	E1
FIELDBROOK	HUM	95521		10	A4
FIELDS LANDING	HUM	95537		15	E1
* FILLMORE	VEN	93015	12,800	88	D4
FINANCIAL DISTRICT	SFCO	94104		142	E2
FINE GOLD	MAD	93643		49	D5
FINLEY	LAK	95435		31	D3
* FIREBAUGH	FRCO	93622	5,825	56	C3
FISH CAMP	MPA	93623		49	D3
FISH ROCK	MEN	95445		30	D4
FISH SPRINGS	INY	93513		59	E1
FIVE CORNERS	LAKE			7	B1
FIVE CORNERS	SJCO	95336		47	C1
FIVE POINTS	FRCO	93624		57	A5
FIVE POINTS	LACO	91732		R	D4
FLEETRIDGE	SDCO	92106		V	A3
FLETCHER HILLS	SDCO	92020		V	D2
FLINN SPRINGS	SDCO	92021		107	A5
FLORIN	SAC	95828		39	E2
FLOURNOY	TEH	96029		24	B2
FLOWING WELLS	RCO	92254		101	C5
* FOLSOM	SAC	95630	41,450	34	B5
* FONTANA	SBD	92335	103,300	99	B1
FOOTHILL FARMS	SAC	95841		34	A5
FOOTHILL RANCH	ORCO	92610		98	D4
FORBESTOWN	BUT	95963		26	A4
FORD CITY	KER	93268		78	A4
FOREST	SIE	95910		26	D4
FORESTA	MPA	95389		49	C2
FORESTHILL	PLA	95631		34	D3
FOREST FALLS	SBD	92339		100	A2
FOREST GLEN	TRI	96030		17	A3
FOREST HOME	AMA	95640		40	C2
FOREST KNOLLS	MAR	94933		38	A5
FOREST KNOLLS	SFCO	94116		141	D5
FOREST LAKE	LAK	95461		32	A4
FOREST RANCH	BUT	95942		25	C2
FOREST SPRINGS	NEV	95945		34	C2
FORESTVILLE	SON	95436		37	D2
FORKS OF SALMON	SIS	96031		11	A2
FORREST PARK	LACO	91350		89	C4
FORT BIDWELL	MOD	96112		7	D3
* FORT BRAGG	MEN	95437	6,200	22	C5
FORT DICK	DN	95538		1	D3
FORT IRWIN	SBD	92310		82	B3
* FORT JONES	SIS	96032	610	3	D5
FORT ROSS	SON	95450		37	B1
FORT SEWARD	HUM	95438		16	D5
* FORTUNA	HUM	95540	9,825	15	E2
FOSTER	SDCO	92040		V	E1
* FOSTER CITY	SMCO	94404	29,300	N	D1
FOSTER PARK	VEN	93001		88	A5
FOUNTAIN SPRINGS	TUL	93257		68	E4
* FOUNTAIN VALLEY	ORCO	92708	54,300	T	C3
FOUR CORNERS	SHA	96016		13	C4
FOUTS SPRINGS	COL	95979		24	A5
* FOWLER	FRCO	93625	3,740	57	D4
FRANKLIN	SAC	95758		39	E2
FRAZIER PARK	KER	93225		88	D1
FREDALBA	SBD	92382		99	D1
FREDERICKSBURG	ALP	96120		36	B4
FREDS PLACE	ED	95720		35	D4
FREEDOM	SCR	95019		54	B2
FREEMAN	KER	93527		80	C1
FREEPORT	SAC	95832		39	E2
FREESTONE	SON	95472		37	D2
* FREMONT	ALA	94536	78,300	P	A2
FREMONT VALLEY	KER	93519		80	B4
FRENCH CAMP	SJCO	95231		40	B5
FRENCH CORRAL	NEV	95975		34	B1
FRENCH GULCH	SHA	96033		18	A1
FRESH POND	ED	95725		35	B4
FRESHWATER	HUM	95504		16	A1
* FRESNO	FRCO	93706	400,400	57	C3
-- FRESNO COUNTY	FRCO		760,900		
FRIANT	FRCO	93626		57	D2
FROGTOWN	CAL	95222		41	B4
FRUITRIDGE	SAC	95820		39	E1
FRUITVALE	KER	93308		78	C3
FRUTO	GLE	95988		24	B4
FULLER ACRES	KER	93307		78	E3
* FULLERTON	ORCO	92631	122,100	T	C1
FULTON	SON	95439		37	E1
FURNACE CREEK RANCH	INY	92328		62	A5

G

COMMUNITY NAME	CO.	ZIP CODE	POP.	PG.	GD.
GALLINAS	MAR	94903		L	B3
* GALT	SAC	95632	15,400	40	A3
GANNS	CAL	95223		41	D2
GARBERVILLE	HUM	95440		16	C5
* GARDENA	LACO	90247	56,800	S	C1
GARDEN FARMS	SLO	93422		76	B2
* GARDEN GROVE	ORCO	92640	151,400	T	C2
GARDEN PARK	ED	95633		34	D4
GARDEN VALLEY	ED	95633		34	D4
GARDNERVILLE	DGL			36	C3
GAREY	SB	93454		86	C1

*** INDICATES INCORPORATED CITY**

CITIES

CITIES AND COMMUNITIES

COMMUNITY NAME	CO.	ZIP CODE	POP.	PG.	GD.
GARLOCK	KER	93519		80	D2
GARNET	RCO	92258		100	C3
GASQUET	DN	95543		2	A3
GAVIOTA	SB	93117		86	D4
GAZELLE	SIS	96034		4	B5
GENESEE	PLU	95983		26	E1
GENOA	DGL			36	B3
GEORGETOWN	ED	95634		34	E3
GERBER	TEH	96035		24	E1
GEYSERVILLE	SON	95441		31	D5
GIANT FOREST	TUL	93271		59	A4
GIBSONVILLE	SIE	95981		26	D3
GILMAN HOT SPRINGS	RCO	92340		99	E3
* GILROY	SCL	95020	34,000	54	D2
GLAMIS	IMP	92248		109	E4
GLANNVALE	SAC	95758		39	E3
GLEN AVON	RCO	92509		99	A2
GLENBROOK	DGL			36	A2
GLENBURN	SHA	96036		13	D4
GLENCOE	CAL	95232		41	B2
* GLENDALE	LACO	91201	193,500	Q	E3
* GLENDORA	LACO	91740	51,200	U	A1
GLEN ELLEN	SON	95442		38	B2
GLENHAVEN	LAK	95443		31	E3
GLENN	GLE	95943		25	A4
-- GLENN COUNTY	GLE		26,600		
GLENNVILLE	KER	93226		69	A5
GLEN OAKS	SDCO	92001		107	A5
GLEN VALLEY	RCO	92370		99	B3
GLENVIEW	LAK	95451		31	E4
GLENVIEW	LACO	90290		Q	A3
GLENVIEW	SDCO	92021		107	A5
GOFFS	SBD	92332		94	E1
GOLDEN GATE HEIGHTS	SFCO	94112		141	D5
GOLDEN HILL	SDCO	92102		216	A3
GOLDEN HILLS	KER	93561		79	C4
GOLDEN SHORES	MOH	92363		95	E1
GOLDEN VALLEY	WSH			28	B3
GOLD HILL	ED	95651		34	D4
GOLD HILL	STOR			36	D1
GOLD RIVER	SAC	95670		40	B1
GOLD RUN	PLA	95717		34	D2
GOLD SPRINGS	TUO	95370		41	C4
GOLETA	SB	93111		87	B4
* GONZALES	MON	93926	6,050	54	E5
GONZALEZ ORTEGA	BAJA			112	C4
GOOD HOPE	RCO	92370		99	B4
GOODSPRINGS	CLK			74	B4
GOODYEARS BAR	SIE	95944		26	D4
GORDONS WELL	IMP			112	A5
GORMAN	LACO	93534		88	E2
GOSHEN	TUL	93227		68	A1
GOTTVILLE	SIS	96050		3	E3
GOVERNMENT FLAT	TEH	95939		23	D2
GRAEAGLE	PLU	96103		27	A3
GRANADA HILLS	LACO	91344		Q	A1
* GRAND TERRACE	SBD	92324	13,200	99	B2
GRANGEVILLE	KIN	93230		67	D1
GRANITEVILLE	NEV	95959		26	E5
GRANT HILL	SDCO	92102		216	B4
GRANTVILLE	SDCO	92120		V	C3
GRAPEVINE	KER	93301		88	D1
* GRASS VALLEY	NEV	95945	9,350	34	C1
GRATON	SON	95444		37	D2
GRAVESBORO	FRCO	93657		58	A3
GRAYSON	STA	95363		47	B3
GRAYS WELL	IMP			112	B5
GREELEY HILL	MPA	95311		48	E1
GREEN ACRES	RCO	92343		99	D4
GREENACRES	KER	93308		78	C3
GREENBRAE	MAR	94904		L	B3
GREENFIELD	KER	93309		78	D3
* GREENFIELD	MON	93927	9,325	65	B1
GREENHAVEN	SAC	95831		39	D1
GREEN POINT	MAR	94945		L	B2
GREEN VALLEY	LACO	91350		89	C3
GREEN VALLEY ESTATES	SOL	94585		38	D3
GREEN VALLEY FALLS	SDCO	92016		107	C5
GREEN VALLEY LAKE	SBD	92341		91	D5
GREENVIEW	SIS	96037		3	D5
GREENVILLE	PLU	95947		20	C5
GREENWOOD	ED	95635		34	D3
GRENADA	SIS	96038		4	B4
* GRIDLEY	BUT	95948	4,780	25	C5
GRIMES	COL	95950		33	B2
GRIZZLY FLAT	ED	95636		35	B5
GROSSMONT	SDCO	92041		V	D3
GROVELAND	TUO	95321		48	E1
* GROVER BEACH	SLO	93433	12,100	76	A4
GROVERS HOT SPRINGS	ALP	96120		36	B5
* GUADALUPE	SB	93434	6,250	76	B5
GUALALA	MEN	95445		30	D4
GUASTI	SBD	91743		U	E2
GUATAY	SDCO	92031		107	C5
GUERNEVILLE	SON	95446		37	C2
GUERNEWOOD PARK	SON	95446		37	C2
GUINDA	YOL	95637		32	D4
* GUSTINE	MCO	95322	4,140	47	C5

H

COMMUNITY NAME	CO.	ZIP CODE	POP.	PG.	GD.
HACIENDA	SON	95436		37	D1
HACIENDA HEIGHTS	LACO	91745		R	E5
HAIGHT-ASHBURY	SFCO	94117		142	A4
* HALF MOON BAY	SMCO	94019	10,600	N	C2
HALLELUJAH JUNCTION	LAS	96135		27	E2
HALLWOOD	YUB	95901		33	D2
HAMBURG	SIS	96045		3	C4
HAMILTON BRANCH	PLU	96137		20	C4
HAMILTON CITY	GLE	95951		24	E3
HAMMOND	TUL	93271		58	E5
HAMMONTON	YUB	95901		33	E2
HAM'S STATION	AMA	95666		41	C1
* HANFORD	KIN	93230	38,450	67	D1
HAPPY CAMP	SIS	96039		3	A4
HARBIN SPRINGS	LAK	95461		32	A4
HARBISON CANYON	SDCO	92021		107	A5
HARBOR	CUR			1	D2
HARBOR CITY	LACO	90710		S	C2
HARDWICK	KIN	93230		67	D1
HARMONY	SLO	93435		75	C2
HARMONY GROVE	SDCO	92025		106	D3
HARRIS	HUM	95447		16	D5
HARRISBURG	INY	92328		71	C1
HARRISON PARK	SDCO	92036		107	C4
HART PARK	KER	93306		78	E2
HASKELL CREEK	SIE	96124		27	B3
HAT CREEK	SHA	96040		13	D5
HATFIELD	SIS	96134		5	D2
HAVILAH	KER	93518		79	C2
* HAWAIIAN GARDENS	LACO	90716	14,500	T	A2
HAWKINSVILLE	SIS	96097		4	A4
* HAWTHORNE	LACO	90250	76,700	Q	D5
HAWTHORNE	MIN			44	B1
HAYES VALLEY	SFCO	94102		142	B4
HAYFORK	TRI	96041		17	B2
* HAYWARD	ALA	94544	122,200	L	E5
HAZEL CREEK	SHA	96017		12	C4
* HEALDSBURG	SON	95448	9,575	37	D1
HEBER	IMP	92249		112	A3
HELENA	TRI	96042		17	B1
HELENDALE	SBD	92342		91	B2
HELLS GATE	INY	92328		61	E3
HELM	FRCO	93627		57	A5
* HEMET	RCO	92343	52,600	99	E4
* HENDERSON	CLK		120,196	74	E3
HENDERSON VILLAGE	SJCO	95240		40	A4
HENLEY	KLAM			5	C1
HENLEY	SIS	96044		4	A3
HENLEYVILLE	TEH	96021		24	C1
HERALD	SAC	95632		40	B3
* HERCULES	CC	94547	18,800	L	C3
HERMIT VALLEY	ALP	95314		42	B1
* HERMOSA BEACH	LACO	90254	18,700	S	A1
HERNANDEZ	SBT	95043		65	E1
HERNDON	FRCO	93721		57	B3
* HESPERIA	SBD	92345	59,400	91	B4
HESSEL	SON	95472		37	E3
HICKMAN	STA	95323		47	E2
HIDDEN GLEN	SDCO	92001		112	B1
* HIDDEN HILLS	LACO	91302	1,860	97	A1
HIDDEN MEADOWS	SDCO	92026		106	D3
HIDDEN VALLEY	PLA	95650		34	B4
HIDDEN VALLEY LAKE	LAK	95461		32	B4
HIGGINS CORNER	NEV	95603		34	C3
* HIGHLAND	SBD	92346	40,500	99	C1
HIGHLAND PARK	LACO	90042		R	A3
HIGHLANDS HARBOR	LAK	95457		32	A3
HIGHTS CORNER	KER	93308		78	C2
HIGHWAY CITY	FRCO	93705		57	C3
HILLCREST	SHA	96065		13	B5
HILL HAVEN	MAR	94920		L	B4
* HILLSBOROUGH	SMCO	94010	11,200	N	C1
HILMAR	MCO	95324		47	E4
HILT	SIS	96043		4	A2
HINKLEY	SBD	92347		91	C1
HOAGLIN	TRI	95495		16	E5
HOBART MILLS	NEV	95734		27	D5
HOBERGS	LAK	95496		31	E4
HODSON	CAL	95228		41	A5
HOLLAND	JOS			2	D1
* HOLLISTER	SBT	95023	24,700	54	E3
HOLLOW TREE	MEN	95455		22	B2
HOLLYWOOD	LACO	90028		Q	D3
HOLLYWOOD BEACH	VEN	93035		96	A1
HOLLYWOOD-BY-THE-SEA	VEN	93035		96	A1
HOLMES	HUM	95569		16	B3
HOLT	SJCO	95234		39	E5
* HOLTVILLE	IMP	92250	5,500	109	B5
HOLY CITY	SCL	95026		P	B5
HOME GARDENS	RCO	91720		99	A3
HOMELAND	RCO	92348		99	D4
HONCUT	BUT	95965		33	D1
HONEYDEW	HUM	95545		15	E4
HOOD	SAC	95639		39	D2
HOOPA	HUM	95546		10	C4
HOPETON	MCO	95369		48	B3
HOPE VLY FOREST CAMP	ALP	96120		36	B5
HOPLAND	MEN	95449		31	B3
HORNBROOK	SIS	96044		4	B3
HORNITOS	MPA	95325		48	E3
HORSE CREEK	SIS	96045		3	C3
HOT SPRINGS	KLAM			6	A1
HOUGH SPRINGS	LAK	95443		32	A2
HOWLAND FLAT	SIE	95981		26	D3
HUASNA	SLO	93402		76	D4
* HUGHSON	STA	95326	3,530	47	E2
HULBURD GROVE	SDCO	92016		107	C5
HULLVILLE	LAK	95469		23	C5
-- HUMBOLDT COUNTY	HUM		125,500		
HUME	FRCO	93628		58	E3
HUMPHREYS STATION	FRCO	93612		58	A2
* HUNTINGTON BEACH	ORCO	92646	187,200	T	B4
HUNTINGTON LAKE	FRCO	93629		50	B5
* HUNTINGTON PARK	LACO	90255	60,200	R	A5
HURLETON	BUT	95962		25	E4
* HURON	FRCO	93234	5,525	67	A2
HYAMPOM	TRI	96046		16	E2
HYDESVILLE	HUM	95547		15	E2

I

COMMUNITY NAME	CO.	ZIP CODE	POP.	PG.	GD.
IDYLLWILD	RCO	92349		100	B4
IDYLWILD	SCL	95030		P	B4
IGNACIO	MAR	94947		L	B2
IGO	SHA	96047		18	B3
ILLINOIS VALLEY	JOS			2	C2
* IMPERIAL	IMP	92251	6,950	109	A5
* IMPERIAL BEACH	SDCO	92032	27,850	V	B5
-- IMPERIAL COUNTY	IMP		140,100		
IMPERIAL GABLES	IMP	92266		110	A3
INCLINE	MPA	95318		49	C2
INCLINE VILLAGE	WSH			36	A1
INDEPENDENCE	CAL	95245		41	B2
INDEPENDENCE	INY	93526		60	A3
INDIAN FALLS	PLU	95952		26	C1
INDIAN SPRINGS	SDCO	92035		112	A1
* INDIAN WELLS	RCO	92260	3,080	100	E4
* INDIO	RCO	92201	42,100	101	A4
INDIO HILLS	RCO			101	B3
* INGLEWOOD	LACO	90301	116,000	Q	D5
INGOT	SHA	96008		18	E1
INSKIP	BUT	95921		25	D1
INVERNESS	MAR	94937		37	D4
INVERNESS PARK	MAR	94937		37	D4
INWOOD	SHA	96088		19	A2
-- INYO COUNTY	INY		18,500		
INYOKERN	KER	93527		80	D1
* IONE	AMA	95640	7,200	40	D2
IOWA HILL	PLA	95713		34	D2
* IRVINE	ORCO	92715	127,200	T	E4
IRVING'S CREST	SDCO	92065		107	A4
IRVINGTON	ALA	94538		P	A2
IRWIN	MCO	95380		47	E4
* IRWINDALE	LACO	91706	1,090	R	E3
ISLA VISTA	SB	93117		87	B4
* ISLETON	SAC	95641	830	M	D2
IVANHOE	TUL	93235		68	B1
IVANPAH	SBD	92364		84	C3

J

COMMUNITY NAME	CO.	ZIP CODE	POP.	PG.	GD.
* JACKSON	AMA	95642	3,880	40	E2
-- JACKSON COUNTY	JKSN		164,400		
JACKSON GATE	AMA	95642		40	E2
JACUMBA	SDCO	92034		111	B4
JAMACHA	SDCO	92035		106	E4
JAMESBURG	MON	93924		64	D1
JAMESTOWN	TUO	95327		41	C5
JAMUL	SDCO	92035		112	A1
JANESVILLE	LAS	96114		21	A4
JARBO GAP	BUT	95916		25	D3
JEAN	CLK			74	C5
JENNER	SON	95450		37	B2
JENNY LIND	CAL	95252		40	D4
JESMOND DENE	SDCO	92026		106	D3
JIMTOWN	SON	95959		31	E5
JOHANNESBURG	KER	93528		80	D3
JOHNSON PARK	SHA	96013		13	C5
JOHNSONDALE	TUL	93236		69	C4
JOHNSONS	HUM	95546		10	B2
JOHNSTONVILLE	LAS	96130		21	A3
JOHNSTOWN	SDCO	92021		107	A5
JOHNSVILLE	PLU	95921		26	E3
JOLON	MON	93928		65	B4
JONESVILLE	BUT	95921		19	E5
JORDAN HTS/LAUREL HTS	SFCO	94118		141	E3
-- JOSEPHINE COUNTY	JOS		71,100		
JOSHUA TREE	SBD	92252		100	E1
JULIAN	SDCO	92036		107	C3
JUNCTION CITY	TRI	96048		17	C1
JUNE LAKE	MNO	93529		50	D1
JUNE LAKE JUNCTION	MNO	93529		50	D1
JUNIPER FLATS	RCO	92367		99	D3
JUNIPER LAKE RESORT	LAS	96020		20	A3

K

COMMUNITY NAME	CO.	ZIP CODE	POP.	PG.	GD.
KAGEL CANYON	LACO	91342		Q	D1
KANE SPRING	IMP	92227		108	D3
KARNAK	SUT	95676		33	C4
KAWEAH	TUL	93237		58	E5
KEARNEY PARK	FRCO	93706		57	B3
KEARNY MESA	SDCO	92111		V	B2
KEARSARGE	INY	93526		60	A3
KEDDIE	PLU	95952		26	C1
KEELER	INY	93530		60	C5
KEENE	KER	93531		79	B4
KELLOGG	SON	94515		31	E5
KELSEY	ED	95643		34	D4
KELSEYVILLE	LAK	95451		31	D3
KELSO	SBD	92351		83	E5
KENO	KLAM			5	A1
KENSINGTON	CC	94708		L	D3
KENSINGTON	SDCO	92116		V	C3
KENTFIELD	MAR	94904		L	A3
KENTWOOD IN THE PINES	SDCO	92036		107	C4
KENWOOD	SON	95452		38	B2
KEOUGH HOT SPRINGS	INY	93514		51	D4
KERBY	JOS			2	D1
KERCKOFF POWERHOUSE	FRCO	93602		57	E1
* KERMAN	FRCO	93630	6,725	57	A3
KERN CITY	KER	93309		78	C3
-- KERN COUNTY	KER		624,700		
KERNVALE	KER	93240		79	C1
KERNVILLE	KER	93238		69	C5
KESWICK	SHA	96001		18	B2
KETTLEMAN CITY	KIN	93239		67	B3
KEYES	STA	95328		47	D3
KILKARE	ALA	94586		P	B1
* KING CITY	MON	93930	9,900	65	C2
KING COLE	KLAM			4	D1
KINGS BEACH	PLA	95719		36	A1
* KINGSBURG	FRCO	93631	8,450	57	D5
KINGSBURY	DGL			36	B3
-- KINGS COUNTY	KIN		118,900		
KINGS MOUNTAIN	SMCO	94062		N	C3
KINGSVILLE	ED	95623		34	D5
KINGVALE	NEV	95728		35	C1
KINSLEY	MPA	95311		49	B2
KIRKVILLE	SUT	95645		33	B3
KIRKWOOD	ALP	95646		36	A5
KIRKWOOD	TEH	96021		24	D2
KIT CARSON	AMA	95644		35	E5
KLAMATH	DN	95548		2	A5
-- KLAMATH COUNTY	KLAM		61,600		
-- KLAMATH FALLS	KLAM		18,680	5	B1
KLAMATH GLEN	DN	95548		2	A5
KLAMATH RIVER	SIS	96050		3	D3
KLAU	SLO	93465		75	D1
KNEELAND	HUM	95549		16	B1
KNIGHTS FERRY	STA	95367		48	A1
KNIGHTS LANDING	YOL	95645		33	C4
KNIGHTSEN	CC	94548		M	D3
KNOB	SHA	96076		17	C3
KNOWLES	MAD	93653		49	B5
KNOWLES CORNER	SON	95472		37	D2
KNOXVILLE	NAPA	95637		32	C4
KONO TAYEE	LAK	95458		31	E3
KORBEL	HUM	95550		10	B5
KORBEL	SON	95550		37	D1
KRAMER	SBD	93516		80	E5
KYBURZ	ED	95720		35	D4

L

COMMUNITY NAME	CO.	ZIP CODE	POP.	PG.	GD.
LA BARR MEADOWS	NEV	95945		34	C2
* LA CANADA FLINTRIDGE	LACO	91011	20,000	R	B2
LA CONCHITA	VEN	93001		87	E5
LA COSTA	SDCO	92008		106	C3
LA CRESCENTA	LACO	91214		R	A2
LADERA	SMCO	94025		N	D3
* LAFAYETTE	CC	94549	23,550	L	E4
LA GRANGE	STA	95329		48	C2
* LAGUNA BEACH	ORCO	92651	23,800	T	E5
LAGUNA CREEK	SAC	95758		39	E2
* LAGUNA HILLS	ORCO	92653	25,000	98	D5
* LAGUNA NIGUEL	ORCO	92677	55,600	98	D5
LAGUNA WEST	SAC	95758		39	E2
LAGUNITAS	MAR	94938		38	A5
* LA HABRA	ORCO	90631	54,100	R	E5
* LA HABRA HEIGHTS	LACO	90631	6,550	R	D5
LA HONDA	SMCO	94020		45	D4
LA HONDA PARK	CAL	94020		41	B4
LAIRDS CORNER	TUL	93257		68	B3
LA JOLLA	SDCO	92037		105	G3
LA JOLLA AMAGO	SDCO	92060		107	A2
LA JOLLA SHORES	SDCO	92037		211	A1
LAKE	SFCO	94118		141	D3
LAKE ALPINE	ALP	95235		42	A1
LAKE ARROWHEAD	SBD	92352		91	C5
LAKE BERRYESSA ESTATES	NAPA	94567		32	C5
LAKE CITY	MOD	96115		7	D5
LAKE CITY	NEV	95959		26	D5
-- LAKE COUNTY (CA)	LAE		55,300		
-- LAKE COUNTY (OR)	LAKE		7,550		
* LAKE ELSINORE	RCO	92330	25,600	99	B4
* LAKE FOREST	ORCO	92630	57,600	98	D4
LAKE FOREST	PLA	95730		35	E2
* LAKE HAVASU CITY	MOH		36,285	96	B4
LAKEHEAD	SHA	96051		12	C5
LAKE HENSHAW	SDCO	92070		107	B3
LAKE HILLS EST	ED	95630		34	C5
LAKE HUGHES	LACO	93532		89	C3
LAKE ISABELLA	KER	93240		79	C1
LAKELAND VILLAGE	RCO	92330		99	B5
LAKE OF THE WOODS	KER	93225		88	C2
* LAKEPORT	LAK	95453	4,580	31	D3
LAKE RIVERSIDE	RCO	92302		100	B5
LAKESHORE	FRCO	93634		50	C5
LAKESHORE	SHA	96051		12	B5
LAKESIDE	SDCO	92040		V	E2
* LAKEVIEW	LAKE		2,645	7	C1
LAKEVIEW	RCO	92353		99	D3
LAKEVIEW	SDCO	92040		107	A5
LAKEVIEW TERRACE	LACO	91340		Q	D1
LAKEVILLE	SON	95954		L	B1
* LAKEWOOD	LACO	90712	77,100	S	E2
LA LOMA	STA	95354		47	D2
* LA MESA	SDCO	92041	56,600	V	D3
* LA MIRADA	LACO	90638	45,800	T	B1
LA MOINE	SHA	96017		12	C4
LAMONT	KER	93241		78	E3
LANARE	FRCO	93656		57	B5
* LANCASTER	LACO	93534	121,000	90	A3
LANDERS	SBD	92284		92	E5
LANGELL VALLEY	KLAM			6	B2
* LA PALMA	ORCO	90623	15,500	T	B2
-- LA PAZ COUNTY	LPAZ		16,550		
LA PLAYA	SDCO	92106		V	A3
LA PORTE	PLU	95981		26	C3
LA PRESA	SDCO	92077		V	E4
* LA PUENTE	LACO	91744	40,400	R	E4
* LA QUINTA	RCO	92253	18,050	100	E4
* LARKSPUR	MAR	94939	11,600	L	A3
LAS CRUCES	SB	93117		86	D4
LA SIERRA	RCO	92505		99	A3
LAS LOMAS	MON	95076		54	C3
LAS LOMAS	SON	95412		31	B5
-- LASSEN COUNTY	LAS		31,050		
* LAS VEGAS	CLK	89114	383,369	74	D2
* LATHROP	SJCO	95330	8,850	47	B1
LATON	FRCO	93242		57	D5
LATROBE	ED	95682		40	C1
LAUGHLIN	CLK			85	D4
LAUREL HEIGHTS	SFCO	94118		141	E3
* LA VERNE	LACO	91750	32,300	U	B2
* LAWNDALE	LACO	90260	29,450	S	B1
LAYTONVILLE	MEN	95454		22	D3
LE GRAND	MCO	95333		48	D5
LEBEC	KER	93243		88	D1
LEE VINING	MNO	93541		43	C5
LEESVILLE	COL	95987		32	B2
LEGGETT	MEN	95455		22	C2
LEISURE TOWN	SOL	95688		39	A2
LEISURE WORLD	ORCO	90740		98	A4
LEISURE WORLD	ORCO	92653		98	D5
LELITER	KER	93527		70	D5
LEMONCOVE	TUL	93244		68	D1
* LEMON GROVE	SDCO	92045	24,700	V	D3
LEMON HEIGHTS	ORCO	92705		T	E3
LEMON VALLEY	WSH	96109		28	B3
* LEMOORE	KIN	93245	16,350	67	C1
LENWOOD	SBD	92311		91	D1
LEONA VALLEY	LACO	93551		89	D3
LEUCADIA	SDCO	92024		106	B3
LEWISTON	TRI	96052		17	D1
LIBERTY FARMS	SOL	95647		39	C3
LIDO ISLE	ORCO	92660		T	C4
LIKELY	MOD	96116		8	B3
LINCOLN	JKSN			4	C2
* LINCOLN	PLA	95648	7,950	34	A3
LINCOLN ACRES	SDCO	92050		V	D4
LINCOLN VILLAGE	SJCO	95207		40	A5
LINDA	YUB	95961		33	D2

* INDICATES INCORPORATED CITY

CITIES AND COMMUNITIES

I

COMMUNITY NAME	CO.	ZIP CODE	POP.	PG.	GD.
LINDA MAR	SMCO	94044		N	B1
LINDA VISTA	SDCO	92111		V	B3
LINDCOVE	TUL	93221		68	C1
LINDEN	SJCO	95236		40	C5
LINDSAY	TUL	93247	8,825	68	D2
LINGARD	MCO	95340		48	C5
LITCHFIELD	LAS	96117		21	C3
LITTLE LAKE	INY	93542		70	C4
LITTLE RIVER	MEN	95456		30	B1
LITTLEROCK	LACO	93543		90	B3
LITTLE SHASTA	SIS	96064		4	C4
LITTLE VALLEY	LAS	96053		14	B5
LIVE OAK	SUT	95953	5,275	33	C1
LIVE OAK PARK	SDCO	92028		106	C2
LIVE OAK SPRINGS	SDCO	92005		112	E1
LIVERMORE	ALA	94550	65,400	M	C5
LIVINGSTON	MCO	95334	10,450	48	A4
LOCH LOMOND	LAK	95426		31	E4
LOCKE	SAC	95690		39	D3
LOCKEFORD	SJCO	95237		40	B4
LOCKWOOD	MON	93932		65	C4
LOCKWOOD VALLEY	VEN	93225		88	C2
LODGE POLE	TUL	93271		59	B4
LODI	SJCO	95240	54,500	40	A4
LODOGA	COL	95979		32	B1
LOGAN HEIGHTS	SDCO	92113		V	B4
LOG CABIN	YUB	95922		26	C5
LOG SPRING	TEH	96074		14	E4
LOLETA	HUM	95551		15	E2
LOMA LINDA	SBD	92354	21,200	99	C2
LOMA MAR	SMCO	94021		N	C4
LOMA PARK	KER	93306		78	E3
LOMA RICA	YUB	95901		33	E1
LOMITA	LACO	90717	20,100	S	C2
LOMO	BUT	95942		25	C1
LOMPOC	SB	93436	41,000	86	B3
LONDON	TUL	93631		58	A5
LONE MOUNTAIN	SFCO	94118		141	E3
LONE PINE	INY	93545		60	B4
LONG BARN	TUO	95335		41	E4
LONG BEACH	LACO	90801	437,800	S	D3
LONGVALE	MEN	95490		22	E4
LONGVIEW	LACO	93553		90	C4
LOOKOUT	MOD	96054		18	A3
LOOMIS	PLA	95650	6,025	34	B4
LOOMIS CORNERS	SHA	96003		18	C2
LORAINE	KER	93518		79	D3
LORELLA	KLAM			6	A1
LOS ALAMITOS	ORCO	90720	12,300	T	A2
LOS ALAMOS	SB	93440		86	C2
LOS ALTOS	SCL	94022	27,300	N	E3
LOS ALTOS HILLS	SCL	94022	7,800	N	E3
LOS ANGELES	LACO	90001	3,638,100	R	A4
LOS ANGELES COUNTY	LACO		9,369,800		
LOS BANOS	MCO	93635	20,100	55	E1
LOS GATOS	SCL	95030	28,950	P	A4
LOS MOLINOS	TEH	96055		24	E1
LOS OLIVOS	SB	93441		86	E3
LOS OSOS	SLO	93402		75	E3
LOS RANCHITOS	MAR	94903		L	A3
LOS SERRANOS	SBD	91709		U	C3
LOS TRANCOS WOODS	SMCO	94025		N	D3
LOST HILLS	KER	93249		77	D1
LOTUS	ED	95651		34	D4
LOVELOCK	BUT	95978		25	D2
LOWER LAKE	LAK	95457		32	A4
LOYALTON	SIE	96118	890	27	C3
LUCERNE	LAK	95458		31	D2
LUCERNE VALLEY	SBD	92356		91	E4
LUCIA	MON	93920		64	D3
LUDLOW	SBD	92357		93	B2
LUNDY	MNO	93541		43	B4
LUNING	MIN			44	E1
LYNWOOD	LACO	90262	65,900	S	D1
LYNWOOD HILLS	SDCO	92010		V	D4
LYON COUNTY	LYON		20,001		
LYONSVILLE	TEH	96075		19	C4
LYTLE CREEK	SBD	92358		91	A5
LYTTON	SON	95448		31	D5

M

COMMUNITY NAME	CO.	ZIP CODE	POP.	PG.	GD.
MACDOEL	SIS	96058		4	E3
MADELINE	LAS	96119		8	B4
MADERA	MAD	93637	34,650	57	A2
MADERA COUNTY	MAD		108,900		
MADISON	YOL	95653		33	A5
MAD RIVER	TRI	95552		16	E3
MADRONE	SCL	95037		P	D5
MAGALIA	BUT	95954		25	C2
MAGUNDEN	KER	93306		78	E3
MALAGA	FRCO	93725		57	D4
MALIBU	LACO	90265	12,200	97	B2
MALIBU BEACH	LACO	90265		97	B2
MALIN	KLAM		730	5	E2
MAMMOTH LAKES	MNO	93546	5,275	50	D2
MANCHESTER	MEN	95459		30	C3
MANHATTAN BEACH	LACO	90266	33,900	S	A1
MANKAS CORNER	SOL	94533		L	E1
MANTECA	SJCO	95336	44,950	47	B1
MANTON	TEH	96059		19	A3
MANZANITA	SDCO	92005		111	A4
MAPLE CREEK	HUM	95550		16	B1
MARCH AFB	RCO	92508		99	C3
MARICOPA	KER	93252	1,240	78	A5
MARINA	MON	93933	17,750	54	B4
MARINA	SFCO	94123		142	B1
MARINA DEL REY	LACO	90291		Q	B5
MARIN CITY	MAR	94965		L	B4
MARIN COUNTY	MAR		239,500		
MARINWOOD	MAR	94903		L	A3
MARIPOSA	MPA	95338		49	B3
MARIPOSA COUNTY	MPA		16,050		
MARIPOSA PINES	MPA	95338		49	B2
MARKLEEVILLE	ALP	96120		36	C5
MARK WEST	SON	95492		37	E2

COMMUNITY NAME	CO.	ZIP CODE	POP.	PG.	GD.
MARK WEST SPRINGS	SON	95492		37	E1
MARSHALL	MAR	94950		37	D4
MARSHALL STATION	FRCO	93651		57	E2
MARTELL	AMA	95654		40	E2
* MARTINEZ	CC	94553	35,150	L	E3
MARTINS FERRY	HUM	95556		10	C3
MAR VISTA	LACO	90066		Q	C4
* MARYSVILLE	YUB	95901	62,200	33	D2
MASONIC	MNO	93517		43	C2
MATHER	TUO	95339		42	B5
MAXWELL	COL	95955		32	D1
MAYFAIR	KER	93307		78	E3
* MAYWOOD	LACO	90270	29,150	R	A4
MCARTHUR	SHA	96056		13	E4
MCCANN	HUM	95569		16	B4
MCCAULEY	MPA	93518		49	C2
MCCLOUD	SIS	96057		12	D2
* MCFARLAND	KER	93250	7,950	78	B1
MCKAYS POINT	TUL	93286		68	D1
MCKEE BRIDGE	JKSN			3	C1
MCKINLEYVILLE	HUM	95521		9	E4
MCKITTRICK	KER	93251		77	D3
MCMULLIN	FRCO	93706		57	B4
MEADOW LAKES	FRCO	93602		58	A1
MEADOW VALLEY	PLU	95956		26	B2
MEADOW VISTA	PLA	95722		34	C3
MECCA	RCO	92254		101	C5
MEEKS BAY	ED	95723		35	E2
MEINERS OAKS	VEN	93023		88	A4
MELOLAND	IMP	92243		112	B3
MENDOCINO	MEN	95460		30	B1
MENDOCINO COAST	MEN	95459		30	C3
-- MENDOCINO COUNTY	MEN		84,500		
* MENDOTA	FRCO	93640	7,400	56	D3
* MENLO PARK	SMCO	94025	30,200	N	D2
MENTONE	SBD	92359		99	D2
* MERCED	MCO	95340	61,000	48	C4
MERCED COUNTY	MCO	95369	198,800	48	D3
MERCED FALLS	MCO	95369		48	D3
MERCY HOT SPRINGS	FRCO	95043		55	E4
MERIDIAN	SUT	95957		33	B2
* MERRILL	KLAM		837	5	D2
MESA GRANDE	SDCO	92070		107	B3
MESQUITE SPRING	INY	92328		61	B2
METTLER	KER	93301		78	E5
MEXICALI	BAJA			112	B4
MEYERS	ED	95731		36	A4
MI-WUK VILLAGE	TUO	95346		41	E4
MICHIGAN BAR	SAC	95683		40	C1
MICHIGAN BLUFF	PLA	95631		35	A2
MIDDLE RIVER	SJCO	95234		39	D5
MIDDLETOWN	LAK	95461		32	A5
MIDDLETOWN	SDCO	92103		215	D2
MIDLAND	KLAM			5	B1
MIDLAND	RCO	92255		103	B3
MIDPINES	MPA	95345		49	B3
MIDWAY	ALA	94550		M	E5
MIDWAY	SHA	96088		19	A2
MIDWAY CITY	ORCO	92655		T	C3
MIDWAY WELL	IMP			112	E3
MILFORD	LAS	96121		21	C5
* MILLBRAE	SMCO	94030	21,250	N	C1
MILL CREEK	TEH	96061		19	D4
MILLERS CORNER	MAD	93614		57	C1
MILLS ORCHARDS	COL	95955		32	C1
* MILL VALLEY	MAR	94941	13,750	L	A3
MILLVILLE	SHA	96062		18	D2
MILO	TUL	93265		68	E2
* MILPITAS	SCL	95035	59,700	P	B3
MILTON	CAL	95230		40	E4
MINA	MIN			44	E2
* MINDEN	DGL		1,441	36	C3
MINERAL	TEH	96063		19	C4
-- MINERAL COUNTY	MIN		6,475		
MINERAL KING	TUL	93271		59	B5
MINKLER	FRCO	93657		58	A3
MINNESOTA	SHA	96001		18	B2
MINTER VILLAGE	KER	93301		78	C2
MIRABEL PARK	SON	95436		37	D2
MIRACLE HOT SPRINGS	KER	93288		79	C1
MIRA LOMA	RCO	91752		98	E2
MIRAMAR	SDCO	92145		V	B1
MIRAMAR	SMCO	94019		N	B2
MIRAMONTE	FRCO	93641		58	C3
MIRA MONTE	VEN	93023		88	A4
MIRANDA	HUM	95553		16	C4
MIRA VISTA	LAK	95461		31	E4
MISSION BAY PARK	SDCO	92109		212	C4
MISSION BEACH	SDCO	92109		V	A3
MISSION DELORES	SFCO	94110		142	C5
MISSION HILLS	SDCO	92103		V	B3
MISSION SAN JOSE	ALA	94538		P	B2
MISSION VALLEY	SDCO	92108		214	A3
* MISSION VIEJO	ORCO	92690	89,900	98	D5
MISSION VILLAGE	SDCO	92123		V	C2
MITCHELL MILL	CAL	95255		41	B2
MOCCASIN	TUO	95347		48	D1
* MODESTO	MDO	95350	178,700	47	D2
MODJESKA	ORCO	92669		98	E4
-- MODOC COUNTY	MOD	95350	10,150	47	D2
-- MOHAVE COUNTY	MOH		124,500		
MOJAVE	KER	93501		80	A5
MOKELUMNE HILL	CAL	95245		41	A3
MONARCH BEACH	ORCO	92677		98	D5
MONMOUTH	FRCO	93725		57	C4
MONO CAMP	MPA	95338		49	B3
MONO CITY	MNO	93541		43	C4
MONO HOT SPRINGS	FRCO	93642		50	D4
MONO LAKE	MNO	93541		43	C5
MONOLITH	KER	93548		79	D4
MONO VISTA	TUO	95370		41	D4
* MONROVIA	LACO	91016	38,900	R	D3
MONSON	TUL	93618		58	B5
* MONTAGUE	SIS	96064	1,370	4	B4
MONTALVO	VEN	93003		88	B5
MONTARA	SMCO	94037		N	B2

COMMUNITY NAME	CO.	ZIP CODE	POP.	PG.	GD.
MONTCLAIR	ALA			L	D4
* MONTCLAIR	SBD	91763	29,950	U	C2
* MONTEBELLO	LACO	90640	62,100	R	C4
MONTECITO	SB	93108		87	D4
MONTE MARIA	MAR	94947		L	A2
MONTE NIDO	LACO	91302		97	B2
* MONTEREY	MON	93940	32,200	54	B4
-- MONTEREY COUNTY	MON		364,500		
MONTEREY HILLS	LACO	90032		R	B3
* MONTEREY PARK	LACO	91754	64,000	R	B4
MONTE RIO	SON	95462		37	C2
* MONTE SERENO	SCL	95030	3,280	P	A4
MONTEZUMA	SOL	94512		39	B4
MONTGOMERY CREEK	SHA	96065		13	A5
MONTROSE	LACO	91020		Q	E2
MOONRIDGE	SBD	92315		92	A5
MOONSTONE	HUM	95570		9	E4
* MOORPARK	VEN	93021	27,750	88	D5
MOORPARK HOME ACRES	VEN	93021		88	D5
* MORAGA	CC	94556	16,300	L	E4
MORENA VILLAGE	SDCO	92006		112	D1
MORENO	SDCO	92040		107	A5
* MORENO VALLEY	RCO	92388	133,400	99	D3
MORETTIS	SDCO	92070		107	B3
* MORGAN HILL	SCL	95037	27,950	P	D5
MORMON BAR	MPA	95338		49	B3
MORONGO VALLEY	SBD	92256		100	C2
* MORRO BAY	SLO	93442	9,675	75	E3
MOSS BEACH	SMCO	94038		N	B2
MOSS LANDING	MON	95039		54	B3
MOUNTAIN CENTER	RCO	92361		100	B4
MOUNTAIN GATE	SHA	96003		18	C1
MOUNTAIN HOME VILLAGE	SBD	92359		99	E1
MOUNTAIN HOUSE	ALA	94550		46	D2
MOUNTAIN MESA	KER	93240		79	D1
MOUNTAIN RANCH	CAL	95246		41	B3
MOUNTAIN REST	FRCO	93667		58	B1
MOUNTAIN SPRINGS	CLK			74	A3
* MOUNTAIN VIEW	SCL	94040	71,300	N	E3
MOUNTAIN VIEW	SDCO	92102		216	D4
MOUNT AUKUM	ED	95656		40	E1
MOUNT BALDY VILLAGE	SBD	91759		90	E5
MOUNT BULLION	MPA	95338		49	A3
MOUNT CHARLESTON	CLK			74	A2
MOUNT HEBRON	SIS	96066		5	A4
MOUNT HELIX	SDCO	92041		V	D3
MOUNT HERMON	SCR	95041		P	A5
MOUNT HOPE	SDCO	92102		216	D3
MOUNT LAGUNA	SDCO	92048		107	E5
* MOUNT SHASTA	SIS	96067	3,520	12	C2
MOUNT SIGNAL	IMP	92231		112	A4
MOUNT VIEW	JKSN			4	C1
MOUNT WILSON	LACO	91023		R	C2
MUGGINSVILLE	SIS	96032		3	C5
MUIR BEACH	MAR	94965		L	A4
MULFORD GARDENS	ALA			L	D5
MURPHYS	CAL	95247		41	C4
MURPHYS RANCH	CAL	95247		41	C4
* MURRIETA	RCO	92362	34,550	99	C5
MURRIETA HOT SPRINGS	RCO	92362		99	C5
MUSCOY	SBD	92405		99	B1
MYERS FLAT	HUM	95554		16	B4

N

COMMUNITY NAME	CO.	ZIP CODE	POP.	PG.	GD.
NAIRN	MCO	95340		48	B4
NANCEVILLE	TUL	93257		68	D3
* NAPA	NAPA	94558	66,900	L	D1
-- NAPA COUNTY	NAP		119,000		
NAPLES	LACO	90803		S	E3
NAPLES	SB	93117		87	A4
NASHVILLE	ED	95675		40	E1
* NATIONAL CITY	SDCO	92050	54,700	V	C4
NATOMA	SAC	95630		34	B5
NAVARRO	MEN	95463		30	D2
NAVELENCIA	FRCO	93654		58	A4
* NEEDLES	SBD	92363	5,750	95	D2
NEENACH	LACO	93534		89	B2
NELSON	BUT	95958		25	B4
NESTOR	SDCO	92154		V	C5
* NEVADA CITY	NEV	95959	2,830	34	C1
-- NEVADA COUNTY	NEV		87,000		
NEW ALMADEN	SCL	95042		P	C4
NEW AUBERRY	FRCO	93602		57	E1
* NEWARK	ALA	94560	40,000	P	A2
NEWBERRY SPRINGS	SBD	92365		92	B2
NEWBURY PARK	VEN	91320		96	D1
NEWCASTLE	PLA	95658		34	C4
NEW CUYAMA	SB	93254		87	C1
NEWELL	MOD	96134		5	E3
NEWHALL	LACO	91321		89	C5
NEWHOPE LANDING	SJCO			39	D3
NEW IDAHO	LAKE			7	B1
NEW IDRIA	SBT	95027		66	A1
* NEWMAN	STA	95360	5,750	47	C4
NEW PINE CREEK	MOD	97635		7	C2
* NEWPORT BEACH	ORCO	92660	69,100	T	C4
NEWPORT CENTER	ORCO	92660		T	D4
NEWTOWN	ED	95709		35	A5
NEWVILLE	GLE	95963		24	B3
NEW WASHOE CITY	WSH	95611		36	C1
NICASIO	MAR	94946		37	E4
NICE	LAK	95464		31	D2
NICHOLLS WARM SPRINGS	RCO	92225		103	C5
NICHOLS	CC	94565		39	A4
NICOLAUS	SUT	95659		33	D3
NILAND	IMP	92257		109	B2
NIMBUS	SAC	94536		40	B1
NIPINNAWASSEE	MAD	93601		49	C4
NIPOMO	SLO	93444		76	C5
NIPTON	SBD	92364		84	C2
NIXON	WSH	96109		28	E2
NOB HILL	SFCO	94108		142	D2
NOE VALLEY	SFCO	94114		142	A5
* NORCO	RCO	91760	24,500	U	E4

COMMUNITY NAME	CO.	ZIP CODE	POP.	PG.	GD.
NORD	BUT	95926		25	A3
NORDEN	NEV	95724		35	C1
NORMAN	GLE	95988		24	D5
NORTH BEACH	SFCO	94133		142	D1
NORTH BLOOMFIELD	NEV	95959		26	D5
NORTH COLUMBIA	NEV	95959		26	C5
NORTH EDWARDS	KER	93523		80	D5
NORTH FORK	MAD	93643		49	E5
NORTH HIGHLANDS	SAC	95660		34	A5
NORTH HILLS	LA	91335		Q	B2
NORTH HOLLYWOOD	LACO	91601		Q	C2
NORTH JAMUL	SDCO	92035		112	A1
* NORTH LAS VEGAS	CLK		80,991	74	D2
NORTH LONG BEACH	LACO	90805		S	D2
NORTH PARK	SDCO	92104		216	B1
NORTH RICHMOND	CC	94807		L	C3
NORTHRIDGE	LACO	91324		Q	B2
NORTH SAN JUAN	NEV	95960		26	B5
NORTH SHORE	RCO	92254		101	D5
NORTHSTAR	PLA	95732		35	E1
NORTH WATERFRONT	SFCO	94113		142	D1
NORTHWOOD	ORCO	92714		T	E3
NORTHWOOD	SON	95462		37	C2
* NORWALK	LACO	90650	99,800	T	A1
* NOVATO	MAR	94949	46,500	L	A2
NOYO	MEN	95437		22	C5
NUBIEBER	LAS	96068		14	B3
NUEVO	RCO	92367		99	D3
-- NYE COUNTY	NYE		17,781		
NYLAND ACRES	VEN	93030		88	C5

O

COMMUNITY NAME	CO.	ZIP CODE	POP.	PG.	GD.
* OAKDALE	STA	95361	14,300	47	D1
OAK GLEN	SBD	92399		99	E2
OAK GROVE	SDCO	92302		107	B1
OAKGROVE	TUL	93271		59	A5
OAKHURST	MAD	93644		49	D4
* OAKLAND	ALA	94601	383,900	L	C4
OAKLEY	CC	94561		M	D3
OAK PARK	SDCO	92105		V	C3
OAK RUN	SHA	96069		18	E1
OAK VIEW	VEN	93022		88	A4
OAKVILLE	NAPA	94562		38	B2
OASIS	RCO	92274		108	B1
OATMAN	MOH			85	E5
OBRIEN	JOS			2	C2
O'BRIEN	SHA	96070		12	C5
OCCIDENTAL	SON	95465		37	C2
OCEAN BEACH	SDCO	92107		V	A3
OCEANO	SLO	93445		76	B5
* OCEANSIDE	SDCO	92054	147,200	106	B3
OCEAN VIEW	SON	95450		37	C2
OCOTILLO	IMP	92259		111	C3
OCOTILLO WELLS	SDCO	92004		108	B3
OGILBY	IMP	92222		110	B5
OILDALE	KER	93308		78	D2
* OJAI	VEN	93023	8,075	88	B4
OLANCHA	INY	93549		70	B1
OLD BORREGO	SDCO	92004		107	E3
OLD RIVER	KER	93307		78	C3
OLD STATION	SHA	96071		19	D1
OLD TOWN	LAS	96137		20	C4
OLEMA	MAR	94950		37	E4
OLENE	KLAM			5	C1
OLINDA	ORCO	92621		T	D1
OLINDA	SHA	96007		18	C3
OLINGHOUSE	WSH			28	E3
OLIVE	ORCO	92665		T	D2
OLIVEHURST	YUB	95961		33	D2
OLIVENHAIN	SDCO	92024		106	C4
OLIVE VIEW	LACO	91342		Q	C1
OLYMPIC VALLEY	PLA	95730		35	D1
OMO RANCH	ED	95661		41	B1
ONEALS	MAD	93645		57	D1
ONO	SHA	96072		18	A3
* ONTARIO	SBD	91761	142,400	U	D2
ONYX	KER	93255		69	E5
OPHIR	PLA	95603		34	C4
* ORANGE	ORCO	92666	119,700	T	D2
-- ORANGE COUNTY	ORCO		2,624,300		
* ORANGE COVE	FRCO	93646		58	B4
ORANGE PARK ACRES	ORCO	92669		U	C5
ORANGEVALE	SAC	95662		34	B5
ORCHARD SHORES	LAK	95423		32	A3
ORCUTT	SB	93455		86	C1
ORDBEND	GLE	95943		25	A3
OREGON HOUSE	YUB	95962		26	A5
ORICK	HUM	95555		10	A2
* ORINDA	CC	94563	16,850	L	D4
ORINDA VILLAGE	CC	94563		L	D4
* ORLAND	GLE	95963	5,625	24	D3
ORLEANS	HUM	95556		10	D2
ORO FINO	SIS	96032		3	D5
ORO GRANDE	SBD	92368		91	B3
ORO LOMA	FRCO	93622		56	A2
OROSI	TUL	93647		58	B4
* OROVILLE	BUT	95965	12,400	25	C4
ORR SPRINGS	MEN	95482		31	A1
OTAY	SDCO	92011		V	C5
OUTINGDALE	ED	95684		34	E5
* OXNARD	VEN	93030	153,300	96	B1

P

COMMUNITY NAME	CO.	ZIP CODE	POP.	PG.	GD.
PACHECO	CC	94553		L	E3
* PACIFICA	SMCO	94044	39,150	N	B1
PACIFIC BEACH	SDCO	92109		V	A2
* PACIFIC GROVE	MON	93950	17,150	54	A4
PACIFIC HEIGHTS	SFCO	94115		142	B2
PACIFIC HOUSE	ED	95725		35	B4
PACIFIC PALISADES	LACO	90272		Q	B4
PACOIMA	LACO	91331		Q	C1
PAHRUMP	NYE			73	C2
PAICINES	SBT	95043		55	B3

*** INDICATES INCORPORATED CITY**

CITIES

CITIES AND COMMUNITIES

COMMUNITY NAME	CO.	ZIP CODE	POP.	PG.	GD.
PAINTED HILLS	RCO	92282		100	C2
PAINTERSVILLE	SAC	95615		39	D3
PAJARO	MON	95076		54	C2
PALA	SDCO	92059		106	D2
PALA MESA VILLAGE	SDCO	92028		106	D2
PALERMO	BUT	95968		25	D5
PALISADES HIGHLANDS	LACO	90272		Q	B4
PALM CITY	SDCO	92154		V	C5
* PALMDALE	LACO	93550	112,000	90	A3
* PALM DESERT	RCO	92260	33,450	100	D4
PALMS	LACO	90034		Q	C4
* PALM SPRINGS	RCO	92262	41,700	100	D3
* PALO ALTO	SCL	94301	58,500	N	E2
PALO CEDRO	SHA	96073		18	D2
PALOMA	CAL	95252		40	E3
PALOMAR MOUNTAIN	SDCO	92060		107	A2
* PALOS VERDES ESTATES	LACO	90274	13,950	S	A2
PALO VERDE	IMP	92266		110	C1
PALO VERDE	SDCO	92001		107	B5
PANAMA	KER	93309		78	D3
PANAMINT SPRINGS	INY	93545		71	A1
PANOCHE	SBT	95043		55	D4
PANORAMA CITY	LACO	91402		Q	C2
* PARADISE	BUT	95969	25,950	25	C3
PARADISE CAY	MAR	94920		38	B5
PARADISE VALLEY	SCL	95037		P	D5
PARAISO SPRINGS	MON	93960		64	E1
* PARAMOUNT	LACO	90723	53,900	S	E1
PARK VILLAGE	INY	92328		62	A5
* PARKER	LPAZ		2,950	104	B1
PARKFIELD	MON	93451		66	C4
* PARLIER	FRCO	93648	9,450	57	E4
PARNASSUS/ASHBURY HTS	SFCO	94117		142	A4
* PASADENA	LACO	91101	137,100	R	B3
PASKENTA	TEH	96074		24	B2
PASO PICACHO	SDCO	92036		107	C4
* PASO ROBLES	SLO	93446	21,450	76	A1
PATRICK CREEK	DN	95543		2	B3
* PATTERSON	STA	95363	9,600	47	B3
PATTON VILLAGE	LAS	96113		21	D5
PAUMA VALLEY	SDCO	92061		106	E2
PAYNES CREEK	TEH	96075		19	B4
PAYNESVILLE	ALP	96120		36	B4
PEANUT	TRI	96041		17	B3
PEARBLOSSOM	LACO	93553		90	C4
PEARDALE	NEV	95945		34	C1
PEARLAND	LACO	93550		90	B3
PEARSONVILLE	INY	93542		70	C5
PEBBLE BEACH	MON	93953		54	A4
PECWAN	HUM	95546		10	B2
PEDLEY	RCO	92509		99	A2
PELICAN CITY	KLAM			5	B1
PENNGROVE	SON	94951		38	A3
PENNINGTON	SUT	95953		33	C1
PENTZ	BUT	95965		25	D3
PEPPERWOOD	HUM	95565		16	A3
PERKINS	SAC	95826		39	E1
* PERRIS	RCO	92370	30,500	99	C4
PESCADERO	SMCO	94060		N	C4
* PETALUMA	SON	94952	47,700	L	A1
PETER PAM	TUO	95335		41	E4
PETERS	SJCO	95236		40	C5
PETROLIA	HUM	95558		15	D4
PHELAN	SBD	92371		90	E4
PHILLIPS	ED	95735		35	E4
PHILLIPSVILLE	HUM	95558		16	B5
PHILO	MEN	95466		30	E3
PICACHO	IMP	92222		110	D4
* PICO RIVERA	LACO	90660	61,100	R	C4
* PIEDMONT	ALA	94611	11,150	L	D4
PIERCY	MEN	95467		22	C1
PIERPONT BAY	VEN	93003		175	D4
PIKE	SIE	95922		26	C5
PILOT HILL	ED	95664		34	C4
PINE COVE	RCO	92349		100	B4
PINECREST	TUO	95364		42	A3
PINEDALE	FRCO	93650		57	C3
PINE FLAT	TUL	93207		69	B4
PINE GROVE	AMA	95665		41	A2
PINE GROVE	LAK	95426		31	E4
PINE GROVE	MEN	95460		30	B1
PINE GROVE	SHA	96003		18	C2
PINE HILLS	SDCO	92036		107	C4
PINEHURST	FRCO	93641		58	D3
PINEHURST	JKSN			4	C1
PINELAND	PLA	95718		35	E2
PINE MEADOW	RCO	92361		100	C5
PINE MOUNTAIN CLUB	KER	93225		88	B1
PINE RIDGE	FRCO	93602		58	B1
PINE VALLEY	SDCO	92062		107	D5
PINO GRANDE	ED	95634		35	A4
* PINOLE	CC	94564	18,100	L	C3
PINOLE ESTATES	CC	94564		L	D3
PINON PINES	KER	93225		88	C1
PINYON PINES	RCO	92361		100	D5
PIONEER STATION	AMA	95666		41	B2
PIONEERTOWN	SBD	92268		100	D1
PIRU	VEN	93040		88	E4
* PISMO BEACH	SLO	93449	8,175	76	B4
* PITTSBURG	CC	94565	50,400	M	B3
PITTVILLE	SHA	96056		13	E4
PIXLEY	TUL	93256		68	B4
* PLACENTIA	ORCO	92670	45,000	T	D1
-- PLACER COUNTY	PLA		206,000		
* PLACERVILLE	ED	95667	8,825	34	E5
PLAINSBURG	MCO	95333		48	D5
PLAINVIEW	TUL	93267		68	C2
PLANADA	MCO	95365		48	D4
PLASSE	AMA	95666		35	E5
PLASTER CITY	IMP	92269		108	D5
PLATINA	SHA	96076		17	D3
PLAYA DEL REY	LACO	90291		97	C2
PLEASANT GROVE	SUT	95668		33	D4
* PLEASANT HILL	CC	94523	31,450	L	E3
* PLEASANTON	ALA	94566	57,800	P	B1
PLEASANT VALLEY	ED	95709		35	A5
-- PLUMAS COUNTY	PLU		20,450		
* PLYMOUTH	AMA	95669	830	40	D2
* POINT ARENA	MEN	95468	420	30	C4
POINT LOMA	SDCO	92106		V	A3
POINT PLEASANT	SAC	95758		39	D3
POINT REYES STATION	MAR	94956		37	D4
POLLARD FLAT	SHA	96017		12	C4
POLLOCK PINES	ED	95726		35	A4
POMINS	ED	95733		35	E2
POMO	MEN	95469		31	C1
* POMONA	LACO	91766	139,800	U	C2
POND	KER	93280		68	B5
PONDEROSA	TUL	93208		69	C3
PONDEROSA BASIN	MPA	95338		49	C3
PONDEROSA SKY RANCH	TEH			19	B4
PONDOSA	SIS	96077		13	C3
POPE VALLEY	NAPA	94567		32	C5
POPLAR	TUL	93257		68	C3
POPPET FLATS	RCO			100	A3
PORT COSTA	CC	94569		L	D3
PORTER RANCH	LACO	91311		Q	A1
* PORTERVILLE	TUL	93257	34,550	68	D3
* PORT HUENEME	VEN	93041	22,250	96	B1
* PORTOLA	PLU	96122	2,140	27	B2
PORTOLA HILLS	ORCO	92679		98	D4
* PORTOLA VALLEY	SMCO	94025	4,410	N	D3
POSEY	TUL	93260		69	B5
POSTON	LPAZ			104	A2
POSTON 2	LPAZ			104	A3
POTRERO	SDCO	92063		112	C2
POTTER VALLEY	MEN	95469		31	B1
* POWAY	SDCO	92064	45,450	V	D1
POZO	SLO	93453		76	D3
PRATHER	FRCO	93651		57	E1
PRATTVILLE	PLU	95923		20	B4
PRESIDIO HEIGHTS	SFCO	94118		141	D2
PRESIDIO OF SAN FRAN	SFCO	94129		141	D2
PRESTON	SON	95425		31	C4
PRIEST	TUO	95305		48	D1
PRINCETON	COL	95970		25	A5
PRINCETON BY THE SEA	SMCO	94018		N	B2
PROBERTA	TEH	96078		24	D1
PROGRESO	BAJA			112	A4
PROJECT CITY	SHA	96079		18	C1
PRUNEDALE	MON	93901		54	C3
PUERTA LA CRUZ	SDCO	92086		107	C2
PULGA	BUT	95965		25	D2
PUMPKIN CENTER	KER	93309		78	D3

Q

COMMUNITY NAME	CO.	ZIP CODE	POP.	PG.	GD.
QUAIL VALLEY	RCO	92380		99	C4
QUAKING ASPEN	TUL	93208		69	C3
QUARTZ HILL	LACO	93536		89	E3
QUARTZSITE	LPAZ		2,005	104	B4
QUINCY	PLU	95971		26	C1
QUINCY JUNCTION	PLU	95971		26	D1

R

COMMUNITY NAME	CO.	ZIP CODE	POP.	PG.	GD.
RACKERBY	YUB	95972		25	E5
RAFAEL VILLAGE	MAR	94949		L	A2
RAILROAD FLAT	CAL	95248		41	B2
RAINBOW	SDCO	92028		106	D1
RAISIN CITY	FRCO	93652		57	B4
RAMONA	SDCO	92065		107	A4
RAMSEY	LPAZ			104	D4
RANCHITA	SDCO	92066		107	D3
RANCHO BERNARDO	SDCO	92128		106	D4
RANCHO CALIFORNIA	RCO	92390		106	D1
RANCHO CORDOVA	SAC	95670		40	B1
* RANCHO CUCAMONGA	SBD	91730	115,900	U	D2
* RANCHO MIRAGE	RCO	92270	10,550	100	D4
RANCHO MURIETA	SAC	95683		40	C1
* RANCHO PALOS VERDES	LACO	90274	42,650	S	B3
RANCHO PENASQUITOS	SDCO	92129		106	D4
RANCHO SAN DIEGO	SDCO	92078		V	E3
RANCHO SANTA FE	SDCO	92067		106	C4
RCHO SANTA MARGARITA	ORCO	92688		989	E4
RANCHO TEHAMA	TEH	96021		24	C1
RANDOLF	SIE	96126		27	C4
RANDSBURG	KER	93554		80	D3
RAVENDALE	LAS	96123		8	C5
RAYMOND	MAD	93653		49	B5
RED APPLE	CAL	95224		41	C3
REDBANK	TEH	96080		18	B5
* RED BLUFF	TEH	96080	13,050	18	C5
REDCREST	HUM	95569		16	A3
* REDDING	SHA	96001	76,700	18	C2
RED HILL	ORCO	92705		T	E3
* REDLANDS	SBD	92373	65,600	99	C2
RED MOUNTAIN	SBD	93558		80	E3
* REDONDO BEACH	LACO	90277	63,900	S	A2
REDWAY	HUM	95560		16	B5
* REDWOOD CITY	SMCO	94061	71,800	N	D2
REDWOOD ESTATES	SCL	95044		P	B4
REDWOOD SHORES	SMCO	94065		N	D2
REDWOOD VALLEY	MEN	95470		31	B1
* REEDLEY	FRCO	93654	19,100	58	A4
RENO	WSH		158,249	28	B4
RENO-STEAD	WSH			28	B3
REPRESA	SAC	95671		34	B5
REQUA	DN	95561		1	E5
RESCUE	ED	95672		34	D5
RESEDA	LACO	91335		Q	B2
REWARD	INY	93526		60	B3
RHEEM VALLEY	CC	94556		L	E4
* RIALTO	SBD	92376	80,300	99	B1
RICARDO	KER	93519		80	B3
RICE	SBD	92280		103	B2
RICHARDSON SPRINGS	BUT	95978		25	B2
RICH BAR	PLU	95915		26	B1
RICHFIELD	TEH	96083		24	D1
RICHGROVE	TUL	93261		68	C5
* RICHMOND	CC	94801	90,900	L	C3
RICHMOND	SFCO	94121		141	B4
RICHVALE	BUT	95974		25	C4
* RIDGECREST	KER	93555	29,000	80	D1
RIMFOREST	SBD	92378		99	C1
RIMROCK	SBD	92268		100	D1
RINCON	SDCO	92082		106	E2
RIO BRAVO	KER	93306		78	E2
* RIO DELL	HUM	95562	2,890	15	E3
RIO DELL	SON	95486		37	D2
RIO LINDA	SAC	95673		33	E5
RIO NIDO	SON	95471		37	D1
RIO OSO	SUT	95674		33	D3
* RIO VISTA	SOL	94571	3,660	M	D2
RIPLEY	RCO	92272		103	D5
* RIPON	SJCO	95366	9,100	47	C2
* RIVERBANK	STA	95367	13,350	47	D2
RIVERDALE	FRCO	93656		57	B5
RIVER KERN	KER	93238		69	D5
RIVER PINES	AMA	95675		40	E1
* RIVERSIDE	RCO	92501	243,400	99	B2
-- RIVERSIDE COUNTY	RCO		1,381,900		
RIVERTON	ED	95806		35	B4
RIVIERA	MOH			85	D4
RIVIERA HEIGHTS	LAK	95443		31	D3
RIVIERA WEST	LAK	95422		31	E3
ROADS END	TUL	93236		69	C4
ROBBINS	SUT	95676		33	C4
ROBINSONS CORNER	BUT	95948		25	C5
ROBLA	SAC	95673		33	E5
ROCKAWAY BEACH	SMCO	94044		N	B1
ROCK HAVEN	SDCO	92065		106	E4
* ROCKLIN	PLA	95677	26,900	34	B4
ROCKPORT	MEN	95488		22	B3
ROCKVILLE	SOL	94585		38	E3
RODEO	CC	94572		L	D3
ROGERS LANDING	MOH			85	D4
* ROHNERT PARK	SON	94928	38,350	38	A2
ROHNERVILLE	HUM	95540		15	E2
ROLANDO	SDCO	92115		V	C3
ROLINDA	FRCO	93705		57	B3
* ROLLING HILLS	LACO	90274	1,980	S	B3
* ROLLING HILLS ESTATES	LACO	90274	8,200	S	B2
ROMOLAND	RCO	92380		99	D4
ROSAMOND	KER	93560		90	A1
ROSEDALE	KER	93308		78	C3
* ROSEMEAD	LACO	91770	54,500	R	C3
ROSEMONT	SAC	95826		40	A1
ROSEMONT	SDCO	92065		106	E4
* ROSEVILLE	PLA	95678	59,700	34	A4
ROSEVILLE	SDCO	92106		V	A3
ROSEWOOD	TEH	96022		18	B4
* ROSS	MAR	94957	2,240	L	A3
ROSSMOOR	ORCO	90720		T	A2
ROUGH AND READY	NEV	95975		34	B1
ROUND MOUNTAIN	SHA	96084		13	A5
ROVANA	INY	93514		51	B3
ROWLAND HEIGHTS	LACO	91745		U	A3
RUBIDOUX	RCO	92509		99	A2
RUCH	JKSN			3	C1
RUCKER	SCL	95020		P	D5
RUMSEY	YOL	95679		32	D4
RUNNING SPRINGS	SBD	92382		99	D1
RUSSIAN HILL	SFCO	94133		142	C2
RUTH	TRI	95526		17	A4
RUTHERFORD	NAPA	94573		38	B2
RYDE	SAC	95680		M	E1

S

COMMUNITY NAME	CO.	ZIP CODE	POP.	PG.	GD.
SABRE CITY	PLA	95660		34	A5
* SACRAMENTO	SAC	95801	384,800	39	E1
-- SACRAMENTO COUNTY	SAC		1,123,400		
* SAINT HELENA	NAPA	94574	5,575	38	B1
SALIDA	STA	95368		47	C2
* SALINAS	MON	93901	122,500	54	C4
SALMON CREEK	SON	94923		37	C2
SALT CREEK LODGE	SHA	96051		12	C5
SALTDALE	KER	93519		80	C3
SALTON	RCO	92257		108	D1
SALTON CITY	IMP	92274		108	C2
SALTON SEA BEACH	IMP	92274		108	C1
SALVADOR	NAPA	94558		38	C3
SALYER	TRI	95563		10	D5
SAMOA	HUM	95560		9	D5
SAN ANDREAS	CAL	95249		41	A3
* SAN ANSELMO	MAR	94960	12,150	L	A3
SAN ANTONIO HEIGHTS	SBD	91786		U	D1
SAN ARDO	MON	93450		65	D3
SAN BENITO	SBT	95023		55	C5
-- SAN BENITO COUNTY	SBT		43,350		
* SAN BERNARDINO	SBD	92402	181,700	99	C1
-- SAN BERNARDINO COUNTY	SBD		1,589,500		
SANBORN	KER	93501		80	A5
* SAN BRUNO	SMCO	94066	40,450	N	C1
SAN CARLOS	SDCO	92119		V	D2
* SAN CARLOS	SMCO	94070	27,800	N	D2
* SAN CLEMENTE	ORCO	92672	46,600	105	D1
SANDBERG	LACO	93532		89	A2
* SAND CITY	MON	93955	190	54	B4
* SAN DIEGO	SDCO	92101	1,183,100	V	B3
SAN DIEGO COUNTRY EST	SDCO	92065		107	A4
-- SAN DIEGO COUNTY	SDCO		2,690,300		
* SAN DIMAS	LACO	91773	35,100	U	B2
SANDY	CLK			74	A5
SAN FELIPE	SDCO	92086		107	C3
* SAN FERNANDO	LACO	91341	23,600	Q	C1
* SAN FRANCISCO	SFCO	94101	755,300	L	B4
-- SAN FRANCISCO COUNTY	SFCO		755,300		
* SAN GABRIEL	LACO	91776	39,600	R	C3
* SANGER	FRCO	93657	18,300	57	E3
SAN GERONIMO	MAR	94963		38	A5
SAN GORGONIO	RCO	92282		100	B3
SAN GREGORIO	SMCO	94074		N	C3
* SAN JACINTO	RCO	92383	23,900	99	E3
* SAN JOAQUIN	FRCO	93660	2,920	56	E4

COMMUNITY NAME	CO.	ZIP CODE	POP.	PG.
* SAN JOSE	SCL	95103	849,400	P
* SAN JUAN BAUTISTA	SBT	95045	1,620	54
* SAN JUAN CAPISTRANO	ORCO	92675	28,950	98
SAN JUAN HOT SPRINGS	ORCO	92675		98
* SAN LEANDRO	ALA	94577	71,500	L
SAN LORENZO	ALA	94580		L
SAN LUCAS	MON	93954		65
* SAN LUIS OBISPO	SLO	93401	41,950	76
-- SAN LUIS OBISPO COUNTY	SLO		232,400	
SAN LUIS REY	SDCO	92068		106
SAN LUIS REY HEIGHTS	SDCO	92028		106
* SAN MARCOS	SDCO	92069	48,100	106
SAN MARIN	MAR	94945		L
* SAN MARINO	LACO	91108	13,400	R
SAN MARTIN	SCL	95046		P
* SAN MATEO	SMCO	94401	91,200	N
-- SAN MATEO COUNTY	SMCO		691,500	
SAN MIGUEL	SLO	93451		66
SAN ONOFRE	SDCO	92672		105
* SAN PABLO	CC	94806	25,950	L
SAN PASQUAL	SDCO	92025		106
SAN PEDRO	LACO	90731		S
SAN PEDRO TERRACE	SM	94044		45
SAN QUENTIN	MAR	94964		L
* SAN RAFAEL	MAR	94901	52,400	L
* SAN RAMON	CC	94583	40,650	M
SAN SIMEON	SLO	93452		75
* SANTA ANA	ORCO	92701	305,800	T
* SANTA BARBARA	SB	93101	89,400	87
-- SANTA BARBARA COUNTY	SB		394,600	
* SANTA CLARA	SCL	95050	98,000	P
-- SANTA CLARA COUNTY	SCL		1,612,300	
* SANTA CLARITA	LACO	91321	129,900	89
* SANTA CRUZ	SCR	95060	52,700	53
-- SANTA CRUZ COUNTY	SCR		243,000	
* SANTA FE SPRINGS	LACO	90670	15,700	R
SANTA MARGARITA	SLO	93453		76
* SANTA MARIA	SB	93454	68,900	86
* SANTA MONICA	LACO	90402	90,300	Q
SANTA NELLA	MCO	95322		55
* SANTA PAULA	VEN	93060	26,700	88
SANTA RITA	ALA	94566		M
SANTA RITA PARK	MER	93660		56
* SANTA ROSA	SON	95402	125,700	37
SANTA SUSANA	VEN	93063		89
SANTA VENETIA	MAR	94903		L
SANTA YNEZ	SB	93460		86
SANTA YSABEL	SDCO	92070		107
* SANTEE	SDCO	92071	54,400	V
SAN YSIDRO	SDCO	92073		V
* SARATOGA	SCL	95070	29,600	P
SATICOY	VEN	93004		88
SATTLEY	SIE	96124		27
SAUGUS	LACO	91350		89
* SAUSALITO	MAR	94965	7,650	L
SAWYERS BAR	SIS	96027		11
SCALES	SIE	95981		26
SCHELLVILLE	SON	95476		L
SCISSORS CROSSING	SDCO	92036		107
SCOTIA	HUM	95565		16
SCOTT BAR	SIS	96085		3
SCOTT DAM	LAK	95469		23
SCOTTS CORNER	ALA	94586		P
* SCOTTS VALLEY	SCR	95060	9,825	P
SCOTTYS CASTLE	INY	92328		61
SCRIPPS MIRAMAR RANCH	SDCO	92131		V
SEACLIFF	SFCO	94121		141
SEACLIFF	VEN	93001		87
* SEAL BEACH	ORCO	90740	26,350	T
SEA RANCH	SON	95497		30
SEARCHLIGHT	CLK			85
SEARCHLIGHT JUNCTION	SBD	92332		95
SEARS POINT	SON	95476		L
* SEASIDE	MON	93955	28,300	54
* SEBASTOPOL	SON	95472	7,525	37
SEDCO HILLS	RCO	92330		99
SEELEY	IMP	92273		108
SEIAD VALLEY	SIS	96086		3
* SELMA	FRCO	93662	17,300	57
SENECA	PLU	95923		20
SERENE LAKES	PLA	95728		35
SERENO DEL MAR	SON	94923		37
SERRA MESA	SDCO	92123		V
SEVEN PINES	INY	93526		59
SHADY DELL	SDCO	92065		V
SHADY GLEN	PLA	95713		34
* SHAFTER	KER	93263	11,000	78
SHANDON	SLO	93461		76
SHASTA	SHA	96087		18
-- SHASTA COUNTY	SHA		161,600	
* SHASTA LAKE	SHA	96079	9,200	18
SHAVER LAKE	FRCO	93664		58
SHAVER LAKE POINT	FRCO	93664		50
SHEEP RANCH	CAL	95250		41
SHEFFIELD VILLAGE	ALA			L
SHELDON	SAC	95624		40
SHELL BEACH	SLO	93449		76
SHELTER VALLEY RANCHOS	SDCO	92036		107
SHERIDAN	SON	95462		37
SHERIDAN DUNCAN MILLS	SON	95462		37
SHERMAN HEIGHTS	SDCO	92102		216
SHERMAN OAKS	LACO	91403		Q
SHINGLE MILL	SON	95480		31
SHINGLE SPRINGS	ED	95682		34
SHINGLETOWN	SHA	96088		19
SHIVELY	HUM	95565		16
SHOSHONE	INY	92384		73
SHUMWAY	LAS			21
SIERRA BROOKS	SIE	96135		27
SIERRA CITY	SIE	96125		27
-- SIERRA COUNTY	SIE		3,390	
* SIERRA MADRE	LACO	91024	11,150	R
SIERRA VILLAGE	TUO			41
SIERRAVILLE	SIE	96126		27
* SIGNAL HILL	LACO	90806	8,775	S
SILVERADO	ORCO	92676		98

*** INDICATES INCORPORATED CITY**

CITIES

COMMUNITY NAME	CO.	ZIP CODE	POP.	PG.	GD.
SILVERADO CANYON	ORCO	92676		98	E4
SILVER CITY	LYON			36	C1
SILVER CITY	TUL	93271		59	B5
SILVER FORK	ED	95728		35	C4
SILVER LAKE	LACO	90039		Q	E3
SILVER PEAK	ESM			52	D1
SILVER STRAND	VEN	93030		96	B1
SIMI VALLEY	VEN	93065	103,200	89	A5
SIMMLER	SLO	93453		77	B3
SISKIYOU COUNTY	SIS		44,600		
SISQUOC	SB	93454		86	C1
SITES	COL	95979		32	C1
SKAGGS SPRINGS	SON	95448		31	C5
SKIDOO	INY	92328		61	D5
SKYFOREST	SBD	92385		99	C1
SKY LONDA	SMCO	94062		N	D3
SKY VALLEY	RCO	92240		100	E3
SLEEPY HOLLOW	MAR	94960		L	A3
SLEEPY HOLLOW	SBD			U	C4
SLEEPY VALLEY	LACO	91350		89	D4
SLIDE INN	TUO	95335		41	E4
SLOAN	CLK			74	D4
SLOAT	PLU	96127		26	E2
SLOUGHHOUSE	SAC	95683		40	B1
SMARTVILLE	YUB	95977		34	A2
SMITHFLAT	ED	95727		34	E5
SMITH RIVER	DN	95567		1	E3
SMITH STATION	TUO	95321		49	A1
SNELLING	MCO	95369		48	C3
SOBOBA HOT SPRINGS	RCO	92383		99	E3
SODA BAY	LAK	95443		31	D3
SODA SPRINGS	NEV	95728		27	C5
SODA SPRINGS	SON	95412		31	A5
SOLANA BEACH	SDCO	92075	13,600	106	B4
SOLANO COUNTY	SOL		373,100		
SOLEDAD	MON	93960	15,700	55	A5
SOLVANG	SB	93463	5,100	86	E3
SOMERSET	ED	95684		35	A5
SOMES BAR	SIS	95568		10	E2
SOMIS	VEN	93066		88	D5
SONOMA	SON	95476	8,750	L	B1
SONOMA COUNTY	SON		421,500		
SONORA	TUO	95370	4,280	41	C5
SONORA JUNCTION	MNO	93517		42	E2
SOQUEL	SCR	95073		54	A2
SORRENTO VALLEY	SDCO	92121		V	B1
SOULSBYVILLE	TUO	95372		41	D5
SOUSA CORNERS	SON	95444		37	D2
SOUTH BELRIDGE	KER	93251		77	D2
SOUTHCREST	SDCO	92113		216	D5
SOUTH DOS PALOS	MCO	93665		56	A2
SOUTH EL MONTE	LACO	91733	21,750	R	C4
SOUTH FORK	MAD			49	E5
SOUTH FORK	MPA	95318		49	B2
SOUTH GATE	LACO	90280	91,100	R	A5
SOUTH LAGUNA	ORCO	92677		T	E5
SOUTH LAKE	KER	93283		79	D1
SOUTH LAKE TAHOE	ED	95705	23,100	36	A3
SOUTH OF MARKET	SFCO	94103		143	C4
SOUTH OROVILLE	BUT	95965		25	D4
SOUTH PARK	SON	95404		38	A2
SOUTH PASADENA	LACO	91030	24,850	R	B3
SOUTH SAN FRANCISCO	SMCO	94080	57,000	N	C1
SOUTH SAN GABRIEL	LACO	91770		R	B4
SOUTH SHORE	ALA			L	D5
SOUTH TAFT	KER	93268		78	A4
SPANISH CREEK	PLU	95971		26	D1
SPANISH FLAT WOODLNDS	NAPA	94558		38	D1
SPANISH RANCH	PLU	95956		26	C1
SPARKS	WSH		62,118	28	C4
SPAULDING	LAS	96130		20	D1
SPENCEVILLE	NEV	95945		34	B2
SPRECKELS	MON	93962		54	D4
SPRING GARDEN	PLU	95971		26	E2
SPRING TOWN	ALA	94550		M	C5
SPRING VALLEY	SDCO	92077		V	D3
SPRINGVILLE	TUL	93265		68	E2
SQUAW VALLEY	FRCO	93646		58	B3
SQUIRREL MTN VALLEY	KER	93240		79	D1
STAFFORD	HUM	95565		16	A3
STAGECOACH	LYON			28	E5
STANDISH	LAS	96128		21	B3
STANFIELD HILL	YUB	95918		34	A1
STANFORD	SCL	94305		N	D2
STANISLAUS	TUO	95247		41	C4
- STANISLAUS COUNTY	STA		415,300		
STANTON	ORCO	90680	31,900	T	B2
STATELINE	DGL			36	B3
STENT	TUO	95347		41	C5
STEVINSON	MCO	95374		47	E4
STEWART	CRSN			36	C2
STEWART-LENNOX	KLAM			5	B1
STEWARTS POINT	SON	95480		30	E5
STINSON BEACH	MAR	94970		L	A4
STIRLING CITY	BUT	95978		25	D2
STOCKTON	SDCO	92102		216	C3
STOCKTON	SJCO	95201	233,600	40	B5
STONYFORD	COL	95979		24	B5
- STOREY COUNTY	STOR		2,526		
STOVEPIPE WELLS	INY	92328		61	D4
STRATFORD	KIN	93266		67	C2
STRATHMORE	TUL	93267		68	D2
STRAWBERRY	ED	95735		35	D2
STRAWBERRY	TUO	95375		42	A3
STRAWBERRY VALLEY	YUB	95981		26	B4
STRONGHOLD	MOD	96431		5	E3
STUDIO CITY	LACO	91604		Q	C3
SUGAR LOAF	SBD	92386		92	A5
SUGARLOAF VILLAGE	TUL	93260		69	B4
SUGAR PINE	MAD	95389		49	D3
SUGARPINE	TUO	95346		41	D4
* SUISUN CITY	SOL	94585	25,500	M	A1
SULTANA	TUL	93666		58	B5
SUMMERHOME PARK	SON	95436		37	D2
SUMMERLAND	SB	93067		87	D4
SUMMIT	VEN	93023		88	C4
SUMMIT CITY	SHA	96089		18	B1
SUN CITY	RCO	92381		99	C4
SUNLAND	LACO	91040		Q	D1
SUNNYBROOK	AMA	95640		40	D2
SUNNYSIDE	SDCO	92002		V	D4
SUNNYSLOPE	RCO	93656		99	A2
* SUNNYVALE	SCL	94086	126,100	P	A3
SUNNY VISTA	SDCO	92010		V	D2
SUNOL	ALA	94586		P	B1
SUNSET	SFCO	94122		141	B5
SUNSET BEACH	ORCO	90742		T	A3
SUNSET ESTATES	PLA	95678		33	E4
SUN VALLEY	LACO	91352		Q	D2
SUN VALLEY	WSH			28	B4
SURFSIDE	ORCO	90743		T	A3
* SUSANVILLE	LAS	96130	14,700	20	E3
SUTCLIFFE	WSH			28	C1
SUTTER	SUT	95982		33	C2
-- SUTTER COUNTY	SUT		74,100		
* SUTTER CREEK	AMA	95685	2,060	40	E2
SWANSBORO COUNTRY	ED	95727		35	A4
SWANSEA	INY	93545		60	C5
SWEETBRIER	SHA	96017		12	C3
SWEETLAND	NEV	95959		26	B5
SYCAMORE	COL	95957		33	A2
SYLMAR	LACO	91342		Q	B1
SYLMAR SQUARE	LACO	91342		Q	C1
SYLVIA PARK	LACO	90290		Q	A3

T

COMMUNITY NAME	CO.	ZIP CODE	POP.	PG.	GD.
* TAFT	KER	93268	6,600	78	A4
TAFT HEIGHTS	KER	93268		77	E4
TAHOE CITY	PLA	95730		35	E2
TAHOE PINES	PLA	95718		35	D2
TAHOE VILLAGE	DGL	25		36	B3
TAHOE VISTA	PLA	95732		36	A1
TAHOMA	PLA	95733		35	E2
TAKILMA	JOS			2	D2
* TALENT	JKSN		3,650	3	E1
TALMAGE	MEN	95481		31	B2
TAMALPAIS VALLEY	MAR	94941		L	A4
TAMARACK	CAL	95223		41	E2
TANCRED	YOL	95606		32	D5
TARZANA	LACO	91356		Q	A3
TASSAJARA	CC	94526		46	B1
TASSAJARA HOT SPGS	MON	93924		64	D2
TAYLORSVILLE	PLU	95983		20	D5
TECATE	BAJA			112	C2
TECATE	SDCO	92080		112	C2
TECOPA	INY	92389		73	A4
TECOPA HOT SPRINGS	INY	92389		73	A4
* TEHACHAPI	KER	93561	6,550	79	D4
TEHACHAPI EAST	KER	93561		79	D4
* TEHAMA	TEH	96090	430	24	D1
-- TEHAMA COUNTY	TEH		54,400		
TELEGRAPH CITY	CAL	95228		40	E5
TELEGRAPH HILL	SFCO	94133		142	D1
* TEMECULA	RCO	92390	41,850	106	C1
* TEMPLE CITY	LACO	91780	33,050	R	C3
TEMPLETON	SLO	93465		76	A2
TENNANT	SIS	96012		5	B5
TERMINAL ISLAND	LACO			S	C3
TERMINOUS	SJCO	95240		39	E4
TERMO	LAS	96132		8	B5
TERRA BELLA	TUL	93270		68	D3
TERRA LINDA	MAR	94903		L	A3
THE HIGHLANDS	SMCO	94402		N	C2
THE NARROWS	SDCO	92004		108	A3
THE WILLOWS	SDCO	92001		107	B5
THERMAL	RCO	92274		101	B5
THERMALANDS	PLA	95648		34	B3
THORNE	MIN			44	B1
THORNTON	SJCO	95686		39	E3
* THOUSAND OAKS	VEN	91360	112,000	96	E1
THOUSAND PALMS	RCO	92276		100	E3
THREE ARCH BAY	ORCO	92677		98	D5
THREE RIVERS	TUL	93271		58	D5
* TIBURON	MAR	94920	8,400	L	B4
TIERRA BUENA	SUT	95991		33	C2
TIERRA DEL SOL	SDCO	92005		112	E2
TIERRASANTA	SDCO	92124		V	C2
TIJUANA	BAJA			111	D2
TIMBER LODGE	MPA	95345		49	B3
TIPTON	TUL	93272		68	B3
TISDALE	SUT	95957		33	B3
TOBIN	PLU	95965		26	A1
TOLLHOUSE	FRCO	93667		58	A2
TOMALES	MAR	94971		37	D3
TOMS PLACE	MNO	93546		51	B3
TOPANGA	LACO	90290		Q	A3
TOPANGA PARK	LACO	90290		97	B1
TOPAZ	MNO	96133		36	D5
TOPOCK	MOH			95	E2
* TORRANCE	LACO	90505	139,800	S	B2
TOWER HOUSE	SHA	96095		18	A1
TOYON	SHA	96019		18	C1
TRABUCO CANYON	ORCO	92679		98	E4
* TRACY	SJCO	95376	44,900	46	E2
TRAIL PARK	ED	95651		34	E4
TRANQUILLITY	FRCO	93668		56	D4
TRAVER	TUL	93673		57	E5
TRAVIS AIR FORCE BASE	SOL	94535		39	A3
TRES PINOS	SBT	95075		55	A3
* TRINIDAD	HUM	95570	360	9	E4
TRINITY CENTER	TRI	96091		11	E4
-- TRINITY COUNTY	TRI		13,400		
TRONA	SBD	93562		71	B5
TROPICO	KER	93560		89	E1
TROWBRIDGE	SUT	95687		33	D3
TROY	PLA	95728		35	B1
* TRUCKEE	NEV	95734	2,400	35	D1
TUDOR	SUT	95991		33	C3
TUJUNGA	LACO	91042		Q	E1
* TULARE	TUL	93274	39,750	68	A2
-- TULARE COUNTY	TUL		351,500		
* TULELAKE	SIS	96134	920	5	D2
TUOLUMNE	TUO	95379		41	D5
-- TUOLUMNE COUNTY	TUO		52,700		
TUOLUMNE MEADOWS	TUO	95379		43	A5
TUPMAN	KER	93276		78	B3
* TURLOCK	STA	95380	49,200	47	E3
TURTLE ROCK	ORCO	92715		98	C4
* TUSTIN	ORCO	92680	63,600	T	E3
TUTTLE	MCO	95340		48	D4
TUTTLETOWN	TUO			41	C5
TWAIN	PLU	95984		26	B1
TWAIN HARTE	TUO	95383		41	D4
TWAIN HARTE VALLEY	TUO	95383		41	D4
* TWENTYNINE PALMS	SBD	92277	14,800	101	B1
TWIN BRIDGES	ED	95735		35	E4
TWIN CITIES	SAC	95632		40	A3
TWIN OAKS	SDCO	92083		106	C3
TWIN PEAKS	SBD	92391		91	C5
TWIN PEAKS	SFCO	94116		142	A5
TWIN PINES	RCO			100	B3
TYNDALL LANDING	YOL	95698		33	B4

U

COMMUNITY NAME	CO.	ZIP CODE	POP.	PG.	GD.
* UKIAH	MEN	95482	14,700	31	B2
ULTRA	TUL	93256		68	D3
* UNION CITY	ALA	94587	58,300	P	A1
UNIVERSAL CITY	LACO	91608		Q	D3
UNIVERSITY CITY	SDCO	92122		V	A2
UNIVERSITY HEIGHTS	SDCO	92116		214	A4
* UPLAND	SBD	91786	66,200	U	D2
UPPER LAKE	LAK	95485		31	D2
UPTOWN	SDCO	92103		213	B5

V

COMMUNITY NAME	CO.	ZIP CODE	POP.	PG.	GD.
VACATION BEACH	SON	95446		37	C2
* VACAVILLE	SOL	95688	84,200	39	A2
VALENCIA	LACO	91355		89	B4
VALERIE	RCO	92274		101	A5
VALINDA	LACO	91744		R	E4
VALLECITO	CAL	95251		41	C4
VALLECITO	SDCO	92036		107	E4
* VALLEJO	SOL	94590	112,300	L	D2
VALLEJO HEIGHTS	SOL	94590		38	D4
VALLE VISTA	RCO	92343		99	E4
VALLEY ACRES	KER	93268		78	A4
VALLEY CENTER	SDCO	92082		106	E2
VALLEY FORD	SON	94972		37	D3
VALLEY HOME	STA	95384		47	D1
VALLEY OF ENCHANTMENT	SBD	92322		91	B5
VALLEY SPRINGS	CAL	95252		40	D3
VALLEY WELLS	INY	92366		71	C4
VAL VERDE	LACO	91350		89	A4
VANDENBERG VILLAGE	STB	93436		86	B2
VAN NUYS	LACO	91408		Q	C2
VENICE	LACO	90291		Q	B5
VENTUCOPA	SB	93252		87	E1
VEN-TU PARK	VEN	91320		96	D1
* VENTURA	VEN	93001	100,300	88	B5
-- VENTURA COUNTY	VEN		716,100		
VERDEMONT	SBD	92407		99	B1
VERDI	WSH			28	A4
VERDI SIERRA PINES	SIE	95737		27	E4
VERDUGO CITY	LACO	91046		Q	E2
* VERNON	LACO	90058	80	R	A4
VERONA	SUT	95659		33	D4
VICHY SPRINGS	MEN	95482		31	B2
VICHY SPRINGS	NAPA	94558		38	D3
VICTOR	SJCO	95253		40	B4
VICTORIA	SDCO	92001		107	B5
* VICTORVILLE	SBD	92392	60,000	91	C3
VIDAL	SBD	92280		103	E1
VIDAL JUNCTION	SBD	92280		103	D1
VILLA GRANDE	SON	95486		37	C2
* VILLA PARK	ORCO	92667	6,375	T	E2
VINA	TEH	96092		24	E2
VINEBURG	SON	95487		L	C1
VINTON	PLU	96135		27	D2
VIOLA	SHA	96088		19	C2
VIRGILIA	PLU	95984		26	B1
* VIRGINIA CITY	STOR		950	36	D1
* VISALIA	TUL	93277	91,300	68	B1
* VISTA	SDCO	92083	80,000	106	C3
VISTA VERDE	SMCO	94025		N	D3
VOLCANO	AMA	95689		41	A2
VOLCANOVILLE	ED	95634		34	E3
VOLLMERS	SHA	96051		12	B4
VOLTA	MER	93635		55	D1
VORDEN	SAC	95690		M	E1

W

COMMUNITY NAME	CO.	ZIP CODE	POP.	PG.	GD.
WAHTOKE PARK	FRCO	93654		58	A4
WALKER	MNO	96107		42	E1
WALLACE	CAL	95254		40	D3
* WALNUT	LACO	91789	31,600	U	A3
* WALNUT CREEK	CC	94595	62,000	M	A4
WALNUT GROVE	SAC	95690		M	E1
WALSH LANDING	SON	95450		37	A1
WARM SPRINGS	ALA	94538		P	B2
WARNER SPRINGS	SDCO	92086		107	C2
* WASCO	KER	93280	18,200	78	B1
WASHINGTON	NEV	95986		26	E5
WASHOE	SON	94931		37	E3
WASHOE CITY	WSH			28	B5
-- WASHOE COUNTY	WSH		254,667		
* WATERFORD	STA	95386	6,375	48	A2
WATERLOO	SJCO	95201		40	B4
* WATSONVILLE	SCR	95076	34,250	54	C2
WATTS	LACO	90002		Q	E5
WAWONA	MPA	95389		49	D3
WEAVERVILLE	TRI	96093		17	D1
* WEED	SIS	96094	3,080	12	C1
WEED PATCH	KER	93307		78	E4
WEIMAR	PLA	95736		34	D3
WEITCHPEC	HUM	95546		10	C3
WELDON	KER	93283		79	D1
WELLSONA	SLO	93446		76	A1
WENDEL	LAS	96136		21	D3
WENTWORTH SPRINGS	ED	95725		35	C3
WEOTT	HUM	95571		16	B4
WEST BRANCH	BUT	95941		25	C1
WEST BUTTE	SUT	95953		33	B2
* WEST COVINA	LACO	91790	101,900	U	A2
WESTERN ADDITION	SFCO	94115		143	A4
WEST HAVEN	FRCO	93234		67	B2
* WEST HOLLYWOOD	LACO	90069	37,200	Q	D3
* WESTLAKE VILLAGE	LACO	91361	7,825	96	E1
WESTLEY	STA	95387		47	B3
WEST LOS ANGELES	LACO	90025	82,500	Q	C4
* WESTMINSTER	ORCO	92683	82,500	T	B4
* WESTMORELAND	IMP	92281	1,690	109	A4
WEST OF TWIN PEAKS	SFCO	94122		141	D5
WEST POINT	CAL	95255		41	B2
WESTPORT	MEN	95488		22	C4
* WEST SACRAMENTO	YOL	95691	30,250	39	D1
WEST SIDE	LAKE			7	B1
WESTVILLE	PLA	95631		35	A2
WESTWOOD	LAS	96137		20	C4
WESTWOOD	LACO	90024		97	C2
* WHEATLAND	YUB	95692	1,960	33	E3
WHEATON SPRINGS	SBD	92364		84	B2
WHEATVILLE	FRCO	93656		57	A5
WHEELER RIDGE	KER	93284		78	D5
WHEELER SPRINGS	VEN	93023		88	A4
WHISKEYTOWN	SHA	96095		18	A2
WHISPERING PINES	LAK	95461		32	A4
WHITE HALL	ED	95725		35	C4
WHITE HORSE	MOD	96054		13	E2
WHITE PINES	CAL	95223		41	C3
WHITE RIVER	TUL	93257		68	E4
WHITETHORN	HUM	95489		22	B1
WHITEWATER	RCO	92282		100	C3
WHITLEY GARDENS	SLO	93451		76	C1
WHITLOW	HUM	95554		16	C4
WHITMORE	SHA	96096		19	A2
* WHITTIER	LACO	90605	82,500	R	D5
WILBUR SPRINGS	COL	95987		32	C3
WILDOMAR	RCO	92395		99	C5
WILDROSE	INY	93562		71	C2
* WILLIAMS	COL	95987	3,020	32	D2
WILLIAMS	JOS			3	A1
* WILLITS	MEN	95490	5,100	23	A5
WILLOW CREEK	HUM	95573		10	D5
WILLOW RANCH	MOD	96138		7	C3
* WILLOWS	GLE	95988	6,350	24	D4
WILLOW SPRINGS	KER	93550		89	D1
WILMINGTON	LACO	90744		S	C2
WILSEYVILLE	CAL	95257		41	B2
WILSONIA	TUL	93633		58	E3
WILTON	SAC	95693		40	B2
WINCHESTER	RCO	92396		99	D4
WINCHUCK	CUR			1	D2
* WINDSOR	SON	95492	18,750	37	E1
WINTER GARDENS	SDCO	92040		V	E2
WINTERHAVEN	IMP	92283		112	C5
* WINTERS	YOL	95694	5,175	39	A1
WINTERWARM	SDCO	92028		106	C2
WINTON	MER	95388		48	A4
WISHON	MAD	93669		49	E4
WITCH CREEK	SDCO	92065		107	B3
WOFFORD HEIGHTS	KER	93285		69	C5
WOLF	NEV	95945		34	B2
WONDER VALLEY	FRCO	93657		58	B3
WOODACRE	MAR	94973		L	A3
WOODBRIDGE	ORCO	92714		T	E4
WOODCREST	RCO	92504		99	B3
WOODFORD	KER	96120		79	B4
WOODFORDS	ALP	96120		36	B4
* WOODLAKE	TUL	93286	6,175	58	D5
* WOODLAND	YOL	95695	43,250	33	B5
WOODLAND HILLS	LACO	91364		Q	A3
* WOODSIDE	SMCO	94062	5,375	N	D2
WOODSIDE VILLAGE	LACO	91792		U	A3
WOODVILLE	TUL	93257		68	C3
WOODY	KER	93287		69	A5
WOOLSEY	SON	95436		37	D2
WORDEN	KLAM			5	B2
WRIGHTS LAKE	ED	95720		35	D4
WRIGHTWOOD	SBD	92397		90	E5
WYANDOTTE	BUT	95965		25	D5
WYNOLA	SDCO	92036		107	C3

Y

COMMUNITY NAME	CO.	ZIP CODE	POP.	PG.	GD.
YANKEE HILL	BUT	95969		25	D3
YANKEE JIMS	PLA	95631		34	D3
YERMO	SBD	92398		92	A1
YETTEM	TUL	93670		58	B5
YOLO	YOL	95697		33	B5
-- YOLO COUNTY	YOL		152,100		
* YORBA LINDA	ORCO	92686	57,600	T	D1
YORKVILLE	MEN	95494		31	B4
YOSEMITE FORKS	MAD	93644		49	D4
YOSEMITE VILLAGE	MPA	95389		49	D1
YOUNGSTOWN	SJCO	95220		40	B4
* YOUNTVILLE	NAPA	94599	3,460	38	C2
* YREKA	SIS	96097	7,175	4	A4
* YUBA CITY	SUT	95991	33,900	33	C2
-- YUBA COUNTY	YUB		62,200		
* YUCAIPA	SBD	92399	37,450	99	D2
* YUCCA VALLEY	SBD	92284	18,650	100	E1
* YUMA	YUMA		60,475	112	D5
-- YUMA COUNTY	YUMA		121,875		

Z

COMMUNITY NAME	CO.	ZIP CODE	POP.	PG.	GD.
ZAMORA	YOL	95698		33	B4
ZENIA	TRI	95495		16	E4
ZEPHYR COVE	DGL			36	A3

*** INDICATES INCORPORATED CITY**

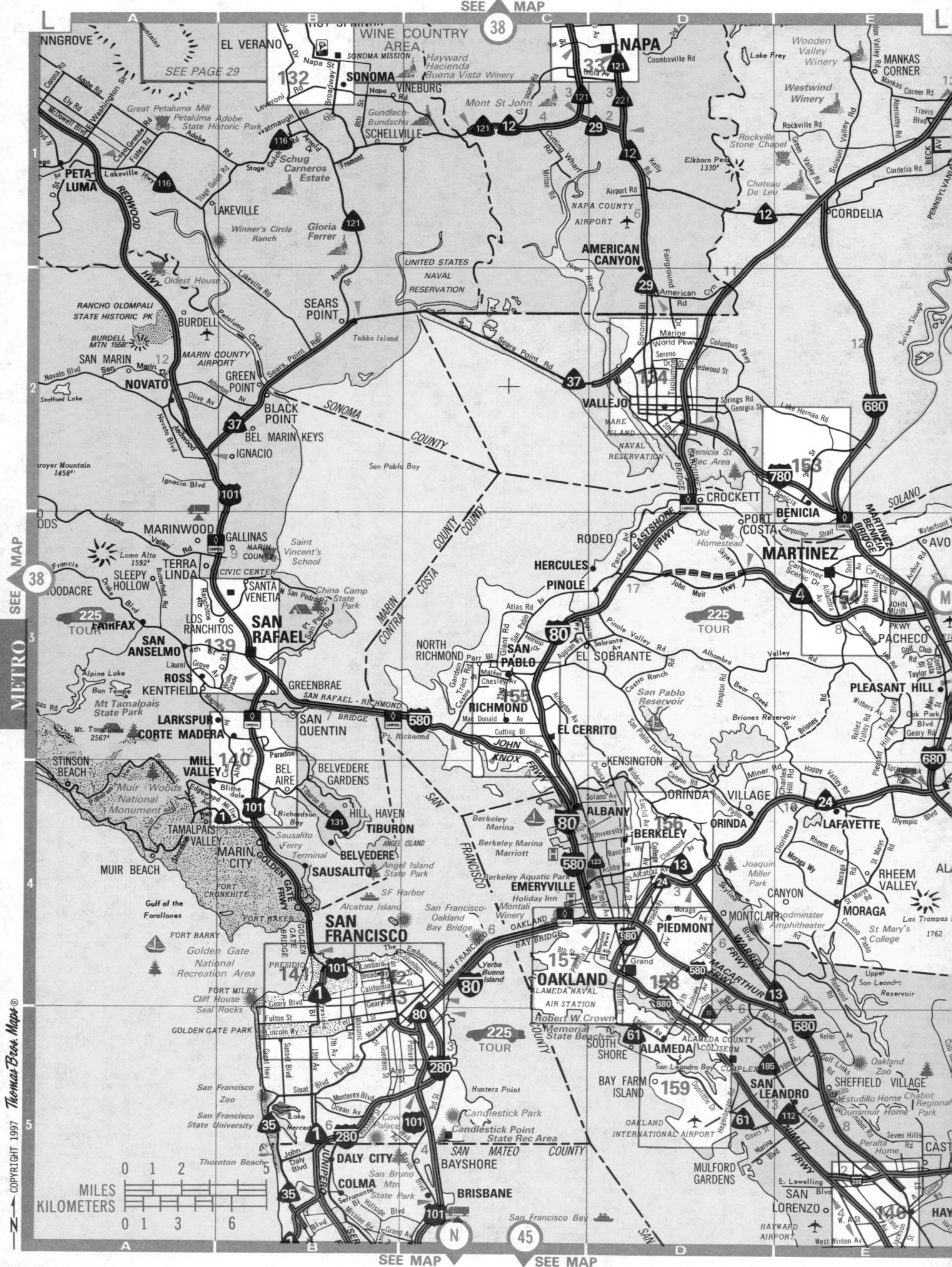

39

MANKAS CORNER
VACAVILLE AIRPORT
Travis Blvd
Air Base Pkwy
Grange Rd
Peabody Rd
Scandia Rd
TRAVIS AIR FORCE BASE
Sutter Island
Victory Hwy
Vorden Rd
VORDEN
LOCKE
WALNUT GROVE

FAIRFIELD
SUISUN CITY
12

RYDE
Grand Island
Walker Landing Rd
Poverty Rd

Grizzly Island Rd
Western Railway Museum
Grizzly Island
Suisun Slough
Montezuma Slough

80

Suisun Bay
Ryer Island
Honker Bay

RIO VISTA
ISLETON
12
Brannan Island Rd
Brannan Island State Rec Area
Twitchell Island
Staten Island
Bouldin Island

EMMATON
Sherman Island
160
Venice Island
Mandeville Island
Franks Tract State Rec Area

SOLANO COUNTY
Sacramento River
Browns Island

AVON
NICHOLS
CLYDE
BAY POINT
Willow Pass Rd
PITTSBURG
ANTIOCH
ANTIOCH BRIDGE
BETHEL ISLAND
Big Break
Holland Tract

4
20
Buchanan Rd
OAKLEY
Cypress Rd
KNIGHTSEN
39

PACHECO
CONCORD
Concord Pavilion
Salvio Pacheco Adobe
Fernando Pacheco Adobe
CONTRA LOMA RESERVOIR
Antioch Airport
Lone Tree Wy
Delta Rd

PLEASANT HILL
CLAYTON
225 TOUR
Pine Hollow Rd
Marsh Creek Rd
BRENTWOOD
Balfour Rd
4

680
WALNUT CREEK
Marriott
Embassy Suites
MT DIABLO STATE PARK
Mt Diablo 3849'
DISCOVERY BAY
Victoria Island
4

ALAMO
RHEEM VALLEY
Eugene O'Neill Nat'l Hist Site 1762
DIABLO
MT DIABLO STATE PARK
BYRON
Camino Diablo

MILES
KILOMETERS
0 1 2 5
0 3 6

DANVILLE
BLACKHAWK
Tassajara Rd
TASSAJARA
Bethany Res State Rec Area
Brushy Peak 1675'
MOUNTAIN HOUSE
J4

SAN RAMON
Marriott
Highland Rd
CONTRA COSTA COUNTY
ALAMEDA COUNTY
Manning Rd
ALTAMONT
Altamont
205

CASTRO VALLEY
DUBLIN
Pleasanton
Dublin Hilton
SPRING TOWN
20
MIDWAY
4
12

580
HAYWARD
Sheraton
Holiday Inn
SANTA RITA
Livermore Airport
Retzlaff Vineyards
84
LIVERMORE
Lawrence Livermore National Laboratory
Concannon Vineyard
Wente Bros

Calif State University Hayward
Veterans Memorial Monument
J2
46
SANTON

SEE MAP METRO SEE 39

N — A — B — C — D — E — N

PACIFIC

COLMA
BRISBANE
SAN LORENZO
HAYWARD AIRPORT
HAY

35
101
82
380
144
35

Pacifica State Beach
PACIFICA
Serramonte Bl
Hillside Blvd
Mission Rd
Grant Av
SOUTH SAN FRANCISCO
SAN BRUNO
Skyline Blvd
Sneath
Sharp Park Beach
ROCKAWAY BEACH
San Pedro Point
SAN PEDRO TERRACE
LINDA MAR
DEVILS SLIDE
Graywhale Cove State
Montara State Beach
MONTARA
MOSS BEACH
Moss Beach
EL GRANADA
AIRPORT
PRINCETON BY THE SEA
Pillar Pt.
MIRAMAR
Half Moon Bay
Half Moon Bay Beach
HALF MOON BAY
Higgins Purisima Rd
SKYLINE

San Francisco Airport Marriott
San Francisco International Airport
San Francisco Bay
MILLBRAE
Broadway
Hyatt
Peninsula Av
Poplar Av
Holiday Inn
Radisson Hotel SF Airport
BURLINGAME
HILLSBOROUGH
Ralston Av
San Francisco State Fish and Game Refuge
Montara Mountain
Pilarcitos Lake
Lower Crystal Springs Reservoir
THE HIGHLANDS
Crystal Springs
Upper Crystal Springs Reservoir
Obester Winery
92
BELMONT
Ralston Av
SAN CARLOS
Hillsdale
HILLSDALE
FOSTER CITY
San Mateo Bridge
YOUNGER FRWY
SAN MATEO
82
280
REDWOOD SHORES
Marine World Pkwy
REDWOOD CITY
ATHERTON
MENLO PARK
EAST PALO ALTO
PALO ALTO AIRPORT
San Francisco Bay Nat'l Wildlife Refuge
DUMBARTON BRIDGE
84

101
Whipple Av
Woodside Rd
De Las Pulgas
WOODSIDE
Kings Mtn Rd
KINGS MOUNTAIN
Star Hill Rd
Bear Gulch Rd
SKY LONDA
PORTOLA VALLEY
35
84
LADERA
Searsville Lake
ALPINE HILLS
LOS TRANCOS WOODS
VISTA VERDE
Alpine Rd
LA HONDA
Mindego Hill 2127'
Black Mountain 2750'
MONTA VISTA
STANFORD
FOOTHILL
PALO ALTO
MOUNTAIN VIEW
LOS ALTOS
LOS ALTOS HILLS
85
280

SAN GREGORIO
San Gregorio State Beach
Pomponio State Beach
84
Pomponio Creek
LOMA MAR
Portola State Park
Ridge Vineyards
Sunrise Cellars
Stevens Cr Reservoir
9
SARA
Mariani Vineyards

Pescadero State Beach
Pescadero Marsh Natural Pres
PESCADERO
North St
Pescadero
Cloverdale Rd
Butano State Park
PORTOLA STATE PARK
SAN MATEO
SANTA CRUZ
Castle Rock State Park

Bean Hollow State Beach
Pebble Beach
Lake Lucerne
Artichoke Rd
Bean Hollow Lakes
Canyon
Gazos Creek Rd
225 TOUR
236
9
EAGLE ROCK LOOKOUT 2488'
BOULDER CREEK
BROOKDALE

Pigeon Point Lighthouse
Gazos Creek Angling Acess
Big Basin Redwoods State Park
THEODORE J HOOVER NATURAL PRESERVE
Ano Nuevo State Reserve
BEN LOMON
Bonny Doon Vineyards
Hallcrest Vineyards
FELTON
Henry Cowell Redwoods State
1

OCEAN

MILES
KILOMETERS
0 1 2 5
0 1 3 6

METRO

Thomas Bros. Maps ®
COPYRIGHT 1997

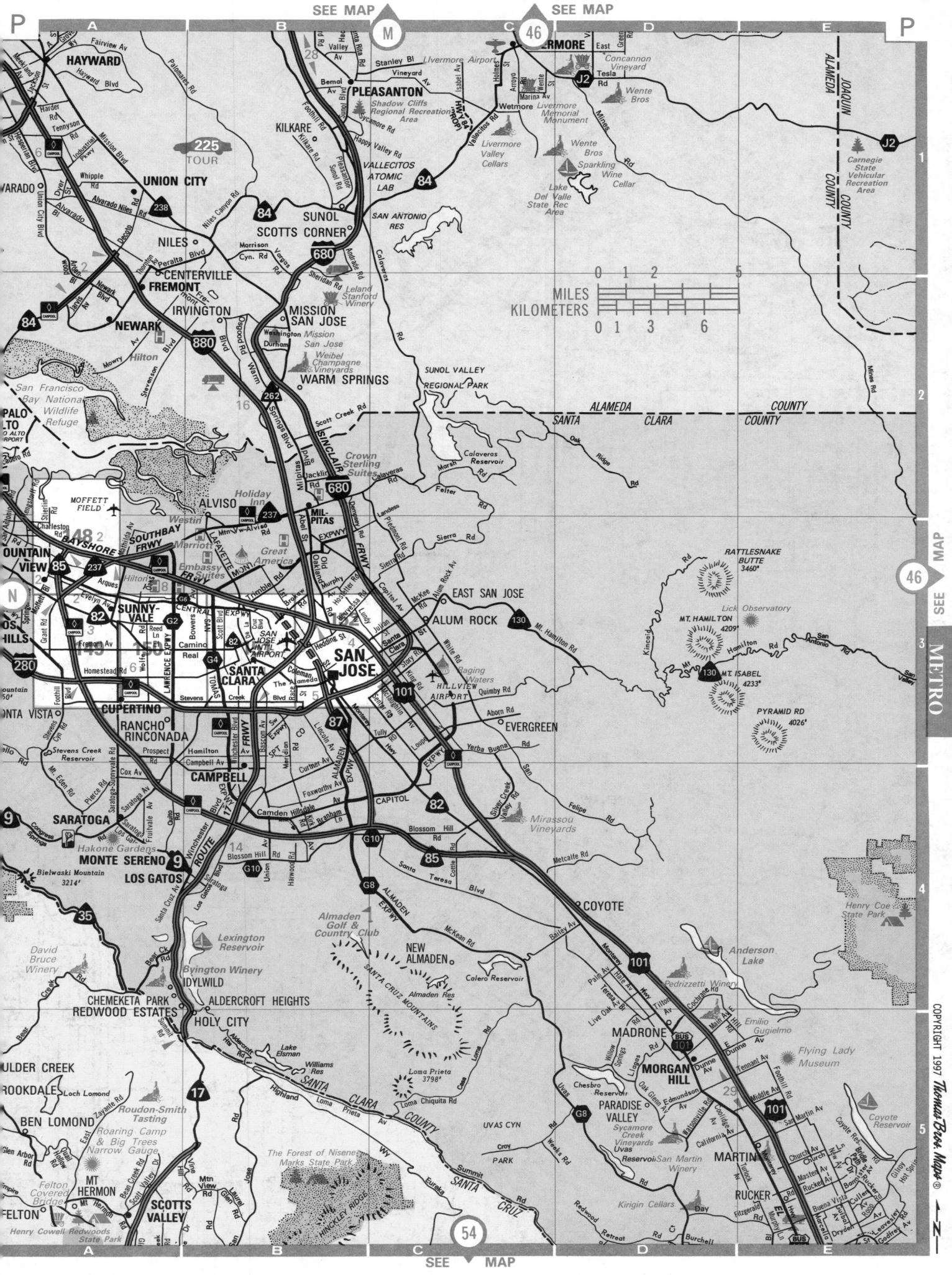

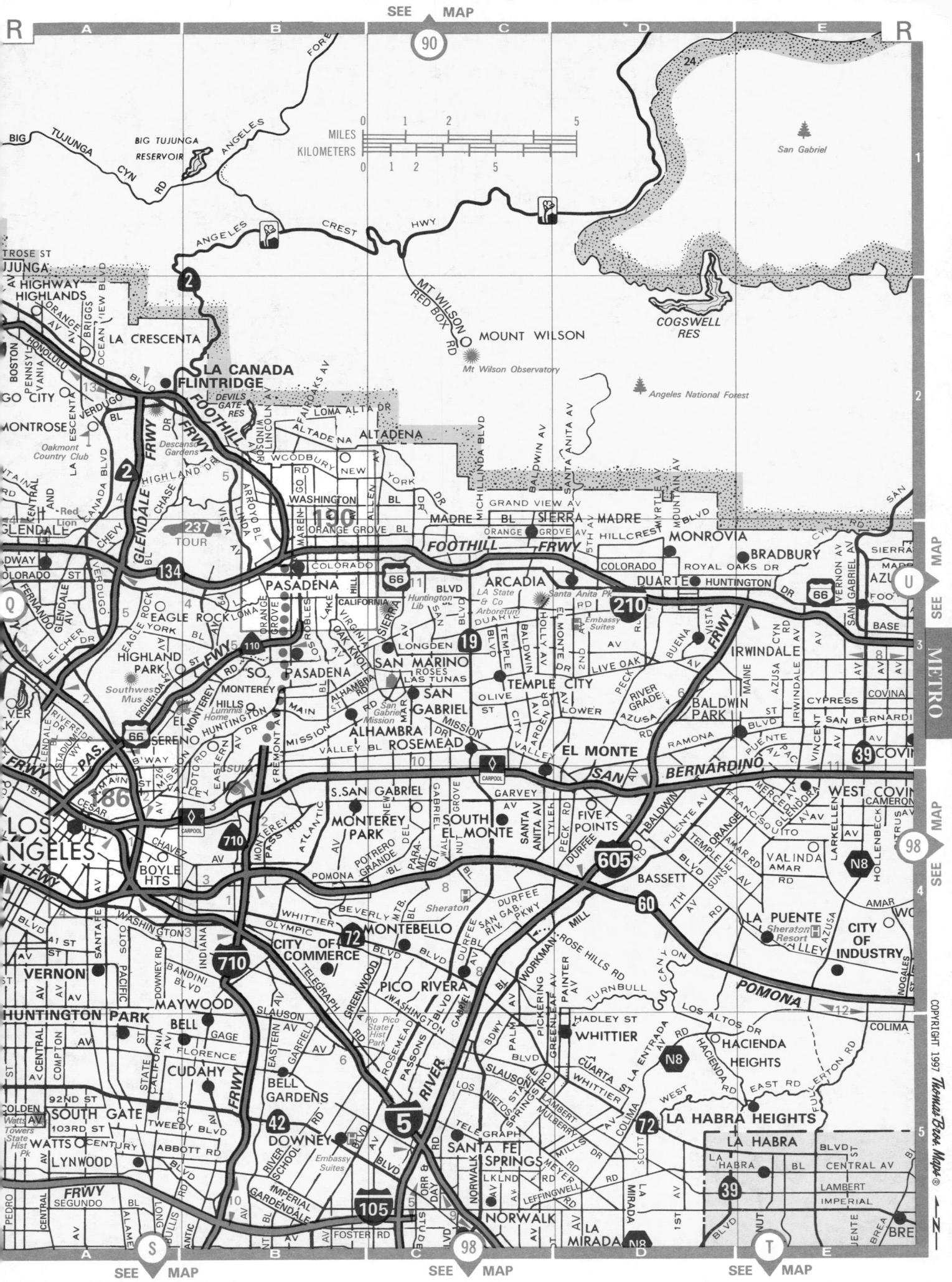

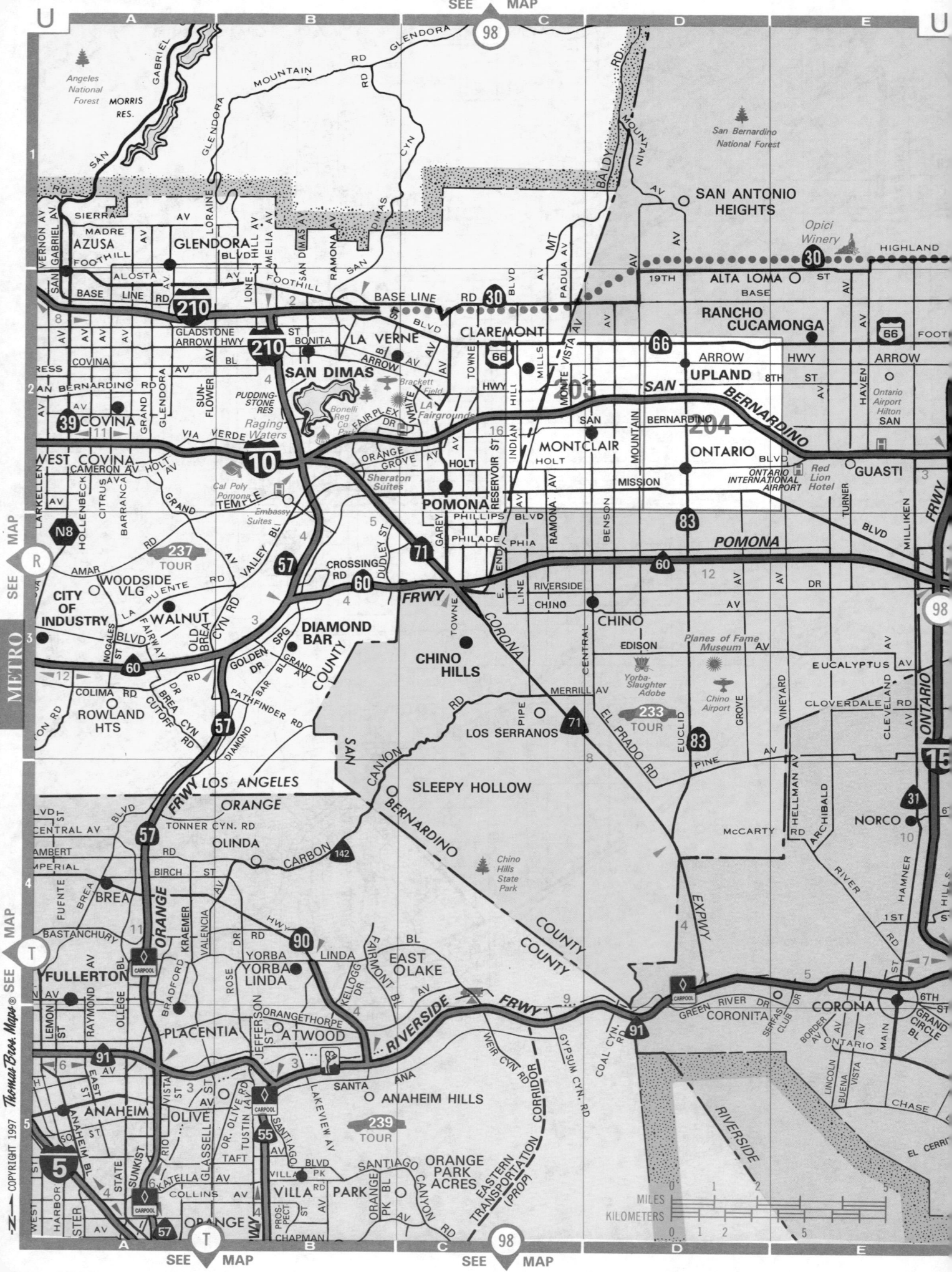

SEE MAP 106
SEE MAP 107
SEE MAP 112
SEE MAP 111
METRO
V
A
B
C
D
E
1
2
3
4
5
DEL MAR
CARMEL VALLEY
POWAY
SHADY DELL
LOS PENASQUITOS CANYON PRESERVE
Torrey Pines State Reserve
San Diego La Jolla Underwater Park
Torrey Pines State Beach
Torrey Pines Golf Course
Sheraton
Univ of Calif, San Diego
Hyatt Regency
La Jolla Marriott
Embassy Suites
SCRIPPS MIRAMAR RANCH
MIRA MESA
SORRENTO VALLEY
MIRAMAR NAVAL AIR STATION
San Vicente Reservoir
SYCAMORE CYN CO PARK
EUCALYPTUS HILLS
Carlton Oaks Lodge & Country Club
MISSION TRAILS REGIONAL PARK
LA JOLLA BAY
SOLEDAD FRWY
KEARNY MESA
CLAIREMONT MESA
TIERRASANTA
SANTEE
GILLESPIE FIELD
LAKESIDE
WNTR GRDNS
FLETCHER HILLS
BOSTONIA
GLENVIEW
MISSION VILLAGE
PACIFIC BEACH
CROWN POINT
MISSION BEACH
MISSION BAY
LINDA VISTA
GENESEE
BAY PARK
MSN HILLS
SERRA MESA
GRANTVILLE
ALLIED GARDENS
SAN CARLOS
DEL CERRO
MURRAY RES
GROSSMONT
EL CAJON
SD State Univ
KENSINGTON
TALMADGE
Open Air Theatre
LA MESA
Pacific SW Railway Museum (La Mesa Depot)
MT HELIX
CASA DE ORO
RANCHO SAN DIEGO
OCEAN BEACH
POINT LOMA
ROSEVILLE
LA PLAYA
SAN DIEGO
CITY HTS
ROLANDO
OAK PARK
LEMON GROVE
SPRING VALLEY
KENWOOD
LINDBERGH FIELD
NORTH ISLAND NAVAL AIR STATION
ENCANTO
LA PRESA
SWEETWATER RESERVOIR
Cabrillo National Monument
Old Spanish Lighthouse
Point Loma
CORONADO
Hotel Del Coronado
LOGAN HTS
NATIONAL CITY
Holiday Inn
LINCOLN ACRES
SUNNYSIDE
San Diego Bay
BONITA
SUNNY VISTA
LYNWOOD HILLS
EASTLAKE
UPPER OTAY RES
CHULA VISTA
Chula Vista Nature Interpretive Center
Silver Strand State Beach
Loews Coronado Bay Resort
Otay Reservoir
CASTLE PARK
LOWER OTAY CO PARK
OTAY
PALM CITY
IMPERIAL BEACH
NAVAL AIR STATION IMPERIAL BEACH
NESTOR
BROWN FIELD
SAN YSIDRO
TIJUANA
Border Field State Park
0 1 2 5 MILES
0 1 2 5 KILOMETERS
JACOB DEKEMA FRWY
SAN DIEGO FRWY
CABRILLO FRWY
MISSION FRWY
241 TOUR
COPYRIGHT 1997 Thomas Bros. Maps®

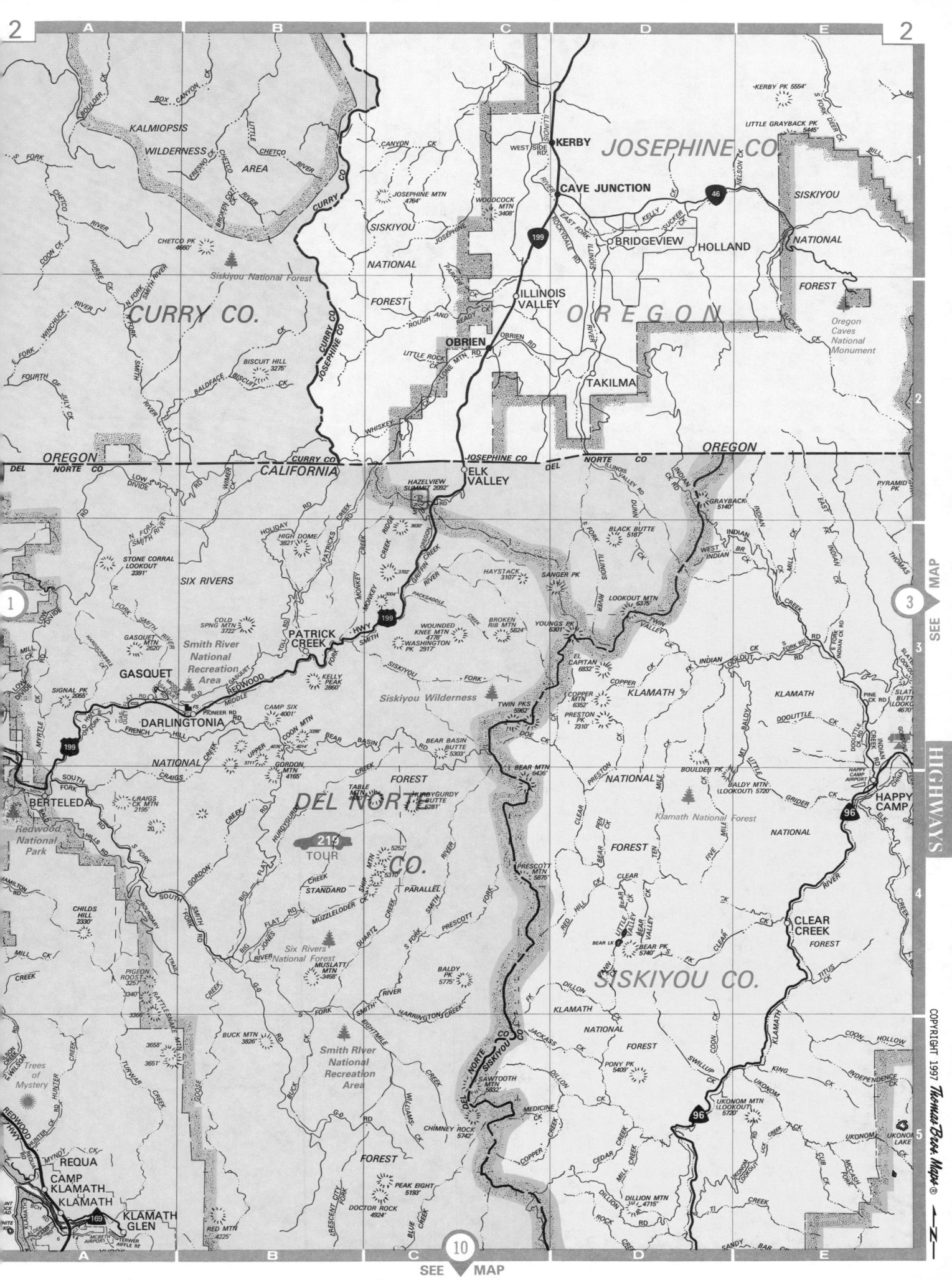

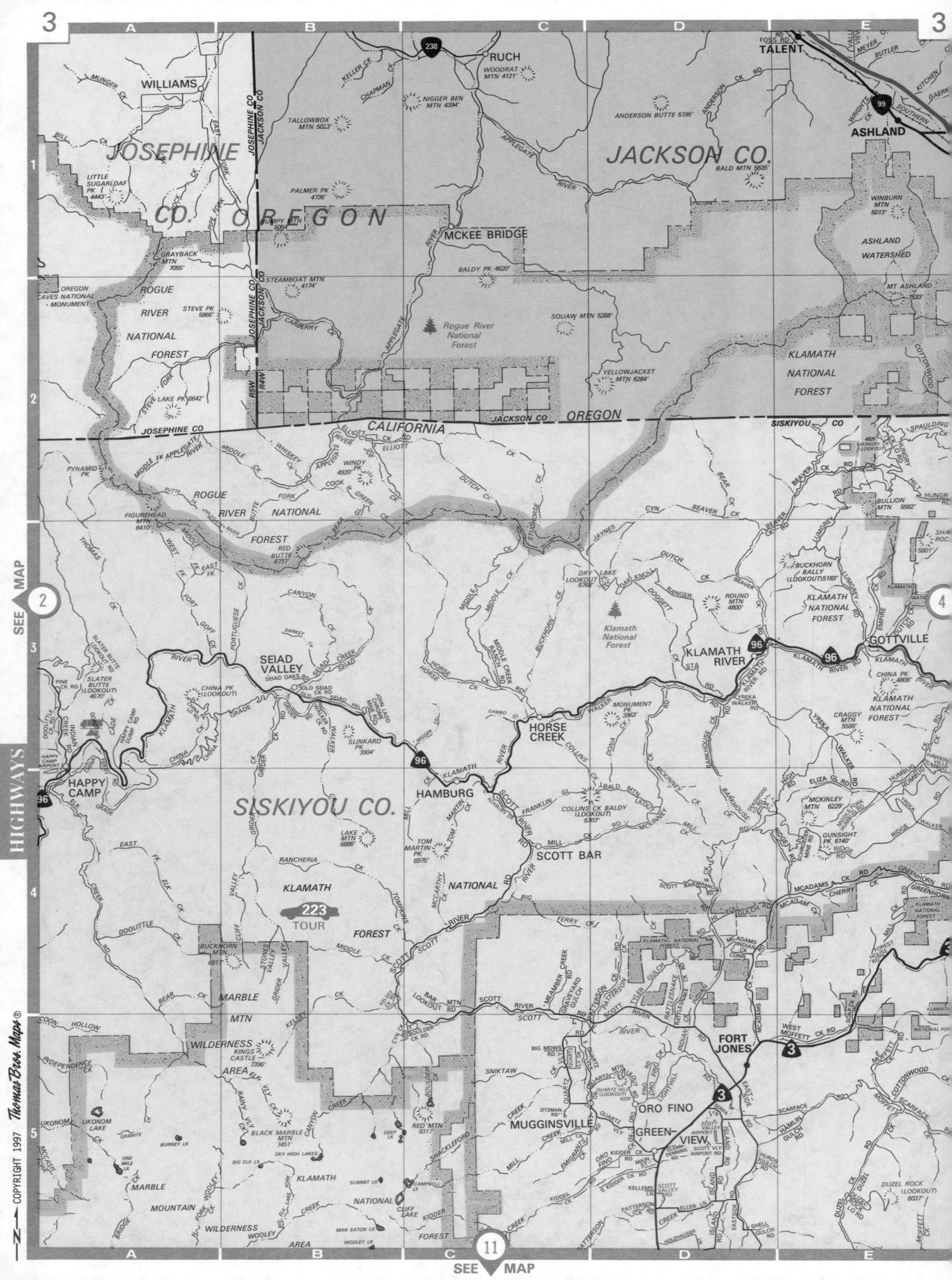

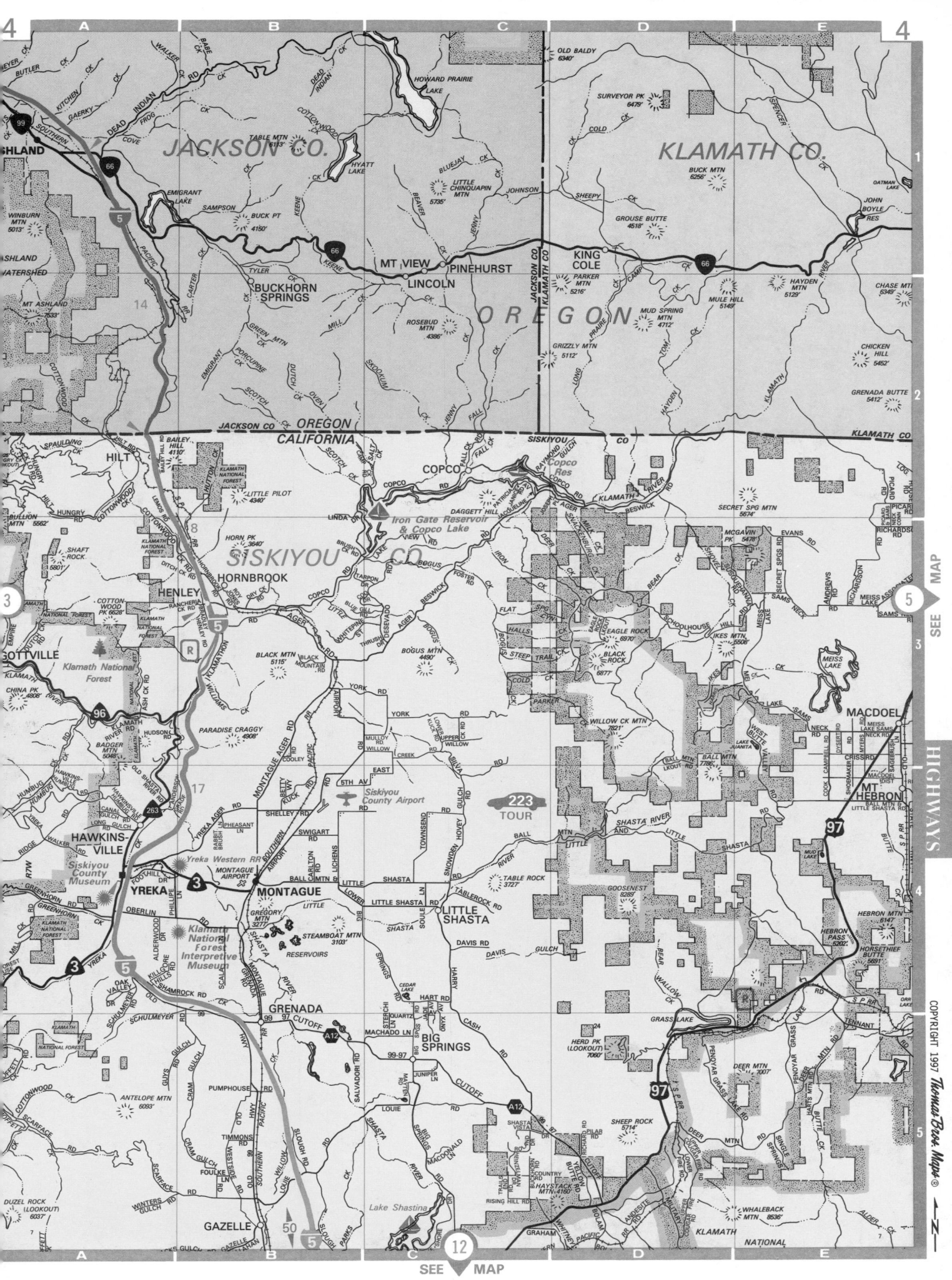

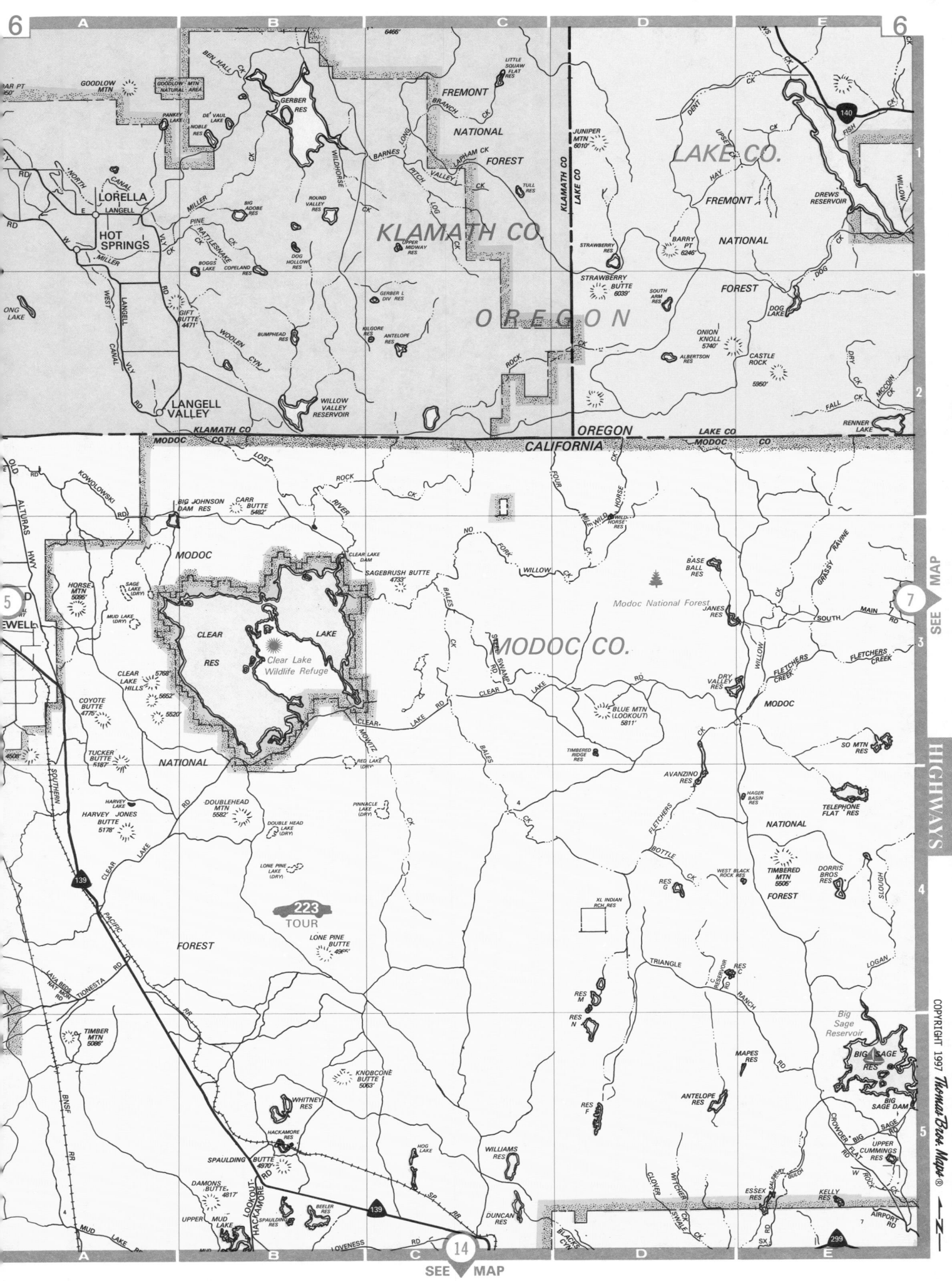

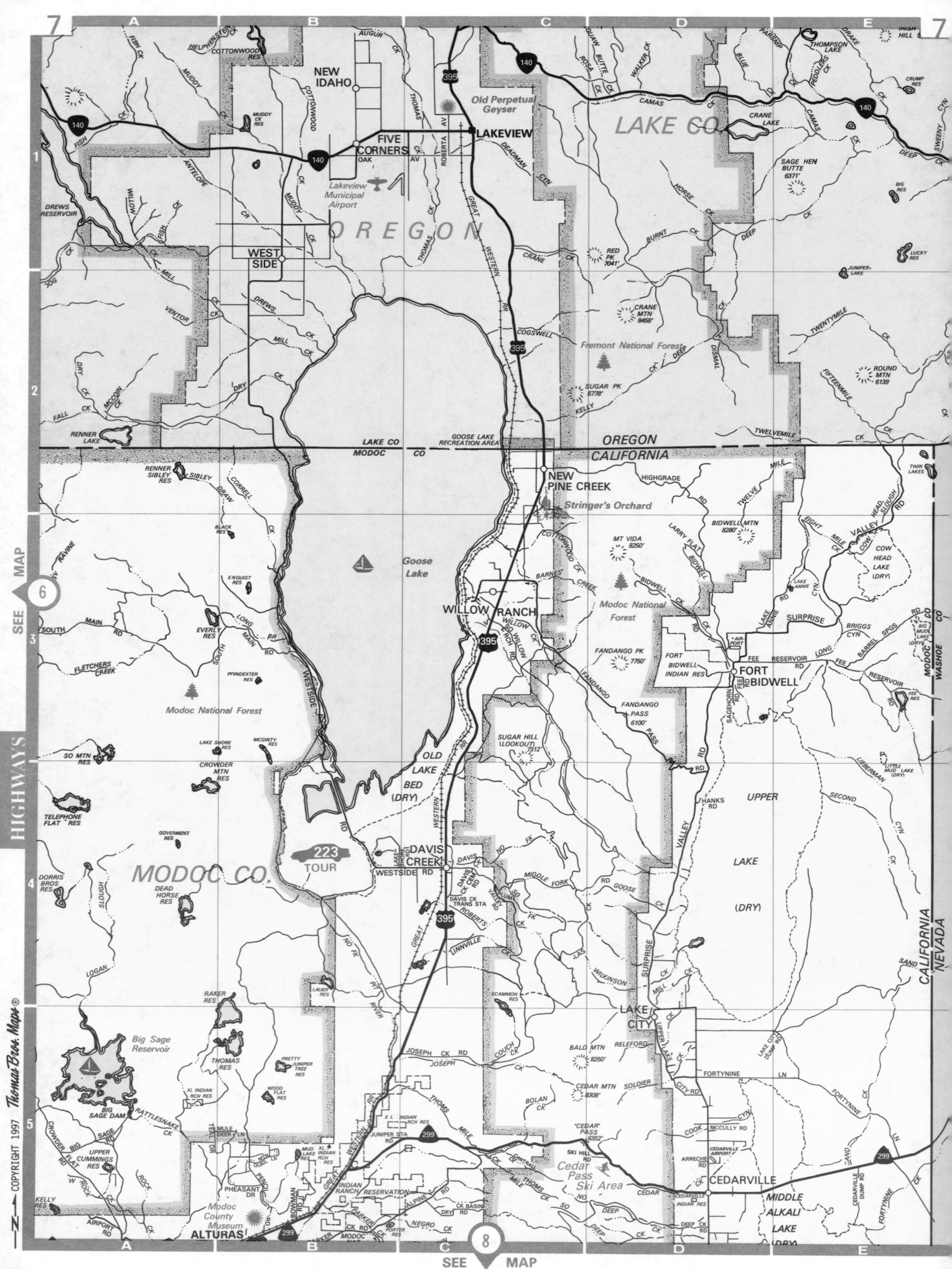

SEE MAP 7

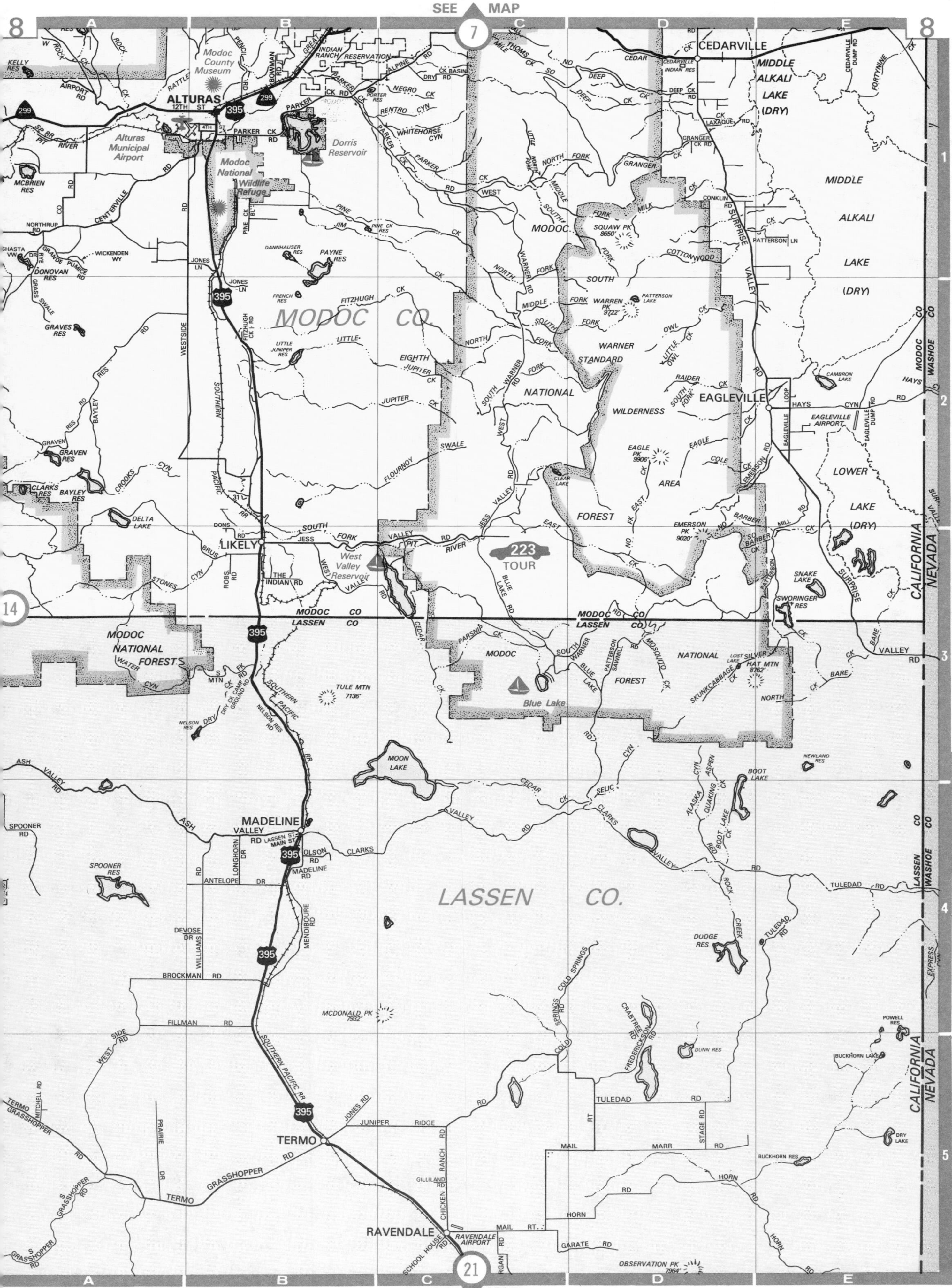
ALTURAS
Modoc County Museum
Alturas Municipal Airport
Modoc National Wildlife Refuge
Dorris Reservoir
CEDARVILLE
MIDDLE ALKALI LAKE (DRY)
MODOC CO
SQUAW PK 8650'
WARREN PK 9722'
PATTERSON LAKE
SOUTH WARNER NATIONAL STANDARD WILDERNESS AREA
MODOC NATIONAL FOREST
EAGLE PK 9906'
EMERSON PK 9020'
EAGLEVILLE
EAGLEVILLE AIRPORT
LOWER LAKE (DRY)
LIKELY
West Valley Reservoir
223 TOUR
DELTA LAKE
CLARKS RES
BAYLEY RES
GRAVEN RES
GRAVES RES
DONOVAN RES
SHASTA VW
MCBRIEN RES
KELLY RES
PAYNE RES
DANNHAUSER RES
FRENCH RES
LITTLE JUNIPER RES
PINE CK RES
SNAKE LAKE
SWORINGER RES
CAMBRON LAKE
MODOC CO
LASSEN CO
TULE MTN 7136'
Blue Lake
LOST LAKE
SILVER
HAT MTN 8762'
NELSON RES
MOON LAKE
MADELINE
SPOONER RES
NEWLAND RES
BOOT LAKE
LASSEN CO.
DODGE RES
MCDONALD PK 7932'
DUNN RES
POWELL RES
BUCKHORN LAKE
BUCKHORN RES
DRY LAKE
TERMO
RAVENDALE
RAVENDALE AIRPORT
OBSERVATION PK 7964'
CALIFORNIA
NEVADA
MODOC CO
WASHOE CO
LASSEN CO
WASHOE CO
A B C D E
1 2 3 4 5
14
395
299
HIGHWAYS

SEE MAP 21

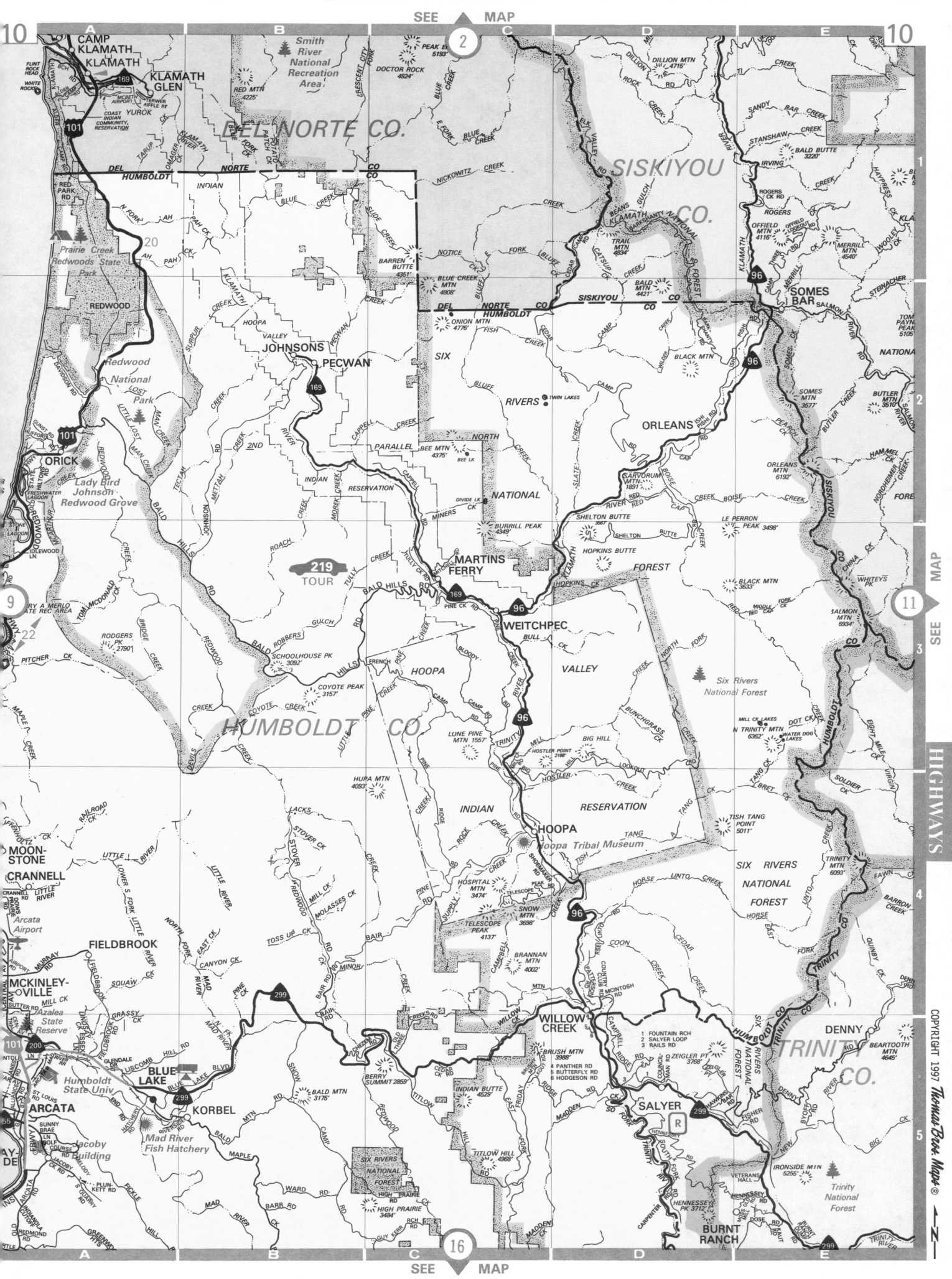

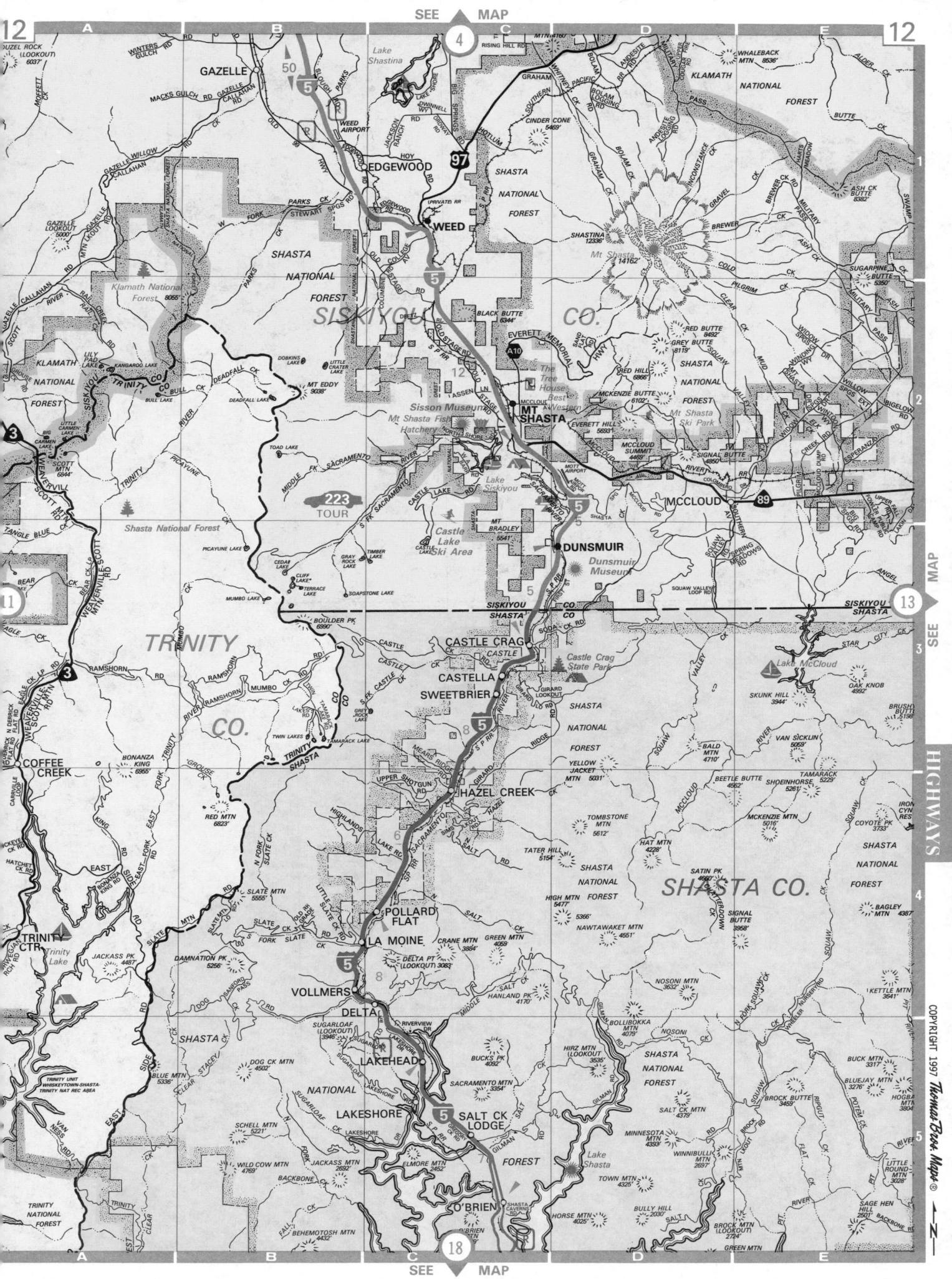

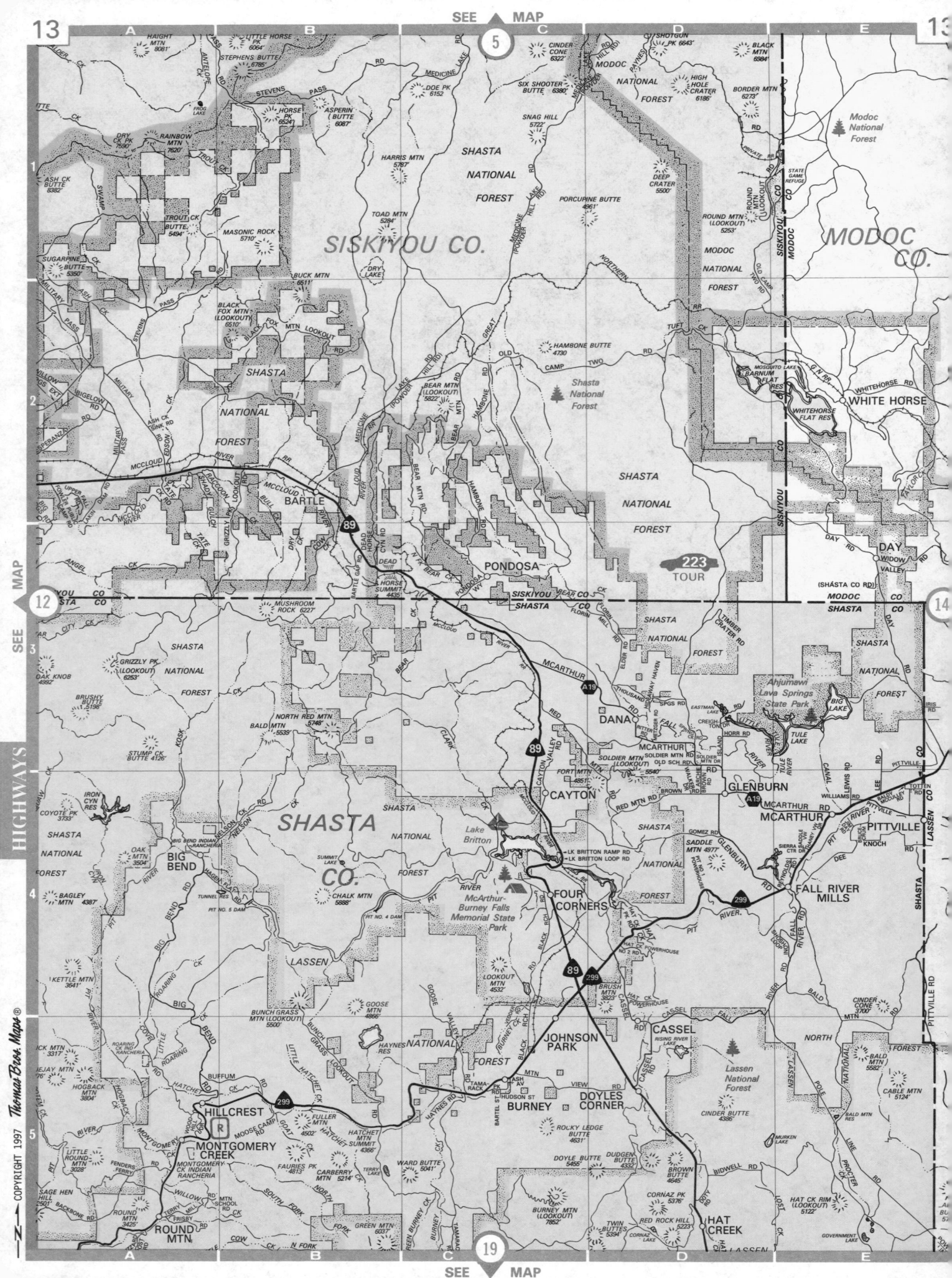

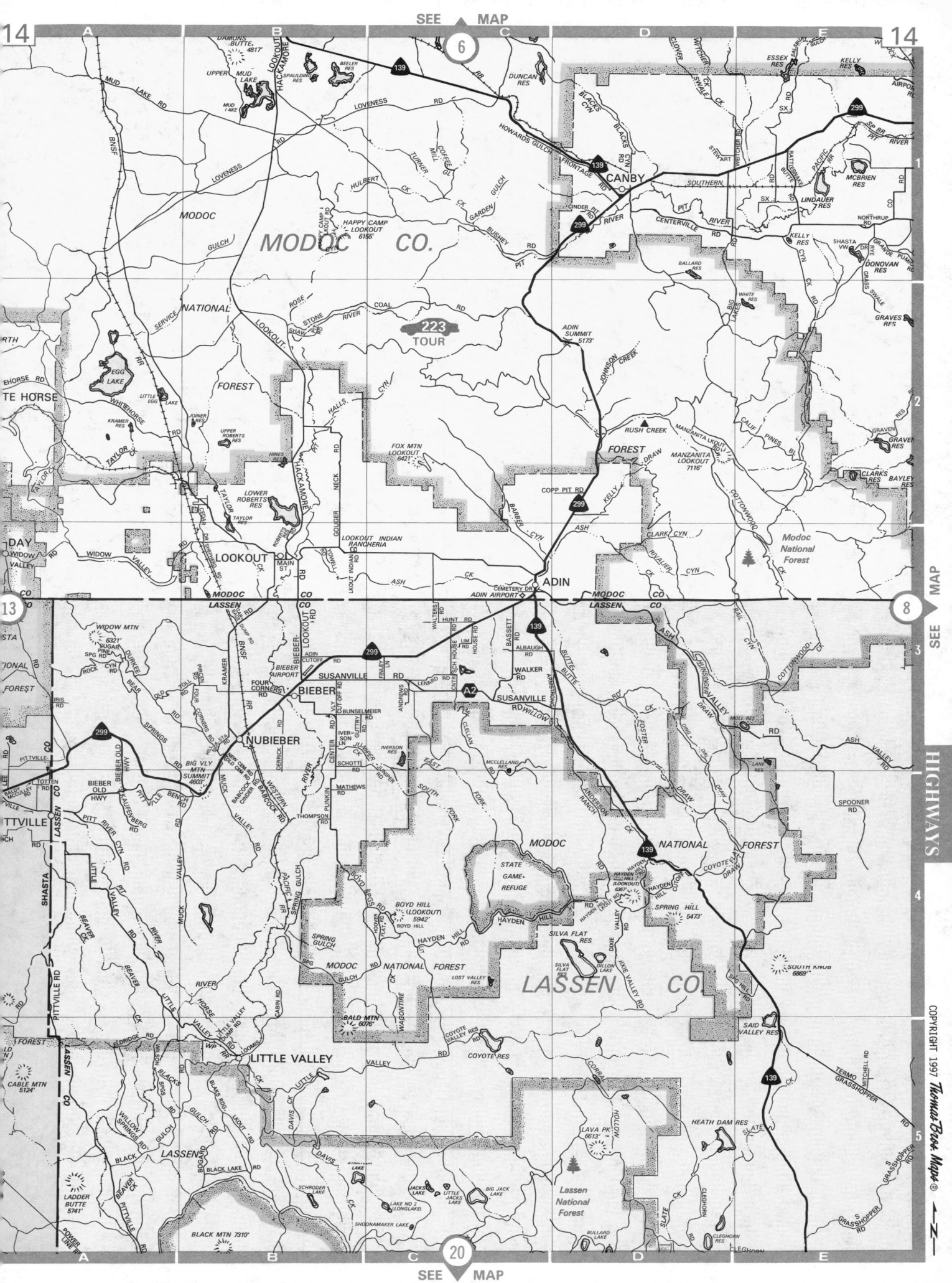

SEE MAP 9

A
B
C
D
E
1
2
3
4
5
SAMOA
HUMBOLDT CO AIRPORT
FAIR-HAVEN
EUREKA AIRPORT
EUREKA
5TH ST
HARRIS ST
CUT-TEN
BAY
HUMBOLDT
HUMBOLDT BAY
S JETTY RD
FIELDS LANDING
RIVER
N FORK
ELK RIVER
PACIFIC
TABLE BLUFF
INDIANOLA RESERVATION
COPENHAGEN
TOMPKINS HILL RD
SALMON
CANNIBAL
COCK ROBIN ISL
LOLETA
101
EEL RIVER
SINGLEY RD
OIL WELL RD
NORTHWESTERN PACIFIC
GOBLE LN
211
PALMER CK RD
FORTUNA
219 TOUR
ROHNERVILLE
OCEAN
CENTERVILLE
FERNDALE
SALT RIVER
WADDINGTON RD
POOLE RD
FERNDALE DUMP DR
QUAIL HILL RD
36
HYDESVILLE
ALTON
FALSE CAPE
MATTOLE RD
BEAR RIVER RDG
RIO DELL
SCOTIA
16
REDWOOD HWY
EEL RIVER
CENTENNIAL RD
UPPER BEAR RIVER
CAPETOWN
CAPE MENDOCINO
SUGAR LOAF ISLAND
HUMBOLDT CO
LOWERY RD
RIVER RIDGE RD
MT PIERCE 3188'
N FK MATTOLE RIVER
TAYLOR PK 3390'
OLD MATTOLE RD
N FORK
MATTOLE RIVER
BIG HILL 3040'
PETROLIA
CHAMBERS RD
MOORE HILL 1245'
CONKLIN CK RD
LIGHTHOUSE RD
CATHEYS PK 3070'
LITTLE CHAPARRAL MTN 2650'
COOSKIE MTN 2951'
HONEYDEW
KING RANGE NATIONAL CONSERVATION AREA
SQUAW CK
OAT HILL 2350'
NORTH SLIDE PK 3512'
HONEYDEW CK
UPPER EAST FK
WILDER RIDGE
HADLEY PK 3020'
King Range National Conservation Area
KINGS PK 4087'
SHUBRICK PK 2797'
SADDLE MTN 3290'
HORSE MTN 1929'
S KINGS PK RD

HIGHWAYS

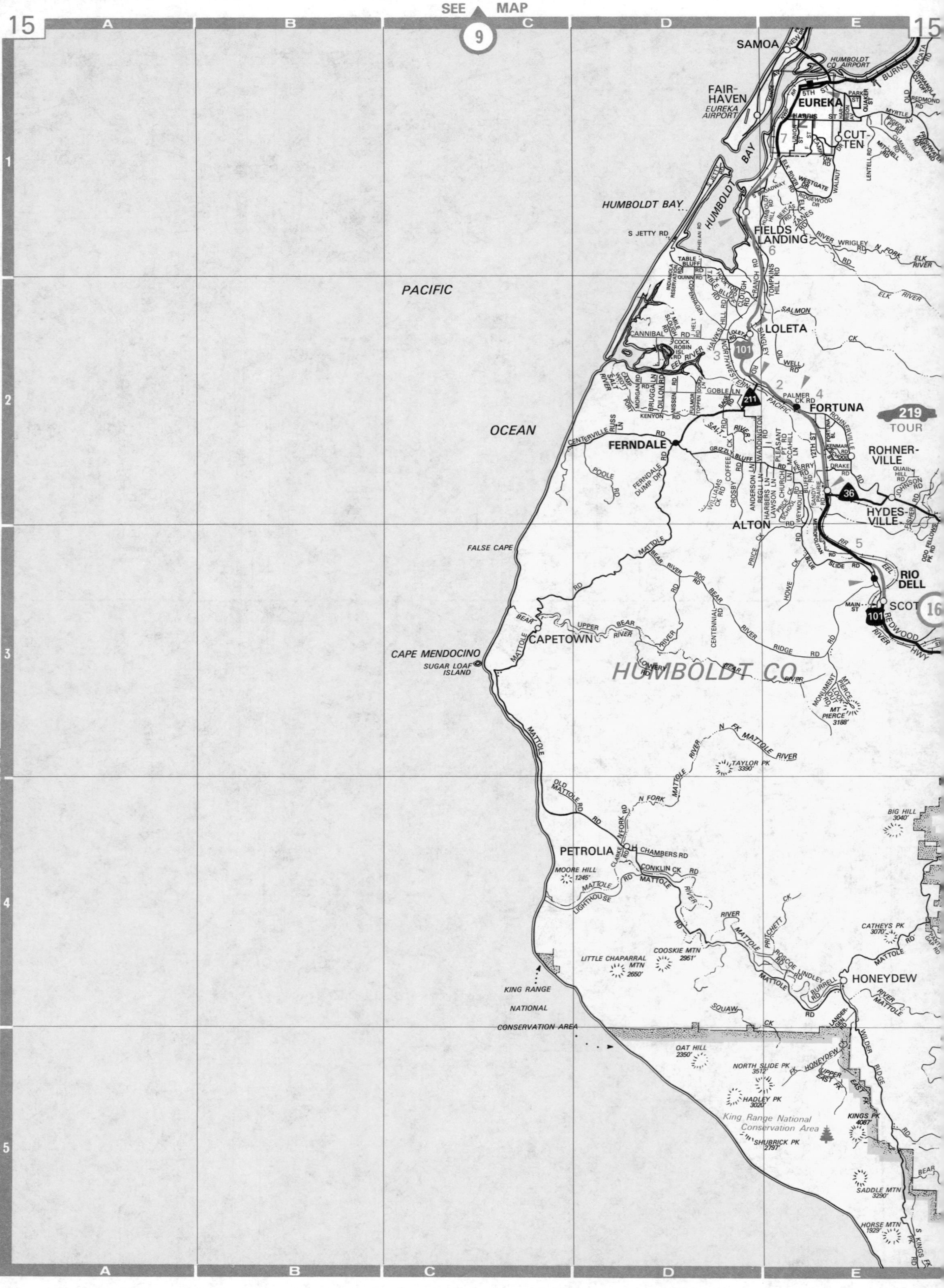

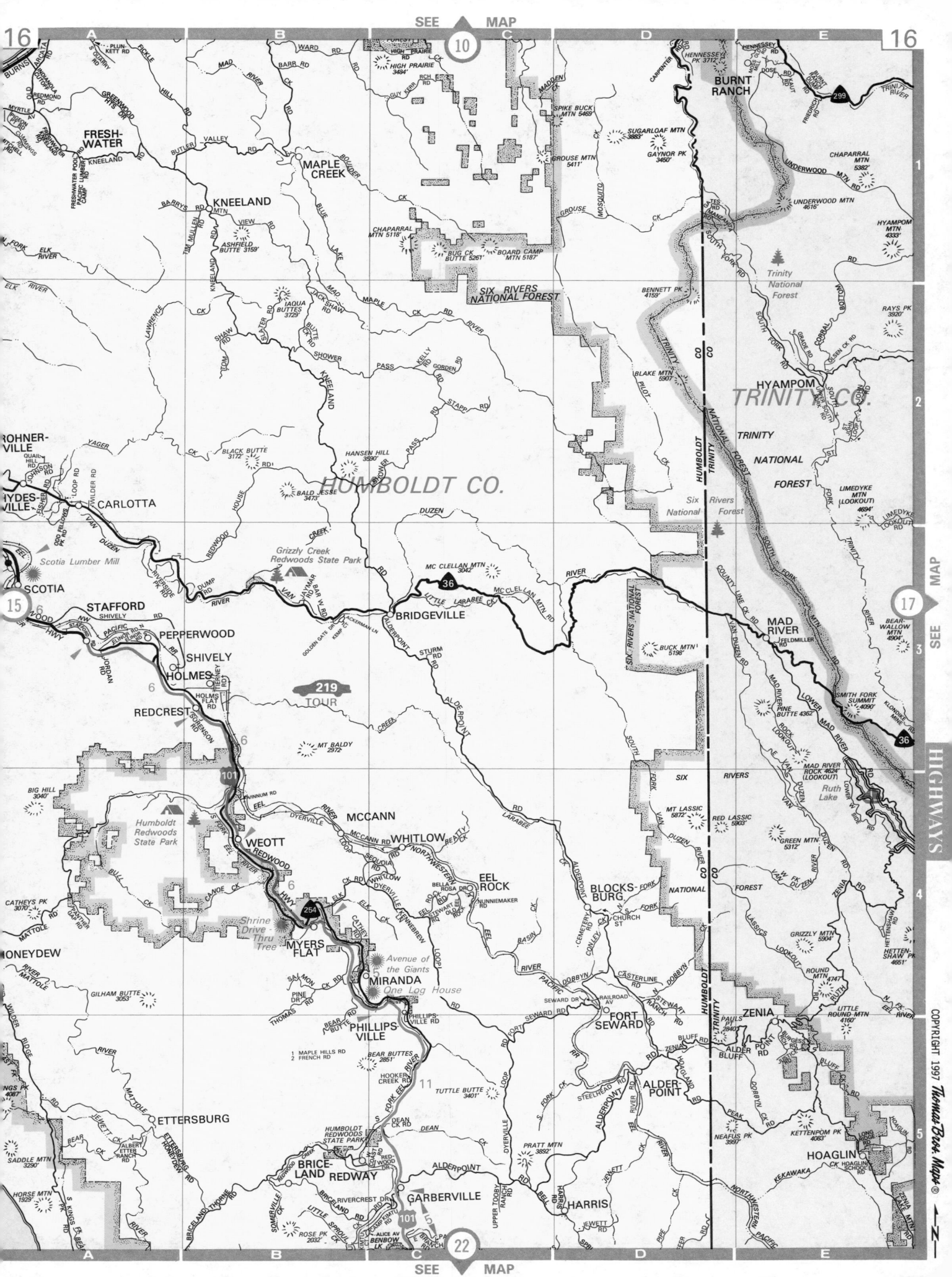

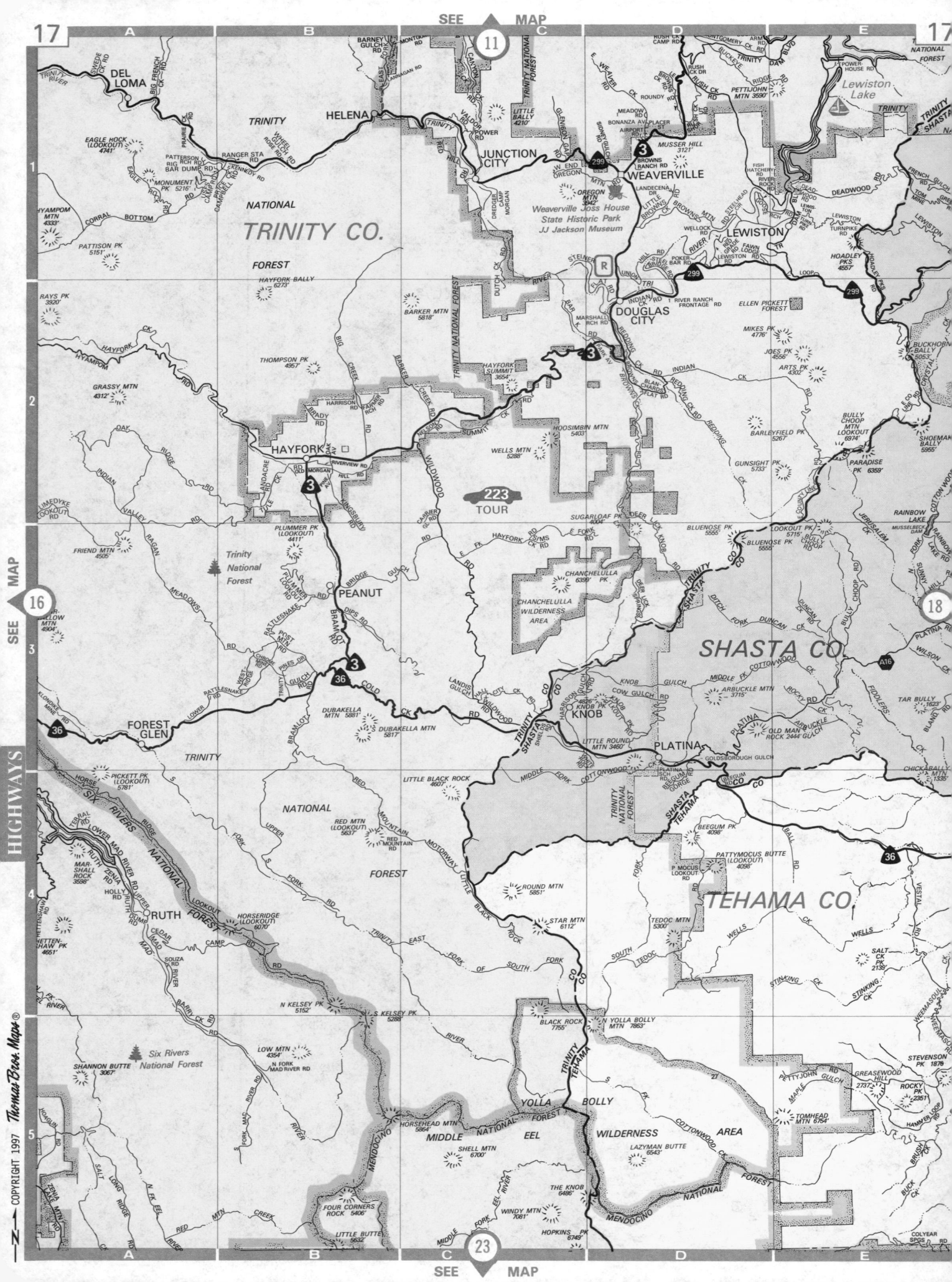

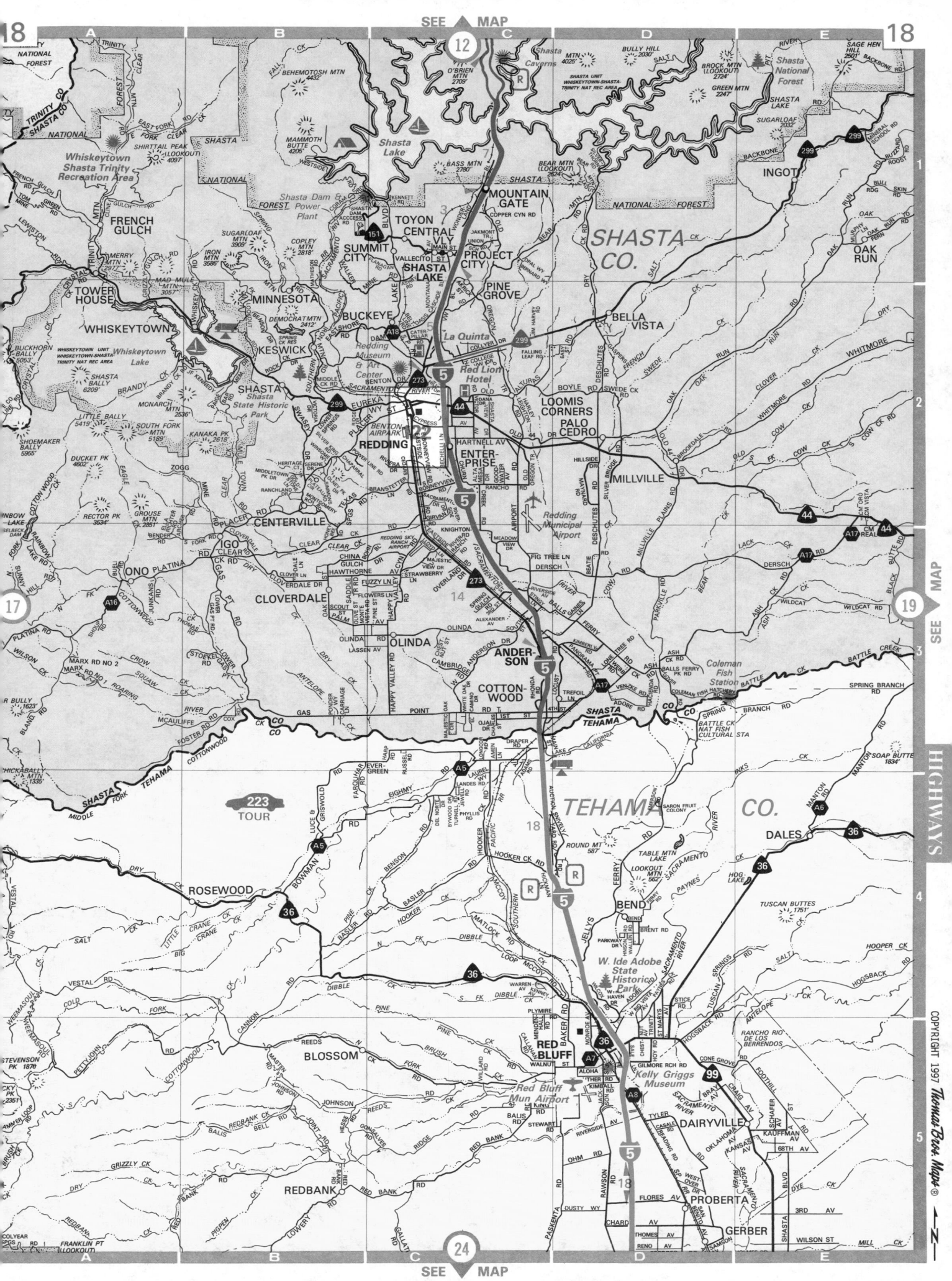

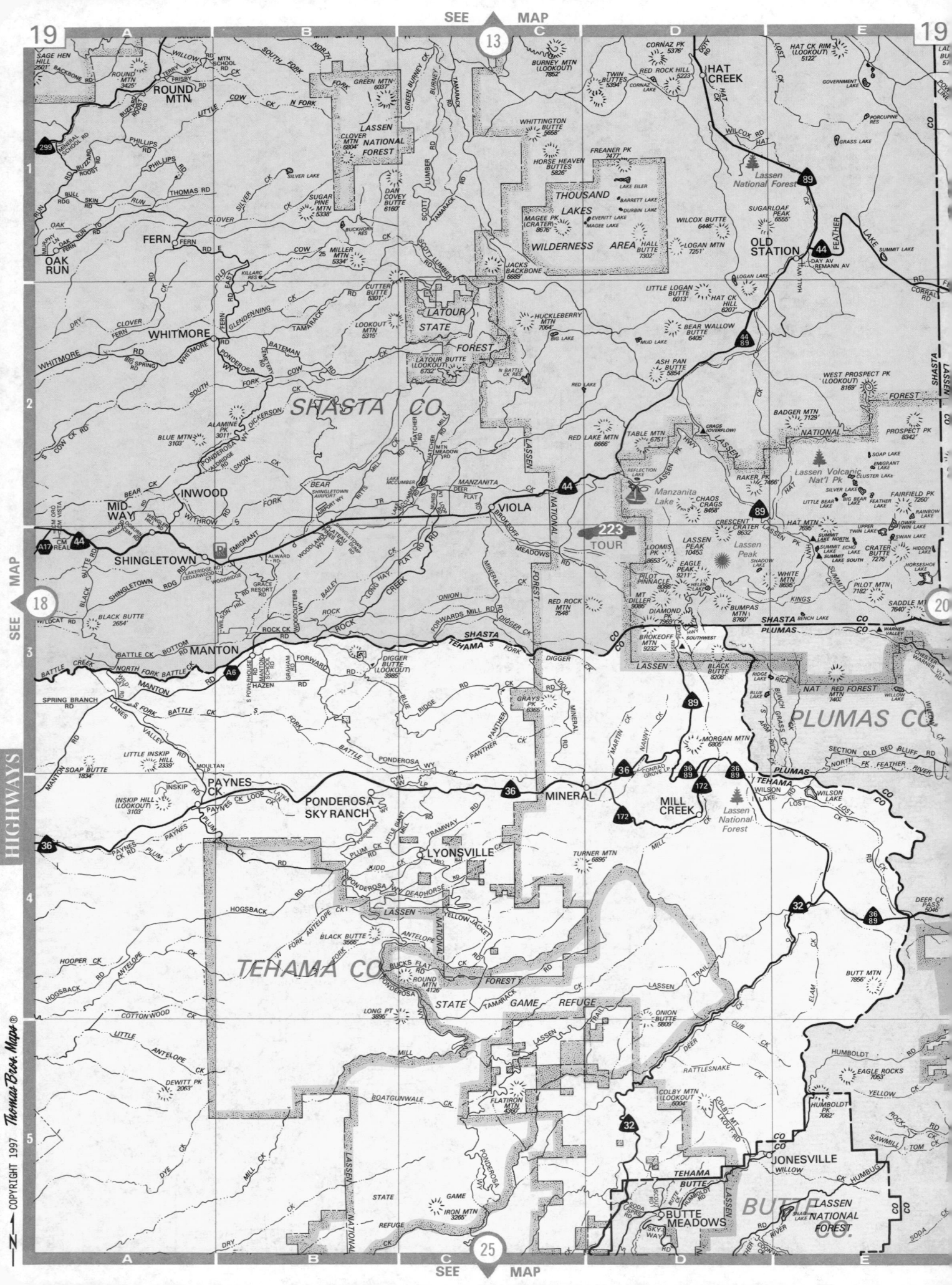

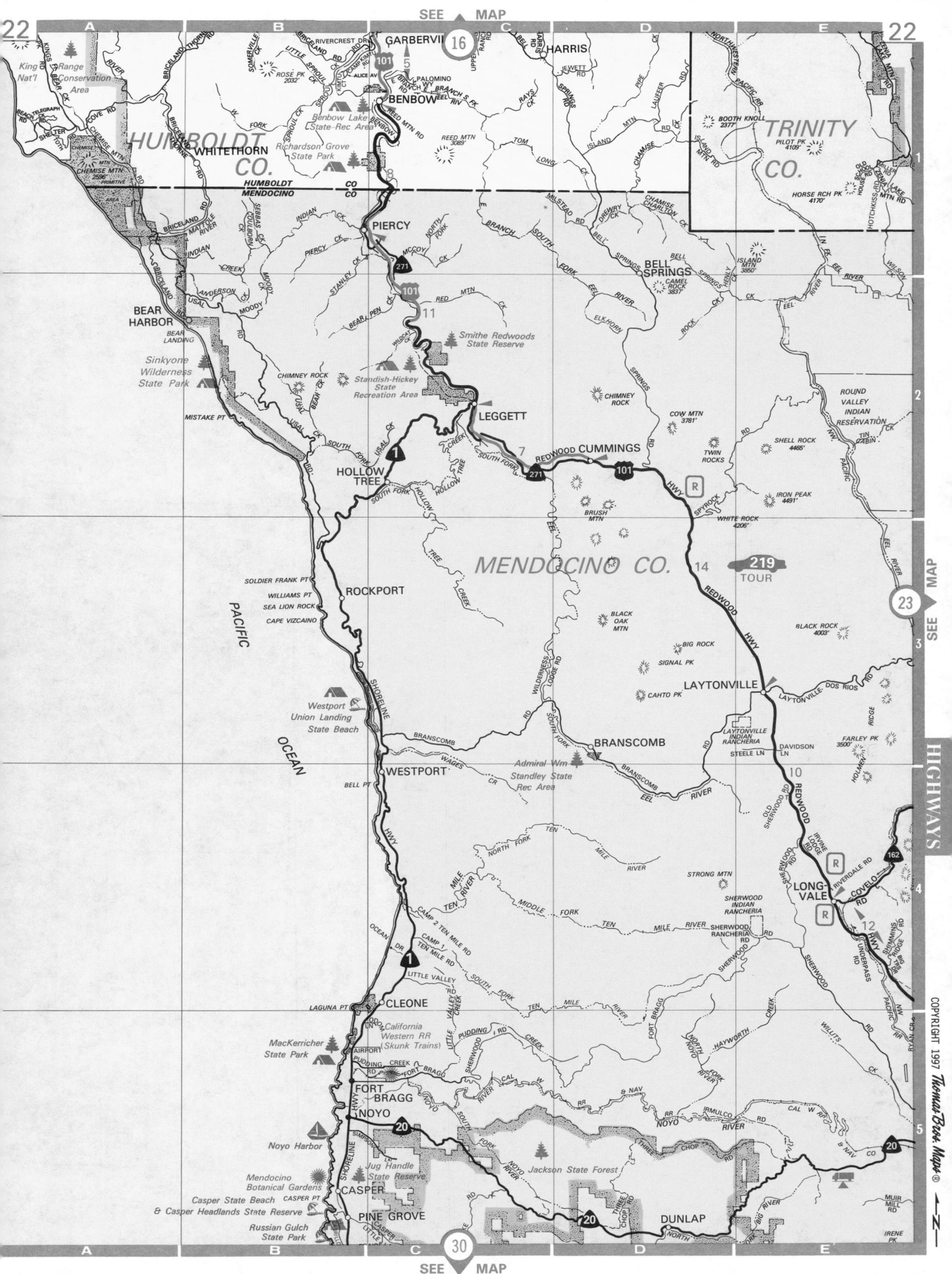

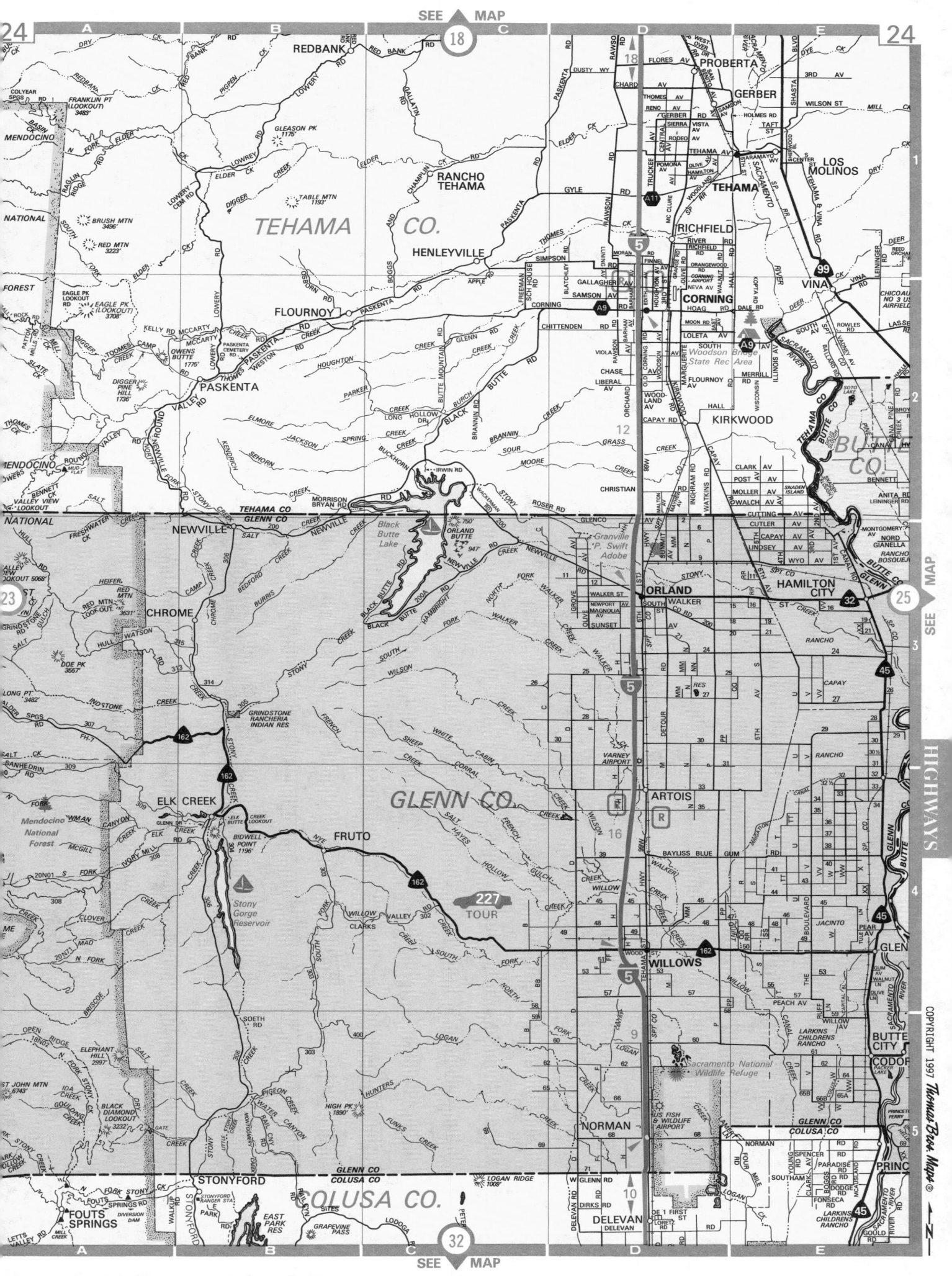

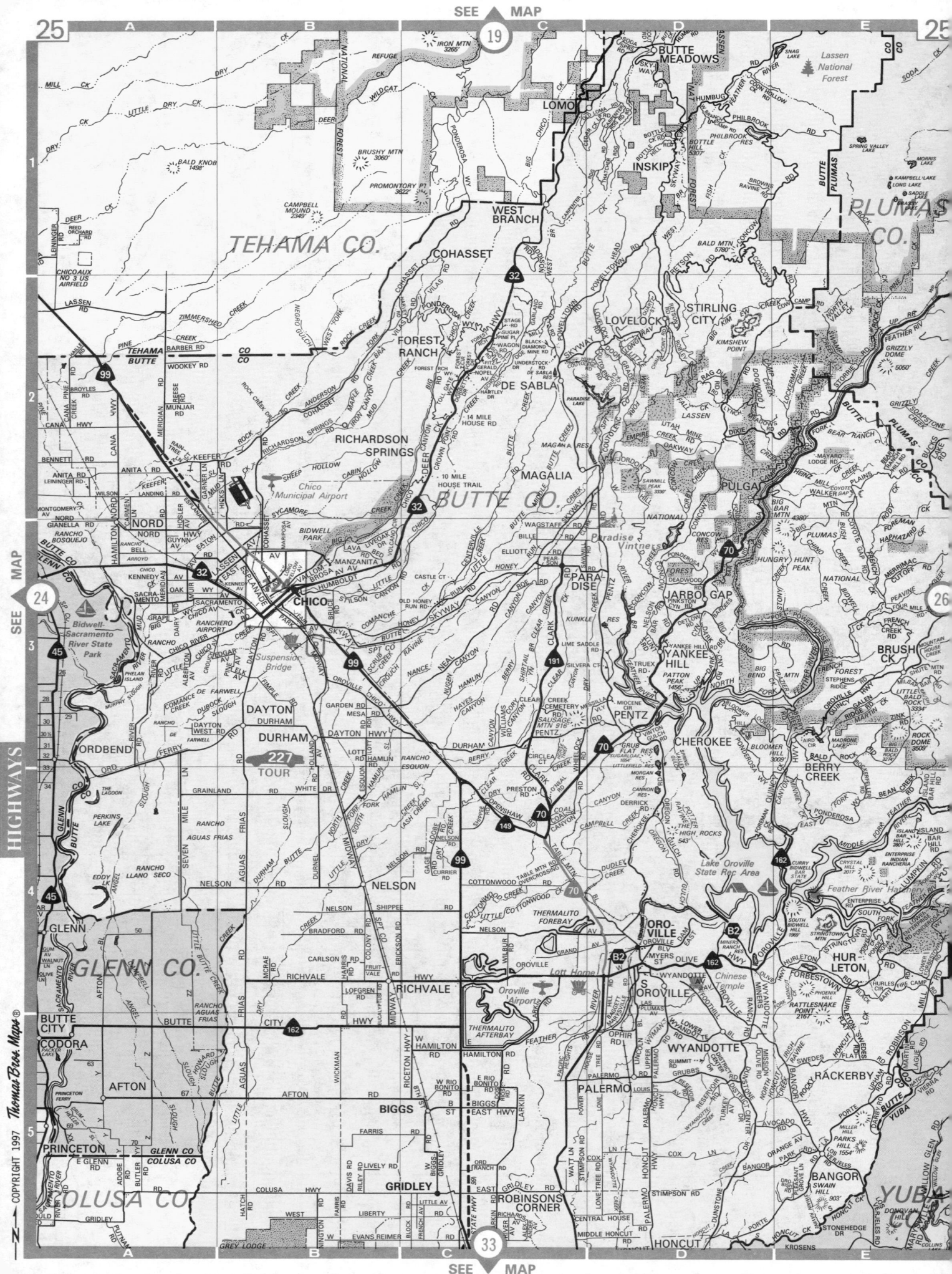

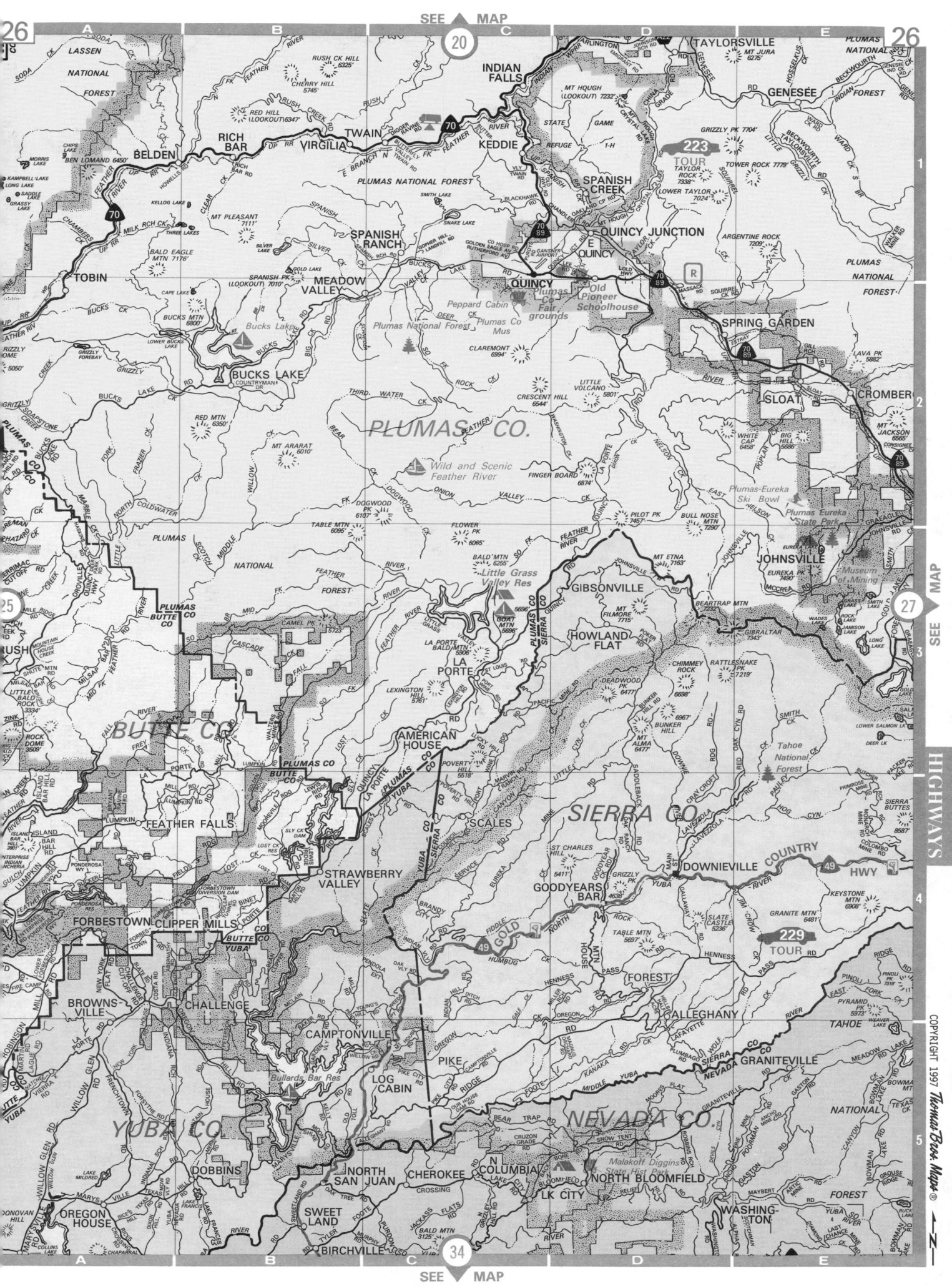

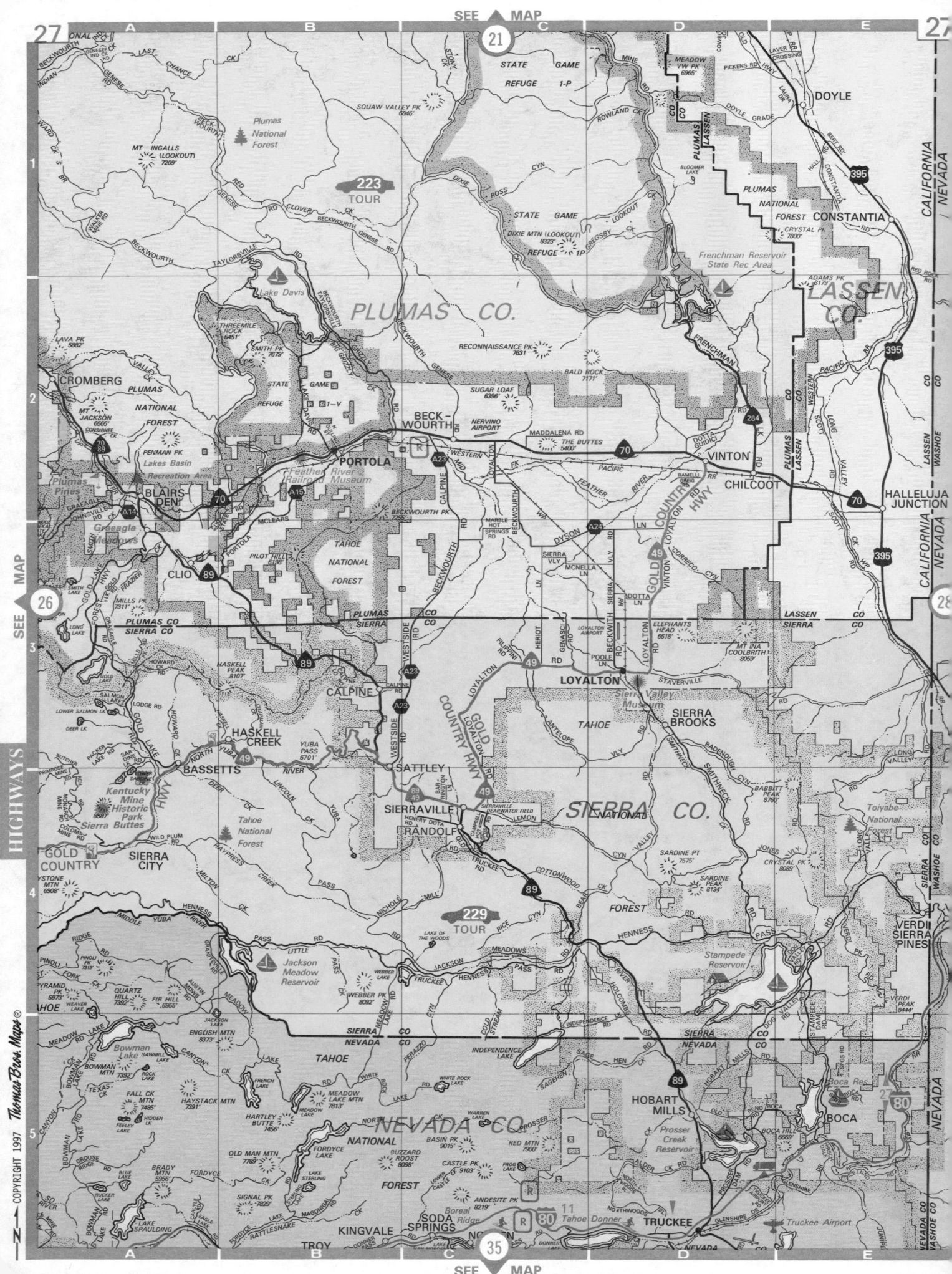

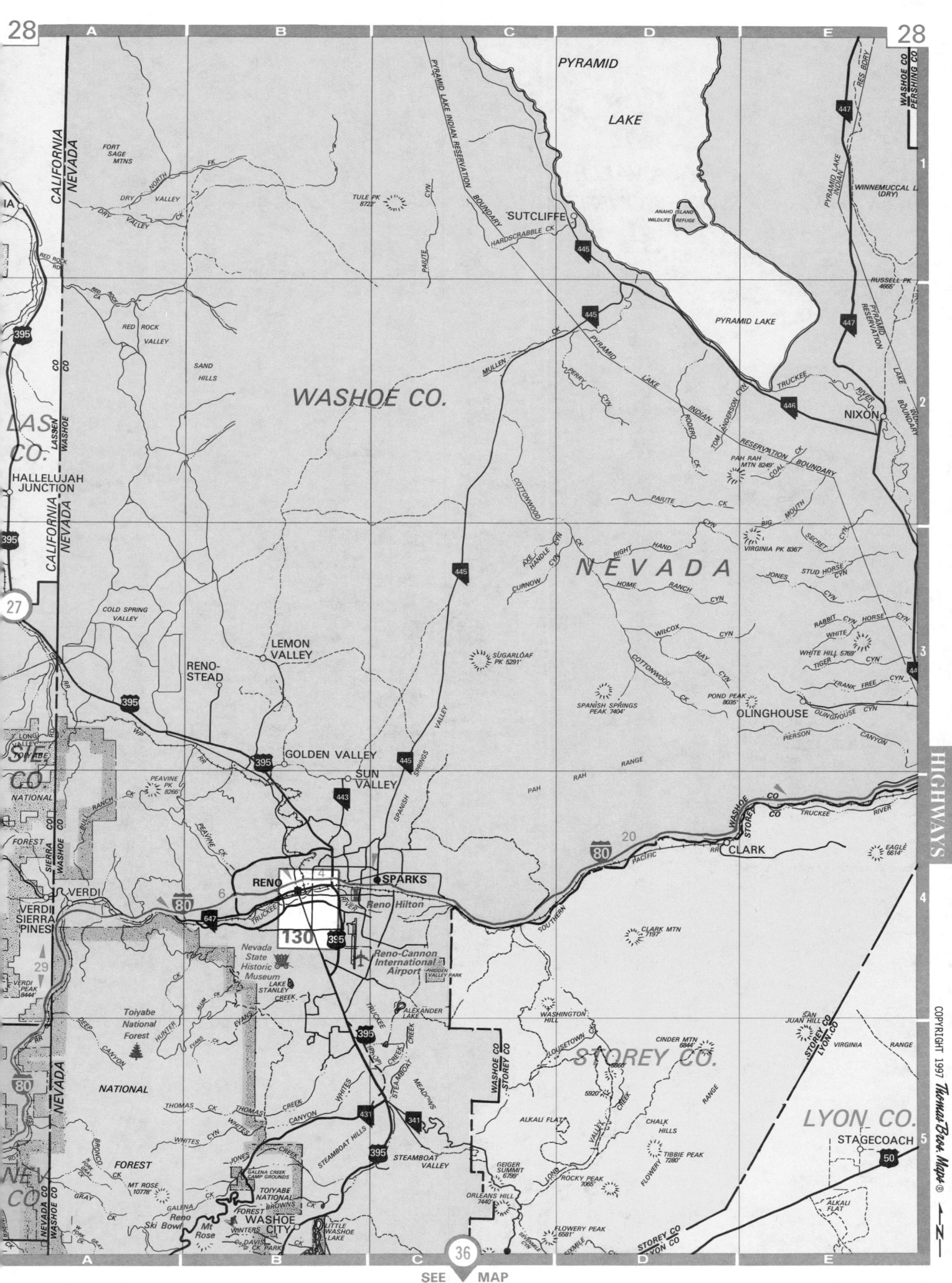

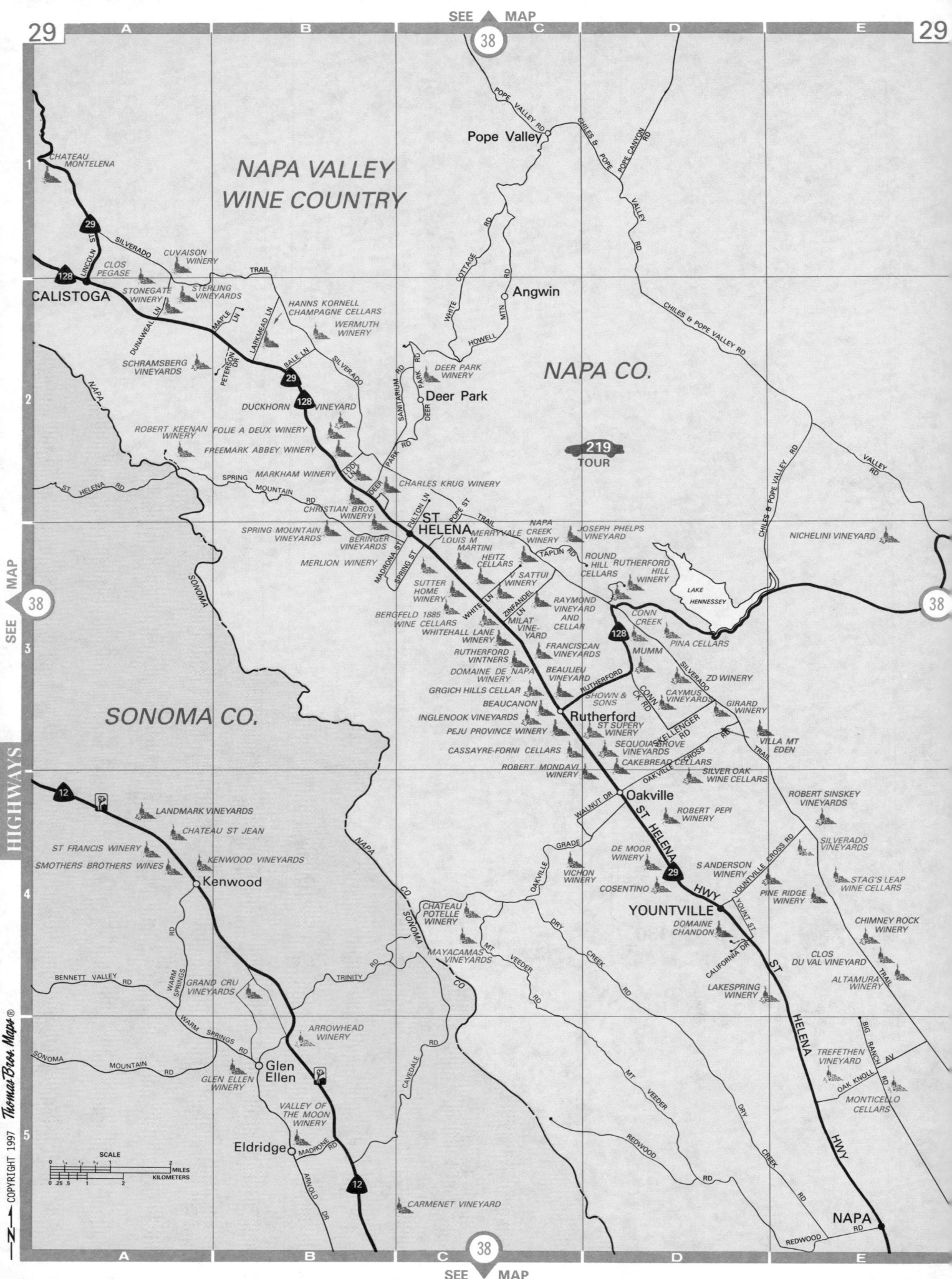

SEE MAP 23

A   B   C   D   E

HIGHWAYS

COLUSA CO.

SNOW MTN W

POTATO HILL

MILL VALLEY
STIRRUP SPILLWAY
BIG SPRINGS
SADDLE
LETTS

Frey Vineyards
RIDGE WOOD
TOMKI RD
HESSMAN AIRPORT
NORTH BUSCH LN
CUTOFF RD
EEL RIVER
PINE MTN
LITTLE ROUND MTN
ELK MOUNTAIN
RICE CREEK
RICE FORK
BEAR CREEK
BEAR CREEK STA
LAKE CO / COLUSA CO
COLUSA COUNTY RD
HORSE GLADE
CEDAR CAMP
GOAT MTN

IMPASSABLE ROCKS
IRENE PK
REEVES RD
CANYON
WALKER RD
17
REDWOOD NW
101 PACIFIC HWY
EAST SIDE RUSSIAN RD
WEST RD
POWER HOUSE RD
BUSCH GIBSON LN
CROSS CENTERVILLE
SPRING VALLEY RD
WEST POTTER RD
POTTER VALLEY
POMO
PINE AV
BURRIS LN
GATE
HOWARD MILL STA
HORSE MTN
POGES PK
MIDDLE CREEK
ELK MTN
MOUNTAIN
DEER VALLEY
SUMMER RIDGE
Mendocino Nat'l Forest
SKY ROCK GATE
HIGH GLADE
N FORK CACHE
TWIN VALLEY RD
WILSON

1

REDWOOD VALLEY
Olson Vineyards
RANCHO YOKAYO
Wiebel Vineyards
CALPELLA
MARINA DR
Lake Mendocino
MENDOCINO CO / LAKE CO
HELLS PK
HUNTER PT
BACHELOR
BACHELOR VALLEY
VALLEY
GATE
YOUNGS RD
GATE
BARTLETT FLAT STA
BARTLETT SPGS
RTLETT SPGS RD
MENDOCINO
NATIONAL
FOREST
TWIN VALLEY RD

ORR SPRINGS
ORR SPRINGS RD
Montgomery Woods State Reserve
Parducci Wine Cellars
Mendocino Vineyards
VICHY SPRINGS
20
OLD WITTER SPRING RD
Blue Lakes
SARATOGA SPRINGS
UPPER LAKE
W ROBINSON RANCHERIA
RECLAMATION RD
NICE
BRIDGE ARBOR RD
SPRING TR
LADDER RIDGE RD
CLOVER RD
GATE
LAKE CO
LONG VLY CREEK
GATE

2

123
UKIAH
8
LOOKOUT PK
VICHY SPGS RD
KNOB HILL RD
RESERVOIR RD
BLUE LAKES
SCHINDLER RD
SCOTTS
WHITE ROCK MTN
North Cow Mountain Recreation Area
EICKHOFF RD
HENDRICKS RD
29
PARK WY
ROCKY PT
Clear Lake
LUCERNE
BERGER BAY
20
BALDY MTN
GLEN HAVEN
CLEAR LAKE OAK

SEE MAP 30

BRANCH RIVER
PINE RIDGE
NAVARRO RIVER
TALMAGE
GIELOW LN
CUNNINGHAM RD
CANYON RD
FERN
MILL
TINDALL RNCH RD
COW
RANCHO YOKAYO
Hidden Cellars Winery
Whaler Vineyard
South Cow Mountain OHV Rec Area
SCOTTS
DESSIE
Lakeport Historic Museum
11TH ST
LAKEPORT
George G Hoberg Vista Pt
Lake County Museum
RUMSEY BAY
SHAG ROCK
QUERCUS PT
HENDERSON
SODA BAY
KONO TAYEE
KONOCTI BAY

UKIAH RD
ROMERS DAIRY RD
PACIFIC
101 REDWOOD HWY
RUSSIAN RIVER
Rancho De Sanel
Jepson Vineyards
Fetzer Vineyards
12
PRATT RNCH
McDowell Valley Vineyards
175
Lake Co. Fairgrounds
LAKEPORT BL
MARTIN ST
Kendall-Jackson
Konocti Cellars
SODA BAY
BIG VALLEY
FINLEY
FINLEY RD
SODA RIVIERA HEIGHTS
RIVIERA WEST
KELSEYVILLE
MT KONOCTI
KONOCTI
CLEAR LAKE

3

UKIAH BOONVILLE RD
253
BOONVILLE
UKIAH BOONVILLE RD
HUTSELL
RANCHERIA
MENDOCINO CO.
HOPLAND
CR RD
Milano Winery
WARD MTN
SQUAW ROCK
MOUNTAIN HOUSE RD
TOLL RD
RED ROCK
Lampson Airport
ARGONAUT
MERRITT
HIGHLAND SPGS RES
ADOBE RES
PETERSON LN
HIGHLAND SPGS RD
WIGHT WY
KELSEY CREEK
GLEN VIEW
29
175
THURSTON LAKE
LOWER LAKE RD
KONOCTI BAY
281
SEGLER SPGS RD
NORTH DIENER RD
LOCH LOMOND
LOMOND

SEE MAP 32

GRIZZLY PK
128
YORKVILLE
Mailliard Redwoods State Reserve
GARCIA RIVER
FISH ROCK RD
HIBBARD RD
BIG OAK DR
ELKHORN RD
13
GUBE MTN
PARDALOE PK
ROCKPILE PK
BLACK MTN
WHITE MTN
MTN TOM
BUCK MTN
MORRIS PK
SKY HIGH
CHERRY
RED MTN
Fritz Cellars
ROCKPILE RD
128
PRESTON
Bandiera Winery
GEYSERS RD
CLOVERDALE
CREEK
MENDOCINO CO / SONOMA CO
RANCHO CASLAMAYOMI
GEYSER PK
GEYSER RESORT RD
ANDERSON CR
GEYSERS RD
ADAMS
HOBERGS
COBB
Boggs Mtn State Forest
PINE GROVE
COBB MTN
FOREST
WHISPERING PINES
ANDERSON SPRINGS
SUGARLOAF

4

MENDOCINO CO
SONOMA CO

SONOMA CO.
ANNA-POLIS
FULLER MTN
HAYFIELD HILL
LAS LOMAS
Lake Sonoma Recreation Area
LAKE SONOMA
Warm Springs Dam & Fish Hatchery
SKAGGS SPRINGS
STEWARTS POINT SKAGGS SPGS RD
BUCK MTN
ASTI
Ferrari-Carano Winery
DRY CREEK
Pedroncelli Winery
Pastori
Geyser Peak Winery
Chateau Souverain
DRY CREEK INDIAN RANCHERIA
Diamond Oaks Vineyards
Murphy-Goode
BLACK MTN
Lake Sonoma Winery
COZZENS CORNERS
CANYON RD
GEYSERVILLE
RANCHO TZABACO
Nervo
101
Trentadue
128
JIMTOWN
Sausal Winery
RANCHO ALLACOMES OR MORISTUL

5

SHINGLE MILL
SODA SPRINGS
STEWARTS POINT SPGS RD
STEWARTS POINT INDIAN RANCHERIA
TIN BARN
COAST GER
OAK MTN
KING RIDGE
SKYLINE
Robert Stemmler
Lambert Bridge
Lytton Springs
WINE CREEK
BRACK
Souverain
LYTTON
ALEXANDER
Healdsburg Municipal Airport
River Oaks Simi Winery
Soda Rock
ALEXANDER VLY
Field Stone
Alexander Valley
Johnson's ALEXANDER VALLEY RANCHERIA
CHALK HILL RD
RANCHO KELLOGG
MALLA COMES OR MORISTUL Y PLAN DE AGUA
128
DEL RIO
POWELL AV
HEALDSBURG
THOMAS RD

A   B   C   D   E

SEE MAP 37

Thomas Bros. Maps®
COPYRIGHT 1997
N

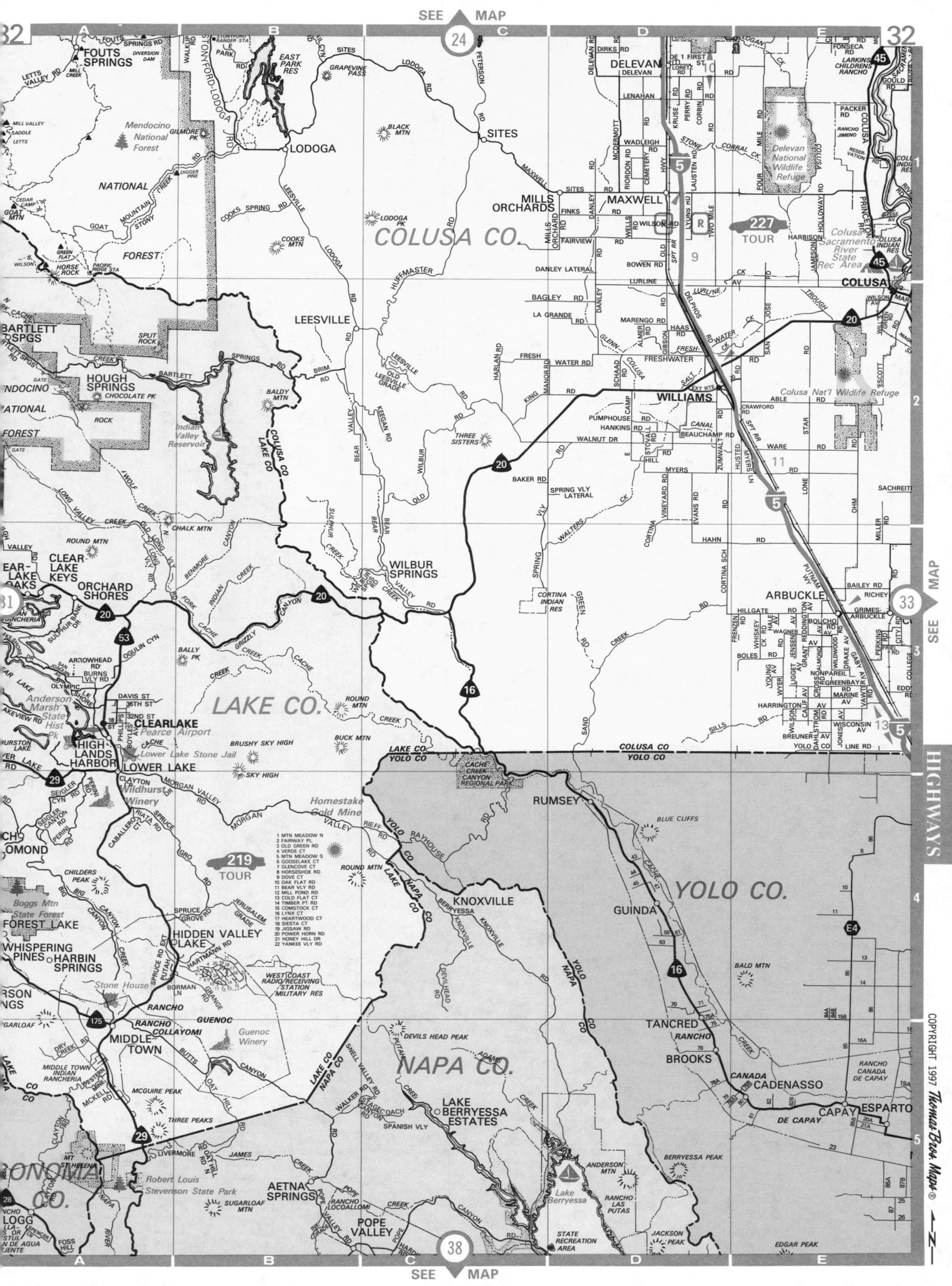

SEE MAP 26

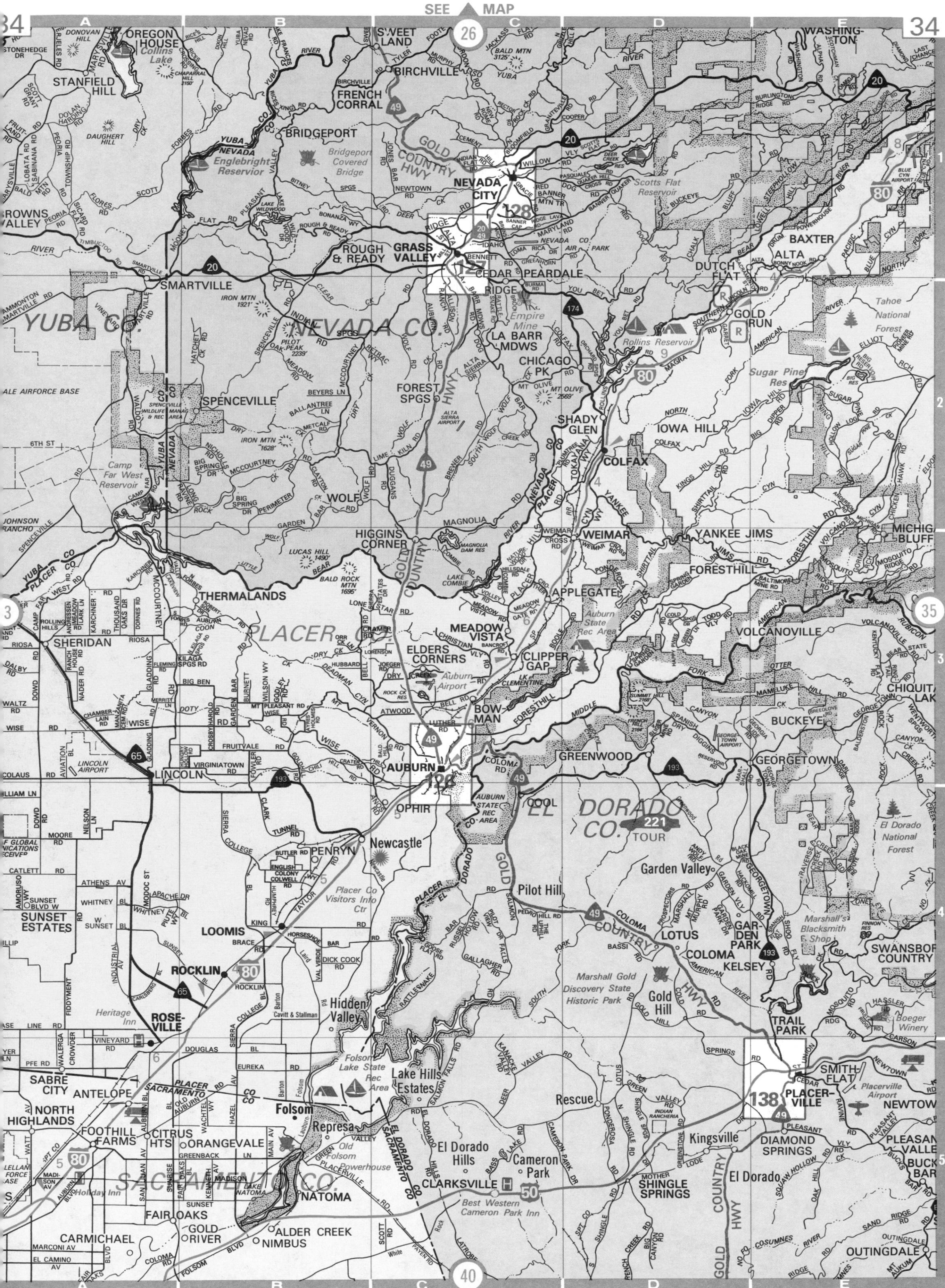

SEE MAP 35

SEE MAP 40

HIGHWAYS

28

PLACER CO.

WASHOE CITY

Mt Rose
Slide Mountain Ski
NATIONAL FOREST BROWNS
WINTERS

NEW WASHOE CITY

Little Washoe Lake

STOREY CO.

VIRGINIA CITY
GOLD HILL

LYON CO.

431

Diamond Peak

INCLINE VILLAGE

Hyatt Lake Tahoe Resort Hotel
Ponderosa Ranch

Bowers Mansion

429

WASHOE LAKE

Nevada State Park

WASHOE CO.

MT DAVIDSON 7864

The Castle

FLOWERY PEAK 6581

EMMA 6462 CYN

LYON CO.

SILVER CITY

KATE PEAK 6122

341 DAYTON

Dayton State Park

NORTHSTAR
267
TAHOE VISTA
NORTH SHORE
MARTIS
ROSEKNOB 9600
OPHIR CK PRICE LAKE

KINGS BEACH
28
CRYSTAL BAY

Lake Tahoe Nevada State Park

MARLETTE PK 8780

HOBART CREEK RES

MARLETTE LAKE

SCRIPPS WILDLIFE MNGMT AREA

MCCLELLAN PEAK 7456

SILVER CITY

BULL CANYON

MILL CANYON

AGATE BAY
CARNELIAN BAY

Kings Beach State
Beach Rec Area

WASHOE CO

WASHOE

CARSON CITY

RAWE PEAK 8348

PINE NUT MOUNTAINS

MILL CANYON

DRY LAKE

PLACER CO.

CALIFORNIA NEVADA

PLACER WASHOE

WASHOE CO

Nevada State Capitol

Warren Fire Museum

State Mus

512

CARSON CITY

513

CARSON CITY

CARSON CITY

PINE NUT

LYON PEAK 8774

1

Lake Tahoe

28

SNOW VALLEY PK 9214

State Railroad Mus

SUNRISE PASS

SUNRISE PASS

PLACER EL DORADO CO CO

CARSON CITY

50

KINGS CYN

Stewart

Stewart Indian Mus

MCTARNAHAN HILL 6856

INDIAN OWNED

CARSON CITY
DOUGLAS CO

BISMARK PEAK 7529

DRY LAKE

GLENBROOK

50

Spooner Lake
Cross Country

DUANE BLISS PK

JACKS VALLEY

INDIAN SCHOOL LANDS

CREEK

JACKS VALLEY RD

HOT SPRINGS MTN 5951

N E V A D A

8316

6108

RANGE

2

DOUGLAS CO

Toiyabe Nat'l Forest

INDIAN CYN

SCHOOL LANDS

HOBO HOT SPGS

MINERAL PEAK 8317

INDIAN OWNED

MT COMO 9005

Mormon Station State Historic Monument

JAMES CYN

206

STEPHANIE LN

JOHNSON LN

MINERAL PEAK

INDIAN OWNED LANDS

LINCOLN CK

SIBERT CYN

VICKY LN

BUCKSKIN RANGE

ARTESIA 69

ZEPHYR COVE

GENOA

CARSON VALLEY

AIRPORT RD

Douglas County Airport

759

INDIAN OWNED LANDS

INDIAN OWNED LANDS

ARTESIA LAKE

DOUGLAS CO

GENOA LN

BUCKEYE CK

5280

PINE NUT

3

35

Best Western Station House Inn

Emerald Bay State Park

TAHOE VILLAGE
Caesars Tahoe
KINGSBURY STATELINE

395

MULLER LN

FISH SPRING FLAT

MT SIEGEL 9450

MCFAUL

DOUGLAS

FOOTHILL RD

MINDEN

88

GARDNERVILLE

395

PINE NUT

OREANA PK 9309

SOUTH LAKE TAHOE

129

207

CARSON RIVER

WATERLOO LN

DOUGLAS CO LYON CO

89

50

MONUMENT PK 10085

206

CENTERVILLE LN

DOUGLAS CO.

INDIAN OWNED LANDS

50

Heavenly Valley

COLD CK

CENTERVILLE

WASHOE INDIAN RES

4

89

Fallen Leaf Lake

Tahoe Airport

88

EAST FORK CARSON RIVER

FALLEN LEAF

MEYERS

FREEL PK 10900

JOBS SISTER 10823

206

MUD LAKE RES

INDIAN OWNED LANDS

EL DORADO CO.

JOBS PK 10580

GOLD HILL 6363

ECHO LAKE

El Dorado National Forest

FREDERICKS-BURG

FREDERICKSBURG RD

CHAMBERS RD

208

ECHO LAKE

229 TOUR

88

PAYNESVILLE

395

PHILLIPS

ECHO SUMMIT 7382

LUTHER PASS 7740

DIAMOND VALLEY RD

CARSON RIVER

EAGLE MTN 8951

89

Echo Summit

KIT CARSON CAMP GND

WOOD FORDS
Old Pony Express

PONY EXPRESS REMOUNT STATION

DARDANELLES LAKE

WATERHOUSE PK 9500

SNOWSHOE SPGS RD

88
89

WEST

Indian Creek Res

INDIAN CEM RD

RILEY

MOUNTAINEER RD

DOUGLAS CO MONO CO

SCOTTS LAKE

89

RANDALL CK

STEVENS LK

NEVADA HILL 9035

SONORA CO OF CA

STEVENS PK 10100

88

PICKETT PK 9170

Hope Valley Cross-Country

HAWKINS PK 10060

89

Alpine County Airport

HIGH PK 9465

LEVIATHAN PK 8963

GOLD HILL

5

Caples Lake 8572

RED LAKE PK 9950

LUTHER CREEK

BURNSIDE

RED LAKE

BLUE LAKES RD

HOPE VALLEY FOREST CAMP

Grover Hot Springs State Park

Alpine County Historic Complex

CURTZ LK

SHAY CK

89

BARNEY CK

LEVIATHAN LOOKOUT RD

POISON FLAT

208

Topaz Lake

KIRKWOOD

DOGWOOD LAKE RD

WOODS LAKE RD

ELEPHANTS BACK 9635

E1

MARKLEEVILLE

MARKLEEVILLE LOOKOUT RD

LEVIATHAN PK 8565

MONITOR PASS 8314

Odd Fellows Memorial

Kirkwood Cross-Country

Kirkwood Ski Resort

MARKLEEVILLE PK 9465

GROVERS HOT SPRINGS

POOR BOY CREEK RD

INDIAN CK

SILVER HILL RD

89

WALKER RIVER

WEST

DOUGLAS CO MONO CO

NEVADA CALIFORNIA

AMADOR CO ALPINE CO

A L P I N E   C O.

THE NIPPLE 9390

UPPER BLUE LAKE

PLEASANT VALLEY

RAYMOND PK 10025

RAYMOND CANYON

HEENAN LK

LOOPE CYN

MORNING STAR

HEENAN RD

TOPAZ

89

MOKELUMNE WILDERNESS AREA

MEADOW LAKE

TWIN LAKE

TAMARACK PK

PENNSYLVANIA

SILVER CK

EAST FORK CARSON RIVER

WOLF CK

DIXON MINE RD

MONO CO.

TOIYABE NATIONAL FOREST

EASTSIDE

CUNNINGHAM LN

4

SILVER CK CAMPGROUN

HIGHWAYS

SONOMA CO.

A B C D E

HEALDSBURG

WINE CREEK RD
Bellerose Vineyard
Mill Creek
BRACK
Healdsburg Municipal Airport
RANCHO SOTOYOME
EXANDER VALLEY RANCHERIA
CHALK HILL RD
Field Stone
RANCHO KELLOG MALLA-COMES OR MORISTO Y PLAN DE CALIENTE
Stephen Zellerbach
128
37

Ewarts IT Indian Rancheria
Kruse Rhododendron State Reserve
GERMAN
COAST HWY
FISK MILL COVE
SKYLINE
KING RIDGE RD
OAK MTN
MILL CREEK RD
POWELL AV
FITCH MTN RD
DEL RIO WOODS
Du Bois
White Oak Vineyards
J.W. Morris Winery
Wheeler Winery
STEPHEN
FRANZ
PORTER CREEK RD

SALT PT GERSTLE COVE
WALSH LANDING
Salt Point State Park
TABLE MTN
Sea Ridge Winery
King Ridge RD
219 TOUR
Armstrong Redwoods State Reserve
ROCKY MT
Korbel MT JACKSON Champagne Cellars
Piper Sonoma Cellars
Belvedere Winery
Rodney Strong
Windsor
1
CHALK HILL VALLEY
WINDSOR
MARK WEST SPRINGS

OCEAN COVE Stillwater Cove
Ft Ross State Historic Park
BLACK MTN
BIG OAT MTN
POLE MTN
CAZADERO
BERKELEY CAMP
EL BONITA
RIO NIDO
HACIENDA
KORBEL
Davis Bynum Winery
SWEETWATER SPRINGS
WINDSOR
Mark West
Windsor Water-Works
MARK WEST SPRINGS

TIMBER COVE WINDERMERE PT
FORT ROSS
FORT ROSS COVE
1
MEYERS GRADE RD
RANCHO MUNIZ
FOX MTN
Austin Creek State Rec Area
EAST GUERNEWOOD
GUERNEWOOD PARK
VACATION BEACH
GUERNE-VILLE
SUMMER HOME PARK
DELL
WOOL-SEY
Dehlinger
Martini & Prati Winery
De Loach Vineyards
101
SANTA ROSA
COLLEGE AV
MARK WEST

JENNER
COAST HWY
GOAT ROCK
VILLA GRANDE
NORTH WOOD
MONTE RIO
SHERIDAN
DUNCANS MILLS
FORESTVILLE
116 HWY
GRATON
SOUSA CORNERS
GUERNEVILLE
12
2
SOUTH PARK

OCEAN VIEW
RED HILL
Rancho Bodega
OCCIDENTAL
CAMP MEEKER
Sea Ridge Winery
GRATON
Rancho Sebastopol
SEBASTOPOL
RANCHO LLANO DE SANTA ROSA
Healdsburg Indian Rancheria
Eagle Ranch Regional Park

BRIDGE HAVEN
SERENO DEL MAR
CARMET
IRISH HILL
Sonoma Coast State Beach
SALMON CREEK
RANCHO BODEGA
FREESTONE
KNOWLES CORNER
CUN-NINGHAM
CADWELL
HESSEL
116
Red Lion
ROHNERT PARK

DUNCAN POINT
BODEGA BAY
MUSSEL PT
Saint Teresa's Church
BODEGA
1
VALLEY FORD
BLOOM-FIELD
WASHOE
116
COTATI
38

Doran Regional Park
Bodega Harbor
BODEGA HEAD
BODEGA BAY
FALLON
TWO ROCK
RANCHO BLUCHER
10

MCCLURES BEACH
DILLON BEACH
TOMALES
DILLON BEACH RD
TOMALES
PETALUMA RD
RANCHO ROBLAR DE LA MISERIA
MIDDLE TWO ROCK RD

3

TOMALES BLUFF
BIRD ROCK
TOMS PT
RANCHO SAN ANTONIO

PACIFIC OCEAN

PIERCE POINT
RANCHO NICASIO
MARSHALL
MARSHALL-

POINT REYES BEACH
Tomales Bay State Park
MARIN CO.
225 TOUR
RANCHO NICASIO

4

INVERNESS
1
PT REYES STATION
INVERNESS PARK
NICASIO
NICASIO RES
S.P. Taylor State Park
FOREST KNOL
LAGUNITA

DRAKES ESTERO
POLEMA
Golden Gate
5

PT REYES
SEA LION COVE
CHIMNEY ROCK
DRAKES BEACH
Point Reyes
PT RESISTANCE
National Seashore
DRAKES BAY
MILLERS PT
KENT LAKE
RANCHO TOMAL

DOUBLE PT
ABALONE PT
BOLINAS

A B C D E

WINE COUNTRY AREA

YOLO CO.

NAPA CO.

SONOMA CO.

SOLANO CO.

MARIN CO.

CONTRA COSTA CO.

Cities & Towns:
CALISTOGA, ST HELENA, ANGWIN, DEER PARK, RUTHERFORD, OAKVILLE, YOUNTVILLE, SALVADOR, NAPA, VICHY SPRINGS, BERRYESSA PINES, BERRYESSA HIGHLANDS, CIRCLE OAKS, FAIRFIELD, ROCKVILLE, CORDELIA, SUISUN CITY, GREEN VALLEY ESTATES, MANKAS CORNER, AMERICAN CANYON, VALLEJO, VALLEJO HTS, BENICIA, CARQUINEZ HTS, CROCKETT, PORT COSTA, RODEO, HERCULES, MARTINEZ, PACHECO, PLEASANT HILL, CLYDE, PINOLE, EL SOBRANTE, SAN PABLO, NORTH RICHMOND, RICHMOND, EL CERRITO, KENSINGTON, ORINDA, LAFAYETTE, WALNUT CREEK

SANTA ROSA, SOUTH PARK, ROHNERT PARK, KENWOOD, GLEN ELLEN, ELDRIDGE, AGUA CALIENTE, FETTERS HOT SPRINGS, BOYES HOT SPRINGS, EL VERANO, SONOMA, VINEBURG, SCHELLVILLE, BIG BEND, LAKEVILLE, PENNGROVE, PETALUMA, SEARS POINT, GREEN POINT, BLACK POINT, IGNACIO, NOVATO, MARINWOOD, SAN RAFAEL, SAN VENETIA, SANTA VENETIA, NICASIO, WOODACRE, SLEEPY HOLLOW, SAN GERONIMO, FAIRFAX, SAN ANSELMO, ROSS, LARKSPUR, CORTE MADERA, MILL VALLEY, SAN QUENTIN, PARADISE CAY, TIBURON, STINSON

Parks & Landmarks:
STEVENSON MEM STATE PARK, SUGARLOAF MTN, Old Faithful Geyser of California, Napa Valley Railroad Depot, Petrified Forest, Mud Baths, Bothe-Napa Valley State Park, Bale Grist Mill St Historic Park, Hurd Candle Factory, Napa Co Hist Mus, Silverado Museum, LAS POSADAS STATE FOREST, SPANISH FLAT WOODLANDS, Lake Berryessa, Lake Solano Co Park, Annadel State Park, Rancho Los Guilicos, Caswell Vineyards, St Francis Las Montanas Winery, Smothers Brothers Wines, Grand Cru, Glen Ellen Winery, Jack London St Hist Pk, Sonoma State Hosp, Hacienda Cellars, Gundlach Bundschu Winery, Viansa Winery, Sonoma Creek Winery, Mt St John Cellars, Bay View, Las Amigas, Napa County Airport, MARINE WORLD PKWY, Skyline County Park, SILVERADO COUNTRY CLUB RESORT, Napa Valley Lodge Best Western, SONOMA STATE UNIV, Matanzas Creek Winery, Petaluma Adobe State Historical Monument, US NAVAL RESERVATION, SONOMA CREEK, Samuel P Taylor State Park, Nicasio Redwoods, Hamilton Field, Audubon Canyon Ranch, Muir Woods Natl Mon, Mt Tamalpais State Park, Alpine Lake, BRIONES REGIONAL PARK, TILDEN REGIONAL PARK, SAN PABLO RES, US NAVAL MAGAZINE, MONTEZUMA SLOUGH, GRIZZLY ISLAND, SUISUN BAY, SAN PABLO BAY

PUTNAM PEAK, ATLAS PEAK, MT VACA, TWIN SISTERS, MT ST HELENA, JACKSON PEAK, EDGAR PEAK, ELKHORN PEAK, VETERANS PEAK, BUZZARD PEAK, HOGBACK MTN, WILDCAT MTN

Highways: 128, 29, 12, 121, 116, 101, 37, 221, 219, 32, 580, 4, 80, 680, 780, 242, 24, 225

AIR BASE PKWY

For Detail Page Locations SEE PAGE 29

For Detail Page Locations SEE PAGE L

SEE MAP 39

HIGHWAYS

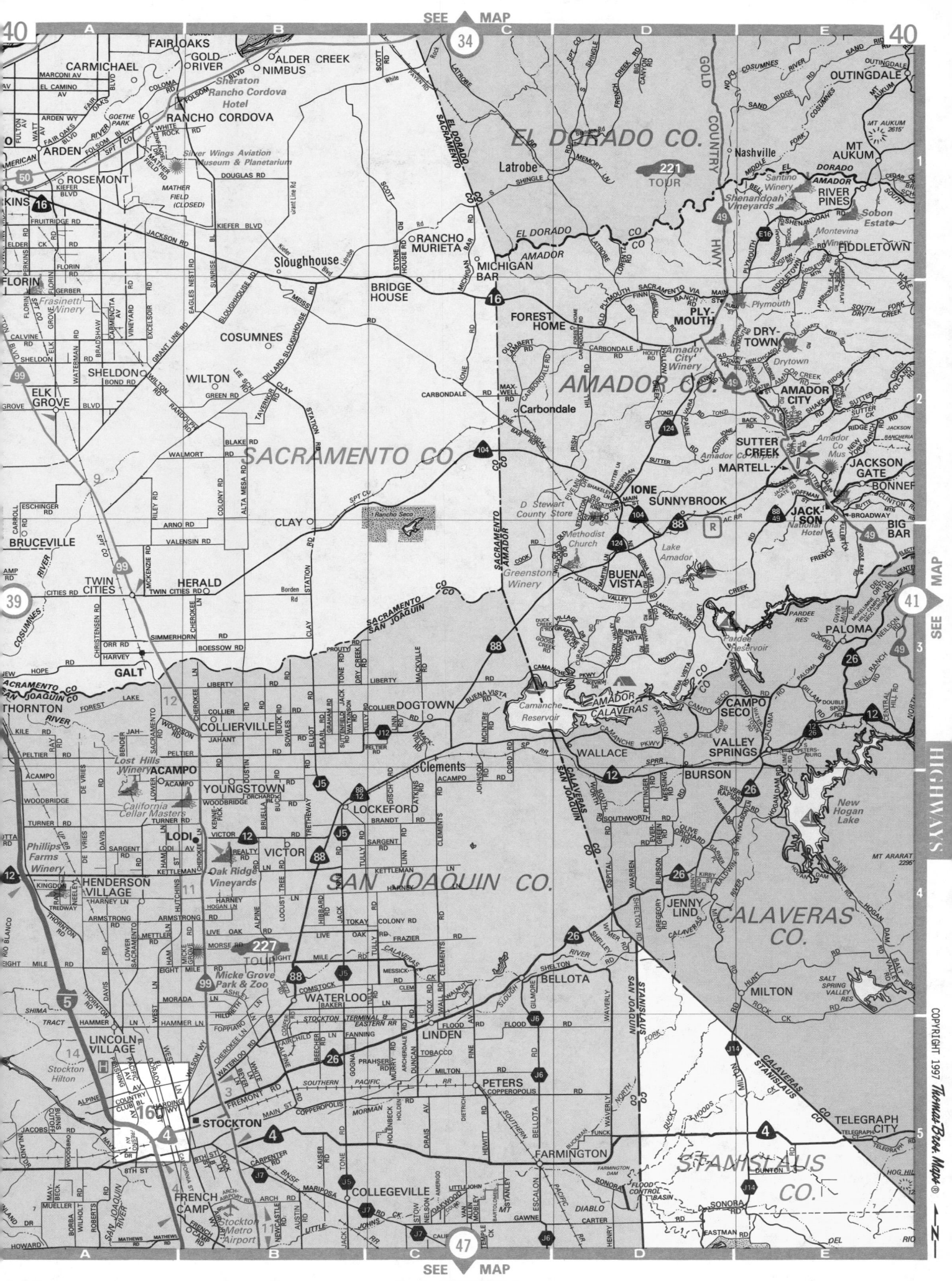

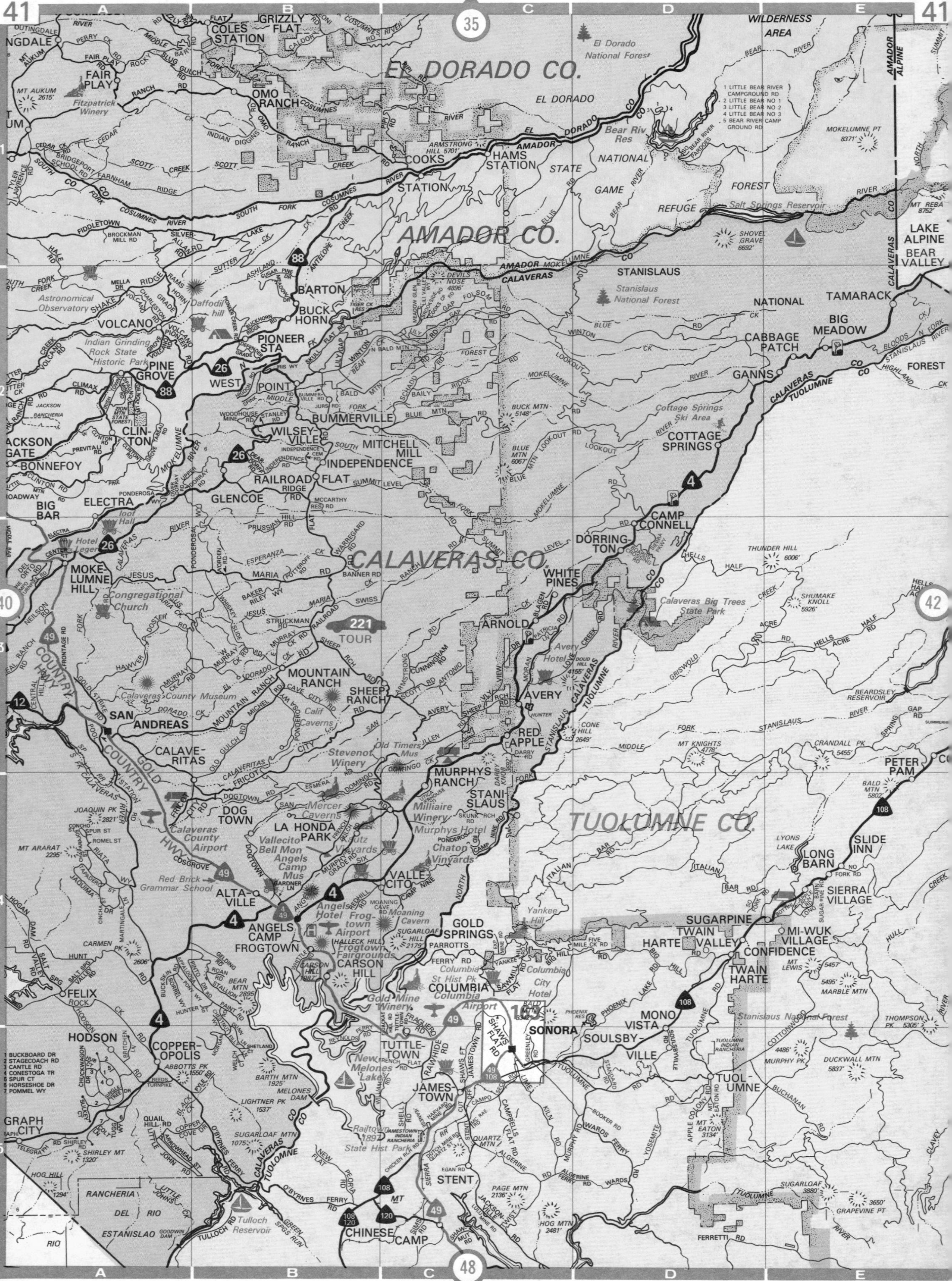

HIGHWAYS

© COPYRIGHT 1997 Thomas Bros. Maps®

EL DORADO CO.

El Dorado National Forest

WILDERNESS AREA

AMADOR ALPINE

1 LITTLE BEAR RIVER CAMPGROUND RD
2 LITTLE BEAR NO 1
3 LITTLE BEAR NO 2
4 LITTLE BEAR NO 3
5 BEAR RIVER CAMP GROUND RD

MOKELUMNE PT 8371'

NGDALE
OUTINGDALE

MT AUKUM 2615'
FAIR PLAY
Fitzpatrick Winery

COLES STATION
GRIZZLY FLAT
OMO RANCH
Indian Diggins

ARMSTRONG HILL 5701'
COOKS STATION
HAMS STATION

AMADOR CO.

EL DORADO

STATE GAME REFUGE

NATIONAL

Bear Riv Res

Salt Springs Reservoir

SHOVEL GRAVE 6692'

FOREST

MT REBA 8752'

LAKE ALPINE
BEAR VALLEY

Astronomical Observatory
VOLCANO
Indian Grinding Rock State Historic Park
PINE GROVE
88
WEST POINT

BARTON
BUCK HORN
PIONEER STA
26

BUMMERVILLE
WILSEY-VILLE
MITCHELL MILL
INDEPENDENCE

DEVILS NOSE 4896'

STANISLAUS
Stanislaus National Forest

NATIONAL

TAMARACK
BIG MEADOW
CABBAGE PATCH
GANNS

JACKSON GATE
BONNEFOY
CLINTON

ELECTRA
GLENCOE
RAILROAD FLAT

BLUE MTN 6067'
BLUE MTN LOOKOUT

Cottage Springs Ski Area
COTTAGE SPRINGS
4

BIG BAR
Hotel Leger
26
MOKE LUMNE HILL

Congregational Church

CALAVERAS CO.

WHITE PINES
DORRINGTON
CAMP CONNELL

THUNDER HILL 6006'

SHUMAKE KNOLL 5926'

42

SEE MAP 40

49
COUNTRY HWY
12

Calaveras County Museum

221 TOUR

ARNOLD
Calaveras Big Trees State Park

SAN ANDREAS
CALAVE-RITAS

MOUNTAIN RANCH
SHEEP RANCH

AVERY
Avery Hotel

RED APPLE

BEARDSLEY RESERVOIR

GOLD COUNTRY HWY

DOG TOWN
Calaveras County Airport

LA HONDA PARK
Mercer Caverns
Stevenot Winery

MURPHYS RANCH
STANI SLAUS
Milliaire Winery
Murphys Hotel

PETER PAM

BALD MTN 5802'
108

MT ARARAT 2295'

Red Brick Grammar School
ALTA-VILLE
49

ANGELS CAMP
FROGTOWN
4
Angels Hotel
Frogtown Fairgrounds

VALLE-CITO
Moaning Cave

TUOLUMNE CO.

LYONS LAKE
LONG BARN
SLIDE INN

SIERRA VILLAGE

FELIX
HODSON
COPPER-OPOLIS
4

CARSON HILL
Gold Mine Winery

GOLD SPRINGS
Columbia St Hist Pk
COLUMBIA
Columbia City Hotel
Columbia Airport

SUGARPINE
TWAIN HARTE
CONFIDENCE
MI-WUK VILLAGE
TWAIN HARTE

MT LEWIS 5457'
MARBLE MTN 5495'

GRAPH CITY

1 BUCKBOARD DR
2 STAGECOACH RD
3 CANTLE RD
4 CONESTOGA TR
5 SPUR CT
6 HORSESHOE DR
7 POMMEL WY

New Melones Lake

TUTTLETOWN
49 108
SONORA
163

JAMESTOWN
Railtown 1897 State Hist Park

MONO VISTA
SOULSBY VILLE

TUOL-UMNE

DUCKWALL MTN 5837'

RANCHERIA DEL RIO
ESTANISLAO

Tulloch Reservoir

STENT
CHINESE CAMP
108 120
49

THOMPSON PK 5305'

SUGARLOAF 3880'

GRAPEVINE PT

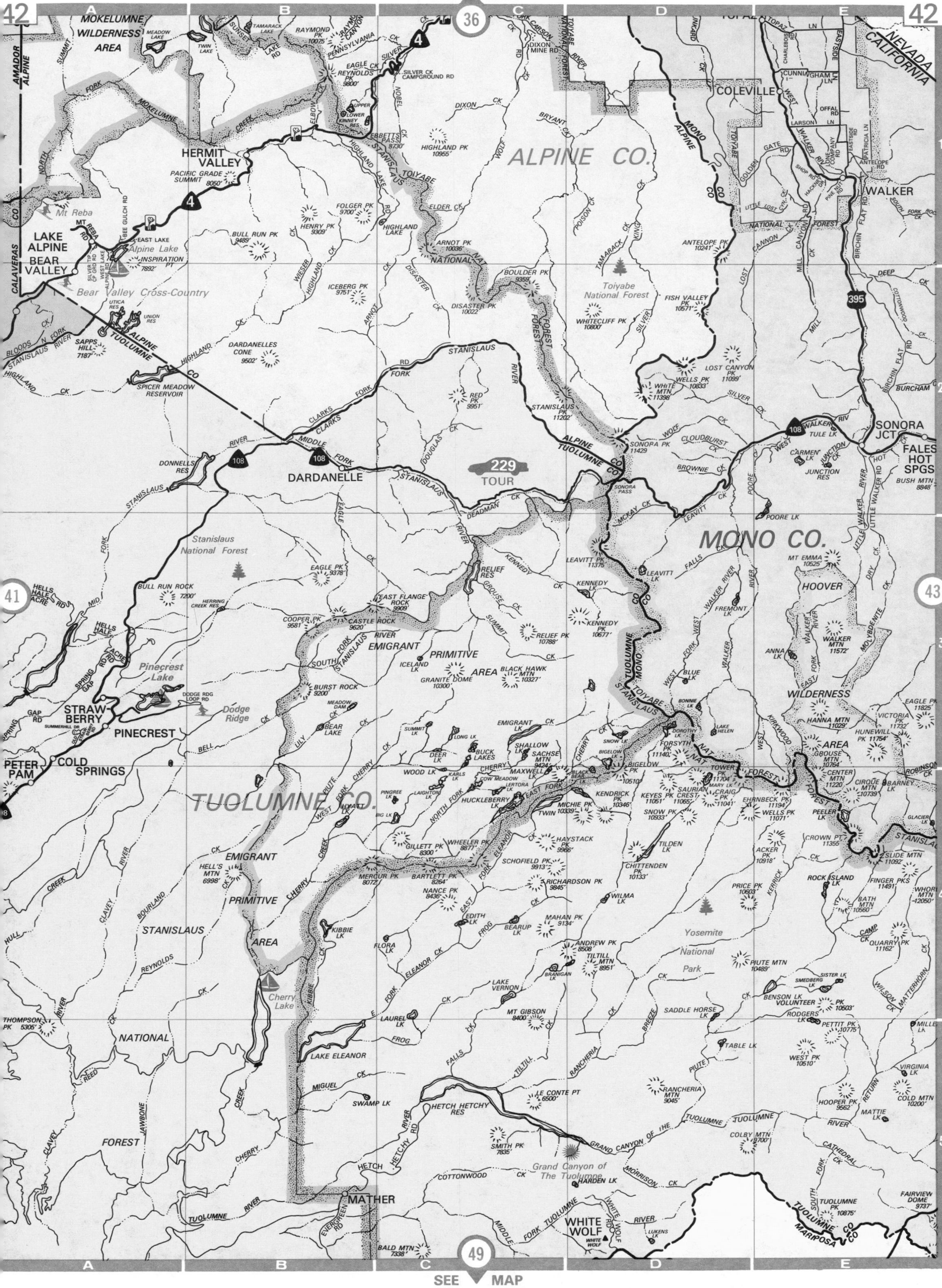

MAP LABELS

MOKELUMNE WILDERNESS AREA

NEVADA
CALIFORNIA

AMADOR ALPINE

COLEVILLE

ALPINE CO.

WALKER

HERMIT VALLEY

Pacific Grade Summit 8050'

LAKE ALPINE
BEAR VALLEY

CALAVERAS CO.

Mt Reba

Alpine Lake
INSPIRATION PT 7892'
East Lake

SAPPS HILL 7187'

Bear Valley Cross-Country

Spicer Meadow Reservoir

Donnells Res.

Toiyabe National Forest

ALPINE TUOLUMNE CO.

Dardanelles Cone 9502'

DARDANELLE

108

STANISLAUS

NATIONAL FOREST

229 TOUR

SONORA JCT.
FALES HOT SPGS

MONO CO.

HOOVER WILDERNESS

41

Stanislaus National Forest

EMIGRANT PRIMITIVE AREA

Pinecrest Lake

Dodge Ridge

STRAW BERRY

PINECREST

PETER PAM

COLD SPRINGS

TUOLUMNE CO.

EMIGRANT PRIMITIVE AREA

STANISLAUS

NATIONAL FOREST

Cherry Lake

Lake Eleanor

Hetch Hetchy Res.

MATHER

Grand Canyon of The Tuolumne

Yosemite National Park

WHITE WOLF

43

HIGHWAYS

TUOLUMNE MARIPOSA CO.

FAIRVIEW DOME 9731'

COPYRIGHT 1997 Thomas Bros. Maps®

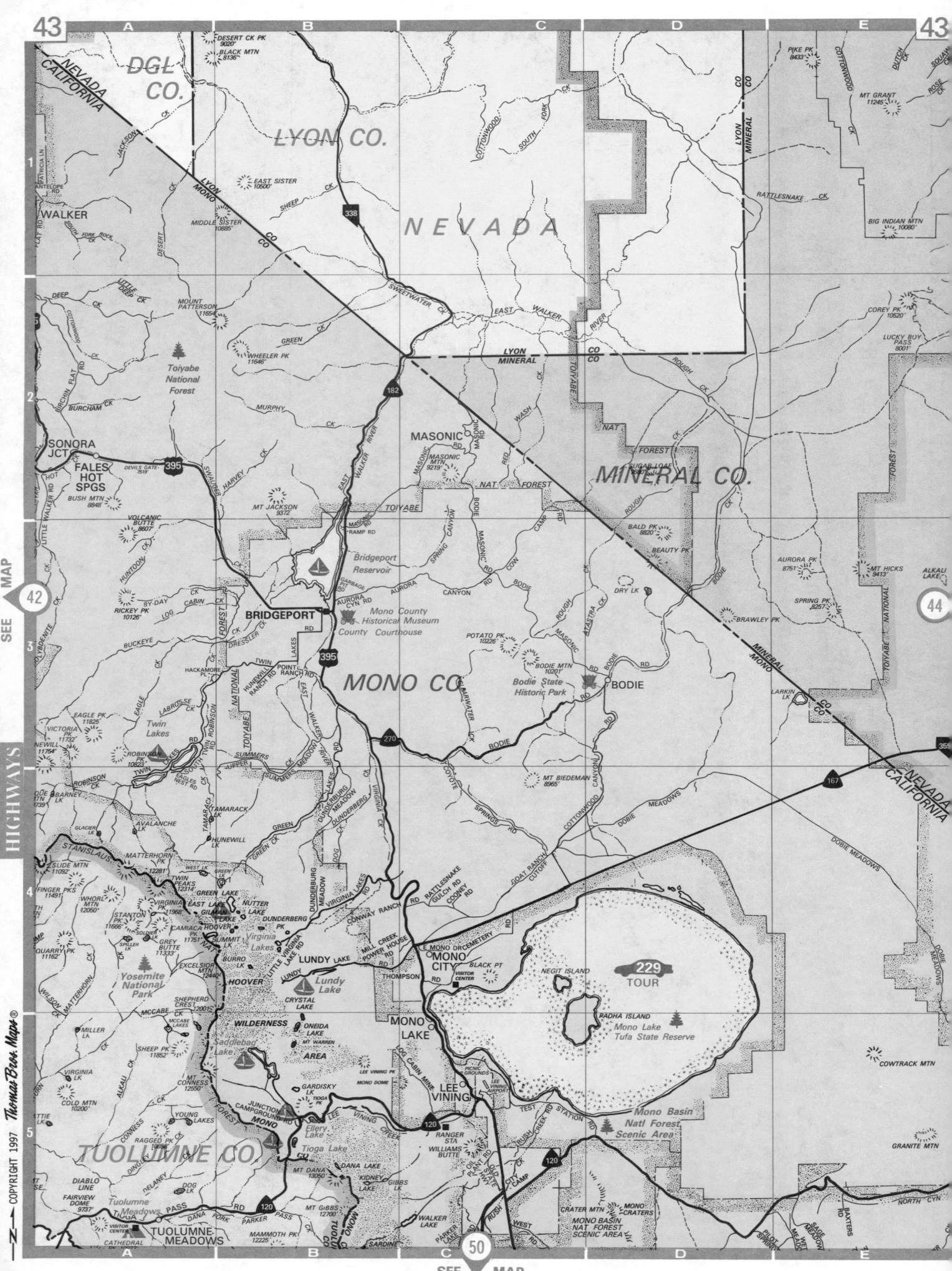

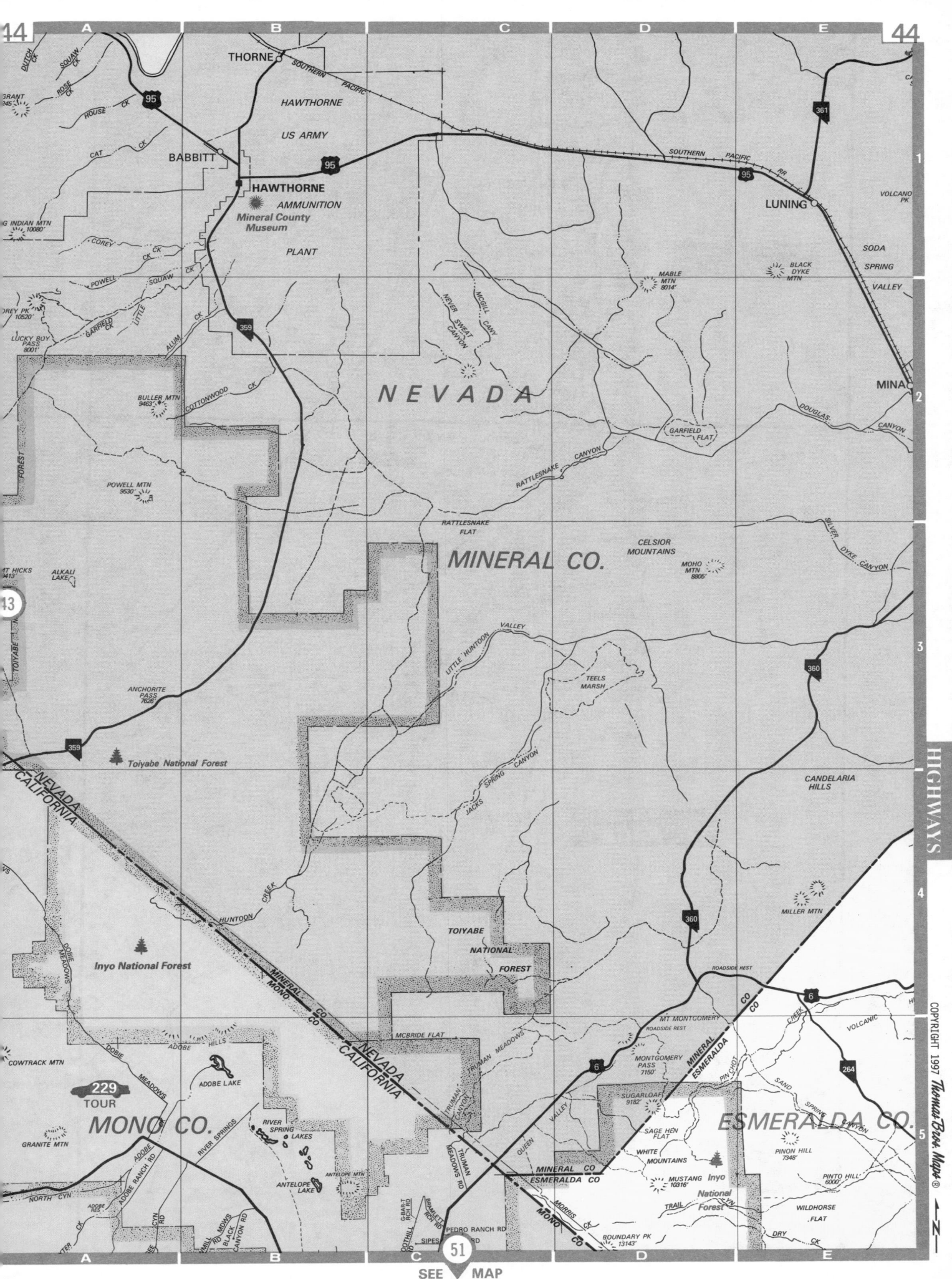

A **B** **C** **D** **E**

LINAS

STINSON
BEACH

MUIR BEACH

MARIN

SAUSALITO

VALLEY
CITY

TIBURON
BELVEDERE

PARADISE
CAY

ANGEL
ISLAND

PT
CHAUNCEY

IRA COSTA CO
FRANCISCO CO

ALAMEDA CO
FLEMING
PT

RICHMOND
INNER HARBOR

WILDCAT
LAFAYETTE
WATER TUNNEL

TON
CONTRA
COSTA CO
ALAMEDA CO

ORINDA

LAFA-
YETTE

WALL
CREEK

24

ALBANY

BERKELEY

EMERYVILLE

80

580

ORINDA
VILLAGE

Canyon

Mont-
clair

Rheem
Valley

MORAGA

Alamo

MORAGA

DANVILLE

1

GOLDEN GATE
BRIDGE

SAN FRANCISCO

101

OAKLAND
BAY
BRIDGE

80

OAKLAND

PIEDMONT

13

980

580

77

SKYLINE

CONTRA COSTA CO
ALAMEDA CO

UPPER
SAN LEANDRO
RES

For Detail Page Locations
SEE PAGE L

LOMBARD ST
CALIFORNIA ST

GEARY BL
FULTON ST
LINCOLN

101

1

WEBSTER ST

ENCINAL

13TH AV

FRUITVALE AV

MACARTHUR FWY

580

ALAMEDA

61

South
Shore

185

SEMINARY AV

98TH BL

MACARTHUR

SAN LEANDRO

Sheffield
Village

Castro
Valley

SAN FRANCISCO
CO.

SUNSET WY
19TH AV

PORTOLA

MONTEREY
BL

OCEAN AV

1

35

280

Bay Farm
Island

OAKLAND
INTERNATIONAL
AIRPORT

DOOLITTLE DR

DAVIS

Mulford
Gardens

112

SEVEN
HILLS

LAKE CHABOT RD

DALY
CITY

COLMA

SAN FRANCISCO CO
SAN MATEO CO

Bayshore

BAYSHORE BL

HILLSIDE BL

880

238

ALAMEDA CO.
CO.

San
Lorenzo

A ST

JACKSON

HAYWARD

2

PACIFICA

MISSION RD
GRAND AV

82

380

BRISBANE

SOUTH SAN FRANCISCO

SAN BRUNO

225
TOUR
SAN FRANCISCO
INTERNATIONAL
AIRPORT

ALAMEDA CO
SAN MATEO CO

W WINTON AV

HARDER
RD
TENNYSON RD

238

HESPERIAN BL

INDUSTRIAL PKWY
MISSION

UNION CITY

46

Rockaway
Beach

SHARP
PK RD

SKYLINE

SWEATH

SAN
BRUNO
AV

SAN
ANDREAS
LAKE

101

MILLBRAE

YOUNGER FWY

SAN MATEO TOLL
BRIDGE

92

SAN

Alvarado

ALVARADO
NILES RD

San Pedro
Terrace

Linda Mar

HILLCREST

HILLSIDE DR

BURLINGAME

SAN MATEO

FOSTER CITY

84

THORNTON AV

NEWARK

3

Montara

Moss Beach

CABRILLO

HILLSBOROUGH

The Highlands

LOWER CRYSTAL
SPRINGS RES

BLACK
MTN

CRYSTAL SPRINGS RD

CHATEAU

BELMONT

RALSTON AV

SAN CARLOS

Redwood
Shores

84

109

DUMBARTON
BRIDGE

EAST
PALO
ALTO

114

MENLO
PARK

Princeton
By The Sea

El Granada

HALF
MOON BAY

92

CANADA RD

SAN
CARLOS

REDWOOD
CITY

ATHERTON

82

101

WILLOW

PALO
ALTO

280

Miramar

HALF MOON BAY

HIGGINS PURISIMA

Skyline

SKYLINE BL

SKYLINE

WOODSIDE

Ladera

PORTOLA
VALLEY

Stanford

OREGON EXPWY

MOUNTAIN
VIEW

CHARLESTON
RD

G6

G3

LOS
ALTOS

237

For Detail Page Locations
SEE PAGE N

1

PURISIMA CK RD

CABRILLO

TUNITAS CK

Kings
Mtn

KINGS MTN RD

84

SAND HILL RD

JUNIPERO
SERRA

ALAMEDA
DE LAS PULGAS

PORTOLA
RD

ALPINE RD

35

G5

LOS
ALTOS
HILLS

FOOTHILL EXPWY

MONTE

SPRINGER

85

82

SU

FREMONT

4

SAN
MATEO
CO.

Sky Londa

SKYLINE

LA HONDA RD

La Honda

SANTA
CLARA
CO.

CUPERTINO
Monte
Vista

SUNNYVALE

SAN GREGORIO

San
Gregorio

STAGE RD

LA HONDA RD

84

ALPINE RD

SKYLINE BL

PORTOLA STATE PK RD

PIERCE RD

SARATOGA

SANTA
CLARA
CO.

FS

BELLO

STEVENS CYN RD

Loma Mar

9

CONGRESS SPRINGS RD

MONTE SERE
LOS G

Pescadero

PESCADERO CK RD

BUTANO CUT-OFF

CLOVERDALE RD

CANYON RD

BEAR
HOLLOW RD

ARTICHOKE RD

SAN MATEO CO
SANTA CRUZ CO

PORTOLA STATE

ALAZOS CK RD

GRISON RD

236

9

35

Redwood

5

SANTA CRUZ CO.

A **B** **C** **D** **E**

HIGHWAYS

N

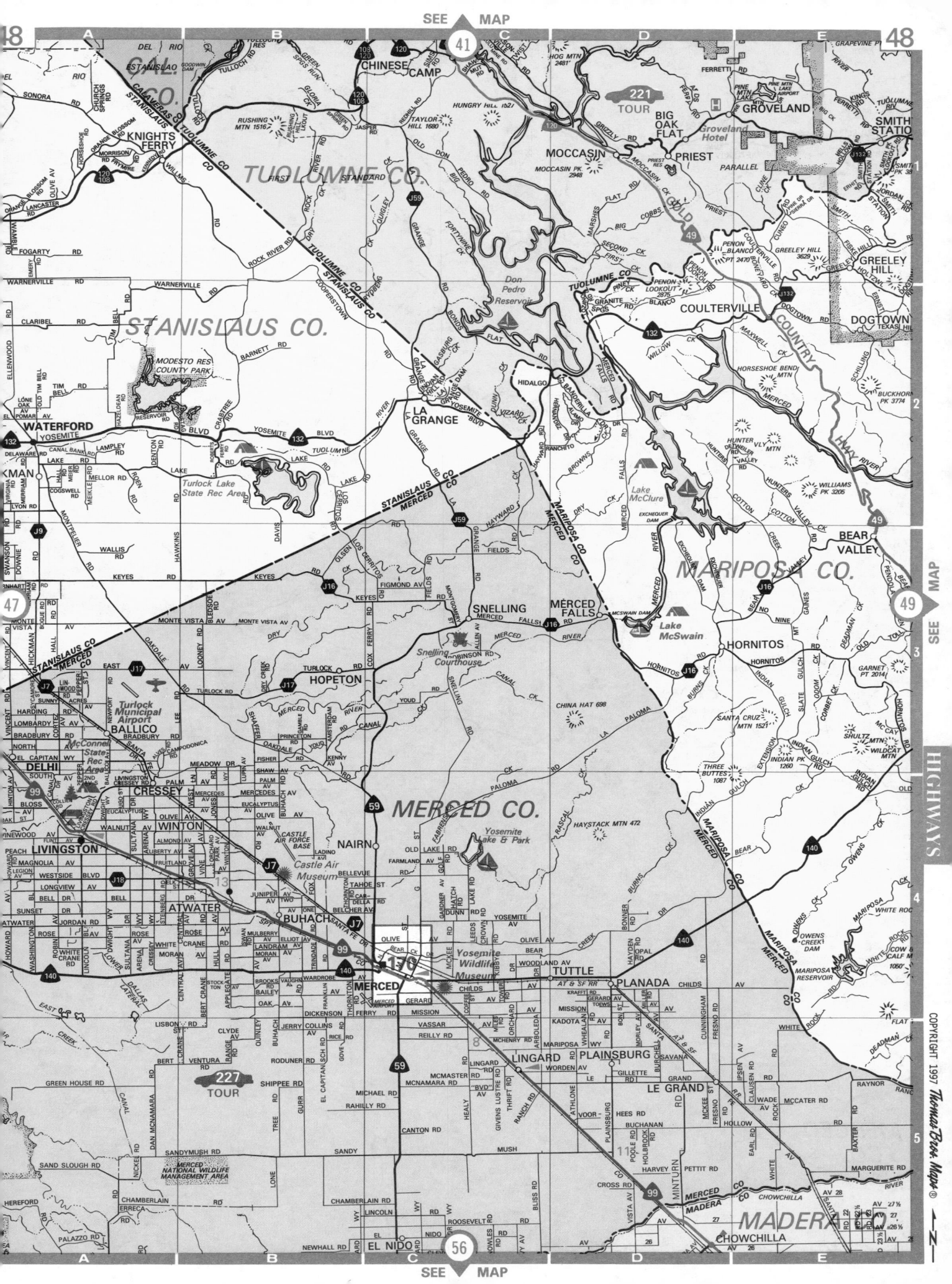

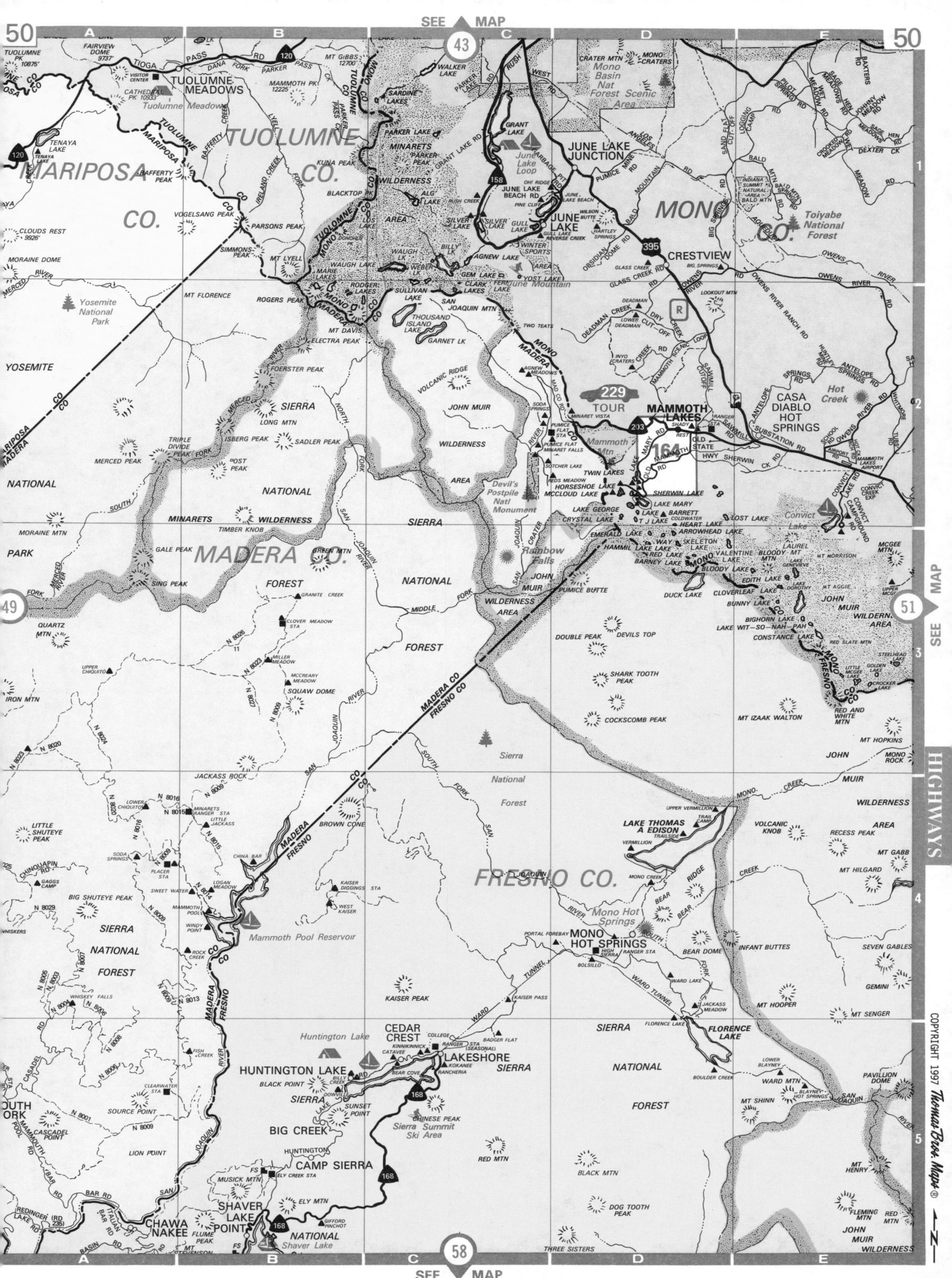

SEE MAP 44

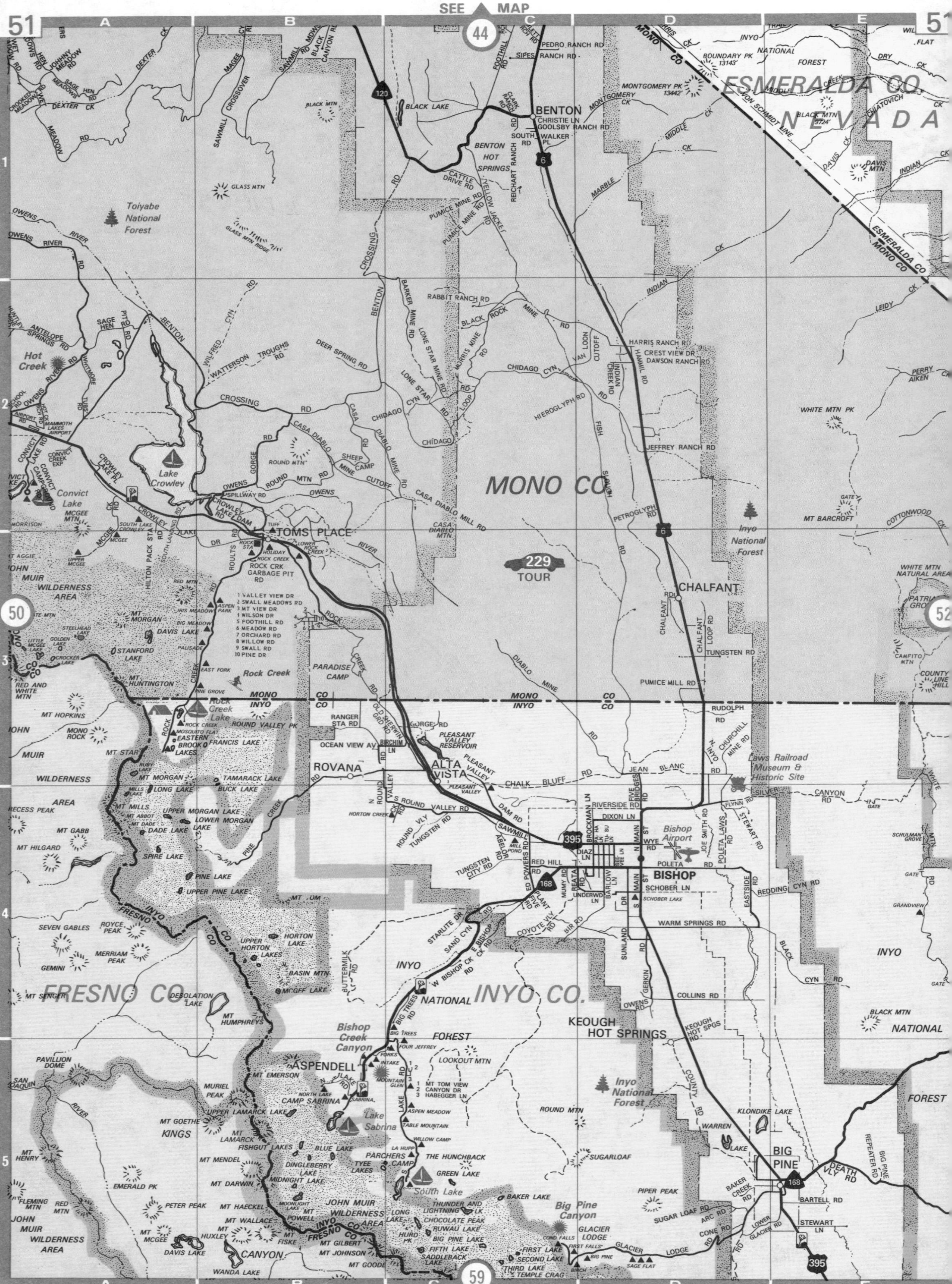

SEE MAP 50

SEE MAP 52

HIGHWAYS

N

Thomas Bros. Maps®
© COPYRIGHT 1997

ESMERALDA CO.
NEVADA

MONO CO.

INYO CO.

FRESNO CO.

BENTON

BENTON HOT SPRINGS

TOMS PLACE

CHALFANT

ROVANA

ALTA VISTA

BISHOP

Bishop Airport

ASPENDELL

BIG PINE

Toiyabe National Forest

Inyo National Forest

John Muir Wilderness Area

John Muir Wilderness

Kings Canyon

Keough Hot Springs

Hot Creek

Lake Crowley

Convict Lake

Rock Creek Lake

Lake Sabrina

South Lake

Klondike Lake

Laws Railroad Museum & Historic Site

Mammoth Lakes Airport

Glass Mtn

Black Mtn

Montgomery Pk 13442'

Boundary Pk 13143'

White Mtn Pk

Mt Barcroft

Patriarch Grove

White Mtn Natural Area

Schulman Grove

Bishop Creek Canyon

Big Pine Canyon

Glacier Lodge

229 TOUR

395

6

120

168

59

SEE MAP 59

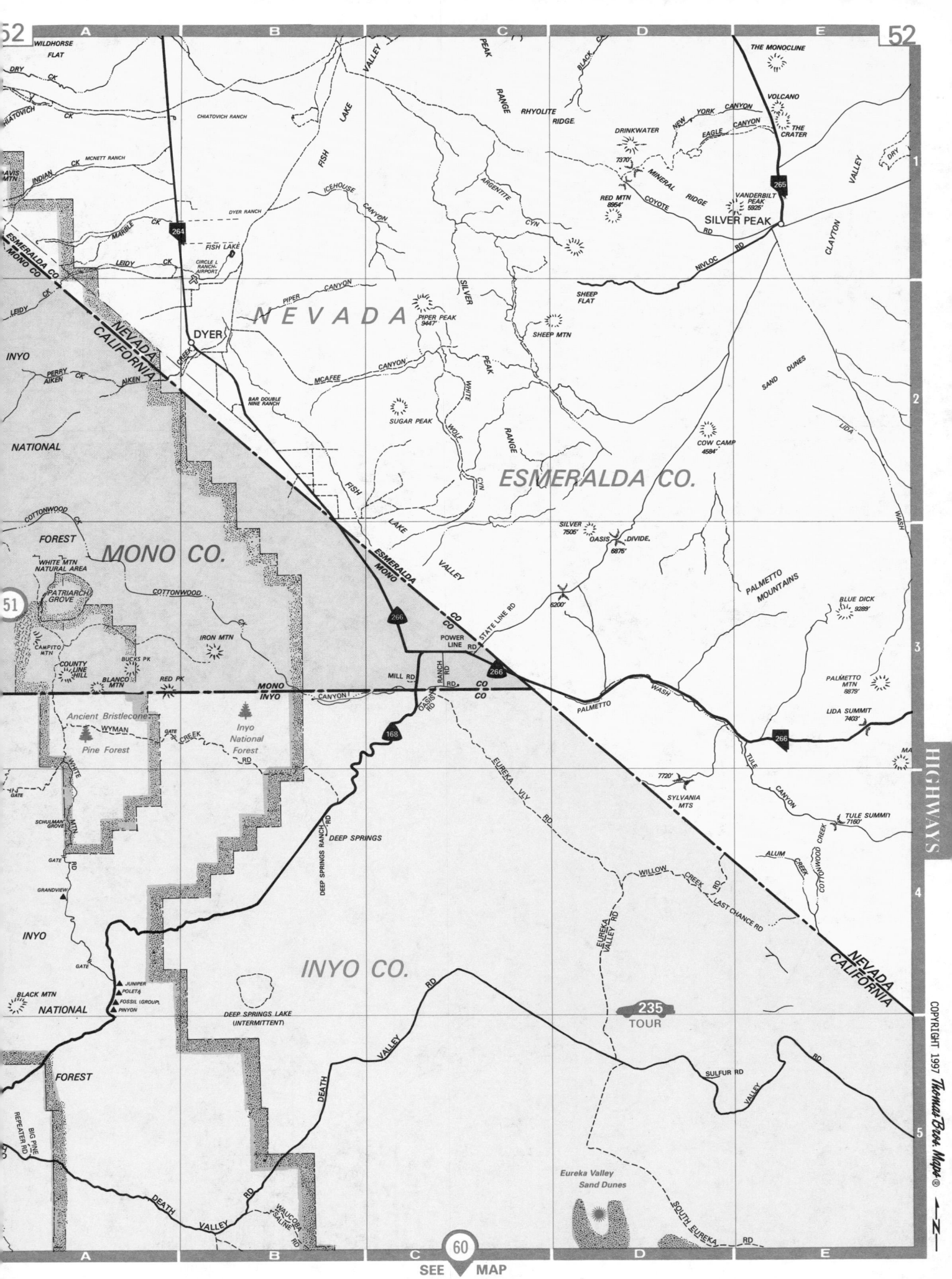

SEE MAP 45
For Detail Page Locations
SEE PAGE N
SANTA CRUZ CO.
225 TOUR
Redwood Estates
Boulder Creek
Brookdale
Ben Lomond
Mt Hermon
Felton
Hallcrest Vineyards
Davenport
Bonny Doon Vineyard
SANTA CRUZ
Wilder Ranch State Park
169
SEE MAP 167
17 MILE DRIVE
POINT JOE
MONTEREY PENINSULA COUNTRY CLUB
PRESIDIO OF MONTEREY
MONTEREY
231 TOUR
MONTEREY CO.
BIRD ROCK
SEAL ROCK
FAN SHELL BEACH
CYPRESS POINT
Spyglass Hill Golf Club
Cypress Point Country Club
Pebble Beach
PENINSULA COMMUNITY HOSP
HIGHWAY 1 GATE (TOLL)
SUNSET POINT
LONE CYPRESS TREE
MIDWAY POINT
The Lodge At Pebble Beach
PEBBLE BEACH
STILLWATER COVE
PESCADERO ROCKS
ARROWHEAD POINT
Pebble Beach Golf Links
PESCADERO POINT
CARMEL GATE (TOLL)
PACIFIC
OCEAN
CARMEL
BAY
CARMEL BY THE SEA
CARMEL HS
SEE MAP 168

COPYRIGHT 1997 Thomas Bros. Maps ®

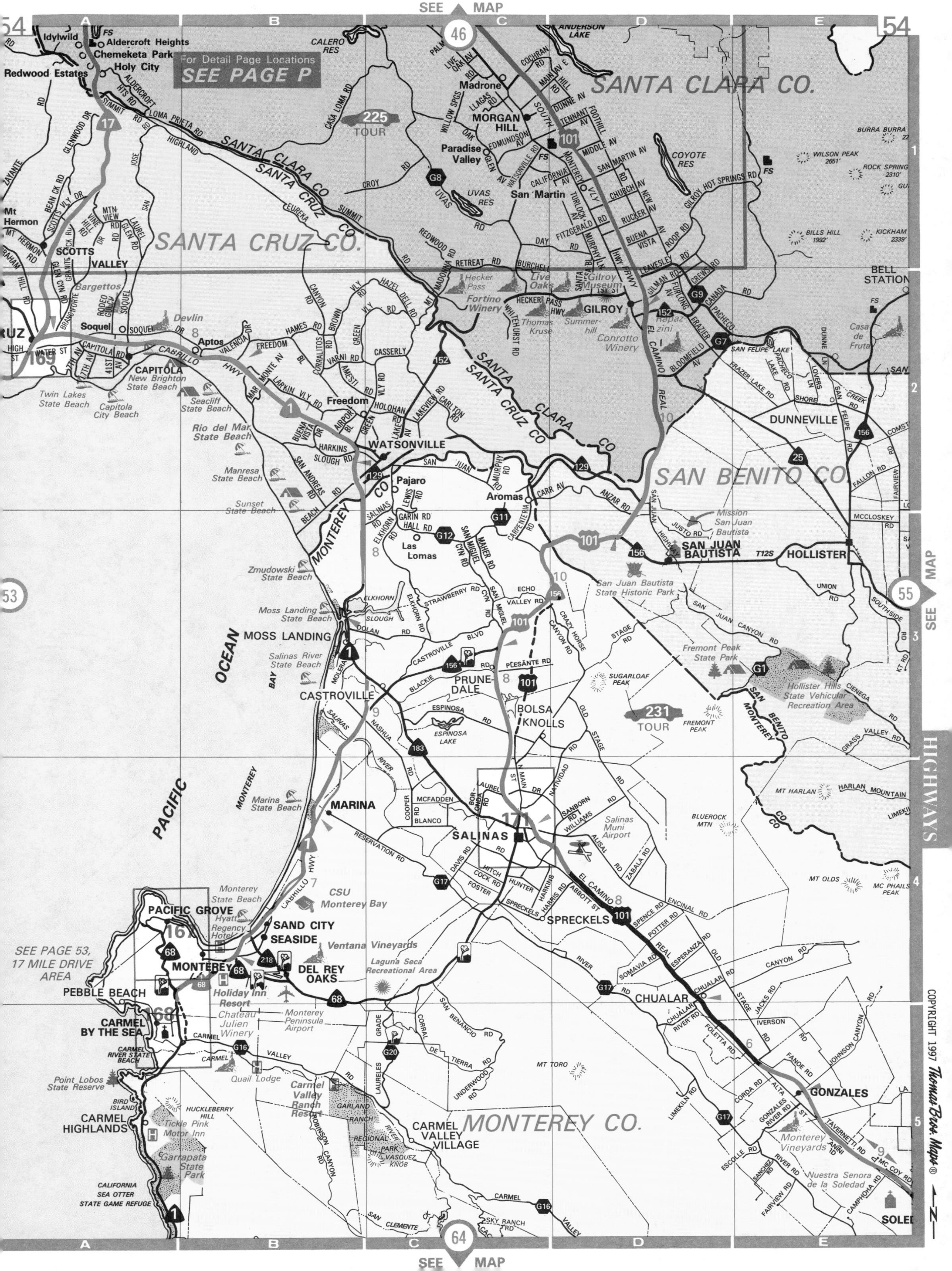
SEE MAP 46
SEE MAP 55
SEE MAP 64
53
For Detail Page Locations
SEE PAGE P
SEE PAGE 53, 17 MILE DRIVE AREA
SANTA CLARA CO.
SANTA CRUZ CO.
SAN BENITO CO.
MONTEREY CO.
PACIFIC OCEAN
MONTEREY BAY
Idylwild
Aldercroft Heights
Chemeketa Park
Holy City
Redwood Estates
Mt Hermon
SCOTTS VALLEY
Bargettos
Soquel
Devlin
Aptos
CAPITOLA
New Brighton State Beach
Twin Lakes State Beach
Capitola City Beach
Seacliff State Beach
Rio del Mar State Beach
Manresa State Beach
Sunset State Beach
Zmudowski State Beach
Moss Landing State Beach
MOSS LANDING
Salinas River State Beach
CASTROVILLE
Freedom
WATSONVILLE
Pajaro
Aromas
Las Lomas
PRUNEDALE
BOLSA KNOLLS
MARINA
Marina State Beach
SALINAS
Salinas Muni Airport
SPRECKELS
CSU Monterey Bay
Monterey State Beach
PACIFIC GROVE
Hyatt Regency Hotel
SAND CITY
SEASIDE
MONTEREY
DEL REY OAKS
Ventana Vineyards
Laguna Seca Recreational Area
PEBBLE BEACH
Holiday Inn Resort
Chateau Julien Winery
Monterey Peninsula Airport
CARMEL BY THE SEA
CARMEL RIVER STATE BEACH
Quail Lodge
Point Lobos State Reserve
BIRD ISLAND
CARMEL HIGHLANDS
Tickle Pink Motor Inn
Garrapata State Park
CALIFORNIA SEA OTTER STATE GAME REFUGE
Carmel Valley Ranch Resort
GARLAND RANCH REGIONAL PARK
VASQUEZ KNOB
CARMEL VALLEY VILLAGE
MT TORO
CHUALAR
GONZALES
Monterey Vineyards
Nuestra Senora de la Soledad
SOLED
CALERO RES
ANDERSON LAKE
Madrone
MORGAN HILL
Paradise Valley
UVAS RES
San Martin
COYOTE RES
BURRA BURRA
WILSON PEAK 2651'
ROCK SPRING 2310'
BILLS HILL 1992'
KICKHAM 2339'
BELL STATION
Hecker Pass
Fortino Winery
Live Oaks
Gilroy Museum
GILROY
Thomas Kruse
Summerhill
Conrotto Winery
Hapazzini
Casa de Fruta
DUNNEVILLE
HOLLISTER
Mission San Juan Bautista
SAN JUAN BAUTISTA
San Juan Bautista State Historic Park
Fremont Peak State Park
SUGARLOAF PEAK
FREMONT PEAK
ESPINOSA LAKE
Hollister Hills State Vehicular Recreation Area
MT HARLAN
BLUEROCK MTN
MT OLDS
MC PHAILS PEAK
225 TOUR
231 TOUR
HIGHWAYS
COPYRIGHT 1997 Thomas Bros. Maps ®

SEE MAP 50

Map

FRESNO CO.

TULARE CO.

Sierra National Forest

Sequoia National Forest

Sequoia National Park

JOHN MUIR WILDERNESS AREA

JOHN MUIR WILDERNESS AREA

SIERRA NATIONAL FOREST

SEQUOIA NATIONAL FOREST

Pine Flat Reservoir Rec Area

Shaver Lake

Wishon Res

Courtright Res

Hume Lake

Cities and places:
NEW AUBERRY, CHAWANAKEE, SHAVER LAKE POINTS, SHAVER LAKE, ALDER SPRINGS, PINE RIDGE, MTN REST, TOLL HOUSE, HUMPHREYS STATION, MDW LAKES, DINKEY CREEK, BALCH CAMP, HUME, WILSONIA, CEDAR BROOK, PINEHURST, BETHEDA SPRINGS, MIRAMONTE, DUNLAP, SQUAW VALLEY, WONDER VALLEY, GRAVESBORO, MINKLER, NAVELENCIA, WAHTOKE PK, ORANGE COVE, REEDLEY, DINUBA, SULTANA, DELFT COLONY, CUTLER, OROSI, EAST OROSI, YETTEM, MONSON, LONDON, TRAVER, ELDERWOOD, BADGER, WOODLAKE, NARANJO, LOMITAS, KAWEAH, HAMMOND, THREE RIVERS

Mountains and peaks:
ELY MTN, GIFFORD PINCHOT, MT STEVENSON, DOG TOOTH PEAK, THREE SISTERS, BROWN PEAK, MAXON DOME, CORRAL MTN, DINKEY DOME, MARBLE POINT, NELSON MTN, EAGLE PEAK, BEAR MTN, VOYAGER ROCK, MARMOT ROCK, LOST PEAK, LOPER PEAK, CASTLE PEAK, VOLCANIC CO, CROWN ROCK, BLACK ROCK, SPANISH MTN, OBELISK, SUGARLOAF HILL, BLACK MTN, BRANFORD MTN, CATS HEAD MTN, HACKER MTN, HOG MTN, WILDCAT MTN, HUGHES MTN, HARMON PEAK, DALTON MTN, BALD MTN, LUCKETT MTN, CONVERSE MTN, LAVA BUTTE, BUCK ROCK, MITCHELL PEAK, BEAR MTN, CURTIS MTN, SHADEQUARTER MTN, PATTEE ROCKS, YUCCA MTN, COLONY PEAK, ASH PEAKS

NOTE: ALL NUMBERED STREETS ARE PRIVATE

1 BARBERRY	51 HIDDEN	68 GERANIUM	80 WILDMINT LN
2 WAXBERRY	52 BUTTERNUT	69 MARIGOLD	81 ROUNDTREE LN
3 HAWTHORNE	53 REDWING	70 SESAME	82 TOTEM LN
4 CARDINAL	54 DANDELION	71 THISTLE	83 WINESAP LN
5 MIMOSA	55 HIGHOAKS	72 RED BUD	84 ASTER LN
6 MALLOW	56 BLUEBELL	73 HUMMINGBIRD	
7 SPEARMINT	57 ROSEMARY	74 MISTLETOE	85 CROW LN
8 BAY RD	58 BEAR CLOVER	75 COSTA LN	86 HONEYSUCKLE LN
9 SUMAC	59 BRAMBLE	76 SIMON LN	87 BRYSON RD
10 BOXELDER	60 SUNDEW	77 PECK LN	
11 PRIMROSE	61 CHUCKWAGON	78 LULLABY LN	
12 SWEETBRIAR	62 BALDPATE	79 BLOSSOM LN	
13 DEERBROOK	63 MOUND		
14 BAYWOOD	64 DAFFODIL		
15 ARTESIA	65 LAVENDER		
16 FEATHER	66 PINTAIL		
17 ARGENBRIGHT	67 GREENHILL		
18 SQUAW VALLEY			
19 CLEAR VIEW			
20 MISTLETOE LN			
21 PEBBLE			
22 SCOUT			
23 RIPPLE			
24 SHADYBROOK			
25 LOGAN BERRY			
26 SHOREWOOD			
27			
29 WILLOWOOD			
30 RUSTIC			
32 PEPPERWOOD			
33 KNOLLGLEN			
34 LONG VIEW			
35 PARTRIDGE			
36 BADGER			
37 IRIS			
38 CLOVER			
39 CORNFLOWER			
40 COLUMBINE			
41 TASSLE			
42 BOBCAT			
43 BUTTERFLY			
44 CREEKSIDE			
45 OAKLEAF			
46 DIABLO			
47 THUNDERHILL			
48 PANORAMA			
49 SASSAFRAS			
50 WISTERIA			

TOUR 229

TOUR 227

HIGHWAYS

SEE MAP 51

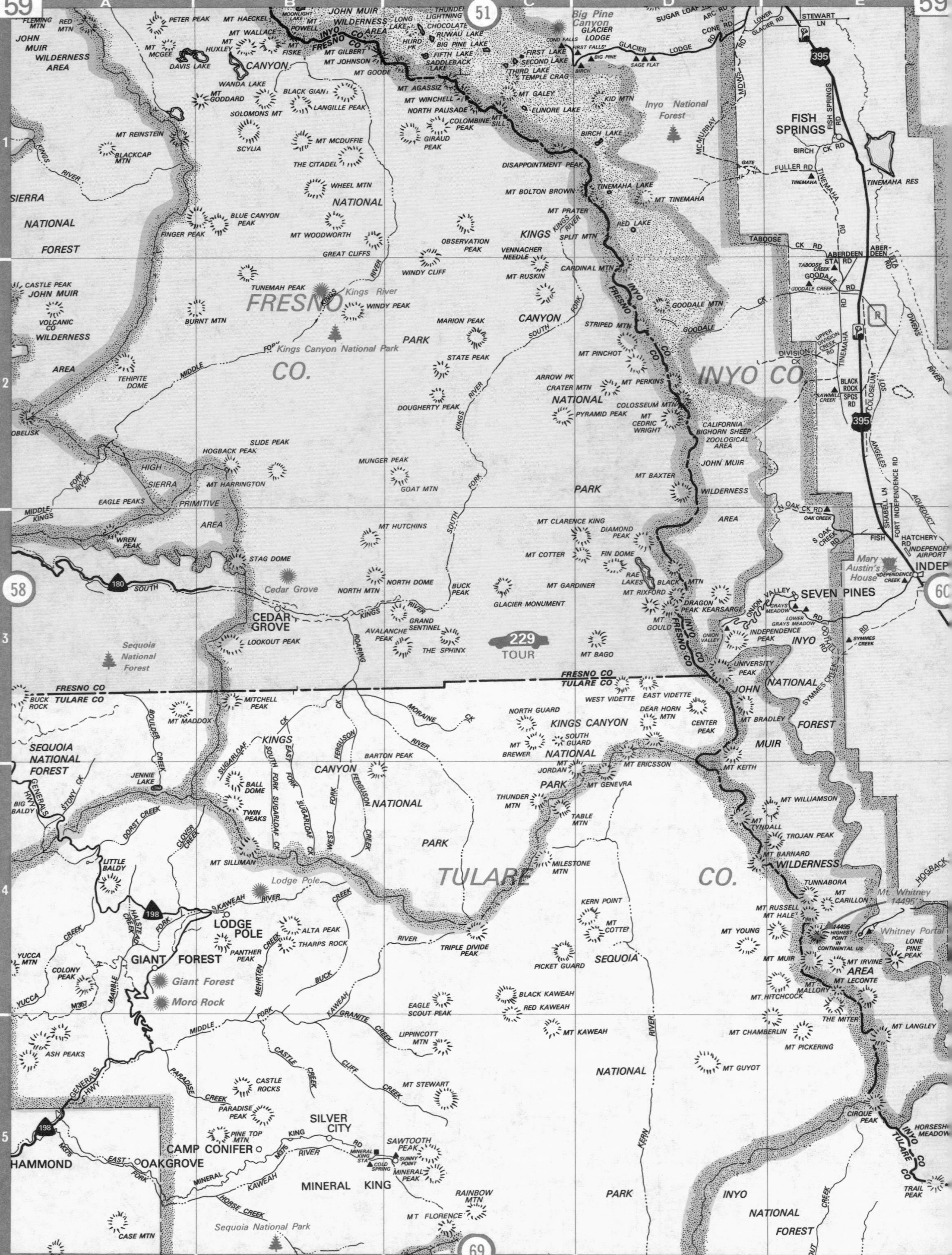

SEE MAP 58

SEE MAP 60

SEE MAP 69

JOHN MUIR WILDERNESS AREA

FLEMING MTN
RED MTN
PETER PEAK
MT HAECKEL
MT WALLACE
MT POWELL
MOONLIGHT
THUNDER
LONG LAKE
LIGHTNING
CHOCOLATE
RUWAU LAKE
BIG PINE LAKE
FIFTH LAKE
SADDLEBACK LAKE
HURD
HELEN PK
FIRST LAKE
SECOND LAKE
THIRD LAKE
TEMPLE CRAG
Big Pine Canyon Glacier Lodge
SUGAR LOAF
STEWART
LOWER GLACIER RD
CONE RD
ARC RD

MT MCGEE
DAVIS LAKE
MT HUXLEY
MT FISKE
MT GILBERT
MT JOHNSON
MT GOODE
CANYON
WANDA LAKE
MT GODDARD
BLACK GIANT
SOLOMONS MT
LANGILLE PEAK
MT AGASSIZ
MT WINCHELL
NORTH PALISADE
MT SILL
COLOMBINE PEAK
MT GALEY
ELINORE LAKE
KID MTN
BIRCH
SAGE FLAT
Inyo National Forest
FISH SPRINGS
BIRCH CK RD
FULLER RD
TINEMAHA

MT REINSTEIN
BLACKCAP MTN
SCYLIA
MT MCDUFFIE
THE CITADEL
GIRAUD PEAK
DISAPPOINTMENT PEAK
BIRCH LAKE
TINEMAHA LAKE
MT TINEMAHA
TABOOSE CK RD
ABERDEEN
STA RD
TINEMAHA RES

SIERRA NATIONAL FOREST
WHEEL MTN
NATIONAL
MT BOLTON BROWN
MT PRATER
RED LAKE
GOODALE
GOODALE CREEK

BLUE CANYON PEAK
FINGER PEAK
MT WOODWORTH
OBSERVATION PEAK
GREAT CLIFFS
WINDY CLIFF
SPLIT MTN
KINGS RIVER
GOODALE MTN
DIVISION CK
UPPER DIVISION CK RD

CASTLE PEAK
JOHN MUIR
VOLCANIC CO WILDERNESS AREA
TEHIPITE DOME
TUNEMAH PEAK
Kings River
WINDY PEAK
FRESNO
CO.
PARK
MARION PEAK
STATE PEAK
VENNACHER NEEDLE
MT RUSKIN
CARDINAL MTN
STRIPED MTN
MT PINCHOT
ARROW PK
CRATER MTN
MT PERKINS
COLOSSEUM MTN
INYO CO
CALIFORNIA BIGHORN SHEEP ZOOLOGICAL AREA
SAWMILL CREEK
BLACK ROCK SPGS RD
395

OBELISK
BURNT MTN
Kings Canyon National Park
KINGS CANYON
NATIONAL
DOUGHERTY PEAK
PYRAMID PEAK
MT CEDRIC WRIGHT
JOHN MUIR

MIDDLE FORK KINGS RIVER
HIGH SIERRA PRIMITIVE AREA
HOGBACK PEAK
SLIDE PEAK
MT HARRINGTON
EAGLE PEAKS
MUNGER PEAK
GOAT MTN
PARK
MT BAXTER
WILDERNESS
AREA
OAK CK RD
N OAK CK RD

WREN PEAK
STAG DOME
MT HUTCHINS
BUCK PEAK
MT CLARENCE KING
DIAMOND PEAK
FIN DOME
MT COTTER
AREA
S OAK CREEK
FISH HATCHERY RD
INDEPENDENCE AIRPORT
INDEP
180
SOUTH
Cedar Grove
NORTH MTN
NORTH DOME
MT GARDINER
GLACIER MONUMENT
RAE LAKES
MT RIXFORD
BLACK MTN
DRAGON PEAK
KEARSARGE
Mary Austin's House
SEVEN PINES

CEDAR GROVE
LOOKOUT PEAK
GRAND SENTINEL
AVALANCHE PEAK
ROARING RIVER
THE SPHINX
MT BAGO
229 TOUR
MT GOULD
ONION VALLEY
GRAYS MEADOW
LOWER GRAYS MEADOW
INDEPENDENCE PEAK
INYO
SYMMES CREEK

FRESNO CO
TULARE CO
UNIVERSITY PEAK
JOHN
NATIONAL
FRESNO CO TULARE CO

BUCK ROCK
TULARE CO
MITCHELL PEAK
MORAINE CK
WEST VIDETTE
EAST VIDETTE
DEAR HORN MTN
CENTER PEAK
MT BRADLEY
FOREST

MT MADDOX
SUGARLOAF
KINGS EAST FORK
FERGUSON CK
BARTON PEAK
NORTH GUARD
KINGS CANYON
SOUTH GUARD
MT BREWER
MT ERICSSON
MT KEITH
MUIR

SEQUOIA NATIONAL FOREST
JENNIE LAKE
BALL DOME
CANYON
NATIONAL
MT JORDAN
MT GENEVRA
MT WILLIAMSON
WILDERNESS

BIG BALDY
GENERALS HWY
STONY CK
TWIN PEAKS
SOUTH FORK SUGARLOAF CK
WEST FORK
PARK
THUNDER MTN
TABLE MTN
MT TYNDALL
TROJAN PEAK
MT BARNARD

LITTLE BALDY
MT SILLIMAN
CLOVER CREEK
TULARE
CO.
TUNNABORA
MT CARILLON
MT RUSSELL
Mt. Whitney 14495
HOGBACK

Lodge Pole
KAWEAH RIVER
MILESTONE MTN
KERN POINT
MT HALE
14495 HIGHEST POINT CONTINENTAL US
Whitney Portal

198
LODGE POLE
ALTA PEAK
THARPS ROCK
MT COTTE?
MT YOUNG
MT IRVINE
LONE PINE PEAK

GIANT FOREST
PANTHER PEAK
BUCK
TRIPLE DIVIDE PEAK
PICKET GUARD
SEQUOIA
MT MUIR
AREA
MT LECONTE
MT MALLORY

YUCCA MTN
COLONY PEAK
Giant Forest
Moro Rock
MEHRTEN CREEK
EAGLE SCOUT PEAK
BLACK KAWEAH
RED KAWEAH
MT HITCHCOCK
THE MITER
MT LANGLEY

YUCCA
M357
MARBLE FORK
MIDDLE FORK
GRANITE CREEK
LIPPINCOTT MTN
MT KAWEAH
NATIONAL
MT CHAMBERLIN
MT PICKERING

ASH PEAKS
KAWEAH
CASTLE ROCKS
CASTLE CREEK
MT STEWART
MT GUYOT
CIRQUE PEAK

GENERALS HWY
PARADISE CREEK
CLIFF CREEK
SEQUOIA NATIONAL PARK
HORSESHOE MEADOW

198
HAMMOND
OAKGROVE
EAST FORK
PARADISE PEAK
PINE TOP MTN
SILVER CITY
KERN RIVER
CAMP CONIFER
SAWTOOTH PEAK
SUNNY POINT
MINERAL KING
PARK
INYO
TRAIL PEAK

MINERAL
KAWEAH
HORSE CREEK
MINERAL KING
MINERAL KING STA
COLD SPRING
MINERAL PEAK
RAINBOW MTN
MT FLORENCE
NATIONAL FOREST

CASE MTN
Sequoia National Park

HIGHWAYS

Thomas Bros. Maps
COPYRIGHT 1997
N

395
59
51
58
60
69

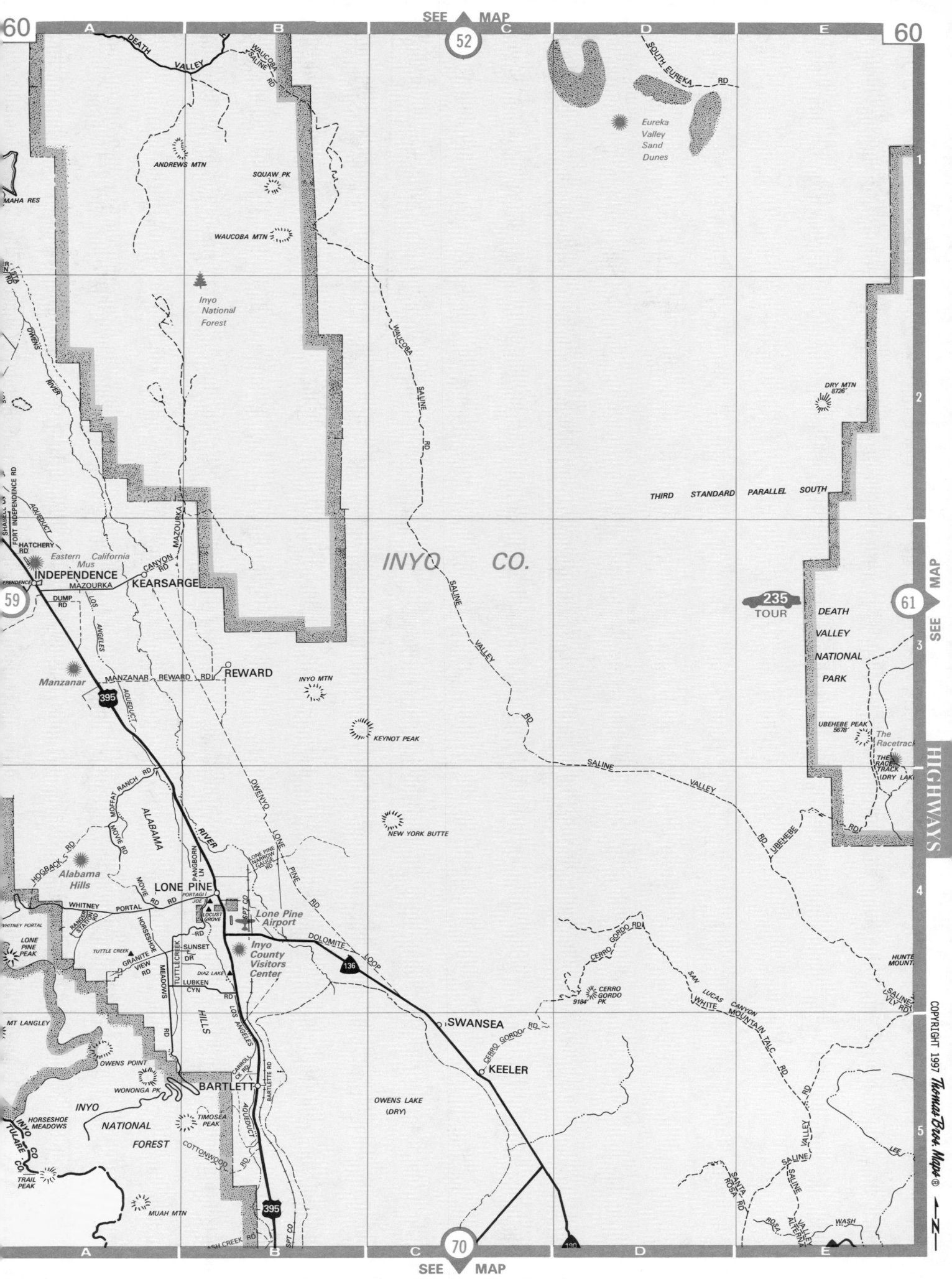

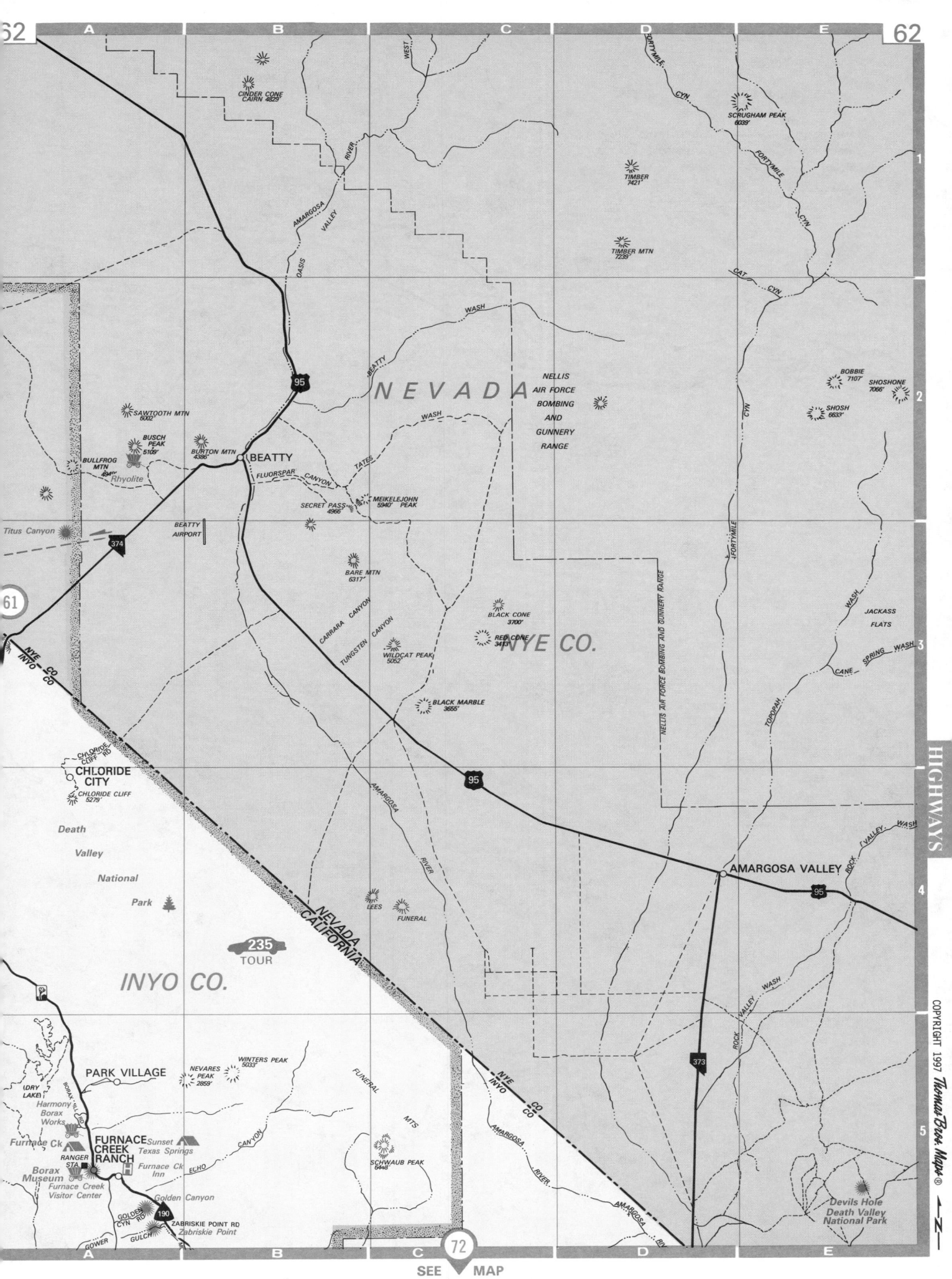

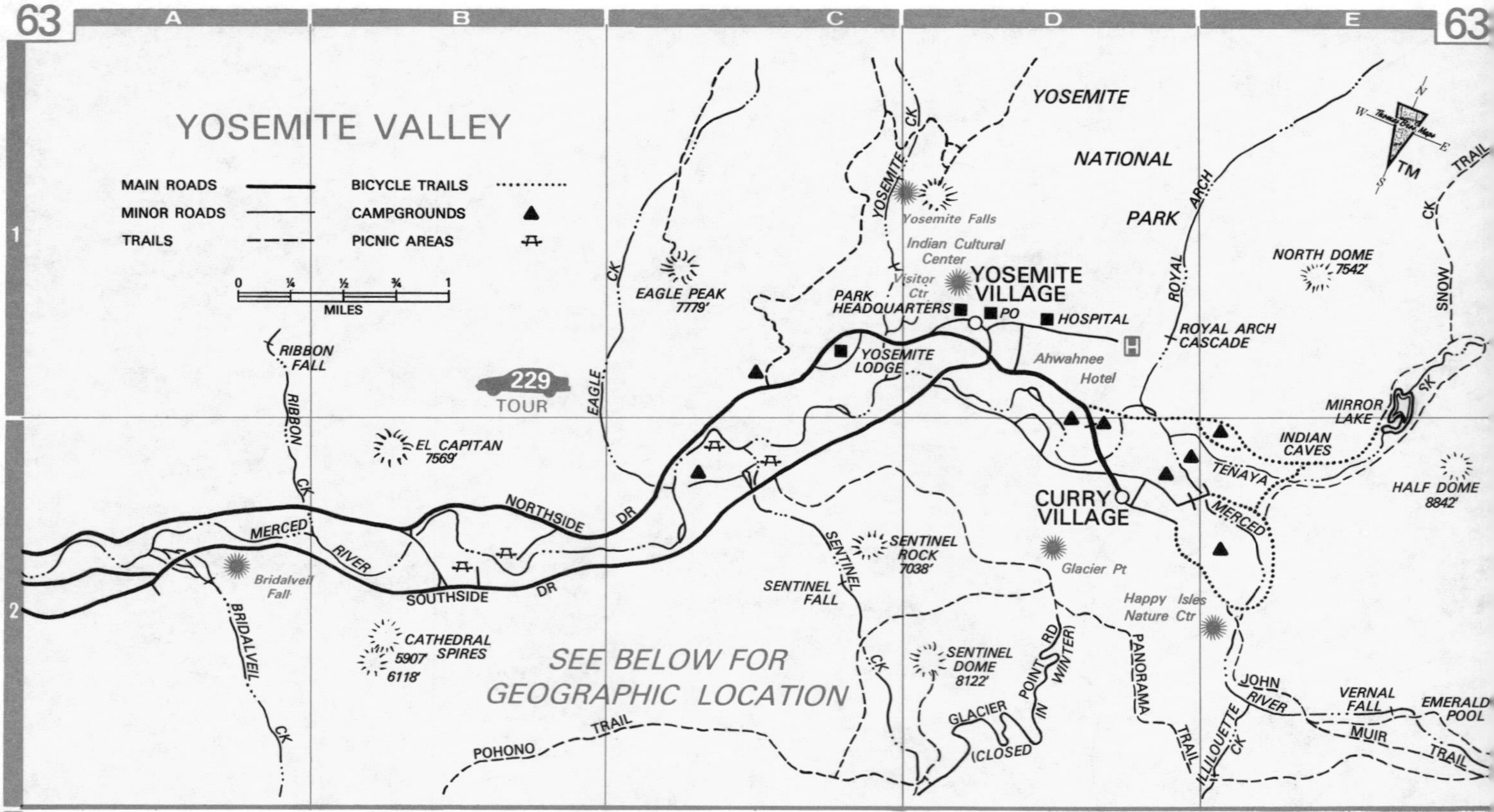

YOSEMITE VALLEY

MAIN ROADS —   BICYCLE TRAILS ·······
MINOR ROADS —   CAMPGROUNDS ▲
TRAILS - - -   PICNIC AREAS ⛩

0   ¼   ½   ¾   1
MILES

YOSEMITE NATIONAL PARK

RIBBON FALL
RIBBON CK
EAGLE CK
EAGLE PEAK 7779'
PARK HEADQUARTERS
Visitor Ctr
PO
HOSPITAL
YOSEMITE LODGE
Ahwahnee Hotel
Yosemite Falls
Indian Cultural Center
YOSEMITE VILLAGE
YOSEMITE NATIONAL PARK
NORTH DOME 7542'
ROYAL ARCH
ROYAL ARCH CASCADE
SNOW CK
TM
MIRROR LAKE
INDIAN CAVES
TENAYA CK
HALF DOME 8842'
CURRY VILLAGE
MERCED
229 TOUR
EL CAPITAN 7569'
NORTHSIDE DR
MERCED RIVER
Bridalveil Fall
BRIDALVEIL CK
SOUTHSIDE DR
CATHEDRAL 5907 SPIRES 6118'
SEE BELOW FOR GEOGRAPHIC LOCATION
SENTINEL CK
SENTINEL FALL
SENTINEL ROCK 7038'
SENTINEL DOME 8122'
GLACIER (CLOSED)
POINT RD (WINTER)
Glacier Pt
Happy Isles Nature Ctr
PANORAMA TRAIL
ILLILOUETTE CK
JOHN RIVER
MUIR TRAIL
VERNAL FALL
EMERALD POOL
POHONO TRAIL

YOSEMITE NATIONAL PARK

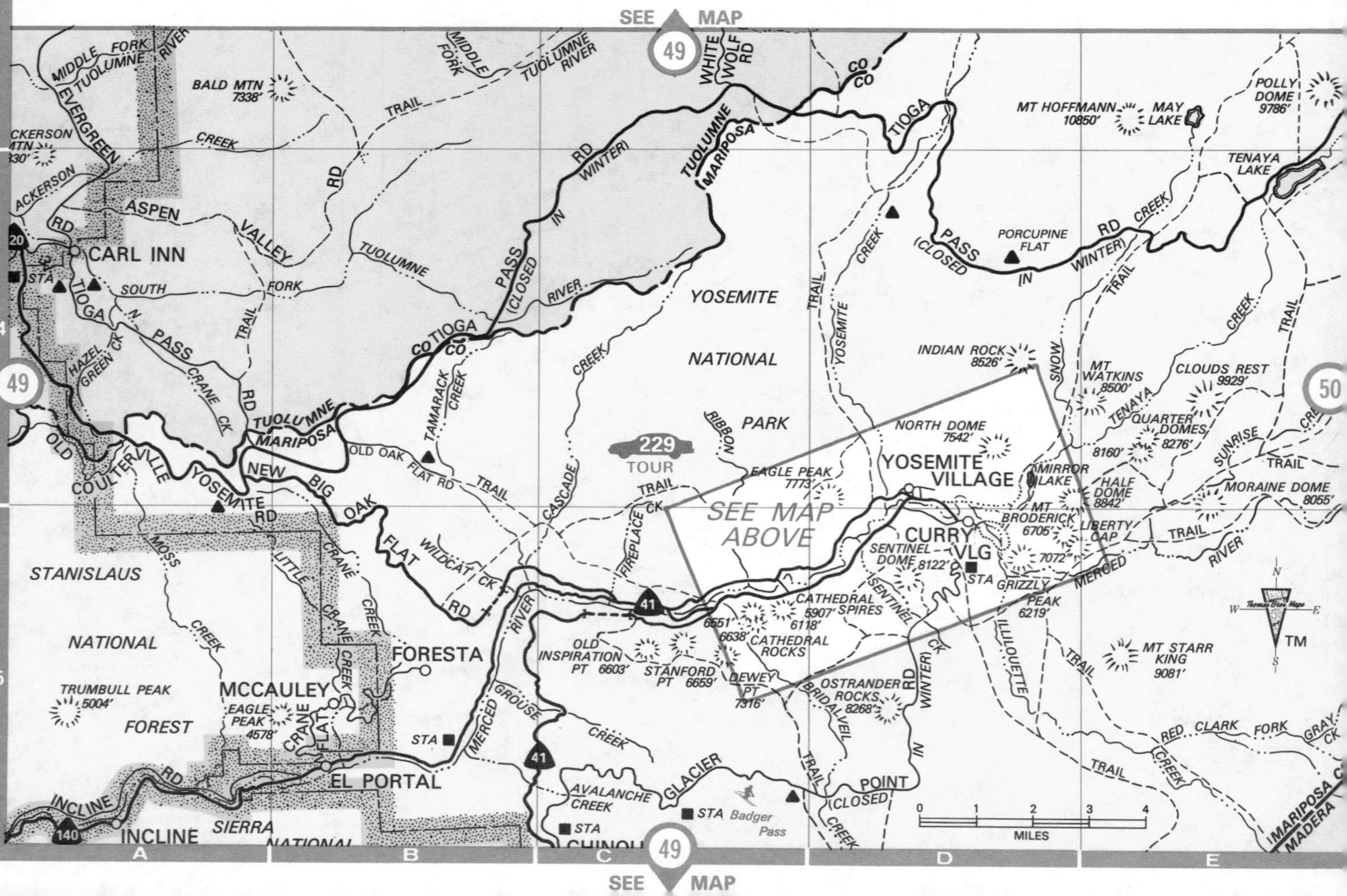

SEE MAP 49
WHITE WOLF RD
MIDDLE FORK TUOLUMNE RIVER
BALD MTN 7338'
MIDDLE FORK
TUOLUMNE RIVER
EVERGREEN
ACKERSON MTN 30'
ASPEN
ACKERSON RD
CARL INN
STA
20
TIOGA RD
HAZEL GREEN CK
SOUTH FORK
TUOLUMNE
CRANE CK
TUOLUMNE MARIPOSA
PASS (CLOSED) IN (WINTER)
RD
TIOGA RD
CO TIOGA CO
TUOLUMNE RIVER
CREEK
CO CO
TIOGA PASS (CLOSED) RD IN (WINTER)
MT HOFFMANN 10850'
MAY LAKE
POLLY DOME 9786'
TENAYA LAKE
PORCUPINE FLAT
YOSEMITE NATIONAL PARK
INDIAN ROCK 8526'
MT WATKINS 8500'
SNOW CREEK
TENAYA
CLOUDS REST 9929'
QUARTER DOMES 8276'
SUNRISE TRAIL
MORAINE DOME 8055'
MT STARR KING 9081'
OLD COULTERVILLE RD
OLD BIG OAK FLAT RD
NEW BIG OAK FLAT RD
YOSEMITE RD
STANISLAUS NATIONAL FOREST
MOSS CREEK
LITTLE CRANE CREEK
CRANE CREEK
FORESTA
MCCAULEY
TRUMBULL PEAK 5004'
EAGLE PEAK 4578'
TAMARACK CREEK
OLD OAK FLAT RD
WILDCAT CK
CASCADE TRAIL
FIREPLACE CK
RIBBON CK
229 TOUR
EAGLE PEAK 7773'
NORTH DOME 7542'
SEE MAP ABOVE
YOSEMITE VILLAGE
MIRROR LAKE
HALF DOME 8842'
LIBERTY CAP
MT BRODERICK 6705'
CURRY VLG
SENTINEL DOME 8122'
STA
GRIZZLY PEAK 6219'
7072'
MERCED RIVER
41
OLD INSPIRATION PT 6603'
STANFORD PT 6659'
6551'
6638'
CATHEDRAL ROCKS
CATHEDRAL 5907 SPIRES 6118'
DEWEY PT 7316'
OSTRANDER ROCKS 8268'
BRIDALVEIL CK
ILLILOUETTE CK
POINT (CLOSED) RD (WINTER)
TM
MERCED RIVER
RED CLARK FORK
GRAY CK
EL PORTAL
MERCED RIVER
GROUSE CREEK
AVALANCHE CREEK
GLACIER
STA Badger Pass
STA
CHINQ
INCLINE
140
SIERRA NATIONAL FOREST
0 1 2 3 4 MILES
MARIPOSA CO MADERA CO

SEE MAP ▲ 49   SEE MAP ◀ 49   SEE MAP ▶ 50   SEE MAP ▼ 49

HIGHWAYS

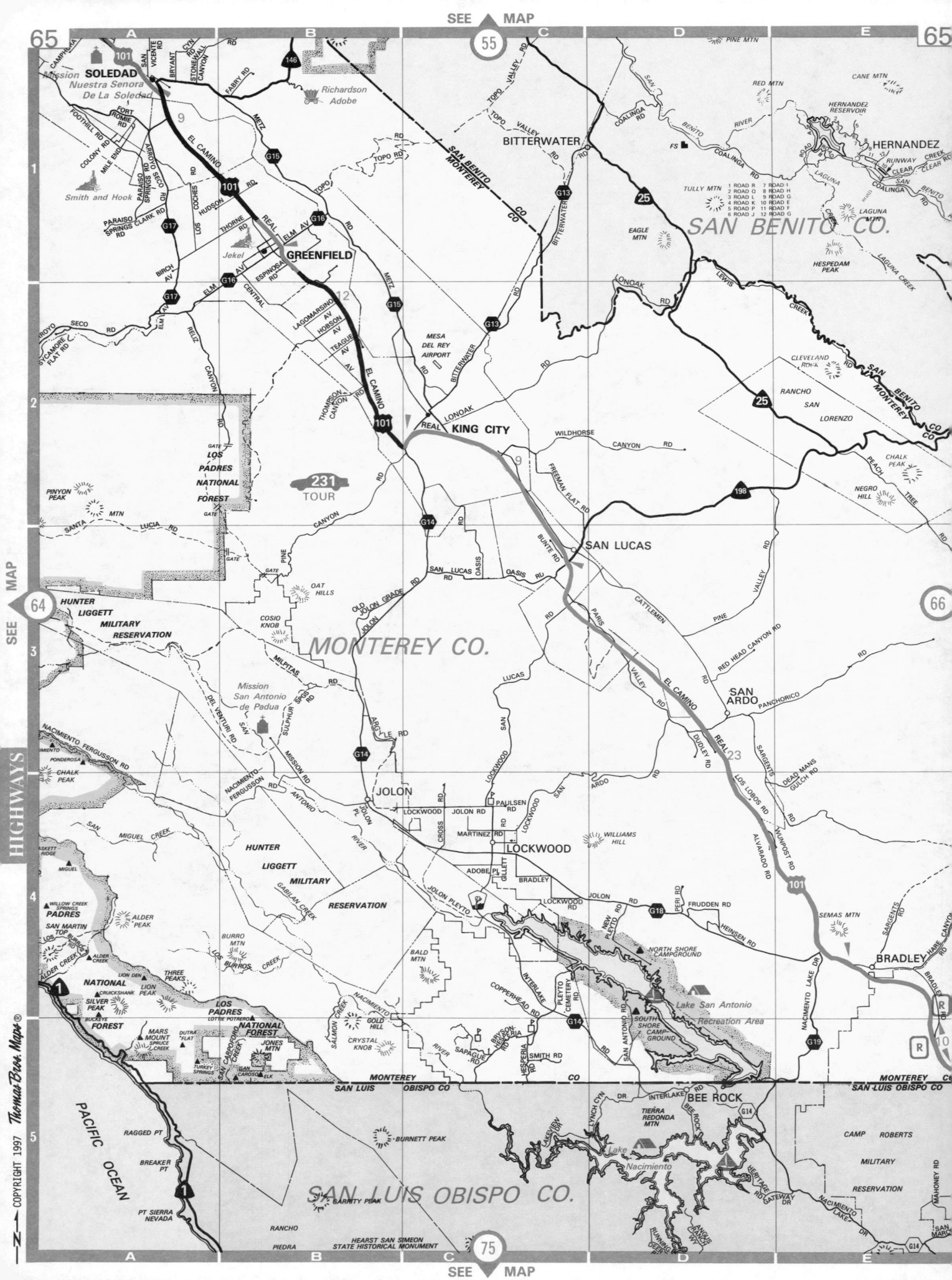

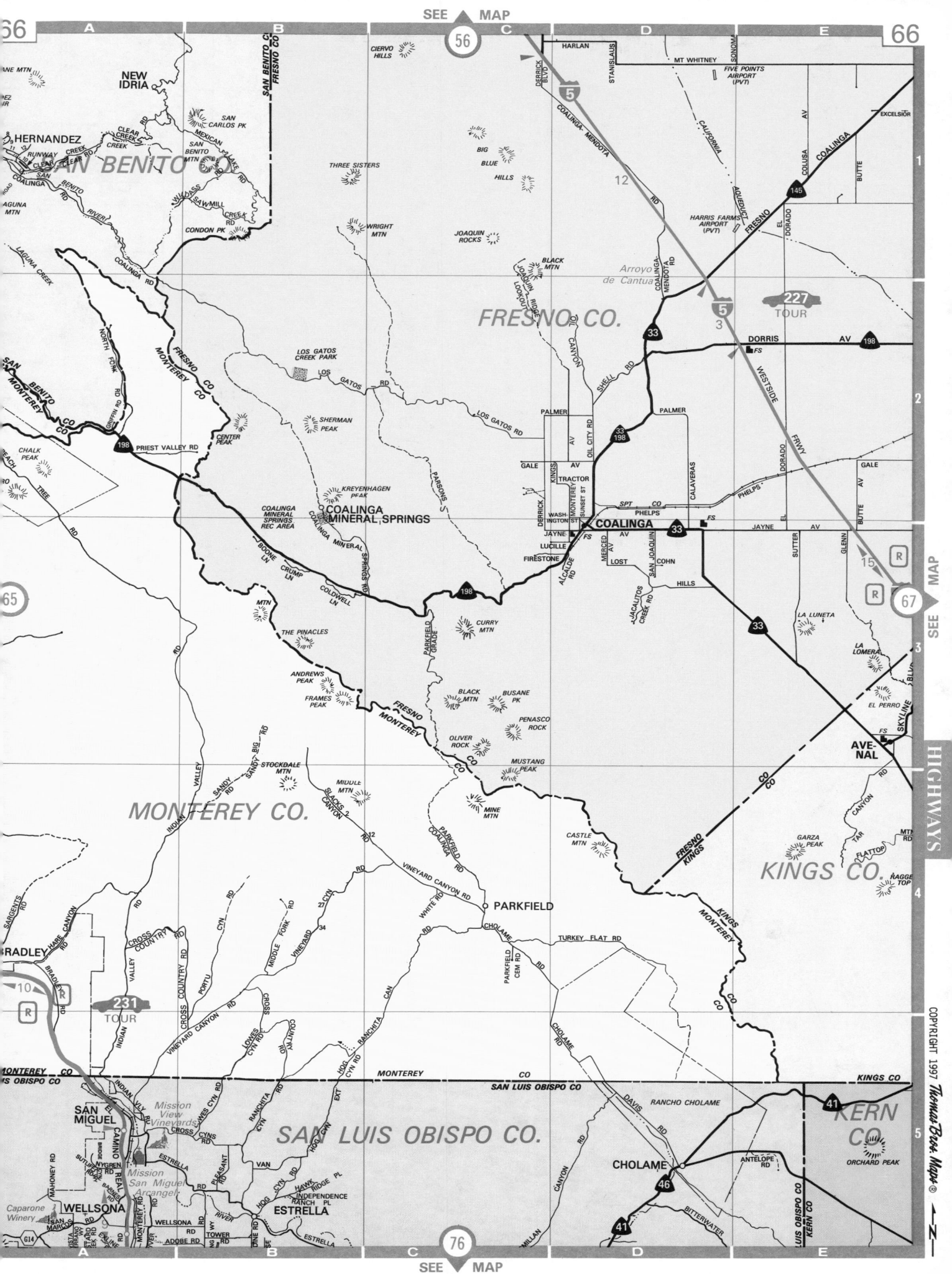

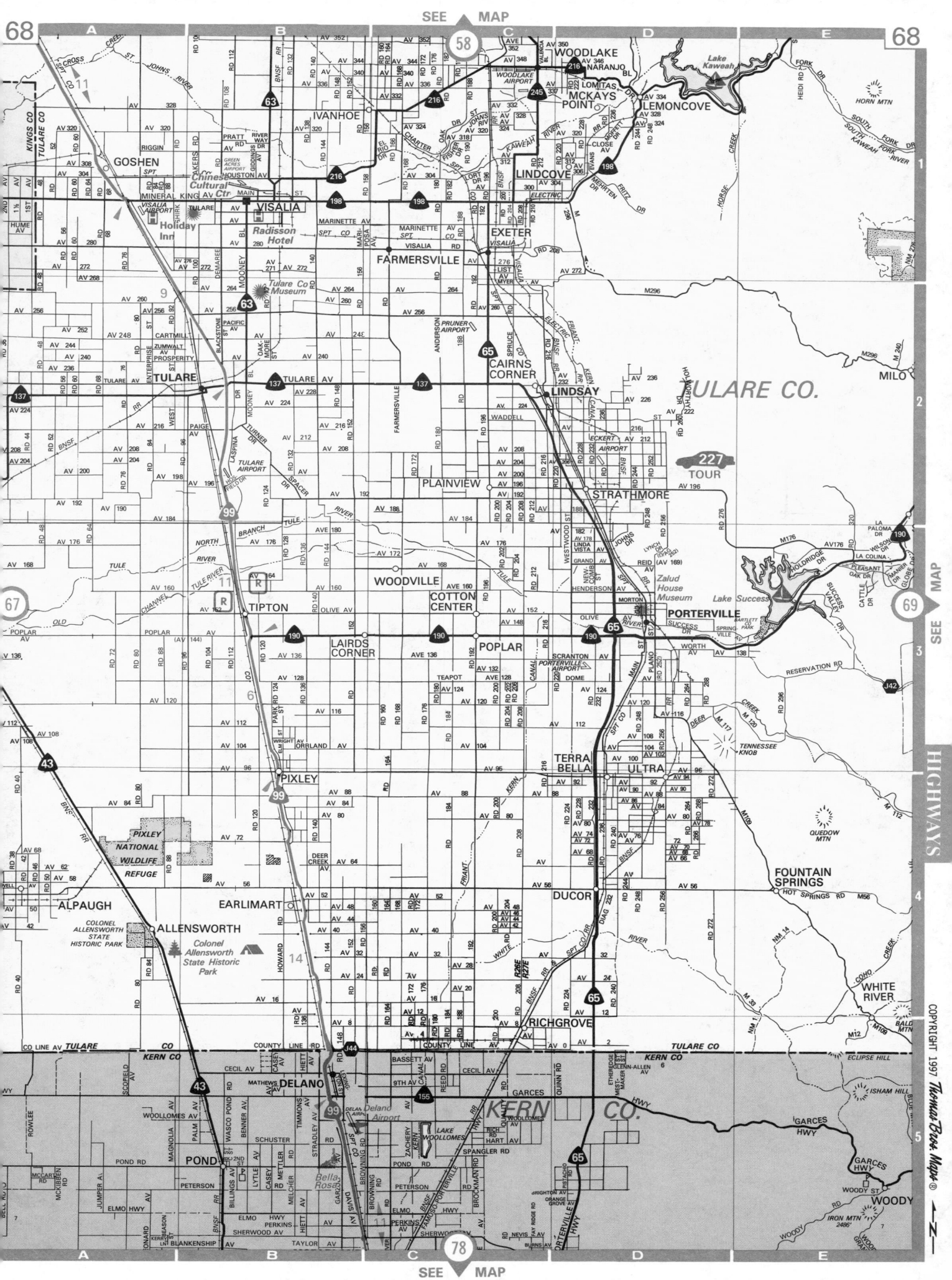

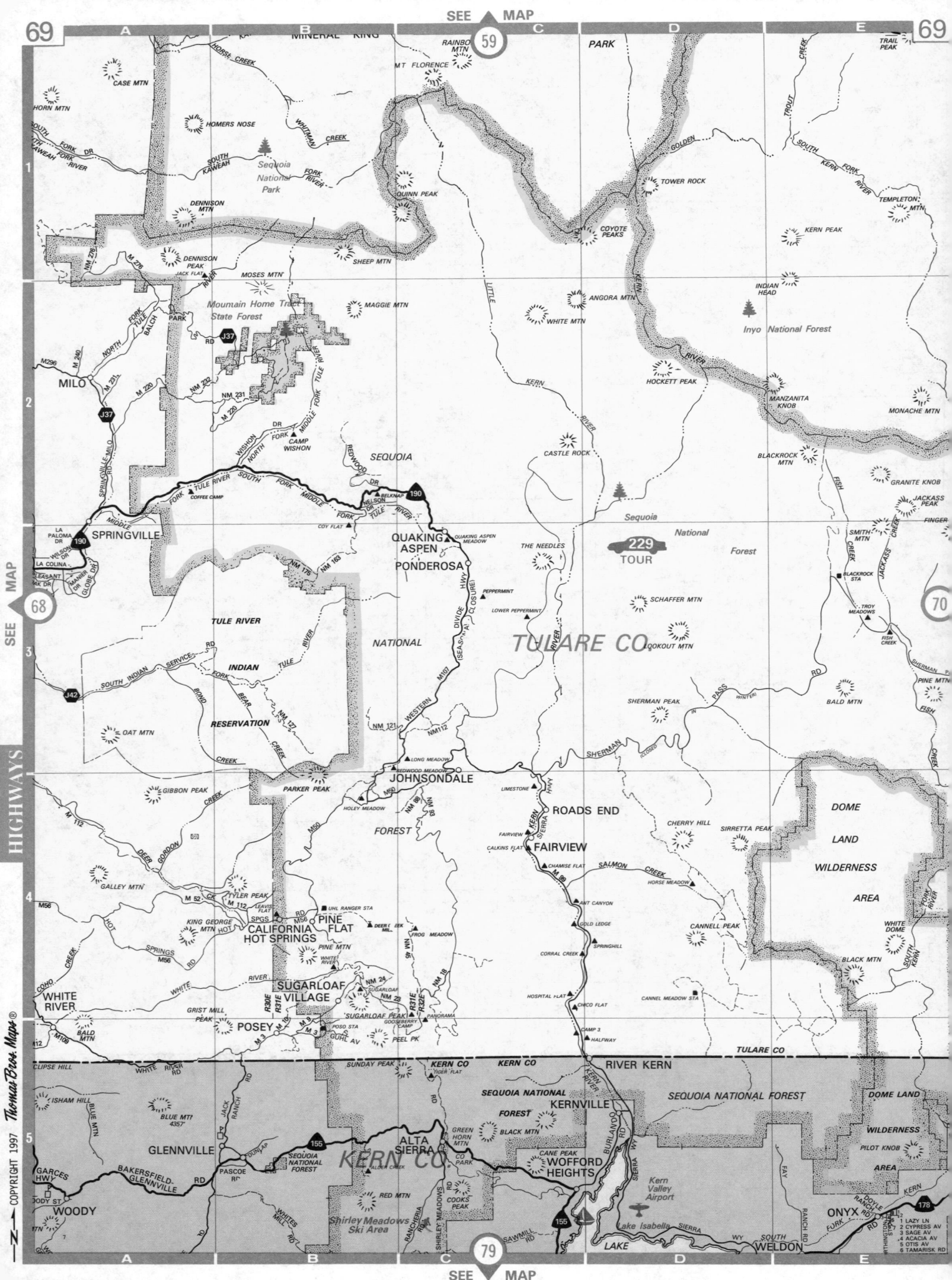

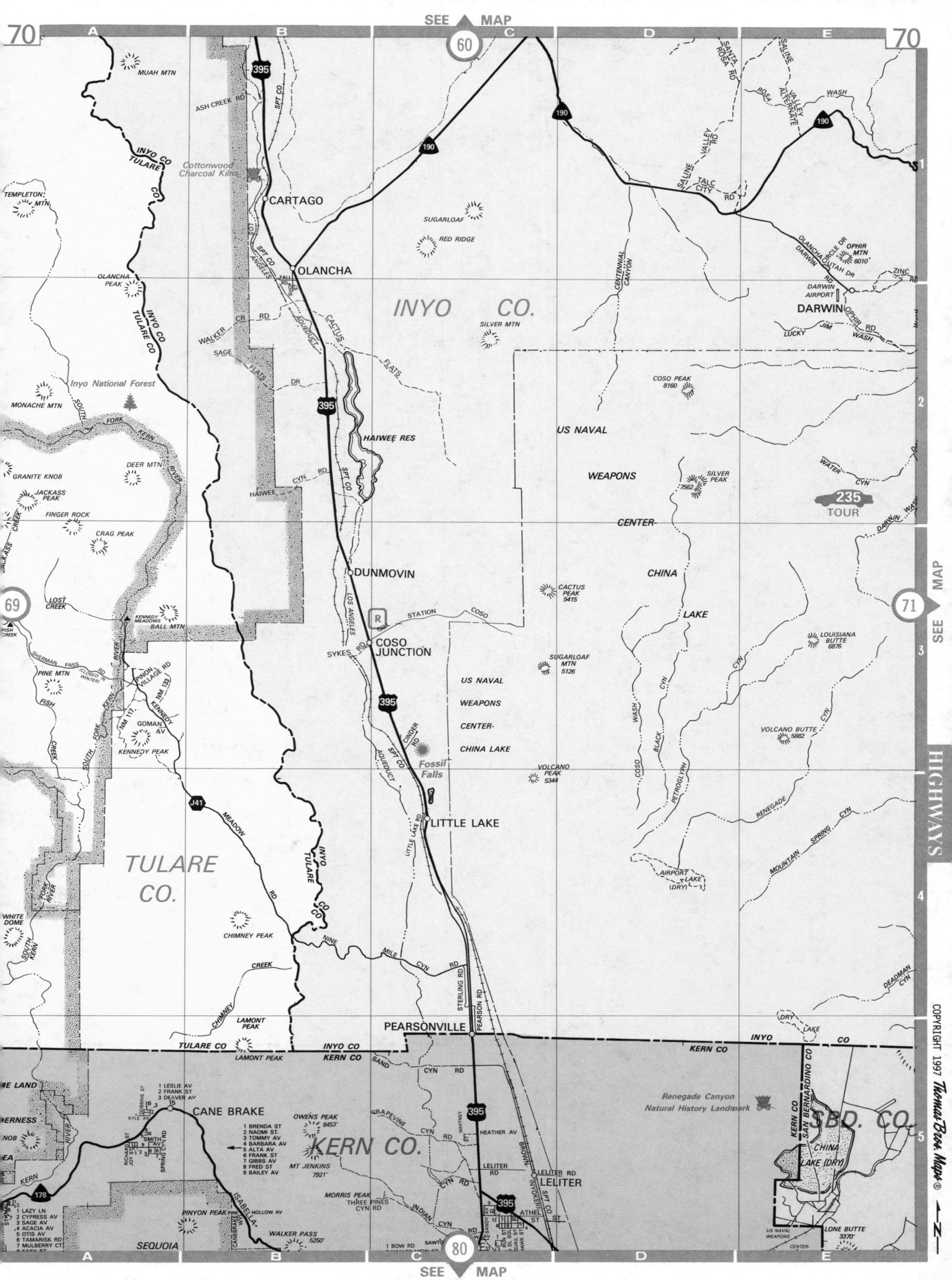

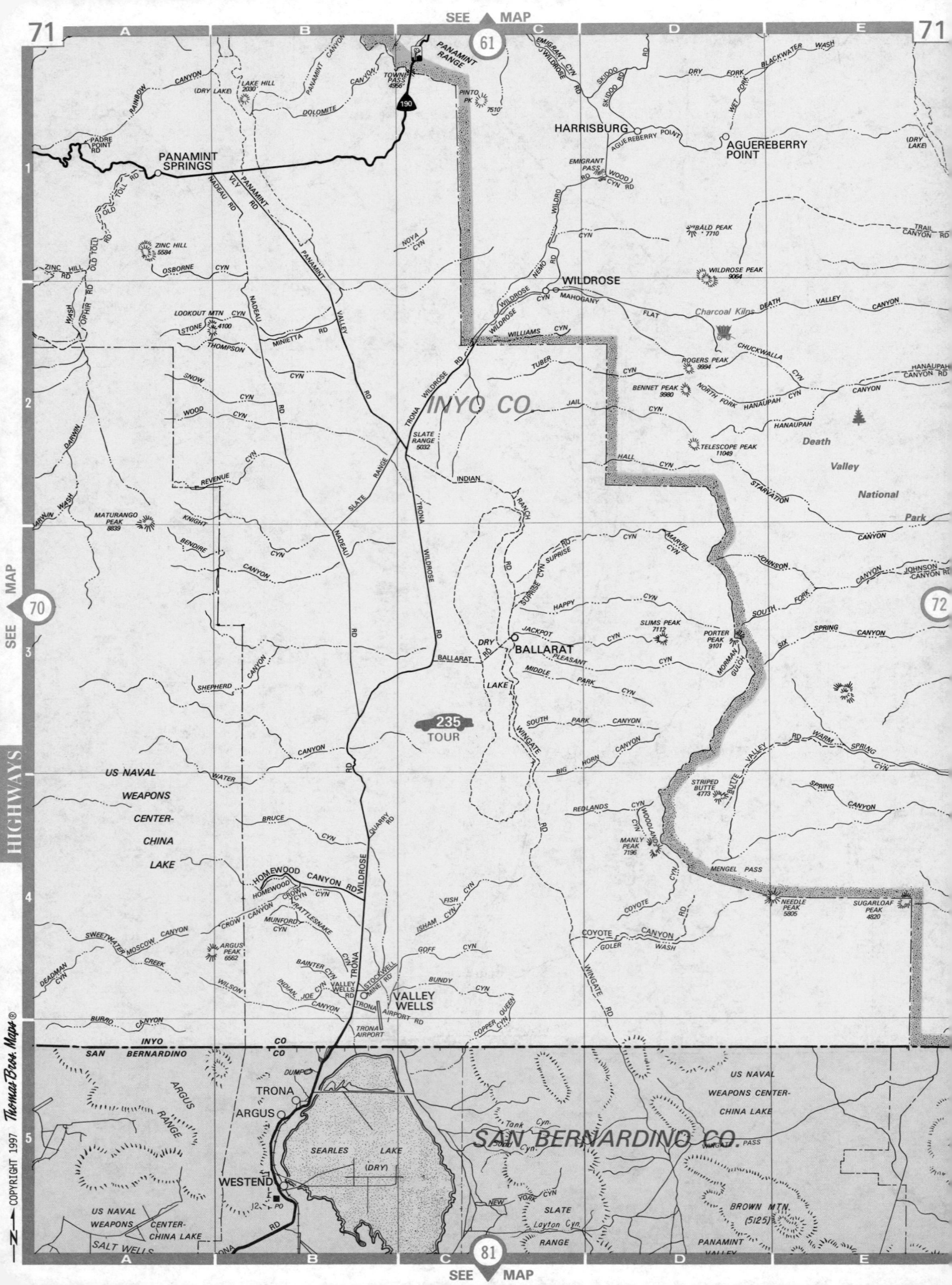

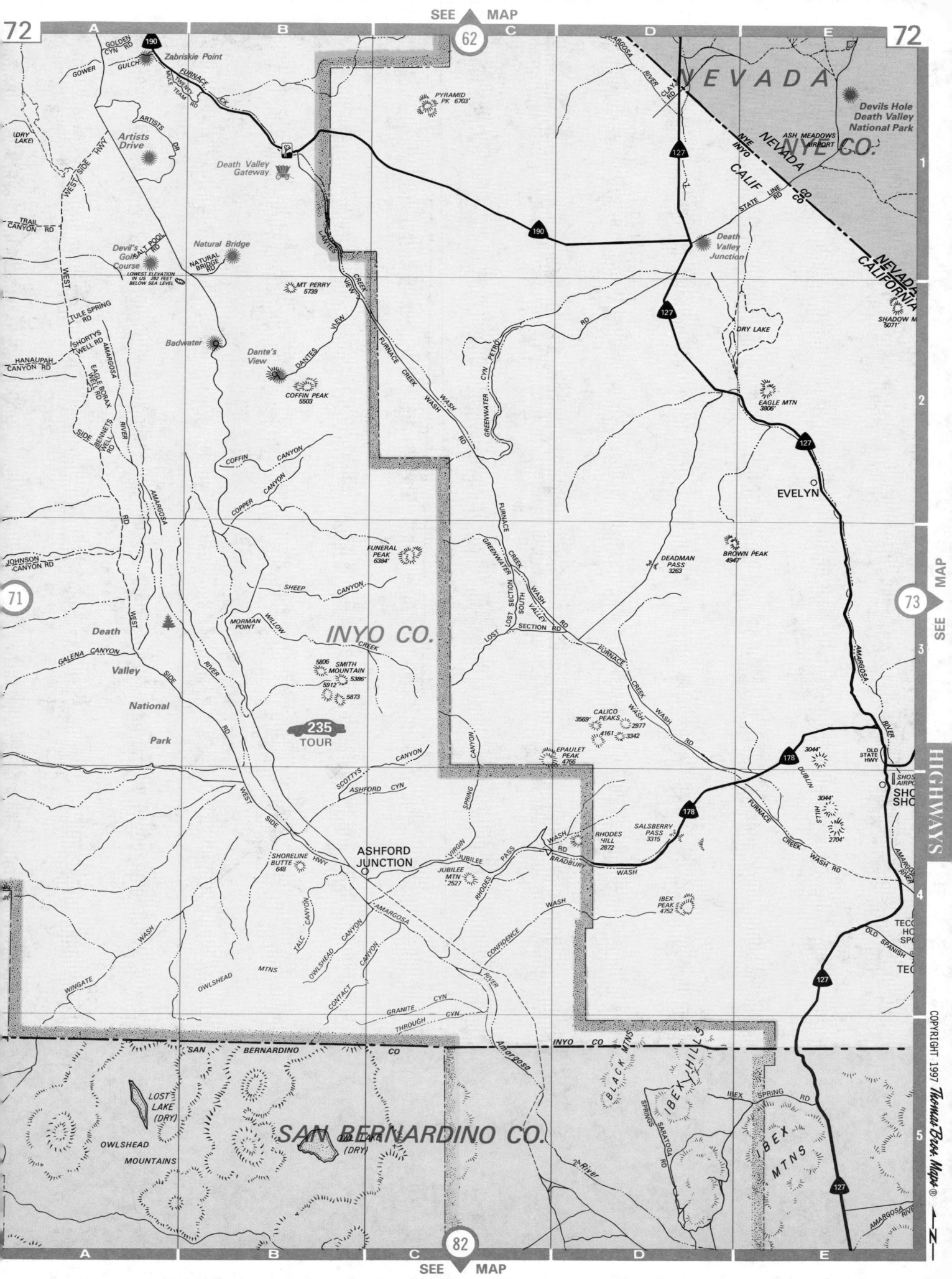

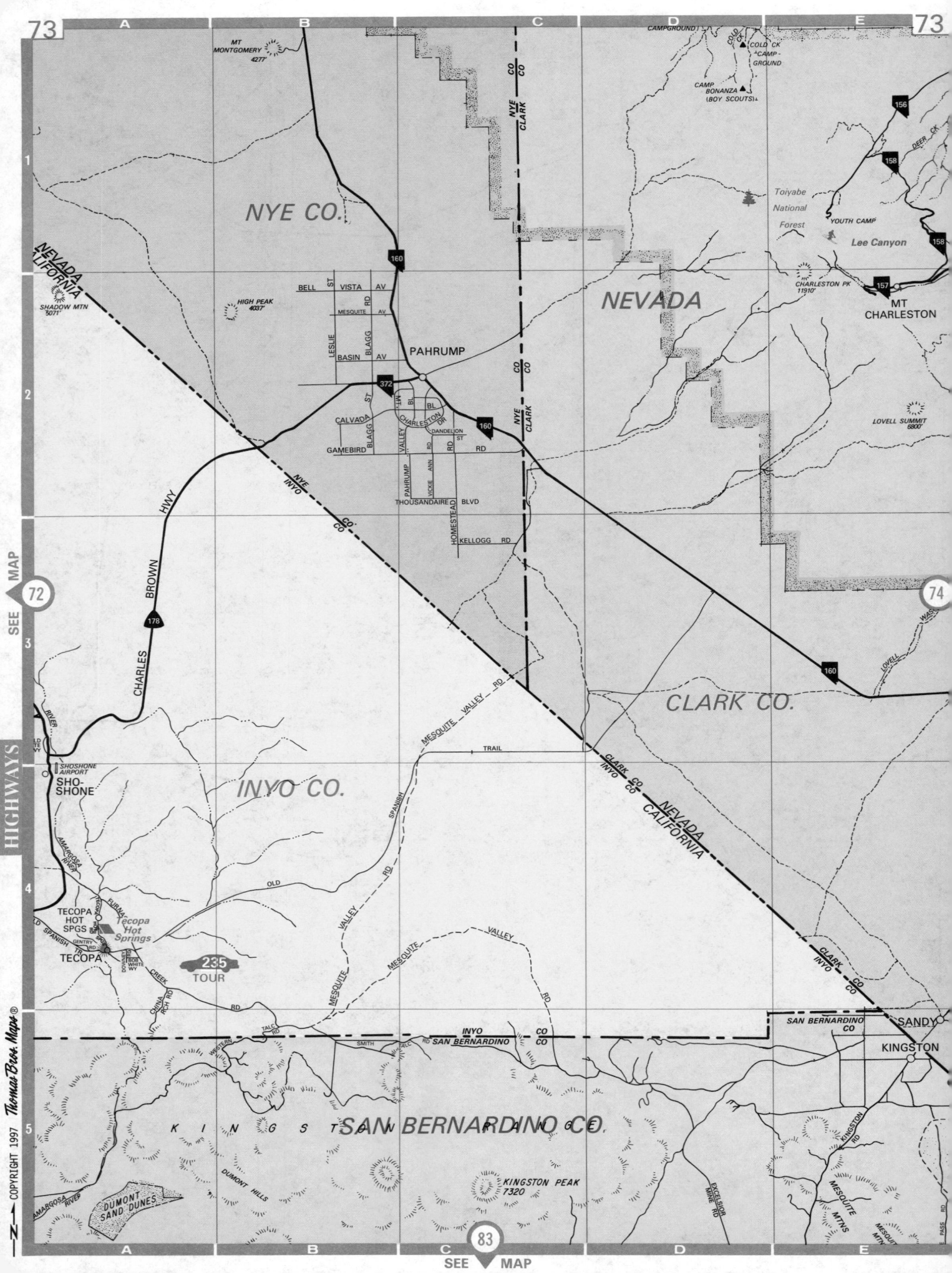

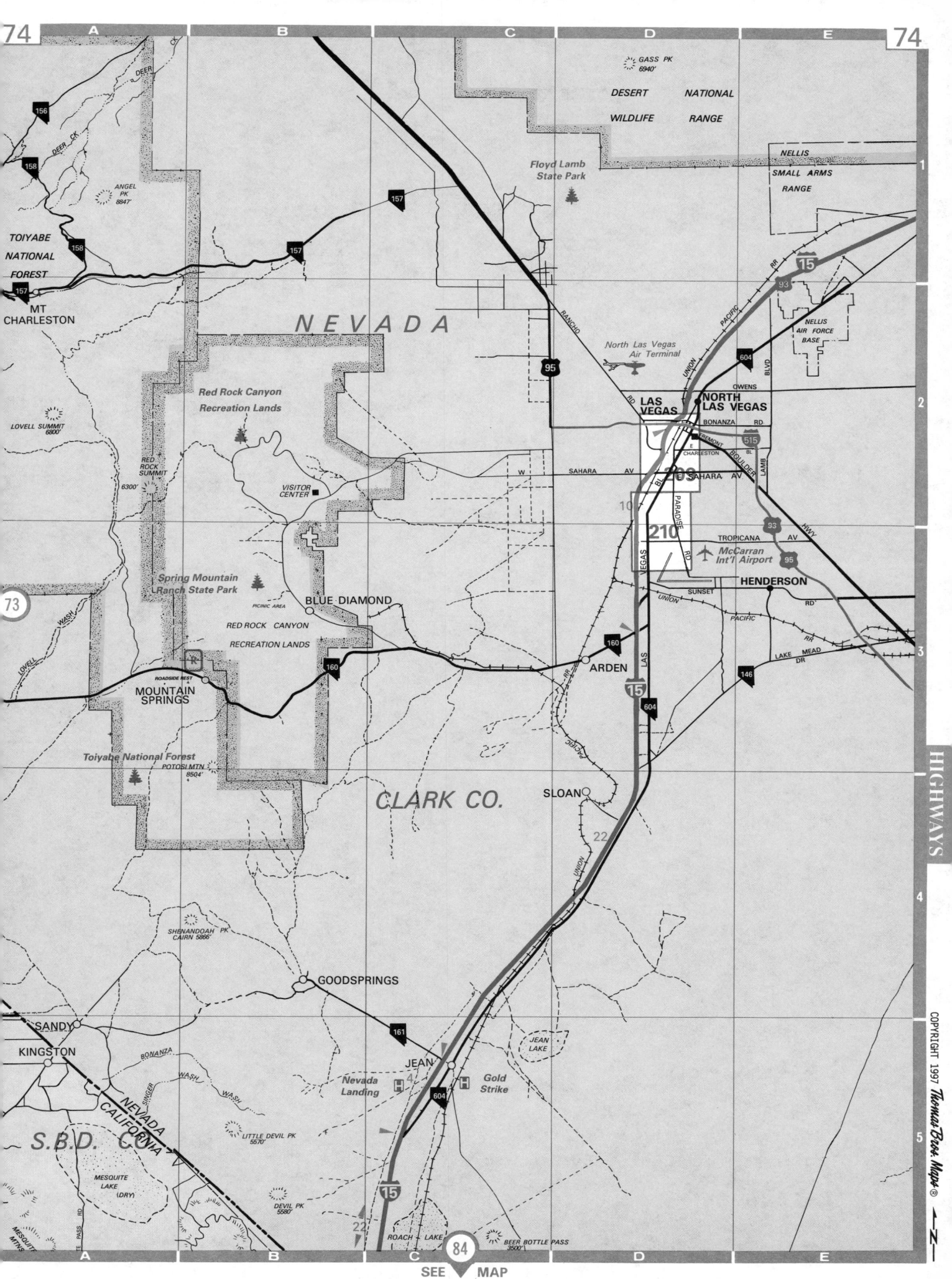

SEE MAP
(65)

SAN LUIS OBISPO CO.

PACIFIC OCEAN

PT SIERRA NEVADA

PT PIEDRAS BLANCAS

CABRILLO

Hearst San Simeon State Historic Monument

RANCHO PIEDRA BLANCA

GARRITY PEAK

PINE MTN

BLACK OAK MTN ROCKY BUTTE

RED MTN

NACIMIENTO RES

LIME MTN

CYPRESS MTN

ADELAIDA

Adelaida Cellars

CHIMNEY ROCK

KLAU

SAN SIMEON

SAN SIMEON PT

SAN SIMEON BAY

HWY

SAN SIMEON

Wm. Randolph Hearst State Beach

San Simeon State Beach

SCOTT ROCK

CAMBRIA

Moonstone Inn Motel
Mariners Inn

MAIN ST

RANCHO

CAMBRIA AIR FORCE STA

Santa Rosa

GREEN

HARMONY VLY RD

HARMONY

Harmony Cellars

SAN GERONIMO

VILLA CREEK RD

NORTHERLY BRANCH GREEN VLY RD

SANTA ROSA CREEK

VALLEY

BLACK MTN RD

231 TOUR

46

York Mountain

Mastantuono Winery

CAYUCOS CREEK

THUNDER CYN RD

PICACHIO RD

COTTONTAIL CK RD

WHALE ROCK RES

RANCHO ASUNCION

TORO CREEK

PARK RANGE PEAK

CAYUCOS

Cayucos State Beach

Morro Strand State Beach

MONTECITO RD

RANCHO MORO Y CAYUCOS

TORO CREEK

OLD

Atascadero State Beach

ESTERO

Breakers Motel

MORRO BAY

Morro Rock

Morro Bay Aquarium

Morro Bay Museum Of Natural History

Morro Bay State Park

CUESTA BY-THE-SEA

MORRO BAY

9TH ST

CABRILLO HWY

HOLLISTER PEAK

Santa Ysabel Rd

SAN BERNARDO CK RD

76

BAYWOOD PARK

LOS OSOS

Los Osos Oaks State Reserve

LOS OSOS VALLEY

RANCHO CANADA DE LOS Y PECHO Y ISLAY

Montana De Oro State Park

RANCHO

CANADA DE

SADDLE PEAK

LOS OSOS

GREEN PEAK

PG&E NUCLEAR POWER PLANT

Y PECHO Y ISLAY

SAN LUIS HILL

PT SAN LU

PACIFIC OCEAN

N

SEE MAP 68

WOODY

MCFARLAND

WASCO 46

FAMOSO

SHAFTER 43

MINTER VILLAGE

HIGHTS CORNER

BUTTON WILLOW 58

ROSEDALE 58

GREENACRES

BAKERSFIELD

KERN CITY

OILDALE

FRUITVALE

EAST BAKERSFIELD

HART PARK

CHOCTAW VALLEY

RIO BRAVO

LOMA PARK

MAGUNDEN

EDISON

MAY-FAIR

FULLER ACRES

TUPMAN

Tule Elk State Reserve

KERN CO.

OLD RIVER

PUMPKIN CENTER

PANAMA

GREENFIELD

LAMONT

DI GIOR

WEED PATCH

ARVIN

DUSTIN ACRES

VALLEY ACRES

Buena Vista Aquatic Recreation Area

Buena Vista Lake Bed

PALOMA OIL FIELD

FORD CITY

TAFT HTS

TAFT

MARICOPA 166

METTLER

Kern Lake Bed

WHEELER RIDGE

33

HIGHWAYS

SEE MAP

77 79

SEE MAP 88

227 TOUR

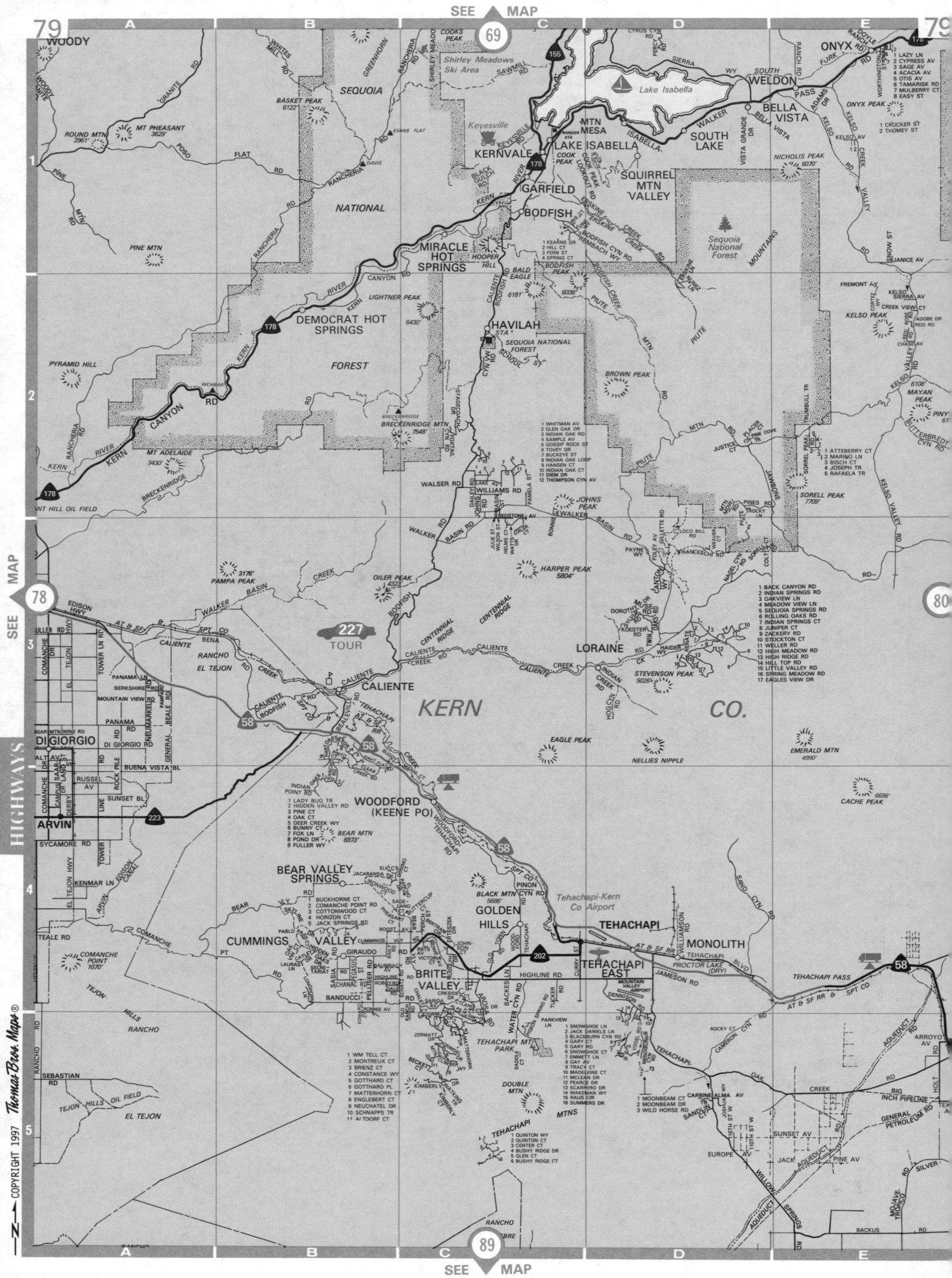

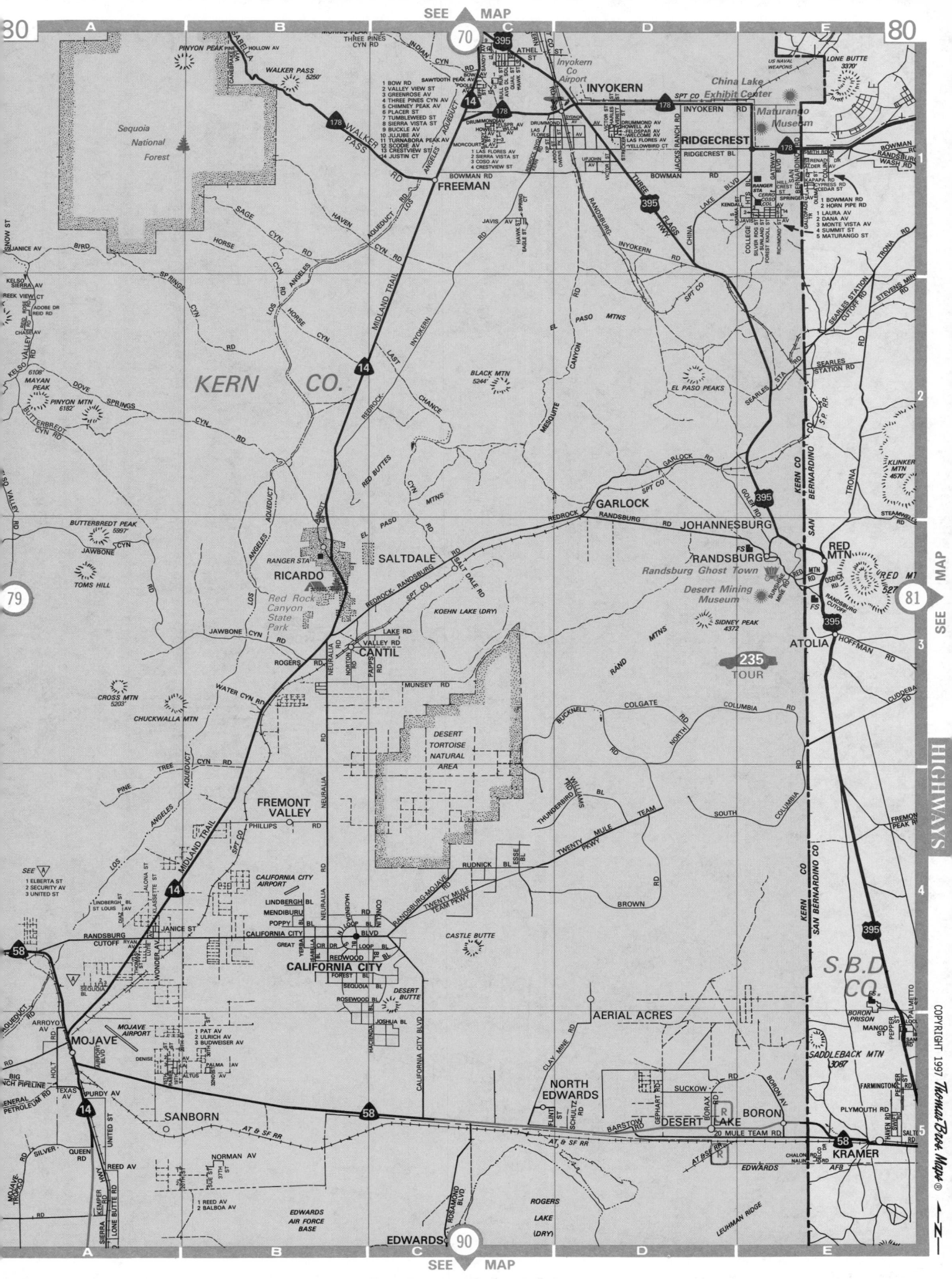

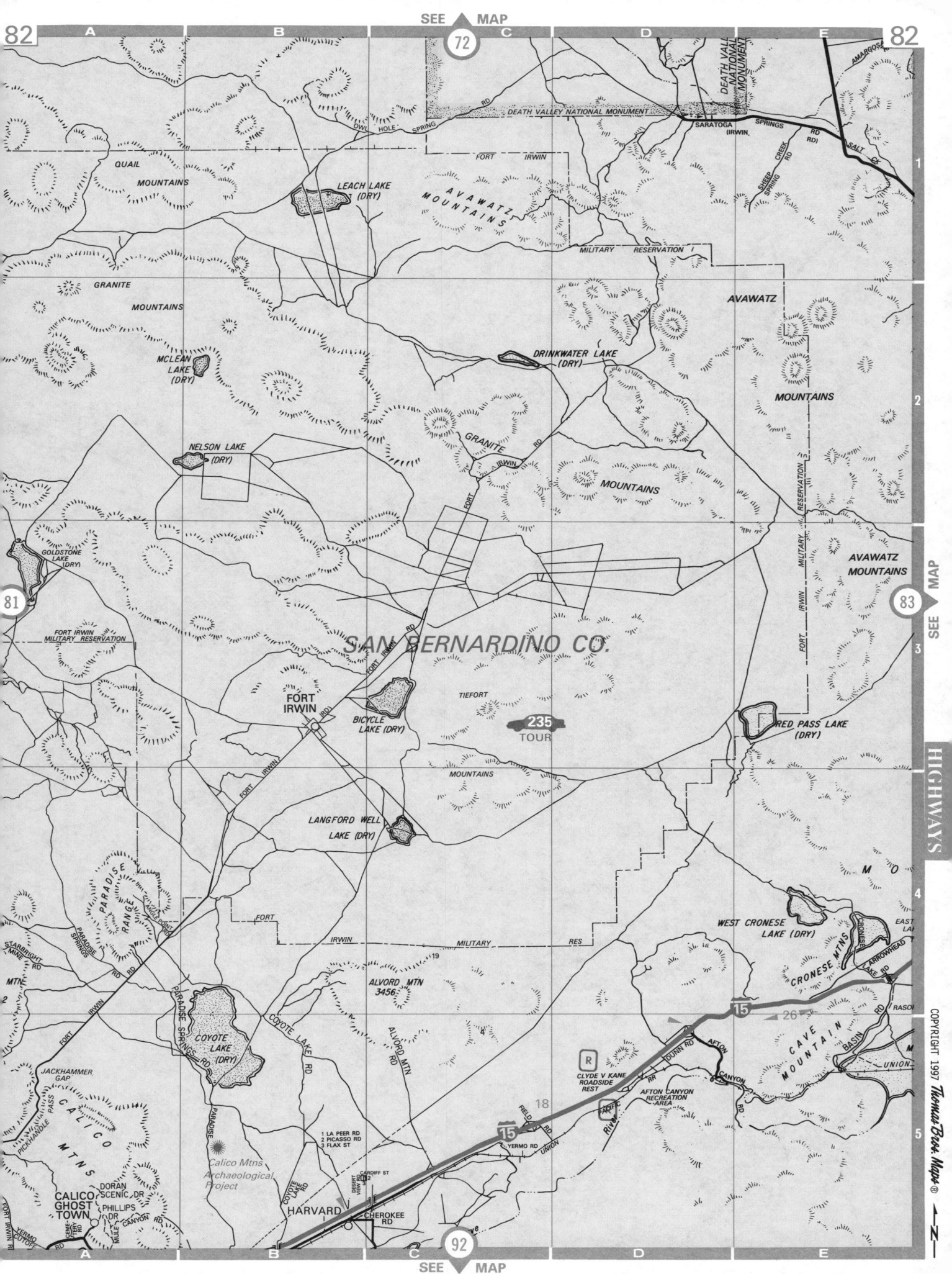

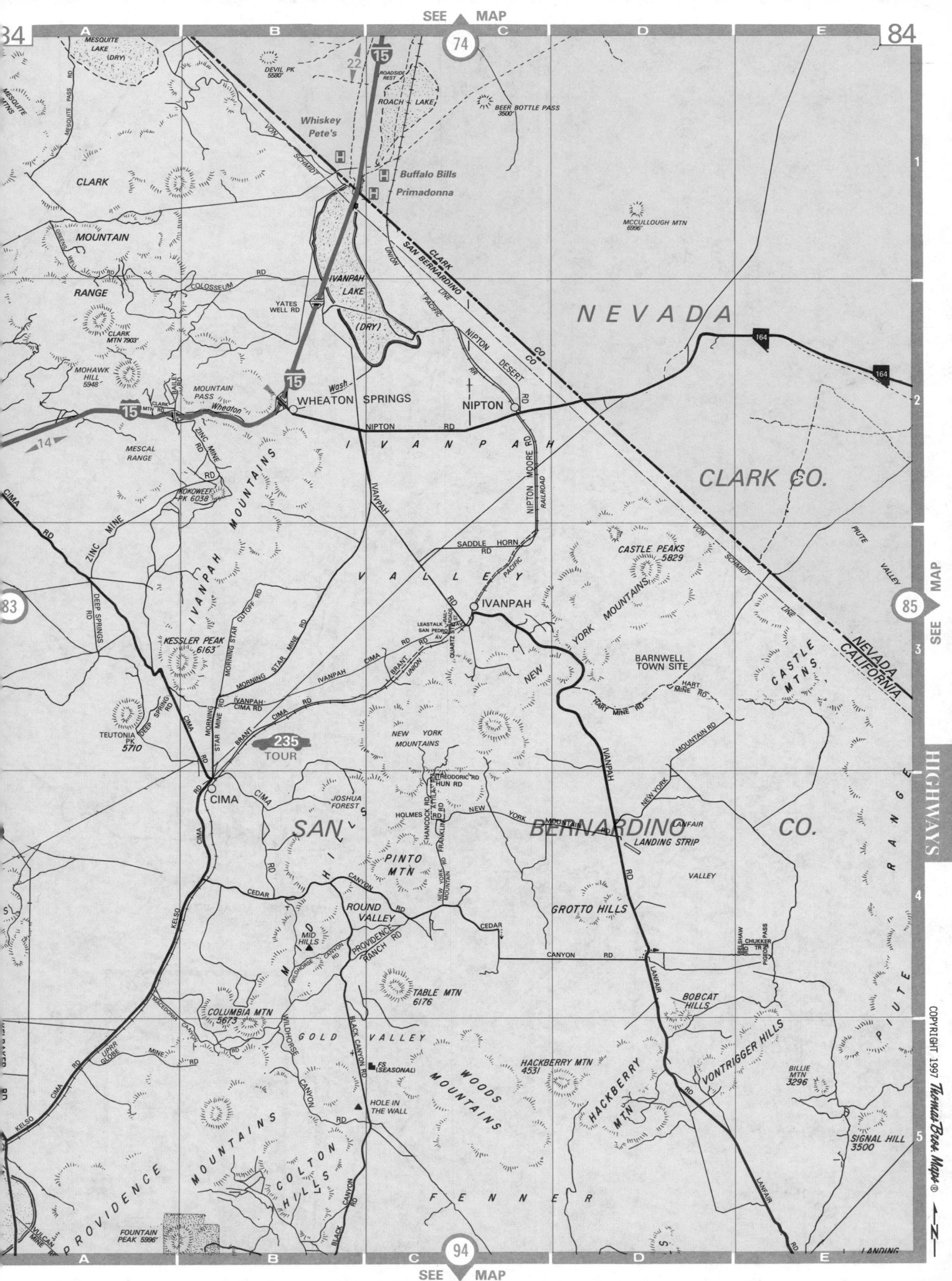

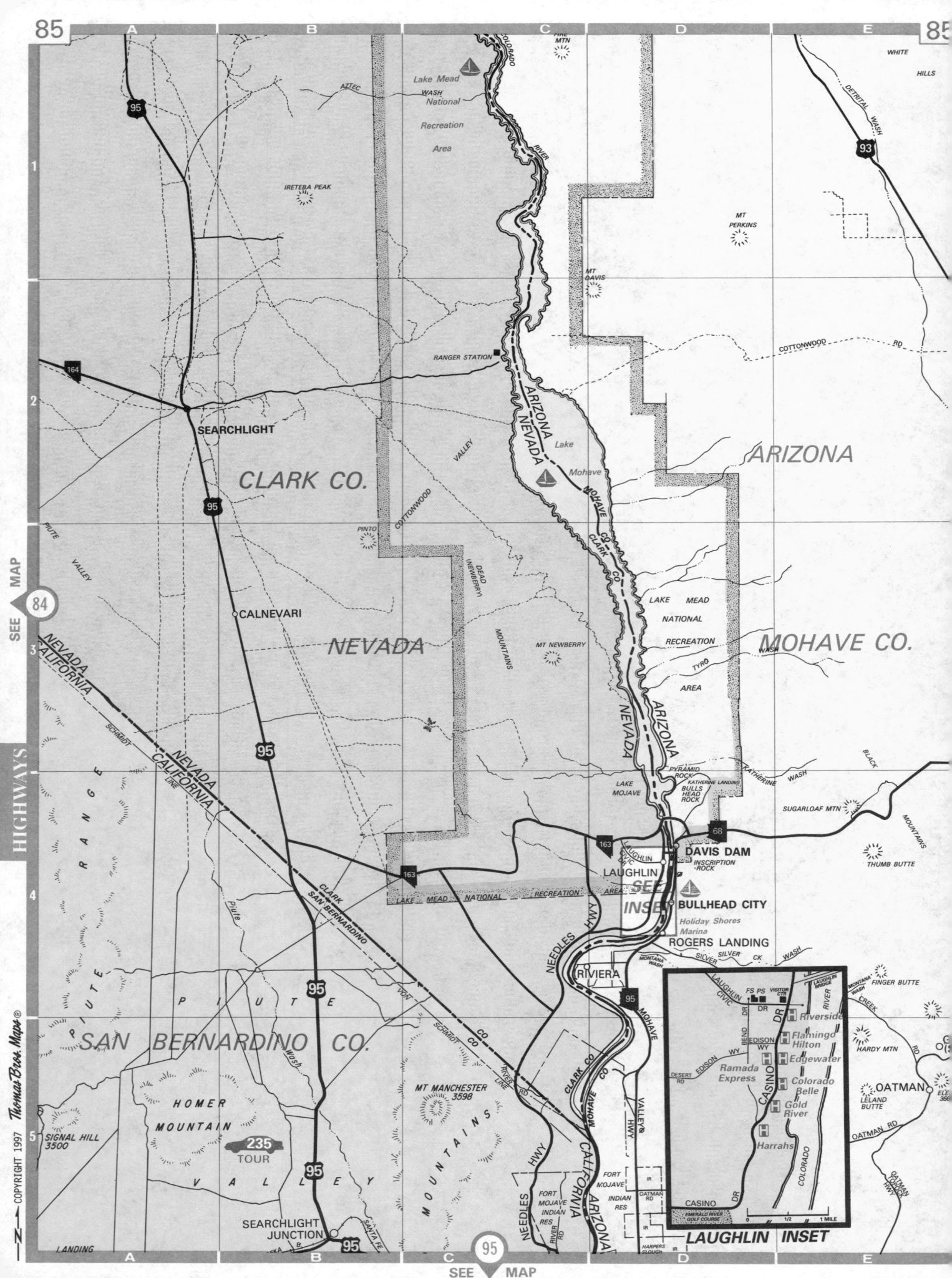

A B C D E

1

2

3

4

5

A B C D E

HIGHWAYS

SEE △ MAP
84

SEE ▽ MAP
95

95

164

SEARCHLIGHT

CLARK CO.

NEVADA

CALNEVARI

IRETEBA PEAK

Lake Mead
WASH
National
Recreation
Area

RANGER STATION

VALLEY

PINTO

COTTONWOOD

DEAD
(NEWBERRY)
MOUNTAINS

MT NEWBERRY

ARIZONA
NEVADA

Lake
Mohave

ARIZONA

MOHAVE CO.

LAKE MEAD
NATIONAL
RECREATION
AREA

TYRO

WASH

MT
PERKINS

MT
DAVIS

COTTONWOOD RD

US 93

WHITE
HILLS

DETRITAL WASH

NEVADA
CALIFORNIA

SCHMIDT LINE

NEVADA
CALIFORNIA
LINE

PIUTE
VALLEY

RANGE

PIUTE

SAN BERNARDINO CO.

HOMER
MOUNTAIN

SIGNAL HILL
3500

235
TOUR

95

VALLEY

MT MANCHESTER
3598

MOUNTAINS

SEARCHLIGHT
JUNCTION

95

CLARK
SAN BERNARDINO

PIUTE

WASH

VON

SCHMIDT
RIVER RD

CLARK CO
MOHAVE CO

NEEDLES HWY

MOHAVE
VALLEY
HWY

CALIFORNIA
ARIZONA

FORT
MOJAVE
INDIAN
RES

NEEDLES HWY

FORT MOJAVE
INDIAN RES

RIVER RD

OATMAN RD

IR

IR

HARPERS
SLOUGH

163

163

LAUGHLIN
CIVIC
AREA

RIVIERA

95

DAVIS DAM

LAUGHLIN

BULLHEAD CITY

Holiday Shores
Marina

ROGERS LANDING

SEE
INSET

68

PYRAMID
ROCK

KATHERINE LANDING

BULLS
HEAD
ROCK

INSCRIPTION
ROCK

KATHERINE
WASH

SUGARLOAF MTN

BLACK

MOUNTAINS

THUMB BUTTE

HARDY MTN

OATMAN

LELAND
BUTTE

FINGER BUTTE

COLORADO RIVER

LAUGHLIN INSET

LAUGHLIN
CIVIC
DR

BEND

DESERT
RD

EDISON WY

EDISON
WY

Ramada
Express

CASINO DR

FS PS
DR

VISITOR
CTR

LAUGHLIN
BRIDGE

Riverside

Flamingo
Hilton

Edgewater

Colorado
Belle

Gold
River

Harrahs

CASINO DR

EMERALD RIVER
GOLF COURSE

MONTANA
WASH

SILVER CK

WASH

CREEK

OATMAN
HWY

0   1/2   1 MILE

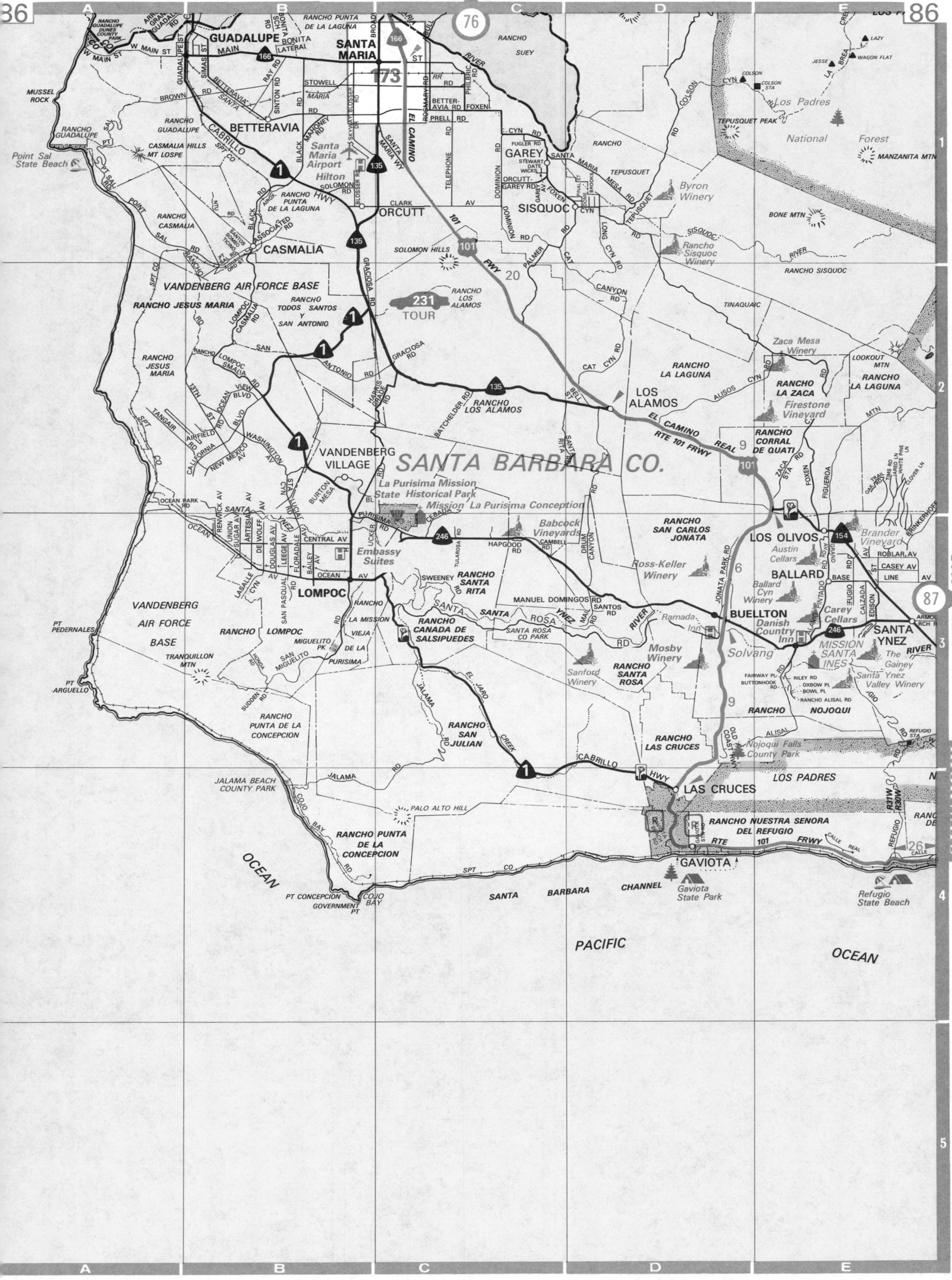

GUADALUPE
SANTA MARIA
173
166
160
BETTERAVIA
Santa Maria Airport
Hilton
ORCUTT
135
CASMALIA
VANDENBERG AIR FORCE BASE
RANCHO JESUS MARIA
RANCHO TODOS SANTOS Y SAN ANTONIO
231 TOUR
101 FWY
20
GAREY
SISQUOC
Byron Winery
Bone Mtn
Rancho Sisquoc Winery
RANCHO SISQUOC
RANCHO LA LAGUNA
Zaca Mesa Winery
RANCHO LA ZACA
Firestone Vineyard
Lookout Mtn
RANCHO LA LAGUNA
LOS ALAMOS
EL CAMINO RTE 101 REAL
RANCHO CORRAL DE QUATI
RANCHO LOS ALAMOS
SANTA BARBARA CO.
VANDENBERG VILLAGE
La Purisima Mission State Historical Park
Mission La Purisima Conception
Babcock Vineyards
RANCHO SAN CARLOS JONATA
Ross-Keller Winery
LOS OLIVOS
Austin Cellars
BALLARD
Ballard Cyn Winery
154
Brander Vineyard
246
LOMPOC
Embassy Suites
RANCHO SANTA RITA
Manuel Domingos Rd
Carey Cellars
BUELLTON
Danish Country Inn
SANTA YNEZ
MISSION SANTA INES
87
Solvang
The Gainey
Santa Ynez Valley Winery
VANDENBERG AIR FORCE BASE
RANCHO LOMPOC
RANCHO CANADA DE SALSIPUEDES
Santa Rosa Co Park
RANCHO SANTA ROSA
Mosby Winery
Ramada Inn
Sanford Winery
RANCHO NOJOQUI
PT PEDERNALES
TRANQUILLON MTN
RANCHO PUNTA DE LA CONCEPCION
RANCHO SAN JULIAN
JALAMA BEACH COUNTY PARK
PALO ALTO HILL
RANCHO LAS CRUCES
Nojoqui Falls County Park
LOS PADRES
PT ARGUELLO
CABRILLO HWY
LAS CRUCES
RANCHO NUESTRA SENORA DEL REFUGIO
RTE 101 FRWY
26
GAVIOTA
Gaviota State Park
Refugio State Beach
PT CONCEPCION GOVERNMENT PT
COJO BAY
OCEAN
SANTA BARBARA CHANNEL
PACIFIC OCEAN

Point Sal State Beach
MUSSEL ROCK
RANCHO GUADALUPE
RANCHO GUADALUPE
CASMALIA HILLS
MT LOSPE
RANCHO CASMALIA
RANCHO PUNTA DE LA LAGUNA

HIGHWAYS

SEE MAP

A | B | C | D | E

S.L.O. CO.

KERN CO.

White Oaks Sta
Bates Canyon

PEAK MTN

MC PHERSON PEAK

HOG PEN SPRING

Aliso Park
FOOTHILL

Rancho Cuyama No 2

NEW CUYAMA
SANTA BARBARA CO
SAN LUIS OBISPO CO
CUYAMA

WASHINGTON ST
Branch Canyon Sta
Cuyama No 2
FOOTHILL

Rancho

BELL
PERKINS RD
ALISO RD
CYN RD
JOHNSON ST
CUYAMA ST
WYLIE ST
KIRSCHENMANN RD
SCHAEFFER RD

KERN CO
BARBARA CO / VENTURA CO

SANTA

33
166

BALLINGER
BALLINGER CYN

SAN RAFAEL WILDERNESS

SAN RAFAEL WILDERNESS

WHEAT PEAK

BALD MTN

MONTGOMERY POTRERO

FOX MTN

VENTUCOPA

LA PANZA AV
EL ROBLAR
QUATAL CYN

SANTA BARBARA CO
VENTURA CO

CUYAMA RIVER

ZACA LAKE
LOS PADRES NATIONAL FOREST
FIGUEROA MTN
CATWAY RD
PINO ALTO
FIGUEROA STA
NIRA
LOST VALLEY
CACHUMA RD
DAVY BROWN
CACHUMA SADDLE STA

Los Padres National Forest

CUYAMA PEAK
UPPER TINTA
MORRO HILL

VEN CO.

RANCHO LA LAGUNA (GUTIERREZ)

CACHUMA MTN
SAN RAFAEL MTN
McKINLEY MTN
CACHUMA MTN
FIGUEROA MTN

SAN RAFAEL

SISQUOC CONDOR SANCTUARY

SAMON PEAK

LOS PADRES

BIG PINE MTN
MADULCE PEAK
LIZARD HEAD
DEAL JUNCTION

WILDERNESS

SANTA BARBARA CO.

LOMA PELONA

VEN CO.

SEE MAP 86

RANCHO DE CANADA LOS PINOS

BRINKERHOFF AV
LINDA VISTA DR
AV
HAPPY CYN RD
ALISOS AV

RANCHO SAN MARCOS

RANCHO TEQUEPIS

231 TOUR

LITTLE PINE MTN

NATIONAL

CREEK

HILDRETH PEAK

SEE MAP 88

ARMOUR RCH RD

Lake Cachuma Recreation Area

154

RANCHO TEQUEPIS

LOMA ALTA

NINETEEN OAKS

FOREST

RANCHO LOS PRIETOS Y NAJALAYEGUA

RANCHO LOMAS LA PURIFICACION

LAKE CACHUMA

HIDDEN POTRERO
MIDDLE CAMUESA POTRERO
GATE

CAMUESA PEAK

GATE

BIG CAUENTE
LOWER CALIENTE

MONTE ARIDO

SANTA VENTURA CO

RIVER

SAN MARCOS PASS RD
SANTA STAGECOACH RD
YNEZ RIVER PARADISE

GIBRALTAR RD
FALLS
SANTA YNEZ LIVE OAK
NORTH PORTAL
MATIAS POTRERO

GIBRALTAR DAM

REDROCK

MONO
CAMUESA

P-BAR FLATS
MTN STA YNEZ
AGUA CALIENTE
PENDOLA STA

OLD MAN MTN
MATILIJA
MURIETTA

REFUGIO STA
CAMINO
CIELO
SANTA YNEZ PEAK
BROADCAST PEAK
CONDOR PEAK

NATIONAL FOREST

RANCHO CANADA DEL CORRAL

AVD DEL CAPITAN
CALLE QUEBRADA
CALLE REAL

WATER TUNNEL
CAMINO CIELO
KINEVAN RD
HIDDEN VLY RD

154
PAINTED CAVE RD
Chumash Painted Caves State Hist Park
LA CUMBRE PEAK
CATHEDRAL PEAK
PAINTED CAVE RD

CAMINO CIELO
BARBARA WATER TUNNEL
FORBUSH FLAT
BLUE CANYON
UPPER BLUE CANYON

GIBRALTAR RES

GATE
ROMERO CYN
MONTECITO PEAK

SANTA

JAMESON LAKE
JUNCAL RD
UPPER SANTA YNEZ

GIBRALTAR

DAULTON WATER TUNNEL
GATE

DIVIDE PEAK
NOON PARK

WHITE LEDGE

26

RANCHO LOS DOS PUEBLOS

Pepper Tree Inn

FOOTHILL RD

Pepper Tree Inn

Montecito Inn
SYCAMORE

MONTECITO

SNOWBALL MTN

CHISMAHO MTN

El Capitan State Beach
NAPLES 101 ELLWOOD GOLETA

HOLLISTER
Sta Barbara Airport
217

ISLA VISTA
COAL OIL PT
Isla Vista Co Beach Park
Univ of Calif Santa Barbara

SPT
CO
AV

101
8
STATE ST

SANTA BARBARA
192
144

SB Zoo

225
225

Radisson Hotel Santa Barbara

GOLETA PT
Goleta Beach County Park
Arroyo Burro Beach County Park

174

Stearns Wharf
SANTA

Clark Bird Refuge
12

SUMMERLAND
Four Seasons Biltmore

BARBARA

192
101 SPT CO
224

Carpinteria State Beach

CARPINTERIA

150
FRWY
101 8
RANCHO EL RINCON
W CASITAS PASS

RINCON PT
PUNTA GORDA
LA CONCHITA
SEACLIFF
VENTURA CO
10

PITAS PT

Channel Islands National Park

SAN MIGUEL ISL
SANTA ROSA ISL
SANTA CRUZ ISL
SANTA BARBARA ISL

INSET NOT TO SCALE

HIGHWAYS

A | B | C | D | E

SEE MAP 78

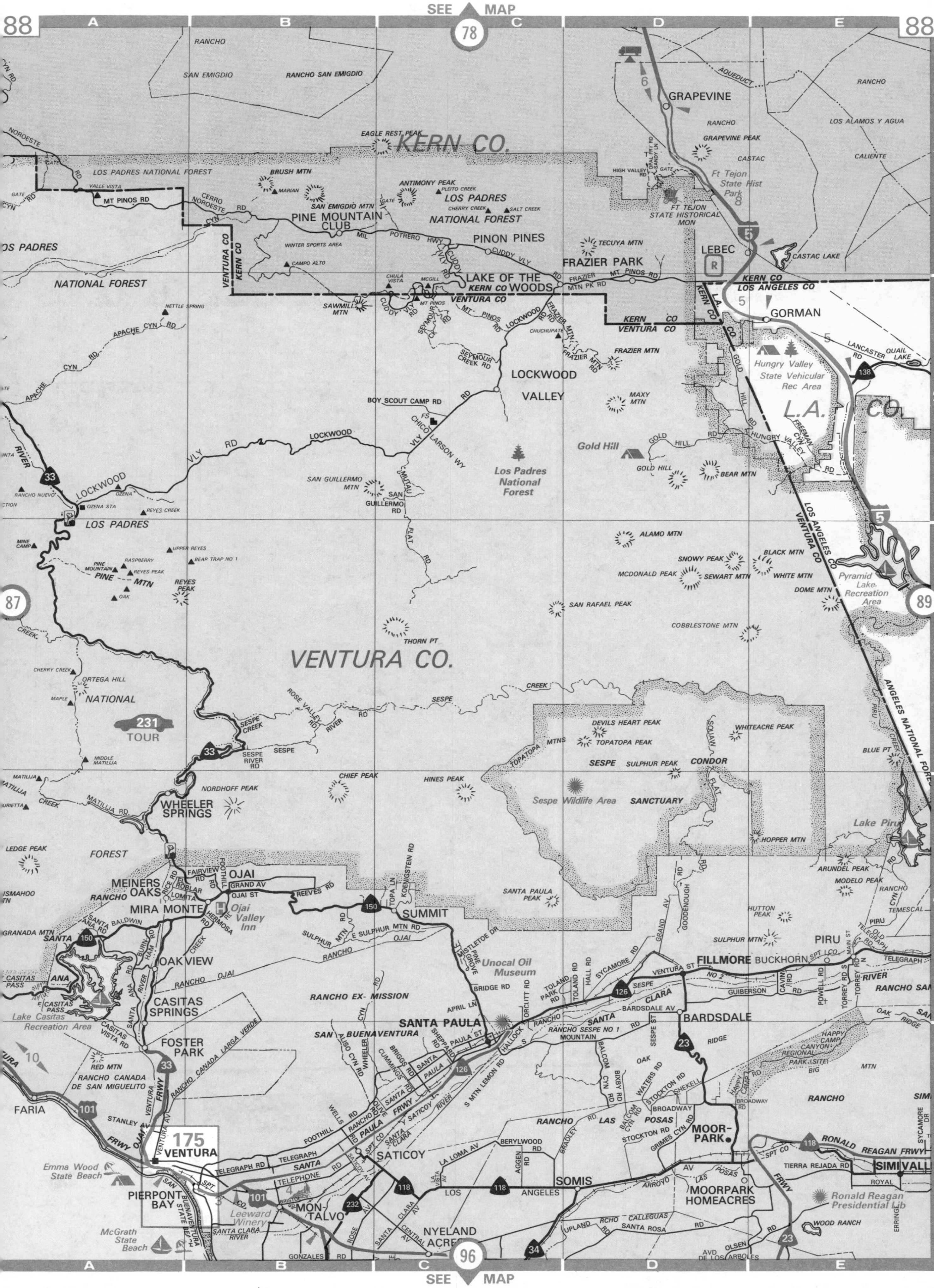

KERN CO.
VENTURA CO.
L.A. CO.
LOS PADRES NATIONAL FOREST
LOS PADRES NATIONAL FOREST
Los Padres National Forest
GRAPEVINE
Ft Tejon State Hist Park
FT TEJON STATE HISTORICAL MON
LEBEC
CASTAC LAKE
GORMAN
Hungry Valley State Vehicular Rec Area
PINE MOUNTAIN CLUB
PINON PINES
FRAZIER PARK
LAKE OF THE WOODS
LOCKWOOD VALLEY
Gold Hill
EAGLE REST PEAK
GRAPEVINE PEAK
ANTIMONY PEAK
SAN EMIGDIO MTN
BRUSH MTN
TECUYA MTN
SAWMILL MTN
FRAZIER MTN
MAXY MTN
BEAR MTN
GOLD HILL
ALAMO MTN
SNOWY PEAK
BLACK MTN
SEWART MTN
WHITE MTN
MCDONALD PEAK
DOME MTN
SAN RAFAEL PEAK
COBBLESTONE MTN
THORN PT
SAN GUILLERMO MTN
Pyramid Lake Recreation Area
LOS ANGELES CO
VENTURA CO
ANGELES NATIONAL FOREST
PINE MTN
REYES PEAK
ORTEGA HILL
NORDHOFF PEAK
CHIEF PEAK
HINES PEAK
DEVILS HEART PEAK
TOPATOPA PEAK
WHITEACRE PEAK
SESPE CONDOR SANCTUARY
Sespe Wildlife Area
HOPPER MTN
Lake Piru
BLUE PT
ARUNDEL PEAK
MODELO PEAK
HUTTON PEAK
SULPHUR MTN
SANTA PAULA PEAK
WHEELER SPRINGS
OJAI
MEINERS OAKS
MIRA MONTE
Ojai Valley Inn
SUMMIT
OAK VIEW
CASITAS SPRINGS
Lake Casitas Recreation Area
FOSTER PARK
RED MTN
RANCHO CANADA DE SAN MIGUELITO
FARIA
VENTURA
Emma Wood State Beach
PIERPONT BAY
McGrath State Beach
Leeward Winery
MONTALVO
SATICOY
NYELAND ACRES
SOMIS
SANTA PAULA
Unocal Oil Museum
RANCHO EX-MISSION
SAN BUENAVENTURA
FILLMORE
BUCKHORN
PIRU
BARDSDALE
MOORPARK
MOORPARK HOMEACRES
Happy Camp Canyon Regional Park (Site)
Ronald Reagan Presidential Lib
SIMI VALLEY
RONALD REAGAN FRWY
VENTURA FRWY
OJAI FRWY
231 TOUR

SEE MAP 87

SEE MAP 89

SEE MAP 96

HIGHWAYS

HIGHWAYS

Thomas Bros. Maps®
COPYRIGHT 1997

KERN CO.

WILLOW SPRINGS
TROPICO
ROSAMOND

KERN CO.
LOS ANGELES CO.

LANCASTER
QUAIL LAKE
RANCHO
NEENACH (PROP)
SANDBURG
LA LIEBRE MTN
BURNT PEAK
SAWMILL MTN
SAWTOOTH MTN
REDROCK MTN

FAIRMONT
FAIRMONT BUTT
Antelope Valley California Poppy Reserve
ANTELOPE ACRES
FAIRMONT RES

LAKE HUGHES
ELIZABETH LAKE
GREEN VALLEY
GRASS MTN
JUPITER MTN
RED MTN

LEONA VALLEY
QUARTZ HILL

Pyramid Lake Recreation Area
WHITAKER PEAK
TOWNSEND PEAK
Angeles National Forest
WARM SPRING LOOKOUT

LOS ANGELES CO.

SLEEPY VALLEY
AGUA DULCE

SIERRA
PELONA

PALMDALE LAKE

Lake Piru
RANCHO TEMESCAL
VERDE LOMA
Lake Castaic
Castaic Lake State Rec Area
CASTAIC

BOUQUET CANYON
FORREST PARK

PARKER MTN
ACTON

237 TOUR

VAL VERDE
Six Flags Magic Mountain
Six Flags Hurricane Harbor
Hilton Garden

CANYON COUNTRY
SAUGUS
SANTA CLARITA
VALENCIA
NEWHALL

MAGIC MTN

RANCHO SAN FRANCISCO

Wm. S. Hart Park
Placerita Cyn State Park
GLEASON MTN

SAN GABRIEL MTNS

VENTURA
Sylmar
IRON MTN

SIMI VALLEY STA SUSANA
SANTA SUSANA MTNS
SIMI
SAN FERNANDO

REAGAN FRWY
118
Granada Hills
Chatsworth
DEVONSHIRE
Pacoima
Sunland
Tujunga

For Detail Page Locations
SEE PAGE Q

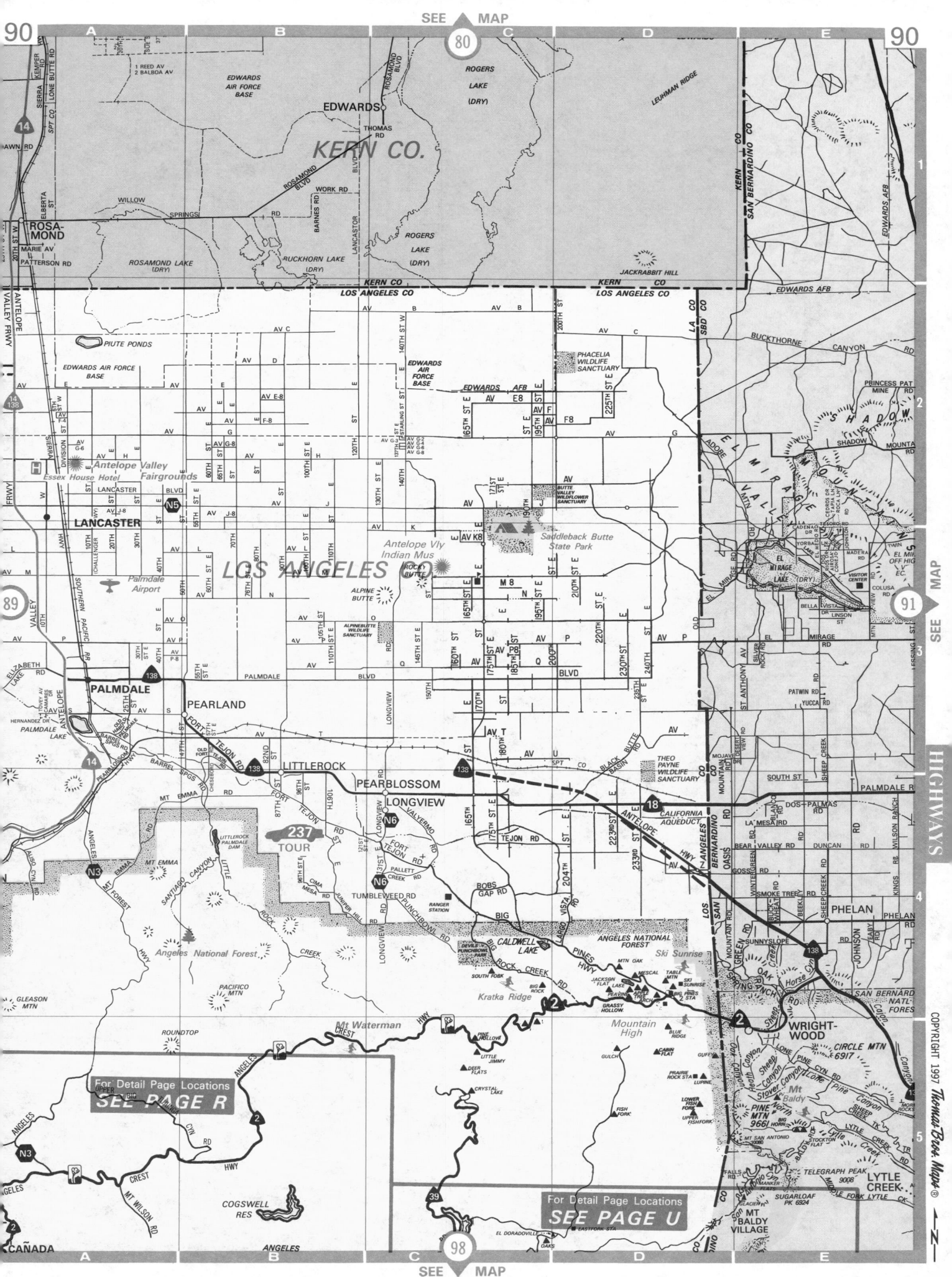

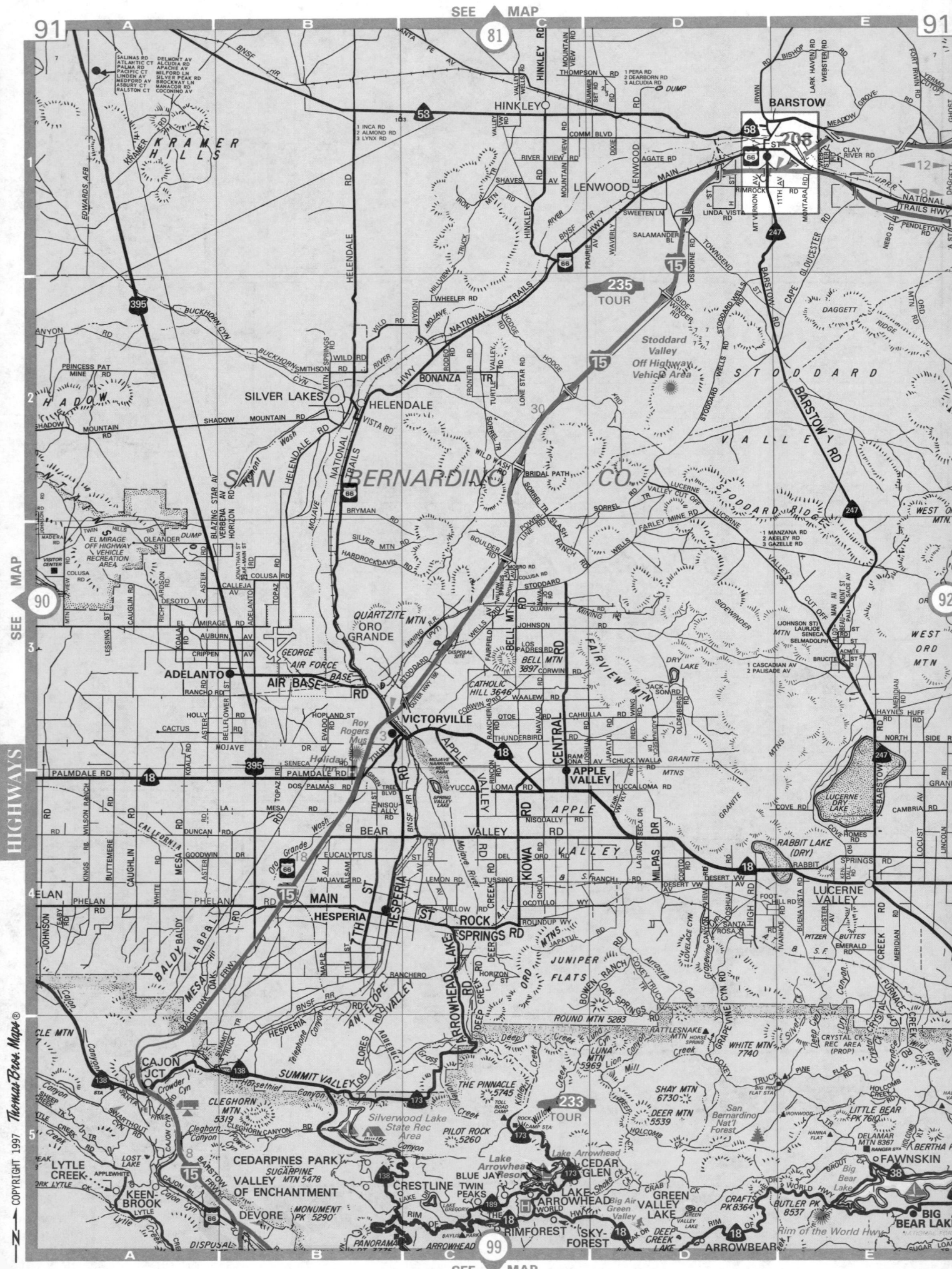

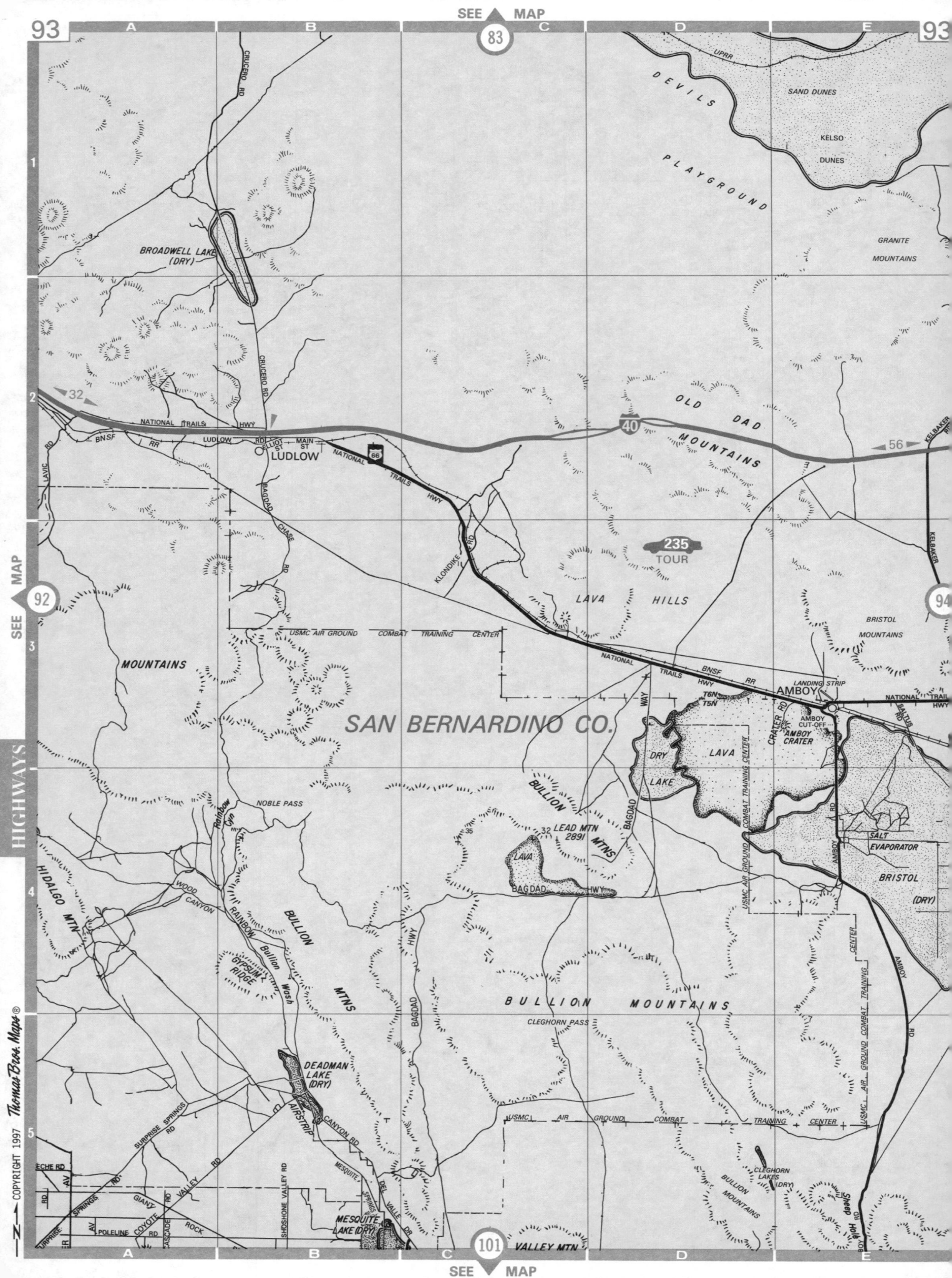

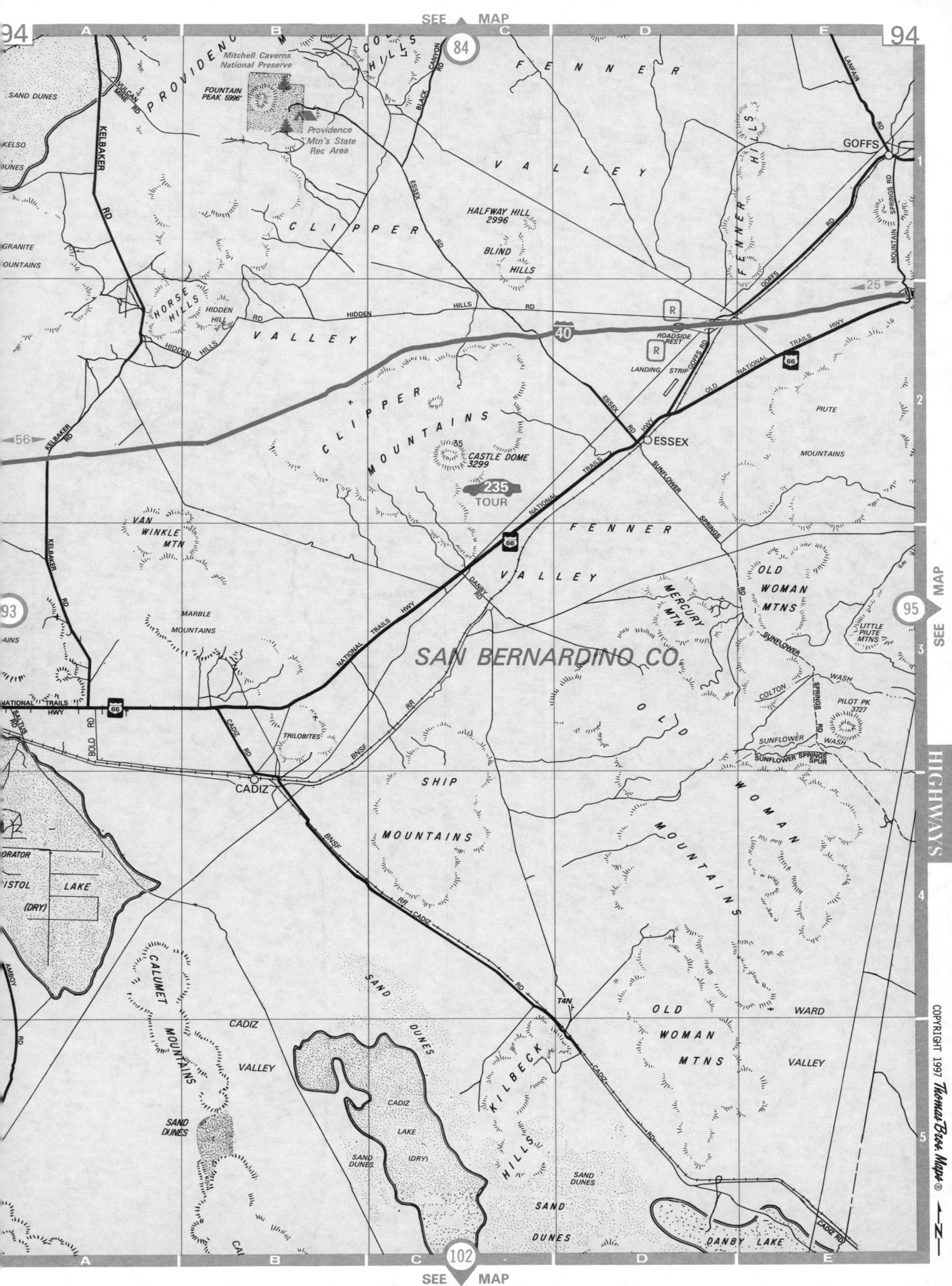

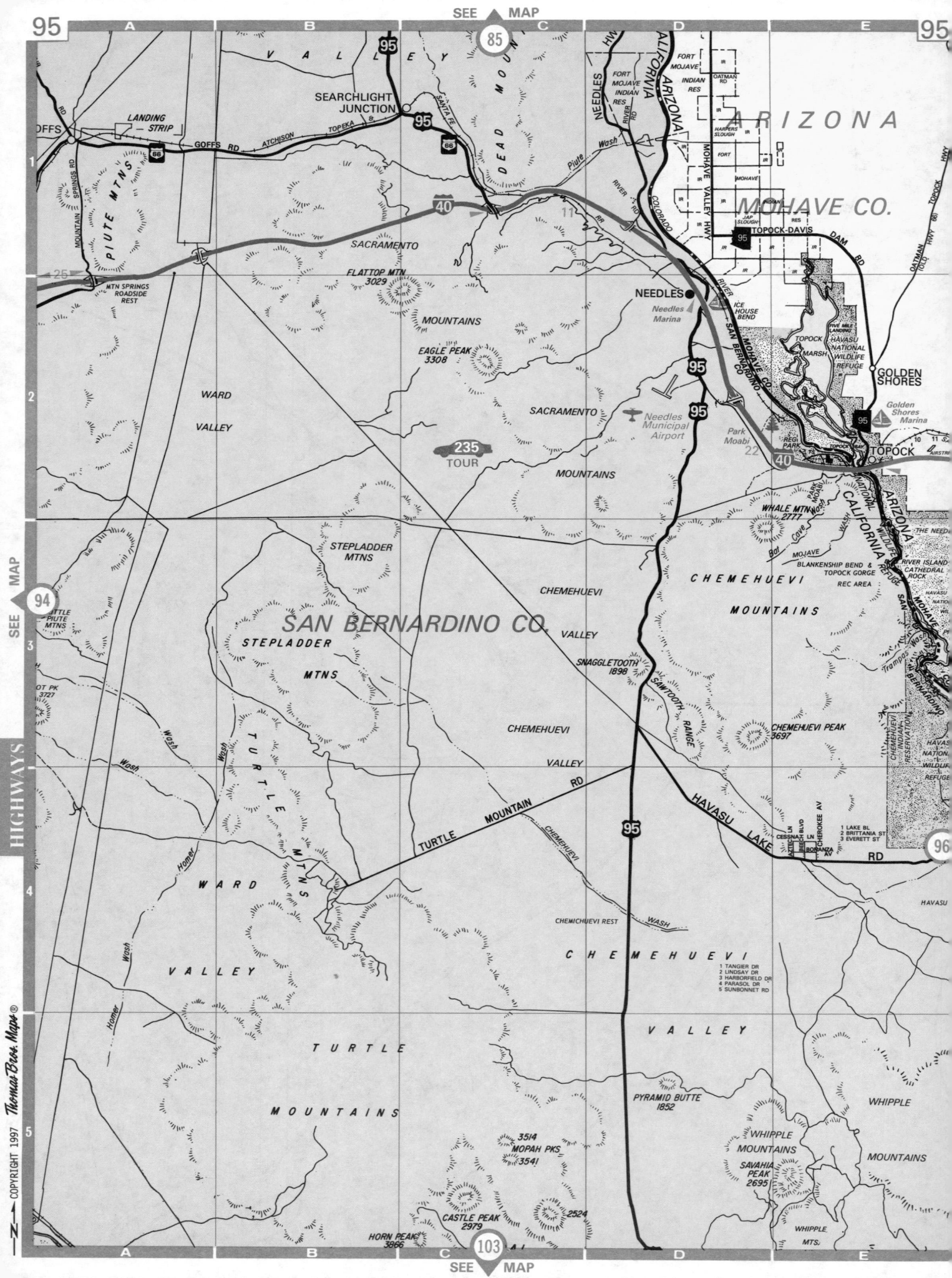

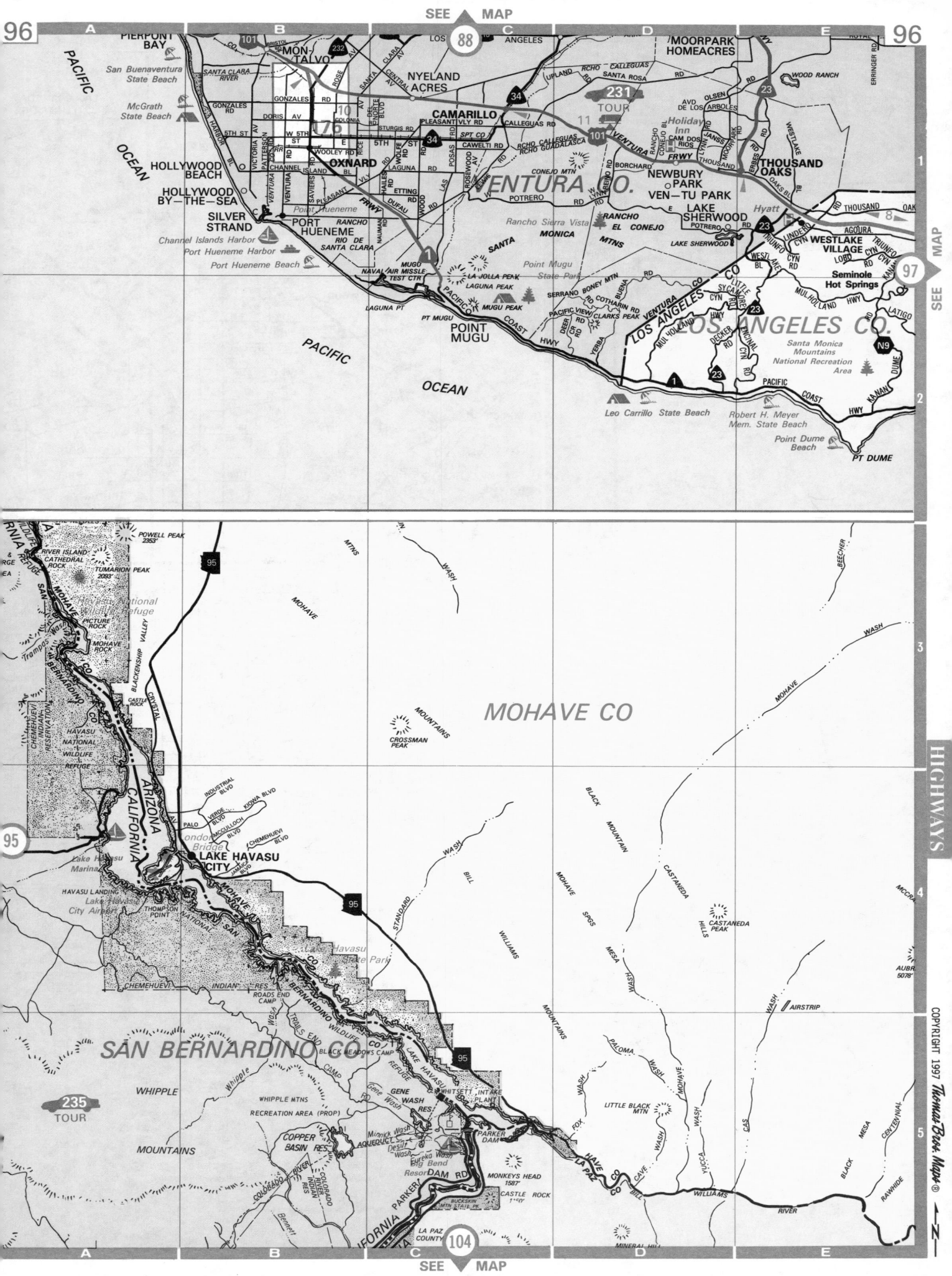

A B C D E

VENTURA CO.

Chatsworth
West Hills
Bell Canyon
Northridge
Roscoe
Reseda
Sherman
Canoga Park
Woodland Hills
Tarzana
Encino
Van Nuys
North Hollywood
Pacoima
Sunland
Tujunga
La Crescenta
LA CAÑADA FLINTRIDGE
BURBANK
Burbank Airport

HIDDEN HILLS
Woodland Hills
CALABASAS
Glenview
Topanga Park
AGOURA HILLS
Agoura
Malibu Lake
Topanga
Monte Nido
Leonis Adobe & Plummer House

LOS ANGELES CO.

GLENDALE
Universal City
Hollywood
Eagle Rock
Highland Park
SOUTH PASADENA
ALHAMBRA
PASADENA

WEST HOLLYWOOD
BEVERLY HILLS
Westwood
Country Club Park
Sherman Oaks
LOS ANGELES
CITY OF

Malibu Creek State Park
Pepperdine University
MALIBU
Malibu Beach
Coral Beach
Dan Blocker Beach
Malibu Lagoon State Beach
SANTA MONICA
Venice
Ocean Park
CULVER CITY
Crenshaw
VERNON
MAYWOOD
HUNTINGTON PARK
BELL
CUDAHY
SOUTH GATE
LYNWOOD

Marina Del Rey
237 TOUR
Playa Del Rey
LOS ANGELES INTERNATIONAL AIRPORT

For Detail Page Locations
SEE PAGE Q

EL SEGUNDO
HAWTHORNE
INGLEWOOD
Manchester
Century
Imperial

MANHATTAN BEACH
HERMOSA BEACH
REDONDO BEACH
LAWNDALE
GARDENA
TORRANCE
CARSON
COMPTON
LONG BEACH
Long Beach Airport
SIGNAL HILL

PALOS VERDES ESTATES
LOMITA
RANCHO PALOS VERDES
ROLLING HILLS ESTATES
ROLLING HILLS
San Pedro
Los Angeles Harbor

For Detail Page Locations
SEE PAGE S

AVALON

1 LA PALOMA
2 GAVIOTA
3 MAR DE CORTEZ

0 ¼ ½
MILES

HAMILTON BEACH
DESCANSO BAY
Catalina Island Museum
CASINO PT
Casino
AVALON BAY
Catalina Yacht Harbor
Visitors Service Center
PACIFIC OCEAN
LOVERS COVE
ABALONE PT
PEBBLY
Wrigley Estate
MT ADA
USC Conference Center
CHIMES TOWER RD
COUNTRY CLUB

1 LOWER E TER RD
2 MIDDLE E TER RD
3 UPPER E TER RD

Pebbly Beach
Amphibious Air Terminal
Pebbly Beach Village Rd

CATALINA ISLAND GOLF COURSE

RIFLE RANGE
QUAIL CYN RD

Wrigley Memorial & Botanical Garden

LOS ANGELES CO.

SANTA CATALINA ISLAND

LANDS END
ARROW PT
EMERALD BAY
SILVER PEAK
ISTHMUS COVE
IRON BOUND BAY
RIBBON ROCK
MT TORQUEMADA
LOBSTER BAY
Catalina Harbor
LITTLE HARBOR
MT ORIZABA
MT BANNING
BLACK JACK MTN
EAGLES NEST
WHITLEY'S PEAK
THOMPSON RES
BULLRUSH
CACTUS PEAK
EAST PEAK

PACIFIC OCEAN
SAN PEDRO CHANNEL
OUTER SANTA BARBARA PASSAGE
LONG PT
WHITE COVE
STAGE RD
AVALON
PALISADES

0   5   10 MILES
0   5   10 KILOMETERS

Thomas Bros. Maps®
COPYRIGHT 1997

HIGHWAYS

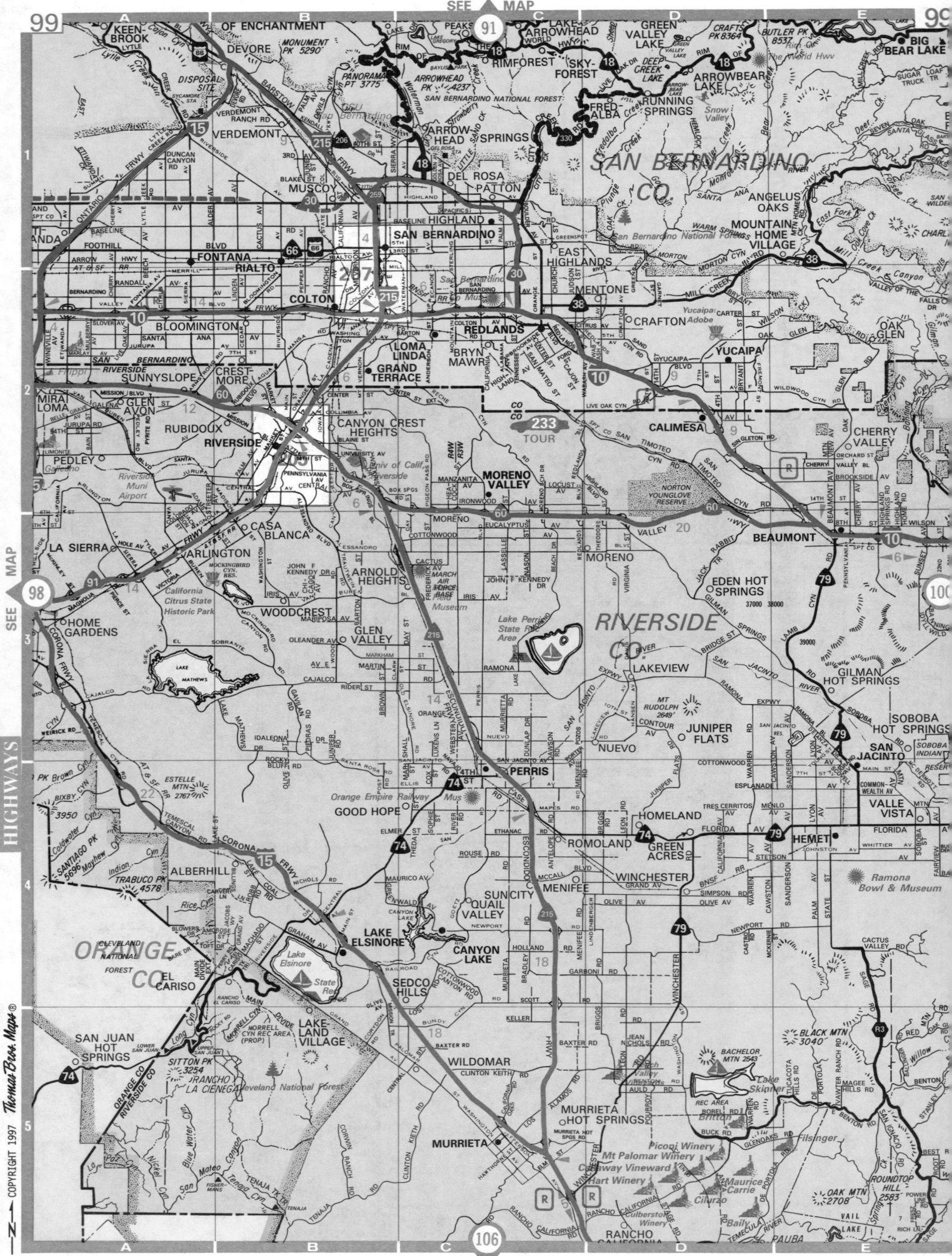

A   B   C   D   E

BIG BEAR CITY
MOONRIDGE
BIG BEAR LAKE
SUGAR LOAF
Snow Summit Ski Area
Bear Mtn Ski Area
San Bernardino
BARTON FLATS
National Forest
38

BLACK MTN 6148
ERWIN LAKE (DRY)
Lake Williams

BLACK MTN 6148
BLACK LAVA BUTTES
FLATTOP
RIMROCK
BLACK HILL

NAPA RD
WINTERS
GATOS TR
YUCCA VALLEY
TWENTYNINE
1

San Gorgonio Wilderness Area
CHARLTON PK 10815
DOLLAR LAKE
FISH CREEK MTN 9722

SAN BERNARDINO CO.

CHAPARROSA PEAK 5541
PIONEER TOWN
Hi-Desert Nature Museum

YUCCA VALLEY
Yucca Valley Airport
JOSHUA TREE
247

SAN GORGONIO MTN 11502
FOREST FALLS
OAK GLEN

Middle Fork
Whitewater River

MORONGO VALLEY
PALO VERDE

BIG MORONGO CANYON PRESERVE
235 TOUR
DESERT HOT SPRINGS
Cabots Pueblo Museum
Joshua Tree National Park
2

BERNARDINO CO
RIVERSIDE CO
THE SINK 5880'
FRED DOME 3331'
KITCHING PK 6000'
MISSION CREEK
INDIAN RESERVATION
PAINTED HILLS

MORONGO INDIAN RESERVATION
Wood Cyn

62
SAN GORGONIO
WHITEWATER
WHITE WATER
N PALM SPRINGS

SKY VALLEY
10
3

10
BANNING
CABAZON
TWIN PINES
San Bernardino National Forest
243

GARNET
111
R
EL DORADO

SEVEN PALMS VALLEY
DESERT HAVEN
EDOM HILL
INDIO
THOUSAND PALMS
COACHELLA

99

SOBOBA HOT SPRINGS
SAN JACINTO
SOBOBA INDIAN RESERVATION
VALLE VISTA
FLORIDA
74

POPPET FLAT
San Jacinto Wilderness Area
Mt San Jacinto State Park
MARION MTN
LAKE FULMOR
243

La Siesta Villas
Palm Springs Aerial Tramway
206 PALM SPRINGS
RAMON
AGUA CREEK

Oasis Water Park
The Autry Hotel
Westin Hotel
Mission Hills Country Club
Marriott Desert Springs Resort
COUNTRY CLUB
4

PINE COVE
TAHQUITZ PK 8826
TAHQUITZ FALLS
San Jacinto Wilderness Area
243
IDYLLWILD
Mt San Jacinto State Park
San Bernardino National Forest
74

INDIAN CANYONS
Canyon Hotel Racquet & Golf Resort
CATHEDRAL CITY
Tamarisk Country Club
RANCHO MIRAGE
PALM DESERT
Marriott Rancho Las Palmas Resort
Embassy Suites
74

Indian Wells Country Club
Marriott Desert Springs Resort
INDIAN WELLS
Hyatt
LA QUINTA
Eldorado Country Club
Hwy
111

MTN CENTER
74
HEMET LAKE
HEMET RES
San Bernardino National Forest
Lake Hemet
RED MTN 4610

NEEDLES EYE
BULLSEYE ROCK
GARNET RIDGE
CONE PK 6694
PINE MTN 7054
DEVILS ROCKPILE
BALD MTN 4454
HELLS KITCHEN

The Living Desert
UNIVERSITY OF CALIFORNIA DESERT RESEARCH AREA
CALLE TECATE
La Quinta Country Club
CALLE TECATE
5

233 TOUR
CAHUILLA MTN 5624
THOMAS MTN 6812
HOG LAKE
PINE MEADOW
LITTLE CAHUILLA MTN 5024

PINYON PINES
SUGAR LOAF MTN
Santa Rosa Indian Res
SANTA ROSA MTN
San Bernardino National Forest
LITTLE PINYON FLAT
MARTINEZ MTN 6548

CAHUILLA
LAKE RIVERSIDE
CAHUILLA INDIAN RESERVATION
371
ANZA
74
Cahuilla Indian Reservation

A   B   C   D   E

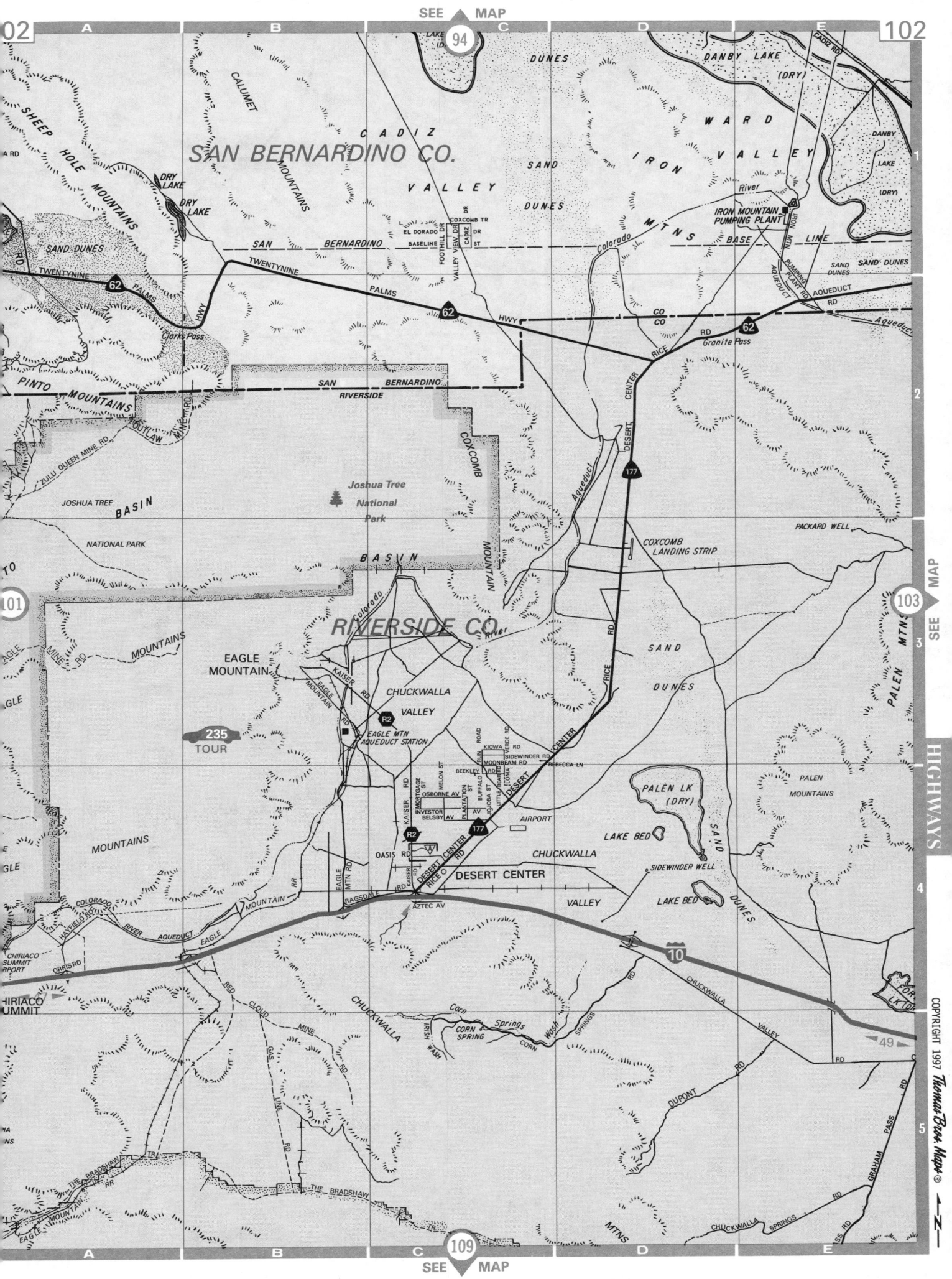

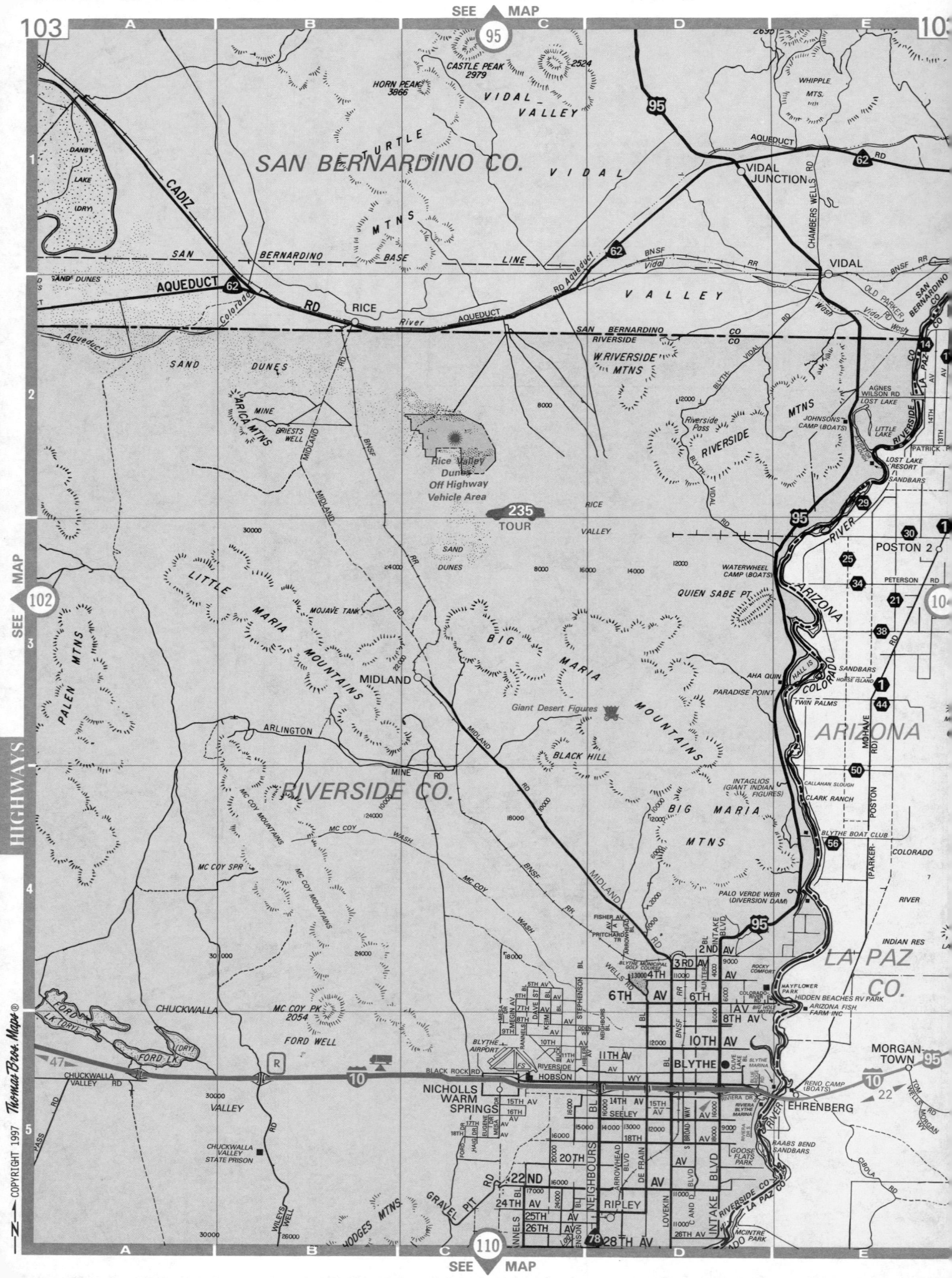

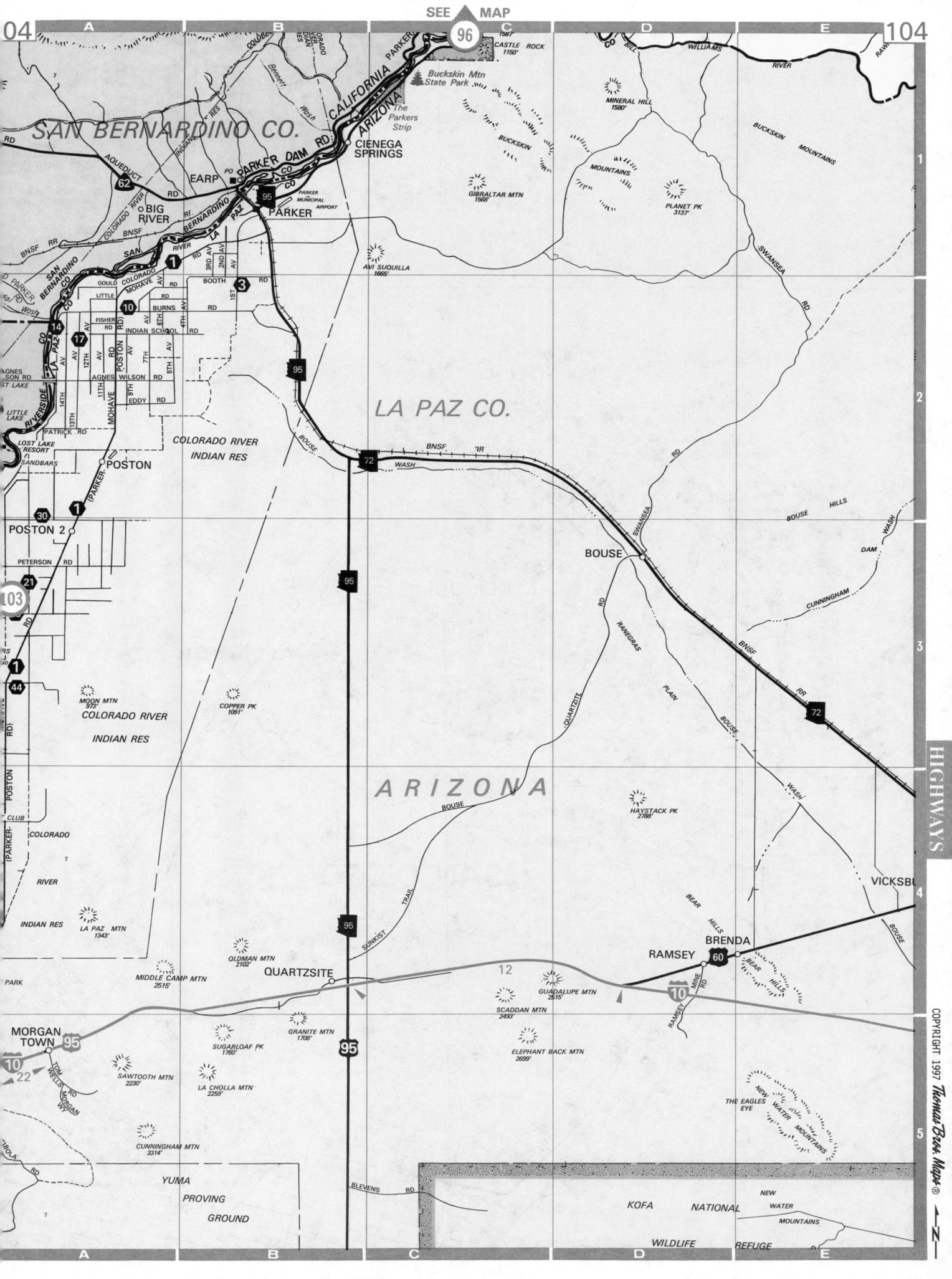

SEE MAP
96

SAN BERNARDINO CO.

CASTLE ROCK
1150'

BILL WILLIAMS RIVER

Buckskin Mtn State Park

MINERAL HILL
1590'

BUCKSKIN MOUNTAINS

CALIFORNIA
ARIZONA

PARKER DAM RD

CIENEGA SPRINGS

The Parkers Strip

BUCKSKIN MOUNTAINS

GIBRALTAR MTN
1568'

PLANET PK
3137'

EARP
62
95
BIG RIVER
PARKER MUNICIPAL AIRPORT

PARKER

SWANSEA RD

1

BNSF RR

SAN BERNARDINO CO.
LA PAZ CO

1

AVI SUQUILLA
1665'

BOOTH RD
3

GOULD MOHAVE AV
COLORADO RD
10
LITTLE
BURNS RD
FISHER
INDIAN SCHOOL RD
14
17
AGNES WILSON RD
EDDY RD

95

LA PAZ CO.

LITTLE LAKE
RIVERSIDE CO

PATRICK RD
LOST LAKE RESORT
SANDBARS
POSTON
COLORADO RIVER INDIAN RES

BOUSE WASH
72

BNSF RR

BOUSE HILLS
WASH

30
1
POSTON 2

PETERSON RD
21
103

BOUSE
SWANSEA RD
CUNNINGHAM
DAM

RANEGRAS RD

1
44
MOON MTN
973'
COPPER PK
1091'
COLORADO RIVER
INDIAN RES

QUARTZITE
PLAIN

BNSF RR
72

A R I Z O N A

BOUSE

HAYSTACK PK
2788'

WASH

POSTON RD

CLUB
COLORADO

RIVER
7

INDIAN RES
LA PAZ MTN
1343'

BOUSE

BEAR HILLS

VICKSBU

BOUSE

4

QLDMAN MTN
2102'
QUARTZSITE
95
SUNKIST TRAIL
12
GUADALUPE MTN
2515'
SCADDAN MTN
2493'
RAMSEY
BRENDA
60
10
RAMSEY MINE RD
BEAR HILLS

PARK
MIDDLE CAMP MTN
2515'

GRANITE MTN
1708'

MORGAN TOWN
95
10
22
TOM WELLS MORGAN RD
SAWTOOTH MTN
2230'
SUGARLOAF PK
1760'
LA CHOLLA MTN
2259'
ELEPHANT BACK MTN
2639'

THE EAGLES EYE

NEW WATER MOUNTAINS

5

CUNNINGHAM MTN
3314'

7

YUMA PROVING GROUND

BLEVENS RD

KOFA NATIONAL

NEW WATER MOUNTAINS

WILDLIFE REFUGE

A   B   C   D   E

HIGHWAYS

SEE MAP 98

SEE MAP V

SEE MAP 212
SEE MAP

PACIFIC OCEAN

HIGHWAYS

Thomas Bros. Maps®
COPYRIGHT 1997

N

Inset (upper right)

South Laguna
Three Arch Bay
Ritz Carlton Hotel
DANA POINT
SAN JUAN CAPISTRANO
ORANGE CO.
Capistrano Beach
239 TOUR
SAN CLEMENTE
San Clemente State Beach
San Onofre Visitor's Ctr
San Mateo Campground
San Onofre State Beach
SAN ONOFRE
PENDLETON

La Jolla area

LA JOLLA AREA
LA JOLLA BAY
LA JOLLA SHORES BEACH
ECOLOGICAL RESERVE
SAN DIEGO – LA JOLLA UNDERWATER PARK
PT LA JOLLA
LA JOLLA COVE
ELLEN SCRIPPS PARK
Boomer Beach
La Jolla Caves
ALLIGATOR HEAD
GOLD FISH PT
Spindrift Golf Course
CHILDREN'S POOL SHELL BEACH
Colonial Inn
Wipeout Beach
ELLEN BROWNING SCRIPPS PARK
COAST BLVD PK
La Jolla Mus of Contemporary Art
The Empress Hotel Of La Jolla
Casa Beach
NICHOLSON PT PARK
La Jolla
La Jolla Country Club
Marine Street Beach
VISTA DE LA PLAYA
Windansea Beach
Playa
PLAYA DEL SUR
KOLMAR ST
ROSEMONT
La Jolla Strand Park
WINAMAR
HERMOSA TERRACE
BIG ROCK REEF
La Jolla Hermosa Park
Bird Rock
CORTEZ PL
SAN DIEGO
MUIRLANDS DR
NAUTILUS ST
LA JOLLA SCENIC
SOLEDAD MTN RD
KATE O SESSIONS MEMORIAL PARK
TURQUOISE ST
TOURMALINE ST
OPAL ST
LORING ST
BERYL ST
241 TOUR
211

PROSPECT
COAST BLVD
PEARL ST
FAY AV
NAUTILUS ST
LA JOLLA BLVD

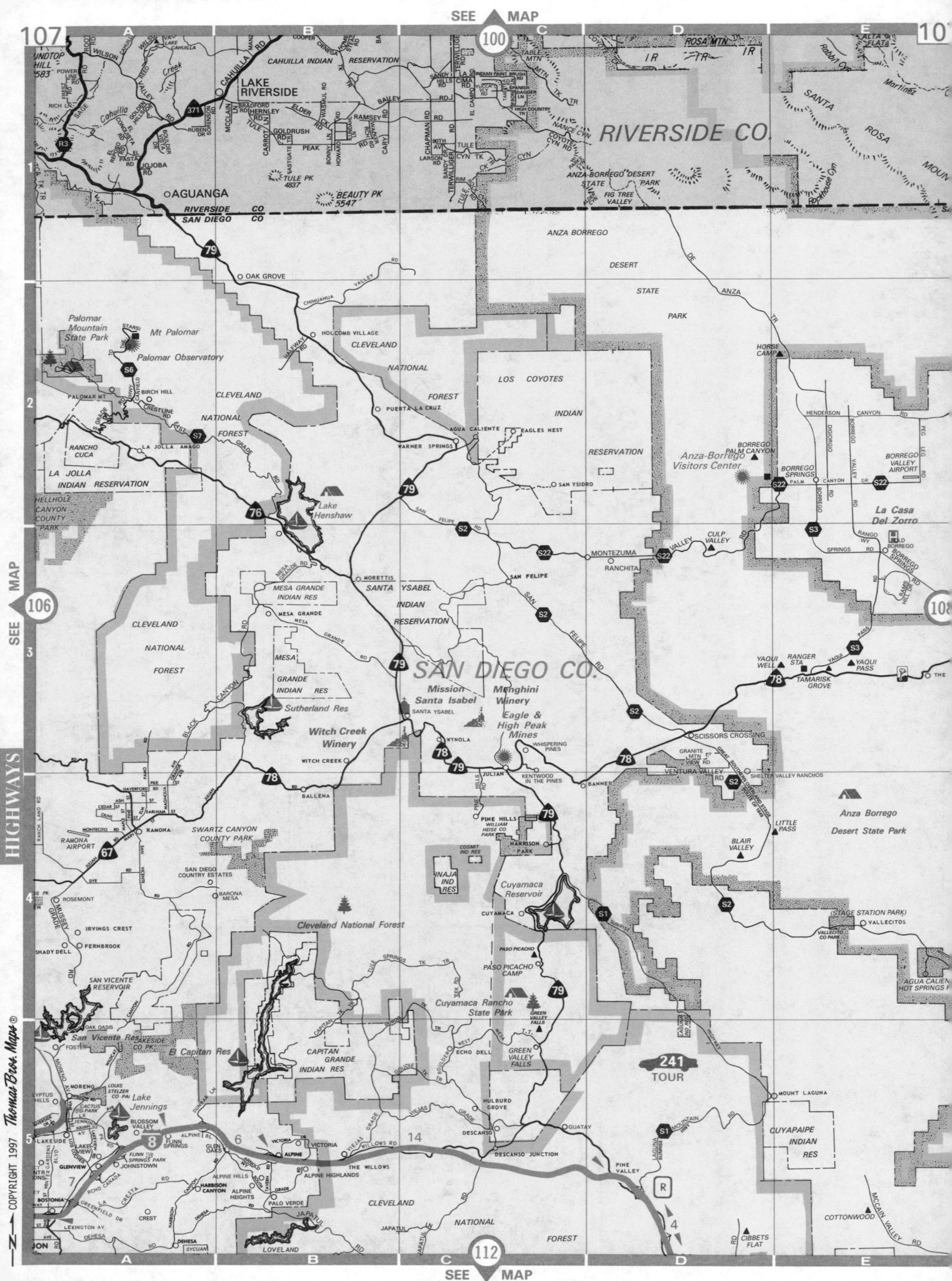

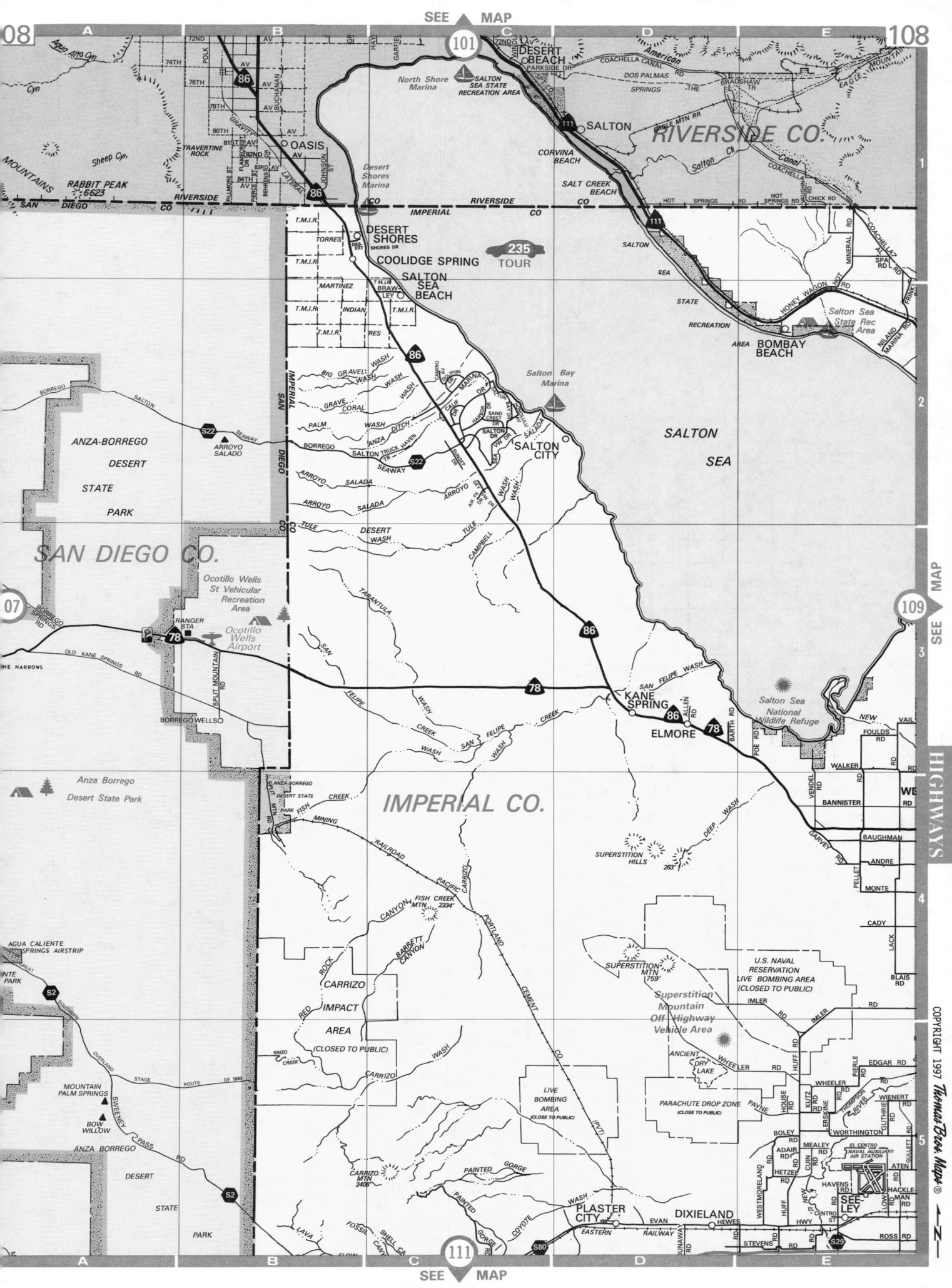

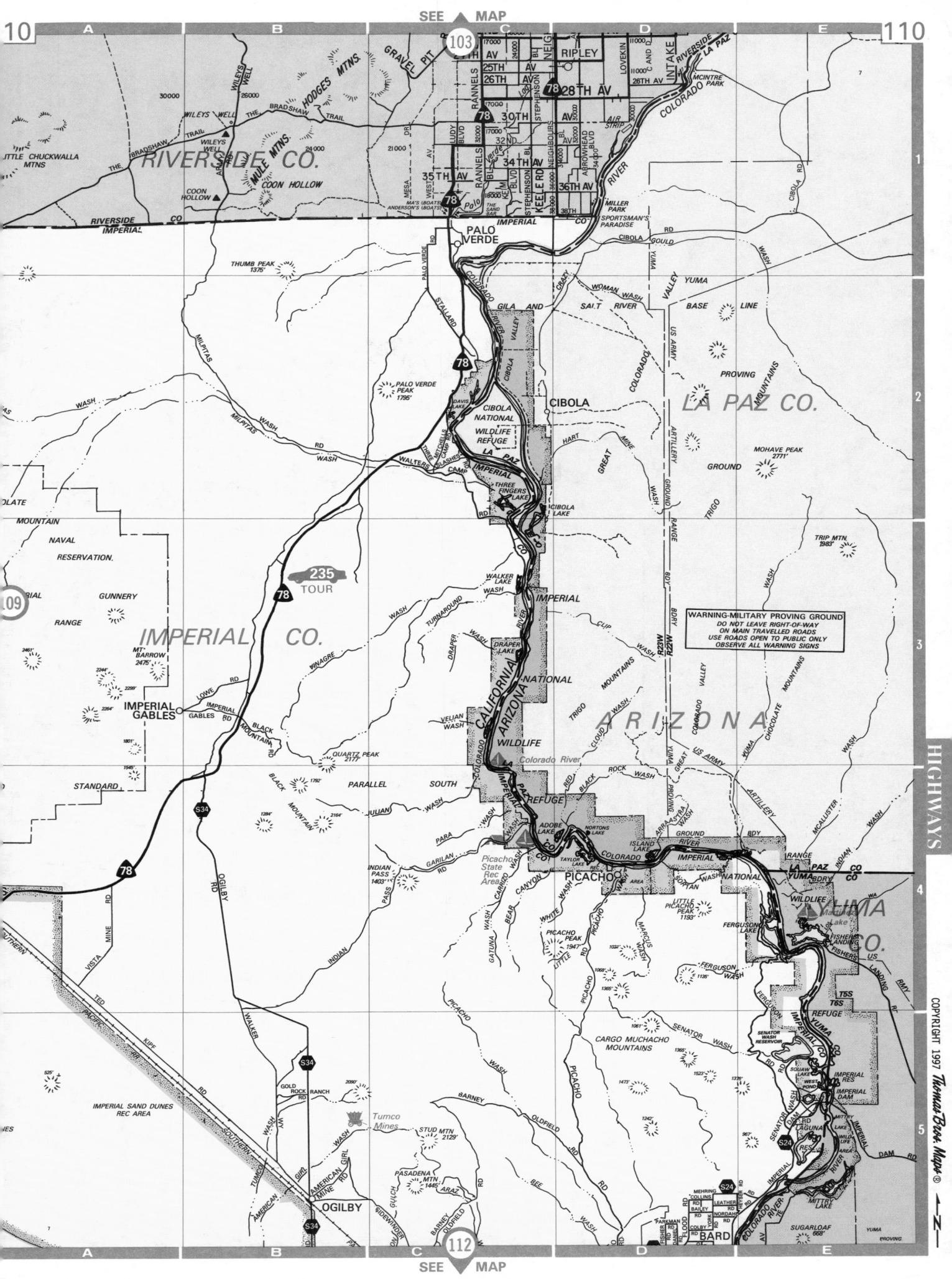

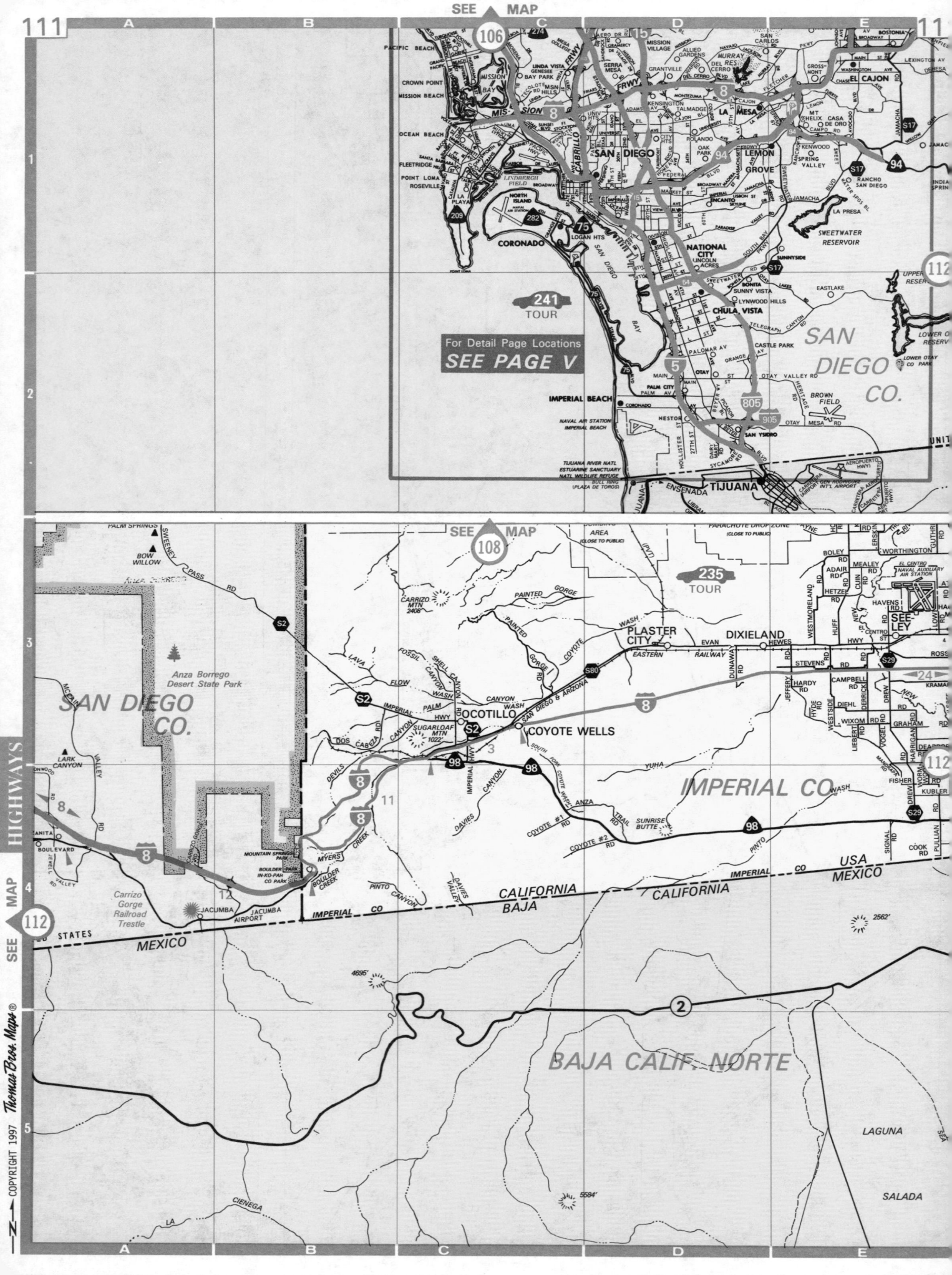

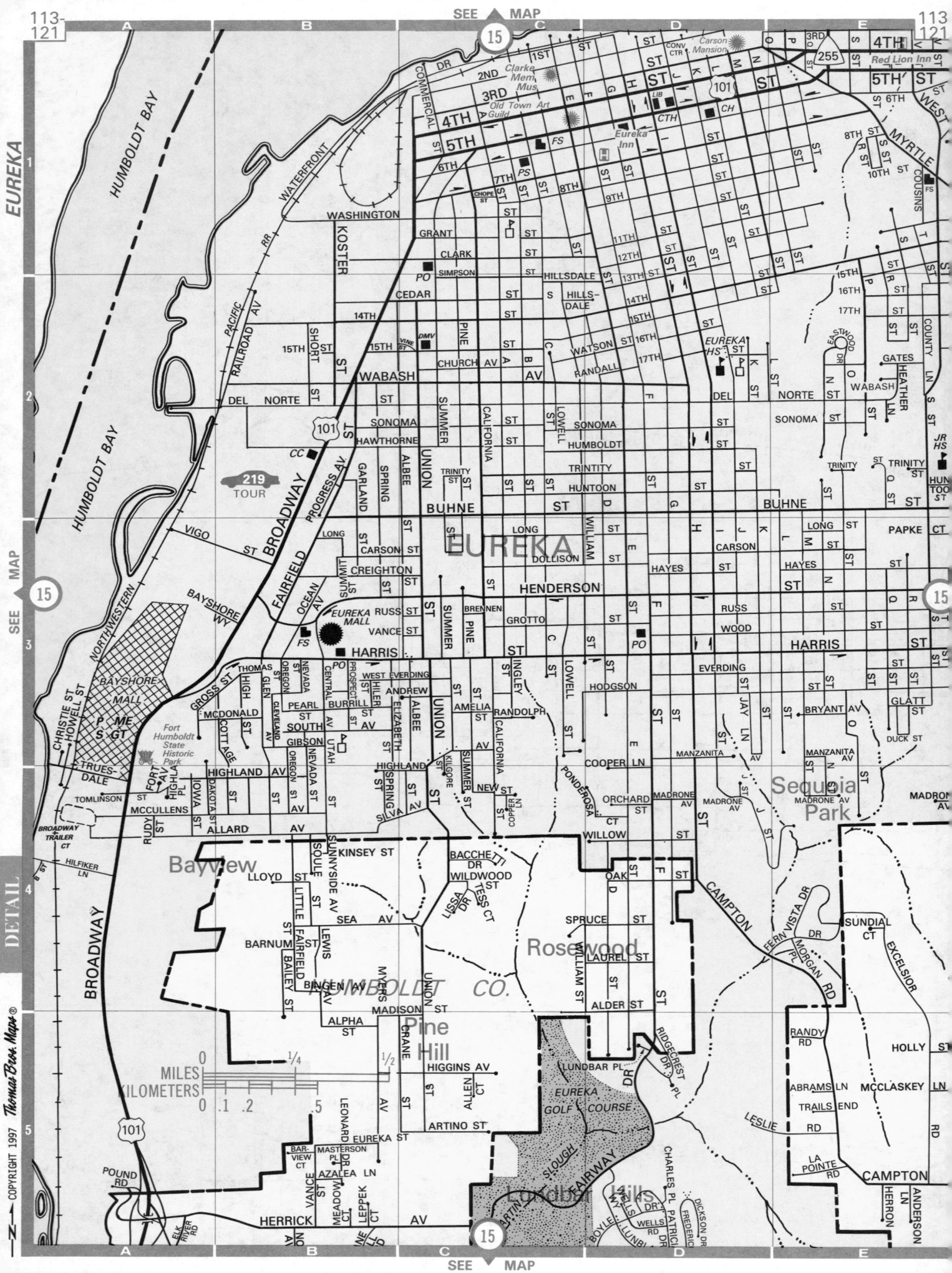

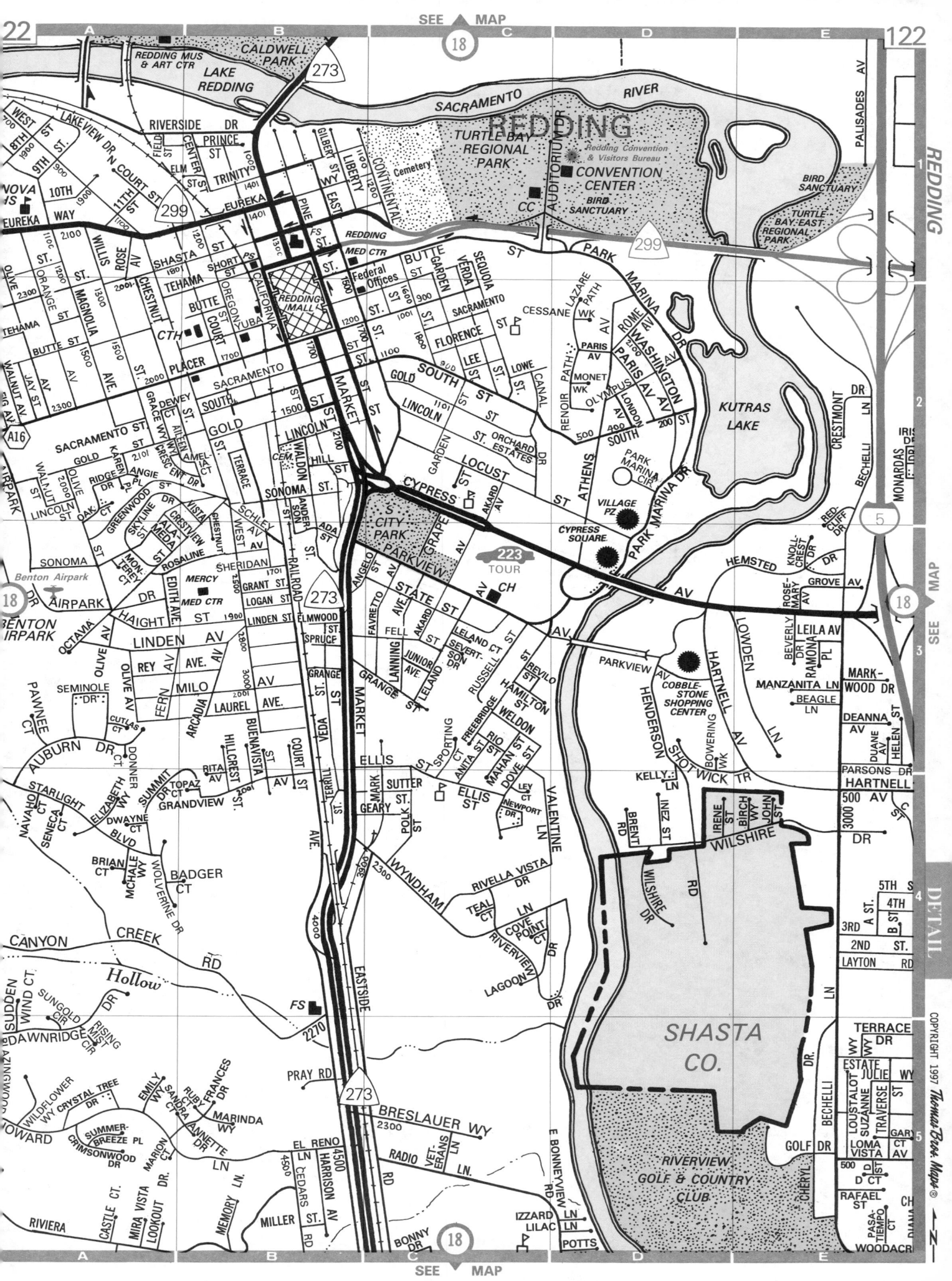

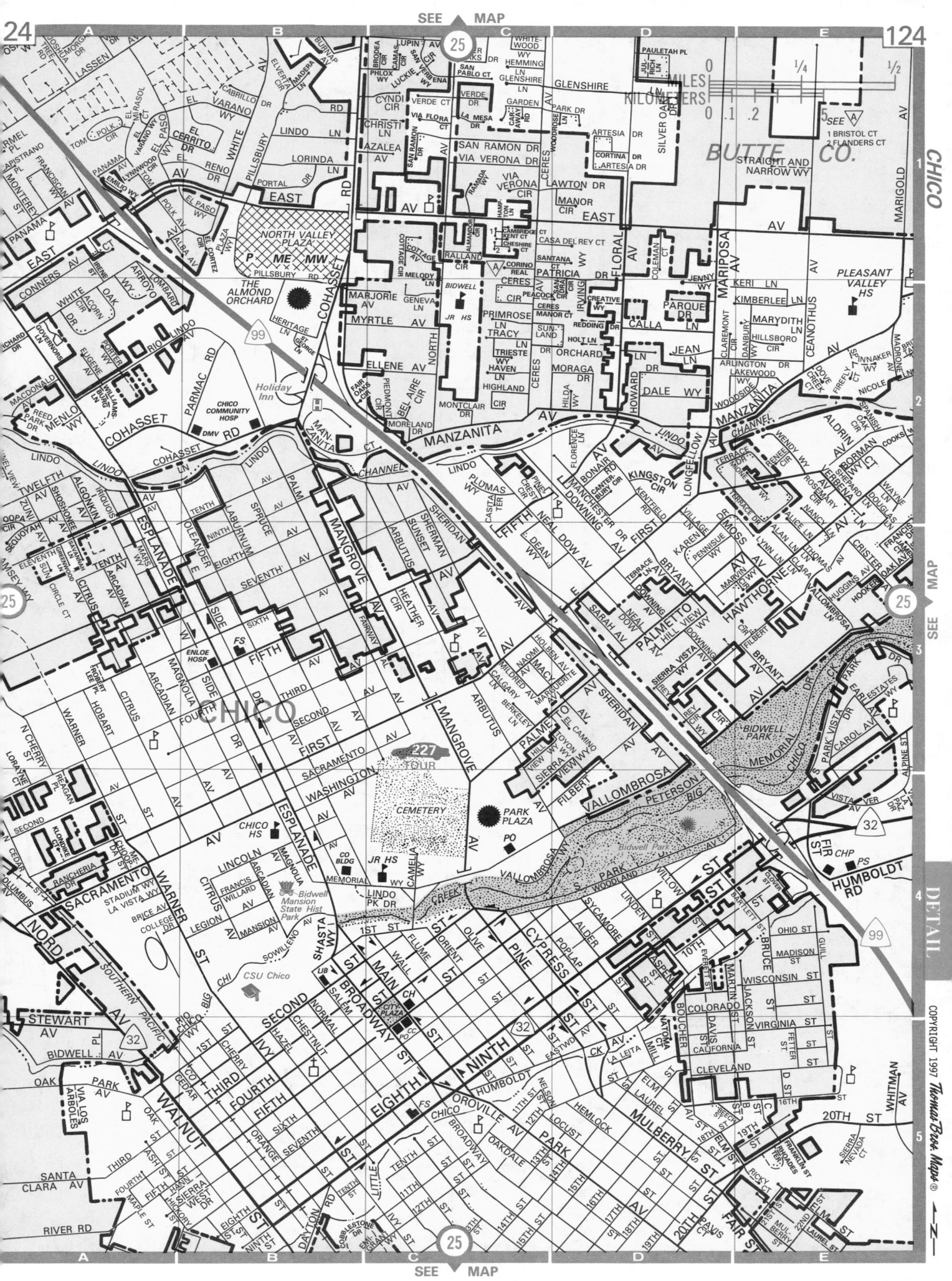

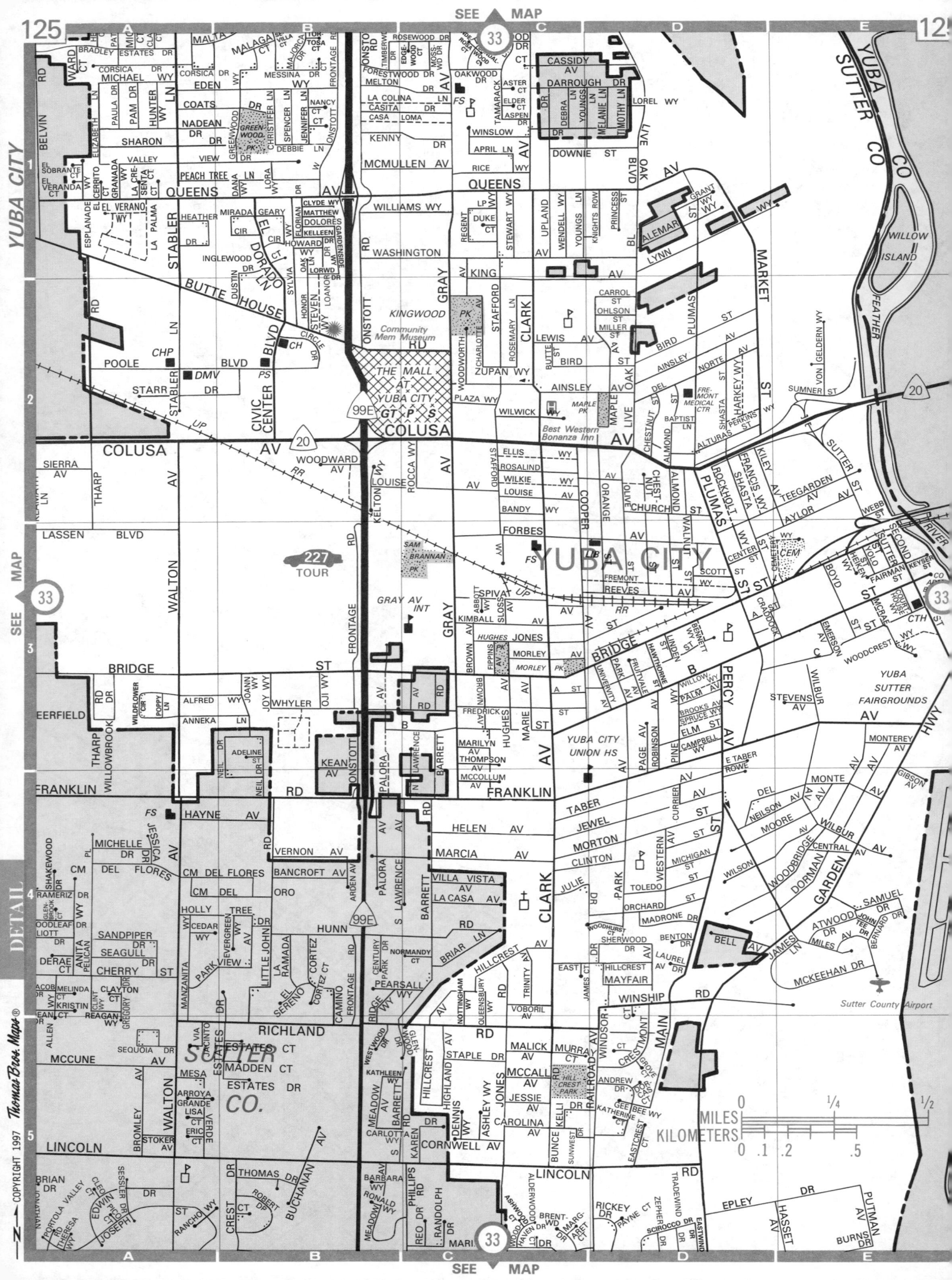

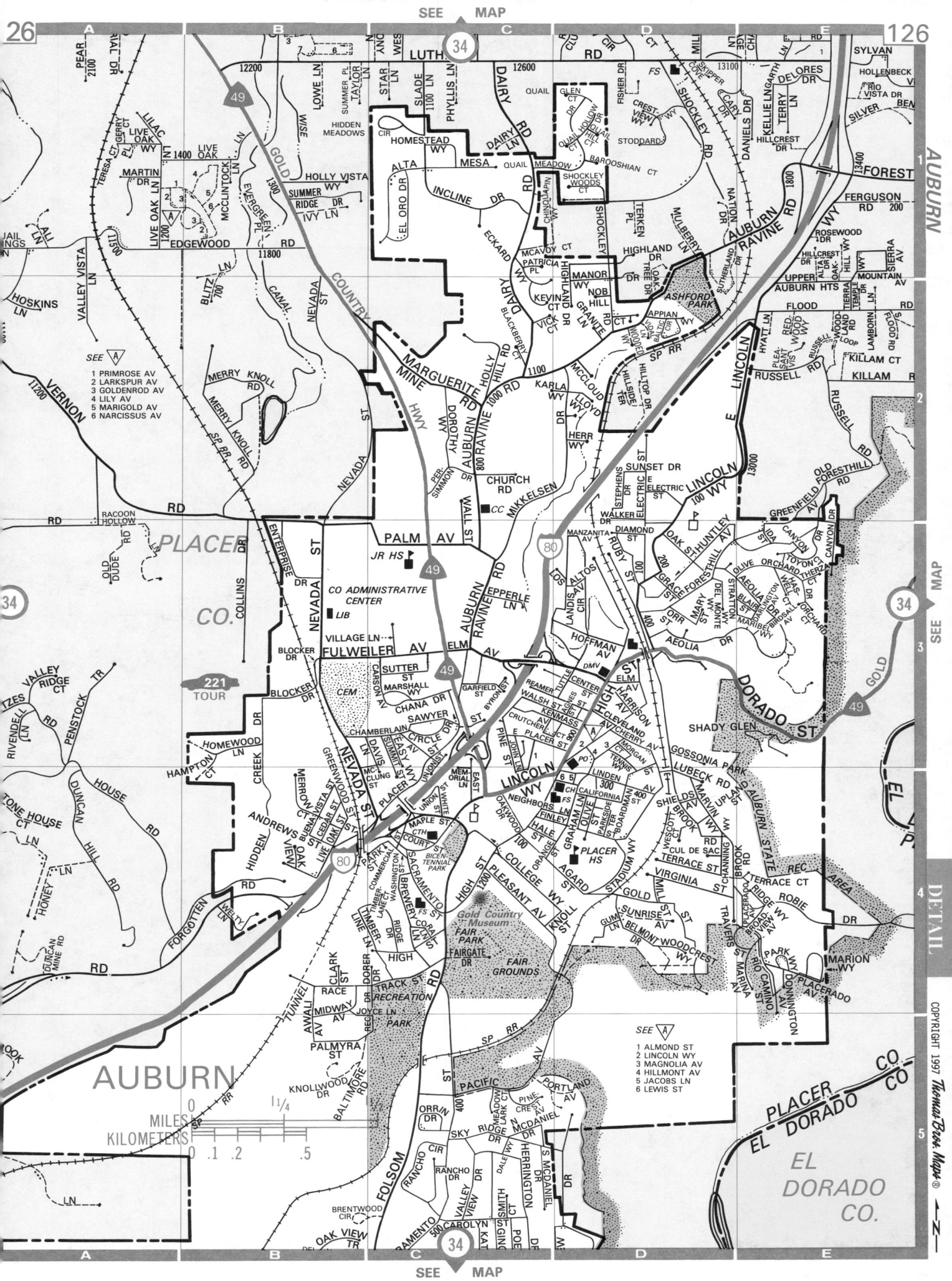

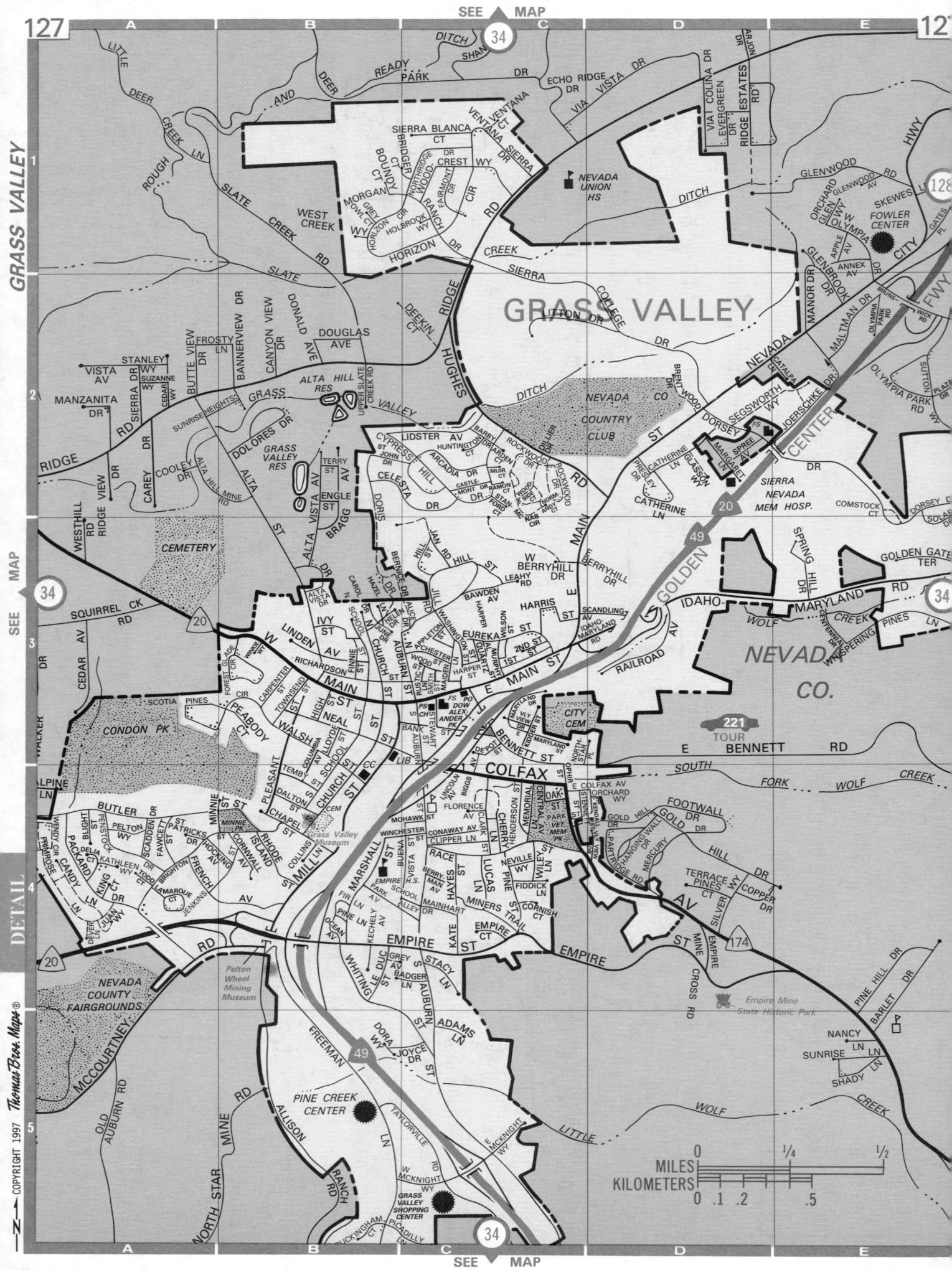

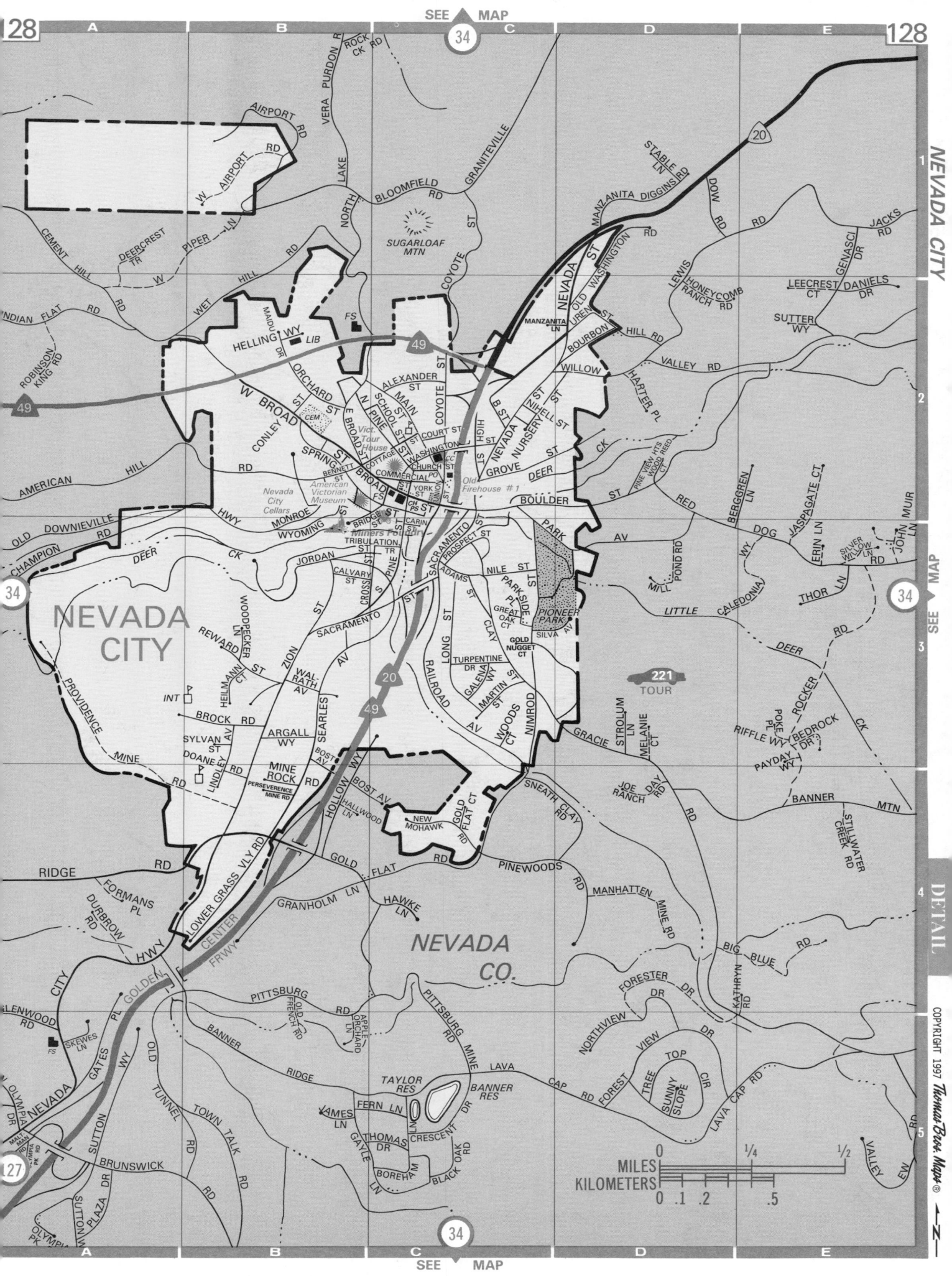

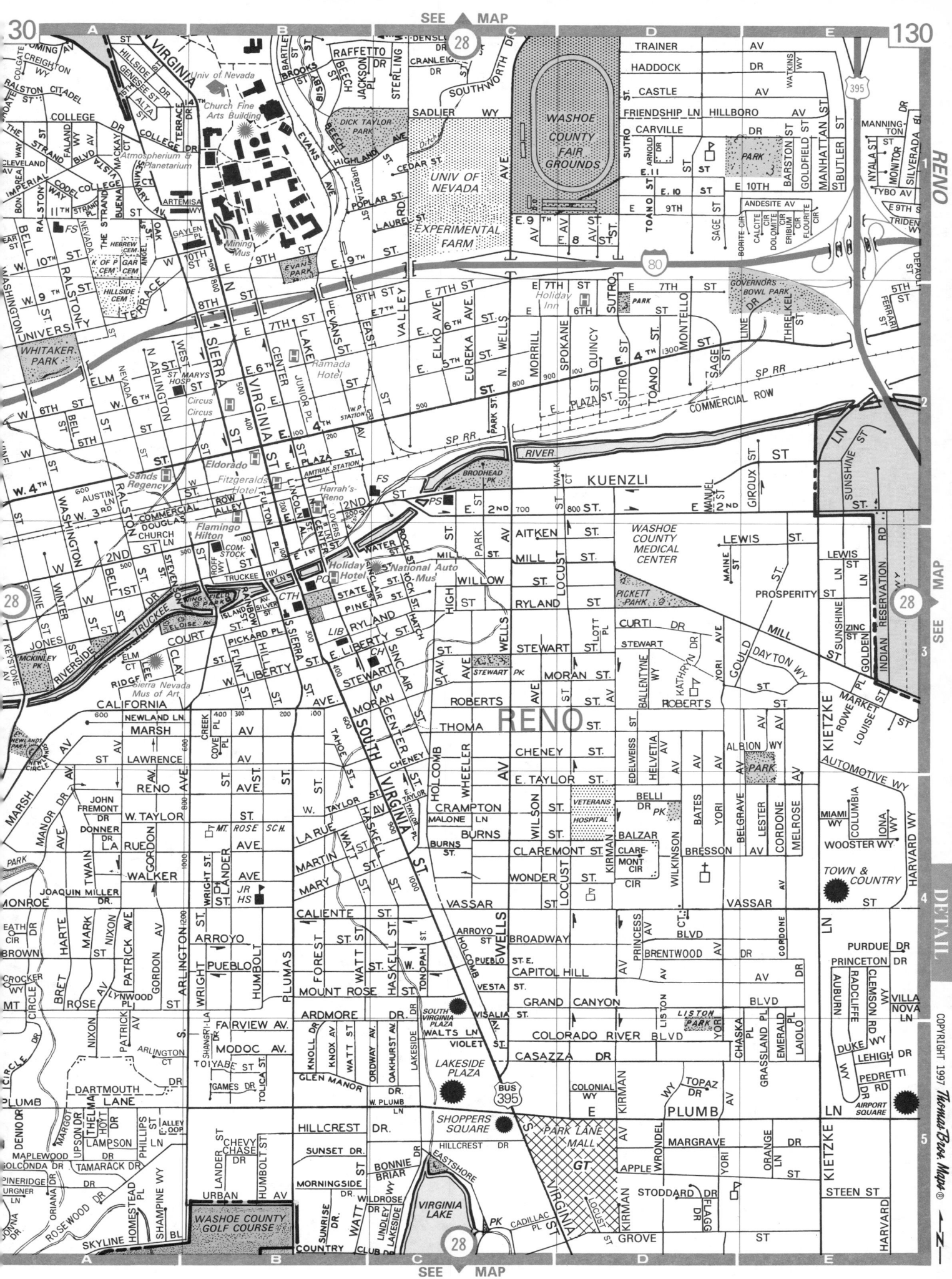

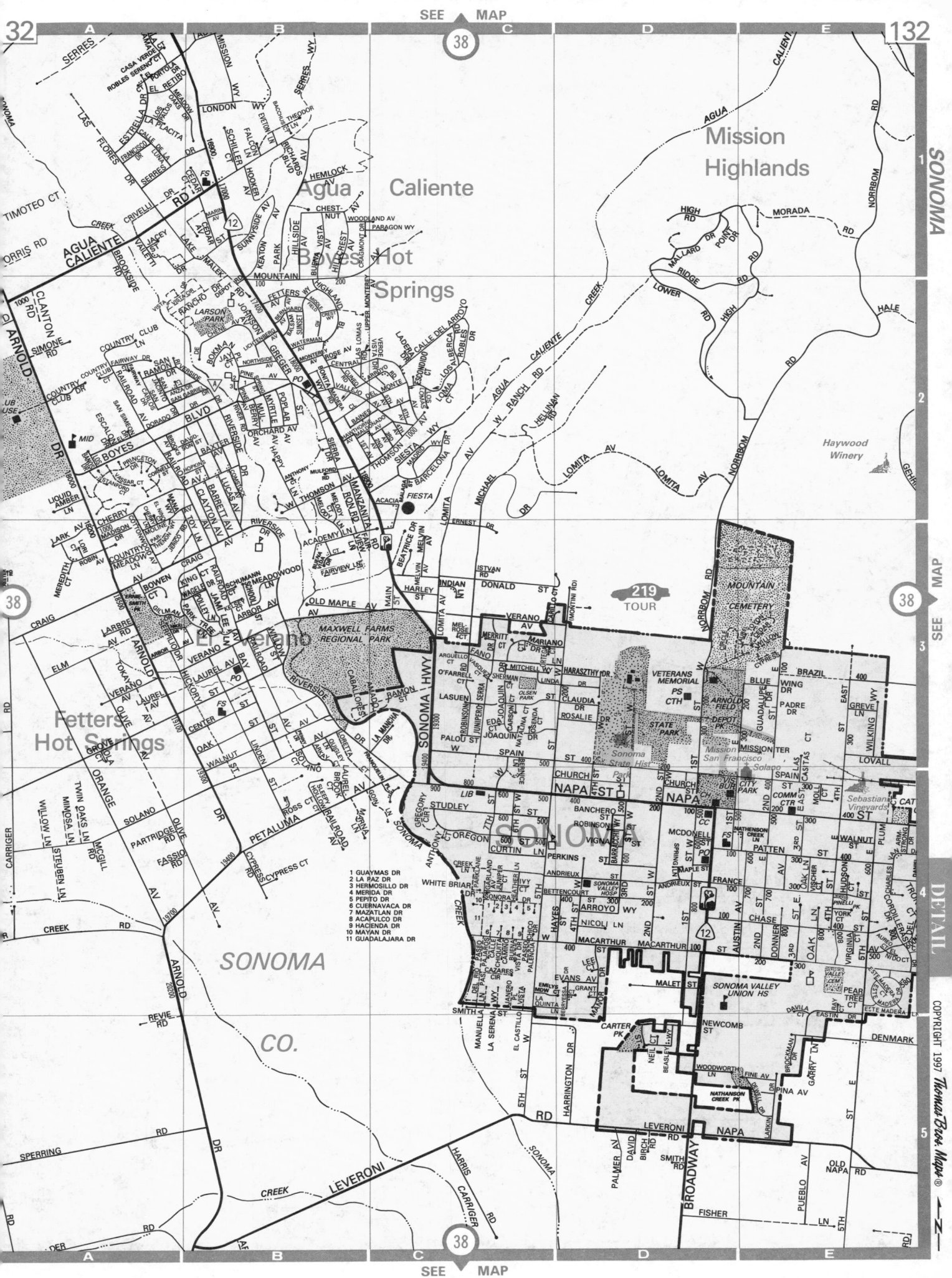

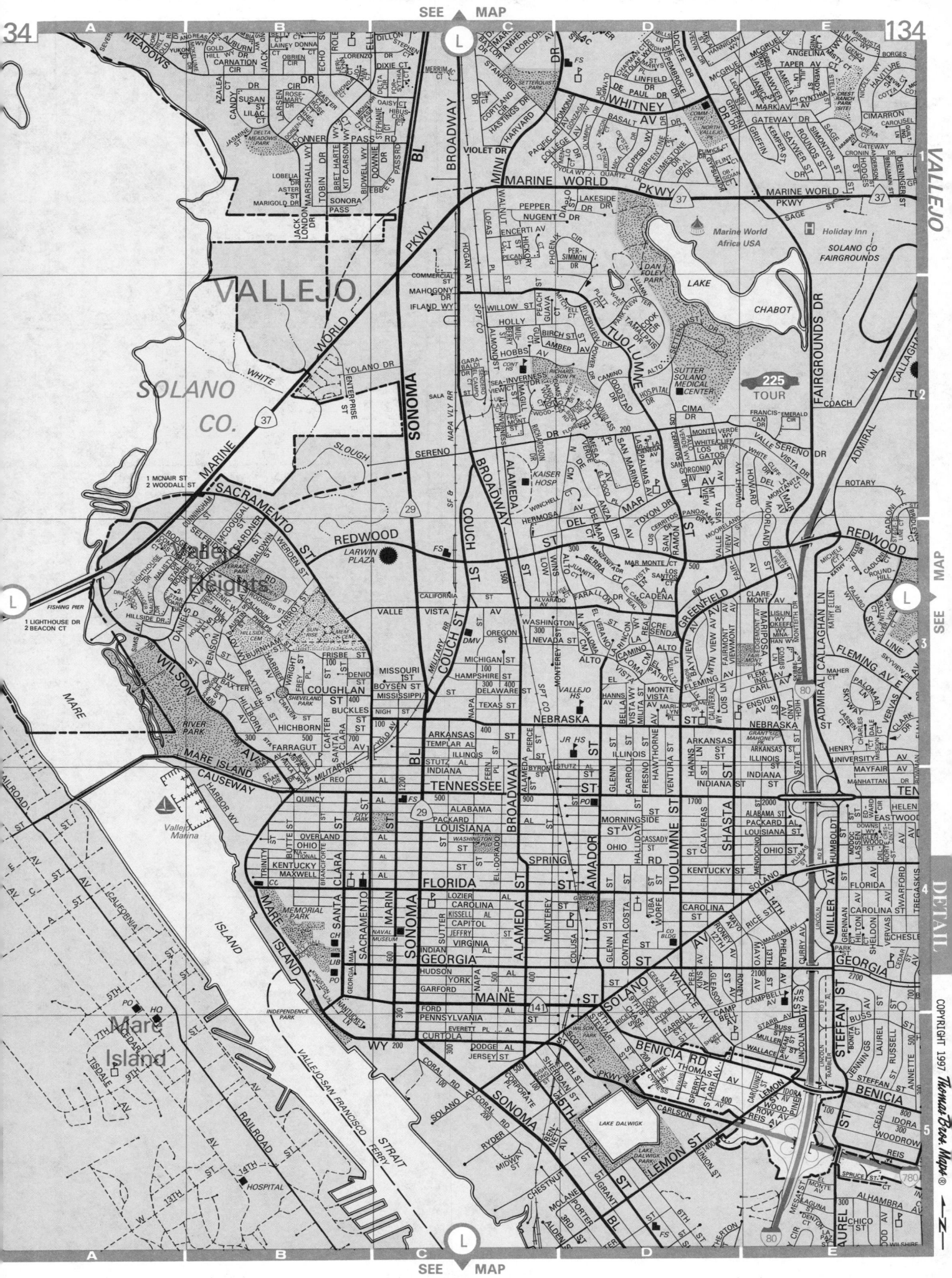

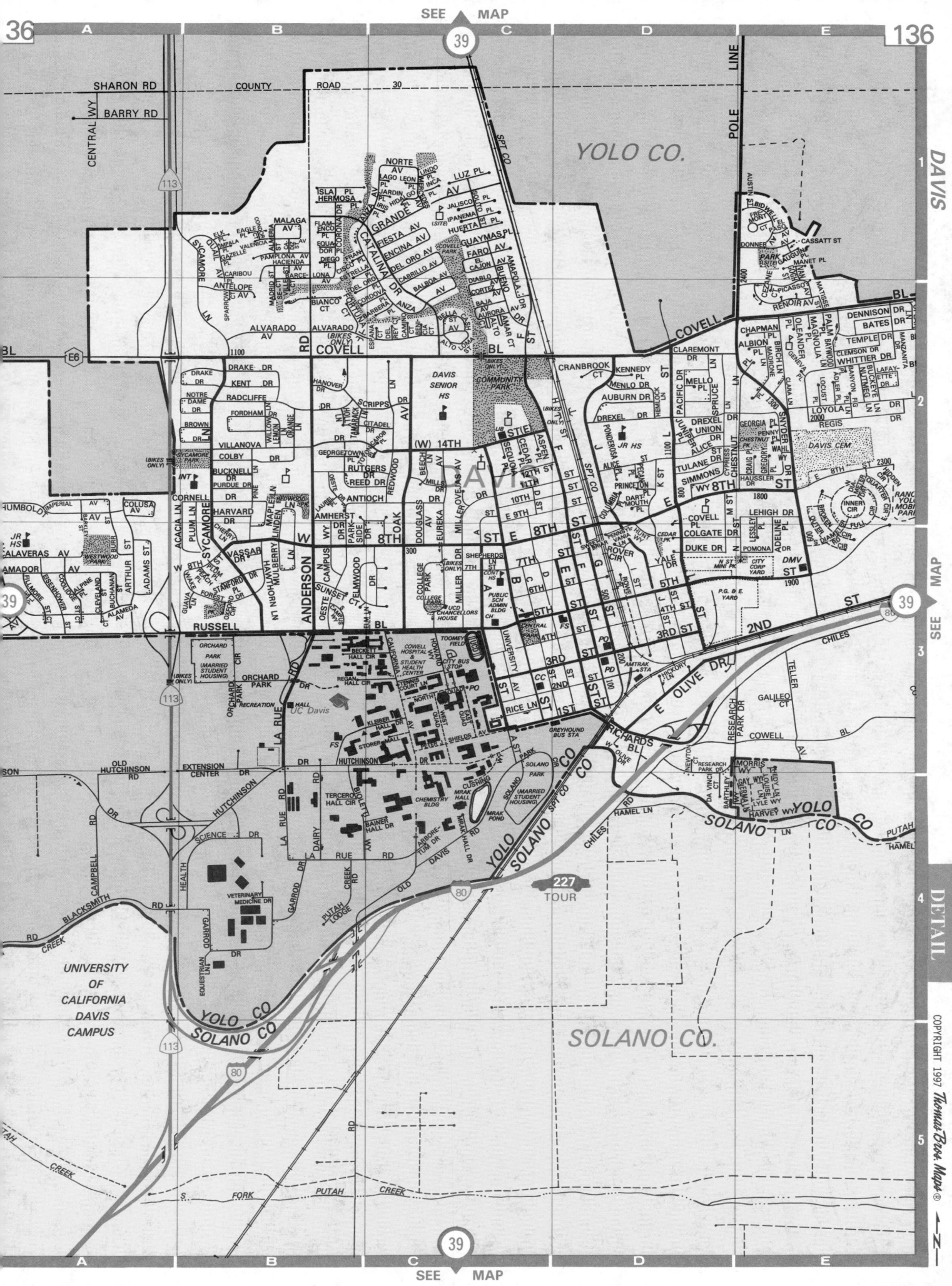

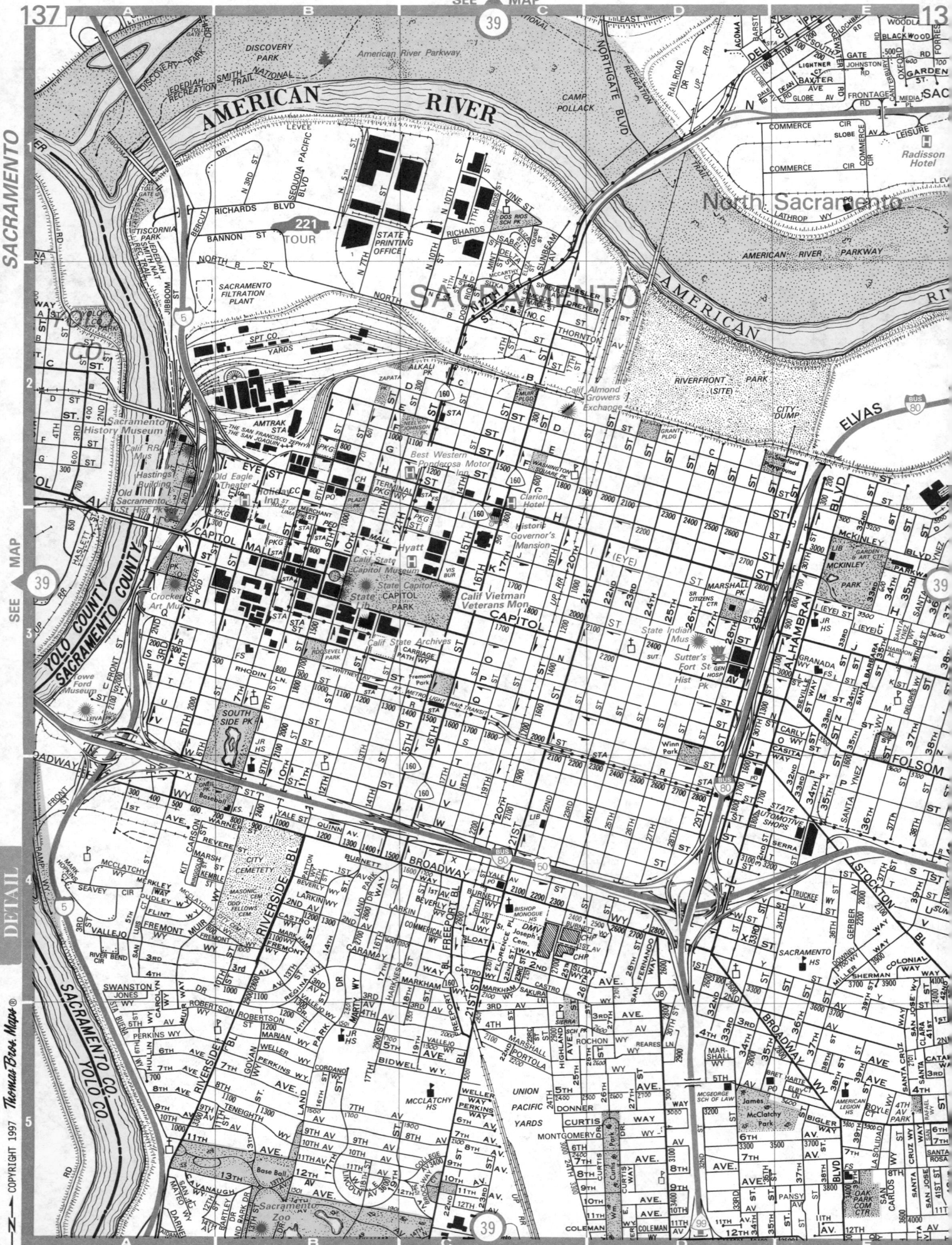

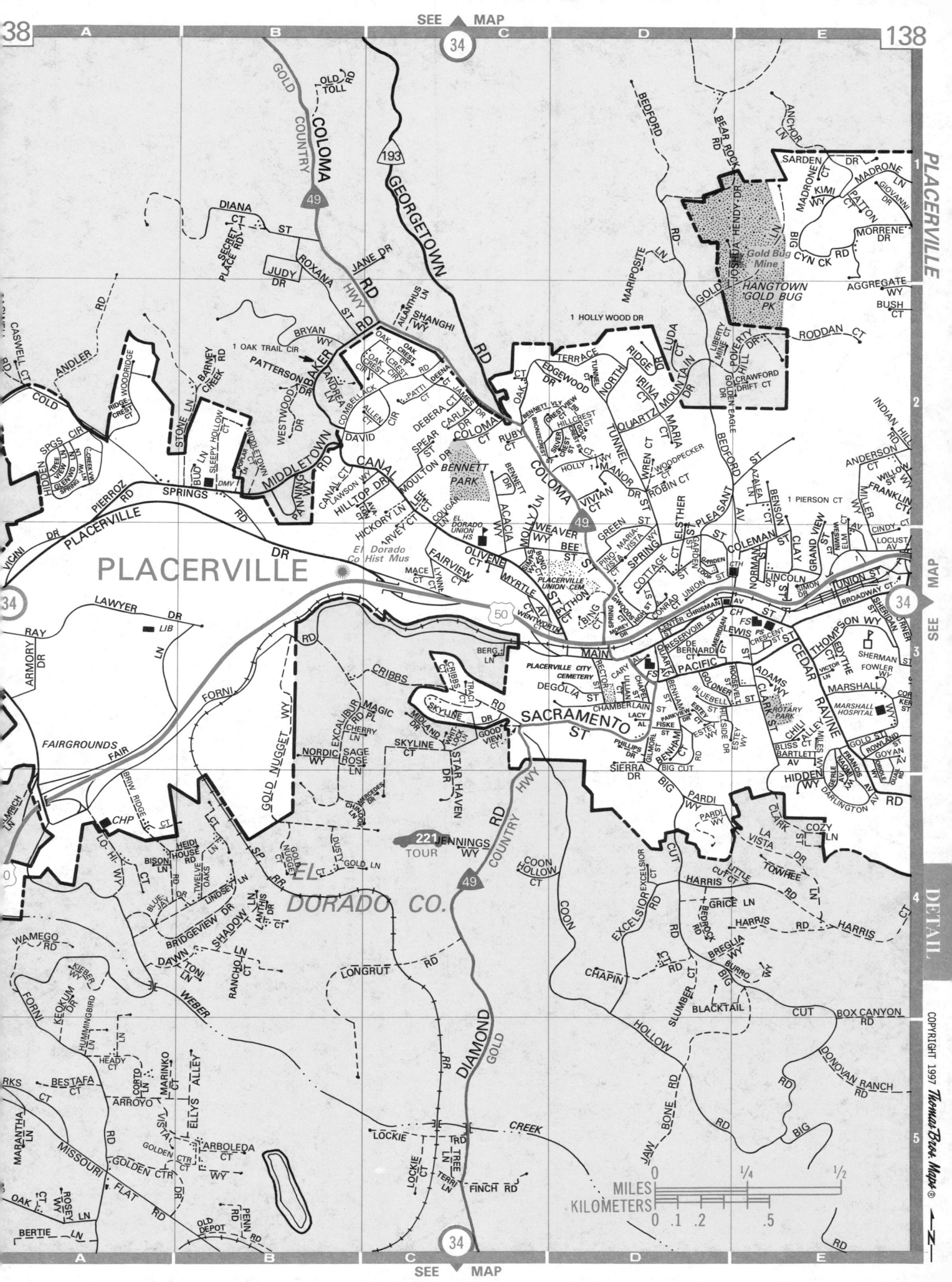

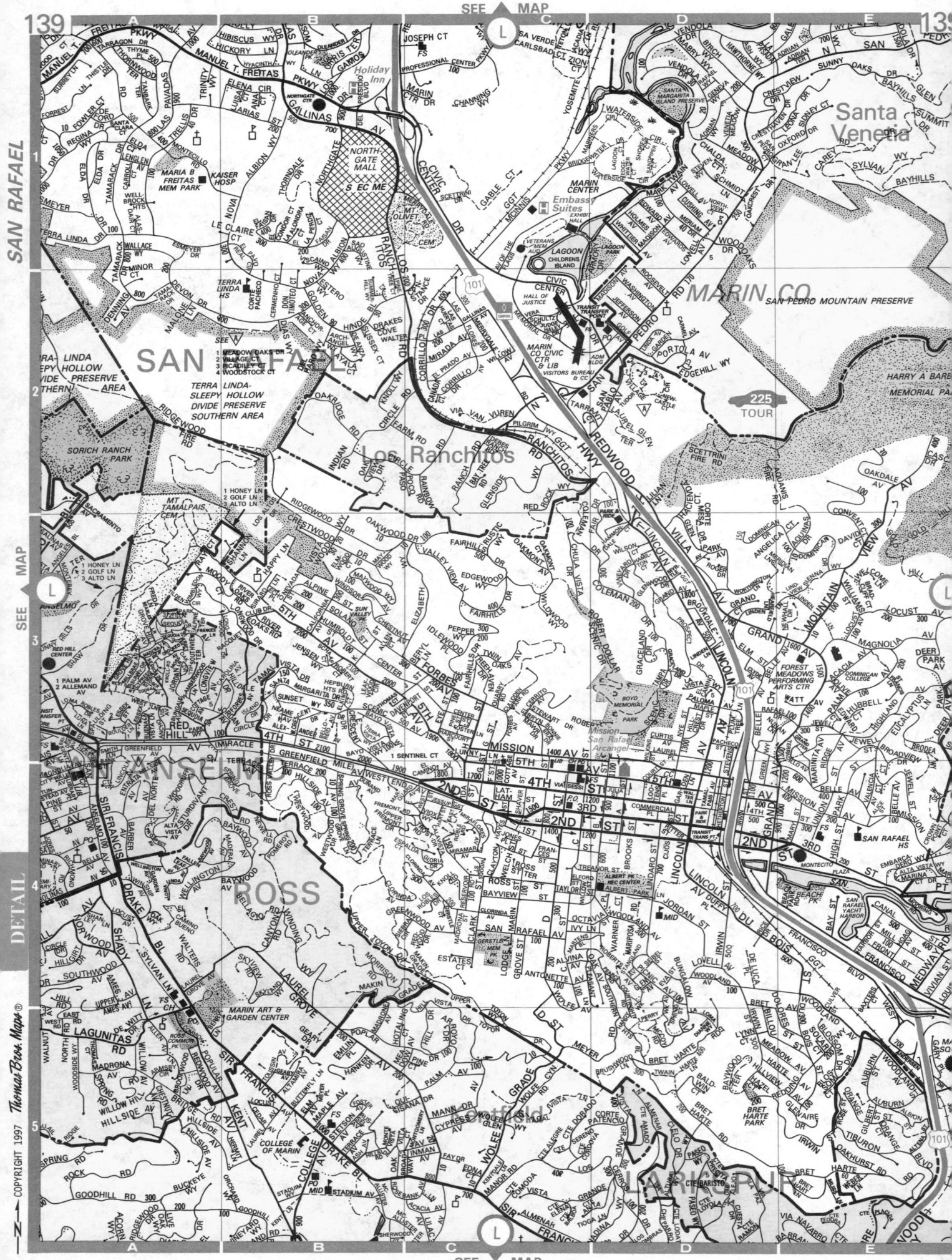

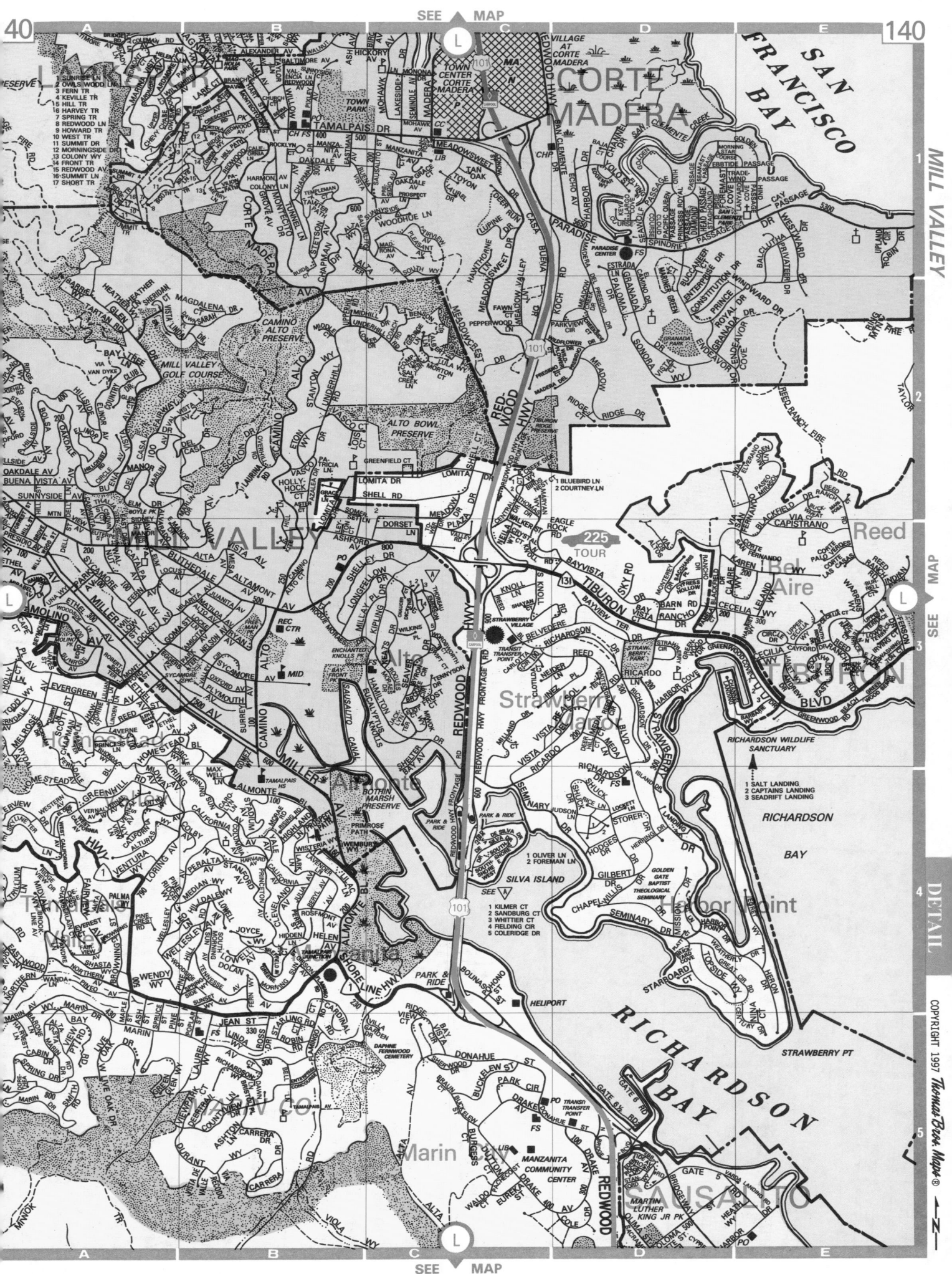

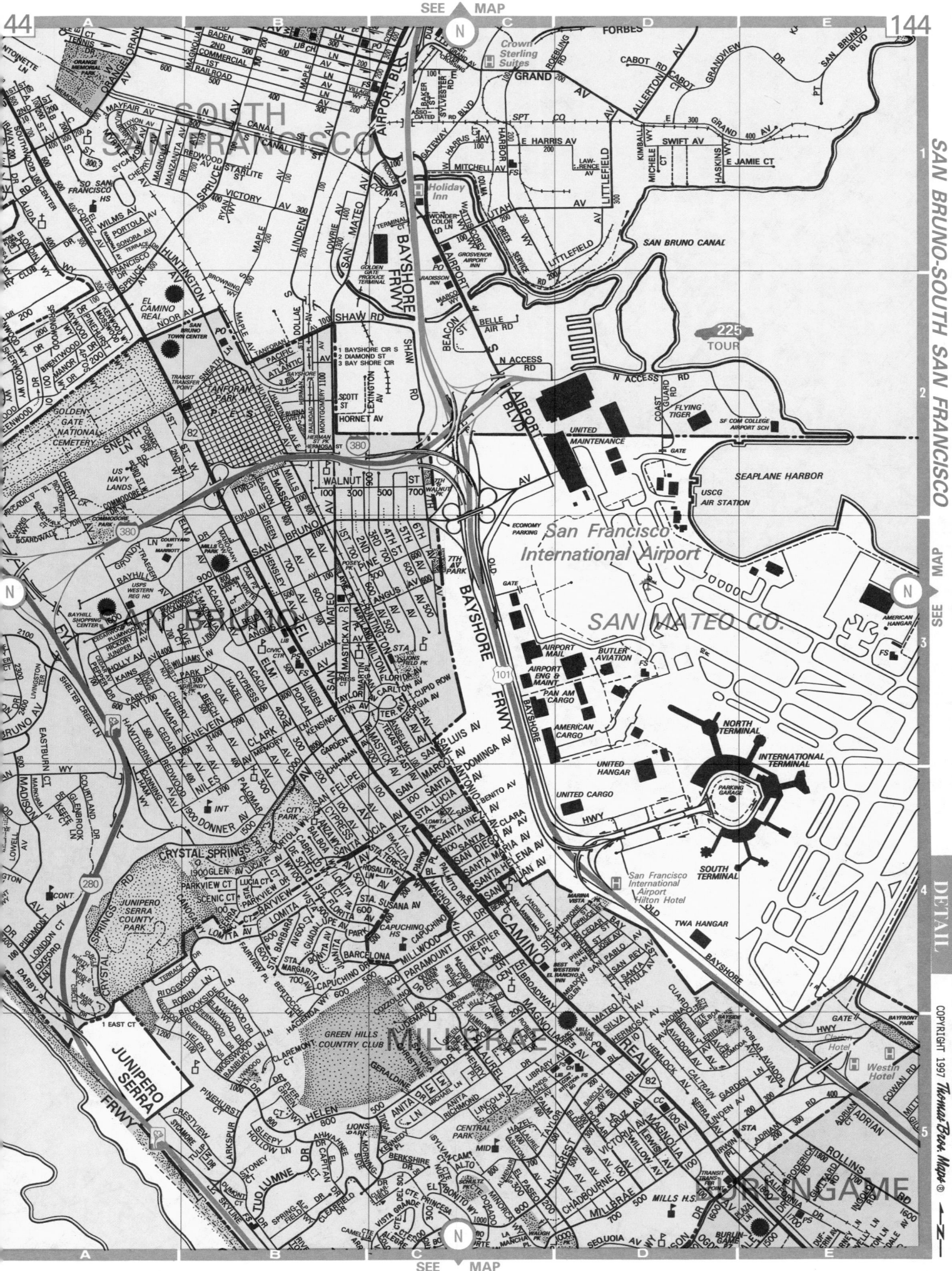

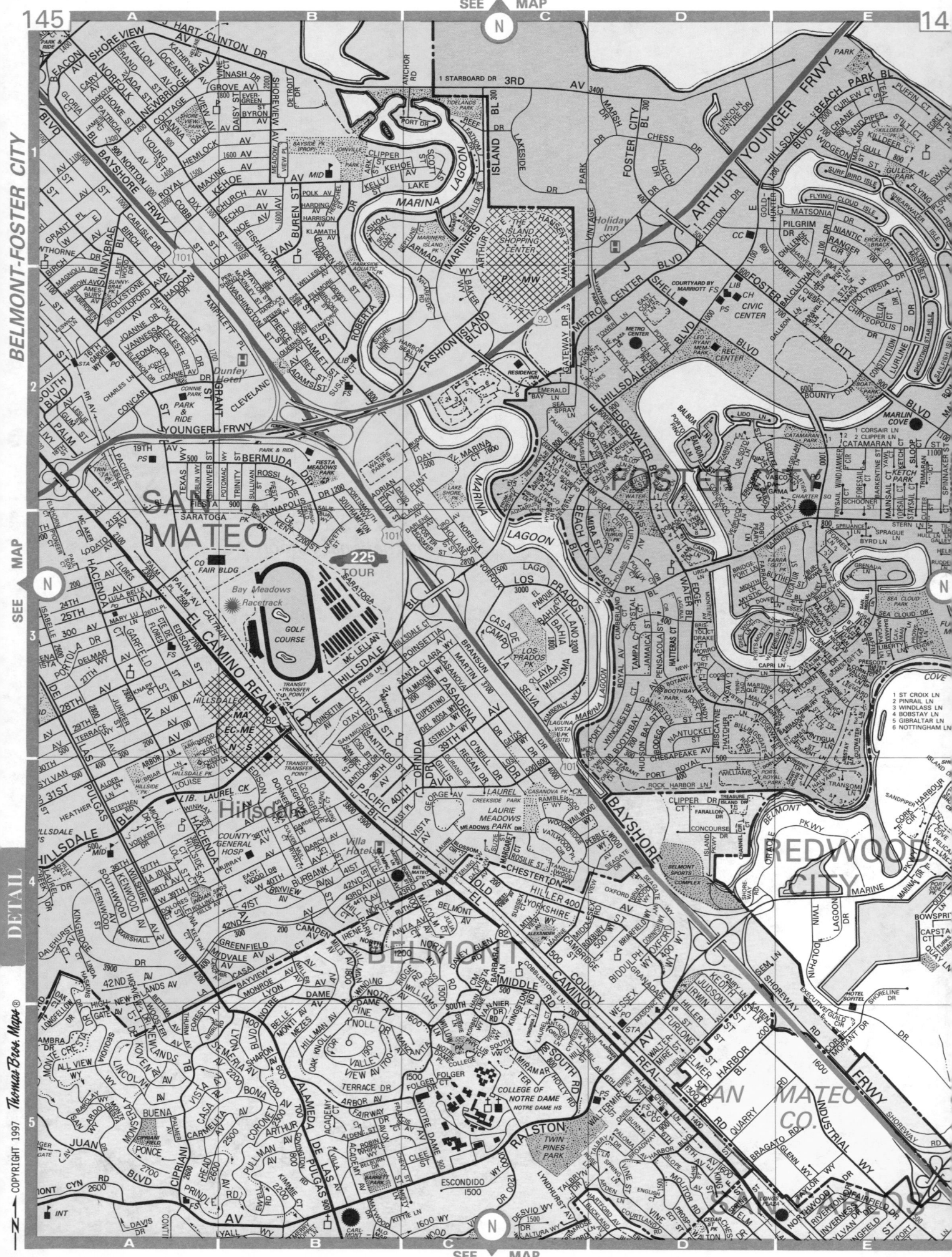

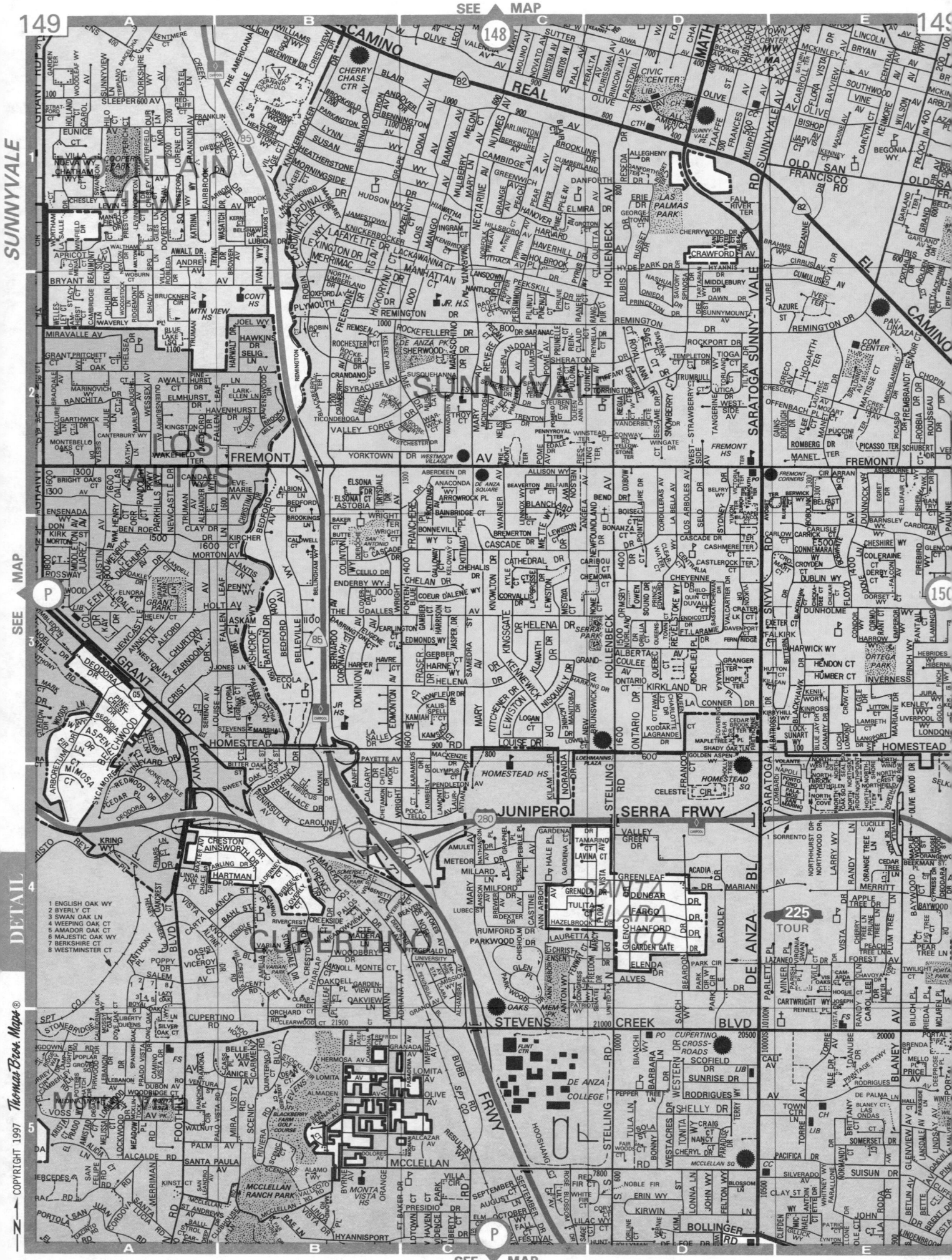

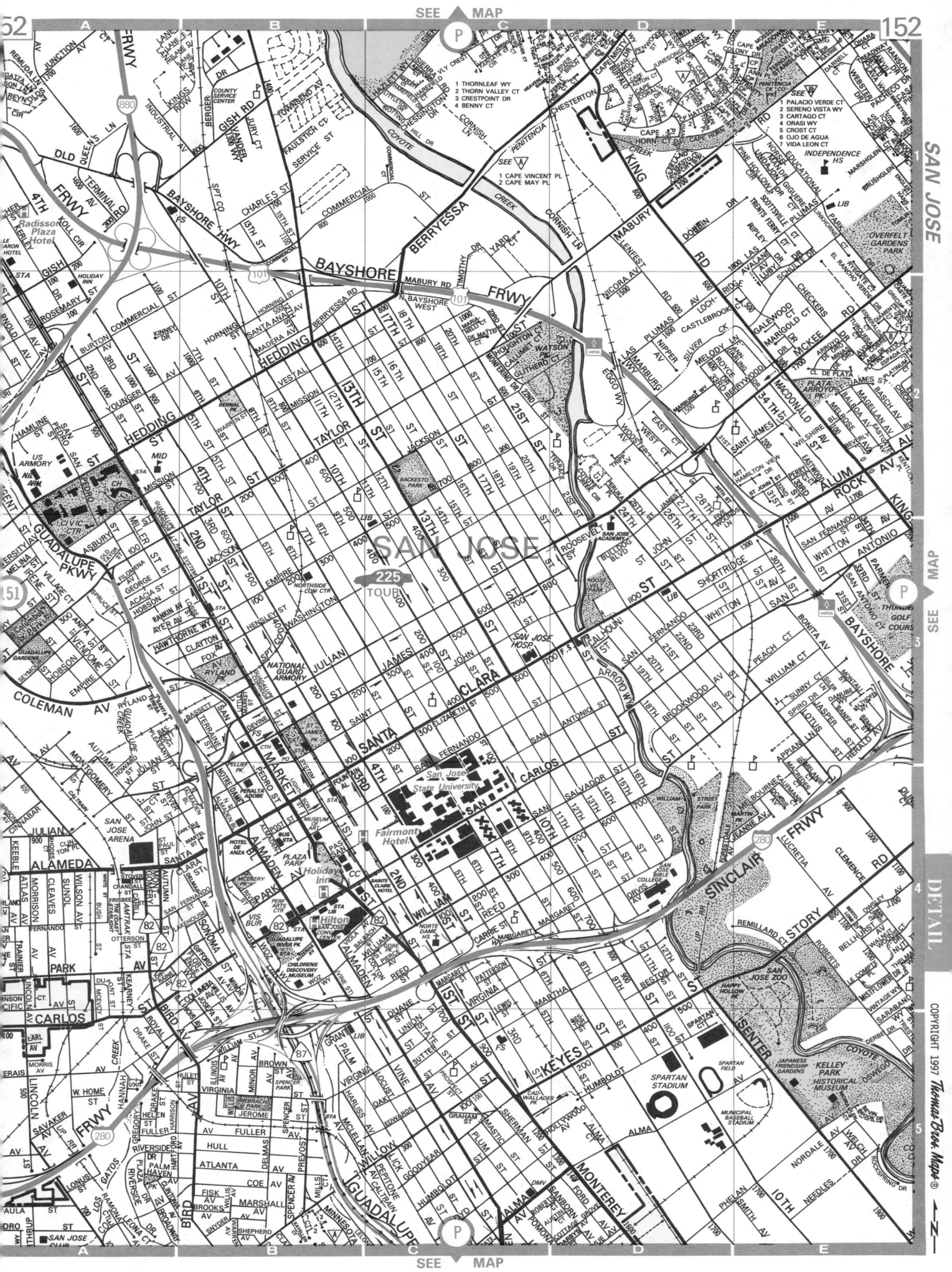

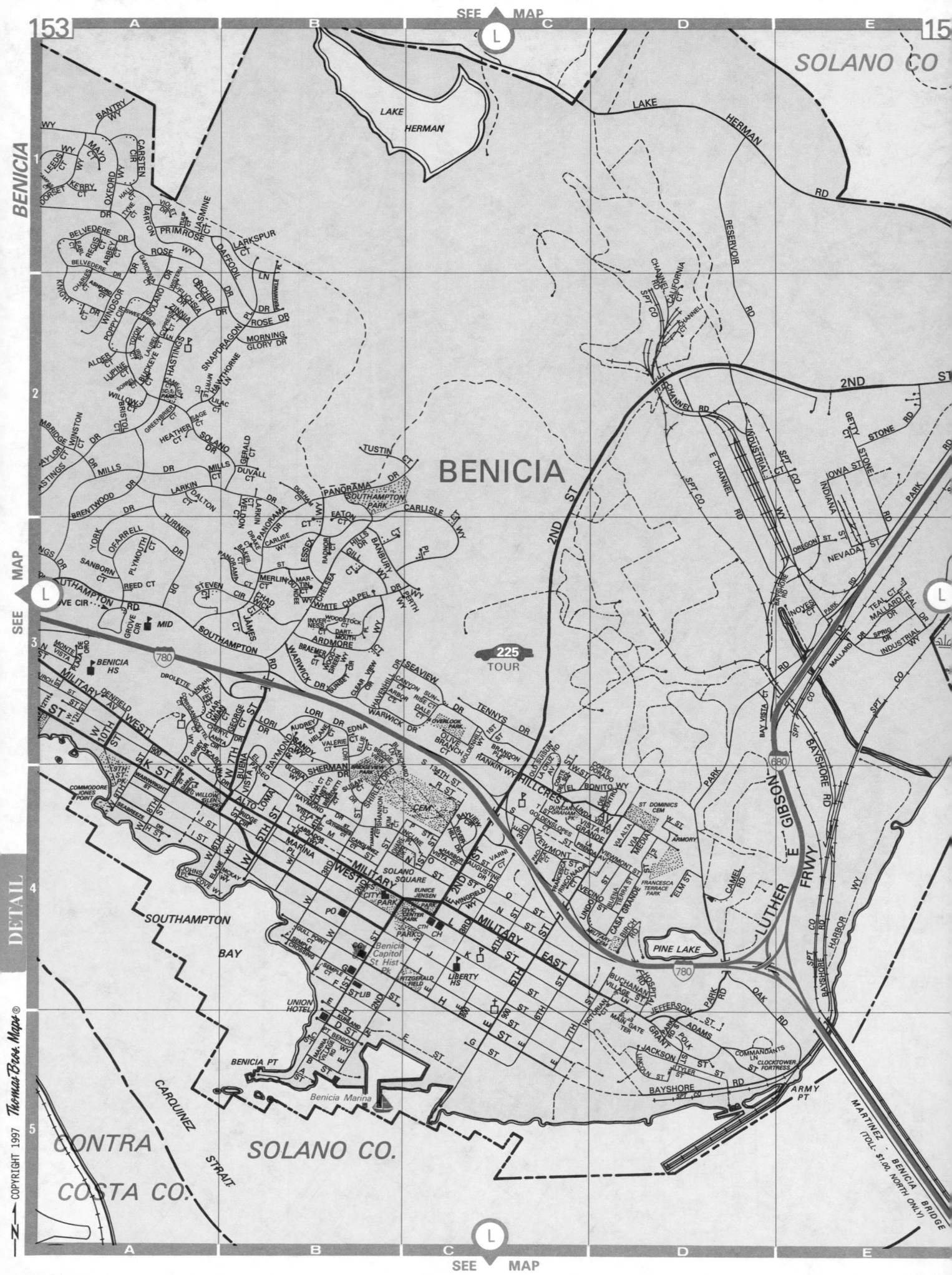

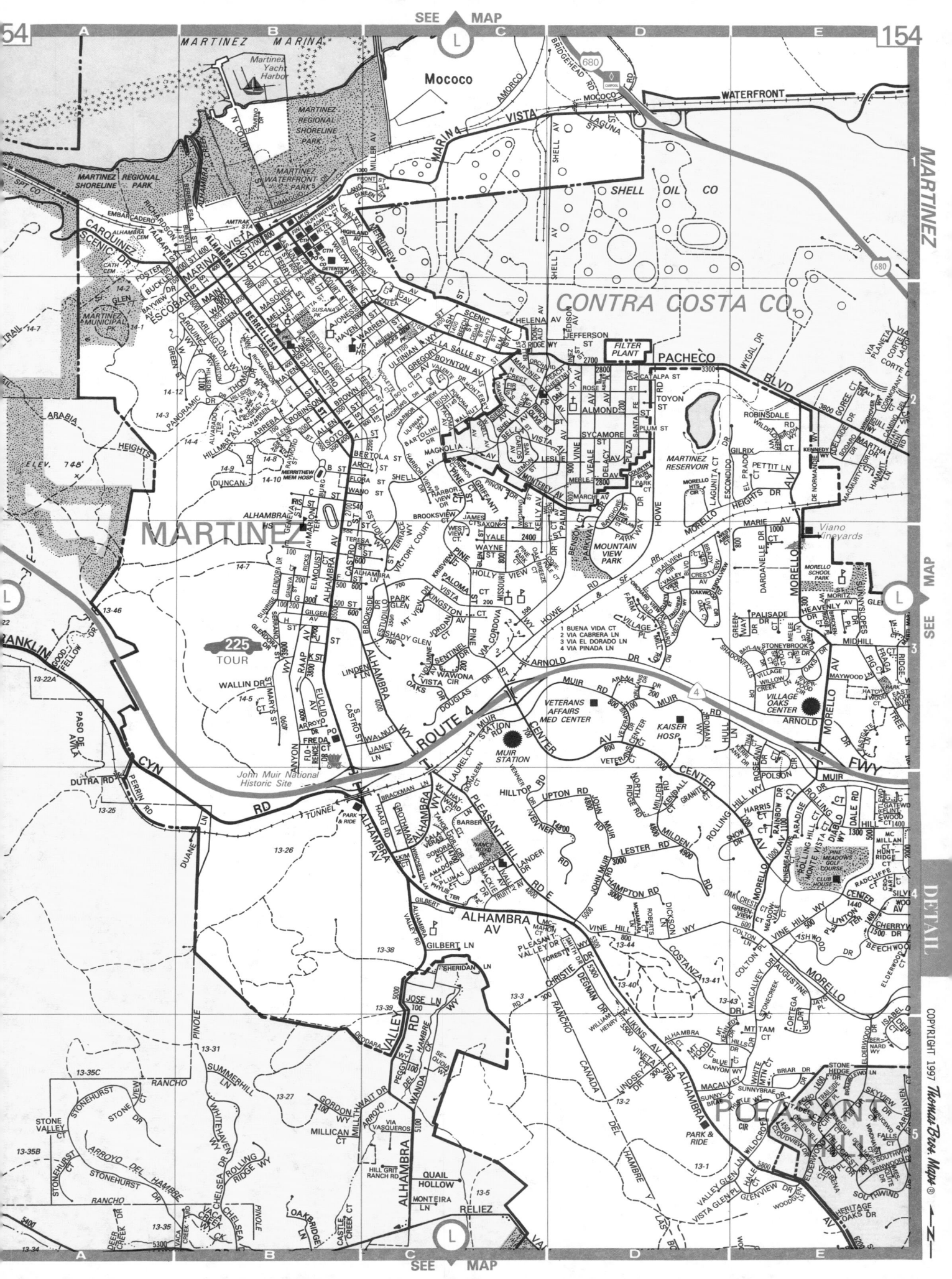

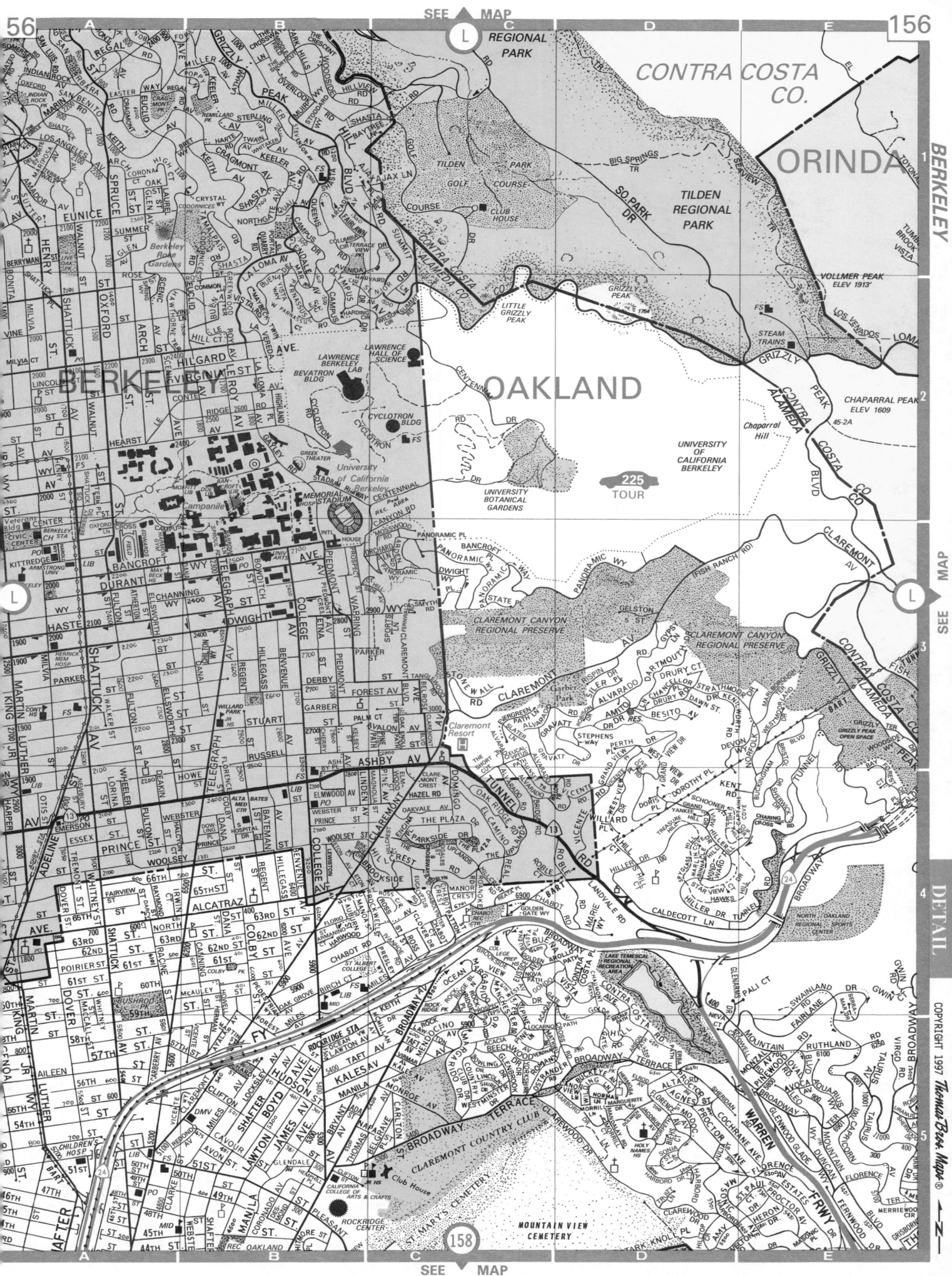

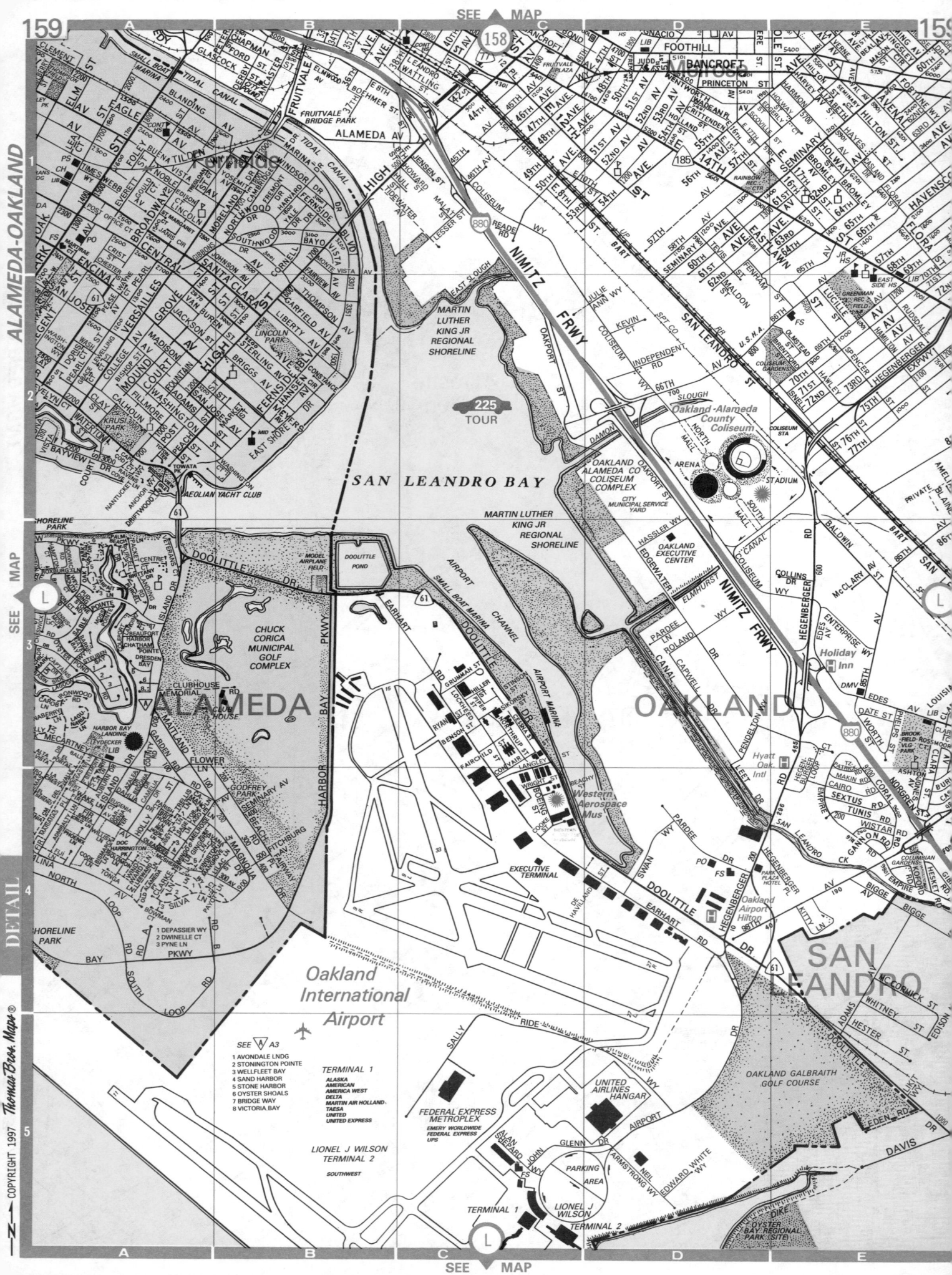

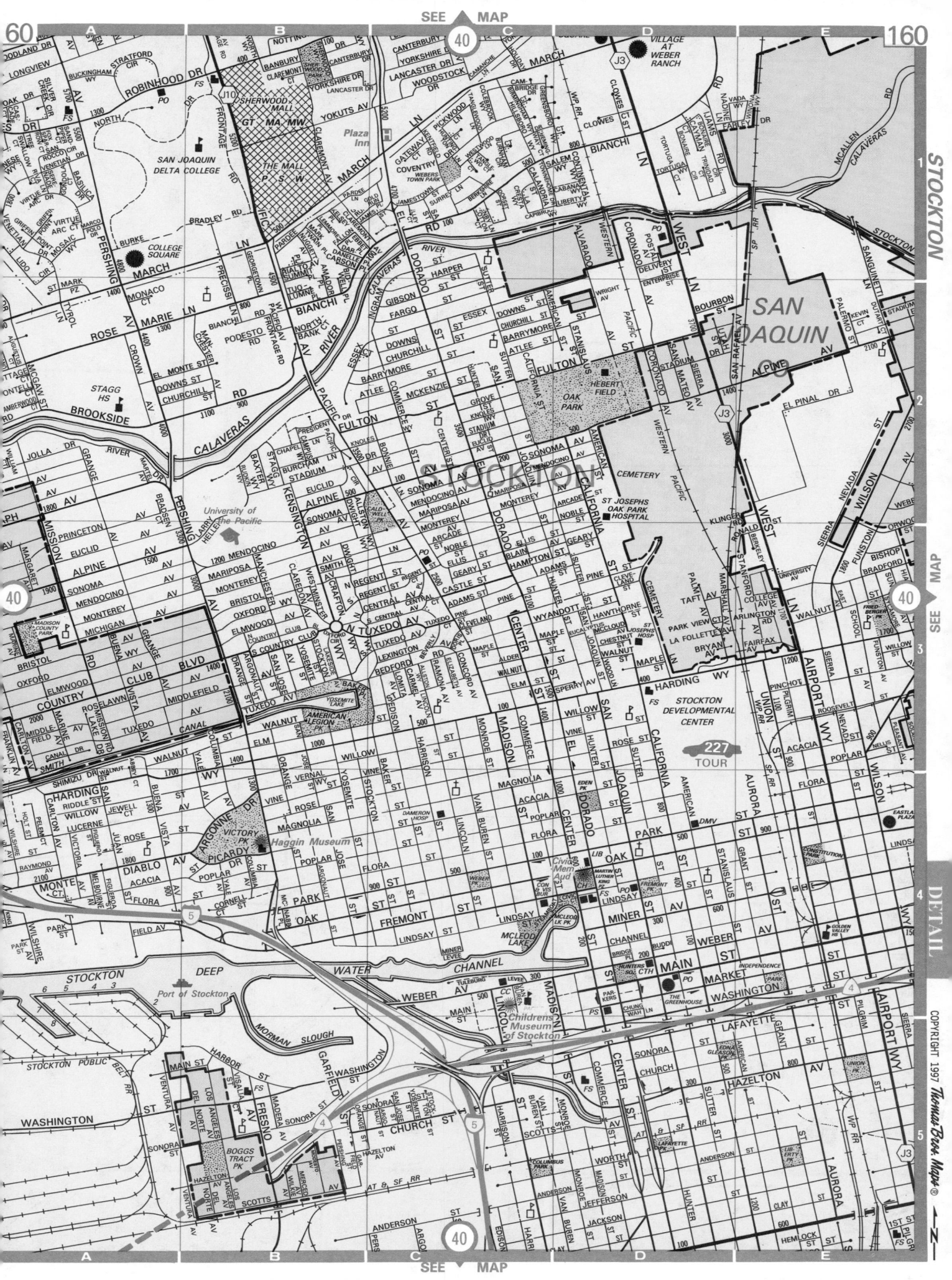

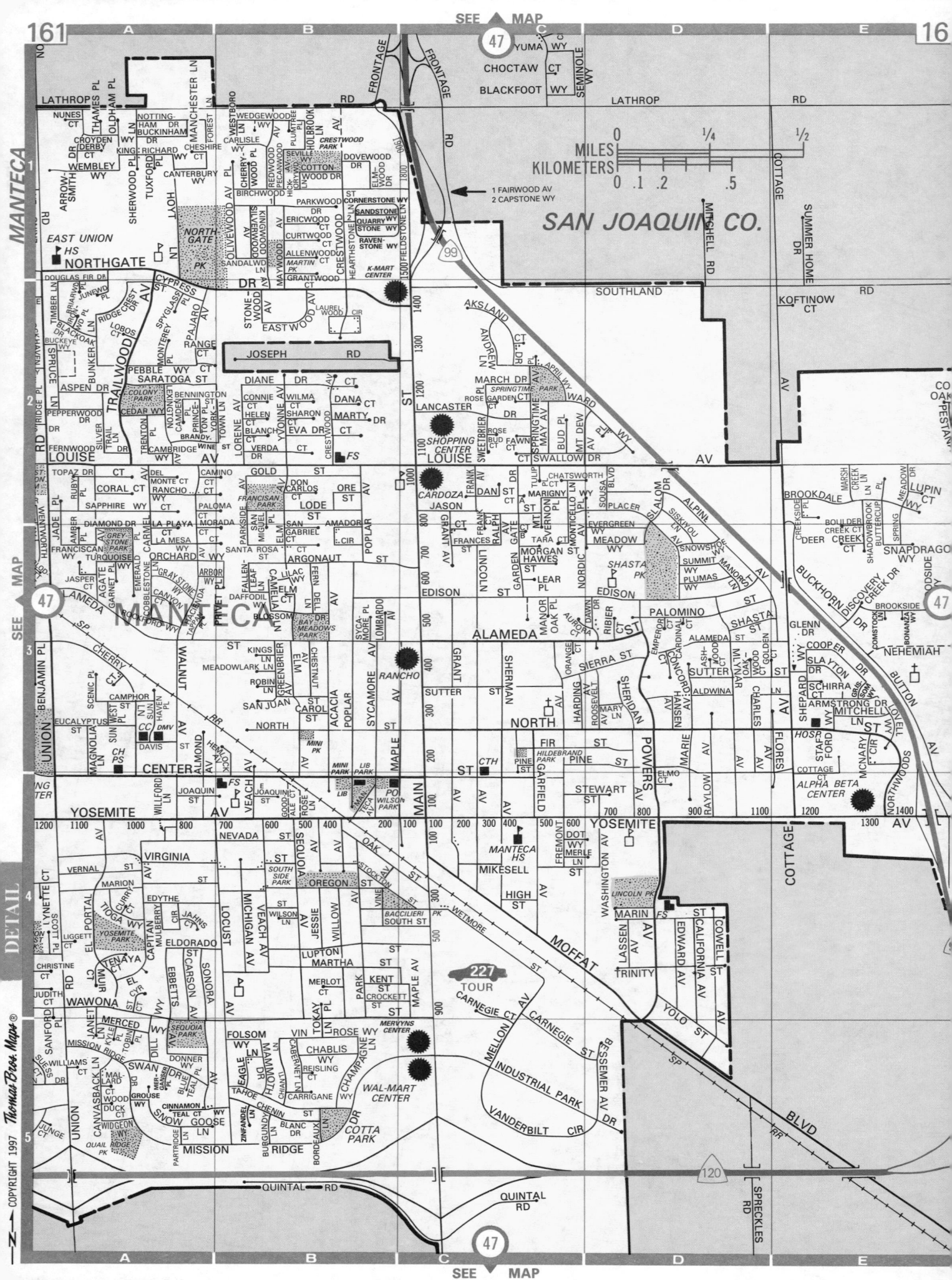

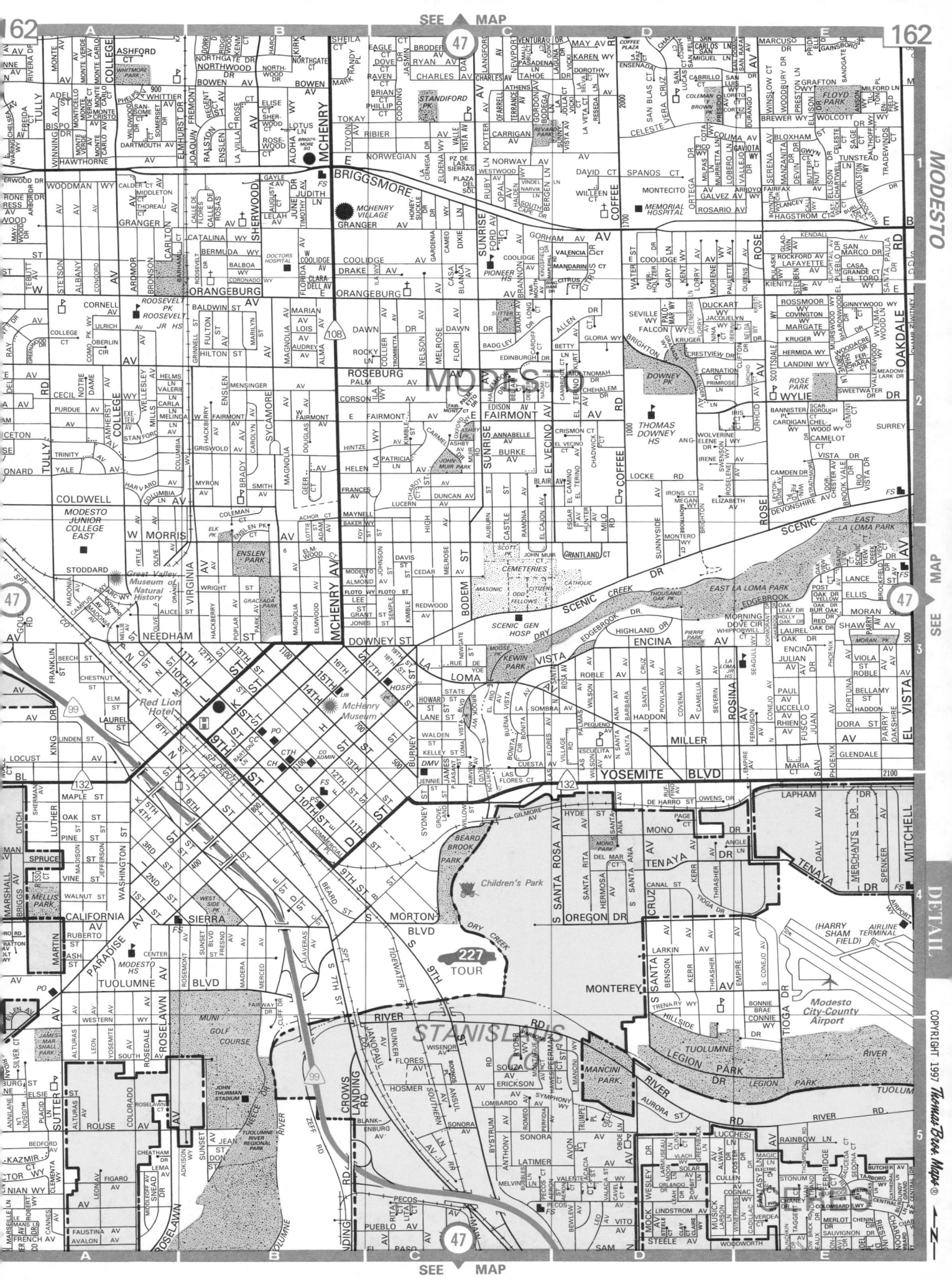

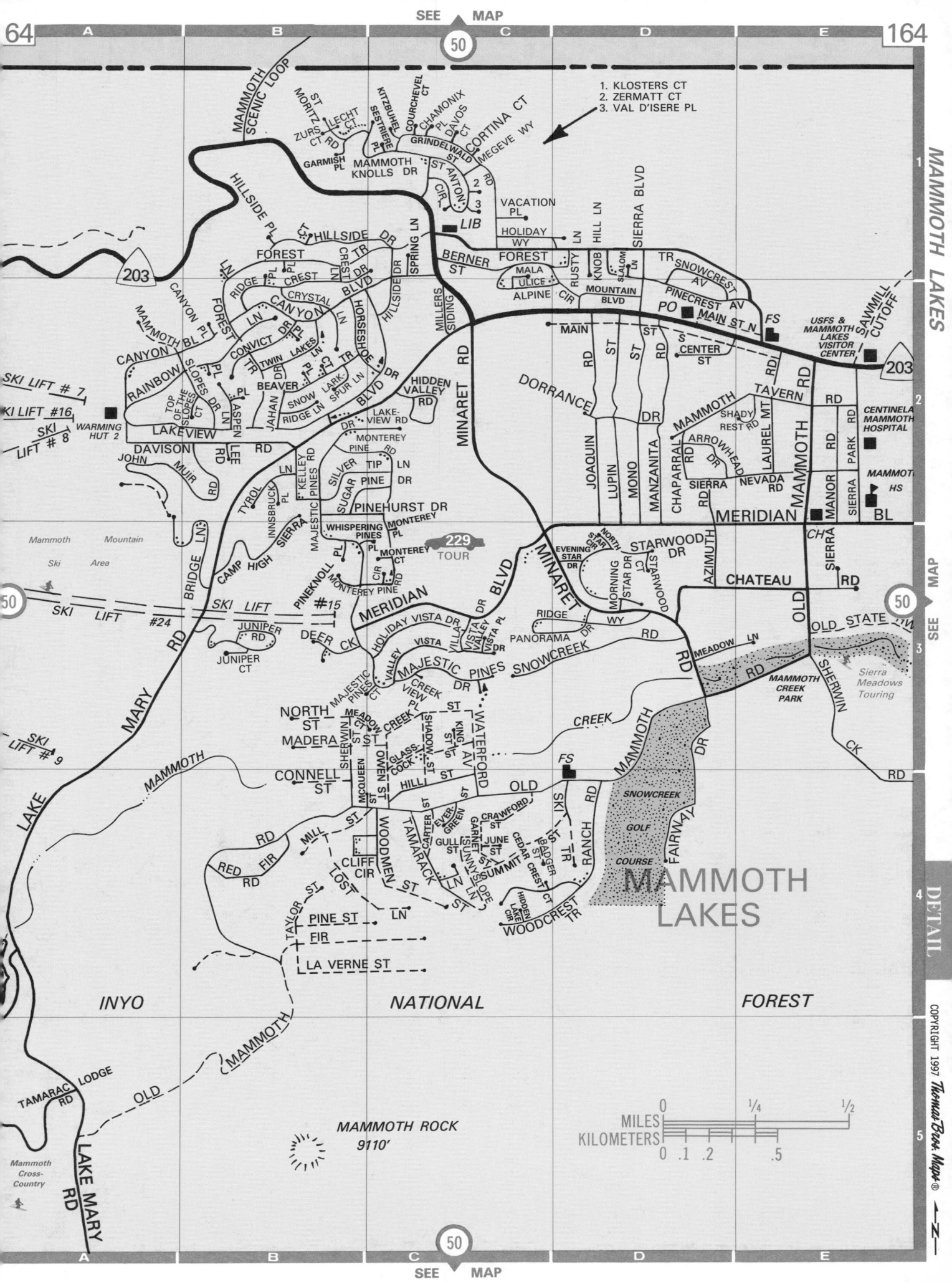

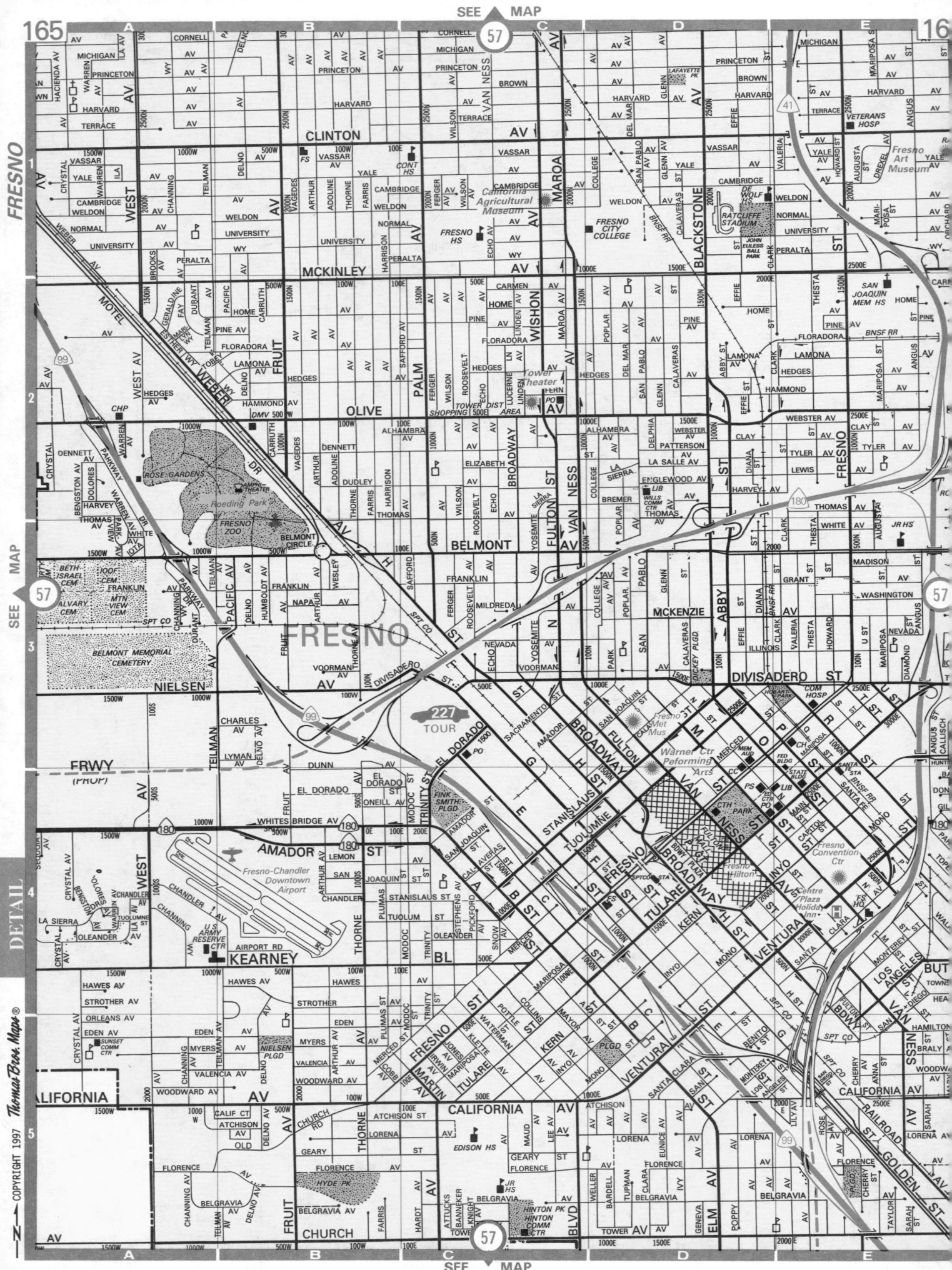

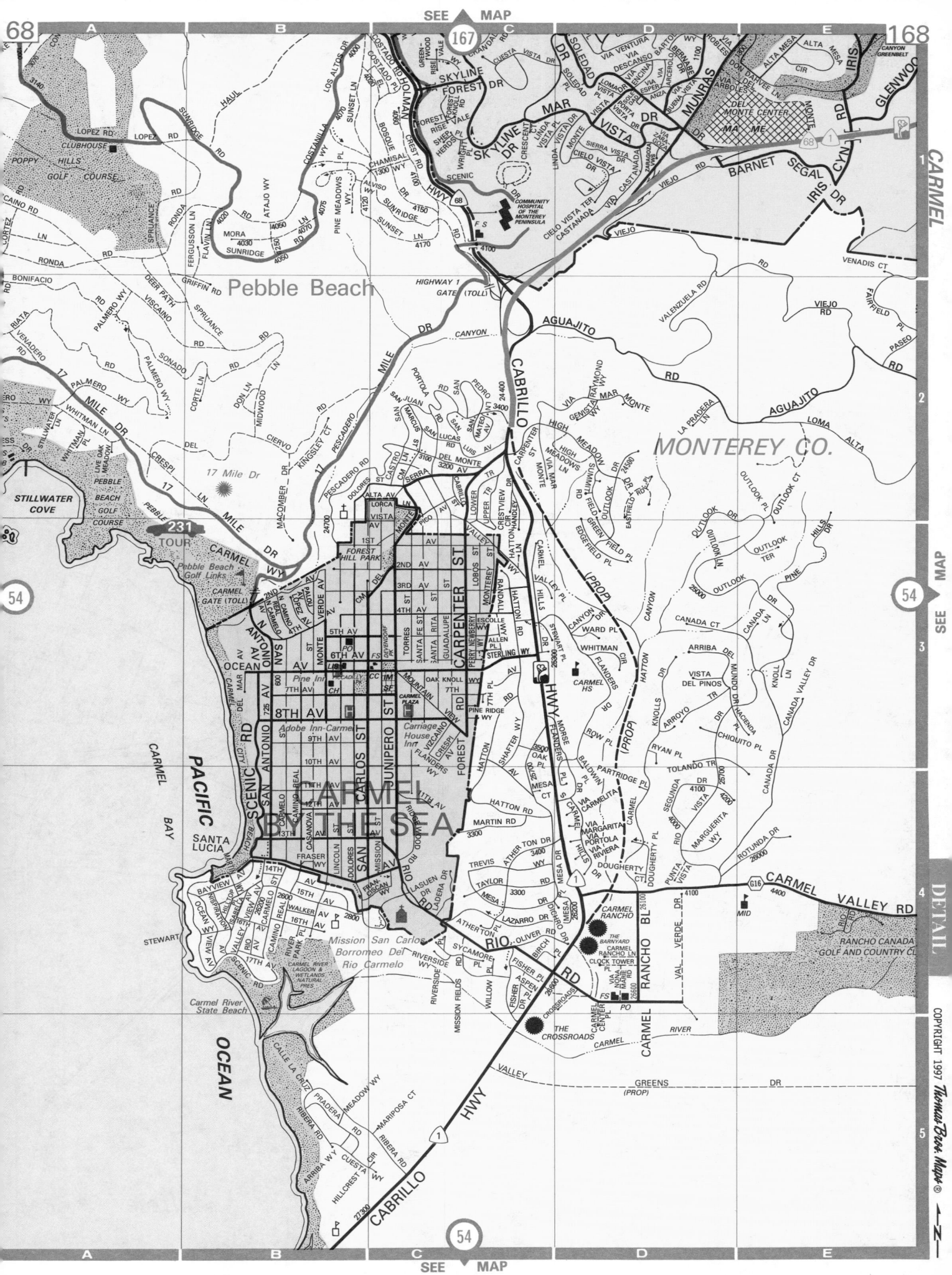

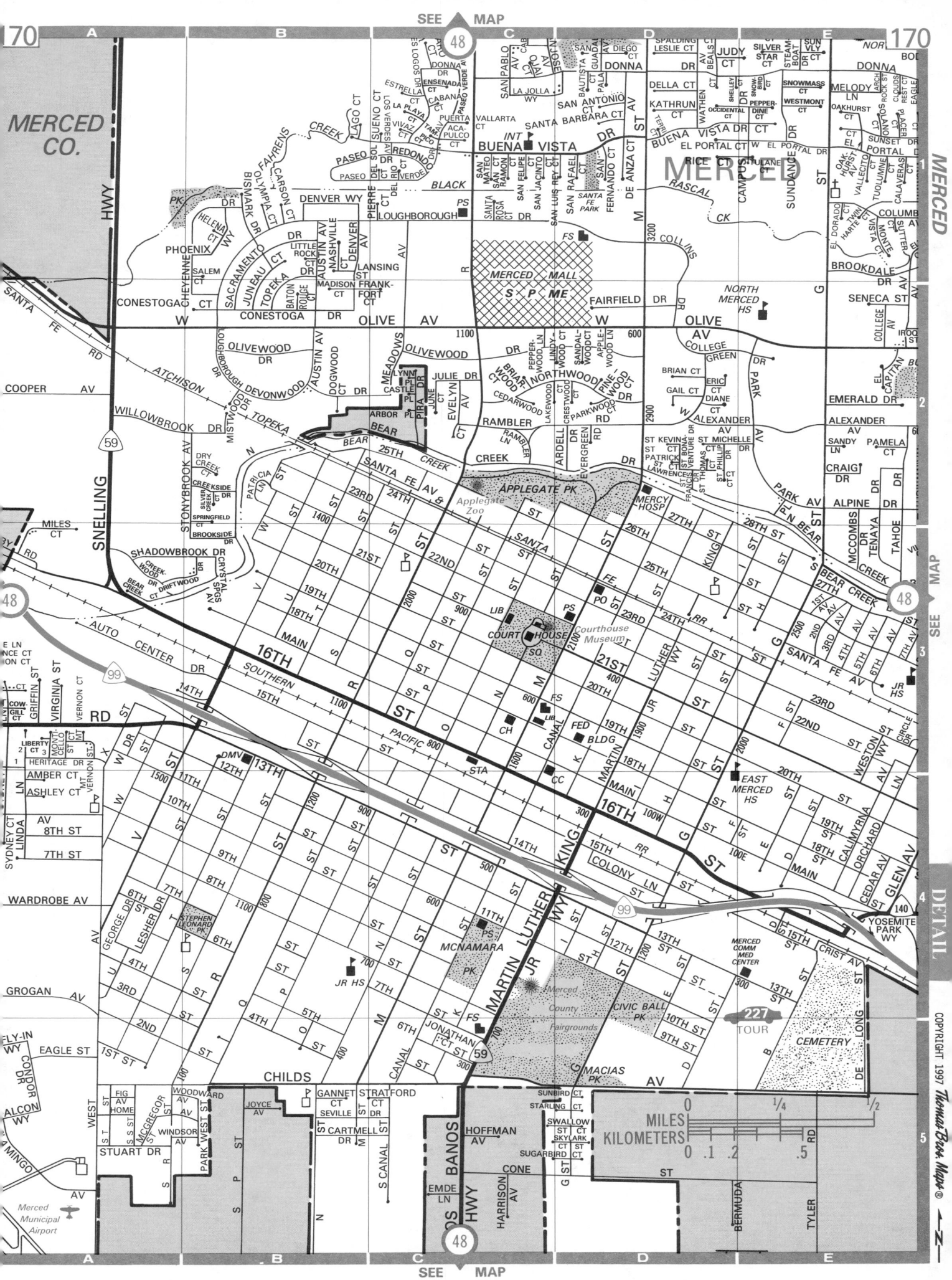

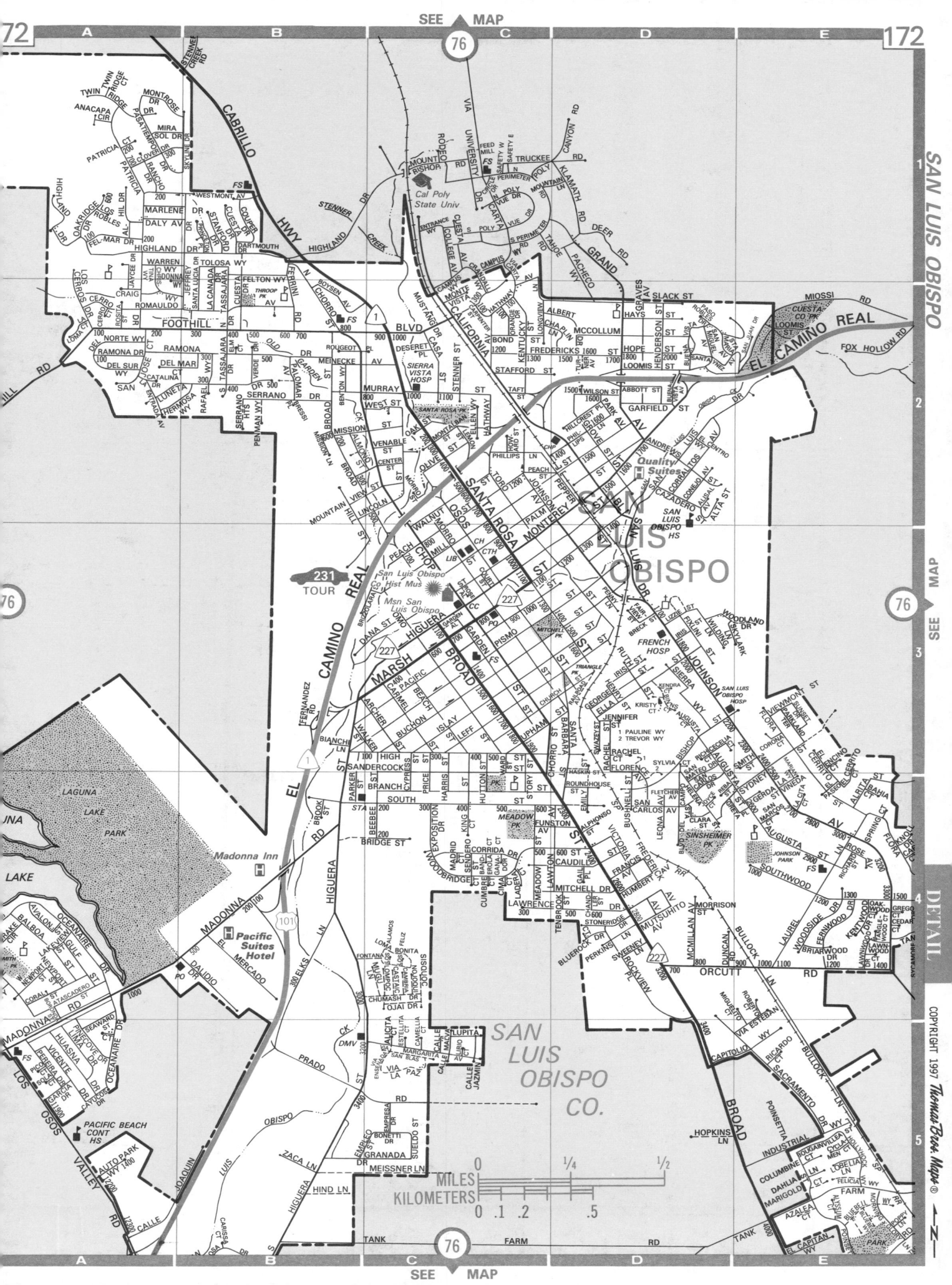

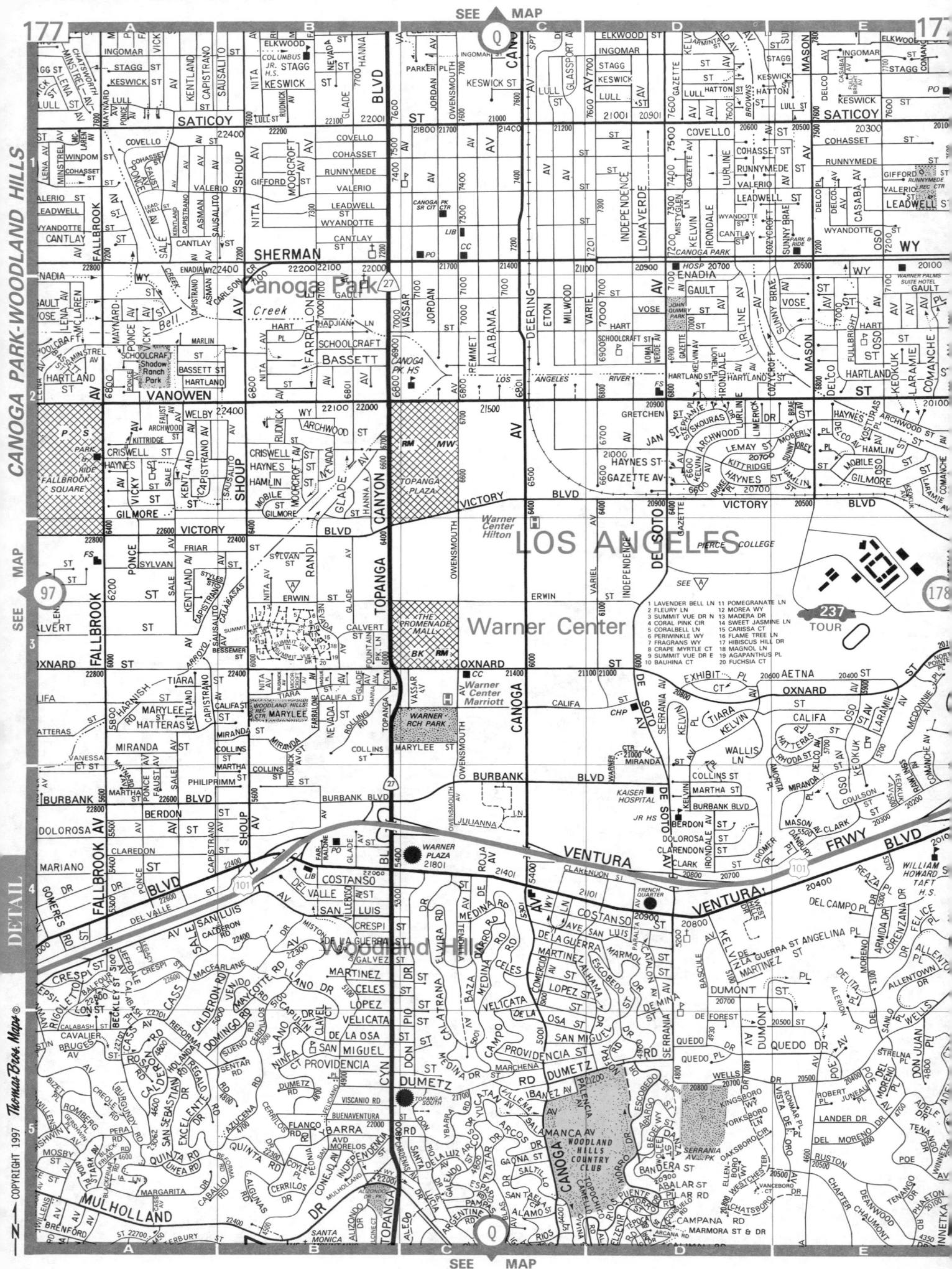

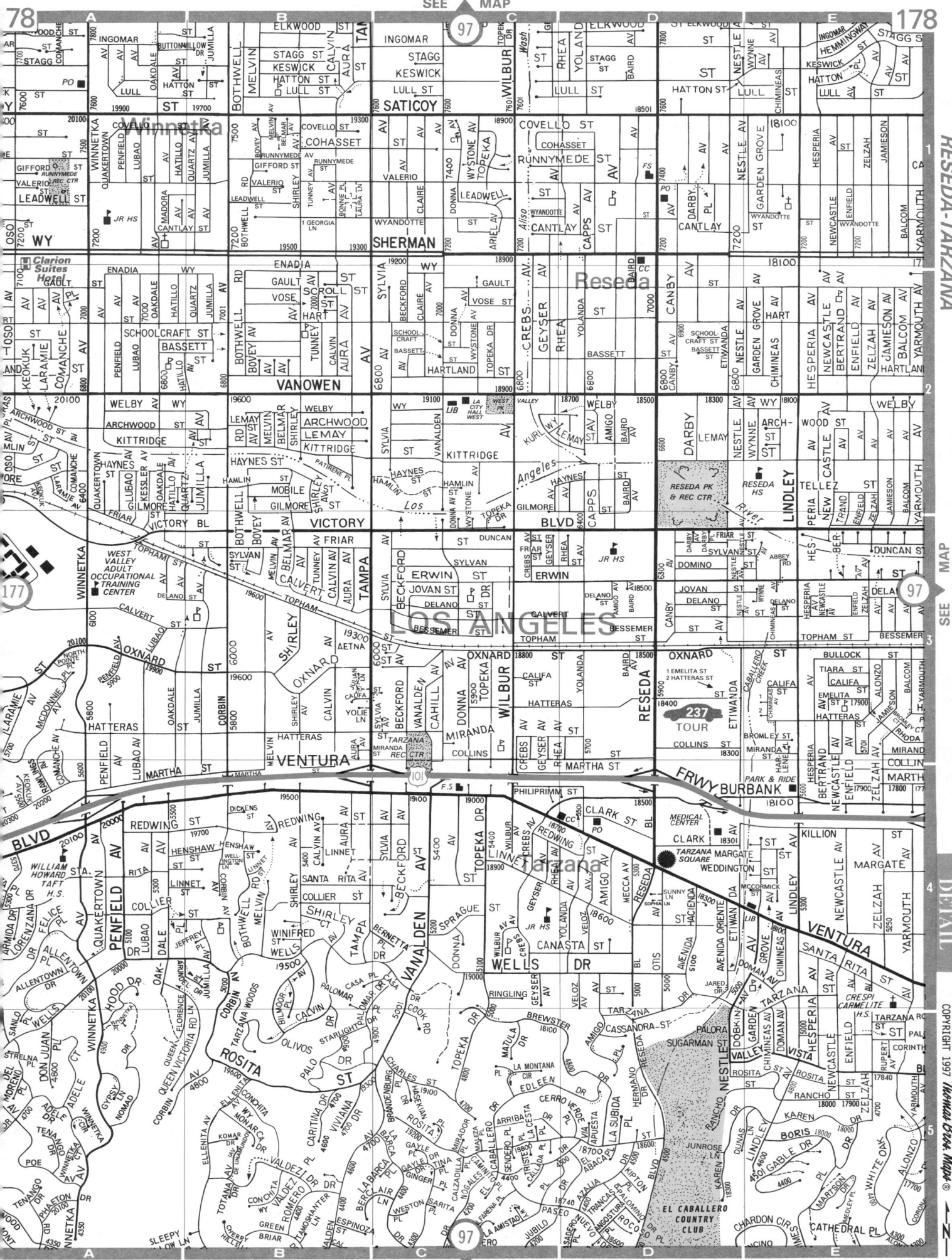

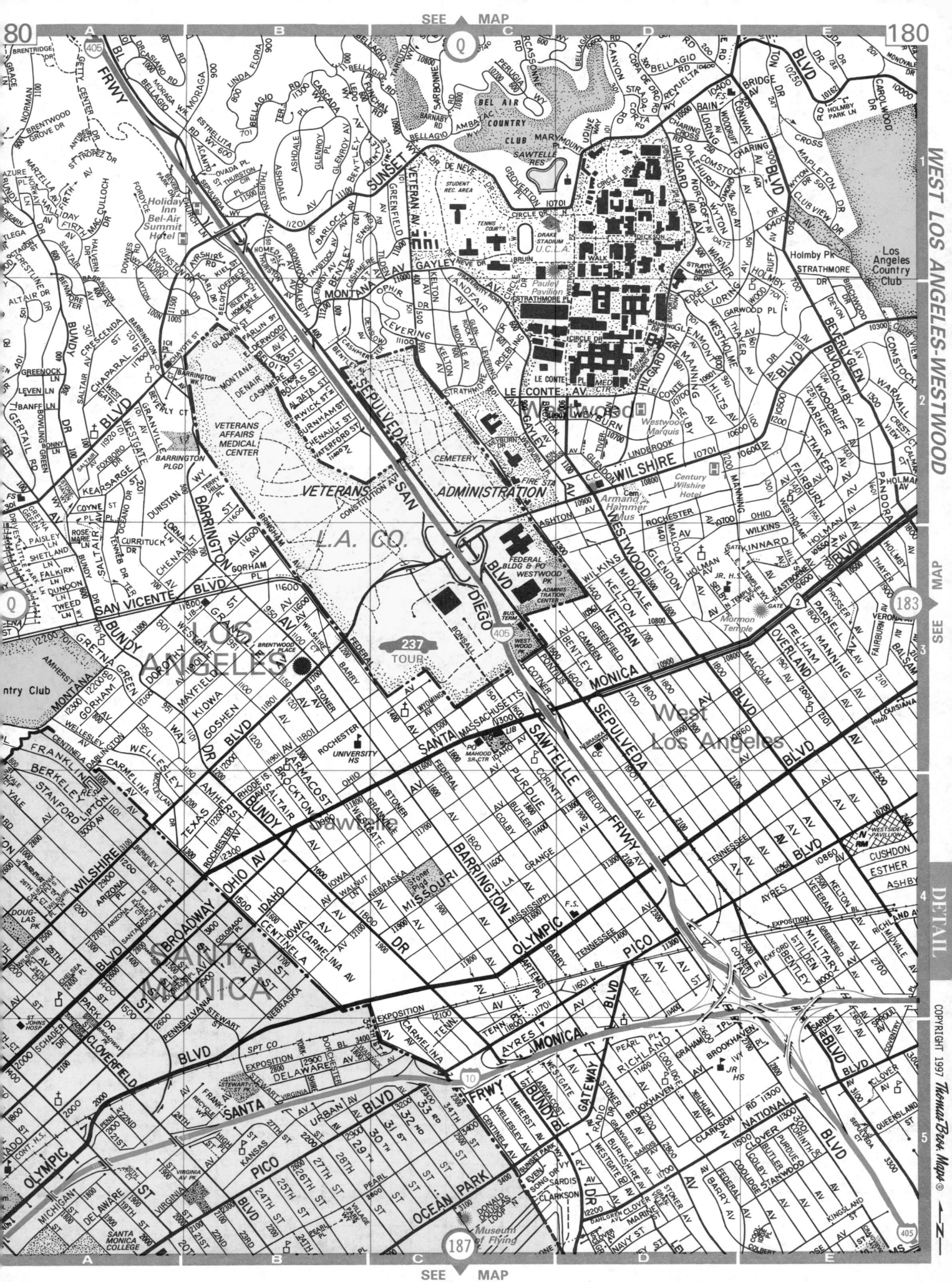

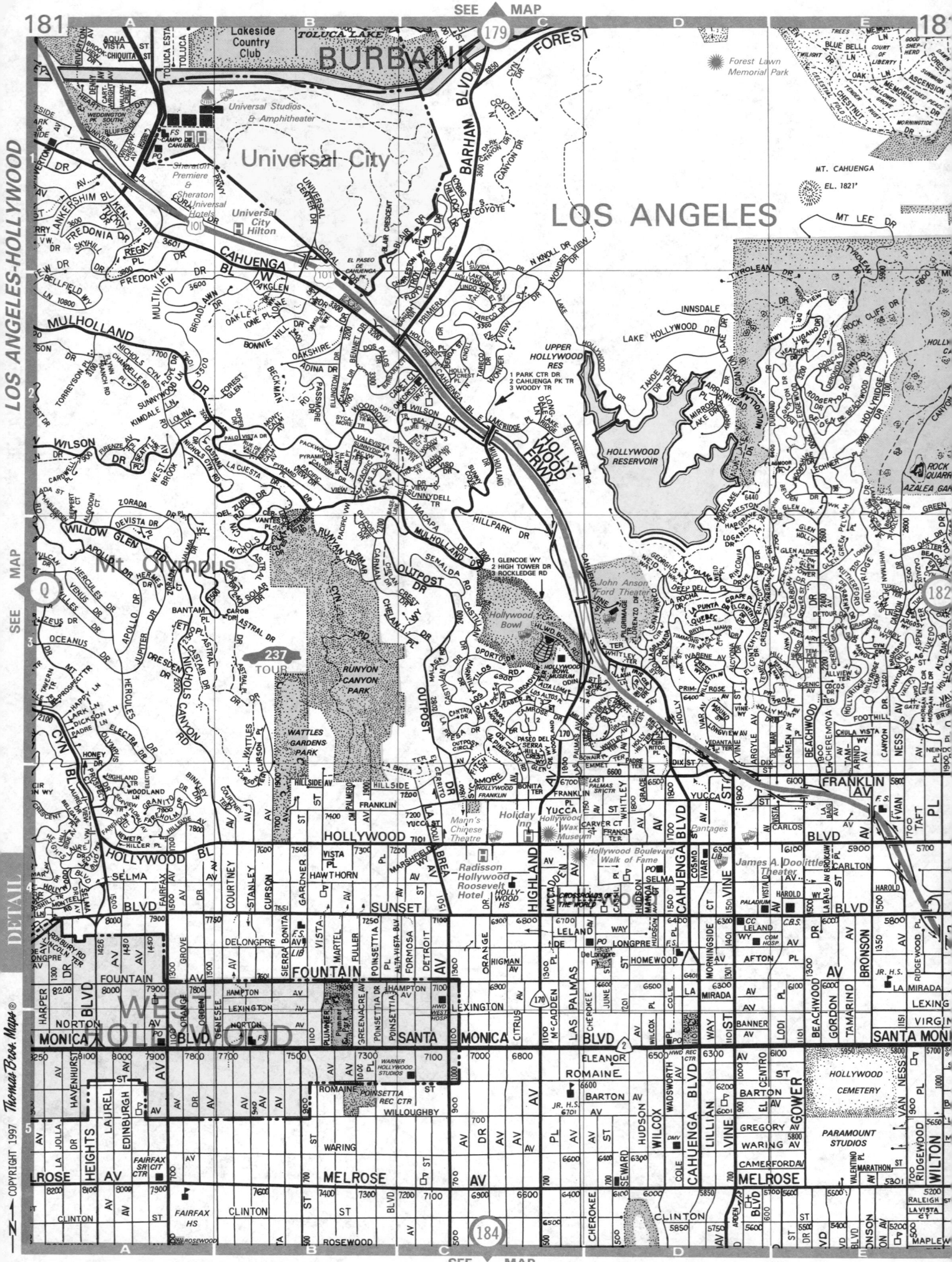

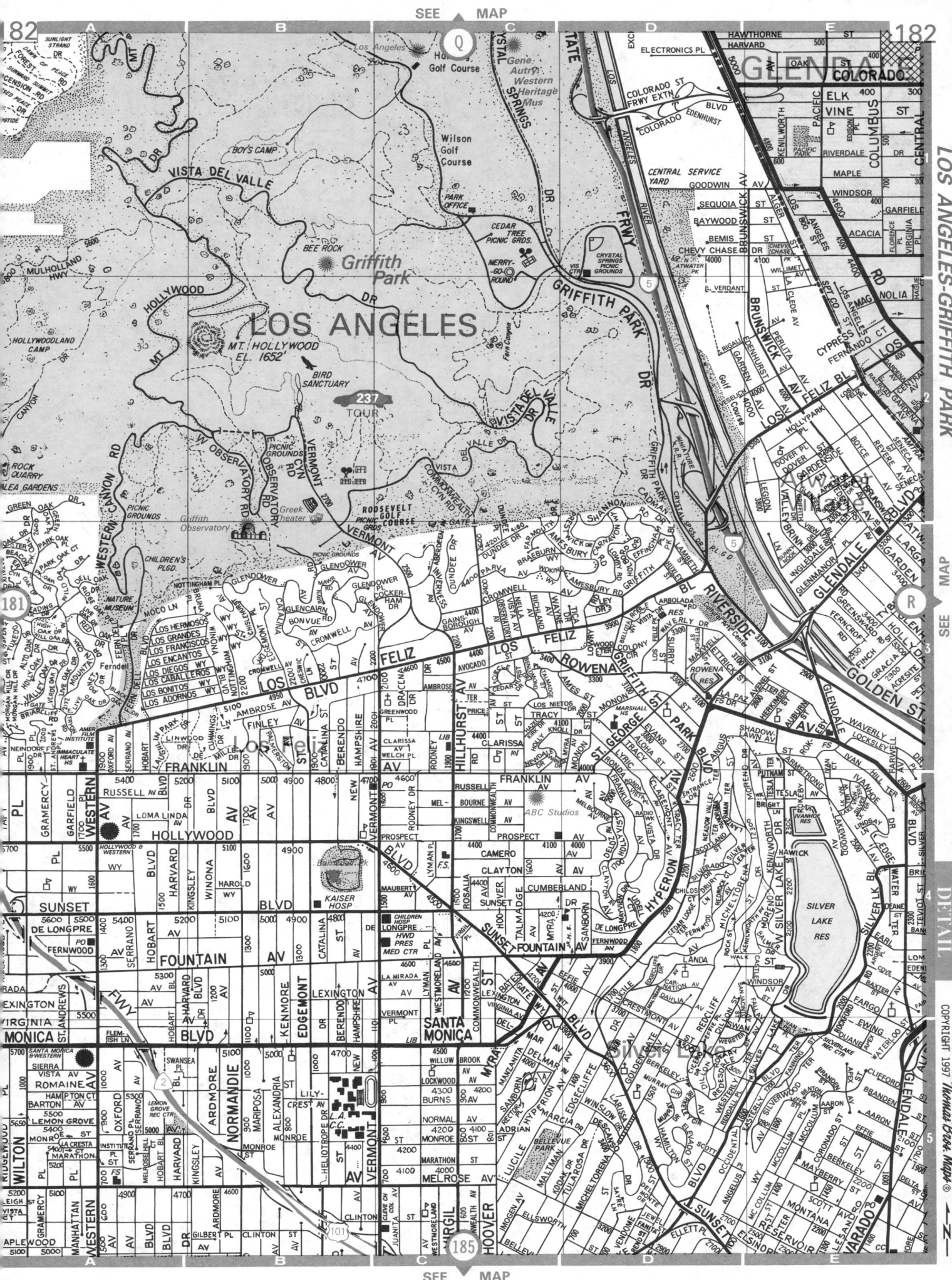

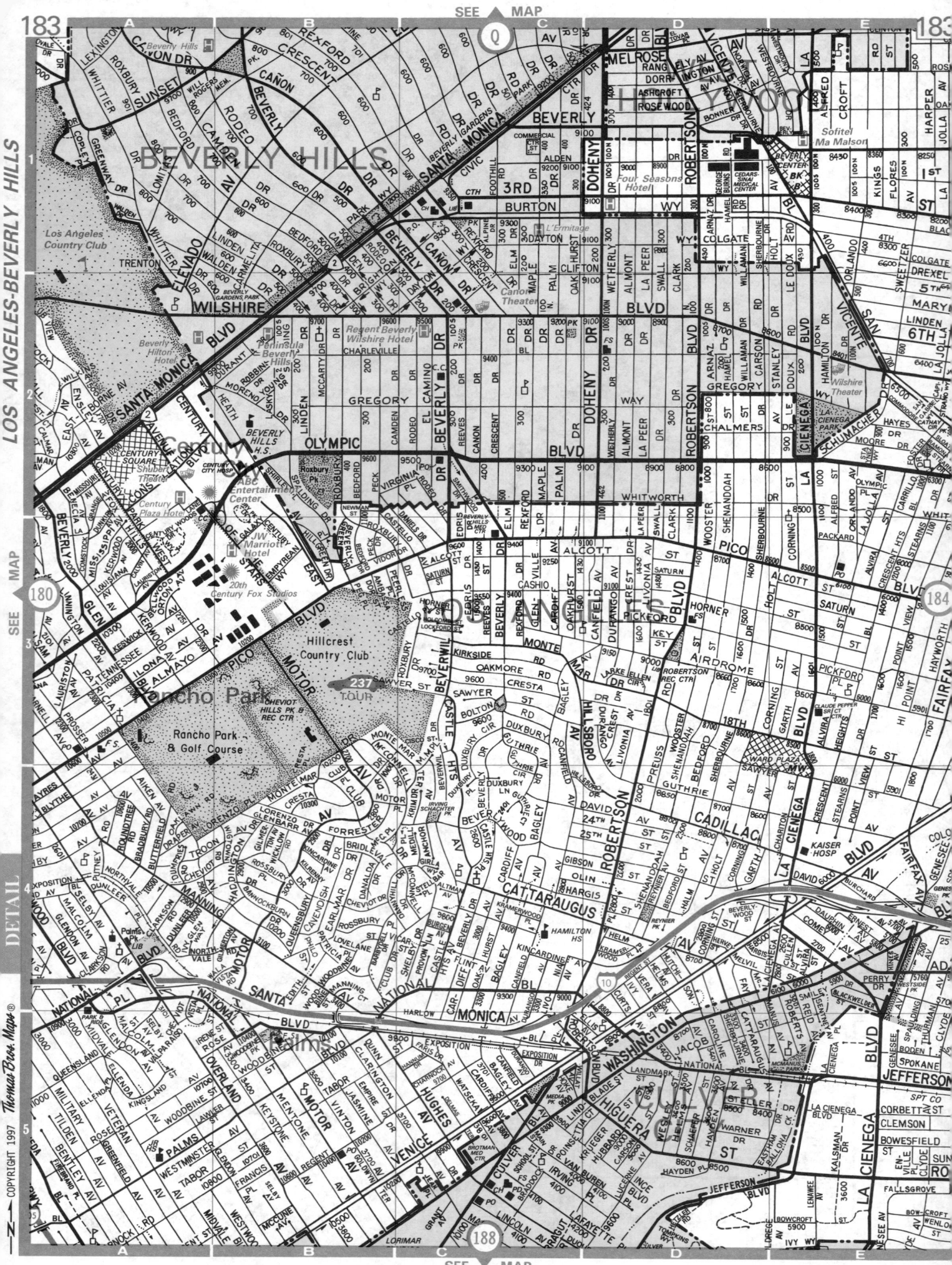

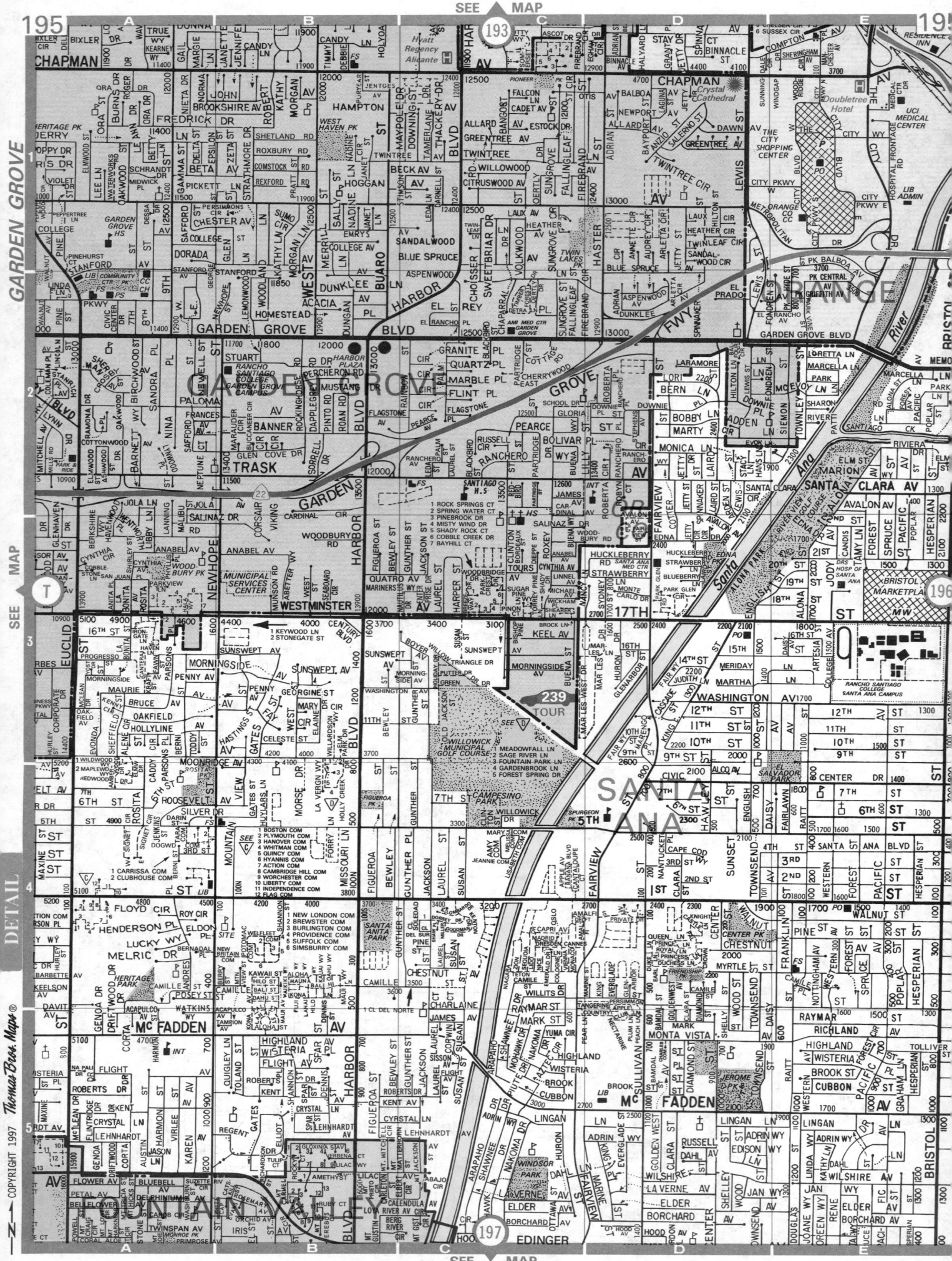

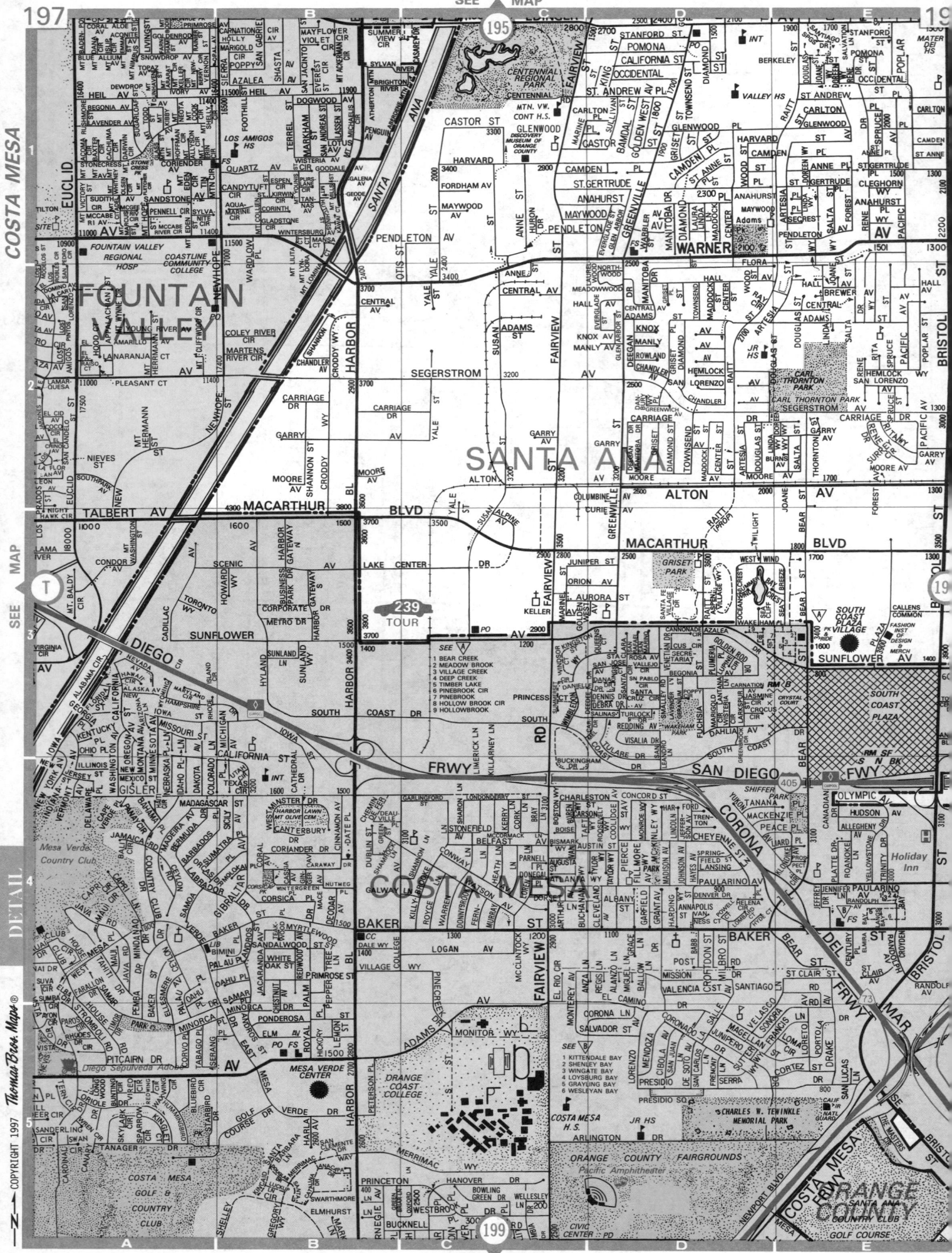

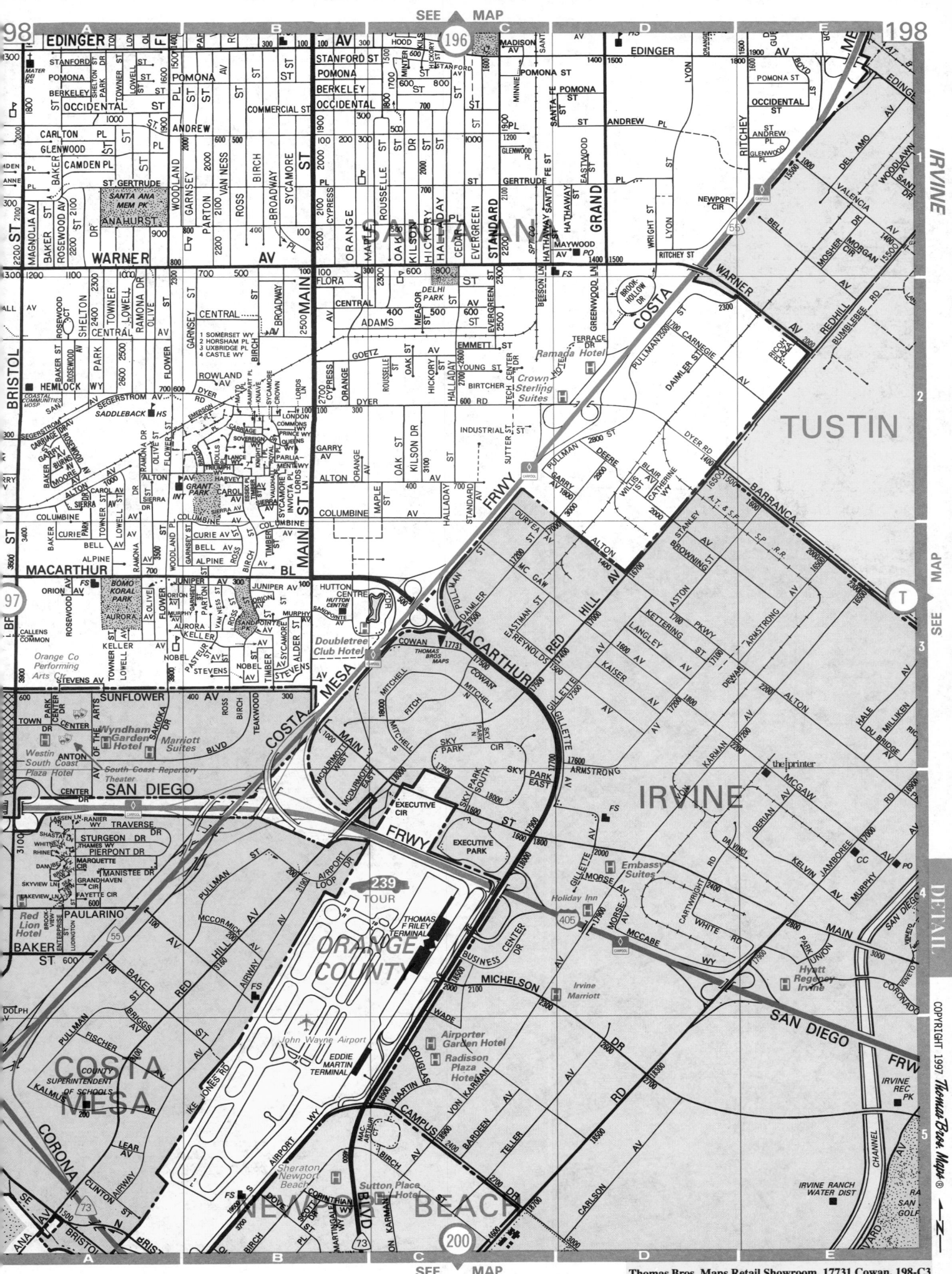

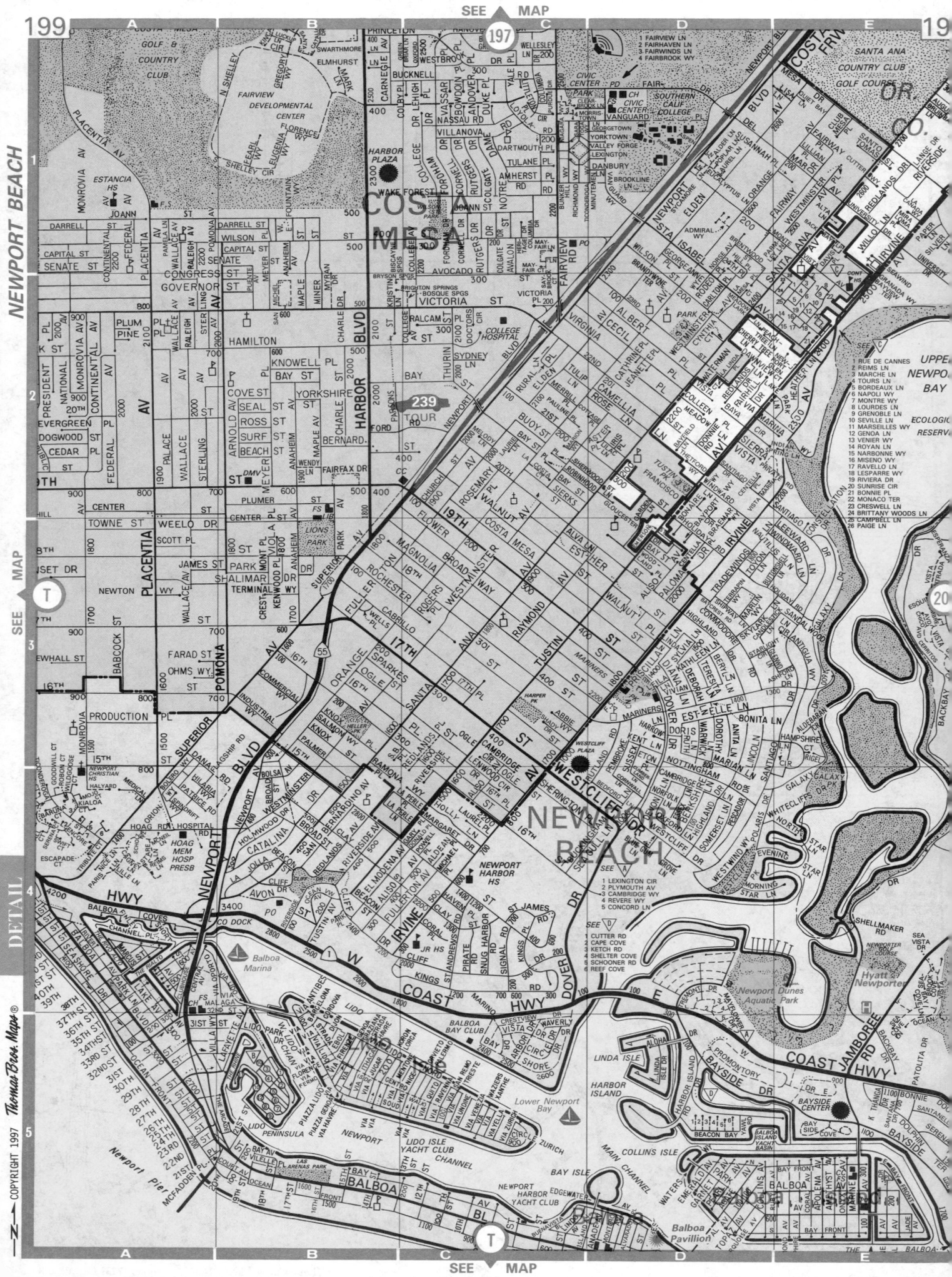

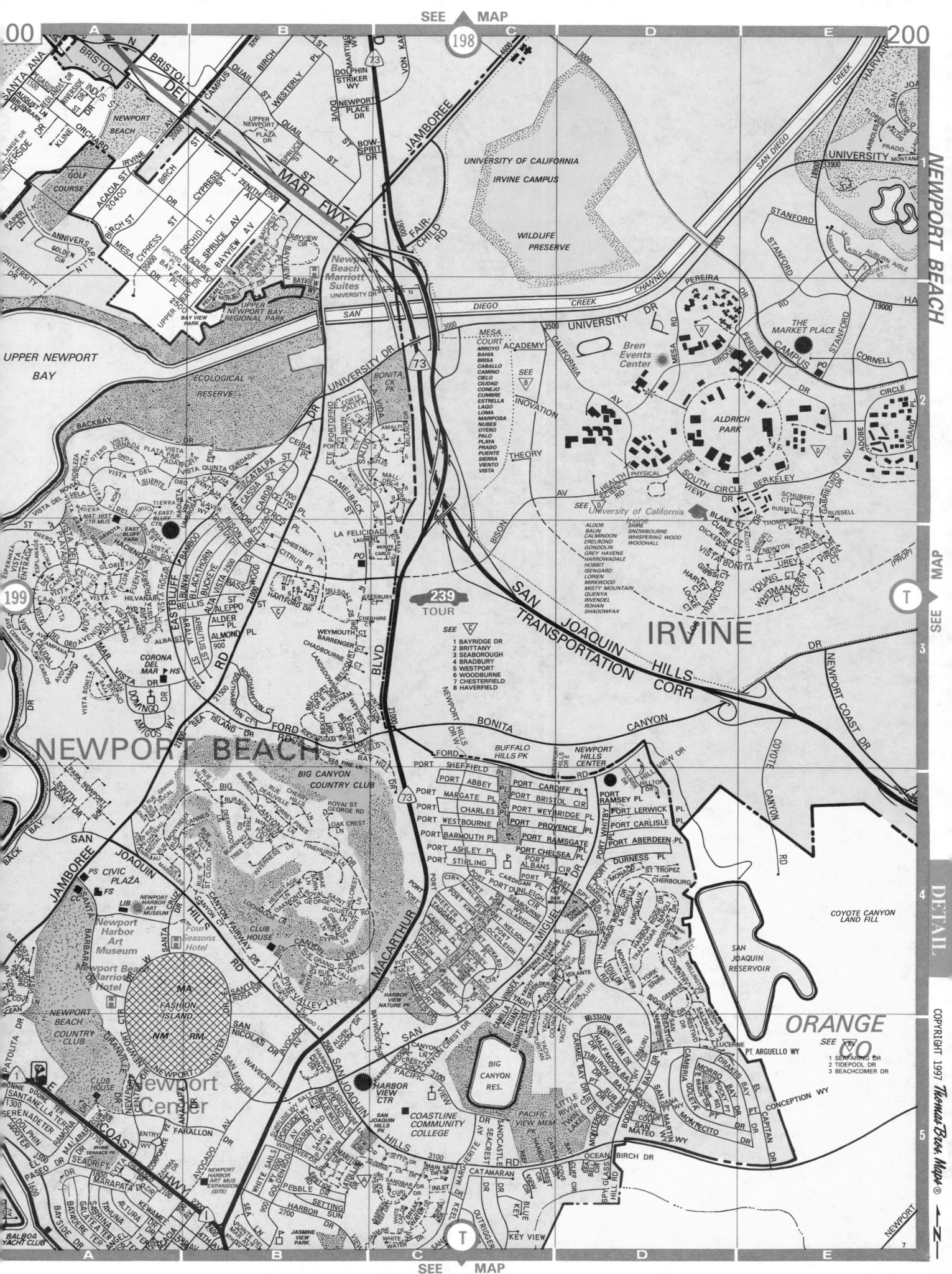

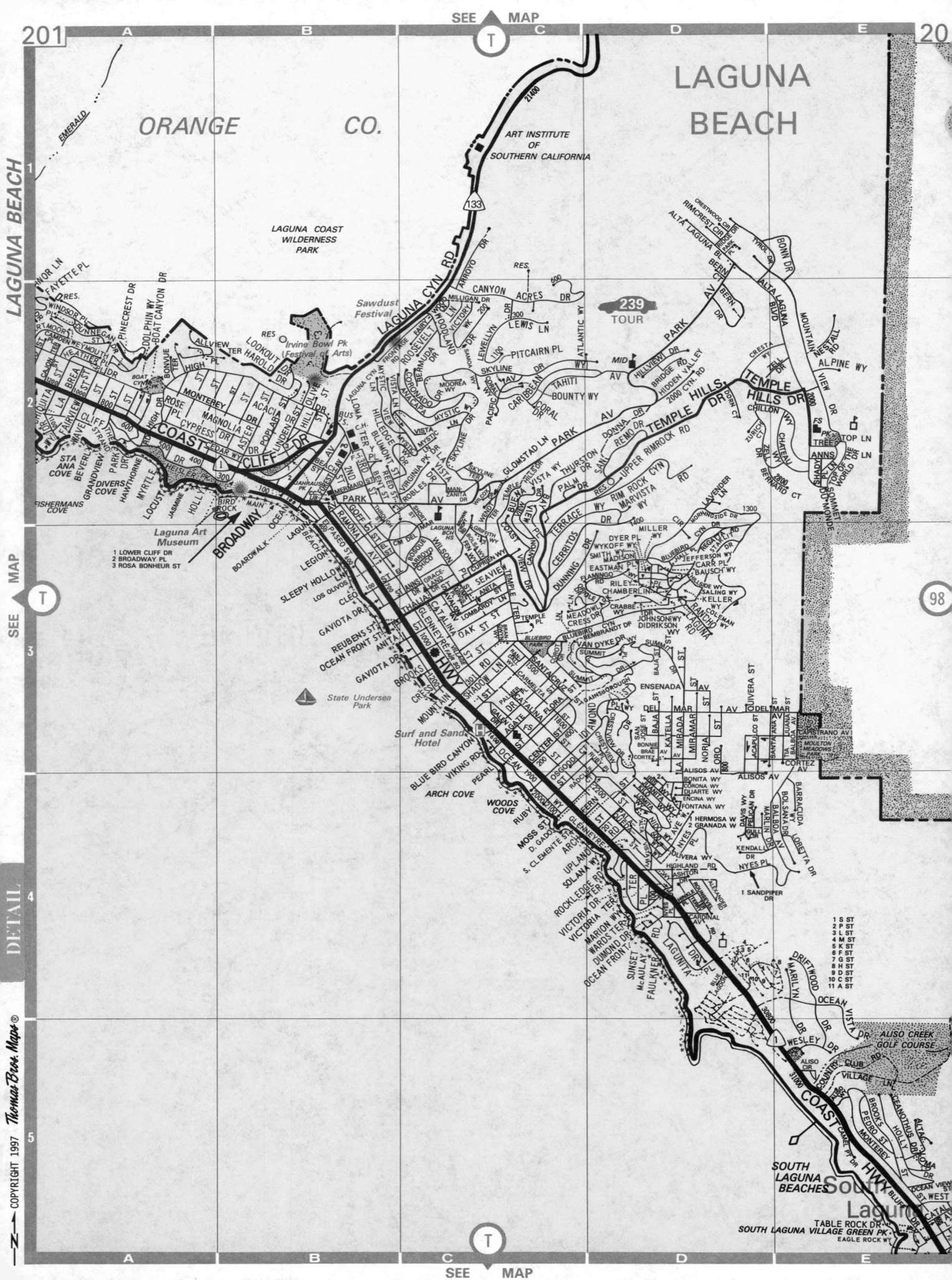

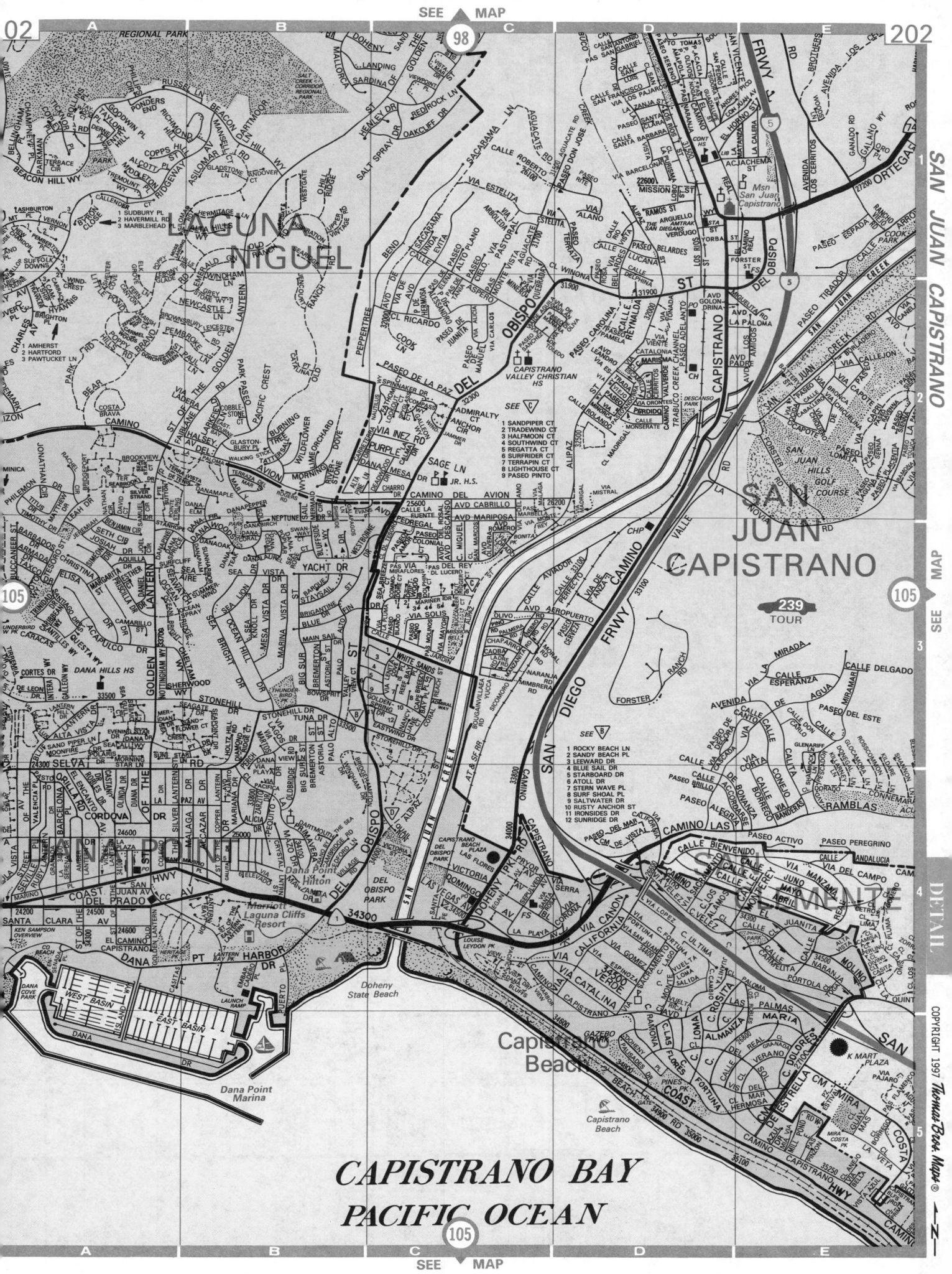

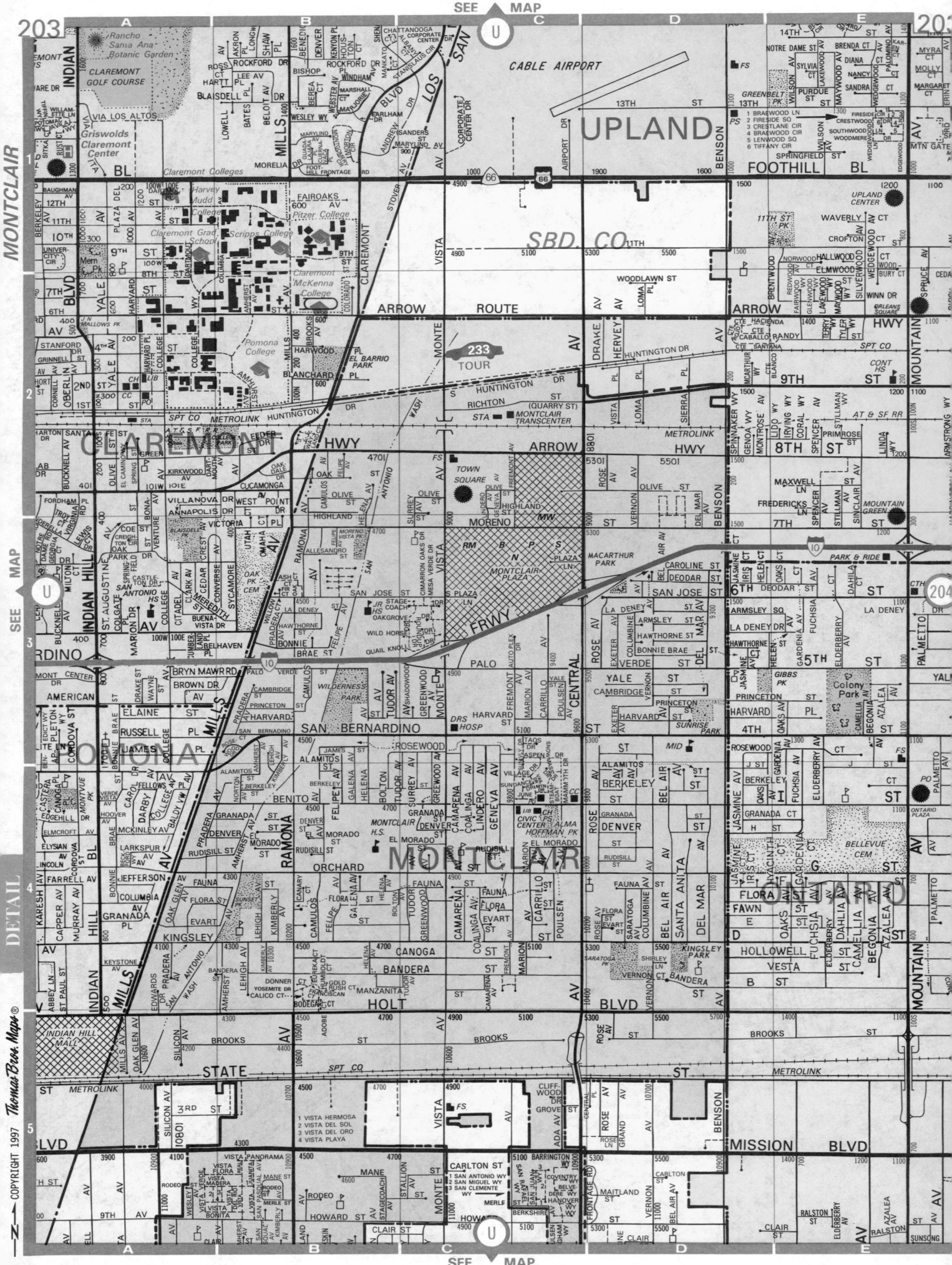

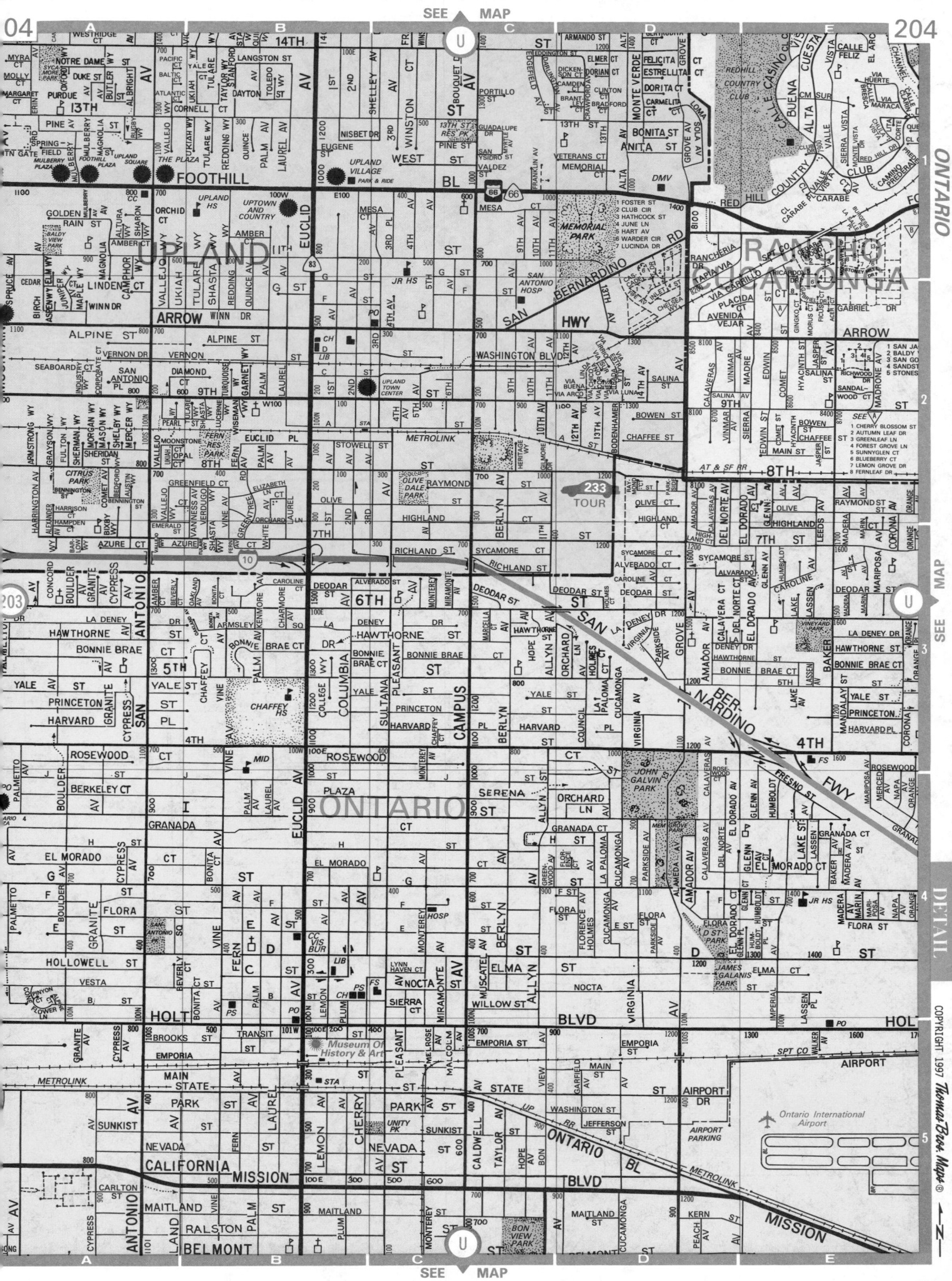

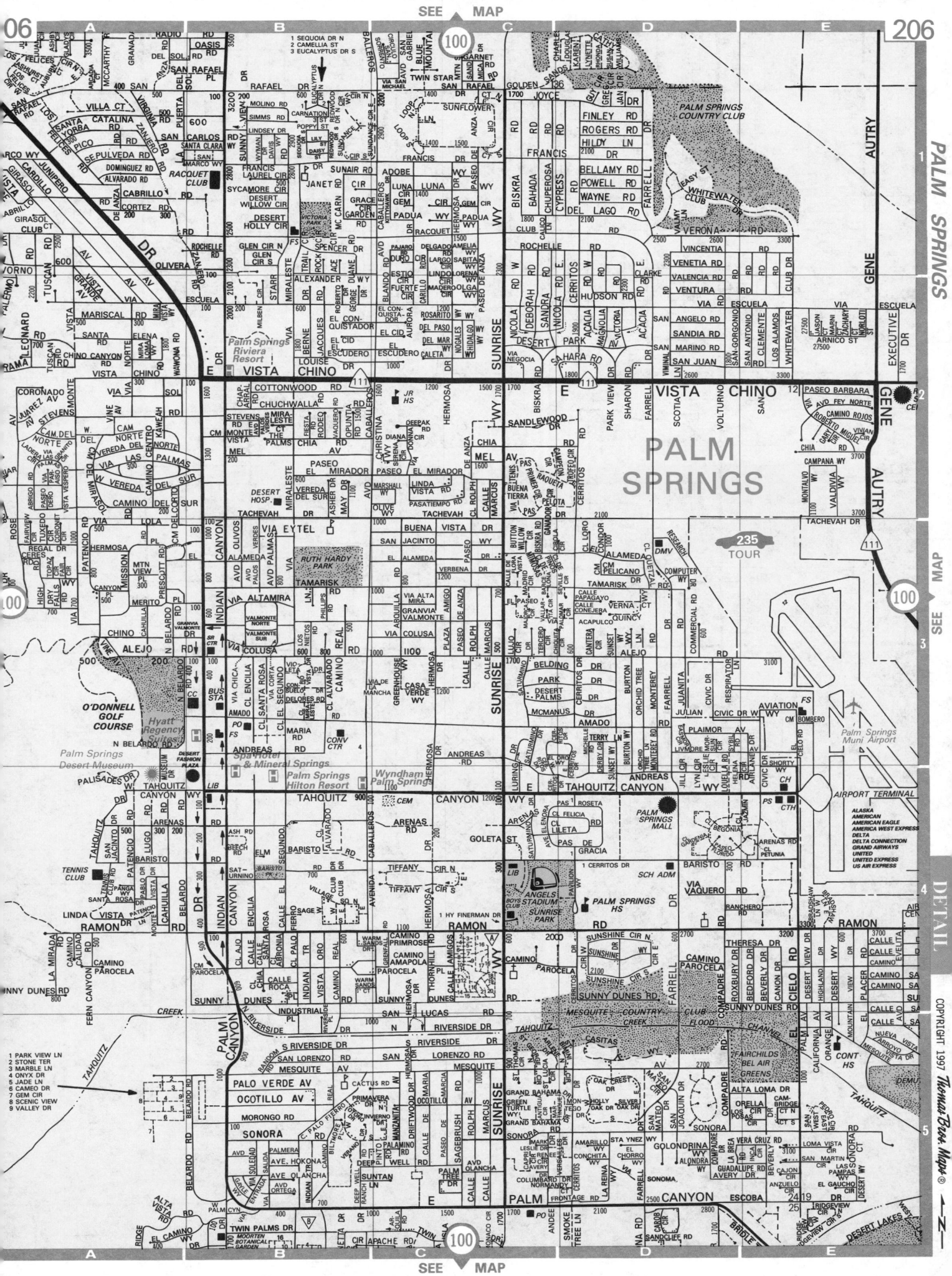

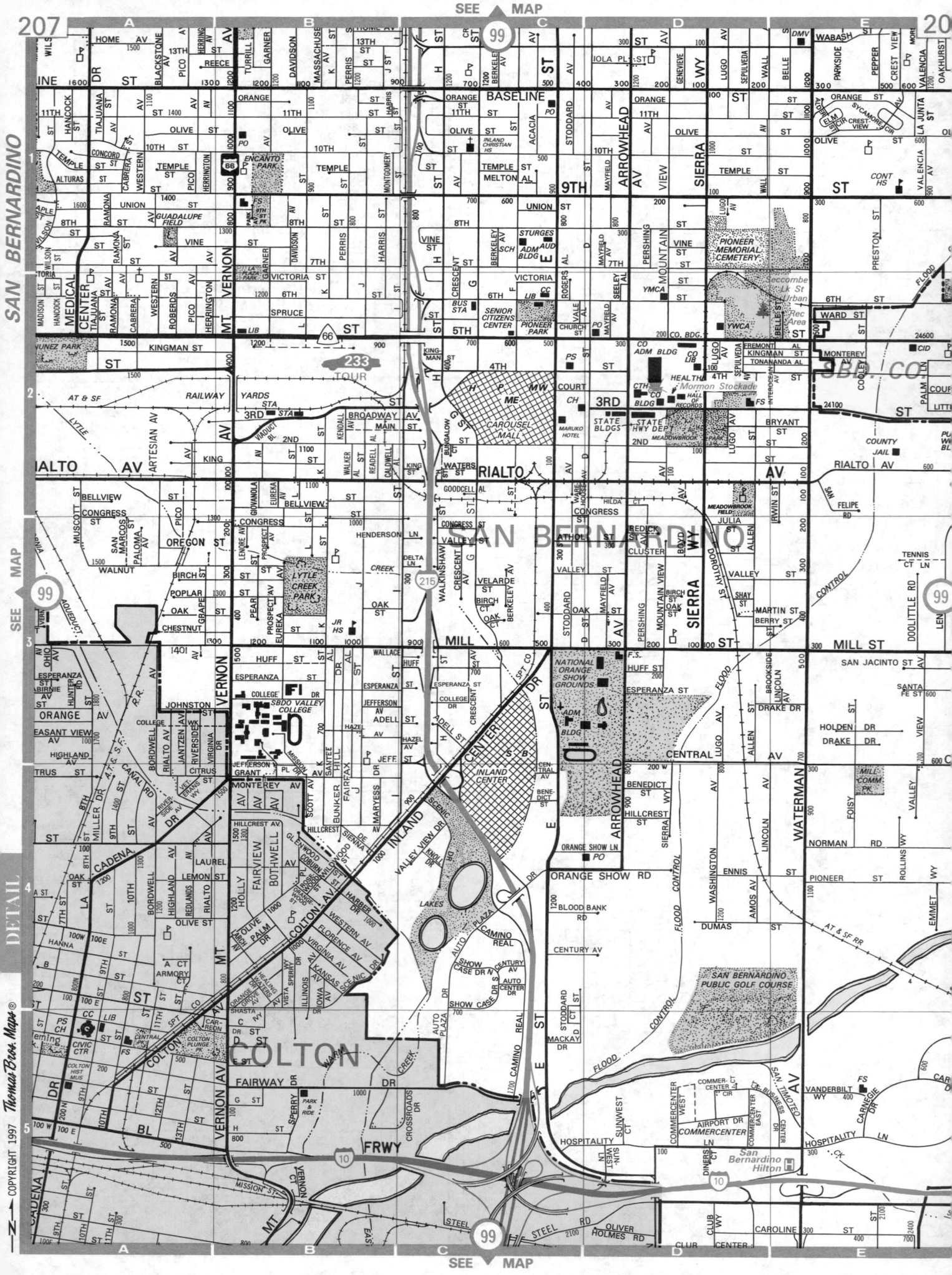

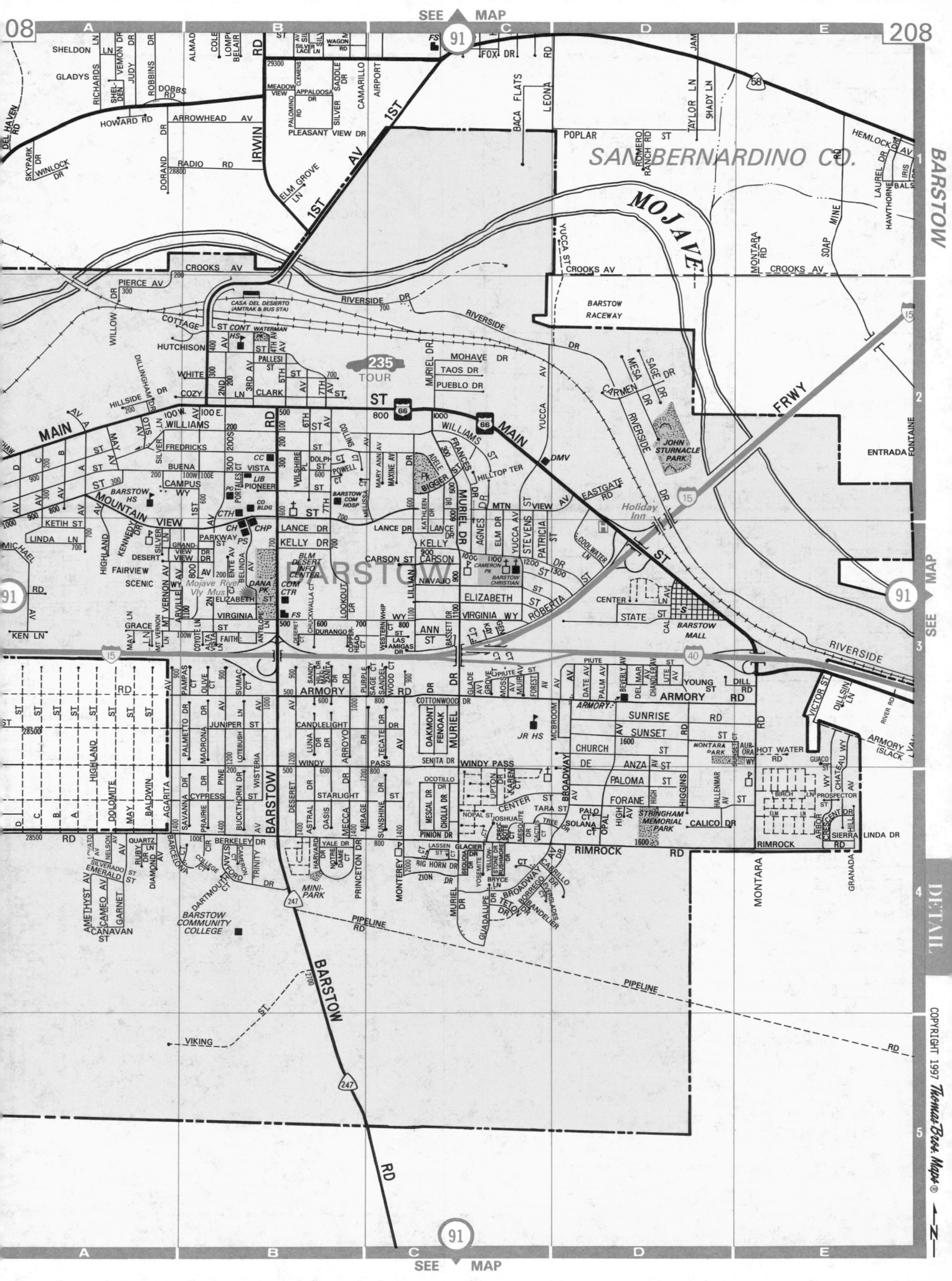

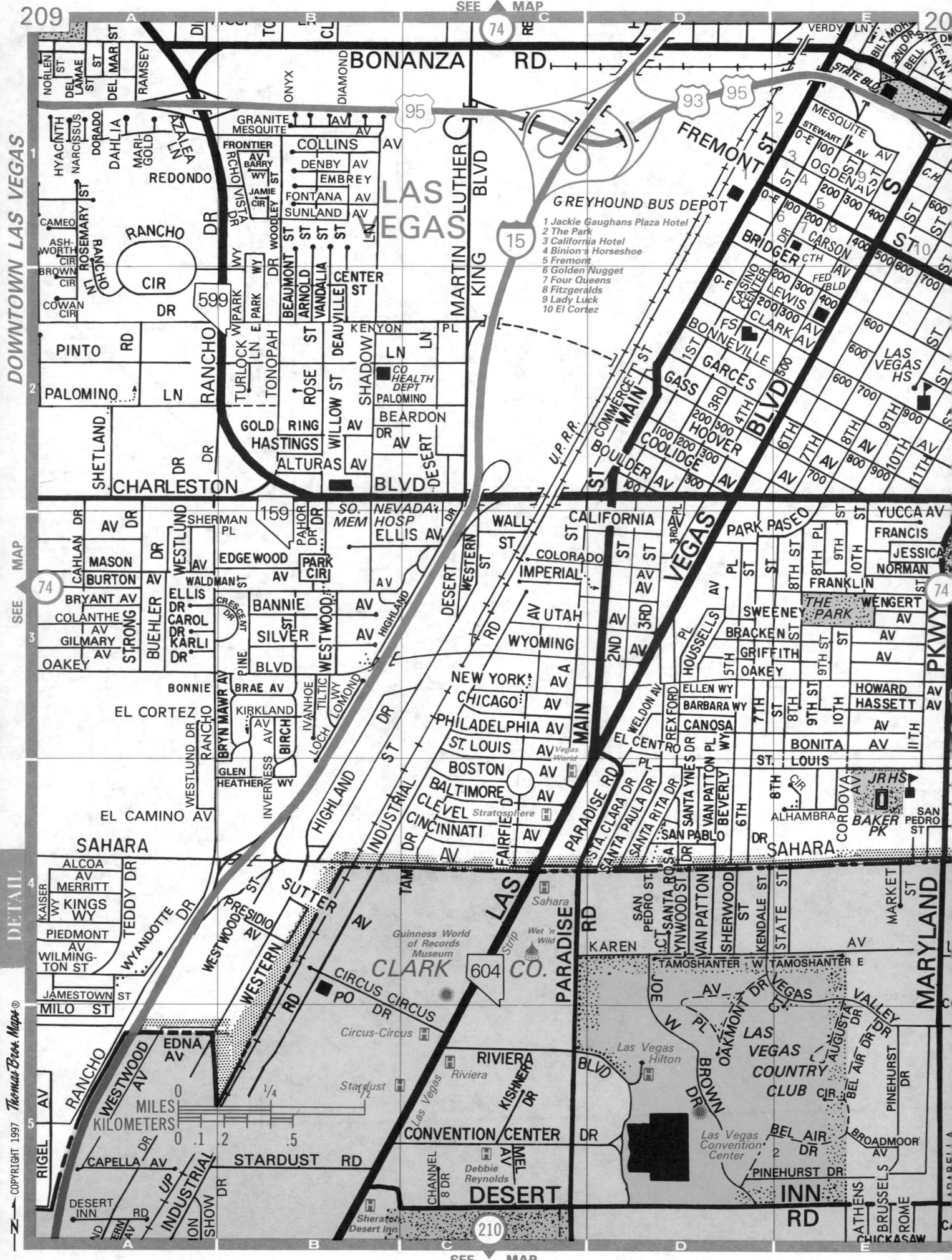

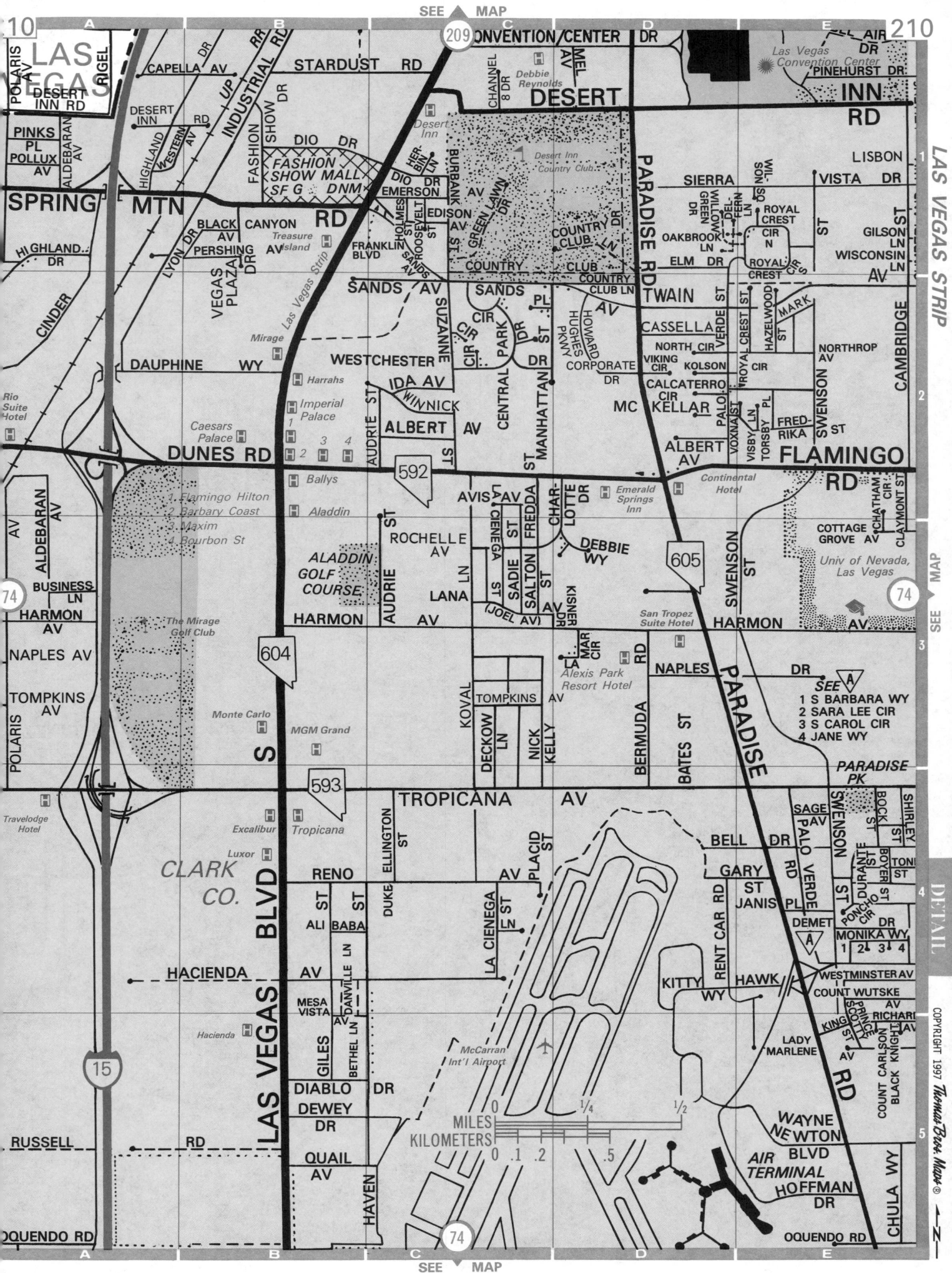

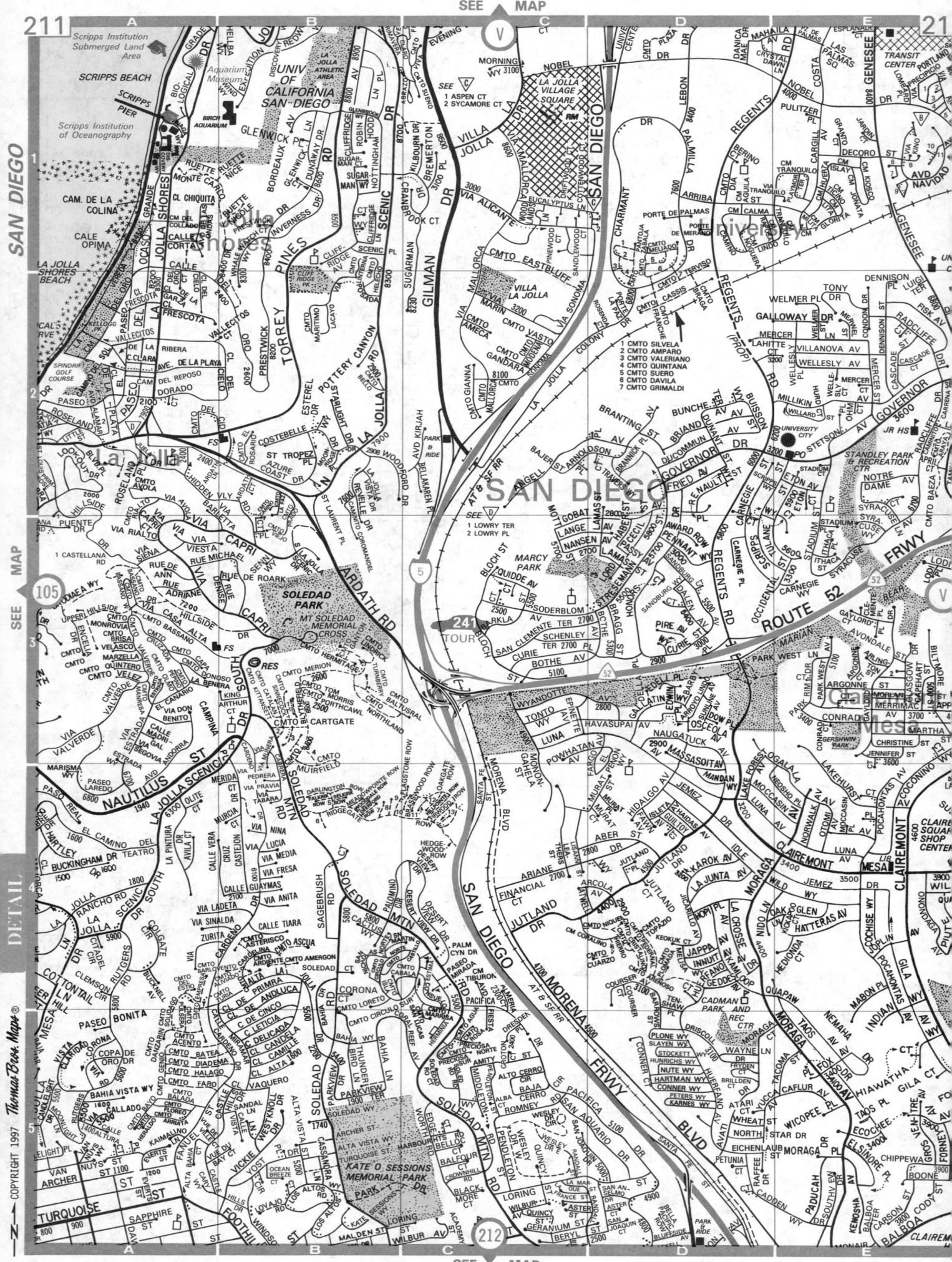

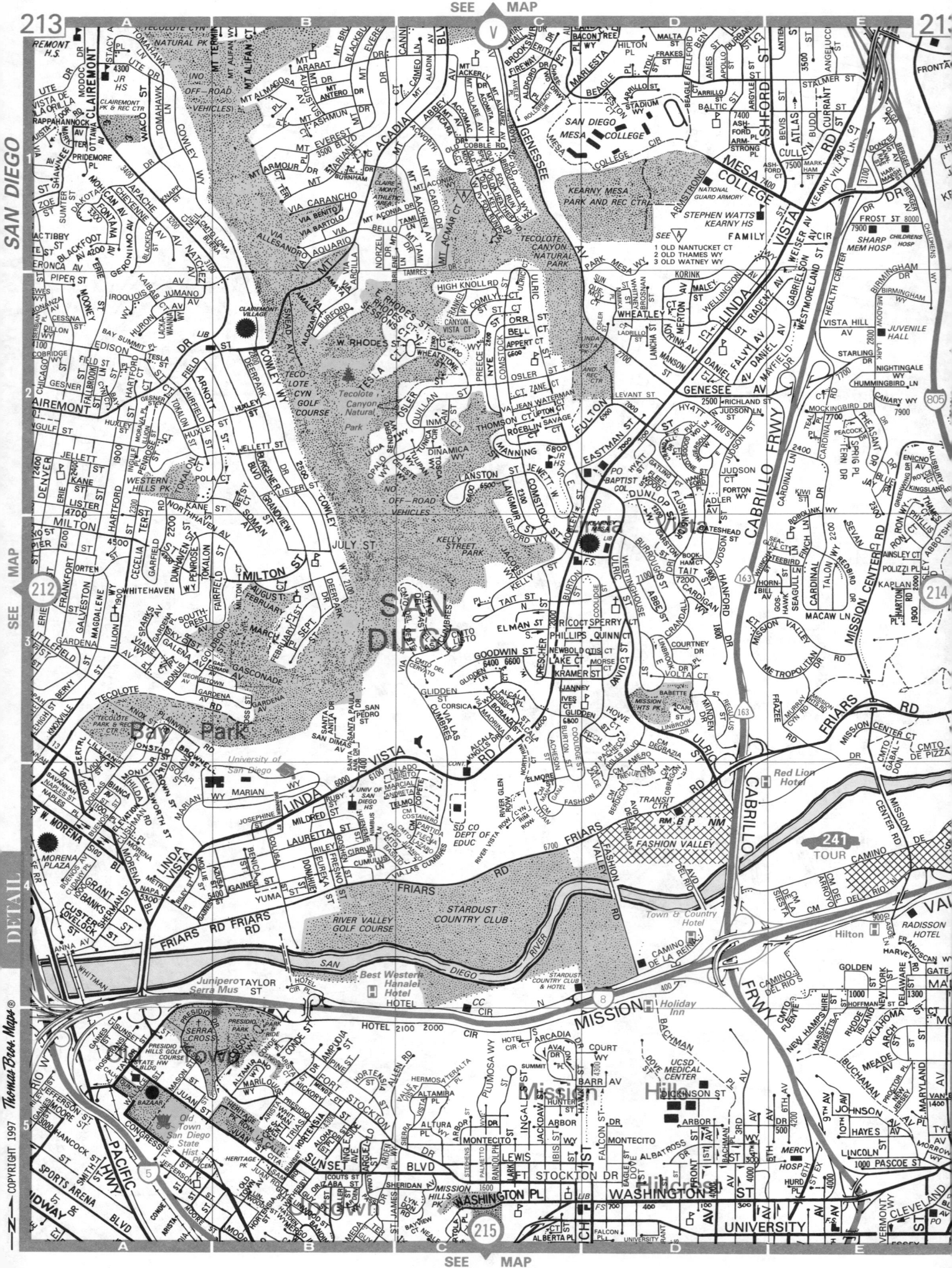

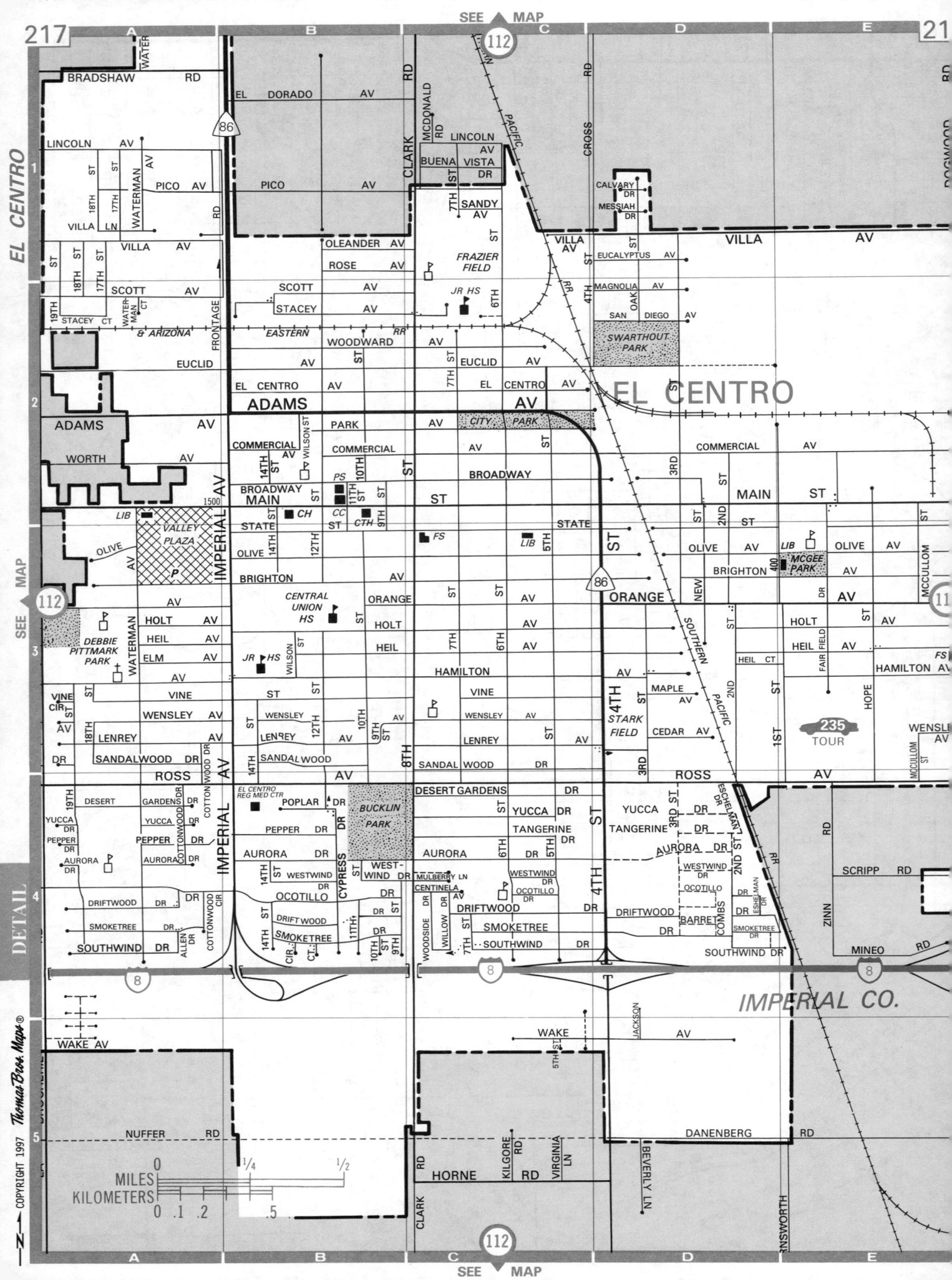

Discover California

The following special Driving Tours will guide you through a variety of routes covering the splendor of California's mountains and deserts, its pounding surf and beautiful beaches. The quiet beauty of the Wine Country and the Redwoods contrast with the exciting hubbub of its fabulous cities and their diverse cultures, as well as entertainment extravaganzas, theme parks, and historical and cultural landmarks. Whether you're a visitor, a newcomer, or longtime resident, these tours are sure to please, excite, and enlighten you.

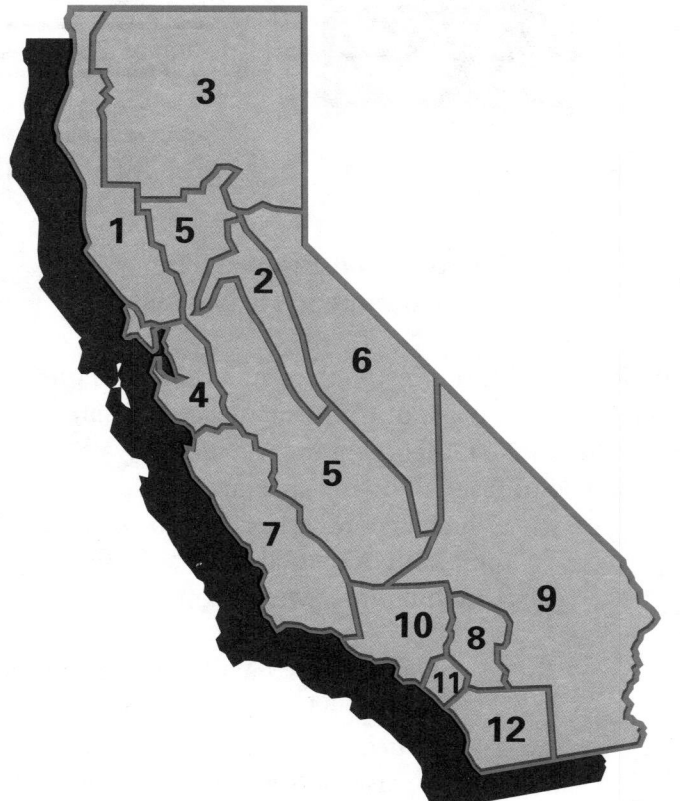

Table of Contents

Instructions and General Information Numbers

This section shows twelve Driving Tours which highlight different regions of California. Each Tour designates a scenic route, and briefly describes some of the points of interest along the way. In addition to the designated Tours, each of the twelve regions is filled with points of interest, some of which are listed on the pages accompanying each Tour section.

The map in each section shows the tours highlighted in yellow. Each Tour section also shows the page in this Atlas to refer to for a more detailed map. Also, the extensive indexes and the fold-out map in the back of the Atlas will provide additional information.

We hope that you will have the opportunity to take all of the Tours, or at least integrate parts of them into your own travel plans.

California Road Conditions Information
Caltrans 24-Hour Service
❖On a touchtone phone, press Highway Number & Pound (#) Key
❖Northern California Conditions: (916) 445-7623
❖Southern California Conditions: (213) 628-7623

General Tourism and Traveling Information
California Trade & Commerce Agency, Office of Tourism
(916) 322-2881

We invite your comments and recommendations. Please write to:

Thomas Bros. Maps®
17731 Cowan, Irvine, CA 92614
c/o CRA Driving Tours

Thomas Bros. Maps® updates this Atlas annually based on field research and available sources, but changes can and do occur. We hope that you will not be inconvenienced by any information that becomes obsolete or inaccurate.

SMITH
RIVER

199

SISKIYOU
MTNS

CRESCENT
CITY

TREES OF
MYSTERY
INDIAN
MUSEUM

SIX

RIVERS

REQUA

REDWOOD
KLAMATH

101

NATIONAL

PARK

ORICK

RIVERS
ORLEANS

PRAIRIE
CREEK
REDWOODS
STATE
PARK

96

NATIONAL

PATRICKS POINT
STATE PARK

TRINIDAD

HOOPA TRIBAL
MUSEUM

FOREST

MCKINLEYVILLE

ARCATA

299

WILLOW
CREEK

EUREKA

BLUE
LAKE

FT HUMBOLDT
STATE HISTORIC
PARK

LOLETA

FORTUNA

FERNDALE

211

SCOTIA LUMBER
MILL

RIO DELL

36

SCOTIA

CAPE
MENDOCINO

HUMBOLDT
REDWOODS
STATE
PARK

WEOTT

AVE OF THE
GIANTS

MYERS FLAT

KING
RANGE
NATIONAL
CONSERVATION
AREA

REDWAY

GARBERVILLE

RICHARDSON
GROVE
STATE PARK

BENBOW

SHELTER
COVE

STANDISH HICKEY
STATE REC AREA

SINKYONE
WILDERNESS
STATE PARK

LEGGETT

MENDOCINO

DRIVE-THRU
TREE
PARK

1

101

EEL

PACIFIC

LAYTONVILLE

RIVER

MAC KERRICHER
STATE PARK

SKUNK TRAIN

MENDOCINO
COUNTY MUSEUM

NATIONAL

FORT BRAGG

NOYO

20

WILLITS

MENDOCINO COAST
BOTANICAL GARDENS

RUSSIAN GULCH
STATE PARK

VAN DAMME
STATE PARK

MENDOCINO

MENDOCINO HEADLANDS
STATE PARK

128

UKIAH

20

FOREST

HENDY WOODS
STATE PARK

LAKE COUNTY
MUSEUM

CLEAR LAKE
STATE PARK

BOONVILLE

253

LAKE-
PORT

CLEAR
LAKE

RUSSIAN

HOPLAND

CLEARLAKE

POINT ARENA
LIGHTHOUSE
MUSEUM

POINT ARENA

ANDERSON MARSH
STATE HISTORIC
PARK

29

CLOVERDALE

GUALALA

ROBERT LOUIS
STEVENSON
STATE PARK

LAKE
BERRYESSA

1

101

SALT POINT
STATE PARK

GEYSERVILLE

HEALDSBURG

PETRIFIED
FOREST

CALISTOGA

FT ROSS STATE
HISTORIC PARK

ARMSTRONG REDWOODS
STATE RESERVE

BOTHE-NAPA VALLEY
STATE PARK

OCEAN

GUERNEVILLE

LUTHER
BURBANK
HOME

SANTA
ROSA

ST HELENA

128

JENNER

SEBASTOPOL

JACK
LONDON
STATE
HISTORIC
PARK

MISSION
SOLANO

YOUNTVILLE

BODEGA BAY

ROHNERT
PARK

SONOMA

NAPA

PETALUMA

NAPA VLY
WINE TRAIN

The Redwood Empire from Wine Country to Redwoods

The Redwood Empire stretches more than 400 miles along the north coast of California, north of San Francisco to the Oregon border. Several days should be allowed to fully enjoy the spectacular scenery, which encompasses rugged coastline, majestic redwood forests, lush valleys and premier wine country.

The **North Coast** is the California of rugged shores and pounding surf, of towering redwoods and rushing streams, of verdant hills and bountiful vineyards.

T H E

**NORTH
COAST**

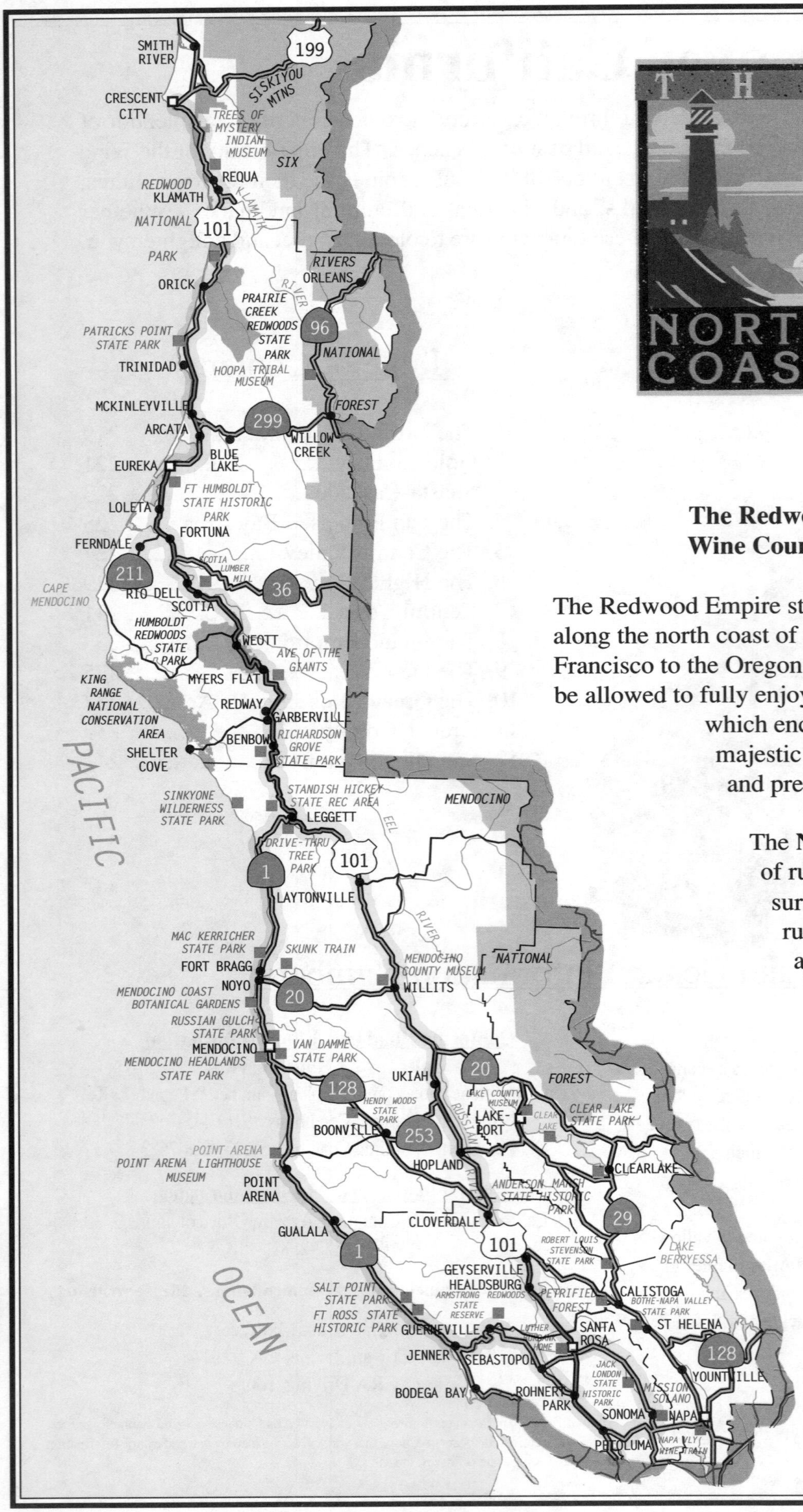

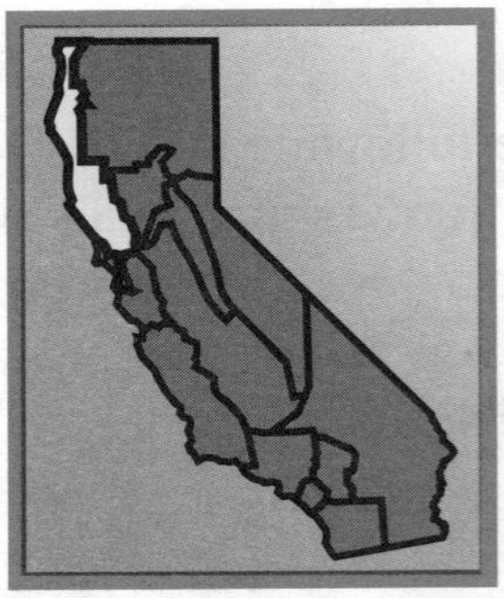

1 Inch to 28 Miles

Scale

0   Miles   28

TOURS

Driving Tour Points of Interest:

BODEGA BAY - *(Page 37, C3)* The bay was discovered in 1775 by Spanish explorers. Russian fur hunters settled at nearby Bodega in 1809. Fishing, landmark Catholic church, hillside and waterfront lodgings and restaurants abound. Golf is available at Bodega Harbor Golf Links, an 18-hole championship course overlooking the ocean. At Spud Point Marina, you'll find boat charters for cruises, whale watching, and deep-sea fishing. **Doran Regional Park** is on the bay sand-spit (swim, camp, fish). **Westside Park** is in the inner-bay (camp, fish, boat launch). The UC Marine Lab offers tours Fridays 2-4 p.m., groups by reservation: (707) 875-2211. At **Bodega Head State Park** at the north end of Bodega Bay, a three-mile trail climbs north and down to Salmon Creek Beach at Sonoma Coast State Beach.

SONOMA COAST STATE BEACH - *(Page 37, C2)* Broad, shining beaches and secluded coves, rocky coastline, and tide pools are protected and maintained by the State. Open to the public at several access points with fire rings on the sand and numerous developed campsites. (707) 875-3483

The drive along the Russian River, named for the fur traders who flourished there in the 19th century, is dotted with small towns, wineries and peaceful orchards. The road winds through forests of redwoods which have been preserved rather than destroyed for the sake of the pavement.

FORT ROSS STATE HISTORIC PARK - *(Page 37, A1)* 11 miles north of Jenner on Highway 1. In the early 1800's Ross, a Russian word for "Russia," was established as a base to hunt otter and seal and to grow food for the Russian colonies in Alaska. The Russians competed with the Spanish in Bodega Bay for control of this rich hunting ground and the verdant Russian River valley. Today, you'll see restored and reconstructed redwood structures: the stockade, block-houses, a Russian chapel, officers' barracks, a Russian well and a storehouse. Living history events, Orthodox Easter church service and Ranch Day events are presented annually. Call for information about the picnic area: (707) 847-3286. See Bufano's 72-foot Peace statue on the access trail from Highway 1, north of the fort.

MOUNT KONOCTI - *(Page 31, E3)* This 4,300-foot dormant volcano with four peaks last erupted within the last few thousand years, and is a landmark for the entire Clear Lake area and the subject of Native American legends. Many enjoy rockhounding for Lake County "diamonds," semi-precious stones of volcanic origin found only in the county. This area also offers golf courses, tennis courts at resorts and parks, and a country club at the lakeside base of the mountain.

SINKYONE WILDERNESS STATE PARK - *(Page 22, B2)* The south gateway to the spectacular isolated Lost Coast, 50 miles north of Fort Bragg. Exit Highway One above Rockport, following unpaved Usal Road (County Road No. 431) to primitive campsites at Usal Creek. Rugged Lost Coast Trail winds 21 miles north through a 7,000-acre coastal plateau, with ocean vistas, waterfalls, cliffs, access to black sand beaches, tide pools and trail campsites. The Visitor Center in ranch house at Needle Rock is open in summer. (707) 986-7711

HUMBOLDT REDWOOD STATE PARK - *(Page 16, A4)* A 51,222 acre park that protects 2,000-year-old trees in a 20 million-year-old forest, the largest remaining stand of virgin redwoods in the world. Camping is permitted. (707) 946-2409

Avenue of the Giants - *(Page 16, C4)* World famous 31-mile scenic drive parallels Highway 101. The road meanders through solemn groves of redwoods, some 300 feet tall. There are numerous attractions and gift shops along the way. Contact The Avenue of the Giants Association at (707) 923-2555

SCOTIA - *(Page 16, A3)* A stylized "company town" built almost entirely of redwood. The sprawling mill, **Pacific Lumber**, offers free, self-guided tours of their redwood-processing plant and museum. (707) 764-2222

FERNDALE - *(Page 15, D2)* Five miles west of Highway 101, a Victorian town of splendid gingerbread style homes and shops. The entire town is a designated State Historical Landmark. (707) 786-4477

EUREKA - *(Page 15, E1)* In the Old Town historic district are specialty shops, art galleries and studios, Humboldt Cultural Center and antiques. The Carson Mansion is the 1885 redwood Queen of Victorians.

PATRICK'S POINT STATE PARK - *(Page 9, E3)* A gorgeous, 630-acre park with 12 hiking trails that allow visitors to walk out near the edge of steep bluffs or onto the sandy beach. For camping information, call (707) 677-3570

PRAIRIE CREEK REDWOODS STATE PARK - *(Page 10, A1)* A large meadowland of tall grasses bordered by dense redwoods and fern canyons. Elk may be seen in the open areas. The Visitors Center has displays and information. (707) 488-2171

GOLD COUNTRY

1 Inch to 22 Miles

Scale

0   Miles   22

MALAKOFF DIGGINS STATE HIST PARK

ROUGH & READY

NEVADA CITY
GRASS VALLEY

EMPIRE MINE STATE HISTORIC PARK

COLFAX

AUBURN

NEWCASTLE

OLD TOWN AUBURN

COLOMA

MARSHALL GOLD DISCOVERY STATE HIST PARK

GOLD BUG MINE

PLACERVILLE

FOREST GENETICS RESEARCH CENTER

FOLSOM

FOLSOM LAKE ST REC AREA

SUTTER'S FORT

RAILROAD MUSEUM

RANCHO CORDOVA

EL DORADO HILLS

DIAMOND SPRINGS

SACRAMENTO
OLD STATE CAPITAL

OLD SACRAMENTO

FIDDLETOWN

PLYMOUTH

VOLCANO

INDIAN GRINDING ROCK STATE HIST PK

AMADOR
SUTTER CREEK

WEST POINT

IONE

JACKSON

MOKELUMNE HILL

CALIFORNIA CAVERNS

SAN ANDREAS

MURPHYS

MERCER CAVES

ANGELS CAMP

COLUMBIA STATE HIST PK

COPPEROPOLIS

MOANING CAVERNS

SONORA

RAILTOWN 1897 STATE HIST PARK

JAMESTOWN

CHINESE CAMP

MOCCASIN

GROVELAND

COULTERVILLE

DON PEDRO RES

LAKE McCLURE

MARIPOSA COUNTY COURTHOUSE

MARIPOSA

CATHEYS VALLEY

CALIF STATE MINING AND MINERAL MUSEUM

WASSAMA ROUND HOUSE STATE HIST PK

OAKHURST

COARSEGOLD

RAYMOND

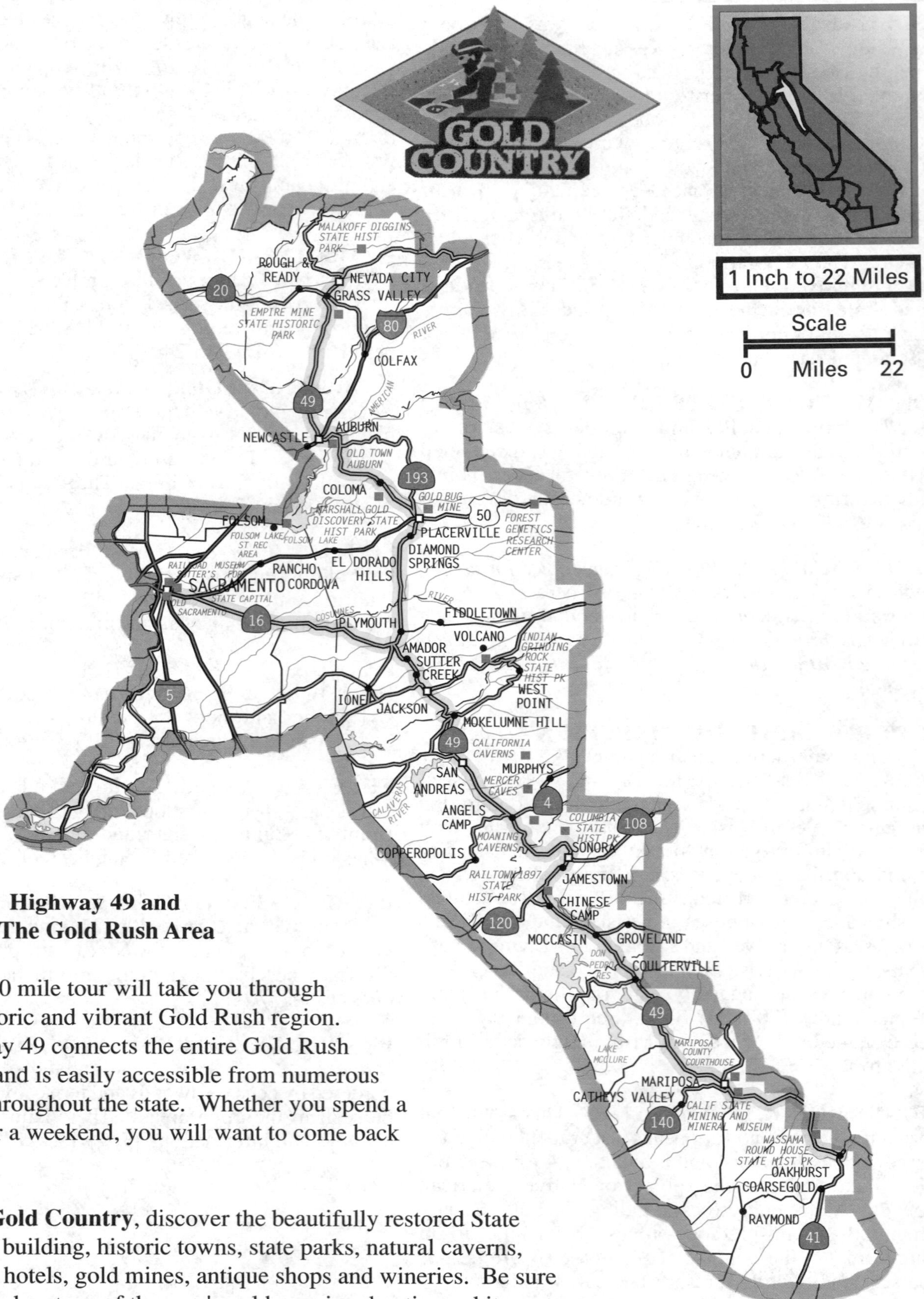

Highway 49 and The Gold Rush Area

This 300 mile tour will take you through the historic and vibrant Gold Rush region. Highway 49 connects the entire Gold Rush region and is easily accessible from numerous roads throughout the state. Whether you spend a week or a weekend, you will want to come back often.

In the **Gold Country**, discover the beautifully restored State Capitol building, historic towns, state parks, natural caverns, historic hotels, gold mines, antique shops and wineries. Be sure to take advantage of the area's gold panning, boating, white water rafting, camping, picnicking and a wide variety of recreational activities.

Driving Tour Points of Interest:

JAMESTOWN - *(Page 41, C5)* Affectionately called "Jimtown" by its residents. This gold camp had an especially bawdy reputation as a rough and tumble town. Visit the **Railtown 1897 State Park**. (209) 984-3953

COLUMBIA - *(Page 41, C4)* "The Gem of the Southern Mines" once attracted 15,000 fortune-seeking miners. Today, Columbia invites visitors to experience that heyday by taking part in Living Histories and special events, or to stroll through town on a walking tour led by authentically-costumed guides. (209) 532-4301 or 532-0150

ANGELS CAMP - *(Page 41, B4)* Made famous twice, first as an important Gold Rush center and again by Mark Twain's short story "The Celebrated Jumping Frog of Calaveras County." Each May, the town hosts its Jumping Frog Jubilee and frog-jumping contest. (209) 754-4009

Mercer Caverns - *(Page 41, B4)* 1.5 miles west of Murphys. Open since 1885, the caves invite explorers into 8 rooms of crystalline formations. (209) 728-2101

The Sierra foothills from Jackson to Plymouth (Page 40) *are blanketed with oak trees and vineyards. Amador County is gaining recognition for its premium wineries. Amador County Chamber of Commerce: (209) 223-0350*

SACRAMENTO - *(Page 39, E1)* The State Capital since 1854. The city has a colorful history, well-preserved amid a modern and dynamic environment of current political activity.

Old Sacramento State Historic Park - *(Page 137, A2)* A 10-block district along the Sacramento River which re-creates the flavor of the Gold Rush days. Museums, saloons and shops line the western-style streets. The **California State Railroad Museum** features dozens of historic exhibits and 21 lavishly restored locomotives and cars. **Old Sacramento Visitors Center**, located in the Old Sacramento State Historic Park, provides information and walking tours of the city. (916) 442-7644

Sutter's Fort - *(Page 137, D3)* Site of the first settlement founded by Captain John Sutter in 1839. The Fort has been restored and houses exhibits and memorabilia of the Gold Rush days. (916) 445-4209

State Capitol - *(Page 137, B3)* Constructed between 1861 and 1874. The main building is a formidable structure with a 210-foot gold dome, marble floors and radiant, crystal chandeliers. It is the dominant landmark among the state buildings in the area, and is surrounded by a 40-acre park of trees and plants from around the world. Tours of the main building, its chambers and some executive offices are available, as well as historical exhibits, murals and a film. (916) 324-0333

COLOMA - *(Page 34, D4)* "Birthplace of the Gold Rush." John Marshall discovered gold here on January 24, 1848. The **James W. Marshall Gold Discovery Park** is a 300-acre State Park that captures the spirit of the Old West through living history exhibits, museums and walking tours. (916) 622-3470

AUBURN - *(Page 34, C3)* One of the first mining camps in California. Old Town Auburn boasts California's oldest operating post office and the oldest volunteer fire department "West of Boston", both established in 1852.

GRASS VALLEY - *(Page 34, C1)* An active mining town for 100 years. The large, commercial operations continued into the 1950's.

Empire Mine State Park - *(Page 127, D4)* Documents 107 years of mining history with displays, exhibits, films and tours. Call the Visitors Center at (916) 273-8522

NEVADA CITY - *(Page 34, C1)* "Queen City of the Northern Mines," once the third largest city in California. Many fine buildings and homes remain, including California's oldest, still-operating hotel and the state's oldest theatre building.

Thomas Bros. Maps ®
COPYRIGHT 1997

SHASTA · CASCADE

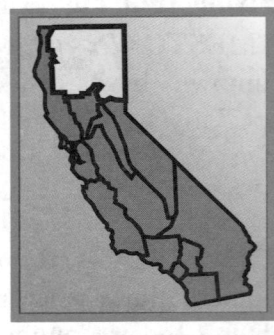

Scale

0   Miles   35

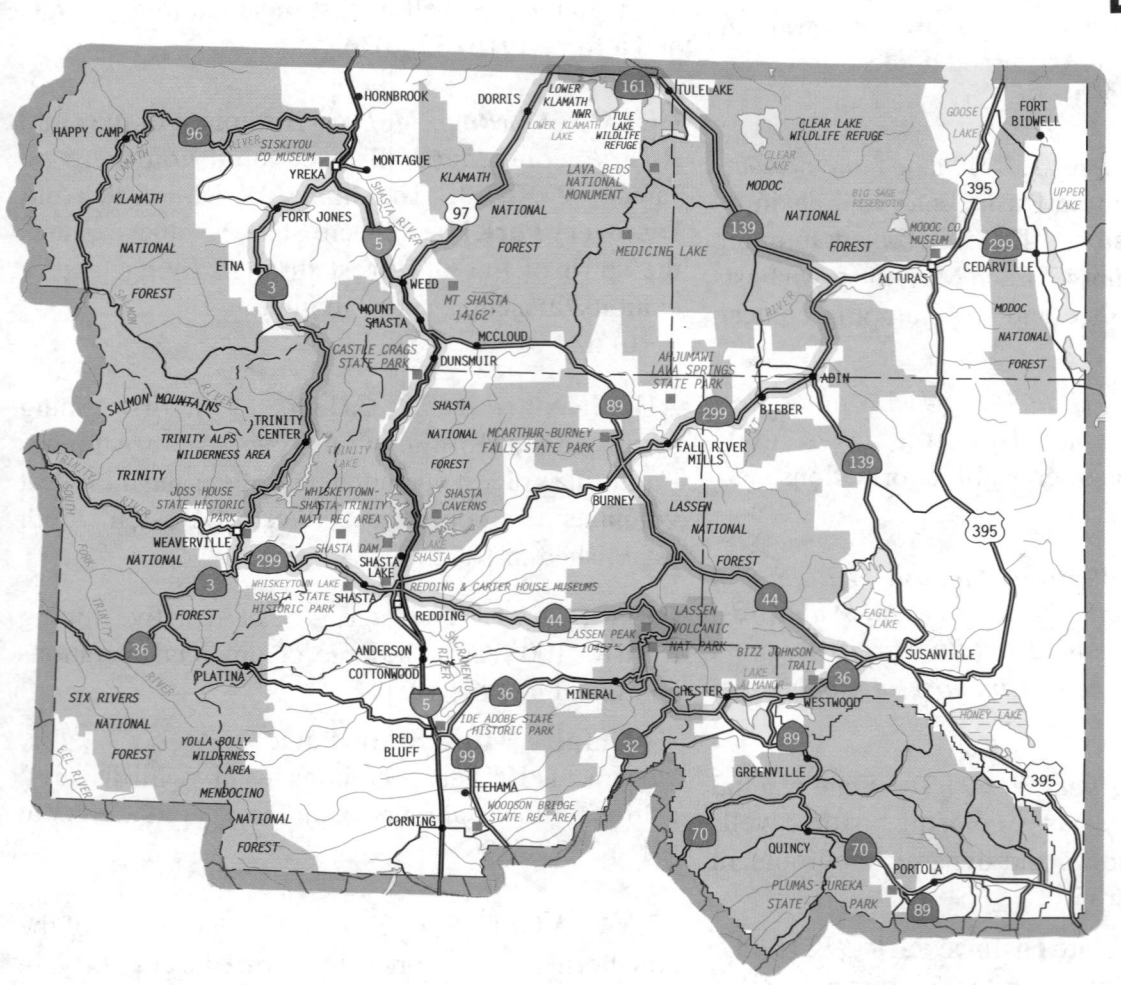

Towering Mountains, Caves and Crags

This approximately 560-mile round trip provides a lovely drive through countryside dotted with historical sites and natural wonders. If you take time to stop and visit some of each, allow at least two extra days.

The **Shasta-Cascade** is big country - over 28,000 square miles with snow capped mountains, volcanoes, glaciers, waterfalls, white water rivers, dense forests, alpine lakes, and rugged canyons. It is home to seven national forests, one national park, one national monument, six state parks, the Trinity Alps, and the California Cascade Range.

TOURS

Driving Tour Points of Interest:

LASSEN VOLCANIC NATIONAL PARK - *(Page 19, E2)* Located 45 minutes east of Redding and Red Bluff. The park encompasses a remarkable wilderness area scarred by massive volcanic eruptions which occurred a mere 75 years ago. The park's scenic 35-mile main road winds through conifer forests, among clear lakes and hydrothermal areas of boiling mud pots and steaming sulphur vents. The park features over 150 miles of hiking trails, camping, fishing and boating facilities, plus special naturalist activities throughout the summer months. (916) 595-4444

REDDING - *(Page 18,C2)* Gateway city to Northern California and vital crossroads for travelers and commerce.

Shasta-Cascade Wonderland Association, provides extensive maps, brochures and detailed information of the area. 1-800-474-2782

SHASTA STATE HISTORIC PARK - *(Page 18,B2)* Three miles west of Redding. This town of restored buildings depicts the Gold Rush days when the area was a thriving center for wagon trains. (916) 243-8194

WHISKEYTOWN LAKE - *(Page 18, A2)* A man-made Alpine lake popular with water sports enthusiasts. Camping is available.

WEAVERVILLE - *(Page 17, D1)* A Chamber of Commerce walking-tour map of this Gold Rush town highlights 116 historic points on interest. Especially noteworthy are the **Joss House** and **Jackson Memorial Museum**. (916) 623-6101

LAKE SHASTA CAVERNS - *(Page 18, C1)* A fascinating and educational two-hour excursion for all ages. The tour includes a 15-minute catamaran cruise across Lake Shasta, a shuttle bus ride up the mountainside and a tour through the natural caverns. Guides tell the history, folklore and geological development of the area. 1-800-795-CAVE

MOUNT SHASTA CITY - *(Page 12, C2)* An Alpine-like town nestled at the foot of the "Friendly Giant," Mount Shasta.

Mt. Shasta/Sisson Museum - (916) 926-5508 Located on the grounds of California's oldest fish hatchery (est. 1888). Antiques and photographs document the history of the hatchery and Mt. Shasta city. Self-Guided tours only of the hatchery grounds (feeding the fish is encouraged). (916) 926-2215

McARTHUR-BURNEY FALLS MEMORIAL STATE PARK - *(Page 13, C4)* One hour north of Lassen Volcanic National Park. The main attractions are the spectacular **Burney Falls** that cascade over a 129-foot cliff into an emerald pool. A one-mile, self-guided nature trail highlights numerous geological formations, local fauna and lush flora. The 875-acre park is open year round and offers 118 family campsites, six miles of hiking trails, fishing and boat launch facilities onto adjoining Lake Britton. (916) 335-2777

From Highway 89, follow the roadway signs for Medicine Lake. At the junction of Medicine Lake Hwy (Page 5, D5), *the road turns north to the Lava Beds National Monument. This stretch of remote highway slices through thick forests and ancient lava flows. The drive from Highway 89 at Bartle to the Visitors Center at Lava Beds takes about 1-1/2 hours. The nearest food and gas are at Canby or Tulelake.*

LAVA BEDS NATIONAL MONUMENT - *(Page 5, D4)* A surreal area of lava flows, mud holes and caves. The Visitors Center at the south entrance is open during the summer months and provides maps and information highlighting the park's fascinating historical and geological points of interest. Just outside the north entrance is the Petroglyph Section (intriguing Rock Art), etched into the cliffs over 2,000 years ago. (916) 667-2282

TULE LAKE AND LOWER KLAMATH WILDLIFE REFUGES - *(Page 5, D3 & C3)* Vast lake areas which sustain massive concentrations of waterfowl. Several turnouts along Highway 161 enable bird watchers to observe this unique nature reserve.

Highway 97 to Weed cuts through wide open spaces and tranquil farmlands. There are few towns, with limited services, along this 56-mile stretch.

Other Points of Interest:

Highway 96 follows 150 miles of the wild and scenic Klamath River. The area is a recreational paradise where salmon and steelhead fishing, rafting, canoeing, kayaking and wilderness horse packing challenge rugged sportsmen from around the world.

HAPPY CAMP - *(Page 2, E4)* A small, friendly, rural mountain community with full services. The Ranger Station provides maps and camping information. (916) 493-2900

TOURS

San Francisco Bay Area Sampler...
"The Scenic City" Natural Wonders
and Family Fun

This three-day tour begins with a full day exploring the highlights of San Francisco along the city's Scenic 49 Mile Drive. Circle the Bay on day two, visiting the East and North Bay regions. The route includes the cities of Oakland, Berkeley and Vallejo as well as Marin County's seaside villages and the historic redwood forest, Muir Woods. Conclude the day with an evening drive across the Golden Gate Bridge into San Francisco. Head south on day three along I-280. Visit the Silicon Valley cities of San Jose and Santa Clara filled with high-tech and high adventure. Family attractions abound in the natural wonders of the California coastline including the beachside communities of Santa Cruz and Half Moon Bay.

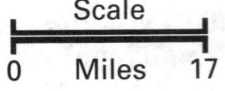

1 Inch to 17 Miles

Scale

0   Miles   17

With a population of more than 6 million, the **San Francisco Bay Area** is the nation's fourth largest metropolitan area. It is a bounty of beaches, historical sites and parks - all in one of the most exquisite natural settings on earth.

1 FISHERMAN'S WHARF
2 THOMAS BROS MAPS
3 CHINATOWN
4 PRESIDIO OF SAN FRANCISCO
5 JACK LONDON WATERFRONT
6 OAKLAND MUSEUM
7 SAN FRANCISO ZOO
8 MT TAMALPAIS STATE PARK

TOURS

BODEGA HEAD
TOMALES BLUFF
TOMALES BAY STATE PARK
POINT REYES NATIONAL SEASHORE
POINT REYES
DRAKES BAY
NOVATO
SAMUEL P TAYLOR STATE PARK
MARINE WORLD AFRICA USA
SAN PABLO BAY
VALLEJO
BENICIA CAPITOL ST HIST PK
BENICIA
101
MISSION SAN RAFAEL
SAN RAFAEL
JOHN MUIR NATL HIST SITE
CONCORD
80
4
STINSON BEACH
RICHMOND
AUDUBON CANYON RANCH
BERKELEY
WALNUT CREEK
MT DIABLO STATE PARK
MUIR WOODS NATIONAL MONUMENT
580
GOLDEN GATE NATL REC AREA
ALCATRAZ ISLAND
24
DANVILLE
BEHRING AUTO MUSEUM
TIBURON
EUGENE ONEILL NATL HIST SITE
SAN RAMON
GOLDEN GATE BRIDGE
OAKLAND
80
GOLDEN GATE PARK
MISSION DOLORES
ALAMEDA
SAN LEANDRO
680
SAN FRANCISCO
CANDLESTICK PARK
DALY CITY
SAN FRANCISCO BAY
HAYWARD
580
LIVERMORE
PACIFICA
PLEASANTON
92
SAN MATEO
FREMONT
280
MISSION SAN JOSE
101
84
880
PARAMOUNT'S GREAT AMERICA
MILPITAS
HALF MOON BAY
REDWOOD CITY
LICK OBSERVATORY
WOODSIDE
PALO ALTO
MOUNTAIN VIEW
MISSION SANTA CLARA
SUNNYVALE
SAN JOSE
84
WINCHESTER MYSTERY HOUSE
PESCADERO
35
87
SARATOGA
85
LOS GATOS
MORGAN HILL
HENRY COE STATE PARK
BIG BASIN REDWOODS STATE PARK
BOULDER CREEK
1
9
17
101
FELTON
ROARING CAMP BIG TREES RAILROAD
SANTA CRUZ
CAPITOLA
GILROY
152
NATURAL BRIDGES STATE BEACH
MISSION SANTA CRUZ
APTOS
SANTA CRUZ BOARDWALK
WATSONVILLE
PACIFIC OCEAN

Driving Tour Points of Interest:

SANTA CRUZ - *(Page 169, E4)* Enjoys a natural setting between ocean and forest with close proximity to the big cities. The **Boardwalk**, (408) 423-5590, is California's only operating seaside amusement park. Visitors Center: (408) 425-1234.

BIG BASIN REDWOODS STATE PARK - *(Page 53, E1)* Towering redwoods, some over 330 feet tall and 18 feet in diameter, create a lush canopy over the road; rich green mosses thrive on the stone bridges, wooden fences and tree trunks. Unfortunately, the road is not suitable for trailers or large RVs. (408) 338-8860

SAN JOSE - *(Page 46, B4)* Located in a region known equally for fine wines and high-technology industries.

Winchester Mystery House - *(Page 151, B5)* Created by the heiress of the Winchester Rifle fortune. The 160-room mansion and 6 acres of gardens were designed according to the bizarre superstitious obsessions of their eccentric owner. (408) 247-2101

Rosicrucian Park - *(Page 151, D4)* Contains elaborate fountains, tiled walkways, gardens and statues in the style of ancient Egypt. The Rosicrucian Museum features the largest collection of ancient Egyptian relics in the western U.S. (408) 947-3636

MISSION SAN FRANCISCO DE ASIS (Mission Dolores) - *(Page 142, C4)* Established in 1776 as the 6th in the chain of 21 Franciscan missions. It is the oldest building in San Francisco. (415) 621-8203

GOLDEN GATE PARK - *(Page 141)* Formerly 1,000 acres of sand dunes. This park has been transformed into one of the most beautiful metropolitan parks in the world featuring miles of pleasant drives, green lawns, playing fields, bridle paths, and bicycle routes. There are also lakes and gardens, a stadium, and a golf course.

California Academy of Sciences - (415) 750-7145; **Conservatory of Flowers; Japanese Tea Garden; Strybing Arboretum; M.H. De Young Memorial Museum.**

SAN FRANCISCO ZOO - *(Page L, B5)* Ranks among the top city zoos in the U.S. The collection boasts over 1,000 animals and birds. (415) 753-7083

CIVIC CENTER - *(Page 143, B4)* Includes an impressive group of federal, state and city buildings: City Hall, Civic Auditorium, Performing Arts Center, War Memorial, Opera House, Main Public Library, and San Francisco Museum of Modern Art.

UNION SQUARE - *(Page 143, C3)* The heart of downtown shopping. This attractive outdoor square is used for many civic events, fashion shows, rallies, and concerts. Around the square and spreading southward are many of San Francisco's fine shops and department stores.

JAPANTOWN - *(Page 143, A3)* Traditional shops, restaurants, a theatre, teahouses, sushi bars, Japanese baths and a five-tiered, 35-foot Peace Pagoda reflect the spirit of the 12,000 San Francisco residents of Japanese descent.

CHINATOWN - *(Page 143, C2)* A 24-block area of pagoda-style architecture, curio shops, street markets, restaurants, and temples. Home to the largest Chinese community outside the Orient.

During your visit, please stop by **Thomas Bros. Maps and Books**, *550 Jackson Street, (415) 981-7520*

FISHERMAN'S WHARF - *(Page 143, B1)* The famous waterfront area of seafood restaurants, harbor cruises, excellent shopping, galleries, and entertainment. The refurbished brick buildings of Ghirardelli Square, The Cannery, and Pier 39 are especially popular restaurant and shopping meccas.

LOMBARD STREET - *(Page 143, B2)* Called "The Crookedest Street in the World." The steep, one-way, brick avenue, trimmed in flowers, is open to all vehicles except motorhomes and trailers.

TELEGRAPH HILL - *(Page 143, C2)* Includes **Coit Tower**, a 210-foot monument built in 1934 as a memorial to the city's volunteer firemen. An elevator takes visitors to the top for a panoramic view of San Francisco, the East Bay, the waterfront, the bay bridges, and Alcatraz Island.

FORT MASON CENTER - *(Page 143, A1)* A former Army base converted into a cultural center. This artisan's showplace includes 45 studios, 3 theatres, and 5 museums. (415) 979-3010

PALACE OF FINE ARTS - *(Page 142, A1)* Built for the 1915 Panama-Pacific International Exposition. It has been beautifully restored and now houses the **Exploratorium**, a science museum, (415) 561-0362, and the 1,000-seat **Palace of Fine Arts Theatre**. (415) 567-6642

PRESIDIO OF SAN FRANCISCO - *(Page 141, C2)* U.S. Sixth Army headquarters. The 1,500 acres of park-like hills and beaches are open to the public. The Presidio Army Museum chronicles over 100 years of San Francisco military history. (415) 561-4323

SAUSALITO - *(Page L, B4)* Historic artist's colony. Its picturesque marina is filled with over 350 houseboats, while the hillsides are filled with unusual homes perched precariously above the bay. Sausalito is a popular retreat offering numerous restaurants with spectacular day and evening views of the bay.

MUIR WOODS NATIONAL MONUMENT - *(Page L, A4)* Located 2 miles off the Panoramic Highway. A network of trails threads the 553 acres of redwood forests. No camping, picnicking or fishing permitted. (415) 388-2595

STINSON BEACH - *(Page L, A4)* A small town and popular park now a part of the Golden Gate National Recreation Area. The sandy beaches and good surf attract over one million visitors each year. (415) 868-0942

Audubon Canyon Ranch - *(Page 38, A5)* Wildlife sanctuary and educational center. Open March through July. (415) 868-9244

MT. TAMALPAIS STATE PARK - *(Page L, A3)* Beautiful area of redwoods laced with roads and trails. The view from "Mt. Tam" encompasses the Pacific Ocean and Farallon Islands, San Francisco Bay, and on a clear day, as far as the great Central Valley. Hiking and camping are available, and a natural amphitheater seats 3,750 people.

SAN RAFAEL - *(Page L, B3)* Visit the **Mission San Rafael Archangel**, a replica built in 1949 on the approximate site of the original 1817 mission. (415) 456-3016

Marin County Civic Center - Designed by Frank Lloyd Wright. The 140-acre complex is a combination of futuristic structures and landscapes. (415) 499-7407

BERKELEY - *(Page L, D4)* Notoriously described as "radical," "revolutionary" and "avante garde." It is regarded as one of the nation's leading educational centers with the **University of California** *(Page 156, B2)* and its academic populace having shaped the city through the decades. The top of the 307-foot Campanile affords a view of the campus, the East Bay area and San Francisco. Campus information: (510) 642-5215.

OAKLAND - *(Page L, C4)* Named for the extensive groves of live oak trees that once flourished here. The city has grown into a major urban center with one of the largest commercial ports in the world. It is also a residential district for thousands of bay area commuters. Call the Visitors Center at (510) 839-9000.

Lake Merritt - *(Page 158, B3)* A 155-acre body of salt water in the center of the city surrounded by Lakeside Park. It is a favorite recreation spot with a garden center, Children's Fairyland, Gamebird Refuge, Natural Science Center, sailboats for rent, and 122 acres of green lawns. At night, the entire lake is adorned with a string of white lights called the "necklace of lights" which gives an enchanting radiance to the park.

Oakland Museum - *(Page 158, A3)* Covering 4 square blocks, this three-tiered complex is really 3 different museums in one: history, natural science and art, with exhibits as intriguing as the building's architecture. (510) 238-3401

Jack London Square - *(Page 157, E4)* A 10-block area of waterfront considered the historical center of Oakland. Fine restaurants and shops line the wharf where the famous adventure writer spent much of his time.

Paramount Theatre - *(Page 158, A2)* A sublime example of Art Deco form. The 3,000-seat theatre, built in 1931, has been restored and is an active facility. Tours are available by calling (510) 465-6400.

MARINE WORLD AFRICA USA - *(Page 134, E1)* A unique combination of wildlife park and oceanarium, 160-acre Marine World Africa USA is home to more than 100 species of animals. Other attractions include the largest display of robotic dinosaurs in the U.S., water-ski and boat shows, a playground, restaurants, snack bars and picnic areas. (707) 643-6722 or (707) 644-4000

TOURS

THE CENTRAL VALLEY

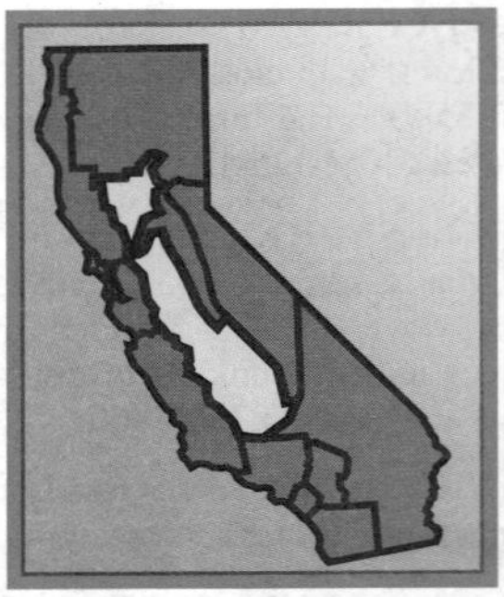

1 Inch to 47 Miles

Scale

0   Miles   47

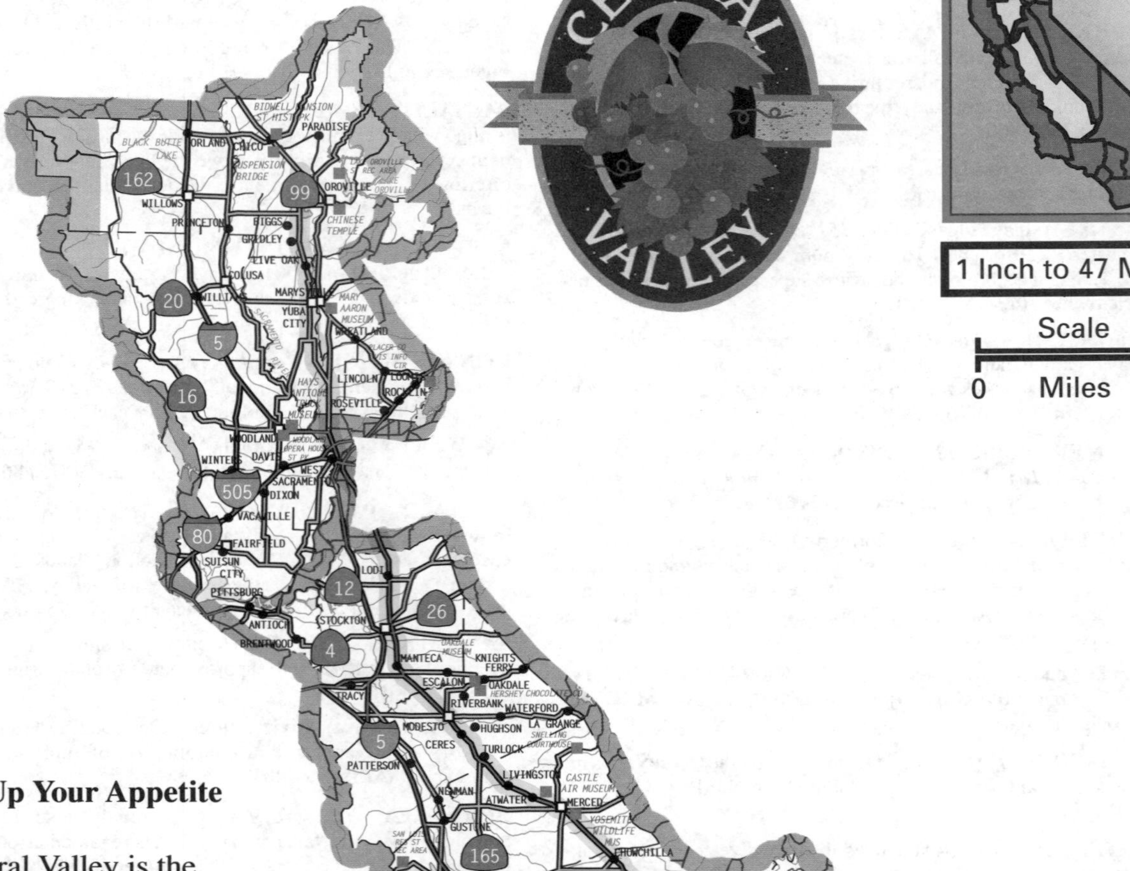

Pack Up Your Appetite

The Central Valley is the nation's leading agricultural area, with more than 11 million acres of irrigated land planted in cotton, grapes, figs, grain, almonds, asparagus, carrots, raisins, kiwi fruit, corn and more. This driving tour introduces you to some of the friendliest people in the world in such landmark cities as Chico, Stockton, Modesto, Merced, Fresno, and Selma. Enjoy "just picked" fresh fruit and vegetables from roadside fields and be sure to take in an agricultural tour if time permits.

In the sunny **Central Valley**, recreation is plentiful. Enjoy fishing from the many lakes and rivers or take a houseboat out along the thousands of miles of the Delta's waterways.

COPYRIGHT 1997 Thomas Bros. Maps ®

Driving Tour Points of Interest:

BAKERSFIELD

Kern County Museum - *(Page 166, C2)* The museum's 16-acre outdoor complex is the beginning of a walk through history. With over 60 structures, the museum displays a wide variety of historic buildings depicting scenes from the past. Diverse artifacts relating to Kern County life between the 1860's and 1930's are displayed in genuine and recreated residences, businesses, and civic buildings. (805) 861-2132

VISALIA

Tulare County Museum - *(Page 68, B2)* Beautifully landscaped and home to the remainder of a great oak forest that once existed in the area, Mooney Grove Museum is the largest and most complete museum in the county with many historical items. The original "End of the Trail" statue was on display in the park until 1968, when it was moved to the Cowboy Hall of Fame and replaced by a bronze replica. (209) 733-6616

Chinese Cultural Center - *(Page 68, B1)* Guarding the entrance to the center are two 12-ton marble TZU-SHIH lions which are used in China to act as guards for important buildings. Inside, the center features ongoing arts and crafts exhibits as well as unique artifacts of China and its culture. To visit the Chinese Cultural Center is to experience over 12,000 years of Chinese culture. Free, but call ahead for reservations. (209) 625-4545

FRESNO

Wild Water Adventures - *(Page 57, D3)* A family water amusement park with more than 52 acres of grass, trees and "Wet and Wild" water fun, Wild Water Adventures has more than 17 rides and attractions including 15,000 gallons of splashin' kiddie areas and the West's largest wave pool. Open daily mid-June through Labor Day. Limited days and hours in May and September. (209) 297-6540

Chaffee Zoological Gardens - *(Page 165, B2)* Located in Roeding Park, the zoological and botanical gardens have more than 600 specimens of mammals, birds and reptiles. Highlights include the Tropical Rainforest, the Asian Elephant Compound and the world's first computerized Reptile House. Open every day of the year from 10:00 a.m. (209) 498-2671

Fresno Art Museum - *(Page 165, E1)* The Fresno Art Museum is the area's only modern-art museum. Featuring up to 22 separate exhibitions per year, the museum collects and exhibits American sculpture, Californian art, Mexican art and works on paper. An extensive collection of Ansel Adams photographs, Robert Cremean sculpture, French post-Impressionist graphics and pre-Columbian Mexican sculpture makes the collection unique in the West. (209) 485-4810

Shaver and Huntington Lakes - *(Page 58, B1)* This beautiful resort area has it all. Camping, fishing, sailing/boating, four-wheeling and horse pack trips in the summer, downhill, cross-country skiing and snowmobiling in the winter. Services include lodging and condominium rentals, restaurants and shopping. The Shaver Lake Chamber of Commerce also sponsors several special events throughout the year. (209) 841-3350

MERCED

Castle Air Museum - *(Page 48, B4)* This museum is a history lesson that the whole family can share. It alone houses one of the country's finest collections of World War II aircraft along with planes of recent vintage restored to their original appearance. Displays of military equipment, uniforms, medals, and other memorabilia can be viewed at an indoor museum. (209) 723-2178

Courthouse Museum - *(Page 170, D3)* This three-story courthouse, which was built in 1875, was designed by Albert A. Bennett, one of the architects of the State Capitol. In the architectural style of Italianate, it is situated in the center of beautiful Courthouse Park. The museum houses 8,500 square feet of exhibits which depict the history of early settlers to the Great Central Valley. (209) 723-2401

Lake Yosemite - *(Page 48, C4)* Lake Yosemite County Park is a favorite with sailors, boaters and windsurfers alike. The lake is used for fishing, boating, swimming, and waterskiing while shaded picnic and sports areas dot the rest of the park. A paved bike path leads from the park back into Merced, connecting into the twelve miles of class one, grade-separated bike trails. In all, 29 tree-shaded parks enhance the city. (209) 384-3333

MODESTO

Hershey's Chocolate Company & Visitors Center - *(Page 47, E1)* Visitors can watch chocolate being made during a free factory tour of the Hershey plant in Oakdale. Tours are offered Monday - Friday, 8:30 a.m. to 3:00 p.m. (209) 848-8126

McHenry Mansion and Museum - *(Page 162, B3)* Catch a glimpse of turn-of-the-century living at both the McHenry Mansion and McHenry Museum in Modesto. The mansion is a fully-restored and furnished Victorian house built in 1883, offering free tours Tuesdays-Thursdays and Sundays, 1:00 p.m. to 4:00 p.m., (209) 577-5344. The museum is open Tuesdays-Sundays, 12:00 p.m. to 4:00 p.m. (209) 577-5366

STOCKTON - *(Page 40, B5)* Surrounded by 1,000 miles of winding California Delta waterways, Stockton is the state's largest inland seaport, providing large ocean-going vessels with access from the San Francisco Bay to the Port of Stockton. The Delta provides outdoor and water recreation such as houseboating, swimming and water skiing, fishing, waterfowl hunting, and bird watching. (209) 547-2770.

Children's Museum of Stockton - *(Page 160, C4)* A center of learning and discovery for children, providing interactive exhibits in a warm, inviting environment. Exhibits encourage creative play and expression among children and provide insight into people and cultures. (209) 465-4386

TOURS

THE HIGH SIERRA

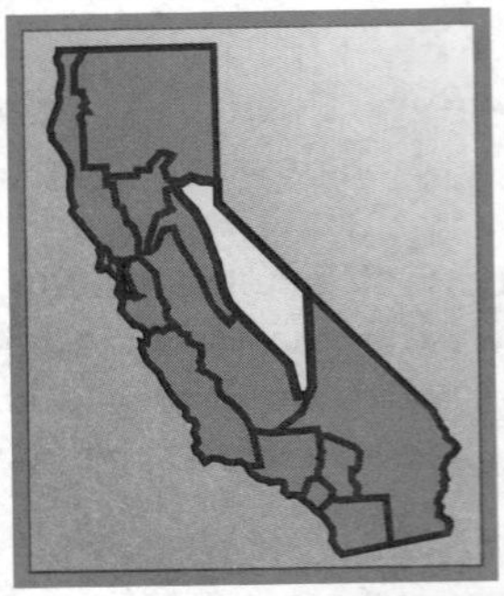

1 Inch to 39 Miles

Scale — 0 Miles 39

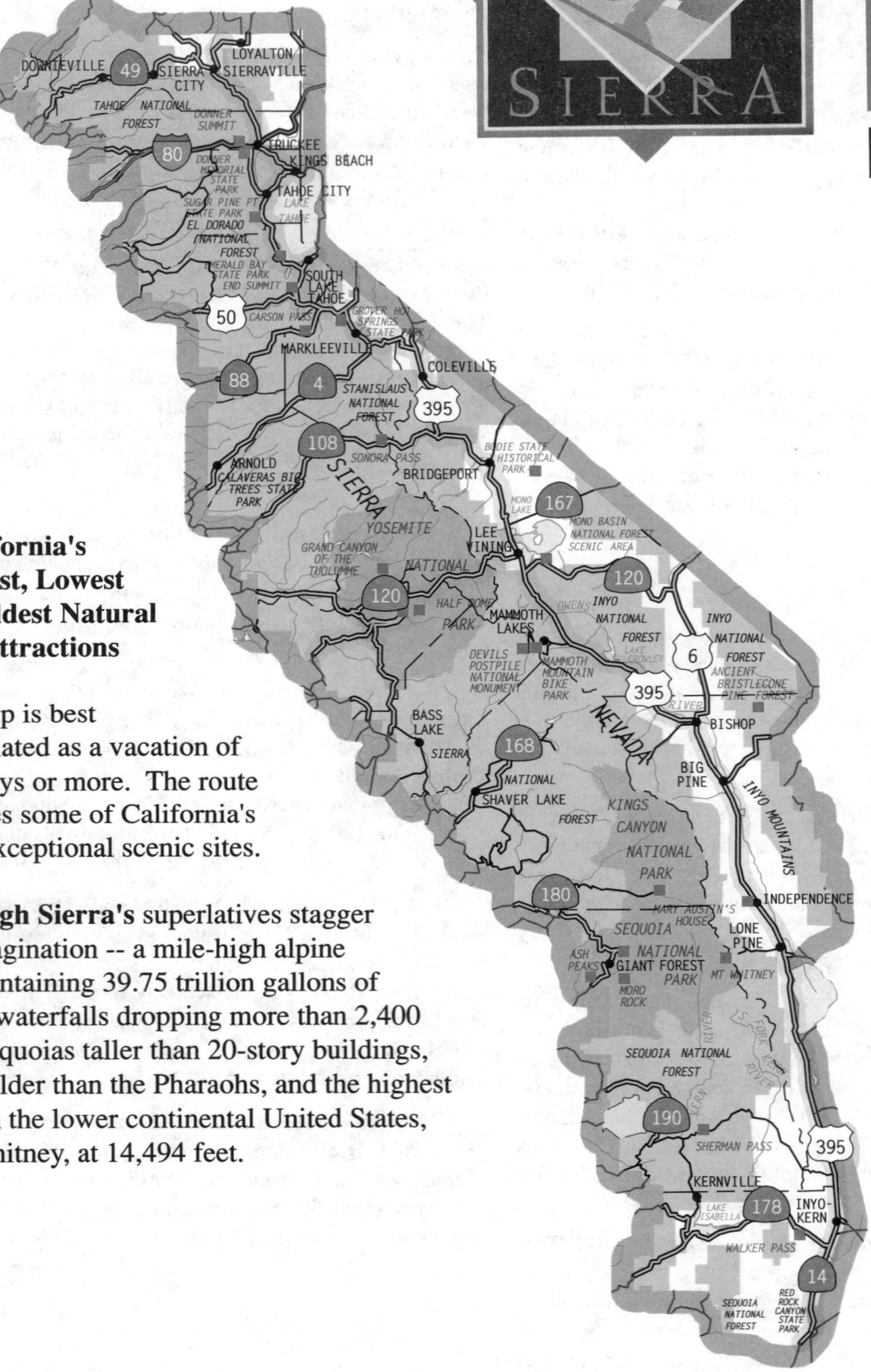

California's Highest, Lowest and Oldest Natural Attractions

This trip is best appreciated as a vacation of four days or more. The route includes some of California's most exceptional scenic sites.

The **High Sierra's** superlatives stagger the imagination -- a mile-high alpine lake containing 39.75 trillion gallons of water, waterfalls dropping more than 2,400 feet, sequoias taller than 20-story buildings, pines older than the Pharaohs, and the highest peak in the lower continental United States, Mt. Whitney, at 14,494 feet.

Driving Tour Points of Interest:

KINGS CANYON / SEQUOIA NATIONAL PARK - Perhaps one of the most beautiful and peaceful places on earth. The headquarters for both parks, Ash Mountain, is located 7 miles north of Three Rivers on Highway 198 *(Page 58, E5)*. The Visitors Center provides information, maps and brochures of the parks. (209) 565-3341

Along the 46-mile Generals Highway which links the two parks, there are numerous *points of interest*. The main attractions, of course, are the incredible Sequoias, the largest living things on earth. They have survived the last ice age and are found only along the western slope of the Sierra Nevada. Unbelievably, these 2,000-year-old giants were in danger of being destroyed by greedy loggers. Evidence of this careless harvest is on display at Big Stump Basin and should be a reminder to us of our responsibility to protect these and all natural wonders.

At **Moro Rock** *(Page 59, A4)* climbers can get a 100-mile panorama of surrounding mountains and valleys. At **Giant Forest** *(Page 59, A4)* the 2,500-year-old General Sherman Tree stands 272 feet high, the largest living thing on earth. The Congress Trail is a two-mile hike through several stands of sequoias; park rangers lead groups of visitors and explain the history of the trees. **Grant Grove** is the location of 4 or 5 of the largest sequoias in the world.

There are several full-service campgrounds within the two parks. Hiking and fishing are popular and horses may be rented for trips into the backcountry. The parks are open all year, although some roads are closed in the winter.

WESTERN SLOPE - The western portion of the Southern Sierra is dominated by Kings Canyon and Sequoia National Parks, twin treasures joined end to end. The main entrance for both parks, Ash Mountain, can be reached by main road, Highway 180 east from Fresno *(Page 58, D3)*; but if time allows, we recommend taking the zigzag route that threads through the Sequoia National Forest from Lake Isabella. Forests of tall trees, craggy granite rocks, waterfalls and numerous campgrounds line the way. The county-maintained road is closed during the winter. Call CALTRANS for road conditions. (916) 445-1534

EASTERN SLOPE - Highway 395 is a straight course due north and south through the Owens Valley, flanked by dramatic granite walls of the Sierra Nevada to the west and the Inyo-White mountains and Mojave Desert to the east. Joshua trees and volcanic rock pepper the roadside landscape.

Visitors Center - Located at the Junction of Highway 395 and Highway 136. This excellent center provides extensive information, maps, exhibits, and information concerning the Eastern Sierras & High Desert. Books and gift items are also for sale.

LONE PINE - *(Page 60, A4)* Gateway to both Death Valley and Mt. Whitney. This is a great place to stock up on provisions before tackling either of these formidable giants.

Alabama Hills - A rocky area northwest of town that has been used in countless movie westerns.

Whitney Portal - *(Page 59, E4)* 13 miles west of Lone Pine, it is the trail head for hikers attempting to ascend Mt. Whitney. Mt. Whitney Ranger District: (619) 876-6200

BISHOP - *(Page 51, D4)* Business and recreational center of the Owens Valley. Visitors Information: (619) 873-8405

Laws Railroad Museum - Splendid restoration of the once-active town of Laws. In addition to a locomotive and cars, the 11-acre area has several buildings which display antique collections of everything from bottles to baggage. (619) 873-5950

MAMMOTH LAKES - *(Page 50, D2)* One of California's year-round getaways. While snow skiing is the wintertime focus, the area offers such summertime activities as hiking, camping, pack trips, water sports and excellent trout fishing. Mammoth Lakes Visitors Bureau: (800) 367-6572

DEVIL'S POSTPILE NATIONAL MONUMENT - *(Page 50, C2)* The monument consists of a sheer wall of symmetrical basaltic columns more than 60 feet high. The unusual formation was created eons ago by the crystallization of volcanic matter. A trail leads to the top where the surface resembles mosaic tiles. (619) 934-2289

YOSEMITE NATIONAL PARK - *(Page 49)* The grandeur cannot be adequately captured in the words of John Muir or the photographs of Ansel Adams. Yosemite must be experienced first-hand. The park covers nearly 1,200 square miles of glacier-carved valleys, massive cliffs and Alpine wilderness. It is one of the nation's most popular attractions with nearly 3 million visitors each year. Summer (June-Sept.) is the busiest time. Check with park service for seasonal road closures and trail information as well as accommodations, campsite reservations and activities. Park headquarters *(Page 63, D1)* in Yosimite Valley provides guides, maps and information.

MONO LAKE - Tufa State Reserve *(Page 43, D5)* A surrealistic landscape of limestone formations rise from the lake. The area has scant vegetation and the water is three times as salty as the ocean. The salt water sustains a unique ecosystem of algae, brine shrimp and brine flies which in turn attract 80 species of waterfowl. Some of the tufa has been exposed by the declining water level and walking trails allow a close-up view. (619) 647-6331

BODIE STATE HISTORIC PARK - *(Page 43, C3)* A "genuine" gold-mining ghost town. What remains of the original town has been left to natural decay and presents an authentic glimpse of the once booming Old West Town. The road to Bodie is partially unpaved, so call for road conditions. (619) 647-6445

SOUTH LAKE TAHOE - *(Page 36, A3)* The more populated end of the lake with luxury hotels, restaurants and shops. The Nevada side allows gambling casinos.

Vikingsholm - *(Page 35, E3)* A private residence built in 1929, in classic Scandinavian design. A steep, one-mile hike is necessary to tour this lovely, secluded estate.

LAKE TAHOE - *(Page 35 & 36)* "The Lake of the Sky." This is a premier resort area offering a full spectrum of outdoor activities for the entire family. The 72 miles of shoreline provide access to the incredibly clear blue lake; the surrounding mountains are dotted with everything from campsites to casinos. Lake Tahoe's Visitor Authority: (916) 544-5050

TAHOE CITY - *(Page 35, E2)* The north shore of Lake Tahoe includes many popular ski resorts. Pine forests and mountain lodges dominate, making it a quieter, more rustic experience.

DOWNIEVILLE - *(Page 26, D4)* Once a boom town of 5,000 miners. Today, an audio walking-tour highlights 23 historic sites and buildings. The museum and courthouse exhibits are especially interesting. Call for hours: (916) 289-3261

Other Points of Interest:

ANCIENT BRISTLECONE PINE FOREST - *(Page 52, A3)* A 28,000 acre area of the White Mountains that contains the oldest living things on earth. These gnarled pine trees are over 4,000 years old. (619) 873-2500

The view southwest provides a spectacular panorama of the Sierra Nevada and Mount Whitney.

CALAVERAS BIG TREES STATE PARK *(Page 41, D3)* Two groves of giant redwoods and pines. These sequoias were the first of their kind to receive world-wide attention. Scientists and journalists flocked to the forests in the 1850's to examine and report on these natural phenomena. (209) 795-2334

The Enchanting Middle Kingdom and a Castle on the Hill

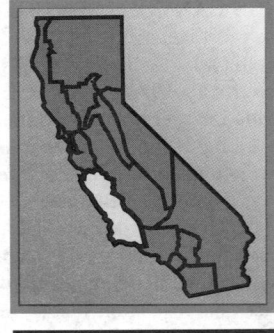

1 Inch to 29 Miles

Scale

Miles

0   29

Plan a minimum of three to five days to fully enjoy all the attractions and points of interest that this 388 mile round trip offers. From Ventura Harbor to the red tile roofs of Santa Barbara, to walnut groves, to a Danish Hamlet and the Lompoc Flower Fields, through the "Barbecue Capital of the World" to the home of the Pismo Clam, from the state's burgeoning new wine regions to Hearst's famous Castle to Monterey's Aquarium by-the-bay and world class golf, you'll be amazed at the stunning sites of this tour.

The **Central Coast**, with its austere cypress trees, fog-shrouded cliffs, and crashing surf immortalized in photographs by Ansel Adams and Edward Weston, continues to draw vacationers year after year.

MONTEREY BAY

MARINA
Monterey Bay
Aquarium
PACIFIC GROVE
17 MILE DRIVE
PEBBLE BEACH
CARMEL-BY-THE-SEA
PT LOBOS STATE RESERVE
GARRAPATA STATE PARK
CANNERY ROW
FISHERMANS WHARF
MONTEREY
MISSION SAN CARLOS BORROMEO

HOLLISTER
SAN JUAN BAUTISTA
MISSION SAN JUAN BAUTISTA
SALINAS
101
25
PINNACLES NATIONAL MONUMENT
GONZALES
MISSION NUESTRA SENORA
SOLEDAD
NEW IDRIA
GREENFIELD

POINT SUR
BIG SUR
ANDREW MOLERA STATE PARK
NEPENTHE
PFEIFFER-BIG SUR STATE PARK
LOS PADRES
JULIA PFEIFFER BURNS STATE PARK
LOPEZ POINT
COAST
NATIONAL
FOREST
RANGE
KING CITY
198
SAN LUCAS
MISSION SAN ANTONIO
JOLON
SAN ANTONIO RES
PARKFIELD

CAPE SAN MARTIN
LAKE NACIMIENTO
CAMP ROBERTS MILITARY RES
MISSION SAN MIGUEL
SAN MIGUEL
41
SHANDON

POINT PIEDRAS BLANCAS
POINT SAN SIMEON
SAN SIMEON
HEARST SAN SIMEON STATE HISTORICAL MONUMENT
CAMBRIA
46
PASO ROBLES
ATASCADERO
101
58

CAYUCOS
MORRO BAY
41
ESTERO BAY
MORRO BAY STATE PARK
MONTANA DE ORO STATE PARK
1
LOS OSOS
MISSION SAN LUIS OBISPO
SAN LUIS OBISPO

PISMO BEACH
GROVER BEACH
PISMO DUNES STATE VEHICULAR REC AREA
GUADALUPE
POINT SAL
ARROYO GRANDE
TWITCHELL RESERVOIR
NIPOMO
SANTA MARIA

PACIFIC

LA PURISIMA MISSION
LOS ALAMOS
135
101
CUYAMA
166
SIERRA MADRE MOUNTAINS
LOS
VENTUCOPA
33
PADRES
NATIONAL
FOREST
LAKE PIRU

POINT ARGUELLO
LOMPOC
246
BUELLTON
1
SOLVANG
MISSION SANTA INES
SANTA YNEZ
NOJOQUI FALLS CO PK
154
MTNS
LAKE CACHUMA
GOLETA
SUMMERLAND
OJAI
150
SANTA PAULA
FILLMORE
126
MOORPARK
SIMI VALLEY

POINT CONCEPCION
GAVIOTA STATE PARK
MISSION SANTA BARBARA
SANTA BARBARA
CARPINTERIA
MISSION SAN BUENAVENTURA
VENTURA
CHANNEL ISLAND NATIONAL PARK VISITOR CENTER
118
OXNARD
23
RONALD REAGAN PRESIDENTIAL LIB & CTR
THOUSAND OAKS
1

OCEAN
CHANNEL ISLANDS NATIONAL PARK
SAN MIGUEL ISLAND
SANTA ROSA ISLAND
SANTA CRUZ ISLAND
ANACAPA ISLAND
PORT HUENEME
LAGUNA POINT

TOURS

Driving Tour Points of Interest:

SANTA BARBARA - *(Page 87, C4)* A charming city of adobe buildings, red tile roofs and palm trees. Among the fine galleries, restaurants and shops in the downtown area, there are many historical plaques and markers identifying early buildings *(Page 174)*. The Visitors Center, 1 Santa Barbara Street, (805) 965-3021, provides copies of a Red Tile Walking Tour which will guide you to over a dozen points of interest in a 12-block area.

CACHUMA LAKE RECREATION AREA - *(Page 87, A3)* A large, full-service campground. In addition to 600 campsites, there are hiking trails, a boating and fishing marina, horseback riding, bicycle rentals, a general store, Weekend Fireside Theatre and special 2-hour cruises on the lake to view migrating eagles. (805) 688-4658

SOLVANG - *(Page 86, D3)* A Danish village established in 1911 with old-country architecture, windmills, cobblestone sidewalks, and good-luck storks. This enchanting town celebrates its Hans Christian Andersen heritage with authentic shops, bakeries, and many fine restaurants. Solvang Information Center: (805) 688-6144

Old Mission Santa Ines - Located a short distance from the heart of downtown Solvang. Established in 1804, it is the 19th Franciscan mission and one of the best preserved.

NOJOQUI FALLS COUNTY PARK - *(Page 86, E3)* A 164-foot waterfall, 7 miles south of Solvang. This unique local "natural wonder" is a popular picnic and hiking spot.

LOMPOC - *(Page 86, B3)* Lompoc Valley is known as the "Flower Seed Capital of the World." Experts agree that 50-75% of all flower seeds in the world come from this tiny area. A map outlining a 19-mile self-guided tour called the "Valley Flower Drive" is available from the Lompoc Chamber of Commerce. (805) 736-4567

La Purisima Mission - *(Page 86, C2)* Founded in 1787, it was the 11th Franciscan mission and well known as the most fully restored, located in the most original setting. It has 9 buildings with 900 acres of park and 12 miles of foot trails. (805) 733-3713

PISMO BEACH - *(Page 76, B4)* Bordered by groves of tall eucalyptus trees which were planted at the turn of the century and today are a haven for migrating Monarch butterflies that travel from as far away as Canada each Fall to seek protection until Spring. The sand dunes are the most extensive coastal dunes remaining in California. **Pismo** is a Chumash Indian word for "blobs of tar," known today as Pismo clams.

Pismo Dunes State Vehicular Recreation Area - Provides access to 12 miles of beach where you may drive your car. Camping, hiking, surf fishing, and clam digging are permitted on the dunes. (805) 473-7220

SAN LUIS OBISPO - *(Page 76, B3)* The County Seat and bustling town of 43,900 residents. For county-wide visitors information call (805) 541-8000

Mission San Luis Obispo de Tolosa - *(Page 172, C3)* Established in 1772, it is named for a 13th century French saint. The mission is 5th in the chain of 21 missions and still serves as a parish church. (805) 543-6850 or (805) 781-8220

MORRO BAY - *(Page 75, E3)* The huge dome-shaped rock, for which Morro Bay is named, is actually a centuries-old, 576-foot volcanic dome. The Chamber of Commerce, (805) 772-4467, provides a map of the city and other helpful information. Walk along the Embarcadero to watch the fishermen at work, or browse through the interesting shops.

CAMBRIA - *(Page 75, C2)* This quiet village, tucked away among the pines, was a former lumbering, shipping, mining, and whaling station. Today, the restored town is a popular artist colony, filled with unique galleries, antique stores, and gift shops. (805) 927-3624

HEARST SAN SIMEON STATE HISTORICAL MONUMENT - *(Page 75, B1)* Popularly known as the "Hearst Castle." The gargantuan estate of the late William Randolph Hearst with its lavish architecture, furnishings and landscaping was donated to the state and is open to the public. Tours are conducted and reservations are necessary. (800) 444-4445

PFEIFFER BIG SUR STATE PARK - *(Page 64, B2)* Pine trees, chaparral and redwoods create a peaceful refuge. Though the park is not large, 807 acres, it provides access to the Los Padres National Forest and the Ventana Wilderness. Combined, there are over 300,000 acres for hiking, camping and fishing along Big Sur River. (408) 667-2315

Nepenthe - Means "no sorrow." This fine restaurant was designed by a student of Frank Lloyd Wright. Redwood and adobe were used so that the building became "one with the landscape and the earth it stands on." Located on the ocean side of the highway, three miles south of Big Sur State Park.

POINT LOBOS - *(Page 54, A5)* One of the most strikingly beautiful areas of California coastline. This state reserve takes special care to preserve the unspoiled shoreline and natural flora. The area is strictly for day use and the number of visitors is limited.

CARMEL BY THE SEA - *(Page 54, A5)* The village flavor of Carmel reflects the creativeness and individuality of its many artists and writers. Hilly streets, whimsical architecture and natural landscaping combine to create a storybook aura.

Mission San Carlos Borromeo - *(Page 168, B4)* Founded in 1770 as the 2nd in the eventual chain of 21 missions. Father Serra, the "Father of the Missions," has his final resting place located here. It is a fine example of the typical mission architecture. (408) 624-3600

17-Mile Drive - *(Page 53)* Beginning at the north end of Carmel, it winds through scenic wooded areas of the Del Monte Forest and fabulous shoreline, past the famous **Pebble Beach Golf Course** and on to Monterey.

MONTEREY - *(Page 54, A4)* A favorite year-round resort. The Chamber of Commerce, (408) 649-1770, can provide detailed information and walking-tour maps. **Cannery Row** and **Fisherman's Wharf** are popular areas for restaurants and shopping. The scenic peninsula along Ocean View Boulevard to the Pt. Pinos Lighthouse is lined with Victorian homes, many converted into Bed and Breakfast Inns.

Monterey Bay Aquarium - *(Page 167, E2)* This "hands -on" aquarium is one of the largest in the world with special exhibits and habitats for over 5,000 sea creatures. (408) 648-4888

MISSION SAN JUAN BAUTISTA - *(Page 54, D3)* The 15th Franciscan Mission. It is well preserved and still an active Catholic church. The beautiful plaza where it sits also has several other historic buildings. (408) 623-4528

PINNACLES NATIONAL MONUMENT - *(Page 55, B5)* This area is a geological phenomenon, created from an ancient volcano that erupted along the San Andreas Rift Zone, just east of the park. Hiking, rock climbing, cave exploring, picnicking and camping are permitted. Since crags and spires create a ridge through the center of the park, there is no road connecting both entrances. (408) 389-4485

SOLEDAD MISSION - *(Page 65, A1)* The **Mission Nuestra Senora de la Soledad**, "Our Lady of Solitude," was founded in 1791 as the 13th in a chain of 21 California Missions. It has been restored and offers a museum and chapel. (408) 678-2586

TOURS

THE **INLAND EMPIRE**

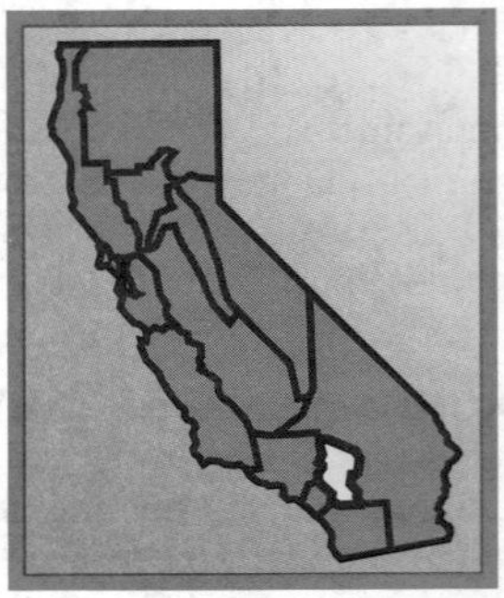

1 Inch to 14 Miles

Scale

0   Miles   14

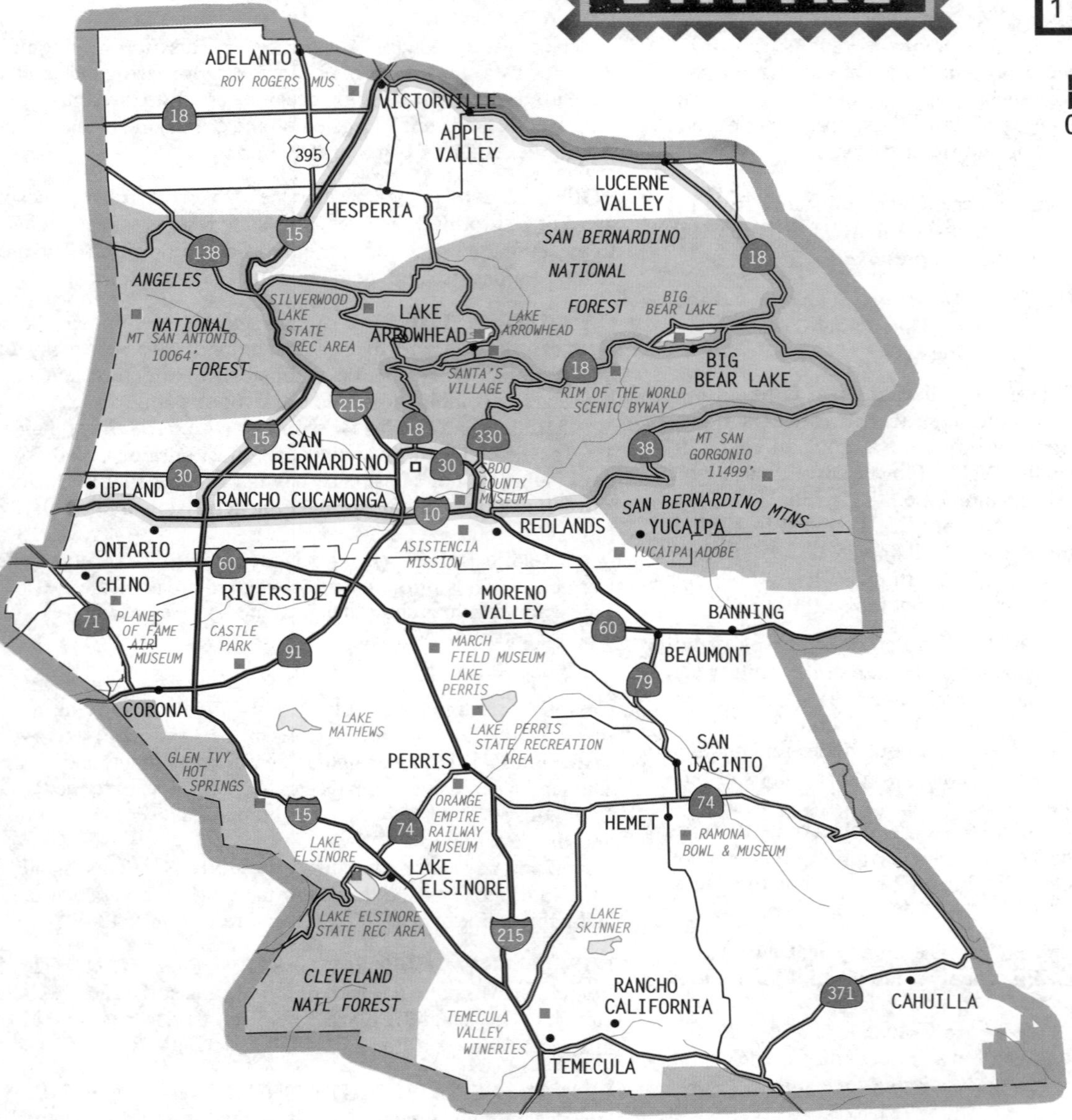

ADELANTO
ROY ROGERS MUS
18
VICTORVILLE
APPLE
VALLEY
395
HESPERIA
LUCERNE
VALLEY
138
15
SAN BERNARDINO
NATIONAL
18
ANGELES
SILVERWOOD
LAKE
STATE
REC AREA
FOREST
BIG
BEAR LAKE
NATIONAL
MT SAN ANTONIO
10064'
FOREST
LAKE
ARROWHEAD
LAKE
ARROWHEAD
18
BIG
BEAR LAKE
SANTA'S
VILLAGE
RIM OF THE WORLD
SCENIC BYWAY
215
15
18
330
38
MT SAN
GORGONIO
11499'
SAN
BERNARDINO
30
30
SBDO
COUNTY
MUSEUM
UPLAND
RANCHO CUCAMONGA
10
SAN BERNARDINO MTNS
ONTARIO
REDLANDS
YUCAIPA
ASISTENCIA
MISSION
YUCAIPA ADOBE
60
CHINO
RIVERSIDE
MORENO
VALLEY
BANNING
71
PLANES
OF FAME
AIR
MUSEUM
CASTLE
PARK
91
60
BEAUMONT
MARCH
FIELD MUSEUM
LAKE
PERRIS
79
CORONA
LAKE
MATHEWS
LAKE PERRIS
STATE RECREATION
AREA
SAN
JACINTO
GLEN IVY
HOT
SPRINGS
PERRIS
HEMET
74
RAMONA
BOWL & MUSEUM
15
ORANGE
EMPIRE
RAILWAY
MUSEUM
74
LAKE
ELSINORE
LAKE
ELSINORE
215
LAKE
SKINNER
LAKE ELSINORE
STATE REC AREA
CLEVELAND
NATL FOREST
RANCHO
CALIFORNIA
371
CAHUILLA
TEMECULA
VALLEY
WINERIES
TEMECULA

Valleys and Peaks of the Inland Empire

Southern California's Inland Empire is a land of towering mountain peaks, fertile valleys and vibrant communities. The region is rich in history and provides a wealth of recreational opportunities. This tour requires a minimum of two days to fully enjoy the diverse attractions found in the area.

The **Inland Empire** gave rise to the popular conception that in Southern California, one can water-ski and snow-ski in the same day... it's really possible. Lakes for warm weather sports are just a short trip from snow-clad mountains. Wine tasting from local vineyards, picking apples in season or camping in a national forest, or shopping at its best, this region has it all.

Driving Tour Points of Interest:

ROY ROGERS MUSEUM - *(Page 91, B3)* Western film stars Roy Rogers and Dale Evans, family memorabilia including Roy's famous horse, Trigger; walk-thru exhibits. Open seven days a week 9 a.m. to 5 p.m., except Thanksgiving and Christmas.
(619) 243-4547

SILVERWOOD LAKE STATE RECREATION AREA - *(Page 91, B5)* On Highway 138. The park is a forest of Ponderosa pine, cedar, oak and fir. The area provides excellent camping and picnicking while the man-made lake offers fishing, swimming, water-skiing and boating. (619) 389-2303

RIM OF THE WORLD HIGHWAY - *(Page 99, C1)* A 40-mile scenic drive along Highway 18 north of San Bernardino. The route threads along the 5,000 to 7,000-foot crest of the San Bernardino Mountains, through several rustic communities and resort areas.

Lake Arrowhead - *(Page 91, C5)* A beautiful man-made lake in an Alpine setting. It is a year-round resort for nature lovers and sports enthusiasts. Restaurants, both quaint and luxurious, lodges, shops and theatres complete the vacation package.

Big Bear Lake - *(Page 91, E5)* Known for crisp air and spectacular scenery, a wide range of accommodations, restaurants and activities. In the summer, the 7-mile lake is a playground for water sports; in the winter, the surrounding mountains offer several snow-skiing areas and cozy cabin retreats.

San Bernardino County Museum - *(Page 99, C2)* An especially exciting place for children because of "hands-on" exhibits of small animals and reptiles. The Museum also boasts a collection of 100,000 bird eggs. Located in Redlands. (909) 798-8570

Other Points of Interest:

RIVERSIDE ART MUSEUM - *(Page 205, C2)* Built in 1929 in the Mission Revival tradition, the museum offers art exhibits, gallery and restaurant. Placed on the National Register of Historic Places in 1982. Open Mon.-Sat. 10:00 a.m. to 4 p.m. (909) 684-7111

RIVERSIDE MUNICIPAL MUSEUM - *(Page 205, B2)* Italian Renaissance structure contains a large collection of native American Indian artifacts and exhibits of the citrus industry's early days and local history. (909) 782-5273

MARCH FIELD MUSEUM - *(Page 99, C3)* Static displays of aircraft, flying memorabilia and vintage planes. With prior notice, a film titled "The March Field Story" can be viewed. Open Mon - Fri. 10 a.m. to 4 p.m.; Sat. and Sun. noon to 4 p.m. Closed holidays.

LAKE PERRIS STATE RECREATIONAL AREA - *(Page 99, C3)* Boating, camping, fishing, swimming, water slide, wind surfing, jet skiing, water skiing. Boat rentals available, sailing, bicycling, horseback riding trails, hiking trails, rock climbing and picnicking. (909) 657-0676

ORANGE EMPIRE RAILWAY MUSEUM - *(Page 99, B4)* Railroad and trolley memorabilia. Walk-thru exhibits, picnicking. Trolley rides on weekends. All-day passes. Open Sat., Sun. and major holidays. Grounds open daily. Closed Thanksgiving and Christmas. (909) 943-3020

LAKE ELSINORE RECREATION AREA - *(Page 99-B4)* This 2,954-acre area includes 600 developed campsites; fishing, swimming, boating and food service available. (909) 674-3177

PLANES OF FAME MUSEUM - *(Page U, D3)* The museum houses a unique collection of World War II airplanes and fighter jets, many of them flyable and exhibits of military aviation memorabilia. Open daily except Christmas, 9 a.m. to 5 p.m. (909) 597-3722 or 597-3514

SKI AREAS

Bear Mountain - *(Page 92, A5)* P.O. Box 6812, Big Bear Lake 92315, (909) 585-2519. 2 quad chairs, 5 double chairs, 3 triple chairs, 3 pomas. Summit elevation 8,800 ft. Downhill

Mountain High - *(Page 90, D5)* P.O. Box 428, Wrightwood 92397, (619) 249-5477. 11 chairs, 1 tow. Summit elevation 8,200 ft. Downhill

Ski Sunrise - *(Page 90, D4)* P.O. Box 645, Wrightwood 92397, (619) 249-6150. Off Hwy. 2. Summit elevation 7,600 ft. Downhill

Snow Summit - *(Page 100, A1)* 880 Summit Blvd., P.O. Box 77, Big Bear Lake 92315, (909) 866-5766. 11 chairs, 230 skiable acres, 3 food service lodges, ski school and rentals. Summit elevation 8,200 ft. Downhill

Snow Valley - *(Page 99, D1)* P.O. Box 2337, Running Springs 92382, (909) 867-2751. Located in the San Bernardino Mountains off Highway 18, 4 miles east of Running Springs. 13 chair lifts and 230 acres of skiing terrain. Just 85 miles from Los Angeles. Group rates available. Downhill

COPYRIGHT 1997 ◄—N—►

Thomas Bros. Maps®

TOURS

THE

DESERTS

1 Inch to 43 Miles

Scale

0 Miles 43

168

SCOTTYS CASTLE

EUREKA DUNES

GRAPEVINE MOUNTAINS

DEATH

INYO COUNTY VISITORS CENTER

KEELER

OWENS LAKE

190

VALLEY

FURNACE CREEK

AMARGOSA

DEATH VALLEY JUNCTION

FUNERAL MOUNTAINS

OLANCHA

HAIWEE RESERVOIR

NATIONAL

BADWATER -282'

RANGE

CHINA LAKE NAVAL WEAPONS CENTER

395

PARK

178

SHOSHONE

TECOPA HOT SPRINGS

TECOPA

COUNTY PARK

TRONA

SEARLES LAKE

RIDGECREST

178

CHINA LAKE

TRONA PINNACLES

127

CHINA LAKE NAVAL WEAPONS CENTER

FORT IRWIN MILITARY RESERVATION

JOHANNESBURG

RANDSBURG GHOST TOWN

SILVER DRY LAKE

BAKER

EAST MOJAVE NATIONAL SCENIC AREA

RED ROCK CANYON STATE PARK

FORT IRWIN

SODA DRY LAKE

SODA SPRINGS

MITCHELL CAVERNS NATURAL PRESERVE

CALIFORNIA CITY

RAINBOW BASIN

CALICO GHOST TOWN

15

KELSO

US 95

MOJAVE

BORON

58

BARSTOW

DESERT

NEEDLES

NEEDLES MARINA

14

EDWARDS AIR FORCE BASE

ROGERS LAKE

395

CALICO MTNS ARCHAEOLOGICAL PROJECT

LUDLOW

40

AMBOY

CADIZ

CHEMEHUEVI VALLEY INDIAN RESERVATION

247

TWENTYNINE PALMS MARINE CORPS BASE

BRISTOL LAKE

PARKER DAM

247

LUCERNE LAKE

CADIZ LAKE

DANBY LAKE

1 OASIS WATER PARK
2 DESERT MUSEUM
3 INDIAN CANYONS
4 LIVING DESERT
5 PAINTED GORGE

TWENTYNINE PALMS

YUCCA VALLEY

62

PUEBLO MUSEUM

DESERT HOT SPRINGS

JOSHUA TREE NATIONAL PARK

62

95

177

PALM SPRINGS AERIAL TRAMWAY

PALM SPRINGS

CATHEDRAL CITY

RANCHO MIRAGE

10

DESERT CENTER

BLYTHE

JACINTO PK

IDYLLWILD

SAN JACINTO STATE PARK

INDIAN WELLS

INDIO

COACHELLA

COLORADO RIVER

PALM DESERT

195

LA QUINTA

74

SANTA ROSA MTNS

SALTON SEA

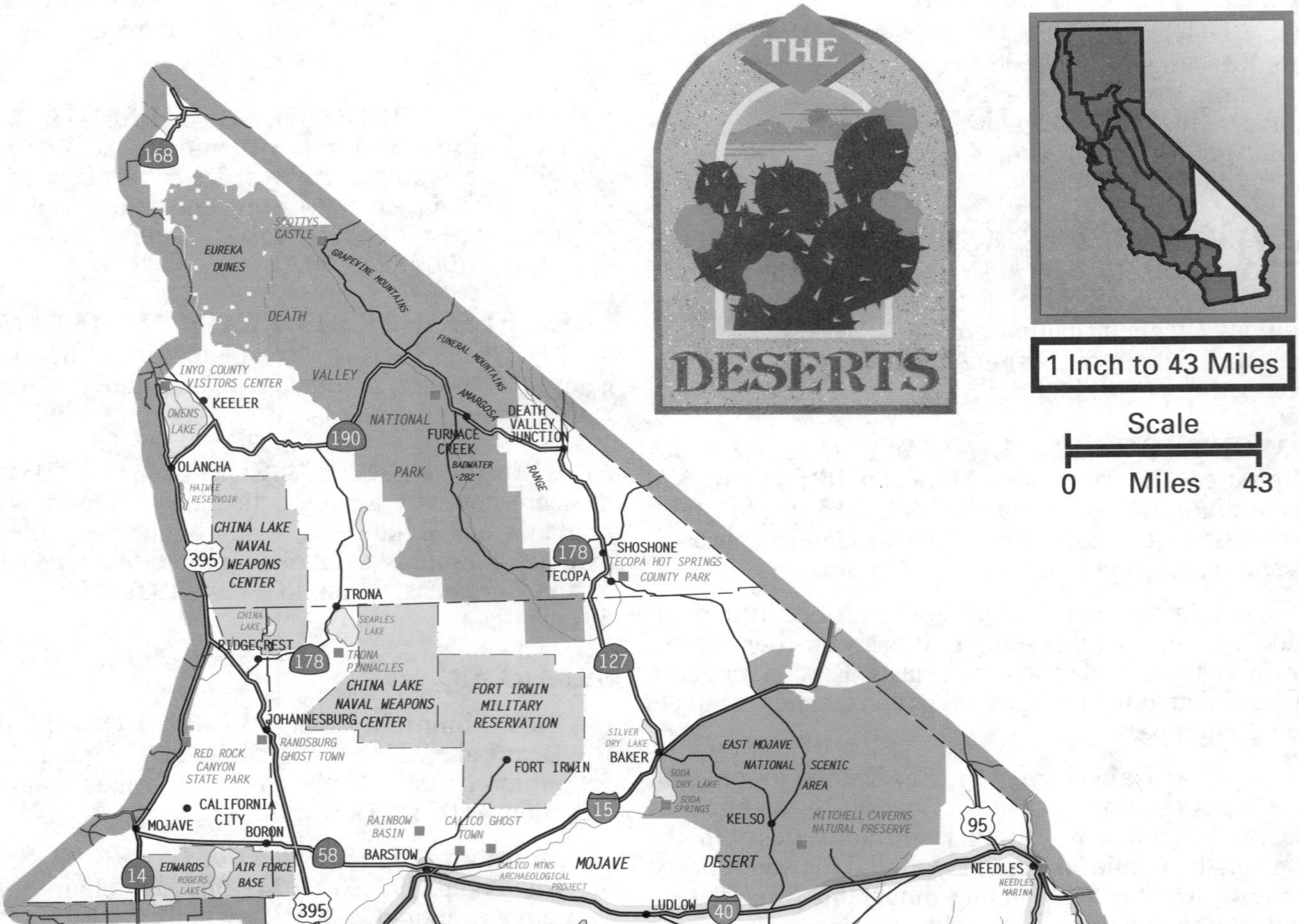

Deserts, Resorts,
Joshua Trees and the
Old West

This 3 to 5-day tour takes you
through California's vast Mojave
desert to the Arizona and Nevada
borders and returns through historic
gold and silver mining country.

Miles of sand and cactus suddenly come alive
in an explosion of color in the **Deserts**; the
warm desert in bloom is unforgettable. But most
of the year the vast expanses of cholla, prickly pear,
and Joshua trees create a desolate grandeur.

86

SALTON SEA NATIONAL WILDLIFE REFUGE

111

CALIPATRIA

78

PICACHO STATE RECREATION AREA

115

WESTMORELAND

BRAWLEY

FORT YUMA INDIAN RES

IMPERIAL

EL CENTRO

HOLTVILLE

8

98

CALEXICO

Driving Tour Points of Interest:

PALMS-TO-PINES HIGHWAY - The 64-mile scenic drive through the San Bernardino National Forest and San Jacinto Mountains.

Idyllwild - *(Page 100, B4)* Small, mountain community with lots of shops and restaurants. The Idyllwild Visitors Center has a splendid museum and a wealth of information. (909) 659-3850

INDIO - *(Page 101, A4)* "The Date Capital of the World." 200,000 date palms yield 40 million pounds of many varieties of dates. Stop at Shield's Date Gardens for blackdate ice cream and a 20-minute slide show on the romance of the date. (619) 347-0996

LIVING DESERT - *(Page 100, E4)* A 1,200-acre park containing the plants and animals of various desert regions. Fascinating exhibits and 6 miles of trails introduce visitors to desert life beyond the civilized world. Closed in August only. (619) 346-5694

PALM SPRINGS - *(Page 206)* World-class resort with exclusive shops, fine restaurants and luxury hotels galore. Nicknamed the "Golf Capital of the World," Palm Springs also boasts 8,000 swimming pools and an average of 330 days of sunshine each year. Call the Visitors Bureau for information. (619) 770-9000

Desert Museum - *(Page 206, A3)* A unique structure which houses an eclectic combination of contemporary art exhibits, regular concerts and dance performances. (619) 325-7186

Moorten Botanical Garden - *(Page 206, B5)* A 4-acre garden filled with 3,000 varieties of desert plants representing several regions of the world. (619) 327-6555

Aerial Tramway - *(Page 100, C3)* Called the "Eighth Engineering Wonder of the World," it is the longest singlelift passenger tramway in the world. Two 80-passenger trams rise from the desert floor to 8,516 feet for a breathtaking view of Palm Springs, the Coachella Valley and the Salton Sea. At the top is a restaurant, gift shop and picnic area. A 6-mile hike leads to the top of Mt. San Jacinto (10,840') where on a clear day the view extends to the mountain ranges of Las Vegas. (619) 325-1391

Mt. San Jacinto State Park - *(Page 100, B3)* Combines granite peaks and sub-Alpine forests of mostly untouched wilderness. Camping and extensive hiking and riding trails are available. (909) 659-2607

Indian Canyons - *(Page 100, C4)* Four canyons, once inhabited by the Agua Caliente Cahuilla Indians. Palm and Andreas Canyons have the most and second-most palm trees in the world, with Murray Canyon listed as fourth. Tahquitz Canyon is noted for its magnificent waterfalls and pools. Each canyon is a lush and tranquil oasis. Excellent for hiking, picnicking and birdwatching.

DESERT HOT SPRINGS - *(Page 100, D2)* Another popular resort, just northeast of Palm Springs, across Highway 10. It is known for natural hot mineral waters which reach temperatures of 200 degrees F. (800) FIND-DHS

Cabot's Old Indian Pueblo Museum - *(Page 100, D2)* A 35-room, Hopi-style pueblo filled with odd memorabilia, Indian artifacts, arts and crafts collected by the late owner, Cabot Yerxa. Closed July and August. (619) 329-7610

JOSHUA TREE NATIONAL PARK - *(Page 101, A2)* Encompasses two desert regions:

The Eastern Half is representative of the "low" Colorado Desert, arid and rocky, with the distinctive Ocotillo Cacti and numerous other plants and wildlife unique to the region.

The Western Half is the "high" Mojave Desert where Joshua Trees grow to 40 feet tall. A giant member of the lily family, it was supposedly named by the Mormons for its upstretched "praying" arms. The **Keys View** provides a dramatic view of the Coachella Valley and San Jacinto Mountains. There are no services within the park, but the well-maintained roads provide turnouts with information plaques and picnic tables. The unusual rock formations have been used as protection by Indians and hideouts by cattle rustlers in the past, and more recently were the backdrop to a private ranch.

Brochures and trail maps are available at the West Entrance Information Station. There are two visitor centers in the park. **The Oasis Visitor Center** at the Twenty-nine Palms entrance has a museum and short self-guided nature walk, (619) 367-7511. The **Cottonwood Visitor Center** is at the south entrance *(Page 101, D4)*.

Other Points of Interest:

DEATH VALLEY NATIONAL PARK - *(Page 61)* Far from desolate, this reserve is home to countless species of flora and fauna. The desert bighorn, golden eagle, mountain lion and desert tortoise also find sanctuary here. Highway 190 crosses a series of peaks and salt bogs, multi-colored vistas and unspoiled wilderness. There is a distinct drop in elevation as the road descends to **Badwater**, *(Page 72, A2)* the lowest spot in the western hemisphere, 282 feet below sea level. A few communities survive in the harsh desert where summer temperatures may reach 130 degrees F and average less than 2" of rainfall each year. The Visitors Center provides information, brochures and exhibits concerning the 2 million acres of national park. (619) 786-2331

Scotty's Castle - *(Page 61, B1)* Lavishly decorated Spanish/Moorish estate built in the 1920's now owned by the National Park Service. Daily tours are conducted.

Stovepipe Wells - *(Page 61, D4)* A small town with a motel and store. Nearby is a great location to play on the huge sand dunes.

SALTON SEA STATE RECREATION AREA - *(Page 108)* Created in 1905 when the Colorado River flooded. This 35-mile long inland sea is 230 feet below sea level and is one of the world's largest bodies of inland salt water. Gradual leaching of minerals from the land has made the water several times saltier than the ocean. Fish originally introduced in the 1950's by the Department of Fish and Game have adapted and survived . Seventy-five species of birds make this their permanent home while as many as 300 other species have migrated here at one time or another. The 17,868-acre Salton Sea area is undeveloped but is a popular area for boaters and fishermen. Campsites are available. (619) 393-3052

L.A.'s The Place

This driving tour is designed to capture the diversity of the Los Angeles area. From Pacific Coast Highway, to the magic of Hollywood, to historic landmarks and to various ethnic communities of the downtown, you'll enjoy shopping, dining, accommodations and the friendly people that make up this world-class destination.

1 Inch to 15 Miles

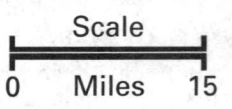
Scale
0   Miles   15

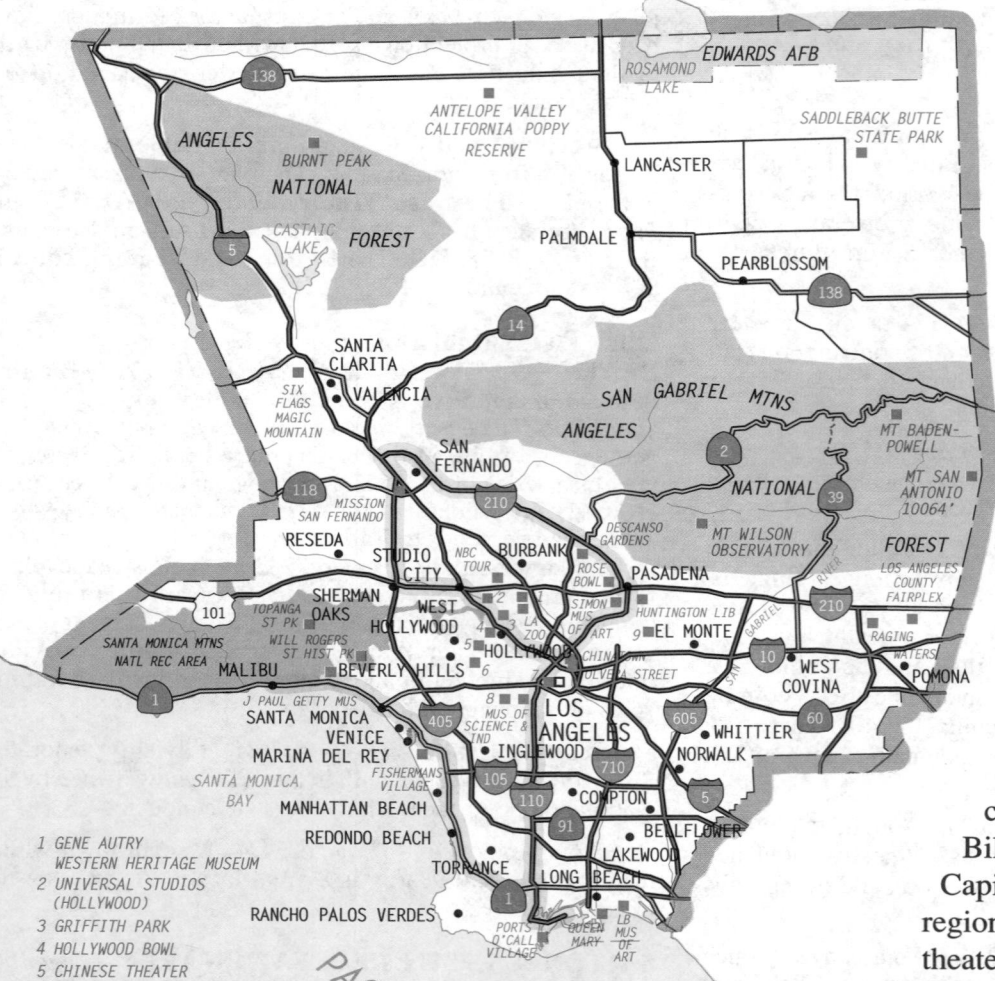

1 GENE AUTRY
  WESTERN HERITAGE MUSEUM
2 UNIVERSAL STUDIOS
  (HOLLYWOOD)
3 GRIFFITH PARK
4 HOLLYWOOD BOWL
5 CHINESE THEATER
6 LA BREA TAR PITS
  AND LA COUNTY MUSEUM
7 THOMAS BROS MAPS
8 EXPOSITION PARK
9 MISSION SAN GABRIEL

Los Angeles County is 4,083 square miles filled with an infinite variety of recreational and cultural opportunities.

Billed as the "Entertainment Capital of the World", the region features the best in theater and music, art and museums, television and motion pictures, sporting events and world-famous attractions.

Driving Tour Points of Interests:

While the people of other cities talk about the local weather, the people of Los Angeles and Orange County talk about the local traffic. The Southland has the most intricate freeway system in the world. Driving the freeways is often compared to an amusement park ride and a visit to Southern California would not be complete, or possible, without it (See Pages Q, R, S, and T or the fold-out map for an overview).

QUEEN MARY - *(Page 192, E4)* One of the largest passenger ships ever built. (310) 435-3511.

RANCHO PALOS VERDES - *(Page S, B3)* An area of rolling hills and exclusive homes. The **Wayfarer's Chapel** is an inspiring glass church designed by Lloyd Wright in 1946. (310) 377-1650

Highway 1 provides access to many beach cities, each with a unique personality (Page 97). *Redondo Beach has the surfers, Manhattan Beach has the yuppies, Marina Del Rey has the yachts and Venice has the bizarre.*

SANTA MONICA - *(Page 97, C2)* A broad, sparkling beach community with a very special pier. **Santa Monica Pier** - built in 1908, is a popular California landmark. Souvenir shops, restaurants, an arcade and historic carousel share this unique setting. It is a popular Hollywood film location. (310) 458-8900

J. PAUL GETTY MUSEUM - *(Page Q, A4)* The museum and surrounding gardens are a re-creation of an ancient Roman country villa. The museum houses a permanent collection of Greek and Roman antiquities and pre-twentieth century Western European art. Parking reservations are necessary. (310) 458-2003

TOPANGA - *(Page 97, B2)* This rustic mountain town and canyon became a popular mecca for the "counterculture" in the 1960's. The **Topanga State Park** is the nation's second largest urban park and the world's largest wildland situated within the boundaries of a major city. (310) 455-2465

Universal Studios - *(Page 181, B1)* A tram ride through the backlots and stages of a movieland park: (818) 777-3801; **Hollywood Bowl** - *(C3)* Magnificent outdoor amphitheatre and park: (213) 850-2000; **Mann's Chinese Theatre** - *(C4)* Hosts gala movie premieres: (213) 464-8111; **Hollywood Wax Museum** - *(C4)* Movie legends immortalized in wax, (213) 462-8860; **Walk of Fame** - *(D4)* The stars of the stars.

BEVERLY HILLS - *(Page 183)* One of the most glamorous celebrity residential communities in Southern California and one of the world's most exclusive shopping districts. Visitors Bureau: (310) 271-8174

HANCOCK PARK AREA - *(Page 184)* Another cluster of intriguing and diverse points of interest is only moments away: **Los Angeles County Museum of Art** - *(A2)* One of the most comprehensive art collections in the world: (213) 857-6000; **George C. Page Museum of La Brea Discoveries** - *(B2)* Showcases the research and outstanding fossils recovered from the adjacent Rancho La Brea Tar Pits: (213) 936-2230; **Farmer's Market** - *(A1)* Open-air market since 1934: (213) 933-9211; **CBS Studios** - *(A1)* Television programs in production.

EXPOSITION PARK - *(Page 185, C5)* South of the downtown area on Highway 110, take the Exposition Blvd. exit. **Natural History Museum** - More than 14,000,000 specimens, artifacts, and 300 million years of earth history on display in the nation's fourth largest natural history museum. (213) 744-3414

Also in this area: **California State Museum of Science and Industry, Aerospace Building, Los Angeles Memorial Coliseum, Sports Arena** and **Exposition Park Rose Gardens.** (213) 748-6131.

Nearby is the **University of Southern California Campus** and the **Shrine Civic Auditorium**.

DOWNTOWN LOS ANGELES - *(Page 185 & 186)* The "City of Angels." The first two stops should be the **Los Angeles Visitors Information Center** at the LA Hilton Hotel *(Page 185, E3)* and **Thomas Bros. Maps and Books**, 521 W. 6th St., *(Page 186, A3)*. (213) 627-4018

Olvera Street and El Pueblo de Los Angeles Historic Monument - *(Page 186, B2)* Founding site of Los Angeles includes 27 historic buildings. (213) 628-1274

Museum of Contemporary Art - *(Page 186, A3)* Sleek and geometric, devoted to the art and culture from 1940 to the present. (213) 626-6222

Music Center - *(Page 186, A2)* Performing arts complex which includes three major theatres. Tour information: (213) 972-7211.

GRIFFITH PARK - *(Page 182)* One of the world's largest municipal parks. In addition to hiking and horseback riding trails, a golf course and lots of picnic areas, the 4,000-acre park encompasses numerous other attractions:

Los Angeles Zoo - Features a new children's exploration park: (213) 666-4090; **Gene Autry Western Heritage Museum** - Bringing the excitement of the Old West back to life: (213) 667-2000; **Griffith Observatory** - For a close-up view of the stars: (213) 664-1191

TOURS

Sunshine, Beaches, Attractions, Resorts and More!

If you're searching for some of the world's finest restaurants and shopping experiences, look no further. The same goes for charming seaside communities, world-class theme parks, prime surfing and original art work. Again, look no further. Add to that outstanding recreational facilities, numerous parks and museums and it all adds up to this special driving tour of Orange County.

Orange County has long been famous for its family-oriented theme parks, 42 miles of shoreline and the citrus groves that gave the area its name. Today, the region has taken on an international sophistication undreamed of 50 years ago.

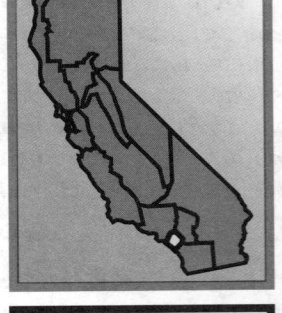

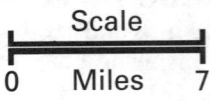

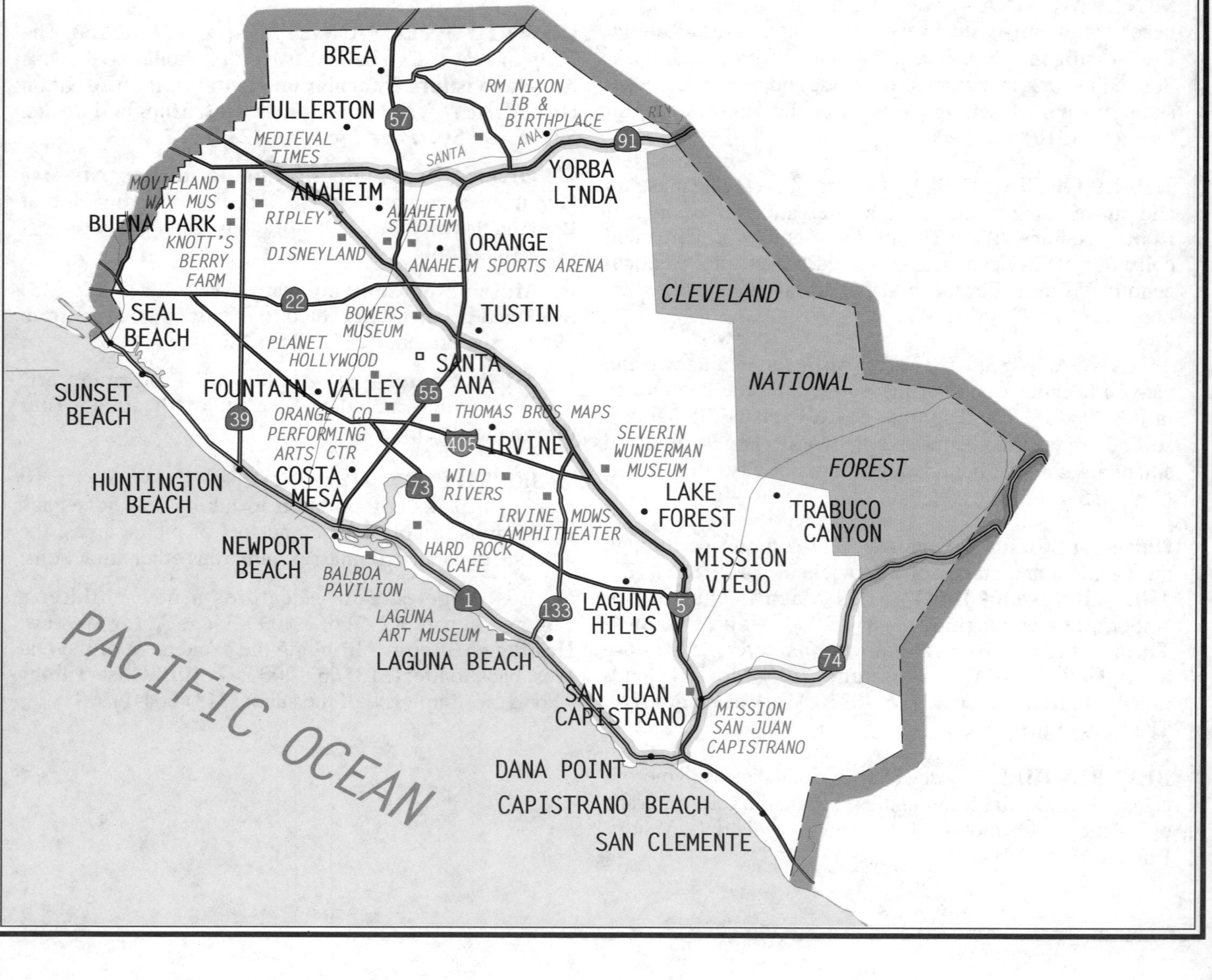

1 Inch to 7 Miles

Scale

0   Miles   7

TOURS

BREA

FULLERTON

RM NIXON LIB & BIRTHPLACE

57

MEDIEVAL TIMES

SANTA ANA

91

MOVIELAND WAX MUS

ANAHEIM

YORBA LINDA

BUENA PARK

RIPLEY'S

ANAHEIM STADIUM

KNOTT'S BERRY FARM

DISNEYLAND

ORANGE

ANAHEIM SPORTS ARENA

CLEVELAND

SEAL BEACH

22

BOWERS MUSEUM

TUSTIN

NATIONAL

SUNSET BEACH

PLANET HOLLYWOOD

FOUNTAIN VALLEY

SANTA ANA

55

39

ORANGE CO PERFORMING ARTS CTR

THOMAS BROS MAPS

SEVERIN WUNDERMAN MUSEUM

FOREST

HUNTINGTON BEACH

405

IRVINE

COSTA MESA

73

WILD RIVERS

LAKE FOREST

TRABUCO CANYON

IRVINE MDWS AMPHITHEATER

NEWPORT BEACH

HARD ROCK CAFE

MISSION VIEJO

BALBOA PAVILION

1

133

LAGUNA HILLS

5

LAGUNA ART MUSEUM

LAGUNA BEACH

74

SAN JUAN CAPISTRANO

MISSION SAN JUAN CAPISTRANO

PACIFIC OCEAN

DANA POINT

CAPISTRANO BEACH

SAN CLEMENTE

Driving Tour Points of Interest:

SAN JUAN CAPISTRANO - *(Page 105, D1)* Home of the **Mission San Juan Capistrano** - *(Page 202, E1)* Founded in 1776. The restored structure contains a museum; a self-guided tour explains the Mission's history. The famous Mission is the place where thousands of swallows return each year on St. Joseph's Day, March 19th. (714) 248-2047

DOHENY STATE BEACH - *(Page 202, B4)* 120 developed campsites and large beach area. (714) 496-6172

LAGUNA BEACH *(Page 201)* A captivating town with an emphasis on art. The attractive streets are lined with galleries, shops and cafes. Chamber of Commerce: (714) 494-1018

Laguna Art Museum - *(Page 201, B2)* Exhibitions highlight historical and contemporary American art, with special emphasis on works produced in California. Open Tues.-Sun. 11 a.m. to 5 p.m. (714) 494-6531

WILD RIVERS WATERPARK - *(Page 98, D4)* Family waterpark with 40 rides and attractions for all ages. Open mid-May thru Sept. Call for schedule and hours. (714) 768-WILD

CRYSTAL COVE STATE PARK - *(Page T, D5)* Between Corona Del Mar and Laguna Beach. 2,800 acres, with three miles of beach and an underwater preserve for divers to explore. Open 6 a.m. to sunset. (714) 494-3539

BALBOA ISLAND - *(Page 199, D5)* A tiny island jammed with cozy, pricey, beach houses. The main street is lined with boutiques and cafes selling everything from bikinis to frozen bananas. Take the car ferry across to the **"Fun Zone"** for a ride on the ferris wheel, a cruise of the harbor or an ocean cruise to Catalina Island.

Balboa Pavilion - *(Page 199, D5)* Designated a California Historical Landmark, built in 1905, Balboa Pavilion has been restored to authentic "waterfront Victorian." (714) 673-5245

NEWPORT HARBOR ART MUSEUM - *(Page 200, A4)* Offers modern and contemporary art. Changing exhibitions and a permanent collection of post-WWII California art. Gift shop, restaurant. Call for group discount (10 or more). Handicapped access. Open Tues.-Sat. 10 a.m. to 5 p.m. Sun. 12 p.m. to 5 p.m. (714)759-1122

NEWPORT BEACH FASHION ISLAND - *(Page 200, A4)* More than 200 shops located in an open-air Mediterranean-style village atmosphere. Ocean view dining. Handicapped facilities. (714) 721-2000

UPPER NEWPORT BAY ECOLOGICAL RESERVE - *(Page 199, E2)* Meandering coastal lagoon surrounded by prominent bluffs and cliffs. Nature study, photography, hiking, bicycling, boating. Kayak and canoe tours, campfire programs monthly. (714) 640-6746

HUNTINGTON STATE BEACH - *(Page T, B4)* Fire rings, cold showers, bicycle trail, paved ramp for beach wheelchair access. Popular beach area. (714) 536-1454

BOLSA CHICA STATE BEACH - *(Page T, B3)* 3 miles up the coast from Huntington Beach on Hwy. 1. A popular swimming and surfing beach that has fire rings, dressing rooms, cold showers, bicycle trails and a paved ramp for beach wheelchair access. (714) 846-3460

ORANGE COUNTY PERFORMING ARTS CENTER - *(Page 198, A3)* Includes a 3,000-seat, three-tiered main theatre for musical theatre, symphony, opera and dance. (714) 556-ARTS

SOUTH COAST PLAZA - *(Page 197, E3)* Contains finest collection of shops and restaurants including Gucci, Cartier, Saks, Tiffany, Emporio Armani, Chanel, and Escata. (714) 435-2000

SOUTH COAST REPERTORY THEATRE - *(Page 198, A3)* This Tony Award-winning professional resident theatre presents an 11-month season, Sept. thru July, of 12 classic contemporary plays on two stages. (714) 957-4033

THOMAS BROS. MAPS RETAIL SHOWROOM - *(Page 198, C3)* Corporate headquarters and retail showroom. Please stop by and say "hello". 17731 Cowan, Irvine. (714) 863-1984 or (800) 899-6277

BOWERS MUSEUM OF CULTURAL ART - *(Page 196, B3)* Housed in a recently expanded Spanish-style 1930's building, the museum specializes in the cultural arts of the Americas and Pacific Rim and has permanent galleries on the arts of Native America, Africa and Oceania. (714) 567-3600

ANAHEIM STADIUM - *(Page 194, A5)* Is the home of the California Angels baseball club. Guided tours of stadium daily except Sunday. Parking for tour guests free. (714) 254-3100

ARROWHEAD POND OF ANAHEIM - *(Page 194, A4)* Known as "The Pond" home of The Mighty Ducks National League Hockey team. Opened in 1993, this state-of-the-art arena is open year round for many other sporting events and concerts. For general information call (714) 704-2400.

DISNEYLAND - *(Page 193, B4)* The "Magic Kingdom" known throughout the world as the spectacular showcase for Mickey Mouse and all the Disney characters. The $200 million amusement park is divided into several theme "lands". A full day is needed to enjoy all of the attractions. (714) 999-4565

HOBBY CITY DOLL AND TOY MUSEUM - *(Page T, B2)* Dolls from all over the world are exhibited inside this half-scale replica of the White House. 21 hobby, craft and collector shops are located within the complex. Open 10 a.m.-6 p.m. Closed major holidays. (714) 527-2323

KNOTT'S BERRY FARM - *(Page T, B2)* A popular family amusement park with six theme areas, shows and over 150 rides. In addition, the Market Place has restaurants and specialty shops featuring the original Mrs. Knott's jams and preserves. Located at 8039 Beach Blvd. in Buena Park. (714) 220-5200

MOVIELAND WAX MUSEUM - *(Page T, B2)* Features more than 258 wax likenesses of movie and TV stars. Facilities for the handicapped. Free parking. Open every day and night of the year. (714) 522-1154

RICHARD NIXON LIBRARY - *(Page T, E1)* Museum archives and birthplace offers exhibits on Vietnam, China, the Soviet Union, the White House and Watergate. Gift shop. Open 10 a.m. to 5 p.m. daily. Handicapped access. (714) 993-3393

One of the Most Ideal Climates in the Nation

San Diego's 59 mile scenic drive is a beautiful way to spend a day. It can be driven in three hours with few stops, or one could spend days visiting the many museums, parks, restaurants, shops and countless attractions.

Highlights of this tour include Coronado, Fort Rosecrans Cemetery, Cabrillo National Monument, Sunset Cliffs, Mission Bay Park, Sea World, La Jolla, Old Town, Balboa Park, the San Diego Zoo and the zoo's sister park - the Wild Animal Park, Escondido, Seaport Village, the San Diego Convention Center and the Gaslamp Quarter.

San Diego, the hub of this region, is famous for its mild, temperate climate and 70 miles of sandy beaches.

For history buffs, San Diego offers preserved historic sections to tour. In the mountains east of San Diego is the gold-mining town of Julian. The eastern portion of San Diego County comprises the Anza-Borrego Desert State Park.

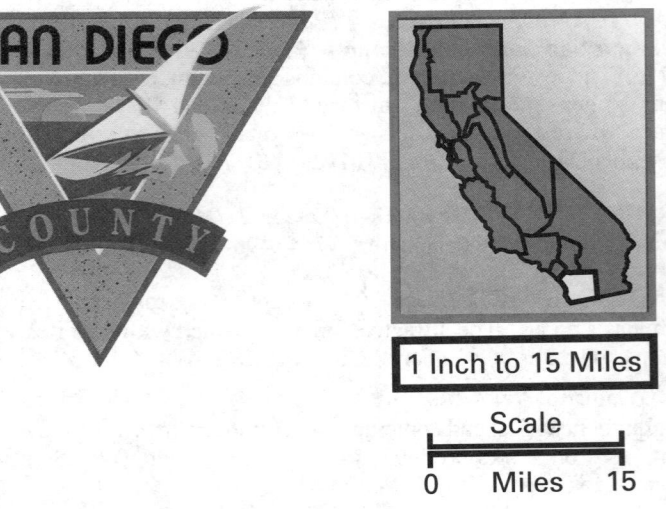

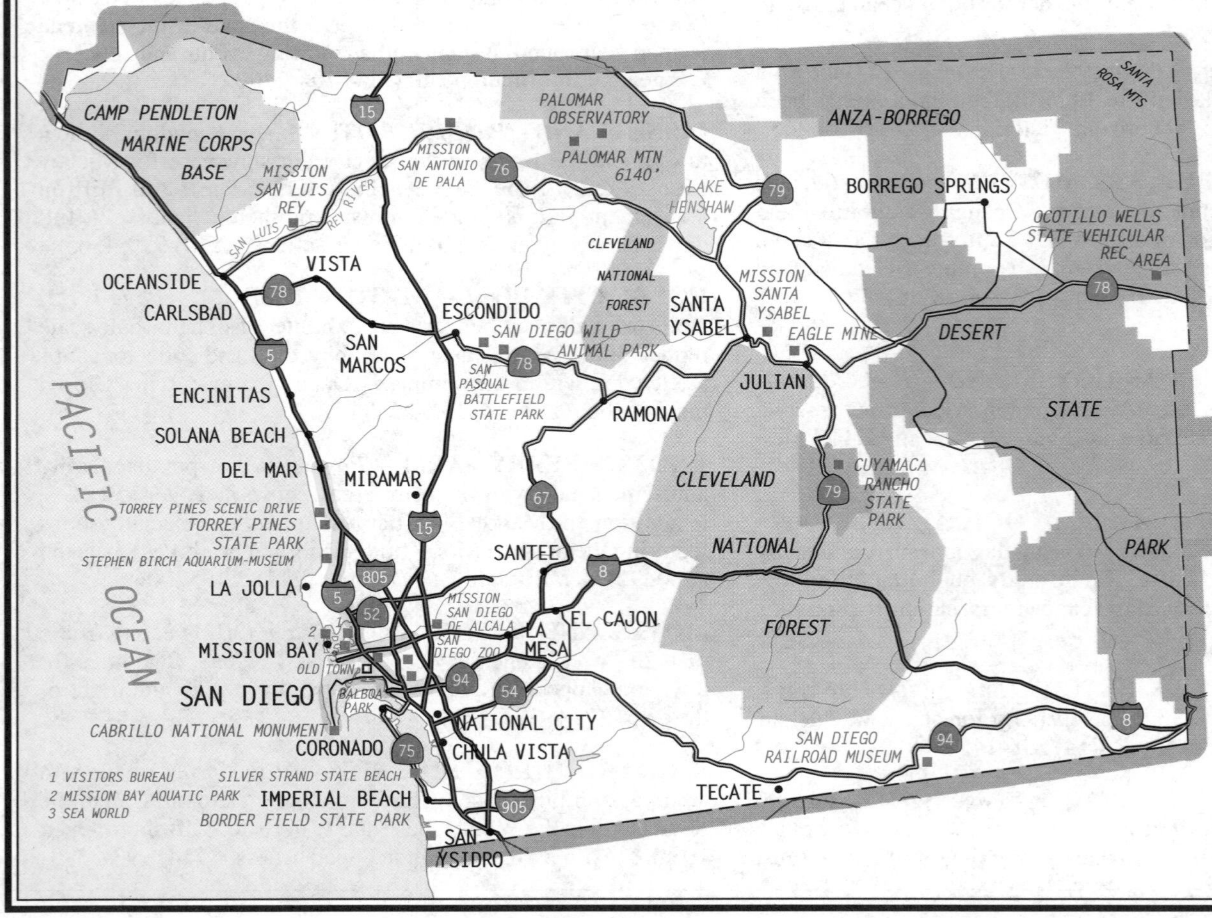

1 Inch to 15 Miles

Scale

0   Miles   15

TOURS

PACIFIC OCEAN

CAMP PENDLETON MARINE CORPS BASE

MISSION SAN LUIS REY

PALOMAR OBSERVATORY

PALOMAR MTN 6140'

MISSION SAN ANTONIO DE PALA

ANZA-BORREGO

SANTA ROSA MTS

REY RIVER

SAN LUIS

15

76

LAKE HENSHAW

79

BORREGO SPRINGS

OCOTILLO WELLS STATE VEHICULAR REC. AREA

VISTA

CLEVELAND

MISSION SANTA YSABEL

OCEANSIDE
CARLSBAD

78

ESCONDIDO

NATIONAL

FOREST

SANTA YSABEL

EAGLE MINE

DESERT

78

SAN MARCOS

5

SAN DIEGO WILD ANIMAL PARK

78

JULIAN

STATE

ENCINITAS

SAN PASQUAL BATTLEFIELD STATE PARK

RAMONA

SOLANA BEACH

DEL MAR

MIRAMAR

CLEVELAND

CUYAMACA RANCHO STATE PARK

PARK

TORREY PINES SCENIC DRIVE
TORREY PINES STATE PARK
STEPHEN BIRCH AQUARIUM-MUSEUM

67

79

LA JOLLA

15

SANTEE

NATIONAL

5

805

52

MISSION SAN DIEGO DE ALCALA

8

MISSION BAY

OLD TOWN

SAN DIEGO ZOO

EL CAJON

FOREST

SAN DIEGO

2

94

LA MESA

BALBOA PARK

54

CORONADO

75

NATIONAL CITY

CHULA VISTA

SAN DIEGO RAILROAD MUSEUM

94

8

1 VISITORS BUREAU
2 MISSION BAY AQUATIC PARK
3 SEA WORLD

SILVER STRAND STATE BEACH

IMPERIAL BEACH

BORDER FIELD STATE PARK

905

TECATE

SAN YSIDRO

Driving Tour Points of Interest:

CABRILLO NATIONAL MONUMENT - *(Page V, A4)* Named for the Portuguese explorer Juan Rodriguez Cabrillo, who claimed the area for Spain in 1542. Point Loma provides a view of the city and the bay as well as a vantage point to watch migratory whales at certain times of the year. A lighthouse, museum and hiking trails are maintained year-round. (619) 557-5450

DOWNTOWN - *(Page 215, D3)* Easy to navigate by car, on foot or the Old Town Trolley Tours. Start at the International Visitors Information Center (619) 236-1212, located at **Horton Plaza Center**, a multi-tiered shopping complex with 160 shops, restaurants and cinemas. The **Embarcadero** is the busy waterfront area where visitors can watch the fleets come in, tour a Navy ship or take a harbor cruise. The **Maritime Museum** features three restored ships, including the Star of India, the oldest merchant vessel afloat. (619) 234-9153

BALBOA PARK - *(Page 216)* Over 1,000 acres of fascinating museums, theatres, gardens, shops and restaurants. This unique park was the site of two World's Fairs and continues to greet millions of visitors from around the world. The **San Diego Zoo**, located within the park, proudly exhibits a renowned collection of rare birds and animals in natural habitats. (619) 234-3153

OLD TOWN SAN DIEGO STATE HISTORIC PARK - *(Page 213, A5)* The location of the first permanent Spanish settlement in what is now California. The small cluster of adobe buildings has been restored and the area revitalized into a charming plaza of museums, galleries, shops and restaurants. A walking tour map is available at the Visitors Center. (619) 220-5422

MISSION SAN DIEGO DE ALCALA - *(Page 214, E3)* Established in 1769 as the first Franciscan Mission. The restored church and impressive bell tower are surrounded by attractive gardens. Open year round. (619) 281-8449

MISSION BAY PARK - *(Page 212)* An aquatic playground for water sports enthusiasts. Twenty-seven miles of shoreline are open for public swimming, fishing and picnicking. Several boat launches are located around the bay as motor-boating, water skiing and sailing are popular.

Sea World - *(Page 212, C4)* One of California's most popular theme parks, featuring 135 acres of entertaining and educational marine exhibits and performances. This is an all-day excursion in itself. (619) 226-3901

LA JOLLA - *(Page 105, C3)* The "jewel" of San Diego. Reminiscent of the French Riviera, this gorgeous residential community has a village area along Prospect Street *(Page 105, B2)* with swank restaurants, boutiques and galleries.

La Jolla Cave - *(Page 105, B5)* Wave eroded sandstone cliffs have formed several impressive caves, one of which can be reached by an 80-foot staircase through a curio shop. (619) 454-6080

Stephen Birch Aquarium/Museum - *(Page 211, A1)* Several displays emphasize those fish and animals found in the Southern California waters. Changing displays explore the latest oceanography developments. (619) 534-3474

TORREY PINES SCENIC DRIVE - *(Page V, A1)* Curves north of La Jolla to **Torrey Pines State Reserve**. The clifftop park protects over 7,000 gnarled Torrey pines which exist naturally only one other place in the world, on Santa Rosa Island. Several short, interpretive nature trails, a museum and Visitors Center provide information. (619) 755-2063

DEL MAR - *(Page V, A1)* Where "The Turf Meets the Surf." The oceanside **Del Mar Racetrack** was founded in 1937 by a group of Hollywood celebrities. Each year, July through September, the pink and green art deco grandstand is open to the public for championship thoroughbred racing. Other events are held throughout the year. (619) 755-1141

Other Points of Interest:

ENCINITAS - *(Page 106, B4)* Take the Encinitas Boulevard exit to the **Quail Botanical Gardens,** a peaceful setting of foot trails that meander through 30 acres of rare and exotic plants, trees and flowers. Nationally recognized for its diverse and botanically important plant collections. Gift shop and plant sales. (619) 436-3036

SAN DIEGO WILD ANIMAL PARK - *(Page 106, D3)* Located 6 miles south of Escondido. This wildlife sanctuary exists in conjunction with the San Diego Zoo. Animals are often relocated from one park to the other. Within the compound, many of the 2,400 animals are allowed to roam freely in natural settings. A special monorail takes visitors on a one-hour safari-like adventure. (619) 480-0100

PALOMAR MOUNTAIN STATE PARK - *(Page 107, A2)* Thick fir and cedar forests resemble the Sierra Nevada. Fishing and camping are permitted.

PALOMAR OBSERVATORY - *(Page 107, A2)* Showcases a 200-inch Hale telescope, one of the largest in the world. There is a visitors gallery, photographs, a videotape and a small gift shop. (619) 742-2119

JULIAN - *(Page 107, C3)* A turn-of-the-century mining town and self-proclaimed "Apple Capital of San Diego." Old west storefronts harbor quaint shops and home-style restaurants. The Chamber of Commerce provides information, local maps and a calendar of events. (619) 765-1857

Eagle & High Peak Mines - *(Page 107, C3)* Visitors travel 1,000 feet into an authentic gold mine. There is a Museum and displays of tools, machinery and antique engines. (619) 765-0036

CUYAMACA RANCHO STATE PARK - *(Page 107, C4)* A peaceful area of oak and pine trees, meadows and streams. There are hundreds of miles of riding and hiking trails within the park. The 3-1/2 mile Cuyamaca Peak trail leads to the 6,512 foot summit where the view encompasses the Pacific Ocean, the desert, Mexico and the Salton Sea. Camping is permitted. (619) 765-0755

ANZA-BORREGO DESERT STATE PARK - *(Page 107, D2)* 600,000 acres of peaceful, isolated desert, the largest in the State. Even though the area may appear desolate, it is actually a complex and fragile ecosystem; steep canyon walls and feathery palms protect numerous bird and wildlife species. In the spring, the desert is a carpet of colorful wildflowers. Camping is permitted. The Visitors Center, just west of Borrego Springs, provides trail maps and information. (619) 767-5311

TOURS

LIST OF ABBREVIATIONS

ABBR	NAME	ABBR	NAME	ABBR	NAME	ABBR	NAME
AL	ALLEY	CRES	CRESCENT	L	LA	RIV	RIVER
AR	ARROYO	CSWY	CAUSEWAY	LN	LANE	RV	RIVER
ARR	ARROYO	CT	COURT	LP	LOOP	RO	RANCHO
AV	AVENUE	CTE	CORTE	LS	LAS, LOS	S	SOUTH
AVD	AVENIDA	CTO	CUT OFF	MDW	MEADOW	SN	SAN
AVD D LS	AVENIDA DE LOS	CTR	CENTER	MHP	MOBILE HOME PARK	SPG	SPRING
BCH	BEACH	CV	COVE	MNR	MANOR	SPGS	SPRINGS
BL	BOULEVARD	CY	CANYON	MT	MOUNT	SQ	SQUARE
BLVD	BOULEVARD	CYN	CANYON	MTN	MOUNTAIN	SRA	SIERRA
CEM	CEMETERY	D	DE	MTWY	MOTORWAY	ST	SAINT
CIR	CIRCLE	DL	DEL	MTY	MOTORWAY	ST	STREET
CK	CREEK	DR	DRIVE	N	NORTH	STA	SANTA
CL	CALLE	DS	DOS	PAS	PASEO	STA	STATION
CL DL	CALLE DEL	E	EAST	PAS DE	PASEO DE	TER	TERRACE
CL D LS	CALLE DE LAS	EST	ESTATE	PAS DL	PASEO DEL	THTR	THEATER
	CALLE DE LOS	EXWY	EXPRESSWAY	PAS D LS	PASEO DE LAS	TKTR	TRUCK TRAIL
CL EL	CALLE EL	EXT	EXTENSION		PASEO DE LOS	TR	TRAIL
CLJ	CALLEJON	FRWY	FREEWAY	PGD	PLAYGROUND	VIA D	VIA DE
CL LA	CALLE LA	FWY	FREEWAY	PK	PARK	VIA D LS	VIA DE LAS
CL LS	CALLE LAS	FY	FREEWAY	PK	PEAK		VIA DE LOS
	CALLE LOS	GN	GLEN	PKWY	PARKWAY	VIA DL	VIA DEL
CM	CAMINO	GRDS	GROUNDS	PL	PLACE	VIS	VISTA
CM D	CAMINO DE	GRN	GREEN	PT	POINT	VLG	VILLAGE
CM D LA	CAMINO DE LA	GRV	GROVE	PY	PARKWAY	VLY	VALLEY
CM D LS	CAMINO DE LAS	HTS	HEIGHTS	PZ	PLAZA	VW	VIEW
	CAMINO DE LOS	HWY	HIGHWAY	RCH	RANCH	W	WEST
CMTO	CAMINITO	HY	HIGHWAY	RCHO	RANCHO	WK	WALK
CN	CANAL	JCT	JUNCTION	RD	ROAD	WY	WAY
COM	COMMON	KPN	KEY PENINSULA NORTH	RDG	RIDGE		
CR	CRESCENT	KPS	KEY PENINSULA SOUTH	RES	RESERVOIR		

INDEX OF CITIES

CITY NAME	ABBR	PAGE	CITY NAME	ABBR	PAGE
ALAMEDA	A	157	NEVADA CITY	NEVC	128
ANAHEIM	ANA	193	NEWPORT BEACH	NB	199
AUBURN	AUB	126	OAKLAND	O	157
AVALON	AVLN	97	ONTARIO	ONT	204
BAKERSFIELD	BKD	166	ORANGE	ORA	194
BARSTOW	BARS	208	OXNARD	OXN	176
BELMONT	BLMT	145	PACIFIC GROVE	PAC	167
BENICIA	BEN	153	PALM SPRINGS	PMSP	206
BERKELEY	B	156	PALO ALTO	PA	147
BEVERLY HILLS	BH	183	PASADENA	PAS	190
BURBANK	BUR	179	PIEDMONT	P	158
CARMEL BY THE SEA	CAR	168	PLACERVILLE	PLCV	138
CHICO	C	124	POMONA	POM	203
CLAREMONT	CLA	203	RANCHO CUCAMONGA	ROC	204
COLTON	CLTN	207	REDDING	RED	122
CORONADO	COR	215	REDWOOD CITY	RC	145
CORTE MADERA	CRTM	140	RENO	RENO	130
COSTA MESA	CM	197	RICHMOND	R	155
CULVER CITY	CUL	188	RIVERSIDE	RIV	205
CUPERTINO	CPTO	149	ROSS	ROSS	139
DANA POINT	DPT	202	SACRAMENTO	SCTO	137
DAVIS	DVS	136	SALINAS	SAL	171
EL CENTRO	EC	217	SAN ANSELMO	SANS	139
EL CERRITO	ELC	155	SAN BERNARDINO	SBDO	207
EL SEGUNDO	ELS	189	SAN BRUNO	SBR	144
EUREKA	EUR	121	SAN CLEMENTE	SCL	202
FAIRFIELD	FRFD	135	SAN DIEGO	SD	211
FOSTER CITY	FCTY	145	SAN FRANCISCO	SF	141
FOUNTAIN VALLEY	FTNV	197	SAN JOSE	SJ	152
FRESNO	FRE	165	SAN JUAN CAPISTRANO	SJC	202
GARDEN GROVE	GG	195	SAN LUIS OBISPO	SNLO	172
GRASS VALLEY	GV	127	SAN MATEO	SM	145
HAWTHORNE	HAW	189	SAN PABLO	SP	155
HAYWARD	H	146	SAN RAFAEL	SR	139
INGLEWOOD	ING	189	SANTA ANA	SA	196
IRVINE	IRV	198	SANTA BARBARA	STB	174
LAGUNA BEACH	LAG	201	SANTA CLARA	SCLR	150
LAGUNA NIGUEL	LN	202	SANTA CRUZ	SC	169
LAS VEGAS	LV	209	SANTA MARIA	SMA	173
LONG BEACH	LB	192	SANTA MONICA	SMON	180
LOS ALTOS	LSAL	149	SANTA ROSA	STR	131
LOS ANGELES	LA	177	SONOMA	SNMA	132
MANHATTAN BEACH	MB	189	SONORA	SNRA	163
MAMMOTH LAKES	ML	164	SOUTH LAKE TAHOE	SLT	129
MANTECA	MAN	161	SOUTH SAN FRANCISCO	SSF	144
MARTINEZ	M	154	STOCKTON	S	160
MENLO PARK	MP	147	SUISUN CITY	SUIS	135
MERCED	MER	170	SUNNYVALE	SVL	149
MILLBRAE	MLBR	144	TUSTIN	TUS	198
MILL VALLEY	MV	140	UKIAH	U	123
MODESTO	MDO	162	UPLAND	UPL	204
MONTCLAIR	MTCL	203	VALLEJO	VAL	134
MONTEREY	MONT	167	VENTURA	VENT	175
MOUNTAIN VIEW	MVW	148	WEST HOLLYWOOD	WHOL	181
NAPA	NAP	133	YUBA CITY	YUBA	125

INDEX OF COUNTIES

COUNTY NAME	ABBR	PAGE	COUNTY NAME	ABBR	PAGE
CALIFORNIA			SANTA CLARA	SCL	46
			SANTA CRUZ	SCR	53
ALAMEDA	ALA	45	SHASTA	SHA	18
ALPINE	ALP	42	SIERRA	SIE	27
AMADOR	AMA	40	SISKIYOU	SIS	4
BUTTE	BUT	25	SOLANO	SOL	39
CALAVERAS	CAL	41	SONOMA	SON	37
COLUSA	COL	32	STANISLAUS	STA	47
CONTRA COSTA	CC	38	SUTTER	SUT	33
DEL NORTE	DN	2	TEHAMA	TEH	18
EL DORADO	ED	35	TRINITY	TRI	17
FRESNO	FRCO	57	TULARE	TUL	68
GLENN	GLE	24	TUOLUMNE	TUO	42
HUMBOLDT	HUM	16	VENTURA	VEN	88
IMPERIAL	IMP	109	YOLO	YOL	33
INYO	INY	59	YUBA	YUB	33
KERN	KER	78			
KINGS	KIN	67	**ARIZONA**		
LAKE	LAE	31			
LASSEN	LAS	20	LA PAZ	LPAZ	104
LOS ANGELES	LACO	97	MOHAVE	MOH	85
MADERA	MAD	49	YUMA	YUMA	112
MARIN	MAR	38			
MARIPOSA	MPA	49	**NEVADA**		
MENDOCINO	MEN	22			
MERCED	MCO	48	CARSON CITY	CRSN	36
MODOC	MOD	6	CLARK	CLK	74
MONO	MNO	43	DOUGLAS	DGL	36
MONTEREY	MON	64	ESMERALDA	ESM	52
NAPA	NAPA	38	LYON	LYON	43
NEVADA	NEV	34	MINERAL	MIN	43
ORANGE	ORCO	98	NYE	NYE	62
PLACER	PLA	34	STOREY	STOR	28
PLUMAS	PLU	26	WASHOE	WSH	28
RIVERSIDE	RCO	99			
SACRAMENTO	SAC	39	**OREGON**		
SAN BENITO	SBT	54			
SAN BERNARDINO	SBD	91	CURRY	CUR	1
SAN DIEGO	SDCO	106	JACKSON	JKSN	3
SAN FRANCISCO	SFCO	45	JOSEPHINE	JOS	2
SAN JOAQUIN	SJCO	40	KLAMATH	KLAM	5
SAN LUIS OBISPO	SLO	75	LAKE	LAKE	7
SAN MATEO	SMCO	45	**MEXICO**		
SANTA BARBARA	SB	86	BAJA CALIFORNIA	BAJA	111

STREET INDEX

A

STREET	CO.	PAGE	GRID
A ST	ALA	L	E5
A ST	ALA	45	E2
A ST	DVS	136	C3
A ST	DN	1	D4
A ST	H	146	E2
A ST	SBD	92	A1
A ST	SD	215	D3
A ST	TEH	18	E5
A ST W	ALA	L	E5
A ST W	ALA	N	E1
A ST W	H	146	B3
ABBOTT DR	KER	80	B3
ABBOTT RD	LACO	R	A5
ABBOTT ST	MON	54	D4
ABBOTT ST	SAL	171	D4
ABBY ST	FRE	165	D3
ABEL ST	SCL	P	B3
ABELIA ST	SBD	92	B3
ABELOR RD	INY	51	C4
ABERDEEN DR	SBD	100	E1
ABERDEEN STA RD	INY	59	E1
ABERNATHY RD	SOL	L	E1
ABERNATHY RD	SOL	M	A1
ABERNATHY RD	SOL	38	E3
ABERNATHY RD	YUB	26	A4
ABLE RD	COL	32	E2
ABORN RD	SCL	P	C3
ABORN RD	SCL	46	C4
ABRAM DR	RCO	100	A5
ACACIA AV	ANA	193	D1
ACACIA AV	STA	47	C3
ACACIA AV	SUT	33	C2
ACACIA ST	SAL	171	A4
ACADEMY AV	FRCO	57	E4
ACAMPO RD	SJCO	39	E4
ACARI RD	KER	78	B3
ACKERMAN LN	HUM	16	B3
ACME RD	SUT	33	B3
ACMITE ST	KER	91	E3
ACOMA TR	SBD	100	D1
ADA RD	KER	78	B3
ADAIR RD	IMP	108	E5
ADAIR RD	STA	47	C2
ADAM FOX FRM RD	HUM	9	E4
ADAMS AV	CM	197	C5
ADAMS AV	EC	217	B2
ADAMS AV	FRCO	56	D4
ADAMS AV	FRCO	57	C4
ADAMS AV	FRCO	58	A4
ADAMS AV	ORCO	T	C4
ADAMS AV	SD	214	B4
ADAMS AV	SDCO	V	C3
ADAMS AV	SDCO	111	D1
ADAMS BLVD	LA	184	A4
ADAMS BLVD	LA	185	C4
ADAMS BLVD	LACO	Q	D4
ADAMS DR	KER	79	E1
ADAMS RD	TEH	18	C4
ADAMS ST	IMP	109	A5
ADAMS ST	RCO	99	A2
ADAMS ST	RCO	101	A4
ADDISON RD	BUT	25	C1
ADELAIDA RD	SLO	75	E1
ADELAIDA RD	SLO	76	A1
ADELINE ST	B	156	A4
ADELINE ST	O	157	D2
ADELANTO RD	SBD	91	B3
ADIN CUTOFF RD	LAS	14	B3
ADML CALLAHN LN	VAL	134	E3
ADOBE DR	KER	79	E2
ADOBE DR	KER	80	A2
ADOBE PL	MON	65	C4
ADOBE RD	BUT	25	C4
ADOBE RD	COL	25	A5
ADOBE RD	KER	78	D4
ADOBE RD	SBD	101	B1
ADOBE RD	SLO	76	A1
ADOBE RD	SHA	18	D3
ADOBE RD	SON	L	A1
ADOBE RD	SON	38	A3
ADOBE RD	TEH	18	D4
ADOBE CREEK RD	LAK	31	D3
ADOBE MTN RD	SBD	90	D2
ADOBE RANCH RD	MNO	44	A5
ADOHR RD	KER	78	A3
ADOLFO LOPEZ BL	BAJA	112	B4
AERO DR	SD	214	A1
AERO DR	SDCO	V	B2
AERO DR	SDCO	111	D1
AEROPUERTO HWY	BAJA	111	E2
AFTON BLVD	GLE	25	A4
AFTON RD	BUT	25	B5
AFTON CANYON RD	SBD	82	D5
AGATE RD	SBD	91	D1
AGER RD	SIS	4	B3
AGER RD	SIS	5	D2
AGER BESWICK RD	SIS	4	C3
AGGEN RD	VEN	88	C5
AGNES WILSON RD	LPAZ	104	A2
AGNES WILSON RD	RCO	103	E2
AGOURA RD	LACO	96	E1
AGUA CALIENT BL	BAJA	111	E3
AGUA CALIENT RD	SB	87	D4
AQUA CALIENT RD	SON	132	A1
AGUA DULCE CYN	LACO	89	D4
AGUA FRIA RD	MPA	49	A3
AGUAJITO RD	MON	53	E4
AGUAJITO RD	MON	168	D2
AGUA MANSA RD	RCO	99	B2
AGUAS FRIAS RD	BUT	25	B4

STREET	CO.	PAGE	GRID
AGUEREBERRY PT	INY	71	D1
AHERN RD	SJCO	47	A2
AHLF RD	SUT	33	C2
AIKENS MINE RD	SBD	83	D4
AINSWORTH PL	RCO	107	A1
AIR BASE PKWY	FRFD	135	C2
AIR BASE PKWY	SOL	M	A1
AIR BASE PKWY	SOL	38	E3
AIR BASE RD	SBD	91	B3
AIRD CIR	BUT	25	E3
AIROLA	CAL	41	B4
AIROSA DR	SBD	90	E3
AIROX RD	SB	86	B1
AIR PARK DR	IMP	108	C2
AIRPORT BLVD	KER	80	A5
AIRPORT BLVD	LA	188	D5
AIRPORT BLVD	LA	189	D1
AIRPORT BLVD	LACO	Q	D5
AIRPORT BLVD	RCO	101	A4
AIRPORT BLVD	SAL	171	E5
AIRPORT BLVD	SMCO	N	C1
AIRPORT BLVD	SF	144	C1
AIRPORT BLVD	SJ	151	E2
AIRPORT BLVD	SCR	54	B2
AIRPORT BLVD	SON	37	E1
AIRPORT BLVD S	SSF	144	C2
AIRPORT DR	O	159	D5
AIRPORT RD	ALP	36	C4
AIRPORT RD	DGL	36	C3
AIRPORT RD	HUM	9	E4
AIRPORT RD	KER	78	A4
AIRPORT RD	MEN	22	B5
AIRPORT RD	MEN	30	C1
AIRPORT RD	MOD	8	A1
AIRPORT RD	MNO	50	E2
AIRPORT RD	NAPA	L	D1
AIRPORT RD	NAPA	38	C3
AIRPORT RD	O	159	D4
AIRPORT RD	SLO	76	B1
AIRPORT RD	SHA	18	C3
AIRPORT RD	SIS	4	B3
AIRPORT RD	SOL	M	D1
AIRPORT RD	SOL	39	C3
AIRPORT RD	TRI	17	D1
AIRPORT WY	SJCO	40	B5
AIRPORT WY	SJCO	47	B2
AIRWAY DR	KLAM	5	C1
AKER AV	STA	47	C1
AKERS RD	TUL	68	B1
AKINS RD	SIS	5	D2
AKRICH ST	SHA	18	C2
ALABAMA ST	SBD	99	C2
ALAMEDA AV	BUR	179	C5
ALAMEDA AV	LACO	Q	D3
ALAMEDA AV	O	159	B1
ALAMEDA AV	SAL	171	C5
ALAMEDA AV	YOL	39	D2
ALAMEDA ST	LA	186	B4
ALAMEDA ST	LACO	97	E2
ALAMEDA ST	LACO	S	D2
ALAMEDA ST	MAN	161	C3
ALAMEDA ST	VAL	134	C4
ALAMEDA, THE	SJ	151	C2
ALAMEDA, THE	SJ	152	A4
ALAMEDA, THE	SCLR	151	C2
ALAM D LS PULGS	BLMT	145	A4
ALAM D LS PULGS	SMCO	N	C1
ALAM D LS PULGS	SMCO	N	D2
ALAM D LS PULGS	SM	145	A4
ALAM D LS PULGS	SMCO	45	D4
ALAMEDA PAD SER	STB	174	C2
ALAMITOS AV	LACO	S	D3
ALAMO DR	MPA	48	D2
ALAMO RD	IMP	109	B5
ALAMO ST	LACO	88	E5
ALAMO ST	SIS	5	A2
ALAMO ST	VEN	88	E5
ALAMO ST	VEN	89	A5
ALAMO CREEK RD	SLO	76	D5
ALAMO PINTADO	SB	86	E3
ALBA RD	SCR	N	E5
ALBA RD	SCR	53	E1
ALBAUGH RD	LAS	14	C3
ALBERS RD	STA	47	E2
ALBRT ETTER RCH	HUM	16	A5
ALBERTON AV	BUT	25	A3
ALBION LTL RIV	MEN	30	B1
ALBION RIDGE RD	MEN	30	C1
ALBRIGHT RD	IMP	109	B3
ALCALDE RD	FRCO	66	D3
ALCATRAZ AV	ALA	L	D4
ALCATRAZ AV	O	156	B4
ALCOSTA BLVD	CC	M	B5
ALDEN ST	KER	78	E4
ALDER AV	SBD	80	E1
ALDER AV	SBD	99	B1
ALDER ST	PAC	167	B2
ALDER CAMP RD	DN	1	E5
ALDER CAMP RD	DN	9	E1
ALDER CAMP RD	DN	10	A1
ALDER CREEK RD	NEV	27	D5
ALDER CK BCH RD	MEN	30	C3
ALDRCRFT HTS RD	SCL	P	B5
ALDRCRFT HTS RD	SCL	54	C1
ALDERPOINT RD	HUM	16	C3
ALDER PT BLUFF	TRI	16	D5
ALDER SPGS RD	GLE	23	D3
ALDER SPGS RD	GLE	24	A3
ALDERWOOD DR	SIS	4	A4
ALDINE DR	SD	214	E4
ALDINE DR	SDCO	V	C3
ALDINE DR	SDCO	111	D1
ALDRIDGE RD	SHA	19	A2

STREET	CO.	PAGE	GRID
ALEJO DR	RCO	100	C3
ALESSANDRO BLVD	RCO	99	B3
ALEXANDER AV	BUT	33	C1
ALEXANDER AV	SHA	18	C3
ALEXANDER LN	LAS	21	C3
ALEXANDR VLY RD	SON	31	D5
ALFALFA AV	STA	47	C4
ALFRD HARRL HWY	KER	78	D2
ALGA RD	SDCO	106	C3
ALGERINE RD	TUO	41	C5
ALGODON RD	YUB	33	D3
ALGRN WRDS FRRY	TUO	41	C5
ALGOMAN AV	SBD	91	C5
ALHAMBRA	CC	38	E5
ALHAMBRA AV	CC	L	E3
ALHAMBRA AV	M	154	B1
ALHAMBRA BLVD	SCTO	137	E3
ALHAMBRA RD	LACO	R	B3
ALHAMBRA WY	M	154	C3
ALHAMBRA VLY RD	CC	L	D3
ALHAMBRA VLY RD	CC	38	D5
ALHAMBRA VLY RD	CC	154	C5
ALHAMBRA VLY RD	M	154	C4
ALICE AV	HUM	16	C5
ALICIA AV	YUB	33	D2
ALICIA PKWY	ORCO	98	D5
ALISAL RD	MON	54	D4
ALISAL RD	SB	86	E3
ALISAL ST E	SAL	171	D4
ALISAL ST W	SAL	171	B4
ALISO CANYON RD	LACO	89	E4
ALISO CANYON RD	SB	87	C1
ALISO CANYON RD	VEN	88	B5
ALISO PARK RD	SB	87	C1
ALISOS AV	SB	87	A3
ALISOS CYN RD	SB	86	D2
ALLAN RD	AMA	41	A1
ALLEGHANY RD	YUB	26	C5
ALLEN AV	LACO	R	C2
ALLEN AV	MCO	48	C3
ALLEN RD	IMP	108	D3
ALLEN RD	KER	78	C3
ALLEN RD	SJCO	47	C1
ALLENDALE RD	SOL	39	A2
ALLERTON AV	SSF	144	D1
ALLIANCE RD	HUM	9	E5
ALLIANCE RD	HUM	10	A5
ALLISON RCH RD	NEV	34	C2
ALLUVIAL AV	FRCO	57	C3
ALMA AV	KER	79	D5
ALMA ST	PA	147	A2
ALMA ST	SJ	152	C5
ALMA ST	SCL	N	E2
ALMA ST	SCL	45	D4
ALMADEN AV	SJ	152	B4
ALMADEN BLVD	SJ	152	B4
ALMADEN EXPWY	SCL	P	B4
ALMADEN EXPWY	SCL	46	B5
ALMANOR DR W	PLU	20	B4
ALMER RD	COL	32	D2
ALMOND AV	CLO	32	E3
ALMOND AV	MCO	48	A4
ALMOND AV	STA	47	C3
ALMOND DR	MCO	55	D2
ALMOND DR	MCO	56	A2
ALMOND DR	SLO	76	B2
ALMOND RD	KER	77	B1
ALMND ORCHRD RD	SUT	33	B1
ALMONDWOOD DR	SJCO	47	B2
ALMONTE BLVD	MAR	140	B4
ALOHA ST	TEH	18	D5
ALONA ST	KER	80	A4
ALONDRA BLVD	LACO	97	E3
ALONDRA BLVD	LACO	98	A3
ALOSTA AV	LACO	98	C1
ALOSTA AV	LACO	U	A2
ALPHA RD	NEV	26	E5
ALPINE AV	FRCO	56	D4
ALPINE AV	SJCO	40	D5
ALPINE AV	S	160	A3
ALPINE BLVD	SDCO	107	A5
ALPINE RD	MOD	7	C5
ALPINE RD	MOD	8	C1
ALPINE RD	SJCO	40	B4
ALPINE RD	SMCO	N	D3
ALPINE RD	SMCO	45	D4
ALPINE MINE RD	ALP	36	A4
ALPS DR	KER	79	C5
ALT CT	RCO	107	C1
ALTA	FRCO	58	A4
ALTA ST	MON	54	E5
ALTA ST	NEV	34	C1
ALTA BONNY NOOK	PLA	34	E1
ALTADENA DR	LACO	98	A1
ALTADENA DR	LACO	R	B2
ALTAMONT PS RD	ALA	M	D5
ALTA SIERRA DR	NEV	34	C2
AL TAHOE BLVD	SLT	129	A4
ALTAIR AV	SDCO	106	D5
ALTA LOMA DR	SBD	100	E1
ALTA MESA RD	SHA	18	C2
ALTA MESA RD	SAC	40	B2
ALTAMONT PSS RD	ALA	46	C2
ALTA VISTA	AVLN	97	A4
ALTA VISTA	BKD	166	E2
ALTA VISTA DR	KER	78	D3
ALTHEA AV	FRCO	56	A2
ALTON AV	SA	197	D3
ALTUS AV	KER	80	B5
ALUM ROCK AV	SCL	P	C3
ALUM ROCK AV	SCL	46	B4
ALVARADO BLVD	ALA	N	E2
ALVARADO BLVD	ALA	P	A1

STREET	CO.	PAGE	GRID
ALVARADO BLVD	ALA	45	E3
ALVARADO RD	MON	65	D4
ALVARADO RD	STA	47	E2
ALVARADO ST	LA	185	C3
ALVARADO ST	LACO	Q	E4
ALVARADO ST	SDCO	106	C2
ALVARADO ST	MCO	55	D2
ALVARADO TR	MCO	48	C4
ALVARADO-NLS RD	ALA	45	E3
ALVARADO-NLS RD	ALA	P	A1
ALVES RD	MCO	48	A3
ALVIN AV	SMA	173	B2
ALVIN DR E	SAL	171	D1
ALVIN DR W	SAL	171	C1
ALVISO-MLPTS RD	SCL	46	A4
ALVORD MTN RD	SBD	82	C5
ALWARD RD	SHA	19	B3
AMADOR AV	FRCO	56	D5
AMADOR ST	FRE	165	B4
AMADOR ST	VAL	134	B5
AMADOR CREEK RD	AMA	40	E2
AMAR RD	LACO	98	D5
AMAR RD	LACO	R	E4
AMARGOSA RD	SBD	91	B3
AMARGOSA ST	SBD	92	C2
AMBOY RD	SBD	93	D4
AMBOY RD	SBD	101	C1
AMBROSE DR	SAL	171	A4
AMBOY CUTOFF	SBD	93	E3
AMEDEE RD	LAS	21	D4
AMELIA AV	LACO	U	B1
AMEN LN	TEH	18	C3
AMERICAN AV	FRCO	57	A5
AMERICAN AV	FRCO	58	B4
AMERICAN AV	MCO	47	D4
AMERICAN AV	STA	47	C2
AMERICAN CYN RD	NAPA	L	D2
AMERICAN CYN RD	NAPA	38	D4
AMERICN FLAT RD	AMA	40	E2
AMRICAN FLT SDE	AMA	40	E1
AMERICN GIRL MN	IMP	110	B5
AMERICN MINE RD	SHA	18	A1
AMERIGO	SJCO	40	C5
AMES ST	ALA	M	D5
AMES ST	ALA	46	C2
AMESTI RD	SCR	54	B2
AMOROSE ST	RCO	99	B4
AMSTERDAM RD	MCO	48	B3
ANAHEIM BLVD	ANA	193	C1
ANAHEIM BLVD	ORCO	98	C3
ANAHEIM BLVD	ORCO	T	C2
ANAHEIM ST	LB	192	D2
ANAHEIM ST	LA	191	A1
ANAHEIM ST	LA	192	D1
ANAHEIM ST	LACO	97	D4
ANAHEIM ST	LACO	S	C2
ANAPAMU ST	STB	174	C3
ANCHO ERIE MINE	NEV	26	E5
ANCHO MINE RD	NEV	26	E5
ANCHOR	FRCO	58	B4
ANDERHOLT RD	IMP	112	B4
ANDERSON DR W	SHA	18	C3
ANDERSON LN	HUM	15	D2
ANDERSON RD	DVS	136	B3
ANDERSON RD	SLO	76	A1
ANDERSON RD	SOL	39	C4
ANDERSON RD	STA	47	C4
ANDERSON RD	TUL	68	C2
ANDERSON ST	SBD	99	C2
ANDERSON CK RD	JKSN	3	D1
ANDERSON GRADE	SIS	4	A4
ANDERSON RCH RD	LAS	14	D4
ANDERSON VLY WY	MEN	30	E3
ANDESITE RD	SIS	4	D5
ANDESITE RD	SIS	12	B1
ANDESITE LOG RD	SIS	12	D1
ANDRADE RD	ALA	P	B1
ANDRADE RD	ALA	46	B3
ANDRE RD	IMP	109	A4
ANDRESSEN RD	PLA	34	B3
ANDREW AV	SB	86	C1
ANDREWS RD	LAS	14	C3
ANDREWS RD	SIS	4	E3
ANGELES CRST HY	LACO	R	B1
ANGELES FRST HY	LACO	90	A4
ANGELES FRST HY	LACO	R	B1
ANITA RD	BUT	25	A2
ANNADALE AV	FRCO	57	B4
ANNADALE AV	FRCO	58	A3
ANNAPOLIS RD	SON	30	E5
ANNAPOLIS RD	SON	31	A5
ANNETTE RD	KER	76	E1
ANNIN AV	KER	78	B1
ANTELOPE DR	LAS	8	B4
ANTELOPE HWY	LACO	90	D4
ANTELOPE RD	MNO	42	E1
ANTELOPE RD	MNO	43	A1
ANTELOPE RD	RCO	99	C4
ANTELOPE RD	SAC	34	A5
ANTELOPE RD	SLO	66	E5
ANTELOPE SPGS	MNO	50	E2
ANTELOPE VLY FY	LACO	89	E2
ANTELOPE VLY RD	SIE	27	C3
ANTHONY RD	LACO	89	D4
ANTOLA RD	LAS	21	C3
ANTONIO PKWY	ORCO	98	E5
ANZA RD	IMP	112	A4
ANZA RD	RCO	106	D1
ANZAR RD	SBT	54	D2
ANZA TRAIL RD	IMP	111	C4
APACHE TR	RCO	100	B3
APACHE CYN RD	VEN	88	A2
APPALOOSA RD	CAL	41	A4
APPIAN WY	CC	L	C3

STREET	CO.	PAGE	GRID
APPIAN WY	CC	38	C5
APPLE AV	STA	47	C3
APPLE RD	TEH	24	C2
APPLE CANYON RD	RCO	100	C4
APPLE COLONY RD	TUO	41	D5
APPLEGATE RD	MCO	48	B4
APPLE RANCH RD	TUO	41	E4
APPLE SEED LN	RCO	100	A5
APPLE VALLEY RD	SBD	91	C3
APPLEWHITE	SBD	91	A5
APRICOT AV	STA	47	C3
APRIL LN	VEN	88	C4
AQUEDUCT RD	KER	79	E5
AQUEDUCT RD	KER	80	A5
AQUEDUCT RD	SBD	103	A2
AQUEDUCT RD	SBD	104	A1
ARAMAYO WY	TEH	24	E1
ARASTRADERO RD	PA	147	E5
ARATA LN	SON	37	E1
ARBINI RD	STA	47	E1
ARBOGA RD	YUB	33	D2
ARBOLEDA DR	MCO	48	C5
ARBOR AV	BLMT	145	B5
ARBOR RD	SLO	76	A1
ARBOR WY	MCO	56	C1
ARBORETUM RD	PA	147	A3
ARBOR VITAE ST	ING	189	D1
ARBOR VITAE ST	LA	189	D1
ARBOR VITAE ST	LACO	Q	D5
ARBURUA RD	MCO	55	D2
ARC RD	INY	51	D5
ARCH RD	SJCO	40	B5
ARCH AIRPORT RD	SJCO	40	B5
ARCHER AV	SUT	33	C1
ARCHER RD	SHA	18	A3
ARCHERDALE RD	SJCO	40	C5
ARCHIBALD AV	RCO	98	E3
ARCHIBALD AV	SBD	U	E4
ARCHIE BROWN RD	SHA	13	D4
ARDATH RD	SD	211	B3
ARDATH RD	SDCO	V	A2
ARDATH RD	SDCO	106	C5
ARDEN DR	LACO	R	C3
ARDEN WY	SAC	40	A1
ARDENWOOD BLVD	ALA	N	E1
ARDENWOOD BLVD	ALA	P	A1
ARENA WY	MCO	48	A4
ARGO ST	KER	80	D1
ARGONAUT RD	LAK	31	D3
ARGONNE DR	S	160	B4
ARGUELLO BL	SF	141	D2
ARGYLE RD	MON	65	B3
ARLINGTON AV	CC	L	C3
ARLINGTON AV	LA	184	E5
ARLINGTON AV	LACO	Q	D4
ARLINGTON AV	LACO	S	B2
ARLINGTON AV	RIV	205	A5
ARLINGTON AV	RCO	99	A2
ARLINGTON AV S	RENO	130	A5
ARLINGTON RD	PLU	20	D5
ARLINGTON MN RD	RCO	103	B3
ARMORY RD	BARS	208	B3
ARMOUR RD	SUT	33	C4
ARMOUR RANCH RD	SB	86	E3
ARMOUR RANCH RD	SB	87	A3
ARMSTRONG	SJCO	40	A4
ARMSTRONG AV	FRCO	57	D2
ARMSTRONG AV	FRCO	57	D3
ARMSTRONG RD	CAL	41	C3
ARMSTRONG RD	LAS	14	D3
ARMSTRONG RD	RCO	99	A2
ARMSTRONG RD	STA	47	C4
ARMSTRONG RD	YUB	33	D1
ARMSTRNG WDS RD	SON	37	C1
ARMY RD	RCO	110	B1
ARMY ST	SFCO	L	B5
ARMY ST	SFCO	45	C2
ARNO RD	SAC	40	A3
ARNOLD DR	SON	L	B2
ARNOLD DR	SON	38	B3
ARNOLD DR	SON	132	A3
ARNOLD RD	IMP	112	C5
ARNOLD WY	SDCO	107	B5
AROSA RD	KER	79	C4
ARQUES AV	SVL	148	E5
ARQUES RD	SCL	P	A3
ARRECHE RD	MOD	7	D5
ARRELLAGA ST	STB	174	B3
ARROW HWY	CLA	203	C2
ARROW HWY	LACO	98	B1
ARROW HWY	LACO	U	A2
ARROW HWY	MTCL	203	C2
ARROW HWY	ROC	204	A2
ARROW HWY	SBD	98	D1
ARROW HWY	SBD	U	D2
ARROW HWY	UPL	204	A2
ARROW ROUTE	SBD	203	B2
ARROWHEAD AV	SBDO	207	D4
ARROWHEAD BLVD	RCO	103	D5
ARROWHEAD BLVD	RCO	110	D1
ARROWHEAD RD	LAK	32	A3
ARROWHEAD ST	CAL	41	A5
ARROWHEAD TR	SBD	82	E4
ARROWHEAD TR	SBD	83	A4
ARROWHEAD LK RD	SBD	91	C5
ARROYA AV	MCO	56	A1
ARROYO AV	KER	79	E5
ARROYO AV	KER	80	A5
ARROYO BLVD	LACO	R	B2
ARROYO BLVD	PAS	190	A4
ARROYO PKWY	PAS	190	C5
ARROYO RD	ALA	P	C1
ARROYO RD	ALA	46	C2

STREET INDEX

STREET	CO.	PAGE	GRID
ARROYO RD	SBD	92	A4
ARROYO BURRO RD	SB	87	C4
ARROYO GR GUADL	SLO	76	B5
ARROYO GR GUADL	SLO	86	A1
AROYO GR HUASNA	SLO	76	D4
ARROYO SECO RD	MON	64	E2
ARROYO SECO RD	MON	65	A1
ARTESIA AV	SB	86	B3
ARTESIA BLVD	LACO	97	D3
ARTESIA BLVD	LACO	98	A3
ARTESIA BLVD	LACO	S	B1
ARTESIA FRWY	LACO	98	A3
ARTESIA FRWY	LACO	S	D1
ARTESIA FRWY	LACO	T	A1
ARTHUR	SJCO	47	C1
ARTHUR RD	CC	L	E3
ARTHUR RD	CC	M	A3
ARTHUR ST	RCO	101	C5
ARTICHOKE RD	SMCO	N	C4
ARTICHOKE RD	SMCO	45	C5
ARTIC MINE RD	NEV	26	E5
ARTISTS DR	INY	72	A1
ASH AV	SHA	13	C5
ASH AV	STA	47	C3
ASH ST	SD	215	D3
ASH ST	SDCO	107	A4
ASHBY AV	ALA	L	D4
ASHBY AV	B	156	B3
ASHBY RD	SHA	18	C2
ASH CREEK RD	INY	60	B5
ASH CREEK RD	SHA	18	E3
ASH CREEK RD	SIS	4	A3
ASH CK SINK RD	SIS	13	A2
ASHE RD	KER	78	D4
ASHLAN AV	FRCO	56	C3
ASHLAN AV	FRCO	57	A5
ASHLEY LN	SJCO	40	B4
ASH VALLEY RD	LAS	8	A3
ASH VALLEY RD	LAS	14	D3
ASHWORTH RD	MPA	49	B3
ASILOMAR AV	PAC	167	A2
ASPEN VALLEY RD	TUO	49	C1
ASPEN VALLEY RD	TUO	63	A4
ASSOCIATED RD	SB	86	B1
ASSOCIATED RD	SIS	4	E3
ASSOCIATED RD	SIS	5	A3
ASTER RD	SBD	91	A3
ASTORIA AV	KER	89	C1
ATEN RD	IMP	109	A5
ATHEL ST	KER	80	C1
ATHERTON AV	MAR	L	A2
ATHERTON BLVD	MAR	38	B4
ATHERTON ST	LACO	S	E2
ATHERTON ST	LACO	T	A2
ATHLONE RD	MCO	48	D5
ATKINS RD	SJCO	40	C4
ATLANTIC AV	A	157	D5
ATLANTIC AV	FRFD	135	C1
ATLANTIC AV	LB	192	E2
ATLANTIC AV	LACO	97	E3
ATLANTIC AV	LACO	S	D1
ATLANTIC AV	LACO	S	D2
ATLANTIC AV E	FRFD	135	D1
ATLANTIC BLVD	LACO	98	A2
ATLANTIC BLVD	LACO	R	B4
ATLAS	CC	38	C5
ATLAS RD	CC	L	C3
ATLAS PEAK RD	NAPA	38	D2
ATTERBERRY CT	KER	79	E2
ATTILA RD	SBD	84	C4
ATWATER	MCO	47	E4
ATWELL AV	TUL	67	E4
ATWELL AV	TUL	68	A4
ATWOOD	PLA	34	C3
AUBERRY RD	FRCO	57	E1
AUBERRY RD	FRCO	58	A1
AUBERRY RD	MAD	49	E5
AUBREY AV	MCO	56	A2
AUBURN BLVD	SAC	34	A5
AUBURN RD	NEV	34	C2
AUBURN RD	PLA	34	B3
AUBURN RAVNE RD	AUB	126	C3
AUBURN RAVNE RD	PLA	126	C3
AUCTION SNIVELY	TEH	18	D4
AUDUBON DR	FRCO	57	C2
AUGUST AV	MCO	47	D4
AUGUST RD	STA	47	D4
AUGUSTINE RD	RCO	109	C1
AUKLET RD	SBD	92	C1
AULD RD	RCO	99	D5
AURORA CYN RD	MNO	43	B3
AUSTIN RD	IMP	109	A5
AUSTIN RD	SJCO	40	B5
AUSTIN RD	SJCO	47	B1
AUSTIN CREEK RD	SON	37	C2
AUSTIN MDWS RD	NEV	27	A4
AUSTRIAN RD	CAL	41	B4
AUTOPSTA TIJ-EN	BAJA	111	D3
AVALON AV	SBD	100	E1
AVALON BLVD	LA	191	C1
AVALON BLVD	LACO	97	E3
AVALON BLVD	LACO	S	C1
AVALON CYN RD	AVLN	97	A5
AVENA	SJCO	47	C1
AVENAL CUTOFF	KIN	67	A3
AVD BERMUDAS	RCO	100	E4
AVD DEL CAPITAN	SB	87	A4
AVD D LS ARBLES	VEN	88	D5
AVD D LS ARBLES	VEN	96	D1
AVENIDA DEL SOL	KER	80	C1
AVENIDA ENCINO	RCO	100	D5
AVD LA CUMBRE	RCO	100	D5
AVD LOS FELIZ	RCO	100	D5

STREET	CO.	PAGE	GRID
AVENIDA OBREGON	RCO	100	E4
AVENUE A	KER	89	E1
AVENUE A	YUMA	112	D5
AVENUE B	LACO	89	D2
AVENUE B	LACO	90	C2
AVENUE C	LACO	89	D2
AVENUE C	LACO	90	D2
AVENUE C	YUMA	112	C5
AVENUE D	LACO	90	B2
AVENUE E	LACO	89	E2
AVENUE E	LACO	90	A2
AVENUE E	RCO	99	B3
AVENUE E	YUMA	112	C5
AVENUE E-8	LACO	90	B2
AVENUE F	LACO	89	B2
AVENUE F	LACO	89	D2
AVENUE F	LACO	90	C2
AVENUE F	SBD	99	D2
AVENUE F-4	LACO	89	E2
AVENUE F-4	LACO	90	A2
AVENUE F-8	LACO	89	C2
AVENUE F-8	LACO	90	D2
AVENUE G	LACO	89	E2
AVENUE G-2	LACO	90	C2
AVENUE G-3	LACO	90	C2
AVENUE G-4	LACO	90	C2
AVENUE G-6	LACO	90	C2
AVENUE G-8	LACO	90	B2
AVENUE H	LACO	89	E2
AVENUE I	LACO	89	E2
AVENUE J	LACO	89	E3
AVENUE J	LACO	90	C2
AVENUE J-8	LACO	90	A2
AVENUE K	LACO	89	E3
AVENUE K	LACO	90	C3
AVENUE K-8	LACO	89	D3
AVENUE L	LACO	89	E3
AVENUE L	LACO	90	B3
AVENUE L	RCO	99	D2
AVENUE M	LACO	89	E3
AVENUE M	LACO	90	B3
AVENUE M-8	LACO	89	E3
AVENUE N	LACO	89	E3
AVENUE N	LACO	90	C3
AVENUE O	LACO	90	A3
AVENUE ONE	MCO	48	B4
AVENUE P	LACO	89	E3
AVENUE P	LACO	90	A3
AVENUE P	LACO	90	D3
AVENUE P-8	LACO	90	A3
AVENUE P-8	LACO	90	C3
AVENUE Q	LACO	90	C3
AVENUE Q	LACO	90	C3
AVENUE S	LACO	89	E3
AVENUE S	LACO	90	A3
AVENUE SAN LUIS	LA	177	B4
AVENUE STANFORD	LACO	89	B4
AVENUE T	LACO	90	B3
AVENUE T	LACO	90	C3
AVENUE TWO	MCO	48	B4
AVENUE U	LACO	90	C3
AVENUE Z	LACO	90	D4
AVENUE 2	TUL	68	D5
AVENUE 4 1/2	MAD	56	E3
AVENUE 5	MAD	56	E3
AVENUE 5 1/2	MAD	56	E3
AVENUE 5 1/2	MAD	57	A3
AVENUE 6	MAD	56	E3
AVENUE 6	MAD	57	A3
AVENUE 6 1/2	MAD	57	A3
AVENUE 7 1/2	MAD	56	D3
AVENUE 7 1/2	MAD	56	E3
AVENUE 7 1/2	MAD	57	C3
AVENUE 8	MAD	56	E3
AVENUE 8	MAD	57	A2
AVENUE 8	MAD	57	C2
AVENUE 8	TUL	68	B5
AVENUE 8 1/2	MAD	57	A2
AVENUE 9	MAD	56	E2
AVENUE 9	MAD	57	C2
AVENUE 9 1/2	MAD	56	E2
AVENUE 10	MAD	56	E2
AVENUE 10	MAD	57	B2
AVENUE 10 1/2	MAD	56	E2
AVENUE 10 1/2	MAD	57	A2
AVENUE 11	MAD	56	E2
AVENUE 11	MAD	57	A2
AVENUE 11 1/2	MAD	56	E2
AVENUE 11 1/2	MAD	57	A2
AVENUE 12	MAD	56	E2
AVENUE 12	MAD	57	B2
AVENUE 12	TUL	68	B5
AVENUE 12	TUL	68	C5
AVENUE 12 1/2	MAD	57	B2
AVENUE 13	MAD	56	E2
AVENUE 13 1/2	MAD	56	E2
AVENUE 13 1/2	MAD	57	A2
AVENUE 14	MAD	56	D2
AVENUE 14	MAD	57	C2
AVENUE 14 1/2	MAD	56	E2
AVENUE 14 1/2	MAD	57	A2
AVENUE 14 1/2	MAD	57	C2
AVENUE 15	MAD	56	E2
AVENUE 15 1/2	MAD	56	E2
AVENUE 15 1/2	MAD	57	B2
AVENUE 16	MAD	56	E2
AVENUE 16	TUL	68	B4
AVENUE 16	TUL	68	C4
AVENUE 16 1/2	MAD	56	E2
AVENUE 17	MAD	56	D2
AVENUE 17 1/2	MAD	56	E2
AVENUE 18	MAD	56	D2
AVENUE 18 1/2	MAD	56	D2

STREET	CO.	PAGE	GRID
AVENUE 19	MAD	56	D1
AVENUE 19 1/2	MAD	56	D1
AVENUE 20	LA	186	D2
AVENUE 20	MAD	56	D1
AVENUE 20 1/2	MAD	56	D1
AVENUE 21	MAD	56	D1
AVENUE 21	MAD	57	A1
AVENUE 21 1/2	MAD	56	D1
AVENUE 22	MAD	56	D1
AVENUE 22 1/2	MAD	56	D1
AVENUE 23 1/2	MAD	56	D1
AVENUE 24	MAD	56	D1
AVENUE 24	TUL	68	B4
AVENUE 24 1/2	MAD	56	E1
AVENUE 25	MAD	56	D1
AVENUE 25 1/2	MAD	56	D1
AVENUE 26	MAD	56	D1
AVENUE 26 1/2	MAD	56	E1
AVENUE 27	MAD	48	D5
AVENUE 27 1/2	MAD	48	E5
AVENUE 28	MAD	48	E5
AVENUE 28	TUL	68	C4
AVENUE 32	TUL	68	B4
AVENUE 40	TUL	68	C4
AVENUE 42	TUL	67	E4
AVENUE 42	TUL	68	C4
AVENUE 42	TUL	68	A4
AVENUE 44	TUL	68	B4
AVENUE 46	TUL	67	E4
AVENUE 46	TUL	68	C4
AVENUE 50	TUL	67	E4
AVENUE 52	TUL	68	B4
AVENUE 52	TUL	68	C4
AVENUE 54	TUL	67	E4
AVENUE 56	TUL	68	B4
AVENUE 58	TUL	68	A4
AVENUE 62	TUL	68	A4
AVENUE 64	TUL	68	D4
AVENUE 66	TUL	68	D4
AVENUE 68	TUL	68	A4
AVENUE 68	TUL	68	D4
AVENUE 70	TUL	68	D4
AVENUE 74	TUL	68	D4
AVENUE 76	TUL	68	D4
AVENUE 78	TUL	68	D4
AVENUE 80	TUL	68	B4
AVENUE 80	TUL	68	C4
AVENUE 84	TUL	68	A4
AVENUE 86	TUL	68	D4
AVENUE 88	TUL	67	E4
AVENUE 88	TUL	68	A4
AVENUE 88	TUL	68	D4
AVENUE 90	TUL	68	D4
AVENUE 92	TUL	68	D4
AVENUE 94	TUL	68	D4
AVENUE 95	TUL	68	C4
AVENUE 96	TUL	68	D4
AVENUE 100	TUL	68	D3
AVENUE 102	TUL	68	D3
AVENUE 104	TUL	67	E3
AVENUE 104	TUL	68	C3
AVENUE 108	TUL	68	A3
AVENUE 108	TUL	68	D3
AVENUE 112	TUL	67	E3
AVENUE 112	TUL	68	D3
AVENUE 116	TUL	68	B3
AVENUE 116	TUL	68	D3
AVENUE 120	TUL	67	E3
AVENUE 120	TUL	68	D3
AVENUE 124	TUL	68	C3
AVENUE 128	TUL	67	E3
AVENUE 128	TUL	68	C3
AVENUE 132	TUL	68	C3
AVENUE 136	TUL	67	E3
AVENUE 136	TUL	68	C3
AVENUE 138	TUL	68	E3
AVENUE 144	TUL	68	A3
AVENUE 152	TUL	68	B3
AVENUE 152	TUL	68	C3
AVENUE 156	TUL	68	D3
AVENUE 160	TUL	68	A3
AVENUE 160	TUL	68	D3
AVENUE 164	TUL	68	B3
AVENUE 168	TUL	68	A3
AVENUE 168	TUL	68	C3
AVENUE 169	TUL	68	D3
AVENUE 172	TUL	68	C3
AVENUE 176	TUL	68	A3
AVENUE 176	TUL	68	C3
AVENUE 178	TUL	68	D3
AVENUE 180	TUL	68	B3
AVENUE 182	TUL	68	D3
AVENUE 184	TUL	68	C2
AVENUE 188	TUL	68	D2
AVENUE 190	TUL	68	A2
AVENUE 192	TUL	68	A2
AVENUE 192	TUL	68	B2
AVENUE 196	TUL	68	B2
AVENUE 196	TUL	68	D2
AVENUE 198	TUL	68	A2
AVENUE 199	TUL	67	E2
AVENUE 200	TUL	68	A2
AVENUE 200	TUL	68	C2
AVENUE 204	TUL	67	E2
AVENUE 204	TUL	68	A2
AVENUE 204	TUL	68	C2
AVENUE 204	TUL	68	C4
AVENUE 206	TUL	68	D2
AVENUE 208	TUL	67	E2
AVENUE 208	TUL	68	A2
AVENUE 208	TUL	68	C2
AVENUE 212	TUL	68	B2
AVENUE 212	TUL	68	D2

STREET	CO.	PAGE	GRID
AVENUE 216	TUL	68	A2
AVENUE 216	TUL	68	D2
AVENUE 222	TUL	68	D2
AVENUE 224	TUL	68	B2
AVENUE 226	TUL	68	D2
AVENUE 228	TUL	68	B2
AVENUE 232	TUL	68	D2
AVENUE 236	TUL	68	A2
AVENUE 236	TUL	68	D2
AVENUE 240	TUL	68	A2
AVENUE 244	TUL	68	A2
AVENUE 248	TUL	68	A2
AVENUE 252	TUL	68	A2
AVENUE 256	TUL	67	E2
AVENUE 260	TUL	68	A2
AVENUE 264	TUL	68	B2
AVENUE 268	TUL	68	A2
AVENUE 271	TUL	68	B1
AVENUE 272	TUL	68	A1
AVENUE 272	TUL	68	D1
AVENUE 276	TUL	68	C1
AVENUE 280	TUL	68	A1
AVENUE 300	TUL	68	C1
AVENUE 304	TUL	68	A1
AVENUE 306	TUL	68	D1
AVENUE 308	TUL	68	A1
AVENUE 312	TUL	68	D1
AVENUE 318	TUL	68	C1
AVENUE 320	TUL	68	A1
AVENUE 320	TUL	68	D1
AVENUE 324	TUL	68	C1
AVENUE 328	TUL	68	A1
AVENUE 328	TUL	68	C1
AVENUE 332	TUL	68	C1
AVENUE 332	TUL	58	C5
AVENUE 334	TUL	58	D5
AVENUE 334	TUL	68	D1
AVENUE 336	TUL	68	B1
AVENUE 336	TUL	58	C5
AVENUE 337	TUL	68	C1
AVENUE 340	TUL	68	B1
AVENUE 340	TUL	58	C5
AVENUE 344	TUL	68	B1
AVENUE 344	TUL	58	C5
AVENUE 346	TUL	68	D1
AVENUE 348	TUL	68	C1
AVENUE 350	TUL	58	D5
AVENUE 352	TUL	57	E5
AVENUE 352	TUL	58	C5
AVENUE 356	TUL	58	B5
AVENUE 356	TUL	58	C5
AVENUE 360	TUL	57	E5
AVENUE 360	TUL	58	C5
AVENUE 364	TUL	58	C5
AVENUE 368	TUL	58	B5
AVENUE 368	TUL	58	C5
AVENUE 376	TUL	57	E5
AVENUE 376	TUL	58	C5
AVENUE 380	TUL	58	C5
AVENUE 384	TUL	58	A5
AVENUE 386	TUL	58	C5
AVENUE 388	TUL	58	C5
AVENUE 390	TUL	57	E5
AVENUE 390	TUL	58	C5
AVENUE 392	TUL	58	A5
AVENUE 394	TUL	58	C5
AVENUE 396	TUL	57	E5
AVENUE 396	TUL	58	A5
AVENUE 398	TUL	58	C5
AVENUE 400	TUL	58	B5
AVENUE 404	TUL	58	B5
AVENUE 404	TUL	58	C5
AVENUE 408	TUL	57	E5
AVENUE 408	TUL	58	B5
AVENUE 410	TUL	57	E5
AVENUE 416	TUL	58	C5
AVENUE 424	TUL	58	A4
AVENUE 428	TUL	58	B4
AVENUE 432	TUL	58	B4
AVENUE 436	TUL	58	B4
AVENUE 438	TUL	58	B4
AVENUE 440	TUL	58	B4
AVENUE 444	TUL	58	B4
AVENUE 448	TUL	58	B4
AVENUE 450	TUL	58	B4
AVENUE 452	TUL	58	B4
AVENUE 456	TUL	58	B4
AVENUE 460	TUL	58	B4
AVENUE 464	TUL	58	B4
AVENUE 468	TUL	58	B4
AVENUE 472	TUL	58	B4
AVERY RD	FRCO	55	E3
AVERY RD	MCO	55	D3
AVERY SHEEP RCH	CAL	41	C3
AVIATION BLVD	ELS	189	E3
AVIATION BLVD	HAW	189	E3
AVIATION BLVD	ING	189	E3
AVIATION BLVD	LA	188	E5
AVIATION BLVD	LA	189	E3
AVIATION BLVD	LACO	97	D3
AVIATION BLVD	LACO	S	B1
AVIATION BLVD	RB	189	E3
AVOCADO BLVD	SDCO	V	E3
AVOCADO BLVD	SDCO	111	E1
AVOCADO RD	BUT	25	E5
AYERS AV	SJCO	47	C1
AYRES HOLMES RD	PLA	34	B3
AZALEA TR	RCO	100	B3
AZEVEDO	MCO	47	D5
AZEVEDO RD	SOL	39	C4
AZEVEDO RD	STA	47	C4
AZTEC AV	RCO	102	C4
AZUSA AV	LACO	98	B2

STREET	CO.	PAGE	GRID
AZUSA AV	LACO	R	E4
AZUSA CANYON RD	LACO	R	E3
B			
B ST	BUT	25	C5
B ST	DVS	136	C3
B ST	FRE	165	C4
B ST	H	146	E2
B ST	IMP	109	A4
B ST	KER	68	B5
B ST	LA	191	B1
B ST	LACO	97	E4
B ST	LACO	S	C2
B ST	SCTO	137	C2
B ST	SD	215	D3
B ST	SJCO	40	B5
B ST	YUBA	125	D3
B ST	YUB	33	D2
B ST N	SCTO	137	B2
BABCOCK RD	LAS	14	B4
BABCOCK CNDR RD	LAS	14	B4
BABEL SLOUGH RD	YOL	39	D2
BACHELOR VLY RD	LAK	31	C2
BACK BONE RD	NEV	26	D5
BACKBONE RD	SHA	13	A5
BACKBONE RD	SHA	18	E1
BACKES LN	KER	79	C4
BACKUS RD	KER	79	E5
BACON RD	STA	47	B2
BACON ST	SDCO	V	A3
BACON ST	SDCO	111	C1
BACON ISLAND	SJCO	39	E5
BADDAGE RD	RCO	107	B1
BADENOUGH CY RD	SIE	27	D3
BADGER RD	SON	38	A2
BADGER FLAT	MCO	55	D1
BAGDAD HWY	SBD	93	C4
BAGDAD HWY	SBD	101	C1
BAGDAD WY	SBD	93	D4
BAGDAD CHASE RD	SBD	93	B2
BAGGTT MARYSVLL	BUT	25	D5
BAGLEY RD	COL	32	D2
BAILEY AV	KER	70	A5
BAILEY AV	MCO	48	B4
BAILEY AV	SB	86	B3
BAILEY AV	SCL	P	D4
BAILEY RD	COL	32	E3
BAILEY RD	CC	M	B3
BAILEY RD	CC	39	A5
BAILEY RD	DN	1	D3
BAILEY RD	IMP	110	D5
BAILEY RD	RCO	107	B1
BAILEY RD	SBD	84	A2
BAILEY RD	SCL	46	C5
BAILEY RD	SUT	33	C3
BAILEY FLATS RD	MAD	49	B5
BAILEY HILL RD	SIS	4	A2
BAILY RD	KER	79	B4
BAILY RIDGE RD	CAL	41	C2
BAIN ST	RCO	99	A2
BAIR RD	HUM	10	B4
BAIRD RD	SON	38	A2
BAKER AV	ONT	204	E3
BAKER AV	ORCO	T	C3
BAKER AV	ROC	204	E3
BAKER RD	COL	32	C2
BAKER RD	MCO	55	E1
BAKER RD	PLCV	138	B2
BAKER RD	SJCO	40	B4
BAKER RD	STA	47	C3
BAKER RD	TEH	18	D5
BAKER RD	SUT	33	C4
BAKER RD	YUB	26	B5
BAKER ST	CM	197	B4
BAKER ST	CM	198	A4
BAKER CREEK RD	INY	51	D5
BAKER RILEY WY	CAL	41	B3
BKRSFLD-GLNVLLE	KER	68	E5
BKRSFLD-GLNVLLE	KER	69	A5
BKRSFLD-GLNVLLE	KER	78	D2
BAKRSFLD-MCKITT	KER	78	A3
BALBOA AV	SD	211	E5
BALBOA AV	SD	212	C1
BALBOA AV	SDCO	V	A2
BALBOA AV	SDCO	106	C5
BALBOA BLVD	LACO	97	C1
BALBOA BLVD	LACO	Q	B1
BALBOA BLVD	NB	199	B5
BALBOA BLVD	ORCO	T	C4
BALCH PARK RD	TUL	69	A2
BALCOM CYN RD	VEN	88	D5
BALDERSTON	ED	34	E3
BALD HILL RD	PLA	34	C3
BALD HILLS RD	DN	1	E4
BALD HILLS RD	DN	2	A4
BALD HILLS RD	HUM	10	A2
BALD MTN RD	CAL	41	B2
BALD MTN RD	HUM	10	B5
BALD MTN RD	MEN	23	A2
BALD MTN RD	MNO	50	D1
BALD MTN RD	SHA	13	E4
BALD MTN RD	YUB	33	E1
BALD MTN RD N	CAL	41	C2
BALD MTN LKOUT	SIS	3	D4
BALD MT SPGS RD	MNO	50	E1
BALD ROCK RD	BUT	25	E3
BALDWIN AV	LACO	R	C3
BALDWIN RD	STA	47	D2
BALDWIN RD	STA	47	B3
BALDWIN RD	VEN	88	A4
BALDWIN ST	CAL	40	D4
BALDWIN PARK BLVD	LACO	R	D4

STREET INDEX

STREET	CO.	PAGE	GRID
BALDY RD	SBD	90	E5
BALDY MCCULY RD	SHA	13	E4
BALDY MESA RD	SBD	91	A4
BALE LN	NAPA	29	B2
BALFOUR RD	CC	M	C3
BALFOUR RD	CC	39	C5
BALIS BELL RD	TEH	18	B5
BALL RD	ANA	193	A3
BALL RD	ANA	194	A3
BALL RD	ORCO	98	B3
BALL RD	ORCO	T	B2
BALL RD	TEH	17	E4
BALL MT LTL SHA	SIS	4	B4
BALL MT LTL SHA	SIS	5	A4
BALL MTN LKOUT	SIS	4	D3
BALL ROCK RD	TEH	23	E1
BALLANTREE LN	NEV	34	B2
BALLARAT RD	INY	71	C3
BALLARD RD	TEH	24	E2
BALLICO AV	MCO	48	A4
BALLINGER RD	RCO	99	E5
BALLINGR CYN RD	VEN	87	E1
BALIS RD	TEH	18	C5
BALLS FERRY RD	SHA	18	D3
BALL FERRY PK RD	SHA	18	D3
BALSAM RD	SBD	91	B4
BALSAMO RD	SBD	81	A5
BALTIMORE MN RD	PLA	34	E3
BANCROFT AV	O	159	D1
BANCROFT DR	SDCO	V	D3
BANCROFT DR	SDCO	111	E1
BANCROFT RD	CC	M	A3
BANCROFT RD	STA	47	C3
BANCROFT WY	ALA	L	D4
BANCROFT WY	B	156	A3
BANDERILLA DR	MPA	48	D2
BANDINI BLVD	LACO	R	A4
B & R LN	SOL	39	C3
BANDUCCI RD	KER	79	B4
BANGOR AV	KIN	57	E5
BANGOR PARK RD	BUT	25	D5
BANGOR PARK CTO	BUT	25	E5
BANGS AV	STA	47	C2
BANNER RD	CAL	41	B3
BANNER QUAKR HL	NEV	34	D1
BANNER RDG LAVA	NEV	34	C1
BANNING IDYLLWD	RCO	100	A4
BANNISTER AV	SCL	P	E5
BANNISTER RD	IMP	108	E4
BANTA RD	SJCO	47	E2
BAR RD	MAD	49	E5
BAR RD	MAD	50	A5
BARBARA WRTH RD	IMP	112	B4
BARBER	SJCO	39	E3
BARBER LN	RCO	107	B1
BARBER RD	ALP	36	B4
BARBER RD	TEH	25	A2
BARBER MTN RD	SDCO	112	B1
BARD RD	IMP	110	D5
BARDSDALE AV	VEN	88	D4
BARHAM AV	TEH	24	D2
BARHAM BLVD	LA	181	C1
BARHAM BLVD	LACO	Q	D3
BAR K RD	TRI	17	C2
BARKER RD	KER	67	B5
BARKER CREEK RD	TRI	17	B2
BARKER MINE RD	MNO	51	C2
BARKHOUSE CK RD	SIS	3	D3
BARKSHANTY RD	SIS	10	D2
BARLOW LN	INY	51	D4
BAR MTN LOOKOUT	SIS	3	C4
BARNES LN	MEN	23	B2
BARNES RD	KER	90	B1
BARNES RD	SBD	92	D4
BARNES RD	SLO	66	A5
BARNES RD	SLO	76	A1
BARNETT AV	SDCO	V	B3
BARNETT RD	STA	48	B2
BARNEY GULCH RD	TRI	11	B5
BARNHART RD	STA	47	C5
BARNY OLDFLD RD	IMP	110	C5
BARR RD	HUM	10	B5
BARRANCA AV	LACO	U	A3
BARRANCA PKWY	ORCO	98	C4
BARRANCA PKWY	ORCO	T	D3
BARRANCA RD	TUS	198	E2
BARREL SPGS RD	LACO	90	A3
BARREL SPGS RD	MOD	7	E3
BARRETT	CC	38	C5
BARRETT AV	FRCO	57	B5
BARRETT AV	FRCO	57	C5
BARRETT LAKE RD	SDCO	112	B2
BARRINGTON AV	LACO	180	B2
BARRINGTON LN	SIE	27	C4
BARRY RD	SUT	33	D2
BARRYS RD	HUM	16	A1
BARSTOW AV	FRCO	57	A3
BARSTOW AV	FRCO	57	C3
BARSTOW AV	KIN	57	E5
BARSTOW FRWY	SBD	91	A5
BARSTOW FRWY	SBD	99	B1
BARSTOW RD	BARS	208	B3
BARSTOW RD	KER	80	D5
BARSTOW RD	SBD	91	E2
BARSTOW RD	SBD	92	A4
BARTEL ST	SHA	13	C5
BARTELL RD	INY	51	E5
BARTH RD	IMP	108	E3
BARTLE GAP RD	SIS	13	B3
BARTLETT RD	SOL	39	B3
BARTLETTE RD	INY	60	B5
BARTLETT SPG RD	LAK	31	E2
BARTOLOMEI	SJCO	40	C5
BARTOLOMEI	SJCO	47	C1
BARTON	PLA	34	B5
BARTON RD	SBD	99	C2
BARTON ST	RCO	99	B3
BARTON HILL RD	YUB	26	B4
BAR W RD	HUM	16	B3
BASCOM AV	SCL	46	B4
BASCOM AV	SJ	151	C4
BASCOM AV	SCL	P	B3
BASE LINE AV	SB	86	E3
BASELINE RD	LACO	98	D1
BASE LINE RD	LACO	U	A2
BASE LINE RD	PLA	33	E5
BASELINE RD	SBD	U	D2
BASELINE RD	SBD	98	E1
BASELINE RD	SBD	101	C1
BASELINE ST	SBDO	207	B1
BASELINE ST	SBD	102	C1
BASIC SCHOOL RD	KER	78	B5
BASILONE RD	SDCO	105	E1
BASIN RD	SBD	82	E5
BASIN ST	KER	79	C2
BASLER RD	TEH	18	B4
BASS	FRCO	56	C3
BASSET RD	LAS	14	C3
BASSETT AV	KER	68	C5
BASS HILL RD	LAS	21	A3
BASS LAKE RD	ED	34	C5
BASS VALLEY RD	MAD	49	D4
BASTANCHURY RD	ORCO	T	C1
BATAVIA RD	SOL	39	B2
BATCHELDER RD	SB	86	C2
BATEMAN RD	SHA	19	B2
BATES	SUT	33	C4
BATTL CK BTM RD	SHA	19	A3
BAUGHMAN RD	IMP	108	E4
BAUMBACH AV	KER	79	B4
BAUTISTA RD	RCO	100	A4
BAXTER AV	NAP	133	B2
BAXTER RD	MCO	48	E5
BAXTER RD	RCO	99	C5
BAXTERS RD	MNO	43	E5
BAXTERS RD	MNO	50	E1
BAY DR	SC	169	A3
BAY HWY	SON	37	C3
BAY RD	SMCO	N	D2
BAY RD	SMCO	45	D3
BAY ST	SF	142	B1
BAY ST	SF	143	A2
BAY ST	SC	169	B4
BAYLEY RES RD	MOD	8	A2
BAYLIS BLUE GUM	GLE	24	D4
BAYOU RD	SAC	33	D5
BAYSHORE BLVD	SMCO	L	C5
BAYSHORE BLVD	SMCO	45	C2
BAYSHORE FRWY	BLMT	145	B3
BAYSHORE FRWY	BURL	144	C3
BAYSHORE FRWY	MLBR	144	C3
BAYSHORE FRWY	MVW	148	A3
BAYSHORE FRWY	SJ	151	D1
BAYSHORE FRWY	SJ	152	B1
BAYSHORE FRWY	SM	145	B3
BAYSHORE FRWY	SMCO	45	D3
BAYSHORE FRWY	SMCO	144	C3
BAYSHORE FRWY	SMCO	145	B3
BAYSHORE FRWY	SSF	144	C1
BAYSHORE FRWY	SVL	148	D3
BAYSIDE DR	NB	199	D5
BAYSIDE DR	NB	200	A5
BAY VIEW AV	NAPA	38	C3
BAY VIEW RD	MCO	55	C1
BEACH BLVD	ORCO	98	B3
BEACH BLVD	ORCO	T	B1
BEACH RD	HUM	22	A1
BEACH RD	IMP	109	A2
BEACH RD	MPA	49	B4
BEACH RD	SCR	54	B3
BEACH ST	SF	143	A2
BEACH PARK BL	FCTY	145	D3
BEACON RD	SLO	76	B1
BEACON ST	AVLN	97	B4
BEAL RD	IMP	109	B2
BEALE RD N	YUB	33	D2
BEALE RD S	YUB	33	E3
BEALE ST	SF	143	D4
BEAL RANCH RD	CAL	40	E3
BEALEVILLE RD	KER	79	B3
BEAMER ST	YOL	33	B5
BEAN CLIPPER RD	YUB	26	B4
BEAN CREEK RD	BUT	25	E4
BEAN CREEK RD	SCR	P	A5
BEAN CREEK RD	SCR	54	A1
BEAN HOLLOW RD	SMCO	N	C4
BEAN HOLLOW RD	SMCO	45	C5
BEAR ST	CM	197	E4
BEAR ST	ORCO	T	D3
BEAR BASIN RD	DN	2	B3
BEAR BUTTE RD	HUM	16	B5
BEAR CANYON RD	FRCO	66	B2
BEAR CREEK DR N	MCO	48	C4
BEAR CREEK DR S	MCO	48	C4
BEAR CREEK LOOP	TRI	12	A3
BEAR CREEK RD	CC	L	D3
BEAR CREEK RD	CC	38	D5
BEAR CREEK RD	LAK	31	D1
BEAR CREEK RD	SCL	P	A4
BEAR CREEK RD	SCR	N	E5
BEAR CREEK RD	SCR	P	A5
BEAR CREEK RD	SCR	45	E5
BEARD RD	NAP	133	C2
BEAR GULCH RD	SMCO	N	C3
BEAR MTN BLVD	KER	78	D4
BEAR MTN RD	FRCO	58	B3
BEAR MTN RD	SHA	18	C1
BEAR MTN RD	SIS	13	C2
BEAR MTN LKOUT	SHA	18	D1
BEAR MT WINE RD	KER	78	E3
BEAR MT WINE RD	KER	79	A3
BEAR RANCH HILL	BUT	25	E2
BEAR RIVER	AMA	41	D1
BEAR RIVER S	AMA	41	D1
BEAR RIVER DR	SUT	33	D3
BEAR RIV RDG RD	HUM	15	D3
BEAR SPRINGS RD	LAS	14	A3
BEAR TRAP DR	MPA	49	A3
BEAR TRAP RD	NEV	26	C5
BEAR VALLEY	MPA	48	E3
BEAR VLY PKWY	SDCO	106	D4
BEAR VALLEY RD	COL	32	B2
BEAR VALLEY RD	KER	79	B4
BEAR VALLEY RD	SBD	90	E4
BEAR VALLEY RD	SIE	27	D4
BEAR VLY CUTOFF	SBD	91	B4
BEASON ST	KER	78	A1
BEASORE RD	MAD	49	E4
BEATIE RD	SHA	18	D3
BEAUCHAMP RD	COL	32	D2
BEAUMONT AV	RCO	99	E3
BEAUMONT ST	SBD	91	E3
BEAVER CREEK RD	SIS	3	D3
BECHELLI LN	RED	122	E2
BECHELLI LN	SHA	18	C2
BECK AV	SOL	L	E1
BECK AV	SOL	M	A1
BECKER	SUT	33	C4
BECKER RD	SOL	39	C1
BECKET CT	KER	79	C5
BECKWITH RD	SIE	27	D3
BECKWITH RD	STA	47	B2
BECKWRTH CALPNE	PLU	27	C3
BECKWRTH GENESE	PLU	26	E1
BECKWRTH GENESE	PLU	27	B1
BECKWRTH LOYLTN	PLU	27	C3
BCKWRTH TYLRSVL	PLU	26	E1
BCKWRTH TYLRSVL	PLU	27	B1
BEDFORD DR	SBD	92	B1
BEE CANYON RD	RCO	100	A4
BEECH AV	KER	78	B2
BEECH AV	SBD	99	A2
BEECH ST	BKD	166	B2
BEECH ST	SDCO	106	C2
BEECHER RD	SJCO	40	B5
BEE GULCH RD	ALP	42	A1
BEEGUM RD	SHA	17	D4
BEEGUM GORGE RD	SHA	17	D4
BEEKLEY RD	RCO	102	C4
BEEKLEY RD	SBD	90	E4
BEEROCK RD	SLO	65	D5
BEHYMER	FRCO	56	C2
BEHYMER AV	FRCO	57	D2
BELCHER AV	MCO	48	B4
BELFAST RD	LAS	21	B3
BELFIELD RD	SBD	92	E5
BELL	MCO	48	A4
BELL LN	PLU	26	D1
BELL RD	AMA	40	E1
BELL RD	BUT	25	A3
BELL RD	KER	77	E2
BELL RD	KER	78	A2
BELL RD	PLA	34	B3
BELL RD	SB	87	C1
BELL RD	STA	47	C4
BELL ST	SB	86	D2
BELLA ROSA DR	HUM	16	C4
BELLA VISTA DR	KER	79	D1
BELLE TER	KER	166	D5
BELLE GRAVE AV	RCO	99	A2
BELLEVUE AV	SUT	33	D3
BELLEVUE RD	MCO	48	B4
BELLFLOWER BLVD	LACO	98	A3
BELLFLOWER BLVD	LACO	S	E2
BELLFLOWER BLVD	LACO	T	A2
BELLFLOWER ST	SBD	91	B3
BELL HILL RD	LAK	31	D3
BELL MTN RD	SBD	91	C3
BELL SPRINGS RD	HUM	16	C5
BELL SPRINGS RD	MEN	22	D1
BELLVIEW RD	MAD	57	C1
BELMONT AV	FRE	165	C3
BELMONT AV	FRCO	56	C3
BELMONT AV	FRCO	57	C3
BELOMY ST	SCLR	151	B3
BELSBY AV	RCO	102	C4
BELTLINE RD	SHA	18	C2
BELVIN RD	YUBA	125	A1
BENA RD	KER	79	A3
BENBOW DR	HUM	22	C1
BEND	TEH	18	D4
BENDER	SJCO	40	A3
BENDER AV	KER	78	B2
BENDER RD	SHA	18	A3
BENDLER RD	STA	47	E2
BENEDICT CYN DR	LACO	Q	C3
BENHAM LN	CUR	1	D2
BEN HUR RD	MPA	49	B4
BENICIA AV	KIN	57	E5
BENICIA RD	SOL	38	D4
BENICIA RD	VAL	134	D5
BENIT JUAREZ BL	BAJA	112	B4
BENNER AV	KER	68	B5
BENNET RD	LACO	89	A5
BENNET RD	VEN	88	E5
BENNETS WELL RD	INY	72	A2
BENNETT RD	BUT	25	A2
BENNETT RD	MCO	55	E2
BENNETT RD	NEV	34	C1
BENNETT RD	RCO	100	D3
BENNETT VLY RD	SON	38	A2
BENNETT VLY RD	STR	131	D4
BENSON AV	MTCL	203	D3
BENSON AV	ONT	203	D5
BENSON AV	SBD	U	D3
BENSON AV	SBD	203	D3
BENSON AV	UPL	203	D1
BENSON DR	SHA	18	B2
BENSON RD	TEH	18	C4
BENT RD	STA	47	D2
BENTLEY RD	STA	47	D2
BENTON DR	SHA	18	C2
BENTON RD	RCO	99	D5
BENTON RD E	RCO	99	E5
BENTON ST	SCLR	150	C3
BENTON CROSSING	MNO	51	B2
BERDOO CYN RD	RCO	101	B3
BERKELEY AV	STA	47	E3
BERKSHIRE RD	KER	79	A3
BERMUDA DR	SM	145	B2
BERNAL AV	ALA	M	B5
BERNAL AV	ALA	P	B1
BERNAL DR E	SAL	171	C3
BERNARD ST	KER	78	D3
BERNARD WY	SHA	18	C1
BERRELLESA ST	M	154	B2
BERRY AV	H	146	E4
BERRY RD	SUT	33	D3
BERRY CREEK RD	BUT	25	E3
BERRYESSA RD	SJ	152	C1
BERRYESSA RD	SCL	P	B3
BERRYESSA RD	SCL	46	B4
BERRYSSA KNX RD	NAPA	32	C4
BERT RD	LAS	27	E1
BERTAS RD	HUM	15	E1
BERT CRANE RD	MCO	48	B5
BERTRAM CIR	KER	79	C4
BERYL ST	LACO	97	D3
BERYL ST	LACO	S	B1
BERYL ST	SD	212	A1
BERYLWOOD RD	VEN	88	C5
BESSEMR MINE RD	SBD	92	B4
BIRD RD	IMP	109	B4
BEST RD	MPA	49	C3
BEST RD	RCO	99	E5
BEST RD	SUT	33	C3
BEST RANCH RD	YOL	33	C5
BETHANY RD	SJCO	46	D1
BETHEL AV	FRCO	57	E4
BETHEL RD	SLO	76	A2
BETHEL ISLND RD	CC	M	D3
BETHEL ISLND RD	CC	39	C5
BETTERAVIA RD	STB	173	C5
BETTERAVIA RD	SB	86	B1
BETTERAVIA RD	SMA	173	C5
BETTS RD	TRI	23	A1
BETTY WY	SIS	4	B4
BETZ RD	SUT	33	D3
BEVERLY BLVD	BH	183	C1
BEVERLY BLVD	LA	183	C1
BEVERLY BLVD	LA	184	B1
BEVERLY BLVD	LA	185	C1
BEVERLY BLVD	LACO	97	D2
BEVERLY BLVD	LACO	98	A2
BEVERLY BLVD	LACO	183	C1
BEVERLY BLVD	LACO	Q	D4
BEVERLY DR	BH	183	B1
BEVERLY DR	LAS	20	E3
BEVERLY DR	LA	183	B1
BEVERLY DR	LACO	Q	C3
BEVERLY GLEN BL	LA	180	E2
BEVERLY GLEN BL	LA	183	A3
BEVERLY GLEN BL	LACO	97	C1
BEVERLY GLEN BL	LACO	Q	C3
BEVERWIL DR	BH	183	C3
BEVERWIL DR	LA	183	C3
BEYER BLVD	SDCO	V	D5
BEYER BLVD	SDCO	111	D2
BEYER LN	SJCO	40	B5
BEYER WY	SDCO	V	C5
BEYER WY	SDCO	111	D2
BEYERS LN	NEV	34	B2
BIANCHI RD	S	160	B1
BIDDLE	SLO	76	B4
BIDWELL RD	SHA	13	D5
BIDWELL CK RD	MOD	7	D3
BIEBER LKOUT RD	LAS	14	B3
BIG BAR DUMP RD	TRI	17	A1
BIG BAR MTN RD	BUT	25	E2
BIG BEN	PLA	34	B3
BIG BEND DR	CLK	85	D5
BIG BEND RD	BUT	25	D3
BIG BEND RD	SHA	13	A4
BIG CANYON	LAK	32	A4
BIG CREEK RD	PLU	26	B2
BIG CREEK RD	TRI	17	B2
BIG CK SHAFT RD	TUO	48	E1
BIG COVE RD	PLU	20	B4
BIG DIPPER	PLA	34	E2
BIGELOW RD	SIS	13	A2
BIGELOW RD	SUT	33	B1
BIG FLAT RD	DN	2	B4
BIG FRCH CK RD	TRI	17	A1
BIGGAR LN	MEN	23	A2
BIGGS EAST HWY	BUT	25	C5
BIG HILL RD	TUO	41	D4
BIG HILL LOOKUT	HUM	10	C3
BIG HORN DR	RCO	100	D5
BIG INCH PIPELN	KER	79	E5
BIG INCH PIPELN	KER	80	A5
BIG LAKES RD	MOD	14	D2
BIG MEADOWS RD	SIS	3	C5
BIG OAK DR	MEN	31	B3
BIG PINES HWY	LACO	90	C4
BIG PN REPTR RD	INY	51	E5
BIG RANCH RD	NAPA	29	E5
BIG RANCH RD	NAPA	38	C2
BIG RANCH RD	NAPA	133	C2
BIG RESRVOIR RD	PLA	34	E2
BIG ROCK CK RD	LACO	90	C4
BIG SAGE RD	MOD	6	E5
BIG SAGE RD	MOD	7	A5
BIG SANDY RD	MON	66	B4
BIG SPRING DR	NEV	34	B2
BIG SPRING RD	SHA	19	A2
BIG SPRINGS RD	MNO	50	D1
BIG SPRINGS RD	SIS	4	C5
BIG SPRINGS RD	SIS	12	E2
BIG SPRINGS CTO	PLU	20	B4
BIG STUMP RD	SIS	5	A2
BIG TRAILS DR	MEN	22	E4
BIG TREES RD	INY	51	C4
BIG TUJUNGA BL	LACO	Q	E1
BIG TUJUNGA CYN	LACO	89	E5
BIG VALLEY RD	LAK	31	D3
BILBY RD	SAC	39	E2
BILLE RD	BUT	25	C3
BILLIE ST	KER	78	D4
BILLINGS AV	KER	78	B1
BILLINGS LN	RCO	99	B4
BILLY WRIGHT RD	MCO	55	C2
BINET RD	BUT	26	B4
BINGHAMTON RD	SOL	39	B2
BIOLA AV	FRCO	57	B3
BIR RD	INY	51	C4
BIRCH AV	MON	65	A1
BIRCH ST	ORCO	98	C3
BIRCH ST	ORCO	T	D1
BIRCH ST	ORCO	U	A4
BIRCH CREEK RD	INY	59	E1
BIRCHIM LN	INY	51	C3
BIRCHIN FLAT RD	MNO	42	E2
BIRCHIN FLAT RD	MNO	43	A2
BIRCHVILLE RD	NEV	26	B5
BIRD AV	SJ	152	B5
BIRD RD	SJCO	47	A2
BIRDS LANDNG RD	SOL	39	B4
BIRD SPG CYN RD	KER	80	A1
BIRKHEAD	FRCO	57	C2
BIRMINGHAM DR	SDCO	106	B4
BISCH CT	KER	79	E2
BISHOP AV	FRCO	57	B4
BISHOP AV	FRCO	67	B1
BISHOP AV	SUT	33	C1
BISHOP ST	SNLO	172	D4
BISHOP CK RD E	INY	51	C4
BISHOP CK RD W	INY	51	C4
BISIGNANI RD	MCO	55	E1
BISSET STN RD	MAD	49	D4
BITNEY SPGS RD	NEV	34	B1
BITTERWATER RD	MON	65	C2
BITTRWTR VLY RD	KER	77	A1
BIXBY RD	VEN	88	D5
BIXLER RD	CC	39	D5
BLACK RD	SB	86	B1
BLACK BART RD	BUT	25	E4
BLACK BEAR RD	SIS	11	B2
BLACK BUTTE RD	GLE	24	B3
BLACK BUTTE RD	SHA	19	A3
BLACK BUTTE RD	TEH	24	C2
BLK BTTE BSN RD	LACO	90	D3
BLACK CANYON RD	INY	51	E4
BLACK CANYON RD	MNO	44	B5
BLACK CANYON RD	MNO	51	B1
BLACK CANYON RD	SBD	81	C5
BLACK CANYON RD	SBD	84	B5
BLACK CANYON RD	SBD	94	C1
BLACK CANYON RD	SDCO	107	A3
BLACK DIAMND WY	CC	39	B5
BLACK DIAMND MN	BUT	25	D1
BLK EAGLE MN RD	RCO	101	E3
BLACK FOX MTN	SIS	13	B2
BLACK GULCH RD	KER	79	C1
BLACK GULCH RD	LAS	14	A5
BLACK HAWK RD	CC	M	B4
BLACK HAWK RD	CC	46	A1
BLACKHAWK RD	PLU	26	C1
BLACK HILLS RD	RCO	100	D4
BLACKIE RD	MON	54	C3
BLACK LAKE RD	LAS	14	B5
BLACKMER RD	SUT	33	B2
BLACKMORE	SJCO	47	C1
BLACK MTN RD	IMP	110	B3
BLACK MTN RD	SDCO	106	D4
BLACK MTN RD	SMCO	N	C2
BLACK MTN RD	SMCO	45	C3
BLACK MTN RD	SIS	4	B3
BLACK MTN TR	RCO	100	B3
BLACK MTN LO RD	SLO	76	D3
BLACK RANCH RD	SHA	13	C4
BLACK ROCK RD	RCO	103	C5
BLACK ROCK CYN	SBD	100	E2
BLACK RCK MN RD	MNO	51	C2
BLACK ROCK SPGS	INY	59	E2
BLACKS CYN RD	MOD	14	D1
BLACKS RDG LKOT	LAS	14	B5
BLACKSTONE AV	FRE	165	D1
BLACKSTONE ST	TUL	68	B2
BLACKWELL LN	DN	1	D4
BLAGEN RD	CAL	41	C3
BLAINE ST	RCO	99	B2
BLAIR RD	IMP	109	B3
BLAIS RD	IMP	109	A4
BLAKE RD	SAC	40	B2
BLAKE ST	SBD	99	B1

STREET	CO.	PAGE	GRID
BLAKER RD	STA	47	D3
BLANCHARD FT RD	TRI	17	D2
BLANCO	MON	54	C4
BLANCO RD	MPA	48	D2
BLANCO RD E	MON	171	C5
BLANCO RD E	SAL	171	C5
BLANCO RD W	MON	171	A5
BLANCO RD W	SAL	171	A5
BLAND RD	SHA	17	E3
BLANEY AV	CPTO	149	E5
BLANKENSHIP AV	KER	78	A1
BLANKO RD	SBD	90	E4
BLATCHLEY RD	TEH	24	D2
BLAZING STAR AV	SBD	91	A3
BLEDSOE RD	MCO	48	B3
BLEVENS RD	LPAZ	104	C5
BLEWETT RD	STA	47	B2
BLICKENSTAFF RD	LAS	21	B4
BLISS DR	RCO	107	C1
BLISS RD	MCO	48	C5
BLISS RD	YUB	33	D2
BLITHEDALE AV	MAR	L	B4
BLITHEDALE AV E	MV	140	A3
B L M DUMP RD	LAS	20	E1
BLOCK RD	BUT	25	C5
BLOCK RD	BUT	33	C1
BLODGETT RD	IMP	109	B5
BLOODY CAMP RD	HUM	10	C3
BLOOMR HLL LKOT	BUT	25	D3
BLOOMFIELD AV	LACO	T	A2
BLOOMFIELD AV	SCL	54	D2
BLOOMFIELD RD	SON	37	D3
BLOOMFLD GRNTVL	NEV	26	D5
BLOOMINGTON RD	SBD	99	B2
BLOSS AV	MCO	47	D4
BLOSSER RD	STB	173	A2
BLOSSER RD	SB	86	B1
BLOSSER RD	SMA	173	A4
BLOSSOM	SJCO	39	E3
BLOSSOM AV	MCO	56	A2
BLOSSOM RD	STA	47	E2
BLOSSOM HILL RD	SCL	P	B4
BLOSSOM HILL RD	SCL	46	A5
BLOWERS DR	RCO	99	A4
BLUE GILL RD	SIS	4	B3
BLUE GULCH RD	SIS	11	B3
BLUE GUM AV	STA	47	C2
BLUE LAKE BLVD	HUM	10	A5
BLUE LAKE RD	MOD	8	C3
BLUE LK MPLE CK	HUM	16	B1
BLUE LAKES RD	ALP	36	B5
BLUE LAKES RD	LAK	31	C2
BLUE MTN RD	CAL	41	C2
BLUE MTN RD	KER	69	A5
BLUE MTN LKT RD	CAL	41	C2
BLUE RIDGE RD	SOL	38	E2
BLUE RIDGE RD	TEH	19	C3
BLUE SLIDE RD	HUM	15	E3
BLUFF ST	RCO	100	A2
BLUFF CREEK RD	TRI	16	E5
BLYTHE AV	FRCO	57	C3
BLYTHE AV	FRCO	67	B1
BLYTHE-VIDAL RD	RCO	103	D2
BOARDER ST	RCO	100	A3
BOARTS RD	IMP	109	A4
BOAT HARBOR RD	LAS	20	E2
BOBCAT TR	RCO	100	A5
BOB HOPE DR	RCO	100	E4
BOBS GAP RD	LACO	90	C4
BOB WHITE WY	INY	73	A4
BOCA RD	NEV	27	E5
BOCA SPRINGS RD	NEV	27	E5
BOCA SPGS RD E	NEV	27	E5
BOCKMAN RD	ALA	146	A2
BODEGA AV	SON	38	A3
BODEGA HWY	SON	37	D2
BODEM ST	MDO	162	D2
BODFISH CYN RD	KER	79	D1
BODIE RD	MNO	43	C3
BODIE MASONC RD	MNO	43	C3
BOESSOW RD	SAC	40	B3
BOGARD RD	LAS	14	B5
BOGGS RD	COL	24	E5
BOGGS & CHAMLIN	TEH	24	C2
BOGUE RD	STA	47	E3
BOGUE RD	STA	48	A3
BOGUE RD	SUT	33	C2
BOHAN DILLON RD	SON	37	B1
BOHEMIAN HWY	SON	37	C2
BOHN BLVD	SHA	18	B3
BOLAM RD	SIS	4	D5
BOLAM RD	SIS	12	D1
BOLAM LOGGNG RD	SIS	12	D1
BOLES RD	COL	32	E3
BOLEY RD	IMP	108	E5
BOLLINGER CY RD	CC	M	A4
BOLLINGER CY RD	CC	M	B5
BOLINGER CYN RD	CC	45	E1
BOLINGER CYN RD	CC	46	A1
BOLO RD	SBD	94	A3
BOLSA AV	ORCO	98	B4
BOLSA CHICA RD	ORCO	98	B4
BOLSA CHICA RD	ORCO	T	B3
BON ST	MCO	48	D5
BONANZA AV	TRI	17	D1
BONANZA RD	CLK	74	D2
BONANZA RD	LV	209	B1
BONANZA RD	SBD	101	A1
BONANZA TR	SBD	91	C2
BONANZA WY	NEV	34	B1
BONANZA KING RD	TRI	12	A4
BOND RD	SJCO	40	A2
BOND RD	STA	47	E2

STREET	CO.	PAGE	GRID
BONDS CORNER RD	IMP	112	C4
BONDS FLAT RD	TUO	48	C2
BONDURANT	MPA	49	A2
BONE STEEL RD	IMP	112	C4
BONETTI RD	SJCO	46	D1
BONITA AV	LACO	98	C1
BONITA AV	LACO	U	B2
BONITA RD	MCO	55	D2
BONITA RD	SDCO	V	D4
BONITA RD	SDCO	111	D2
BONITA CYN DR	IRV	200	C3
BONITA CYN DR	ORCO	98	C4
BONITA CYN DR	ORCO	T	D4
BONITA LATERAL	SB	76	C5
BONITA LATERAL	SB	86	B1
BONITA SCHL RD	SLO	76	C5
BONITA SCHL RD	SB	76	C5
BONITA SCHL RD	SB	86	B1
BONITA VISTA RD	RCO	100	C4
BONNER RD	MCO	48	D4
BONNEYVIEW RD E	SHA	18	C2
BONNEYVIEW RD S	SHA	18	C2
BONNIE CT	KER	79	C3
BONNY LN	RCO	107	B1
BONNY DOON RD	SCR	53	D2
BOOKER RD	TUO	41	D5
BOONE LN	FRCO	66	B3
BOONE ST	SMA	173	A3
BOOTH RD	LPAZ	104	B2
BOOT JACK	MPA	49	C3
BORAX RD	KER	80	D5
BORAX MILL RD	INY	62	A5
BORBA	SJCO	40	A5
BORBA	SJCO	47	A1
BORCHARD	VEN	96	D1
BORDEN RD	SAC	40	B3
BORDEN ST	MAD	57	A2
BORDER AV	RCO	U	E5
BORDER AV	SBD	100	E1
BOREL RD	RCO	99	D5
BORMAN LN	LAK	32	B4
BORNT RD	IMP	112	C4
BORON AV	KER	80	E5
BORREGO SLTN SEA	SDCO	108	A2
BORREGO SPGS RD	SDCO	107	E2
BORREGO VLY RD	SDCO	107	E2
BOSCOVICH RD	IMP	112	D5
BOSTON AV	LACO	Q	E2
BOTTINI	TUO	41	E4
BOTTLE CREEK RD	BUT	25	D1
BOTTLE HILL RD	BUT	25	D1
BOTTLE ROCK RD	LAK	31	E4
BOUCHO RD	COL	32	E3
BOULDER AV	SBD	99	C1
BOULDER HWY	CLK	74	D2
BOULDER RD	SBD	91	C3
BOULDER CK RD	SDCO	107	C5
BOULDER CK RD	SIS	3	E5
BOULEVARD, THE	GLE	24	C5
BL D L AMERICAS	BAJA	112	B4
BOULTON RD	SUT	33	C3
BOUNDARY ST	SD	216	C1
BOUNDARY TR	DN	2	A4
BOUNDARY CONE RD	MOH	85	D5
BOUQUET CYN RD	LACO	89	C4
BOUSE QUARTZITE	LPAZ	104	C5
BOW AV	KER	80	C1
BOWEN RD	COL	32	D1
BOWEN RANCH RD	SBD	91	C4
BOWERS AV	SCL	P	B3
BOWERS AV	SCLR	150	D1
BOWKER RD	IMP	112	B3
BOWKER RD	IMP	112	B4
BOWL PL	SB	86	E3
BOWMAN RD	KER	80	D1
BOWMAN RD	MOD	7	B5
BOWMAN RD	SBDO	81	A1
BOWMAN RD	SJCO	47	A1
BOWMAN RD	TEH	18	B4
BOWMAN LAKE RD	NEV	27	A5
BOWMAN LAKE RD	NEV	35	A1
BOX CANYON RD	RCO	101	C5
BOX CAR RD	MCO	55	E1
BOX ELDER ST	RCO	100	C4
BOX SPRINGS BL	RCO	99	B2
BOX SPRINGS RD	RCO	99	C2
BOYCE RD	SOL	39	A1
BOYD	CC	38	E5
BOYD DR	TUL	58	C4
BOYD RD	IMP	109	B5
BOYD SPRINGS RD	LAS	14	B4
BOYER RD	MPA	49	C3
BOYER RD	YUB	33	D1
BOYES BLVD	SON	132	A2
BOYLE RD	IMP	109	A3
BOYLE RD	SHA	18	D2
BOYLES AV	LAK	32	A3
BOY SCOUT CP RD	VEN	88	B2
BRACE RD	PLA	34	B4
BRACK RD	SON	31	D5
BRACK RD	SON	37	D1
BRADBURY RD	MCO	47	E3
BRADBURY RD	MCO	48	A3
BRADBURY RD	STA	47	C3
BRADFORD AV	ORCO	T	D1
BRADFORD RD	BUT	25	B4
BRADFORD RD	RCO	107	B1
BRADLEY AV	SDCO	V	E2
BRADLEY AV	SDCO	106	E5
BRADLEY RD	MON	65	E4
BRADLEY RD	RCO	99	C4
BRADLEY RD	VEN	88	C5
BRADLY HENLY RD	SIS	4	B3

STREET	CO.	PAGE	GRID
BRADLEY LOCK RD	MON	65	C4
BRADSHAW RD	IMP	109	A5
BRADSHAW RD	SAC	40	A2
BRADSHAW RD	YUB	33	E3
BRADSHW TR, THE	RCO	102	A5
BRADSHW TR, THE	RCO	110	B1
BRADY RD	TRI	17	B2
BRAGG RD	RCO	100	A5
BRAMLETT RCH RD	MNO	44	C5
BRAMLOT RD	TRI	17	B3
BRANCH RD	SLO	76	B1
BRANCH RD E	HUM	22	C1
BRANCH RD W	SIS	3	D4
BRANCH CAMP W	BUT	25	D1
BRANCH MILL RD	SLO	76	B4
BRANCIFORTE DR	SCR	54	A2
BRANCO RD	MCO	55	E1
BRAND BLVD	LACO	Q	E2
BRANDON RD	ED	40	D1
BRANDT	IMP	109	A3
BRANDT RD	SJCO	40	C4
BRANDT RD	KER	78	A2
BRANDY CITY RD	SIE	26	C4
BRANDY CREEK RD	SHA	18	A2
BRANFORD ST	LACO	Q	C2
BRANHAM LN	SCL	P	B4
BRANHAM LN	SCL	46	B5
BRANNAN ST	SF	143	D5
BRANNAN ISLD RD	SAC	39	C4
BRANNAN ISLD RD	SAC	M	D2
BRANNAN MTN RD	HUM	10	C4
BRANNIGAN MN RD	SBD	83	C4
BRANNIN RD	TEH	24	C2
BRANNON AV	FRCO	56	B2
BRANSCOMB RD	MEN	22	D4
BRANSTETTER LN	SHA	18	C2
BRANT RD	SBD	84	C3
BRANT CIMA RD	SBD	84	B3
BRAWLEY	IMP	108	C2
BRAWLEY AV	FRCO	57	C5
BRAY AV	TEH	18	D5
BRAZO RD	MCO	47	C4
BREA BLVD	ORCO	98	C3
BREA BLVD	ORCO	U	A4
BREA BLVD	ORCO	T	C1
BREA CANYON RD	LACO	98	C2
BREA CYN CUTOFF	LACO	U	A3
BREA CYN CUTOFF	LACO	98	C2
BRECKENRIDGE RD	KER	78	E3
BRECKENRIDGE RD	KER	79	A2
BREEDLOVE RD	ED	34	E3
BRENDA ST	KER	70	A5
BRENT RD	TEH	18	D4
BRENTWOOD AV	CC	M	D3
BRENNAN	SJCO	47	C1
BRENTWOOD AV	CC	39	C5
BRETZ RD	FRCO	58	B1
BREUING RD	MCO	55	D1
BREUNER AV	COL	32	E3
BREWER RD	NEV	34	C2
BREWER RD	PLA	33	E4
BREWER CREEK RD	SIS	12	E1
BRICELAND RD	HUM	16	B5
BRICELAND RD	MEN	22	A1
BRICELND THORNE	HUM	16	B5
BRIDESTEIN RD	IMP	109	C5
BRIDGE RD	VEN	88	C4
BRIDGE ST	COL	33	A2
BRIDGE ST	RCO	99	D3
BRIDGE ST	SUT	33	C2
BRIDGE ST	SUT	125	A3
BRIDGE ST	YUBA	125	D3
BRIDGE ARBOR	LAK	31	D2
BRIDGE CK SPGS	LAS	20	C2
BRIDGE GULCH RD	TRI	17	B3
BRDGPORT SCH RD	ED	41	A1
BRIDGEWAY	MAR	140	D5
BRIDLE PATH DR	SCL	P	E5
BRIGGS AV	LACO	R	A2
BRIGGS RD	RCO	99	D4
BRIGGS RD	VEN	88	C5
BRIGGS GRIDLY W	BUT	25	C5
BRIGGSMORE AV	STA	47	C2
BRIGHTON AV	MDO	162	E1
BRIGHTWOOD	MAD	57	B1
BRIM RD	COL	32	B2
BRIMHALL RD	KER	78	B3
BRINKERHOFF AV	SB	86	E3
BRINKERHOFF AV	SB	87	A3
BRIONES VLY RD	CC	39	B5
BRISTOL RD	VEN	88	B5
BRISTOL ST	CM	197	E4
BRISTOL ST	CM	198	A4
BRISTOL ST	ORCO	98	C4
BRISTOL ST	ORCO	197	E4
BRISTOL ST	ORCO	T	D3
BRISTOL ST	SA	195	B5
BRISTOL ST	SA	196	A2
BRISTOL ST	SA	197	E2
BRISTOL ST	SA	198	B1
BRISTOL ST N	NB	200	B1
BRITE RD	KER	78	A3
BRITTO RD	MCO	56	A2
BROAD ST	NEVC	128	B2
BROAD ST	SNLO	172	C3
BROAD ST	SLO	172	D5
BROAD ST W	NEVC	128	B2
BROADWAY	A	157	E3
BROADWAY	ALA	L	D4
BROADWAY	ALA	45	D1
BROADWAY	AMA	40	E2
BROADWAY	ANA	193	B2
BROADWAY	EUR	121	A4

STREET	CO.	PAGE	GRID
BROADWAY	FRE	165	C3
BROADWAY	LB	192	D3
BROADWAY	LA	185	E5
BROADWAY	LA	186	A3
BROADWAY	LACO	Q	E3
BROADWAY	LACO	S	C1
BROADWAY	LACO	S	D2
BROADWAY	O	156	C5
BROADWAY	O	158	A2
BROADWAY	SCTO	137	A4
BROADWAY	SBD	92	D5
BROADWAY	SD	215	E3
BROADWAY	SD	216	A3
BROADWAY	SDCO	V	E2
BROADWAY	SDCO	V	B3
BROADWAY	SDCO	106	D3
BROADWAY	SDCO	106	E5
BROADWAY	SDCO	111	D1
BROADWAY	SDCO	111	D2
BROADWAY	SF	143	A3
BROADWAY	SFCO	L	B4
BROADWAY	SB	76	C5
BROADWAY	SC	169	E3
BROADWAY	SMA	173	C3
BROADWAY	SMON	180	A4
BROADWAY	SOL	134	C1
BROADWAY	SNMA	132	D5
BROADWAY	SON	L	B1
BROADWAY	SUT	33	C2
BROADWAY	VAL	134	C2
BROADWAY	YUB	33	D3
BROADWAY N	LA	186	C1
BROADWAY N	LACO	R	A3
BROADWAY RD	LACO	R	C5
BROADWAY RD	VEN	88	D5
BROADWAY ST	C	124	B4
BROADWAY ST	FRFD	135	B4
BROADWAY ST	SBD	101	A1
BROADWAY TER	O	156	C5
BROCK RD	IMP	112	A3
BROCKMAN LN	INY	51	D4
BROCKMAN RD	KER	78	C1
BROCKMAN RD	LAS	8	A4
BROCKMAN MLL RD	AMA	41	A1
BROCK MTN LKOUT	SHA	12	E5
BROKAW RD	SJ	151	D1
BROKAW RD	SCL	P	B3
BROKAW RD	SCL	46	B4
BROKEOFF MDWS	SHA	19	C2
BROOKDALE RD	SHA	18	D2
BROOKHILL RD	MAD	57	C2
BROOKHURST ST	ORCO	98	B4
BROOKHURST ST	ORCO	T	C2
BROOKS RD	MCO	48	B4
BROOKS ST	SB	86	D1
BROOKSIDE	FRCO	58	D4
BROOKSIDE AV	RCO	99	E2
BROOKSIDE AV	SBD	99	C2
BROOKSIDE DR	SP	155	A1
BROOKSIDE RD	CAL	41	C2
BROOKSIDE RD	S	160	A2
BROPHY RD	YUB	33	D2
BROWN RD	KER	70	C5
BROWN RD	KER	80	C1
BROWN RD	SB	86	A1
BROWN RD	SHA	13	D4
BROWN RD	SOL	39	B3
BROWN RD	SUT	33	C3
BROWN ST	NAP	133	C3
BROWN ST	RCO	99	B3
BROWNLL LAVA BD	SIS	5	D3
BROWNING	PLA	33	E5
BROWNING RD	COL	33	B3
BROWNING RD	KER	68	C5
BROWNING RD	SUT	33	C3
BROWN MATERL RD	KER	77	C1
BROWNS CREEK RD	TRI	17	D2
BROWNS MTN RD	TRI	17	D1
BROWNS RANCH RD	TRI	17	D1
BROWNS RAVINE	BUT	25	D1
BROWNS VALLEY	SBT	55	B4
BROWNS VLY RD	NAP	133	A3
BROWN VALLEY RD	SOL	39	A2
BROWN VALLEY RD	SCR	54	B2
BROYLE RD	STA	47	C3
BROYLES RD	BUT	25	A2
BROYLES RD	STA	47	C2
BRUCE RD	BUT	25	B3
BRUCE CRUM	SHA	13	E4
BRUCEVILLE RD	SAC	39	E3
BRUCITE ST	KER	91	E3
BRUELLA RD	SJCO	40	B4
BRUGGA LN	HUM	15	D2
BRUNDAGE LN	BKD	166	C5
BRUNDAGE LN	KER	166	C5
BRUNSWICK AV	LA	182	E2
BRUNSWICK RD	NEV	34	C1
BRUS	MOD	8	B3
BRUSH LN	STA	47	C3
BRUSH CREEK RD	SIS	4	B3
BRUSH CREEK RD	SON	38	A2
BRUSHY MTN LKOT	HUM	10	C5
BRYAN AV	FRCO	57	B5
BRYANT	FRCO	56	B2
BRYANT ST	SBD	99	D2
BRYANT ST	SF	142	D4
BRYANT ST	SF	143	D5
BRYANT RAVIN RD	BUT	26	A4
BRYANTS CYN RD	MON	55	A5
BRYANTS CYN RD	MON	65	A1
BUARO ST	GGR	195	B2
BUCHANAN RD	CC	M	B3
BUCHANAN RD	CC	39	B5

STREET	CO.	PAGE	GRID
BUCHANAN RD	MAD	49	B5
BUCHANAN RD	TUO	41	E5
BUCHANAN ST	RCO	101	B5
BUCHANAN HLW RD	MCO	48	D5
BUCK RD	RCO	99	D5
BUCK RD	SJCO	40	B3
BUCKEYE RD	MPA	49	A3
BUCKEYE RD	NEV	34	D1
BUCKEYE ARM RD	TRI	11	D5
BUCKEYE CK RD	SON	31	A5
BUCKEYE CK RD	TRI	12	A4
BUCKEYE RDG RD	TRI	11	D5
BUCKHORN	TEH	24	C2
BUCKHORN AV	KER	89	C1
BUCKHORN RD	SIS	4	C5
BUCKHORN RDG RD	AMA	41	B2
BUCKHORN STA LP	TRI	17	E1
BUCKLEY RD	SLO	76	B4
BUCKMAN FUNCK	SJCO	40	D5
BUCK MEADOWS	MPA	49	A1
BUCKNELL RD	KER	80	D3
BUCKS BAR RD	ED	34	E5
BUCKS FLAT RD	TEH	19	B4
BUCKSKIN RD	CAL	41	A4
BUCKS LAKE RD	PLU	26	C1
BUCKTHRN CYN RD	SBD	90	E2
BUCKWHEAT RD	SBD	90	E4
BUDDY CT	KER	79	B3
BUELL RD	SHA	18	A3
BUENA CREEK RD	SDCO	106	C3
BUENA VISTA	AMA	40	D3
BUENA VISTA	LACO	97	D1
BUENA VISTA	SCL	54	D1
BUENA VISTA AV	A	157	D5
BUENA VISTA AV	A	158	B5
BUENA VISTA AV	MV	140	A2
BUENA VISTA AV	RIV	205	A2
BUENA VISTA AV	RCO	U	E5
BUENA VISTA AV	SCL	P	E5
BUENA VISTA BL	KER	78	D4
BUENA VISTA BL	KER	79	A4
BUENA VISTA DR	MER	170	C1
BUENA VISTA DR	SBD	100	E1
BUENA VISTA DR	SLO	76	A1
BUENA VISTA DR	SCR	54	B2
BUENA VISTA RD	AMA	40	D3
BUENA VISTA RD	KER	78	C3
BUENA VISTA RD	SBD	91	E4
BUENA VISTA RD	SJCO	40	C3
BUENA VISTA ST	BUR	179	C2
BUENA VISTA ST	LACO	Q	D2
BUENA VISTA ST	LACO	R	D3
BUENA VISTA ST	VEN	88	D5
BUERER LN	SJCO	47	C1
BUERKLE RD	KER	78	A3
BUFFALO RUN RD	RCO	102	C4
BUFFUM LN	LAS	21	B3
BUFFUM RD	SHA	13	A5
BUHACH RD	MCO	48	B5
BUHNE ST	EUR	121	C2
BULKLEY RD	SOL	39	C2
BULLARD AV	FRCO	56	C3
BULLARD AV	FRCO	57	B3
BULL CANYON RD	SLO	76	D5
BULL CREEK RD	MPA	49	B2
BULLION MTN RD	SBD	101	C1
BULLIS RD	LACO	S	D1
BULLRIDGE WHEEL	KIN	67	B4
BULL RUN ST	KER	80	C1
BULL SKIN RIDGE	SHA	19	A1
BULLY CHOOP RD	SHA	17	E3
BULS RD	KER	87	E1
BUMMERVILLE RD	CAL	41	B2
BUNCE RD	SUT	33	D2
BUNCH GRASS LKT	SHA	13	B5
BUNDY DR	LA	180	B4
BUNDY DR	LACO	Q	C4
BUNDY CANYON RD	RCO	99	C5
BUNKER RD	MCO	47	C5
BUNKER RD	MCO	55	C1
BUNKER HILL RD	SIE	26	D3
BUNKER STATN RD	SOL	39	C3
BUNNY LN	RCO	100	C5
BUNSELMEIER RD	LAS	14	B3
BUNTE RD	MON	65	C3
BUNTGVLL CUMMGS	LAS	21	B4
BURBANK BLVD	BUR	179	B3
BURBANK BLVD	LA	179	B3
BURBANK BLVD	LACO	97	C1
BURBANK BLVD	LACO	Q	C2
BURBANK ST	KER	78	A2
BURCH RD	SUT	33	C3
BURCHELL AV	MCO	48	D5
BURCHELL RD	SCL	54	C1
BURCH HAVEN RD	MCO	55	B2
BURGESS RCH RD	TRI	16	E5
BURKE LN	SOL	39	B3
BURLANDO RD	KER	69	D5
BURLINGAME AV	SMCO	N	C1
BURLNGTN RDG RD	NEV	34	E1
BURMA RD	NEV	34	C2
BURNETT	PLA	34	B3
BURNHAM RD	VEN	88	A4
BURNS AV	KER	78	C1
BURNS FRWY	HUM	9	E5
BURNS FRWY	HUM	10	A5
BURNS RD	LPAZ	104	A2
BURNS CANYON RD	SBD	100	B1
BURNS CUTOFF	SJCO	40	A5
BURNSIDE LK RD	ALP	36	B4
BURNS VALLEY RD	LAK	32	A3
BURNT RCH DUMP	TRI	10	E5
BURNT TREE RD	SBD	81	C5

STREET	CO.	PAGE	GRID
BURRELL RD	HUM	15	E4
BURRIS LN	MEN	31	C1
BURRIS RD	SUT	33	B2
BURROUGH N RD	FRCO	58	A2
BURROUGH VLY RD	FRCO	58	A2
BURSON RD	CAL	40	D4
BURTON WY	BH	183	C1
BURTON WY	LA	183	C1
BURTON MESA BL	SB	86	B2
BURWOOD RD	SJCO	47	D2
BUSH ST	AMA	40	D2
BUSH ST	SF	142	A3
BUSH ST	SF	143	C4
BUSHARD ST	ORCO	T	C3
BUSHEY RD	MOD	14	C1
BUSSEL RD	KER	78	B2
BUSTER RD	COL	33	A2
BUTANO CUTOFF	SMCO	N	C4
BUTANO CUTOFF	SMCO	45	C5
BUTCHER RCH RD	SIE	26	E3
BUTLER AV	FRCO	57	C3
BUTLER RD	COL	25	A5
BUTLER RD	STA	47	B2
BUTLER VLY RD	HUM	16	A1
BUTTE AV	FRCO	66	E1
BUTTE AV	SUT	33	C2
BUTTE RD	LAS	14	D3
BUTTE RD E	SUT	33	C2
BUTTE RD N	SUT	33	B1
BUTTE RD S	SUT	33	B2
BUTTE RD W	SUT	33	B1
BUTTE CITY HWY	BUT	25	A5
BUTTE CREEK RD	HUM	16	B2
BUTTE HOUSE RD	SUT	33	C2
BUTTE HOUSE RD	YUBA	125	A2
BUTTEMER RD	SBD	90	E4
BUTTE MTN RD	AMA	40	E2
BUTTE MTN RD	TEH	24	C2
BUTTERBREDT CYN	KER	79	E2
BUTTERBREDT CYN	KER	80	A2
BUTTERCUP CT	KER	79	C4
BUTTERFIELD RD	MAR	L	A3
BUTTRFLD STG RD	MAD	49	D5
BUTTRFLD STG RD	MAD	57	D1
BUTTRFLD STG RD	RCO	99	D5
BUTTERFLY PK RD	RCO	100	C5
BTRFLY VLY TWAN	PLU	26	C1
BUTTERMILK RD	INY	51	B4
BUTTERS RD	IMP	109	C4
BUTTE SLOUGH RD	COL	33	A2
BUTTE VALLEY RD	INY	72	A3
BUTTE VLY RD E	SIS	5	A3
BUTTE VLY RD W	SIS	4	E3
BUTTE VLY AIRPT	SIS	5	A3
BUTTONHOOK RD	SB	86	D3
BUTTONWILLOW AV	FRCO	58	A4
BUTTONWILLOW DR	KER	77	E3
BUTTONWILLOW DR	KER	78	A3
BUTTS RD	MCO	47	C5
BUTTS RD	MCO	55	C1
BUTTS CANYON RD	LAK	32	B5
BUZZARD ROOST	SHA	19	A1
BVD AV	MCO	48	C5
BYERS PASS RD	LAS	21	B3
BYINGTON RD	SUT	33	C4
BYOFF RD	TRI	10	E5
BYRON HWY	CC	M	D3
BYRON HWY	CC	39	C5
BYRON RD	SJCO	46	D1
BYRON RD	CC	M	E4
BYRON RD	CC	46	D1
BYSTRUM RD	STA	47	D3
BYWOOD DR	TEH	18	C4

C

STREET	CO.	PAGE	GRID
C ST	KER	68	B5
C ST	SD	215	D3
C ST	YOL	137	A2
CABALLERO CT	LAK	32	A4
CABIN RD	LAS	14	B4
CABRILLO AV	LACO	S	C2
CABRILLO BLVD	STB	174	E4
CABRILLO DR	AVLN	97	B5
CABRILLO FRWY	SD	213	D3
CABRILLO FRWY	SD	215	E2
CABRILLO FRWY	SDCO	V	B3
CABRILLO HWY	MONT	167	D5
CABRILLO HWY	MONT	168	C2
CABRILLO HWY	MON	53	E5
CABRILLO HWY	MON	54	B4
CABRILLO HWY	MON	168	C2
CABRILLO HWY	SNLO	172	B1
CABRILLO HWY	SLO	75	B1
CABRILLO HWY	SLO	76	B5
CABRILLO HWY	SLO	172	B1
CABRILLO HWY	SMCO	N	B2
CABRILLO HWY	SMCO	45	B3
CABRILLO HWY	SB	86	B1
CABRILLO HWY	SC	169	A4
CABRILLO HWY	SCR	N	D5
CABRILLO HWY	SCR	53	D1
CABRILLO HWY	SCR	54	A2
CACHAGUA RD	MON	54	C5
CACHAGUA RD	MON	64	C1
CACHUMA RD	SB	87	A2
CACTUS AV	RCO	99	C3
CACTUS AV	SBD	99	B1
CACTUS DR	MCO	55	D2
CACTUS FLATS	INY	70	B2
CACTUS VLY RD	RCO	99	E4
CADET RD	KER	78	A4
CADILLAC AV	LA	183	D4
CADIZ DR	SBD	102	C1
CADIZ RD	SBD	94	B3
CADIZ RD	SBD	103	A1
CADY RD	IMP	109	A4
CAHUENGA BLVD	LA	179	A3
CAHUENGA BLVD	LA	181	D5
CAHUENGA BLVD	LACO	Q	D3
CAHUENGA BLVD W	LA	181	B2
CAHUILLA RD	RCO	100	B5
CAHUILLA RD	SBD	91	C3
CAHUILLA HTS RD	RCO	100	A5
CAIRO	KIN	57	D5
CAJALCO RD	RCO	99	A3
CAJON BLVD	SBD	91	A5
CAJON ST	SBD	99	C2
CALAVERAS AV	FRCO	56	D4
CALAVERAS AV	FRCO	66	D2
CALAVERAS RD	ALA	P	C1
CALAVERAS RD	ALA	46	B3
CALAVERAS RD	SCL	46	B4
CALAVERITAS RD	CAL	41	A3
CALDOR RD	ED	41	B1
CALICO BLVD	SBD	92	A1
CALICO RD	SBD	92	A1
CALIENT-BODF RD	KER	79	B3
CALIENT-BODF RD	KER	79	C2
CALIENTE CK RD	KER	79	C3
CALIFORNIA AV	BKD	166	B3
CALIFORNIA AV	COL	32	E3
CALIFORNIA AV	FRE	165	A5
CALIFORNIA AV	FRCO	56	C3
CALIFORNIA AV	FRCO	57	C3
CALIFORNIA AV	KER	78	D3
CALIFORNIA AV	LACO	R	A5
CALIFORNIA AV	MDO	162	A4
CALIFORNIA AV	RENO	130	A3
CALIFORNIA AV	RCO	98	E3
CALIFORNIA AV	RCO	99	D4
CALIFORNIA AV	SCL	P	D5
CALIFORNIA AV	SCL	54	A2
CALIFORNIA AV	SC	169	C4
CALIFORNIA AV	STA	47	B2
CALIFORNIA BLVD	LACO	R	B3
CALIFORNIA BLVD	NAP	133	B2
CALIFORNIA BLVD	PAS	190	A4
CALIFORNIA BLVD	SNLO	172	C2
CALIFORNIA BLVD	SLO	172	C2
CALIFORNIA DR	IMP	108	C2
CALIFORNIA DR	NAPA	29	D4
CALIFORNIA ST	BUR	179	C3
CALIFORNIA ST	EUR	121	C2
CALIFORNIA ST	LACO	98	A1
CALIFORNIA ST	ONT	204	A5
CALIFORNIA ST	RED	122	B1
CALIFORNIA ST	SBD	99	B1
CALIFORNIA ST	SDCO	106	B3
CALIFORNIA ST	SF	141	C3
CALIFORNIA ST	SF	142	A3
CALIFORNIA ST	SF	143	D4
CALIFORNIA ST	SFCO	L	B4
CALIFORNIA ST	SFCO	45	B1
CALIFORNIA ST	SJCO	40	A5
CALIFORNIA ST	S	160	D2
CALIF CITY BLVD	KER	80	B4
CALIFRNIA FARMS	SJCO	47	C1
CALIF PINES BL	MOD	14	E2
CALISTOGA RD	SON	38	A1
CALKINS RD	FRCO	57	E1
CALLAHAN RD	TEH	18	C5
CALLAHAN RD E	SIS	11	D1
CALLE DEL SOL	AVLN	97	B4
CALLE ECUESTRE	SB	87	A4
CALLEGUAS RD	VEN	96	C1
CALLE H COLEGIO	BAJA	112	B4
CALLE LIPPIZANA	SB	87	A4
CALLENDR BLK LK	SLO	76	B5
CALLE QUEBRADA	SB	87	A4
CALLE REAL	SB	86	E4
CALLE REAL	SB	87	A4
CALLOWAY DR	KER	78	C3
CALNEVA RD	LAS	21	E5
CALPACK RD	SJCO	46	E1
CALPINE RD	SIE	27	B3
CALPINE LO RD	SIE	27	B3
CALVIN CREST RD	MAD	49	D4
CALVINE RD	SAC	39	E2
CALVINE RD	SAC	40	A2
CALZ	BAJA	112	B4
CALZADA AV	SB	86	C3
CAMANCHE PKWY N	AMA	40	C3
CAMANCHE PKWY S	CAL	40	D3
CAMARES DR	LACO	90	A3
CAMARILLO ST	LA	179	B4
CAMARILLO ST	LACO	Q	D3
CAMBRIA AV	FRCO	56	A2
CAMBRIA RD	SBD	91	E4
CAMBRIDGE DR	BUR	179	E2
CAMBRIDGE RD	SHA	18	C3
CAMBRIDGE ST	ORA	196	D1
CAMBRIDGE ST	SA	196	D1
CAMDEN AV	SCL	P	B4
CAMDEN AV	SCL	46	A5
CAMERON AV	LACO	98	C2
CAMERON AV	LACO	U	A2
CAMERON RD	MEN	30	C2
CAMERON CYN RD	KER	79	D5
CAMERON PARK DR	ED	34	C5
CAMINO AV	IMP	108	C2
CAMINO ALTO	MAR	L	B4
CAMINO ALTO	MV	140	B3
CM CAPISTRANO	SJC	202	D3
CAMINO CIELO	SB	87	A3
CM DE FLORES	AVLN	97	B4
CAMINO DL MONTE	AVLN	97	A4
CAMINO DL MONTE	CAR	53	D5
CAMINO DL MONTE	CAR	168	C3
CAMINO DL MONTE	MON	168	C3
CAMINO DIABLO	CC	M	D4
CAMINO DIABLO	CC	46	C1
CM DOS RIOS	VEN	96	D1
CM LAS RAMBLAS	SJC	202	D4
CM MIRA COSTA	SCL	202	E5
CAMINO ORO	SHA	19	A2
CAMINO PABLO	CC	L	D4
CAMINO PABLO	CC	L	E4
CAMINO REAL	LACO	S	A2
CAMINO REAL	SHA	19	A3
CAMINO SANTA FE	SDCO	106	C5
CM SANTA FE DR	SDCO	V	B2
CM TASSAJARA RD	CC	M	B4
CM TASSAJARA RD	CC	46	A1
CAMINO VISTA	SHA	19	A2
CAMMATTI-SHN RD	SLO	76	D1
CAMP RD	SAC	39	E3
CAMP RD E	COL	32	D2
CAMPBELL	SJCO	47	D1
CAMPBELL AV	BUT	33	C1
CAMPBELL AV	SCL	P	B3
CAMPBELL AV	SCL	46	A5
CAMPBELL DR	KER	78	E4
CAMPBELL RD	IMP	111	E3
CAMPBELL RD	SBD	101	D1
CAMPBELL RD	SB	86	C3
CAMPBELL RD	SOL	39	B1
CAMPBL HOT SPGS	SIE	27	C4
CAMPBELL RDG RD	TRI	10	D5
CAMPBLLS FLT RD	TUO	41	C5
CAMP CREEK RD	BUT	25	E2
CAMP CREEK RD	SIS	4	B2
CAMP FAR WST RD	PLA	34	A3
CAMPHORA RD	MON	54	E5
CAMPHORA RD	MON	55	A5
CAMP KIMTU RD	HUM	16	C5
CAMP NINE RD	CAL	41	C4
CAMPO RD	SDCO	V	D3
CAMPO RD	SDCO	111	E1
CAMPODONICA RD	MCO	48	A3
CAMPOS LN	SOL	39	A1
CAMP ROCK RD	SBD	92	A1
CAMPO SECO RD	CAL	40	D3
CAMPO SECO RD	TUO	41	C5
CAMP THREE RD	SIS	10	E2
CAMPTON RD	EUR	121	D4
CAMPTON RD	HUM	15	E1
CAMPTONVILLE RD	SIE	26	C5
CAMPUS AV	ONT	204	C3
CAMPUS AV	UPL	204	C3
CAMPUS DR	IRV	198	C5
CAMPUS DR	KER	78	E4
CAMPUS DR	ORCO	198	C5
CAMPUS DR	SCL	147	A3
CAMP WEOTT RD	HUM	15	D2
CMP 1 TEN MI RD	MEN	22	C4
CMP 2 TEN MI RD	MEN	22	C4
CAMP 8 RD	SLO	76	C2
CAMUESA RD	SB	87	D3
CANA HWY	BUT	25	A2
CANADA BLVD	LACO	97	E1
CANADA BLVD	LACO	R	A2
CANADA RD	SMCO	N	D2
CANADA RD	SMCO	45	C3
CANADA RD	SCL	54	D2
CANAL AV	FRCO	57	E1
CANAL BLVD	SJCO	46	E1
CANAL BLVD	SJCO	47	A1
CANAL DR	MCO	47	E4
CANAL DR	MCO	48	A4
CANAL RD	GLE	24	E3
CANAL RD	KER	77	E2
CANAL RD	KER	78	A2
CANAL ST	PLCV	138	C3
CANAL BANK RD	STA	47	E2
CANAL BANK RD	STA	48	A2
CANAL GULCH RD	SIS	4	A4
CANAL SCHOOL RD	MCO	47	C4
CANA PINE CREEK	BUT	25	A2
C AND D BLVD	RCO	103	D5
CANFIELD RD	SDCO	107	A2
CANFIELD RD	SON	37	E3
CANNIBAL RD	HUM	15	D2
CANNON RD	SDCO	106	B3
CANNON RD	TEH	18	B5
CANNON ST	SDCO	V	A3
CANOGA AV	LA	177	C3
CANON DR	BH	183	B1
CANON RD	SOL	39	A3
CANON ST	SDCO	111	C1
CANON PERDIDO	STB	174	C4
CANRIGHT RD	SOL	39	C3
CANTELOW RD	SOL	38	E2
CANTELOW RD	SOL	39	A2
CANTON RD	MCO	48	C5
CANYON DR	RCO	100	C3
CANYON DR	SBD	82	A5
CANYON RD	INY	52	B3
CANYON RD	MEN	23	A5
CANYON RD	MNO	52	B3
CANYON RD	SBD	93	B5
CANYON RD	SBD	100	C2
CANYON RD	SMCO	N	C4
CANYON RD	SMCO	45	C5
CANYON RD	SR	139	B4
CANYON RD	SHA	18	C3
CANYON RD	SON	31	D5
CANYON WY	PLA	34	D2
CANYON CREEK RD	MOD	14	E1
CANYON CREEK RD	SIS	3	B5
CANYON CREEK RD	TRI	17	C1
CANYON CREST DR	RCO	99	B2
CANYON VW LOOP	TEH	19	B4
CANYON VIEW RD	SBD	91	D4
CAPAY AV	GLE	24	E3
CAPAY RD	TEH	24	D2
CAPE GLOUCESTER	SBD	91	E2
CAPEZZOLI LN	LAS	21	C4
CAPITAL BLVD	GLE	24	E4
CAPITAN TK TR	SDCO	107	B5
CAPITOL AV	SCTO	137	C3
CAPITOL AV	SCL	P	C3
CAPITOL AV	SCL	46	B4
CAPITOL AV	YOL	137	A2
CAPITOL AV	YOL	39	D1
CAPITOL EXPWY	SCL	P	C4
CAPITOL EXPWY	SCL	46	B5
CAPITOL ST	SAL	171	B3
CAPITOLA RD	SCR	54	A2
CAPPELL RD	HUM	10	C2
CAPPS CROSSING	ED	35	B5
CAPRI AV	MCO	55	D1
CARBINE TR	KER	79	D5
CARBON CYN RD	ORCO	98	C3
CARBON CYN RD	ORCO	T	E1
CARBON CYN RD	ORCO	U	B4
CARBON CYN RD	SBD	98	C3
CARBON CYN RD	SBD	U	B4
CARBONDALE RD	AMA	40	C2
CARBONDALE RD	SAC	40	C2
CARDELLA RD	MCO	48	B4
CARDIFF ST	SDCO	V	D3
CAREY RD	IMP	109	A4
CARGIL LN	RCO	107	C1
CARIBOU RD	SIS	11	C3
CARLETON RD	MPA	49	B3
CARLIN RD	SJCO	46	E1
CARLSBAD BLVD	SDCO	106	B3
CARLSON	CC	38	C5
CARLSON BLVD	CC	L	C3
CARLSON BLVD	R	155	B3
CARLSON RD	BUT	25	B4
CARLSON RD	SUT	33	C3
CARLTON RD	SCR	54	C2
CARLTON RD	SIS	4	B4
CARLUCCI RD	MCO	56	A1
CARLYLE RD	NEV	27	A5
CARMEL RD	KER	77	D1
CARMELLIA AV	FRCO	56	B2
CARMEL MTN RD	SDCO	106	D4
CARMEL RCHO BL	MON	168	D5
CARMEL VLY RD	MON	54	B5
CARMEL VLY RD	MON	64	C1
CARMEL VLY RD	MON	168	E4
CARMEL VLY RD	SDCO	V	A1
CARMEL VLY RD	SDCO	106	C4
CARMEN LN	BUT	25	A3
CARMENCITA AV	SJCO	40	A2
CARMENITA AV	LACO	T	B1
CARNATION RD	MCO	47	D5
CARNELIAN BAY	PLA	35	E1
CARNEROS AV	NAPA	38	C3
CARPENTER RD	HUM	10	D5
CARPENTER RD	SJCO	40	B5
CARPENTER RD	STA	47	C3
CARPENTER ST	CAR	53	D5
CARPENTER ST	CAR	168	C3
CARPENTER ST	MON	168	C3
CARPENTERIA	MON	54	C3
CARPINTERIA ST	STB	174	E3
CARPENTER RIDGE	BUT	25	D1
CARQUINEZ SC DR	CC	L	E3
CARR AV	SBT	54	C2
CARRIAGE LN	SHA	18	B3
CARRIER GLCH RD	TRI	17	C3
CARRILLO ST	STB	174	B4
CARRIZO GRGE RD	SDCO	111	A4
CARROLL RD	SAC	39	E3
CARROLL CK RD	INY	60	B5
CARROLTON	SJCO	47	C1
CARROT LN	RCO	107	B1
CARRVILLE LOOP	TRI	11	E4
CARRVILLE LOOP	TRI	12	A4
CARSON RD	ED	34	E5
CARSON ST	LACO	97	D3
CARSON ST	LACO	S	B2
CARSTENS RD	MPA	49	B3
CARTER RD	MPA	49	B3
CARTER ST	SBD	99	D2
CARTMILL AV	TUL	68	A2
CARUTHERS AV	FRCO	57	C5
CARVER LN	RCO	99	B4
CASADEL RD	MAD	49	E5
CASADEL RD	MAD	50	A5
CASA DIABLO CTO	MNO	51	B2
CASA DIABLO MN	MNO	51	B2
CASA GRANDE RD	SON	L	A1
CASALE RD	TEH	18	D5
CASA LOMA RD	SCL	P	C5
CASA LOMA RD	SCL	54	B1
CASCADE BLVD	SHA	18	C2
CASCADE RD	SBD	101	A1
CASCADIAN AV	SBD	91	D3
CASE RD	RCO	99	C4
CASEY AV	KER	68	B5
CASEY AV	SB	86	E3
CASEY RD	IMP	109	B5
CASEY RD	SOL	39	B2
CASINO DR	CLK	85	D5
CASITAS VIS RD	VEN	88	A5
CASSPR LTL LK RD	MEN	22	C5
CASS ST	MONT	167	E4
CASS ST	MON	53	E3
CASS ST	SDCO	V	A2
CASS ST	SDCO	106	C5
CASSEL RD	SHA	13	D5
CASSEL FALL RIV	SHA	13	D4
CASSERLY RD	SCR	54	C2
CASSIDY ST	SDCO	106	B3
CASTAIC RD	LACO	89	B4
CASTAIC CYN RD	LACO	89	B3
CASTERLINE RD	HUM	16	D4
CASTLE CT	BUT	25	C3
CASTLE ST	S	160	C3
CASTLE CREEK RD	SHA	12	C3
CASTLE LAKE RD	SIS	12	C2
CASTRO	CC	38	C5
CASTRO RD	CC	38	D5
CASTRO RD	RCO	99	D4
CASTRO RANCH RD	CC	L	D3
CASTRO VLY BL	ALA	146	D1
CASTROVILLE BL	MON	54	C3
CATALINA AV	AVLN	97	B5
CATALINA BLVD	SDCO	V	A3
CATALINA DR	DVS	136	C1
CAT CANYON RD	SB	86	D2
CATERPILLAR RD	SHA	18	C2
CATFISH BCH RD	PLU	20	B4
CATHEDRAL RD	ED	36	A3
CATHEY RD	HUM	16	B4
CATLETT RD W	SUT	33	D4
CATRINA RD	MCO	56	B1
CATTARAUGUS AV	CUL	183	C4
CATTARAUGUS AV	LA	183	C4
CATTLE DR	TUL	68	E3
CATTLE DRIVE RD	MNO	51	C1
CATTLEMEN RD	MON	65	D3
CATWAY RD	SB	87	A2
CAUGHLIN RD	SBD	91	A3
CAVE CITY RD	CAL	41	B3
CAVEDALE RD	SON	38	B2
CAVIN RD	VEN	88	E4
CAVITT & STLLMN	PLA	34	B4
CAWELTI RD	VEN	96	C1
CAWSTON AV	RCO	99	E4
CAYLEY DR	KER	79	B4
CAYTON VLY RD	SHA	13	C4
CAYUCOS CK RD	SLO	75	D2
CAZADERO HWY	SON	37	C1
CCMO RD	KER	77	D3
CEBADA CYN RD	SB	86	C3
CECIL AV	KER	68	B5
CECIL RD	COL	33	B3
CECILVILLE RD	SIS	11	C3
CEDAR AV	FRCO	57	C3
CEDAR AV	FRCO	57	C5
CEDAR AV	RCO	100	C4
CEDAR AV	SBD	99	B2
CEDAR DR	MOD	14	B2
CEDAR ST	SBD	80	E1
CEDAR ST	SDCO	107	A4
CEDAR CAMP RD	HUM	10	C2
CEDAR CAMP RD	SIS	10	C1
CEDAR CAMP RD	TRI	17	A4
CEDAR CANYON RD	SBD	84	B4
CEDAR CREEK RD	ED	41	A1
CEDAR CREEK RD	HUM	10	C5
CEDAR CK LP RD	BUT	25	C1
CEDAR GROVE RD	SIS	5	A2
CEDAR RAVINE RD	ED	34	E5
CEDAR RAVINE ST	PLCV	138	E3
CEDARVILLE DUMP	MOD	8	E1
CEDAR WELL	SIS	5	A4
CEDARWOOD CT	SHA	19	A3
CEDROS DR	SBD	90	E2
CEMENT HILL RD	FRFD	135	C1
CEMENT HILL RD	NEV	34	C1
CEMETERY DR	MOD	14	C3
CEMETERY RD	COL	32	D1
CEMETERY RD	HUM	16	D4
CEMETERY RD	MCO	47	D4
CEMETERY RD	MNO	43	C4
CEMETERY RD	SBD	82	A5
CEMETERY RD	SHA	19	B2
CEMETERY RD	SIS	5	A2
CENTENNIAL RD	HUM	15	D3
CENTER AV	MCO	56	B2
CENTER RD	LAS	21	A3
CENTER RD	STA	47	B2
CENTER ST	CAL	41	A3
CENTER ST	MAN	161	A4
CENTER ST	RCO	99	B2
CENTER ST	SBD	99	C2
CENTER ST	SC	169	D3
CENTER ST	S	160	D3
CENTER ST EXT	RCO	99	C2
CENTER ST S	TEH	24	E1
CTR SCH HOUSE	LAS	14	C3
CENTER VLY RD	MEN	23	A5
CENTERVILLE LN	DGL	36	B3
CENTERVILLE RD	BUT	25	C3
CENTERVILLE RD	HUM	15	D2
CENTERVILLE RD	MOD	8	A1
CENTERVILLE RD	MOD	14	D1
CENTINELA AV	CUL	187	D1
CENTINELA AV	ING	188	B3
CENTINELA AV	LA	187	D1
CENTINELA AV	LACO	Q	C4
CENTINELLA RD	MCO	55	C1
CENTRAL AV	A	158	A5
CENTRAL AV	A	159	A1
CENTRAL AV	FRCO	56	D4
CENTRAL AV	FRCO	57	B4
CENTRAL AV	HUM	9	E4
CENTRAL AV	HUM	10	A4

STREET INDEX

STREET	CO.	PAGE	GRID
CENTRAL AV	KER	78	A2
CENTRAL AV	LA	186	B5
CENTRAL AV	LACO	97	E2
CENTRAL AV	LACO	Q	E2
CENTRAL AV	LACO	S	C1
CENTRAL AV	MCO	47	D4
CENTRAL AV	MON	65	B2
CENTRAL AV	MTCL	203	C3
CENTRAL AV	ORCO	T	C1
CENTRAL AV	ORCO	U	A4
CENTRAL AV	PAC	167	C2
CENTRAL AV	RCO	99	B2
CENTRAL AV	RCO	205	B5
CENTRAL AV	SAL	171	A4
CENTRAL AV	SBD	U	D3
CENTRAL AV	SBD	98	D2
CENTRAL AV	RCO	99	B4
CENTRAL AV	SBD	203	C3
CENTRAL AV	SB	86	B3
CENTRAL AV	STA	47	D3
CENTRAL AV	SUT	33	B3
CENTRAL AV	TEH	24	D1
CENTRAL AV	VEN	88	C5
CENTRAL AV	YOL	39	D2
CENTRAL RD	SBD	91	C3
CENTRAL EXPWY	MVW	148	B4
CENTRAL EXPWY	SCL	N	E2
CENTRAL EXPWY	SCL	P	B3
CENTRAL EXPWY	SVL	148	B4
CENTRAL FRWY	SF	143	A5
CENTRAL SKYWAY	SF	142	C4
CENTRAL ST	RCO	99	C5
CENTRAL CAMP RD	MAD	49	E4
CENTRAL HILL RD	CAL	40	E3
CENTRAL HILL RD	CAL	41	A3
CENTRL HOUSE RD	BUT	25	D5
CENTRALIA ST	LACO	S	E2
CENTRALIA ST	LACO	T	A2
CENTRAL VLY HWY	KER	78	B1
CENTURY BLVD	LA	189	D1
CENTURY BLVD	LACO	97	D2
CENTURY BLVD	LACO	Q	D5
CERINI AV	FRCO	57	B5
CERINI AV	FRCO	57	C5
CERRITOS AV	ANA	193	D4
CERRITOS AV	ORCO	T	B2
CERRO GORDO RD	INY	60	C5
CERRO GORDO RD	INY	60	D4
CERRO NOROESTE	KER	78	A5
CERRO NOROESTE	KER	87	E1
CERVANTES BLVD	SF	142	A1
CESAR CHAVEZ AV	LACO	R	A4
CHABOT RD	VAL	134	D1
CHADBOURNE RD	CC	39	B5
CHADBOURNE RD	SOL	38	E3
CHADWICK RD	SBD	101	E1
CHAHLIP LN	FRCO	58	C1
CHALET DR	KER	79	C4
CHALFANT RD	MNO	51	D3
CHALFANT LP RD	MNO	51	D3
CHALK BLUFF RD	INY	51	C4
CHALK BLUFF RD	NEV	34	D1
CHALK HILL RD	SON	37	E1
CHALLNGE CTO RD	YUB	26	A4
CHALLENGER WY	LACO	90	A3
CHALONE RD	SBT	55	A5
CHAMBERLAIN	PLA	34	A3
CHAMBERLAIN RD	MCO	48	B5
CHAMBERS RD	HUM	15	D4
CHAMBERS WLS RD	SBD	103	E1
CHAMPAGNE AV	KER	89	C1
CHAMPS FLAT RD	LAS	20	C2
CHANAC RD	KER	79	B4
CHANDLER	YUB	33	D1
CHANDLER BLVD	BUR	179	C5
CHANDLER BLVD	LA	179	A4
CHANDLER BLVD	LACO	Q	C2
CHANDLER RD	PLU	26	D1
CHANDON AV	BUT	33	C1
CHANNEL ISLD BL	VEN	96	B1
CHAPARAJOS ST	CAL	41	A4
CHAPARRAL DR	SHA	18	B2
CHAPMAN AV	GGR	195	A1
CHAPMAN AV	ORA	195	D1
CHAPMAN AV	ORA	196	B1
CHAPMAN AV	ORCO	98	C3
CHAPMAN AV	ORCO	T	B2
CHAPMAN AV	ORCO	T	C1
CHAPMAN DR	CRTM	140	B2
CHAPMAN RD	RCO	107	C1
CHAPPIUS LN N	LAS	21	B3
CHAPPIUS LN S	LAS	21	B4
CHAPULNIK RD	IMP	109	B4
CHARD AV	TEH	18	D5
CHARLEBOIS RD	MNO	42	E1
CHARLES ST	KER	80	D1
CHARLES ST	SHA	18	C3
CHARLES HILL RD	CC	L	E4
CHARLESTON BLVD	LV	209	A2
CHARLESTON BL E	CLK	74	D2
CHARLESTON RD	MCO	55	D2
CHARLESTON RD	SCL	N	E3
CHARLESTON RD	SCL	P	A3
CHARLESTON RD	SCL	45	E4
CHARLESTON RD W	PA	147	E5
CHRLSTN VOLCANO	AMA	41	A2
CHAROLAIS RD	SLO	76	A1
CHARTER WY	SJCO	40	B5
CHARTER OAK DR	TUL	68	C1
CHASE AV	KER	79	E2
CHASE AV	KER	80	A2
CHASE AV	SDCO	V	E3
CHASE AV	SDCO	111	E1

STREET	CO.	PAGE	GRID
CHASE AV	TEH	24	D2
CHASE DR	RCO	98	E3
CHASE SCHOOL RD	RCO	100	E3
CHATEAU DR	SMCO	45	C3
CHATEAU RD	ML	164	D3
CHATEAU FRESNO	FRCO	57	B4
CHATEAU FRESNO	FRCO	57	B5
CHATSWORTH BLVD	SDCO	V	A3
CHATSWORTH BLVD	SDCO	111	C1
CHECKMATE RD	RCO	100	A5
CHELSEY AV	CC	L	C3
CHEMEHUEVI BLVD	MOH	96	B4
CHEMISE MTN RD	HUM	22	A1
CHEROKEE LN	SAC	40	B3
CHEROKEE LN	SJCO	40	B3
CHEROKEE RD	BUT	25	D4
CHEROKEE RD	MCO	55	D1
CHEROKEE RD	SBD	82	C5
CHEROKEE RD	SJCO	40	B5
CHERRY AV	FRCO	57	C4
CHERRY AV	FRCO	57	C5
CHERRY AV	KER	78	B2
CHERRY AV	LACO	97	E4
CHERRY AV	LACO	S	D2
CHERRY AV	RCO	99	E3
CHERRY AV	SBD	99	A2
CHERRY AV	STA	47	C4
CHERRY ST	SUT	33	C2
CHERRY CREEK RD	SON	31	C4
CHERRY GLEN RD	SOL	38	E3
CHERRY VLY BLVD	RCO	99	E2
CHERT RD	RCO	107	B1
CHESEBORO RD	LACO	90	B4
CHESTER AV	BKD	166	C4
CHESTER AV	KER	78	D3
CHESTER LN	BKD	166	B4
CHESTER JUNIPR-			
-LAKE RD	PLU	20	A3
CHESTER SKI RD	PLU	20	A4
CHESTR WRNR VLY	PLU	19	E3
CHESTER WARNER-			
-VALLEY RD	PLU	20	A3
CHESTNUT AV	FRCO	57	C2
CHESTNUT AV	FRCO	57	C5
CHESTNUT AV	SMCO	N	B1
CHESTNUT AV	SA	196	B4
CHESTNUT AV	TEH	18	D5
CHESTNUT ST	SF	143	A3
CHESTNUT ST	SHA	18	C3
CHESTNUT WY	CAL	41	B5
CHEVALIER RD	KER	78	D4
CHEVY CHASE DR	LACO	97	E1
CHEVY CHASE DR	LACO	R	A3
CHEZEM RD	HUM	10	B5
CHICAGO AV	RIV	205	E4
CHICAGO AV	STA	47	C2
CHICK RD	IMP	112	B3
CHICK RD	RCO	108	E1
CHICKEN HAWK RD	PLA	34	E2
CHICKEN RCH RD	LAS	8	C5
CHICKEN RCH RD	TUO	41	C5
CHICO AV	KIN	57	E5
CHICO CANYON RD	BUT	25	C2
CHICORB LN	SOL	39	B2
CHICO RIVER RD	BUT	25	A3
CHIDAGO LOOP	MNO	51	C2
CHIDAGO CYN RD	MNO	51	B2
CHIHUAHUA VLY	SDCO	107	B2
CHILD RD	TUO	163	D3
CHILDS AV	MER	170	B5
CHILDS AV	MCO	48	C4
CHILE CAMP RD	CAL	40	D3
CHILENO VLY RD	SON	37	E3
CHILENO VLY RD	SON	38	A3
CHILES RD	YOL	39	C1
CHILES POPE VLY	NAPA	29	D1
CHILES POPE VLY	NAPA	38	C1
CHILI HILL RD	PLA	34	B3
CHIMNEY ROCK RD	SLO	75	D1
CHINA CAMP RD	MCO	55	D1
CHINA CREEK RD	MAD	49	D4
CHINA GRADE	SIS	3	A3
CHINA GRADE LP	KER	78	D2
CHINA GRADE RD	PLU	26	D1
CHINA GULCH DR	SHA	18	B3
CHINA LAKE BLVD	KER	80	D1
CHINA PK LO RD	SIS	3	A3
CHINA POINT RD	BUT	25	D2
CHINA RANCH RD	INY	73	A5
CHINO AV	SBD	U	C3
CHINO AV	SBD	98	D2
CHINQUAPIN RD	MAD	49	E4
CHINQUAPIN RD	MAD	50	A4
CHINQUAPIN DR	MEN	23	A5
CHIRIACO RD	RCO	101	E4
CHITTENDEN RD	TEH	24	C2
CHLORIDE RD	SBD	92	B1
CHLORIDE CLF RD	INY	62	A3
CHOLAME RD	MON	66	C4
CHOLAME VLY RD	SLO	66	D5
CHOLLA RD	SBD	91	C4
CHOLLA RD	SBD	92	C5
CHORRO ST N	SNLO	172	B2
CHORRO ST S	SNLO	172	C3
CHOWCHILLA	MAD	56	D3
CHOWCHILLA BLVD	MAD	56	D1
CHOWCHILLA MTN	MPA	49	C3
CHRISMAN RD	SJCO	47	A2
CHRISTENSEN RD	SAC	40	A3
CHRISTIAN RD	TEH	24	D2
CHRISTIE LN	MNO	51	C1
CHRISTN VLY RD	PLA	34	C3
CHROME MINE RD	TRI	17	B3

STREET	CO.	PAGE	GRID
CHUALAR RD	MON	54	D4
CHUALAR CYN RD	MON	54	E4
CHUALAR RIV RD	MON	54	D5
CHUCKWAGON DR	CAL	41	A5
CHUCKWALLA RD	SBD	91	D3
CHUCKWL SPGS RD	RCO	102	D5
CHUCKWLA VLY RD	RCO	102	D4
CHUCKWLA VLY RD	RCO	103	A5
CHURCH AV	FRE	165	B5
CHURCH AV	FRCO	57	A3
CHURCH AV	FRCO	57	D3
CHURCH AV	SCL	54	D1
CHURCH AV	SCL	P	E5
CHURCH LN	HUM	15	E2
CHURCH LN	SCL	P	E5
CHURCH RD	SOL	M	D2
CHURCH RD	SOL	39	C4
CHURCH ST	HUM	16	D4
CHURCH ST	SBD	99	C2
CHURCH ST	STA	47	D2
CHURCH ST	S	160	C5
CHURCH HILL RD	CAL	41	A3
CHURCHILL MN RD	INY	51	D3
CHURCH SPGS RD	STA	48	A1
CHURN CREEK RD	SHA	18	C2
CIBOLA RD	LPAZ	103	E5
CIBOLA RD	LPAZ	110	D1
CIENAGA RD	KER	78	A5
CIENEGA RD	SBT	54	E3
CIENEGA RD	SBT	55	A4
CIMA RD	SBD	83	E2
CIMA RD	SBD	84	A2
CIMA MESA RD	LACO	90	B4
CINCHA ST	CAL	41	A4
CINDER RD	INY	70	C3
CINDER PIT RD	MOD	14	D1
CIRCLE DR	INY	70	E1
CIRCLE DR	RCO	100	B4
CIRCLEA CT	BUT	25	C3
CIRCLE C LN	SOL	39	B2
CITRACADO PKWY	SDCO	106	D3
CITRON ST	ANA	193	B1
CITRUS AV	LACO	98	C2
CITRUS AV	LACO	U	A2
CITRUS AV	SBD	99	A2
CITRUS AV	SBD	99	D2
CITRUS AV	SDCO	106	C3
CITRUS AV	SDCO	106	D3
CITY DR, THE	ORA	195	E2
CITY CAMP	MNO	43	C5
CIVIC CENTER DR	SR	139	C1
CIVIC CENTER DR	SA	196	A3
CLAIREMONT DR	SD	211	E4
CLAIREMONT DR	SD	213	A1
CLAIREMONT DR	SDCO	V	B2
CLAIREMONT DR	SDCO	106	C5
CLAIREMONT MESA	SD	211	D4
CLAIRMNT MSA BL	SDCO	V	B2
CLAIREMONT MESA	SDCO	106	C5
CLARATINA AV	STA	47	D2
CLAREMONT AV	ALA	L	D4
CLAREMONT AV	B	156	C4
CLAREMONT AV	O	156	B5
CLAREMONT BLVD	CLA	203	B2
CLARIBEL RD	STA	47	D2
CLARISSA AV	AVLN	97	B5
CLARK AV	COL	24	E5
CLARK AV	LACO	S	E2
CLARK AV	SB	86	C1
CLARK AV	TEH	24	E2
CLARK AV	YUBA	125	C4
CLARK RD	BUT	25	C3
CLARK RD	IMP	109	A5
CLARK RD	IMP	112	A4
CLARK RD	MEN	30	D2
CLARK RD	MON	65	A1
CLARK RD	SLO	76	C1
CLARK RD	SOL	39	B2
CLARK RD	STA	47	C2
CLARK RD	SUT	33	C1
CLARK ST	NAP	133	E3
CLARKE RD	HUM	15	D4
CLARK MTN RD	SBD	84	A2
CLARK RANCH RD	MNO	51	C1
CLARKSBURG	YOL	39	D2
CLARKS FORK RD	ALP	42	B2
CLARKSON AV	FRCO	56	D5
CLARKSON AV	FRCO	57	C5
CLARKS VLY RD	GLE	24	B4
CLARKS VLY RD	LAS	8	D4
CLAUS RD	STA	47	D2
CLAUSEN RD	MCO	48	E5
CLAWITER RD	ALA	45	E2
CLAWITER RD	ALA	146	B4
CLAWITER RD	ALA	N	E1
CLAWITER RD	H	146	B4
CLAY RD	INY	72	D1
CLAY ST	SAL	171	B4
CLAY ST	U	123	B3
CLAY BANK RD	SOL	39	A3
CLAY MINE RD	KER	80	C5
CLAY RIVER RD	SBD	91	E1
CLAY STATION RD	SAC	40	B3
CLAYTON AV	FRCO	56	D4
CLAYTON AV	FRCO	58	A4
CLAYTON RD	CC	39	A5
CLAYTON RD	NEV	34	B2
CLAYTON RD	SON	32	A5
CLAYTON RD	STA	47	D3
CLAYTON CREEK	LAK	32	A4
CLEAR CREEK RD	KER	79	B4
CLEAR CREEK RD	SBT	65	E1
CLEAR CREEK RD	SBT	66	A1

STREET	CO.	PAGE	GRID
CLEAR CREEK RD	SHA	18	B3
CLEARFIELD DR	MLBR	144	B5
CLEAR LAKE RD	MOD	6	C3
CLEGHORN RD	LAS	14	D5
CLEGHORN CYN RD	SBD	91	B5
CLEM	SJCO	40	C4
CLEMENCEAU AV	FRCO	57	D5
CLEMENTE AV	AVLN	97	B5
CLEMENTS RD	SJCO	40	C4
CLEMENTS RD	SUT	33	C2
CLEVELAND AV	MAD	57	A2
CLEVELAND AV	SBD	U	E3
CLEVELAND AV	SD	213	E5
CLEVELAND AV	STA	47	D1
CLEVELAND RD	MCO	56	C1
CLEVELAND ST	RCO	101	C5
CLIFF DR	LAG	201	B2
CLIFF DR	NB	199	C4
CLIFF DR	STB	174	A5
CLIFF DR W	SC	169	D4
CLIFF RIDGE RD	MEN	30	C2
CLIFTON CT RD	SJCO	46	D1
CLINE GULCH RD	SHA	18	A1
CLINTON AV	FRE	165	B1
CLINTON AV	FRCO	56	E3
CLINTON AV	FRCO	57	A3
CLINTON AV	KIN	57	E5
CLINTON AV S	SJCO	47	B1
CLINTON RD	AMA	41	A2
CLINTON RD	STA	47	D2
CLINTON RD E	AMA	41	A2
CLINTON RD W	AMA	41	A2
CLINTN KEITH RD	RCO	99	C5
CLIO STATE RD	PLU	27	B3
CLOSE AV	TUL	68	D1
CLOUGH RD	HUM	15	D2
CLOUTIER ST	DN	1	D3
CLOVER LN	SB	86	E2
CLOVER LN	SB	87	A2
CLOVER LN	SHA	18	B3
CLOVER CREEK RD	KLAM	5	A1
CLOVERDALE DR	SHA	18	B3
CLOVERDALE RD	RCO	U	E3
CLOVERDALE RD	RCO	98	E2
CLOVERDALE RD	SMCO	N	C4
CLOVERDALE RD	SMCO	45	C5
CLOVERFIELD BL	SMON	180	A5
CLOVERLEAF DR	MAD	57	B2
CLOVER VLY RD	LAK	31	D2
CLOVIS AV	FRCO	57	D5
CLUB DR	DN	1	E3
CLYDE AV	MCO	48	B5
COACHELLA CANAL	RCO	108	D1
COACHLA CN RD	IMP	109	B2
COACHLLA CYN RD	RCO	101	D5
COAL RD	RCO	99	B4
COAL CANYON RD	BUT	25	C4
COAL CANYON RD	ORCO	U	D5
COAL CANYON RD	ORCO	98	D3
COALINGA RD	SBT	65	D1
COALINGA RD	SBT	66	A1
COALNGA MNL SPG	FRCO	66	B3
COAL MINE RD	AMA	40	D3
COAST HWY	LAG	201	A2
COAST HWY	ORCO	201	A2
COAST HWY	ORCO	202	D5
COAST HWY	SON	30	D5
COAST HWY E	NB	199	D4
COAST HWY E	NB	200	A5
COAST HWY W	NB	199	C4
COAST RD	MON	64	B1
COAST RIDGE TR	MON	64	E4
COCHRANE RD	SCL	P	D4
COCHRAN RD	SCL	54	C1
COCK RBN ISL RD	HUM	15	D2
COCOPAH RD	IMP	112	D5
COD DR	SIS	4	B3
CODONI AV	STA	47	D2
COFFEE RD	KER	78	C2
COFFEE RD	MDO	162	E2
COFFEE RD	STA	47	D2
COFFEE ST	MCO	48	C5
COFFEE CREEK RD	HUM	15	D2
COFFEE CREEK RD	TRI	11	D3
COGSWELL RD	STA	47	E2
COGSWELL RD	STA	48	A2
COHASSET RD	BUT	25	B2
COHASSET RD	C	124	A2
COHEN RD	SJCO	47	A1
COHN AV	FRCO	66	D3
COLBY RD	IMP	110	D5
COLBY MTN LKOUT	TEH	19	D5
COLDEN AV	LACO	Q	E5
COLD CANYON RD	LACO	97	B2
COLD CREEK RD	TRI	17	B3
COLD SPRINGS RD	ED	34	D4
COLD SPRINGS RD	LAS	8	C4
COLDWATR CYN AV	LACO	97	C1
COLDWATR CYN AV	LACO	Q	C2
COLDWATR CYN DR	LACO	97	D1
COLDWELL AV	MDO	162	A2
COLDWELL LN	FRCO	66	B3
COLE AV	LACO	181	D5
COLE RD	IMP	112	B4
COLE RD	MPA	49	B3
COLE GRADE RD	SDCO	106	D2
COLEMAN AV	MP	147	A1
COLEMAN AV	SMCO	147	A1
COLEMAN AV	SCL	P	B3
COLEMAN AV	SCLR	151	C2
COLEMN FSH HTCH	SHA	18	D3
COLEMAN VLY RD	SON	37	C2
COLES RD	SUT	33	B3

STREET	CO.	PAGE	GRID
COLES LEVEE RD	KER	78	B4
COLEY RD	IMP	112	D5
COLFAX	PLA	34	D2
COLFAX AV	GV	127	C4
COLFAX AV	LACO	Q	D3
COLFAX AV	NEV	127	C4
COLGATE RD	KER	80	D3
COLIMA RD	LACO	98	B3
COLIMA RD	LACO	R	D5
COLIN RD	SBD	80	E1
COLLEGE AV	ALA	L	D4
COLLEGE AV	B	156	B3
COLLEGE AV	MAR	139	B5
COLLEGE AV	MDO	162	A2
COLLEGE AV	O	156	B5
COLLEGE AV	SDCO	V	C3
COLLEGE AV	SDCO	111	D1
COLLEGE AV	SIS	12	C1
COLLEGE AV	SON	37	E2
COLLEGE AV	STR	131	C3
COLLEGE AV W	STR	131	B3
COLLEGE BLVD	SDCO	106	B3
COLLEGE DR	SAL	171	A4
COLLEGE DR	SMA	173	D4
COLLEGE CITY RD	COL	33	A3
COLLEGE HTS BL	KER	80	E1
COLLIER RD	MCO	47	E4
COLLIER RD	MCO	48	A4
COLLIER RD	SJCO	40	B3
COLLIER CYN RD	ALA	46	B2
COLLINS AV	ORA	194	D4
COLLINS AV	ORCO	T	D2
COLLINS RD	IMP	110	D5
COLLINS RD	INY	51	D4
COLLINSVILLE RD	SOL	M	B2
COLLINSVILLE RD	SOL	39	B4
COLLYER DR	SHA	18	C2
COLOMA RD	ED	34	D4
COLOMA RD	ED	138	B1
COLOMA RD	SAC	40	A1
COLOMA ST	PLCV	138	C2
COLOMBERO DR	SIS	12	D2
COLOMBO MINE RD	SIE	26	E4
COLOMBO MINE RD	SIE	27	A4
COLOMBUS AV	MCO	47	D4
COLONY RD	BUT	25	B4
COLONY RD	MON	64	E1
COLONY RD	MON	65	A1
COLONY RD	SAC	40	B2
COLORADO AV	RCO	99	A3
COLORADO AV	SCL	N	E2
COLORADO AV	SMON	180	A5
COLORADO BLVD	LACO	97	E1
COLORADO BLVD	LACO	98	A1
COLORADO BLVD	LACO	R	D3
COLORADO BLVD	PAS	190	B4
COLORADO RD	FRCO	57	A5
COLORADO RD	MPA	49	B3
COLORADO ST	GLEN	182	E1
COLORADO ST	LACO	Q	E3
COLORADO ST	LACO	S	E2
COLORADO ST	LACO	T	A2
COLORADO RV RD	RCO	103	D4
COLOSEUM	INY	59	E2
COLOSSEUM RD	SBD	84	B2
COLSEN CYN RD	SB	86	D1
COLT LN	CAL	41	A5
COLTON AV	CLTN	207	B4
COLTON AV	SBD	99	B2
COLUMBIA AV	RCO	99	B2
COLUMBIA RD N	KER	80	D3
COLUMBIA RD S	KER	80	D4
COLUMBINE RD	SIS	12	C2
COLUMBUS AV	SF	143	B2
COLUMBUS AV	SFCO	45	C1
COLUMBUS PKWY	SOL	L	D2
COLUMBUS PKWY	SOL	38	D4
COLUMBUS ST	KER	78	D3
COLUSA AV	CC	L	D4
COLUSA AV	FRCO	56	E4
COLUSA AV	FRCO	66	E1
COLUSA AV	SUT	125	A2
COLUSA AV	YUBA	125	A2
COLUSA HWY	BUT	25	B5
COLUSA RD	SBD	91	B3
COLUSA CO RD	COL	31	E1
COLUSA-PRNTN RD	COL	32	E1
COLYEAR SPGS RD	TEH	17	E5
COMANCHE DR	KER	78	E4
COMANCHE DR	KER	79	A3
COMANCHE PT RD	KER	79	A4
COMBIE RD	NEV	34	C3
COMBIE RD	PLA	34	C3
COMETA RD	SJCO	47	D1
COMM BLVD	SBD	91	C1
COMMERCE AV	LACO	Q	E1
COMMERCIAL ST	SD	216	A4
COMMONS RD	STA	47	D3
COMMONWEALTH	ORCO	98	B3
COMMONWEALTH AV	ORCO	T	B1
COMMONWEALTH AV	RCO	99	E4
COMPTCHE UKIAH	MEN	30	B1
COMPTON AV	LACO	Q	E5
COMPTON BLVD	LACO	S	B1
COMSTOCK	WSH	130	B3
COMSTOCK RD	SBT	55	A2
COMSTOCK RD	SJCO	40	B4
CONARD RD	LAS	20	D3
CONCHO ST	CAL	41	A4
CONCORD AV	CC	39	C5
CONCORD BLVD	CC	M	A3
CONCORD BLVD	CC	39	A5
CONCOW RD	BUT	25	D1

STREET	CO.	PAGE	GRID
CONDIT AV	STA	47	B3
CONDOR RD	SBD	92	B1
CONDOR RD	SBD	101	C1
CONDUIT	SUT	33	C3
CONE RD	INY	51	D5
CONE RD 3	LAS	20	B1
CONE GROVE RD	TEH	18	D5
CONEJO AV	FRCO	57	B5
CONEJO AV	FRCO	57	C5
CONEJO DR	SBD	90	E3
CONE PEAK RD	MON	64	E3
CONFER RD	SJCO	40	B5
CONGRESS AV	MONT	53	D3
CONGRESS AV	PAC	167	B3
CONGRESS ST	SD	213	A5
CONGRSS SPGS RD	SCL	45	E5
CONGRSS SPGS RD	SCL	N	E4
CONGRSS SPGS RD	SCL	P	A4
CONKLIN BLVD	KER	80	C4
CONKLIN RD	MOD	8	D1
CONKLIN CK RD	HUM	15	D4
CONKLING RD	IMP	112	A3
CONN CREEK RD	NAPA	29	D4
CONNECTION	LAS	21	E4
CONNELLY RD	IMP	112	C3
CONRAD GROVE LP	TEH	19	D3
CONSTANCE AV	STB	174	A2
CONSTANTIA RD	LAS	27	E1
CONSTELLATN AV	KER	89	C1
CONSUMNES MINE	ED	35	B5
CONTADAS	CC	45	D1
CONTOUR AV	RCO	99	D3
CONTRA COSTA AV	FRCO	56	D4
CONTRA COSTA BL	CC	L	E3
CONTRA COSTA BL	CC	M	A3
CONTRA LOMA BL	CC	M	C3
CONVENTN CTR DR	CLK	209	C5
CONVICT CPGD RD	MNO	50	E2
CONVICT CPGD RD	MNO	51	A2
CONVICT CK EXP	MNO	51	A2
CONVICT LAKE RD	MNO	50	E2
CONVICT LAKE RD	MNO	51	A2
CONVOY ST	SDCO	V	B2
CONVOY ST	SDCO	106	D5
CONWAY RANCH RD	MNO	43	B4
COOK LN	SOL	39	B3
COOK RD	AMA	40	C3
COOK ST	RCO	100	E4
COOK ST	SMA	173	A3
COOK CAMPBLL RD	SIS	4	E4
COOK PEAK LKOUT	KER	79	D1
COOKS CAMP RD	CAL	41	C2
COOKS SPRING RD	COL	32	B1
COOLEY RD	IMP	109	B5
COOLEY RD	SIS	4	B3
COOLGARDIE RD	SBD	81	D4
COOLIDGE AV	O	158	E4
COOLIDGE AV	SCL	P	D5
COOMBSVILLE RD	NAPA	L	D1
COOMBSVILLE RD	NAPA	38	D3
COON HOLLOW CK	BUT	25	D1
COOPER RD	IMP	109	C5
COOPER RD	MON	54	C4
COOPER RD	NEV	34	D1
COOPR CIENG T T	RCO	100	B5
COOPERSTOWN RD	STA	48	B2
COPA DE ORA AV	MCO	55	D1
COPCO RD	SIS	4	B3
COPENHAGEN	HUM	15	D2
COPP AV	KER	89	B1
COPPER	FRCO	57	D2
COPPER AV	FRCO	56	A2
COPPER CYN RD	SHA	18	C1
COPPER CITY RD	SBD	81	D4
COPPER COVE DR	CAL	41	A5
COPPER HEAD RD	MON	65	C4
COPPER MTN RD	SBD	101	B1
COPPEROPOLIS	SJCO	40	C5
COPPER VISTA WY	SDCO	106	C3
COPP PIT RD	MOD	14	D2
COPUS RD	KER	78	B4
CORAL RD	MCO	47	E5
CORAL RD	MCO	55	E1
CORAM RD	SHA	18	B1
CORBETT CYN RD	SLO	76	B4
CORBIN AV	LA	178	B3
CORBIN RD	COL	32	D1
CORCORAN RD	KER	77	E1
CORD	SJCO	40	C3
CORDA RD	MON	54	E5
CORDELIA RD	SOL	L	E1
CORDELIA RD	SOL	M	A1
CORDELIA RD	SOL	38	E3
CORDELIA RD	SOL	135	B5
CORDELIA RD	SUIS	135	B5
CORE RD	SAC	39	E2
CORKILL RD	RCO	100	D3
CORN CAMP RD	KER	77	E3
CORNELIA AV	FRCO	57	B4
CORNELIUS AV	SUT	33	D3
CORNING RD	TEH	24	C2
CORN SPRINGS RD	RCO	102	C5
CORONA AV	KIN	57	E5
CORONA EXPWY	RCO	98	D2
CORONA EXPWY	SBD	98	D2
CORONA FRWY	RCO	98	E3
CORONA RD	SON	L	A1
CORONA RD	SON	38	A3
CORONA D MAR FY	CM	197	D4
CORONA D MAR FY	ORCO	98	C4
CORONADO AV	SDCO	V	C5
CORONADO AV	SDCO	111	D2
CORRAL RD	SHA	19	E2

STREET	CO.	PAGE	GRID
COPPEROPOLIS RD	TRI	17	B5
CORRAL CYN RD	SDCO	112	C1
CORRL DE TIERRA	MON	54	C5
CORRAL HOLLW RD	SJCO	46	E2
CORRALITOS RD	SCR	54	B2
CORREIA RD	SJCO	39	E4
CORRELL RD	SUT	33	B3
CORTE MADERA AV	CRTM	140	B1
CORTEZ AV	MCO	47	E3
CORTEZ AV	MCO	48	A3
CORTEZ WY	KER	79	E2
CORTINA SCH RD	COL	32	D3
CORTINA VNYD RD	COL	32	D3
CORTO RD	SBD	91	D4
CORWIN RD	SBD	91	C3
CORWIN RANCH RD	RCO	99	B5
CORYDON RD	RCO	99	B5
COSGROVE	CAL	41	B4
COSTA RD	YUB	26	A4
COSTA MESA FRWY	ORCO	98	B4
COSTA MESA FRWY	ORCO	T	C4
COSTNER RD	STA	47	C2
COTA ST	STB	174	C4
COTHARIN RD	VEN	96	D2
COTTA RD	SJCO	39	E4
COTTAGE AV	MAN	161	E1
COTTAGE AV	SJCO	161	E1
COTTLE RD	STA	47	D1
COTTON RD	MCO	55	E2
COTTON CREEK	MPA	48	D2
COTTON GIN RD	MCO	55	E2
COTTNTAIL CK RD	SLO	75	D2
COTTONWOOD AV	RCO	99	C3
COTTONWOOD AV	RCO	99	D4
COTTONWOOD DR	SBD	92	C1
COTTONWOOD RD	BUT	25	C4
COTTONWOOD RD	INY	60	B5
COTTONWOOD RD	KER	78	D3
COTTONWOOD RD	MCO	47	C5
COTTONWOOD RD	RCO	100	A2
COTTONWOOD RD	SBT	55	B4
COTTONWD CYN RD	MNO	43	C4
COTTONWD CYN RD	RCO	99	C4
COTTONWD CYN RD	SB	77	B5
COTTONWD CK RD	SIS	4	A2
COTTONWD SPG RD	RCO	101	D4
COUCH ST	VAL	134	C3
COUGHLAN ST	VAL	134	B3
COULTERVILLE RD	MPA	49	C2
COUNCIL HILL RD	SIE	26	C4
COUNCILMAN RD	HUM	10	D5
COUNTRY	SJCO	40	C5
COUNTRY RD	SIS	4	C5
COUNTRY CLUB BL	SJCO	40	A5
COUNTRY CLUB BL	SJCO	160	A3
COUNTRY CLUB DR	RCO	100	D4
COUNTRY CLUB RD	AVLN	97	A5
COUNTRY CLUB RD	HUM	10	D4
COUNTRY CLUB RD	YUB	33	D3
COUNTRYMAN DR	PLU	26	B2
COUNTY RD	INY	51	D5
COUNTY RD	MOD	8	A1
COUNTY RD	MOD	14	E1
COUNTY RD B	GLE	24	C4
COUNTY RD BB	GLE	24	C4
COUNTY RD C	GLE	24	C3
COUNTY RD D	GLE	24	D4
COUNTY RD F	GLE	24	D3
COUNTY RD H	GLE	24	D3
COUNTY RD H	GLE	24	D4
COUNTY RD I	GLE	24	D3
COUNTY RD J	GLE	24	D3
COUNTY RD M	GLE	24	D4
COUNTY RD MM	GLE	24	D3
COUNTY RD N	GLE	24	D4
COUNTY RD NN	GLE	24	D3
COUNTY RD P	GLE	24	D4
COUNTY RD PP	GLE	24	D4
COUNTY RD QQ	GLE	24	D3
COUNTY RD R	GLE	24	E4
COUNTY RD RR	GLE	24	E3
COUNTY RD S	GLE	24	E4
COUNTY RD SS	GLE	24	E4
COUNTY RD T	GLE	24	E4
COUNTY RD TT	GLE	24	E4
COUNTY RD U	GLE	24	E3
COUNTY RD V	GLE	24	E3
COUNTY RD V	GLE	24	E4
COUNTY RD VV	GLE	24	E3
COUNTY RD VV	GLE	24	E4
COUNTY RD W	GLE	24	E4
COUNTY RD WW	GLE	24	E4
COUNTY RD XX	GLE	24	E3
COUNTY RD XX	GLE	25	A5
COUNTY RD Y	GLE	25	A5
COUNTY RD YY	GLE	25	A5
COUNTY RD Z	GLE	25	A4
COUNTY RD ZZ	GLE	25	A4
COUNTY RD 5	YOL	33	A4
COUNTY RD 6	YOL	33	A4
COUNTY RD 7	YOL	33	A4
COUNTY RD 8	YOL	32	E4
COUNTY RD 9	GLE	24	D3
COUNTY RD 10	YOL	32	E4
COUNTY RD 11	GLE	24	E3
COUNTY RD 11	YOL	32	E4
COUNTY RD 11	YOL	33	B4
COUNTY RD 11A	YOL	33	B4
COUNTY RD 11B	YOL	33	B4
COUNTY RD 12	YOL	33	B4
COUNTY RD 12A	YOL	33	A4
COUNTY RD 13	YOL	32	E4
COUNTY RD 14	YOL	33	A4

STREET	CO.	PAGE	GRID
COUNTY RD 14A	YOL	33	B4
COUNTY RD 15	GLE	24	E3
COUNTY RD 15	YOL	33	B4
COUNTY RD 15B	YOL	32	E4
COUNTY RD 16	GLE	24	E3
COUNTY RD 16	YOL	33	A5
COUNTY RD 16A	YOL	32	E5
COUNTY RD 17	YOL	33	A5
COUNTY RD 18	GLE	24	E3
COUNTY RD 18	YOL	33	B5
COUNTY RD 18B	YOL	33	C5
COUNTY RD 18C	YOL	33	C5
COUNTY RD 19	GLE	24	E3
COUNTY RD 19	YOL	33	B5
COUNTY RD 19A	YOL	33	A5
COUNTY RD 20	GLE	24	E3
COUNTY RD 20	YOL	33	C5
COUNTY RD 20A	YOL	32	E5
COUNTY RD 21	GLE	24	E3
COUNTY RD 21A	YOL	32	E5
COUNTY RD 23	GLE	25	A3
COUNTY RD 23	YOL	33	A5
COUNTY RD 24	GLE	24	D3
COUNTY RD 24	YOL	33	B5
COUNTY RD 25	GLE	24	D3
COUNTY RD 25	YOL	33	A5
COUNTY RD 25A	YOL	33	A5
COUNTY RD 26	GLE	24	C3
COUNTY RD 26	YOL	33	A5
COUNTY RD 26A	YOL	33	C5
COUNTY RD 27	GLE	24	D3
COUNTY RD 27	YOL	33	B5
COUNTY RD 28	GLE	24	D3
COUNTY RD 28	YOL	39	A1
COUNTY RD 28H	YOL	39	C1
COUNTY RD 29	GLE	24	E3
COUNTY RD 29	GLE	25	A3
COUNTY RD 29	YOL	39	A1
COUNTY RD 29A	YOL	39	A1
COUNTY RD 30	GLE	24	D3
COUNTY RD 30	GLE	25	A3
COUNTY RD 30	YOL	39	B1
CO RD 30 1/2	GLE	25	A3
COUNTY RD 31	GLE	24	D4
COUNTY RD 31	GLE	25	A3
COUNTY RD 31	YOL	39	A1
COUNTY RD 32	GLE	24	E4
COUNTY RD 32	GLE	25	A4
COUNTY RD 32	YOL	39	B1
CO RD 32 1/2	GLE	24	E4
COUNTY RD 33	GLE	24	D4
COUNTY RD 33	GLE	25	A4
COUNTY RD 34	GLE	24	E4
COUNTY RD 34	GLE	25	A4
COUNTY RD 35	GLE	24	D4
COUNTY RD 36	GLE	24	E4
COUNTY RD 36	YOL	39	C2
COUNTY RD 37	GLE	24	E4
COUNTY RD 38	GLE	24	E4
COUNTY RD 38	YOL	39	C2
COUNTY RD 38A	YOL	39	C2
COUNTY RD 39	GLE	24	D4
COUNTY RD 40	GLE	24	E4
COUNTY RD 41	GLE	24	E4
COUNTY RD 43	GLE	24	E4
COUNTY RD 43	YOL	32	D4
COUNTY RD 44	GLE	24	E4
COUNTY RD 44	YOL	32	D4
COUNTY RD 45	GLE	24	D4
COUNTY RD 45	YOL	32	D4
COUNTY RD 46	GLE	24	E4
COUNTY RD 47	YOL	32	D4
COUNTY RD 48	GLE	24	D4
COUNTY RD 49	GLE	24	D4
COUNTY RD 50	GLE	24	E4
COUNTY RD 50	GLE	25	A4
COUNTY RD 53	GLE	24	E4
COUNTY RD 57	GLE	24	D4
COUNTY RD 58	GLE	24	C4
COUNTY RD 59	GLE	24	C5
COUNTY RD 59	YOL	32	D4
COUNTY RD 60	GLE	24	D5
COUNTY RD 61	GLE	24	E5
COUNTY RD 61	YOL	32	D4
COUNTY RD 62	GLE	24	C5
COUNTY RD 63	GLE	25	A5
COUNTY RD 63	YOL	32	D4
COUNTY RD 64	GLE	24	E5
COUNTY RD 65A	GLE	24	E5
COUNTY RD 65B	GLE	24	E5
COUNTY RD 65C	GLE	24	C5
COUNTY RD 66A	GLE	24	D5
COUNTY RD 66B	GLE	24	E5
COUNTY RD 67	GLE	25	A5
COUNTY RD 68	GLE	24	D5
COUNTY RD 69	GLE	24	C5
COUNTY RD 69	GLE	25	A5
COUNTY RD 70	GLE	25	A5
COUNTY RD 70	YOL	32	D4
COUNTY RD 71	GLE	24	D5
COUNTY RD 71	YOL	32	D4
COUNTY RD 75A	YOL	32	D4
COUNTY RD 76	YOL	32	D5
COUNTY RD 78	YOL	32	D5
COUNTY RD 78A	YOL	32	D5
COUNTY RD 79	YOL	32	D5
COUNTY RD 79A	YOL	32	E5
COUNTY RD 79B	YOL	32	E5
COUNTY RD 80	YOL	32	E5
COUNTY RD 81	YOL	32	E5
COUNTY RD 82	YOL	32	E5
COUNTY RD 82B	YOL	32	E5
COUNTY RD 84A	YOL	32	E4

STREET	CO.	PAGE	GRID
COUNTY RD 84B	YOL	32	E4
COUNTY RD 85	YOL	32	E5
COUNTY RD 85B	YOL	32	E5
COUNTY RD 86	YOL	32	E4
COUNTY RD 86A	YOL	33	A5
COUNTY RD 87	YOL	33	A5
COUNTY RD 87B	YOL	33	A5
COUNTY RD 88	YOL	33	A4
COUNTY RD 88A	YOL	33	A5
COUNTY RD 88B	YOL	33	A5
COUNTY RD 89	YOL	33	A4
COUNTY RD 90	YOL	39	A1
COUNTY RD 90A	YOL	33	A5
COUNTY RD 91	YOL	33	A5
COUNTY RD 91A	YOL	39	A1
COUNTY RD 91B	YOL	33	A4
COUNTY RD 92	YOL	33	B4
COUNTY RD 92B	YOL	33	A4
COUNTY RD 92C	YOL	33	B5
COUNTY RD 92F	YOL	39	B1
COUNTY RD 93	YOL	33	B5
COUNTY RD 93A	YOL	33	B4
COUNTY RD 93B	YOL	33	B4
COUNTY RD 94	YOL	33	B4
COUNTY RD 94A	YOL	33	B5
COUNTY RD 94B	YOL	33	B5
COUNTY RD 95	YOL	33	B4
COUNTY RD 95A	YOL	39	B1
COUNTY RD 96	YOL	33	B5
COUNTY RD 96B	YOL	33	B5
COUNTY RD 97	YOL	33	B5
COUNTY RD 97D	YOL	39	B1
COUNTY RD 98	YOL	33	B4
COUNTY RD 99	YOL	33	B5
COUNTY RD 99E	YOL	33	C5
COUNTY RD 100	YOL	33	C5
COUNTY RD 101	YOL	33	C5
COUNTY RD 101A	YOL	39	C1
COUNTY RD 102	YOL	33	C5
COUNTY RD 102B	YOL	33	C5
COUNTY RD 103	YOL	33	C5
COUNTY RD 104	YOL	39	C1
COUNTY RD 105	YOL	39	C2
COUNTY RD 106	YOL	39	C2
COUNTY RD 107	YOL	33	C4
COUNTY RD 107A	YOL	33	D4
COUNTY RD 108	YOL	33	B4
COUNTY RD 116	YOL	33	C4
COUNTY RD 119	YOL	33	D5
COUNTY RD 122	YOL	33	D5
COUNTY RD 124	YOL	33	D5
COUNTY RD 126	YOL	39	D1
COUNTY RD 128A	YOL	39	D1
COUNTY RD 152	YOL	39	C2
COUNTY RD 155	YOL	39	C2
COUNTY RD 200	GLE	24	D3
COUNTY RD 303	GLE	24	B4
COUNTY RD 304	GLE	24	B4
COUNTY RD 307	GLE	24	A3
COUNTY RD 310	GLE	23	E4
COUNTY RD 314	GLE	24	B3
COUNTY RD 315	GLE	24	A3
COUNTY RD 400	GLE	24	B5
COUNTY HOSP RD	PLU	26	C1
COUNTY LINE RD	KER	68	B5
CO LINE RD E	TRI	17	E2
CO LINE CK RD	TRI	16	D3
COURCHEVEL RD	PLA	35	D2
COURSE RD	KER	78	B4
COURT ST	RED	122	B2
COURTLAND RD N	YOL	39	D2
COURTLANDT CT	KER	79	C4
COUTOLENC RD	BUT	25	D2
COVE AV	FRCO	58	B4
COVE RD	SBD	91	E4
COVE RD	SHA	13	A5
COVELL BLVD	DVS	136	B2
COVELO RD	MEN	23	A3
COVELO RD	MEN	22	E4
COVELO RFUSE RD	MEN	23	A2
COVERT RD	STA	47	C2
COVINA BLVD	LACO	R	E3
COWBOY CNTRY TR	RCO	107	B1
COWBOY JOE RD	LAS	21	D5
COW CAMP RD	BUT	25	E2
COW CAMP RD	MNO	43	C3
COW CREEK RD S	SHA	18	E2
COW CREEK RD S	SHA	19	A2
COWEL RD	CC	38	E5
COW GULCH RD	SHA	17	D3
COW HAVEN CY RD	KER	80	B1
COW MTN ACCESS	MEN	31	B2
COX AV	SCL	P	A4
COX AV	SCL	45	E5
COX LN	BUT	25	D5
COX RD	IMP	109	A3
COX RD	SJCO	40	C4
COX RD	SHA	18	B3
COX RD	STA	47	B3
COX ST	RCO	99	C4
COXCOMB TR	SBD	102	C1
COXEY	SBD	91	D4
COX FERRY RD	MCO	48	B3
COYOTE RD	MCO	56	B1
COYOTE RD	SBD	101	A2
COYOTE #1 RD	IMP	111	C4
COYOTE #2 RD	IMP	111	C4
COYOTE CYN RD	INY	71	D4
COYOTE CYN RD	RCO	107	C1
COYOTE GAP RD	BUT	25	E2
COYOTE LAKE RD	SBD	82	B5
COYOTE RES RD	SCL	P	E5
COYOTE SPGS RD	MNO	43	C4

STREET	CO.	PAGE	GRID
COYOTE VLY RD	INY	51	C4
COYOTE VLY RD	SBD	93	A5
COYOTE VLY RES	LAS	14	C5
COZZI AV	MCO	56	A1
CRABTREE RD	LAS	8	D4
CRABTREE RD	STA	48	B2
CRAFTON AV	SBD	99	D2
CRAIG	SJCO	47	C1
CRAIG AV	SON	132	B3
CRAIG AV	TEH	18	E5
CRAIG RD	SUT	33	B1
CRAMER	PLA	34	B3
CRAM GULCH RD	SIS	4	B5
CRANE AV	MCO	47	D4
CRANE RD	STA	47	D2
CRANE CANYON RD	SON	38	A2
CRANE FLAT	MPA	63	B5
CRANE FLAT RD	MPA	49	C2
CRANE VALLEY RD	MAD	49	E5
CRANMORE RD	SUT	33	B3
CRANMORE RD	SUT	33	C4
CRANNELL RD	HUM	9	E4
CRANNELL RD	HUM	10	A4
CRATER RD	SBD	93	E3
CRATER HILL RD	PLA	34	B3
CRAWFORD AV	FRCO	58	A4
CRAWFORD RD	CLO	32	E2
CRAWFORD RD	MEN	23	A3
CRAWFORD RD	STA	47	D2
CRAY CROFT RDG	SIE	26	D4
CRAZY HORSE CYN	MON	54	D3
CREED RD	SOL	39	B3
CREEK RD	MCO	55	D2
CREEK RD	RED	122	A4
CREEK RD	VEN	88	B4
CREEKSIDE CT	KER	79	C4
CREEKSIDE LN	STA	47	E2
CREIGHTON DR	SHA	13	D3
CRENSHAW BLVD	LACO	97	D3
CRENSHAW BLVD	LACO	Q	D5
CRENSHAW BLVD	LACO	S	B2
CREOLE MINE RD	SBD	92	E4
CRESCENT AV	AVLN	97	B4
C RESERVOIR RD	MOD	6	D4
CRESSEY WY	MCO	48	A4
CRESSMAN RD	FRCO	58	B1
CREST DR	RCO	99	B2
CREST RD	LACO	S	B2
CRESTLINE RD	SDCO	107	A2
CRESTON RD	SLO	76	B1
CRESTON EUREKA	SLO	76	B2
CRESTN ODONOVAN	SLO	76	C2
CRESTVIEW DR	MNO	51	D2
CRESTVIEW ST	KER	80	C1
CREWS RD	SCL	54	D2
CRIPE RD	FRCO	58	A1
CRIPPEN AV	SBD	91	A3
CRIPPLE CK RD	SLO	76	B2
CRISPIN RD	MEN	30	C3
CRISS RD	SIS	4	E3
CRISS RD	SIS	5	A3
CRISTIANITOS RD	SDCO	105	E1
CRISWELL AV	MCO	55	E1
CROCKER RD	SJCO	46	E1
CROCKER SPGS RD	KER	77	D4
CRONESE LAKE RD	SBD	82	E4
CRONESE LAKE RD	SBD	83	A4
CROOKED MDW RD	MNO	50	E1
CROSBY RD	HUM	15	D2
CROSBY ST	SD	216	A5
CROSBY HAROLD	PLA	34	B3
CROSS RD	COL	32	E3
CROSS RD	MON	65	C4
CROSS CYNS RD	SLO	66	B5
CROSS CTRVILLE	MEN	31	B1
CROSS CNTRY RD	MON	66	B4
CROUCH AV	BUT	25	A3
CROW RD	STA	47	E2
CROW CANYON RD	ALA	M	A5
CROW CANYON RD	ALA	45	E2
CROWDER	PLA	33	E5
CROWDER FLAT RD	MOD	6	E5
CROWLEY RD	SUT	33	C3
CROWLEY LAKE DR	MNO	51	A3
CROWLEY LAKE PL	MNO	51	A2
CROWLY LK DM RD	MNO	51	B2
CROWN RD	MCO	48	C4
CROWN & PICKLE	SBD	92	D5
CROWN POINT RD	BUT	25	C2
CROWN VLY PKWY	ORCO	98	D5
CROWN VALLEY RD	LACO	89	E4
CROWS LANDNG RD	MDO	162	C5
CROWS LANDNG RD	STA	47	C4
CROWS LANDNG RD	STA	162	C5
CROY RD	SCL	P	C5
CROY RD	SCL	54	C1
CRUCERO RD	SBD	83	A5
CRUCERO RD	SBD	93	B1
CRUICKSHANK RD	IMP	112	B3
CRUMP LN	FRCO	66	B3
CRUZON GRADE RD	NEV	26	C5
CRYSTAL AV	MOH	96	A3
CRYSTAL CK RD	SHA	18	A2
CRYSTAL SPGS AV	SBR	144	A4
CRYSTAL SPGS DR	LA	182	C1
CRYSTAL SPGS DR	LACO	Q	E3
CRYSTAL SPGS RD	KLAM	5	C1
CRYSTAL SPGS RD	SMCO	N	C2
CRYSTAL SPGS RD	SMCO	45	C3
CUDA DR	KER	78	E4
CUDDEBACK RD	SBD	80	E3
CUDDEBACK RD	SBD	81	A3
CUDDY VALLEY RD	KER	88	C1

COPYRIGHT 1997 Thomas Bros. Maps ®

251
CUDDY VALLEY RD
STREET INDEX
DUNCAN RD

STREET	CO.	PAGE	GRID
CUDDY VALLEY RD	VEN	88	C2
CUFF RD	IMP	109	B2
CUIN RD	IMP	108	E5
CULL CANYON RD	ALA	M	A5
CULL CANYON RD	ALA	45	E1
CULLEN AV	SCL	P	E5
CULVER BLVD	CUL	183	C5
CULVER BLVD	CUL	188	A3
CULVER BLVD	LA	183	C5
CULVER BLVD	LA	188	A3
CULVER BLVD	LACO	97	C2
CULVER BLVD	LACO	187	D5
CULVER DR	ORCO	98	C4
CULVER DR	ORCO	T	E4
CUMMINGS RD	HUM	15	E1
CUMMINGS RD	VEN	88	B5
CUMMINGS SKYWAY	CC	38	D4
CUMMINGS VLY RD	KER	79	B4
CUNEO RD	MPA	48	E1
CUNNINGHAM LN	MNO	42	E1
CUNNINGHAM RD	CAL	41	C3
CUNNINGHAM RD	MCO	48	D5
CUNNINGHAM RD	MEN	31	B2
CURLEW ST	SD	215	D1
CURRAN RD	AMA	40	D3
CURREY RD	SOL	39	B1
CURRIE RD	SOL	39	B4
CURRIER RD	BUT	25	C4
CURTIS ST	SM	145	B3
CURTIS ST W	SAL	171	C2
CURTNER AV	SCL	P	B4
CURTNER AV	SCL	46	B5
CUSTER AV	FRCO	56	B2
CUSTER AV	SBD	91	E4
CUTCA TRUCK TR	RCO	106	E1
CUTLER AV	GLE	24	E3
CUT OFF RD	LAS	21	C3
CUTOFF RD	MEN	23	C5
CUTTING	CC	38	C5
CUTTING AV	GLE	24	E3
CUTTING BLVD	CC	L	C3
CUTTING BLVD	R	155	A4
CUTTNGS WHRF RD	NAPA	L	C1
CUTTNGS WHRF RD	NAPA	38	C3
CUYAMA ST	SB	87	D1
CYA RD	MPA	49	A3
CYPRESS AV	LACO	R	E3
CYPRESS AV	RED	122	C2
CYPRESS AV	SHA	18	C2
CYPRESS AV	SUT	33	D3
CYPRESS RD	CC	M	D3
CYPRESS RD	CC	39	C5
CYPRESS RD	MCO	56	A1
CYPRESS RD	SBD	80	E1
CYPRESS ST	C	124	C4
CYPRESS ST	LACO	98	C2
CYPRESS MTN DR	SLO	75	D1
CYPRUS AV	U	123	B2
CYRMIC RD	KER	77	D3
CYRUS CANYON RD	KER	79	D1
D			
D ST	MAR	L	B3
D ST	MDO	162	C4
D ST	ONT	203	D4
D ST	SR	139	C4
D ST	SON	L	A1
D ST	SON	38	A3
DAGGETT YERMO	SBD	92	A1
DAGNINO RD	ALA	M	C5
DAGNINO RD	ALA	46	C2
DAHLIN RD	SJCO	47	C1
DAHLSTROM RD	COL	32	E3
DAILEY RD	KER	79	C2
DAINTY AV	CC	M	D3
DAINTY AV	CC	39	C5
DAIRY AV	LACO	S	D1
DAIRY LN	MCO	56	A1
DAIRY RD	BUT	25	A3
DAIRY RD	KER	78	A3
DAIRY RD	STA	47	B2
DAIRY RD	YUB	33	E3
DAIRY MART RD	SDCO	V	C5
DAIRY MART RD	SDCO	111	D2
DAKIN RD	LAS	21	C4
DAKOTA AV	FRCO	57	C3
DAKOTA AV	FRCO	56	E3
DAKOTA AV	STA	47	C2
DALBY	PLA	33	E3
DALE LN	SHA	18	B3
DALE RD	KER	79	B4
DALE RD	STA	47	C2
DALE RD	TEH	24	E2
DALE TR	SBD	101	E1
DALE VISTA RD	SBD	101	E1
DALLY RD	SOL	39	B3
DALTON AV	ALA	M	D5
DALTON AV	ALA	46	C1
DALY ST	LA	186	D1
DAMIEN AV	LACO	98	C1
DANA DR	SHA	18	C2
DANA FOOTHLL RD	SLO	76	C5
DANBY RD	SBD	101	D1
DANENBERG RD	IMP	112	B3
DANIELS AV	VAL	134	A3
DANLEY LATERAL	COL	32	C1
DANLEY RD	COL	32	D1
DAN MCNAMARA RD	MCO	48	A5
DANTES VIEW	INY	72	B1
DANVILLE BLVD	CC	M	A4
DANVILLE BLVD	CC	45	E1
DARBY RD	BUT	25	E5
DARBY RD	CAL	41	C3
DARGATE RD	KER	77	E2
DARK CANYON RD	BUT	25	D3
DARLING RD	LACO	89	D4
DARLING RDG RD	ED	34	E4
DARMS LN	NAPA	38	C2
DARRAH RD	MPA	49	B3
DATE ST	SB	86	C1
DATE PALM DR	RCO	100	D4
DATONI RD	YUB	33	D2
DAUBENBERGER RD	STA	47	E3
DAULTON RD	MAD	56	B1
DAULTON RD	MAD	57	B1
DA VALL DR	RCO	100	D3
DAVENPORT RD	LACO	89	D4
DAVEY GLEN RD	SM	145	C4
DAVID AV	MONT	53	C3
DAVID AV	MONT	167	B3
DAVID AV	PAC	167	B3
DAVID RD	KER	78	E5
DAVIDSON	FRCO	56	B2
DAVIDSON RD	HUM	9	E2
DAVIDSON RD	HUM	10	A2
DAVIS AV	FRCO	57	A5
DAVIS AV	FRCO	57	C5
DAVIS AV	KER	78	B1
DAVIS RD	BUT	25	B5
DAVIS RD	IMP	109	A2
DAVIS RD	KER	76	E1
DAVIS RD	MON	54	C4
DAVIS RD	MON	171	A4
DAVIS RD	RCO	99	D3
DAVIS RD	SJCO	40	A4
DAVIS RD	SIS	4	C4
DAVIS RD	SIS	5	C4
DAVIS RD	STA	47	C4
DAVIS RD	STA	48	B3
DAVIS RD	SUT	33	B2
DAVIS ST	ALA	L	D5
DAVIS ST	ALA	45	D2
DAVIS ST	LAK	32	A3
DAVIS CK CEM RD	MOD	7	C4
DVS CK TRNS STA	MOD	7	C4
DAWN RD	KER	89	E1
DAWN RD	KER	90	A1
DAWSON RD	RCO	99	C3
DAWSON RANCH RD	MNO	51	D2
DAY AV	SHA	19	E1
DAY RD	MOD	13	E3
DAY RD	SCL	54	C1
DAY RD	SHA	13	E3
DAY ST	RCO	99	C3
DAY RD	SCL	P	E5
DAYBREAK CT	TUO	163	D3
DAYLIGHT PASS	INY	61	E4
DAYLIGHT PS CTO	INY	61	E3
DAYTON RD	BUT	25	B3
DAYTON WEST RD	BUT	25	A3
DEAD HRSE CY RD	SIS	13	B3
DEAD INDIAN RD	JKSN	4	A1
DEADMAN CK RD	MNO	50	D2
DEAD MANS GULCH	MON	65	E4
DEADWOOD RD	BUT	25	D3
DEADWOOD RD	PLA	35	A2
DEADWOOD RD	TRI	17	E1
DEADWOOD LO RD	SIS	3	D4
DEALWOOD RD	IMP	109	B5
DEAN CREEK RD	HUM	16	C5
DE ANGELIS RD	MCO	47	D4
DE ANZA BLVD	CPTO	149	D4
DE ANZA DR	RCO	99	E3
DE ANZA TR	SDCO	107	D1
DEARBORN RD	IMP	111	E3
DEARDORFF RD	CAL	41	B2
DEARWOOD DR	MEN	31	B2
DEATH VALLEY RD	INY	52	B5
DEAVER AV	KER	70	A5
DECPTION CYN RD	RCO	100	E3
DECKER AV	SBD	92	E5
DECKER RD	SUT	33	B2
DECORD DR	LACO	89	A4
DECOTO RD	ALA	P	A1
DECOTO RD	ALA	45	E3
DEE KNOCH RD	SHA	13	E4
DEEP CREEK RD	MOD	8	D1
DEEP CREEK RD	SBD	91	C5
DEEP SPRINGS RD	SBD	84	A3
DEEP SPGS RANCH	INY	52	B4
DEEP WELL RD	MCO	55	E1
DEER WY	RCO	100	B5
DEER CREEK AV	TUL	68	B5
DEER CREEK RD	SBD	91	C4
DEER CREEK RD	VEN	96	D2
DEER FLAT RD	SHA	19	C2
DEERHORN VLY RD	SDCO	112	B1
DEER LICK KNOB	TRI	17	D2
DEER LICK SPGS	TRI	17	D3
DEER MTN RD	SIS	4	D5
DEER PARK RD	BUT	26	A3
DEER PARK RD	NAPA	29	B2
DEER PARK RD	NAPA	38	B1
DEER SPRING RD	MNO	51	B2
DEER VALLEY	ED	34	C5
DEER VALLEY RD	CC	M	C3
DEER VALLEY RD	CC	39	B5
DEETZ RD	SIS	12	C2
DEFENDER GRADE	AMA	41	B2
DEFRAIN BLVD	RCO	103	D5
DE HARVEY ST	KER	78	A4
DEHESA RD	SDCO	107	A5
DE LA CRUZ BL	SCL	P	B3
DE LA CRUZ BL	SCLR	151	C2
DE LA GUERRA ST	STB	174	D3
DEL AMO BLVD	LACO	98	A3
DEL AMO BLVD	LACO	S	D2
DE LA VINA ST	STB	174	B3
DELAWARE AV	SC	169	A5
DELAWARE RD	STA	47	E2
DELAWARE ST	SM	N	C1
DELCERRO BLVD	SDCO	V	C3
DELCERRO BLVD	SDCO	111	D1
DEL DIOS HWY	SDCO	106	D4
DELEVAN RD	COL	32	D1
DELFATTI LN	KLAM	5	B1
DELFERN RD	KER	77	D2
DELFIND RD	KER	77	D2
DELHI RD	SOL	39	C2
DELIMA RD	SJCO	47	A1
DEL MAR AV	LACO	R	C4
DEL MAR AV	VAL	134	D3
DEL MAR BLVD	PAS	190	C4
DEL MAR HTS RD	SDCO	106	C4
DEL MAR HTS RD	SDCO	V	A1
DEL MONTE AV	SUT	33	C4
DEL MONTE BLVD	MONT	167	B1
DEL NORTE AV	FRCO	57	A4
DEL NORTE DR	TEH	18	C4
DEL OBISPO ST	ORCO	98	D5
DEL OBISPO ST	DPT	202	B4
DEL OBISPO ST	SJC	202	C2
DEL ORO RD	SBD	91	C4
DEL ORTO RD	CAL	40	E3
DEL ORTO RD	CAL	41	A3
DEL PASO RD	SAC	33	D5
DELPHOS RD	CLO	32	D2
DEL PUERTO AV	STA	47	C3
DEL PUERTO CYN	STA	46	E4
DEL PUERTO CYN	STA	47	A3
DEL REY AV	FRCO	57	E3
DEL REY AV	FRCO	57	E5
DEL ROSA AV	SBD	99	C1
DELTA AV	SJCO	46	E1
DELTA AV	SJCO	47	A1
DELTA RD	CC	M	D3
DELTA RD	CC	39	C5
DELTA RD	MCO	55	E1
DE LUZ RD	SDCO	106	B1
DEMAREE RD	TUL	68	B1
DEMAREST MNE RD	CAL	41	A4
DEMPSEY RD	SCL	P	B2
DENISE AV	KER	80	A5
DENNETT ST	PAC	167	B2
DENNISON RD	KER	79	D4
DENNY RD	TRI	10	E5
DENNY RD	TRI	11	A4
DENTON RD	MCO	56	A1
DENTON RD	STA	48	A2
DENTN & LEAK RD	MCO	56	B1
DENVER AV	FRCO	56	E4
DENVER AV	KIN	57	E5
DEVERTON RD	SOL	39	B3
DE PORTOLA RD	RCO	99	E5
DEPOT AV	SB	86	C1
DEPOT RD	ALA	146	B5
DEPOT RD	H	146	B5
DEPOT ST	SMA	173	B3
DERBY ST	B	156	B3
DERRICK BLVD	FRCO	66	C2
DERRICK RD	BUT	25	D4
DERRICK RD	IMP	111	E3
DERRICK RD	LAS	14	B3
DERRICK FT RD N	TRI	11	E3
DERRICK FT RD N	TRI	12	A3
DERRICK FT RD S	TRI	12	A3
DERSCH RD	SHA	18	C3
DESCANSO AV	AVLN	97	B5
DESCHUTES RD	SHA	18	D2
DESERT RD	CLK	85	D5
DESERT RD	IMP	112	D3
DESERT CTR RICE	RCO	102	C4
DESERT INN RD	CLK	209	C5
DESERT INN RD	CLK	210	C1
DSRT SHORES DR	IMP	108	C1
DESERT VIEW AV	SBD	91	D4
DESERT WILLW TR	SBD	100	D2
DESEVADO RD	SIS	4	C3
DE SOTO AV	LA	177	D3
DE SOTO AV	LACO	177	D4
DESSIE DR	LAK	31	C3
DETLOW RD	BUT	25	D3
DETOUR RD	GLE	24	D3
DETWEILER RD	MPA	48	D2
DEVILS CORRL RD	LAS	20	D3
DEVILS DEN RD	KIN	67	B5
DEVOE RD	SUT	33	C4
DEVONSHIRE BLVD	LACO	97	C1
DEVORE RD	SBD	99	B1
DEVOSE DR	LAS	8	A4
DE VRIES	SJCO	40	A4
DEWITT RD	STA	47	D2
DE WOLF AV	FRCO	57	D2
DE WOLF AV	FRCO	57	D5
DE WOLF AV	SB	86	B3
DE 1 FIRST ST	COL	32	D1
DIABLO RD	CC	M	B4
DIABLO RD	CC	46	A1
DIABLO MINE RD	INY	51	C3
DIABLO MINE RD	MNO	51	C3
DIABLO OASIS DR	RCO	100	C3
DIAGONAL 7	MAD	56	C3
DIAGONAL 11	MAD	56	D1
DIAGONAL 232	TUL	68	D4
DIAGONAL 252	TUL	68	D3
DIAGONAL 254	TUL	68	D3
DIAMOND RD	ED	138	C5
DIAMOND BAR BL	LACO	98	C2
DIAMOND BAR BL	LACO	U	B3
DIAMOND MTN RD	PLU	20	E4
DIAMOND VLY RD	ALP	36	C4
DIAZ LN	INY	51	D4
DIAZ ST	KER	80	A4
DICK COOK	PLA	34	B4
DICKERMAN RD	IMP	109	B4
DICKINSON AV	FRCO	57	B4
DICKINSON AV	FRCO	67	B1
DICKNSN FRRY RD	MCO	48	B5
DIDO AV	SBD	92	A3
DIEHL RD	IMP	111	E3
DIEHL RD	STA	47	C4
DIENSTAG RD	STA	48	A2
DIERSSEN RD	SAC	39	E3
DIETRICH	SJCO	40	C5
DIETRICH RD	IMP	109	B4
DIGGER RAVNE RD	PLU	26	C1
DI GIORGIO RD	KER	78	D3
DI GIORGIO RD	KER	79	A3
DIGIORGIO RD	SDCO	107	E2
DILLARD RD	SAC	40	A3
DILLION RD	SIS	10	D1
DILLON RD	HUM	15	D2
DILLON RD	RCO	100	E3
DILLON RD	RCO	100	C3
DILLON BEACH RD	MAR	37	D3
DINKELSPIEL RD	SOL	39	B4
DINKEY CREEK RD	FRCO	58	B1
DINKY AV	KER	89	B1
DINUBA AV	FRCO	56	E4
DINUBA AV	FRCO	57	C4
DINUBA AV	FRCO	58	A4
DIPS RD	TRI	17	B3
DIRKS RD	COL	24	D5
DISCH RD	SJCO	40	C4
DISTELRATH DR	DN	1	D3
DISTRICT CTR DR	BUT	25	D5
DITCH RD	KER	78	A5
DITCH RD	SIE	26	C4
DITCH CREEK RD	SIS	4	A3
DIVISADERO ST	FRE	165	B3
DIVISADERO ST	SF	142	A2
DIVISION ST	LACO	89	E2
DIVISION ST	SDCO	V	C4
DIVISION ST	SDCO	111	D1
DIVISION ST	SLO	76	B5
DIVISION CK RD	INY	59	E2
DIXIE RD	BUT	25	D2
DIXIE RD	SBD	91	D1
DIXIE CANYON-			
-ROUND VALLEY	PLU	20	C5
DIXIE VALLEY RD	LAS	14	D4
DIXON AV E	SOL	39	B2
DIXON AV W	SOL	39	B2
DIXON LN	INY	51	D4
DIXON HILL RD	YUB	26	A5
DIXON MINE RD	ALP	42	C1
DOBBINS ST	KER	70	A5
DOBIE LN	MEN	23	B3
DOBIE MEADOWS	MNO	43	D4
DOBIE MEADOWS	MNO	43	E4
DOBIE MEADOWS	MNO	44	A4
DOBSON RD	SBD	81	E4
DODDS	SJCO	47	C1
DODDS RD	STA	47	C4
DODGE RD	COL	24	E5
DODGE RDG LP RD	TUO	42	A3
DOE MILL RD	BUT	25	C2
DOERKSEN RD	STA	47	E3
DOG BAR RD	NEV	34	C2
DOG CREEK RD	SHA	12	B4
DOGGIE TR	SBD	101	A2
DOGTOWN RD	CAL	41	B4
DOGTOWN RD	MPA	48	E2
DOGTOWN RD	MPA	49	A2
DOG VALLEY RD	SIE	27	E5
DOGWOOD DR	EC	217	E4
DOGWOOD RD	ALP	36	A5
DOGWOOD RD	IMP	109	A5
DOGWOOD RD	IMP	112	A4
DOHENY DR	BH	183	D2
DOHENY DR	LA	183	D2
DOHENY DR	LACO	Q	D4
DOHENY PARK RD	DPT	202	C4
DOLAN RD	MON	54	B3
DOLAN HARDNG RD	YUB	34	A1
DOLLARHIDE RD	NAPA	38	C1
DOLORES ST	SF	142	C5
DOLPHIN AV	KER	80	C1
DOLPHIN DR	IMP	108	C2
DOME AV	TUL	68	D3
DOME ST	SB	86	D1
DOMINION RD	SB	86	C1
DOMINO CT	KER	79	B4
DON RD	SBD	101	D1
DONAHUE RD	SUT	33	C4
DONKIN RD	STA	47	B3
DONLON,JAMES BL	CC	M	C3
DONNER PASS RD	NEV	27	B5
DONOVAN RD	SMA	173	A2
DON PEDRO RD	STA	47	C3
DONS RD	MOD	8	B2
DOOLITTLE DR	A	159	A3
DOOLITTLE DR	ALA	L	D5
DOOLITTLE DR	ALA	45	D2
DOOLITTLE DR	O	159	C3
DOOLITTLE CK RD	SIS	2	E3
DOON GRADE	BUT	25	D2
DORA RD	SUT	33	B2
DORA ST	U	123	C3
DORAN SCENIC DR	SBD	82	A5
DORFF LN	HUM	15	D2
DORIS AV	VEN	96	B1
DORNES RD	PLA	34	A3
DORRETT DR	BUT	25	C2
DORRIS AV	FRCO	66	E2
DORRIS BROWNELL	SIS	5	B3
DORRIS TEHNER	SIS	5	A3
DORSEY RD	STA	47	D1
DOS CABEZA RD	IMP	111	B3
DOSE RD	TRI	10	E5
DOS PALMAS RD	SBD	90	E4
DOS REIS RD	SJCO	47	A1
DOS RIOS DR	SBD	90	E3
DOS RIOS LN	STA	47	B3
DOS RIOS RD	BUT	25	C5
DOSTER RD	CAL	41	A3
DOTTA LN	PLU	27	D3
DOTTA GUIDCI RD	PLU	27	D2
DOTY RD	SHA	13	D5
DOUBLE SPGS RD	CAL	40	E3
DOUGHERTY RD	CC	M	B4
DOUGHERTY RD	CC	46	B1
DOUGHERTY RD	SUT	33	C3
DOUGLAS	KIN	67	D1
DOUGLAS AV	FRCO	56	C4
DOUGLAS AV	SB	86	B3
DOUGLAS LN	SBD	100	E1
DOUGLAS RD	SAC	40	B1
DOUGLAS ST	ELS	189	D3
DOUGLAS RGR STA	MAD	49	E5
DOVE	SJCO	47	D1
DOVER AV	FRFD	135	D3
DOVER AV	KIN	67	E1
DOVER DR	NB	199	C4
DOVER DR	ORCO	T	C4
DOVER CANYON RD	SLO	75	E1
DOVE SPG CYN RD	KER	80	A2
DOW BUTTE RD	LAS	20	D1
DOW BUTTE LO RD	LAS	20	D1
DOWD RD	PLA	34	A3
DOWD RD	PLA	33	E4
DOWDEN RD	IMP	109	B3
DOWER AV	FRCO	57	B3
DOWER AV	FRCO	57	B5
DOW FLAT RD	LAS	20	D1
DOWNEY AV	LACO	S	E1
DOWNEY RD	INY	73	A4
DOWNEY RD	LACO	R	A4
DOWNEY ST	MDO	162	C3
DOWNIE RD	STA	47	E3
DOWNIE RD	STA	48	A3
DOWS PRAIRIE RD	HUM	9	E4
DOYLE DR	SF	141	D1
DOYLE GRADE	LAS	27	D1
DOYLE RD	MCO	47	C5
DOYLE RANCH RD	KER	69	E5
DOYLE RANCH RD	KER	79	E1
DRAIN 10 RD	SIS	5	E2
DRAIS AV	SJCO	40	C5
DRAKE AV	COL	32	E3
DRAKE RD	HUM	15	E2
DRAPER RD	STA	47	C4
DRAPER RD	TEH	18	C3
DREDGR CP MORGN	TRI	17	C1
DRESSER AV	KER	78	A2
DREW RD	IMP	111	E3
DREXLER	SUT	33	B2
DRIVE 212	TUL	58	C5
DRIVE 244	TUL	68	D2
DRIVE 254	TUL	58	D4
DRIVER AV	LACO	97	A1
DRIVER RD	KER	68	C5
DRIVER RD	KER	78	C1
DRIVER RD	KER	78	C2
DROBISH RD	BUT	25	E5
DROGE	SJCO	47	C1
DRUM CANYON RD	SB	86	D3
DRUMMOND AV	KER	80	C1
DRY CREEK RD	LAK	32	A5
DRY CREEK RD	MCO	48	B3
DRY CREEK RD	MNO	50	D2
DRY CREEK RD	NAPA	29	C4
DRY CREEK RD	NAPA	38	B2
DRY CREEK RD	PLA	34	C3
DRY CREEK RD	SJCO	40	B3
DRY CREEK RD	SLO	76	B1
DRY CREEK RD	SHA	18	D1
DRY CREEK RD	SIS	4	B3
DRY CREEK RD	SON	31	C5
DRY CREEK RD	TUL	58	D5
DRY CREEK RD W	SON	31	D5
DRY CREEK RD W	SON	37	D1
DRY CK BASIN RD	MOD	8	C1
DRY CK CMP GRND	LAS	8	B3
DRY CREEK CTO	MNO	50	D2
DRYDEN AV	SCL	P	E5
DRY GENESEO RD	SLO	76	B1
DRY SLOUGH RD	COL	33	A2
DRYTOWN AMADOR-			
-VIA BUNKERHILL	AMA	40	E2
DU BOIS ST	SR	139	D4
DUBOIS TK TR	SDCO	107	B5
DUCK CREEK RD	AMA	40	C3
DUCK LAKE RD	LAS	21	E4
DUDLEY RD	MON	65	D3
DUFAU	VEN	96	C1
DUGGANS RD	NEV	34	C2
DUMETZ RD	LA	177	C5
DUMP RD	HUM	16	B3
DUMP RD	INY	60	A3
DUNAWAY RD	IMP	111	D3
DUNAWEAL LN	NAPA	29	A2
DUNBAR LN	SDCO	107	A5
DUNCAN RD	SBD	90	E4

INDEXES

STREET	CO.	PAGE	GRID
DUNCAN RD	SJCO	40	C5
DUNCAN ST	KER	78	E4
DUNCAN CYN RD	SBD	99	A1
DUNCAN CREEK RD	SHA	17	E3
DUNDERBURG MDW	MNO	43	B4
DUNE RD	SBD	92	B1
DUNES RD	CLK	210	B2
DUNFORD RD	KER	78	A3
DUNLAP DR	RCO	99	C3
DUNLAP RD	FRCO	58	C3
DUNLAP RD	KER	69	B5
DUNN LN	CAL	41	B5
DUNN RD	MCO	48	C4
DUNN RD	SBD	82	D5
DUNN RD	STA	47	B2
DUNNE AV	SCL	P	D5
DUNNE AV E	SCL	P	D5
DUNSTONE DR	BUT	25	D5
DUNTON RD	STA	40	E5
DUPONT RD	RCO	102	D5
DURANT AV	B	156	A3
DURBROW RD	NEV	128	A4
DURFEE AV	LACO	R	C4
DURHAM HWY	BUT	25	C3
DURHAM RD	ALA	P	B2
DURHAM RD	SIS	5	A3
DURHAM DAYTN HY	BUT	25	B3
DURHAM FERRY RD	SJCO	47	A2
DURKEE RD	LAS	14	A3
DURNEL RD	BUT	25	B4
DUSK LN	TUO	163	D3
DUSTIN RD	SJCO	40	B4
DUSTIN AKERS RD	KER	78	A4
DUSTY LN	STA	47	D2
DUSTY WY	TEH	18	D5
DUSTY MILE RD	SBD	92	D5
DUTCH CREEK RD	SIS	3	E3
DUTCH CREEK RD	TRI	17	C2
DUTCHER CK RD	SON	31	C5
DUTCH MINE RD	TUO	41	C5
DUTTON AV	SON	131	C4
DUTTON AV N	STR	131	B3
DUVALL ST	KER	78	A4
DUZEL CREEK RD	SIS	3	E5
DUZEL CREEK RD	SIS	11	E1
DUZEL RCK LO RD	SIS	3	E5
DUZEL RCK LO RD	SIS	11	E1
DWIGHT WY	MCO	48	A4
DWINNELL WY	SIS	12	C1
DWINNELL WY	SIS	12	C1
DYE RD	SDCO	107	A4
DYER DR	PLU	20	C4
DYER LN	PLA	33	E5
DYER RD	ORCO	T	D3
DYER ST	ALA	N	E1
DYER ST	ALA	P	A1
DYER ST	ALA	45	E3
DYERVILLE LOOP	HUM	16	B4
DYERVILLE LP RD	HUM	16	C4
DYSERT RD	SIS	4	E3
DYSON LN	PLU	27	C3
E			
E ST	DVS	136	D3
E ST	EUR	121	C1
E ST	FRE	165	C4
E ST	H	146	E2
E ST	SCTO	137	C2
E ST	SBDO	207	C4
E ST	SBD	99	B2
E ST	SDCO	V	C4
E ST	SDCO	111	D2
E ST	YUB	33	D2
EABY RD	SBD	90	E4
EADY RD	IMP	112	A4
EAGER RD	SUT	33	C2
EAGLE AV	FRCO	56	A2
EAGLE BORAX WLL	INY	72	E2
EAGLE CK LP RD	TRI	11	E3
EAGLE CK LP RD	TRI	12	A3
EAGLE FIELD RD	MCO	55	E2
EAGLE LAKE RD	NEV	27	A5
EAGLE MTN RD	RCO	102	B4
EAGLE PK LKOUT	TEH	24	A2
EAGLE ROCK BLVD	LACO	R	A3
EAGLE ROCK RD	TRI	17	A1
EAGLE RCK LKOUT	SIS	4	B3
EAGLES NEST RD	MNO	43	A4
EAGLES NEST RD	SAC	40	B2
EAGLEVL DUMP RD	MOD	8	E2
EAGLEVILLE LOOP	MOD	8	E2
EARDLEY AV	PAC	167	C2
EARHART RD	O	159	D4
EARLHAM ST	SDCO	107	A4
EARP RD	COL	33	A2
EAST AV	ALA	M	D5
EAST AV	ALA	46	C2
EAST AV	BUT	25	B3
EAST AV	BUT	124	B1
EAST AV	C	124	A1
EAST AV	FRCO	57	C5
EAST AV	MCO	48	A3
EAST AV	TEH	24	D2
EAST LN	MEN	23	B3
EAST RD	LACO	R	E5
EAST ST	ANA	193	D1
EAST ST	AUB	126	C3
EAST ST	ORCO	T	D2
EAST ST	RED	122	B1
EASTBLUFF DR	NB	200	A3
EAST END RD	SBD	92	A4
EASTERN AV	LACO	98	A2

STREET	CO.	PAGE	GRID
EASTERN AV	LACO	R	B5
EAST FORK RD	SHA	18	A1
EAST FORK RD	TRI	11	B5
EAST FORK RD	TRI	12	A4
EAST FORK RD	TRI	17	C3
EAST GRADE RD	SDCO	107	A2
EAST GRADE RD	TRI	16	E2
E FK HAYFORD RD	TRI	17	C3
E FK INDIAN CK	SHA	2	E3
E FK STUART CPG	TRI	11	E5
EASTIN RD	STA	47	C5
EASTMAN RD	STA	40	D5
EASTMAN RD	STA	47	D1
EASTMONT RD	KER	78	E2
EASTSHORE FRWY	ELC	155	D3
EASTSHORE FRWY	R	155	D3
EASTSHORE FRWY	SP	155	D3
EASTSHORE RD	SHA	18	B2
EAST SIDE	PLU	20	D5
EASTSIDE LN	MNO	42	E1
EASTSIDE RD	INY	51	D4
EASTSIDE RD	MEN	23	A5
EAST SIDE RD	MEN	31	B2
EASTSIDE RD	MNO	42	E1
EASTSIDE RD	RED	122	B4
EASTSIDE RD	SHA	18	C2
EASTSIDE RD	SHA	18	C3
EASTSIDE RD	SIS	3	D5
EASTSIDE RD	SIS	11	D1
EAST SIDE RD	TRI	12	A4
E SIDE CALPELLA	MEN	31	B1
E SDE PORTR VLY	MEN	31	B1
E SDE REDWD VLY	MEN	31	B1
EAST WEST RD	SIS	5	D2
EASY ST	KER	79	C4
EASY ST	SHA	18	D2
EATON RD	BUT	25	A3
EATON RD	STA	47	E1
EBERLE RD	KER	78	C4
ECHO PARK AV	LA	185	E1
ECHO PARK AV	LA	186	A1
ECHO VALLEY RD	MON	54	C3
EDDINS RD	IMP	109	A3
EDDY RD	COL	33	A3
EDDY RD	LPAZ	104	A2
EDDY ST	SF	143	B5
EDDY GULCH RD	SIS	11	B2
EDDY GLH LKOUT	SIS	11	B3
EDEN PLAINS RD	CC	M	D3
EDGAR AV	BUT	25	B3
EDGEMONT ST	LA	182	B5
EDGER RD	IMP	108	E5
EDGEWATER BLVD	FCTY	145	D2
EDGEWOOD AV	MAR	L	A4
EDGEWOOD RD	SMCO	N	C2
EDGEWOOD RD	SMCO	45	D3
EDGEWOOD RD	SIS	12	C1
EDINGER AV	ORCO	98	B4
EDINGER AV	ORCO	T	B3
EDINGER AV	SA	196	A5
EDINGER AV	SA	197	C1
EDINGER AV	SA	198	A1
EDINGER ST	FTNV	195	C5
EDINGER ST	SA	195	C5
EDISON AV	SBD	98	D2
EDISON AV	SBD	U	D3
EDISON BLVD	BUR	179	B3
EDISON HWY	KER	78	E3
EDISON HWY	KER	79	A3
EDISON RD	KER	78	E3
EDISON ST	SB	86	E3
EDISON WY	CLK	85	D5
EDITH AV	TEH	24	D2
EDMINSTER RD	MCO	47	D4
EDMUNDSON AV	SCL	P	D5
EDMUNDSON AV	SCL	54	C1
ED POWERS RD	INY	51	C4
ED RAU RD	SAC	39	E2
EDSEL LN	STA	47	C2
EDWARD ST	KER	79	B5
EDWARDS	SJCO	47	D1
EDWARDS ST	ORCO	T	B3
EEL RIVER RD	MEN	23	B5
EEL RIVER RD	MEN	31	C1
EEL ROCK RD	HUM	16	C4
EGAN RD	TUO	41	C5
EGGERT RD	SOL	39	C2
EHRLICH RD	STA	47	C3
EICKHOFF RD	LAK	31	D2
EIGHMY RD	TEH	18	C4
EIGHTH ST	C	124	C5
EIGHT MILE RD	SJCO	39	E4
EISENHOWER DR	RCO	100	E5
EISENHOWER ST	FRFD	135	D3
ELBERTA ST	KER	89	E1
EL CAJON BLVD	SD	214	A5
EL CAJON BLVD	SDCO	V	D3
EL CAJON BLVD	SDCO	111	D1
EL CAMINO AV	SAC	40	A1
EL CAMINO DR	SHA	18	C3
EL CAMINO RD	SBD	101	D1
EL CAMINO CIELO	SB	87	C4
EL CAMINO REAL	BLMT	145	C4
EL CAMINO REAL	BURL	144	B3
EL CAMINO REAL	MP	147	A2
EL CAMINO REAL	MLBR	144	C4
EL CAMINO REAL	MON	54	D4
EL CAMINO REAL	MON	65	A1
EL CAMINO REAL	MON	66	A5
EL CAMINO REAL	MON	171	B1
EL CAMINO REAL	MVW	148	B5
EL CAMINO REAL	PA	147	B3
EL CAMINO REAL	SAL	171	D3

STREET	CO.	PAGE	GRID
EL CAMINO REAL	SBT	54	D2
EL CAMINO REAL	SBR	144	B3
EL CAMINO REAL	SDCO	106	B3
EL CAMINO REAL	SNLO	172	B4
EL CAMINO REAL	SLO	66	A5
EL CAMINO REAL	SLO	76	B2
EL CAMINO REAL	SLO	172	E2
EL CAMINO REAL	SM	145	A3
EL CAMINO REAL	SMCO	N	D2
EL CAMINO REAL	SMCO	45	C3
EL CAMINO REAL	STB	173	D5
EL CAMINO REAL	SB	86	C1
EL CAMINO REAL	SCL	P	A3
EL CAMINO REAL	SCLR	150	B2
EL CAMINO REAL	SCLR	151	A2
EL CAMINO REAL	SCL	46	A4
EL CAMINO REAL	SCL	54	D2
EL CAMINO REAL	SMA	173	C1
EL CAMINO REAL	SSF	144	B3
EL CAMINO REAL	SVL	150	B2
EL CAMPO RD	MCO	55	E2
EL CAMPO RD	RCO	100	C5
EL CAMPO RD	SLO	76	B5
EL CAPITAN WY	MCO	47	E4
EL CAPITAN WY	MCO	48	A3
EL CAPTN SCH RD	MCO	48	B5
EL CARISO TK TR	RCO	99	B4
EL CENTRO AV	NAPA	38	C3
EL CENTRO BLVD	SUT	33	D3
EL CENTRO RD	SAC	33	D5
EL CENTRO ST	IMP	111	E3
EL CERRITO RD	RCO	98	E3
EL CERRO BLVD	CC	M	A4
EL CIELITO RD	STB	174	D1
EL CIELO DR	RCO	100	D3
EL CIELO RD	PMSP	206	E5
EL CONQUISTA RD	RCO	107	A1
ELDER AV	KIN	67	B1
ELDER CREEK RD	RCO	107	B1
ELDER CREEK RD	SAC	40	A1
EL DIABLO RD	SBD	92	E5
EL DORADO AV	FRCO	56	E4
EL DORADO AV	FRCO	66	E2
EL DORADO AV	S	160	C1
EL DORADO DR	RCO	100	C3
EL DORADO DR	SBD	102	C1
EL DORADO ST	AUB	126	D3
EL DORADO ST	FRE	165	C3
EL DORADO ST	MONT	167	E4
EL DORADO ST	SJCO	40	A5
EL DRDO HLLS RD	ED	34	C5
EL DORADO MN RD	RCO	101	C2
ELDRIDGE RD	LAS	14	A5
ELEANOR AV	STA	47	D2
ELEVADO AV	BH	183	A2
ELEVADO RD	SBD	91	B3
ELDER ST	SDCO	106	C2
ELDER CREEK RD	SAC	39	E1
ELECTRA RD	AMA	41	A3
ELEVATOR RD	SOL	39	D3
ELFERS RD	STA	47	B3
ELGIN	MCO	56	B1
ELGIN AV	KIN	67	B1
ELHOLM RD	MCO	47	C5
ELINOR RD N	HUM	16	A3
ELINOR RD S	HUM	16	A3
ELIZA GULCH RD	SIS	3	E4
ELIZABETH LK RD	LACO	89	C3
ELIZABETH LK RD	LACO	90	A3
ELZBTH LK P CYN	LACO	89	B2
ELK	MCO	48	A4
ELK AV	BUT	25	B3
ELK CT	KER	79	B4
ELK CREEK RD	HUM	16	B4
ELK CREEK RD	SIS	3	A4
ELK GROVE BLVD	SAC	39	E2
ELK GRV FLRN RD	SAC	39	E2
ELK HILLS RD	KER	77	E3
ELK HILLS RD	KER	78	A3
ELKHORN AV	FRCO	56	D5
ELKHORN AV	FRCO	57	D5
ELKHORN BLVD	SAC	33	D5
ELKHORN RD	MEN	31	A4
ELKHORN RD	MON	54	C3
ELKHORN RD	SLO	77	D4
ELKHORN GRAD RD	KER	78	A5
ELKHORN GRADE	FRCO	57	B5
ELK MOUNTAIN RD	LAK	23	C5
ELK MOUNTAIN RD	LAK	31	C1
ELK RIVER RD	HUM	121	A5
ELK RIVER RD	HUM	15	E1
ELK VALLEY RD	DN	1	D4
ELK VALLEY RD	SIS	10	D1
ELK VLY CRSS RD	DN	1	D3
ELLA AV	YUB	33	D2
ELLA RICHTER RD	SHA	18	A3
ELLENA ST	FRCO	57	B5
ELLENWOOD DR	STA	47	E2
ELLENWOOD RD	STA	48	A2
ELLER LN	SIS	3	D5
ELLER LN	SIS	11	D1
ELLIOT	SJCO	40	B3
ELLIOT AV	MCO	48	B4
ELLIOT ST	SBD	93	B2
ELLIOT RCH RD	PLA	34	E2
ELLIOTT RD	BUT	25	C3
ELLIOTT CK RD	SIS	3	B2
ELLIOTT RCH RD	SAC	39	E2
ELLIS AV	RCO	99	C4
ELLIS RD	AMA	41	C1
ELLIS RD	YUB	33	D2
ELLIS ST	SF	143	B5
ELLSWORTH ST	B	156	A3

STREET	CO.	PAGE	GRID
ELM AV	FRCO	57	C4
ELM AV	MON	65	B1
ELM AV	SBR	144	B3
ELM AV	SDCO	106	B3
ELM ST	BKD	166	B2
ELM ST	RCO	99	C5
ELM ST	SDCO	107	A4
ELM ST	TUL	68	B3
EL MARGARITA RD	SUT	33	C2
EL MEDIO RD	SBD	90	E3
ELMER AV	SUT	33	C2
ELMER ST	RCO	99	B4
ELMIRA RD	SOL	39	A2
EL MIRAGE RD	SBD	90	E3
EL MIRAGE RD	SBD	91	A3
ELMO HWY	KER	78	A1
EL MONTE AV	LACO	R	D3
EL MONTE AV	TUL	58	A4
EL MONTE RD	SCL	N	E3
EL MONTE RD	SCL	45	E4
ELNA RD	INY	59	E1
EL NIDO RD	MCO	48	C5
EL NORTE PKWY	SDCO	106	D3
ELORDY LN	SUT	33	E4
EL PASTA RD	RCO	107	A1
EL POMAR AV	STA	47	E2
EL POMAR DR	SLO	76	A2
EL POMAR RD	SLO	76	B2
EL POMAR RO RD	SLO	76	B2
EL PORTAL	CC	38	C5
EL POZO GRADE	SLO	76	D3
EL RANCHO DR	KER	79	C4
EL REPOSO RD	RCO	107	A1
EL RIO DR	TUL	68	C1
EL ROBLAR	VEN	88	A4
EL ROBLAR ST	SB	87	E1
EL SEGUNDO BLVD	ELS	189	D4
EL SEGUNDO BLVD	LACO	97	D3
EL SEGUNDO BLVD	LACO	Q	D5
EL SEGUNDO BLVD	LACO	S	C1
EL SERENO RD	MCO	55	C2
EL SOBRANTE RD	RCO	99	B3
EL TEJON HWY	KER	78	E4
EL TEJON HWY	KER	79	A4
EL TORO DR	BKD	166	C5
EL TORO RD	ORCO	98	D5
ELVAS FRWY	SCTO	137	E2
ELVERTA RD	SAC	33	D5
EL VICINO AV	MDO	162	D2
ELWOOD RD	FRCO	58	B3
ELY RD	SON	L	A1
ELY RD	SUT	33	C4
ELYSIAN VLY RD	LAS	21	A4
EMBARCADRO, THE	SF	143	B2
EMBARCADERO RD	PA	147	C2
EMBARCADERO RD	SCL	N	E2
EMERALD AV	RCO	100	E3
EMERALD AV	STA	47	C2
EMERALD DR	SDCO	106	C3
EMERALD RD	SBD	91	E4
EMERSON RD	MOD	8	D2
EMERSON RD	TEH	18	D4
EMERY RD	STA	47	E2
EMERY RD	STA	48	A2
EMIGH RD	SOL	39	C4
EMIGRANT RD	PLU	26	D1
EMIGRANT TR	SHA	19	B3
EMMERT RD	COL	33	A3
EMMIGRANT TR	ALP	36	B4
EMPIRE	CC	39	C5
EMPIRE AV	BUR	179	B2
EMPIRE AV	CC	M	D3
EMPIRE AV	GV	127	B4
EMPIRE ST	NEV	127	C4
EMPIRE CREEK RD	SIS	3	E3
EMPIRE GRADE	SCR	N	E5
EMPIRE GRADE	SCR	53	D1
EMPIRE MINE RD	CC	M	C3
EMPIRE MINE RD	CC	39	B5
ENCHNTD FRST RD	RCO	100	A4
ENCINAL	MON	54	D4
ENCINAL AV	ALA	L	D5
ENCINAL AV	ALA	45	D1
ENCINAL RD	SUT	33	C1
ENCINITAS BLVD	SDCO	106	C4
ENCINITAS RD	SDCO	106	C3
END RD W	HUM	10	A5
ENDERTS BCH RD	DN	1	E4
ENGLEHART AV	FRCO	58	A4
ENGLISH RD	IMP	109	A3
ENGLISH COLONY	PLA	34	B4
ENGLISH HILLS	SOL	39	A2
ENNIS RD	FRCO	58	C3
ENNIS RD	SUT	33	B2
ENOS LN	KER	78	B3
ENSLEY RD	SUT	33	C4
ENTERPRISE	SJCO	47	D1
ENTERPRISE RD	BUT	25	E4
ENTERPRISE ST	TUL	68	A2
ERBES RD	VEN	96	E1
EREISTIN DR	SBD	92	D5
ERHIT RD	TUO	48	E1
ERHIT RD	TUO	49	A1
ERICKSON RD	BUT	25	B4
ERLE RD	MCO	48	E5
ERNST	MPA	48	E2
ERNST	MPA	49	A2
ERRECA RD	MCO	48	A5
ERRINGER RD	VEN	88	E5
ERRINGER RD	VEN	89	A5
ERRINGER RD	VEN	96	E1
ERRINGER RD	VEN	97	A1
ERSKINE RD	IMP	108	E5

STREET	CO.	PAGE	GRID
ERSKINE CK RD	KER	79	D1
ERTESZEK DR	KER	79	C4
ERWIN ST	LA	178	C3
ESCALON BELLOTA	SJCO	40	C5
ESCALON BELLOTA	SJCO	47	C1
ESCHINGER RD	SAC	39	E2
ESCHINGER RD	SAC	40	A2
ESCOBAR ST	M	154	A2
ESCOLLE RD	MON	54	D5
ESCONDIDO AV	SDCO	106	C3
ESCONDIDO FRWY	RCO	99	C3
ESCONDIDO FRWY	SD	216	D3
ESCONDIDO FRWY	SDCO	106	D2
ESCONDIDO RD	LACO	89	D4
ESMERALDA RD	CAL	41	B4
ESPERANZA AV	RCO	100	B3
ESPERANZA RD	MON	54	D4
ESPERANZA RD	SIS	13	A2
ESPINOSA RD	MON	54	C3
ESPINOSA RD	MON	65	B1
ESPLANADE	BUT	25	A2
ESPLANADE AV	RCO	99	D4
ESPLANADE, THE	C	124	B3
ESPOLA RD	SDCO	106	D4
ESQUON RD	BUT	25	B4
ESSEX LN	HUM	10	A5
ESSEX RD	SBD	94	D2
ESTHER AV	MCO	56	B2
ESTRELLA RD	SLO	66	A5
ESTRELLA RD	SLO	76	B1
ESTUDILLO AV	ALA	L	E5
ETHANAC RD	RCO	99	C4
ETHEREDGE ST	KER	68	D5
ETIWANDA AV	SBD	98	E2
ETTERBG HONEYDW	HUM	16	A5
ETTING RD	VEN	96	C1
ETZEL RD	SOL	39	C2
EUCALYPTUS AV	MCO	48	A4
EUCALYPTUS AV	RCO	99	C3
EUCALYPTUS AV	SBD	U	E3
EUCALYPTUS AV	STA	47	B3
EUCALYPTUS RD	BUT	25	B5
EUCALYPTUS RD	MCO	56	A2
EUCALYPTUS ST	AVLN	97	B5
EUCALYPTUS ST	SBD	91	B4
EUCLID AV	ALA	L	D4
EUCLID AV	ONT	204	B4
EUCLID AV	SBD	U	D3
EUCLID AV	SBD	98	D2
EUCLID AV	SDCO	V	C3
EUCLID AV	SDCO	111	D1
EUCLID AV	SF	141	E3
EUCLID AV	STA	47	E3
EUCLID AV	UPL	204	B1
EUCLID ST	FTNV	197	A3
EUCLID ST	GGR	195	A3
EUCLID ST	ORCO	98	B3
EUCLID ST	ORCO	T	C2
EUCLID ST	SA	195	A5
EUREKA RD	PLA	34	B5
EUREKA RD S	INY	52	D5
EUREKA WY	RED	122	B1
EUREKA WY	SHA	18	C2
EUREKA CYN RD	SCR	P	C5
EUREKA CYN RD	SCR	54	B1
EUREKA HILL RD	MEN	30	C3
EUREKA MINE RD	SIE	26	C4
EUREKA VLY RD	INY	52	D4
EUROPE AV	KER	79	D5
EVAN HEWES HWY	IMP	111	D3
EVAN HEWES HWY	IMP	112	D3
EVANS	TUL	68	D1
EVANS AV	FRCO	56	B2
EVANS RD	COL	32	D2
EVANS RD	RCO	107	C1
EVANS RD	SIS	4	E3
EVNS REIMR RD W	BUT	25	B5
EVELYN AV	MVW	148	B4
EVELYN AV	SCL	P	A3
EVELYN AV	SVL	148	E5
EVELYN AV	SVL	150	A1
EVERETT AV	KIN	67	C1
EVERETT ST	KER	80	D1
EVERETT MEM HWY	SIS	12	C2
EVERGLADE	SUT	33	C3
EVERGREEN RD	CAL	40	D4
EVERGREEN RD	TEH	18	C3
EVERGREEN RD	TUO	42	B5
EVERGREEN RD	TUO	63	A3
EVERITT RD	SUT	33	C2
EXCELSIOR AV	FRCO	66	E1
EXCELSIOR AV	FRCO	67	C1
EXCELSIOR AV	KIN	67	D1
EXCELSIOR RD	SAC	40	A2
EXCELSIOR MN RD	SBD	73	D5
EXCELSIOR MN RD	SBD	83	D1
EXCELSIOR PT RD	NEV	34	E1
EXCHEQUER	MPA	48	D3
EXCHEQUER DR	FRCO	58	C1
EXCHEQUER DAM	MPA	48	D3
EXP MINE RD	TUO	41	C4
EXPOSITION BLVD	LA	184	C5
EXPOSITION BLVD	LA	185	C5
EXPOSITION BLVD	LACO	97	D2
EXPOSITION BLVD	LACO	Q	D4
EXPOSITION BLVD	SAC	39	E1
F			
F ST	DVS	136	D2
F ST	EUR	121	D3
F ST	FRE	165	D4
F ST	HUM	15	E1

STREET	CO.	PAGE	GRID
F ST	SBD	99	B1
F ST	SDCO	V	C4
F ST	SDCO	111	D2
FABRY RD	MON	55	B5
FAHEY RD	MCO	55	C1
FAIR ST	BUT	25	B3
FAIR ST	BUT	124	E5
FAIRBANKS RD	MEN	23	A3
FAIRCHILD LN	SJCO	40	B5
FAIRFAX	FRCO	56	B3
FAIRFAX AV	KIN	67	C1
FAIRFAX AV	LA	181	A4
FAIRFAX AV	LA	184	A3
FAIRFAX AV	LACO	Q	D4
FAIRFAX AV	LACO	181	A4
FAIRFAX RD	KER	78	E3
FAIRFAX BOLINAS	MAR	38	A5
FAIRFIELD AV	FRFD	135	B3
FAIRFIELD AV	SBD	91	C3
FAIRFIELD ST	EUR	121	B3
FAIRGROUND DR	NAPA	L	D1
FAIRGROUNDS DR	VAL	134	E2
FAIRHAVEN AV	ORA	196	C2
FAIRHAVEN AV	ORCO	T	E2
FAIRHAVEN AV	SA	196	C2
FAIRLANE RD	SBD	92	A4
FAIRMEAD BLVD	MAD	56	E1
FAIRMONT AV	SDCO	V	C3
FAIRMONT AV	SDCO	111	D1
FAIRMONT AV E	MDO	162	D1
FAIRMONT RD	LACO	89	C2
FAIRMOUNT AV	SD	214	E5
FAIRMOUNT AV	SD	216	E1
FAIROAKS AV	LACO	R	B2
FAIR OAKS AV	LACO	190	B2
FAIR OAKS AV	PAS	190	B4
FAIR OAKS AV	SCL	45	E4
FAIR OAKS AV	SCL	46	A4
FAIR OAKS AV	SVL	149	E1
FAIR OAKS BLVD	SAC	40	A1
FAIR OAKS BLVD	SAC	34	A5
FAIR PLAY RD	ED	41	A1
FAIRVIEW AV	ALA	P	A1
FAIRVIEW AV	CC	M	D3
FAIRVIEW AV	CC	39	C5
FAIRVIEW AV	RCO	100	A4
FAIRVIEW AV	SB	87	B4
FAIRVIEW RD	COL	32	D1
FAIRVIEW RD	CM	199	C1
FAIRVIEW RD	MON	54	E5
FAIRVIEW RD	ORCO	98	C4
FAIRVIEW RD	ORCO	T	C4
FAIRVIEW RD	SBT	54	E2
FAIRVIEW RD	SBT	55	A2
FAIRVIEW RD	SBD	92	C1
FAIRVIEW RD	VEN	88	B4
FAIRWAY DR	CLTN	207	B5
FAIRWAY DR	EUR	121	C5
FAIRWAY PL	SB	86	E3
FAITH HOME RD	MCO	47	D4
FAITH HOME RD	STA	47	D3
FALL RD	INY	70	B2
FALLBROOK AV	LA	177	A4
FALL CREEK RD	SIS	4	C2
FALLEN LEAF RD	ED	35	E3
FALLING LEAF RD	SHA	18	C2
FALLON RD	SBT	54	E2
FALLON RD	SBT	55	A2
FALL RIVER RD	SHA	13	E4
FALLS CYN RD	AVLN	97	A5
FAMOSO HWY	KER	78	A1
FAMOSO-PRTVL HY	KER	78	C1
FANDANGO PSS RD	MOD	7	D3
FANNING	SJCO	40	B5
FANOE RD	MON	54	E5
FARGO AV	KIN	67	C1
FARGO CANYON RD	RCO	101	B4
FARINA ST	RCO	100	A5
FARLEY MINE RD	SBD	91	D3
FARMER RANCH RD	TRI	17	B2
FARMERSVILLE RD	TUL	68	C2
FARM HILL BLVD	SMCO	N	D2
FARM HILL BLVD	SMCO	45	D3
FARMLAN RD	SUT	33	B2
FARMLAND AV	MCO	48	C4
FARNHAM RDG RD	ED	41	A1
FARQUHAR RD	TEH	18	B4
FARRIS DR	CAL	40	D4
FARRIS RD	BUT	25	B5
FARRIS RD	BUT	33	B1
FASIG RD	SUT	33	B3
FAUST RD	STA	47	C2
FAWCETT RD	IMP	112	A3
FAWN LODGE RD	TRI	17	D1
FAXON RD	COL	33	B3
FAY LN	SIS	11	D1
FAY RD	MCO	47	D4
FAY RANCH RD	KER	69	E5
FAY RANCH RD	KER	79	E1
FAY RIDGE RD	KER	78	C1
FEATHER LAKE HY	LAS	20	A2
FEATHER LAKE RD	SHA	19	E1
FEATHER RIV BL	YUB	33	D3
FEDERAL BLVD	SDCO	V	C3
FEDERAL BLVD	SDCO	111	D1
FEE RD	MOD	7	D3
FEENSTRA RD	SLO	76	B2
FEE RESRVOIR RD	MOD	7	D3
FELCIANA MTN RD	MPA	49	B3
FELDMILLER RD	TRI	16	E3
FELDSPAR AV	KER	80	D1
FELICITA RD	SDCO	106	D3
FELIZ CREEK RD	MEN	31	B3
FELL ST	SFCO	L	B5
FELL ST	SF	141	E4
FELL ST	SF	142	B4
FELL ST	SFCO	45	B1
FELLOWSHIP RD	STB	174	A5
FELTER RD	SCL	46	B4
FELTON EMPRE RD	SCR	53	E1
FENDERS FERRY	SHA	13	A5
FENSLER RD	SIS	5	D2
FENTEM RD	MCO	47	C5
FERGUSON RD	IMP	110	E4
FERN RD	SHA	19	A2
FERN RD E	SHA	19	A1
FERN ST	SD	216	B3
FERN ST	SDCO	V	C3
FERN ST	SDCO	111	D1
FERN CANYON DR	MEN	31	B2
FERNDALE DMP RD	HUM	15	D2
FERRELL RD	IMP	112	A4
FERRETTI RD	TUO	41	D5
FERRETTI RD	TUO	48	D1
FERRY RD	TEH	18	D4
FERRY RD E	HUM	15	C2
FESLER ST	SMA	173	B2
FICKLE HILL RD	HUM	10	A5
FIDDLETOWN RD	AMA	40	E2
FIDLTWN QTZ MTN	AMA	40	E1
FIDDLTWN SLV LK	AMA	41	A1
FIDDYMENT	PLA	33	E4
FIELD RD	SBD	82	C5
FIELDBROOK RD	HUM	10	A4
FIELDS RD	MCO	48	C3
FIELDS RD	RCO	100	A3
FIELDS RIDGE RD	BUT	26	B4
FIESTA ISLND RD	SD	212	E4
FIFIELD RD	IMP	109	B4
FIFIELD RD	SUT	33	D4
FIFTH AV	C	124	B3
FIFTH ST	C	124	B5
FIG AV	FRE	165	C5
FIG AV	FRCO	57	C4
FIG AV	FRCO	57	C5
FIG AV	STA	47	C3
FIGMOND AV	MCO	48	C3
FIG TREE LN	SHA	18	C3
FIGUEROA ST	LA	185	D5
FIGUEROA ST	LA	191	B1
FIGUEROA ST	LACO	R	A3
FIGUEROA ST	LACO	S	C2
FIGUEROA ST	MONT	167	E3
FIGUEROA MTN RD	SB	87	B2
FILBURN AV	KER	78	A1
FILIPPINI RD	SIE	27	C3
FILLMAN RD	LAS	8	A4
FILLMORE ST	RCO	101	B5
FILLMORE ST	SF	142	B2
FILLY LN	CAL	41	B5
FIMPLE RD	BUT	25	B3
FINCK RD	SJCO	46	E1
FINE AV	SJCO	40	C5
FINE AV	STA	47	D2
FINK RD	STA	47	C4
FINKS RD	COL	32	D1
FINLEY LN	LAS	14	C3
FINNEL AV	TEH	24	D1
FINNEY RD	IMP	109	B5
FINNEY RD	STA	47	C2
FINNING HILL RD	PLA	34	E2
FIR ST	C	124	E4
FIR ST	RCO	100	C4
FIRE CAMP RD	BUT	25	E4
FIRESTONE	FRCO	66	C3
FIRESTONE BLVD	LACO	97	E2
FIRESTONE BLVD	LACO	R	A5
FIRETHORN RD	SBD	92	B3
FIRST AV	C	124	D3
FIRST AV	STA	47	C3
FIRST AV E	C	124	D3
FIRST ST	SIS	12	D3
FISCHER RD	IMP	111	E4
FISH & GAME RD	LAS	21	C3
FISHER AV	KER	89	C1
FISHER DR	TUL	68	C1
FISHER RD	HUM	15	E2
FISHER RD	IMP	110	D5
FISHER RD	LPAZ	104	A2
FISHER RD	MCO	48	B4
FISHER RD	TRI	10	E5
FISHERS LANDING	YUMA	110	E4
FISH HATCHRY RD	INY	59	E3
FISH ROCK RD	MEN	31	A4
FISH ROCK RD	MEN	30	D4
FISH SLOUGH RD	MNO	51	D2
FISH SPRINGS RD	INY	59	E1
FISKE	MPA	48	E1
FISKE	MPA	49	A1
FITCH MTN RD	SON	37	D1
FITZGERALD DR	BUT	25	C2
FITZGERALD RD	SCL	P	D5
FITZGERALD RD	SCL	54	D1
FITZHUGH CK RD	MOD	8	B2
FIVE BRIDGES RD	INY	51	D4
FIVE MILE DR	AMA	40	D2
FIVE MILE CK RD	TUO	41	D4
FIVE MI STA RD	SBD	95	D2
FLAMINGO RD	CLK	210	C2
FLANAGAN RD	SHA	18	C1
FLANNERY RD	SOL	39	B3
FLATTOP MTN RD	KIN	67	A4
FLEA VALLEY RD	BUT	25	D2
FLEMING AV E	VAL	134	E3
FLEMING RD	PLA	34	A3
FLETCHER DR	LACO	Q	E3
FLETCHER PKWY	SDCO	V	D3
FLETCHER PKWY	SDCO	111	E1
FLINT AV	KIN	67	C1
FLINT AV	MCO	47	E5
FLINT AV	MCO	48	A4
FLINT ST	KER	80	C5
FLOOD RD	IMP	110	D5
FLOOD RD	SJCO	40	C5
FLORADALE AV	SB	86	B3
FLORAL AV	C	124	D1
FLORAL AV	FRCO	56	D4
FLORAL AV	FRCO	57	B4
FLORENCE AV	ING	188	E5
FLORENCE AV	LACO	97	D2
FLORENCE AV	LACO	Q	D5
FLORES AV	TEH	18	D5
FLORES RD	YUB	34	A1
FLORIDA AV	RCO	99	D4
FLORIDA DR	SD	216	A2
FLORIDA ST	VAL	134	C4
FLORIN RD	SAC	40	A1
FLORIN MILL RD	SHA	13	D3
FLORIN PERKINS	SAC	40	A2
FLOURNOY AV	TEH	24	D2
FLOWER ST	LA	185	E4
FLOWER ST	SA	196	A3
FLOWERS LN	SHA	18	B3
FLOWING WELLS	IMP	109	B3
FLOYD AV	FRCO	57	B3
FLOYD AV	STA	47	D2
FLYNN RD	INY	51	D4
FLYNN CREEK RD	MEN	30	D2
FOAM ST	MONT	167	E2
FOAM ST	MON	53	E2
FOBES RANCH RD	RCO	100	C4
FOGARTY RD	STA	47	E1
FOGARTY RD	STA	48	A1
FOGG RD	SAC	39	E2
FOLETTA RD	MON	54	D5
FOLEY AV	KER	79	D3
FOLSOM AV	AUB	126	C5
FOLSOM AV	FRCO	56	B2
FOLSOM BLVD	SAC	34	B5
FOLSOM BLVD	SAC	39	E1
FOLSOM BLVD	SAC	40	A1
FOLSOM BLVD	SCTO	137	E4
FONSECA RD	COL	24	E5
FONTANA AV	SBD	99	A2
FOOLISH PLSR RD	RCO	107	A1
FOOTE RD	SIE	26	C5
FOOTHILL AV	O	159	D1
FOOTHILL BLVD	ALA	146	D1
FOOTHILL BLVD	BUT	25	D4
FOOTHILL BLVD	CLA	203	C1
FOOTHILL BLVD	CPTO	149	A5
FOOTHILL BLVD	H	146	E2
FOOTHILL BLVD	LACO	89	C5
FOOTHILL BLVD	LACO	89	E5
FOOTHILL BLVD	LACO	98	B1
FOOTHILL BLVD	LACO	Q	B1
FOOTHILL BLVD	LACO	U	A1
FOOTHILL BLVD	NAP	133	B4
FOOTHILL BLVD	O	158	B3
FOOTHILL BLVD	ORCO	T	E3
FOOTHILL BLVD	ROC	204	B1
FOOTHILL BLVD	SBD	99	A1
FOOTHILL BLVD	SD	212	B1
FOOTHILL BLVD	SDCO	V	A2
FOOTHILL BLVD	SDCO	106	C5
FOOTHILL BLVD	SNLO	172	A2
FOOTHILL BLVD	UPL	203	C1
FOOTHILL BLVD	UPL	204	B1
FOOTHILL DR	SBD	102	C1
FOOTHILL DR	SIS	4	A4
FOOTHILL DR	SOL	39	A2
FOOTHILL EXPWY	PA	147	C5
FOOTHILL EXPWY	SCL	N	E3
FOOTHILL EXPWY	SCL	45	E4
FOOTHILL EXPWY	SCCO	149	A4
FOOTHILL FRWY	LACO	97	D1
FOOTHILL FRWY	LACO	98	A1
FOOTHILL FRWY	LACO	R	B2
FOOTHILL FRWY	LACO	R	C3
FOOTHILL FRWY	PAS	190	B2
FOOTHILL RD	ALA	P	B1
FOOTHILL RD	ALA	46	B2
FOOTHILL RD	DGL	36	B3
FOOTHILL RD	INY	59	E3
FOOTHILL RD	MNO	51	C1
FOOTHILL RD	MON	64	E1
FOOTHILL RD	MON	65	A1
FOOTHILL RD	SBD	91	D4
FOOTHILL RD	SBD	92	A4
FOOTHILL RD	SLO	76	A3
FOOTHILL RD	STB	174	B1
FOOTHILL RD	SB	87	D1
FOOTHILL RD	SB	174	B1
FOOTHILL RD	SCL	P	E5
FOOTHILL RD	SCL	54	D1
FOOTHILL RD	TEH	18	E5
FOOTHILL RD	VEN	88	B4
FOOTHILL RD	VEN	88	B5
FOOTHILL TRANS-			
-CORRRIDOR	ORCO	98	E4
FOPPIANO LN	SJCO	40	B5
FORBES N	PLA	34	B3
FORBES S	PLA	34	A3
FORBES AV	SR	139	C3
FORBESTOWN RD	BUT	25	E4
FORBESTOWN RD	BUT	26	A4
FRBSTOWN RES RD	BUT	26	A4
FORD RD	NB	200	B3
FORD ST	RCO	100	E3
FORD ST	SBD	99	C2
FORDYCE LAKE RD	NEV	27	B5
FOREMAN CIR RD	BUT	25	D4
FOREST	MPA	49	D3
FOREST AV	MONT	53	D2
FOREST AV	PAC	167	C3
FOREST BLVD	KER	80	B4
FOREST CIR	BUT	25	C2
FOREST DR	BUT	25	C2
FOREST RD	CAR	168	C4
FOREST TR	ML	164	B1
FOREST HOME BL	SBD	99	E2
FORST HM CRBNDL	AMA	40	D2
FOREST HOUSE	SIS	3	E4
FOREST LAKE	SJCO	40	A3
FOREST LAWN DR	LA	179	E5
FOREST LAWN DR	LA	181	C1
FOREST LAWN DR	LACO	Q	D3
FOREST RANCH RD	BUT	25	C2
FOREST RANCH WY	BUT	25	C2
FORGAY RD	PLU	20	D5
FORREST ST	BKD	166	C4
FORRESTER RD	IMP	109	A4
FORSMANS PL	NEV	128	A4
FORSYTHE RD	YUB	26	A5
FT BRAGG SHERWD	MEN	22	C5
FT CADY RD	SBD	92	C1
FORT INDEPNDNCE	INY	59	E3
FORTNA RD	SUT	33	C2
FORT ROMIE RD	MON	64	E1
FORT ROMIE RD	MON	65	A1
FORT ROSS RD	SON	37	B1
FORT SAGE RD	LAS	21	E5
FORT SEWARD RD	HUM	16	C5
FORT STOCKTN DR	SD	213	B5
FORT STOCKTN DR	SDCO	V	B3
FORT STOCKTN DR	SDCO	111	C1
FORT TEJON RD	LACO	90	B3
FORTUNA BLVD	HUM	15	E2
FORTY MILE RD	YUB	33	D3
FORTYNINE LN	MOD	7	D3
FORTYNINE PALMS	SBD	101	B1
FORWARD RD	TEH	19	B3
FORWARDS MILL	SHA	19	C3
FOSS RD	JKSN	3	D1
FOSS HILL	SON	32	A5
FOSSIL BED RD	SBD	81	C5
FOSTER	MON	54	C4
FOSTER RD	LACO	R	B5
FOSTER RD	LACO	S	E1
FOSTER RD	LACO	T	A1
FOSTER RD	NAP	133	B5
FOSTER RD	SHA	18	B3
FOSTER RD	SIS	4	C3
FOSTER CITY BL	FCTY	145	D2
FOSTER CITY BL	SMCO	N	D3
FOSTER CITY BL	SMCO	45	D3
FOSTER MTN RD	MEN	23	B5
FOULDS RD	IMP	108	E3
FOULKE LN	SIS	4	B5
FOUNTAIN AV	LA	182	A4
FOUNTN HOUSE RD	YUB	26	B5
FOUR CORNERS RD	LAS	14	B3
FOUR MILE RD	COL	24	E5
FOUR MILE RD	COL	32	E1
FOUR MIL RDG RD	BUT	25	E3
FOURTEENTH ST	EUR	121	B2
FOURTH AV	SUT	33	D3
FOURTH ST	C	124	B5
FOUSSAT RD	SDCO	106	B3
FOUTS SPGS RD	COL	24	A5
FOWLER AV	FRCO	57	D2
FOWLER AV	FRCO	57	D5
FOWLER RD	PLA	34	B3
FOWLER PBLC CMP	SIS	13	A2
FOX RD	LAS	21	B4
FOX RD	MCO	48	B4
FOX RD	STA	47	D2
FOX RD	SOL	39	B2
FOXEN CANYON RD	SB	86	D1
FOXWORTHY AV	SCL	P	B4
FOXWORTHY AV	SCL	46	B5
FRAGUERO RD	TUO	41	C5
FRANCESCHI RD	KER	79	D3
FRANCISCO ST	SF	143	A3
FRANCISQUITO AV	LACO	R	E4
FRANCISQITO CYN	LACO	89	C3
FRANCIS SPGS RD	SBD	83	C2
FRANCO WSTRN RD	KER	77	D3
FRANK AV	KER	70	A5
FRANK COX RD	STA	47	B3
FRANKENHEIMR RD	STA	47	E1
FRANKLIN AV	LA	181	E4
FRANKLIN AV	LA	182	A4
FRANKLIN AV	LACO	Q	C4
FRANKLIN AV	YUBA	125	C4
FRANKLIN BLVD	SAC	39	E2
FRANKLIN BLVD	SCTO	137	D5
FRANKLIN RD	MCO	48	B4
FRANKLIN RD	SBD	84	C4
FRANKLIN RD	SUT	33	B2
FRANKLIN RD	SUT	125	A4
FRANKLIN ST	MDO	162	A4
FRANKLIN ST	MONT	167	D3
FRANKLIN ST	MON	53	E3
FRANKLIN ST	SF	143	A4
FRANKLIN CYN RD	M	154	A3
FRANKLIN LEVEE	SUT	33	B2
FRANK SNATRA DR	RCO	100	D4
FRANKWOOD AV	FRCO	58	A4
FRASER RD	KER	78	C3
FRATES RD	SON	L	A1
FRATES RD	SON	38	A3
FRAZIER LN	MEN	23	B2
FRAZIER RD	FRCO	57	E1
FRAZIER RD	SJCO	40	C4
FRAZIER MTN RD	VEN	88	C2
FRAZR MTN PK RD	KER	88	C2
FRAZIER PK RD	SCL	54	D2
FRAZINE RD	STA	47	D2
FREDERICK AV	SJCO	47	B2
FREDERICK ST	RCO	99	C3
FREDERICKSBURG	ALP	36	C4
FREDERICKSON LN	CC	M	C3
FREDERICKSON RD	LAS	8	D5
FRED HAIGHT DR	DN	1	E3
FREDRICKS RD	IMP	109	A4
FREEBORN RD	KER	78	A3
FREEDOM BLVD	SCR	54	B2
FREEMAN FLAT RD	MON	65	C2
FREEMN SCH HSE	TEH	24	C2
FREEMONT BLVD	ALA	P	B2
FREEPORT BLVD	SCTO	137	C5
FREITAS PKWY	MAR	38	B5
FREITAS RD	STA	47	C4
FREMONT AV	KER	79	E2
FREMONT AV	KIN	67	B1
FREMONT AV	LSAL	149	B2
FREMONT AV	LACO	R	B4
FREMONT AV	SCL	P	A3
FREMONT AV	SCL	45	E4
FREMONT AV	SVL	149	B2
FREMONT BLVD	ALA	46	A3
FREMONT DR	SON	L	B1
FREMONT RD	SBD	92	C1
FREMONT RD	SJCO	40	B5
FREMONT ST	CLK	74	D2
FREMONT ST	LV	209	D1
FREMONT ST	SBD	99	D2
FREMONT ST	SF	143	D4
FREMONT ST	S	160	A4
FREMONT PEAK RD	SBD	81	A4
FRENCH AV	BUT	33	C1
FRENCH RD	HUM	16	B5
FRENCH&SUGAR CK	SIS	11	D2
FRENCH BAR RD	AMA	40	E3
FRENCH CAMP RD	HUM	10	C3
FRENCH CAMP RD	SJCO	40	B5
FRENCH CAMP RD	SJCO	47	B1
FRENCH CREEK RD	BUT	25	E3
FRENCH CREEK RD	ED	40	D1
FRENCH CREEK RD	SIS	11	D2
FRENCH FLAT RD	TUO	41	B5
FRENCH GULCH RD	CAL	41	B4
FRENCH GULCH RD	SHA	18	A1
FRENCH HILL RD	DN	2	A3
FRENCHMAN LK RD	PLU	27	D2
FRENCHTOWN RD	YUB	26	A5
FRENZEN RD	COL	32	E3
FRESHWATER RD	COL	32	C2
FRESHWTR KNEELD	HUM	15	E1
FRESHWATER POOL	HUM	16	A1
FRESNO AV	KER	78	B2
FRESNO AV	KER	78	C2
FRESNO AV	SJCO	40	A5
FRESNO RD	MCO	48	D5
FRESNO ST	FRE	165	E2
FRESNO ST	FRCO	57	C3
FRESNO-COALINGA	FRCO	66	E1
FRESNO FLAT RD	MAD	49	D4
FRESZ RD	RCO	106	E1
FREWERT RD	SJCO	47	A1
FREY AV	KER	77	E2
FREY AV	KER	78	A2
FREY RANCH RD	BUT	26	B3
FRIANT RD	FRCO	57	C2
FRIANT RD	MAD	57	D2
FRIARS RD	SD	213	A4
FRIARS RD	SD	214	D2
FRIARS RD	SDCO	V	B3
FRIARS RD	SDCO	111	D1
FRIARS RD	SDCO	214	B3
FRICOT CITY RD	CAL	41	B4
FRIDAY RIDGE RD	HUM	10	C5
FRIEDRICH RD	TRI	16	E1
FRIEL RD	CLO	33	A3
FRINK RD	IMP	109	A2
FRISBY RD	SHA	19	A1
FRITZ DR	TUL	68	D1
FRONT ST	DN	1	D4
FRONT ST	LA	191	A3
FRONT ST	SAL	171	C4
FRONT ST	SF	143	D3
FRONT ST	SC	169	D3
FRONT ST	SOL	39	C4
FRONTAGE RD	CAL	41	A3
FRONTIER RD	SBD	91	C2
FRUCHTENICHT RD	COL	33	B3
FRUDDEN RD	MON	65	D4
FRUIT AV	FRE	165	B2
FRUIT AV	FRCO	57	C4
FRUIT AV	FRCO	57	C5
FRUIT AV	STA	47	B3
FRUIT ST	SA	196	D3
FRUITLAND AV	MCO	48	A4
FRUITLAND RD	YUB	33	D1
FRUITRIDGE RD	SAC	39	E1
FRUITRIDGE RD	SAC	40	A1
FRUITVALE AV	ALA	L	D4
FRUITVALE AV	ALA	45	D1
FRUITVALE AV	KER	78	D3
FRUITVALE AV	O	158	E4
FRUITVALE AV	O	159	B1
FRUITVALE AV	SCL	P	A4
FRUITVALE RD	BUT	25	B4
FRUITVALE RD	PLA	34	B3

STREET	CO.	PAGE	GRID
FRY RD	SOL	39	B2
FRYMIRE RD	STA	48	A1
FUENTE ST	ORCO	T	C1
FUERTE DR	SDCO	V	E3
FUERTE DR	SDCO	111	E1
FUGLER RD	SB	86	C1
FULKERTH RD	STA	47	C3
FULLEN RD	CAL	41	C3
FULLER LN	AMA	40	E3
FULLER RD	INY	59	E1
FULLERTON RD	LACO	98	B2
FULLERTON RD	LACO	R	E5
FULMOR RD	HUM	15	D2
FULMOR TOPPEN	HUM	15	D2
FULTON AV	SAC	40	A1
FULTON LN	NAPA	29	C2
FULTON RD	SON	37	E2
FULTON ST	B	156	A3
FULTON ST	SF	141	D4
FULTON ST	SF	142	A3
FULTON ST	SF	143	A5
FULTON ST	SFCO	L	B5
FULTON ST	SFCO	45	B1
FULTON ST	S	160	B2
FULTON ST N	FRE	165	C3
FULWEILER AV	AUB	126	B3
FURLONG AV	SCL	54	D2
FURNACE CK RD	SBD	91	E4
FURNC CK WSH RD	INY	72	C2
FURNC CK WSH RD	INY	73	A4
FUZZY LN	SHA	18	C3
G			
G ST	DVS	136	D3
G ST	FRE	165	C4
G ST	HUM	9	E5
G ST	HUM	10	A5
G ST	MER	170	D4
G ST	MCO	48	C4
G ST	MCO	48	C4
G ST	SCTO	137	C2
GABY AV	COL	32	E3
GADDINI	SOL	39	A1
GAFFERY RD	STA	47	A3
GAFFEY ST	LA	191	A5
GAFFEY ST	LACO	S	C3
GAFFNEY RD	YOL	39	D2
GAGE AV	LACO	Q	E5
GAGE RD	BUT	25	C4
GAINES LN	SHA	18	D3
GALE AV	FRCO	66	C2
GALE RD	SBD	91	E2
GALENA ST	RCO	99	A2
GALENA CYN RD	INY	72	A3
GALEPPI RD	LAS	21	C4
GALLAGHER AV	TEH	24	D2
GALLAGHER RD	SUT	33	E3
GALLATIN RD	LAS	20	D2
GALLATIN RD	TEH	24	C1
GALLAWAY RD	SIE	26	D4
GALLINAS AV	SR	139	B1
GALLOPADE TR	SBD	80	E1
GALVEZ AV	FRCO	56	B2
GAMBLE RD	MCO	48	B3
GAMMA GULCH RD	SBD	100	D1
GAMMEL RD	SBD	101	C1
GANESHA BLVD	LACO	U	B2
GANGER RD	SIS	5	D2
GANN RD	CAL	40	E4
GAP FOLSOM RD	CAL	41	C2
GARAPATOS RD	MON	64	B1
GARATE RD	LAS	8	C5
GARBAGE DUMP RD	LAS	14	B3
GARBAGE PIT RD	MNO	43	B3
GARBAGE PIT RD	MNO	50	D1
GARBONI RD	RCO	99	D4
GARCES HWY	KER	67	E5
GARCES HWY	KER	68	C5
GARCES HWY	KER	69	A5
GARCIA RIVER RD	MEN	30	C3
GARDEN DR	LAK	31	D2
GARDEN HWY	SAC	39	D1
GARDEN HWY	SUT	33	D2
GARDEN HWY	SUT	125	D5
GARDEN HWY	YUBA	125	E4
GARDEN RD	SDCO	106	E4
GARDEN ST	STB	174	B3
GARDENA BLVD	LACO	S	C1
GARDEN BAR RD	PLA	34	B3
GARDEN BAR RD	NEV	34	B2
GARDENDALE ST	LACO	R	B5
GARDENDALE ST	LACO	S	E1
GARDEN GROVE BL	GGR	195	A2
GARDEN GROVE BL	ORA	195	D2
GARDEN GROVE BL	ORCO	98	B4
GARDEN GROVE BL	ORCO	T	C2
GARDEN GROVE FY	GGR	195	B2
GARDEN GROVE FY	ORA	195	B2
GARDEN GROVE FY	ORA	196	C1
GARDEN GROVE FY	ORCO	98	B4
GARDEN GROVE FY	ORCO	T	C3
GARDEN TRACT RD	CC	L	C3
GARDEN VLY RD	ED	34	D4
GARDEN VLY RD	YUB	26	B5
GARDINER FRY RD	TEH	24	E2
GARDNER AV	MCO	48	C4
GARDNER LN	CAL	41	B4
GARDNER ST	LA	184	B1
GARDNER ST	VAL	134	B3
GARDNER FLD RD	KER	78	A4
GAREY AV	LACO	98	D2
GAREY AV	LACO	U	C3
GAREY AV	SB	86	C1
GARFIELD AV	FRCO	57	B3
GARFIELD AV	FRCO	57	B5
GARFIELD AV	LACO	98	A2
GARFIELD AV	LACO	R	B5
GARFIELD AV	LACO	S	D1
GARFIELD AV	ORCO	98	B4
GARFIELD AV	ORCO	T	B3
GARFIELD AV	SAC	34	A5
GARFIELD ST	RCO	101	C5
GARIN RD	MON	54	C2
GARLAND RD	BUT	25	C2
GARLOCK RD	KER	80	D2
GARMIRE RD	SUT	33	B2
GARNER LN	BUT	25	A2
GARNER PL	CAL	40	D4
GARNER RD	STA	47	D2
GARNET AV	SD	212	A1
GARNET AV	SDCO	V	A2
GARNET AV	SDCO	106	C5
GARNET ST	SBD	99	D2
GARNETT LN	SOL	39	B2
GARNIER RD	LAS	21	D5
GARRARD	CC	38	C5
GARRET	PLA	34	D2
GARRETT DR	RCO	100	A5
GARRISON AV	STA	47	C2
GARST RD	IMP	109	A3
GARST RD	STA	47	D2
GARVEY AV	LACO	98	A2
GARVEY AV	LACO	R	C4
GARVEY RD	IMP	108	E4
GARWOOD RD	SUT	33	D4
GARZOLI AV	KER	78	B1
GAS COMPANY RD	KER	78	A4
GASKELL RD	KER	89	B2
GASKELL RD	KER	89	D1
GAS LINE RD	RCO	102	B5
GASPERS RD	SHA	18	D2
GAS POINT RD	SHA	18	B3
GASQUET FLAT RD	DN	2	A3
GASTENBIDE RD	MCO	55	C2
GASTON RD	NEV	26	E5
GATES RD	STA	47	B2
GATES RD	TRI	16	D1
GATES CANYON RD	SOL	38	E2
GATEWAY	CC	39	D5
GATEWAY BLVD	LA	180	D5
GATEWAY BLVD	KER	80	E1
GATEWAY RD	CC	M	D3
GATOS TR	SBD	100	E1
GAVILAN DR	RCO	99	B3
GAVIOTA	AVLN	97	A4
GAVIOTA BCH RD	SB	86	D4
GAVIOTA STA RD	SB	86	D4
GAVILAN RD	SDCO	106	C1
GAWNE CARTER RD	SJCO	40	C5
GAWNE CARTER RD	SJCO	47	C1
GAZELLE CALLAHN	SIS	4	B5
GAZELLE CALLAHN	SIS	11	E2
GAZELLE CALLAHN	SIS	12	A1
GAZELLE MTN LKT	SIS	12	A1
GAZOS CREEK RD	SMCO	N	C4
GAZOS CREEK RD	SMCO	45	C5
G-BAR-T RCH RD	MNO	44	C5
G-BAR-T RCH RD	MNO	51	C1
GEARY BLVD	SF	141	A3
GEARY BLVD	SF	142	A3
GEARY BLVD	SFCO	L	B4
GEARY BLVD	SFCO	45	B1
GEARY RD	CC	L	E3
GEARY RD	CC	M	A3
GEARY RD	CC	38	E5
GEARY ST	SF	143	A4
GECKO RD	IMP	109	D4
GEER AV	MCO	47	D4
GEER RD	STA	47	E3
GELDING RD	CAL	41	B4
GENASCI RD	SIE	27	C3
GENE AUTRY TR	PMSP	206	E2
GENERL BEALE RD	KER	79	A3
GENRL PETROLEUM	KER	79	E5
GENRL PETROLEUM	KER	80	A5
GENRL PETROLEUM	KER	89	C1
GENERALS HWY	TUL	58	E3
GENERALS HWY	TUL	59	A5
GENESEE AV	SD	211	E1
GENESEE AV	SD	213	C1
GENESEE AV	SDCO	V	B2
GENESEE AV	SDCO	106	C5
GENESEE RD	PLU	26	D1
GENESEE INDN CK	PLU	26	E1
GENESEO RD	SLO	76	B1
GENEVA AV	KIN	67	C1
GENOA LN	DGL	36	C3
GENTRY RD	IMP	109	A3
GENTRY RD	INY	72	E4
GENTRY RD	INY	73	A4
GEORGE RD	IMP	112	A4
GEORGE SMITH RD	FRCO	58	B3
GEORGETOWN	ED	34	E3
GEORGETOWN RD	ED	34	E4
GEORGETOWN RD	PLCV	138	C1
GEO WSHNTN BL S	SUT	33	C3
GEORGIA LN	STA	47	E2
GEORGIA RD	SBD	81	C5
GEORGIA ST	VAL	134	C4
GEORGIA ST	SOL	L	D2
GEORGIA SLID RD	ED	34	E3
GEPHART RD	KER	80	D5
GERARD AV	MCO	48	C4
GERBER RD	SAC	40	A2
GERBER RD	TEH	24	D1
GERKIN RD	INY	51	D4
GERRIE LN	RCO	107	C1
GETTYSBURG AV	FRCO	56	C3
GETTYSBURG AV	FRCO	57	A3
GEYSERS RD	SON	31	C4
GEYSRS RESRT RD	SON	31	D4
GHOST TOWN RD	SBD	92	A1
GIANT RD	CC	L	C3
GIANT ROCK RD	SBD	92	E5
GIANT ROCK RD	SBD	93	A5
GIBRALTAR RD	SB	87	C3
GIBSON RD	COL	32	D2
GIBSON RD	YOL	33	B5
GIBSON CYN RD	SOL	39	A2
GIDDINGS AV	TUL	68	B1
GIELOW LN	MEN	31	B2
GIFFORD RD	SUT	33	C4
GILBERT RD	STA	47	D1
GILLAM RD	CAL	40	E3
GILLESPIE RD	IMP	109	A2
GILLESPIE ST	STB	174	A4
GILLETT RD	IMP	109	B5
GILLETT RD	MON	65	C4
GILLETTE RD	KER	79	D3
GILLETTE RD	MCO	48	D5
GILLILAND RD	LAS	8	C5
GILLIS CYN RD	SLO	76	D1
GILLMAN AV	KER	89	D1
GILL RANCH RD	PLU	26	E2
GILL STA COSO	INY	70	C3
GILMAN DR	SD	211	C2
GILMAN DR	SDCO	V	A2
GILMAN DR	SDCO	106	C5
GILMAN RD	SCL	54	D2
GILMAN RD	SHA	12	D4
GILMAN SPGS RD	RCO	99	D3
GILMORE	SJCO	40	C4
GILMORE RCH RD	TEH	18	D5
GILROY HT SP RD	SCL	54	D1
GIRARD LO RD	SHA	12	C3
GIRARD LOOKOUT	SHA	12	C3
GIRARD RIDGE RD	SHA	12	C4
GIRAUDO RD	KER	79	B4
GIRD RD	SDCO	106	C2
GIRDNER RD	SUT	33	B2
GIRVAN RD	SHA	18	C2
GISH ST	SJ	152	A2
GIVENS LUSTR RD	MCO	48	C5
GLACIER LODG RD	INY	51	D5
GLACIER PT RD	MPA	49	D2
GLACIER PT RD	MPA	63	C5
GLADDING RD	PLA	34	A3
GLADSTONE ST	LACO	U	A2
GLASSCOCK RD	SJCO	39	D4
GLASSELL ST	ORA	194	C4
GLASSELL ST	ORA	196	C1
GLASSELL ST	ORCO	98	C3
GLASSELL ST	ORCO	T	D2
GLASS FLOW RD	MNO	50	D1
GLEASON RD	SBD	92	D5
GLEN AV	MER	170	E4
GLEN RD	SB	87	B4
GLEN ALPINE RD	ED	35	E4
GLEN ANNIE RD	SB	87	B4
GLEN ARBOR RD	SCR	N	E5
GLEN ARBOR RD	SCR	P	A5
GLEN ARBOR RD	SCR	53	E1
GLENBURN RD	SHA	13	D4
GLEN CANYON RD	SCR	54	A1
GLENCO AV	GLE	24	D3
GLENDALE AV	LACO	97	E1
GLENDALE AV	LACO	Q	E3
GLENDALE BLVD	LA	182	E3
GLENDALE BLVD	LA	185	E2
GLENDALE BLVD	LACO	Q	E3
GLENDALE DR	HUM	10	A5
GLENDALE FRWY	LACO	R	A3
GLENDORA AV	LACO	98	B2
GLENDORA AV	LACO	U	A2
GLENDORA MTN RD	LACO	98	C1
GLENDORA MTN RD	LACO	U	A1
GLENISON GAP RD	TRI	17	C1
GLENN AV	FRCO	66	E3
GLENN DR	GLE	24	A4
GLENN RD	TEH	24	C2
GLENN RD E	COL	25	A5
GLENN RD W	COL	24	D5
GLENN-ALLEN AV	KER	68	D5
GLENN COOLDG DR	SC	169	A2
GLENN COOLDG DR	SCR	169	A2
GLENNDENNING RD	SIS	3	D5
GLENN M ANDERSN			
-FWY & TRANSIT	LACO	Q	C5
GLENOAKS BLVD	BUR	179	C1
GLENOAKS BLVD	LA	179	C1
GLENOAKS BLVD	LACO	89	D5
GLENOAKS BLVD	LACO	97	D1
GLENOAKS BLVD	LACO	Q	C1
GLENOAKS RD	RCO	99	D5
GLENSHIRE DR	NEV	27	D5
GLENWOOD DR	SCR	54	A1
GLENWOOD LN	FRCO	58	B1
GLOBE DR	TUL	69	A3
GLOBE MINE RD	SBD	84	A5
GLORIA RD	MON	54	E5
GLORIA RD	MON	55	A5
GLORIETTA BLVD	CC	L	E4
GLORIETTA BLVD	CC	45	D1
G-O RD	DN	2	B4
GOAT MTN RD	COL	32	A1
GOAT MTN RD	SBD	100	E1
GOBBI ST	U	123	C4
GOBLE LN	HUM	15	D2
GODDELL RD	CAL	40	E3
GODFREY AV	SCL	P	E5
GODFREY RCH RD	SLO	75	E1
GODLEY RD	PLA	34	B3
GODWIN RD	SBD	101	C1
GOETZ RD	RCO	99	C4
GOFFS RD	SBD	94	D2
GOFFS RD	SBD	95	A1
GOGNA	SJCO	40	B5
GOLD CROWN RD	RCO	101	E2
GOLD CROWN RD	SBD	101	E1
GOLDEN AV	SBD	99	C1
GOLDEN RD	SIS	5	D2
GOLDEN ST	SBD	100	E1
GOLDEN CYN RD	INY	72	A1
GOLDEN CTR FRWY	GV	127	D3
GOLDEN CTR FRWY	NEV	128	A4
GOLDEN EAGLE AV	PLU	26	C1
GOLDEN GATE AV	SF	142	A3
GOLDEN GATE AV	SF	143	A5
GOLDEN GATE DR	HUM	16	B3
GOLDEN GATE RD	MNO	42	D1
GOLDENROD AV	FRCO	57	A4
GOLDEN SPGS DR	LACO	U	B3
GOLDEN STATE AV	BKD	166	C2
GOLDEN STATE BL	FRCO	57	E5
GOLDEN STATE BL	STA	47	D3
GOLDEN STATE DR	MAD	57	A2
GOLDEN STATE FY	BUR	179	C1
GOLDEN STATE FY	LA	179	C1
GOLDEN STATE FY	LA	182	D1
GOLDEN STATE FY	LA	186	D3
GOLDEN STATE FY	LACO	89	B4
GOLDEN STATE FY	LACO	97	D1
GOLDEN STATE FY	LACO	Q	B1
GOLDN TROUT CRS	BUT	26	B4
GOLDENWEST AV	ORCO	98	B4
GOLDEN WEST ST	ORCO	T	B3
GOLD HILL RD	ED	34	D4
GOLDHILL RD	PLA	34	B3
GOLD HILL RD	SOL	38	D4
GOLD HILL RD	VEN	88	D2
GOLD LAKE RD	PLU	27	A3
GOLD LAKE RD	SIE	27	A3
GOLD LK FOREST	PLU	26	E3
GOLD PARK	SBD	101	C2
GOLD RCK RCH RD	IMP	110	B5
GOLD RUN RD	LAS	20	E3
GOLDRUSH RD	RCO	107	B1
GOLDSBOROUGH GL	SHA	17	D3
GOLD STONE LN	SHA	18	B2
GOLDSTONE RD	SBD	81	E3
GOLD STRIKE RD	CAL	41	A3
GOLER RD	KER	80	E2
GOLF RD	MCO	48	C4
GOLF CLUB RD	CC	L	E3
GOLF CLUB RD	CC	M	A3
GOLF COURSE RD	HUM	10	A5
GOLF LINKS RD	AVLN	97	B5
GOLF LINK RD	MCO	47	E4
GOLF LINKS RD	ALA	L	E5
GOLF LINKS RD	ALA	45	E1
GOMAN AV	TUL	70	A3
GOMER AV	KER	78	A1
GOMEZ RD	SHA	13	D4
GONDER RD	IMP	109	B4
GONSALVES RD	TEH	18	C5
GONZAGA RD	MCO	55	C1
GONZALES RD	MCO	55	C2
GONZALES RD	VEN	88	B5
GONZALES RD	VEN	96	B1
GONZALES RIV RD	MON	54	E5
GOODALE RD	INY	59	E2
GOODE HILL RD	LACO	89	E3
GOODENOUGH RD	VEN	88	D4
GOODFELLOW AV	FRCO	57	E4
GOODWATER AV	SHA	18	C2
GOODWIN DR	SBD	91	A4
GOODWIN RD	STA	47	D2
GOODYEAR RD	SOL	38	E4
GOODYEAR CK RD	SIE	26	D4
GOOLSBY RCH RD	MNO	51	C1
GOOSE CREEK RD	AMA	40	C3
GOOSE HAVEN RD	SOL	39	B3
GOOSE RANCH RD	TRI	17	D1
GOOSE VALLEY RD	SHA	13	C4
GOPHER CYN RD	SDCO	106	C2
GOPHR HLL LNDFL	PLU	26	C1
GORDEN RD	HUM	16	C2
GORDONS FRRY RD	SIS	3	A3
GORDON VLY RD	NAPA	38	E3
GORDON VLY RD	SOL	L	E1
GORDON VLY RD	SOL	38	E3
GORGE RD	INY	51	C3
GORMAN RANCH	PLA	34	E3
GOSFORD RD	KER	78	C3
GOSS RD	SBD	90	E4
GOUDIE TRUCK TR	SDCO	107	C5
GOUGER NECK RD	MOD	14	B3
GOUGH ST	SF	142	C2
GOUGH ST	SF	143	A4
GOULD AV	LACO	S	B1
GOULD RD	COL	32	E1
GOULD RD	LPAZ	104	A2
GOVE RD	MCO	48	B5
GOVER RD	SHA	18	D3
GOVERNOR DR	SD	211	D2
GOVERNOR DR	SDCO	V	B2
GOVERNOR DR	SDCO	106	C5
GOVERNOR MN RD	LACO	89	E4
GOWER ST	LA	181	E5
GOWLING RD	IMP	109	B5
G P RD	KER	77	C1
GRACE RESORT RD	SHA	19	B3
GRACIE RD	NEV	34	C1
GRACIOSA RD	SB	86	C2
GRAEAGLE RD	SIE	26	E3
GRAEAGLE RD	SIE	27	A3
GRAEAGL JHNSVLL	PLU	26	E2
GRAESER RD	IMP	112	C3
GRAHAM	SIS	12	C1
GRAHAM AV	RCO	99	B4
GRAHAM RD	FRCO	57	A4
GRAHAM RD	IMP	111	E3
GRAHAM RD	SJCO	40	B3
GRAHAM RD	TEH	19	B3
GRAHAM HILL RD	SC	169	D1
GRAHAM HILL RD	SCR	54	A1
GRAHAM HILL RD	SCR	169	D1
GRAHAM PASS RD	RCO	109	E1
GRAINLAND RD	BUT	25	A4
GRAMERCY DR	SD	214	B1
GRAMERCY DR	SDCO	V	C2
GRAMERCY DR	SDCO	111	D1
GRANADA AV	SAL	171	D2
GRAND AV	ALA	L	D4
GRAND AV	BUT	25	C4
GRAND AV	ELS	189	A3
GRAND AV	LA	185	D4
GRAND AV	LACO	97	E2
GRAND AV	LACO	98	C2
GRAND AV	LACO	Q	C5
GRAND AV	LACO	U	A2
GRAND AV	LACO	S	A1
GRAND AV	O	158	A2
GRAND AV	ORCO	98	C4
GRAND AV	ORCO	T	D3
GRAND AV	PAS	190	A5
GRAND AV	P	158	C1
GRAND AV	RCO	99	D4
GRAND AV	RCO	99	B4
GRAND AV	RCO	99	E4
GRAND AV	SA	196	D4
GRAND AV	SA	198	D1
GRAND AV	SD	212	B2
GRAND AV	SDCO	V	A3
GRAND AV	SNLO	172	D1
GRAND AV	SLO	76	B4
GRAND AV	SMCO	L	B5
GRAND AV	SMCO	N	B1
GRAND AV	SMCO	45	C2
GRAND AV	SR	139	D3
GRAND AV	SB	86	E3
GRAND AV	TUL	68	D3
GRAND AV	VEN	88	D4
GRAND AV	YUB	33	D2
GRAND AV E	SSF	144	C1
GRAND AV W	O	157	D2
GRAND ST	MDO	162	C3
GRAND CIRCLE BL	RCO	U	E5
GRANDE AV	DVS	136	C1
GRANDE PUMICE	MOD	8	A1
GRAND ISLAND RD	SAC	M	E1
GRAND ISLAND RD	SAC	39	C4
GRANDON RD	RCO	107	C1
GRAND VIEW AV	LACO	R	C2
GRANDVILLE RD	MCO	56	B2
GRANGE RD	LAK	32	B4
GRANGE RD	SOL	M	A1
GRANGE RD	SON	38	A2
GRANGE RD	TEH	24	D2
GRANGER CK RD	MOD	8	D1
GRANGEVILLE BL	KIN	67	C1
GRANGEVLLE BYPS	KIN	67	B1
GRANITE RD	KER	78	D1
GRANITE RD	KER	79	A1
GRANITE RD	MAD	49	B5
GRANITE RD	SBD	92	A4
GRANITE CK RD	SCR	54	A2
GRNIT MTN VW RD	SDCO	107	D3
GRANITE SPGS RD	MPA	48	D2
GRANITE VIEW RD	INY	60	A4
GRANITEVILLE RD	NEV	27	A4
GRANIT WELLS RD	SBD	81	A3
GRANT AV	ALCO	146	A2
GRANT AV	COL	32	E3
GRANT AV	SF	143	C2
GRANT RD	LSAL	149	A3
GRANT RD	MCO	56	C1
GRANT RD	MVW	148	A5
GRANT RD	SCL	N	E3
GRANT RD	SCL	P	A3
GRANT RD	SCL	45	E4
GRANT ST	RCO	101	C5
GRANT ST	SM	145	A2
GRANT ST	SMA	173	B1
GRANT LAKE RD	MNO	50	C1
GRANTLAND AV	FRCO	57	B2
GRANTLAND AV	FRCO	67	B1
GRANT LINE RD	SAC	40	A2
GRANT LINE RD	SJCO	47	A2
GRAPE WY	BUT	25	A3
GRAPEFRUIT BLVD	RCO	101	B4
GRAPEVNE CYN RD	KER	70	C5
GRAPEVNE CYN RD	SBD	91	D5
GRAPEVINE GULCH	AMA	40	D3
GRAPP LN	RCO	107	C1
GRASS RD	SBD	100	A1
GRASSHOPPR RD S	LAS	8	A5
GRASSHOPPR RD S	LAS	14	E5
GRASSHOPPER FLT	TRI	11	C5
GRASS VALLEY RD	SBT	54	E3
GRASS VALLEY RD	SBT	55	A3
GRATON RD	SON	37	D2
GRATTON RD	STA	47	E3
GRAVEL PIT RD	RCO	103	C5

255
GRAVEN RES RD

STREET INDEX

HESPERIAN BLVD

Thomas Bros. Maps® COPYRIGHT 1997

STREET	CO.	PAGE	GRID
GRAVEN RES RD	MOD	8	A2
GRAVEN RES RD	MOD	14	E2
GRAVES RD	SJCO	47	B1
GRAVEYARD GULCH	SIS	3	C4
GRAY AV	YUBA	125	C2
GRAYSON	CC	38	E5
GRAYSON RD	STA	47	B3
GREAT CIR DR	KER	80	B4
GREAT HWY	SFCO	L	B5
GREAT HWY	SFCO	45	B2
GREAT NORTHERN	MOD	5	E3
GREAT SO OVRLND	SDCO	108	A5
GREELEY RD	KER	78	C3
GREELY HILL RD	MPA	48	E1
GREELY HILL RD	MPA	49	A1
GREEN RD	COL	32	D3
GREEN RD	IMP	109	C4
GREEN RD	SAC	40	B2
GREEN RD	SBD	90	D4
GREENBACK LN	SAC	34	B5
GREENBAY RD	COL	32	E3
GREENFIELD AV	VAL	134	D3
GREENFIELD DR	SDCO	107	A5
GREEN HILL RD	SON	37	D2
GREENHORN RD	NEV	34	C1
GREENHORN RD	SIS	4	A4
GREEN HOUSE RD	MCO	47	E5
GREEN HOUSE RD	MCO	48	A5
GREEN LAKES RD	MNO	43	B4
GREENLEAF AV	LACO	R	C5
GREENLEY RD	TUO	41	C5
GREENLEY RD	TUO	163	D3
GREEN MTN RD	MAD	49	B5
GREEN MTN LKOUT	MPA	49	B5
GREEN RIVER RD	RCO	U	D5
GREEN RIVER RD	RCO	98	D3
GREENSPOT RD	SBD	99	C1
GREENSPOT RD	SBD	99	D2
GREEN SPRING RD	TUO	48	B1
GREENSTONE	ED	34	D5
GREENS WELL RD	SBD	84	A1
GREENTREE BLVD	SBD	91	B4
GREEN VALLEY RD	CC	M	B4
GREEN VALLEY RD	CC	46	A1
GREEN VALLEY RD	ED	34	D5
GREEN VALLEY RD	ED	34	C5
GREEN VALLEY RD	SAC	34	C5
GREEN VALLEY RD	SCR	54	B2
GREEN VALLEY RD	SOL	L	E1
GREEN VALLEY RD	SOL	38	D3
GREEN VALLEY RD	SON	37	D2
GREENVILLE RD	ALA	46	C2
GREENVILLE ST	ORCO	T	C3
GREENVILLE ST	SA	197	D3
GREENVILLE-			
-ROUND VLY RD	PLU	20	C5
GREENVILLE-			
-WOLF CREEK RD	PLU	20	C5
GREENWALD AV	RCO	99	B4
GREENWOOD AV	FRCO	57	E4
GREENWOOD AV	LACO	R	B4
GREENWOOD RD	ED	34	D4
GREENWOOD RD	SJCO	47	A2
GREENWD HTS DR	HUM	10	A5
GREEN, W S RD	COL	32	E2
GREGORY AV	YOL	39	D1
GREGORY RD	CAL	40	D4
GREGORY CK RD	SHA	12	C5
GREILICH RD	AMA	40	D2
GREVIE RD	COL	33	A3
GREY OWL CT	NEV	127	B1
GRIDER RD	SIS	3	B3
GRIDER CREEK RD	SIS	3	B4
GRIDLEY RD	COL	25	A5
GRIFFIN AV	LA	186	E2
GRIFFIN RD	IMP	109	B4
GRIFFIN RD	STA	47	C2
GRIFFIN ST	SAL	171	D3
GRIFFITH AV	KER	78	B2
GRIFFITH AV	MCO	47	E4
GRIFFITH AV	YUB	33	D2
GRIFFITH PK BL	LA	182	D3
GRIFFITH PK DR	LA	182	D2
GRIFFITH PK DR	LACO	Q	E3
GRIMES AV	STA	47	C2
GRIMES RD	SJCO	46	E1
GRIMES-ARBKL RD	CLU	32	E3
GRIMES CYN RD	VEN	88	D5
GRIMSEL DR	KER	79	C5
GRINDSTONE RD	GLE	23	E3
GRINDSTONE RD	GLE	24	A3
GRIZZLY RD	PLU	27	B2
GRIZZLY RD	TUO	48	D1
GRIZZLY BLUF RD	HUM	15	D2
GRIZZLY GLCH RD	SHA	18	A2
GRIZLY HLL RD N	NEV	26	C5
GRIZZLY ISLD RD	SOL	M	A1
GRIZZLY ISLD RD	SOL	38	E3
GRIZZLY ISLD RD	SOL	39	A3
GRIZZLY ISLD RD	SOL	135	D5
GRIZZLY PEAK BL	B	156	B1
GRIZZLY PEAK BL	CC	156	E2
GRIZZLY PEAK BL	O	156	B1
GRZZLY PK LKOUT	SIS	13	B3
GROOMS	SJCO	47	D1
GROSJEAN	MPA	49	B3
GROTTO CANYON	INY	61	D4
GROUSE CREEK RD	SIS	11	E2
GROUSE RIDGE RD	NEV	27	A5
GROVE AV	GLE	24	D3
GROVE AV	MCO	48	B4
GROVE AV	ONT	204	D3
GROVE AV	ROC	204	D3
GROVE AV	SBD	U	D3
GROVE AV	SBD	98	E2
GROVE AV	U	123	B3
GROVE RD	SUT	33	D3
GROVE ST	ALA	M	A5
GROVE ST	SON	132	A3
GROVE WY	ALA	L	E5
GROVE WY	ALA	P	A1
GROVE WY	ALCO	146	D2
GROVE SHFTR FWY	O	156	B5
GROVE SHFTR FWY	O	157	E3
GROVE SHFTR FWY	O	158	A2
GRUB GULCH RD	MAD	49	B5
GRUBBS RD	BUT	25	D5
GSCHWEND RD	MEN	30	D2
GUADALUPE PKWY	SJ	151	D1
GUADALUPE PKWY	SJ	152	A3
GUADALUPE ST	SB	86	A1
GUALALA LOOKOUT	MEN	30	D4
GUALALA RDG RD	MEN	30	D4
GUERNEVILLE HWY	SON	37	C1
GUERNEVILLE RD	STR	131	A2
GUERNEVILLE RD	SON	37	E2
GUERRERO ST	SF	142	C4
GUERRERO ST	SFCO	L	B5
GUERRERO ST	SFCO	45	C2
GUIBAL AV	SCL	P	E5
GUIBERSON RD	VEN	88	D4
GUIDIVILLE RES	MEN	31	B2
GUINTOLI LN	HUM	9	E5
GULCH RD	TRI	17	B3
GULLETT RD	IMP	109	A5
GULLEY VIEW DR	RCO	107	C1
GULLING ST N	PLU	27	B2
GULLING ST S	PLU	27	B2
GUM AV	GLE	25	A4
GUN CLUB RD	KER	77	E2
GUN CLUB RD	MCO	47	D5
GUNN AV	LACO	R	C5
GUNST RD	HUM	9	E2
GUNST RD	HUM	10	A2
GURR RD	MCO	48	B5
GUTHERIE RD	IMP	108	E5
GUTIERREZ ST	STB	174	C4
GUTTRY RD	LAS	14	B3
GUY KERR RCH RD	HUM	10	C5
GUYS GULCH RD	SIS	4	A5
GWIN MINE RD	CAL	40	E3
GYLE RD	TEH	24	D1
GYPSUM CYN RD	ORCO	U	C5
GYPSUM CYN RD	ORCO	98	D3
H			
H ST	BKD	166	C4
H ST	BEN	153	C5
H ST	EUR	121	D1
H ST	FRE	165	B3
H ST	IMP	109	A4
H ST	KER	78	D3
H ST	MCO	55	D1
H ST	SCTO	137	B2
H ST	SAC	39	E1
H ST	SBD	91	D1
H ST	SDCO	V	C4
H ST	SDCO	106	B4
H ST	SDCO	111	D2
H ST	SR	139	C3
H ST	SB	86	B3
HAAS RD	COL	32	D2
HACIENDA AV	RCO	100	D2
HACIENDA AV	SM	145	A3
HACIENDA BLVD	LACO	98	B2
HACIENDA BLVD	LACO	R	D5
HACIENDA BLVD	KER	80	B4
HACIENDA RD	SHA	18	D3
HACKAMORE PL	MNO	43	A3
HACKETT RD	STA	47	C3
HACKLEMAN RD	IMP	109	A5
HACKMAN RD	SOL	39	C2
HACKNEY DR	MNO	42	E1
HACKSTAFF RD	LAS	21	E5
HAGATA RD	LAS	21	A2
HAGEMAN RD	KER	78	C3
HAGEMAN RD	SUT	33	B2
HAGEN RD	NAPA	38	D3
HAGEN RD	NAPA	133	E2
HAGEN FLAT RD	SHA	13	A4
HAHN RD	COL	32	D3
HAIGHT MTN RD	SIS	5	A5
HAILES RD	VEN	96	C1
HAILLE RD	TEH	25	A2
HALE AV	COL	32	E3
HALE AV	SCL	P	D4
HALE RD	AMA	41	A1
HALEY RD	IMP	109	C3
HALEY RD	MCO	47	C5
HALEY ST	STB	174	C4
HLF MOON BAY RD	SMCO	45	C3
HALFWAY RD	SDCO	107	B2
HALL AV	SJCO	47	D1
HALL RD	LAS	27	E1
HALL RD	MON	54	C3
HALL RD	SON	37	E2
HALL RD	STA	47	E3
HALL RD	STA	48	A2
HALL RD	TEH	24	D2
HALL RD	VEN	88	D4
HALL WY	SHA	19	E2
HALL CITY CK RD	TRI	17	C3
HALLEY RD	SOL	39	A2
HALLOCK	VEN	88	C5
HALLORAN SPG RD	SBD	83	B3
HALLORAN SUMMIT	SBD	83	D2
HALLOWELL RD	STA	47	C4
HALLS FLAT RD	LAS	20	A2
HALLS GRADE RD	RCO	100	B3
HALLWOOD BLVD	YUB	33	D2
HALLWOOD BLVD W	YUB	33	D2
HALSTEAD	SBD	81	C5
HAM LN	SJCO	40	A4
HAMBONE RD	SIS	13	C2
HAMBURG RD	MCO	55	E2
HAMES RD	SCR	54	B4
HAMILTON	ORCO	98	B4
HAMILTON	YOL	39	D2
HAMILTON AV	ORCO	T	B4
HAMILTON AV	SCL	P	B3
HAMILTON AV	SCL	46	A4
HAMILTON AV	TEH	24	D1
HAMILTON RD	DN	1	E4
HAMILTON RD	KER	89	D1
HAMILTON RD	STA	47	B3
HAMILTON RD E	BUT	25	C5
HAMILTON RD W	BUT	25	C5
HAMLTN NORD CNA	BUT	25	A3
HAMLIN RD	BUT	25	C3
HAMLIN GULCH RD	SIS	3	E5
HAMLOW RD	STA	47	E3
HAMMER LN	SJCO	40	A5
HAMMER LOOP RD	TEH	18	A5
HAMMETT RD	STA	47	C2
HAMMIL RD	MNO	51	D2
HAMMONTON RD	YUB	33	E2
HAMMNTN SMRTVLL	YUB	33	E2
HAMNER AV	RCO	U	E4
HAMNER AV	RCO	98	E3
HAMPTON RD	CC	L	D3
HANAUPAH CYN RD	INY	72	A2
HANAWALT AV	KER	78	A1
HANCOCK RD	SBD	84	C4
HANEY VIEW DR	SHA	13	E4
HANFORD ARMONA	KIN	67	C1
HANKINS RD	COL	32	D2
HANKS RD	MOD	7	D4
HANSEN	FRCO	58	B4
HANSEN AV	RCO	99	D3
HANSEN RD	LAS	21	B1
HANSEN RD	SJCO	46	D2
HANSEN ST	SAL	171	E5
HAPGOOD RD	SB	86	C3
HAPPY TR	SBD	92	D5
HAPPY CAMP LKOT	MOD	14	B1
HAPPY CAMP RD	VEN	88	D5
HAPPY CAMP DUMP	SIS	3	A3
HAPPY CANYON RD	SB	87	A3
HAPPY GAP RD	TUL	58	D3
HAPPY VALLEY RD	ALA	P	B1
HAPPY VALLEY RD	CC	L	E4
HAPPY VALLEY RD	ED	35	A5
HAPPY VALLEY RD	SHA	18	C3
HARBERS LN	HUM	15	E2
HARBISON RD	COL	32	E1
HARBISON CYN RD	SDCO	107	A5
HARBOR	YOL	39	D1
HARBOR BLVD	ANA	193	B1
HARBOR BLVD	CM	197	B5
HARBOR BLVD	CM	199	B2
HARBOR BLVD	FTNV	195	B5
HARBOR BLVD	FTNV	197	B2
HARBOR BLVD	GGR	195	B3
HARBOR BLVD	LA	191	B3
HARBOR BLVD	LACO	S	C3
HARBOR BLVD	ORCO	98	B3
HARBOR BLVD	ORCO	T	C2
HARBOR BLVD	SMCO	N	D2
HARBOR BLVD	SA	195	B5
HARBOR BLVD	SA	197	B2
HARBOR BLVD	VENT	175	E4
HARBOR BLVD	VEN	96	B1
HARBOR DR	IMP	108	C2
HARBOR DR	SD	215	D4
HARBOR DR	SD	216	B5
HARBOR DR	SDCO	V	B4
HARBOR DR N	SD	215	B2
HARBOR FRWY	LA	185	D4
HARBOR FRWY	LA	191	A2
HARBOR FRWY	LACO	97	D4
HARBOR FRWY	LACO	S	C2
HARBOR WY	R	155	A3
HARBOR SCNIC DR	LB	192	C3
HARDEN FLAT	TUO	49	B1
HARDER RD	ALA	N	E1
HARDER RD	ALA	P	A1
HARDER RD	ALA	45	E2
HARDER RD W	H	146	D4
HARDIN RD	NAPA	38	C1
HARDING AV	STA	47	D3
HARDING RD	MCO	47	E3
HARDING RD	MCO	48	A3
HARDING WY	SJCO	40	E5
HARDING WY	S	160	A4
HARDMAN AV	NAPA	38	D2
HARDRK DAVIS RD	SBD	91	B3
HARDY RD	IMP	111	E3
HARE CANYON RD	MON	65	E4
HARE CANYON RD	MON	66	A4
HARKINS	MON	54	C4
HARKINS RD	SAL	171	E5
HARKINS SLGH RD	SCR	54	B2
HARKNESS DR	PLU	20	A2
HARKNESS ST	NAP	133	B2
HARLAN AV	FRCO	66	D1
HARLAN AV	FRCO	57	C5
HARLAN RD	COL	32	C2
HARLAN MTN RD	SBT	54	E4
HARLAN MTN RD	SBT	55	A4
HARLEY LEIGHTON	SHA	18	C2
HARMON RD	MCO	56	B1
HARMON RD	TUL	67	E2
HARMONY GRVE RD	SDCO	106	C3
HARMONY VLY RD	SLO	75	C2
HARNEY	SJCO	40	A4
HARP RD	TEH	18	C3
HARPER LN	MCO	55	C2
HARPER LN	SOL	39	B2
HARPER RD	IMP	112	D5
HARPER LAKE RD	SBD	81	B5
HARPOLD RD	KLAM	5	D1
HARRIGAN RD	IMP	111	E3
HARRINGTON AV	COL	32	E3
HARRIS	MPA	49	C3
HARRIS RD	BUT	25	B4
HARRIS RD	HUM	16	D5
HARRIS RD	IMP	109	B5
HARRIS RD	MON	54	C4
HARRIS RD	SUT	33	C3
HARRIS ST	EUR	121	B3
HARRIS ST	HUM	9	E5
HARRIS ST	HUM	15	E1
HARRISON AV	HUM	9	E5
HARRISON AV	HUM	15	E1
HARRISON RD	TRI	17	B2
HARRISON ST	O	158	B2
HARRISON ST	RCO	101	B5
HARRISON ST	SF	143	D5
HARRISN GLCH RD	SHA	17	C3
HARRIS RANCH RD	MNO	51	D2
HARROD RD	SBD	92	A4
HARROLD RD	SJCO	47	D1
HARRY CASH RD	SIS	4	C4
HART AV	KER	68	C5
HART RD	IMP	109	C4
HART RD	SIS	4	C4
HART RD	STA	47	C2
HART FLAT RD	KER	79	B3
HARTLEY DR	BUT	25	C2
HARTMANN RD	LAK	32	B4
HART MINE RD	SBD	84	D3
HARTNELL	RED	122	E4
HARTNELL AV	SHA	18	C2
HART OAKS DR	KER	79	B3
HARTSHORN RD	IMP	109	C5
HARTS MEADOW	SIS	12	E1
HARTS MTN RD	SIS	4	E5
HARTVICKSON LN	CAL	40	E4
HARVARD AV	IRV	200	E1
HARVARD AV	ORCO	T	E3
HARVARD RD	SBD	92	C1
HARVARD MINE RD	TUO	41	C5
HARVEY RD	BUT	25	C2
HARVEY RD	SAC	40	A3
HARVEY RD	STA	47	C4
HARVEY RD 1	LAS	20	C1
HARVEY RD 2	LAS	20	C1
HARVEY RD 4	LAS	20	C1
HARVY MTN LO RD	LAS	20	C1
HARVY PETTIT RD	MCO	48	D5
HARVEY VLY RD	LAS	20	C1
HARWOOD RD	SCL	P	B4
HARWOOD RD	SCL	46	B5
HASKELL AV	LACO	Q	B2
HASKINS RD	SIS	5	D2
HASKINS VALLEY	BUT	26	A3
HASLEY CYN RD	LACO	89	A4
HASSLER RD	ED	34	E4
HASTAIN RD	IMP	109	B4
HASTE ST	B	156	A3
HASTER ST	ANA	193	D5
HASTER ST	ANA	195	C1
HASTER ST	ORCO	T	C2
HATCHET CK RD	TRI	11	E4
HAT CREEK PK RD	SHA	13	D4
HAT CK PWRHOUSE	SHA	13	D4
HAT CK PWRHS #2	SHA	13	D4
HATCH RD	BUT	25	B5
HATCH RD	MCO	48	C4
HATCH RD	STA	47	C2
HATCHET CK RD	NEV	34	B2
HATCHET CK RD	TRI	12	A4
HATHAWAY ST	RCO	100	A3
HAUSER BLVD	LA	184	B3
HAUSER BR RD	SON	37	A1
HAVASU LAKE RD	SBD	95	D4
HAVEN AV	SBD	U	E2
HAVEN AV	SBD	98	E2
HAVEN RD	SBD	80	E5
HAVENS RD	IMP	108	E5
HAVERFORD RD	SDCO	107	A4
HAVLINA ST	SIS	5	D2
HAWEE CANYON RD	INY	70	B2
HAWKEYE AV	STA	47	E3
HAWKINS RD	SOL	39	B2
HAWKINS RD	STA	48	A3
HAWKINS BAR RD	TRI	10	D5
HAWKNSVLLE HMBG	SIS	3	E3
HAWKNSVLLE HMBG	SIS	4	A4
HAWKS HILL RD	HUM	15	D2
HAWLEY GRADE	ED	36	A4
HAWTHORNE AV	C	124	B3
HAWTHORNE AV	SHA	18	D3
HAWTHORNE BLVD	LACO	97	D3
HAWTHORNE BLVD	LACO	S	B3
HAWTHORNE ST	MONT	167	D3
HAWTHORNE ST	RCO	99	C5
HAWVER RD	CAL	41	A3
HAYDEN RD	MCO	48	D4
HAYDEN HILL RD	LAS	14	C4
HAYDN HLL CTO	LAS	14	D4
HAYDN HLL LKOUT	LAS	14	D4
HAYES AV	FRCO	57	B3
HAYES AV	FRCO	57	B5
HAYES ST	NAP	133	C3
HAYES ST	RCO	101	C5
HAYNES RD	SBD	91	E3
HAYNES RD	SHA	13	C5
HAYS CANYON RD	MOD	8	E2
HAYWARD BLVD	ALA	M	A5
HAYWARD BLVD	ALA	P	A1
HAYWARD RD	MCO	48	C2
HAZEL AV	SAC	34	B5
HAZELDEAN RD	STA	48	A2
HAZEL DELL RD	SCR	54	C2
HAZEL VALLEY RD	ED	35	B4
HAZELTINE AV	LACO	Q	C2
HAZELTON AV	S	160	E5
HAZEN RD	TEH	19	B3
HEACOCK ST	RCO	99	C2
HEAD DAM RD	BUT	25	D1
HEALDSBURG AV	SON	37	D2
HEALY RD	MCO	48	C5
HEARST RD	MCO	47	D5
HEARST RD	MCO	55	D1
HEARST POST OFC	MEN	23	B4
HEARST WLLTS RD	MEN	23	A5
HEATH RD	KER	78	C3
HEATHER AV	KER	70	C5
HEATHER AV	MAD	57	B1
HEATHER DR	FRFD	135	C2
HEBER RD	IMP	112	B3
HECKER PASS HWY	SCL	54	C2
HECTOR RD	SBD	92	D2
HEDDING ST	SJ	151	C4
HEDDING ST	SJ	152	B2
HEDDING ST	SCL	P	B3
HEDGER RD	SUT	33	C1
HEFFERNAN AV	IMP	112	A4
HEGAN LN	BUT	25	B3
HEGENBRGR EXPWY	ALA	45	D2
HEGENBRGR EXPWY	O	159	E2
HEGENBERGER RD	ALA	L	D5
HEGENBERGER RD	ALA	45	D2
HEGENBURGER RD	O	159	E3
HEIDI RD	TUL	68	E1
HEINSEN RD	MON	65	D4
HEINZELMAN DR	SIS	4	C5
HEISKELL DR	MAD	57	B1
HEITT AV	KER	68	B5
HELEN DR	MLBR	144	B5
HELENA AV	STA	47	E2
HELENDALE RD	SBD	91	B2
HELLMAN AV	RCO	U	E4
HELLMAN AV	RCO	98	E3
HELLS HALF ACRE	SIE	26	D4
HELLS HALF ACRE	TUO	41	D3
HELLS HALF ACRE	TUO	42	A3
HELLS HOLLOW RD	TUO	48	E1
HELMS CT	KER	79	C3
HEMET LAKE RD	RCO	100	B4
HEMPHILL RD	LAS	21	B4
HENDERSON AV	TUL	68	D3
HENDERSON RD	FRCO	57	B4
HENDERSON RD	FRCO	57	C4
HENDERSON RD	RED	122	D3
HENDERSON ST	EUR	121	C3
HENDERSN CYN RD	SDCO	107	E2
HENDRICKS DR	SBD	101	E1
HENDRICKS RD	LAK	31	C2
HENLEY RD	KLAM	5	C1
HENNESSEY RD	HUM	10	D5
HENNESSEY RD	TRI	10	E5
HENNESS PASS RD	SIE	26	D4
HENNESS PASS RD	SIE	27	A4
HENRY RD	SBD	101	D1
HENRY RD	SJCO	40	D5
HENRY RD	SJCO	47	D1
HENRY ST	B	156	A1
HENRY DOTA RD	SIE	27	C4
HENRY FORD AV	LA	191	E1
HENRY FORD AV	LB	191	E2
HENRY MILLER AV	MCO	56	A1
HENRY MILLER RD	MCO	55	C1
HENSLEY RD	MAD	57	B1
HEREFORD RD	MCO	47	E5
HEREFORD RD	MCO	48	A5
HEREFORD RD	MCO	55	E1
HEREFORD RD	SBD	92	B1
HERIOT LN	PLU	27	C3
HERIOT LN	SIE	27	C3
HERITAGE CT	SHA	18	B2
HERITAGE RD	SDCO	V	D5
HERITAGE RD	SDCO	111	E2
HERLONG ACCESS	LAS	21	D5
HERMOSA AV	LACO	S	A1
HERMOSA RD	KER	78	E3
HERMOSA RD	VEN	88	B4
HERNANDEZ DR	LACO	90	A3
HERNANDEZ DR	MPA	48	C2
HERNDON AV	FRCO	56	B3
HERNDON AV	FRCO	57	C3
HERNLEY RD	RCO	107	B1
HERON AV	SBD	101	A1
HERRICK RD	HUM	121	B5
HERRING RD	KER	78	C4
HERZOG RD	SAC	M	E1
HERZOG RD	SAC	39	D3
HESPELER RD	SOL	38	E2
HESPERIA RD	MON	65	C5
HESPERIA RD	SBD	91	B4
HESPERIAN BLVD	ALA	N	E1
HESPERIAN BLVD	ALA	P	A1
HESPERIAN BLVD	ALA	45	E2

INDEXES

COPYRIGHT 1997 Thomas Bros. Maps ®

STREET	CO.	PAGE	GRID
HESPERIAN BLVD	ALCO	146	A2
HESPERIAN BLVD	H	146	A2
HESSE RD	TEH	18	B5
HETCH HETCHY RD	TUO	42	B5
HETTENSHAW RD	TRI	16	E4
HETZEL RD	IMP	108	E5
HEWES AV	ORCO	98	C4
HEWES AV	ORCO	T	E3
HEWITT RD	SJCO	40	C5
HEWLTT STURTVNT	MEN	31	B3
HEYSER RD	IMP	110	D5
HIALEAH WY	RCO	100	C5
HIATT RD	SUT	33	B4
HIAWATHA AV	AVLN	97	B4
HIBBARD RD	MEN	31	A4
HIBBARD RD	SJCO	40	B4
HICKEY BLVD	SMCO	N	B1
HICKEY BLVD	SMCO	45	B2
HICKMAN LN	TEH	18	C4
HICKMAN RD	STA	47	E3
HICKMAN RD	STA	48	A3
HICKS	LAS	21	B4
HICKS LN	BUT	25	B2
HICKS RD	SUT	33	E3
HIDALGO ST	MPA	48	C2
HIDDEN HILLS RD	SBD	94	A2
HIDDEN OAKS DR	KER	79	B4
HIDDEN VLY RD	SB	87	B4
HIDEAWAY HAVEN	SHA	13	D3
HIEROGLYPH RD	MNO	51	C2
HIETT AV	KER	78	B1
HIGDON RD	CAL	41	B2
HIGGINS AV	BUT	33	C1
HIGGNS PRSMA RD	SMCO	N	B2
HIGGNS PRSMA RD	SMCO	45	C3
HIGH RD	SBD	91	D4
HIGH RD	SIS	3	E4
HIGH ST	ALA	L	D4
HIGH ST	A	159	A2
HIGH ST	AUB	126	D3
HIGH ST	MONT	167	D3
HIGH ST	MON	53	E3
HIGH ST	O	159	B1
HIGH ST	SC	169	B3
HIGH ST	SCR	53	E2
HIGHGRADE RD	MOD	7	D2
HIGHLAND AV	FRCO	57	D2
HIGHLAND AV	LA	181	C4
HIGHLAND AV	LA	184	C1
HIGHLAND AV	LACO	97	D3
HIGHLAND AV	LACO	Q	D4
HIGHLAND AV	LACO	S	A1
HIGHLAND AV	MB	189	A5
HIGHLAND AV	SBD	98	E1
HIGHLAND AV	SBD	99	C2
HIGHLAND AV	SDCO	V	C4
HIGHLAND AV	SDCO	111	D1
HIGHLAND AV	U	123	B3
HIGHLAND BLVD	RCO	99	D2
HIGHLAND DR	CLK	209	A5
HIGHLAND DR	LACO	R	A2
HIGHLAND DR	SNLO	172	A1
HIGHLAND RD	CC	M	C5
HIGHLAND RD	CC	46	B1
HIGHLAND WY	SCR	P	B5
HIGHLAND WY	SCR	54	B1
HIGHLND HOME RD	RCO	99	E3
HIGHLAND LK RD	ALP	42	B1
HIGHLAND SPG RD	LAK	31	D3
HIGHLND SPGS RD	RCO	99	E3
HIGHLAND VLY RD	SDCO	106	E4
HIGHLANDS LK RD	SHA	12	B4
HIGHLANDS VW DR	TUO	163	D3
HIGHLINE RD	IMP	109	C5
HIGHLINE RD	KER	79	B4
HIGHLINE RD	KER	79	C4
HIGH PRAIRIE RD	HUM	10	C5
HIGHRIDGE RD	LACO	S	B3
HIGH ROCK RD	LAS	21	E4
HIGH SCHOOL RD	SON	37	D2
HIGH VALLEY RD	KER	88	D1
HIGH VALLEY RD	LAK	31	E2
HIGH VALLEY RD	LAK	32	A3
HY TO THE STARS	SDCO	107	A2
HIGUERA ST	SLO	76	A4
HIGUERA ST	SNLO	172	B3
HILBORN RD	NAPA	135	B1
HILDRETH LN	SJCO	40	B4
HILDRETH RD	MAD	57	D1
HILL	FRCO	58	B4
HILL AV	PAS	190	E2
HILL RD	COL	32	D2
HILL RD	CC	38	E5
HILL RD	KER	78	C4
HILL RD	KLAM	5	C2
HILL RD	MEN	23	B3
HILL RD	SMCO	N	C4
HILL RD	SCL	P	D5
HILL RD	SCL	54	D1
HILL RD	SIS	5	A3
HILL RD E	MEN	23	A5
HILL ST	AVLN	97	B4
HILL ST	LA	185	D5
HILL ST	LA	186	A3
HILL ST	LACO	S	D2
HILL ST	ML	164	C4
HILL ST	SDCO	V	A3
HILL ST	SDCO	106	B3
HILL ST	SDCO	111	D2
HILLCREST AV	BEN	153	C4
HILLCREST AV	CC	39	B5
HILLCREST BLVD	LACO	R	D3
HILLCREST BLVD	MLBR	144	D5

STREET	CO.	PAGE	GRID
HILLCREST BLVD	SMCO	N	C1
HILLCREST BLVD	SMCO	45	B3
HILLCREST RD	CC	M	C3
HILLCREST ST	KER	80	E1
HILLDALE AV	MCO	55	C1
HILLDALE AV	MCO	86	E1
HILLER RD	HUM	9	E4
HILLER ST	BLMT	145	C4
HILLGATE RD	COL	32	E3
HILLHURST AV	LA	182	C3
HILLMAN AV	BLMT	145	B4
HILLSBORO AV	LA	183	D3
HILLSDALE AV	SCL	P	B4
HILLSDALE BLVD	SMCO	N	C2
HILLSDALE BL E	FCTY	145	D2
HILLSDALE BL E	SM	145	B3
HILLSDALE BL W	SM	145	A4
HILLS FERRY RD	MCO	47	C4
HILLSIDE AV	RCO	98	E3
HILLSIDE BLVD	SMCO	L	B5
HILLSIDE BLVD	SMCO	N	B1
HILLSIDE BLVD	SMCO	45	C2
HILLSIDE DR	MPA	49	C3
HILLSIDE DR	SMCO	N	C1
HILLSIDE DR	SMCO	45	C3
HILLSIDE DR	SHA	18	D2
HILL SIDE STA	LAS	14	B3
HILLSIDE VIS RD	RCO	107	C1
HILLS VALLEY RD	FRCO	58	B4
HILLTOP	SHA	18	C2
HILLTOP DR	CC	L	C3
HILLTOP RD	SIS	5	A2
HILL VIEW TK TR	SBD	91	C2
HILMAR RD	STA	47	D4
HILT RD	SIS	4	A2
HILT HUNGRY RD	SIS	4	A2
HILTON PACK STA	MNO	51	A3
HILTONS RD	HUM	9	E2
HILTONS RD	HUM	10	A2
HIME RD	IMP	112	A3
HI MOUNTAIN RD	SLO	76	C3
HINDS RD	STA	47	D1
HINKLEY RD	SBD	81	C5
HINTON AV	MCO	47	E4
HIRSCH RD	MPA	49	B4
HIRSCHDALE RD	NEV	27	E5
HITCHCOCK RD	MON	54	C4
HI YOU GULCH RD	SIS	3	D4
HOADLEY PKS RD	SHA	17	E1
HOAG RD	TEH	24	D2
HOAGLAND RD	HUM	16	D5
HOAGLIN RD	TRI	16	E5
HOAGLIN SCH RD	TRI	16	E5
HOBART AV	FRCO	56	B2
HOBART MILLS RD	NEV	27	D5
HOBBS RD	IMP	109	A2
HOBBS RD	SUT	33	C3
HOBO GULCH RD	TRI	11	B5
HOBSON AV	MON	65	B2
HOBSON WY	RCO	103	C5
HOFFMAN BLVD	R	155	A4
HOFFMAN LN	CC	46	C1
HOFFMAN RD	SBD	80	E3
HOFFMAN RD	SBD	81	A3
HOFFMAN RD	YUB	33	D3
HOFFMAN ST	AMA	40	E2
HFMN PLUMAS RD	YUB	33	D3
HOGAN	FRCO	58	A4
HOGAN LN	SJCO	40	B4
HOGAN DAM RD	CAL	40	E4
HOGBACK RD	INY	60	A4
HOG CANYON RD	KER	79	D3
HOG CANYON RD	SLO	76	B1
HOG CANYON EXT	SLO	66	B5
HOGIN RD	STA	47	C4
HOG LAKE TK TR	RCO	100	B5
HOGSBACK RD	TEH	18	D5
HOGSBACK RD	TEH	19	B4
HOKE RD	SUT	33	D2
HOLBROOK RD	MCO	48	D5
HOLBROOK WY	NEV	127	C1
HOLCOMB CK RD	SBD	91	E5
HOLCOMB VLY RD	SBD	91	E5
HOLCOMBS RD	SIE	27	D4
HOLDEN	SJCO	40	C5
HOLDNER RD	SOL	39	B2
HOLDRIDGE DR	TUL	68	E3
HOLDRIDGE RD	IMP	112	C3
HOLE AV	RCO	99	A3
HOLENBECK	SJCO	40	C5
HOLIDAY AV	KER	89	C1
HOLIDAY RD	DN	2	B3
HOLLAND	YOL	39	D2
HOLLAND AV	BUT	25	B3
HOLLAND RD	RCO	99	C4
HOLLAND RD	SOL	39	C3
HOLLND TRACT RD	CC	39	D5
HOLLENBECK AV	LACO	U	A3
HOLLENBECK AV	SVL	149	D2
HOLLISTER AV	SB	87	B4
HOLLISTER ST	SDCO	V	C5
HOLLISTER ST	SDCO	111	D2
HOLLOW LN	SHA	18	C2
HOLLOW RD	CC	39	A5
HOLLOWAY RD	COL	32	E1
HOLLOWAY RD	KER	77	C1
HOLLOW LOG RD	PLA	34	E2
HOLLY AV	LACO	R	C3
HOLLY RD	SBD	91	A3
HOLLY RD	TRI	17	A4
HOLLY ST	SMCO	N	D2
HOLLYWOOD BLVD	LA	181	A4
HOLLYWOOD BLVD	LA	182	A4

STREET	CO.	PAGE	GRID
HOLLYWOOD BLVD	LACO	97	D2
HOLLYWOOD BLVD	LACO	Q	D3
HOLLYWOOD FRWY	LA	181	B2
HOLLYWOOD FRWY	LA	185	D1
HOLLYWOOD FRWY	LA	186	A2
HOLLYWOOD FRWY	LACO	97	D1
HOLLYWOOD FRWY	LACO	Q	D3
HOLLYWOOD LN	SBD	101	D1
HOLLYWOOD WY	BUR	179	B3
HOLLYWOOD WY	LA	179	B3
HOLLYWOOD WY	LACO	97	D1
HOLLYWOOD WY	LACO	Q	D2
HOLMAN HWY	MONT	167	C5
HOLMAN HWY	MON	53	D4
HOLMAN HWY	MON	168	C1
HOLMES AV	KER	78	B5
HOLMES LN	SOL	39	A2
HOLMES RD	SBD	84	C4
HOLMES RD	TEH	24	E1
HOLMES ST	ALA	P	C1
HOLMES ST	ALA	46	B2
HOLMS FLAT RD	HUM	16	B3
HOLOHAN RD	SCR	54	C2
HOLSTEAD RD	SBD	81	C5
HOLT AV	LACO	U	C2
HOLT BLVD	MTCL	203	B5
HOLT BLVD	ONT	203	B5
HOLT BLVD	ONT	204	A5
HOLT BLVD	POM	203	B5
HOLT BLVD	SBD	U	C2
HOLT BLVD	SBD	98	D2
HOLT RD	IMP	109	C5
HOLT RD	KER	79	E5
HOLT RD	KER	80	A5
HOLTON RD	IMP	109	B5
HOLTVLE DUMP RD	IMP	109	C5
HOLTZWL	MPA	48	E2
HOLTZWL	MPA	49	A2
HOLWORTHY DR	TUL	68	D2
HOLZHAUSER LN	SIS	11	D1
HOME AV	SD	216	D3
HOME AV	SDCO	V	C3
HOME AV	SDCO	111	D1
HOMEDALE RD	KLAM	5	C1
HOMES RD	SBD	91	E4
HOMESTEAD AV	SAL	171	B4
HOMESTEAD RD	SLO	76	B2
HOMESTEAD RD	SCL	P	A3
HOMESTEAD RD	SCL	45	E4
HOMESTEAD RD	SCLR	150	C3
HOMESTEAD RD	SCLR	151	A3
HOMESTEAD RD	SVL	150	C3
HOMEWOOD CYN RD	INY	71	B4
HONDA RD	SB	86	B3
HONEY BEE RD	SHA	18	B3
HONEY RUN RD	BUT	25	C3
HONEY SPGS RD	SDCO	112	B1
HONEY WAGON RD	IMP	108	E2
HONOLULU AV	IMP	108	C2
HONOLULU AV	LACO	Q	E2
HONOLULU RD	KER	78	A4
HOOD FRANKLN RD	SAC	39	E2
HOOKER CREEK RD	HUM	16	C5
HOOKER CREEK RD	TEH	18	C4
HOOKTON RD	HUM	15	D1
HOOPER RD	SUT	33	C2
HOOPER RD	YUB	33	D2
HOOVER RD	MCO	56	C1
HOOVER ST	LA	185	C3
HOOVER ST	LACO	Q	E4
HOOVER FLAT RD	LAS	14	C4
HOPE ST	KLAM	5	C1
HOPE ST	LA	185	E4
HOPKINS ST	ALA	L	C4
HOPLAND ST	SBD	91	B3
HOPPER RD	STA	47	E2
HOPYARD RD	ALA	M	B5
HOPYARD RD	ALA	46	B2
HORIZON CIR	NEV	127	B1
HORIZON RD	SBD	91	B3
HORIZON ST	SBD	91	C4
HORN LN	SIS	11	D1
HORN RD	LAS	8	D5
HORNBROOK RD	SIS	4	B3
HORNITOS RD	MPA	48	D3
HORR RD	SHA	13	D3
HORSE CANYON RD	KER	80	B1
HORSE CREEK RD	SIS	3	C3
HORSE LAKE RD	LAS	21	B1
HORSE LINTO RD	HUM	10	D4
HORSE RDG LKOUT	TRI	17	A4
HORSESHOE RD	STA	47	E1
HORSESHOE RD	STA	48	A1
HORSESHOE BR RD	PLA	34	B4
HORSESHOE HL RD	MAR	37	E5
HORSESHOE MDWS	INY	60	A4
HORTON CREEK RD	INY	51	C4
HOSFIELD DR	TUL	68	B2
HOSKING RD	KER	78	D3
HOSLER AV	BUT	25	A3
HOSTETTER RD	SCL	P	B3
HOTCHKISS RD	TRI	22	E1
HOT CK RANCH RD	MNO	50	E2
HOT CK RANCH RD	MNO	51	A2
HOTLUM	SIS	12	C1
HOT SPRINGS RD	ALP	36	B5
HOT SPRINGS RD	RCO	108	D1
HOT SPRINGS RD	TUL	68	E4
HOT SPRINGS RD	TUL	69	A4
HOUGHTON AV	TEH	24	D2
HOUGHTON RD	KER	78	C4
HOUSE RD	IMP	108	E5
HOUSE RD	LAS	14	C3

STREET	CO.	PAGE	GRID
HOUSTON AV	KIN	67	D1
HOUSTON AV	TUL	68	B1
HOUT RD	AMA	40	D2
HOVLEY RD	IMP	109	A4
HOWARD	SJCO	47	A1
HOWARD AV	FRCO	57	A5
HOWARD AV	FRCO	57	A3
HOWARD AV	MCO	47	E4
HOWARD AV	MCO	48	A4
HOWARD AV	SD	214	A5
HOWARD RD	MCO	47	E4
HOWARD RD	RCO	107	B1
HOWARD RD	STA	47	B3
HOWARD RD	SJCO	47	A1
HOWARD RD	TUL	68	B4
HOWARD ST	MEN	23	A3
HOWARD CREEK RD	SIE	27	A3
HOWRDS GLCH FTG	MOD	14	C1
HOWE RD	CC	L	E3
HOWE CREEK RD	HUM	15	E3
HOWELL AV	KER	80	C1
HOWELL AV	SIS	11	D1
HOWELL RD	IMP	109	A2
HOWELL MTN RD	NAPA	29	C2
HOWELL MTN RD	NAPA	38	B1
HOWELLS RD	PLU	26	B1
HOWLAND HILL RD	DN	1	D4
HOWSLEY RD	SUT	33	D4
HOY RD	SIS	12	C1
HOY RD	TEH	18	D5
HOYER RD	STA	47	C4
HUASNA RD	SLO	76	C4
HUASNA TOWNSITE	SLO	76	D4
HUB CT	CAL	41	A5
HUBBARD	PLA	34	B3
HUBBARD RD	LACO	89	E4
HUBBARD ST	LACO	89	C5
HUBBARD ST	LACO	Q	C1
HUDSON AV	FRCO	56	B2
HUDSON RD	MON	65	A1
HUDSON RD	SIS	4	A3
HUDSON RD	SUT	33	E3
HUDSON ST	SMCO	N	D2
HUDSON ST	SHA	13	C5
HUERHUERO L PNZ	SLO	76	C2
HUEY RD	SLO	76	A1
HUFF RD	IMP	108	E5
HUFF RD	SBD	91	E3
HUFF ST	RCO	107	C1
HUFFAKER RD	SUT	33	E3
HUFFMASTER RD	COL	32	C2
HUFFORD RD	HUM	9	E2
HUFFORD RD	HUM	10	A2
HUGHES AV	CUL	183	C5
HUGHES AV	FRCO	57	C4
HUGHES AV	FRCO	67	C1
HUGHES AV	LA	183	C5
HUGHES LN	KER	78	D3
HUGHES RD	GV	127	C2
HUGHES RD	NEV	127	C2
HUGHES RD	SUT	33	C2
HULEN RD	MCO	47	C5
HULEN RD	MCO	55	C1
HULL AV	MCO	48	B4
HULL RD	GLE	24	A3
HULL CREEK RD	TRI	23	A1
HULL MTN RD	LAK	23	D5
HULL VALLEY RD	MEN	23	A2
HULTBERG RD	MCO	47	D4
HULTBERG RD	STA	47	D3
HUMBOLDT AV	FRCO	56	E3
HUMBOLDT AV	FRCO	57	A3
HUMBOLDT RD	BUT	19	D5
HUMBOLDT RD	BUT	25	B3
HUMBOLDT RD	C	124	E4
HUMBOLDT RD	DN	1	D4
HUMBOLDT RD	PLU	19	E5
HUMBOLDT RD	PLU	20	A5
HUMBLDT HILL RD	HUM	15	E1
HUMBUG RD	PLU	19	E5
HUMBUG RD	PLU	20	A5
HUMBUG CREEK RD	SIS	4	A4
HUMBUG HUMBOLDT	PLU	20	B4
HUME AV	KIN	67	E1
HUME RD	FRCO	58	E3
HUMPHREY CIR	PLU	20	D5
HUMPHREY RD	SUT	33	C2
HUN RD	SBD	84	C4
HUNEWILL RCH RD	MNO	43	B3
HUNGRY CK LO RD	SIS	4	A2
HUNGRY CK MTWY	PLU	20	E5
HUNGRY VLY RD	VEN	88	D2
HUNT RD	CAL	40	E4
HUNT RD	CAL	41	A4
HUNT RD	IMP	112	B3
HUNT RD	LAS	14	C3
HUNT RD	MCO	47	C5
HUNTER	MON	54	C4
HUNTER BLVD	RCO	103	D4
HUNTER CREEK RD	DN	1	E5
HUNTER CREEK RD	DN	2	A5
HUNTER MTN RD	INY	61	A4
HUNTERS VLY RD	MPA	48	E2
HUNTINGTON AV	SBR	144	C3
HUNTINGTON DR	LACO	97	E2
HUNTINGTON DR	LACO	R	B3
HUNTINGTON RD	MAD	57	C2
HUNTINGTON RD	STA	47	B2
HUTCHINS ST	SJCO	40	A4
HUTCHINSON RD	SJCO	47	B2
HUTCHINSON RD	SUT	33	C3
HUNTLEY MINE RD	MNO	50	E2
HUNTSMAN AV	FRCO	56	E4

STREET	CO.	PAGE	GRID
HUNTSMAN AV	FRCO	57	C4
HUNTSMAN AV	FRCO	58	A4
HUPP COUTOLENC	BUT	25	D2
HURDS GULCH RD	SIS	3	D5
HURLES CIR	BUT	25	E4
HURLETON RD	BUT	25	E4
HURLTN SWDS FLT	BUT	25	E4
HURLEY FLATS RD	RCO	100	B3
HURRICANE RD	SLO	77	D4
HUSMAN RD	MCO	47	C5
HUSMAN RD	MCO	55	C1
HUSTED RD	COL	32	E2
HUSTON RD	IMP	109	B5
HUTCHINS	MCO	56	B1
HUTSELL RD	MEN	30	E3
HYAMPOM RD	TRI	17	A2
HYDE RD	IMP	111	E3
HYDE ST	FRCO	57	B5
HYDRIL RD	KIN	67	A3
HYPERION AV	LA	182	D4
I			
I AV	SBD	91	C4
I ST	BEN	153	A4
I ST	EUR	121	D1
I ST	MDO	162	B3
IBEX SPRING RD	SBD	72	D5
ICE HOUSE RD	ED	35	C3
ICE HOUSE RD	ED	35	C4
ICELAND RD	NEV	27	E5
IDAHO AV	KIN	67	D2
IDAHO RD	STA	47	D3
IDAHO ST	SDCO	V	C3
IDAHO ST	SDCO	111	D1
IDAHO-MARYLD RD	GV	127	D3
IDAHO-MARYLD RD	NEV	34	C1
IDAHO-MARYLD RD	NEV	127	D3
IDALEONA DR	RCO	99	B3
IDLEWOOD LN	HUM	9	E3
IDLEWOOD LN	HUM	10	A3
IGNACIO BLVD	MAR	L	A2
IKE CROW RD	STA	47	C4
ILLINOIS AV	STA	47	C2
ILLINOIS AV	TEH	24	E2
ILLINOIS VLY RD	DN	2	D2
IMLER RD	IMP	108	E4
IMOLA AV	NAPA	L	D1
IMOLA AV	NAP	133	C5
IMOLA AV W	NAP	133	B5
IMPERIAL AV	EC	217	B4
IMPERIAL AV	IMP	109	A5
IMPERIAL AV	SD	216	A4
IMPERIAL AV	SDCO	V	C3
IMPERIAL AV	SDCO	111	D1
IMPERIAL HWY	IMP	111	B3
IMPERIAL HWY	LA	189	B2
IMPERIAL HWY	LACO	97	D3
IMPERIAL HWY	LACO	98	B3
IMPERIAL HWY	LACO	Q	C5
IMPERIAL HWY	LACO	R	E5
IMPERIAL HWY	LACO	S	A1
IMPERIAL HWY	ORCO	R	E5
IMPERIAL HWY	ORCO	T	C1
IMPERIAL ST	KER	77	E2
IMPERIAL ST	KER	78	B2
IMPERIAL DAM RD	IMP	110	E5
IMPERL GABLS RD	IMP	110	B3
INCLINE RD	MPA	49	B2
INCLINE RD	MPA	63	A5
INDEPENDENCE RD	CAL	41	B2
INDPNDCE CEM RD	CAL	41	B2
INDEPNDNC LK RD	SIE	27	C5
INDEPNDNCIA MAT	BAJA	112	B4
INDIA ST	SD	215	C1
INDIAN AV	PMSP	206	B4
INDIAN AV	RCO	100	C3
INDIAN RD	LAS	21	A4
INDIAN TR	SBD	91	C2
INDIAN TR	SBD	101	B1
INDIANA AV	MCO	56	B1
INDIANA AV	STA	47	E2
INDIANA ST	LACO	R	B4
INDIANA RCH RD	YUB	26	A5
INDIANA SCH RD	YUB	26	A5
INDIAN CYN RD	KER	70	C5
INDIAN CYN RD	KER	80	C1
INDIAN CEM RD	ALP	36	B4
INDIAN COVE CIR	SBD	101	B2
INDIAN CV E RD	SBD	101	B2
INDIAN CV W RD	SBD	101	B2
INDIAN CV MT RD	SBD	101	B2
INDIAN CREEK RD	ALP	36	C5
INDIAN CREEK RD	KER	79	D3
INDIAN CREEK RD	MNO	51	D2
INDIAN CREEK RD	PLU	21	A5
INDIAN CREEK RD	RCO	100	A4
INDIAN CREEK RD	SIS	2	D2
INDIAN CREEK RD	SIS	3	D4
INDIAN CREEK RD	TRI	17	D2
INDIAN DIGGINS	ED	41	B1
INDIAN FLAT RD	NEV	34	C1
INDIAN GUIDE	FRCO	58	B3
INDIAN GULCH RD	MPA	48	E3
INDIAN GULCH RD	MPA	49	A4
INDIAN GLCH EXT	MPA	48	D4
INDIAN HILL BL	CLA	203	A3
INDIAN HILL BL	LACO	98	D1
INDIAN HILL BL	POM	203	A5
INDIAN HILL RD	RCO	100	C5
INDIAN HILL RD	SIE	26	C4
INDIAN HILL RD	STA	48	C2
INDIANOLA AV	FRCO	57	E4

257
INDIANOLA CTO

STREET INDEX

KENDALL RD

STREET	CO.	PAGE	GRID
INDIANOLA CTO	HUM	9	E5
INDIANOLA CTO	HUM	10	A5
INDIANOLA RESRV	HUM	15	D2
INDIAN OLE RD	LAS	20	C4
INDIAN PAINT DR	RCO	100	C5
INDIAN PASS RD	IMP	110	B4
INDIAN PEAK RD	MPA	49	B3
INDIAN POINT RD	KER	79	B4
INDIAN RANCH RD	INY	71	C2
INDIAN RES RD	AMA	40	D3
INDIAN ROCK RD	IMP	112	D5
INDIANS RD	MON	64	D2
INDIAN SCHL RD	LPAZ	104	A2
INDIAN SERVICE RD	TUL	69	A3
INDIAN SPRINGS RD	ALP	36	D5
INDIAN SPRINGS RD	NEV	34	B2
INDIAN SPRINGS RD	SBD	81	D4
INDIAN TOM LAKE	SIS	5	B2
INDIAN VALLEY RD	MAR	38	A4
INDIAN VLY RD	MON	66	A5
INDIAN VLY RD	SIE	26	C4
INDIAN VLY RD	SLO	66	A5
INDIAN VLY RD	TRI	17	A2
INDIAN WELLS ST	KER	80	D1
INDIO AV	SBDO	100	E1
INDUSTRIAL BLVD	MOH	96	B4
INDUSTRIAL PKWY	ALA	N	E1
INDUSTRIAL PKWY	ALA	P	A1
INDUSTRIAL PKWY	ALA	45	E2
INDSTRL FARM RD	KER	78	C2
INGHRAM RD	TEH	24	D2
INGLEWOOD AV	LACO	S	B1
INGLEWOOD BLVD	LA	188	A2
INGOMAR GRADE	MCO	55	D1
INGOMAR RD	MCO	47	D5
INGOMAR RD	MCO	55	D1
INGRAHAM ST	SD	212	B1
INGRAHAM ST	SDCO	V	A3
INGRAM LN	SUT	33	B1
INGRAM CREEK RD	STA	47	A3
INK GRADE	NAPA	32	B5
INK GRADE	NAPA	38	B1
INLAND DR	SJCO	39	E5
INLAND CTR DR	SBDO	207	B4
INSKIP RD	TEH	19	A4
INTAKE BLVD	RCO	103	D5
INTERLAKE RD	SLO	65	D5
INTERNATIONL AV	FRCO	57	D2
INTERNATIONL AV	IMP	109	B3
INVESTOR AV	RCO	102	C4
INWOOD RD	SHA	19	A3
INYO N	INY	51	D3
INYO ST	DN	1	D4
INYOKERN RD	KER	80	D1
IONA AV	KIN	67	D2
IONE RD	SAC	40	C2
IONE MICHIGAN BR	AMA	40	C2
IOWA AV	RCO	99	B2
IOWA AV	STA	47	C3
IOWA CITY RD	YUB	33	D1
IOWA HILL RD	PLA	34	E2
IRIS AV	RCO	99	B3
IRIS CT	KER	79	C1
IRIS DR	SAL	171	C2
IRIS LN	SDCO	106	B3
IRIS WY	CAL	41	B2
IRIS CANYON RD	MONT	167	E5
IRIS CANYON RD	MONT	168	E1
IRISH HILL RD	AMA	40	D2
IRISH TOWN PNE-			
-GRV WIELAND RD	AMA	41	A2
IRMULCO RD	MEN	22	D5
IRONAGE RD	SBD	101	E1
IRONE AV	KER	89	C1
IRON MTN RD	SBD	91	C1
IRON MTN RD	SHA	18	B1
IRON MTN PUMPNG	SBD	102	E1
IRONWOOD AV	RCO	99	C2
IRONWOOD CT	KER	79	B4
IRVINE AV	CM	199	C4
IRVINE AV	NB	199	C4
IRVINE AV	ORCO	199	E1
IRVINE BLVD	ORCO	98	C4
IRVINE BLVD	ORCO	T	E3
IRVINE RD	IMP	109	C4
IRVINE CTR DR	ORCO	98	C4
IRVINE CTR DR	ORCO	T	E3
IRVINE LODGE RD	MEN	22	E4
IRWIN RD	SBD	81	E5
IRWIN RD	SBD	82	A5
IRWIN RD	SBD	208	B1
IRWIN RD	TEH	24	C2
IRWINDALE AV	LACO	R	E3
ISABELLA BLVD	KER	80	B4
ISABELA-WLKR PS	KER	79	D1
ISABELA-WLKR PS	KER	80	B1
ISHI PISHI RD	HUM	10	D2
ISLAND RD	SHA	13	D3
ISLAND RD	SIS	3	D5
ISLAND RD	SIS	11	D1
ISLAND BAR HILL	BUT	25	E4
ISLAND MTN RD	HUM	22	D1
ISLAND MTN RD	TRI	22	D1
ISLAND PARK RD	FRCO	58	B2
ISLETON RD	SAC	M	E1
ISPEN AV	MCO	48	E5
ITALIAN BAR RD	FRCO	50	A5
ITALIAN BAR RD	TUO	41	C4
IVANHOE RD	SBD	91	E4
IVANPAH RD	SBD	84	C2
IVANPAH CIMA RD	SBD	84	B3
IVERSON LN	LAS	14	B3
IVERSON RD	MEN	30	D4

STREET	CO.	PAGE	GRID
IVERSON RD	MON	54	E5
IVERSON ST	SAL	171	B4
IVESGROVE DR	LACO	89	D3
IVORY MILL RD	GLE	24	A4
IVY AV	MCO	56	C1
IVY ST	C	124	B5
J			
J ST	DVS	136	D2
J ST	MDO	162	B3
J ST	MER	170	C5
J ST	SCTO	137	E3
J ST	SDCO	V	C4
J ST	SDCO	111	D2
JACALITOS CK RD	FRCO	66	D3
JACARANDA DR	KER	79	B4
JACK AV	KER	78	B2
JACKASS FLTS RD	NEV	26	C5
JACKASS GRADE	SBT	55	E4
JACKASS GRADE	SBT	56	A4
JACKASS HILL RD	TUO	41	C5
JACK CREEK RD	SLO	75	E2
JACK CREEK RD	SLO	76	A2
JACKLIN RD	SCL	P	B2
JACKLIN RD	SCL	46	B3
JACK PINE AV	KER	79	E5
JACK RABBIT TR	RCO	99	D3
JACK RANCH RD	KER	69	B5
JACK RANCH RD	KER	80	D1
JACKS RD	MON	54	E5
JACK SHAW RD	HUM	16	B2
JACK SLOUGH RD	YUB	33	D2
JACKSNIPE RD	SOL	38	E3
JACKSON	PLA	33	E4
JACKSON AV	KER	77	E1
JACKSON AV	KER	78	B1
JACKSON AV	KIN	67	D2
JACKSON AV	SJCO	47	D1
JACKSON DR	SDCO	V	D2
JACKSON DR	SDCO	106	D5
JACKSON RD	IMP	109	B4
JACKSON RD	SAC	40	A1
JACKSON RD	SBD	91	D3
JACKSON RD	STA	47	C2
JACKSON ST	ALA	L	E5
JACKSON ST	ALA	M	A5
JACKSON ST	ALA	N	E1
JACKSON ST	ALA	P	A1
JACKSON ST	ALA	45	E2
JACKSON ST	RCO	99	A3
JACKSON ST	RCO	101	A4
JACKSON ST	SF	143	D3
JACKSON ST	TEH	18	D5
JACKSON ST W	ALA	N	E1
JACKSON ST W	H	146	D4
JACKSON GATE RD	AMA	40	E2
JACKSON MDWS RD	SIE	27	C4
JACKSON RCH RD	HUM	9	E5
JACKSON SLGH RD	SAC	M	D2
JACKSON VLY RD	AMA	40	D3
JACKSONVILLE RD	TUO	41	C5
JACKS VALLEY RD	DGL	36	B2
JACK TONE RD	SJCO	40	B4
JACOB DEKEMA FY	SD	214	A3
JACOB DEKEMA FY	SD	216	C1
JACOB DEKEMA FY	SDCO	V	D4
JACOB DEKEMA FY	SDCO	106	C5
JACOB DEKEMA FY	SDCO	111	D2
JACOBS	FRCO	58	B4
JACOBS RD	SJCO	40	A5
JACOBS WY	RCO	99	B4
JACOBY CREEK RD	HUM	10	A5
JACQUELINE	SIS	4	C2
JADE AV	SIS	4	C4
JAHANT	SJCO	40	A3
JAHANT RD	SJCO	40	B3
JAIL RD	AVLN	97	B5
JAKE RD	RCO	100	A5
JALAMA RD	SB	86	B4
JAMACHA BLVD	SDCO	V	E3
JAMACHA RD	SDCO	V	E3
JAMACHA RD	SDCO	111	D1
JAMAICA BLVD	MOH	96	E4
JAMBOREE RD	IRV	198	E4
JAMBOREE RD	IRV	200	C1
JAMBOREE RD	NB	200	A4
JAMBOREE RD	ORCO	98	C5
JAMBOREE RD	ORCO	T	E3
JAMES RD	FRCO	56	E4
JAMES RD	IMP	109	B5
JAMES RD	KER	78	D2
JAMES DONLON BL	CC	M	C3
JAMES LICK FRWY	SF	142	E5
JAMES LICK FRWY	SFCO	45	C2
JAMES LICK SKWY	SF	142	D4
JAMES LICK SKWY	SF	143	D5
JAMESON AV	FRCO	57	B5
JAMESON AV	FRCO	57	B4
JAMESON RD	COL	32	E1
JAMESON RD	KER	79	D4
JAMISON CK RD	SCR	N	D5
JAMISON CK RD	SCR	53	D1
JANE RD	SBD	92	D4
JANES RD	HUM	10	A5
JANESVLLE GRADE	LAS	21	B4
JANICE AV	KER	79	E1
JANICE AV	KER	80	A1
JANICE RD	SIS	4	C2
JANICE ST	KER	80	A4
JANOPAUL AV	STA	162	C5
JANSS RD	VEN	96	D1
JAPATUL LN	SDCO	107	B5

STREET	CO.	PAGE	GRID
JAPATUL LN	SDCO	112	B1
JAPATUL RD	SBD	91	C4
JAPATUL RD	SBD	91	D3
JAPATUL RD	SDCO	107	B5
JAPATUL RD	SDCO	112	B1
JAPATUL VLY RD	SDCO	107	C5
JAPATUL VLY RD	SDCO	112	C1
JAQUIMA DR	CAL	41	A4
JARDINE RD	SLO	76	B1
JARED LN	SB	86	E2
J ARTHR YNGR FY	FCTY	145	D1
J ARTHR YNGR FY	SM	145	D1
J ARTHR YNGR FY	SMCO	45	D3
JARVIS AV	ALA	N	E2
JARVIS AV	ALA	P	A2
JARVIS AV	ALA	45	E3
JARVIS RD	ALP	36	C4
JASMINE RD	SBD	92	B3
JASPER LN	YUB	33	E2
JASPER RD	IMP	112	B4
JASPER RD	TUO	48	B1
JASPER SEARS BR	MCO	55	C1
JASPER SEARS RD	MCO	55	C1
JAVA AV	KIN	67	C2
JAVA DR	SVL	148	E2
JAVIS AV	KER	80	C1
JAVIS AV	KER	80	E1
JAWBONE CYN RD	KER	79	E2
JAWBONE CYN RD	KER	80	B3
JAY DEE LN	RCO	100	C5
JAYMAR RD	HUM	16	B3
JAYNE AV	FRCO	66	D3
JAYNE AV	FRCO	67	A2
JEAN BLANC RD	INY	51	D3
JEANESE	TUO	41	C5
JEAN NICHOLS RD	RCO	99	D5
JEFF ST	KER	80	C1
JEFFERSON AV	FRCO	56	E4
JEFFERSON AV	FRCO	57	C4
JEFFERSON AV	FRCO	58	A4
JEFFERSON AV	RCO	99	C5
JEFFERSON AV	SM	N	D2
JEFFERSON BLVD	CUL	183	D5
JEFFERSON BLVD	CUL	188	C1
JEFFERSON BLVD	LA	183	D5
JEFFERSON BLVD	LA	185	A5
JEFFERSON BLVD	LACO	97	D2
JEFFERSON BLVD	LACO	Q	D4
JEFFERSON BLVD	LACO	187	D4
JEFFERSON BLVD	LACO	188	A4
JEFFERSON BLVD	YOL	39	D2
JEFFERSON ST	MONT	167	D4
JEFFERSON ST	NAP	133	C4
JEFFERSON ST	ORCO	T	D1
JEFFERSON ST	RCO	101	A4
JEFFERSON ST	SDCO	106	B3
JEFFERSON ST	SF	143	A2
JEFFERSON ST N	NAP	133	B1
JEFFERY RD	IMP	111	E3
JEFFREY RD	ORCO	98	C4
JEFFREY RD	ORCO	T	E4
JEFFREY RCH RD	MNO	51	D2
JELLYS FERRY RD	TEH	18	D4
JENEVEIN AV	SBR	144	B3
JENKINS RD	KER	78	C3
JENKS LAKE RD	SBD	100	A1
JENNINGS RD	STA	47	C3
JENNY LIND RD	CAL	40	D4
JENSEN AV	COL	32	E3
JENSEN AV	FRCO	56	C4
JENSEN AV	FRCO	57	A3
JENSEN RD	SLO	75	E1
JERROLD AV	FRCO	56	B2
JERRY COLLNS AV	MCO	48	B5
JERSEY	MCO	55	E2
JERSEY AV	KIN	67	C2
JERSEYDALE RD	MPA	49	C3
JERSEY ISLAND	CC	39	C4
JERSEY ISLND RD	CC	M	D3
JERUSALEM GRADE	LAK	32	B4
JESS VALLEY RD	MOD	8	B3
JESSICA DR	SUT	125	A4
JESUS MARIA RD	CAL	41	A3
JETTY RD S	HUM	15	D1
JEWELL AV	PAC	167	A1
JEWELL RD	TEH	18	C4
JEWELL VLY RD	SDCO	111	A4
JEWETT RD	HUM	16	D5
JEWETT RD	SUT	33	C3
JEWETTA AV	KER	78	C3
J HELT RD	HUM	15	D2
JIM DAY RD	SHA	13	E4
JIM HARVEY RD	SHA	18	C2
JIMMY DURNTE BL	SDCO	106	C4
JIM NEGRA RD	MCO	55	C2
JOAQUIN RD	ML	164	D2
JOAQUIN RDG LKT	FRCO	66	C2
JOEGER	PLA	34	C3
JOE SMITH RD	INY	51	D4
JOHANSEN RD	STA	47	D2
JOHN ST	RCO	100	E3
JOHN ST	SAL	171	C4
JOHN DALY BLVD	SMCO	L	B5
JOHN DALY BLVD	SMCO	45	B2
J F KENNEDY DR	RCO	99	C3
J F KENNEDY DR	SF	141	B4
JOHN FOX RD	STA	47	E2
JOHN GIBSON BL	LA	191	A2
JOHN LADD CHROM	SIS	3	B3
JOHN MUIR PKWY	CC	L	D3
JOHN MUIR PKWY	CC	38	D5
JOHNNY MDW RD	MNO	43	E5
JOHNNY MDW RD	MNO	50	E1

STREET	CO.	PAGE	GRID
JOHNNY MDW RD	MNO	51	A1
JOHNS DR	TUL	68	D3
JOHNS RD	KER	79	C3
JOHN SCHOOL RD	COL	33	A3
JOHN SCHOOL RD	YOL	33	A3
JOHN SMITH RD	SBT	55	A3
JOHNSON AV	MCO	47	D4
JOHNSON AV	SDCO	V	E2
JOHNSON AV	SDCO	106	E5
JOHNSON AV	SNLO	172	D3
JOHNSON AV	SLO	76	B3
JOHNSON CT	KER	79	C4
JOHNSON DR	TUL	58	B4
JOHNSON LN	DGL	36	C3
JOHNSON RD	HUM	10	B3
JOHNSON RD	HUM	15	E2
JOHNSON RD	KER	78	C3
JOHNSON RD	LAS	21	B3
JOHNSON RD	LACO	89	D3
JOHNSON RD	LACO	89	D4
JOHNSON RD	MCO	55	E1
JOHNSON RD	SBD	90	E3
JOHNSON RD	SBD	90	E4
JOHNSON RD	SBD	91	C3
JOHNSON RD	SJCO	40	C4
JOHNSON RD	TEH	18	B5
JOHNSON RD	TEH	18	D4
JOHNSON RD N	MCO	55	D1
JOHNSON ST	RCO	101	B5
JOHNSON ST	RCO	108	B1
JOHNSON ST	SBD	91	E3
JOHNSON ST	SB	87	D1
JOHNSON CYN RD	INY	72	A3
JOHNSON CYN RD	MON	54	E5
JOHNSON CYN RD	MON	55	A5
JOHNSON RCH RD	PLU	20	D5
JOHNSON SCH RD	LAS	21	B3
JOHNSTON AV	KER	80	D1
JOHNSTON AV	RCO	99	E4
JOHNSVILLE RD	SIE	26	D3
JOHNSVLL MCCREA	PLU	26	E3
JOHN WEST RD	MAD	49	D4
JOINES RD	YUB	33	E1
JOINT HWY 14	LAS	21	A3
JOINT HWY 14	LAS	21	A3
JOINT RD	TEH	18	B5
JOJOBA RD	RCO	107	A1
JOJOBA RD E	RCO	107	A1
JOJOBA ST	RCO	102	C4
JOLON RD	MON	65	B3
JOLON PLEYTO	MON	65	B4
JONATA PARK RD	SB	86	D3
JONATHAN ST	SBD	91	B3
JONES AV	COL	32	E3
JONES LN	MOD	8	B1
JONES RD	LAS	8	B5
JONES RD	MCO	48	B4
JONES RD	SJCO	47	D1
JONES ST	FRCO	57	B5
JONES ST	SF	143	B2
JONES ST	SMA	173	D3
JONES BAR RD	NEV	34	C1
JONES BRADWAY	SBD	92	A3
JONES VALLEY RD	SIE	27	E4
JORDAN RD	HUM	16	A3
JORDAN RD	MCO	47	E4
JORDAN RD	MCO	48	A4
JORDAN CREEK RD	MPA	48	E1
JORDAN CREEK RD	MPA	49	A1
JORDON HILL RD	BUT	25	D2
JORGENSEN RD	MCO	47	C5
JORGENSEN RD	STA	47	C4
JOSE BASIN RD	FRCO	50	A5
JOSE BASIN RD	MAD	58	A1
JOSEPH PL	SIS	4	C2
JOSEPH CREEK RD	MOD	7	C5
JOSHUA BLVD	KER	80	C5
JOSHUA DR	SBD	100	D2
JOSHUA LN	SBD	100	E2
JOSHUA RD	SBD	91	C3
JOSHUA RD	SBD	91	D4
JOSHUA WY	KER	79	D5
JOSHUA TREE RD	SBD	92	C5
JOY RD	SON	37	C2
JOY ST	KER	70	A5
J T CROW RD	STA	47	C4
JUAN ST	SD	213	A5
JUAN ST	SDCO	V	B3
JUAN DIEGO-			
-FLATS RD	RCO	100	A5
JUBILEE PASS RD	INY	72	C4
JUDSON ST	SBD	99	C2
JULIAN AV	KER	89	D1
JULIAN AV	SDCO	107	A5
JULIAN RD	SDCO	107	A4
JULIAN ST	SCL	P	C3
JULIAN ST	SCL	46	B4
JULIAN ST	SJ	152	A4
JULIE ST	KER	79	C3
JUMAR CT	RCO	107	B1
JUMPER AV	KER	78	A2
JUNCAL RD	SB	87	D4
JUNE ST	SBD	99	B1
JUNE LK BCH RD	MNO	50	C1
JUNIPER AV	MCO	48	B4
JUNIPER LN	SIS	4	C5
JUNIPER RD	LAS	14	C3
JUNIPER RD	RCO	99	B3
JUNIPER ST	SDCO	106	C2
JUNIPER FLTS RD	RCO	99	D4
JUNIPER FLTS RD	RCO	101	A2
JUNIPER HILL RD	LACO	90	B4
JUNIPR KNOLL RD	SIS	5	A3

STREET	CO.	PAGE	GRID
JUNIPER LAKE RD	LAS	20	A3
JUNIPERO ST	CAR	168	C4
JUNIPERO SRA BL	SCL	N	D3
JUNIPERO SRA BL	SCL	45	D4
JUNIPERO SRA FY	CPTO	149	C4
JUNIPERO SRA FY	CPTO	150	A4
JUNIPERO SRA FY	MLBR	144	A5
JUNIPERO SRA FY	SJ	150	A4
JUNIPERO SRA FY	SMCO	45	C3
JUNIPERO SRA FY	SCL	149	C4
JUNIPER RDG RD	LAS	8	C5
JUNIPER STA RD	MOD	7	B5
JUNKANS RD	SHA	18	A3
JURS RD	CAL	41	B2
JURUPA AV	RCO	99	A2
JURUPA AV	SBD	99	A2
JURUPA RD	RCO	99	A2
JUSTICE CT	KER	79	D2
JUSTICE RD	TRI	16	E5
JUTLAND DR	SD	211	C4
K			
K ST	BEN	153	A4
K ST	MDO	162	B3
KADOTA AV	MCO	48	D5
KAGEL CANYON RD	LACO	Q	D1
KAISER	SJCO	40	B5
KAISER RD	IMP	109	C3
KAISER RD	RCO	102	C4
KAISER RD	STA	47	D3
KALIN RD	IMP	109	A4
KAMM AV	FRCO	56	E5
KAMM AV	FRCO	57	C5
KAMM AV	TUL	57	D5
KAMM RD	IMP	109	C5
KANDRA RD	SIS	5	D2
KANE RD	HUM	9	E3
KANE RD	SBD	91	E2
KANSAS AV	KIN	67	D2
KANSAS AV	MDO	162	A3
KANSAS AV	STA	47	C2
KANSAS AV	TEH	18	E5
KAPAPA RD	SBD	80	E1
KAPRANOS RD	LAK	23	C5
KARCHNER RD	PLA	34	A3
KAREN AV	RCO	100	C3
KARLO RD	LAS	21	C2
KARNAK RD	SUT	33	C4
KASSON RD	SJCO	47	A2
KATELLA AV	ANA	193	C4
KATELLA AV	ANA	194	B4
KATELLA AV	ORA	194	B4
KATELLA AV	ORCO	98	B3
KATELLA AV	ORCO	T	D2
KATHERINE RD	VEN	97	A1
KAUFENBERG RD	LAS	14	A4
KAUFFMAN AV	TEH	18	E5
KAUFMAN RD	STA	47	E2
KAUT RD	TRI	10	E5
KAVANAUGH RD	IMP	112	C3
KEARNEY AV	FRCO	57	A3
KEARNEY BLVD	FRE	165	B4
KEARNY ST	SF	143	C2
KEARNY VILLA RD	SD	213	E1
KEARNY VILLA RD	SD	214	A1
KEARNY VILLA RD	SDCO	V	C2
KEARNY VILLA RD	SDCO	106	D5
KEATON RD	MCO	47	D4
KECKS RD	KER	77	A1
KEEFER RD	BUT	25	A2
KEEGAN RD	COL	32	C2
KEELE RD	RCO	110	C1
KEIM BLVD	RCO	110	C1
KELBAKER RD	SBD	83	C3
KELBAKER RD	SBD	84	A5
KELBAKER RD	SBD	93	E2
KELBAKER RD	SBD	94	A1
KELLEMS LN	SIS	3	D5
KELLEMS LN	SIS	11	D1
KELLER RD	RCO	99	C5
KELLEY RD	SBD	101	D1
KELLOG RD	SUT	33	B2
KELLOGG DR	ORCO	98	C3
KELLOGG DR	ORCO	T	E1
KELLOGG RD	DN	1	D3
KELLOGG SRRA BL	RCO	100	C3
KELLY	SJCO	47	D1
KELLY RD	HUM	16	C2
KELLY RD	NAPA	L	D1
KELLY RD	NAPA	38	D3
KELLY RD	TEH	24	A2
KELLY RD	YUB	26	B5
KELLY GULCH RD	SIS	11	B2
KELSEY CREEK RD	SIS	3	B4
KELSEY CREEK RD	LAK	31	D3
KELSO AV	KER	79	E1
KELSO RD	ALA	M	E4
KELSO RD	ALA	46	D1
KELSO RD	KER	79	E1
KELSO RD	SBD	83	C4
KELSO CIMA RD	SBD	83	E5
KELSO CIMA RD	SBD	84	A4
KELSO CK VLY RD	KER	79	E1
KELSO VALLEY RD	KER	79	E2
KELSO VALLEY RD	KER	80	A2
KEMP CT	HUM	16	B3
KEMPER RD	KER	80	A5
KEMPER RD	STA	47	D2
KEMPTON RD	SUT	33	D3
KENDALL AV	KER	80	D1
KENDALL DR	SBD	99	B1
KENDALL RD	SBD	91	E4

STREET INDEX

STREET	CO.	PAGE	GRID
KENDLE RD	IMP	109	C4
KENMAR LN	KER	79	A4
KENMAR RD	HUM	15	E2
KENNEBRAW LN	HUM	16	C4
KENNEDY AV	BUT	25	A3
KENNEDY RD	STA	48	A1
KENNEDY RD	TRI	17	B1
KENNEDY MEADOW	TUL	70	A3
KENNEDY MEM DR	SHA	18	B2
KENNEFICK RD	SJCO	40	B4
KENNETH AV	SAC	34	B5
KENNETH RD	LACO	Q	D2
KENNETT RD	SHA	18	C1
KENNEY AV	TEH	18	C4
KENNY AV	MCO	48	B4
KENNY CAMP RD	TRI	11	D5
KENO WORDEN RD	KLAM	5	A1
KENSINGTON WY	S	160	B2
KENT AV	KIN	67	B2
KENT AV	KIN	67	C2
KENT AV	MAR	139	B5
KENT AV	SUT	33	C1
KENTUCKY AV	YOL	33	B5
KENTUCKY ST	FRFD	135	B3
KENWOOD	SDCO	111	E1
KENWOOD DR	SDCO	V	D3
KEOUGH HOT SPGS	INY	51	D5
KERN RD	SBD	101	D1
KERN ST	SAL	171	D4
KERN CANYON RD	KER	79	A2
KERN RIV CYN RD	KER	79	B2
KERTO RD	KER	78	A5
KERSHAW RD	IMP	109	B4
KESTER AV	LACO	Q	C3
KETTLEMAN LN	SJCO	40	A4
KETTNER BLVD	SD	215	D4
KETTNER BLVD	SDCO	V	B3
KEYES RD	MCO	48	B3
KEYES RD	STA	47	D3
KEYES RD	STA	48	A3
KEYES ST	SJ	152	D5
KEYS RD	SUT	33	D4
KEYSTONE RD	IMP	109	A5
KEYSVILLE RD	KER	79	C1
KEZAR DR	SF	141	D4
KIBBE RD	YUB	33	D1
KICKAPOO TR	SBD	100	D2
KIDDER AV	FRFD	135	C3
KIDDER CREEK RD	SIS	3	C5
KIDDER CK RD S	SIS	3	D5
KIDDER CK RD S	SIS	11	D1
KID LAKES	PLA	35	C1
KIDWELL RD	SOL	39	B1
KIEFER BLVD	SAC	39	E1
KIEFER BLVD	SAC	40	B1
KIEFER RD	IMP	112	C4
KIELY BLVD	SJ	150	E5
KIELY BLVD	SCLR	150	D3
KIERNAN AV	STA	47	B2
KIETZKE LN	RENO	130	E3
KIFER RD	SCLR	150	D1
KIFER RD	SVL	150	A1
KILAGA SPGS RD	PLA	34	B3
KILAGA SPG RD N	PLA	34	B3
KILBURN AV	NAP	133	A4
KILBURN RD	STA	47	C4
KILE RD	SJCO	39	E3
KILER CANYON RD	SLO	75	E1
KILER CANYON RD	SLO	76	A1
KILGORE RD	SUT	33	A2
KILKARE RD	ALA	46	B2
KILLGORE HLS RD	SIS	4	A4
KILROY	STA	47	D3
KILROY RD	MCO	47	D4
KIMBALL LN	YUB	33	D2
KIMBALL RD	TEH	18	D5
KIMBERLINA RD	KER	78	B1
KIMBERLY CT	KER	79	C5
KIMBERLY DR	KER	79	C5
KIMBERLY RD	SHA	18	D3
KIMTU CT	HUM	16	B5
KINCAID RD	SCL	P	D3
KINCAID RD	SCL	46	C4
KINE AV	RCO	99	C3
KINEVAN RD	SB	87	B4
KING AV	KIN	67	C2
KING RD	COL	32	C2
KING RD	IMP	112	C3
KING RD	KER	67	C5
KING RD	PLA	34	B4
KING RD	SJ	152	D1
KING RD	SCL	P	C3
KING RD	SCL	46	B4
KING RD	SCL	152	D1
KING RD	SOL	39	C2
KING RD	TEH	18	C5
KING RD	TRI	12	A4
KING ST	BKD	166	E4
KING CITY RD	SBT	65	C1
KINGDON	SJCO	40	A4
KING RANCH RD	BUT	25	E5
KING RIDGE RD	SON	37	A1
KINGS AV	FRCO	66	D2
KINGS RD	SBD	90	E4
KINGS RD	TUO	48	E1
KINGS RD	TUO	49	A1
KINGSBURY RD	TRI	17	B2
KINGS CANYON RD	FRCO	58	A3
KINGS HILL RD	PLA	34	D2
KINGSLEY ST	MTCL	203	A4
KINGS MTN RD	SMCO	N	D2
KINGS MTN RD	SMCO	45	C4
KINGS PEAK RD	HUM	16	A5

STREET	CO.	PAGE	GRID
KINGSTON RD	SBD	83	E2
KINGS VALLEY RD	DN	1	E3
KINNEY RD	MEN	30	C3
KIOWA BLVD	MOH	96	B4
KIOWA RD	RCO	102	C3
KIOWA RD	SBD	91	C4
KIP ST	KER	80	C1
KIRBY RD	MCO	48	C4
KIRBY ST	CAL	40	D4
KIRK RD	SCL	P	B4
KIRKER PASS RD	CC	M	B3
KIRKVILLE RD	SUT	33	C3
KIRSCHENMANN RD	SB	87	D1
KIT CARSON RD	AMA	35	E5
KIT CARSON CPGD	ALP	36	B4
KITCHEN CK RD	SDCO	112	D1
KLAMATH BCH RD	DN	1	E5
KLAMATH BCH RD	DN	9	E1
KLAMATH BCH RD	DN	10	A1
KLAMATH MILL RD	DN	2	A5
KLAMATHON RD	SIS	4	B3
KLAMATH RIV RD	SIS	3	D3
KLASSETTE ST	KER	80	A4
KLAU MINE RD	SLO	75	D1
KLIPSTEIN ST	KER	78	A5
KLIPSTEIN CY RD	KER	78	A5
KLOKE RD	IMP	112	B4
KLONDIKE RD	SBD	93	C3
KLONDKE MINE RD	TRI	17	A3
KNEELAND RD	HUM	16	B1
KNIEBES RD	MCO	47	D5
KNIGHTON RD	SHA	18	C3
KNIGHTS RD	SUT	33	C3
KNIGHTSEN AV	CC	M	D3
KNIGHTSEN AV	CC	39	C5
KNOB HILL RD	MEN	31	B2
KNOB PK LKOT RD	SHA	17	D3
KNOTT AV	ORCO	98	B3
KNOTT AV	ORCO	T	B2
KNOWLES RD	MAD	49	B5
KNOWLES RD	MCO	56	C1
KNOX RD	STA	47	E1
KNOXVL DVLHD RD	NAPA	32	C4
KOALA RD	SBD	91	A3
KOCH RD	KER	78	B2
KOENIGSTEIN RD	VEN	88	C4
KOESTER RD	KER	79	D3
KONOCTI RD	LAK	31	D3
KOPTA RD	TEH	24	E2
KOSTER RD	SJCO	47	A2
KOSTER ST	EUR	121	B1
KOWOLOWSKI RD	MOD	6	A2
KRAEMER BLVD	ORCO	T	D1
KRAFFT RD	MCO	48	D4
KRAFT RD	KER	78	E5
KRAMAR RD	IMP	111	E3
KRAMER BLVD	ORCO	98	C3
KRAMER RD	LAS	14	B3
KRAMER RD	SBD	91	A1
KRATZMEYER RD	KER	78	C2
KREHE RD	SUT	33	C1
KROSENS RD	YUB	25	E5
KRUSE RD	COL	32	D1
KT RD	SBT	54	E3
KT RD	SBT	55	A3
KUBLER RD	IMP	111	E4
KUCK RD	SIS	4	B4
KUENZLI ST	RENO	130	D2
KUMBERG RD	IMP	112	C4
KUNA AV	SBD	92	E5
KURT RD	KER	77	E1
KUTZ RD	IMP	108	E5
KYLE AV	KER	70	A5
KYTE AV	KER	78	C2
L			
L ST	CC	M	C3
L ST	DVS	136	D3
L ST	DN	1	D4
L ST	MDO	162	B3
L ST	SCTO	137	B3
L ST	SDCO	V	C4
L ST	SDCO	111	D2
LA BARR MDWS RD	NEV	34	C2
LABP & L RD	SBD	91	A4
LA BREA AV	LA	181	C4
LA BREA AV	LA	184	C3
LA BREA AV	LACO	97	D2
LA BREA AV	LACO	Q	D5
LA BREA CK RD	SB	77	A5
LA BRISA DR	SBD	100	E1
LA BRISTA DR	SBD	100	D1
LA BRUCHERIE RD	IMP	112	A3
LA CADENA DR	CLTN	207	A4
LA CADENA DR	SBD	90	E3
LA CADENA DR	SBD	99	B2
LACEY BLVD	KIN	67	C1
LA CIENEGA BLVD	BH	183	E2
LA CIENEGA BLVD	CUL	183	E5
LA CIENEGA BLVD	ING	188	E4
LA CIENEGA BLVD	ING	189	E2
LA CIENEGA BLVD	LA	183	E4
LA CIENEGA BLVD	LACO	97	D2
LA CIENEGA BLVD	LACO	Q	D4
LA CIENEGA BLVD	LACO	183	E2
LA CIENEGA BLVD	LACO	188	E1
LA CIENEGA BLVD	LACO	189	E2
LAC JAC	FRCO	58	A4
LACK RD	IMP	109	E4
LA COLINA	TUL	68	E3
LA COLINA LN	RCO	107	C1
LA CONTENTA RD	SBD	100	E2

STREET	CO.	PAGE	GRID
LA COSTA AV	SDCO	106	C3
LA CRESCENTA AV	LACO	R	A2
LA CRESTA DR	SDCO	107	A5
LA CUARTA ST	LACO	R	D5
LADD RD	STA	47	C2
LADDER RIDGE RD	LAK	31	D2
LADINO AV	MCO	48	B4
LA ENTRADA AV	LACO	R	D5
LAFAYETTE RD	SIE	26	D5
LAFAYETTE ST	SCLR	151	B1
LAFAYETTE ST	S	160	D5
LA GLORIA RD	SBT	55	B5
LAGOMARSINO AV	MON	65	B2
LAGOON DR	KER	78	A2
LA GRANADA	SDCO	106	C4
LA GRANDE RD	COL	32	C2
LA GRANGE RD	DN	1	E5
LA GRANGE RD	MCO	48	C2
LA GRANGE RD	STA	48	C2
LA GRANGE RD	TUO	48	C1
LA GRANGE DM RD	STA	48	C2
LAGUE RD	YUB	26	A5
LAGUNA AV	FRCO	67	B1
LAGUNA FRWY	ORCO	98	D4
LAGUNA FRWY	ORCO	T	E4
LAGUNA RD	SON	37	D2
LAGUNA RD	VEN	96	C1
LAGUNA CYN RD	LAG	201	B2
LAGUNA CYN RD	ORCO	98	C5
LAGUNA CYN RD	ORCO	T	E5
LAGUNA CREEK TR	SOL	38	E3
LAGUNA MTN RD	SDCO	107	D5
LAGUNA SECA DR	SBD	91	D4
LAGUNA SECA RD	MCO	55	D3
LA HABRA BLVD	ORCO	R	E5
LA HABRA BLVD	ORCO	T	C1
LA HONDA RD	SMCO	N	C3
LA HONDA RD	SMCO	45	C4
LAIRD RD	PLA	34	B4
LAIRD RD	STA	47	C3
LAIRO RED ROCK	SIS	5	C3
LA JOLLA AV	SDCO	106	C5
LA JOLLA BLVD	SDCO	V	A2
LA JOLLA BLVD	SDCO	106	C5
LA JOLLA AMAGO	SDCO	107	A2
LA JOLLA S DR N	SD	211	B2
LA JOLLA S RD S	SD	211	A4
LA JOLLA SHR DR	SD	211	A2
LA JOLLA VLG RD	SDCO	V	A2
LAKE AV	FRCO	56	E3
LAKE AV	FRCO	57	A3
LAKE AV	KER	79	C2
LAKE AV	LACO	98	A1
LAKE AV	LACO	R	B3
LAKE AV	PAS	190	D4
LAKE AV	SCR	54	C2
LAKE BLVD	SHA	18	C2
LAKE DR	SBD	91	C5
LAKE RD	FRCO	50	B5
LAKE RD	KER	80	C3
LAKE RD	MCO	48	C4
LAKE RD	STA	47	E2
LAKE RD	STA	48	A2
LAKE RD N	INY	51	B5
LAKE RD S	INY	51	C5
LAKE RD S	KER	78	B4
LAKE RD S	KER	78	C4
LAKE ST	MAD	57	A2
LAKE ST	RCO	99	B4
LK ALMANOR W DR	PLU	20	B4
LK ALMANR RD E	PLU	20	C4
LK ALPINE RD E	ALP	42	A1
LK ALPINE RD W	ALP	42	A2
LK ANNIE RD	MOD	7	D3
LK BRITTON LOOP	SHA	13	C4
LK BRITTON RAMP	SHA	13	C4
LAKE CALIF DR	TEH	18	D3
LAKE CANYON RD	LACO	89	B3
LAKE CANYON RD	LACO	89	C3
LAKE CITY RD	NEV	26	C5
LK CITY DUMP RD	MOD	7	D5
LAKE CREST RD	LAS	21	B4
LAKE DAVIS RD	PLU	27	B2
LAKE EARL DR	DN	1	D4
LAKE FOREST DR	ORCO	98	D4
LAKE FRANCES RD	YUB	26	B5
LAKE HERMAN RD	SOL	L	E2
LAKE HERMAN RD	SOL	38	D4
LAKE HERMAN RD	SOL	153	C1
LK JENNINGS PK	SDCO	107	A5
LAKELAND RD	LACO	R	C5
LAKELAND RD	LACO	T	A1
LAKE LEAVITT RD	LAS	21	B3
LAKE MARY RD	ML	164	A4
LAKE MARY RD	MNO	50	D2
LAKE MATHEWS DR	RCO	99	B3
LAKE MCCUMBER	SHA	19	B2
LAKE MEAD DR	CLK	74	E3
LAKE MORENA DR	SDCO	112	D1
LAKE MURRAY BL	SDCO	V	D3
LAKE MURRAY BL	SDCO	106	D5
LAKEPORT BLVD	LAK	31	D3
LAKE POWAY RD	SDCO	106	D4
LAKERIDGE RD	SHA	19	A3
LAKE SHORE AV	O	158	B3
LAKESHORE BLVD	LAK	31	D3
LAKESHORE DR	KLAM	5	B1
LAKESHORE DR	LAK	32	A3
LAKESHORE DR	SHA	12	C5
LAKE SHORE DR	SIS	12	C1
LAKESHORE RD	MOD	7	B4
LAKESIDE DR	O	158	A3
LAKE SIDE LN	SIS	4	C2
LAKE STATION RD	KER	78	B4

STREET	CO.	PAGE	GRID
LAKE TAHOE BLVD	SLT	129	A4
LAKEVIEW	KIN	67	C2
LAKEVIEW	PLA	34	A3
LAKEVIEW AV	ORCO	T	E2
LAKEVIEW AV	RCO	99	D3
LAKEVIEW DR	AMA	40	D3
LAKEVIEW DR	LAK	31	D2
LAKE VIEW DR	LAS	21	B4
LAKE VIEW DR	SLO	75	D1
LAKEVIEW RD	MPA	49	B3
LAKEVIEW RD	SCR	54	C2
LAKEVIEW RD	SDCO	107	A5
LAKE VIEW RD	SIS	4	C3
LAKEVIEW RD	SON	38	B3
LAKEVIEW CEM RD	SIS	5	A3
LAKEVILLE HWY	SON	L	A1
LAKEVILLE RD	SON	L	B2
LK WILDWOOD DR	NEV	34	B1
LAKEWOOD BLVD	LACO	98	A3
LAKEWOOD BLVD	LACO	S	E2
LAKEWOOD DR	MEN	23	A5
LAKIN DAM RD	SIS	13	A2
LA LOMA AV	B	156	B2
LA LOMA AV	MDO	162	C3
LA LOMA AV	VEN	88	C5
LA LOMA RD	LACO	R	B3
LA LOMA RD	PAS	190	A5
LAMB BLVD	CLK	74	E2
LAMB CANYON RD	RCO	99	E3
LAMBERT LN	LAS	21	C4
LAMBERT RD	LACO	R	C5
LAMBERT RD	ORCO	U	A4
LAMBERT RD	ORCO	T	C1
LAMBERT RD	SAC	39	D3
LAMBIE RD	SOL	39	B3
LAMBUTH RD	STA	47	D1
LAMERT LN	GLE	24	D5
LA MESA RD	SBD	90	E4
LA MIRADA AV	LACO	R	D5
LA MIRADA AV	LACO	T	B1
LA MIRADA BLVD	LACO	98	B3
LAMMERS RD	SJCO	46	E2
LAMPLEY RD	STA	48	A2
LAMPSON AV	GGR	195	A1
LAMPSON AV	ORCO	T	B2
LANCASTER BLVD	KER	90	B1
LANCASTER BLVD	LACO	90	A2
LANCASTER RD	LACO	88	E2
LANCASTER RD	LACO	89	A2
LANCASTER RD	STA	47	E1
LANCASTER RD	STA	48	A1
LANCHA PLANA-			
-BUENA VISTA RD	AMA	40	D3
LANDACRE RD	TRI	17	B2
LANDAU BLVD	RCO	100	D3
LANDECENA DR	TRI	17	D1
LANDER AV	MCO	47	D5
LANDER AV	STA	47	E3
LANDERGEN RD	HUM	15	E4
LANDES RD	TEH	18	C4
LANDESS RD	SCL	46	B4
LANDIS GULCH	TRI	17	C3
LANDRAM AV	MCO	48	B4
LANES RD	FRCO	57	C2
LANES VALLEY RD	TEH	19	A3
LANFAIR RD	SBD	84	D3
LANFAIR RD	SBD	94	E1
LANGDON RD	MCO	55	D2
LANGLL VLY RD E	KLAM	5	E1
LANGLL VLY RD E	KLAM	6	A1
LANGLL VLY RD W	KLAM	5	E1
LANGLL VLY RD W	KLAM	6	A1
LANGWORTH RD	STA	47	D2
LANINI RD	MON	54	E5
LANINI RD	MON	55	A5
LANKERSHIM BLVD	LA	179	A5
LANKERSHIM BLVD	LACO	97	D1
LANKERSHIM BLVD	LACO	Q	C3
LANNAGAN RD	TRI	11	B5
LANNAGAN RD	TRI	17	B1
LANPHERE RD	HUM	9	E5
LANSING AV	KIN	67	C2
LA PALMA AV	ANA	193	D1
LA PALMA AV	ANA	194	A1
LA PALMA AV	KER	80	A5
LA PALMA AV	ORCO	98	A3
LA PALMA AV	ORCO	T	B2
LA PALOMA	AVLN	97	A4
LA PALOMA DR	TUL	68	E3
LA PALOMA RD	MCO	48	C4
LA PANZA AV	SB	87	E2
LA PAZ RD	ORCO	98	D5
LA PORTE RD	BUT	25	D5
LA PORTE RD	BUT	26	B4
LA PORTE RD	YUB	26	A5
LA POSTA RD	SDCO	112	D1
LA PUENTE RD	LACO	U	A3
LARCHMONT BLVD	LA	184	E1
LARGO GRANDE	RCO	107	B1
LARGO VISTA RD	LACO	90	D4
LARKELLEN AV	LACO	R	E4
LARKIN RD	BUT	25	C4
LARKIN RD	SUT	33	C1
LARKIN VALLEY	SCR	54	B2
LARKMEAD LN	NAPA	29	B5
LARKSPUR DR	MLBR	144	B5
LARREA AV	SBD	101	B1
LARRY FLAT	MOD	7	D3
LARSEN RD	IMP	109	A5
LARSON LN	MNO	42	E1
LARSON RD	RCO	107	C1
LA RUE RD	YOL	136	B3
LA SALLE CANYON	SB	86	B3

STREET	CO.	PAGE	GRID
LAS AMIGAS RD	NAPA	38	C3
LAS ANIMAS RD	SCL	46	C5
LAS FLORES AV	KER	80	C1
LA SIERRA AV	RCO	99	A3
LAS LOMAS AV	AVLN	97	A5
LAS PALMAS AV	STA	47	C3
LASPINA DR	TUL	68	B2
LAS PLUMAS AV	BUT	25	D4
LAS POSAS	VEN	96	C1
LS PULGAS CY RD	SDCO	106	A2
LAS ROCAS	RCO	100	D4
LASSELLE ST	RCO	99	C3
LASSEN AV	BUT	25	B3
LASSEN AV	FRCO	67	A1
LASSEN AV	FRCO	57	A3
LASSEN LN	SIS	12	C2
LASSEN RD	TEH	25	A2
LASSEN ST	LAS	8	B4
LASSEN ST	NAP	133	A1
LASSEN TRAIL	TEH	19	D4
LASSEN CREEK RD	MOD	7	C4
LASSEN PARK HWY	SHA	19	D2
LASSICS LKOT RD	TRI	16	E4
LAST CHANCE CYN	KER	80	C2
LAST CHANCE MNE	NEV	26	E5
LAST CHANCE MNE	NEV	35	A1
LAS TUNAS DR	LACO	R	C3
LAS VARAS RD	SB	87	A4
LAS VEGAS BLVD	CLK	74	D3
LAS VEGAS BL S	CLK	209	C4
LAS VEGAS BL S	CLK	210	B5
LAS VEGAS BL S	LV	209	C4
LAS VIRGENES RD	LACO	97	A1
LATHAM RD	SUT	33	B3
LATHROP RD	MAN	161	A1
LATHROP RD	SJCO	47	A1
LATHROP RD	SJCO	161	D1
LATIGO CYN RD	LACO	97	A2
LA TIJERA BLVD	LA	188	C5
LA TIJERA BLVD	LACO	Q	D5
LATKA LN	TEH	19	B4
LATROBE RD	AMA	40	D1
LATROBE RD	ED	40	C1
LATROBE RD	SAC	40	B1
LA TUNA CYN RD	LACO	97	D1
LA TUNA CYN RD	LACO	Q	D2
LAUFFER RD	HUM	22	D1
LAUGHLIN RD	STA	47	E2
LAUGHLIN CVC DR	CLK	85	D4
LAURA DR	LAS	27	E1
LAUREL AV	KIN	67	B2
LAUREL AV	MLBR	144	C5
LAUREL AV	SUT	33	D3
LAUREL DR E	MON	171	E2
LAUREL DR E	SAL	171	E2
LAUREL DR W	SAL	171	A2
LAUREL DR W	MON	171	A2
LAUREL LN	YUB	33	D1
LAUREL ST	NAP	133	A4
LAUREL ST	SD	215	D2
LAUREL ST	SDCO	V	B3
LAUREL ST	SC	169	C3
LAUREL WY	TEH	18	C4
LAUREL CYN BLVD	LACO	97	D1
LAUREL CYN BLVD	LACO	Q	C1
LAUREL DELL RD	LAK	31	C2
LAURELES GRADE	MON	54	C5
LAUREL GLEN RD	SCR	P	B5
LAUREL GLEN RD	SCR	54	A1
LAUREL GROVE AV	MAR	139	B4
LAUREL GROVE AV	MAR	L	A3
LAUREL GROVE AV	ROSS	139	A4
LAURELLEN RD	YUB	33	D2
LAURENT ST	SC	169	B3
LAURJOE RD	SBD	91	E3
LAUSTEN RD	COL	32	D1
LAUX RD	COL	33	A1
LAVA BED RD	BUT	25	B3
LAVA BDS NAT MN	MOD	6	A4
LAVA BDS MED LK	SIS	5	C5
LAVAL RD	KER	78	E5
LAVER CROSSING	LAS	21	D5
LAVERNE AV	MAR	140	A3
LA VETA AV	ORA	196	B1
LAVEZZOLA RD	SIE	26	D4
LAVIC RD	SBD	92	E2
LA VISTA AV	VEN	88	C5
LAWRENCE EXPWY	SCL	P	A3
LAWRENCE EXPWY	SCLR	150	C4
LAWRENCE EXPWY	SJ	150	C4
LAWRENCE EXPWY	SVL	150	C4
LAWSON LN	HUM	15	E2
LAXAQUE RD	MOD	8	D1
LAYTNVL DOS RIO	MEN	22	E3
LAZARO CARDENAS	BAJA	112	B4
LAZARUS LN	RCO	100	A5
L B CROW RD	STA	47	C4
LEACH RD	YUB	33	D3
LEAR AV	SBD	101	B1
LEARY RD	SAC	M	E1
LEARY RD	SAC	39	D3
LEASTALK AV	SBD	84	C3
LEATHER RD	IMP	110	D5
LEAVENWORTH ST	SF	143	B2
LEAVESLEY RD	SCL	P	E5
LEAVESLEY RD	SCL	54	D1
LEAVITT RD	LAS	21	B3
LEE RD	MCO	48	A3
LEE RD	PLU	26	D1
LEE RD	SHA	13	E4
LEE RD	SUT	33	D4
LEEDS	MCO	48	C4
LEEGE AV	SB	86	B3

STREET	CO.	PAGE	GRID
LEEK RD	STA	47	D2
LEE SCHOOL RD	SAC	40	B2
LEESVILLE RD	COL	32	C2
LEESVL-LODGA RD	COL	32	B1
LEFF RD	RCO	107	B1
LEFFINGWELL RD	LACO	R	C5
LEFFINGWELL RD	LACO	T	B1
LEGION AV	MCO	47	E4
LEGION AV	MCO	48	A4
LEGION PARK DR	MDO	162	E5
LE GRAND RD	MCO	48	D5
LEGRAY RD	KER	78	E5
LEIGHTON, H RD	SHA	18	C2
LEILA LN	SBD	101	E1
LEIMERT BLVD	LACO	Q	D4
LEININGER RD	TEH	25	A1
LEISER RD	SUT	33	C4
LEISURE TOWN RD	SOL	39	A2
LELITER RD	KER	70	C5
LEMON AV	SDCO	V	D3
LEMON AV	SDCO	111	E1
LEMON AV	SJCO	47	D1
LEMON AV	STA	47	B3
LEMON RD	SBD	91	C4
LEMON ST	ORCO	T	C1
LEMON ST	VAL	134	D5
LEMON CANYON RD	SIE	27	C4
LEMOS RD	SIS	4	A2
LENAHAN RD	COL	32	D1
LENARD RD	LAS	14	C3
LENINGER RD	BUT	25	A2
LENTELL RD	HUM	15	E1
LENWOOD RD	SBD	91	D1
LEO RD	RCO	107	A1
LEON AV	MCO	56	B2
LEON RD	RCO	99	D4
LEONA AV	LACO	89	D3
LEONARD AV	FRCO	57	D4
LEONARD AV	KER	78	A2
LEONARD RD	MPA	49	C3
LEONI RD	ED	35	B5
LEOTA ST	MCO	55	D1
LEPRECHAUN LN	RCO	107	B1
LERDO HWY	KER	77	D2
LERDO HWY	KER	78	A2
LEROY AV	SJCO	47	B1
LESSING ST	SBD	91	A3
LETTS VALLEY RD	COL	31	E1
LEVEE RD	FRCO	56	E4
LEVEE RD	IMP	112	D5
LEVEE RD	YOL	39	C2
LEVERONI RD	SON	L	B1
LEVERONI RD	SON	38	B3
LEVERONI RD	SON	132	B5
LEVIATHAN LKOUT	ALP	36	D5
LEVIATHAN RD	ALP	36	D5
LEWELLING BLVD	ALA	146	B1
LEWELLING BL E	ALA	L	E5
LEWIS RD	MON	54	C2
LEWIS RD	SHA	13	E4
LEWIS RD	SOL	39	B3
LEWIS RD	STA	47	C4
LEWIS RD	VEN	96	C1
LEWIS RD	YUB	33	E3
LEWIS CREEK RD	MON	65	D2
LEWIS RIDGE RD	BUT	26	B4
LEWISTON AV	FRCO	67	C1
LEWISTON RD	SHA	18	A1
LEWISTON RD	TRI	17	D1
LEWISTON TURNPK	TRI	17	E1
LEXINGTON AV	MCO	56	A2
LEXINGTON AV	SDCO	106	E5
LEXINGTON ST	SCLR	151	B3
LEXINGTN HLL RD	PLU	26	C3
LIBERAL AV	TEH	24	D2
LIBERTY AV	MCO	48	A4
LIBERTY RD	SJCO	40	B3
LIBERTY RD W	BUT	25	B5
LIBERTY ISLD RD	SOL	M	D1
LIBERTY ISLD RD	SOL	39	C3
LIBRAMIENTO SUR	BAJA	111	D3
LIBRAMNT ORIENT	BAJA	111	D2
LICHEN WY	RCO	107	B1
LICHENS RD	SIS	4	B4
LIEBERT RD	IMP	111	E3
LIGGET AV	COL	32	E3
LIGHTHILL RD	SIS	3	D5
LIGHTHOUSE AV	MONT	167	D2
LIGHTHOUSE AV	MON	53	E2
LIGHTHOUSE AV	PAC	167	B2
LIGHTHOUSE RD	HUM	15	D4
LIGHTHOUSE RD	MEN	30	C3
LILI VALLEY WY	CAL	41	C2
LILLEY MTN DR	MAD	49	C5
LILY GAP RD	CAL	41	C2
LIM RD	LAS	14	C3
LIME CREEK RD	CAL	40	E3
LIMEDYKE LKOUT	TRI	16	E2
LIMEKILN RD	MON	54	D5
LIME KILN RD	NEV	34	C2
LIMEKILN RD	SBT	54	E4
LIMEKILN RD	SBT	55	A4
LIME KILN RD	TUO	41	C5
LIME SADDLE RD	BUT	25	C3
LIMONITE AV	RCO	99	A2
LINCOLN	LACO	97	C2
LINCOLN	MCO	48	B5
LINCOLN AV	ANA	193	B2
LINCOLN AV	ANA	194	B2
LINCOLN AV	FRCO	56	D4
LINCOLN AV	FRCO	57	A4
LINCOLN AV	FRCO	58	A4
LINCOLN AV	KIN	67	C2

STREET	CO.	PAGE	GRID
LINCOLN AV	LACO	R	B2
LINCOLN AV	LACO	190	B1
LINCOLN AV	ORA	194	E2
LINCOLN AV	ORCO	98	B3
LINCOLN AV	ORCO	T	B2
LINCOLN AV	PAS	190	B1
LINCOLN AV	RCO	U	E5
LINCOLN AV	RCO	98	E3
LINCOLN AV	SAL	171	C4
LINCOLN AV	SD	214	A5
LINCOLN AV	SDCO	106	D3
LINCOLN AV	SR	139	D3
LINCOLN AV	SA	196	C3
LINCOLN AV	SCL	P	B3
LINCOLN AV	SCL	46	B4
LINCOLN AV	YUB	33	E1
LINCOLN AV W	NAP	133	A3
LINCOLN BLVD	BUT	25	D5
LINCOLN BLVD	LA	187	A1
LINCOLN BLVD	LA	189	A1
LINCOLN BLVD	LACO	Q	B4
LINCOLN BLVD	LACO	187	D3
LINCOLN BLVD	MCO	47	E4
LINCOLN BLVD	MCO	48	A4
LINCOLN BLVD	SF	141	B2
LINCOLN BLVD	SMON	187	A1
LINCOLN RD	SBD	91	E4
LINCOLN RD	SUT	33	C2
LINCOLN RD	SUT	125	A5
LINCOLN RD	YUBA	125	A5
LINCOLN ST	NAPA	29	A1
LINCOLN ST	RCO	101	B5
LINCOLN ST	SC	169	D3
LINCOLN ST	S	160	D5
LINCOLN ST N	KER	77	E4
LINCOLN ST N	KER	78	A4
LINCOLN WY	AUB	126	D2
LINCOLN WY	SFCO	L	B5
LINCOLN WY	SF	141	C4
LINCOLN WY	SFCO	45	B1
LINCOLN WY E	AUB	126	D2
LINCOLN WY E	PLA	126	D2
LINDA DR	SIS	4	B2
LINDA VISTA AV	LACO	98	A1
LINDA VISTA AV	LACO	R	B2
LINDA VISTA AV	NAP	133	A2
LINDA VISTA AV	PAS	190	A3
LINDA VISTA AV	TUL	68	D3
LINDA VISTA DR	SB	87	A3
LINDA VISTA RD	SBD	91	D1
LINDA VISTA RD	SD	213	B4
LINDA VISTA RD	SDCO	V	B3
LINDA VISTA RD	SDCO	111	C1
LINDBERGH BLVD	KER	80	B4
LINDBLOOM RD	MCO	55	D3
LINDEN AV	MCO	56	A1
LINDEN AV	SBD	99	B2
LINDEN AV	SSF	144	B1
LINDENBERGER RD	RCO	99	D4
LINDERO CYN RD	LACO	96	E1
LINDLEY AV	LA	178	E4
LINDLEY AV	LACO	97	C1
LINDLEY RD	HUM	15	E4
LINDSAY RD	IMP	109	A3
LINDSAY RD	KER	78	C4
LINDSEY AV	GLE	24	E3
LINE RD	YOL	39	D2
LINEA DEL CIELO	SDCO	106	C4
LINGARD RD	MCO	48	C5
LINN RD	SJCO	40	C4
LINNE RD	SJCO	46	E2
LINNE RD	SLO	76	B1
LINSON AV	SBD	91	A3
LINWOOD AV	STA	47	C3
LINWOOD RD	MCO	47	E3
LINWOOD RD	MCO	48	A3
LISBON ST	MCO	48	A5
LISBON ST	SDCO	V	D3
LISCOMB HILL RD	HUM	10	A5
LIST AV	TUL	68	C1
LITT RD	STA	47	D2
LITTLE AV	BUT	25	C5
LITTLE RD	LPAZ	104	A2
LITTLE BEAR RD	RCO	102	C4
LITL BLACK ROCK	TRI	17	C4
LTL BRWNS CK RD	TRI	17	D1
LTL BRWNS CK RD	TRI	17	D1
LTL GIANT MILL	TEH	19	B4
LTL GRASS VLY	PLU	26	C3
LITTL HONKR BAY	SOL	39	B3
LITTLE JOHN	SJCO	40	C5
LITTLE JOHN RD	CAL	41	A5
LITTLE LAKE RD	INY	70	C4
LITTLE LAKE RD	MEN	30	C1
LITL MORONGO DR	SBD	100	D1
LITL PANOCHE RD	FRCO	55	D4
LITL PANOCHE RD	SBT	55	D4
LITTLE RIVER	MEN	30	B1
LTL SLATE CK RD	SHA	12	B4
LTL SYCAMOR CYN	LACO	96	D2
LITL TUJUNGA RD	LACO	89	D5
LITTLE VLY RD	LAS	14	A4
LITTLE VLY RD	MEN	22	C4
LITTLE VLY DUMP	LAS	14	B5
LITL VIRGNIA LK	MNO	43	B4
LITTLE WALKR RD	MNO	42	E3
LITTLE WALKR RD	MNO	43	A3
LITTON DR	NEV	127	C2
LIVELY RD	BUT	25	B5
LIVE OAK	FRCO	58	B3
LIVE OAK AV	LACO	98	B1
LIVE OAK AV	SBD	99	A2
LIVE OAK AV	SCL	P	D5

STREET	CO.	PAGE	GRID
LIVE OAK AV	SCL	54	C1
LIVEOAK DR	BUT	25	B3
LIVE OAK DR	SBD	99	D1
LIVE OAK RD	SBT	55	B4
LIVE OAK RD	SJCO	40	B4
LIVEOAK RD	SLO	76	A1
LIVE OAK RD	TEH	18	C5
LIVE OAK CYN RD	ORCO	98	E4
LIVE OAK CYN RD	SBD	99	D2
LIVERMORE RD	NAPA	32	A5
LIVNGSTN CRESSY	MCO	47	E4
LIVNGSTN CRESSY	MCO	48	A4
LIVORNA RD	CC	M	A4
LLAGAS RD	SCL	P	D5
LLAGAS RD	SCL	54	C1
LLANO RD	SON	37	E2
LLOYD LN	SHA	18	C3
LOBATA RD	YUB	33	E1
LOCAN AV	FRCO	57	D3
LOCH LOMOND RD	LAK	31	E4
LOCKHART RD	SBD	81	B4
LOCKWOOD RD	STA	47	D3
LOCKWOOD CEM RD	MON	65	C4
LOCKWD JOLON RD	MON	65	C4
LOCKWD SAN ARDO	MON	65	C4
LOCKWD SN LUCAS	MON	65	C3
LOCKWOOD VLY RD	VEN	88	C2
LOCO BILL RD	KER	79	D3
LOCUST AV	RCO	99	C2
LOCUST AV	SBD	81	A5
LOCUST AV	SBD	91	E4
LOCUST AV	STA	47	C3
LOCUST RD	SHA	18	D3
LOCUST TREE RD	SJCO	40	B4
LODGE RD	FRCO	58	A1
LODI LN	NAPA	29	B2
LODI RD	COL	33	A3
LOFGREN RD	BUT	25	B4
LOGAN AV	SD	216	E5
LOGAN LN	MEN	23	B2
LOG CABIN MINE	MNO	43	C5
LOGGING CAMP RD	MNO	50	E1
LOG HOUSE RD	SIS	4	E2
LOKERN RD	KER	77	D3
LOKOYA RD	NAPA	38	B2
LOLETA AV	TEH	24	D2
LOLETA RD	HUM	15	D2
LOMA AV	MCO	56	B1
LOMA ALTA DR	LACO	98	A1
LOMA ALTA DR	LACO	R	B2
LOMA ALTA DR	STB	174	B4
LOMA PRIETA AV	SCR	P	B5
LOMA PRIETA RD	SCR	54	A1
LOMA RICA DR	NEV	34	C1
LOMA RICA RD	YUB	33	D1
LOMAS CANTADAS	CC	156	E2
LOMAS SANTA FE	SDCO	106	C4
LOMA VERDE RD	RCO	102	C4
LOMA VISTA DR	NAPA	38	C2
LOMBARD ST	SFCO	L	B4
LOMBARD ST	SF	142	A2
LOMBARD ST	SF	143	A3
LOMBARD ST	SFCO	45	B1
LOMBARDY AV	MCO	47	E3
LOMBARDY AV	MCO	48	A3
LOMITA	VEN	88	A4
LOMITA AV	MLBR	144	B4
LOMITA BLVD	LACO	97	D3
LOMITA BLVD	LACO	S	B2
LOMITAS DR	TUL	58	D5
LOMITAS DR	TUL	68	D1
LOMPOC-CASML RD	SB	86	B2
LONDALE RD	STA	47	D1
LONE BUTTE RD	KER	80	A5
LONE COMPANY RD	MNO	42	E1
LONE HILL AV	LACO	U	B2
LONE MTN RD	JOS	2	C2
LONE OAK AV	STA	47	E2
LONE PINE LN	SON	38	A1
LONE PINE CYN	SBD	90	E5
LONE PN NRRW GG	INY	60	B4
LONE STAR MN RD	MNO	51	C2
LONE STAR RD	COL	32	E2
LONE STAR RD	MNO	51	C2
LONE STAR RD	PLA	34	B3
LONE STAR RD	SBD	91	C2
LONE TREE	SJCO	47	C1
LONE TREE RD	BUT	25	D5
LONE TREE RD	MCO	48	B5
LONE TREE RD	SBT	55	A2
LONE TREE RD	SHA	18	D3
LONE TREE WY	CC	M	C3
LONE TREE WY	CC	39	B5
LONG BARN	TUO	41	E4
LONG BEACH BLVD	LB	192	E3
LONG BEACH BLVD	LACO	97	E3
LONG BEACH BLVD	LACO	S	D1
LONG BEACH BL N	LACO	S	D1
LONG BEACH FRWY	LB	192	C2
LONG BEACH FRWY	LACO	97	E3
LONG CANYON RD	SB	86	D1
LONG CANYON RD	RCO	100	D3
LONGCOR RD	TEH	18	C3
LONGDEN AV	LACO	R	C3
LONG FELLOW AV	BUT	25	B3
LONG GULCH RD	SIS	4	A4
LONG HAY FLAT	SHA	19	B3
LONG HOLLOW DR	MAD	49	C5
LONG HOLLOW DR	TEH	24	C2
LONGHORN DR	LAS	8	B4
LONGHORN LN	KER	79	B4
LONG PRAIRIE RD	SIS	5	A5
LONG RAVINE RD	NEV	34	B2

STREET	CO.	PAGE	GRID
LONG RIDGE RD	TRI	16	E5
LONG VALLEY RD	ALP	36	C4
LONG VALLEY RD	LAK	32	A3
LONG VALLEY RD	SIE	27	E3
LONG VALLEY RD	PLU	20	C5
LONGVIEW AV	MCO	47	E4
LONGVIEW AV	MCO	48	A4
LONGVIEW RD	LACO	90	C3
LONOAK RD	MON	65	C2
LOOKOUT RD	CAL	41	C2
LKOUT-HACKMR RD	MOD	6	B5
LKOUT-HACKMR RD	MOD	14	B1
LKOUT INDIAN RD	MOD	14	B3
LOOKOUT MTN RD	SLO	76	C3
LOONEY RD	MCO	48	B3
LOOP BLVD N	KER	80	B4
LOOP BLVD S	KER	80	B4
LOOP RD	HUM	16	A2
LOOP RD	RCO	101	B2
LOOP RD	SHA	19	C2
LOPES RD	SOL	38	E4
LOPEZ DR	SLO	76	B4
LOPEZ CANYON RD	LACO	Q	C1
LOPEZ CANYON RD	SLO	76	C4
LOQUAT AV	STA	47	B3
LORAINE AV	LACO	U	A1
LORENSON	PLA	34	B3
LORENTZ RD	AMA	40	D1
LORENZEN RD	SJCO	47	A2
LORETZ RD	CLO	32	D1
LORRAINE RD	SBD	92	E5
LORT DR	TUL	68	C1
LOS ALAMITOS BL	ORCO	T	A2
LOS ALAMOS RD	RCO	99	C5
LOS ALTOS DR	LACO	R	D4
LOS ANGELES AV	VEN	88	C5
LOS ANGELES AV	VEN	89	A5
LOS ANGELES ST	KER	78	A2
LOS ANGELES ST	LA	185	E5
LS ANGLS AQDUCT	KER	80	B2
LS BERROS ARRYO	SLO	76	B4
LOS BURROS RD	MON	64	E4
LOS BURROS RD	MON	65	A4
LOS CERRITOS RD	MCO	48	B3
LOS CERRITOS RD	STA	48	B2
LOS COCHES RD	MON	65	A1
LOS COCHES RD	SDCO	V	E2
LOS COCHES RD	SDCO	107	A5
LS COYOTES DIAG	LACO	S	E2
LS COYOTES DIAG	LACO	T	A2
LOS FELIZ BLVD	GLEN	182	E2
LOS FELIZ BLVD	LA	182	B3
LOS FELIZ BLVD	LACO	97	D1
LOS FELIZ BLVD	LACO	Q	E3
LOS FLORES RD	SBD	91	B5
LOS GATOS BLVD	SCL	P	B4
LOS GATOS BLVD	SCL	46	A5
LOS GATOS RD	FRCO	66	C2
LOS LOBOS RD	MON	65	D4
LOS NIETOS RD	LACO	98	A2
LOS NIETOS RD	LACO	R	C5
LOS OLIVOS ST	STB	174	A3
LOS OSOS VLY RD	SLO	75	E3
LOS OSOS VLY RD	SLO	76	A3
LOS PADRES RD	SBD	91	C3
LOS PALOS DR	SAL	171	D5
LOS PINOS DR	RCO	100	D5
LOS PINOS RD	SDCO	112	D1
LOS PRADOS	SM	145	C3
LS RANCHITOS RD	SR	139	B1
LOS ROBLES RD	LACO	98	A1
LOS ROBLES AV	LACO	R	B3
LOS ROBLES AV	PAS	190	C2
LOST RD	RCO	99	C4
LOST CREEK RD	TEH	19	E4
LOST CK DAM RD	YUB	26	B4
LOST HILLS AV	FRCO	66	D3
LOST HILLS RD	KER	77	D2
LOST LAKE RD	ALP	36	A5
LOST LAKE RD	FRCO	57	D2
LOST SECTION S	INY	72	C3
LOST SECTION RD	INY	72	C3
LOS VERJELES RD	BUT	25	E5
LOS VERJELES RD	YUB	25	E5
LOTT RD	BUT	25	B3
LOTUS RD	ED	34	D5
LOUIE RD	SIS	4	C5
LOUIS AV	BUT	25	D5
LOUISE AV	MAN	161	A2
LOUISE AV	SJCO	47	C1
LOUISIANA ST	SUIS	135	C4
LOUISIANA ST	VAL	134	C4
LOUMAS LN	KER	79	C4
LOUPE AV	SCL	P	C3
LOUPE AV	SCL	46	B4
LOVE CREEK RD	CAL	41	C3
LOVEKIN BLVD	RCO	103	D5
LOVELAND RD	IMP	109	A4
LOVELOCK RD	BUT	25	D2
LOVENESS RD	MOD	14	B1
LOW RD	IMP	111	E3
LOWDEN RD	RED	122	E3
LOWDEN RD	SHA	122	E3
LOW DIVIDE RD	DN	1	E3
LOW DIVIDE RD	DN	2	A3
LOWE RD	IMP	110	B3
LOWELL ST	SDCO	V	A3
LOWELL HILL RD	NEV	34	E1
LOWER RD	AVLN	97	B5
LOWER AZUSA RD	LACO	98	A2
LOWER AZUSA RD	LACO	R	D3
LOWR CHILES VLY	NAPA	29	E2
LOWR CHILES VLY	NAPA	38	C1

STREET	CO.	PAGE	GRID
LOWER COLFAX RD	NEV	34	C2
LOWER DORRAY RD	CAL	41	A2
LOWER E TER	AVLN	97	B5
LOWR ENTRPRS RD	BUT	25	E4
LOWER FIRE RD	SIS	4	D5
LOWER FORBESTWN	BUT	26	A4
LOWER GAS PT RD	SHA	18	B3
LOWR GLACIER RD	INY	51	E5
LOWER HONCUT RD	BUT	25	D5
LOWER JONES	SJCO	39	D5
LOWER KLAMTH HY	KLAM	5	B1
LOWER KUCK RD	SIS	4	C3
LOWER LAKE RD	DN	1	D3
LOWER LAKE RD	LAK	31	E3
LOWER LAKE RD	LAK	32	A3
LWR LITL SHASTA	SIS	4	B4
LOWER MAD RIVER	TRI	16	E3
LOWER RATLSNAKE	TRI	17	A3
LOWER SACRAMNTO	SJCO	40	A4
LOWER SPGS RD	SHA	18	B2
LWR WESTSIDE RD	TRI	16	E4
LOWR WYANDTT RD	BUT	25	D5
LOWERY RD	HUM	15	D3
LOWERY RD	TEH	18	B5
LOWERY CEM RD	TEH	24	A1
LOWES CANYON RD	SLO	66	B5
LOW GAP RD	MEN	30	D1
LOW GAP RD	MEN	31	A2
LOW GAP RD	MEN	123	A2
LOW GAP RD	U	123	A2
LOYALTON RD	SIE	27	D3
LOYALTON RD	SIE	27	C3
LOZANO RD	MPA	48	D2
LOZANOS RD	PLA	34	B4
LUBKEN RD	INY	60	B4
LUCAS VALLEY RD	MAR	L	A3
LUCAS VALLEY RD	MAR	38	A4
LUCE GRISWLD RD	TEH	18	B4
LUCERNE VLY CTO	SBD	91	D2
LUCILLE	FRCO	66	D3
LUCILLE LN	RCO	107	C1
LUCINDA RD	SBD	81	C5
LUCKEHE RD	SUT	33	C1
LUCKY HILL RD	SIE	26	C3
LUCY BROWN RD	SLO	76	D1
LUDLOW RD	SBD	93	A2
LUDY BLVD	RCO	110	C1
LUIS AV	MCO	55	C1
LUISENO RD	RCO	107	B1
LUKENS LN	RCO	99	C3
LULU MINE RD	TUO	41	C5
LULU MINE RD	TUO	48	C1
LUMGREY RD	SIS	3	E3
LUMPKIN RD	BUT	25	E4
LUMPKIN RD	BUT	26	B4
LUMPKIN-			
-LA PORTE RD	BUT	26	A4
LUMPKIN RDG RD	BUT	26	B3
LUNA RD	IMP	109	B3
LUNA VISTA LN	SBD	100	D1
LUNDY AV	SCL	P	B3
LUNDY LAKE RD	MNO	43	B4
LUNING AV	TEH	24	D1
LUNT RD	BUT	25	D3
LUPIN AV	MCO	48	B4
LUPINE	FRCO	58	B3
LUPINE LN	RCO	100	C5
LURLINE AV	COL	32	D2
LUTHER RD	PLA	34	C3
LUTHER RD	TEH	18	D5
LUTHER E GIBSON	SOL	38	E4
LUTHER GIBSN FY	BEN	153	D4
LUTIE AV	KER	80	A4
LUX AV	MCO	56	B1
LYERLY RD	IMP	109	B3
LYNCH RD	NAPA	38	D3
LYNCH CANYON DR	SLO	65	D5
LYNCH MDWS RD	BUT	25	D2
LYNN RD	VEN	96	D1
LYNN RD W	VEN	96	D1
LYON AV	FRCO	56	C2
LYON AV	RCO	99	E3
LYON RD	STA	47	E2
LYON RD	STA	48	A2
LYONS AV	LACO	89	B4
LYONS AV	SLT	129	A3
LYONS RD	IMP	111	E4
LYONS RD	IMP	112	A4
LYONS ST	SNRA	163	C3
LYTLE AV	KER	68	B5
LYTLE CREEK RD	SBD	90	E5
LYTLE CREEK RD	SBD	99	A1
LYTTON ST	SDCO	V	A3
M			
M ST	EUR	121	D1
M ST	FRE	165	D3
M ST	MCO	48	C4
M ST	MER	170	C5
M 1	TUL	69	A5
M 3	TUL	69	B5
M 8	LACO	90	C3
M 9	TUL	69	B5
M 10	TUL	69	B5
M 15	TUL	69	A4
M 33	TUL	68	E4
M 52	TUL	69	A4
M 56	TUL	69	B4
M 99	TUL	69	C4
M 107	TUL	69	C3
M 109	TUL	68	E4
M 109	TUL	69	A4

STREET	CO.	PAGE	GRID
M 112	TUL	69	A4
M 117	TUL	68	D3
M 120	TUL	68	E3
M 176	TUL	68	E3
M 220	TUL	69	A2
M 231	TUL	69	A2
M 240	TUL	68	E2
M 276	TUL	69	A1
M 296	TUL	68	D1
M 348	TUL	68	E1
M 357	TUL	58	E5
M 357	TUL	59	A4
M 375	TUL	59	B5
M 453	TUL	58	D4
M 461	TUL	58	D4
M 465	TUL	58	D4
M 468	TUL	58	D4
M 469	TUL	58	D4
MABURY RD	SJ	152	D1
MABURY ST	SA	196	D3
MAC RD	RCO	107	C1
MACARTHUR BLVD	ALA	L	D5
MACARTHUR BLVD	ALA	45	D1
MACARTHUR BLVD	CM	197	B3
MACARTHUR BLVD	IRV	198	C3
MACARTHUR BLVD	IRV	200	B5
MACARTHUR BLVD	NB	198	C3
MACARTHUR BLVD	NB	200	B5
MACARTHUR BLVD	O	157	E1
MACARTHUR BLVD	O	158	B2
MACARTHUR BLVD	ORCO	98	C4
MACARTHUR BLVD	ORCO	T	C3
MACARTHUR BLVD	ORCO	198	C3
MACARTHUR BLVD	SA	197	D3
MACARTHUR BLVD	SA	198	A3
MACARTHUR FRWY	ALA	45	D1
MACARTHUR FRWY	O	157	D1
MACARTHUR FRWY	O	158	B2
MACDOEL DIST RD	SIS	4	E4
MACDOEL DIST RD	SIS	5	A3
MACDONALD AV	CC	L	C3
MACDONALD AV	R	155	B3
MACDONALD LN	SIS	4	C5
MACE BLVD	YOL	39	C1
MACEDONA CYN RD	SBD	84	A4
MACHADO LN	SIS	4	C5
MACHADO ST	RCO	99	B4
MACKERT RD	SUT	33	C4
MACKS GULCH RD	SIS	4	A5
MACKS GULCH RD	SIS	12	A1
MACKVILLE RD	SJCO	40	C3
MACLAY AV	LACO	89	D5
MACLAY AV	LACO	Q	C1
MACY ST	LA	186	C3
MACY ST	LACO	97	E2
MACY ST	LACO	R	A4
MADDALENA RD	PLU	27	C2
MADDEN AV	SUT	33	C2
MADDOCK RD	SUT	33	C4
MADEIRA AV N	MON	171	D3
MADEIRA AV N	SAL	171	D3
MADELINE RD	LAS	8	B4
MADERA AV	FRCO	57	A4
MADERA AV	KER	78	B2
MADERA AV	KER	78	C2
MADERA AV	MAD	57	A2
MADERA RD	MCO	55	D1
MADERA RD	SBD	90	E3
MADERA ST	SDCO	V	D3
MADERA ST	SDCO	111	D1
MADISON AV	KIN	67	C2
MADISON AV	SAC	34	A5
MADISON AV	SAC	34	B5
MADISON AV	SBR	144	A4
MADISON AV	SD	214	A4
MADISON ST	KER	166	E5
MADISON ST	RCO	99	B2
MADISON ST	RCO	101	A4
MADISON ST	S	160	D3
MADONNA RD	SLO	76	A4
MADONNA RD	SNLO	172	B4
MAD RIVER RD	HUM	9	E5
MAD RIVER ROCK	TRI	16	E3
MADRONA ST	NAPA	29	B3
MADRONE RD	SON	38	B3
MADSEN	FRCO	57	E2
MADSEN AV	FRCO	57	E5
MAGEE CANYON RD	MNO	44	A5
MAGEE CANYON RD	MNO	51	B1
MAGEE HILLS RD	RCO	99	E5
MAGIC MTN PKWY	LACO	89	B4
MAGNOLIA	MAR	38	B5
MAGNOLIA	SJCO	47	D1
MAGNOLIA AV	FRCO	57	C5
MAGNOLIA AV	GLE	24	D3
MAGNOLIA AV	KER	78	A2
MAGNOLIA AV	LB	192	D3
MAGNOLIA AV	MAR	L	A3
MAGNOLIA AV	MCO	47	E4
MAGNOLIA AV	MCO	48	A4
MAGNOLIA AV	ONT	203	E5
MAGNOLIA AV	ORCO	98	B4
MAGNOLIA AV	ORCO	T	C2
MAGNOLIA AV	RCO	99	A3
MAGNOLIA AV	RIV	205	A4
MAGNOLIA AV	SDCO	V	E2
MAGNOLIA AV	SDCO	106	E5
MAGNOLIA AV	SDCO	107	A4
MAGNOLIA AV	MLBR	144	C4
MAGNOLIA AV	STA	47	B3
MAGNOLIA BLVD	BUR	179	B4
MAGNOLIA BLVD	LA	179	B4
MAGNOLIA BLVD	LACO	Q	C3

STREET	CO.	PAGE	GRID
MAGNOLIA RD	YUB	33	D1
MAGNUS ORCHD RD	SIE	26	D5
MAGONIGAL RD	NEV	27	B5
MAHER RD	MON	54	C3
MAHOGANY WY	LAS	20	E2
MAHOGANY FLAT	INY	71	C2
MAHOGANY PK RD	SIS	5	B3
MAHON AV	SJCO	47	D1
MAHONEY RD	SLO	75	E1
MAHONEY RD	SB	86	B1
MAIDEN LN	AVLN	97	B4
MAIL RD	SB	86	D3
MAIL RT	LAS	8	C5
MAIN AV E	SCL	P	D5
MAIN AV E	SCL	54	C1
MAIN RD N	KLAM	5	E2
MAIN RD S	MOD	7	A3
MAIN ST	A	157	C4
MAIN ST	AMA	40	D2
MAIN ST	BARS	208	A2
MAIN ST	CC	L	E4
MAIN ST	CC	M	A3
MAIN ST	CC	M	A4
MAIN ST	EC	217	B2
MAIN ST	ELS	189	A3
MAIN ST	GV	127	C3
MAIN ST	HUM	15	E3
MAIN ST	IMP	109	A5
MAIN ST	IMP	109	B2
MAIN ST	INY	51	D4
MAIN ST	IRV	198	B3
MAIN ST	KER	78	E3
MAIN ST	LAK	31	D3
MAIN ST	LAS	8	B4
MAIN ST	LAS	21	B4
MAIN ST	LV	209	C3
MAIN ST	LA	185	E5
MAIN ST	LA	186	A3
MAIN ST	LACO	88	E4
MAIN ST	LACO	Q	C5
MAIN ST	LACO	Q	E5
MAIN ST	LACO	R	B3
MAIN ST	LACO	S	A1
MAIN ST	LACO	S	C2
MAIN ST	MAN	161	C4
MAIN ST	MEN	30	C4
MAIN ST	MOD	14	B3
MAIN ST	NAP	133	C2
MAIN ST	NAPA	38	A1
MAIN ST	ORCO	98	B4
MAIN ST	ORCO	T	D3
MAIN ST	PLCV	138	D3
MAIN ST	RCO	U	E5
MAIN ST	RCO	98	E3
MAIN ST	RCO	99	B4
MAIN ST	RCO	99	E4
MAIN ST	RCO	205	C2
MAIN ST	SAL	171	C4
MAIN ST	SBD	91	B4
MAIN ST	SBD	91	D1
MAIN ST	SBD	93	B2
MAIN ST	SD	216	B5
MAIN ST	SDCO	V	C5
MAIN ST	SDCO	V	E3
MAIN ST	SDCO	106	C2
MAIN ST	SDCO	107	A4
MAIN ST	SDCO	111	D2
MAIN ST	SF	143	E4
MAIN ST	SJCO	40	B5
MAIN ST	SLO	75	C2
MAIN ST	SLO	76	A2
MAIN ST	SA	196	B4
MAIN ST	SA	198	A3
MAIN ST	SB	76	C5
MAIN ST	SB	86	B1
MAIN ST	STB	173	A3
MAIN ST	SMA	173	A3
MAIN ST	SHA	18	C1
MAIN ST	SIE	26	D4
MAIN ST	SIS	3	D5
MAIN ST	SON	37	C2
MAIN ST	STA	47	B3
MAIN ST	S	160	E4
MAIN ST	SUIS	135	C4
MAIN ST	TEH	18	D3
MAIN ST	TUL	68	B1
MAIN ST	TUL	68	D3
MAIN ST	VENT	175	A2
MAIN ST	YUBA	125	D5
MAIN ST E	STA	47	D4
MAIN ST N	AMA	40	E2
MAIN ST N	LA	186	C2
MAIN ST N	LACO	R	A4
MAIN ST N	MON	54	C4
MAIN ST N	SAL	171	C2
MAIN ST S	SAL	171	B5
MAIN ST W	GV	127	A3
MAIN ST W	SB	76	B5
MAIN ST W	SB	86	A1
MAIN ST W	STA	47	D3
MAIN DRAIN RD	KER	77	D2
MAINE AV	LACO	R	E3
MAINE ST	SOL	38	D4
MAINE ST	VAL	134	C4
MAIN EAST WEST	MOD	5	E3
MAIN PRAIRIE RD	SOL	39	B3
MAJESTC OAK CIR	SHA	18	E3
MAJESTIC VW DR	SHA	18	C3
MALAGA AV	FRCO	56	E4
MALAGA AV	FRCO	57	C4
MALAGA RD	KER	78	E3
MALIBU CYN RD	LACO	97	A2
MALIN HWY	MOD	5	E2

STREET	CO.	PAGE	GRID
MALLARD RD	MCO	55	E2
MALLARD RD	YOL	39	D2
MALLOTT RD	SUT	33	C2
MALTON AV	TEH	24	D2
MALUM RIDGE RD	MAD	49	E4
MALVERN AV	ORCO	T	C1
MAMELUKE HLL RD	ED	34	E3
MAMMTH POOL RD	MAD	49	E5
MAMMTH POOL RD	MAD	50	A5
MAMMTH SCNC LP	MNO	50	D2
MAMMOTH TVRN RD	ML	164	D2
MANCHESTER AV	ANA	193	A2
MANCHESTER AV	ING	188	D5
MANCHESTER AV	LA	187	D5
MANCHESTER AV	LA	188	A5
MANCHESTER AV	LACO	97	D2
MANCHESTER AV	LACO	Q	D5
MANCHESTER AV	SDCO	106	C4
MANDEVLL CYN RD	LACO	97	C2
MANDRAPA RD	IMP	111	E4
MANGALAR RD	RCO	100	C5
MANGO ST	SBD	80	E5
MANGROVE AV	BUT	124	B2
MANGROVE AV	C	124	C3
MANHATTAN AV	LACO	97	D3
MANHATTAN AV	LACO	S	A1
MANHATTAN BLVD	LACO	97	D3
MANHATTAN BLVD	LACO	S	B1
MANIER DR	TUL	69	A3
MANKAS CORNR RD	SOL	L	E1
MANKAS CORNR RD	SOL	M	A1
MANKAS CORNR RD	SOL	38	E3
MANLY RD	KER	89	D1
MANNING RD	ALA	M	C5
MANNEL AV	KER	78	B2
MANNING AV	FRCO	56	B4
MANNING AV	FRCO	57	E4
MANNING RD	ALA	46	C1
MANOR RD	COL	32	C2
MANOR ST	KER	78	D2
MANTECA AV	KIN	67	C2
MANTECA RD	SJCO	47	B2
MANTON RD	TEH	18	E4
MANTON RD	TEH	19	A3
MANTON SCH RD	TEH	19	B3
MANUAL DOMINGOS	SB	86	C3
MANZANA DR	RCO	100	D3
MANZANITA AV	BUT	25	B3
MANZANITA AV	BUT	124	C2
MANZANITA AV	RCO	99	C2
MANZANITA RD	ML	164	D2
MANZANITA RD	RCO	100	B5
MANZANITA RD	TRI	16	D1
MANZANITA LK RD	MAD	49	E5
MANZANITA LKOUT	MOD	14	D2
MANZNR REWRD RD	INY	60	A3
MAPES RD	LAS	21	C3
MAPES RD	RCO	99	C4
MAPLE AV	FRCO	57	C2
MAPLE AV	FRCO	67	C1
MAPLE AV	SBD	91	B4
MAPLE AV	STR	131	D4
MAPLE LN	NAPA	29	B2
MAPLE LN	SBD	100	A1
MAPLE ST	RCO	98	E3
MAPLE ST	SAL	171	C4
MAPLE ST	SDCO	107	A4
MAPLE CREEK RD	HUM	10	B5
MAPLE HILLS RD	HUM	16	B5
MARBLE HOT-			
-SPRINGS RD	PLU	27	C2
MARCH LN	S	160	A1
MARCIEL DR	MAD	57	B2
MARCONI AV	SAC	40	A1
MARCO POLO AV	RCO	100	A5
MARCUM RD	SUT	33	D4
MARCUSE RD	SUT	33	D3
MAR DE CORTEZ	AVLN	97	A4
MARE ISLAND BL	VAL	134	B4
MARE ISL CAUSWY	VAL	134	B3
MARENGO AV	LACO	R	B3
MARENGO RD	COL	32	D2
MARENGO ST	LA	186	E2
MARGUERITE AV	TEH	24	D2
MARGUERITE PKWY	ORCO	98	D5
MARGUERITE RD	MCO	48	E5
MARGUERTE MN RD	AUB	126	C2
MARICOPA HWY	KER	78	B5
MARIE AV	KER	89	E1
MARIE DR	PLU	20	D5
MARILLA AV	AVLN	97	B4
MARIN AV	FRCO	56	D4
MARIN ST	VAL	134	C4
MARINA AV	ALA	P	C1
MARINA AV	ALA	46	C2
MARINA BLVD	ALA	L	D5
MARINA BLVD	ALA	45	D2
MARINA BLVD	SF	142	A1
MARINA BLVD	SUIS	135	C4
MARINA DR	IMP	108	C2
MARINA DR	MEN	31	B1
MARINA EXPWY	LACO	187	D3
MARINA FRWY	CUL	188	A3
MARINA FRWY	LA	188	A3
MARINA FRWY	LACO	97	C2
MARINA VISTA	M	154	B2
MARIPOSA ST	VAL	134	E3
MARINE AV	COL	32	E3
MARINE AV	MB	189	C5
MARINE AV	RB	189	C5
MARINE PKWY	RC	145	E4
MARINERS ISL BL	SM	145	C2
MARINETTE	TUL	68	B1

STREET	CO.	PAGE	GRID
MARINE WORLD PY	SMCO	N	D2
MARINE WORLD PY	SMCO	45	D3
MARINO LN	KER	79	E2
MARIPOSA AV	BUT	25	B3
MARIPOSA AV	C	124	D2
MARIPOSA AV	RCO	99	B3
MARIPOSA AV	TUL	68	B1
MARIPOSA RD	SJCO	40	B5
MARIPOSA RD	SJCO	47	C1
MARIPOSA RD	STA	47	D2
MARIPOSA ST	FRE	165	C4
MARIPOSA ST	SFCO	142	E4
MARIPOSA WY	MCO	48	C5
MARIPOSA DUMP	MPA	49	B3
MARITIME ST	O	157	B2
MARKET AV	CC	L	C3
MARKET ST	COL	33	A2
MARKET ST	O	157	E2
MARKET ST	RED	122	B3
MARKET ST	RIV	205	B3
MARKET ST	RCO	99	B2
MARKET ST	SD	215	E4
MARKET ST	SD	216	A4
MARKET ST	SFCO	L	B5
MARKET ST	SF	142	B4
MARKET ST	SF	143	D4
MARKET ST	SFCO	45	C1
MARKET ST	SJ	152	B3
MARKET ST	SCLR	151	B3
MARKET ST	S	160	E5
MARKET ST	YUBA	125	D1
MARKET ST W	MON	171	B3
MARKET ST W	SAL	171	B3
MARKHAM ST	RCO	99	B3
MARK HOPKINS AV	SUT	33	D3
MARKLEEVLLE LKT	ALP	36	C5
MARKS	FRCO	57	C5
MARKS AV	FRCO	57	C4
MARKS RD	SBD	101	D1
MARK SPGS W RD	SON	37	E1
MARKWEST STA RD	SON	37	D1
MARLAY AV	SBD	99	A2
MAR MONTE AV	SCR	54	B2
MARNI CT	KER	79	C4
MAROA AV	FRE	165	C1
MAROA AV	FRCO	57	C3
MARQUARDT AV	LACO	T	B1
MARR RD	LAS	8	D5
MARSH RD	SCL	46	B3
MARSH RD	SMCO	N	D2
MARSH ST	SNLO	172	C3
MARSH ST	SLO	76	A3
MARSHALL RD	ED	34	D4
MARSHALL RD	MCO	55	C1
MARSHALL RD	STA	47	C4
MARSHALL ST	RCO	99	C4
MARSHALL-PETALMA	MAR	37	D4
MARSHALL RCH RD	TRI	17	C2
MARSH CREEK RD	CC	M	B3
MARSH CREEK RD	CC	M	D4
MARSH CREEK RD	CC	39	A5
MARSH CREEK RD	CC	39	A5
MARSHES FLAT RD	TUO	48	D1
MARSHVIEW RD	SOL	38	E4
MART AV	STA	47	E2
MARTIN AV	FRE	165	C5
MARTIN AV	KER	78	B2
MARTIN LN	AMA	40	D3
MARTIN RD	FRCO	56	B5
MARTIN RD	IMP	109	A4
MARTIN RD	MON	64	D1
MARTIN RD	YUB	25	E5
MARTIN ST	LAK	31	D3
MARTIN ST	MONT	167	D4
MARTIN ST	MON	53	E3
MARTIN ST	RCO	99	B3
MARTINEZ RD	MON	65	C4
MARTINEZ CYN RD	LACO	89	A4
MARTINGALE LN	CAL	41	A4
MRTN LTHR KG BL	LA	184	C5
MRTN LTHR KG BL	LACO	Q	D4
M L KING JR WY	ALA	L	D4
MARTIS PEAK RD	PLA	35	E1
MARTY RD	SUT	33	A2
MARVIN RANCH RD	SIE	26	C4
MAR VISTA	SDCO	106	C3
MAR VISTA DR	MONT	168	D1
MAR VISTA DR	MONT	167	D4
MAR VISTA DR	MON	53	E3
MARX RD NO 1	SHA	18	A3
MARX RD NO 2	SHA	18	A3
MARYLAND ST	VAL	134	B5
MARYSVILLE BLVD	SAC	33	E5
MARYSVILLE RD	YUB	26	A5
MARYSVILLE RD	YUB	33	E1
MASON ST	SF	143	C1
MASON ST	STB	174	E3
MASON DIXON RD	SBD	100	E1
MASONIC AV	SFCO	L	B5
MASONIC AV	SF	142	A3
MASONIC RD	MNO	43	C2
MASSACHUSTTS AV	SDCO	V	D3
MASSACHUSTTS AV	SDCO	111	D1
MASSACK RD	PLU	26	D2
MASSEY RD	MPA	49	C3
MAST AV	KER	78	B1
MASTEN AV	SCL	P	E5
MASTEN RD	TEH	18	B5
MASTERS AV	FRCO	56	D4
MASTERSONS RD	SIS	11	E2
MATHER ST	O	158	B1
MATHER FIELD RD	SAC	40	A1
MATHESON RD	SHA	18	B2

STREET	CO.	PAGE	GRID
MATHEWS RD	LAS	14	B4
MATHEWS RD	SJCO	40	A5
MATHEWS RD	SJCO	47	A1
MATHEWS RD	SIS	5	A2
MATHILDA AV	SCL	P	A3
MATHILDA AV	SCL	45	E4
MATHILDA AV	SVL	148	D5
MATILIJA RD	VEN	88	A4
MATLOCK LP	TEH	18	C4
MATTERHORN DR	KER	79	C5
MATTHEWS LN	YUB	33	D1
MATTOLE RD	HUM	15	C3
MATTOLE RD	HUM	15	E4
MAUI RD	SBD	92	C1
MAURICO AV	RCO	99	C4
MAWSON RD	SUT	33	A2
MAXSON RD	FRCO	58	B2
MAXWELL LN	SOL	39	C2
MAXWELL RD	AMA	40	C2
MAXWELL CYN RD	NAPA	38	C1
MAXWLL SITES RD	COL	32	C1
MAY	CC	38	C5
MAYARADA	SBD	101	E1
MAYARO LODGE RD	BUT	25	E2
MAYBECK	SJCO	40	A5
MAYBERT RD	NEV	26	E5
MAYER AV	KER	78	B2
MAYER RD	YUB	33	D2
MAYFIELD RD	RCO	102	A4
MAYHEW AV	TEH	24	D2
MAYNARD RD	SHA	18	D2
MAY SCHOOL RD	ALA	M	C5
MAY SCHOOL RD	ALA	46	C2
MAYS CANYON RD	SON	37	C2
MAYTEN RD	SIS	4	C5
MAZE BLVD	MDO	162	A3
MAZE BLVD	STA	47	C2
MAZOURKA CANYON	INY	60	A3
MCADAMS CK RD	SIS	3	D5
MCADAMS INDN CK	SIS	3	D4
MCARTHUR RD	SHA	13	C3
MCARTHUR RD	SUT	33	B2
MCAULIFFE RD	SHA	18	A3
MCAUSLAND RD	COL	24	E5
MCBEAN PKWY	LACO	89	B4
MCCABE RD	IMP	112	A3
MCCABE RD	MCO	47	B5
MCCABE RD	MCO	55	B1
MCCAHILL LN	HUM	15	E2
MCCAIN BLVD	COR	215	B5
MCCAIN VLY RD	SDCO	111	A3
MCCALL AV	FRCO	57	D3
MCCALL BLVD	RCO	99	C4
MCCANN RD	HUM	16	B4
MCCART RD	KER	68	A5
MCCARTHY RES RD	CAL	41	B2
MCCARTY RD	RCO	U	D4
MCCARTY RD	TEH	24	B2
MCCATER RD	MCO	48	E5
MCCAY	MPA	48	E3
MCCLAIN LN	RCO	107	B1
MCCLATCHY RD	SUT	33	B2
MCCLELLAN RD	CPTO	149	B5
MCCLELLAN RD	LAS	14	C3
MCCLELLAND LN	LAS	21	C3
MCCLELLN MTN RD	HUM	16	C3
MCCLINTOCK RD	STA	47	C4
MCCLOSKEY RD	SBT	54	E3
MCCLOSKEY RD	SBT	55	A3
MCCLOSKEY RD	SOL	39	C3
MCCLOUD DUMP RD	SIS	12	E2
MCCLURE AV	TEH	24	D1
MCCLURE RD	STA	47	D2
MCCLURE SUB RD	MEN	31	B2
MCCOMBS RD	KER	77	E1
MCCOMBS RD	KER	78	B1
MCCONAHUE GL RD	SIS	11	E1
MCCONNELL RD	IMP	109	B5
MCCORMACK RD	SOL	39	B3
MCCOURTNEY RD	NEV	34	B2
MCCOURTNEY RD	NEV	127	A5
MCCOURTNEY RD	PLA	34	A3
MCCOY AV	KER	77	E1
MCCOY RD	LAS	20	C3
MCCOY RD	MON	54	E5
MCCOY RD	MON	55	A5
MCCOY RD	TEH	18	C4
MCCRACKEN RD	STA	47	B3
MCCREERY RCH RD	SBT	55	C3
MCCRORY RD	SOL	39	A3
MCCULLACH RD	MCO	47	D4
MCCULLOCK BLVD	MOH	96	B4
MCCULLY RD	MOD	7	D5
MCCUNE RD	SOL	39	A2
MCDANIEL RD	IMP	112	D5
MCDERMOTT RD	COL	32	D1
MCDERMOTT RD	RCO	99	E4
MCDOEL DORRS RD	SIS	5	A3
MCDONALD	SJCO	39	E5
MCDONALD AV	STA	47	C2
MCDONALD RD	IMP	109	A3
MCDOWELL BLVD	SON	L	A1
MCEWEN RD	CC	L	D3
MCEWEN RD	CC	38	D5
MCEWEN RD	STA	47	E2
MCFADDEN	MON	54	C4
MCFADDEN AV	SA	195	A5
MCFADDEN AV	SA	196	C5
MCFARLND-WDY RD	KER	78	C1
MCGARY RD	SOL	38	D4
MCGEE AV	STA	47	D2
MCGEE CREEK RD	MNO	51	A3
MCGOWAN	YUB	33	D2

261
MCGRATH RD
STREET INDEX
MORENA RES DR

INDEXES

STREET	CO.	PAGE	GRID
MCGRATH RD	SUT	33	B2
MCHENRY AV	MDO	162	C3
MCHENRY AV	SJCO	47	C2
MCHENRY RD	MCO	48	C5
MCINTIRE RD	SJCO	40	C3
MCINTOSH RD	HUM	10	D4
MCKEAN RD	SCL	P	C4
MCKEAN RD	SCL	46	C5
MCKEE RD	MCO	48	C4
MCKEE RD	SJ	152	E2
MCKEE RD	SCL	P	C3
MCKEE RD	SCL	46	B4
MCKEE ST	MCO	48	D5
MCKEEN RD	SIS	11	D2
MCKELL RD	LAK	32	A5
MCKENZIE AV	FRE	165	D3
MCKENZIE RD	SAC	40	A3
MCKERNIE ST	RCO	99	E4
MCKIBBEN RD	KER	78	A1
MCKIM RD	IMP	109	B5
MCKINLEY AV	FRE	165	B2
MCKINLEY AV	FRCO	57	A3
MCKINLEY AV	SJCO	47	A1
MCKINLEY ST	RCO	99	A3
MCKINLEYVLLE AV	HUM	9	E4
MCKINNEY CK RD	SIS	3	D4
MCKNNEY RUBICN	PLA	35	D2
MCLAIN RD	YUB	26	B4
MCLAUGHLIN AV	LA	187	E1
MCLAUGHLIN AV	SCL	P	C3
MCMASTER RD	MCO	48	D5
MCMILLAN CYN RD	SLO	76	C1
MCMULLIN	SJCO	47	A2
MCMULLIN GRADE	FRCO	57	A4
MCMURRY MDWS RD	INY	59	D1
MCNAMARA RD	MCO	48	C5
MCNEILL LN	SOL	39	B1
MCNELLA LN	PLU	27	C3
MCNERNEY RD	IMP	109	A3
MCRAE RD	BUT	25	B4
MCRAE RD	TUO	41	C5
MCSWAIN RD	MER	170	A3
MCSWAIN RD	MCO	170	A3
MEACHAM RD	KER	78	B3
MEAD RD	IMP	109	B4
MEADE AV	SD	214	B5
MEADOW DR	AMA	41	B2
MEADOW DR	MCO	48	A4
MEADOW RD	TRI	17	D1
MEADOW GLEN RD	CAL	41	C2
MEADOW LAKE RD	NEV	26	E5
MEADOW LAKE RD	NEV	27	B4
MEADOW LAKE RD	SIE	27	B5
MEADOW RIDGE RD	MAD	49	D5
MEADOWS DR	VAL	134	A1
MEADOWS RD	IMP	112	B4
MEADOWSWEET DR	CRTM	140	C1
MEADOW VLY RD	YUB	26	E5
MEADOW VIEW DR	SHA	18	C3
MEADOWVIEW RD	SAC	39	D2
MEADOW VISTA RD	PLA	34	C3
MEALEY RD	IMP	108	E5
MEAMBER CK RD	SIS	3	C4
MEARS RIDGE RD	SHA	12	C3
MECCA DALE RD	RCO	101	E3
MECHAM RD	SON	37	E3
MEDFORD AV	KIN	67	C2
MEDFORD RD	FRCO	57	E1
MEDICINE LK HWY	MOD	5	E5
MEDICINE LK HWY	SIS	5	D5
MEDICINE LK RD	SIS	5	C5
MEDICINE LK RD	SIS	13	B2
MEDLIN RD	STA	47	C4
MEEKLAND AV	ALA	L	E5
MEEKLAND AV	ALA	M	A5
MEEKLAND AV	ALA	N	E1
MEEKLAND AV	ALA	P	A1
MEEKS RD	SBD	92	D5
MEHRING RD	IMP	110	D5
MEHRTEN DR	TUL	68	D1
MEIER RD	STA	47	E2
MEIER RD	STA	48	A2
MEIGS RD	STB	174	A5
MEIKLE RD	STA	47	E2
MEIKLE RD	STA	48	A2
MEISS RD	SAC	40	B2
MEISS LAKE-			
-SAMS NECK RD	SIS	4	E3
MEISS LAKE-			
-SAMS NECK RD	SIS	5	A3
MELCHER RD	KER	78	B1
MELLA DR	AMA	41	A2
MELLO AV	SJCO	47	C1
MELLOR RD	STA	48	A2
MELODY CT	HUM	10	A5
MELOLANO RD	IMP	109	B5
MELON ST	RCO	102	C4
MELONES CT	TUO	41	B5
MELROSE AV	LA	181	B5
MELROSE AV	LA	182	C5
MELROSE AV	LACO	Q	D3
MELROSE AV	LACO	183	D1
MELROSE AV	SDCO	106	C3
MELROSE DR	SDCO	106	C3
MEMORY LN	SA	195	E2
MEMORY LN	SA	196	A2
MENALTO AV	MP	147	C1
MENDENHALL RD	TEH	18	C5
MENDIBOURE RD	LAS	8	B4
MENDIBURN	KER	79	D5
MENDIBURN RD	KER	80	B4
MENDOCINO AV	FRCO	57	E1
MENDOCINO AV	STR	131	C1
MENDOCINO PASS	MEN	23	B2
MENIFEE RD	RCO	99	C4
MENLO AV	RCO	99	E4
MERCED AV	FRCO	66	D3
MERCED AV	KER	78	A2
MERCED AV	LACO	R	E4
MERCED AV	MCO	47	E4
MERCEDES AV	MCO	48	B4
MERCED FALLS RD	MPA	48	D3
MERCED FALLS RD	TUO	48	D2
MERIDIAN AV	SCL	151	E5
MERIDIAN BLVD	ML	164	C3
MERIDIAN RD	BUT	25	A3
MERIDIAN RD	SBD	91	E2
MERIDIAN RD	SCL	P	B3
MERIDIAN RD	SCL	46	B4
MERIDIAN RD	SOL	39	B3
MERIDIAN RD	SUT	33	A2
MERIDIAN ST	SJ	151	E5
MERLE AV	STA	47	D2
MERRIAM RD	STA	47	E3
MERRIAM RD	YUB	26	B5
MERRILL AV	FRCO	56	B2
MERRILL RD	TEH	24	E2
MERRILL RD S	KLAM	5	C2
MERRILL ST	SBD	99	A2
MERRILL FLAT RD	LAS	20	D2
MERRILLVILLE RD	LAS	20	E2
MERRIMAC CTO RD	BUT	25	E3
MERRITT	LAK	31	D3
MERRITT DR	TUL	57	E5
MERRITT DR	TUL	58	A5
MERRITT LN	PLA	34	A3
MERVEL AV	MCO	55	E2
MESA DR	RCO	103	C5
MESA DR	RCO	110	C1
MESA DR	SBD	100	E1
MESA DR	SDCO	106	B3
MESA RD	MAR	37	E5
MESA RD	SBD	92	E5
MESA TK TR W	SDCO	107	C5
MESA COLLEGE DR	SD	213	D1
MESA COLLEGE DR	SDCO	V	B2
MESA GRANDE RD	SDCO	107	B3
MESQUITE RD	INY	61	B2
MESQUITE CYN RD	KER	80	C2
MESQUITE PSS RD	SBD	84	A1
MESQUITE SPG RD	SBD	101	B1
MESQUITE VLY RD	INY	73	C3
MESSICK	SJCO	40	C4
MESSICK RD	SUT	33	D3
MESSILLA VLY RD	BUT	25	D3
MESSING RD	CAL	40	D4
MESTMAKER ST	KER	68	D5
METCALF RD	NEV	34	B2
METCALFE RD	SCL	P	D4
METCALFE RD	SCL	46	C5
METROPOLE AV	AVLN	97	B5
METROPOLITAN RD	HUM	15	E2
METTER RD	SUT	33	C1
METTLER AV	KER	68	B5
METTLER AV	KER	78	B2
METTLER RD	SJCO	40	A4
METTLER RD	STA	47	D1
METZ RD	MON	65	B1
METZGER RD	SHA	13	D3
MEXICAN LAKE RD	SBT	66	B1
MEYER RD	LACO	R	D5
MEYER RD	LACO	T	B1
MEYERS LN	SUT	33	B1
MEYERS GRADE RD	SON	37	B1
MICA RD	RCO	107	C1
MICHAEL RD	MCO	48	B5
MICHEL RD	CAL	41	B3
MICHELLE DR	SUT	125	A4
MICHELSON DR	IRV	198	C4
MICHELTORENA ST	STB	174	B3
MICHIGAN BAR RD	SAC	40	C2
MICHILLINDA BL	LACO	R	C2
MICHOACAN AVD	BAJA	112	B4
MICKE GROVE RD	SJCO	40	B4
MIDDLE AV	SCL	P	E5
MIDDLE AV	SCL	54	D1
MIDDLE RD	BLMT	145	C4
MIDDLE RD	MAR	37	D3
MIDDLE RD	SJCO	46	E1
MIDDLE BAR RD	AMA	40	E3
MIDDLE CREEK RD	SHA	18	B2
MIDDLE CREEK RD	SIS	3	C3
MIDDLE CK RCH	SIS	3	C3
MIDDLE E TER	AVLN	97	B5
MIDDLEFIELD RD	MP	147	A1
MIDDLEFIELD RD	PA	147	E3
MIDDLEFIELD RD	SCL	N	E2
MIDDLEFLD RD E	MVW	148	B4
MIDDLE FORK RD	MON	66	B4
MDDL FK GASQUET	DN	2	A3
MID FK HUMBG RD	SIS	3	E4
MIDDLE HARBR RD	O	157	C3
MIDDL HONCUT RD	BUT	25	D5
MIDDLE RIDGE RD	MEN	30	B2
MIDDLETON DR	DN	1	D3
MIDDLETON RD	SUT	33	B2
MIDDLETON RD	TRI	11	E3
MIDDLETOWN RD	PLCV	138	B2
MIDDLETWN PK DR	SHA	18	B2
MDL TWO ROCK RD	SON	37	E3
MIDLAND AV	SDCO	106	D4
MIDLAND RD	RCO	103	B2
MIDLAND TR	KER	80	C2
MIDOIL RD	KER	77	E4
MIDWAY	BUT	25	B5
MIDWAY DR	SD	213	A5
MIDWAY DR	SDCO	V	A3
MIDWAY RD	ALA	M	E5
MIDWAY RD	KER	77	E4
MIDWAY RD	SBD	101	D1
MIDWAY RD	SOL	39	A2
MIDWAY WELLS	INY	61	D3
MIKISHA BLVD	SBD	92	D5
MILAN RD	KER	77	E2
MILE END	MON	64	E1
MILE END	MON	65	A1
MILES RD	MCO	48	C5
MILFORD RD	SBDO	81	A1
MILFORD CEM RD	LAS	21	C5
MILFORD GRADE	LAS	21	C5
MILGEO RD	SJCO	47	C2
MIL-GOR RD	SBD	101	E1
MILHAM AV	KIN	67	B3
MILITAR	BAJA	112	B4
MILITARY E	BEN	153	C4
MILITARY W	BEN	153	B4
MILITARY W	SOL	38	D4
MILITARY RD	SIS	13	A2
MILITARY PASS	SIS	12	D1
MILITARY PASS	SIS	13	A2
MILL AV	KER	78	B1
MILL RD	BUT	26	B4
MILL RD	MNO	52	C3
MILL RD	SLO	76	B1
MILL RD	TEH	19	C4
MILL RD	YUB	26	B4
MILL ST	GV	127	B4
MILL ST	NEV	34	C1
MILL ST	RENO	130	C3
MILL ST	SBD	99	C2
MILL ST	SBDO	207	C3
MILL ST	U	123	C3
MILLARD CYN RD	RCO	100	B2
MILLBRAE AV	MLBR	144	D5
MILLBRAE AV	SMCO	N	C1
MILLBRAE AV	SMCO	45	C3
MILLBROOK AV	FRCO	57	C2
MILL CANYON RD	MNO	42	E2
MILL CREEK RD	HUM	10	C3
MILL CREEK RD	MEN	31	B2
MILL CREEK RD	SBD	99	E1
MILL CREEK RD	SIS	3	C5
MILL CREEK RD	SIS	3	E4
MILL CREEK RD	SON	37	D1
MILL CK PWR HS	MNO	43	B4
MILLER	MAR	45	B1
MILLER AV	CPTO	150	A5
MILLER AV	FRCO	56	B2
MILLER AV	MAR	L	B4
MILLER AV	MV	140	A3
MILLER AV	VAL	134	E4
MILLER RD	COL	32	A3
MILLER RD	IMP	112	C3
MILLER RD	MCO	48	D4
MILLER RD	TRI	22	E1
MILLER RD	YOL	39	C2
MILLER ST	SMA	173	C3
MILL ST	U	123	C3
MILLER RANCH RD	SIE	26	D4
MILLERTON RD	FRCO	57	D2
MILLERTON RD	MAD	57	D1
MILLIKEN AV	SBD	U	E3
MILLIKEN AV	SBD	98	E2
MIL POTRERO HWY	KER	88	B1
MILLS AV	CLA	203	A4
MILLS AV	LACO	R	D5
MILLS AV	MTCL	203	A4
MILLS RD	MCO	47	C5
MILLS RD	SOL	39	C2
MILLS RD	SUT	33	B2
MILLS ORCHRD RD	COL	32	D1
MILLS PARK RD	SIE	27	A3
MILLUX AV	FRCO	56	B2
MILLUX RD	KER	78	C4
MILLVL PLAIN RD	SHA	18	D3
MILLWOOD DR	TUL	58	C5
MILLWOOD RD	FRCO	58	C3
MILNES RD	STA	47	D2
MILPAS DR	SBD	91	D4
MILPAS ST	STB	174	D3
MILPITAS BLVD	SCL	P	B2
MILPITAS BLVD	SCL	46	B4
MILPITAS RD	MON	64	E3
MILPITAS RD	MON	65	B3
MILPITAS WSH RD	IMP	110	B2
MILSAP BAR RD	BUT	25	E3
MILSAP BAR RD	BUT	26	A3
MILSTEAD RD	MEN	22	D1
MILTON RD	CAL	40	E5
MILTON RD	NAPA	L	C1
MILTON RD	NAPA	38	C3
MILTON RD	SJCO	40	C5
MILTON RD	STA	40	E5
MINA RD	MEN	23	A1
MINE RD	VEN	89	A5
MINER RD	CC	L	D4
MINER ST	S	160	E4
MINERAL RD	IMP	108	E1
MINERAL RD	SHA	19	C3
MINERAL KING AV	TUL	68	A1
MINERAL KING RD	TUL	59	B5
MINERAL SCHOOL	SHA	19	A1
MINERET RD	ML	164	C2
MINERS CREEK RD	SIS	11	D2
MINES RD	ALA	P	D1
MINES RD	ALA	46	C2
MINES RD	SCL	46	D3
MING AV	KER	78	C3
MINI DR	VAL	134	C1
MINNEOLA RD	SBD	92	B1
MINNESOTA ST	SDCO	106	C2
MINNEWAWA AV	FRCO	57	D2
MINNEWAWA AV	FRCO	57	D5
MINNIEAR RD	STA	47	B3
MINNIETTA RD	INY	71	B2
MINT RD	MCO	56	B1
MINTURN RD	MCO	48	D5
MIRABEL RD	SON	37	D2
MIRAMAR RD	SDCO	V	B1
MIRAMAR RD	SDCO	106	D5
MIRAMAR WY	SDCO	V	B2
MIRAMAR WY	SDCO	106	D5
MIRA MESA BLVD	SDCO	V	B1
MIRA MESA BLVD	SDCO	106	C5
MIRANDA AV	CC	M	A4
MIRASOL AV	KER	77	E3
MIRASOL AV	KER	78	A3
MISSION AV	MCO	48	C5
MISSION AV	SD	214	A5
MISSION AV	SDCO	106	B3
MISSION AV	SR	139	C3
MISSION BLVD	ALA	45	E2
MISSION BLVD	ALA	146	C1
MISSION BLVD	H	146	D2
MISSION BLVD	MTCL	203	A5
MISSION BLVD	ONT	203	D5
MISSION BLVD	ONT	204	B5
MISSION BLVD	POM	203	A5
MISSION BLVD	RCO	99	A2
MISSION BLVD	SBD	U	D2
MISSION BLVD	SBD	98	D2
MISSION BLVD	SBD	203	A5
MISSION BLVD	SD	212	A1
MISSION BLVD	SDCO	V	A2
MISSION BLVD	SDCO	106	C5
MISSION DR	LACO	R	C3
MISSION FRWY	SDCO	V	A3
MISSION RD	LA	186	D2
MISSION RD	LACO	98	A2
MISSION RD	LACO	R	B3
MISSION RD	MON	65	B3
MISSION RD	SDCO	106	C2
MISSION RD	SMCO	L	B5
MISSION RD	SMCO	N	B1
MISSION RD	SMCO	45	B2
MISSION ST	SFCO	L	B5
MISSION ST	SF	142	C5
MISSION ST	SF	143	C5
MISSION ST	STB	174	A3
MISSION ST	SC	169	A4
MISSION TR	RCO	99	B5
MISSION BAY DR	SD	212	D1
MISSN BAY DR W	SD	212	B4
MISSION CTR RD	SD	213	E3
MISSION CK RD	RCO	100	C2
MISSION GRGE RD	SDCO	V	C2
MISSION GRGE RD	SDCO	106	E5
MISSION LKS BL	RCO	100	C2
MISSN OLIVE RD	BUT	25	E5
MISSION RDGE RD	STB	174	D2
MISSION VLY FWY	SD	213	C5
MISSION VLY FWY	SD	214	A4
MISSION VLGE DR	SD	214	C1
MISSION VLGE DR	SDCO	V	C2
MISSION VLGE DR	SDCO	106	D5
MISSOURI AV	STA	47	E2
MISTLETOE DR	VEN	88	C4
MITCHELL RD	HUM	10	C3
MITCHELL RD	HUM	15	E1
MITCHELL RD	LAS	8	A5
MITCHELL RD	LAS	14	E5
MITCHELL RD	STA	47	D4
MITCHLLS CMP RD	IMP	110	C2
MIX CANYON RD	SOL	38	E2
MOANING CAVE RD	CAL	41	B4
MOBLEY	SJCO	40	C5
MOBLEY	SJCO	47	C1
MOCAL RD	KER	77	E4
MOCAL RD	KER	78	D4
MOCKINGBIRD CYN	RCO	99	B3
MODJESKA CYN RD	ORCO	98	E4
MODOC AV	FRCO	57	A3
MODOC COUNTY RD	MOD	5	D3
MOFFAT BLVD	MAN	161	C4
MOFFAT BLVD	SJCO	161	C4
MOFFAT RANCH RD	INY	60	A4
MOFFATT RD	MCO	47	D5
MOFFETT BLVD	MVW	148	A4
MOFFETT BLVD	SCL	N	E3
MOFFETT BLVD	SCL	P	A3
MOFFETT DR	TUL	68	D1
MOFFETT RD	STA	47	D3
MOFFETT CK RD E	SIS	3	E5
MOFFETT CK RD W	SIS	3	E5
MOHAVE RD	LPAZ	103	E3
MOHAVE ROSE DR	LACO	89	D3
MOHAVE VLY HWY	MOH	85	D5
MOHLER RD	SJCO	47	B2
MOJAVE AV	KER	89	C1
MOJAVE DR	SBD	91	B3
MOJAVE RD	SBD	91	B4
MOJAVE RD	SBD	101	C1
MOJAVE-RANDSBRG	KER	80	C4
MOJVE TRPICO RD	KER	79	E5
MOJVE TRPICO RD	KER	80	A5
MOJVE TRPICO RD	KER	89	E1
MOKELUMNE HILL-			
-CMP SECO TP RD	CAL	41	C3
MOLERA RD	MON	54	B3
MOLINO AV	MV	140	A3
MOLLER AV	TEH	24	E2
MONARCH MINE RD	SIE	26	E4
MONARCH MINE RD	SIE	27	A4
MONO DR E	MONO	43	C4
MONO WY	TUO	163	D4
MONROE	MCO	55	D1
MONROE AV	FRCO	57	B3
MONROE AV	FRCO	57	B5
MONROE AV	TEH	18	D5
MONROE ST	RCO	101	A4
MONROE ST	SCLR	150	C1
MONSON	FRCO	58	B4
MONTGUE AGER RD	SIS	4	B4
MONTAGUE EXPWY	SCL	P	B3
MONTAGUE GRNADA	SIS	4	B4
MONTANA AV	LA	180	A3
MONTANA AV	LACO	97	C2
MONTANA AV	SHA	18	C2
MONTANA ST	PAS	190	A1
MONTARA RD	SBD	91	E1
MONTE RD	IMP	109	A4
MONTEBELLO BLVD	LACO	R	C4
MONTE BELLO RD	SCL	N	E3
MONTE BELLO RD	SCL	45	E4
MONTE BLOYD RD	MEN	30	D2
MONTECITO RD	SDCO	107	A4
MONTECITO RD	SLO	75	E2
MONTECITO ST	STB	174	D3
MONTE DIABLO AV	S	160	A4
MONTEREY AV	FRCO	56	D4
MONTEREY AV	FRCO	66	D2
MONTEREY AV	MDO	162	D4
MONTEREY AV	RCO	100	E4
MONTEREY BLVD	SFCO	L	B5
MONTEREY BLVD	SFCO	45	B2
MONTEREY HWY	SCL	P	D4
MONTEREY HWY	SCL	54	D1
MONTEREY RD	LACO	R	B3
MONTEREY RD	SLO	76	A1
MONTEREY RD	SLO	76	A2
MONTEREY HWY	SCL	46	B4
MONTEREY ST	SAL	171	C4
MONTEREY ST	SNLO	172	C3
MONTEREY PSS RD	LACO	R	B4
MONTE VERDE AV	CAR	168	B3
MONTE VISTA AV	MCO	48	A3
MONTE VISTA AV	SBD	U	C2
MONTE VISTA AV	SBD	80	E1
MONTE VISTA AV	STA	47	C3
MONTE VISTA AV	STA	48	A3
MONTE VISTA DR	SDCO	106	C3
MONTE VISTA RD	SHA	18	B3
MONTEZUMA RD	SDCO	V	C3
MONTEZUMA RD	SDCO	111	D1
MONTEZUMA HL RD	SOL	39	B4
MONTFORD AV	MV	140	A3
MONTGOMERY AV	BUT	25	A3
MONTGOMERY DR	STR	131	D3
MONTGOMERY RD	IMP	109	B3
MONTGOMERY RD	TRI	11	B5
MONTGOMERY ST	SF	143	C2
MONTGOMERY ST	MCO	48	C3
MONTGOMRY CK RD	TRI	11	D5
MONTGMRY RCH RD	SHA	18	B2
MONTICELLO RD	NAPA	133	E1
MONTPELIER RD	STA	47	E3
MONTPELIER RD	STA	48	A3
MONUMENT BLVD	CC	M	A3
MONUMENT RD	HUM	15	E3
MOODY RD	MEN	22	B2
MOODY ST	ORCO	T	B2
MOONEY BLVD	TUL	68	B2
MOONEY RD	LAS	20	C2
MOONEY RD	LAS	20	C3
MOONEY FLAT RD	NEV	34	A1
MOONRIDGE RD	SBD	100	A1
MOONSHINE RD	YUB	26	B5
MOONWIND ST	KER	80	D1
MOORE RD	LAS	21	E4
MOORE RD	PLA	33	E4
MOORE RD	PLA	34	A4
MOORE RD	SUT	33	B2
MOOREHEAD RD	STA	47	C5
MOORES FLAT RD	NEV	26	D5
MOORPARK RD	VEN	96	D1
MOORPARK ST	LACO	Q	C3
MOORVILL RDG RD	BUT	26	B4
MOOSE CAMP RD	SHA	13	B5
MORADA LN	SJCO	40	A4
MORAGA AV	ALA	L	D4
MORAGA AV	ALA	45	D1
MORAGA AV	MCO	55	D1
MORAGA AV	O	158	E1
MORAGA AV	P	158	D1
MORAGA AV	SD	211	E5
MORAGA RD	CC	L	E4
MORAGA RD	CC	45	E1
MORAGA WY	CC	L	E4
MORAN AV	MCO	48	A4
MORAN RD	CAL	41	C3
MORAN RD	STA	47	C4
MORAN RD	TEH	24	D1
MORCOURT AV	KER	80	C1
MOREHEAD RD	DN	1	D3
MOREHEAD RD	SUT	33	B2
MORELLO AV	CC	L	E3
MORELLO AV	CC	154	E3
MORELLO AV	M	154	E4
MORENA BLVD	SD	211	C4
MORENA BLVD	SD	212	E1
MORENA BLVD	SD	213	A4
MORENA BLVD	SDCO	V	A2
MORENA BLVD	SDCO	111	C1
MORENA BLVD W	SD	213	A4
MORENA RES DR	SDCO	112	D1

MORENO AV

STREET INDEX

262

NTU RD

STREET	CO.	PAGE	GRID
MORENO AV	SDCO	V	E1
MORENO AV	SDCO	106	E5
MORENO RD	STB	174	C2
MORENO ST	MTCL	203	C3
MORENO BEACH DR	RCO	99	C2
MORGAN RD	CAL	41	B5
MORGAN RD	HUM	15	D2
MORGAN RD	LAS	21	C1
MORGAN RD	SBD	101	D1
MORGAN RD	STA	47	D3
MORGAN WY	LPAZ	104	A5
MORGAN CYN RD	FRCO	57	E2
MORGAN TERRITRY	CC	46	B1
MORGAN VLY RD	LAK	32	B4
MORLEY AV	MCO	48	D5
MORMON ST	LA	191	C3
MORMN EMGRNT TR	ED	35	C5
MORNING DR	KER	78	E3
MORNING STAR CT	TUO	163	C3
MORNING STAR CTO	SBD	84	B3
MORNING STAR DR	TUO	163	C4
MORNING STAR MN	SBD	84	B3
MORNING STAR RD	ALP	36	C5
MORONGO RD	RCO	100	A3
MORONGO RD	SBD	101	B1
MORONI RD	SUT	33	B2
MORRETTI CYN RD	SLO	76	B4
MORRILL RD	STA	47	D2
MORRIS AV W	MDO	162	A2
MORRIS RD	COL	33	A2
MORRIS RD	KER	78	A3
MORRIS RD	STA	47	C4
MORRIS MINE RD	MNO	51	C2
MORRISON RD	STA	48	A1
MORRISN BRYN RD	TEH	24	B2
MORRISON CYN RD	ALA	P	B1
MORRISON CYN RD	ALA	46	A3
MORRIS RANCH RD	RCO	100	C5
MORRO RD	KER	91	C3
MORSE RD	SJCO	40	B4
MORSE RD	YOL	39	D3
MORTON AV	TUL	68	D3
MORTON BL S	MDO	162	C4
MOSAIC CANYON	INY	61	D4
MOSELEY RD	DN	1	D3
MOSHER	MPA	49	D3
MOSQUITO RD	ED	34	E4
MOSQUITO RDG RD	PLA	34	E3
MOSS OLD MILL RD	TRI	10	E5
MOTHER LODE DR	ED	34	D5
MOTHER LODE TR	MAD	49	C4
MOTOR AV	LA	183	B3
MOTOR AV	LACO	Q	C4
MOTT AIRPORT RD	SIS	12	D2
MOULTAN LOOP	TEH	19	A3
MOULTON PKWY	ORCO	98	D5
MOUND SPGS RD	SBD	100	C1
MT ACADIA BLVD	SD	213	B2
MOUNTAIN AV	LACO	R	D2
MOUNTAIN AV	RCO	100	A4
MOUNTAIN AV	SBD	U	D2
MOUNTAIN AV	SBD	98	D1
MOUNTAIN AV	UPL	203	E2
MOUNTAIN BLVD	O	156	E5
MOUNTAIN DR	STB	174	B2
MOUNTAIN RD	SBD	90	D4
MOUNTAIN RD S	VEN	88	C5
MOUNTAIN ST	LACO	Q	E2
MTN CLIMBER WY	KER	79	C5
MTN HOME CK RD	SBD	99	E1
MTN HOME RCH RD	SON	38	A1
MTN HOUSE RD	ALA	M	E4
MTN HOUSE RD	ALA	46	D1
MTN HOUSE RD	MEN	31	B4
MTN HOUSE RD	SIE	26	D4
MTN LEMON RD S	VEN	88	C5
MTN MEADOW RD	SHA	19	C2
MTN QUAIL LN	MOD	7	B5
MOUNTAIN RCH RD	CAL	41	B3
MTN SCHOOL RD	SHA	13	B5
MTN SPRINGS RD	SBD	91	B2
MTN SPRINGS RD	SBD	94	E1
MTN SPRINGS RD	SLO	76	A1
MOUNTAIN VW AV	FRCO	56	C5
MOUNTAIN VW AV	FRCO	57	D5
MOUNTAIN VW AV	SBD	99	C2
MOUNTAIN VW AV	RCO	99	E2
MOUNTAIN VW RD	HUM	16	B1
MOUNTAIN VW RD	KER	78	E3
MOUNTAIN VW RD	KER	79	A3
MOUNTAIN VW RD	MEN	30	E3
MOUNTAIN VW RD	RCO	100	D3
MOUNTAIN VW RD	SBD	90	E3
MOUNTAIN VW RD	SBD	91	C1
MOUNTAIN VW RD	SBD	92	B1
MOUNTAIN VW RD	STB	174	A4
MOUNTAIN VW RD	SCR	P	B5
MOUNTAIN VW RD	SCR	54	A1
MOUNTAIN VW RD	SHA	13	C5
MOUNTAIN VW RD	STA	47	D3
MOUNTAIN VW ST	BARS	208	A2
MTN VW-ALVSO RD	MVW	148	A5
MTN VW-ALVSO RD	SCL	P	B3
MTN VIEW RCH RD	SON	31	C5
MT AUKUM RD	ED	40	E1
MT AUKUM RD	ED	41	A1
MT BALDY LKOUT	SIS	2	E3
MT BULLION CTO	MPA	49	A3
MT DIABLO SC BL	CC	M	B4
MT EATON RD	TUO	41	D5
MT EDEN RD	SCL	N	E4
MT EDEN RD	SCL	P	A4
MT EDEN RD	SCL	45	E5

STREET	CO.	PAGE	GRID
MT EMMA RD	LACO	90	A4
MT GAINES	MPA	48	E3
MT GLEASON AV	LACO	Q	E2
MT HAMILTON RD	SCL	P	C3
MT HAMILTON RD	SCL	46	C4
MT HERMON RD	SCR	P	A5
MT HERMON RD	SCR	53	E1
MT HOUGH CRYSTL	PLU	26	D1
MT HOLLYWOOD DR	LA	182	A2
MT HOUSE RD	YUB	26	C5
MT MADONNA RD	SCL	54	C2
MT OLIVE RD	NEV	34	C2
MT OPHIR RD	MPA	49	A3
MT PIERCE LKOUT	HUM	15	E3
MT PINOS RD	KER	88	D2
MT PINOS RD	VEN	88	A1
MT PINOS RD	VEN	88	C2
MT REBA RD	ALP	42	A1
MT SHASTA DR	SIS	12	E2
MT VEEDER RD	NAPA	29	C4
MT VEEDER RD	NAPA	38	C2
MT VERNON AV	CLTN	207	B4
MT VERNON AV	KER	78	D3
MT VERNON AV	RCO	99	B2
MT VERNON AV	SBD	91	D1
MT VERNON AV	SBD	99	B2
MT VERNON AV	SBDO	207	B2
MT VERNON RD	PLA	34	B3
MT WHITNEY	FRCO	57	C5
MT WHITNEY AV	FRCO	66	D1
MT WHITNEY ST	KER	70	C5
MT WILSON	LACO	98	A1
MT WILSON RD	LACO	R	C2
MT ZION RD	AMA	41	A2
MOVIE RD	INY	60	A4
MOWRY AV	ALA	P	A2
MOWRY AV	ALA	46	A3
M T FREITAS PKY	SR	139	A1
MUCK VALLEY RD	LAS	14	B4
MUDD RD	IMP	109	A5
MUD LAKE RD	ALP	36	C4
MUD LAKE RD	MOD	6	A5
MUD LAKE RD	MOD	14	A1
MUELLER	SJCO	40	A5
MUELLER	SJCO	47	A1
MUIR AV	BUT	25	A3
MUIR MILL RD	MEN	22	E5
MUIR WOODS RD	MAR	L	A4
MUIR WOODS RD	MAR	45	A1
MULBERRY AV	MCO	48	B4
MULBERRY AV	RCO	99	A2
MULBERRY DR	LACO	R	C5
MULBERRY ST	C	124	D5
MULE BRIDGE RD	SIS	11	C2
MULE CANYON RD	SBD	92	A1
MULE CREEK RD	TRI	11	D5
MULE DEER LN	MOD	7	B5
MULE TOWN RD	SHA	18	B2
MULHOLLAND DR	LA	177	A5
MULHOLLAND DR	LA	181	A2
MULHOLLAND DR	LACO	97	C1
MULHOLLAND DR	LACO	Q	D1
MULHOLLAND HWY	LACO	97	A1
MULLER LN	DGL	36	B3
MULLER RD	KER	78	C3
MULLER RD	KER	79	A3
MULLOY RD	SIS	4	C3
MUMMA RD	COL	33	A3
MUMY RD	INY	51	C4
MUNCY RD	STA	47	C3
MUNJAR RD	BUT	25	A2
MUNRAS AV	MONT	167	D5
MUNRAS AV	MON	53	E4
MUNSEY RD	KER	80	C3
MUNRAS AV	MONT	168	D1
MUNZER RD	KER	78	B3
MURCHISON DR	MLBR	144	D5
MURIEL DR	BARS	208	C2
MURPHY AV	SCL	P	B3
MURPHY LN	SCL	P	E5
MURPHY LN	SCL	54	D1
MURPHY LN	SHA	19	A1
MURPHY RD	IMP	112	A3
MURPHY RD	MON	54	C2
MURPHY RD	NEV	26	C5
MURPHY RD	SBT	55	B3
MURPHY RD	SCR	54	C2
MURPHY RD	SJCO	47	C1
MURPHY RD	STA	47	C2
MURPHY RD	TUO	41	C5
MURPHYS GRD RD	CAL	41	B4
MURRAY RD	HUM	9	E4
MURRAY RD	HUM	10	A4
MURRAY RD	SJCO	40	C5
MURRAY RD	SUT	33	C3
MURRAY CK RD E	CAL	41	B3
MURRAY CK RD W	CAL	41	B3
MURRAY RIDGE RD	SD	214	A2
MURRIETA HT SPG	RCO	99	C5
MURRIETTA RD	RCO	99	C3
MUSCAT AV	FRCO	57	B4
MUSCAT AV	FRCO	57	D4
MUSCOTT ST	SBDO	207	A2
MUSTANG RD	RCO	100	A5
MUSTANG SPGS RD	SLO	76	A1
MUTAU FLAT RD	VEN	88	C5
MYER AV	TUL	68	C2
MYERS LN	COL	32	E2
MYERS RD	COL	32	D2
MYERS RD	SIS	4	E3
MYERS RD	SIS	5	A3
MYERS ST	BUT	25	D4
MYKLE OAKS RD	MPA	49	A3

STREET	CO.	PAGE	GRID
MYRA AV	LA	182	C5
MYRTLE AV	DN	1	E5
MYRTLE AV	EUR	121	E1
MYRTLE AV	HUM	9	E5
MYRTLE AV	HUM	15	E1
MYRTLE AV	LACO	R	D2
MYRTLEWOOD DR	MAD	57	C2
N			
NABORLY RD	SBD	101	D1
NACIMNTO-FER RD	MON	64	E3
NACIMNTO-FER RD	MON	65	A3
NACIMIENTO LAKE	MON	65	E4
NACMIENTO LK DR	SLO	75	E1
NACMIENTO LK DR	SLO	76	A1
NACIONAL ST	SAL	171	A3
NADEAU RD	INY	71	B1
NADER RD	PLA	34	A3
NAGEL CANYON RD	KER	79	D3
NAGLEE AV	SJ	151	D4
NANTES AV	MCO	55	E1
NAPA AV	FRCO	56	E5
NAPA RD	SBD	92	E5
NAPA RD	SON	38	B3
NAPA RD	SON	L	B1
NAPA RD	SON	132	D5
NAPA ST	SON	L	B1
NAPA ST E	SNMA	132	E4
NAPA ST E	SON	38	B3
NAPA ST W	SNMA	132	C4
NARANJO BLVD	TUL	58	D5
NARANJO BLVD	TUL	68	D1
NARBONNE AV	LACO	S	B2
NARRAGANSETT AV	SDCO	V	A3
NARRAGANSETT AV	SDCO	111	C1
NASHUA RD	MON	54	C3
NASON RD	MON	64	C1
NASON ST	RCO	99	C3
NATIONAL AV	SD	216	A4
NATIONAL AV	SDCO	V	C4
NATIONAL AV	SDCO	111	D1
NATIONAL BLVD	CUL	183	D5
NATIONAL BLVD	LA	180	E5
NATIONAL BLVD	LA	183	C4
NATIONAL BLVD	LACO	Q	C4
NATL TRAILS HWY	SBD	91	B2
NATL TRAILS HWY	SBD	92	A1
NATL TRAILS HWY	SBD	93	A2
NATL TRAILS HWY	SBD	94	A3
NATIVIDAD RD	MON	54	D4
NATOMAS RD	SUT	33	D4
NATURAL BRDG RD	INY	72	B1
NAUMAN RD	VEN	96	B1
NAUTILUS ST	SD	211	A4
NAVAJO DR	SAL	171	C1
NAVAJO RD	RCO	99	C4
NAVAJO RD	SBD	91	C3
NAVAJO RD	SDCO	V	D2
NAVAJO RD	SDCO	111	D1
NAVARO ST	SDCO	V	A3
NAVARRO RDG RD	MEN	30	C2
NAVELENCIA AV	FRCO	58	A4
NAVY DR	SJCO	40	A5
NEAL SPRING RD	SLO	76	B1
NEBO ST	SBD	92	A1
NEBRASKA AV	FRCO	57	B4
NEBRASKA AV	FRCO	57	C4
NEBRASKA AV	TUL	58	A4
NEBRASKA ST	VAL	134	C3
NECKLE RD	IMP	112	A3
NECTAR RD	RCO	107	B1
NEEDHAM RD	STA	47	B3
NEEDHAM ST	MDO	162	A3
NEEDLE PEAK RD	SLT	129	D4
NEELEY	SJCO	40	A4
NEENACH RD	LACO	89	E2
NEES AV	FRCO	56	C3
NEES AV	FRCO	57	C3
NEGRO CREEK DR	TUL	58	C4
NEGRO HOLE RD	SIS	5	C4
NEIGHBORS BLVD	RCO	103	D5
NEIGHBORS BLVD	RCO	110	D1
NEILSON RD	CAL	40	E3
NELANDER	MCO	47	E4
NELSON	SJCO	47	C1
NELSON AV	BUT	25	C4
NELSON DR	TUL	69	B2
NELSON RD	BUT	25	B4
NELSON RD	TRI	17	C2
NELSON BAR RD	BUT	25	D3
NELSON CREEK RD	SHA	13	E4
NELSON PIT RD	IMP	112	C3
NELSON RES RD	LAS	8	B3
NELSONS CROSSNG	BUT	26	A3
NELSN SHPPEE RD	BUT	25	B4
NEROLY RD	CC	39	C5
NEROLY RD	CC	M	C5
NESTLE AV	LA	178	D5
NETHERLANDS RD	YOL	39	D2
NETHERTON RD	MCO	47	C5
NEUGERBAUER	SJCO	39	E5
NEUMARKEL RD	KER	79	A3
NEURALIA RD	KER	80	B4
NEVA AV	TEH	24	D2
NEVADA AV	KIN	67	B2
NEVADA AV	KIN	67	C2
NEVADA ST	AUB	126	B3
NEVADA ST	NEVC	128	C2
NEVADA ST	NEV	128	D2
NEVADA CITY HWY	GV	127	D2
NEVADA CITY HWY	NEV	127	D2
NEVADA CITY HWY	NEV	128	A5

STREET	CO.	PAGE	GRID
NEVIS AV	KER	78	C1
NEW AV	LACO	R	C4
NEW AV	SCL	P	E5
NEW AV	SCL	54	D1
NEWARK BLVD	ALA	P	A2
NEWARK BLVD	ALA	45	E3
NEWBERRY RD	SBD	92	C1
NEW BIG OAK FLT	MPA	49	C1
NEW BIG OAK FLT	MPA	63	B4
NEWCASTLE	PLA	34	C3
NEWCASTLE RD	SJCO	40	B5
NEW CEMETERY RD	LAS	14	B3
NEW CHESTR DUMP	PLU	20	B4
NW CHG QRTZ MTN	AMA	40	E2
NEWCOMB AV	FRCO	56	C4
NEWCOMB ST	TUL	68	D3
NEW DIXIE MN RD	SBD	92	C5
NEW DOCK ST	LA	191	C2
NEW DOCK ST	LACO	S	C3
NEWHALL AV	LACO	89	B4
NEWHALL RD	MCO	48	B5
NEWHALL RD	SUT	33	B2
NEWHALL ST	SJ	151	D3
NEW HOPE RD	SAC	39	E3
NEW HOPE RD	SAC	40	A3
NEWHOPE ST	FTNV	197	B2
NEWHOPE ST	GGR	195	A3
NEWHOPE ST	ORCO	T	C3
NEWHOPE ST	SA	195	A3
NEW IDRIA RD	SBT	55	E5
NEW IDRIA RD	SBT	56	A4
NEWLAND ST	ORCO	T	B3
NEWMARK AV	FRCO	57	E4
NEW PLEYTO RD	MON	65	D4
NEW PEORIA FLAT	TUO	41	B5
NEWPORT AV	GLE	24	D3
NEWPORT AV	ORCO	98	C4
NEWPORT AV	ORCO	T	E2
NEWPORT BLVD	CM	199	C2
NEWPORT BLVD	NB	199	A4
NEWPORT FRWY	CM	197	E5
NEWPORT FRWY	CM	198	B3
NEWPORT FRWY	ORA	194	E3
NEWPORT FRWY	ORA	196	E3
NEWPORT FRWY	ORCO	196	E3
NEWPORT FRWY	SA	196	E4
NEWPORT FRWY	TUS	196	E4
NEWPORT RD	MCO	48	A3
NEWPORT RD	RCO	99	C4
NEWPORT RD	RCO	99	D4
NEWPORT CST DR	ORCO	T	D5
NEWPORT CST DR	IRV	200	E3
NEWPORT CST DR	ORCO	98	C5
NEWPORT CST DR	ORCO	T	D5
NEWRIVER RD	TRI	11	A4
NEW ROME RD	NEV	34	C1
NEWSOM RD	MCO	47	C5
NEWSOM RD	MCO	55	C1
NEWTON AV	KIN	67	C3
NEWTOWN RD	ED	34	E5
NEWVILLE RD	GLE	24	B3
NEWVILLE RD	TEH	24	A2
NEW YORK DR	LACO	R	B2
NEW YRK FLAT RD	YUB	26	A4
NEW YRK HOUS RD	YUB	26	A5
NEW YORK MTN RD	SBD	84	C4
NEW YORK RCH RD	AMA	40	E2
NIAGARA AV	COL	33	A2
NICASIO VLY RD	MAR	37	E4
NICE LUCERNE	LAK	31	D2
NICHOLAS RD	MAD	57	E2
NICHOLLS RD	NEV	34	B2
NICHOLS RD	IMP	112	A3
NICHOLS RD	RCO	99	B4
NICHOLS CYN RD	LA	181	A3
NICHOLS MILL RD	SIE	27	B4
NICKEL RD	MCO	48	A5
NICOLAS RD	RCO	99	D5
NICOLAUS	PLA	33	E4
NICOLAUS AV	SUT	33	D3
NIDER RD	IMP	109	B3
NIDERER RD	SLO	75	E1
NIDERER RD	SLO	76	A1
NELSON	SJCO	40	C5
NIELSON AV	FRE	165	A3
NIELSEN AV	FRCO	57	A3
NIELSON RD	CAL	41	A3
NIESTRATH RD	SON	37	B1
NIHELL ST	NEV	128	C2
NILAND AV	IMP	109	B3
NILAND MRINA RD	IMP	109	A2
NILE AV	SJCO	47	B1
NILE RD	SJCO	47	B1
NILES AV	KIN	67	D3
NILES ST	BKD	166	E2
NILES ST	KER	78	E3
NILES CANYON RD	ALA	P	B1
NILES CANYON RD	ALA	46	A3
NILL AV	KER	78	C1
NIMITZ BLVD	SD	212	C5
NIMITZ BLVD	SDCO	V	A3
NIMITZ BLVD	SDCO	111	C1
NIMITZ FRWY	ALA	45	D2
NIMITZ FRWY	ALA	146	C4
NIMITZ FRWY	H	146	C4
NIMITZ FRWY	O	157	D1
NIMITZ FRWY	O	158	B4
NIMITZ FRWY	O	159	C1
NIMITZ FRWY	SJ	152	A1
NINE RD	CAL	41	C4
NINE MILE CYN	INY	70	B4
NINTH ST	C	124	C5
NIPTON RD	SBD	84	C2

STREET	CO.	PAGE	GRID
NIPTON DESRT RD	SBD	84	C2
NIPTON MOORE RD	SBD	84	C2
NISQUALLY RD	SBD	91	B4
NISSEN RD	HUM	15	D2
NM 1	TUL	68	E5
NM 14	TUL	68	E4
NM 18	TUL	69	C4
NM 23	TUL	69	B4
NM 24	TUL	69	B4
NM 45	TUL	69	C4
NM 50	TUL	69	B4
NM 88	TUL	69	C4
NM 93	TUL	69	C4
NM 112	TUL	69	C3
NM 117	TUL	70	A3
NM 121	TUL	69	B3
NM 127	TUL	69	B3
NM 133	TUL	70	A3
NM 163	TUL	69	B3
NM 175	TUL	69	B3
NM 231	TUL	69	B2
NM 232	TUL	69	A2
NM 276	TUL	69	A1
NOBLE RD	YUB	33	D2
NOFFSINGER RD	IMP	109	B3
NOLAN RD	IMP	109	B4
NOLINA CIR	RCO	100	D4
NO NINE	MPA	48	E3
NONPAREIL AV	COL	32	E3
NOPEL AV	BUT	25	C2
NORD AV	BUT	124	A4
NORD AV	KER	78	C3
NORD HWY	BUT	25	A3
NORDAHL RD	IMP	110	D5
NORD GIANELLA	BUT	25	A3
NORDOFF ST	LACO	97	C1
NORFOLK ST	SM	145	A1
NORHAM PL	SBD	101	A1
NORIEGA RD	KER	78	C3
NORIEGA ST	SF	141	C5
NORMA ST S	KER	80	E1
NORMAL ST	SD	214	A5
NORMAL ST	SDCO	V	B3
NORMAL ST	SDCO	111	D1
NORMAN	SUT	33	B2
NORMAN AV	KER	80	B5
NORMAN RD	COL	24	E5
NORMANDIE AV	LA	182	B5
NORMANDIE AV	LA	185	B5
NORMANDIE AV	LACO	Q	E5
NORMANDIE AV	LACO	S	C2
NORMANDY CT	NEV	127	C2
NORMAN HILLS RD	RCO	107	C1
NORRBOM RD W	SON	38	B3
NORRBOM RD	SON	132	D3
NORRIS RD	KER	78	C2
NORRIS CYN RD	CC	M	A5
NORRIS CYN RD	CC	46	A1
NORRISH RD	IMP	109	C5
NORTH AV	FRCO	56	C4
NORTH AV	FRCO	57	B4
NORTH AV	KIN	57	D5
NORTH AV	MCO	47	E3
NORTH AV	MCO	48	A3
NORTH AV	ORCO	T	C2
NORTH AV	SDCO	106	D3
NORTH AV	STA	47	C2
NORTH HWY	INY	61	D3
NORTH RD	STA	47	B2
NORTH ST	MAN	161	C3
NORTH ARM	PLU	20	D5
N BNK CHETKO RD	CUR	1	D2
NORTH BUSCH RD	MEN	23	B5
NORTH BUSCH RD	MEN	31	B1
NORTHCREST DR	DN	1	D4
NORTHRLY BR GRN	SLO	75	D2
NORTH FORK RD	HUM	15	D4
NORTH FORK RD	MAD	49	D5
NORTH FORK RD	SBT	66	A2
NORTH FORK RD	TUO	41	E4
N FK MAD RIV RD	TRI	17	B5
NORTHGATE BLVD	SAC	39	E1
NORTH GATE RD	CC	M	A4
NORTH GATE RD	CC	39	A5
NORTH GATE RD	SOL	39	A3
N LIVERMORE AV	ALA	46	C2
NORTH RIDGE RD	SBD	100	C2
NORTHRUP RD	MCO	47	D4
NORTHRUP RD	MOD	8	A1
NORTHRUP RD	MOD	14	E1
NORTH SHORE	PLA	35	E1
NORTH SHORE DR	SBD	92	A5
NORTH SHORE RD	SIS	12	C2
NORTHSIDE DR	MPA	63	B2
NORTH SIDE RD	SBD	91	E3
NORTH STAR TR	SBD	100	C2
NORTH VALLEY RD	PLU	20	D5
NORTHWOODS BLVD	NEV	27	D5
NORTON RD	KER	80	B3
NORTON RD	SBT	55	E4
NORTON RD	SOL	39	C3
NORTONVILLE	CC	39	B5
NORVEL RD	LAS	20	C3
NORWALK BLVD	LACO	98	A3
NORWALK BLVD	LACO	R	C5
NORWALK BLVD	LACO	T	A2
NORWGIAN RCH RD	TRI	11	E4
NORWOOD AV	SR	139	A4
NOTRE DAME AV	BLMT	145	B5
NOVATO BLVD	MAR	L	A2
NOVATO BLVD	MAR	38	A4
NOYES VALLEY RD	SIS	11	E2
NTU RD	SB	86	B1

INDEXES

STREET INDEX

STREET	CO.	PAGE	GRID
NUESTRO RD	SUT	33	C2
NUEVO RD	RCO	99	C3
NUNES LN	SHA	19	C2
NUNNIEMAKER RD	HUM	16	C4
NURSE SLOUGH LN	SOL	39	A3
NURSERY ST	NEV	128	C2
NYON RD	SBD	100	B1

O

STREET	CO.	PAGE	GRID
O ST	FRE	165	D3
OAHU RD	SBD	92	C1
OAK AV	DVS	136	C3
OAK AV	LAKE	7	B1
OAK AV	MCO	48	B4
OAK AV	SUT	33	D3
OAK AV	TRI	17	B2
OAK DR	SDCO	112	D1
OAK RD	MPA	49	B3
OAK ST	BKD	166	A4
OAK ST	MCO	47	E4
OAK ST	MCO	48	A4
OAK ST	SF	141	E4
OAK ST	SF	142	A4
OAK ST	SHA	18	B3
OAK ST	S	160	B4
OAK ST	U	123	C2
OAK WY	BUT	25	A3
OAK CREEK RD	KER	79	D5
OAK CREEK RD N	INY	59	E3
OAK CREEK RD S	INY	59	E3
OAKDALE RD	MCO	48	A3
OAKDALE RD	MCO	48	B3
OAKDALE RD	STA	47	D2
OAKDL WTRFRD HY	STA	47	E2
OAK FLAT RD	SLO	75	E1
OAK FLAT RD	SLO	76	A1
OAK FLAT RD	STA	47	B4
OAK GLEN AV	SCL	P	D5
OAK GLEN AV	SCL	54	C1
OAK GLEN RD	RCO	100	A5
OAK GLEN RD	SBD	99	E2
OAK GROVE	CC	38	E5
OAK GROVE	MPA	49	B4
OAK GROVE RD	CC	M	A3
OAK GRV SCHOOL	MPA	49	B4
OAK HILL RD	ED	34	E5
OAK HILL RD	SBD	91	A4
OAK KNOLL AV	LACO	R	B3
OAK KNOLL AV	NAPA	29	E5
OAK KNOLL AV	NAPA	38	C2
OAK KNL RNG STA	SIS	3	D3
OAKLAND AV	FRCO	67	A1
OAKLAND AV	O	158	B2
OAKLAND AV	P	158	C1
OAKLAND RD	SJ	152	B1
OAKLAND CP RD	PLU	26	D1
OAKLEA RD	STA	47	B3
OAKLEY LN	YUB	33	E3
OAK MEADOW RD	NEV	34	B2
OAKMONT TR	SHA	18	C1
OAKMORE ST	TUL	68	B2
OAK PARK BLVD	CC	L	E3
OAK PARK BLVD	CC	M	A3
OAK RANCH RD	SIE	26	D4
OAK RIDGE RD	SCL	P	D2
OAK RIDGE RD	TRI	17	A2
OAK RUN RD	SHA	18	D2
OAK RUN RD	SHA	18	E1
OAK RUN TO FERN	SHA	19	A1
OAK SPG RCH RD	SBD	90	E4
OAK SPRINGS RD	SBD	91	D4
OAKS AV	ONT	203	D5
OAKS RANCHO RD	KER	79	B4
OAK TREE RD	NEV	26	B5
OAK VALLEY DR	SIS	4	A4
OAK VALLEY RD	YUB	26	C4
OAK VIEW CT	KER	79	B4
OAKVLLE CRSS RD	NAPA	29	D3
OAKVLLE CRSS RD	NAPA	38	D2
OAKVILLE GRADE	NAPA	29	C4
OAKVILLE GRADE	NAPA	38	C2
OAKWAY	BUT	25	D2
OAKWOOD	SJCO	40	C5
OAKWOOD	SJCO	47	C1
OASIS RD	MON	65	C3
OASIS RD	INY	52	C3
OASIS RD	RCO	102	C4
OASIS RD	SBD	90	D4
OASIS RD	SHA	18	C2
OAT GAP RD	MEN	23	C5
OAT HILL RD	LAK	32	B5
OAT HILL RD N	NAPA	32	B5
OATMN TOPOCK HY	MOH	95	E1
OBANION RD	SUT	33	C3
OBERLIN RD	SIS	4	A4
OBRIEN RD	JOS	2	C2
OBSIDAN DOME RD	MNO	50	D1
O'BYRNES FERRY	TUO	41	B5
OCCIDENTAL RD	SON	37	D2
OCEAN AV	CAR	53	D5
OCEAN AV	CAR	168	B3
OCEAN AV	SFCO	L	B5
OCEAN AV	SFCO	45	B2
OCEAN AV	SB	86	B3
OCEAN BLVD	LB	191	E2
OCEAN BLVD	LB	192	B3
OCEAN BLVD	LACO	98	A4
OCEAN BLVD	LACO	S	D2
OCEAN DR	DN	1	D3
OCEAN DR	HUM	9	E4
OCEAN DR	MEN	22	C4
OCEAN BEACH FWY	SD	212	C5
OCEAN PARK BLVD	LA	180	C5
OCEAN PARK BLVD	LACO	Q	C4
OCEAN PARK BLVD	SMON	180	C5
OCEAN PARK BLVD	SMON	187	A1
OCEAN PARK RD	SB	86	A2
OCEANSIDE BLVD	SDCO	106	B3
OCEAN VIEW AV	INY	51	B3
OCEAN VIEW BLVD	LACO	R	A2
OCEAN VIEW BLVD	PAC	167	A1
OCEAN VIEW BLVD	SD	216	B4
OCEAN VIEW BLVD	SDCO	V	C4
OCEAN VIEW BLVD	SDCO	111	D1
OCEANVIEW DR	CUR	1	D2
OCEAN VIEW DR	DN	1	D3
OCONNOR WY	SLO	76	A3
OCOTILLO WY	SBD	91	C4
ODD FELLW PK RD	HUM	16	A3
ODOM LN	MEN	22	C5
O'FARRELL ST	SF	143	A5
OFFAL RD	MNO	42	E1
OFFIELD LOOKOUT	SIS	10	E1
OFFUTT RD	KER	78	B1
OGBURN CEM RD	SHA	19	A2
OGIER RD	IMP	112	C3
OGILBY RD	IMP	110	B4
OGULIN CANYON	LAK	32	A3
O'HARA AV	CC	M	D3
O'HARA AV	CC	39	C5
OHIO AV	FRCO	56	C3
OHIO AV	LA	180	B4
OHM RD	COL	32	E2
OHM RD	TEH	18	D5
OIL CANYON RD	FRCO	66	D2
OIL CITY RD	FRCO	66	D2
OILER CT	KER	79	C3
OILFIELDS RD	KER	78	D2
OIL PLANT RD	MNO	43	C5
OIL WELL RD	HUM	15	E2
OJAI DR	SHA	18	C3
OJAI FRWY	VEN	88	A5
OJAI FRWY	VENT	175	A2
OJAI FRWY	VEN	175	A2
OJAI ST	VEN	88	B4
O'KEEFE ST	MP	147	B1
O'KEEFE ST E	SMCO	147	C1
OKEEFFE RD	SIS	5	D2
OKLAHOMA AV	TEH	18	D5
OKLAHOMA SCH RD	SIS	5	B3
OLANCHA DRWN RD	INY	70	E1
OLD HWY	COL	32	D1
OLD HWY	LAS	21	D5
OLD HWY	MPA	49	A4
OLD HWY	PLU	26	D1
OLD AIRLINE HWY	SBT	55	B4
OLD ALLRED RD	MPA	49	B3
OLD ALTURAS HWY	MOD	5	E2
OLD ALTURAS HWY	MOD	6	A2
OLD ALTURAS RD	SHA	18	C2
OLD ARCATA RD	HUM	9	E5
OLD ARCATA RD	HUM	10	A5
OLD AUBURN RD	SAC	34	B5
OLD BANNING- -IDYLLWILD RD	RCO	100	A3
OLD BAYSHRE HWY	SJ	152	A1
OLD BREA CYN RD	LACO	U	A3
OLD CAMP TWO RD	SIS	13	C2
OLD CASTLE RD	SDCO	106	D2
OLD CEMETERY RD	LAS	14	B3
OLD CHAMPS FLAT	LAS	20	D1
OLD CHISHOLM DR	SBD	101	B1
OLD COAST HWY	SB	86	D3
OLD COPPER CITY	SBD	81	D3
OLD CORNING RD	TEH	24	D2
OLD COULTRVLLE- -YOSEMITE RD	MPA	49	C1
OLD COULTRVLLE- -YOSEMITE RD	MPA	63	A4
OLD CUTOFF RD	LAS	21	B4
OLD DAVIS RD	SOL	39	C1
OLD DON PDRO RD	TUO	48	C1
OLD DRYTOWN- -PLYMOUTH RDYMT	AMA	40	D2
OLD EEL RIV RD	LAK	23	C5
OLD EEL ROCK	HUM	16	C4
OLD EL MIRAGE	SBD	90	D3
OLD ELSINORE RD	RCO	99	C3
OLDENBERG RD	SBD	91	D3
OLD FT TEJON RD	LACO	90	B3
OLD FRIANT RD	FRCO	57	C2
OLD GASQUET TLL	DN	2	B3
OLD GULCH RD	CAL	41	B4
OLD HRLD PLM RD	LACO	90	A3
OLD HAUN RD	PLU	20	C4
OLD HERNANDZ RD	SBT	55	C5
OLD HIGHWAY 99	SIS	12	B1
OLD HWY 138	LACO	89	D2
OLD HWY RD	LAS	14	A4
OLD HWY RD	PLU	26	C1
OLD HWY RT 29	LAS	21	C5
OLD HWY S FORK	DN	2	A3
OLD HONEY RUN	BUT	25	C3
OLD KANE SPG RD	SDCO	108	A3
OLD KNOX RD	YUB	26	B4
OLD LAMBERT RD	AMA	40	C2
OLD LANDMARK DR	SBD	91	D1
OLD LEESVL GRAD	COL	32	C2
OLD LOMA RD	BUT	25	C1
OLD LONG VLY RD	LAK	32	A3
OLD MAIL RT	LAS	8	C5
OLD MAMMOTH RD	ML	164	A5
OLD MAMMOTH RD	MNO	50	D2
OLD MATTOLE RD	HUM	15	C4
OLD MIDLAND RD	KLAM	5	B1
OLD MILL RD	DN	1	D4
OLD MINE RD	SBD	101	A1
OLD MINE TR	RCO	100	B5
OLD MIRAMAR RD	SDCO	V	B2
OLD MIRAMAR RD	SDCO	106	C5
OLD MORGN HL RD	TRI	17	B2
OLD MORRO RD	SLO	76	A2
OLD NATL TR HWY	SBD	94	D2
OLD OAK FLAT RD	MPA	49	C1
OLD OAKLAND RD	SCL	P	B3
OLD OAKLAND RD	SCL	46	B4
OLD PARKER RD	SBD	103	E2
OLD PIEDMONT RD	SCL	46	B4
OLD PLYMTH SAC- -VIA FIN RCH RD	AMA	40	D2
OLD PONY EXPRSS	ALP	36	B4
OLD RAILROAD GR	SHA	12	B4
OLD RANCH RD	KER	79	C5
OLD REDWOOD HWY	SON	37	E1
OLD RENO RD	NEV	27	D5
OLD RDG ROUTE RD	LACO	89	A2
OLD RIVER RD	KER	78	C3
OLD RIVER RD	KER	78	C4
OLD RIV SCHL RD	LACO	R	B5
OLD SN FRANCSCO	SVL	150	A1
OLD SCHOOL RD	SHA	13	D3
OLD SCH HOUS RD	TRI	22	E1
OLD SEIAD HWY	SIS	3	B3
OLD SEIAD CK RD	SIS	3	B3
OLD SHASTA RIV	SIS	4	A4
OLD SHERWIN GRD	INY	51	B3
OLD SHERWOOD RD	MEN	22	E4
OLD SKYLINE	KIN	67	A3
OLD SONOMA RD	NAP	133	B4
OLD SONOMA RD	NAPA	L	C1
OLD SONOMA RD	NAPA	38	C3
OLD SONOMA RD	NAPA	133	A5
OLD SPANISH TR	INY	72	E4
OLD SPANISH TR	INY	73	B4
OLD STAGE RD	MEN	30	B4
OLD STAGE RD	MON	54	D3
OLD STAGE RD	SIS	12	C2
OLD STAGE RD N	SIS	12	C1
OLD STAGEROAD	MEN	30	D4
OLD STATE HWY	HUM	9	E2
OLD STATE HWY	HUM	10	A2
OLD STATE HWY	INY	72	E3
OLD STATE HWY	INY	73	A3
OLD STATE HWY	KIN	67	B4
OLD STATE HWY	LAK	31	C2
OLD STATE HWY	MNO	43	C5
OLD STATE HWY	MNO	50	D2
OLD STATE HWY	SIS	4	E3
OLD STATE HWY	SIS	5	A4
OLD STEWRTS PT- -SKAGGS SPGS RD	SON	31	B5
OLD STOCKTON RD	AMA	40	D3
OLD STOCKTON- -IONE HWY	AMA	40	D2
OLD STRWBRRY RD	TUO	41	E3
OLD STRWBRRY RD	TUO	42	A3
OLD SUTTER CK- -AMADOR CITY HY	AMA	40	E2
OLD STTR HLL RD	AMA	40	E2
OLD TELEGRPH RD	VEN	88	E4
OLD TELEGRPH RD	VEN	89	A4
OLD THREE CK RD	HUM	10	C5
OLD TIM BELL RD	STA	47	E2
OLD TOLL	MPA	49	A3
OLD TOLL RD	INY	71	A1
OLD TOLL RD	LAS	14	A3
OLD TOLL RD	MEN	31	C3
OLD TOLL RD	YUB	26	B5
OLD TOPANGA CYN	LACO	97	B2
OLD TRUCKEE RD	SIE	27	C4
OLD WESTSIDE RD	SIS	4	B5
OLD WILBUR RD	COL	32	C2
OLD WITR SPG RD	LAK	31	C2
OLD WMN SPGS RD	SBD	92	A4
OLD WMN SPGS RD	SBD	100	D1
OLD YERMO CTO	SBD	91	E1
OLD YOSEMITE RD	MPA	49	A1
OLD 44 DR	SHA	18	C2
OLEANDER	SJCO	47	B2
OLEANDER AV	BKD	166	C4
OLEANDER AV	RCO	99	B3
OLEMA ST	SBD	80	E1
OLINDA RD	SHA	18	C3
OLIVAS LN	SOL	39	A2
OLIVE AV	BUR	179	C5
OLIVE AV	COR	215	B5
OLIVE AV	FRE	165	B2
OLIVE AV	FRCO	57	A3
OLIVE AV	FRCO	57	C3
OLIVE AV	GLE	24	D3
OLIVE AV	MAR	L	A2
OLIVE AV	MCO	48	A4
OLIVE AV	MCO	48	C4
OLIVE AV	RCO	99	B5
OLIVE AV	SDCO	106	C3
OLIVE AV	SJCO	47	B2
OLIVE AV	STA	47	B3
OLIVE AV	STA	47	E1
OLIVE AV	STA	48	A1
OLIVE AV	TEH	24	D1
OLIVE AV	TUL	68	D3
OLIVE AV W	MER	170	B2
OLIVE DR	KER	78	D2
OLIVE DR E	DVS	136	D3
OLIVE HWY	BUT	25	D4
OLIVE LN	GLE	25	A4
OLIVE RD	TEH	24	D2
OLIVE RD	VEN	88	B5
OLIVE ST	AVLN	97	B4
OLIVE ST	LA	185	B5
OLIVE ST	LACO	R	C3
OLIVE ST	MAR	38	B4
OLIVE ST	RCO	99	B4
OLIVE ST	SDCO	107	A4
OLIVE ST	SHA	18	B3
OLIVEHURST	YUB	33	D2
OLIVE LAKE BLVD	RCO	103	D5
OLIVENHAIN RD	SDCO	106	C4
OLIVE ORCHRD RD	CAL	40	D4
OLIVER RD	SBT	55	D4
OLIVERA DR	TUL	58	C5
OLIVE SCHOOL LN	SOL	39	A2
OLIVET RD	SON	37	D2
OLIVEWOOD AV	TEH	24	D2
OLNEY PARK DR	SHA	18	B2
OLSEN RD	MCO	48	B3
OLSEN RD	VEN	88	D5
OLSEN CREEK RD	TRI	16	E2
OLSON RD	LAS	8	B4
OLYMPIC	LAK	32	A3
OLYMPIC BLVD	BH	183	B2
OLYMPIC BLVD	LA	183	B2
OLYMPIC BLVD	LA	184	B2
OLYMPIC BLVD	LA	185	B3
OLYMPIC BLVD	LA	186	B4
OLYMPIC BLVD	LA	180	C4
OLYMPIC BLVD	LACO	97	D2
OLYMPIC BLVD	LACO	Q	D4
OLYMPIC BLVD	SMON	180	A5
OLYMPIC RD	MAD	57	B1
OLYMPIC RD	SBD	100	E1
OMAHA AV	KIN	67	B3
OMAHA AV	KIN	67	E3
OMEGA RD	NEV	26	E5
OMO RANCH RD	ED	41	B1
ONEAL RD	BUT	25	C4
ONEAL RD	MAD	57	D1
ONE HOLE SPG RD	SBD	92	C5
ONION VALLEY RD	ED	35	B3
ONION VALLEY RD	INY	59	E3
ONSTOTT RD	SUT	33	C2
ONTARIO AV	RCO	U	E5
ONTARIO AV	RCO	98	E3
ONTARIO FRWY	SBD	99	A1
ONYX AV	SIS	4	C5
OPAL RD	MCO	48	D4
OPAL WY	SHA	18	C1
OPAL FERRY RD	KER	88	D1
OPAL MTN RD	SBD	81	C4
OPENSHAW RD	BUT	25	C4
OPEN SHAW RD	PLU	20	D5
OPHIR RD	BUT	25	D5
OPHIR RD	INY	71	A2
ORANGE AV	BUT	25	E5
ORANGE AV	EC	217	D3
ORANGE AV	FRCO	57	C4
ORANGE AV	FRCO	57	D4
ORANGE AV	KIN	67	A3
ORANGE AV	KIN	67	D3
ORANGE AV	LACO	Q	E2
ORANGE AV	LACO	R	D4
ORANGE AV	LACO	S	D2
ORANGE AV	ORCO	T	B2
ORANGE AV	RCO	99	C3
ORANGE AV	SD	214	C5
ORANGE AV	SDCO	V	B4
ORANGE AV	SDCO	V	D5
ORANGE AV	SDCO	111	C1
ORANGE AV	SDCO	111	D2
ORANGE AV	SJCO	47	D1
ORANGE AV	SON	132	A4
ORANGE AV	STA	47	C3
ORANGE AV W	SSF	144	A1
ORANGE FRWY	ANA	194	A4
ORANGE FRWY	ORA	196	A1
ORANGE FRWY	ORCO	98	C3
ORANGE FRWY	ORCO	194	A4
ORANGE FRWY	ORCO	T	D1
ORANGE RD	SDCO	107	A3
ORANGE ST	KER	78	B2
ORANGE ST	RCO	99	B2
ORANGE ST	SBD	99	C2
ORANGE BLSSM RD	STA	48	A1
ORANGEBURG AV E	MDO	162	D1
ORANGEBURG AV W	MDO	162	B1
ORANGE GROVE AV	LACO	R	C3
ORANGE GROVE AV	LACO	U	B2
ORANGE GROVE BL	LACO	R	B3
ORANGE GROVE BL	PAS	190	C3
ORANGE-OLIVE RD	ORA	194	C3
ORANGE-OLIVE RD	ORCO	98	C3
ORANGE-OLIVE RD	ORCO	T	D2
ORANGE PARK BL	ORCO	T	E2
ORANGE SHOW RD	CLTN	207	C5
ORANGE SHOW RD	SBDO	207	C5
ORANGETHORPE AV	ORCO	98	B3
ORANGETHORPE AV	ORCO	98	D4
ORANGETHORPE AV	ORCO	T	B1
ORANGEWOOD AV	ORCO	T	B2
ORANGEWOOD RD	TEH	24	D1
ORCHARD AV	H	146	E4
ORCHARD AV	SLO	76	C5
ORCHARD AV	TEH	24	D2
ORCHARD DR	FRCO	58	D4
ORCHARD DR	MCO	48	C5
ORCHARD RD	IMP	112	C3
ORCHARD RD	MCO	47	C5
ORCHARD RD	SJCO	40	B4
ORCHARD RD	STA	47	B2
ORCHARD ST	RCO	99	E2
ORCHARD WY	MCO	56	C1
ORCHARD PARK AV	MCO	48	B4
ORCHARD SPGS RD	NEV	34	D2
ORCUTT RD	SLO	76	B4
ORCUTT RD	SLO	172	D4
ORCUTT RD	SNLO	172	D4
ORCUTT RD	VEN	88	C4
ORCUTT-GAREY RD	SB	86	C1
ORD ST	SB	86	B2
ORD FERRY RD	BUT	25	A4
ORD MOUNTAIN RD	SBD	91	E2
ORD RANCH RD	BUT	25	C5
ORDWAY RD	SIS	12	C1
OREGON DR	MDO	162	D4
OREGON EXPWY	PA	147	D3
OREGON EXPWY	SCL	45	E4
OREGON EXPWY	SCL	N	E2
OREGON CREEK RD	SIE	26	D4
OREGON GULCH RD	BUT	25	D4
OREGON HILL RD	YUB	26	B5
OREGON MTN RD	DN	2	C3
ORESTIMBA RD	STA	47	C4
ORINDA DR	SM	145	C4
ORLEANS AV	FRCO	55	E3
ORMONDE RD	SLO	76	B4
ORMSBY AV	FRCO	56	C2
ORMSBY ST	SDCO	106	C2
ORNBAUN RD	MEN	30	E3
ORO FINO RD	SIS	3	D5
OROVILLE BANGOR	BUT	25	D4
OROVLL CHICO HY	BUT	25	B3
OROVLLE DM BL E	BUT	25	D4
OROVLLE DM BL W	BUT	25	C4
OROVLLE GRIDLEY	BUT	25	C5
OROVLE QUNCY HY	BUT	25	D4
OROVLE QUNCY HY	BUT	25	E3
OROVLE QUNCY HY	BUT	26	A3
ORR RD	SAC	40	A3
ORR & DAY RD	LACO	R	C5
ORR & DAY RD	LACO	T	A1
ORR CREEK LN	PLA	34	B3
ORRIS RD	RCO	102	A4
ORRLAND AV	TUL	68	B3
ORR MTN LOOKOUT	SIS	5	A4
ORR SPRINGS RD	MEN	30	E1
ORR SPRINGS RD	MEN	31	A1
ORSI RD	STA	47	E1
ORTEGA HWY	ORCO	98	E5
ORTEGA HWY	SCL	202	E1
ORTIGALITA RD	MCO	55	D2
OSAGE RD	SOL	39	B2
OSBORN RD	SIS	5	D2
OSBORN RD	TEH	24	B2
OSBORNE AV	RCO	102	C4
OSBORNE RD	SBD	91	D2
OSBORNE ST	LACO	97	C1
OSBORNE ST	LACO	Q	C2
OSBORNE PARK RD	IMP	109	D4
OSDICK RD	SBD	80	E3
OSGOOD RD	ALA	P	B2
OSO PKWY	ORCO	98	D5
OSO FLACO LK RD	SLO	76	B5
OSOS ST	SNLO	172	C2
OSPITAL RD	CAL	40	D4
OSTROM RD	YUB	33	E2
OSWALD RD	SUT	33	B2
OSWELL ST	KER	78	D3
OTAY LAKES RD	SDCO	V	D4
OTAY LAKES RD	SDCO	111	E2
OTAY MESA RD	SDCO	V	D5
OTAY MESA RD	SDCO	111	E2
OTAY VALLEY RD	SDCO	V	D5
OTAY VALLEY RD	SDCO	111	E2
OTIS DR	A	159	A2
OTIS ST	LACO	R	A5
OTOE RD	SBD	91	C3
OUR HSE DAM RD	SIE	26	C5
OUTINGDALE	ED	40	E1
OUTLAW MINE RD	RCO	102	A2
OUTPOST DR	LA	181	C3
OVERLAND AV	CUL	188	C1
OVERLAND AV	LA	183	B5
OVERLAND AV	LACO	Q	C4
OVERLAND AV	MCO	55	D1
OVERLAND DR	SHA	18	C3
OWENS	SJCO	47	D1
OWENS AV	CLK	74	E2
OWENS RD	INY	51	D4
OWENS RD	SIS	5	A2
OWENS GORGE RD	MNO	51	B2
OWENS RIVER RD	MNO	50	E1
OWENS RV RCH RD	MNO	50	E1
OWENYO LONE PNE	INY	60	B4
OWL HOLE SPG RD	SBD	82	B1
OXALIS AV	FRCO	56	B2
OXBOW PL	SB	86	E3
OXFORD AV	FRCO	56	A2
OXFORD RD	SOL	39	D3
OXFORD ST	B	156	A2
OXNARD BLVD	OXN	176	C1

P

STREET	CO.	PAGE	GRID
P ST	BKD	166	D5
P ST	FRE	165	E3
P ST	KER	166	D5
P ST	SCTO	137	A3
P ST	SBD	91	D1
PACHECO BLVD	CC	L	E3
PACHECO BLVD	CC	38	E5
PACHECO BLVD	CC	154	C2
PACHECO BLVD	M	154	C2
PACHECO RD	KER	78	D3

264
PACHECO PASS HY
STREET INDEX
PINE CREEK BLVD

STREET	CO.	PAGE	GRID
PACHECO PASS HY	SCL	54	E2
PACHECO PASS RD	SCL	54	D2
PACIFIC AV	DN	1	D4
PACIFIC AV	LB	192	D3
PACIFIC AV	LA	187	A2
PACIFIC AV	LA	191	A4
PACIFIC AV	LACO	97	D4
PACIFIC AV	LACO	S	C3
PACIFIC AV	LACO	S	D2
PACIFIC AV	PAC	167	C2
PACIFIC AV	SC	169	D3
PACIFIC AV	S	160	B1
PACIFIC AV	SUT	33	D3
PACIFIC AV	SUT	33	D4
PACIFIC AV	TUL	68	B2
PACIFIC BLVD	LACO	97	E2
PACIFIC BLVD	LACO	R	A4
PACIFIC BLVD	SM	145	B4
PACIFIC HWY	SD	213	A5
PACIFIC HWY	SD	215	C2
PACIFIC ST	MONT	167	E4
PACIFIC ST	SBD	99	C1
PACIFIC BCH DR	SD	212	A2
PACIFIC BCH DR	SDCO	V	A3
PACIFIC CST HWY	LB	192	D1
PACIFIC CST HWY	LA	192	D1
PACIFIC CST HWY	LACO	97	B2
PACIFIC CST HWY	LACO	S	B1
PACIFIC CST HWY	LACO	T	A3
PACIFIC CST HWY	ORCO	98	C5
PACIFIC CST HWY	ORCO	T	A3
PACIFIC CST HWY	VEN	96	C2
PACIFC GRV-CRML	MONT	167	B4
PACIFC GRV-CRML	MON	53	D3
PACIFC GRV-CRML	MON	167	B4
PACIFC GRV-CRML	PAC	167	B4
PACIFIC HTS RD	BUT	25	C5
PACIFIC LUMBER	HUM	16	A1
PACIFIC MINE RD	SIE	26	C3
PACIFIC VIEW DR	MEN	30	C3
PACIFIC VIEW RD	VEN	96	C2
PACKER RD	COL	32	E1
PACKER LAKE RD	SIE	26	E3
PACKER LAKE RD	SIE	27	A3
PAC MINE RD	SIE	26	D3
PADUA AV	CLA	203	C1
PADUA AV	UPL	203	C1
PAGE AV	FRCO	67	B1
PAGE RD	STA	47	B2
PAGE MILL RD	PA	147	C5
PAGE MILL RD	SCL	N	E3
PAGE MILL RD	SCL	45	D4
PA HA LN	INY	51	D4
PAIGE AV	TUL	68	B2
PAIGE BAR RD	SHA	18	B2
PAINE RD	AMA	40	D2
PAINT RD	CAL	41	B4
PAINTED CAVE	SB	87	C4
PAINTED GRGE RD	IMP	111	C3
PAINTER AV	LACO	98	B2
PAINTER AV	LACO	R	D4
PAJARO ST	SAL	171	C4
PALA RD	DN	1	D3
PALA RD	RCO	106	D1
PALA TEMECLA RD	SDCO	106	D1
PALAZZO RD	MCO	47	E5
PALAZZO RD	MCO	48	A5
PALAZZO RD	MCO	55	E1
PALERMO RD	BUT	25	D5
PALRMO HONCT HY	BUT	25	D5
PALISADE AV	SBD	91	E3
PALISADES AV	RED	122	E1
PALISADES DR	LACO	97	C2
PALLETT CK RD	LACO	90	C4
PALM AV	AUB	126	C3
PALM AV	COR	215	C5
PALM AV	FRE	165	C2
PALM AV	FRCO	57	C3
PALM AV	KER	78	B1
PALM AV	KER	78	C3
PALM AV	LACO	R	C5
PALM AV	MCO	48	A4
PALM AV	RCO	99	B2
PALM AV	RCO	99	E4
PALM AV	SBD	99	B1
PALM AV	SDCO	V	C5
PALM AV	SDCO	V	D3
PALM AV	SDCO	111	D2
PALM AV	SDCO	111	E1
PALM AV	SCL	P	D4
PALM AV	SCL	54	C1
PALM AV	SHA	18	B3
PALM DR	RIV	206	E1
PALM DR	RCO	100	D3
PALM DR	SDCO	106	C4
PALM DR	SCL	N	E2
PALM ST	BKD	166	B4
PALM CANYON DR	PMSP	206	B5
PALM CANYON DR	RCO	100	D4
PALM CANYON DR	SDCO	107	E2
PALM CYN DR E	PMSP	206	C5
PALM CYN DR N	PMSP	206	A1
PALMDALE BLVD	LACO	90	B3
PALMDALE RD	SBD	90	E4
PALMDALE RD	SBD	91	A3
PALMER AV	FRCO	66	C2
PALMER RD	SB	86	C2
PALMER CREEK RD	HUM	15	E2
PALMETTO AV	BUT	124	C3
PALMETTO AV	C	124	C3
PALMETTO AV	ONT	203	E5
PALMETTO AV	ONT	204	A5
PALMETTO ST	SBD	80	E5

STREET	CO.	PAGE	GRID
PALMETTO ST	SBD	81	A5
PALMETTO WY	LAS	20	D2
PALMS TO PINES	RCO	100	E4
PALO COLORDO RD	MON	64	B1
PALOMA RD	CAL	40	E3
PALOMAR AV	SDCO	V	C5
PALOMAR AV	SDCO	111	D2
PALOMAR ST	RCO	99	C5
PALOMAR APRT RD	SDCO	106	B3
PALOMAR DIV TK	RCO	106	D1
PALOMARES RD	ALA	M	A5
PALOMARES RD	ALA	P	A1
PALOMARES RD	ALA	46	A2
PALOMAS AV	KER	77	E3
PALOMAS AV	KER	78	A3
PALOMINO RD	SDCO	106	C2
PALOMINO WY	HUM	22	C1
PALO PRIETA CHO	SLO	76	D1
PALOS VERDES BL	LACO	S	B2
PALOS VRDS DR E	LACO	97	D4
PALOS VRDS DR E	LACO	S	B3
PALOS VRDS DR N	LACO	97	D3
PALOS VRDS DR N	LACO	S	B2
PALOS VRDS DR S	LACO	S	A3
PALOS VRDS DR S	LACO	97	D4
PALOS VRDS DR W	LACO	97	D4
PALOS VRDS DR W	LACO	S	A2
PALO VERDE AV	LACO	S	E2
PALO VERDE BLVD	MOH	96	B4
PALO VERDE RD	IMP	110	C1
PALO VERDE RD	SBD	100	C2
PALO VERDE ST	MTCL	203	C3
PAMELA ST	KER	79	C2
PAMO RD	SDCO	107	A3
PAMPA RD	KER	79	A3
PANAMA LN	KER	78	B3
PANAMA LN	KER	79	A3
PANAMA RD	KER	78	D3
PANAMA RD	KER	79	A3
PANAMINT VLY RD	INY	71	B1
PANCHO RD	RCO	107	A1
PANCHORICO RD	MON	65	E3
PANGBORN LN	INY	60	B4
PANOCHE RD	FRCO	56	D3
PANOCHE RD	SBT	55	B4
PANOCHE RD	SBT	56	A4
PANORAMA DR	KER	78	E2
PANORAMA PT RD	SHA	18	D3
PANORAMIC HWY	MAR	38	A5
PANORAMIC HWY	MAR	L	A4
PANORAMIC HWY	MAR	45	A1
PANTHER CK RD	TEH	19	C3
PANTHER GAP RD	HUM	16	A4
PAPPAS RD	KER	80	C3
PARADISE AV	MDO	162	A4
PARADISE AV	STA	47	C3
PARADISE DR	CRTM	140	D1
PARADISE DR	MAR	L	B3
PARADISE DR	RCO	100	C5
PARADISE RD	CLK	74	D2
PARADISE RD	CLK	209	C4
PARADISE RD	CLK	210	E3
PARADISE RD	COL	24	E5
PARADISE RD	LV	209	C4
PARADISE RD	SJCO	46	E1
PARADISE RD	SJCO	47	A1
PARADISE RD	SB	87	B3
PARADISE RD	STA	47	C2
PARADISE SPG RD	SBD	81	E4
PARADISE SPG RD	SBD	82	B5
PARADISE VLY RD	SDCO	V	D4
PARADISE VLY RD	SDCO	111	D1
PARAISO SPGS RD	MON	64	E1
PARAISO SPGS RD	MON	65	A1
PARAMOUNT BLVD	LACO	98	A3
PARAMOUNT BLVD	LACO	R	C4
PARAMOUNT BLVD	LACO	S	E1
PARDEE DAM RD	CAL	40	D3
PARDOES	AMA	41	D1
PARIS AV	KIN	67	D3
PARIS VALLEY RD	MON	65	D3
PARK AV	BUT	25	B3
PARK AV	C	124	C5
PARK AV	LAG	201	C2
PARK AV	O	157	D1
PARK AV	SJ	151	D3
PARK AV	SJ	152	B4
PARK AV	SCLR	151	C3
PARK AV	TRI	17	D2
PARK AV W	NAP	133	A3
PARK BLVD	ALA	L	D4
PARK BLVD	ALA	45	D1
PARK BLVD	O	158	D3
PARK BLVD	SD	214	A5
PARK BLVD	SD	215	E3
PARK BLVD	SD	216	A1
PARK BLVD	SDCO	V	B3
PARK BLVD N	SA	196	B2
PARK DR S	CC	156	D1
PARK RD	BEN	153	D4
PARK RD	IMP	109	B4
PARK RD	SBT	55	A3
PARK RD E	COL	24	B5
PARK ST	ALA	L	D5
PARK ST	HUM	9	E5
PARK ST	S	160	B4
PARK ST	TUL	68	B3
PARK WY	LAK	31	D2
PARK CREEK RD	ED	35	B4
PARKER AV	CC	L	D3
PARKER RD	SBD	101	E1
PARKER RD	STA	47	D2
PARKER CREEK RD	MOD	8	C1

STREET	CO.	PAGE	GRID
PARKER CREEK RD	MOD	8	B1
PARKER CK RD W	MOD	8	C1
PARKER DAM RD	SBD	104	B1
PARKER LAKE RD	MNO	43	C5
PARKER LAKE RD	MNO	50	C1
PARKER-POSTN RD	LPAZ	103	E4
PARKFIELD GRADE	FRCO	66	C3
PARKFLD CEM RD	MON	66	C4
PARKFLD-COALNGA	FRCO	66	C4
PARK HILL RD	SLO	76	B3
PARKMAN RD	IMP	110	D5
PARK MARINA DR	RED	122	D1
PARK MOABI	SBD	95	E2
PARKMONT DR	LACO	89	D3
PK PRESIDIO BL	SF	141	C3
PARKS RD	SUT	33	C3
PARKSIDE DR	RCO	101	D5
PARKSIDE DR N	CC	M	B3
PARKVIEW AV	RED	122	C3
PARKVIEW LN	KER	79	C5
PARKVILLE RD	SHA	18	D3
PARKWAY DR	DN	1	D4
PARKWAY DR	TEH	18	D4
PARLIER AV	FRCO	56	E4
PARLIER AV	FRCO	57	D4
PARLIER AV	FRCO	58	B4
PARNASSUS BLVD	SF	141	D5
PARR	CC	38	C5
PARR BLVD	CC	L	C3
PARROTTS FERRY	TUO	41	C4
PARSONS RD	FRCO	66	C2
PASADENA AV	LA	186	D1
PASADENA FRWY	LA	186	B2
PASADENA FRWY	LACO	97	E2
PASADENA FRWY	LACO	R	A3
PASCOE RD	KER	69	B5
PASEO AV	SUT	33	C1
PASEO DEL MAR	LACO	97	D4
PASEO DEL MAR	LACO	S	B3
PASKENTA RD	TEH	18	C5
PASKENTA RD	TEH	24	C1
PASKENTA CEM RD	TEH	24	B2
PASO ST	KER	78	A5
PASO NOGAL	CC	38	E5
PASO ROBLES BL	SLO	76	A1
PASO ROBLES HWY	KER	77	A1
PASQUALE RD	NEV	34	D1
PASS RD	SUT	33	A2
PASSONS BLVD	LACO	R	C5
PAST TIME LN	RCO	100	A5
PATHFINDER RD	LACO	U	B3
PATRICIA AV	SIS	4	C2
PATRICIA LN	CAL	41	C3
PATRICIA LN	MNO	42	E1
PATRICIA LN	MNO	43	A1
PATRICK RD	LPAZ	104	A2
PATRICK WY	SBD	100	E1
PATRICKS CK RD	DN	2	B3
PATRICKS PT	HUM	9	E3
PATTERSON AV	SB	87	B4
PATTERSON LN	MOD	8	E1
PATTERSON RD	HUM	10	D4
PATTERSON RD	KER	89	B1
PATTERSON RD	STA	47	D2
PATTERSON RD	VEN	96	B1
PATTERSON CK RD	SIS	3	D5
PATTERSON CK RD	SIS	11	D1
PATTRSN MILL RD	MOD	8	E3
PATTERSON PS RD	ALA	M	D5
PATTERSON PS RD	ALA	46	C2
PATTERSON PS RD	SJCO	46	D2
PATTERSN RCH RD	TRI	17	A1
PATTERSN SAWMLL	LAS	8	D3
PATTISON RD	CAL	40	D3
PATTON	MCO	55	E1
PATTON MILLS RD	TEH	24	A2
PATTYMOCUS-			
-LOOKOUT RD	TEH	17	D4
PATWIN RD	SBD	90	E3
PAUBA RD	RCO	106	D1
PAUI RD	RCO	107	B1
PAULARINO AV	CM	197	E4
PAULINE AV	STA	47	C2
PAUL NEGRA RD	MCO	55	E3
PAXTON RD	SBDO	100	E1
PAXTON ST	LACO	Q	C1
PAYEN RD	SAC	40	C1
PAYMASTER MN RD	SBD	83	C4
PAYNE AV	CC	39	C5
PAYNE RD	IMP	108	E5
PAYNE RD	SUT	33	B2
PAYNE WY	KER	79	D3
PAYNES CK LOOP	TEH	19	A4
PAYNES CREEK RD	TEH	19	A4
PAYNES CREEK RD	TEH	18	D4
PEABODY CT	NEV	127	B3
PEABODY RD	SOL	M	B1
PEABODY RD	SOL	39	A3
PEACEFUL GLEN	SOL	39	A2
PEACH AV	FRCO	57	D2
PEACH AV	FRCO	57	D5
PEACH AV	GLE	24	E4
PEACH AV	MCO	47	E4
PEACH AV	MCO	48	A4
PEACH AV	SBD	91	C4
PEACH TREE RD	MON	65	E2
PEACH TREE RD	MON	66	A2
PEACHY CYN RD	SLO	75	E1
PEACHY CYN RD	SLO	76	A1
PEAK RD	TRI	16	D5
PEAR AV	GLE	25	A4
PEAR AV	STA	47	C4
PEARBLOSSOM HWY	LACO	90	A4

STREET	CO.	PAGE	GRID
PEARL RD	SJCO	40	B3
PEARL ST	SDCO	V	A2
PEARL ST	SDCO	106	C5
PEAR MAIN ST	SBD	91	B3
PEARSON RD	BUT	25	C3
PEARSON RD	INY	70	C5
PEASE RD	SUT	33	C2
PEAVINE RDG RD	ED	35	B4
PEBBLE BEACH DR	DN	1	D4
PEBBLY BEACH RD	AVLN	97	B5
PECHO VALLEY RD	SLO	75	E3
PECK RD	LACO	98	B1
PECK RD	LACO	R	D4
PEDERSON	FRCO	58	A3
PEDLEY RD	RCO	99	A2
PEDRICK RD	SOL	39	B2
PEDRICK RD	SOL	39	B1
PEDRO RANCH RD	MNO	51	C1
PEDROS RD	STA	47	D3
PEGASUS DR	KER	78	D2
PEGASUS ST	KER	79	B4
PEG LEG RD	SDCO	107	E2
PELGER RD	SUT	33	B3
PELICAN RD	STA	47	B2
PELLERIN RD	STA	47	E2
PELLET RD	IMP	108	E4
PELLISER RD	KER	79	B4
PELTIER RD	SJCO	39	E3
PELTIER RD	SJCO	40	A3
PENCIL RD	MOD	7	B5
PENDLETON RD	SBD	92	A1
PENDOLA RD	YUB	26	B4
PENDOLA EXT	YUB	26	C4
PENDOLA GARDEN	MPA	49	A3
PENFIELD AV	LA	178	A4
PENINSULA AV	SMCO	N	C1
PENINSULA DR	HUM	15	E5
PENINSULA DR	PLU	20	B4
PENMAN SPGS RD	SLO	76	B1
PENNINGTON RD	BUT	33	B1
PENNINGTON RD	SUT	33	C1
PENNSYLVANIA AV	FRFD	135	B3
PENNSYLVANIA AV	LACO	Q	E2
PENNSYLVANIA AV	RIV	205	E3
PENNSYLVANIA AV	RCO	99	E3
PENNSYLVANIA AV	SOL	L	E1
PENNSYLVANIA AV	SOL	M	A1
PENNSYLVANIA AV	SOL	135	B4
PENNSYLV GCH RD	CAL	41	C4
PENON LOOKOUT	MPA	48	D1
PENOYAR GRSS LK	SIS	4	E5
PENROSE ST	LACO	Q	D2
PENTLAND RD	KER	78	B5
PENTZ RD	BUT	25	C3
PEORIA RD	YUB	34	A1
PEPPER AV	SBD	99	B2
PEPPER DR	KER	78	E3
PEPPER RD	SON	37	E3
PEPPER ST	MCO	47	E4
PEPPER ST	MCO	48	A4
PEPPER ST	SBD	80	E5
PEPPER ST	SBD	81	A5
PERALTA BLVD	ALA	P	A1
PERALTA BLVD	ALA	46	A3
PERALTA ST	ALA	L	C4
PERALTA ST	O	157	C2
PERCH ST	KER	79	C4
PERCY AV	YUBA	125	D3
PERCY RD	KER	79	D1
PEREZ RD	IMP	112	D5
PERI RD	MON	65	D4
PERIMETER RD	NEV	34	B2
PERINI RD	LAK	32	A4
PERKINS AV	KER	78	B1
PERKINS RD	CLO	33	A3
PERKINS RD	SB	87	C1
PERKINS ST	U	123	B3
PERRAL RD	KER	77	D2
PERRIN AV	FRCO	57	D2
PERRIN RD	SJCO	47	B2
PERRIS BLVD	RCO	99	C3
PERRY RD	COL	32	D1
PERRY RD	RCO	99	B4
PERRY CREEK RD	ED	41	A1
PERSHING AV	S	160	A1
PERSHING AV	SJCO	40	A5
PERSHING DR	LA	187	D5
PERSHING DR	LACO	Q	C5
PERSHING DR	SD	216	A3
PERSHING DR	SDCO	V	C3
PESCADERO RD	SMCO	N	C4
PESCADERO CK RD	SMCO	45	C5
PETALUMA AV	SON	132	B4
PETALUMA HLL RD	STR	131	D4
PETALUMA HLL RD	SON	38	A2
PETALUMA HLL RD	SON	131	D4
PETE MILLER RD	STA	47	C5
PETERSBOURGH S	CAL	40	E3
PETERSBURG RD	SIS	11	B3
PETERSON DR	NAPA	29	B2
PETERSON LN	LAK	31	D3
PETERSON RD	COL	32	C1
PETERSON RD	FRCO	58	B1
PETERSON RD	IMP	109	B3
PETERSON RD	KER	68	C5
PETERSON RD	KER	77	E1
PETERSON RD	KER	78	B1
PETERSON RD	LPAZ	104	A3
PETERSON RD	LACO	89	D4
PETERSON RDG RD	YUB	26	B5
PETRIFIED FORST	NAPA	38	A1
PETRIFIED FORST	SON	38	A1
PETRO RD	INY	72	C2

STREET	CO.	PAGE	GRID
PETROGLYPH RD	MNO	51	D3
PETRLEUM CLB RD	KER	78	A4
PETTINGER RD	CAL	40	D4
PETTYJOHN RD	TEH	17	E5
PEW RD	SBD	85	C5
PEZZI RD	SJCO	40	B4
PFE RD	PLA	33	E5
PFITZER RD	MCO	47	D5
PHEASANT CT	KER	79	B4
PHEASANT DR	MOD	7	B5
PHEASANT LN	SIS	4	B4
PHELAN RD	HUM	15	D1
PHELAN RD	SBD	91	A4
PHELPS AV	FRCO	66	D2
PHILADELPHIA ST	LACO	98	D2
PHILADELPHIA ST	SBD	U	C3
PHILADELPHIA ST	SBD	98	D2
PHILBRIC RD	SB	86	C1
PHILBROOK RD	BUT	25	D1
PHILDOW RD	LAS	20	E3
PHILIP	PLA	33	E4
PHILIPS RD	MCO	55	E1
PHILLIPE LN	SIS	4	A4
PHILLIPS	LAK	32	A3
PHILLIPS BLVD	SBD	U	C3
PHILLIPS DR	SBD	82	A5
PHILLIPS RD	KER	78	C1
PHILLIPS RD	KER	78	D4
PHILLIPS RD	KER	80	B4
PHILLIPS RD	SHA	19	A1
PHILLIPS RD	SOL	39	B1
PHILLIPSVLLE RD	HUM	16	C4
PHILO GRNWD RD	MEN	30	C2
PHOENIX LAKE RD	TUO	41	D5
PHYLLIS RD	TEH	18	C4
PICACHO RD	IMP	110	D5
PICADOR BLVD	SDCO	V	D5
PICADOR BLVD	SDCO	111	D2
PICARD RD	SIS	4	E2
PICARD RD	SIS	5	A2
PICRD SAMS NECK	SIS	4	E2
PICARDY DR	S	160	B4
PICAYUNE RD	MAD	49	D5
PICKENS RD	LAS	21	D5
PICKERING AV	LACO	R	C5
PICKETT RD	IMP	109	B4
PICO BLVD	LA	180	D4
PICO BLVD	LA	183	B3
PICO BLVD	LA	184	C3
PICO BLVD	LA	185	A3
PICO BLVD	LACO	Q	C4
PICO BLVD	SMON	180	B5
PICO BLVD	SMON	187	A1
PICO CANYON RD	LACO	89	B4
PIEDMONT AV	B	156	B3
PIEDMONT AV	O	158	B1
PIEDMONT RD	SCL	P	C3
PIEDRA RD	FRCO	58	A3
PIEDRA AZUL	MCO	55	D3
PIEDRAS DR	RCO	99	B3
PIER AV	LACO	S	B1
PIERCE LN	SOL	38	E4
PIERCE RD	SCL	P	A4
PIERCE RD	SCL	45	E5
PIERCE RD	SUT	33	C3
PIERCE ST	BKD	166	A2
PIERCE ST	RCO	99	A3
PIERCE ST	RCO	101	B4
PIERCE CK MTWY	PLU	21	A4
PIERCE POINT RD	MAR	37	D4
PIERI RD	KER	78	B4
PIERLE RD	IMP	108	E5
PIERSON BLVD	RCO	100	C2
PIGEON PASS RD	RCO	99	C2
PIGEON POINT RD	HUM	15	E1
PIGEON SPG RD	KER	79	C5
PIKE RD	STA	47	D3
PIKE CITY RD	SIE	26	C5
PIKE CITY RD	YUB	26	C5
PILAR RD	SIS	4	D5
PILE ST	SDCO	107	A4
PILGRIM CK RD	SIS	12	E2
PILITAS HUERHRO	SLO	76	C2
PILOT SPRING RD	MNO	43	D5
PILOT SPRING RD	MNO	50	E1
PIMLICO DR	RCO	100	C5
PINAL ST	SB	86	D1
PINE AV	BUT	25	B3
PINE AV	LB	192	D3
PINE AV	MEN	31	C1
PINE AV	PAC	167	C2
PINE AV	SBD	U	D4
PINE AV	SBD	98	D2
PINE AV	TRI	17	B2
PINE DR	HUM	16	B4
PINE DR	LAS	20	E2
PINE DR	MPA	48	E1
PINE ST	C	124	C4
PINE ST	CC	L	E3
PINE ST	MONT	167	D2
PINE ST	MON	53	E2
PINE ST	NAP	133	B4
PINE ST	RED	122	B1
PINE ST	RCO	100	C4
PINE ST	SDCO	107	A4
PINE ST	SF	142	A3
PINE ST	SF	143	C4
PINE ST	SHA	18	C3
PINE ST	U	123	C2
PINE CANYON RD	MON	65	B3
PINE CANYON RD	SB	76	E5
PINE COVE TR	KER	79	D2
PINE CREEK BLVD	MOD	8	B1

INDEXES

STREET	CO.	PAGE	GRID
PINE CREEK RD	INY	51	B4
PINE CREEK RD	HUM	10	C3
PINE CREEK RD	SIS	2	E3
PINE FLAT	SON	31	E5
PINE FLAT RD	SBD	91	E5
PINE FLAT RD	SCR	N	E5
PINE FLAT RD	SCR	53	D1
PINE GROVE	VEN	88	C4
PINE GROVE RD	KLAM	5	C1
PINE GRV TABEAU	AMA	41	A2
PINE GULCH RD	AMA	40	E2
PINE HILLS RD	SDCO	107	C4
PINE HOLLOW RD	CC	M	B3
PINEHURST RD	CC	45	D1
PINE MTN DR	TUO	48	E1
PINE MTN RD	KER	78	E1
PINE MTN RD	KER	79	A1
PINE MTN RD	MEN	31	D4
PINE NUT RD	MNO	42	E1
PINE RIDGE	FRCO	58	C3
PINE RIDGE RD	HUM	10	C3
PINE RIDGE RD	MEN	31	A2
PINES TO PALMS HWY	RCO	100	B4
PINE TREE CY RD	KER	80	A4
PINE VALLEY RD	MON	65	D3
PINEVISTA CIR	RCO	100	A3
PINEWOOD LN	FRCO	58	B1
PINEY CK LOOP	MON	64	D2
PINKSTON CYN RD	BUT	25	D3
PINNACLE RD	SBD	81	A1
PINOLE VLY RD	CC	L	D3
PINOLI RIDGE RD	NEV	26	E4
PINOLI RIDGE RD	NEV	27	A4
PINON CANYON RD	KER	79	C4
PINON VILLGE RD	TUL	70	A3
PINTO DR	CAL	41	B4
PINTO RD	RCO	101	E4
PINTO BASIN RD	RCO	101	C4
PINTO MTN RD	SBD	101	C3
PIONEER AV	STA	47	D1
PIONEER BLVD	LACO	98	A3
PIONEER BLVD	LACO	T	A2
PIONEER DR	KER	78	E3
PIONEER RD	DN	2	B3
PIONEER RD	MCO	55	D2
PIONEER RD	STA	47	D3
PIONEER TR	SLT	129	C4
PIONEER CK RD	AMA	41	B2
PIONEERTOWN RD	SBD	100	D1
PIONEER TR RD	ED	36	A3
PIPE CREEK RD	RCO	100	C5
PIPE LINE AV	SBD	U	C3
PIPE LINE AV	SBD	98	D2
PIPER RD	CC	M	D3
PIPES RD	SBD	100	C1
PIPES CANYON RD	SBD	100	D1
PIPI RD	ED	41	C1
PIRCEN RD	LAS	14	B3
PIRU CANYON RD	LACO	89	A4
PIRU CANYON RD	VEN	88	E4
PISGAH CRATR RD	SBD	92	E2
PISTACHIO RD	KER	77	B1
PIT RD	MNO	51	A2
PIT #1 PWRHS RD	SHA	13	D4
PITTMAN HILL RD	FRCO	58	A2
PITT RIV CYN RD	LAS	14	A4
PITT SCHOOL RD	SOL	39	B2
PITTVILLE RD	LAS	20	A1
PITTVILLE RD	SHA	13	E4
PITTVILLE BENCH	LAS	14	A4
PITTZER RD	IMP	112	B3
PIUMA RD	LACO	97	A2
PIUTE MTN RD	KER	79	D2
PIUTE PINES RD	KER	79	D3
PLACENTIA AV	CM	199	A3
PLACENTIA AV	NB	199	A3
PLACENTIA AV	ORCO	T	C4
PLACER AV	FRCO	56	E4
PLACER CT	KER	79	D2
PLACER RD	SHA	18	B2
PLACER RD	SUT	33	E3
PLACER ST	RED	122	A2
PLACER ST	SHA	18	B2
PLACER ST	TRI	17	D1
PLACER HILLS RD	PLA	34	C3
PLACERITA CYN	LACO	89	C5
PLACERVILLE DR	PLCV	138	A3
PLACERVILLE RD	SAC	34	B5
PLAINS RD	CC	39	C5
PLAINSBURG RD	MCO	48	D5
PLANO ST	TUL	68	D3
PLANTATION ST	RCO	102	C4
PLANT FIVE RD	INY	51	C4
PLANZ RD	KER	78	D3
PLASKETT RDG RD	MON	64	E4
PLATEAU CIR	SHA	18	B2
PLATEAU PINE RD	SHA	19	B3
PLATFORM RD	MAR	37	E4
PLATINA RD	SHA	18	A3
PLATINA RD	SHA	17	D3
PLATINA SCH RD	SHA	17	D4
PLAYA AZUL	AVLN	97	B4
PLAZA ST	SDCO	106	C4
PLEASANT	CC	38	E5
PLEASANT AV	SON	37	E1
PLEASANT RD	SLO	66	B5
PLEASANT GROVE	PLA	33	D4
PLEASANT GROVE	SUT	33	E4
PLEASANT GRV LN	BUT	25	E5
PLEASANT HILL	SON	37	D2
PLEASANT HLL RD	CC	L	E4
PLEASANT HLL RD	CC	M	A3
PLEASNT HL RD E	M	154	C4

STREET	CO.	PAGE	GRID
PLEASANT OAK DR	TUL	68	E3
PLEASNTN SNL RD	ALA	P	B1
PLEASNTN SNL RD	ALA	46	B2
PLEASANT PT RD	HUM	15	E2
PLEASNTS VLY RD	SOL	38	E2
PLEASANT VLY AV	O	156	B5
PLEASANT VLY RD	ALP	36	C5
PLEASANT VLY RD	ED	34	E5
PLEASANT VLY RD	NEV	34	B1
PLEASANT VLY RD	STA	47	D1
PLEASANT VLY RD	VEN	96	B1
PLEASNT VLY DAM	INY	51	C3
PLESANTE RD	MON	54	C3
PLEYTO CEM RD	MON	65	C4
PLINCO MINE RD	PLU	21	C5
PLUMAS AV	FRCO	57	A3
PLUMAS ST	RENO	130	B4
PLUMAS ARBGA RD	YUB	33	D3
PLUMB LN E	RENO	130	D5
PLUMB LN W	RENO	130	C5
PLUMBAGO RD	SIE	26	D5
PLUM CREEK RD	TEH	19	A4
PLUMMER LKOT RD	TRI	17	B3
PLUM VALLEY RD	MOD	7	C4
PLUNKETT RD	HUM	10	A5
PLYMIRE RD	TEH	18	C3
PLYMOUTH AV	KIN	67	A3
PLYMOUTH RD	SBD	80	E5
PLYMTH SHNDOAH	AMA	40	E1
POCK LN	SJCO	40	B5
POCKET RD	SAC	39	D2
POE RD	IMP	108	E3
POE POWERHOUSE	BUT	25	E3
POINSETTIA LN	SDCO	106	B3
PT CABRILLO DR	MEN	30	B1
PT LAKEVIEW RD	LAK	32	A3
POINT LOMA AV	SDCO	V	A3
POINT LOMA AV	SDCO	111	C1
POINT LOMA BL W	SDCO	V	A3
POINT LOMA BL W	SD	212	B5
PT OF TIMBER RD	CC	39	C5
PT PLEASANT RD	SAC	39	E3
POINT RANCH RD	MNO	43	B3
PT REYES PETLMA	MAR	37	E4
POINT SAL RD	SB	86	A1
PT SAN PEDRO RD	MAR	L	B3
POKER BAR RD	TRI	17	D1
POKER FLAT RD	SIE	26	D3
POLE LINE RD	MCO	55	E2
POLELINE RD	SBD	93	A5
POLE LINE RD	SHA	13	E5
POLETA RD	INY	51	D4
POLETA LAWS RD	INY	51	D4
POLHEMUS RD	SMCO	N	C2
POLI ST	VENT	175	E2
POLK AV	FRCO	57	B3
POLK AV	FRCO	67	B1
POLK AV	FRCO	57	B5
POLK ST	LACO	Q	C1
POLK ST	RCO	101	B5
POLLACK FLAT	SIS	5	A5
POLSON RD	NAPA	38	D3
POMEGRANATE AV	STA	47	C3
POMELO AV	STA	47	C3
POMERADO RD	SDCO	V	C1
POMERADO RD	SDCO	106	D5
POMEROY AV	SCLR	150	C3
POMEROY LS BERS	SLO	76	C5
POMONA AV	COR	215	C5
POMONA AV	CM	199	B5
POMONA AV	TEH	24	D1
POMONA BLVD	LACO	R	B4
POMONA FRWY	LACO	98	A2
POMONA FRWY	LACO	R	E4
POMONA ST	CC	38	D5
POMPONIO CK RD	SMCO	N	C3
POND RD	KER	68	A5
PONDER WY	SHA	18	B3
PONDEROSA BLVD	LAS	21	B4
PONDEROSA RD	CAL	41	C4
PONDEROSA WY	AMA	41	B3
PONDEROSA WY	BUT	25	C2
PONDEROSA WY	BUT	25	D3
PONDEROSA WY	BUT	26	A4
PONDEROSA WY	CAL	41	B3
PONDEROSA WY	MPA	49	B3
PONDEROSA WY	PLA	34	D3
PONDEROSA WY	SHA	19	B2
PONDEROSA WY	TEH	19	B3
PONDOSA WY	SIS	13	C3
PONY RD	SBD	92	C4
PONY WY	CAL	41	A4
PONY EXPRESS TR	ED	35	A4
POOLE AV	KER	80	C1
POOLE LN	SIE	27	D3
POOLE RD	HUM	15	D2
POOLE RD	MCO	48	D5
POOL STATION RD	CAL	41	A3
POONKINNEY RD	MEN	23	A3
POOP OUT HL RD	SBD	100	A1
POOR BOY CK RD	ALP	36	C5
POORE RD	IMP	109	C4
POPE ST	NAPA	29	C2
POPE CANYON RD	NAPA	38	C1
POPE VALLEY RD	NAPA	29	C1
POPE VALLEY RD	NAPA	32	B5
POPE VALLEY RD	NAPA	38	B1
POPLAR AV	KER	78	B2
POPLAR AV	MLBR	144	D5
POPLAR AV	SMCO	N	C1
POPPET FLAT RD	RCO	100	A3
POPPY BLVD	KER	80	B4
PORTAL RD W	MNO	43	C5

STREET	CO.	PAGE	GRID
PORT CHICAGO HY	CC	M	A3
PORTER	FRCO	58	A4
PORTER AV	RCO	99	C3
PORTER RD	SOL	39	B2
PORTER CREEK RD	SON	37	E1
PORTERVILLE HWY	KER	68	D5
PORTERVILLE HWY	KER	78	D1
PORTERVILLE WY	KER	78	C1
PORT KENYON RD	HUM	15	D2
PORTOLA AV	ALA	M	C5
PORTOLA AV	RCO	100	E4
PORTOLA BLVD	ALA	46	C2
PORTOLA DR	SFCO	L	B5
PORTOLA DR	SFCO	45	B2
PORTOLA RD	SLO	76	A2
PORTOLA RD	SMCO	N	D3
PORTOLA RD	SMCO	45	D4
PORTLA ST PK RD	SMCO	45	D5
PORTLA ST PK RD	SMCO	N	D4
PORTOLA MCLEARS	PLU	27	B3
PORTUGUESE BEND	SUT	33	C4
PORTUGUESE CYN	MON	66	B4
PORT WINE RIDGE	PLU	26	C3
PORT WINE RIDGE	SIE	26	C4
PORTY ST	KER	78	D4
POSO AV	KER	77	E1
POSO AV	KER	78	A1
POSO FLAT RD	KER	79	A1
POST AV	TEH	24	E2
POST RD	RCO	99	B4
POST ST	SF	142	B3
POST ST	SF	143	A4
POST MTN RD	TRI	17	B3
POTRERO AV	SF	142	D4
POTRERO RD E	VEN	96	D1
POTRERO RD W	VEN	96	C1
POTRERO ST	SFCO	L	C5
POTRERO GRDE BL	LACO	R	C4
POTTER RD	MON	54	D4
POTTEROFF RD	CAL	41	B3
POUND RD	IMP	109	A3
POUNDSTONE RD	COL	33	B3
POURROY RD	RCO	99	D5
POVERTY RD	SAC	M	E1
POVERTY RD	SAC	39	D3
POVERTY HILL RD	SIE	26	C4
POWAY RD	SDCO	V	C1
POWAY RD	SDCO	106	D4
POWDER HILL RD	SIS	5	C5
POWDER HILL RD	SIS	13	C1
POWELL AV	SON	37	D1
POWELL RD	SBD	92	D5
POWELL RD	SUT	33	B1
POWELL RD	VEN	88	E4
POWELLTOWN RD	BUT	25	D2
POWER RD	TRI	17	C1
POWER HOUSE RD	FRCO	57	E1
POWERHOUSE RD	TRI	11	E5
POWERHOUSE RD S	TEH	19	B3
POWER HSE HL RD	BUT	25	C5
POWER INN RD	SAC	39	E1
POWER LINE RD	LAS	20	A1
POWER LINE RD	MNO	52	C3
POWER LINE RD	RCO	106	E1
POWER LINE RD	SAC	33	D5
POWER LINE RD	SBD	83	A3
POWER LINE RD	SBD	91	C3
POWER LINE RD	SHA	18	B2
POWER LINE RD	SUT	33	D4
POWERS AV	MAN	161	D3
POZOS RD	RCO	99	C3
PRADO RD	SNLO	172	B5
PRAHSER RD	SJCO	40	C5
PRAIRE WY	MEN	30	C1
PRAIRE WY	MEN	30	B1
PRAIRIE AV	LACO	S	B1
PRAIRIE AV	SBD	91	C1
PRAIRIE DR	LAS	8	A5
PRAIRIE CK RD	TRI	17	A1
PRAIRIE FLWR RD	STA	47	D3
PRAIRIE FLWR RD	STA	47	D4
PRATT RD	TUL	68	B1
PRATT RANCH RD	MEN	31	C3
PRATVLL BRT RES	PLU	20	B5
PREFUMO CYN RD	SLO	75	E4
PREFUMO CYN RD	SLO	76	A4
PRELL RD	SB	86	C1
PRESCOTT AV	MONT	167	C3
PRESCOTT AV	MON	53	D3
PRESCOTT AV	PAC	167	C3
PRESCOTT RD	SJCO	47	B1
PRESIDIO AV	SF	142	A2
PRESIDIO BLVD	SFCO	L	B5
PRESIDIO BLVD	SFCO	45	B1
PRESSLEY RD	SON	38	A2
PRESTON	MPA	49	A5
PRESTON RD	BUT	25	C4
PRESTON RD	IMP	111	E4
PRESTON RD	MCO	47	C4
PREVITALI RD	AMA	41	A2
PRICE CREEK RD	HUM	15	D3
PRICE CK CAMPBL	TRI	17	B1
PRICE CK SCH RD	HUM	15	E2
PRICE CANYON RD	SLO	76	B4
PRIEST COLTRVLL	MPA	48	D1
PRIEST COLTRVLL	TUO	48	E1
PRIEST VLY RD	MON	66	A2
PRIM RD	IMP	109	B5
PRIMROSE MN RD	SIE	26	E4
PRINCE AV	FRCO	56	A2
PRINCE RD	MCO	47	C4
PRINCESS PAT MN	SBD	90	E2
PRINCETON	FRCO	58	A3

STREET	CO.	PAGE	GRID
PRINCETON RD	MCO	48	B3
PROGRESS RD	SUT	33	B2
PROSPECT AV	KER	78	A1
PROSPECT AV	ORCO	T	E2
PROSPECT AV	SDCO	V	E2
PROSPECT BLVD	PAS	190	A3
PROSPECT RD	SCL	45	E4
PROSPECT RD	SCL	P	A3
PROSPECT ST	SDCO	V	A2
PROSPECT ST	SDCO	106	C5
PROSPERITY AV	TUL	68	A2
PROSSER DAM RD	NEV	27	D5
PROUTY RD	SJCO	40	B3
PROVIDENCE RCH	SBD	84	B4
PRUNE AV	STA	47	C3
PRUNERIDGE AV	CPTO	150	A4
PRUNERIDGE AV	SJ	151	A4
PRUNERIDGE AV	SCLR	150	C4
PRUNERIDGE AV	SCL	151	A4
PUDDING CK RD	MEN	22	B5
PRUSSIAN HLL RD	CAL	41	B3
PUEBLO AV	KIN	67	C3
PUEBLO AV	NAP	133	B2
PUENTE AV	LACO	98	B2
PUENTE AV	LACO	R	D4
PULGA RD	BUT	25	D2
PULLMAN RD	IMP	111	E4
PUMICE MINE RD	MNO	50	D1
PUMICE MINE RD	MNO	51	C1
PUMICE MILL RD	MNO	51	D3
PUMP RD	MCO	55	E2
PUMP RD	STA	47	C4
PUMPHOUSE RD	COL	32	D2
PUMPHOUSE RD	SIS	4	B5
PUMPHOUSE RD	YOL	39	D2
PUNKIN CTR RD	LAS	14	B4
PURDON RD	NEV	26	C5
PURDY AV	KER	80	A5
PURISIMA RD	SB	86	B3
PURISIMA CK RD	SMCO	45	C4
PURITAN MINE RD	LACO	89	E4
PUTAH LN	LAK	32	A4
PUTAH CREEK RD	SOL	39	A1
PUTNAM RD	COL	25	A5
PUTNAM WY	COL	32	E3
PYLE RD	CAL	41	B5
PYLE RD	LAK	31	D2
PYRAMID HILLS	KIN	67	A5
PYRITE RD	RCO	99	A2
Q			
QUAIL AV	KIN	67	B3
QUAIL DR	RCO	100	B5
QUAIL HILL RD	HUM	16	A2
QUAIL ST	KER	80	C1
QUAIL WY	RCO	100	A5
QUAIL HILL RD	CAL	41	A5
QUAIL HOLLOW RD	SCR	N	E5
QUAIL SPGS RD	SBD	101	A1
QUAIL SPGS SPUR	SBD	101	A2
QUAKER ST	HUM	9	E5
QUAKR HL CRS RD	NEV	34	D1
QUALITY RD	KER	68	C5
QUARRY RD	HUM	9	E4
QUARRY RD	MAD	49	B5
QUARRY RD	PA	147	A3
QUARRY RD	SDCO	V	D4
QUARRY RD	SDCO	111	C1
QUARRY RD S	HUM	10	A5
QUARTZ AV	SIS	4	C5
QUARTZ ST	BUT	25	D2
QUARTZ ST	SBD	84	C3
QUARTZ ST	TUO	41	C5
QUARTZ HILL RD	SHA	18	C2
QUARTZ MT LKOUT	SIS	3	D5
QUARTZ MTN RD	MAD	49	D5
QUARTZ VLY DR	SIS	3	C5
QUARTZ VLY RD	SIS	3	C5
QUARTZ VLY RD E	SIS	3	C5
QUATAL CYN RD	KER	87	E2
QUATAL CYN RD	SB	87	E2
QUATAL CYN RD	VEN	88	A1
QUEBEC AV	KIN	67	E3
QUEBEC AV	KIN	67	A3
QUEEN OF SHEBA	INY	72	A3
QUEENS AV	YUBA	125	A1
QUEENS WY	LB	192	D4
QUESTHAVEN RD	SDCO	106	C3
QUICK RD	IMP	112	C5
QUIEN SABE RD	SBT	55	B3
QUIEN SABE RCH	SBT	55	B3
QUIMBY RD	SCL	P	C3
QUIMBY RD	SCL	46	B4
QUINCY RD	SIE	26	D3
QUINCY RD	STA	47	E3
QUINCY JCT RD	PLU	26	D1
QUINCY LA PORTE	PLU	26	D2
QUINCY LA PORTE	PLU	26	C4
QUINLEY AV	MCO	48	B5
QUINN RD	HUM	15	D1
QUINN RD	KER	68	D5
QUISENBERRY RD	STA	47	C3
QUITO RD	SCL	P	A4
QUITO RD	SCL	46	A5
R			
R ST	FRE	165	E3
R ST	MER	170	B4
RABBIT BRUSH LN	SIS	4	B4
RABBIT RANCH RD	MNO	51	C2
RABBIT SPGS RD	SBD	91	E4

STREET	CO.	PAGE	GRID
RABBIT SPGS RD	SBD	92	A4
RABER ST	KER	80	A5
RACE ST	SJ	151	E4
RACE ST	SCL	P	B3
RACE TRACK RD	SAC	M	E1
RACE TRACK RD	SAC	39	D3
RACE TRACK RD	TUO	163	A3
RACETRACK VLY	INY	61	A2
RACINE AV	KIN	67	E3
RACQUET CLUB DR	SR	139	B3
RADIO LN	RED	122	C5
RADIO STATN RD	SOL	39	B2
RAGAN MEADWS RD	TRI	17	A3
RAG DUMP RD	BUT	25	D2
RAGLIN RIDGE RD	TEH	23	E1
RAGLIN RIDGE RD	TEH	24	A1
RAGSDALE RD	RCO	102	B4
RAHILLY RD	MCO	48	B5
RAIL CANYON RD	COL	24	B5
RAIL CANYON RD	GLE	24	B5
RAIL CREEK RD	SIS	12	A2
RAILROAD AV	CC	M	B3
RAILROAD AV	DN	1	D4
RAILROAD AV	HUM	16	D4
RAILROAD AV	RED	122	B3
RAILROAD AV	SMA	173	B2
RAILROAD AV	SOL	135	E3
RAILROAD AV	SUT	33	D2
RAILROAD AV	VAL	134	A4
RAILROAD ST	SBD	84	C3
RAILROAD CYN RD	RCO	99	C4
RAILRD FLAT RD	CAL	41	B3
RAINBOW	FRCO	57	E3
RAINBOW BASN RD	SBD	81	D5
RAINBOW CYN RD	SBD	93	B4
RAINBOW GLEN RD	SDCO	106	C1
RAINBOW LAKE RD	SHA	18	A3
RAINES RD	STA	47	B3
RAIN TREE LN	BUT	25	A2
RAJNUS RD	KLAM	5	E2
RALPH RD	IMP	109	A5
RALSTON AV	BLMT	145	C5
RALSTON AV	SMCO	N	C1
RALSTON AV	SMCO	45	C3
RAMAL RD	SON	38	C3
RAMBLA PACIFICO	LACO	97	B2
RAMELI GREIG RD	PLU	27	D2
RAMIREZ RD	YUB	33	D1
RAMON RD	PMSP	206	C4
RAMON RD	RCO	100	D3
RAMONA AV	LACO	U	B1
RAMONA AV	MTCL	203	B5
RAMONA AV	SBD	U	C3
RAMONA AV	SBDO	203	B5
RAMONA AV	SBD	91	C3
RAMONA AV	SBD	98	D2
RAMONA BLVD	LACO	R	D3
RAMONA BLVD	RCO	99	E3
RAMONA DR	SNLO	172	A2
RAMONA EXPWY	RCO	99	C3
RAMONA FRWY	SDCO	V	D3
RAMONA FRWY	SDCO	106	E5
RAMOS RD	MCO	55	D1
RAMP RD	MNO	43	B3
RAMSEY RD	RCO	107	B1
RAMSEY RD	SOL	38	E3
RAMSEY MINE RD	LPAZ	104	D4
RAMS HILL DR	SDCO	107	E3
RAMSHORN RD	TRI	12	A3
RAMS HORN GRADE	AMA	41	A2
RAMSHN MUMBO CK	TRI	12	B3
RANCH RD	HUM	15	D2
RANCH RD	MCO	48	C5
RANCH RD	MNO	52	C3
RANCHERIA RD	KER	69	C5
RANCHERIA RD	KER	78	E2
RANCHERIA RD	KER	79	A2
RANCHERIA RD	MEN	30	C3
RANCHERIA CK RD	SIS	4	A3
RANCHERIAS RD	SBD	91	C3
RANCHERIA-SAWML	KER	79	B1
RANCHERO	SBD	91	B4
RANCHITA CYN RD	MON	66	C5
RANCHITA CYN RD	SLO	66	B5
RANCHITO RD	MPA	48	D2
RANCHITOS RD	MAR	L	A3
RANCHLAND DR	SHA	18	B2
RANCH LAND RD	SDCO	106	E4
RANCHO AV	SBD	99	B2
RANCHO DR	KER	78	E4
RANCHO DR	KER	79	A4
RANCHO DR	SBD	91	A3
RANCHO RD	KER	78	E5
RANCHO RD	KER	79	A5
RANCHO RD	LV	209	A2
RANCHO RD	SB	76	C5
RANCHO RD	SB	86	B1
RANCHO RD	SHA	18	C2
RNCHO ALISAL RD	SB	86	E3
RCHO BAUTSTA RD	RCO	100	B5
RO BERNARDO RD	SDCO	106	D4
RANCHO CALIF RD	RCO	99	D5
RANCHO CALIF RD	RCO	106	C1
RANCHO CANADA	SDCO	107	A5
RNCHO CONEJO BL	VEN	96	D1
RO SANTA FE RD	SDCO	106	C3
RANCHO VIEJO RD	SJC	202	E1
RANDALL AV	SBD	99	A2
RANDALL RD	KER	77	E4
RANDOLPH RD	MCO	47	E4
RANDOLPH RD	SAC	40	A2
RANDSBURG RD	SBD	81	C2
RANDSBRG CTO	KER	80	A4

STREET	CO.	PAGE	GRID
RANDSBRG CTO	SBD	80	E3
RANDSBG INYOKRN	KER	80	D1
RANDSBG WASH RD	SBD	80	E1
RANDSBG WASH RD	SBD	81	A1
RANGE RD	MCO	48	B5
RANGER STA RD	INY	51	B3
RANGER STA RD	INY	60	A4
RANGER STA RD	TRI	17	B1
RANGO WY	SDCO	107	E3
RANNELS BLVD	RCO	103	C5
RANNELS BLVD	RCO	110	C1
RASOR RD	SBD	83	A4
RATTLESNAKE RD	NEV	34	C2
RATTLESNAKE RD	TRI	17	B3
RATTLSNK BTT RD	MOD	14	E1
RATTLSNK CYN RD	SBD	92	C5
RATTLSNAK CK RD	SIS	3	D5
RAWHIDE RD	TUO	41	C5
RAWSON RD	TEH	18	D5
RAY	SJCO	40	A3
RAY RD	SB	86	B1
RAYHOUSE RD	YOL	32	C4
RAYMOND AV	ORCO	T	C1
RAYMOND RD	ALA	M	D5
RAYMOND RD	ALA	46	C2
RAYMOND RD	MAD	49	C5
RAYMOND RD	MAD	57	B1
RAYNOR RANCH	MCO	48	E5
READING RD	TEH	18	D5
REAL RD	BKD	166	A4
REAL RD	KER	166	A5
REALTY RD	SJCO	40	B4
REATA RD	INY	51	D4
RECALDE RD	SBT	55	E4
RECHE RD	SBD	92	D5
RECHE RD	SDCO	106	C2
RECHE CANYON RD	RCO	99	C2
RECLAMATION RD	LAK	31	D2
RECLAMATION RD	SUT	33	C3
RECTOR RD	NEV	34	C1
RED BANK RD	TEH	18	B5
RED BANK RD	TEH	24	C1
RED BOX RD	LACO	R	D2
RED CAP RD	HUM	10	D2
RED CLOUD MN RD	RCO	102	B4
REDDING AV	KIN	67	D3
REDDING CYN RD	INY	51	E4
REDDING CK RD	TRI	17	D2
REDDINGTON AV	COL	32	E3
RED DOG RD	NEV	34	C1
RED GRADE RD	TRI	17	D1
RED HEAD CYN RD	MON	65	D3
RED HILL AV	CM	198	A4
RED HILL AV	IRV	198	D3
RED HILL AV	ORCO	98	C4
RED HILL AV	ORCO	T	D3
REDHILL RD	CAL	41	B4
RED HILL RD	IMP	109	A3
RED HILL RD	INY	51	C4
RED HILL RD	TRI	17	C1
REDHILL RD	TUO	48	C1
REDINGER LK RD	MAD	49	E5
REDINGER LK RD	MAD	50	A5
REDLANDS BLVD	RCO	99	C2
REDLANDS BLVD	SBDO	207	D5
REDLANDS BLVD	SBD	99	C2
REDLANDS FRWY	RCO	99	D2
REDLANDS FRWY	SBD	99	D2
REDLANDS ST	SBD	99	D2
REDMEYER RD	MEN	31	B2
REDMOND RD	HUM	9	E5
RED MOUNTAIN RD	KER	80	E3
RED MOUNTAIN RD	MCO	55	B1
RED MOUNTAIN RD	RCO	100	A5
RED MOUNTAIN RD	SBD	80	E3
RED MOUNTAIN RD	SHA	13	C3
RED MOUNTAIN RD	TRI	17	B4
RED MTN LKOUT	GLE	24	A3
RED MTN MTWY	TRI	17	B4
RED MTN TK TR	RCO	106	C1
RED OAK CYN RD	SIE	26	E3
REDONDO AV	LACO	98	A4
REDONDO AV	LACO	S	E2
REDONDO BLVD	LA	184	B4
REDONDO BCH BL	LACO	S	B1
REDPARK RD	HUM	9	E1
RED ROCK RD	LAS	27	E2
RED ROCK RD	SIS	5	A3
REDROCK-INYOKRN	KER	80	C1
REDROCK-INYOKRN	KER	80	C2
REDROCK-RANDSBG	KER	80	B3
RED ROVER MN RD	LACO	89	E4
RED SHANK LN	RCO	100	A5
REDSTONE AV	KER	79	C3
RED TOP RD	SOL	38	D3
RED TOP MTN RD	MAD	57	C1
RED VISTA RD	ALP	36	A5
REDWING RD	SBD	91	D3
REDWOOD BLVD	KER	80	B4
REDWOOD DR	HUM	16	C5
REDWOOD DR	TUL	69	B2
REDWOOD HWY	CRTM	140	C2
REDWOOD HWY	DN	1	E3
REDWOOD HWY	DN	2	A5
REDWOOD HWY	DN	9	E3
REDWOOD HWY	HUM	15	E3
REDWOOD HWY	HUM	16	B4
REDWOOD HWY	MAR	L	A2
REDWOOD HWY	MAR	38	A4
REDWOOD HWY	MAR	140	C2
REDWOOD HWY	MEN	22	C2
REDWOOD HWY	SR	139	D2
REDWOOD HWY	STR	131	C2

STREET	CO.	PAGE	GRID
REDWOOD HWY	SON	31	B3
REDWOOD HWY	SON	37	E2
REDWOOD HWY	SON	38	A3
REDWOOD RD	ALA	L	E4
REDWOOD RD	ALA	45	E1
REDWOOD RD	ALA	47	E1
REDWOOD RD	NAPA	29	D5
REDWOOD RD	NAPA	38	C2
REDWOOD RD	STA	47	D3
REDWOOD ST	SOL	L	D2
REDWOOD ST	VAL	134	B3
REDWD HOUSE RD	HUM	16	B3
REDWD RETREAT RD	SCL	P	D5
REDWD RETREAT RD	SCL	54	C1
REED	FRCO	58	A4
REED AV	KER	80	A5
REED AV	SVL	150	B1
REED LN	SCL	P	A3
REED RD	KER	68	C5
REED RD	SUT	33	C2
REEDER RD	KLAM	5	C1
REED MTN RD	HUM	22	C1
REED ORCHARD RD	TEH	25	A1
REEDS CREEK RD	TEH	18	B5
REEDS TURNPIKE	CAL	41	A5
REED VALLEY RD	RCO	100	A5
REESE AV	COL	33	A1
REESE RD	BUT	25	A2
REEVES RD	VEN	88	B4
REEVES CYN RD	MEN	31	A1
REFUGIO RD	SB	86	E3
REGENTS RD	SD	211	D2
REGENTS RD	SDCO	V	A2
REGENTS RD	SDCO	106	C5
REGLI LN	HUM	15	E2
REICHART RCH RD	MNO	51	C1
REID AV	TUL	68	D3
REID RD	KER	79	E2
REID RD	KER	80	A2
REILLY RD	MCO	48	C5
REINA RD	KER	78	C2
REINO RD	VEN	96	D1
REIS AV	VAL	134	E5
RELIEF HILL RD	NEV	26	D5
RELIEZ RD	CC	38	E5
RELIEZ VLY RD	CC	L	E3
RELIZ CANYON RD	MON	65	A2
REMANN AV	SHA	19	E1
REMBACH WY	KER	79	C1
RENFRO RD	KER	78	C3
RENGSTORFF RD	SCL	N	E2
RENGSTORFF RD	SCL	P	A2
RENO AV	TEH	24	D1
RENWICK AV	SB	86	B3
REQUA RD	DN	1	E5
REQUA RD	DN	2	A5
RESEDA BLVD	LA	178	D3
RESEDA BLVD	LACO	97	C1
RESERVATION RD	COL	32	E1
RESERVATION RD	MON	54	B4
RESERVATION RD	TUL	68	C3
RESERVE RD	KER	77	D3
RESERVOIR RD	BUT	25	D5
RESERVOIR RD	ED	34	D3
RESERVOIR RD	SOL	38	E4
RESERVOIR RD	STA	48	A2
RETRAC WY	NEV	34	C2
RETSON RD	BUT	25	D2
REVIS RD	MAD	49	C5
REWARD RD	KER	77	D3
REYES ADOBE RD	LACO	96	E1
REYNARD WY	SD	215	D2
REYNOLDS AV	MCO	56	B2
REYNOLDS HWY	MEN	23	A5
REYNOLDS RD	SHA	13	E4
REYNLDS FRRY RD	TUO	41	B5
RHEEM BLVD	CC	L	E4
RHELM	CC	38	C5
RHONDA RD	SHA	18	C3
RIALTO AV	SBD	99	B1
RIALTO AV	SBDO	207	C2
RIATA RD	LAK	32	A4
RIATA WY	CAL	41	A4
RICE AV	SBD	101	A1
RICE AV	VEN	96	B1
RICE RD	FRCO	57	C2
RICE RD	MCO	48	B5
RICE RD	STA	47	E2
RICE RD	VEN	88	A4
RICE CANYON RD	LAS	21	B3
RICE CREEK RD	LAK	23	D5
RICE CREEK RD	LAK	31	D1
RICES CRSSG RD	NEV	34	B1
RICES CRSSG RD	YUB	26	A5
RICES TEX HL RD	YUB	26	A5
RICETON HWY	BUT	25	C5
RICH LN	RCO	106	E1
RICH RD	KER	68	C5
RICHARD RD	SIS	4	D5
RICHARD ST	KER	70	A5
RICHARDS AV	BUT	33	C1
RICHARDS BLVD	DVS	136	D3
RICHARDSON AV	SF	142	A1
RICHARDSON RD	SBD	91	A3
RICHARDSON RD	SIS	4	E3
RICHARDSON RD	SIS	5	A2
RICHARDSON SPGS	BUT	25	B2
RICH BAR RD	PLU	26	B1
RICHEY RD	CLO	33	A3
RICHFIELD RD	TEH	24	D1
RICH GULCH RD	PLU	26	B1
RICHLAND RD	SUT	125	B5
RICHMOND RD	LAS	21	A3

STREET	CO.	PAGE	GRID
RICHMOND ST	SD	215	E1
RICHVALE HWY	BUT	25	B4
RIDER ST	RCO	99	B3
RIDGE DR	SHA	18	B2
RIDGE RD	AMA	40	E2
RIDGE RD	CAL	41	B2
RIDGE RD	NEV	34	C1
RIDGE RD	NEV	127	A2
RIDGE RD	NEV	128	A4
RIDGE RD	SIE	26	C5
RIDGE RD	SIS	3	E4
RIDGE RD	TEH	18	C5
RIDGECREST BLVD	KER	80	D1
RIDGE ROUTE RD	ED	34	E4
RIDGEWAY DR	ED	35	B4
RIDGEWAY HWY	MEN	23	B5
RIDGEWOOD	MEN	23	A5
RIDGEWOOD DR	HUM	15	E1
RIDGEWOOD RD	SHA	18	C2
RIEBLI RD	SON	37	E1
RIEBLI RD	SON	38	A1
RIEFF RD	LAK	32	B4
RIEGO RD	SUT	33	D5
RIGGIN AV	TUL	68	A1
RIGGINS RD	SUT	33	C4
RIGGS RD	SBD	83	B2
RIKER ST	SAL	171	B5
RILEY RD	BUT	25	B5
RILEY RD	SB	86	E3
RILEY RD	SAC	40	A2
RIM O T WRLD HY	SBD	91	C5
RIM O T WRLD HY	SBD	99	D1
RIMPAU BLVD	LA	184	C3
RIMROCK RD	BARS	208	D4
RIM ROCK RD	RCO	107	C1
RIMROCK RD	SBD	91	D1
RIMROCK RD	SBD	100	C1
RIM ROCK CANYON	RCO	107	C1
RINCON AV	SDCO	106	D3
RINCON AV	SON	38	A2
RINCON RD	SBD	91	C4
RINCNADA LS PIL	SLO	76	C3
RINGWOOD AV	SMCO	N	E5
RIO RD	CAR	168	C4
RIO RD	MON	168	C4
RIO BLANCO	SJCO	39	E4
RIO BONITO RD E	BUT	25	C5
RIO BONITO RD W	BUT	25	C5
RIO DEL SOL RD	RCO	100	E3
RIOLINDA AV	FRCO	57	B4
RIO LINDA BLVD	SAC	33	E5
RIO OSO RD	SUT	33	D3
RIORDON RD	COL	32	D1
RIOSA RD	PLA	33	E3
RIOSA RD	PLA	34	A3
RIO VISTA AV	FRCO	58	A4
RIO VISTA AV W	TEH	18	D4
RIO VISTA RD	SUIS	135	C4
RIO VISTA ST	ORCO	T	D2
RIPONE RD	STA	47	C2
RIPPON RD N	SJCO	47	C1
RIPPON RD W	SJCO	47	B2
RISING HILL RD	SIS	4	C5
RITCHEY ST	SA	198	E1
RITTER RD	SHA	13	D3
RITTS MILL RD	SHA	19	B2
RIVER AV	BUT	33	C1
RIVER BLVD	KER	78	D3
RIVER RD	BUT	25	A3
RIVER RD	COL	33	E5
RIVER RD	HUM	15	D3
RIVER RD	HUM	16	D5
RIVER RD	MAD	49	C5
RIVER RD	MAD	57	B1
RIVER RD	MCO	47	D4
RIVER RD	MON	54	D4
RIVER RD	RCO	U	E4
RIVER RD	RCO	98	E3
RIVER RD	RCO	99	C4
RIVER RD	SAC	M	E1
RIVER RD	SBD	85	C5
RIVER RD	SBD	95	D1
RIVER RD	SJCO	47	C1
RIVER RD	SLO	66	A5
RIVER RD	SLO	76	A1
RIVER RD	SLO	76	C3
RIVER RD	SON	37	D1
RIVER RD	STA	47	B3
RIVER RD	STA	47	D1
RIVER RD	TEH	24	D1
RIVER RD S	YOL	39	D2
RIVER ST	SC	169	C1
RIVER ST	SCR	169	C1
RIVER ST	SON	31	C4
RIVER BENCH RD	LAS	20	E3
RIVERBEND AV	FRCO	57	E3
RIVERCREST DR	HUM	16	B5
RIVEREDGE RD	SDCO	106	C1
RIVERFORD RD	SDCO	V	E2
RIVERFORD RD	SDCO	106	E5
RIVER GRADE RD	LACO	R	D3
RIV JCT FRMS RD	SJCO	47	B2
RIVER RANCH RD	SHA	18	C3
RIVER ROCK RD	TRI	17	D1
RIVERSIDE	WSH	130	B3
RIVERSIDE AV	MCO	47	D4
RIVERSIDE AV	RCO	103	C5
RIVERSIDE AV	SBD	99	B1
RIVERSIDE AV	SHA	18	C3
RIVERSIDE AV	TEH	18	D5
RIVERSIDE BLVD	SCTO	137	B4
RIVERSIDE BLVD	SAC	39	D1
RIVERSIDE DR	LA	179	B5

STREET	CO.	PAGE	GRID
RIVERSIDE DR	LA	182	D3
RIVERSIDE DR	LACO	Q	E3
RIVERSIDE DR	RED	122	A1
RIVERSIDE DR	RCO	99	B4
RIVERSIDE DR	SBD	U	C3
RIVERSIDE DR	SBD	98	D2
RIVERSIDE DR	SDCO	V	E2
RIVERSIDE DR	SDCO	106	E5
RIVERSIDE DR	SHA	18	C2
RIVERSIDE DR	SON	132	B3
RIVERSIDE DR	STA	47	D2
RIVERSIDE FRWY	ANA	194	C1
RIVERSIDE FRWY	ORCO	98	C3
RIVERSIDE FRWY	ORCO	T	E1
RIVERSIDE FRWY	RCO	99	A3
RIVERSIDE RD	HUM	10	A5
RIVERSIDE RD	INY	51	D4
RIVERSIDE RD	SBD	92	C1
RIVERSIDE ST	KER	78	A2
RIVERSIDE PK RD	HUM	16	A3
RIVER SPRINGS	MNO	44	B5
RIVERVIEW DR	SHA	12	C5
RIVER VIEW RD	SBD	91	C1
RIVERVIEW RD	TRI	17	B2
RIVER WAY DR	TUL	68	B1
RIVIERA	RED	122	A5
RIVIERA DR	SD	212	B2
RIVIERA DR	SDCO	V	A3
RIVIERA DR	SHA	18	C2
RIVIERA RD	SUT	33	C1
ROAD 1	LAS	20	B1
ROAD 1	MAD	56	B1
ROAD 4	LAS	20	B1
ROAD 4	MAD	56	C1
ROAD 5	MAD	56	C1
ROAD 5 1/2	MAD	56	C2
ROAD 6	MAD	56	C1
ROAD 7	MAD	56	C1
ROAD 8	MAD	56	C1
ROAD 8 1/2	MAD	56	C3
ROAD 9	LAS	20	B1
ROAD 9	MAD	56	C1
ROAD 10	MAD	56	D1
ROAD 10 1/2	MAD	56	D2
ROAD 11	MAD	56	D1
ROAD 12	MAD	56	D1
ROAD 12	TUL	57	E5
ROAD 13	MAD	56	D1
ROAD 14	MAD	56	D1
ROAD 14 1/2	MAD	56	D1
ROAD 15	MAD	56	D1
ROAD 15 1/2	MAD	56	D1
ROAD 16	MAD	56	D2
ROAD 16	TUL	57	E5
ROAD 16 1/2	MAD	56	D2
ROAD 17	MAD	56	D2
ROAD 18	MAD	56	E1
ROAD 18 1/2	MAD	56	E1
ROAD 19	MAD	56	E1
ROAD 19 1/2	MAD	56	E2
ROAD 20	MAD	56	E2
ROAD 20 1/2	MAD	56	E2
ROAD 21	MAD	56	E2
ROAD 21 1/2	MAD	56	E2
ROAD 22	MAD	48	E5
ROAD 22 1/2	MAD	48	E5
ROAD 23	MAD	48	E5
ROAD 23 1/2	MAD	56	E1
ROAD 24	MAD	56	E1
ROAD 24	TUL	57	E5
ROAD 24	TUL	67	E2
ROAD 24 1/2	MAD	56	E2
ROAD 24 1/2	MAD	57	A2
ROAD 25	LAS	20	B1
ROAD 25	MAD	57	A2
ROAD 26	MAD	57	A2
ROAD 26 1/2	MAD	57	A2
ROAD 27	MAD	57	A1
ROAD 28	MAD	57	A2
ROAD 28	TUL	57	E5
ROAD 28	TUL	67	E2
ROAD 28 1/2	MAD	57	A2
ROAD 29	MAD	49	B5
ROAD 29 1/2	MAD	57	B2
ROAD 30	MAD	57	B2
ROAD 30 1/2	MAD	57	B2
ROAD 31	MAD	57	B3
ROAD 31 1/2	MAD	57	B2
ROAD 32	MAD	57	B2
ROAD 32	TUL	57	E5
ROAD 33	MAD	57	B2
ROAD 33 1/2	MAD	57	B2
ROAD 34	MAD	57	B3
ROAD 34	TUL	67	E4
ROAD 34	TUL	68	A4
ROAD 34 1/2	MAD	57	B2
ROAD 35	MAD	57	B2
ROAD 36	MAD	57	B2
ROAD 36	TUL	57	E5
ROAD 37	MAD	57	B2
ROAD 37 1/2	MAD	57	C2
ROAD 38	MAD	57	C2
ROAD 38	TUL	67	E4
ROAD 39	MAD	57	C2
ROAD 39 1/2	MAD	57	C2
ROAD 40	MAD	57	C2
ROAD 40	TUL	57	E5
ROAD 40 1/2	MAD	57	C2
ROAD 42	TUL	57	E4
ROAD 44	TUL	57	E5
ROAD 46	TUL	68	A4
ROAD 48	TUL	57	E4
ROAD 48	TUL	68	A1

STREET	CO.	PAGE	GRID
ROAD 50	TUL	68	A4
ROAD 52	TUL	58	A4
ROAD 52	TUL	68	A1
ROAD 56	TUL	58	A5
ROAD 56	TUL	68	A1
ROAD 60	TUL	58	A5
ROAD 60	TUL	68	A1
ROAD 64	TUL	58	A4
ROAD 64	TUL	68	A1
ROAD 68	TUL	58	A5
ROAD 68	TUL	68	A1
ROAD 72	TUL	58	A4
ROAD 74	TUL	58	A5
ROAD 76	TUL	58	A5
ROAD 76	TUL	68	A1
ROAD 78	TUL	58	A4
ROAD 80	TUL	58	A5
ROAD 80	TUL	68	A2
ROAD 84	TUL	58	A5
ROAD 84	TUL	68	A1
ROAD 88	TUL	58	A5
ROAD 88	TUL	68	A3
ROAD 92	TUL	68	A2
ROAD 96	TUL	58	A4
ROAD 100	TUL	58	B5
ROAD 100	TUL	68	B1
ROAD 104	TUL	58	B5
ROAD 108	TUL	68	B1
ROAD 109	TUL	58	B4
ROAD 110	MEN	31	B3
ROAD 112	TUL	58	B5
ROAD 114	TUL	58	B4
ROAD 116	TUL	58	B5
ROAD 120	TUL	58	B5
ROAD 124	TUL	58	B4
ROAD 124	TUL	68	B2
ROAD 128	TUL	58	B4
ROAD 128	TUL	68	B3
ROAD 132	TUL	58	B4
ROAD 132	TUL	68	B1
ROAD 136	TUL	58	B4
ROAD 136	TUL	68	B3
ROAD 138	TUL	68	B1
ROAD 140	TUL	58	B4
ROAD 140	TUL	68	B1
ROAD 143	TUL	58	B4
ROAD 144	TUL	58	B5
ROAD 148	TUL	58	B5
ROAD 148	TUL	68	B1
ROAD 152	TUL	58	B4
ROAD 152	TUL	68	B1
ROAD 156	TUL	58	B5
ROAD 156	TUL	68	B1
ROAD 158	TUL	68	B1
ROAD 164	TUL	68	C1
ROAD 166	TUL	68	C1
ROAD 168	TUL	68	C1
ROAD 172	TUL	68	C2
ROAD 176	TUL	68	C3
ROAD 180	TUL	58	C5
ROAD 180	TUL	68	C1
ROAD 182	TUL	58	C5
ROAD 182	TUL	68	C1
ROAD 184	TUL	58	C5
ROAD 188	TUL	68	C3
ROAD 190	TUL	68	C1
ROAD 192	TUL	68	C1
ROAD 194	TUL	58	C5
ROAD 196	TUL	58	C5
ROAD 196	TUL	68	C1
ROAD 197	TUL	58	C5
ROAD 200	TUL	58	C5
ROAD 200	TUL	68	C1
ROAD 202	TUL	68	C3
ROAD 204	MAD	57	C2
ROAD 204	TUL	58	C5
ROAD 205	MAD	57	C2
ROAD 206	TUL	58	C5
ROAD 208	TUL	58	C5
ROAD 208	TUL	68	C1
ROAD 209	MAD	57	C1
ROAD 210	TUL	68	C1
ROAD 212	TUL	58	C5
ROAD 212	TUL	68	C1
ROAD 216	MAD	57	D1
ROAD 216	TUL	68	C2
ROAD 220	TUL	58	D5
ROAD 220	TUL	68	D1
ROAD 222	TUL	68	D1
ROAD 224	TUL	68	D4
ROAD 228	TUL	68	D1
ROAD 232	TUL	68	D2
ROAD 235	MAD	50	A5
ROAD 236	TUL	68	D1
ROAD 240	TUL	68	D4
ROAD 244	TUL	68	D1
ROAD 248	TUL	68	D1
ROAD 252	TUL	68	D2
ROAD 256	TUL	68	D3
ROAD 260	TUL	68	D2
ROAD 264	TUL	68	D3
ROAD 266	TUL	68	D4
ROAD 268	TUL	68	D3
ROAD 272	TUL	68	D4
ROAD 276	TUL	68	D2
ROAD 296	TUL	68	E3
ROAD 320	TUL	68	E3
ROAD 406	MAD	57	C1
ROAD 434	MAD	49	D4
ROAD 601	MAD	49	D4
ROAD 602	MAD	57	B1
ROAD 612	MAD	49	C5
ROAD 810	MAD	49	C4

STREET INDEX

STREET	CO.	PAGE	GRID
ROAD 812	MAD	49	C4
ROAD RUNNER RUT	SBD	100	D1
ROAN RD	CAL	41	B4
ROBB RD	RCO	99	B4
ROBBEN RD	SOL	39	B3
ROBBEN RD	SOL	39	B2
ROBBINS RD	SUT	33	B3
ROBBINS RCH RD	NEV	26	D5
ROBBY RD	KER	79	B4
ROBERTA AV	LAKE	7	C1
ROBRTNO RIGHETI	SLO	76	B4
ROBERTS LN	KER	78	D2
ROBERTS RD	SJCO	40	A5
ROBERTS RD	SJCO	47	A1
ROBERTS RD	SON	38	A3
ROBERTS FRRY RD	STA	48	B2
ROBERTSON BLVD	BH	183	D2
ROBERTSON BLVD	CUL	183	D5
ROBERTSON BLVD	LA	183	D4
ROBERTSON BLVD	LACO	Q	D4
ROBERTSON BLVD	LACO	183	D2
ROBERTSON BLVD	MAD	56	D1
ROBERTS RES RD	MOD	14	B3
ROBIN AV	MCO	47	E4
ROBIN AV	MCO	48	A4
ROBINSON	SJCO	47	C1
ROBINSON RD	IMP	109	A5
ROBINSON RD	MCO	48	C3
ROBINSON RD	SOL	39	B3
ROBINSON CYN RD	MON	54	B5
ROBINSON CK RD	MEN	31	A2
ROBINSN MILL RD	BUT	25	E5
ROBNSN RCHRIA W	LAK	31	D2
ROBLAR AV	SB	86	E3
ROBLAR RD	SON	37	D3
ROBLEY POINT RD	BUT	25	D2
ROBS RD	MOD	8	B3
ROCA LN	SBD	90	E2
ROCK CANYON RD	LAS	14	A3
ROCK CANYON RD	RCO	107	C1
ROCK CREEK DR	BUT	25	B2
ROCK CREEK RD	CAL	40	E4
ROCK CREEK RD	CAL	41	A4
ROCK CREEK RD	ED	34	E3
ROCK CREEK RD	INY	51	A3
ROCK CREEK RD	MNO	51	A3
ROCK CREEK RD	NEV	34	C1
ROCK CREEK RD	SHA	18	B2
ROCK CREEK RD	SHA	19	B3
ROCK CK GRBG PT	MNO	51	B3
ROCKERFELLER RD	BUT	25	E3
ROCKHAVEN	SBD	101	A2
ROCKING CHR RD	SBD	101	A2
ROE RD	BUT	25	C3
ROCKLIN	PLA	34	B4
ROCK PILE RD	KER	79	A4
ROCKPILE RD	SON	31	B4
ROCKRIDGE RD	RCO	100	A5
ROCK RIVER RD	STA	48	B1
ROCK RIVER RD	TUO	48	B1
ROCK SPRINGS RD	SBD	91	C4
ROCKVILLE RD	SOL	L	E1
ROCKVILLE RD	SOL	38	D3
ROCKWOOD RD	IMP	112	A4
ROCKY CT	KER	79	D5
ROCKY LN	KER	79	D3
ROCKY RD	RCO	99	B5
ROCKY BAR RD	ED	41	A1
ROCKY BLUFF RD	RCO	99	B4
ROCKY CANYON RD	SLO	76	B2
ROCKYDALE RD	JOS	2	D1
ROCKY PT CMPGRD	PLU	20	B4
RODDEN RD	STA	47	E1
RODEO AV	TEH	24	D1
RODEO BLVD	LACO	Q	D4
RODEO RD	LA	184	A5
RODEO RD	SBD	91	C2
RODEO GULCH RD	SCR	54	A2
RODUNER RD	MCO	48	B5
ROEDING RD	STA	47	D3
ROEN RD	STA	48	A2
ROGERS RD	KER	80	B3
ROGERS RD	STA	47	B3
ROGERS CREEK RD	SIS	10	E1
ROHNERVILLE RD	HUM	15	E2
ROLAND DR	SIS	4	C5
ROLINDA AV	FRCO	57	B5
ROLLING HLLS RD	LACO	S	B2
ROLLINS RD	MLBR	144	E5
ROLLINS LAKE RD	PLA	34	D2
ROMEL ST	CAL	41	A4
ROMERO	MCO	55	C1
ROMERO RD	MCO	47	C5
ROMERO CYN RD	SB	87	D4
ROMERS DAIRY RD	MEN	31	B3
ROMIE LN E	SAL	171	C5
RONALD REAGAN FY	LA	89	B5
RONALD REAGAN FY	VEN	88	E5
RONNIE AV	KER	79	B5
ROOP RD	SCL	P	E5
ROOP RD	SCL	54	D1
ROOSEVELT RD	MCO	48	C5
ROOST AV	KER	79	B4
ROOT AV	KER	78	B1
ROOT RD	RCO	99	E5
ROOT RD	STA	47	D2
ROSA RD	MCO	47	D4
ROSAMOND BLVD	KER	89	D1
ROSAMOND BLVD	KER	90	B1
ROSAMND HLLS RD	RCO	107	C1
ROSAMUND BLVD	KER	80	C5
ROSARITA DR	SAL	171	D2
ROSCOE BLVD	LACO	97	C1

STREET	CO.	PAGE	GRID
ROSCOE RD	HUM	15	E4
ROSCOE RD	STA	47	E2
ROSE AV	FRCO	56	E4
ROSE AV	FRCO	57	C4
ROSE AV	LA	187	A2
ROSE AV	MCO	47	E4
ROSE AV	MCO	48	B4
ROSE AV	VEN	88	B5
ROSE AV	VEN	96	B1
ROSE DR	ORCO	T	D1
ROSE RD	KER	79	E2
ROSE RD	KER	80	A2
ROSE RD	SIS	5	D2
ROSE RD	TRI	17	B1
ROSE RD	YOL	39	D2
ROSE ST	SDCO	106	D3
ROSEBURG AV	MDO	162	A1
ROSECRANS	LACO	97	D3
ROSECRANS AV	ELS	189	B5
ROSECRANS AV	MB	189	B5
ROSECRANS AV	ORCO	98	B3
ROSECRANS AV	ORCO	T	C1
ROSECRANS BLVD	SDCO	111	C1
ROSECRANS ST	SDCO	V	A3
ROSE GARDEN RD	MCO	47	C5
ROSEDALE HWY	KER	78	C3
ROSE HILLS RD	LACO	R	D4
ROSE LAWN AV	MCO	47	E3
ROSELAWN AV	MDO	162	A5
ROSE LAWN AV	STA	47	D2
ROSELLE AV	STA	47	D2
ROSE MARIE LN	S	160	A1
ROSEMARY RD	SB	86	C1
ROSEMEAD BLVD	LACO	98	A2
ROSEMEAD BLVD	LACO	R	C5
ROSE MINE RD	SBD	92	B5
ROSEMORE AV	STA	47	C2
ROSER RD	TEH	24	C2
ROSES RD	LACO	R	C3
ROSE VALLEY RD	VEN	88	B3
ROSEWOOD AV	VEN	96	C1
ROSEWOOD BLVD	KER	80	B5
ROSITA ST	LA	178	B5
ROSS AV	EC	217	A4
ROSS RD	IMP	111	E3
ROSS RD	IMP	112	D5
ROSSI ST	SAL	171	C3
ROSSMORE AV	LA	184	D2
ROSSMORE AV	LACO	Q	D4
ROSY RIDGE RD	RCO	107	B1
ROUGH&READY RD	NEV	34	B1
ROULTS RD	MNO	51	B3
ROUND HOUSE RD	MAD	49	D4
ROUND MTN LKOUT	SIS	13	D1
ROUND MTN RD	KER	78	D2
ROUND MTN RD	MNO	51	B2
ROUND ROBIN DR	RCO	100	B4
ROUNDUP WY	SBD	91	C4
ROUND VALLEY RD	SBD	100	B1
ROUND VALLEY RD	TEH	23	D2
ROUND VLY RD N	INY	51	B4
ROUND VLY RD S	INY	51	C4
RND VLY TUNGSTN	INY	51	C4
ROUNDY RD	TRI	17	D1
ROUSE AV	STA	162	A5
ROUSE RD	RCO	99	C4
RT OLYMPC TORCH	LAS	20	D2
ROUTE 4 FRWY	CC	154	D3
ROUTE 4 FRWY	M	154	D3
ROUTE 47 FRWY	LB	191	E2
ROUTE 47 FRWY	LB	192	A2
ROUTE 47 FRWY	LA	191	E2
ROUTE 47 FRWY	LA	192	A2
ROUTE 47 FRWY	LACO	97	E4
ROUTE 47 FRWY	LACO	S	D2
ROUTE 52 FRWY	SD	211	E3
ROUTE 94 FRWY	SD	216	C3
ROUTE 101 FRWY	STB	173	D5
ROUTE 101 FRWY	SB	86	D4
ROUTE 101 FRWY	SB	87	D4
ROUTE 101 FRWY	SMA	173	C1
ROWDY CREEK RD	DN	1	E3
ROWENA AV	LA	182	D3
ROWLEE RD	KER	77	E2
ROWLEE RD	KER	78	A2
ROWLES RD	TEH	24	E2
ROXBURY DR	SIS	3	C4
ROXBURY RD	MCO	56	B1
ROXFORD ST	LACO	89	C5
ROXFORD ST	LACO	Q	B1
ROYAL AV	VEN	88	E5
ROYAL AV	VEN	89	A5
ROYAL OAKS DR	LACO	R	D3
ROY JONES RD	SIS	4	B3
ROYO RNCHERO DR	SUT	33	C2
RUBIDOUX BLVD	RCO	99	B2
RUBLE RD	STA	47	C3
RUCKER AV	SCL	P	E5
RUCKER AV	SCL	54	D1
RUDD RD	KER	78	C3
RUDDICK	MEN	31	B2
RUDGEAR RD	CC	M	A4
RUDNICK RD	KER	80	C4
RUDOLPH DR	KER	79	C4
RUDOLPH RD	INY	51	D3
RUEGGER RD	IMP	109	A3
RUFF LN	GLE	24	E5
RUFFIN RD	SDCO	V	C2
RUFFIN RD	SDCO	106	D5
RUGGED TRAIL RD	RCO	107	C1
RUMBLE RD	STA	47	C2
RUNGE RD	SOL	39	C2
RUSH ST	RCO	107	C1

STREET	CO.	PAGE	GRID
RUSH CREEK DR	TRI	11	D5
RUSH CREEK RD	MNO	43	C5
RUSH CREEK RD	TRI	17	D1
RUSH CK SHORTCT	TRI	17	D1
RUSH CK CAMP RD	TRI	11	D5
RUSHNG HILL LKT	TUO	48	B1
RUSS LN	HUM	15	D2
RUSSEL AV	KER	79	A4
RUSSELL AV	FRCO	56	A3
RUSSELL BLVD	DVS	136	B3
RUSSELL BLVD	YOL	39	A1
RUSSELL RD	CAL	41	A3
RUSSELL RD	SAC	39	D3
RUSSELL RD	STA	47	B2
RUSSELL RD	TEH	18	C3
RUTH AV	BLMT	145	C4
RUTH DUMP RD	TRI	17	A4
RUTHERFORD	NAPA	29	D3
RUTHERFORD RD	IMP	109	A4
RUTH HILL RD	FRCO	58	C3
RUTH HILL RD	FRCO	58	B3
RUTH ZENIA RD	TRI	16	E4
RYAN AV	KER	80	A4
RYAN RD	LAS	21	B3
RYAN RD	SLO	76	C2
RYAN CREEK RD	MEN	23	A5
RYE CANYON RD	LACO	89	B4
RYE GRASS SWALE	MOD	8	A1
RYE GRASS SWALE	MOD	14	E1
RYER RD E	SOL	39	D3
RYER ISLAND RD	SOL	M	D1

S

STREET	CO.	PAGE	GRID
S ST	EUR	121	E2
SABINANA RD	YUB	33	E1
SABODAN ST	KER	78	D5
SACHREITER RD	COL	33	A2
SACRAMENTO AV	BUT	25	A3
SACRAMENTO AV	C	124	A4
SACRAMENTO AV	FRCO	56	D4
SACRAMENTO AV	SUT	33	D3
SACRAMENTO BLVD	SCTO	137	E5
SACRAMENTO DR	SHA	18	C2
SACRAMNTO FWY N	SCTO	137	D1
SACRAMENTO ST	AUB	126	C4
SACRAMENTO ST	PLA	34	D1
SACRAMENTO ST	PLCV	138	C3
SACRAMENTO ST	VAL	134	B2
SACRMNTO VLY BL	SUT	33	C4
SACRMNTO VLY RD	SUT	33	C3
SADDLE CT	KER	79	C5
SADDLEBACK RD	SIE	26	D4
SADDLEHORN RD	SBD	84	C3
SADDLE PEAK RD	LACO	97	B2
SADDLE TRAIL RD	SHA	18	B3
SADDLE VIEW CT	SHA	13	E4
SAGE AV	SBD	100	D1
SAGE RD	HUM	15	D2
SAGE RD	RCO	99	E4
SAGEBRUSH LN	SIS	4	E3
SAGE CANYON RD	KER	80	B1
SAGE FLATS DR	INY	70	B2
SAGE HEN RD	MNO	51	A2
SAGE HEN RD	NEV	27	D5
SAGE HN MDWS RD	MNO	43	E5
SAGE HN MDWS RD	MNO	50	E1
SAGE HN MDWS RD	MNO	51	A1
SAGEHORN RD	MOD	7	D3
SAGELAND CT	KER	79	B4
SAGE VALLEY RD	LAS	21	D5
SAGINAW AV	FRCO	57	E4
SAHARA AV	LV	209	A4
SAHARA AV E	CLK	74	D2
SAHARA AV W	CLK	74	C2
ST CATHERINE WY	AVLN	97	B4
ST FRANCIS AV	STA	47	C2
ST GEORGE ST	LA	182	D3
ST HELENA HWY	NAPA	29	D4
ST HELENA RD	SON	38	A1
ST JAMES ST	SJ	152	C3
ST JOHN RD	TRI	16	E2
ST JOHN LOOP RD	TRI	16	E2
ST LOUIS AV	KER	80	A4
ST LOUIS RD	HUM	9	E5
ST LOUIS RD	HUM	10	A5
ST LOUIS RD	PLU	26	C3
ST MARYS AV	TEH	18	D5
ST MARYS RD	CC	L	E4
ST MARYS RD	CC	M	A4
ST MARYS RD	CC	45	E1
SALE LN	TEH	18	D5
SALEM AV	KIN	67	E3
SALINAS AV	SOL	39	B3
SALINAS RD	MON	54	C2
SALINAS ST	STB	174	E3
SALINE VLY ALT	INY	70	E1
SALINE VLY RD	INY	60	C3
SALINE VLY RD	INY	60	D5
SALMON CREEK RD	HUM	16	B4
SALMON FALLS RD	ED	34	C5
SALMON LAKE RD	SIE	26	E3
SALMON LAKE RD	SIE	27	A3
SALMON RIVER RD	SIS	10	E2
SALMON RIVER RD	SIS	11	A2
SALT RD N	SHA	12	C4
SALT CREEK RD	MCO	55	D2
SALT CREEK RD	SHA	12	D5
SALTDALE RD	KER	80	C3
SALTON DR	IMP	108	C2
SALTON RD	SBD	80	E5
SALTON RD	SBD	81	A5
SALTON BAY DR	IMP	108	C2

STREET	CO.	PAGE	GRID
SALTON VIEW RD	RCO	101	B3
SALT POOL RD	INY	72	A1
SALT SPG VLY RD	CAL	41	A5
SALT SPG VLY RD	CAL	41	A4
SALTUS RD	SBD	93	E3
SALTUS RD	SBD	94	A3
SALVADORI RD	SIS	4	B5
SAM ALLEY RIDGE	LAK	31	D2
SAMEL DR	SBD	100	D2
SAMPLE RD	FRCO	57	E2
SAMPSON ST	SD	216	B5
SAMSON AV	TEH	18	D5
SAMSON AV	TEH	24	D2
SAN ANDREAS RD	SCR	54	B2
SAN ANDREAS RD	SBD	100	E2
SAN ANDREAS ST	STB	174	A3
SN ANTONE CP RD	CAL	41	B4
SAN ANTONIO AV	CAR	53	D5
SAN ANTONIO AV	ONT	204	A3
SAN ANTONIO AV	UPL	204	A3
SN ANTONIO AV N	CAR	168	B4
SAN ANTONIO DR	LACO	S	D2
SAN ANTONIO DR	LACO	T	A1
SAN ANTONIO RD	MON	65	D5
SAN ANTONIO RD	SB	86	B2
SAN ANTONIO RD	SCL	N	E3
SAN ANTONIO RD	SCL	P	A3
SAN ANTONIO RD	SCL	P	E3
SAN ANTONIO RD	SCL	45	E4
SAN ANTONIO ST	SJ	152	E3
SAN ANTONIO VLY	SCL	46	D4
SAN BENACIO RD	MON	54	C4
SAN BENITO AV	FRCO	56	D4
SAN BENITO AV	TEH	18	D5
SN BERNARDNO AV	FRCO	56	C3
SN BERNARDNO AV	SBD	98	D2
SN BERNARDNO FY	CLA	203	A3
SN BERNARDNO FY	LA	186	D3
SN BERNARDNO FY	LACO	98	B2
SN BERNARDNO FY	LACO	R	D4
SN BERNARDNO FY	MTCL	203	A3
SN BERNARDNO FY	ONT	203	D3
SN BERNARDNO FY	ONT	204	B3
SN BERNARDNO FY	SBD	98	D2
SN BERNARDNO FY	UPL	204	B3
SN BERNARDNO RD	LACO	U	A2
SN BERNARDNO RD	SBD	80	E1
SN BERNARDNO RD	UPL	204	C2
SN BERNARDNO ST	MTCL	203	B3
SN BERNARDNO ST	POM	203	C3
SN BERNARDNO ST	SBD	U	D2
SN BERNARDNO CK	SLO	75	E3
SN BERNARDNO CK	SLO	76	A3
SANBORN RD	SUT	33	C2
SANBORN RD S	SAL	171	E5
SAN BRUNO AV	SBR	144	B3
SAN BRUNO AV	SMCO	45	B2
SAN CARLOS AV	SMCO	N	D2
SAN CARLOS AV	SMCO	45	D3
SAN CARLOS RD	MCO	55	D2
SAN CARLOS ST	CAR	168	B4
SAN CARLOS ST	SJ	151	D5
SAN CARLOS ST	SJ	152	C4
SAN CARLOS ST	SCL	151	D5
SANCHES RD	MCO	47	C4
SANCHEZ RD	MON	54	E5
SAND CANYON AV	ORCO	98	C4
SAND CANYON AV	ORCO	T	E4
SAND CANYON RD	INY	51	C4
SAND CANYON RD	KER	70	C5
SAND CANYON RD	KER	79	D4
SAND CANYON RD	LACO	89	C4
SAND CANYON RD	SBD	99	D2
SAND CREEK RD	COL	32	D3
SAND CREEK RD	FRCO	58	B4
SAND CREEK RD	TUL	58	B4
SAND CREST DR	IMP	108	C2
SANDERS RD	STA	47	C3
SANDERS RD	SUT	33	C2
SANDERSON AV	RCO	99	E4
SAND FLAT RD	SIS	12	D2
SAND FLAT CTO	MNO	50	E1
SAND HILL RD	SMCO	N	D3
SAND HILL RD	SMCO	45	D4
SANDIA CREEK DR	SDCO	106	C1
SAN DIEGO AV	FRCO	56	C4
SAN DIEGO AV	SD	213	B5
SAN DIEGO FRWY	CUL	188	A1
SAN DIEGO FRWY	HAW	189	E3
SAN DIEGO FRWY	ING	188	D4
SAN DIEGO FRWY	IRV	198	E5
SAN DIEGO FRWY	LA	180	C2
SAN DIEGO FRWY	LA	188	D4
SAN DIEGO FRWY	LACO	97	C2
SAN DIEGO FRWY	LACO	180	C2
SAN DIEGO FRWY	LACO	189	E3
SAN DIEGO FRWY	LACO	S	B1
SAN DIEGO FRWY	ORCO	98	D4
SAN DIEGO FRWY	ORCO	197	A3
SAN DIEGO FRWY	ORCO	198	A4
SAN DIEGO FRWY	ORCO	202	C4
SAN DIEGO FRWY	ORCO	T	B3
SAN DIEGO FRWY	SD	211	D1
SAN DIEGO FRWY	SD	212	E3
SAN DIEGO FRWY	SD	215	D3
SAN DIEGO FRWY	SD	216	A3
SAN DIEGO FRWY	SDCO	V	A2
SAN DIEGO FRWY	SDCO	106	B3
SAN DIEGO FRWY	SDCO	111	D2
SAN DIEGO FRWY	SJC	202	C4
SAN DIEGO ST	KER	78	B2
SN DIEGO MSN RD	SD	214	D2
SAN DIMAS AV	LACO	U	B1

STREET	CO.	PAGE	GRID
SN DIMAS CYN RD	LACO	U	B1
SANDMOUND BLVD	CC	39	D5
SAN DOMINGO RD	CAL	41	B4
SAND RIDGE RD	ED	34	E5
SAND RIDGE RD	ED	40	E1
SANDRINI RD	KER	78	D4
SANDROCK RD	SD	214	B1
SANDROCK RD	SDCO	V	B3
SANDROCK RD	SDCO	106	D5
SAND SLOUGH RD	MCO	47	E5
SAND SLOUGH RD	MCO	48	A5
SANDY AV	KER	80	C1
SANDY DR	RCO	107	C1
SANDY RD	MON	66	B4
SANDY ST	KER	80	C1
SANDY HILLS RD	RCO	107	C1
SANDY MUSH RD	MCO	48	B5
SANDY PRAIRIE	HUM	15	E2
SAN FELIPE RD	SBT	54	E2
SAN FELIPE RD	SBT	55	A2
SAN FELIPE RD	SDCO	107	C2
SAN FELIPE RD	SCL	P	C3
SAN FELIPE RD	SCL	46	C4
SAN FERNANDO BL	BUR	179	C1
SAN FERNANDO BL	LA	179	C1
SAN FERNANDO RD	BUR	179	E2
SAN FERNANDO RD	GLEN	182	D1
SAN FERNANDO RD	LA	186	D1
SAN FERNANDO RD	LACO	89	B5
SAN FERNANDO RD	LACO	89	C5
SAN FERNANDO RD	LACO	97	E1
SAN FERNANDO RD	LACO	Q	C1
SANFORD RD	SON	37	D2
SANFORD RCH RD	MEN	31	B2
SN FRANCSQT CYN	LACO	89	B4
SAN GABRIEL BL	LACO	98	A2
SAN GABRIEL BL	LACO	R	C3
SAN GABRIEL FWY	LACO	98	A3
SAN GABRIEL FWY	LACO	S	E1
SAN GABRIEL RD	LACO	R	E3
SAN GABRIEL CYN	LACO	98	C1
SN GABRL CYN RD	LACO	R	E3
SN GABRL RIV FY	LACO	T	A1
SN GABRL RIV PY	LACO	R	C4
SN GORGONIO AV	RCO	100	A3
SN GUILLERMO RD	VEN	88	B2
SANHEDRIN RD	GLE	24	A4
SN IGNACIO RD	RCO	99	E5
SANITARIUM RD	NAPA	29	C2
SAN JACINTO RD	RCO	99	C4
SAN JACINTO ST	SBD	100	C2
SAN JACINTO RDG	RCO	100	A4
SAN JOAQUIN AV	FRCO	66	D3
SAN JOAQUIN AV	LAK	32	A3
SAN JOAQUIN RD	ORCO	T	E3
SAN JOAQUIN ST	S	160	D3
SN JQUIN HLS RD	NB	200	A4
SN JQN HLS TRNS COR	ORCO	T	E5
SN JQN HLS TRNS COR	ORCO	98	C5
SN JQN HLS TRNS COR	ORCO	200	C3
SAN JOSE RD	CLO	32	E2
SAN JOSE RD	SCR	P	B5
SN JOSE AVNALES	SLO	76	D3
SN JOSE L PANZA	SLO	76	C3
SN JOSE-STA MAR	SLO	76	B3
SN JS ST MAR LK	SLO	76	C3
SN JS ST MAR MT	SLO	76	D3
SAN JUAN AV	SAC	34	A5
SAN JUAN HWY	SBT	54	D2
SAN JUAN RD	MCO	56	B1
SAN JUAN RD	MON	54	C2
SAN JUAN CYN RD	SBT	54	D3
SAN JUSTO RD	SBT	54	D3
SANKEY RD	SUT	33	D4
SAN LUCAS RD	MON	65	C3
SAN LUIS BAY DR	SLO	76	A4
SAN LUISITO CK	SLO	75	E3
SAN LUISITO CK	SLO	76	A3
SAN MARCOS RD	SLO	76	A1
SAN MARCOS RD	SB	87	B4
SN MARCOS PS RD	SB	87	B3
SAN MARIN DR	MAR	L	A2
SAN MARTIN AV	SCL	P	E5
SAN MARTIN AV	SCL	54	D1
SN MARTNZ CHQT	LACO	89	A4
SN MARTNZ GD CN	LACO	89	A4
SAN MATEO AV	FRCO	56	D5
SAN MATEO AV	SBR	144	B1
SAN MATEO AV	SSF	144	B1
SAN MATEO RD	SDCO	105	E1
SAN MATEO ST	SBD	99	C2
SAN MIGUEL AV	SAL	171	C5
SAN MIGUEL DR	CC	M	A4
SAN MIGUEL DR	NB	200	C5
SN MGUEL CYN RD	MON	54	C3
SN MIGUELITO RD	SB	86	B3
SN PABLO AV	ALA	L	D4
SAN PABLO AV	ALA	45	D1
SAN PABLO AV	CC	L	C3
SAN PABLO AV	CC	38	C5
SAN PABLO AV	ELC	155	E4
SAN PABLO AV	O	157	E2
SAN PABLO AV	R	155	D2
SAN PABLO AV	SP	155	B1
SN PABLO DAM RD	CC	L	D3
SN PABLO DAM RD	CC	38	C5
SN PABLO DAM RD	SP	155	C1
SAN PASQUAL RD	SDCO	106	D3
SAN PASQUAL RD	SB	86	B3
SAN PASQUAL VLY	SDCO	106	E3
SAN PEDRO AV	SBD	84	C3
SAN PEDRO RD N	MAR	L	B3
SAN PEDRO RD N	MAR	38	B5

STREET	CO.	PAGE	GRID
SAN PEDRO RD N	MAR	139	C2
SAN PEDRO RD N	SR	139	C2
SAN PEDRO ST	LA	185	E5
SAN PEDRO ST	LA	186	A4
SAN PEDRO ST	LACO	S	C1
SAN RAFAEL AV	PAS	190	A4
SAN RAFAEL DR	RCO	100	C3
SN RAMON VLY BL	CC	M	B5
SN RAMON VLY BL	CC	46	A2
SANS BAKER RD	FRCO	58	C3
SN SIMEON CK RD	SLO	75	C1
SANTA ANA AV	CM	199	C3
SANTA ANA AV	NB	199	C3
SANTA ANA AV	ORCO	T	C4
SANTA ANA AV	ORCO	199	E1
SANTA ANA AV	SBD	99	A2
SANTA ANA BLVD	SA	196	A4
SANTA ANA FRWY	ANA	193	D4
SANTA ANA FRWY	LA	186	D3
SANTA ANA FRWY	LACO	98	A2
SANTA ANA FRWY	LACO	T	B1
SANTA ANA FRWY	ORCO	98	A2
SANTA ANA FRWY	ORCO	T	B1
SANTA ANA FRWY	SA	196	B2
SANTA ANA RD	VEN	88	A5
SANTA ANA ST	ANA	193	B2
STA ANA CYN RD	ORCO	98	C3
STA ANA CYN RD	ORCO	T	E2
STA ANA VLY RD	SBT	55	A3
SANTA ANITA AV	LACO	98	B2
SANTA ANITA AV	LACO	R	C4
SANTA ANITA AV	LACO	R	D2
SANTA ANITA RD	SBT	55	B3
STA BARBARA ST	SDCO	111	C1
STA BARBARA ST	STB	174	B2
STA BARBARA ST	SDCO	V	A3
STA BARB CYN RD	SB	87	D1
SANTA CLARA	A	159	A1
SANTA CLARA AV	O	158	B2
SANTA CLARA AV	SA	195	E2
SANTA CLARA AV	SA	196	A2
SANTA CLARA AV	VEN	88	B5
SANTA CLARA ST	SJ	152	C3
SANTA CLARA ST	SCL	P	C3
SANTA CLARA ST	SCL	46	B4
SANTA CLARA ST	VAL	134	B4
SANTA CLARA WY	SM	145	C3
SANTA CRUZ AV	SCL	P	A4
STA CRZ GUN CLB	MCO	55	E2
STA CRZ GUN CLB	MCO	56	A2
SANTA FE	MCO	48	C4
SANTA FE AV	KIN	67	E3
SANTA FE AV	LB	192	B2
SANTA FE AV	LA	186	C5
SANTA FE AV	LACO	R	A4
SANTA FE AV	LACO	S	D2
SANTA FE AV	MCO	48	D5
SANTA FE AV	SBD	81	B5
SANTA FE AV	SDCO	106	C2
SANTA FE AV	SJCO	47	D1
SANTA FE AV	STA	47	D2
SANTA FE BLVD	MAD	57	B2
SANTA FE DR	MCO	48	A3
SANTA FE DR	SDCO	106	C4
SANTA FE GRADE	FRCO	56	C3
SANTA FE GRADE	MCO	47	D4
SANTA FE RD	SBD	92	B4
SANTA FE ST	SBD	92	A1
SANTA FE WY	KER	78	B2
STA FE FIRE RD	SBD	91	A5
STA FE SPGS RD	LACO	R	C5
SANTA ISABEL	CM	199	D1
SANTA LUCIA	SBR	144	B4
SANTA LUCIA AV	CAR	168	B4
SANTA LUCIA AV	MCO	55	D1
SANTA LUCIA RD	SLO	76	A2
SANTA MARIA WY	SB	86	C1
STA MAR MESA RD	SB	86	C1
SANTA MONICA BL	BH	183	A2
SANTA MONICA BL	LA	180	C3
SANTA MONICA BL	LA	181	C5
SANTA MONICA BL	LA	182	A5
SANTA MONICA BL	LA	183	A2
SANTA MONICA BL	LACO	97	D2
SANTA MONICA BL	LACO	181	C5
SANTA MONICA BL	LACO	183	A2
SANTA MONICA BL	SMON	180	C5
SANTA MONICA FY	LA	184	A4
SANTA MONICA FY	LA	185	A4
SANTA MONICA FY	LA	186	A4
SANTA MONICA FY	LACO	97	C2
SANTA MONICA FY	LACO	Q	C4
SANTA MONICA FY	SMON	180	B5
SANTA PAULA FWY	VEN	88	C5
SANTA PAULA ST	VEN	88	C5
STA RITA GRADE	MCO	56	B1
SANTA RITA RD	ALA	M	B5
SANTA RITA RD	ALA	46	B2
STA RITA OLD CK	SLO	75	E2
SANTA ROSA AV	SON	37	E2
SANTA ROSA AV	STR	131	D4
SANTA ROSA RD	INY	60	D5
SANTA ROSA RD	RCO	99	B4
SANTA ROSA RD	SBD	91	D4
SANTA ROSA RD	SB	86	C3
SANTA ROSA RD	VEN	88	D5
SANTA ROSA ST	SNLO	172	C2
STA ROSA CK RD	SLO	75	C2
STA ROSA MTN TK	RCO	100	D5
SANTA TERESA BL	SCL	P	C4
SANTA TERESA BL	SCL	46	B5
SANTA TERESA BL	SCL	54	D2
SANTA YSABEL RD	SLO	75	E3
SANTIAGO BLVD	ORA	194	E2
SANTIAGO BLVD	ORCO	98	C3
SANTIAGO BLVD	ORCO	T	E2
SANTIAGO CYN RD	ORCO	98	D3
SANTIAGO CYN RD	ORCO	T	E2
SN TIMTEO CY RD	RCO	99	D2
SN TIMTEO CY RD	SBD	99	D2
SAN TOMAS EXPWY	SJ	150	E5
SAN TOMAS EXPWY	SCL	P	B3
SAN TOMAS EXPWY	SCLR	150	E2
SAN TOMAS EXPWY	SCLR	151	A1
SANTOS AV	SJCO	47	C1
SANTOS RD	SB	86	D3
SANTOS ST	SB	86	B1
SAN VICENTE BL	LA	180	A3
SAN VICENTE BL	LA	183	E2
SAN VICENTE BL	LA	184	B3
SAN VICENTE BL	LACO	97	C2
SAN VICENTE BL	LACO	Q	D4
SAN VICENTE RD	MON	55	A5
SAN VICENTE RD	MON	65	A1
SAN VICENTE RD	SDCO	107	A4
SAN VINCENTE AV	SAL	171	B4
SAPAQUE RD	MON	65	C5
SARATOGA AV	KER	80	E1
SARATOGA AV	SJ	150	E5
SARATOGA AV	SCL	P	A4
SARATOGA AV	SCLR	150	E5
SARATOGA AV	SCLR	151	A4
SARATOGA AV	SCL	46	A5
SARATGA-LS G RD	SCL	P	A4
SARTGA-LS GATOS	SCL	46	A5
SARATOGA SPGS	LAK	31	C2
SARATOGA SPG RD	SBD	72	D5
SARATOGA SPG RD	SBD	82	D1
SARATOGA-SVL RD	SCL	P	A4
SARATOGA-SVL RD	SCL	45	E4
SARATOGA-SVL RD	SVL	149	D2
SARBO RD	MCO	55	D1
SARDINE LAKE RD	SIE	27	A4
SARGENT RD	SJCO	40	A4
SARGENTS RD	MON	65	E4
SARGENTS RD	MON	66	A4
SARIDA AV	KER	79	C4
SARINA RD	DN	1	D3
SARON FRUIT COL	TEH	18	D4
SASIA RD	KER	79	B4
SATICOY AV	VEN	88	B5
SATICOY ST	LA	177	E2
SATICOY ST	LA	178	C1
SAUGUS VNTRA RD	LACO	89	A4
SAVANA	MCO	48	D5
SAVIERS RD	OXN	176	C5
SAWMILL	INY	51	C4
SAW MILL RD	ALP	36	B5
SAWMILL RD	BUT	25	C3
SAWMILL RD	KER	69	C5
SAWMILL RD	KER	79	C1
SAWMILL RD	MNO	50	E2
SAW MILL CREEK	SBT	66	B1
SAWMILL CRSSOVR	MNO	51	B1
SAWMILL CTO	MNO	50	D2
SAWMILL FLAT RD	TUO	41	C4
SAWMILL MDWS RD	MNO	51	B1
SAWTELLE AV	SUT	33	C3
SAWTELLE BLVD	CUL	188	A1
SAWTELLE BLVD	LA	180	C3
SAWTELLE BLVD	LA	188	B2
SAWTOOTH PEAK	KER	80	C1
SAWYER AV	STA	47	D1
SAWYERS BAR RD	SIS	11	C1
SAYLOR RD	STA	47	E3
SAYRE ST	LACO	Q	C1
SCALA LN	SIS	4	B4
SCALES RD	YUB	26	C4
SCANDIA RD	SOL	M	B1
SCANDIA RD	SOL	39	A3
SCARFACE RD	SIS	3	E5
SCARFACE RD	SIS	4	A5
SCARLT BUGLE RD	RCO	100	C5
SCARONI AV	KER	78	B2
SCENIC DR	STA	47	D2
SCENIC DR	MDO	162	D2
SCENIC DR	STA	162	D2
SCENIC RD	CAR	168	B4
SCHAAD RD	COL	32	D2
SCHADD RD	CAL	41	C2
SCHAEFFER RD	SB	87	D1
SCHAFER AV	TEH	18	E5
SCHAGLE RD	SUT	33	C3
SCHALLOCK RD	KER	78	C5
SCHARTZ RD	IMP	109	B4
SCHATZ RD	KER	79	C4
SCHEAFER	MPA	49	B3
SCHEIBER RD	SUT	33	D3
SCHELL RD	IMP	112	C3
SCHILLING	MPA	48	E2
SCHILLING AV	FRCO	67	B1
SCHLAG RD	SUT	33	C2
SCHMIDT DR	RCO	107	A1
SCHMIDT RD	MCO	47	C5
SCHOBER LN	INY	51	D4
SCHOOL RD	IMP	112	D5
SCHOOL RD	MNO	50	E2
SCHOOL RD	MNO	51	A2
SCHOOL ST	HUM	15	E2
SCHOOL ST	MEN	30	C3
SCHOOL ST	U	123	C2
SCHOOLER RD	SBD	101	D1
SCHOOL HOUSE RD	LAS	21	C1
SCHOOL HOUSE RD	MPA	49	A4
SCHLHOUSE HL RD	SIS	4	D3
SCHOTT RD	BUT	25	C2
SCHOTT RD	LAS	14	B3
SCHROEDER AV	SUT	33	C1
SCHROEDER MINE	SIS	3	E4
SCHUETTE RD	LAK	31	C2
SCHULMEYER RD	SIS	4	A5
SCHULTE RD	SJCO	46	E2
SCHULTZ RD	KER	80	D5
SCHUSTER RD	KER	68	B5
SCIARONE RD	ED	35	B5
SCOFIELD AV	KER	78	A1
SCOTIA PINES CIR	NEV	127	A3
SCOTT AV	LACO	R	D5
SCOTT BLVD	SCL	P	B3
SCOTT BLVD	SCLR	151	A2
SCOTT RD	CAL	41	C3
SCOTT RD	LAS	27	E2
SCOTT RD	MPA	49	C3
SCOTT RD	RCO	99	C4
SCOTT RD	SAC	40	C1
SCOTT RD	SIS	5	D2
SCOTT BAR RD	SIS	3	D4
SCOTT CREEK RD	ALA	P	B2
SCOTT CREEK RD	ALA	46	B3
SCOTT DAM RD	LAK	23	C5
SCOTT FORBES RD	YUB	34	A1
SCOTT LUMBER RD	SHA	19	C1
SCOTT MTN RD	SIS	11	E2
SCOTT MTN RD	TRI	11	E2
SCOTT RIVER RD	SIS	3	B4
SCOTTS CREEK RD	LAK	31	C3
SCOTTS FLAT RD	NEV	34	D1
SCOTTS VLY RD	LAK	31	C2
SCOTTS VLY RD	SCR	54	A1
SCOTT VALLEY DR	SCR	P	A5
SCOTT VALLEY RD	SIS	3	D5
SCOTT VALLEY RD	SIS	11	D1
SCOTT VLY AIRPT	SIS	3	D5
SCOUT RD	BUT	19	D5
SCOUT ST	SHA	18	B3
SCOVELL AV	RCO	99	E4
SCRANTON AV	TUL	68	D3
SEAL BEACH BLVD	ORCO	98	A4
SEAL BEACH BLVD	ORCO	T	A3
SEARLES STA RD	KER	80	E2
SEARLES STA RD	SBD	80	E2
SEARLES STA CTO	SBD	80	E2
SEARS RD	LAS	21	B4
SEARS POINT RD	SOL	38	C4
SEARS POINT RD	SOL	134	B2
SEARS POINT RD	SON	L	B2
SEARS POINT RD	VAL	134	B2
SEASIDE AV	LA	191	D3
SEASIDE BLVD	LACO	S	C3
SEATTLE AV	KIN	67	D3
SEA VIEW DR	IMP	108	C2
SEAVIEW RD	SON	37	A1
SEAVW QUARRY RD	SON	37	B1
SEAWARD AV	VENT	175	D3
SEBASTIAN RD	KER	78	E5
SEBASTIAN RD	KER	79	A5
SEBASTOPOL AV	STR	131	C4
SEBASTOPOL FRWY	STR	131	B4
SEBASTOPOL FRWY	SON	131	B4
SEBASTOPOL RD	SON	131	B4
SECO ST	PAS	190	A3
SECOND ST	C	124	B5
SECRETARIAT RD	KER	79	B4
SECRET SPGS RD	SIS	4	E3
SECTION OLD-			
-RED BLUFF RD	PLU	19	E3
SEE CANYON RD	SLO	75	E4
SEE CANYON RD	SLO	76	A4
SEE VEE LN	INY	51	D4
SEIAD CREEK	SIS	3	B3
SEIAD OAKS RD	SIS	3	B3
SEIDNER	SJCO	47	D1
SEIGLER CYN RD	LAK	32	A4
SEIGLER SPGS RD	LAK	31	E4
SEIGLER SPGS			
-NORTH RD	LAK	32	A4
SELLERS AV	CC	M	D4
SELLERS AV	CC	39	C5
SELMADOLPH ST	SBD	91	E3
SELVA RD	DPT	202	A4
SEMINARY AV	ALA	L	D5
SEMINARY AV	ALA	45	D1
SEMINARY AV	O	159	E1
SEMINARY DR	MAR	140	C4
SEMINARY DR	MV	140	C4
SENATOR WASH RD	IMP	110	E5
SENECA RD	PLU	20	B5
SENECA RD	SBD	91	B4
SENECA RD	SBD	91	E3
SENILIS AV	SBD	100	C2
SENTER RD	SJ	152	E5
SENTER RD	SCL	P	C3
SENTER RD	SCL	46	B4
SEPULVEDA BLVD	CUL	188	A1
SEPULVEDA BLVD	ELS	189	C3
SEPULVEDA BLVD	LA	180	D3
SEPULVEDA BLVD	LA	183	A5
SEPULVEDA BLVD	LA	188	C4
SEPULVEDA BLVD	LA	189	C3
SEPULVEDA BLVD	LACO	97	C1
SEPULVEDA BLVD	LACO	Q	C2
SEPULVEDA BLVD	LACO	S	B1
SEPULVEDA BLVD	LACO	180	B2
SEPULVEDA BLVD	MB	189	C3
SEQUOIA BLVD	KER	80	B4
SEQUOIA RD	FRCO	58	D3
SEQUOIA RD	HUM	16	C4
SERENADE DR	SBD	80	E1
SERENE DR	SHA	18	B2
SERENO DR	VAL	134	C2
SERFAS CLUB DR	RCO	U	E5
SERFAS CLUB DR	RCO	98	E3
SERPA LN	SIS	3	D5
SERPA LN	SOL	39	B2
SERRAMONTE BLVD	SMCO	L	B5
SERRAMONTE BLVD	SMCO	N	B1
SERRANO RD	VEN	96	C2
SERVICE RD	SIE	26	C4
SERVICE RD	STA	47	C3
SESPE ST	VEN	88	D5
SESPE RIVER RD	VEN	88	B3
SEVEN HILLS RD	ALA	L	E5
SEVEN HILLS RD	ALA	M	A5
SEVEN MILE LN	BUT	25	A4
SEVEN MILE RD	SLO	77	B3
SEVEN MI SLOUGH	HUM	15	D2
SEVEN OAK RD	SBD	100	A1
SEVERE RD	IMP	109	A3
SEWARD DR	HUM	16	C4
SEXTON	SJCO	47	C1
SEYMOUR RD	SUT	33	B4
SEYMOUR CK RD	VEN	88	C2
SHABELL LN	INY	59	E3
SHACKELFORD RD	STA	47	B2
SHADOW CYN RD	SLO	75	E2
SHADOW MTN RD	SBD	83	D2
SHADOW MTN RD	SBD	90	E2
SHADOW MTN RD	SBD	91	A2
SHADOW MTN RD	SBD	101	D1
SHADY LN	SR	139	A4
SHADY DELL RD	SIS	5	A3
SHAFFER RD	MCO	48	B3
SHAFFER ST	ORA	194	D3
SHAFTER AV	KER	78	B2
SHAFTER RD	KER	78	C4
SHAIN AV	FRCO	56	B2
SHAKELEY LN	AMA	40	D2
SHAKE RIDGE RD	AMA	40	E2
SHAKE RIDGE RD	AMA	41	A2
SHALE RD	KER	77	E4
SHAMROCK RD	SIS	4	A4
SHANDON CEM RD	SLO	76	D1
SHANDON-SN JUAN	SLO	76	D1
SHANK RD	IMP	109	B4
SHANNON DR	SBD	101	D1
SHANNONDALE RD	LACO	89	E4
SHANNON VLY RD	LACO	89	E4
SHARON RD	MCO	55	E2
SHARON RD	YOL	136	A1
SHARP PARK RD	SMCO	N	B1
SHARP PARK RD	SMCO	45	B2
SHASTA AV	FRCO	56	E3
SHASTA AV	FRCO	57	A3
SHASTA BLVD	TEH	18	E5
SHASTA BLVD	TEH	24	E1
SHASTA ST	VAL	134	D4
SHASTA WY	C	124	B4
SHASTA WY	KLAM	5	C1
SHASTA CO RD	MOD	13	E3
SHA DAM ACCS RD	SHA	18	B1
SHA SPG MCCLOUD	SIS	12	D2
SHASTA VIEW DR	MOD	14	E1
SHASTA VIEW DR	SHA	18	C2
SHASTA VISTA DR	SIS	4	C5
SHATTUCK AV	B	156	A2
SHATTUCK AV	O	156	A4
SHAVES AV	SBD	91	C1
SHAW AV	FRCO	57	C3
SHAWMUT RD	TUO	41	C5
SHAWMUT RD	TUO	48	C1
SHAW PIT RD	MOD	14	B2
SHAWS FLAT RD	SNRA	163	A2
SHAWS FLAT RD	TUO	163	A2
SHAWS FLAT RD	TUO	41	C5
SHAWS FT JMSTWN	TUO	41	C5
SHAY CREEK RD	ALP	36	B5
SHEE CAMP RD	MNO	51	B2
SHEEP CREEK RD	SBD	90	E4
SHEEP CK SPG RD	SBD	82	E1
SHEEP CK TK TR	SBD	90	E5
SHEEP MTN RD	SIS	5	A3
SHEEP RANCH RD	CAL	41	B3
SHEEPY CREEK RD	SIS	5	B2
SHEEPY ISLND RD	SIS	5	B2
SHEFFIELD RD	SUT	33	C3
SHEKELL	VEN	88	D5
SHELBY ST	KER	78	B5
SHELDON RD	SAC	39	E2
SHELDON ST	LACO	Q	C2
SHELL AV	CC	L	E3
SHELL AV	MCO	56	A1
SHELL BLVD	CC	38	E5
SHELL BLVD	FCTY	145	D2
SHELL RD	FRCO	66	D2
SHELL RD	TUO	41	C5
SHELL CANYON RD	IMP	111	C3
SHELLCO RD	KER	67	C5
SHELL GULCH RD	SIS	11	D1
SHELL NO 2	YUB	33	D1
SHELLEY	SJCO	40	D4
SHELLEY RD	SIS	4	B4
SHELTER COVE RD	HUM	22	A1
SHELTER ISLD DR	SDCO	V	A3
SHELTON RD	SBD	101	D1
SHELTON RD	SJCO	40	C4
SHELTN BUTTE RD	HUM	10	D3
SHENANDOAH SCHL	AMA	40	E1
SHEPHERD AV	FRCO	57	C2
SHEPHERD RD	MOD	14	B3
SHEPPARD RD	VEN	88	C5
SHERIDAN	FRCO	58	A4
SHERIDAN RD	ALA	P	B2
SHERIDAN RD	ALA	46	B3
SHERIDAN RD	SLO	76	B5
SHERMAN RD	SBD	100	C2
SHERMAN WY	LA	177	B1
SHERMAN WY	LA	178	C1
SHERMAN WY	LACO	97	C1
SHERMAN ISLAND-			
-E LEVEE RD	SAC	M	D2
SHERWIN CK RD	MNO	50	E2
SHERWOOD AV	KER	77	E1
SHERWOOD AV	KER	78	B1
SHERWOOD BLVD	TEH	24	E1
SHERWOOD DR	SAL	171	C3
SHERWOOD RD	MEN	22	E4
SHERWD RNCHERIA	MEN	22	D4
SHETLAND CT	CAL	41	B5
SHIELDS AV	FRCO	56	A3
SHIELDS AV	FRCO	57	A3
SHIELDS RD	SHA	17	C3
SHIELLS RD	STA	47	C4
SHILOH RD	SOL	39	B4
SHILOH RD	SON	37	E1
SHIMMINS RDG RD	MEN	22	E4
SHINGLE RD S	ED	40	C1
SHINGLETWN DUMP	SHA	19	B3
SHINGLETOWN RDG	SHA	19	A3
SHINN RANCH RD	LAS	21	D2
SHIPPEE RD	BUT	25	C4
SHIPPEE RD	MCO	48	B5
SHIRK RD	TUL	68	A1
SHIRLAND	PLA	34	C4
SHIRLEY RD	CAL	41	A5
SHIRLEY MDWS RD	KER	79	C1
SHIRT TAIL CYN	PLA	34	D2
SHIVELY RD	HUM	16	A3
SHOEMAKE AV	STA	47	B2
SHOEMAKER AV	LACO	T	B1
SHOEMAKER RD	HUM	10	C4
SHOEMAKER RD	SIS	4	E4
SHOP RD	MNO	42	E1
SHOP ST	INY	70	B2
SHORE RD	SBT	54	E2
SHORELINE DR	LB	192	D3
SHORELINE DR	STB	174	C5
SHORELINE HWY	MAR	L	A4
SHORELINE HWY	MAR	37	D4
SHORELINE HWY	MEN	22	C3
SHORELINE HWY	MEN	30	C4
SHORELINE HWY	MAR	140	B4
SHORT AV	KER	91	C3
SHORT LN	TUO	163	C3
SHORT RD	KER	78	A5
SHORT CREEK RD	MEN	23	B2
SHORTYS WELL RD	INY	72	A2
SHOSHONE VLY RD	SBD	93	B5
SHOSHONI LOOP	SHA	13	E4
SHOUP AV	LA	177	B3
SHOUP RD	SHA	18	A3
SHOWER PASS RD	HUM	16	B2
SHRODE LN	LAS	21	C3
SHULTZ RD	MCO	56	C1
SHUMWAY RCH RD	RCO	100	D5
SHUTE MTN RD	BUT	25	E3
SHUTT ST	DN	1	D3
SHY ST	MCO	47	C5
SHY ST	MCO	55	C1
SICARD FLAT RD	YUB	34	A1
SIDDING RD	KER	78	B3
SIDEWINDER RD	IMP	110	C5
SIDEWINDER RD	RCO	102	C3
SIDEWINDER RD	SBD	91	D2
SIDNEY GULCH RD	TRI	17	D1
SIERRA AV	FRCO	57	C3
SIERRA AV	NAP	133	A1
SIERRA AV	SBD	99	A2
SIERRA DR	MPA	48	E1
SIERRA DR	MDO	162	B4
SIERRA HWY	KER	80	A5
SIERRA HWY	KER	90	A1
SIERRA HWY	LACO	89	C4
SIERRA PKWY	CAL	41	D3
SIERRA RD	LAS	20	E3
SIERRA RD	SCL	P	C3
SIERRA RD	SCL	46	B4
SIERRA RD	STA	47	E1
SIERRA ST	RENO	130	B2
SIERRA WY	KER	69	D5
SIERRA WY	KER	79	D1
SIERRA WY	SBDO	207	D3
SIERRA WY	SBD	99	C1
SIERRA WY	TUL	58	A5
SIERRA CTR DR	SHA	13	E4
SRA COLLEGE BL	PLA	34	B4
SRA COLLEGE DR	NEV	127	C1
SIERRA DEL SOL	RCO	100	E3
SIERRA MADRE AV	LACO	98	C1
SIERRA MADRE AV	LACO	U	A1
SIERRA MADRE BL	LACO	98	A1
SIERRA MADRE BL	LACO	R	C3
SIERRA MADRE BL	LACO	R	C2
SIERRA VISTA AV	TEH	24	D1
SIERRA VISTA ST	KER	80	C1
SIERRA VLY RD	PLU	27	C3
SIEVERS RD	SOL	39	B1
SIGNAL RD	IMP	111	E4
SIGNAL BUTTE RD	LAS	20	E1
SIGNAL RIDGE RD	MEN	30	D3
SIKES RD	SOL	39	C2
SILAXO AV	FRCO	56	C2
SILLS RD	COL	32	D3
SILSBEE RD	IMP	112	A3
SILURIAN LK RD	SBD	83	B2
SILVA RD	MPA	49	B3

269
SILVA RD
STONE VALLEY RD

STREET INDEX

STREET	CO.	PAGE	GRID
SILVA RD	SIS	4	C3
SILVERA CT	BUT	25	C3
SILVERADO TR	NAP	133	E4
SILVERADO TR	NAPA	29	A1
SILVERADO TR	NAPA	38	C2
SILVER BAR RD	MPA	49	B4
SILVER BRDG RD	SHA	18	D2
SILVER CYN RD	INY	51	E4
SILVRADO CYN RD	ORCO	98	E4
SILVER CREEK RD	MOH	85	D4
SILVER CREEK RD	SCL	P	C5
SILVER CREEK RD	SCL	46	B4
SILVER CK CMPGD	ALP	42	C1
SILVER HILL RD	ALP	36	C5
SILVER KING RD	SHA	18	B2
SILVER LAKE BL	LA	182	E4
SILVER LAKE BL	LA	185	D1
SILVER LAKE BL	LACO	Q	E1
SILVER LAKE RD	LAS	20	B3
SILVER BAR RD	MPA	49	B4
SILVER PUFF DR	KER	89	E3
SILVER QUEEN RD	KER	79	E5
SILVER QUEEN RD	KER	80	A5
SILVR RAPIDS RD	CAL	40	D4
SILVR STRAND BL	SDCO	V	B4
SILVR STRAND BL	SDCO	111	D2
SILVERTHORN RD	SHA	18	D1
SLVR TIP CPGRD	ALP	42	A2
SILVER VLY RD	SBD	92	B1
SILVEYVILLE RD	SOL	39	B2
SIMAS ST	SB	86	B1
SIMMERHORN RD	SAC	40	A3
SIMMLER RD	SLO	77	A2
SIMMLR BITTRWTR	SLO	76	E1
SIMMLR BITTRWTR	SLO	77	A1
SIMMLR SN DIEGO	SLO	77	C4
SIMMONS RD	LAK	23	C5
SIMMONS RD	SHA	18	B2
SIMMONS RD	STA	47	C3
SIMPSON LN	MEN	22	C5
SIMPSON LN	YUB	33	D2
SIMPSON RD	IMP	109	B3
SIMPSON RD	RCO	99	D4
SIMPSON RD	TEH	24	C1
SIMPSN DATNI RD	YUB	33	D2
SIMS RD	TUO	41	C5
SIMS RD	TUO	48	C1
SIMS CREEK RD	TRI	17	C3
SIMS LOOKOUT RD	SHA	12	C4
SINCLAIR FRWY	ALA	46	A3
SINCLAIR FRWY	SJ	151	D5
SINCLAIR FRWY	SCL	46	A3
SINCLAIR FRWY	SCL	151	D5
SINCLAIR RD	IMP	109	A3
SINEX AV	PAC	167	B3
SINGLE SPRINGS	SIS	4	E5
SINGLETON RD	RCO	99	D2
SINGLE TREE	SBD	100	E2
SINGLETREE DR	CAL	41	A5
SINGLEY RD	HUM	15	E2
SINNARD AV	SUT	33	C1
SINTON RD	SB	86	B1
SIR F DRAKE BL	MAR	37	E4
SIR F DRAKE BL	MAR	38	A5
SIR F DRAKE BL	MAR	L	A3
SIR F DRAKE BL	ROSS	139	A4
SIR F DRAKE BL	SANS	139	A4
SISK RD	STA	47	C2
SISKIYOU AV	FRCO	57	A3
SISKIYOU AV	FRCO	67	A2
SITES-LODOGA RD	COL	24	B5
SITES-LODOGA RD	COL	32	B1
SIX MILE RD	CAL	41	B4
SKAGGS ISLND RD	SOL	38	C3
SKAGGS SPGS RD	SON	31	C5
SKIDOO RD	INY	71	D1
SKI HILL RD	MOD	7	C5
SKI RUN BLVD	SLT	129	C3
SKITTONE RD	STA	47	D2
SKULL FLAT RD	CAL	41	B2
SKUNK RANCH RD	CAL	41	C4
SKYLINE BLVD	ALA	L	D4
SKYLINE BLVD	ALA	45	D1
SKYLINE BLVD	KIN	67	A3
SKYLINE BLVD	SMCO	N	B1
SKYLINE BLVD	SMCO	N	C2
SKYLINE BLVD	SMCO	45	C3
SKYLINE BLVD	SCL	N	E4
SKYLINE DR	KER	79	B4
SKYLINE DR	MONT	167	C4
SKYLINE DR	MON	53	D3
SKYLINE DR	SBD	100	E1
SKYLINE DR	SDCO	V	D4
SKYLINE DR	SDCO	111	D1
SKYLINE MTWY	PLU	20	D4
SKYLINE RD	KER	77	E3
SKYLINE RD	KIN	67	A3
SKYLINE RD	SON	31	A5
SKY LINE DR	VAL	134	E3
SKYLINE FRST DR	MONT	167	C5
SKYLINE FRST DR	MONT	168	C1
SKYLINE FRST DR	MON	53	D4
SKYLINE RCH RD	SBD	100	D1
SKY RANCH RD	MON	54	C5
SKY VALLEY RD	RCO	100	E3
SKY VALLEY RD	SOL	38	D4
SKY VIEW DR	IMP	108	C2
SKYVIEW RD	MAD	57	C2
SKYWAY	BUT	25	C2
SKYWAY DR	SB	86	B1
SKYWAY RD	BUT	19	D5
SKYWAY RD	BUT	25	D1
SLACKS CYN RD	MON	66	B3
SLASH X RCH RD	SBD	91	C2
SLATE RD	YUB	26	A4
SLATE CREEK RD	SHA	12	B4
SLATE CREEK RD	TRI	11	D5
SLATE GULCH	MPA	48	E3
SLATE MTN RD	TRI	12	A4
SLATE MTN LO RD	SHA	12	B4
SLATER AV	ORCO	T	B3
SLATER RD	HUM	16	B2
SLATE RANGE	INY	71	B2
SLATER BUTTE LO	SIS	3	A3
SLAUGHTERHOUSE	MPA	49	B3
SLAUSON AV	CUL	188	D3
SLAUSON AV	LACO	97	D2
SLAUSON AV	LACO	Q	E4
SLAUSON AV	LACO	R	C5
SLAUSON AV	LACO	188	D3
SLAYTON RD	IMP	109	C5
SLIGER MINE RD	ED	34	D3
SLOAT BLVD	SFCO	L	B5
SLOAT BLVD	SFCO	45	B2
SLOAT RD	PLU	26	E2
SLOUGH RD	SIS	4	B5
SLOUGH RD	SIS	12	B1
SLOUGHHOUSE RD	SAC	40	B2
SLOVER AV	SBD	99	A2
SLUG GULCH RD	ED	41	A1
SLUSSER RD	SON	37	D2
SLY PARK RD	ED	35	A5
SMALLEY RD	FRCO	57	E1
SMARTS RANCH RD	SBD	92	B5
SMARTVILLE RD	YUB	34	A1
SMITH	YUB	33	E1
SMITH AV	FRCO	57	E4
SMITH AV	KER	78	B1
SMITH AV	KER	70	A5
SMITH GRADE	SCR	53	D1
SMITH RD	MON	65	C5
SMITH RD	SBD	80	E1
SMITH MTN RD	MON	66	B3
SMITH PK LKOUT	TUO	48	E1
SMITH PK LKOUT	TUO	49	A1
SMITHNECK RD	SIE	27	D4
SMITHSON RD	SBD	91	B2
SMITH STA RD	MPA	48	E1
SMITH STA RD	MPA	49	A1
SMITH STA RD	TUO	48	E1
SMITH STA RD	TUO	49	A1
SMITH TALC RD	SBD	73	B5
SMOKE CK RCH RD	LAS	21	D3
SMOKE TREE RD	SBD	90	E4
SNAVELY RD	DN	1	E3
SNEATH LN	SMCO	N	B1
SNEATH LN	SMCO	45	B2
SNEATH LN	SBR	144	A2
SNELL ST	SNRA	163	B3
SNELLING HWY	MER	170	A3
SNELLING RD	MCO	48	C3
SNELL VALLEY RD	NAPA	32	B5
SNOW RD	KER	77	E2
SNOW RD	KER	78	C2
SNOW ST	KER	79	E1
SNOW ST	KER	80	A1
SNOW CAMP RD	HUM	10	B5
SNOWDN HOVEY GL	SIS	4	C4
SNOWS RD	ED	35	A5
SNOWSHOE SPGS	ALP	36	B4
SNOW TENT RD	NEV	26	D5
SNYDER RD	IMP	109	C5
SNYDER RD	MCO	47	C5
SOAP CREEK RD	SIS	3	E5
SOBOBA RD	RCO	99	E3
SOBOBA ST	RCO	100	A4
SOBRANTE AV	CC	L	D3
SOBRANTE AV	CC	38	C5
SODA BAY RD	LAK	31	D3
SODA CANYON RD	NAPA	38	C2
SODA CREEK RD	SHA	12	C3
SODA LAKE RD	KER	78	A5
SODA LAKE RD	KER	87	E1
SODA LAKE RD	SLO	77	C5
SODA LAKE CK RD	SLO	77	B3
SODA LK SN DIEG	SLO	77	B3
SODA LK SN DIEG	SLO	77	D4
SODA ROCK LN W	SON	31	D5
SODA SPRINGS RD	BUT	19	D5
SODA SPRINGS RD	SON	30	E5
SOETH RD	GLE	24	B5
SOLANO AV	ALA	L	D4
SOLANO AV	NAP	133	A2
SOLANO AV	VAL	134	C5
SOLANO WY	CC	M	A3
SOLDIER MTN DR	SHA	13	D3
SOLDIER MTN RD	SHA	13	D3
SOLEDAD DR	MONT	167	D4
SOLEDAD DR	MONT	168	D1
SOLEDAD DR	MON	53	E4
SOLEDAD FRWY	SDCO	V	B2
SOLEDAD FRWY	SDCO	106	C5
SOLEDAD CYN RD	LACO	89	E4
SOLEDAD MTN RD	SD	211	B4
SOLOMAN RD	SB	86	B1
SOMAVIA RD	MON	54	D4
SOMEO ST	SB	86	B1
SOMERSVILLE RD	CC	M	B3
SOMERSVILLE RD	CC	39	B5
SONOMA AV	FRCO	56	D4
SONOMA AV	FRCO	66	D1
SONOMA AV	STR	131	E3
SONOMA BLVD	NAPA	L	D2
SONOMA BLVD	VAL	134	C4
SONOMA HWY	SNMA	132	C3
SONOMA MTN RD	SON	38	A2
SONORA	SJCO	40	D5
SONORA	STA	48	A1
SONORA RD	STA	40	D5
SONORA RD	STA	47	D1
SONORA RD	STA	48	A1
SOPHIE ST	RCO	99	C4
SOQUEL AV	SC	169	D3
SOQUEL DR	SCR	54	A2
SOQUEL-SAN JOSE	SCR	54	A2
SORENSON RD	HUM	16	B3
SORENSON RD	RCO	107	B1
SORREL WY	CAL	41	A4
SORRENTO VLY RD	SDCO	106	C4
SORRENTO VLY RD	SDCO	V	A1
SOSCOL AV	NAP	133	D3
SOSCOL RD	NAPA	38	D3
SOTO ST	LA	186	D5
SOTO ST	LACO	R	A4
SOULE LN	SIS	4	C4
SOULSBYVILLE RD	TUO	41	D5
SOUTH AV	FRCO	56	E4
SOUTH AV	FRCO	57	B4
SOUTH AV	MCO	47	E4
SOUTH AV	MCO	48	A4
SOUTH AV	TEH	24	E2
SOUTH DR	SF	141	B4
SOUTH RD	MNO	51	C1
SOUTH RD	BLMT	145	C5
SOUTH ST	ANA	193	B3
SOUTH ST	ANA	194	A2
SOUTH ST	GLE	24	D3
SOUTH ST	LACO	98	A3
SOUTH ST	LACO	S	D1
SOUTH ST	LACO	T	B1
SOUTH ST	ORCO	T	C2
SOUTH ST	RED	122	B2
SOUTH ST	SBD	90	E4
SOUTH ST	SNLO	172	B4
SOUTH ST	SHA	18	C3
SOUTHAM RD	COL	24	E5
SOUTHAMPTON RD	BEN	153	A3
SOUTH BANK RD	DN	1	E3
S BNK CHETKO RD	CUR	1	D2
SOUTH BAY FRWY	SDCO	V	D4
SOUTH BAY FRWY	SDCO	111	D1
SOUTHBAY FRWY	SVL	148	C4
SOUTHERN AV	SIS	12	D2
S EMBARCADRO FY	SF	142	E4
S EMBARCADRO FY	SFCO	45	C2
SOUTH FORK DR	TUL	58	E5
SOUTH FORK DR	TUL	68	E1
SOUTH FORK DR	TUL	69	A1
SOUTH FORK RD	DN	1	E4
SOUTH FORK RD	DN	2	A4
SOUTH FORK RD	SHA	18	B3
SOUTH FORK RD	SIS	2	E3
SOUTH FORK RD	TRI	10	D5
SOUTH FORK RD	TRI	16	E2
SOUTH FORK RD	TUO	41	D4
S FK LOOKOUT RD	SHA	18	B2
S FK MAD RIV RD	TRI	17	B5
S FORK MTN RD	LAS	8	B3
S FORK MTN RD	TRI	16	E3
S FK SALMON RIV	SIS	11	A2
SOUTH GRADE RD	SDCO	107	A2
SOUTH GRADE RD	SDCO	107	B5
SOUTH LNDG RD	MNO	51	A3
SOUTHSIDE DR	MPA	63	B2
SOUTHSIDE RD	SBT	54	E3
SOUTHSIDE RD	SBT	55	A3
SOUTH VLY FRWY	SCL	54	C1
SW EXPWY	SCL	P	B3
SOUTHWORTH RD	CAL	40	D4
SOUZA RD	TRI	17	A4
SOWLES RD	SJCO	40	B3
SPA RD	IMP	108	E1
SPACER DR	TUL	68	B2
SPANGLE GOLD RD	MAD	49	C5
SPANGLER RD	KER	68	C5
SPANISH DAGGER	RCO	100	C5
SPANISH DRY DGN	ED	34	C5
SPANISH RCH RD	PLU	26	B1
SPANSH RCH BUTE	PLU	25	E2
SPANSH RCH BUTE	PLU	26	A2
SPANISH VALLEY	NAPA	32	C5
SPARKS RD	MCO	47	C5
SPARKS RANCH RD	SOL	39	B1
SPAULDING RD	LAS	20	D1
SPEAR AV	HUM	10	A5
SPECIMAN SPG RD	MAD	49	B4
SPENCE RD	MON	54	B4
SPENCER LN	SON	32	A5
SPENCER LN	SON	38	A1
SPENCER RD	COL	24	E5
SPENCER RD	STA	47	A2
SPENCEVILLE RD	NEV	34	B2
SPENCEVILLE RD	YUB	33	E3
SPERRY AV	STA	47	B3
SPERRY RD	STA	47	E3
SPGNOLI MINE RD	AMA	41	A2
SPICER RD	COL	33	A3
SPILLWAY RD	MNO	51	B2
SPINELLI RD	MAD	49	C5
SPINK RD	CAL	41	B2
SPOONER RD	LAS	8	A4
SPOONER RD	LAS	14	E4
SPORTS ARENA BL	SD	212	D5
SPORTS ARENA BL	SD	213	A5
SPRECKELS BLVD	MON	54	C4
SPRING RD	VAL	134	C4
SPRING ST	LACO	S	E2
SPRING ST	NAPA	29	C3
SPRING ST	U	123	B3
SPRING ST N	LA	186	B2
SPRING TR	LAK	31	D2
SPRING BRNCH RD	TEH	18	D3
SPRING BRNCH RD	TEH	19	A3
SPRINGBROOK RD	CC	L	E4
SPRINGBROOK RD	CC	M	A4
SPRING CREEK RD	SHA	13	D3
SPRINGDALE ST	ORCO	T	B3
SPRINGER RD	SCL	N	E3
SPRINGFIELD AV	FRCO	56	E4
SPRINGFIELD AV	FRCO	57	B4
SPRING GAP RD	TUO	41	E3
SPRING GAP RD	TUO	42	A3
SPRING GARDEN	PLA	34	D3
SPRING GULCH RD	LAS	14	B4
SPRING GULCH RD	SHA	18	C3
SPRING HILL RD	LAS	14	E4
SPRING HILL RD	SON	37	E3
SPRING HILL RD	SON	38	A3
SPRING LAKE RD	KLAM	5	B1
SPRING MDWS RD	SIS	12	E3
SPRING MTN RD	NAPA	29	A2
SPRING MTN RD	NAPA	38	B1
SPRINGS RD	SOL	L	D2
SPRINGS RD	SOL	38	D4
SPRING VLY LTRL	COL	32	D2
SPRING VLY RD	COL	32	C2
SPRING VLY RD	MEN	31	B1
SPRING VLY RD	YUB	33	E1
SPRINGVILLE AV	TUL	68	D3
SPRINGVLLE MILO	TUL	69	A2
SPROUL CREEK RD	HUM	22	B1
SPRUCE AV	SSF	144	B1
SPRUCE RD	TUL	68	C2
SPRUCE RD EXT	LAK	32	A4
SPRUCE ST	B	156	A1
SPRUCE CAMP RD	MCO	55	E2
SPRUCE GROVE RD	LAK	32	B4
SPUNKY CYN RD	LACO	89	C3
SPUR ST	CAL	41	A4
SPYROCK RD	MEN	22	D2
SQUAW BUSH RD	SBD	92	B4
SQUAW FLAT RD	VEN	88	D3
SQUAW GULCH RD	SIS	11	D2
SQUAW VALLEY RD	SIS	12	D3
SQUAW VLY LP RD	SIS	12	D3
SQUIRREL CK RD	PLU	26	D2
STABLER LN	YUBA	125	A1
STADIUM WY	LACO	Q	E3
STADIUM WY	SD	214	B3
STADIUM WY	SDCO	V	B3
STADIUM WY	SDCO	111	D1
STAFFORD RD	HUM	16	A3
STAGE RD	AVLN	97	A4
STAGE RD	BUT	25	C2
STAGE RD	LAS	8	D5
STAGE RD	LACO	T	B1
STAGE RD	SMCO	N	C4
STAGE RD	SMCO	45	C5
STAGE COACH LN	SDCO	106	C2
STAGECOACH RD	HUM	9	E4
STAGECOACH RD	SB	87	B3
STAGECOACH CYN	NAPA	32	C5
STAGE GULCH RD	SON	L	A1
STAGHORN RD	RCO	107	C1
STAHL RD	IMP	109	B4
STALLARD RD	IMP	110	C2
STALLION WY	CAL	41	B4
STAMPEDE DAM RD	SIE	27	E5
STAMPFLI LN RD	PLU	20	D5
STANDARD RD	TUO	41	D5
STANDARD MNE RD	PLU	20	C5
STANDIFORD AV	STA	47	C2
STANDISH PIT RD	LAS	21	B3
STANDLEY ST	U	123	B3
STANISLAUS AV	FRCO	66	D1
STANISLAUS RD W	STA	47	B3
STANLEY	SJCO	40	C5
STANLEY AV	VEN	88	A5
STANLEY BLVD	ALA	M	C5
STANLEY BLVD	ALA	P	C1
STANLEY BLVD	ALA	46	B2
STANLEY RD	CAL	41	B2
STANLEY RD	IMP	109	B3
STANLEY RD	RCO	100	A5
STANWOOD DR	STB	174	E2
STANYAN ST	SF	141	E3
STAPP RD	HUM	16	C2
STAR AV	STA	47	E2
STARBRIGHT MINE	SBD	82	A4
STARDUST RD	CLK	210	B1
STAR HILL RD	SMCO	N	C3
STARK	SJCO	47	A1
STARK RD	STA	47	B3
STARKEY RD	SLO	76	C1
STARLING ST	LACO	90	C2
STARLITE DR	INY	51	C4
STARR RD	IMP	109	C5
STATE LN	SBD	100	B1
STATE ST	LACO	R	A5
STATE ST	MTCL	203	B5
STATE ST	ONT	203	B5
STATE ST	POM	203	B5
STATE ST	RCO	99	E4
STATE ST	SB	87	C4
STATE ST	SD	215	D4
STATE ST	SDCO	V	B4
STATE ST	STB	174	B3
STATE ST N	MEN	31	B2
STATE ST N	U	123	C2
STATE ST S	MEN	123	D3
STATE ST S	U	123	D3
STATE COLLGE BL	ORCO	98	C3
STATE COLLGE BL	ORCO	T	D2
STATE COL BL N	ANA	193	E5
STATE COL BL N	ORA	193	E5
STATE COL PKWY	SBD	99	B1
STATE FRSTRY RD	SON	31	A5
STATE LINE RD	MOD	5	D2
STATE LINE RD	MNO	52	C3
STATE LINE RD	INY	72	D1
STATE LINE RD	SIS	5	B2
STATEN ISLND RD	SJCO	39	D4
STATE RANCH RD	SUT	33	C3
STATION RD	KER	78	A3
STAVERVILLE RD	SIE	27	D3
STEARNS RD	STA	47	E2
STEARNS ST	LACO	S	E2
STEARNS ST	VEN	89	A5
STEEG RD	SBD	101	D1
STEEL BRIDGE RD	TRI	17	D1
STEELE LN	MEN	22	E3
STEELE LN W	STR	131	B2
STEELE CYN RD	NAPA	38	D2
STEELHEAD CIR	TRI	17	D1
STEELHEAD RD	HUM	16	D5
STEEL SWAMP RD	MOD	6	C3
STEFFAN ST	VAL	134	E5
STEIDLMAYER RD	CLU	33	A2
STEINEGUL	SJCO	47	D1
STEINER RD	SUT	33	B3
STEINER FLAT RD	TRI	17	C1
STELLAR RD	SBD	92	A4
STELLING RD N	CPTO	149	C4
STELLING RD S	CPTO	149	D5
STENT CUTOFF	TUO	41	C5
STEPHANIE LN	DGL	36	C2
STEPHENSON BLVD	RCO	110	C1
STEPHENS RIDGE	BUT	25	E3
STERCHI LN	SIS	4	C5
STERLING AV	SBD	99	C2
STERLING RD	INY	70	C4
STERLING LAKE	NEV	27	B5
STETSON AV	RCO	99	E4
STEVEN ST	KER	78	B5
STEVENS RD	IMP	111	E3
STEVENS CK BLVD	CPTO	149	C5
STEVENS CK BLVD	CPTO	150	A5
STEVENS CK BLVD	SCL	P	B3
STEVENS CK BLVD	SCLR	150	A5
STEVENS CK BLVD	SCL	46	A4
STEVENS CK FRWY	MVW	148	A4
STEVENS CK RD	SCL	N	E3
STEVENS CK RD	SCL	P	A3
STEVENS CK RD	SCL	45	E4
STEVENSON BLVD	ALA	P	A2
STEVENSN BDG RD	SOL	39	B1
STEVENS MINE RD	SBD	80	E2
STEVENS MINE RD	SBD	81	A2
STEVENS PASS RD	SIS	5	A5
STEVENS PASS RD	SIS	13	B1
STEWART	MOD	14	D1
STEWART AV	BUT	124	A5
STEWART LN	INY	51	E5
STEWART LN	SOL	39	B4
STEWART RD	HUM	16	C4
STEWART RD	INY	51	D4
STEWART RD	SJCO	47	A1
STEWART RD	SUT	33	D2
STEWART RD	TEH	18	C5
STEWART ST	SB	86	C1
STEWARTS POINT- -SKAGGS SPGS RD	SON	30	E5
STEWARTS POINT- -SKAGGS SPGS RD	SON	31	A5
STEWART RCH RD	HUM	16	D4
STEWART SPGS RD	SIS	12	B1
STICE RD	TEH	18	D4
STIERLIN RD	SCL	N	E2
STIERLIN RD	SCL	P	A2
STILLWELL AV	MONT	167	D3
STILLWELL AV	MON	53	E3
STILSON CYN RD	BUT	25	B3
STIMPSON RD	BUT	25	D5
STIMPSON RD	BUT	33	D1
STINE RD	BKD	166	A5
STINE RD	KER	78	D3
STINGY LN	SHA	18	C3
STOCKDALE HWY	KER	78	A3
STOCKDALE RD	SLO	76	A1
STOCKER ST	LACO	Q	D4
STOCKTON AV	MCO	48	B4
STOCKTON AV	SJ	151	E3
STOCKTON BLVD	SCTO	137	E4
STOCKTON BLVD	SAC	39	E1
STOCKTON RD	VEN	88	D5
STOCKTON ST	SF	143	C2
STOCKTON ST	SNRA	163	A5
STOCKWLL MNE RD	INY	71	B4
STODDARD RD	STA	47	C2
STODDARD RD	STA	47	E2
STODDARD MTN RD	SBD	91	C2
STODDARD WELLS	SBD	91	D2
STOEKEL RD	SHA	18	B3
STONE AV	STA	47	C2
STONE RD	LAS	20	E1
STONE RD	MCO	55	D1
STONEBORO RD	MEN	30	C3
STONE CANYON RD	MON	66	B3
STONE COAL RD	MOD	14	B2
STONEHEDGE DR	YUB	25	E5
STONEHILL DR	DPT	202	B3
STONE HOUSE RD	SAC	40	C1
STONEHURST AV	LACO	Q	D2
STONERIDGE DR	ALA	46	A2
STONE VALLEY RD	CC	M	A4

INDEXES

STONE VALLEY RD
STREET INDEX
270
TIPTOP RD

STREET	CO.	PAGE	GRID
STONE VALLEY RD	CC	46	A1
STONEWLL CYN RD	MON	65	A1
STONEY CREEK RD	LAS	21	D2
STONY CREEK RD	AMA	40	D3
STONYFD-LDGA RD	COL	24	B5
STONY POINT RD	STR	131	A3
STONY POINT RD	SON	37	E2
STONY POINT RD	SON	37	E3
STONY POINT RD	SON	131	A4
STOREY	FRCO	56	C2
STORRIE RD	PLU	25	E2
STORY RD	SJ	152	E4
STORY RD	SCL	P	C3
STORY RD	SCL	46	B4
STORY RD	STA	47	E3
STOVALL RD	COL	32	D2
STOVEPIPE WELLS	INY	61	D4
STOVER RD	HUM	10	B4
STOW	SJCO	40	C5
STOW	SJCO	47	C1
STOWELL RD	STB	173	B4
STOWELL RD	SB	86	B1
STOWELL RD	SMA	173	B4
STRADLEY AV	KER	68	B5
STRAND, THE	LAS	20	E1
STRATTON LN	SOL	39	B4
STRAWBERRY DR	MAR	140	D3
STRAWBERRY LN	SHA	18	C3
STRAWBERRY RD	MON	54	C3
STREETER AV	RCO	99	B2
ST OF GL LNTERN	DPT	202	A4
STREET 200	MAD	57	D1
STREET 225	MAD	50	A5
STREET 600	MAD	49	B1
STREET 600	MAD	49	C4
STREET 603	MAD	57	B1
STREIBY RD	IMP	109	B4
STRINGTOWN RD	BUT	25	E4
STRIPLIN RD	SUT	33	D4
STROUD AV	FRCO	57	C5
STRUCKMAN RD	CAL	41	B3
STUBBLEFIELD RD	KER	78	A5
STUBBLEFIELD RD	KER	87	E1
STUBBY SPGS TR	RCO	101	A2
STUDEBAKER RD	LACO	98	A3
STUDEBAKER RD	LACO	S	E1
STUDEBAKER RD	LACO	S	E2
STUDEBAKER RD	LACO	T	A1
STUHR RD	STA	47	C4
STUKEY ST	DN	1	D3
STUMPFIELD MTN	MPA	49	C3
STUMPTOWN RD	HUM	9	E4
STUNT RD	LACO	97	B2
STURGIS RD	VEN	96	B1
STURM RD	HUM	16	C3
SUBACO RD	SUT	33	B3
SUBSTATION RD	MNO	50	E2
SUCCESS DR	TUL	68	D3
SUCCESS VLY DR	TUL	68	E3
SUCKER RUN RD	BUT	26	A4
SUCKOW RD	KER	80	D5
SUDDEN RD	SB	86	B3
SUE AV	KER	89	C1
SUE ST	KER	80	B5
SUEY RD	SMA	173	E3
SUEY CREEK RD	SLO	76	D5
SUGAR CREEK RD	SIS	11	D2
SUGARLOAF RD	FRCO	58	A1
SUGAR LOAF RD	INY	51	D5
SUGRLF LKSHR RD	SHA	12	B5
SUGRLOAF LKT RD	SHA	12	B5
SUGARLOAF TK TR	SBD	99	E1
SUGAR PINE	PLA	34	E2
SUGAR PINE PL	BUT	25	C2
SUGAR PINE RD	TUO	41	E4
SUGAR PINE SPG	LAS	14	A3
SUISUN VLY RD	SOL	L	E1
SUISUN VLY RD	SOL	38	E3
SULFUR RD	INY	52	D5
SULKEY CT	CAL	41	A5
SULLENGER RD	SUT	33	B2
SULLIVAN RD	KER	78	A2
SULLIVAN RD	MPA	49	B3
SULLIVAN RD	STA	47	C5
SULLIVAN ST	SA	195	D5
SULPHUR BANK DR	LAK	32	A3
SULPHUR MTN RD	VEN	88	B4
SULPHR MTN RD E	VEN	88	B4
SULPHUR SPGS RD	MON	65	B3
SULTANA DR	MCO	48	A4
SULTZE AV	KER	78	B5
SUMMERHILL DR	TUO	42	A3
SUMMER HOMES RD	ML	164	C2
SUMMERS LN	KLAM	5	B1
SUMMERS RD	LAS	21	E5
SUMMERSET RD	SBD	91	C1
SUMMIT AV	GLE	24	D3
SUMMIT AV	SBD	99	A1
SUMMIT RD	BUT	25	D5
SUMMIT RD	KER	79	C4
SUMMIT RD	SCL	P	C5
SUMMIT RD	SCR	P	A5
SUMMIT RD	SCR	54	B1
SUMMIT CREEK RD	TRI	17	C2
SUMMIT LAKE DR	NAPA	38	B1
SUMMIT LEVEL RD	CAL	41	C3
SUMMITROSE ST	LACO	Q	E1
SUMMIT TRUCK TR	SBD	91	B5
SUMMY	SUT	33	B2
SUMNER AV	AVLN	97	B5
SUMNER AV	FRCO	56	E4
SUMNER AV	FRCO	58	B4
SUMNER ST	BKD	166	E3

STREET	CO.	PAGE	GRID
SUNBURST AV	SBD	100	E1
SUNDOWN LN	TUO	163	C3
SUNEVER RD	SBD	101	A1
SUNFAIR RD	SBD	101	A1
SUNFLOWER AV	CM	197	D3
SUNFLOWER AV	CM	198	A3
SUNFLOWER AV	LACO	U	A2
SUNFLOWR SPG RD	SBD	94	D2
SUNFLR SPGS SPR	SBD	94	E3
SUNKIST ST	ANA	194	A2
SUNKIST ST	ORCO	T	D2
SUNKIST TR	LPAZ	104	C4
SUNLAND BLVD	LACO	97	D1
SUNLAND BLVD	LACO	Q	D2
SUNLAND DR	INY	51	D4
SUNNY LN	AVLN	97	B5
SUNNY ACRES AV	MCO	47	E3
SUNNY ACRES AV	MCO	48	A3
SUNNYBRAE BLVD	SM	145	A2
SUNNY BRAE LN	HUM	10	A5
SUNNY HILL RD	SHA	18	A3
SUNNYSIDE AV	FRCO	57	D3
SUNNYSIDE AV	FRCO	57	D4
SUNNYSIDE AV	MAD	57	A1
SUNNYSIDE AV	MV	140	A2
SUNNYSIDE RD	LAS	21	B4
SUNNYSLOPE	FRCO	58	B2
SUNNYSLOPE RD	SBD	90	E4
SUNNYVALE AV	CPTO	149	D1
SUNNYVALE AV	SVL	148	E5
SUNNY VISTA RD	SBD	100	E1
SUNOL BLVD	ALA	P	B1
SUNRISE	SBD	101	B1
SUNRISE BLVD	SAC	34	A5
SUNRISE BLVD	SJCO	40	B1
SUNRISE HWY	SDCO	107	D4
SUNRISE HWY	SDCO	107	D5
SUNRISE WY	PMSP	206	C5
SUNRISE WY	RCO	100	D3
SUNRISE SPGS RD	SBD	93	A5
SUNSET	SAC	34	B5
SUNSET AV	FRFD	135	D3
SUNSET AV	KER	79	E5
SUNSET AV	LACO	R	D4
SUNSET AV	MAD	57	A2
SUNSET AV	MCO	55	D1
SUNSET AV	RCO	99	E3
SUNSET AV	SOL	135	D3
SUNSET BLVD	BH	183	A1
SUNSET BLVD	KER	79	A4
SUNSET BLVD	LA	181	B4
SUNSET BLVD	LA	182	A4
SUNSET BLVD	LA	185	D1
SUNSET BLVD	LA	186	A1
SUNSET BLVD	LACO	97	C2
SUNSET BLVD	LACO	Q	D2
SUNSET BLVD	SD	213	B5
SUNSET BLVD	SDCO	V	B3
SUNSET BLVD	SFCO	L	B5
SUNSET BLVD	SF	141	A5
SUNSET BLVD	SFCO	45	B1
SUNSET BLVD	LA	180	C1
SUNSET BLVD W	PLA	33	E4
SUNSET BLVD W	PLA	34	A4
SUNSET DR	IMP	108	C2
SUNSET DR	INY	60	B4
SUNSET DR	MCO	47	E4
SUNSET DR	MCO	48	A4
SUNSET DR	MONT	53	C2
SUNSET DR	PAC	167	B2
SUNSET DR	SDCO	106	C3
SUNSET PKWY	MAR	38	B4
SUNSET RD	CC	M	D3
SUNSET RD	CC	39	C5
SUNSET RD	CLK	74	D3
SUNSET RD	GLE	24	D3
SUNSET RD	SBD	100	E1
SUNSET ST	FRCO	66	D2
SUNSET CYN DR	LACO	Q	D4
SUNSET CLFFS BL	SD	212	B5
SUNSET CLFFS BL	SDCO	V	A3
SUNSET CLFFS BL	SDCO	111	C1
SUNSET CRSSG RD	LACO	U	B3
SUNSET LAKE RD	ALP	42	B1
SUNSHINE MNE RD	KER	80	E3
SUPERIOR AV	CM	199	A3
SUPERIOR AV	NB	199	A3
SUPERIOR RD	KER	78	B3
SURPRISE CYN RD	INY	71	C3
SURPRISE SPG RD	SBD	100	E1
SURPRISE VLY RD	LAS	8	E3
SURPRISE VLY RD	MOD	7	E3
SURPRISE VLY RD	MOD	8	E3
SUSAN HILLS DR	LAS	20	E3
SUSANVILLE RD	LAS	14	B3
SUSQUEHANNA RD	SIS	4	D3
SUTLIFF RD	SJCO	47	D1
SUTTENFIELD RD	SJCO	40	B3
SUTTER AV	FRCO	56	E4
SUTTER AV	FRCO	66	E3
SUTTER AV	MDO	162	A5
SUTTER LN	AMA	40	D2
SUTTER RD	HUM	9	E4
SUTTER RD	HUM	10	A4
SUTTER RD	YOL	39	D3
SUTTER ST	AMA	40	E2
SUTTER ST	SF	142	B3
SUTTER ST	SF	143	C4
SUTTER CK IONE-			
-BACK CUTOFF RD	AMA	40	D2
SUTTR CK VOLCNO	AMA	40	E2
SUTTER ISLND RD	SAC	M	E1
SUTTER ISLND RD	SAC	39	D3

STREET	CO.	PAGE	GRID
SUTTERVILLE RD	SAC	39	D1
SWAN RD	MCO	48	B4
SWAN RD	SOL	39	C2
SWAN MTN RD	PLU	20	B3
SWANSEA RD	LPAZ	104	D3
SWANSON AV	FRCO	57	B5
SWANSON AV	FRCO	57	C5
SWANSON RD	STA	47	E3
SWANTON RD	SCR	N	D5
SWANTON RD	SCR	53	D1
SWARTHOT CYN RD	SBD	91	A5
SWASEY DR	SHA	18	B2
SWEDE CREEK RD	SHA	18	D2
SWEDE CREEK RD	TRI	11	A5
SWEDES FLAT RD	BUT	25	E5
SWEENEY RD	ED	35	A5
SWEENEY RD	SB	86	C3
SWEENEY RD	SOL	39	A2
SWEENEY PASS RD	SDCO	108	A5
SWEENY RD	MCO	55	C2
SWEET RD	IMP	109	A5
SWEETEN LN	SBD	91	D1
SWEETLAND RD	NEV	26	B5
SWEETSER RD	KER	89	E1
SWEETWATER RD	SDCO	V	C4
SWEETWATER RD	SDCO	111	E1
SWEETWATER RD	SDCO	111	D2
SWEETWR SPGS BL	SDCO	V	E3
SWEETWTR SPG RD	SON	37	D1
SWEITZER LN	SBD	92	D5
SWENSEN RD	MCO	47	D4
SWETZER RD	SUT	33	E3
SWIFT AV	MCO	56	A2
SWIFT RD	SBD	80	E5
SWIFT ST	SC	169	A4
SWIFT CREEK	TRI	11	E4
SWIGART RD	SIS	4	B4
SWISS RANCH RD	CAL	41	B3
SX RD	MOD	14	E1
SYCAMORE AV	FRCO	57	A4
SYCAMORE AV	SDCO	106	C3
SYCAMORE DR	LACO	88	E5
SYCAMORE LN	DVS	136	B3
SYCAMORE RD	ALA	P	B1
SYCAMORE RD	KER	78	E4
SYCAMORE RD	KER	79	A4
SYCAMORE RD	SDCO	V	C5
SYCAMORE RD	SDCO	111	D2
SYCAMORE RD	VEN	88	D4
SYCAMORE ST	ANA	193	B2
SYCAMORE ST	MCO	47	E3
SYCAMORE ST	MCO	48	A3
SYCAMORE CYN RD	SB	87	C4
SYCAMORE CYN RD	STB	174	E3
SYCAMORE CUTOFF	CLU	33	A2
SYCAMRE FLAT RD	MON	65	A2
SYCAMORE SL RD	COL	33	A2
SYCAMORE VLY RD	CC	M	B4
SYCAMORE VLY RD	CC	46	A1
SYDNOR AV	KER	80	D1
SYKES RD	INY	70	B3
SYLVAN AV	STA	47	D2
SYLVESTER RD	MCO	55	D1
SYMMES CREEK RD	INY	59	E3
T			
T ST	BKD	166	D4
T ST	STA	47	C4
TABL MTN OVRCRS	BUT	25	C4
TABLE BLUFF RD	HUM	15	D1
TABLE MTN BL	BUT	25	C4
TABLE MTN RD	FRCO	57	D2
TABLE MTN RD	RCO	100	C5
TABLE MTN TK TR	RCO	107	C1
TABLEROCK RD	SIS	4	C4
TABOOSE CK RD	INY	59	E1
TABOR AV	FRFD	135	B2
TABOR AV	SOL	39	A3
TABOR AV E	FRFD	135	C2
TACKER RD	IMP	109	B4
TAFT AV	ORA	194	C3
TAFT AV	ORCO	98	C3
TAFT AV	ORCO	T	D2
TAFT HWY	KER	78	C3
TAFT ST	TEH	24	E1
TAGE RD	SBD	101	D1
TAGLIO RD	MCO	47	D5
TAHOE ST	MCO	48	B4
TAHQTZ-MCCLM WY	PMSP	206	A4
TALBERT AV	FTNV	197	A3
TALBERT AV	ORCO	98	B4
TALBERT AV	ORCO	T	B3
TALBERT LN	SOL	39	B4
TALBOT ST	SDCO	V	A3
TALC CITY RD	INY	70	D1
TALMAGE RD	U	123	D4
TAMALPAIS AV	MAR	38	B5
TAMALPAIS DR	CRTM	140	B1
TAMARACK AV	SDCO	106	B3
TAMARACK RD	SHA	19	C1
TAMARACK RD	TEH	19	C4
TAMARACK LK RD	TRI	12	B3
TAMARACK PK RD	SHA	13	C5
TAMPA AV	LA	178	B3
TAMPA AV	LACO	97	B1
TANABE RD	YUB	33	D1
TANATEA ST	RCO	107	C1
TANK FARM RD	KER	78	A4
TANK FARM RD	SLO	76	B4
TANNERY GLCH RD	TRI	11	D5
TAPADERO ST	CAL	41	A4
TAPIA LN	SBD	90	E2

STREET	CO.	PAGE	GRID
TAPLIN RD	NAPA	29	C3
TAPO RD	VEN	89	A5
TAPO CANYON RD	VEN	89	A5
TARA AV	KER	69	B5
TAR CANYON RD	KIN	66	E4
TARKE RD	SUT	33	B2
TARPON DR	SIS	4	B3
TASSAJARA RD	ALA	46	B2
TASSAJARA RD	ALA	M	B5
TASSAJARA RD	MON	64	D2
TATE CREEK RD	SIS	13	A2
TAVERN RD	SDCO	107	B5
TAVERNETTI RD	MON	54	E5
TAVERNETTI RD	MON	55	A5
TAVERNOR RD	SAC	40	B2
TAYLOR AV	KER	78	B1
TAYLOR BLVD	CC	L	E3
TAYLOR BLVD	CC	M	A3
TAYLOR BLVD	CC	38	E5
TAYLOR BLVD	MLBR	144	C5
TAYLOR LN	SIS	5	B4
TAYLOR RD	CC	39	C4
TAYLOR RD	STA	47	C3
TAYLOR ST	SF	143	B2
TAYLOR ST	SJ	152	B2
TAYLORSVL TRANS	PLU	20	D5
TEAFORD SDLE RD	MAD	49	E4
TEAGUE AV	FRCO	57	D2
TEAGUE AV	MON	65	B2
TEAL DR	MOD	7	A5
TEALE RD	KER	78	D4
TEALE RD	KER	79	A4
TEAPOT	TUL	68	C3
TECHNR RBSN RD	SIS	5	A4
TECOLOTE RD	SDCO	V	B3
TECOLOTE RD	SDCO	111	C1
TECOPA HOT SPGS	INY	73	A4
TED ELDER RD	SHA	13	D3
TED KIPF RD	IMP	109	C3
TED KIPF RD	IMP	110	A4
TEDOC RD	TEH	17	D4
TEFFT ST	SLO	76	C5
TEGAN RD	SAC	39	E2
TEGNER RD	MCO	47	D4
TEHACHAPI BLVD	KER	79	D4
TEHACHP-WLW SPG	KER	79	D5
TEHAMA AV	KIN	67	A4
TEHAMA AV	TEH	24	D1
TEHAMA ST	GLE	24	D4
TEHAMA & VNA RD	TEH	24	E1
TEJON RD	LACO	90	C4
TELEGRAPH AV	B	156	B3
TELEGRAPH AV	O	156	B3
TELEGRAPH AV	S	160	A2
TELEGRAPH RD	CAL	40	E5
TELEGRAPH RD	CAL	41	A5
TELEGRAPH RD	LACO	89	A4
TELEGRAPH RD	LACO	98	A2
TELEGRAPH RD	LACO	R	B4
TELEGRAPH RD	MPA	49	B3
TELEGRAPH RD	VEN	88	E4
TELEGRPH CYN RD	SDCO	V	D4
TELEGRPH CYN RD	SDCO	111	D2
TELEGRAPH CK RD	HUM	22	A1
TELEGRAPH MN RD	SBD	83	D3
TELEPHONE RD	SB	86	C1
TELEPHONE RD	VEN	88	B5
TELESCOPE PK RD	RD	10	C4
TELL BLVD	DN	1	D3
TEMESCAL CYN RD	RCO	99	A3
TEMPERANCE AV	FRCO	57	D2
TEMPERANCE AV	FRCO	57	D5
TEMPLE AV	LACO	R	D4
TEMPLE AV	LACO	S	E2
TEMPLE ST	LA	185	C1
TEMPLE ST	LA	186	B2
TEMPLE CITY BL	LACO	R	C3
TEMPLE CREEK	SJCO	47	C1
TEMPLE HILLS DR	LAG	201	D2
TEMPLETON RD	SLO	76	A2
TENAJA RD	RCO	99	B5
TENAJA TRUCK TR	RCO	99	B5
TENMILE RD	MEN	30	D4
TENMILE CTO	MEN	30	D4
TENNANT AV	SCL	P	E5
TENNANT AV	SCL	54	D1
TENNANT RD	SIS	4	E5
TENNANT RD	SIS	5	A5
TENNANT LAVA BD	MOD	5	D4
TENNANT LAVA BD	SIS	5	B5
TENNESSEE ST	SBD	99	C2
TENNESSEE ST	VAL	134	C4
TENNESSEE ST E	FRFD	135	C3
TENNYSON RD	ALA	N	E1
TENNYSON RD	ALA	P	A1
TENNYSON RD	ALA	45	E2
TEPUSQUET RD	SB	86	D1
TEQUEPIS CYN RD	SB	87	A3
TERCEIRA RD	MCO	55	E2
TERMINAL IS FWY	LACO	S	D2
TERMINOUS RD	SAC	39	D4
TERMO GRASSHPPR	LAS	8	A5
TERMO GRASSHPPR	LAS	14	E5
TERRA BELLA ST	LACO	Q	C2
TERRACE	FRCO	58	A3
TERRACE RD	RCO	100	D4
TERRY MILL RD	SHA	13	A5
TERWER RIFFL RD	DN	10	A1
TERWILLIGER RD	RCO	107	C1
TESLA RD	ALA	M	D5
TESLA RD	ALA	P	D1
TESLA RD	ALA	46	C2
TESORO RD	SBD	90	E3

STREET	CO.	PAGE	GRID
TEST STATION	MNO	43	C5
TEXAS AV	KER	79	E5
TEXAS AV	KER	80	A5
TEXAS RD	STA	47	C2
TEXAS ST	FRFD	135	A3
TEXAS ST	SD	216	B1
TEXAS ST	SDCO	V	B3
TEXAS ST	SDCO	111	D1
TEXAS ST N	SOL	M	A1
TEXAS ST N	SOL	38	E3
TEXAS ST N	FRFD	135	C3
TEXAS HILL	MPA	48	E2
TEXAS HILL RD	YUB	26	A5
TEXAS SPGS RD	SHA	18	B2
THATCHER RD	SHA	19	C2
THATCHER MLL RD	SHA	19	C2
THATCHER RDG RD	BUT	25	D1
THE BRADSHAW TR	RCO	102	A5
THEDA ST	RCO	99	C4
THE INDIAN RD	MOD	8	B3
THEODORE ST	RCO	99	D3
THEODORIC RD	SBD	84	C4
THING RD	SDCO	112	C2
THIRD ST	C	124	B5
THISSELL RD	SOL	39	B2
THOMAS	SON	31	E5
THOMAS	SON	37	E1
THOMAS RD	HUM	16	B5
THOMAS RD	KER	90	C1
THOMAS RD	MCO	55	C2
THOMAS RD	SBT	55	A3
THOMAS RD	SHA	18	B3
THOMAS RD	SHA	19	A1
THOMAS ST	KER	80	A4
THOME RD	YUB	33	D1
THOMES AV	TEH	24	D1
THOMPSON AV	FRCO	57	D3
THOMPSON AV	FRCO	57	D5
THOMPSON BLVD	VENT	175	B2
THOMPSON RD	IMP	109	A5
THOMPSON RD	LAS	14	B4
THOMPSON RD	MNO	43	B4
THOMPSON RD	SBD	81	C5
THOMPSON RD	SLO	76	C5
THOMPSON RD	SUT	33	C3
THOMPSON CYN AV	KER	79	C2
THOMPSON CYN RD	MON	65	B2
THOMSEN RD	SOL	39	C2
THORNBERRY RD	MAD	49	D4
THORNBURG ST	SMA	173	B3
THORNE AV	FRE	165	B4
THORNTON AV	ALA	P	A1
THORNTON AV	ALA	45	E3
THORNTON AV	ALA	46	A3
THORNTON RD	MCO	48	B4
THORNTON RD	SJCO	40	A4
THOUSND OAKS BL	LACO	96	E1
THOUSND OAKS BL	VEN	96	D1
THOUSND PLMS RD	RCO	100	E3
THOUSAND SPGS	SHA	13	D3
THREE CHOP RD	MEN	22	D5
THREE FLAGS HWY	KER	80	D1
THREE PINES CYN	KER	80	B1
THREE POINTS RD	LACO	89	B2
THREE SLASHS RD	IMP	110	C2
THRIFT RD	MCO	48	C5
THRUSH DR	SIS	4	C3
THUNDER	SDCO	106	B3
THUNDERBIRD BL	KER	80	C4
THUNDERBIRD RD	SBD	91	C3
THUNDER CYN RD	SLO	75	D2
TIBURON BLVD	MAR	L	B4
TIBURON BLVD	MAR	140	E3
TICE VALLEY BL	CC	L	E4
TICE VALLEY BL	CC	M	A4
TICINO ST	SB	86	B1
TIEDEMAN RD	STA	47	B2
TIERNEY RD	HUM	16	B3
TIERRA BUENA RD	SUT	33	C2
TIERRA DEL SOL	SDCO	112	E2
TIERRA RJADA RD	VEN	88	E5
TIERRA SANTA BL	SDCO	V	C2
TIERRA SANTA BL	SDCO	106	D5
TIFFANY RCH RD	SLO	76	B4
TIGER CREEK RD	SIS	11	D2
TILTON AV	SCL	P	D4
TILTON DR	LACO	89	E3
TIM BELL RD	STA	48	A2
TIMBER COVE RD	SON	37	A1
TIMBER CRATER	SHA	13	D3
TIMBUCTOO RD	YUB	34	A1
TIMM RD	SOL	39	A2
TIMMONS AV	KER	68	B5
TIMMONS RD	SIS	4	B5
TIM MULLEN RD	HUM	16	B1
TIMS RD	SB	86	E2
TIN BARN RD	SON	31	A5
TIN BARN RD	SON	37	A1
TINDALL RCH RD	MEN	31	B2
TINEMAHA RD	INY	59	E1
TIOGA PASS RD	MPA	42	E5
TIOGA PASS RD	MPA	43	A5
TIOGA PASS RD	MPA	50	A1
TIOGA PASS RD	MPA	63	D3
TIOGA PASS RD	MNO	43	A5
TIOGA PASS RD	TUO	42	E5
TIOGA PASS RD	TUO	50	A1
TIOGA PASS RD	TUO	63	A4
TIONESTA RD	MOD	5	E5
TIONESTA RD	MOD	6	A4
TIONESTA RD	SIS	5	D5
TIPPECANOE ST	SBD	99	C2
TIPTOP RD	MPA	49	C3

INDEXES

STREET INDEX

STREET	CO.	PAGE	GRID
TISDALE	SUT	33	B3
TITLOW HILL RD	HUM	10	C5
TITSWORTH RD	IMP	109	C4
TIZON RD	RCO	107	B1
TOBACCO	SJCO	40	C5
TOBIN DR	VAL	134	B1
TODCO RD	KER	69	B5
TODD RD	SON	37	E2
TODD EYMANN RD	FRCO	58	D3
TODD VALLEY	PLA	34	D3
TOEWS AV	MCO	48	D4
TOFT DR	RCO	99	A4
TOKAVANA WY	PLA	34	D2
TOKAY COLONY RD	SJCO	40	B4
TOLAND LN	SOL	39	C4
TOLAND RD	VEN	88	C4
TOLAND PARK RD	VEN	88	C4
TOLL GATE WY	BUT	25	C2
TOLL HOUSE RD	FRCO	57	D2
TOLL HOUSE RD	FRCO	58	A2
TOMALES RD	SON	37	E3
TOMALES PETALMA	MAR	37	D3
TOM GREEN MN RD	SHA	18	A1
TOMKI RD	MEN	23	B5
TOMPKNS HILL RD	HUM	15	E2
TOM SHAW RD	HUM	16	B2
TOM WELLS RD	LPAZ	104	A5
TONNER CYN RD	ORCO	U	A4
TONZI RD	AMA	40	D2
TOOBY DR	FRFD	135	A3
TOOME CAMP	TEH	24	A2
TOOMES RD	STA	47	C2
TOPA LN	VEN	88	C4
TOPANGA CYN BL	LA	177	B3
TOPANGA CYN BL	LACO	97	B1
TOPAZ LN	MNO	42	E1
TOPAZ RD	SBD	91	B3
TOPEKA DR	LA	178	C4
TOPO RD	MON	65	B1
TOPO VALLEY RD	SBT	65	C1
TOPOCK DAVIS DM	MOH	95	E1
TOPPEN DORFF LN	HUM	15	D2
TORO CANYON RD	SB	87	D4
TORO CREEK RD	SLO	75	E2
TORO CREEK RD	SLO	76	A2
TORRANCE BLVD	LACO	97	D3
TORRANCE BLVD	LACO	S	B2
TORREY PINES RD	SD	211	B2
TORREY PINES RD	SDCO	V	A2
TORREY PINES RD	SDCO	106	C5
TORREY RD N	VEN	88	E4
TORREY RD S	VEN	88	E4
TOTH RD	HUM	22	A1
TOTTEN RD	SHA	13	E4
TOVEY AV	LACO	90	A3
TOWER RD	MCO	48	C4
TOWER RD	SLO	76	B1
TOWER LINE RD	KER	79	A4
TOWNE AV	LACO	U	C2
TOWNSEND RD	IMP	109	C5
TOWNSEND RD	SIS	4	C4
TOWNSEND ST	SBD	91	D1
TOWNSHIP AV	VEN	88	E5
TOWNSHIP AV	VEN	89	A5
TOWNSHIP RD	KLAM	5	B2
TOWNSHIP RD	YUB	34	A1
TOWNSHIP RD N	SUT	33	C2
TOWNSHIP RD S	SUT	33	C3
TOZER ST	MAD	57	A2
TRABUCO RD	ORCO	98	D4
TRABUCO RD	ORCO	T	E3
TRACTOR AV	FRCO	66	D2
TRACY AV	KER	78	A2
TRACY BLVD	SBD	100	D1
TRACY BLVD	SJCO	46	E1
TRAGEDY SPGS RD	AMA	35	D5
TRAIL CANYON RD	INY	72	A1
TRAILS END LN	RCO	107	C1
TRAILS END RD	SIS	4	C5
TRAILS END CAMP	SBD	96	B5
TRAMPA CYN RD	MON	64	C1
TRAMWAY RD	TEH	19	C4
TRANCAS ST	NAP	133	C2
TRANCAS ST	NAPA	133	D2
TRANSMSN LNE RD	SBD	92	A4
TRASK AV	GGR	195	B2
TRASK AV	ORCO	T	B3
TRAUTWEIN RD	RCO	99	B3
TRAVIS BLVD	FRFD	135	B3
TRAVIS BLVD	SOL	L	E1
TRAVIS BLVD	SOL	M	A1
TRAYNHAM RD	COL	33	A3
TREAT BLVD	CC	M	A3
TREAT BLVD	CC	38	E5
TREDWAY	SJCO	40	E2
TREFOIL LN	SHA	18	D3
TREMONT RD	SOL	39	C1
TREMONT ST	AVLN	97	B5
TRENTHAM RD	IMP	109	B5
TRES CERITOS AV	RCO	99	D4
TRESTLE GLEN	MAR	45	B1
TRESTLE GLEN RD	O	158	C3
TRETHEWAY RD	SJCO	40	B4
TRIANGLE RD	MPA	49	B3
TRIANGLE RCH RD	MOD	6	D4
TRIANGLE RCH RD	STA	47	D2
TRIMBLE RD	SCL	P	B3
TRIMMER SPGS RD	FRCO	58	A3
TRIMMER SPGS RD	INY	58	C2
TRINDADE RD	MCO	48	B4
TRNIDAD SCNC DR	HUM	9	E4
TRINITY	TEH	18	D5
TRINITY AV	FRCO	56	E3
TRINITY AV	FRCO	57	A4
TRINITY RD	SON	38	B2
TRINITY ST	FRE	165	C4
TRINITY ST	RED	122	B1
TRINITY ALPS RD	TRI	11	D5
TRINITY DAM BL	TRI	11	D5
TRINITY DAM BL	TRI	17	D1
TRINITY MTN RD	SHA	18	A1
TRINITY PINE DR	TRI	17	B3
TRIPP FLATS RD	RIV	100	B5
TRIUNFO CYN RD	LACO	96	E1
TRONA RD	SBD	80	E2
TRONA RD	SBD	81	A1
TRONA AIRPRT RD	INY	71	B4
TRONA WLDRSE RD	INY	71	B4
TROPICANA AV	CLK	74	D3
TROPICANA AV	CLK	210	C4
TROWER	MPA	49	A3
TROWER AV	NAP	133	A1
TROY RD	SBD	92	C2
TRUCKEE AV	TEH	24	D1
TRUCKE ARPRT RD	NEV	27	D5
TRUCKE-TAHO ARP	NEV	35	E1
TRUESDALE RD	SLO	76	D1
TRUEX RD	BUT	25	D3
TRUMAN RD	KER	89	D1
TRUMAN MDWS RD	MNO	44	C5
TRUMBULL RD	LAS	21	D2
TRUXTUN AV	BKD	166	B3
TRUXTUN AV	KER	78	D3
TSCHIRKY RD	SIS	5	D2
TUBBS RD	SOL	39	A2
TUCACOTA HLS RD	RCO	99	E5
TUCKER RD	KER	79	C4
TUCKER RD	LAS	21	D5
TUCKER CYN RD	SLO	76	D1
TUCSON AV	KIN	67	D4
TUDOR RD	SUT	33	C3
TUGG WY	CAL	41	A5
TUJUNGA AV	LACO	Q	D3
TUJUNGA CYN BL	LACO	Q	E1
TULARE AV	KER	77	E2
TULARE AV	FRCO	57	C3
TULARE AV	TUL	68	B1
TULARE ST	FRE	165	D4
TULAROSA RD	SB	86	C3
TULE LN	CC	39	C5
TULE LN	GLE	24	E4
TULE RD	COL	33	A3
TULE RD	YOL	39	D2
TULE CYN TK TR	RCO	107	C1
TULE CREEK RD	TRI	17	B2
TULEDAD RD	LAS	8	D5
TULE PEAK RD	RCO	107	B1
TULE SPRING RD	INY	72	A2
TULE SPGS TK TR	SDCO	107	B4
TULIP AV	STA	47	C4
TULLOCH RD	MCO	48	B1
TULLOCH RD	TUO	41	B5
TULLY RD	MDO	162	A2
TULLY RD	SJCO	40	C4
TULLY RD	SCL	P	C3
TULLY RD	SCL	46	B4
TULLY RD	STA	47	C2
TULLY CREEK RD	HUM	10	C3
TUMBLEWEED RD	LACO	90	C4
TUNA CANYON RD	LACO	97	B2
TUNGSTEN RD	MNO	51	D3
TUNGSTEN CTY RD	INY	51	C4
TUNITAS CK RD	SMCO	N	C3
TUNITAS CK RD	SMCO	45	C4
TUNNEL RD	B	156	C4
TUOLUMNE AV	FRCO	56	D4
TUOLUMNE BLVD	MDO	162	A4
TUOLUMNE DR	MLBR	144	B5
TUOLUMNE RD	STA	47	C3
TUOLUMNE ST	SOL	L	D2
TUOLUMNE ST	VAL	134	D2
TUPMAN RD	KER	78	B3
TURK ST	SF	142	A3
TURK ST	SF	143	B5
TURKEY AV	BUT	25	D5
TURKEY FLAT RD	MON	66	D4
TURKEY HILL RD	KLAM	5	E2
TURLOCK AV	SCL	P	E5
TURLOCK AV	SCL	54	D1
TURLOCK RD	MCO	48	B3
TURNBULL CYN RD	LACO	98	B2
TURNBULL CYN RD	LACO	R	D4
TURNELL RD	TEH	18	C4
TURNER AV	BUT	33	C1
TURNER AV	MCO	47	D4
TURNER AV	SBD	U	E2
TURNER DR	TUL	68	B2
TURNER RD	AMA	40	E2
TURNER RD	MCO	47	D4
TURNER RD	SJCO	39	E4
TURNER RD	STA	47	D3
TURNER ISLND RD	MCO	56	A1
TURQUOISE ST	SD	211	A5
TURQUOISE ST	SDCO	V	A2
TURQUOISE ST	SDCO	106	C5
TURRI RD	SLO	75	E3
TURRI RD	SLO	76	A3
TURTLE MTN RD	SBD	95	C4
TURTLE VLY RD	SBD	91	C2
TUSCAN SPGS RD	TEH	18	D4
TUSSING RCH RD	SBD	91	C4
TUSTIN AV	CM	199	C3
TUSTIN AV	NB	199	C3
TUSTIN AV	ORA	194	E3
TUSTIN AV	ORA	196	E2
TUSTIN AV	ORCO	98	C4
TUSTIN AV	ORCO	196	E4
TUSTIN AV	ORCO	199	C3
TUSTIN AV	SA	196	E4
TUSTIN AV	ORCO	T	D2
TU SU LN	INY	51	D4
TUTTLECREEK RD	INY	60	A4
TUTTLETOWN RD	TUO	41	C5
TUXEDO AV N	S	160	C3
TUXFORD ST	LACO	Q	D2
TWEEDY BLVD	LACO	R	A5
TWENTIETH ST	C	124	E5
TWENTY-EIGHT MI	STA	47	E1
TWNTY MULE TEAM	INY	72	A1
TWNTY MULE TEAM	KER	80	C4
TWNTYNINE PALMS	SBD	100	E1
TWNTYNINE PALMS	SBD	101	D1
TWENTY-SIX MILE	STA	47	D1
TWILIGHT CT	TUO	163	D4
TWILIGHT LN	TUO	163	D3
TWIN RD S	MNO	43	A3
TWIN CITIES RD	SAC	39	E3
TWIN CITIES RD	SAC	40	A3
TWIN LAKES RD	MNO	43	B3
TWIN LAKES RD	TRI	12	B3
TWIN LKS CMPST	ALP	35	E5
TWIN OAKES RD	KER	79	D3
TWIN OAKS VLY	SDCO	106	C3
TWIN PEAKS RD	SDCO	106	D4
TWIN PINES RD	RCO	100	A3
TWIN VALLEY RD	LAK	31	E2
TWIN VIEW BLVD	SHA	18	C2
TWISSELMAN RD	KER	67	B5
TWIST RD	TUO	41	C5
TWIST RD	TUO	48	C1
TWITCHLL ISL RD	SAC	M	D2
TWITCHLL ISL RD	SAC	39	C4
TWO MILE RD	COL	32	D1
TWO MILE RD	SBD	101	B1
TYLER AV	LACO	R	C4
TYLER RD	TEH	18	D5
TYLER ST	MONT	167	E3
TYLER ST	RCO	99	A3
TYLER ST	RCO	101	B4
TYLER ST	SAL	171	B2
TYLER ST	SDCO	V	D3
TYLER ST	SDCO	111	D1
TYLER FOOT CRSG	NEV	26	B5
TYLER GULCH RD	SIS	3	D4
TYLER ISLAND RD	SAC	M	E2
TYLER ISLAND RD	SAC	39	D4
U			
U ST	FRE	165	E3
UBEHEBE RD	INY	60	E4
UGO ST	MCO	48	A4
UKIAH RD	MEN	31	B2
UKIAH BOONVILLE	MEN	30	E3
UKIAH BOONVILLE	MEN	31	A3
UKONOM LKOUT RD	SIS	2	E5
ULLREY AV	SJCO	47	C1
ULRIC ST	SD	213	D3
ULRIC ST	SDCO	V	B3
ULRIC ST	SDCO	111	C1
UNDERPASS RD	MEN	22	E4
UNDERSTOCK DR	BUT	25	C2
UNDERWOOD LN	INY	51	D4
UNDERWOOD RD	MON	54	C5
UNDERWD MTN RD	TRI	16	E1
UNDINE RD	SJCO	46	E1
UNION AV	BKD	166	E3
UNION AV	KER	166	E5
UNION AV	FRFD	135	C4
UNION AV	SB	86	C1
UNION AV	SCL	P	B4
UNION AV	SCL	46	A4
UNION AV	SOL	38	E3
UNION RD	KER	78	B4
UNION RD	MAN	161	A3
UNION RD	SBT	54	E3
UNION RD	SJCO	47	B1
UNION RD	SLO	76	B1
UNION ST	EUR	121	C2
UNION ST	HUM	15	E1
UNION CITY BLVD	ALA	N	E1
UNION CITY BLVD	ALA	P	A1
UNION CITY BLVD	ALA	45	E3
UNION HILL RD	TRI	17	D1
UNION RIDGE RD	ED	34	E5
UNION SCHOOL RD	SHA	18	C1
UNION SUGAR AV	SB	86	B3
UNITED ST	KER	80	A5
UNIVERSITY AV	ALA	L	D4
UNIVERSITY AV	KER	78	E2
UNIVERSITY AV	PA	147	B2
UNIVERSITY AV	RIV	205	B2
UNIVERSITY AV	RCO	99	B2
UNIVERSITY AV	SAL	171	A4
UNIVERSITY AV	SD	214	D5
UNIVERSITY AV	SD	215	D1
UNIVERSITY AV	SD	216	D1
UNIVERSITY AV	SDCO	V	B3
UNIVERSITY AV	SDCO	111	D1
UNIVERSITY AV	SMCO	N	E2
UNIVERSITY DR	IRV	200	C2
UNIVERSITY DR	ORCO	98	C4
UNIVERSITY DR	ORCO	T	D4
UPAS ST	SD	216	A1
UPHAM RD	BUT	25	E5
UPHILL RD	SBD	101	A1
UPJOHN RD W	KER	80	D1
UPLAND RD	VEN	88	C5
UPPER E TER	AVLN	97	B5
UPPER BEAR RIV	HUM	15	D3
UPPR COUGR FIRE	SIS	4	D5
UPPR COUGR FIRE	SIS	12	D1
UPPER DIVISN CK	INY	59	E2
UPPER DORRAY RD	CAL	41	A2
UPPER FALL RD	SIS	13	A2
UPPER LK CTY RD	MOD	7	D5
UPR MAD RIV RD	TRI	17	A4
UPPER PALRMO RD	BUT	25	D5
UPPER SHOTGN RD	SHA	12	C4
UPPER S FORK RD	TRI	16	E2
UPPR SUMMRS MDW	MNO	43	B3
UPPER TOBY RCH	HUM	16	C5
UPPER WILLOW CK	SIS	4	C3
USAL RD	MEN	22	B2
USFS CAMP RD	TRI	17	A1
USONA RD	MPA	49	C4
USTICK RD	STA	47	C3
UTAH AV	SSF	144	C1
UTAH DR	INY	70	E1
UTAH ST	FRFD	135	B3
UTAH TR	SBD	101	C1
UTAH MINE RD	BUT	25	D2
UTICA AV	KIN	67	D4
UTICA PWRHSE RD	CAL	41	C4
UVAS RD	SCL	54	C1
UXMAL	BAJA	112	B4
V			
V ST	MER	170	A4
VADNEY AV	TEH	24	E2
VAIL	SJCO	39	E3
VAIL RD	IMP	109	A3
VAIRA RANCH RD	AMA	40	D2
VALDOR RD	TRI	17	C1
VALENCIA AV	LACO	89	B4
VALENCIA AV	ORCO	98	C3
VALENCIA AV	ORCO	T	D1
VALENCIA BLVD	TUL	58	C5
VALENCIA BLVD	TUL	68	C1
VALENCIA RD	SCR	54	B2
VALENSIN RD	SAC	40	A3
VALENTINE AV	FRCO	57	C4
VALENTINE AV	FRCO	67	C1
VALERIA AV	FRCO	56	B2
VALERIO ST	STB	174	B3
VALK RD	STA	47	E2
VALLECITO ST	SHA	18	C1
VALLECITOS RD	ALA	P	C1
VALLECITOS RD	ALA	46	B2
VALLE VISTA AV	VAL	134	C3
VALLE VISTA RD	SBD	101	B1
VALLEY AV	ALA	M	B5
VALLEY AV	ALA	P	B1
VALLEY AV	ALA	46	B2
VALLEY BLVD	LACO	97	E2
VALLEY BLVD	LACO	98	B2
VALLEY BLVD	LACO	R	C3
VALLEY BLVD	SBD	99	A2
VALLEY PKWY	SDCO	106	D3
VALLEY RD	KER	80	C3
VALLEY RD	MEN	23	A5
VALLEY RD	PLA	34	A3
VALLEY RD E	SB	87	D4
VALLEY RD W	MOD	8	B3
VALLEY CTR RD	SBD	92	B1
VALLEY CTR RD	SDCO	106	E3
VALLEY CIR BL	LACO	97	B1
VALLEY CTO RD	LAS	14	B3
VALLEY FORD RD	SON	37	D3
VLY FRD/FRNKLN- -MARSH RD	MAR	37	D3
VLY FRD/FRNKLN- -SCHOOL RD	MAR	37	D3
VALLEY HOME RD	STA	47	D1
VALLEY SAGE RD	LACO	89	D4
VALLEY VIEW DR	CAL	41	C3
VALLEY VIEW DR	SBD	102	C1
VALLEY VIEW RD	JKSN	3	E1
VALLEY VIEW RD	SBD	91	C1
VALLEY VIEW ST	ORCO	98	B3
VALLEY VIEW ST	ORCO	T	B2
VALLEY VW LKOUT	TEH	24	A2
VALLEY VISTA BL	LA	178	E5
VALLEY WELLS RD	INY	71	B4
VALLEY WELLS RD	SBD	81	C5
VALLEY WEST RD	KER	78	A4
VALLOMBROSA AV	BUT	25	B3
VALLOMBROSA AV	BUT	124	D4
VALLOMBROSA AV	C	124	D4
VALOS RD	KER	78	E5
VALPARAISO AV	SMCO	N	D2
VALPARAISO AV	SCL	45	D4
VALPREDO AV	KER	78	D5
VAL VERDE	PLA	34	B4
VALYERMO	LACO	90	C4
VAN ALDEN AV	LA	178	C4
VAN ALLEN	SJCO	40	C5
VAN ALLEN	SJCO	47	C1
VAN ARSDALE RD	MEN	23	B5
VAN BRMMR LKOUT	SIS	5	B4
VAN BUREN BLVD	RCO	99	A2
VAN BUREN ST	MONT	167	E4
VAN BUREN ST	RCO	101	A4
VANCE AV	HUM	15	E1
VAN CLIFF	MCO	47	E5
VANDEGRIFT BLVD	SDCO	106	B2
VANDEGRIFT RD	SDCO	106	B2
VANDEN RD	SOL	39	A3
VANDENBERG RD	SB	86	B2
VANDER LINDN RD	IMP	112	C3
VANDER POEL RD	IMP	112	A3
VANDER VEER RD	RCO	101	C5
VAN DOLLEN RD	SLO	66	B5
VAN DUSEN CYN	SBD	92	A5
VAN DUZEN RD	TRI	16	E4
VAN DUZEN RD E	TRI	16	E3
VAN GORDN CK RD	SLO	75	C1
VAN LOON CUTOFF	MNO	51	D2
VAN NESS AV	FRE	165	D3
VAN NESS AV	FRCO	57	C3
VAN NESS AV	LACO	Q	D5
VAN NESS AV	SF	143	A4
VAN NESS AV	SFCO	L	B4
VAN NESS AV	SFCO	45	C1
VAN NESS AV S	SF	142	C4
VAN NESS RD	TRI	12	A5
VAN NUYS BLVD	LACO	89	C5
VAN NUYS BLVD	LACO	97	C1
VAN NUYS BLVD	LACO	Q	C1
VANOWEN ST	BUR	179	B2
VANOWEN ST	LA	177	A2
VANOWEN ST	LA	178	B2
VANOWEN ST	LA	179	B2
VAN SICKLE RD	SOL	39	A4
VANS RANCH RD	SBD	92	E5
VARGAS RD	ALA	P	B1
VARGAS RD	ALA	46	B3
VARNER RD	RCO	100	D3
VARNI RD	SCR	54	B2
VASCO RD	ALA	M	D5
VASCO RD	ALA	46	C2
VASCO RD	CC	M	D4
VASCO RD	CC	46	C1
VASQUEZ CYN RD	LACO	89	C4
VASQUEZ CK RD	SBT	55	D4
VASSAR AV	MCO	48	C5
VASSAR ST	RENO	130	C4
VAUGHN AV	MCO	48	B4
VAUGHN RD	RCO	108	E1
VAUGHN RD	SOL	39	B2
VAWTER RD	COL	32	E3
VAWTER RANCH RD	RCO	99	E5
VEDDER RD	SHA	13	C5
VEE BEE ST	RCO	100	E3
VENCILL RD	IMP	112	C3
VENDEL RD	IMP	108	E4
VENICE BLVD	LA	183	C5
VENICE BLVD	LA	184	C3
VENICE BLVD	LA	185	C3
VENICE BLVD	LA	187	C2
VENICE BLVD	LA	188	A1
VENICE BLVD	LACO	97	C2
VENICE BLVD	LACO	Q	C4
VENTURA AV	FRCO	57	D3
VENTURA AV	MAD	56	D1
VENTURA AV	VEN	88	A5
VENTURA AV	VENT	175	B2
VENTURA BLVD	LA	177	D4
VENTURA BLVD	LA	178	A4
VENTURA BLVD	LACO	97	C1
VENTURA FRWY	BUR	179	C5
VENTURA FRWY	LA	177	C4
VENTURA FRWY	LA	178	B4
VENTURA FRWY	LA	179	C5
VENTURA FRWY	LACO	97	A1
VENTURA FRWY	VENT	175	C2
VENTURA FRWY	VEN	88	A5
VENTURA FRWY	VEN	96	C1
VENTURA RD	MCO	48	B5
VENTURA RD	OXN	176	A4
VENTURA RD	VEN	96	B1
VENTURA ST	FRE	165	D5
VENTURA ST	VEN	88	D4
VENTURE VLY RD	SDCO	107	D3
VENZKE RD	SHA	18	D3
VERA AV	KER	80	D1
VERANO AV	SON	132	C3
VERBENA AV	C	124	E2
VERBENA AV	SBD	91	B3
VERBENA DR	RCO	100	D2
VERDE AV	MCO	47	D4
VERDEMNT RCH RD	SBD	99	B1
VERDE SCHOOL RD	IMP	112	C3
VERDI PEAK RD	SIE	27	E4
VERDUGO AV	BUR	179	B4
VERDUGO AV	LACO	Q	D3
VERDUGO BLVD	LACO	R	A2
VERDUGO LN	KER	78	C2
VERDUGO RD	LACO	R	A3
VERMICULITE MN	SBD	100	E2
VERMONT AV	ANA	193	C3
VERMONT AV	LA	182	B5
VERMONT AV	LA	185	C5
VERMONT AV	LACO	97	D3
VERMONT AV	LACO	S	C2
VERMONT CYN RD	LA	182	B2
VERNON AV	LACO	97	D2
VERNON AV	LACO	Q	E4
VERNON AV	LACO	U	A1
VERNON RD	SUT	33	D4
VERNON ST	ORG	193	E4
VERSAILLES AV	A	159	A2
VESTA ST	SDCO	111	D1
VESTA ST	SDCO	V	C4
VESTAL RD	TEH	18	A4
VETERAN AV	LACO	Q	C5
VETERANS HALL	TRI	10	E5
VIA CAPRI	SD	211	A3
VIA DE LA VALLE	SDCO	106	C4
VIA DEL REY	MONT	167	D4
VIA DEL REY	MON	53	E3
VIADUCT BLVD	SBDO	207	B2
VIA GAYUBA	MONT	167	D4
VIA PARAISO	MONT	167	D4

VIA RANCHO PKWY

STREET INDEX

272

WHITEHORSE RD

STREET	CO.	PAGE	GRID
VIA RANCHO PKWY	SDCO	106	D4
VIA SECO ST	SBD	92	A3
VIA VERDE	LACO	U	A2
VICHY SPGS RD	MEN	31	B2
VICKREY LN	SOL	38	E2
VICKY LN	DGL	36	C3
VICTOR AV	SHA	18	C2
VICTOR RD	SJCO	40	B4
VICTOR ST	KER	80	D1
VICTORIA AV	RCO	99	A3
VICTORIA AV	RIV	205	C4
VICTORIA CT	KER	79	C4
VICTORIA DR	SDCO	107	B5
VICTORIA DR	SHA	18	B2
VICTORIA ST	LACO	97	E3
VICTORIA ST	LACO	S	C1
VICTORIA ST	ORCO	T	C4
VICTORIA ST	SM	199	A2
VICTORIA ST	STB	174	B4
VICTORY AV	STA	47	D1
VICTORY BLVD	BUR	179	B2
VICTORY BLVD	LA	177	C2
VICTORY BLVD	LA	178	B3
VICTORY BLVD	LA	179	B2
VICTORY BLVD	LACO	97	D1
VICTORY BLVD	LACO	Q	C2
VICTORY HWY	CC	M	C3
VICTORY HWY	CC	39	C5
VICTORY HWY	SAC	M	E1
VICTORY PL	BUR	179	D2
VICTORY PL	LACO	Q	D2
VICTORY RD	SJCO	47	D1
VIEJAS GRADE	SDCO	107	B5
VIERRA RD	YUB	26	A5
VIEUDELOU AV	AVLN	104	B4
VIEW DR	TUL	58	B4
VIEW LAND RD	LAS	21	D3
VILAS RD	BUT	25	C2
VILLA AV	EC	217	C1
VILLA AV	SR	139	D3
VILLA RD	IMP	109	B5
VILLA ST	SAL	171	B3
VILLA CREEK RD	SLO	75	D2
VILLAGE DR	AMA	40	D3
VILLAGE RD	SDCO	106	C5
VLLA L JOLLA DR	SD	211	C1
VLLA MANUCHA RD	STA	47	C4
VILLA PARK RD	ORCO	T	E2
VINA RD	TEH	24	E2
VINCENT AV	LACO	R	E3
VINCENT RD	MCO	47	E3
VINCENT RD	MCO	48	A3
VINCENT RD	STA	47	E3
VINCENT RD	STA	48	A3
VINE AV	MCO	48	B4
VINE AV	SJCO	47	D1
VINE ST	LA	181	D5
VINE ST	LACO	Q	D3
VINE ST	SDCO	V	E2
VINE ST	SDCO	107	A5
VINE ST	SJ	152	B4
VINE WY	KER	79	C1
VINE HILL RD	SCR	P	B5
VINE HILL RD	SCR	54	A1
VINELAND AV	FRCO	57	A4
VINELAND AV	LACO	97	D1
VINELAND AV	LACO	Q	D2
VINELAND RD	KER	78	E4
VINEWOOD AV	MCO	47	E4
VINEWOOD AV	MCO	48	A4
VINEYARD AV	ALA	M	C5
VINEYARD AV	ALA	P	C1
VINEYARD AV	ALA	46	B2
VINEYARD AV	OXN	176	D1
VINEYARD AV	SBD	98	E2
VINEYARD AV	SBD	U	E3
VINEYARD AV	VEN	176	D1
VINEYARD DR	SLO	75	E1
VINEYARD DR	SLO	76	A1
VINEYARD RD	PLA	34	A5
VINEYARD RD	SJCO	40	A2
VINEYARD RD	STA	47	B3
VINEYARD RD	YUB	34	A2
VINEYARD WY	MCO	56	B1
VINEYARD CYN RD	MON	66	B4
VINNUM RD	HUM	16	B4
VINTON GULCH RD	BUT	25	D3
VINTON LOYALTON	PLU	27	D3
VIOLA AV	TEH	24	D2
VIOLA MINERAL	TEH	19	C3
VIRGIL AV	LACO	Q	E4
VIRGINIA	SBD	92	D5
VIRGINIA AV	KIN	67	E4
VIRGINIA AV	MDO	162	B2
VIRGINIA RD	LACO	R	B3
VIRGINIA RD	STA	47	E2
VIRGINIA RD	STA	48	A2
VIRGINIA RD	YUB	33	E1
VIRGINIA ST	RCO	99	B2
VIRGINIA ST N	RENO	130	B2
VIRGINIA ST S	RENO	130	B3
VIRGINIA LK RD	MNO	43	B4
VIRGINIATOWN RD	PLA	34	B3
VISALIA RD	FRCO	58	D4
VISALIA RD	TUL	68	C1
VISTA AV	MCO	48	D5
VISTA LN	LAS	21	B4
VISTA RD	SBD	91	B2
VISTA WY	SDCO	106	B3
VISTA CHINO	PMSP	206	A2
VISTA CHINO	RCO	100	A3
VISTA DEL MAR	LACO	97	C2
VISTA DL MAR BL	ELS	189	A4
VISTA DL MAR BL	LACO	Q	C5
VISTA DEL VALLE	LA	182	B1
VISTA DE ORO	RCO	100	E3
VISTA ENCINA AV	MDO	162	D3
VISTA GRANDE DR	KER	79	D1
VISTA MINE RD	IMP	110	A4
VIVIAN RD	STA	47	C3
VLASNIK RD	KER	77	E2
VOGEL RD	IMP	111	E3
VOGEL RD	KER	79	D5
VOLCANO CIR	BUT	25	B3
VOLCANO PIONEER	AMA	41	A2
VOLCANOVILLE RD	ED	34	E3
VOLLEY RD	PLA	34	C3
VOLTA RD	MCO	55	D1
VOLTAIRE ST	SDCO	V	A3
VOLTAIRE ST	SDCO	111	C1
VON GLAHN	SJCO	47	C1
VOORHESS RD	MCO	48	D5
VORDEN RD	SAC	M	E1
VORDEN RD	SAC	39	D3
VOTAW RD	AMA	40	E1
VULCAN MINE RD	SBD	84	A5
VULCAN MINE RD	SBD	94	A1
W			
WAALEW RD	SBD	91	C3
W A BARR RD	SIS	12	C2
WABASH AV	EUR	121	B2
WABASH AV	SBD	99	D2
WABASH BLVD	SD	214	C5
WABASH BLVD	SD	216	C5
WABASH BLVD	SDCO	111	D1
WABASH BLVD	SDCO	V	C4
WACHTEL WY	SAC	34	B5
WACKERMAN RD	TEH	24	C2
WADDELL ST	TUL	68	C2
WADDINGTON RD	HUM	15	D2
WADE AV	MCO	48	E5
WADLEIGH RD	COL	32	D1
WAGNER	SJCO	47	C1
WAGNER AV	ANA	194	A3
WAGNER AV	COL	32	E3
WAGON RD	BUT	25	C2
WAGON WHEEL	SBD	101	A1
WAGSTAFF RD	BUT	25	C3
WAHL RD	IMP	112	A3
WAINWRIGHT RD	MCO	47	D4
WAKEFIELD	FRCO	58	A4
WALCH AV	TEH	24	E2
WALDO RD	YUB	34	A2
WALERGA	PLA	33	E5
WALGROVE AV	LA	187	C1
WALKER DR	SHA	13	D4
WALKER PL	MNO	51	C1
WALKER RD	DN	1	E3
WALKER RD	IMP	108	E3
WALKER RD	LAS	14	C3
WALKER RD	MEN	23	A5
WALKER RD	MEN	31	A1
WALKER RD	NAPA	32	B5
WALKER RD	PLU	20	B4
WALKER RD	SBD	92	C5
WALKER RD	SIS	3	D3
WALKER RD	SON	37	E3
WALKER ST	GLE	24	D3
WALKER ST	ORCO	T	B2
WALKER WY	IMP	110	B5
WALKER BASIN RD	KER	79	C3
WALKER CREEK RD	INY	70	B2
WALKER CREEK RD	SIS	3	B3
WALKR LANDNG RD	SAC	M	E1
WALKR LANDNG RD	SAC	39	D3
WALKER MINE RD	PLU	26	E1
WALKER MINE RD	SHA	18	B1
WALKER PLAINS	BUT	25	E2
WALKUP RD	COL	32	B1
WALL RD	SJCO	40	C4
WALLACE AV	VAL	134	D4
WALLACE RD	KER	78	C1
WALLACE RD	SON	38	A2
WALLACE CK RD	SON	37	D1
WALLEN RD	TEH	18	D4
WALLER ST	SF	141	E4
WALLER ST	SF	142	A4
WALLIS RD	STA	48	A3
WALLY HILL RD	CAL	41	B4
WALMORT RD	SAC	40	A2
WALNUT AV	CC	M	A3
WALNUT AV	CC	38	E5
WALNUT AV	FRE	165	C5
WALNUT AV	FRCO	57	C4
WALNUT AV	LACO	Q	E2
WALNUT AV	MCO	48	A4
WALNUT AV	ORCO	T	E3
WALNUT AV	STA	47	C3
WALNUT AV	STA	47	D1
WALNUT AV	TUL	68	B1
WALNUT AV	U	123	B3
WALNUT AV	YUB	33	D2
WALNUT BLVD	CC	M	A4
WALNUT BLVD	CC	M	D4
WALNUT BLVD	CC	39	C5
WALNUT BLVD	CC	46	C1
WALNUT DR	COL	32	D2
WALNUT DR	HUM	15	E1
WALNUT DR	NAPA	29	D4
WALNUT DR	SJCO	40	C4
WALNUT LN	GLE	25	A4
WALNUT RD	TEH	24	D2
WALNUT ST	ANA	193	B4
WALNUT ST	C	124	A5
WALNUT ST	ORCO	T	C1
WALNUT ST	PAS	190	B3
WALNUT ST	TEH	18	C5
WALNUT ST	VAL	134	C1
WALNUT GROVE AV	LACO	R	C4
WALNUT GROVE RD	SJCO	39	E4
WALSER RD	KER	79	C2
WALTERS RD	LAS	14	C3
WALTERS RD	SOL	39	A3
WALTERS CAMP RD	IMP	110	C2
WALTERS MINE RD	BUT	26	B3
WALTHERS RD	SOL	M	A1
WALTON AV	SUT	33	C2
WALTON AV	SUT	125	A5
WALTZ RD	PLA	33	E3
WAMBLE RD	STA	47	E1
WAMBLE RD	STA	48	A1
WANGENHEIM RD	STA	47	C4
WARD AV	STA	47	B4
WARD RD	HUM	10	B5
WARD RD	LACO	89	E4
WARD RD	MCO	55	E1
WARD CREEK RD	PLU	26	E1
WARD LAKE RD	LAS	21	B3
WARDLOW RD	LACO	98	A3
WARDLOW RD	LACO	S	E2
WARDLOW RD	LACO	T	A2
WARDROBE AV	MCO	48	B4
WARDS FERRY RD	TUO	41	D5
WARDS FERRY RD	TUO	48	D1
WARE RD	COL	32	E2
WARE RD	IMP	112	B4
WARING RD	SDCO	V	C3
WARING RD	SDCO	111	D1
WARING RD	STA	47	E3
WARM SPGS BLVD	ALA	P	B2
WARM SPGS BLVD	ALA	46	B3
WARM SPRINGS RD	INY	51	D4
WARM SPRINGS RD	SON	38	B2
WARNER AV	FTNV	197	D2
WARNER AV	ORCO	98	B4
WARNER AV	ORCO	T	C3
WARNER AV	ORCO	T	E3
WARNER AV	SA	197	E2
WARNER AV	SA	198	A1
WARNER AV	TUS	198	D2
WARNER RD S	LAS	8	C3
WARNER RD W	MOD	8	C1
WARNER ST	C	124	B3
WARNERVILLE RD	STA	47	E2
WARNERVILLE RD	STA	48	A2
WARREGARD RD	CAL	41	B3
WARREN AV	RCO	99	D4
WARREN AV	TEH	18	C4
WARREN FRWY	ALA	45	D1
WARREN FRWY	O	156	E5
WARREN RD	CAL	40	D4
WARREN RD	RCO	99	D5
WARREN RD	RCO	99	D4
WARREN VISTA AV	SBD	100	E1
WASCO WY	KER	78	A3
WASCO POND RD	KER	68	B5
WASHBURN WY	KLAM	5	B1
WASHINGTON AV	RCO	99	C5
WASHINGTON AV	SBD	99	B2
WASHINGTON AV	SDCO	V	E3
WASHINGTON AV	SDCO	106	E5
WASHINGTON AV	SA	195	D2
WASHINGTON AV	SA	196	A3
WASHINGTON BLVD	ALA	P	B2
WASHINGTON BLVD	CUL	183	D5
WASHINGTON BLVD	CUL	187	C3
WASHINGTON BLVD	CUL	188	A2
WASHINGTON BLVD	DN	1	D4
WASHINGTON BLVD	LA	183	D5
WASHINGTON BLVD	LA	184	D5
WASHINGTON BLVD	LA	185	B4
WASHINGTON BLVD	LA	186	D5
WASHINGTON BLVD	LA	187	A3
WASHINGTON BLVD	LACO	97	E2
WASHINGTON BLVD	LACO	98	A2
WASHINGTON BLVD	LACO	R	B2
WASHINGTON BLVD	LACO	R	A4
WASHINGTON BLVD	MCO	47	E4
WASHINGTON BLVD	MCO	48	A4
WASHINGTON BLVD	PAS	190	A2
WASHINGTON PL	CUL	188	A2
WASHINGTON PL	LA	188	A2
WASHINGTON PL	SD	213	C5
WASHINGTON RD	MCO	56	B1
WASHINGTON RD	NEV	26	D5
WASHINGTON RD	SBD	92	A3
WASHINGTON RD	STA	47	D3
WASHINGTON ST	SB	87	C1
WASHINGTON ST	FRCO	66	D3
WASHINGTON ST	LA	187	B3
WASHINGTON ST	MONT	167	E4
WASHINGTON ST	RCO	99	B3
WASHINGTON ST	RCO	100	E4
WASHINGTON ST	RIV	99	D5
WASHINGTON ST	SD	213	D5
WASHINGTON ST	SD	215	C1
WASHINGTON ST	SDCO	V	B3
WASHINGTON ST	SDCO	111	C1
WASHINGTON ST	SCLR	151	C3
WASHINGTON ST	SNRA	163	B2
WASHINGTON ST	S	160	C5
WASHINGTON ST	TUO	163	B2
WASHINGTON ST E	SON	L	A1
WASHINGTON ST E	SON	38	A3
WASHOE	FRCO	56	C4
WASHOE AV	FRCO	56	C3
WASIOJA RD	SB	77	C5
WASIOJA RD	SB	87	B1
WATER LN	SMCO	N	C4
WATER ST	AMA	40	E2
WATER ST	SC	169	D2
WATER ST	SCR	54	A2
WATER CANYON RD	KER	80	B3
WATER CANYON RD	KER	79	C5
WATERFRONT RD	CC	L	E3
WATERFRONT RD	CC	M	A3
WATERFRONT RD	CC	154	E1
WATERLOO LN	DGL	36	C3
WATERLOO RD	SJCO	40	B5
WATERMAN AV	SBD	99	C2
WATERMAN AV	SBD	207	E3
WATERMAN AV	SBDO	207	E3
WATERMAN BLVD	FRFD	135	A2
WATERMAN RD	AMA	40	D2
WATERMAN RD	SAC	40	A2
WATERS RD	VEN	88	D5
WATERS END RD	SLO	76	C4
WATERTOWN RD	CAL	40	E3
WATER TROUGH RD	SON	37	D2
WATKINS DR	RCO	99	B2
WATKINS RD	TEH	24	D2
WATKINS TR	KER	79	C5
WATKINSON RD	SJCO	40	B3
WATMAUGH RD	SON	L	B1
WATSON RD	MEN	31	B2
WATSONVILLE RD	SCL	P	D5
WATSONVILLE RD	SCL	54	C1
WATT AV	SAC	34	A5
WATT AV	SAC	40	A1
WATT LN	BUT	25	C5
WATTENBURG RD	MEN	23	A3
WATTRSN TROUGHS	MNO	51	B2
WATTS AV	SUT	33	D3
WATTS DR	KER	79	C3
WATTS VALLEY RD	FRCO	57	E3
WATTS VALLEY RD	FRCO	58	A3
WAUCOBA SALINE	INY	60	C2
WAUKEENA RD	YOL	39	D2
WAVERLY	SBD	91	D1
WAVERLY	SJCO	40	D5
WAWONA RD	MPA	49	D2
WAY RD	MCO	55	E1
WAYBUR RD	SUT	33	C3
WEAVER CREEK E	TRI	17	D1
WEAVER CT	KER	79	D3
WEAVER RD	IMP	109	A4
WEAVER HILLS DR	RCO	107	A1
WEAVERVLL SCOTT	TRI	12	A2
WEAVERVLL SCOTT	TRI	11	D5
WEAVERVLL SCOTT	TRI	11	E3
WEBB RD	IMP	109	C5
WEBB RD	SHA	18	D3
WEBB RD	SUT	33	C4
WEBER AV	FRE	165	A2
WEBER AV	S	160	C5
WEBER RD	SOL	39	B2
WEBSTER AV	RCO	99	C3
WEBSTER RD	SBD	91	E1
WEBSTER ST	A	157	E5
WEBSTER ST	ALA	45	D1
WEBSTER ST	FRFD	135	B4
WEBSTER ST	O	158	A3
WEDEL AV	KER	77	E1
WEED RD	IMP	112	A4
WEEDPATCH HWY	KER	78	E3
WEEDS POINT RD	YUB	26	C4
WEEKS RD	SCL	P	C5
WEEMASOUL RD	TEH	18	A5
WEGIS RD	KER	78	C3
WEIMAR CROSS RD	PLA	34	C3
WEINERT RD	IMP	109	A5
WEIR AV	MCO	47	E4
WEIR CANYON RD	ORCO	U	C5
WEIR CANYON RD	ORCO	98	D3
WEISS RD	SUT	33	B2
WEISER RD	KER	77	C1
WEITCHER RD	MOD	14	E1
WELCH CT	CAL	41	B5
WELCOME AV	KER	80	D1
WELDON	FRCO	58	A3
WELLBARN AV	FRCO	57	E1
WELLOCK RD	TRI	17	D1
WELLS AV	RENO	130	C3
WELLS AV N	RENO	130	C2
WELLS DR	LA	178	C4
WELLS RD	COL	32	D1
WELLS RD	MAD	49	C5
WELLS RD	RCO	103	D4
WELLS RD	VEN	88	B5
WELLSFORD RD	STA	47	D2
WELLSONA RD	SLO	76	A1
WELTY RD	STA	47	A3
WENDEL RD	LAS	21	C3
WENGLER HILL RD	SHA	19	A2
WENTE ST	ALA	P	C1
WENTE ST	ALA	46	C2
WENTWORTH ST	LACO	89	D5
WENTWORTH ST	LACO	Q	D1
WENTWTH SPGS RD	ED	34	E3
WENTWTH SPGS RD	ED	35	B3
WERICK RD	RCO	99	A3
WESCOTT RD	COL	33	A2
WEST AV	FRE	165	A1
WEST AV	FRCO	57	C4
WEST AV	FRCO	67	C1
WEST AV	RCO	110	C1
WEST DR	RCO	100	D2
WEST LN	MCO	48	B4
WEST LN	S	160	E1
WEST LN	SJCO	40	A4
WEST LN	SJCO	160	E1
WEST LN	TUO	163	C3
WEST RD	COL	33	A3
WEST RD	LACO	R	D5
WEST RD	MEN	31	B1
WEST RD	STA	47	C4
WEST ST	ANA	193	B4
WEST ST	EUR	121	E1
WEST ST	O	157	E2
WEST ST	ORCO	T	C2
WEST ST	TUL	68	A2
WESTBOROUGH	SMCO	N	B1
WESTBROOK LN	DN	1	D3
WESTCLIFF DR	NB	199	C4
WEST COAST RD	HUM	16	C5
WEST CREEK WY	NEV	127	B1
W END OREGN MTN	TRI	17	C1
WESTERN AV	KER	78	A2
WESTERN AV	LA	182	A4
WESTERN AV	LA	185	A5
WESTERN AV	LACO	97	D3
WESTERN AV	LACO	Q	E5
WESTERN AV	LACO	Q	E2
WESTERN AV	LACO	S	C3
WESTERN AV	ORCO	T	B2
WESTERN CYN RD	LA	182	A3
WESTERN HILL RD	RCO	100	B5
WESTERN MINE	LAK	32	A5
WESTRN MINERALS	KER	78	A5
WESTERN TALC RD	INY	73	A5
WESTERN TALC RD	SBD	73	A5
WESTFALL	MPA	49	C3
WESTFALL W	MPA	49	A4
WESTGATE AV	HUM	9	E3
WESTGATE DR	HUM	15	E1
WESTGATE DR	NAPA	38	D2
WESTHAVEN DR	HUM	9	E4
WESTLAKE BLVD	VEN	96	E1
WEST LAWN AV	FRCO	57	B4
WEST LAWN AV	FRCO	57	B5
WESTMINSTER AV	GGR	195	B3
WESTMINSTER AV	ORCO	98	A4
WESTMINSTER AV	ORCO	T	A3
WESTMINSTER AV	SA	195	B3
WESTMORELAND RD	IMP	108	E5
WESTON RD	TEH	24	B2
WESTOVER DR	TEH	18	D5
WESTOVER DR	TEH	24	D1
WEST PORTAL RD	MNO	50	D1
WESTRIDGE RD	TRI	17	B3
WESTSIDE BLVD	MCO	47	E4
WESTSIDE BLVD	MCO	48	A4
WESTSIDE FRWY	FRCO	56	B4
WESTSIDE FRWY	FRCO	66	E2
WEST SIDE FRWY	KER	77	D1
WEST SIDE FRWY	KER	78	D4
WESTSIDE FRWY	KIN	67	B4
WESTSIDE FRWY	MCO	55	D1
WESTSIDE FRWY	STA	47	B3
WEST SIDE HWY	INY	72	A1
WEST SIDE HWY	KER	67	B5
WEST SIDE HWY	KER	78	A4
WESTSIDE RD	IMP	111	E3
WEST SIDE RD	JOS	2	C1
WEST SIDE RD	LAS	8	A5
WESTSIDE RD	MOD	7	B3
WESTSIDE RD	MOD	8	A2
WESTSIDE RD	SHA	18	B1
WESTSIDE RD	SIE	27	B3
WESTSIDE RD	SON	37	D1
WSIDE POTTR VLY	MEN	31	B1
WESTWOOD BLVD	LA	183	A4
WESTWOOD BLVD	LACO	Q	C4
WESTWOOD ST	TUL	68	D3
WET MEADOW RD	MNO	50	E1
WETMORE RD	ALA	P	C1
WETMORE RD	ALA	46	C2
WEYER RD	STA	47	E2
WEYMOUTH BLUFF	HUM	15	E2
WHEALAN RD	MCO	48	D5
WHEATLAND RD	SUT	33	E3
WHEDBEE DR	SOL	38	E3
WHEELER RD	IMP	108	D5
WHEELER RD	SBD	91	C2
WHEELER CYN RD	VEN	88	B5
WHEELER NURSERY	SHA	12	E5
WHEELER RDG RD	KER	78	E5
WHEEL GULCH RD	TRI	17	B1
WHEELOCK RD	BUT	25	C3
WHIPPLE AV	SMCO	N	D2
WHIPPLE RD	ALA	P	A1
WHISKEY CK RD	COL	32	E3
WHISKEY CK RD	SHA	18	B2
WHSKEY SLIDE RD	CAL	41	B3
WHISLER RD	KER	78	B1
WHITAKER BLF RD	MAR	37	D3
WHITE AV	LACO	U	C2
WHITE DR	BUT	25	B4
WHITE LN	KER	78	D3
WHITE LN	NAPA	29	C3
WHITE LN	SJCO	40	B5
WHITE RD	COL	33	A3
WHITE RD	MCO	47	D3
WHITE RD	MON	66	C4
WHITE RD	SBD	91	A4
WHITE RD	SCL	P	C3
WHITE RD	SCL	46	B4
WHITE COTTGE RD	NAPA	29	C2
WHITE COTTGE RD	NAPA	38	B1
WHITE CRANE RD	MCO	47	E4
WHITE CRANE RD	MCO	48	A4
WHITEHORSE RD	MOD	13	E2
WHITEHORSE RD	MOD	14	A2

INDEXES

STREET	CO.	PAGE	GRID
WHITEHURST RD	SCL	54	C2
WHITE MTN RD	INY	51	E4
WHITE MTN RD	INY	60	D4
WHITE OAK DR	SHA	18	C3
WHITE PINE LN	SB	86	E2
WHITE PINE LN	SB	87	A2
WHITEPINE ST	SIS	4	B3
WHITE RIVER RD	KER	69	A5
WHITE ROCK RD	ED	40	C1
WHITE ROCK RD	MPA	49	A4
WHITE ROCK RD	MPA	48	E5
WHITE ROCK RD	MCO	48	E5
WHITE ROCK RD	SAC	40	A1
WHITE ROCK RD	SHA	17	D3
WHTE ROCK LK RD	NEV	27	B5
WHITES BRDGE AV	FRCO	56	D3
WHITES BRDGE AV	FRCO	57	C3
WHITES GULCH RD	SIS	11	C2
WHITES MILL RD	KER	69	B5
WHITES MILL RD	KER	79	B1
WHITEWTR CYN RD	RCO	100	C2
WHITE WOLF RD	TUO	42	D5
WHITE WOLF RD	TUO	63	C3
WHITLEY AV	KIN	67	D3
WHITLOCK RD	IMP	109	C5
WHITLOCK RD	MPA	49	A3
WHITLOCK RD E	MPA	49	B3
WHITLOW RD	HUM	16	C4
WHITMORE AV	STA	47	D2
WHITMORE RD	SHA	18	E2
WHITMORE RD	SHA	19	A2
WHITMRE TUBS RD	MNO	50	E2
WHITMRE TUBS RD	MNO	51	A2
WHITNEY AV	VAL	134	D1
WHITNY PORTL RD	INY	60	A4
WHITSETT AV	LACO	Q	C3
WHITTIER AV	RCO	99	E4
WHITTIER BLVD	LA	186	D4
WHITTIER BLVD	LACO	98	B2
WHITTIER BLVD	LACO	R	B4
WHITTIER BLVD	LACO	R	D5
WHITTIER BLVD	ORCO	R	D5
WHITTLE RD	CAL	41	B4
WHITTLEY AV E	AVLN	97	B5
WHITWELL WY	RCO	107	C1
WHITWORTH RD	MCO	47	C5
WHITWORTH RD	MCO	55	C1
WIASMUL RD	RCO	107	B1
WIBLE RD	KER	166	B5
WIBLE RD	KER	78	D4
WICKENDEN WY	MOD	8	A1
WICKMAN RD	BUT	25	B5
WICKS ST	SB	86	C1
WIDGEON RD	YOL	39	D3
WIDOW SPGS DR	SIS	12	E2
WIDOW VALLEY RD	MOD	13	E3
WIDOW VALLEY RD	MOD	14	A3
WIGHT WY	LAK	31	D3
WILBUR	CC	39	B5
WILBUR AV	LA	178	C3
WILBUR RD	BUT	25	C4
WILBUR SPGS RD	COL	32	B3
WILCOX RD	SHA	19	D1
WILCOX RD	TEH	18	D4
WILCOX RANCH RD	TUO	41	C5
WILD RD	SBD	91	B2
WILDASS RD	SBT	66	B1
WILDCAT RD	MCO	55	C2
WILDCAT RD	SHA	18	E3
WILDCAT RD	SHA	19	A3
WILDCAT RD	TEH	19	A3
WILD CAT TR	RCO	100	A5
WILDCAT CK RD	SIS	11	D2
WILDCAT CYN RD	CC	L	D4
WILDCAT CYN RD	CC	45	D1
WILDCAT CYN RD	SDCO	107	A5
WILD DUCK RD	MCO	55	E2
WILDER RD	HUM	16	A2
WILDER RD	TEH	18	D5
WLDRNSS LDGE RD	MEN	22	C3
WILDER RIDGE RD	HUM	16	A4
WILDHORSE RD	SBD	92	B1
WILDHRSE CYN RD	MON	65	C2
WILDHRSE CYN RD	SBD	84	B4
WILDMAN RD	KER	78	E4
WILD PLUM RD	SIE	27	A4
WILDROSE RD	INY	61	C5
WILD WASH RD	SBD	91	C2
WILDWOOD AV	SLT	129	D3
WILDWOOD RD	COL	32	E3
WILDWOOD RD	KER	78	A2
WILDWOOD RD	SJCO	47	C1
WILDWOOD RD	TRI	17	C2
WILDWOOD CYN RD	SBD	99	E2
WILEY WELLS RD	RCO	103	B5
WILFRED CYN RD	MNO	51	B2
WILHOLT RD	SJCO	40	A5
WILKIE AV	SUT	33	D3
WILKINS AV	STA	47	D1
WILKINS RD	IMP	109	B2
WILKINS RD	IMP	112	D5
WILKINSON RD	IMP	109	A3
WILLARD RD	TEH	18	C5
WILLARD CK RD	LAS	20	E3
WILLIAM RD	BUT	25	C3
WILLIAM ST	SJ	152	C4
WILLIAMS	SJCO	47	C1
WILLIAMS AV	MCO	47	D4
WILLIAMS RD	IMP	109	B4
WILLIAMS RD	KER	79	C2
WILLIAMS RD	KER	80	D4
WILLIAMS RD	LAS	8	B4
WILLIAMS RD	MON	54	D4

STREET	CO.	PAGE	GRID
WILLIAMS RD	SHA	13	E4
WILLIAMS CK RD	HUM	15	D2
WILLIAMSON RD	KER	79	D4
WILLIAMSON RD	RCO	107	A1
WILLIAMSON RD	TUO	41	B5
WILLIAM TELL TR	KER	79	C5
WILLIAMS VLY RD	PLU	20	C5
WILLIAMS WLL RD	SBD	81	E5
WILLIS RD	MCO	56	B1
WILLISTON RD	SUT	33	C1
WILLMOTT RD	MCO	55	D1
WILLMS RD	STA	48	A1
WILLOUGHBY RD	IMP	112	A4
WILLOW AV	CRTM	140	B1
WILLOW AV	FRCO	57	D2
WILLOW AV	GLE	24	E5
WILLOW AV	KER	89	C1
WILLOW DR	KER	78	A2
WILLOW DR	MAD	57	B1
WILLOW RD	MP	147	A2
WILLOW RD	SBD	91	C4
WILLOW RD	SDCO	107	A5
WILLOW RD	SLO	76	B5
WILLOW RD	SMCO	N	E2
WILLOW RD	SMCO	45	D3
WILLOW ST	LACO	97	E3
WILLOW ST	LACO	S	D2
WILLOW ST	SJ	152	C5
WILLOW WY	LAS	20	E2
WILLOW CREEK RD	AMA	40	D2
WILLOW CREEK RD	INY	52	D4
WILLOW CREEK RD	SBT	55	C5
WILLOW CREEK RD	SLO	75	E1
WILLOW CREEK RD	SLO	76	A1
WILLOW CREEK RD	SIS	4	C3
WILLOW CREEK RD	YUB	26	B5
WLLW CK RED RCK	SIS	5	B3
WILLOW GLEN DR	SDCO	111	E1
WILLOW GLEN RD	YUB	26	A5
WILLOW PASS RD	CC	M	A3
WILLOW PASS RD	CC	M	B3
WILLOW PASS RD	CC	39	A5
WILLOW POINT RD	YOL	39	D2
WILLOW RCH RD S	MOD	7	C3
WILLOWS RD	SDCO	107	B5
WILLOW SPGS EXT	SIS	12	E2
WILLOW SPGS RD	KER	79	D5
WILLOW SPGS RD	KER	89	D1
WILLOW SPGS RD	KER	90	A1
WILLOW SPGS RD	LAS	14	A5
WILLOW SPGS RD	LACO	89	C3
WILLOW SPGS RD	SCL	P	D5
WILLOW SPGS RD	SCL	54	C1
WILLOW VLY RD	NEV	34	C1
WILL S GREEN RD	COL	32	E2
WILMINGTON AV	LACO	97	E3
WILMINGTON AV	LACO	S	D2
WILMINGTON BLVD	LA	191	B1
WILMINGTON BLVD	LACO	S	C2
WILSHIRE AV	SBD	101	C1
WILSHIRE BLVD	BH	183	B2
WILSHIRE BLVD	LA	180	D2
WILSHIRE BLVD	LA	183	B2
WILSHIRE BLVD	LA	185	A2
WILSHIRE BLVD	LACO	97	D2
WILSHIRE BLVD	LACO	Q	D4
WILSHIRE BLVD	LACO	180	D2
WILSHIRE BLVD	SMON	180	A4
WILSHIRE RD	SBD	92	A4
WILSON AV	COL	32	E3
WILSON AV	MAR	38	A4
WILSON AV	VAL	134	A3
WILSON DR	LA	181	A2
WILSON DR	TUL	68	E3
WILSON RD	IMP	112	D5
WILSON RD	KER	78	D3
WILSON RD	MCO	55	D1
WILSON RD	SBD	101	D1
WILSON RD	SUT	33	D3
WILSON ST	KER	79	C3
WILSON ST	RIV	100	A3
WILSON ST	TEH	24	E1
WILSON WY	PLA	34	B3
WILSON WY	SJCO	40	B5
WILSON BEND RD	COL	33	B3
WILSON CREEK RD	DN	1	E5
WILSON HILL RD	MAR	37	E4
WILSON HILL RD	SHA	19	B3
WILSON LAKE RD	TEH	19	D4
WILSON LANDING	BUT	25	A2
WILSON RANCH RD	SBD	90	E4
WILSON SPGS RD	LAS	14	A5
WILSON VLY RD	RCO	107	A1
WILTON PL	LA	181	E5
WILTON PL	LA	182	A5
WILTON PL	LA	184	E3
WILTON PL	LA	185	A3
WILTON RD	SAC	40	A2
WIMER RD	SJCO	40	D4
WINCHESTER BLVD	SCL	P	B3
WINCHESTER BLVD	SCL	46	A5
WINCHESTER RD	RCO	99	D4
WINCHUCK RD	CUR	1	D2
WINDING WY	SR	139	B4
WINDING WY	SIS	12	E2
WINDLASS DR	RCO	101	C5
WINDSONG WY	RCO	107	B1
WINDSOR AV	LACO	R	B2
WINDSOR RIV RD	SON	37	D1
WINE CREEK RD	SON	31	D5
WINE CREEK RD	SON	37	D1
WINEMAN RD	SLO	76	C5
WINEVILLE AV	SBD	99	A2

STREET	CO.	PAGE	GRID
WINGATE RD	INY	71	C3
WINGFIELD RD	LAS	21	A3
WING LEVEE RD	SJCO	46	E1
WINNETKA AV	LA	178	A3
WINNETKA AV	LACO	97	B1
WINSHIP RD	SOL	39	C2
WINSHIP RD	YUBA	125	D4
WINSLOW RD	IMP	109	A2
WINSOME WY	SHA	18	B2
WINTER GRDNS BL	SDCO	V	E2
WINTER GRDNS BL	SDCO	106	E5
WINTERGREEN RD	SBD	90	E4
WINTERS RD	SBD	100	E1
WINTERS RD	SOL	39	A1
WINTRS GULCH RD	SIS	4	A5
WINTON AV	ALA	45	E2
WINTON AV W	H	146	C4
WINTON AV W	ALA	L	E5
WINTON AV W	ALA	N	E1
WINTON RD	CAL	41	B2
WINTON WY	MCO	48	B4
WINTOON WY	SIS	12	E2
WIRT RD	IMP	109	B3
WISCONSIN AV	COL	32	E3
WISCONSIN AV	TEH	24	E2
WISE RD	PLA	33	E3
WISE RD	PLA	34	A3
WISHON AV	FRE	165	C2
WISHON DR	TUL	69	B2
WISTOS LN	LAS	21	B3
WITHERS AV	CC	L	E3
WITHERS AV	CC	38	E5
WITHROW RD	SHA	19	A2
WITTER SPG E RD	LAK	31	C2
WIXOM RD	IMP	111	E3
WOHLFORD RD	SDCO	106	E3
WOLF RD	NEV	34	C2
WOLF CREEK RD	ALP	36	C5
WOLF CREEK RD	NEV	34	C2
WOLFE RD	CPTO	150	A4
WOLFE RD	SCL	P	A3
WOLFE RD	SCL	45	E4
WOLFE RD	SCL	46	A4
WOLFE RD	SVL	150	A3
WOLFE RD	VEN	96	C1
WOLFE GRADE	MAR	L	B3
WOLFE GRADE	MAR	139	C5
WOLFSEN	MCO	47	E5
WOLFSEN	MCO	55	E1
WOLFSKILL	SOL	39	A1
WONDER AV	KER	80	A4
WONDERLAND BLVD	SHA	18	C1
WONDERLAND DR	RCO	100	A3
WONDER STUMP RD	DN	1	D3
WONDERVIEW RD	RCO	100	A3
WOO RD	MCO	55	E2
WOOD RD	RCO	99	B3
WOOD RD	SUT	33	B2
WOOD RD	VEN	96	C1
WOOD ST	GLE	24	D4
WOODBINE RD	RCO	100	C5
WOODBRIDGE RD	SJCO	39	E4
WOODBRIDGE RD	SJCO	40	B4
WOODBURY RD	LACO	R	B2
WOODBURY RD	PAS	190	A1
WOOD CANYON RD	INY	71	D1
WOODCUTTERS WY	SHA	19	B3
WOODEN VLY RD	NAPA	38	D2
WOODFORD-TEH RD	KER	79	C4
WOODHILL DR	SHA	13	A5
WOODHOUSE MINE	CAL	41	B2
WOODLAND AV	MCO	48	C4
WOODLAND AV	SR	139	E5
WOODLAND AV	STA	47	C2
WOODLAND AV	TEH	24	D1
WOODLAND DR	MPA	49	C3
WOODLAND WY	SHA	19	B3
WOODLF TUNNL RD	BUT	26	B4
WOODLEY RD	SDCO	106	C4
WOOLEY RD E	VEN	96	B1
WOODMAN AV	LACO	97	C1
WOODMAN AV	LACO	Q	C2
WOOD RANCH RD	LAS	21	B2
WOODRIDGE RD	SHA	19	B3
WOODROW AV	SC	169	C5
WOODRUFF AV	LACO	S	E2
WOODRUFF AV	LACO	T	A2
WOODRUFF LN	YUB	33	D1
WOODSBRO RD	SJCO	40	A5
WOODSIDE AV	SDCO	V	E2
WOODSIDE AV	SDCO	106	E5
WOODSIDE RD	SMCO	45	D3
WOODSIDE RD	SMCO	N	D2
WOODS LAKE RD	ALP	36	A5
WOODSON AV	TEH	24	D2
WOODSON RD	SJCO	40	A3
WOOD VALLEY RD	SDCO	106	E3
WOODVIEW LN	MPA	49	B4
WOODWARD AV	SJCO	47	A1
WOODY RD	KER	78	D1
WOODY ST	KER	78	E1
WOODY-GRANIT RD	KER	68	E5
WOODY-GRANIT RD	KER	69	A5
WOODY-GRANIT RD	KER	78	E1
WOODY-GRANIT RD	KER	79	A1
WOOKEY RD	BUT	25	A2
WOOLEY RD	OXN	176	A4
WOOLLOMES AV	KER	68	A5
WOOLNER AV	FRFD	135	A4
WORDEN AV	MCO	48	C5
WORDEN RD	CAL	41	B3
WORK RD	KER	90	B1
WORKMAN ST	LACO	Q	C1

STREET	CO.	PAGE	GRID
WORKMAN MILL RD	LACO	98	A2
WORKMAN MILL RD	LACO	R	C4
WORMWOOD RD	IMP	111	E4
WORSLEY RD	RCO	100	C2
WORTH AV	TUL	68	D3
WORTH RD	SUT	33	D4
WORTHINGTON RD	IMP	108	E5
WORTHINGTON RD	MCO	47	C5
WORTHINGTON ST	KER	79	E1
WRAGG CANYON RD	NAPA	38	D2
WRAN RD	LAS	21	C4
WREN RD	STA	47	E2
WRIGHT AV	SVL	149	B3
WRIGHT AV	TUL	68	B3
WRIGHT RD	IMP	109	C5
WRIGHT RD	SIS	5	D3
WRIGHTS LAKE RD	ED	35	D4
WRIGLEY RD	HUM	15	E1
WRIGLEY TER RD	AVLN	97	B5
WUNPOST RD	MCO	65	E4
WYANDOTTE AV	BUT	25	D4
WYNDTT MNRS RCH	BUT	25	D4
WYE RD	INY	51	D4
WYER RD	COL	32	E3
WYLIE DR	MDO	162	E1
WYLIE ST	SB	87	D1
WYMAN CREEK RD	INY	52	A3
WYNCOOP RD	SUT	33	B2
WYNDHAM LN	RED	122	C4
WYNDHAVEN DR	TEH	18	D4
WYO AV	GLE	24	E3
WYSE RD	LACO	89	D4

X

STREET	CO.	PAGE	GRID
XIMENO AV	LACO	S	E3

Y

STREET	CO.	PAGE	GRID
YAJOME ST	NAP	133	C2
YANKEE HILL RD	TUO	41	C4
YAQUI GULCH RD	MPA	49	B3
YAQUI PASS RD	SDCO	107	E3
YARD RD	TEH	18	D4
YELLOW BUTTE RD	SIS	4	D5
YELLW JACKET RD	MNO	51	C1
YELLW JACKET RD	TEH	19	C4
YERBA BLVD	KER	80	B4
YERBA BUENA RD	VEN	96	D2
YERMO RD	SBD	82	C5
YERMO RD	SBD	92	A1
YERMO CUTOFF	SBD	81	E5
YERMO CUTOFF	SBD	82	A5
YGNACIO VLY RD	CC	M	A3
YMCA RD	FRCO	58	D3
YOAKIM BRDG RD	SON	31	C5
YOCUM RD	IMP	109	B3
YOKE ST	SHA	18	C3
YOLANDA AV	KER	89	C2
YOLANO RD	SOL	39	C2
YOLO AV	FRCO	56	E4
YOLO ST	STA	47	C4
YOLO CO LINE RD	COL	32	E3
YOLO CO LINE RD	COL	33	A3
YORBA LN	SBD	90	E3
YORBA LINDA BL	ORCO	98	C3
YORBA LINDA BL	ORCO	T	D1
YORK AV	KIN	67	A5
YORK BLVD	LACO	97	E1
YORK BLVD	LACO	R	A3
YORK RD	IMP	110	D5
YORK RD	SIS	4	C3
YORK ST	NAP	133	C3
YOSEMITE AV	MAN	161	A4
YOSEMITE AV	MCO	48	C4
YOSEMITE AV	SJCO	47	B1
YOSEMITE BLVD	MDO	162	E3
YOSEMITE BLVD	STA	47	D2
YOSEMITE BLVD	STA	48	B2
YOSEMITE RD	TUO	41	D5
YOSEMTE OAKS RD	MPA	49	B3
YSMTE SPGS PKWY	MAD	49	C5
YOU BET RD	NEV	34	D2
YOUD RD	MCO	48	B3
YOUNG AV	COL	32	E3
YOUNG RD	COL	24	E5
YOUNG RD	IMP	109	B3
YOUNG RD	STA	47	C3
YOUNG ST	RCO	99	E4
YOUNG LOVE AV	SC	169	B4
YOUNGS HILL RD	YUB	26	C4
YOUNGSTOWN RD	MCO	47	E4
YOUNT ST	NAPA	29	D4
YOUNTVLL CRS RD	NAPA	29	D4
YOUNTVLL CRS RD	NAPA	38	C2
YOWELL RD	MOD	14	B3
YREKA AGER RD	SIS	4	B4
YREKA WALKER RD	SIS	3	D3
YREKA WALKER RD	SIS	4	A4
YTURRIARTE RD	SBT	55	D4
YUBA AV	FRCO	56	E3
YUBA NEVADA RD	YUB	26	B5
YUBA PASS RD	SIE	27	B4
YUCAIPA BLVD	SBD	99	D2
YUCCA RD	RCO	107	C1
YUCCA RD	SBD	90	E3
YUCCA TR	SBD	100	E1
YUCCA LOMA RD	SBD	91	C4

Z

STREET	CO.	PAGE	GRID
ZABALA RD	MON	54	D4
ZABRISKIE PT RD	INY	72	A1
ZACA STATION RD	SB	86	E2
ZACHARIAS RD	STA	47	B3
ZACHARY AV	KER	78	C1
ZANES RD	HUM	15	E1
ZAYANTE RD	SCR	54	A1
ZAYANTE RD E	SCR	P	A5
ZEDIKER AV	FRCO	57	E3
ZEDIKER AV	FRCO	57	E4
ZEERING RD	STA	47	C3
ZEIGLER PT RD	HUM	10	D5
ZELDA LN	SBD	101	E1
ZENIA RD	MEN	23	A2
ZENIA RD	HUM	16	D5
ZENIA BLUFF RD	TRI	17	A5
ZENIA LK MTN RD	TRI	22	E1
ZENO RD	LAK	31	D2
ZERKER RD	KER	78	C2
ZERMATT DR	KER	79	C5
ZINC HILL RD	INY	70	E1
ZINC MINE RD	SBD	84	A3
ZINFANDEL DR	SAC	40	A1
ZINFANDEL LN	NAPA	29	C3
ZINK RD	BUT	25	E3
ZITZMAN RD	SIS	3	C5
ZLABEK RD	SIS	5	D2
ZOGG MINE RD	SHA	18	B2
ZOO DR	LACO	Q	E3
ZULU QUEN MN RD	RCO	102	A2
ZUMWALT	SJCO	47	C1
ZUMWALT AV	TUL	68	A2
ZUMWALT RD	COL	32	D2
ZZYZX RD	SBD	83	B4

NUMERICAL STREETS

STREET	CO.	PAGE	GRID
1ST AV	BARS	208	B1
1ST AV	BUT	25	B3
1ST AV	GLE	24	E3
1ST AV	IMP	112	D5
1ST AV	LPAZ	104	B2
1ST AV	LACO	R	D5
1ST AV	LACO	T	B1
1ST AV	MCO	47	E4
1ST AV	PLU	20	A4
1ST AV	SBD	208	C1
1ST AV	SD	215	D4
1ST AV	SDCO	V	B3
1ST AV	SDCO	V	C4
1ST AV	SDCO	111	D2
1ST ST	ALA	M	C5
1ST ST	ALA	46	C2
1ST ST	BEN	153	B4
1ST ST	DN	1	D3
1ST ST	DVS	136	D3
1ST ST	FRCO	57	C3
1ST ST	LA	186	A2
1ST ST	LACO	Q	E4
1ST ST	NAPA	L	C1
1ST ST	NAP	133	C4
1ST ST	ORCO	98	C4
1ST ST	ORCO	T	D3
1ST ST	RCO	U	E4
1ST ST	RCO	98	E3
1ST ST	SF	143	D4
1ST ST	SCL	P	B3
1ST ST	SJ	151	E1
1ST ST	SJ	152	B3
1ST ST	SA	195	A4
1ST ST	SA	196	A4
1ST ST	SCL	46	A4
1ST ST	SCL	54	D2
1ST ST	SHA	18	C3
1 1/2 AV	KIN	68	A1
2ND AV	COL	33	B3
2ND AV	GLE	24	E3
2ND AV	KIN	68	A1
2ND AV	LPAZ	104	B1
2ND AV	MCO	47	D4
2ND AV	RCO	103	D4
2ND AV S	MCO	48	A4
2ND ST	FRFD	135	A3
2ND ST	KER	68	B5
2ND ST	LA	186	A2
2ND ST	LACO	S	E3
2ND ST	MER	170	A5
2ND ST	SDCO	106	B3
2ND ST	SDCO	106	E5
2ND ST	SR	139	C4
2ND ST E	BEN	153	C4
2ND ST E	RENO	130	B3
2ND ST E	SOL	38	D4
2ND ST W	RENO	130	A3
2 1/2 AV	KIN	67	E2
3RD AV	FCTY	145	C1
3RD AV	GLE	24	E3
3RD AV	LPAZ	104	B1
3RD AV	MCO	47	D4
3RD AV	NAPA	38	D3
3RD AV	RCO	103	D4
3RD AV	SBD	99	B1
3RD AV	SDCO	V	C4
3RD AV	SDCO	111	D2
3RD AV	SMCO	N	C1
3RD AV	SMCO	45	C3
3RD AV	TEH	18	E5
3RD AV	TEH	24	E1
3RD ST	BH	183	C1
3RD ST	CC	38	C5
3RD ST	COR	215	B5
3RD ST	DVS	136	D3
3RD ST	EUR	121	C1
3RD ST	LB	192	D3
3RD ST	LA	183	C1

STREET	CO.	PAGE	GRID
3RD ST	LA	184	B1
3RD ST	LA	185	A1
3RD ST	LA	186	A3
3RD ST	LACO	Q	D4
3RD ST	NAP	133	C4
3RD ST	RIV	205	C2
3RD ST	SBDO	207	D2
3RD ST	SBD	99	C1
3RD ST	SFCO	L	C5
3RD ST	SF	143	D4
3RD ST	SR	139	C4
3RD ST	SHA	18	C3
3RD ST	TEH	24	D2
3RD ST	YOL	137	A2
4TH AV	CAR	168	C3
4TH AV	GLE	24	E3
4TH AV	KIN	67	E1
4TH AV	MCO	47	D4
4TH AV	MON	168	C3
4TH AV	RCO	103	D4
4TH AV	SD	215	D3
4TH AV	SDCO	V	C4
4TH AV	SDCO	111	D2
4TH ST	ALA	L	D4
4TH ST	BKD	166	C4
4TH ST	COR	215	C5
4TH ST	EC	217	D4
4TH ST	EUR	121	C1
4TH ST	KER	166	C4
4TH ST	LA	186	A3
4TH ST	MAR	L	A3
4TH ST	MAR	38	B5
4TH ST	MOD	8	B1
4TH ST	ONT	203	D3
4TH ST	ONT	204	B3
4TH ST	RCO	99	C4
4TH ST	SBD	99	D2
4TH ST	SDCO	V	C4
4TH ST	SDCO	111	C1
4TH ST	SJ	152	B2
4TH ST	SR	139	B3
4TH ST	SA	196	B4
4TH ST	SCL	54	E3
4TH ST	SHA	18	D3
4TH ST	STR	131	D3
4TH ST E	RENO	130	B2
4TH ST W	RENO	130	A2
5TH AV	CAR	168	B3
5TH AV	GLE	24	E3
5TH AV	GLE	24	E3
5TH AV	KIN	67	E1
5TH AV	LPAZ	104	A2
5TH AV	LACO	R	D3
5TH AV	SBD	92	D5
5TH AV	SBD	99	D2
5TH AV	SDCO	106	D3
5TH AV	SR	139	B3
5TH AV E	SIS	4	B4
5TH ST	DVS	136	C3
5TH ST	EUR	121	C1
5TH ST	HUM	9	E5
5TH ST	LA	186	A3
5TH ST	RCO	99	A3
5TH ST	SCTO	137	A3
5TH ST	SBD	99	C1
5TH ST	SBD	207	C2
5TH ST	SBDO	207	C2
5TH ST	SF	143	C5
5TH ST	SA	195	C4
5TH ST	SOL	L	D2
5TH ST	TEH	24	E1
5TH ST	VAL	134	D5
5TH ST	VEN	96	B1
5TH ST E	BEN	153	C5
5TH ST E	OXN	176	D4
5TH ST E	VEN	176	D4
5TH ST W	LACO	90	A2
5 1/2 AV	KIN	67	E2
6TH AV	CAR	168	B3
6TH AV	GLE	24	E3
6TH AV	KIN	67	E1
6TH AV	MCO	47	E4
6TH AV	RCO	103	D4
6TH AV	SD	215	E3
6TH AV	SDCO	V	B3
6TH ST	GLE	24	D3
6TH ST	LB	192	D3
6TH ST	LA	184	C2
6TH ST	LA	185	C2
6TH ST	LA	186	A3
6TH ST	ONT	203	D3
6TH ST	RCO	99	A3
6TH ST	YUB	33	E2
6 1/2 AV	KIN	67	E2
7TH	CC	38	C5
7TH AV	CAR	168	B3
7TH AV	KIN	67	E1
7TH AV	LPAZ	104	A2
7TH AV	LACO	R	D4
7TH AV	SF	141	D4
7TH AV	SFCO	L	B5
7TH AV	SFCO	45	B1
7TH AV	SCR	54	A2
7TH AV	YUB	33	D2
7TH ST	EUR	121	C1
7TH ST	IMP	109	A4
7TH ST	KER	78	B1
7TH ST	LB	192	D3
7TH ST	LA	185	C2
7TH ST	LA	186	A3
7TH ST	LACO	97	C2
7TH ST	LACO	98	A4
7TH ST	LACO	S	E2
7TH ST	O	157	C3
7TH ST	O	158	A4
7TH ST	RIV	205	B2
7TH ST	RCO	99	B2
7TH ST	RCO	99	E4
7TH ST	SBD	91	B4
7TH ST	SBD	99	B2
7TH ST	SBD	99	D2
7TH ST	SJ	152	B3
7TH ST	SLO	75	E3
7TH ST	STA	47	E3
7TH ST	UPL	203	E3
7TH ST N	MDO	162	B3
7TH ST S	MDO	162	C4
7TH ST S	STA	162	C4
7TH ST W	BEN	153	B4
7TH STANDARD RD	KER	77	C2
7 1/2 AV	KIN	57	E5
8TH AV	CAR	53	D5
8TH AV	CAR	168	B3
8TH AV	KIN	67	D1
8TH AV	RCO	103	D4
8TH AV	SD	215	E3
8TH ST	ALA	L	C4
8TH ST	BKD	166	C4
8TH ST	BUT	25	C5
8TH ST	EC	217	C3
8TH ST	IMP	112	A3
8TH ST	LA	185	A2
8TH ST	LA	186	A3
8TH ST	O	157	C3
8TH ST	RCO	99	E3
8TH ST	SBD	U	E2
8TH ST	SDCO	V	C4
8TH ST	SDCO	106	B3
8TH ST	SDCO	111	D1
8TH ST	SJCO	40	B5
8TH ST	SON	L	B1
8TH ST	UPL	203	E2
8TH ST E	DVS	136	C3
8TH ST W	DVS	136	B3
8 1/2 AV	KIN	57	D5
9TH AV	KER	68	C5
9TH AV	KIN	67	D1
9TH AV	LPAZ	104	A2
9TH AV	SD	215	E4
9TH AV	SDCO	106	D3
9TH ST	GGR	195	A2
9TH ST	LB	192	C2
9TH ST	LA	185	A3
9TH ST	LA	186	A4
9TH ST	LA	191	A4
9TH ST	LACO	S	C3
9TH ST	MDO	162	B3
9TH ST	SBD	203	E2
9TH ST	SBDO	207	C1
9TH ST	SF	143	B5
9TH ST	UPL	203	E2
9TH ST	UPL	204	B2
9TH ST S	MDO	162	C4
9TH ST S	STA	162	C4
9 1/2 AV	KIN	67	D1
10 MI HOUSE TR	BUT	25	C2
10TH	CC	38	C5
10TH AV	KIN	67	D1
10TH AV	RCO	103	D5
10TH ST	LB	192	D2
10TH ST	RCO	99	D3
10TH ST	SF	142	D4
10TH ST	SJ	152	B2
10TH ST	UPL	203	E2
10TH ST	YUB	33	D2
10TH ST E	LACO	90	A3
10TH ST W	BEN	153	A3
10TH ST W	CC	M	C3
10TH ST W	LACO	89	E3
10 1/2 AV	KIN	67	D2
11TH AV	KIN	67	D1
11TH AV	LPAZ	104	A2
11TH AV	RCO	103	D5
11TH AV	SBD	91	E1
11TH AV	SD	215	E4
11TH AV	SDCO	V	B3
11TH ST	LAK	31	D3
11TH ST	MDO	162	B3
11TH ST	SBD	91	B4
11TH ST	SJCO	47	A2
12TH AV	KIN	67	D1
12TH AV	LPAZ	104	A2
12TH AV	SD	215	E4
12TH AV	SDCO	V	B3
12TH ST	BUT	25	C4
12TH ST	HUM	15	E2
12TH ST	MOD	8	A1
12TH ST	O	157	C2
12TH ST	SCTO	137	C3
12TH ST	YUB	33	D2
12TH ST E	O	159	C1
12TH ST N	SCTO	137	C2
12 3/4 AV	KIN	67	D1
13TH AV	ALA	L	D4
13TH AV	ALA	45	D1
13TH AV	CAR	168	B4
13TH AV	KIN	67	D1
13TH AV	LPAZ	104	A2
13TH AV	O	158	C4
13TH ST	CC	38	C5
13TH ST	SJ	152	B2
13 1/4 AV	KIN	67	D1
14 MILE HOUSE	BUT	25	C2
14TH AV	KIN	67	D1
14TH AV	LPAZ	104	A2
14TH AV	O	158	C4
14TH AV	RCO	100	D3
14TH AV	RCO	103	D5
14TH ST E	ALA	L	E5
14TH ST E	CC	M	C3
14TH AV E	O	158	D5
14TH ST	ALA	146	B1
14TH ST	CC	39	B5
14TH ST	EUR	121	B2
14TH ST	MDO	162	B3
14TH ST	O	157	C2
14TH ST	RIV	99	E2
14TH ST	RIV	205	C3
14TH ST	RCO	99	B2
14TH ST	SBD	99	D2
14TH ST E	ALA	45	E2
14TH ST E	DVS	136	C2
14TH ST E	O	159	D1
14TH ST W	DVS	136	C2
14 1/2 AV	KIN	67	D2
15TH AV	KIN	67	D1
15TH AV	RCO	103	C5
15TH AV	SDCO	106	D3
15TH ST	KER	80	A5
15TH ST	MDO	162	B3
15TH ST	SCTO	137	B4
15 1/2 AV	KIN	67	C1
16TH AV	KIN	67	C1
16TH AV	RCO	100	D3
16TH AV	RCO	103	D5
16TH ST	MER	170	B3
16TH ST	SCTO	137	C4
16TH ST	SBD	98	D1
16TH ST	SBD	99	D2
16TH ST	SD	215	E4
16TH ST	SD	216	A4
16TH ST	SDCO	V	B3
16TH ST	YUMA	112	C5
17 MILE DR	MON	53	B3
17 MILE DR	MON	167	A3
17 MILE DR	PAC	167	B2
17TH AV	KIN	67	C1
17TH AV	SCR	54	A2
17TH ST	CM	199	B3
17TH ST	MDO	162	C3
17TH ST	ORCO	98	C4
17TH ST	ORCO	T	B4
17TH ST	ORCO	T	C4
17TH ST	ORCO	T	D3
17TH ST	SF	141	E5
17TH ST	SF	142	A5
17TH ST	SJ	152	C2
17TH ST	SA	195	D3
17TH ST	SA	196	A3
18TH AV	KIN	67	C1
18TH AV	RCO	100	D3
18TH AV	RCO	103	D5
18TH ST	BKD	166	B3
18TH ST	LAK	32	A3
18TH ST	SDCO	V	C4
18TH ST	SDCO	111	D2
18 3/4 AV	KIN	67	C1
19TH AV	KIN	67	C3
19TH AV	SFCO	L	B5
19TH AV	SFCO	45	B2
19TH ST	BKD	166	B3
19TH ST	CM	199	A2
19TH ST	KER	80	A5
19TH ST	ORCO	T	C4
19TH ST	SBD	98	D1
20TH AV	KIN	67	C1
20TH AV	RCO	100	D3
20TH AV	RCO	103	C5
20TH ST	KER	80	B5
20TH ST	KIN	80	A5
20TH ST E	LACO	90	A3
20TH ST W	KER	89	E1
20 1/2 AV	KIN	67	C2
21ST AV	KIN	67	C3
21ST ST	BKD	166	B3
21ST ST	MER	170	D3
21ST ST	SCTO	137	C4
21ST ST	SJ	152	C2
21 1/2 AV	KIN	67	C1
22ND AV	KIN	67	C1
22ND AV	RCO	100	E3
22ND AV	RCO	103	C5
22ND ST	RCO	100	A3
22ND ST	YUB	33	D2
22 1/2 AV	KIN	67	C1
23RD AV	KIN	67	C1
23RD AV	O	158	C4
23RD ST	BKD	166	C3
23RD ST	CC	L	C3
23RD ST	CC	38	C5
23RD ST	R	155	B3
23RD ST	SP	155	B3
23RD ST	SMON	187	B1
23 1/2 AV	KIN	67	B1
24TH AV	KIN	67	B1
24TH AV	RCO	100	E3
24TH AV	RCO	103	C5
24TH ST	BKD	166	C2
24TH ST	KER	78	D3
24TH ST	SAC	39	E1
24TH ST	SDCO	V	C4
24TH ST	SDCO	111	D2
24TH ST	SJ	152	D2
24TH ST	YUMA	112	C5
24 1/2 AV	KIN	67	B1
25TH AV	KIN	67	B1
25TH AV	KIN	67	B4
25TH AV	RCO	103	C5
25TH AV	SF	141	B3
25TH AV	SM	145	A3
25TH ST	LACO	S	C3
25TH ST	SD	216	A4
25TH ST	SDCO	V	B3
25TH ST E	LACO	90	A3
25TH ST W	KER	89	E1
26TH AV	RCO	101	A3
26TH AV	RCO	103	C5
26TH ST	SD	216	B5
26 1/4 AV	KIN	67	B1
27TH AV	KIN	67	B1
27TH ST	SDCO	V	C5
27TH ST	SDCO	111	D2
28TH AV	KIN	67	B2
28TH AV	RCO	101	A3
28TH AV	RCO	110	D1
28TH AV	SM	145	A3
28TH ST	SD	216	B4
28TH ST	SDCO	V	C3
28TH ST	SDCO	111	D1
29TH AV	ALA	L	D4
29TH ST	SCTO	137	D4
30TH AV	KIN	67	B3
30TH AV	RCO	100	D3
30TH AV	RCO	110	C1
30TH ST	BKD	166	D2
30TH ST	KER	80	B5
30TH ST	SD	214	B5
30TH ST	SD	216	B4
30TH ST	SDCO	V	C4
30TH ST	SDCO	111	D1
30TH ST	SDCO	111	D2
30TH ST E	LACO	90	A3
30TH ST W	KER	89	E1
30TH ST W	LACO	89	E2
31ST AV	SM	145	A4
32ND AV	RCO	101	A3
32ND AV	RCO	110	C1
32ND ST	KER	80	B5
32ND ST	LAK	32	A3
32ND ST	SD	216	C4
32ND ST	SDCO	111	D1
32ND ST	YUMA	112	C5
34TH AV	RCO	100	D3
34TH AV	RCO	110	C1
34TH ST	BKD	166	C2
35TH AV	ALA	L	D4
35TH AV	O	158	E5
35TH AV	RCO	110	C1
36TH AV	KIN	67	A4
36TH AV	RCO	100	D4
36TH AV	RCO	110	D1
36TH ST	LAK	32	A3
37TH ST	KER	80	B5
38TH AV	RCO	101	A4
38TH AV	RCO	110	D1
38TH ST	SD	216	D5
39TH AV	SM	145	C3
40TH AV	RCO	101	A4
40TH AV	SF	141	A3
40TH AV	SM	145	B4
40TH ST	SBD	99	B1
40TH ST	SD	214	D5
40TH ST	SDCO	V	C4
40TH ST E	LACO	90	A3
40TH ST W	KER	89	E1
40TH ST W	LACO	89	E2
41ST AV	SCR	54	A2
41ST ST	LACO	Q	E4
42ND AV	RCO	101	A4
42ND AV	SM	145	B4
43RD ST	SD	214	E5
43RD ST	SD	216	E1
44TH AV	RCO	100	E4
47TH AV	RCO	101	A4
47TH AV	SAC	39	E1
47TH ST E	LACO	90	A3
48TH AV	RCO	101	A4
50TH AV	RCO	101	A4
50TH ST E	LACO	90	A3
50TH ST W	KER	89	E1
50TH ST W	LACO	89	E2
51ST ST	LACO	Q	E4
52ND AV	RCO	101	A4
54TH AV	RCO	101	A4
54TH ST	RCO	99	A2
54TH ST	SDCO	V	C3
54TH ST	SDCO	111	D1
55TH ST E	LACO	90	B3
57TH ST E	LACO	90	B3
58TH AV	RCO	101	A5
60TH AV	RCO	101	A5
60TH ST	SDCO	V	C4
60TH ST E	LACO	90	B2
60TH ST W	KER	89	E2
60TH ST W	LACO	89	E2
62ND AV	RCO	101	B5
64TH AV	RCO	101	B5
65TH EXPWY	SAC	39	E1
65TH ST E	LACO	90	B2
65TH ST W	LACO	89	E2
66TH AV	RCO	101	B5
67TH ST	RCO	101	A5
68TH AV	RCO	101	B5
68TH AV	TEH	18	E5
70TH AV	RCO	101	B5
70TH ST	SDCO	V	D3
70TH ST	SDCO	111	D1
70TH ST E	LACO	90	B3
70TH ST W	LACO	89	E2
72ND AV	RCO	101	B5
73RD AV	ALA	L	D5
74TH AV	RCO	101	B5
76TH AV	RCO	101	B5
76TH ST E	LACO	90	B3
78TH AV	RCO	108	B1
80TH AV	RCO	107	C1
80TH AV	RCO	108	B1
80TH ST E	LACO	90	B3
80TH ST W	KER	89	D2
80TH ST W	LACO	89	D3
81ST AV	RCO	108	B1
82ND AV	RCO	108	B1
82ND ST	LACO	90	B3
84TH AV	RCO	108	B1
85TH ST W	LACO	89	D3
87TH ST E	LACO	90	B4
87TH ST W	LACO	89	D3
90TH ST E	LACO	90	B3
90TH ST W	KER	89	D2
90TH ST W	LACO	89	D3
92ND ST	LACO	Q	E5
92ND ST W	LACO	89	D3
95TH ST W	LACO	89	D3
96TH ST E	LACO	90	B4
97TH ST W	LACO	89	D3
98TH AV	ALA	L	E5
98TH AV	ALA	45	D2
98TH AV	O	159	D4
98TH ST W	LACO	89	D3
99-97 CUTOFF	SIS	4	B5
100TH ST E	LACO	90	B2
100TH ST W	KER	89	D2
103RD ST	LACO	Q	E5
105TH ST E	LACO	90	B3
106TH ST E	LACO	90	B4
110TH ST E	LACO	90	B3
110TH ST W	KER	79	D5
110TH ST W	LACO	89	D2
115TH ST W	KER	79	D5
120TH ST E	LACO	90	B2
120TH ST W	LACO	89	D2
121ST ST E	LACO	90	B4
130TH ST E	LACO	90	C2
130TH ST W	LACO	89	D2
131ST ST E	LACO	90	C4
135TH ST	LACO	S	C1
137TH ST E	LACO	90	C2
140TH ST E	LACO	90	C2
140TH ST W	KER	89	D1
145TH ST	KER	89	D1
145TH ST E	LACO	90	C3
146TH ST	KER	89	D1
147TH ST	KER	89	C1
149TH ST	KER	89	C1
150TH ST E	LACO	90	C3
152ND ST W	KER	89	C1
155TH ST	KER	89	C1
157TH ST W	KER	89	C1
160TH ST W	LACO	89	C2
164TH ST	LACO	S	B1
165TH ST E	LACO	90	C3
170TH ST E	LACO	90	C3
170TH ST W	KER	89	C2
170TH ST W	LACO	89	C2
175TH ST E	LACO	90	C3
176TH ST	KER	89	C1
177TH ST	KER	89	C1
180TH ST E	LACO	90	C3
180TH ST W	LACO	89	C2
182ND ST	LACO	S	C1
185TH ST E	LACO	90	C3
185TH ST W	KER	89	C2
190TH ST	LACO	97	D3
190TH ST	LACO	S	B1
190TH ST E	LACO	90	C2
190TH ST W	LACO	89	C2
195TH ST	LACO	S	E2
195TH ST	LACO	T	A2
195TH ST E	LACO	90	C2
195TH ST W	KER	89	C2
200TH ST E	LACO	90	D2
200TH ST E	LACO	90	C3
204TH ST E	LACO	90	D4
210TH ST	KER	89	C1
210TH ST E	LACO	90	D3
215TH ST W	KER	89	C2
220TH ST	LACO	S	C2
220TH ST E	LACO	90	D3
223RD ST	LACO	S	C2
223RD ST E	LACO	90	D4
225TH ST E	LACO	90	D2
228TH ST	LACO	S	C2
230TH ST E	LACO	90	D3
230TH ST W	KER	89	B2
233RD ST E	LACO	90	D4
235TH ST E	LACO	90	D3
235TH ST W	KER	89	B2
235TH ST W	LACO	89	B2
240TH ST E	LACO	90	D3
295TH ST W	KER	89	B2
300TH ST W	KER	89	B2
8001	MAD	50	A5
8003	MAD	50	A4
8004	MAD	50	A4
8005	MAD	50	A4
8006	MAD	50	A4
8007	MAD	50	A4
8008	MAD	50	A5
8009	MAD	50	A4
8009	MAD	50	A5
8013	MAD	50	B4
8014	MAD	50	B4
8015	MAD	50	B4
8016	MAD	50	A4
8020	MAD	50	A4
8021	MAD	49	E4
8023	MAD	50	B3
8024	MAD	50	A3
8026	MAD	50	B3
8027	MAD	50	B3
8029	MAD	50	A4
8041	MAD	49	E4
8042	MAD	49	D3
8046	MAD	49	D3
8063	MAD	57	C1
8066	MAD	57	D1
8067	MAD	57	E1
8080	MAD	57	D1
8081	MAD	49	D5
8082	MAD	49	D5
8083	MAD	49	D5
8086	MAD	49	C5
8087	MAD	57	C1

FEDERAL

ROUTE NO.	CO. ABBR.	PAGE	GRID
6	ESM	44	E4
6	MIN	44	D5
6	MNO	51	C1
50	CRSN	36	B2
50	DGL	36	B2
50	ED	35	B4
50	ED	36	A3
50	LYON	36	D1
50	SAC	40	A1
60	LPAZ	104	D4
93	CLK	74	E2
93	MOH	85	E1
95	CLK	74	D2
95	LPAZ	103	E5
95	MIN	44	A1
95	NYE	62	B2
95	RCO	103	E2
95	SBD	85	B4
95	SBD	95	B1
95	SBD	103	D1
95	YUMA	112	E5
97	KLAM	5	B1
97	SIS	4	D5
97	SIS	5	A3
97	SIS	12	C1
101	CUR	1	C1
101	DN	10	A1
101	HUM	9	E3
101	HUM	10	A2
101	HUM	15	D2
101	HUM	16	B4
101	HUM	22	C1
101	LACO	97	B1
101	LACO	Q	D3
101	MAR	38	B5
101	MAR	45	B1
101	MAR	L	B2
101	MEN	22	C2
101	MEN	31	A1
101	MON	54	C3
101	MON	55	A5
101	MON	65	B2
101	SB	86	C1
101	SB	87	A4
101	SBT	54	D3
101	SCL	46	A4
101	SFCO	45	B1
101	SFCO	L	B4
101	SLO	76	A1
101	SMCO	45	C2
101	SMCO	L	C5
101	SMCO	N	C1
101	SCL	54	D1
101	SCL	P	C3
101	SON	32	D5
101	SON	37	E1
101	SON	33	A3
101	VEN	88	A5
101	VEN	96	D1
197	DN	1	E3
199	DN	1	E3
199	DN	2	C3
395	CRSN	36	C2
395	DGL	36	C3
395	INY	51	C3
395	INY	59	E1
395	INY	60	A3
395	INY	70	B1
395	KER	70	C5
395	KER	80	D1
395	LAKE	7	C1
395	LAS	8	B3
395	LAS	21	B3
395	LAS	27	E1
395	MOD	7	C3
395	MOD	8	B2
395	MNO	42	E2
395	MNO	43	A2
395	MNO	50	D1
395	SBD	80	E3
395	SBD	91	A2
395	WSH	28	A3

INTERSTATE

ROUTE NO.	CO. ABBR.	PAGE	GRID
5	COL	32	D1
5	COL	33	A3
5	FRCO	55	E3
5	FRCO	56	B4
5	FRCO	66	D1
5	GLE	24	D3
5	JKSN	4	A1
5	KER	77	E2
5	KER	78	B3
5	KER	88	D1
5	KIN	67	C4
5	LACO	88	E2
5	LACO	89	A3
5	LACO	97	E1
5	LACO	98	B3
5	LACO	Q	D2
5	LACO	R	C5
5	MCO	47	C5
5	MCO	55	E2
5	ORCO	98	B3
5	ORCO	105	E1
5	ORCO	T	E3
5	ORCO	U	A5
5	SAC	39	E2
5	SDCO	106	A2
5	SDCO	111	D2
5	SDCO	V	A2
5	SJCO	39	E4
5	SJCO	40	A4
5	SJCO	47	A2
5	SHA	12	C3
5	SHA	18	C2
5	SIS	4	B3
5	SIS	12	D2
5	STA	47	A3
5	TEH	18	D4
5	TEH	24	D1
5	YOL	33	A4
8	IMP	111	B4
8	SDCO	107	A5
8	SDCO	111	C1
8	SDCO	112	D1
8	SDCO	V	B3
8	YUMA	112	D5
10	LPAZ	103	E5
10	LACO	97	D2
10	LACO	98	A2
10	LACO	Q	D4
10	LACO	U	B2
10	RCO	99	E3
10	RCO	100	A3
10	RCO	101	A4
10	RCO	102	D4
10	RCO	103	B5
10	SBD	99	A1
10	SBD	U	E2
15	CLK	74	E1
15	RCO	99	B4
15	SBD	82	C5
15	SBD	83	D3
15	SBD	84	A2
15	SBD	91	D2
15	SBD	92	B1
15	SBD	99	A1
15	SBD	98	E2
15	SDCO	106	D3
15	SDCO	V	C1
40	SBD	92	A1
40	SBD	93	D2
40	SBD	94	D2
40	SBD	95	C1
80	ALA	L	C4
80	CC	38	C5
80	CC	L	C3
80	NEV	27	C6
80	NEV	35	D1
80	PLA	34	D2
80	PLA	35	A1
80	SAC	33	E5
80	SAC	34	A5
80	SAC	39	E1
80	SFCO	45	C1
80	SFCO	L	C4
80	SOL	38	E3
80	SOL	39	A2
80	WSH	28	A4
80	YOL	39	D1
105	LACO	Q	D5
105	LACO	S	B1
110	LACO	97	D3
110	LACO	Q	E5
110	LACO	S	C1
205	SJCO	46	D2
210	LACO	89	E5
210	LACO	97	E1
210	LACO	98	B1
210	LACO	Q	C1
210	LACO	R	A2
210	LACO	U	A2
215	SBD	99	B1
238	ALA	45	E2
238	ALA	L	E5
280	SCL	45	E4
280	SCL	N	E3
280	SCL	P	A3
280	SFCO	45	B2
280	SFCO	L	C5
280	SMCO	45	B2
280	SMCO	N	C2
380	SMCO	45	C2
380	SMCO	N	C1
405	LACO	97	C1
405	LACO	Q	B3
405	LACO	S	C2
405	ORCO	98	B4
405	ORCO	T	A2
505	SOL	39	A2
505	YOL	33	A4
505	YOL	39	A1
580	ALA	45	A1
580	ALA	46	A2
580	ALA	L	D4
580	ALA	M	A5
580	CC	L	C3
580	MAR	38	B5
580	SJCO	46	D2
605	LACO	98	B2
605	LACO	R	D4
605	LACO	S	E2
605	LACO	T	A2
680	ALA	46	B2
680	ALA	P	B1
680	CC	38	E5
680	CC	46	A1
680	CC	L	E4
680	CC	M	A3
680	SCL	46	B4
680	SCL	P	B2
680	SOL	38	E4
680	SOL	L	E2
780	SOL	38	D4
780	SOL	L	E2
805	SDCO	106	C5
805	SDCO	111	D2
805	SDCO	V	B1
880	ALA	P	B2
980	ALA	45	D1
980	ALA	L	D4

STATE

ROUTE NO.	CO. ABBR.	PAGE	GRID
1	HUM	15	D3
1	LACO	96	D2
1	LACO	97	B2
1	LACO	Q	C4
1	LACO	S	B2
1	MAR	37	E4
1	MAR	45	A1
1	MAR	L	B4
1	MEN	22	C2
1	MEN	30	C3
1	MON	54	B3
1	MON	64	B2
1	MON	65	A4
1	ORCO	98	C5
1	ORCO	105	D1
1	ORCO	T	B3
1	SFCO	45	B1
1	SFCO	L	B4
1	SLO	65	A5
1	SLO	75	B1
1	SLO	76	A4
1	SMCO	45	B2
1	SMCO	L	B5
1	SMCO	N	B1
1	SB	86	B2
1	SCR	53	C1
1	SCR	54	B2
1	SCR	N	D5
1	SON	30	D5
1	SON	37	B1
1	VEN	96	C1
2	LACO	90	C4
2	LACO	97	E1
2	LACO	Q	C4
2	LACO	R	A1
2	SBD	90	E5
3	SIS	3	D5
3	SIS	4	A4
3	SIS	11	D1
3	SIS	12	A2
3	TRI	11	E4
3	TRI	12	A3
3	TRI	17	B2
4	ALP	36	C5
4	ALP	42	B1
4	CAL	41	D2
4	CC	38	D5
4	CC	39	C5
4	CC	L	E3
4	CC	M	B3
4	SJCO	39	E5
4	SJCO	40	B5
4	STA	40	E5
9	SCL	45	E5
9	SCL	N	E4
9	SCL	P	A4
9	SCR	53	D1
9	SCR	N	E4
9	SCR	P	A5
12	CAL	40	D4
12	CAL	41	A3
12	NAPA	38	C3
12	NAPA	L	C1
12	SAC	39	C4
12	SAC	M	E2
12	SJCO	39	E4
12	SJCO	40	A1
12	SOL	38	E3
12	SOL	39	A3
12	SOL	M	B1
12	SON	37	E2
12	SON	38	A2
13	ALA	45	D1
13	ALA	L	D4
14	KER	80	C1
14	KER	89	E1
14	LACO	89	E2
15	SBD	98	E2
15	SDCO	V	C3
16	COL	32	C3
16	SAC	39	E1
16	SAC	40	A1
16	YOL	32	D4
17	SCR	54	A1
17	SCR	P	B5
18	LACO	90	D4
18	SBD	91	A4
18	SBD	92	A4
18	SBD	99	C1
19	LACO	98	A3
19	LACO	R	C3
19	LACO	S	E1
20	COL	32	E2
20	COL	33	A2
20	LAK	31	E3
20	LAK	32	A3
20	MEN	22	D5
20	MEN	31	C2
20	NEV	34	C1
20	SUT	33	C2
20	YUB	33	E1
22	ORCO	98	B4
22	ORCO	T	A3
23	LACO	96	E2
23	VEN	88	D5
23	VEN	96	E1
24	ALA	L	D4
24	CC	38	E5
24	CC	45	E1
24	CC	L	E4
24	CC	M	A3
25	MON	65	D2
25	SBT	55	A3
25	SBT	65	D1
26	CAL	41	B2
26	SJCO	40	D4
27	LACO	97	B1
27	LACO	Q	A2
28	CRSN	36	B2
28	PLA	35	E1
28	WSH	36	A1
29	LAK	31	D2
29	LAK	32	A4
29	NAPA	38	B1
29	NAPA	L	D1
29	SOL	38	D4
30	LACO	98	D1
30	LACO	U	C2
30	SBD	98	E1
30	SBD	99	B1
30	SBD	U	E1
31	RCO	98	E2
31	RCO	U	E4
32	BUT	25	A3
32	GLE	24	D3
32	TEH	19	E4
33	FRCO	56	B2
33	FRCO	66	D2
33	KER	67	B5
33	KER	77	B1
33	KER	78	A5
33	KIN	67	A4
33	MCO	47	C5
33	MCO	55	C1
33	SJCO	47	A2
33	SLO	87	E1
33	SB	87	E1
33	STA	47	B3
33	VEN	88	A2
34	VEN	88	C5
34	VEN	96	C1
35	LACO	T	A1
35	SFCO	45	B2
35	SFCO	L	B5
35	SMCO	45	C3
35	SMCO	L	B5
35	SMCO	N	B1
35	SCL	46	A5
36	HUM	15	E2
36	HUM	16	C3
36	LAS	20	E3
36	LAS	21	A3
36	PLU	20	A4
36	SHA	17	E4
36	TEH	17	E4
36	TEH	18	C4
36	TEH	19	C4
36	TRI	16	E3
36	TRI	17	A3
37	MAR	L	B2
37	SOL	38	D4
37	SOL	L	C2
37	SON	38	C4
38	SBD	91	E5
38	SBD	92	A5
38	SBD	99	E1
38	SBD	100	B1
39	KLAM	5	C1
39	LACO	98	C1
39	LACO	R	E3
39	LACO	U	A2
39	ORCO	98	B4
39	ORCO	R	D5
39	ORCO	T	C1
41	FRCO	57	C3
41	KIN	67	C2
41	MAD	49	D4
41	MAD	57	C2
41	MPA	63	C5
41	SLO	66	D5
41	SLO	76	A2
42	LACO	97	E2
42	LACO	Q	C5
42	LACO	R	B5
43	FRCO	57	D5
43	KER	68	B5
43	KER	78	B2
43	KIN	67	E2
43	TUL	68	A3
44	LAS	20	A2
44	SHA	18	C2
44	SHA	19	C2
45	COL	32	E1
45	COL	33	A2
45	GLE	24	E3
45	YOL	33	C4
46	JOS	2	D1
46	KER	77	A1
46	KER	78	B1
46	SLO	66	D5
46	SLO	75	E2
46	SLO	76	B1
47	LACO	191	C3
48	LACO	89	A2
49	AMA	40	D1
49	CAL	41	A3
49	ED	34	D4
49	MAD	49	D4
49	MPA	48	E2
49	MPA	49	A3
49	NEV	34	C1
49	PLA	34	C3
49	PLU	27	D3
49	SIE	26	C4
49	SIE	27	C4
49	TUO	41	C5
49	TUO	48	D1
49	YUBA	26	C4
50	ED	34	C5
50	SAC	39	E1
50	SAC	40	A1
52	SDCO	106	C5
52	SDCO	V	B2
53	LAK	32	A3
54	SDCO	111	E1
54	SDCO	V	D4
55	ORCO	98	C4
55	ORCO	T	D3
56	SDCO	106	D4
57	LACO	98	C2
57	LACO	U	B3
57	ORCO	98	C3
57	ORCO	T	D1
58	KER	77	E3
58	KER	78	B3
58	KER	80	A4
58	SBD	91	C1
58	SLO	76	B3
58	SLO	77	A3
59	MCO	48	C4
60	LACO	98	B2
60	LACO	R	D4
60	RCO	99	B2
60	SBD	98	D2
60	SBD	U	E3
61	ALA	45	D2
61	ALA	L	D5
62	RCO	100	C2
62	RCO	102	E2
62	SBD	101	A1
62	SBD	102	A2
62	SBD	103	B2
63	FRCO	58	B4
63	TUL	58	B5
63	TUL	68	B2
65	KER	68	D6
65	KER	78	D2
65	PLA	34	A3
65	TUL	68	C2
65	YUB	33	D3
66	JKSN	4	A1
66	KLAM	4	D1
66	SBD	98	E1
66	SBD	99	B1
66	SBD	U	D2
67	SDCO	106	E4
67	SDCO	107	A4
67	SDCO	V	E2
68	MOH	85	D4
68	MON	54	B4
70	BUT	25	D3
70	KLAM	5	D1
70	LAS	27	E2
70	PLU	26	A1
70	SUT	33	D4
70	YUB	33	D1
71	LACO	98	D2
71	LACO	U	C3
71	RCO	98	D2
71	SBD	98	D2
71	SBD	U	C3
72	LPAZ	104	B2
72	LACO	97	E2
72	LACO	98	A2
72	LACO	R	B4
73	ORCO	98	C4
73	ORCO	T	D4
74	ORCO	98	E5
74	ORCO	99	A5
74	RCO	99	C4
74	RCO	100	A4
75	SDCO	111	C1
75	SDCO	V	B4
76	SDCO	106	D2
76	SDCO	107	B2
77	ALA	L	D5
77	ALA	45	D1
77	ALA	159	C1
78	IMP	108	C3
78	IMP	109	A4
78	IMP	110	C2
78	RCO	103	D5
78	RCO	110	C1
78	SDCO	106	C3
78	SDCO	107	C3
78	SDCO	108	A3
79	RCO	99	E3
79	RCO	106	D1
79	SDCO	107	B1
80	SFCO	L	C5
82	SCL	46	A4
82	SCL	P	A3
82	SMCO	45	C2
82	SMCO	N	B1
83	SBD	98	D2
83	SBD	U	D3
84	ALA	45	E3
84	ALA	46	B3
84	ALA	M	C5
84	SMCO	45	D4
84	SMCO	N	D3
84	YOL	39	D1
85	SCL	45	E4
85	SCL	P	A3
86	IMP	108	C2
86	IMP	109	A4
86	RCO	101	B4
86	RCO	108	B1
87	SCL	46	B4
87	SCL	P	B3
88	ALP	36	C4
88	AMA	35	D5
88	AMA	41	A2
88	DGL	36	C3
88	SJCO	40	C3
89	ALP	36	B4
89	ED	35	E3
89	ED	36	A4
89	MNO	36	D5
89	NEV	27	D5
89	PLA	35	D1
89	PLU	20	A4
89	PLU	26	C1
89	SHA	13	C3
89	SHA	19	E1
89	SIE	27	C4
89	SIS	12	E2
89	SIS	13	B3
89	TEH	19	D3
90	LACO	Q	D4
90	ORCO	98	C3
90	ORCO	T	E1
91	LACO	97	E3
91	LACO	S	C1
91	ORCO	98	C3
91	ORCO	T	C2
91	RCO	99	A3
91	RCO	U	D5
92	ALA	45	D3
92	ALA	N	E1
92	SMCO	45	D3
92	SMCO	N	C2
94	SDCO	111	E1

HIGHWAY INDEX

ROUTE NO.	CO. ABBR.	PAGE	GRID
94	SDCO	112	D2
94	SDCO	V	D3
95	LPAZ	104	B2
95	MOH	85	D5
95	MOH	95	D1
95	MOH	96	B3
96	HUM	10	C3
96	SIS	2	E4
96	SIS	3	C3
96	SIS	10	E1
98	IMP	111	C3
98	IMP	112	C4
99	BUT	25	B3
99	FRCO	57	B3
99	JKSN	3	E1
99	KER	68	B5
99	KER	78	C2
99	MAD	56	D1
99	MAD	57	B2
99	MCO	48	B4
99	MCO	56	D1
99	SAC	39	E2
99	SAC	40	A2
99	SJCO	40	B4
99	SJCO	47	B1
99	STA	47	D3
99	SUT	33	C3
99	TEH	18	D5
99	TUL	57	E5
103	LACO	97	E4
103	LACO	S	D2
104	SAC	40	C2
107	LACO	97	D3
107	LACO	S	B2
108	MNO	42	E2
108	STA	47	D2
108	TUO	41	D4
108	TUO	42	B2
110	LACO	97	E2
110	LACO	R	B3
111	IMP	108	D1
111	IMP	109	B3
111	IMP	112	B3
111	RCO	100	C3
111	RCO	101	A4
111	RCO	108	D1
112	ALA	45	D2
112	ALA	L	E5
113	SOL	39	B2
113	SOL	M	C1
113	SUT	33	C3
113	YOL	33	C5
114	SMCO	N	D2
115	IMP	109	B3
115	IMP	112	C3
116	SON	37	D2
116	SON	38	A3
116	SON	L	A1
117	SDCO	111	E2
117	SDCO	V	D5
118	LACO	89	B5
118	LACO	Q	C1
118	VEN	88	C5
118	VEN	89	A5
119	KER	78	B3
120	MNO	43	C5
120	MNO	51	B1
120	SJCO	47	B1
120	STA	48	A1
120	TUO	41	C5
120	TUO	48	C1
120	TUO	49	B1
121	NAPA	38	D2
121	NAPA	L	C1
121	SON	38	B3
121	SON	L	B1
123	ALA	L	D4
124	AMA	40	D2
125	SDCO	106	E4
125	SDCO	V	D2
126	LACO	89	A4
126	VEN	88	D4
126	VEN	89	A4
127	INY	72	D2
127	SBD	72	E5
127	SBD	83	B2
128	MEN	30	C2

ROUTE NO.	CO. ABBR.	PAGE	GRID
128	MEN	31	B4
128	NAPA	38	B2
128	SON	31	D5
128	SON	38	A1
128	YOL	39	A1
129	SCR	54	D2
130	SCL	46	C4
130	SCL	P	C3
131	MAR	38	B5
131	MAR	45	B1
131	MAR	L	B4
132	MPA	48	D2
132	SJCO	47	A2
132	STA	47	B2
132	STA	48	B2
133	ORCO	98	D5
133	ORCO	T	E4
134	LACO	97	D1
134	LACO	Q	E3
134	LACO	R	A3
135	SB	86	C1
136	INY	60	B4
137	TUL	68	B2
138	LACO	88	E2
138	LACO	89	A2
138	LACO	90	A3
138	SBD	91	A5
139	LAS	14	C3
139	LAS	20	E1
139	LAS	21	A3
139	MOD	5	E3
139	MOD	6	A4
139	MOD	14	D1
139	SIS	5	E3
140	KLAM	5	C1
140	LAKE	7	A1
140	MCO	47	D4
140	MCO	48	A4
140	MPA	48	E4
140	MPA	49	C2
142	ORCO	T	E1
142	ORCO	U	B4
142	SBD	98	D2
144	SB	87	C4
145	FRCO	57	A4
145	FRCO	66	E1
145	MAD	57	B2
146	CLK	74	E3
146	MON	55	B5
146	SBT	55	C5
147	PLU	20	C4
149	BUT	25	C4
150	SB	87	E4
150	VEN	88	B4
151	SHA	18	C1
152	MAD	56	C1
152	MCO	55	E1
152	MCO	56	B1
152	SCL	54	D2
152	SCR	54	C2
154	SB	87	A3
155	KER	68	B5
155	KER	69	B5
155	KER	79	C1
156	CLK	72	E1
156	CLK	74	A1
156	MON	54	C3
156	SBT	54	E2
156	SBT	55	A2
157	CLK	73	E2
157	CLK	74	A2
158	CLK	73	E1
158	CLK	74	A1
158	MNO	50	C1
160	CLK	73	E3
160	CLK	74	B3
160	NYE	73	C2
160	SAC	39	E1
160	SAC	M	D2
161	CLK	74	C5
161	SIS	5	B2
162	BUT	25	B5
162	GLE	24	B4
162	GLE	25	B5
162	MEN	22	E4
162	MEN	23	A3
163	CLK	85	C4

ROUTE NO.	CO. ABBR.	PAGE	GRID
163	SDCO	106	D5
163	SDCO	V	B3
164	CLK	84	E2
164	LACO	98	A1
165	MCO	47	E5
165	MCO	55	E2
166	KER	77	A4
166	KER	78	B5
166	SB	86	B1
166	SLO	76	D5
167	MNO	43	E4
168	FRCO	50	B5
168	FRCO	57	E2
168	FRCO	58	A1
168	INY	51	E5
168	INY	52	C3
168	MNO	52	C3
169	DN	1	E5
169	DN	2	A5
169	DN	10	A1
169	HUM	10	C3
170	LACO	97	D1
170	LACO	Q	C2
172	TEH	19	D4
173	SBD	91	C5
174	NEV	34	D2
175	LAK	31	E3
175	LAK	32	A5
175	MEN	31	C3
176	SB	86	C1
177	RCO	102	D2
178	INY	72	D3
178	INY	73	A3
178	KERN	69	E5
178	KER	70	A5
178	KER	78	E2
178	KER	79	A2
178	KER	80	B1
178	SBD	81	A1
180	FRCO	56	E3
180	FRCO	57	C3
180	FRCO	58	B3
180	FRCO	59	A3
182	MNO	43	C2
183	MON	54	C3
184	KER	78	E3
185	ALA	45	D1
185	ALA	L	D5
188	SDCO	112	C2
189	SBD	91	C5
190	INY	61	D4
190	INY	70	C1
190	INY	72	C1
190	TUL	68	B3
190	TUL	69	A3
191	BUT	25	C3
192	SB	87	C4
193	ED	34	E4
193	PLA	34	B3
195	RCO	101	B5
198	FRCO	66	E2
198	KIN	67	C2
198	MON	65	D2
198	MON	66	A2
198	TUL	58	E5
198	TUL	59	A5
198	TUL	68	B1
200	HUM	9	E5
200	HUM	10	A5
201	TUL	58	B5
202	KER	79	C4
203	MNO	50	D2
204	KER	78	D3
206	DGL	36	B3
206	SBD	99	B1
207	DGL	36	B3
208	DGL	36	E4
208	MEN	22	B2
209	SDCO	111	C1
209	SDCO	V	A4
213	LACO	S	C3
213	LACO	97	D3
215	RCO	99	C3
216	TUL	68	C1
217	SB	87	B4
218	MON	54	B4
219	STA	47	C2

ROUTE NO.	CO. ABBR.	PAGE	GRID
220	SOL	39	D3
221	NAPA	L	D1
221	NAPA	38	D3
223	KER	78	D4
223	KER	79	A4
224	SB	87	E4
225	SB	87	C4
227	SLO	76	B4
229	SLO	76	B2
232	VEN	88	B5
233	MAD	56	D1
236	SCR	53	D1
236	SCR	N	D4
237	SCL	46	B4
237	SCL	P	A3
238	ALA	46	A2
238	ALA	P	A1
241	ORCO	98	D4
242	CC	M	A3
243	RCO	100	A3
245	FRCO	58	D4
245	TUL	58	C4
245	TUL	68	C1
246	SB	86	C3
247	SBD	91	E2
247	SBD	92	B4
247	SBD	100	D1
250	ORCO	98	C3
253	MEN	31	A3
254	HUM	16	B4
255	HUM	9	E5
255	HUM	10	A5
259	SBD	99	B1
262	ALA	46	A3
262	ALA	P	B2
263	SIS	4	A4
264	ESM	52	A1
265	ESM	52	E1
266	MNO	52	C3
267	ESM	61	C1
267	PLA	35	E1
267	PLA	36	A1
269	FRCO	67	A1
270	MNO	43	B3
271	MEN	22	C1
273	SHA	18	C2
274	SDCO	106	C5
274	SDCO	V	B2
281	LAK	31	E3
282	SDCO	111	C1
282	SDCO	V	B4
284	PLU	27	D2
299	HUM	10	B4
299	LAS	14	A3
299	MOD	7	C5
299	MOD	8	B1
299	MOD	14	D1
299	SHA	13	B5
299	SHA	18	B2
299	TRI	10	D5
299	TRI	16	E1
299	TRI	17	D1
330	SBD	99	C1
338	LYON	43	B1
341	LYON	36	D1
341	WSH	28	C5
359	MIN	44	B2
360	MIN	44	E3
371	RCO	100	B5
372	NYE	73	B2
373	NYE	62	D5
374	NYE	62	A3
380	SMCO	N	B1
428	WSH	36	C1
429	WSH	36	B1
430	WSH	28	B4
431	WSH	28	B5
431	WSH	36	B1
445	WSH	28	D1
446	WSH	28	E2
447	WSH	28	E2
512	CRSN	36	C2
513	CRSN	36	C2
604	CLK	74	E2
666	WSH	28	B4
710	LACO	97	E2
710	LACO	R	B5

ROUTE NO.	CO. ABBR.	PAGE	GRID
710	LACO	S	D2
759	DGL	36	C3
880	ALA	45	E2
880	SCL	46	B4
COUNTY			
1	LPAZ	103	E3
1	LPAZ	104	A1
3	LPAZ	104	B2
10	LPAZ	104	A2
14	LPAZ	103	E2
14	LPAZ	104	A2
17	LPAZ	103	E2
17	LPAZ	104	A2
21	LPAZ	103	E3
21	LPAZ	104	A3
25	LPAZ	103	E3
29	LPAZ	103	E2
30	LPAZ	103	E3
30	LPAZ	104	A3
34	LPAZ	103	E3
38	LPAZ	103	E3
44	LPAZ	103	E3
44	LPAZ	104	A3
50	LPAZ	103	E4
56	LPAZ	103	E4
A 1	LAS	20	D2
A 2	LAS	14	C3
A 3	LAS	21	B4
A 5	TEH	18	C3
A 6	TEH	18	E4
A 6	TEH	19	B3
A 7	TEH	18	D5
A 8	TEH	18	D5
A 9	TEH	24	D2
A10	SIS	12	C2
A11	TEH	24	D1
A12	SIS	4	B5
A13	PLU	20	B4
A14	PLU	27	A3
A15	PLU	27	B2
A16	SHA	17	E3
A16	SHA	18	A3
A16	SHA	122	A2
A17	SHA	18	D3
A17	SHA	19	A3
A18	SHA	18	C2
A19	SHA	13	D3
A21	LAS	20	C2
A22	PLU	20	D5
A23	PLU	27	C2
A23	SIE	27	C3
A24	PLU	27	D3
A25	LAS	21	D5
A26	LAS	21	D5
A27	LAS	21	B3
B 2	BUT	25	D4
D 1	DN	1	E3
D 2	DN	1	D4
D 3	DN	1	D3
D 5	DN	1	D2
E 1	ALP	36	C5
E 4	YOL	32	E4
E 4	YOL	33	A4
E 6	YOL	39	B1
E 6	YOL	136	A2
E 7	SOL	39	B1
E 7	YOL	33	B5
E 8	YOL	33	C4
E 8	YOL	39	C1
E 8	YOL	136	E1
E 9	YOL	39	D2
E10	YOL	33	B4
E11	YOL	33	B4
E13	SAC	39	D3
E16	AMA	40	E1
E16	ED	35	B4
G 1	SBT	54	E3
G 2	SCL	46	A4
G 2	SCL	P	A3
G 2	SCLR	150	C2
G 3	PA	147	D3
G 3	SCL	45	D4
G 3	SCL	147	B6
G 3	SCL	N	E3
G 4	SCL	46	A4
G 4	SCL	P	B3

ROUTE NO.	CO. ABBR.	PAGE	GRID
G 4	SCLR	150	E1
G 4	SCLR	151	A1
G 5	PA	147	C6
G 5	SCL	45	E4
G 5	SCL	147	A5
G 5	SCL	149	A3
G 5	SCL	N	E3
G 6	MVW	148	C5
G 6	SCL	45	E4
G 6	SCL	46	A4
G 6	SCL	148	C5
G 6	SCLR	151	B1
G 6	SVL	148	C5
G 7	SCL	54	D2
G 8	SCL	46	B5
G 8	SCL	54	C1
G 8	SCL	P	B4
G 9	SCL	54	D2
G10	SCL	46	B5
G10	SCL	P	B4
G11	MON	54	C3
G12	MON	54	C3
G13	MON	65	C2
G13	SBT	65	C1
G14	MON	65	B3
G15	MON	65	B1
G16	MON	54	B5
G16	MON	64	C1
G16	MON	65	B1
G16	MON	168	E4
G17	MON	54	C4
G17	MON	65	A1
G18	MON	65	D4
G19	MON	65	E5
G20	MON	54	C5
J 1	FRCO	55	E3
J 1	FRCO	56	A3
J 1	SBT	55	B4
J 2	ALA	46	C2
J 2	ALA	M	D5
J 2	ALA	P	D1
J 2	SJCO	46	E1
J 3	S	160	E2
J 3	SJCO	47	B2
J 3	SJCO	160	E2
J 4	CC	46	D1
J 4	SJCO	46	E2
J 4	SJCO	47	A2
J 5	SJCO	40	B4
J 5	SJCO	47	C1
J 6	SJCO	40	C5
J 6	SJCO	47	D1
J 7	MCO	47	E3
J 7	MCO	48	A3
J 7	SJCO	40	B5
J 7	SJCO	47	C1
J 7	STA	47	D2
J 8	SCTO	137	D5
J 9	SJCO	47	C1
J 9	STA	47	D1
J 9	STA	48	A3
J11	SAC	39	D3
J11	SJCO	39	D3
J12	SJCO	40	C3
J13	SJCO	46	E1
J14	STA	40	E5
J14	STA	47	E1
J15	TUL	68	B2
J16	MPA	48	E3
J16	MCO	48	B3
J16	STA	47	D3
J17	MCO	48	A3
J17	STA	47	C3
J18	STA	47	C4
J19	FRCO	58	B4
J19	TUL	58	A5
J20	MPA	48	E2
J20	TUO	48	E1
J21	TUL	58	D5
J22	TUL	68	B4
J23	TUL	58	C5
J23	TUL	68	C2
J24	TUL	68	B4
J25	TUL	68	A1
J27	TUL	68	C2
J28	TUL	68	C2
J29	TUL	68	D2

ROUTE NO.	CO. ABBR.	PAGE	GRID
J30	TUL	68	B1
J32	TUL	68	A1
J34	TUL	68	A1
J38	TUL	57	E5
J38	TUL	58	B5
J40	TUL	58	A5
J41	TUL	70	B4
J42	TUL	68	E3
J42	TUL	69	A3
J44	TUL	68	C5
J59	MCO	48	C2
J59	TUO	48	C1
N 1	LACO	97	B2
N 2	LACO	89	A2
N 3	LACO	89	E5
N 3	LACO	90	A4
N 5	LACO	90	A2
N 6	LACO	90	C4
N 7	LACO	S	B3
N 8	LACO	98	C2
N 8	LACO	R	D5
N 8	LACO	U	A3
N 8	LACO	T	B1
N 9	LACO	96	E2
N 9	LACO	97	A2
R 2	RCO	102	B4
R 3	RCO	99	E5
R 3	RCO	100	A5
R 3	RCO	106	E1
R 3	RCO	107	A1
S 1	SDCO	107	D4
S 1	SDCO	112	D1
S 2	IMP	111	B3
S 2	SDCO	107	C3
S 2	SDCO	108	A4
S 2	SDCO	111	B3
S 3	SDCO	107	E3
S 4	SDCO	106	D4
S 4	SDCO	V	C1
S 5	SDCO	106	D4
S 6	SDCO	106	E2
S 6	SDCO	107	A2
S 7	SDCO	107	A2
S 8	SDCO	106	C4
S 9	SDCO	106	C4
S10	SDCO	106	C3
S11	SDCO	106	C3
S12	SDCO	106	D3
S13	SDCO	106	C1
S14	SDCO	106	C3
S15	SDCO	106	C2
S16	RCO	106	D1
S16	SDCO	106	D1
S17	SDCO	V	E3
S17	SDCO	111	E1
S17	SDCO	112	A1
S18	ORCO	98	D4
S19	ORCO	98	E4
S20	SB	86	B2
S21	SDCO	V	A1
S21	SDCO	106	C5
S22	IMP	108	C2
S22	SDCO	107	E2
S22	SDCO	108	B2
S24	IMP	112	D5
S24	IMP	110	D5
S26	IMP	109	A4
S27	IMP	109	A5
S28	IMP	109	A5
S28	IMP	112	C3
S29	IMP	108	E5
S29	IMP	111	E3
S30	IMP	109	A3
S30	IMP	112	A3
S31	IMP	109	B4
S31	IMP	112	B3
S32	IMP	109	C4
S32	IMP	112	C3
S33	IMP	109	C4
S33	IMP	112	C4
S34	IMP	110	B4
S80	IMP	108	C5
S80	IMP	109	A5
S80	IMP	111	D3
S80	IMP	112	A3

HIGHWAY NAME	HWY NO.	CO. ABBR.	PAGE	GRID
ANDERSON, GLENN FWY	105	LACO	Q	C5
ANGELES CREST HWY	2	LACO	90	B5
ANGELES CREST HWY	2	SBD	90	E5
ANTELOPE VALLEY FWY	14	KER	89	E2
ANTELOPE VALLEY FWY	14	KER	90	A2
ANTELOPE VALLEY FWY	14	LACO	89	D4
ANTELOPE VALLEY FWY	14	LACO	90	A2
ARROYO PKWY	110	LACO	190	C5
ARTESIA FWY	91	LACO	97	E3
ARTESIA FWY	91	LACO	S	C1
ARTESIA FWY	91	ORCO	98	A3
BAKERSFIELD-MCKITTRICK HWY	58	KER	78	A3
BARSTOW FWY	15	SBD	82	C5
BARSTOW FWY	15	SBD	83	D3
BARSTOW FWY	15	SBD	84	A2
BARSTOW FWY	15	SBD	91	B5
BARSTOW FWY	15	SBD	92	B1
BARSTOW FWY	215	SBD	99	B1
BAY HWY	1	SON	37	C3
BAYSHORE FWY	101	SCL	N	E3
BAYSHORE FWY	101	SCL	P	A3
BAYSHORE FWY	101	SCL	46	A4
BAYSHORE FWY	101	SCL	147	D1
BAYSHORE FWY	101	SCL	148	A3
BAYSHORE FWY	101	SCL	151	D1
BAYSHORE FWY	101	SCL	152	B1
BAYSHORE FWY	101	SMCO	L	C5
BAYSHORE FWY	101	SMCO	N	D2
BAYSHORE FWY	101	SMCO	45	D3
BAYSHORE FWY	101	SMCO	144	C1
BAYSHORE FWY	101	SMCO	145	D4
BOULDER HWY	93	CLK	74	E2
BOULDER HWY	95	CLK	74	E2
BURNS FWY	101	HUM	9	E5
BURNS FWY	101	HUM	10	A5
BURNS FWY	101	HUM	15	E1
CABRILLO FWY	163	SDCO	V	B3
CABRILLO FWY	163	SDCO	111	C1
CABRILLO FWY	163	SDCO	213	D3
CABRILLO FWY	163	SDCO	215	E2
CABRILLO HWY	1	MAR	53	D4
CABRILLO HWY	1	MON	54	B4
CABRILLO HWY	1	MON	64	B2
CABRILLO HWY	1	MON	65	A4
CABRILLO HWY	1	MON	168	C2
CABRILLO HWY	1	SB	86	B1
CABRILLO HWY	1	SCR	N	D5
CABRILLO HWY	1	SCR	53	C1
CABRILLO HWY	1	SCR	54	B2
CABRILLO HWY	1	SCR	169	A4
CABRILLO HWY	1	SLO	65	A5
CABRILLO HWY	1	SLO	75	B1
CABRILLO HWY	1	SLO	76	B5
CABRILLO HWY	1	SLO	172	B1
CABRILLO HWY	1	SMCO	L	B5
CABRILLO HWY	1	SMCO	N	B2
CABRILLO HWY	1	SMCO	45	B3
CALF CANYON HWY	58	SLO	76	C2
CENTRAL EXPWY	82	SCL	N	E3
CENTRAL FWY	101	SFCO	142	C5
CENTRAL SKYWAY	101	SFCO	142	C4
CENTRAL SKYWAY	101	SFCO	143	C5
CENTRAL VALLEY HWY	43	KER	78	B1
CENTURY FWY	105	LACO	Q	D5
CHARLES BROWN HWY	178	INY	73	A3
COAST HWY	1	ORCO	105	D1
COAST HWY	1	ORCO	199	C4
COAST HWY	1	ORCO	201	A2
COAST HWY	1	ORCO	202	D5
COAST HWY	1	SON	30	D5
COAST HWY	1	SON	37	B2
COAST HWY E	1	ORCO	200	A5
CORONA DEL MAR FWY	73	ORCO	T	D4
CORONA DEL MAR FWY	73	ORCO	98	C4
CORONA DEL MAR FWY	73	ORCO	197	D4
CORONA DEL MAR FWY	73	ORCO	198	A5
CORONA EXPWY	71	LACO	U	C3
CORONA EXPWY	71	LACO	98	D2
CORONA EXPWY	71	RCO	98	D2
CORONA EXPWY	71	SBD	U	C3

HIGHWAY NAME	HWY NO.	CO. ABBR.	PAGE	GRID
CORONA EXPWY	71	SBD	98	D2
CORONA FWY	15	RCO	99	B4
COSTA MESA FWY	55	ORCO	T	C4
COSTA MESA FWY	55	ORCO	98	C4
COSTA MESA FWY	55	ORCO	194	E3
COSTA MESA FWY	55	ORCO	196	E4
COSTA MESA FWY	55	ORCO	198	D2
DEKEMA, JACOB FWY	805	SDCO	V	D4
DEKEMA, JACOB FWY	805	SDCO	106	C5
DEKEMA, JACOB FWY	805	SDCO	111	D2
DEKEMA, JACOB FWY	805	SDCO	214	A3
DEKEMA, JACOB FWY	805	SDCO	216	C1
EASTSHORE FWY	80	ALA	L	D3
EASTSHORE FWY	80	CC	L	D3
EASTSHORE FWY	80	CC	38	C5
EASTSHORE FWY	80	CC	155	D3
EL CAMINO REAL	101	MON	54	D4
EL CAMINO REAL	101	MON	55	A5
EL CAMINO REAL	101	MON	65	B2
EL CAMINO REAL	101	MON	66	A5
EL CAMINO REAL	101	MON	171	D3
EL CAMINO REAL	101	SB	86	C1
EL CAMINO REAL	101	SB	87	A4
EL CAMINO REAL	101	SBT	54	D2
EL CAMINO REAL	101	SCL	54	D2
EL CAMINO REAL	82	SCL	147	B3
EL CAMINO REAL	82	SCL	149	E2
EL CAMINO REAL	82	SCL	150	B2
EL CAMINO REAL	82	SCL	151	A2
EL CAMINO REAL	101	SLO	66	A5
EL CAMINO REAL	101	SLO	76	A4
EL CAMINO REAL	101	SLO	172	B4
EL CAMINO REAL	82	SMCO	145	A3
EL DORADO FWY	50	SAC	40	A1
ELVAS FWY	80	SAC	137	E2
ESCONDIDO FWY	215	RCO	99	C4
ESCONDIDO FWY	15	SDCO	V	C1
ESCONDIDO FWY	15	SDCO	106	D2
ESCONDIDO FWY	15	SDCO	216	D3
EVAN HEWES HWY	8	IMP	111	B4
EVAN HEWES HWY	8	IMP	112	A5
EVAN HEWES HWY	8	IMP	112	D3
FAMOSO HWY	46	KER	78	A1
FOOTHILL FWY	210	LACO	Q	B1
FOOTHILL FWY	210	LACO	R	B2
FOOTHILL FWY	210	LACO	U	A2
FOOTHILL FWY	210	LACO	89	D5
FOOTHILL FWY	210	LACO	97	D1
FOOTHILL FWY	210	LACO	98	A1
FOOTHILL FWY	210	LACO	190	B2
FOOTHILL TRANS. CORRIDOR	241	ORCO	98	E4
GARDEN GROVE FWY	22	ORCO	T	C3
GARDEN GROVE FWY	22	ORCO	98	B4
GARDEN GROVE FWY	22	ORCO	195	B2
GARDEN GROVE FWY	22	ORCO	196	C1
GIBSON, LUTHER E FWY	680	SOL	L	E2
GIBSON, LUTHER E FWY	680	SOL	38	E4
GIBSON, LUTHER E FWY	680	SOL	153	E4
GLENDALE FWY	2	LACO	R	A3
GLENDALE FWY	2	LACO	97	E1
GLENN ANDERSON FWY	105	LACO	Q	C5
GOLD COUNTRY HWY	49	AMA	40	D1
GOLD COUNTRY HWY	49	CAL	41	A3
GOLD COUNTRY HWY	49	ED	34	C4
GOLD COUNTRY HWY	49	ED	40	A1
GOLD COUNTRY HWY	49	ED	138	B1
GOLD COUNTRY HWY	49	MPA	48	D1
GOLD COUNTRY HWY	49	MPA	49	A3
GOLD COUNTRY HWY	49	NEV	34	C1
GOLD COUNTRY HWY	49	PLA	34	C3
GOLD COUNTRY HWY	49	PLA	126	B1
GOLD COUNTRY HWY	49	PLU	27	D3
GOLD COUNTRY HWY	49	SIE	26	C4
GOLD COUNTRY HWY	49	SIE	27	C3
GOLD COUNTRY HWY	49	TUO	41	A3
GOLD COUNTRY HWY	49	TUO	48	D1
GOLD COUNTRY HWY	49	TUO	163	B1
GOLDEN CENTER FWY	20	NEV	127	D3
GOLDEN CENTER FWY	20	NEV	128	A4
GOLDEN GATE FWY	101	MAR	L	B4

HIGHWAY NAME	HWY NO.	CO. ABBR.	PAGE	GRID
GOLDEN GATE FWY	101	SFCO	L	B4
GOLDEN GATE FWY	101	SFCO	45	B1
GOLDEN STATE FWY	5	LACO	Q	B1
GOLDEN STATE FWY	5	LACO	R	C5
GOLDEN STATE FWY	5	LACO	88	E2
GOLDEN STATE FWY	5	LACO	89	B4
GOLDEN STATE FWY	5	LACO	97	D1
GOLDEN STATE FWY	5	LACO	179	C1
GOLDEN STATE FWY	5	LACO	182	D2
GOLDEN STATE FWY	5	LACO	186	D3
GROVE SHAFTER FWY	980	ALA	L	D4
GROVE SHAFTER FWY	980	ALA	45	D1
GROVE SHAFTER FWY	24	ALA	156	A5
GROVE SHAFTER FWY	980	ALA	158	A2
GUADALUPE PKWY	87	SCL	151	D1
GUADALUPE PKWY	87	SCL	152	A3
HARBOR FWY	110	LACO	Q	E5
HARBOR FWY	110	LACO	S	C2
HARBOR FWY	110	LACO	97	D4
HARBOR FWY	110	LACO	185	D4
HARBOR FWY	110	LACO	191	A2
HOLLYWOOD FWY	170	LACO	Q	C2
HOLLYWOOD FWY	101	LACO	Q	D3
HOLLYWOOD FWY	101	LACO	97	D1
HOLLYWOOD FWY	170	LACO	97	D1
HOLLYWOOD FWY	101	LACO	181	C2
HOLLYWOOD FWY	101	LACO	182	A5
HOLLYWOOD FWY	101	LACO	185	D1
HOLLYWOOD FWY	101	LACO	186	A2
HOLMAN HWY	68	MON	168	C1
IDYLLWILD NATL FOREST HWY	74	RCO	100	A4
JACOB DEKEMA FWY	805	SDCO	V	D4
JACOB DEKEMA FWY	805	SDCO	106	C5
JACOB DEKEMA FWY	805	SDCO	111	D2
JACOB DEKEMA FWY	805	SDCO	214	A3
JACOB DEKEMA FWY	805	SDCO	216	C1
JAMES LICK FWY	60	SFCO	L	C4
JAMES LICK FWY	80	SFCO	45	C1
JAMES LICK FWY	101	SFCO	142	D5
JAMES LICK SKYWY	80	SFCO	142	D4
JAMES LICK SKYWY	101	SFCO	143	C5
JOHN T KNOX FWY	580	CC	L	C3
JOHN T KNOX FWY	580	CC	155	B4
JUNIPERO SERRA FWY	280	SCL	N	D2
JUNIPERO SERRA FWY	280	SCL	P	A3
JUNIPERO SERRA FWY	280	SCL	45	D3
JUNIPERO SERRA FWY	101	SCL	149	C4
JUNIPERO SERRA FWY	101	SCL	150	A4
JUNIPERO SERRA FWY	280	SMCO	N	B1
JUNIPERO SERRA FWY	280	SMCO	45	B2
JUNIPERO SERRA FWY	280	SMCO	144	A5
KNOX, JOHN T FWY	580	CC	L	C3
KNOX, JOHN T FWY	580	CC	155	B4
LAGUNA FWY	133	ORCO	T	E4
LAGUNA FWY	133	ORCO	98	D5
LAKEVILLE HWY	116	SON	L	A1
LICK, JAMES FWY	80	SFCO	L	C4
LICK, JAMES FWY	80	SFCO	45	C1
LICK, JAMES FWY	101	SFCO	142	D5
LICK, JAMES SKYWY	80	SFCO	142	D4
LICK, JAMES SKYWY	101	SFCO	143	C5
LONG BEACH FWY	710	LACO	R	B4
LONG BEACH FWY	710	LACO	S	D2
LONG BEACH FWY	710	LACO	97	E3
LONG BEACH FWY	710	LACO	192	C2
LOS BANOS HWY	59	MCO	170	C5
LUTHER E GIBSON FWY	680	SOL	L	E2
LUTHER E GIBSON FWY	680	SOL	38	E4
LUTHER E GIBSON FWY	680	SOL	153	E4
MACARTHUR FWY	580	ALA	L	D4
MACARTHUR FWY	580	ALA	45	D1
MACARTHUR FWY	580	ALA	158	B2
MARICOPA HWY	166	KER	78	B5
MARINA EXPWY	90	LACO	187	D3
MARINA FWY	90	LACO	Q	C4
MARINA FWY	90	LACO	97	C2
MARINA FWY	90	LACO	188	A3
MARINE WORLD PKWY	37	SOL	134	B2
MIDLAND TRAIL	14	KER	80	C2
MISSION VALLEY FWY	8	SDCO	V	B3

HIGHWAY NAME	HWY NO.	CO. ABBR.	PAGE	GRID
MISSION VALLEY FWY	8	SDCO	111	C1
MISSION VALLEY FWY	8	SDCO	213	E4
NEEDLES FWY	40	SBD	92	A1
NEEDLES FWY	40	SBD	93	D2
NEEDLES FWY	40	SBD	94	D2
NEEDLES FWY	40	SBD	95	C1
NIMITZ FWY	880	ALA	L	E5
NIMITZ FWY	880	ALA	P	B2
NIMITZ FWY	880	ALA	45	D2
NIMITZ FWY	880	ALA	46	A3
NIMITZ FWY	880	ALA	146	C4
NIMITZ FWY	880	ALA	157	D3
NIMITZ FWY	880	ALA	158	B4
NIMITZ FWY	880	ALA	159	C1
NORTH HWY	190	INY	72	B1
OCEAN BEACH FWY	8	SDCO	212	C5
OJAI FWY	33	VEN	88	A5
OJAI FWY	33	VEN	175	A2
ONTARIO FRWY	15	SBD	98	E2
ONTARIO FRWY	15	SBD	99	A1
ORANGE FWY	57	LACO	U	B3
ORANGE FWY	57	LACO	98	C3
ORANGE FWY	57	ORCO	T	D1
ORANGE FWY	57	ORCO	U	A4
ORANGE FWY	57	ORCO	98	C3
ORANGE FWY	57	ORCO	194	A4
ORTEGA HWY	74	ORCO	98	E5
ORTEGA HWY	74	ORCO	99	A5
ORTEGA HWY	74	ORCO	202	E1
PACIFIC COAST HWY	1	LACO	Q	C4
PACIFIC COAST HWY	1	LACO	S	B1
PACIFIC COAST HWY	1	LACO	96	E2
PACIFIC COAST HWY	1	LACO	97	B2
PACIFIC COAST HWY	1	ORCO	T	A3
PACIFIC COAST HWY	1	ORCO	98	C5
PACIFIC COAST HWY	1	VEN	96	C2
PASADENA FWY	110	LACO	R	A3
PASADENA FWY	110	LACO	R	A3
PASADENA FWY	110	LACO	97	E2
PASADENA FWY	110	LACO	186	B2
PASO ROBLES HWY	46	KER	77	A1
PINES TO PALMS HWY	74	RCO	100	B4
POMONA FWY	60	LACO	R	E4
POMONA FWY	60	LACO	98	B2
POMONA FWY	60	SBD	U	D3
POMONA FWY	60	SBD	98	D2
PORTERVILLE HWY	65	KER	68	D5
PORTERVILLE HWY	65	KER	78	D1
PORTERVILLE HWY	65	TUL	68	C2
RAMONA HWY	125	SDCO	V	D2
REDLANDS FWY	10	RCO	99	D2
REDLANDS FWY	10	RCO	100	A3
REDLANDS FWY	10	SBD	99	D2
REDONDO BEACH FWY	91	KER	97	E3
REDONDO BEACH FWY	91	LACO	S	C1
REDWOOD HWY	101	DN	1	E3
REDWOOD HWY	199	DN	2	B3
REDWOOD HWY	101	DN	10	A1
REDWOOD HWY	101	HUM	9	E3
REDWOOD HWY	101	HUM	10	A2
REDWOOD HWY	101	HUM	15	E3
REDWOOD HWY	101	HUM	16	B4
REDWOOD HWY	101	HUM	22	C1
REDWOOD HWY	101	MAR	L	A2
REDWOOD HWY	101	MAR	38	A4
REDWOOD HWY	101	MAR	45	B1
REDWOOD HWY	101	MAR	139	D2
REDWOOD HWY	101	MAR	140	C2
REDWOOD HWY	101	MEN	22	C2
REDWOOD HWY	101	MEN	31	A1
REDWOOD HWY	101	SON	L	A2
REDWOOD HWY	101	SON	31	C4
REDWOOD HWY	101	SON	37	D1
REDWOOD HWY	101	SON	38	A3
REDWOOD HWY	101	SON	131	C2
RIVERSIDE FWY	91	ORCO	T	D2
RIVERSIDE FWY	91	ORCO	U	C5
RIVERSIDE FWY	91	ORCO	98	C3
RIVERSIDE FWY	91	ORCO	194	D1
RIVERSIDE FWY	91	RCO	U	C5

Thomas Bros. Maps ®
COPYRIGHT 1997
INDEXES

HIGHWAY NAME	HWY NO.	CO. ABBR.	PAGE	GRID
RIVERSIDE FWY	91	RCO	99	A3
RIVERSIDE FWY	91	RCO	205	C2
RIVERSIDE FWY	215	RCO	205	D1
RIVERSIDE FWY	215	SBD	99	B2
RONALD REAGAN FRWY	118	LACO	Q	C1
RONALD REAGAN FRWY	118	LACO	89	B5
RONALD REAGAN FRWY	118	VEN	88	E5
RONALD REAGAN FRWY	118	VEN	89	B5
ROSEDALE HWY	58	KER	78	C3
ROUTE 4 FWY	4	CC	M	B3
ROUTE 4 FWY	4	CC	154	C3
ROUTE 8 FWY	8	SDCO	106	D5
ROUTE 8 FWY	8	SDCO	107	A5
ROUTE 8 FWY	8	SDCO	111	A4
ROUTE 8 FWY	8	SDCO	112	D1
ROUTE 17 FWY	17	SCL	46	A5
ROUTE 17 FWY	17	SCR	P	B4
ROUTE 17 FWY	17	SCR	54	A1
ROUTE 52 FWY	52	SDCO	211	E3
ROUTE 67 FWY	67	SDCO	106	E5
ROUTE 78 FWY	78	SDCO	106	C3
ROUTE 94 FWY	94	SDCO	V	D3
ROUTE 94 FWY	94	SDCO	216	D3
ROUTE 101 FWY	101	SB	86	D2
ROUTE 101 FWY	101	SB	173	C1
SAN BERNARDINO FWY	10	LACO	U	B2
SAN BERNARDINO FWY	10	LACO	98	B2
SAN BERNARDINO FWY	10	LACO	186	D3
SAN BERNARDINO FWY	10	SBD	U	D2
SAN BERNARDINO FWY	10	SBD	98	D2
SAN BERNARDINO FWY	10	SBD	99	A1
SAN BERNARDINO FWY	10	SBD	203	B3
SAN BERNARDINO FWY	10	SBD	204	D3
SAN DIEGO FWY	405	LACO	Q	B3
SAN DIEGO FWY	405	LACO	S	B2
SAN DIEGO FWY	405	LACO	97	C2
SAN DIEGO FWY	405	LACO	180	C2
SAN DIEGO FWY	405	LACO	188	D4
SAN DIEGO FWY	405	LACO	189	E5
SAN DIEGO FWY	405	ORCO	T	B3
SAN DIEGO FWY	405	ORCO	98	B4
SAN DIEGO FWY	5	ORCO	98	D4
SAN DIEGO FWY	5	ORCO	105	D1
SAN DIEGO FWY	405	ORCO	197	D4
SAN DIEGO FWY	405	ORCO	198	A4
SAN DIEGO FWY	5	ORCO	202	D3
SAN DIEGO FWY	5	SDCO	V	A2
SAN DIEGO FWY	5	SDCO	106	A2
SAN DIEGO FWY	5	SDCO	111	D2
SAN DIEGO FWY	5	SDCO	211	E3
SAN DIEGO FWY	5	SDCO	212	E3
SAN DIEGO FWY	5	SDCO	215	E3
SAN DIEGO FWY	5	SDCO	216	B5
SAN GABRIEL RIVER FWY	605	LACO	R	D4
SAN GABRIEL RIVER FWY	605	LACO	S	E2
SAN GABRIEL RIVER FWY	605	LACO	T	A2
SAN GABRIEL RIVER FWY	605	LACO	98	A2
SAN JOAQUIN HILLS TRANS CORR	73	ORCO	T	E5
SAN JOAQUIN HILLS TRANS CORR	73	ORCO	98	C5
SAN JOAQUIN HILLS TRANS CORR	73	ORCO	200	C3
SANTA ANA FWY	5	LACO	98	A2
SANTA ANA FWY	5	LACO	186	D3
SANTA ANA FWY	5	ORCO	T	B1
SANTA ANA FWY	5	ORCO	U	A5
SANTA ANA FWY	5	ORCO	98	A2
SANTA ANA FWY	5	ORCO	193	D4
SANTA ANA FWY	5	ORCO	196	B2
SANTA MONICA FWY	10	LACO	Q	C4
SANTA MONICA FWY	10	LACO	97	D2
SANTA MONICA FWY	10	LACO	180	B5
SANTA MONICA FWY	10	LACO	183	B4
SANTA MONICA FWY	10	LACO	184	D4
SANTA MONICA FWY	10	LACO	185	D4
SANTA MONICA FWY	10	LACO	186	A5
SANTA PAULA FWY	126	VEN	88	B5
SAN VICENTE FWY	67	SDCO	106	E5
SEBASTOPOL FWY	12	SON	131	B4
SHORELINE HWY	1	MAR	L	B4
SHORELINE HWY	1	MAR	37	D4
SHORELINE HWY	1	MAR	45	A1
SHORELINE HWY	1	MAR	140	B4
SHORELINE HWY	1	MEN	22	C3
SHORELINE HWY	1	MEN	30	C4
SILVERADO TRAIL	121	NAPA	133	E4
SINCLAIR FWY	680	ALA	P	B2
SINCLAIR FWY	680	ALA	46	B2
SINCLAIR FWY	680	CC	46	A1
SINCLAIR FWY	680	SCL	P	B2
SINCLAIR FWY	680	SCL	46	B4
SINCLAIR FWY	280	SCL	151	D5
SINCLAIR FWY	280	SCL	152	D4
SNELLING HWY	59	MCO	170	C5
SOLEDAD FWY	52	SDCO	V	B2
SOLEDAD FWY	52	SDCO	106	C5
SONOMA HWY	12	SON	132	C3
SOUTH BAY EXPWY	54	SDCO	V	D4
SOUTH BAY EXPWY	54	SDCO	111	D1
SOUTHBAY FWY	237	SCL	P	A3
SOUTHBAY FWY	237	SCL	46	A4
SOUTHBAY FWY	237	SCL	148	C4
SOUTHRN EMBARCADERO FY	280	SFCO	L	C5
SOUTHRN EMBARCADERO FY	280	SFCO	45	C2
SOUTHRN EMBARCADERO FY	280	SFCO	143	E5
SOUTH VALLEY FWY	101	SCL	54	C1
STEVENS CREEK FWY	85	SCL	N	E3
STEVENS CREEK FWY	85	SCL	P	A3
STEVENS CREEK FWY	85	SCL	45	E4
STEVENS CREEK FWY	85	SCL	148	A4
TAFT HWY	119	KER	78	C3
TERMINAL ISLAND FWY	103	LACO	S	D2
TERMINAL ISLAND FWY	103	LACO	192	A2
THREE FLAGS HWY	395	KER	80	D1
TWENTYNINE PALMS HWY	62	RCO	100	C2
TWENTYNINE PALMS HWY	62	RCO	102	C2
TWENTYNINE PALMS HWY	62	SBD	100	C2
TWENTYNINE PALMS HWY	62	SBD	101	C1
TWENTYNINE PALMS HWY	62	SBD	102	A2
VENTURA FWY	134	LACO	Q	E3
VENTURA FWY	134	LACO	R	A3
VENTURA FWY	101	LACO	97	B1
VENTURA FWY	134	LACO	97	B1
VENTURA FWY	101	LACO	177	C4
VENTURA FWY	101	LACO	178	B3
VENTURA FWY	101	LACO	179	D5
VENTURA FWY	101	VEN	87	E5
VENTURA FWY	101	VEN	88	A5
VENTURA FWY	101	VEN	96	D1
VENTURA FWY	101	VEN	175	C3
WARREN FWY	13	ALA	L	D4
WARREN FWY	13	ALA	45	D1
WARREN FWY	13	CC	156	E5
WESTSIDE FWY	5	FRCO	55	E3
WESTSIDE FWY	5	FRCO	56	B4
WESTSIDE FWY	5	FRCO	66	E2
WEST SIDE FWY	5	KER	77	D1
WEST SIDE FWY	5	KER	78	B3
WEST SIDE FWY	5	KER	88	D1
WESTSIDE FWY	5	KIN	67	C4
WESTSIDE FWY	5	MCO	47	C5
WESTSIDE FWY	5	MCO	55	D1
WESTSIDE FWY	5	SAC	39	E2
WESTSIDE FWY	5	SJCO	39	E4
WESTSIDE FWY	5	SJCO	40	A4
WESTSIDE FWY	5	SJCO	47	A2
WESTSIDE FWY	5	STA	47	B3
WESTSIDE FWY	5	YOL	33	A4
WEST SIDE HWY	33	KER	67	B5
WEST SIDE HWY	33	KER	77	C1
WEST SIDE HWY	33	KER	78	A4
YOUNGER FWY	92	ALA	N	D1
YOUNGER FWY	92	ALA	45	D2
YOUNGER FWY	92	SMCO	N	D1
YOUNGER FWY	92	SMCO	45	D2
YOUNGER FWY	92	SMCO	145	D1

AIRPORTS

NAME & ADDRESS	PAGE	GRID
ALTURAS MUNICIPAL AIRPORT, 1 mi W of Alturas	8	A1
AMADOR COUNTY AIRPORT, near Amador	40	D2
ANTIOCH AIRPORT, Lone Tree Wy, Antioch	M	C3
ARCATA AIRPORT, off Hwy 101 at Airport Rd	10	A4
AUBURN AIRPORT, 4 mi N of Auburn	34	C3
BAKERSFIELD AIRPARK, Watts Dr & Union Av	78	D3
BARSTOW-DAGGETT, Nat'l Trails Hwy, Barstow	92	B1
BENTON AIRPARK, Gold St, Redding	122	A3
BIG BEAR CITY AIRPORT, Big Bear City	92	A5
BISHOP AIRPORT, 2 mi E of Bishop	51	D4
BRACKETT FIELD, McKinley Av, La Verne	U	C2
BUCHANAN FIELD AIRPORT, John Glenn Dr, Concord	M	A3
BURBANK-GLENDALE-PASADENA, 2627 N Hollywood Wy	179	B1
CALAVERAS CO AIRPORT, Hwy 49 S of San Andreas	41	A4
CARSON AIRPORT, Carson City, Nevada	36	C1
CATALINA AIR & SEA TERMINAL, Harbor Blvd	191	B3
CHICO MUNICIPAL AIRPORT, 5 mi NW of Chico	25	B2
CHINO AIRPORT, Hwy 83, Chino	U	D3
COLUMBIA AIRPORT off Hwy 49, Columbia	41	C4
COLUSA COUNTY AIRPORT, 3 mi S of Colusa	33	A2
DELANO MUNICIPAL AIRPORT, Hwy 99, Delano	68	B5
DOUGLAS COUNTY AIRPORT, Minden, Nevada	36	C3
FANTASY HAVEN AIRPORT, 2 mi SE of Tehachapi	79	D4
FRESNO AIR TERMINAL, 5175 E Clinton Av	57	D3
FRESNO-CHANDLER DOWNTOWN AIRPORT, Amador & Thorne	165	B4
FROGTOWN AIRPORT, Off Hwy 49, Angels Camp	41	B4
IMPERIAL COUNTY AIRPORT, Hwy 86 at Main, Imperial	109	A5
INYOKERN COUNTY AIRPORT, Hwy 395, Inyokern	80	D1
JOHN MCNAMARA FIELD, nr Crescent City	1	C4
JOHN WAYNE AIRPORT, MacArthur Blvd, Orange Co	198	B5
KERN VALLEY AIRPORT, Sierra Wy N of Lake Isabella	69	D5
LAKEVIEW MUNICIPAL AIRPORT, near jct of 140 & 395	7	B1
LAMPSON AIRPORT, SW of Clear Lake off Hwy 175	31	D3
LIVERMORE AIRPORT, Stanley Blvd, Livermore	M	C5
LONE PINE AIRPORT, 1 mile south of Lone Pine	60	B4
LONG BEACH MUNICIPAL, 4100 Donald Douglas Dr	S	E2
LOS ANGELES INTERNATIONAL, 1 World Wy	189	C2
MADERA AIRPORT, Hwy 99 & Av 17	57	A2
MARIPOSA YOSEMITE AIRPORT, near Mariposa	49	A3
McCARRAN INTERNATIONAL, 5 miles S of Las Vegas	210	C5
MEADOWS FIELD, Skyway & Airport Drs	78	D2
MENDOCINO COUNTY AIRPORT, Hwy 1 S of Little River	30	B1
MERCED MUNICIPAL AIRPORT, 2 mi SW of Merced	170	A5
MONTEREY PENINSULA AIRPORT, off Hwy 68	54	B1
NAPA COUNTY AIRPORT, 2030 Airport Rd, Napa	38	D3
NEEDLES MUNICIPAL, Airport Rd & Hwy 95, Needles	95	D2
NORTH LAS VEGAS AIR TERMINAL, 3.5 miles NW of L V	74	D2
OAKDALE AIRPORT, 8191 Laughlin Rd, Oakdale	47	E1
OAKLAND INTERNATIONAL, Doolittle & Airport Wy	159	B4
OCOTILLO WELLS AIRPORT, HWY 78, Ocotillo	108	B3
ONTARIO INTERNATIONAL AIRPORT, 2 mi E of Ontario	204	E5
OROVILLE AIRPORT, 3 mi SW of Oroville	25	C4
PALMDALE AIRPORT, Sierra Hwy	90	A3
PALM SPRINGS REGIONAL, 2 mi E of Palm Springs	206	E3
PEARCE AIRPORT, Hwy 53 S of Clearlake	32	A3
PLACERVILLE AIRPORT, S of Hwy 50 near Smithflat	34	E5
REDDING MUNICIPAL AIRPORT, 7 miles SE of Redding	18	C2
RENO-CANNON INTERNL AIRPORT, 2 miles from Reno	28	C4
SACRAMENTO CO METRO ARPRT, 12 mi NW of Sacramento	33	D5
SACRAMENTO EXECUTIVE AIRPORT, 6151 Freeport Blvd	39	D1
SALINAS MUNICIPAL AIRPORT, off Hwy 101	54	D4
SAN DIEGO INTERNATIONAL AIRPORT, Lindbergh Field	215	B2
SAN FRANCISCO INTL, Airport Wy off Bayshore Fwy	144	D3
SAN JOSE INTERNATIONAL AIRPORT, 1661 Airport Bl	151	C1
SAN LUIS OBISPO AIRPORT, 901 Airport Dr	76	B4
SANTA BARBARA AIRPORT, James Fowler Rd	87	B4
SANTA MARIA PUBLIC AIRPORT, Skyway Dr, Sta Maria	86	B1
SANTA MONICA MUNICIPAL AIRPORT	187	C1
SHAFTER-KERN COUNTY AIRFIELD, Lerdo Hwy	78	B2
SISKIYOU COUNTY AIRPORT, Montague	4	C4
STOCKTON METRO AIRPORT, 5000 S Airport Wy	40	B5
SUSANVILLE AIRPORT, 5 mi SE of Susanville	21	B3
SUTTER COUNTY AIRPORT, off Samuel Dr	125	E4
TAFT-KERN AIRPORT, West Side Hwy, Taft	78	A4
TAHOE AIRPORT, Pioneer Trail Rd	36	A3
TEHACHAPI-KERN CO AIRPORT, Green & J Sts	79	D4
TRUCKEE AIRPORT, 4 miles E of Truckee	35	E1
TULELAKE MUNI AIRPORT, N of Hw 139 near Newell	5	E3
TURLOCK MUN AIRPORT, 13099 Newport Rd, Ballico	48	A3
UKIAH AIRPORT, State St	123	D5
VENTURA COUNTY AIRPORT, Oxnard	176	A4
WILLITS MUNI AIRPORT, 3 mi N of Wilits on US 101	23	A5
YUBA COUNTY AIRPORT, Olivehurst	33	D2
YUCCA VALLEY AIRPORT, Hwys 62 & 247, Yucca Valley	100	D1

AMUSEMENT PARKS

NAME & ADDRESS	PAGE	GRID
DISNEYLAND, Harbor Blvd, Anaheim	193	B4
Amusement park-8 theme sections, rides, shops.		
GREAT AMERICA, 1 Great America Pkwy, Santa Clara	P	B3
Family amusement park, American history theme.		
KNOTTS BERRY FARM, 8039 Beach Bl, Buena Park	T	B2
Amusement Pk-6 theme areas,rides,shops,rstnts.		
MARINE WORLD AFRICA USA, 1000 Fairgrounds,Vallejo	134	D1
Land & sea animal shows; natural setting		
OASIS WATER PARK, 1500 Gene Autry Tr, Palm Spgs	100	D3
Wave pool, speed slide, hydro tubes, lagoon.		
RAGING WATERS, 111 Via Verde, San Dimas	U	B2
Pools, slides, picnic area.		
RAGING WATERS, off Capitol Expwy, San Jose	P	C3
Pools, slides, picnic area.		
SAN DIEGO WILD ANIMAL PARK, 5 mi W of Escondido	106	D3
Tour through preserve for endangered species.		
SEA WORLD, 1720 S Shores Rd, Mission Bay Park	212	C4
Marine life amusement park, shows and attractions.		
SIX FLAGS HURRICANE HARBOR, I-5 at Valencia Av	89	B4
Theme waterpark, pools and slides.		
SIX FLAGS MAGIC MOUNTAIN, I-5 at Valencia Av	89	B4
Family amusement park; thrill rides and shops.		
UNIVERSAL STUDIOS & AMPHITHEATER, Univ City Plaza	181	B1
Features tours of movie and TV sets; shows.		
WATERWORLD USA, 1600 Exposition Blvd, Sacramento	39	E1
Water amusement park, pools and slides.		
WET 'N WILD, 2600 Las Vegas Blvd, Las Vegas	209	C4
Wave pool, flumes, water roller coaster.		
WILD RIVERS, Irvine Center Dr, Irvine	98	D4
Water slides and activities.		
WILD WATER ADVENTURES, 11413 E Shaw, Clovis	57	D3
Water amusement park with 17 water rides.		
WINDSOR WATERWORKS, 8225 Conde, Windsor	37	E1
Pool, flumes, picnic area.		

BEACHES

NAME & ADDRESS	PAGE	GRID
ARROYO BURRO BEACH COUNTY PARK, 2981 Cliff Dr	87	C4
Swimming, picnicking, surf fishing.		
ASILOMAR STATE BEACH, Sunset Dr, Pacific Grove	167	A1
Conference facilities in a beautiful setting.		
ATASCADERO STATE BEACH, Jct Hwy 1 and Hwy 41	75	D3
Swimming, fishing and camping.		
AVILA STATE BEACH, Front St	76	A4
Fishing, fire rings, swimming.		
BAKER BEACH, NW shore Presidio, San Francisco	141	B2
Fishing, hiking nearby, no swimming.		
BEAN HOLLOW STATE BEACH, S of Half Moon Bay	N	B4
Fishing and camping on the beach.		
BOLSA CHICA STATE BEACH, N of Huntington Beach	T	A3
Sandy beach, body surfing, picnicking.		

NAME & ADDRESS	PAGE	GRID	NAME & ADDRESS	PAGE	GRID
BOOMER BEACH, Coast Blvd, La Jolla Scenic beach, swimming and fishing.	105	B2	MARINE STREET BEACH, La Jolla Fishing, swimming and sunbathing.	105	A3
CABRILLO BEACH, E of Pacific Av, San Pedro Public boat ramp, surf fishing, barbeque pits.	S	C3	MCGRATH STATE BEACH, S of Santa Clara River Hiking, camping, fishing.	96	A1
CAPISTRANO BEACH, San Juan Capistrano Sandy beach, body surfing, picnicking.	202	D5	MONTARA STATE BEACH, N of Half Moon Bay Fishing beach.	N	A2
CAPITOLA CITY BEACH, 30th Av, Capitola Swimming and fishing.	54	A2	MONTEREY STATE BEACH, Park Av Sandy beach, fishing, swimming in summer.	54	B4
CARDIFF STATE BEACH, Cardiff Fine beach for fishing or swimming.	106	B4	MOONLIGHT STATE BEACH, Encinitas Sandy beach for swimming and fishing.	106	B4
CARLSBAD STATE BEACH, 3 mi S of Carlsbad Bl Fish, swim, surf, camp, store, concessions.	106	A3	MORRO STRAND STATE BEACH, end of Yerba Buena Rd Sand dunes, streams; camping permitted.	75	D2
CARMEL RIVER STATE BEACH, Scenic Rd Skin diving, fishing, bird watching sites.	168	B4	MOSS LANDING STATE BEACH, off Hwy 1 Fishing and equestrian trails.	54	B3
CARPINTERIA STATE BEACH, Linden Av Camping, picnicking, fishing pier, boat ramp.	87	D4	NATURAL BRIDGES STATE BEACH, W Cliff Dr Natural sandstone formation; picnics, fishing.	169	A5
CASA BEACH, Coast Blvd, La Jolla Swimming and fishing.	105	A3	NEW BRIGHTON STATE BEACH, off Hwy 1 Sandy beach, tide pools.	54	A2
CASPER HEADLANDS STATE RESERVE, Hwy 1 near Casper Scenic environment with good fishing.	22	A5	NEWPORT DUNES AQUATIC PARK, off Pacific Coast Hwy Swimming and other aquatic recreation.	199	D4
CASPER STATE BEACH, off Hwy 1 near Casper Scenic area for picnicking and fishing.	22	B5	OCEANSIDE CITY BEACH, The Strand & Pacific Popular resort; 4 mi beach, swim, skin dive.	106	A3
CAYUCOS STATE BEACH, on Ocean Front Rd Fishing pier, barbeque & picnic facilities.	75	D2	PACIFICA STATE BEACH, Hwy 1, Pacifica Fishing, hiking, tidepools.	N	B1
CORAL BEACH, Hwy 1 W of Malibu Beach Fishing, swimming and picnicking.	97	A2	PELICAN STATE BEACH, 21 miles N of Crescent City Fishing; no swimming.	1	D2
CORONA DEL MAR STATE BEACH, Corona Del Mar Sandy beach, tidepools, body surfng, picnckng.	T	D5	PESCADERO STATE BEACH, Hwy 1 S of Half Moon Bay Good beach for fishing.	N	B4
DAN BLOCKER BEACH, PCH & Corral Canyon, Malibu Swimming, surfing and sunbathing.	97	A2	PISMO STATE BEACH, off Hwy 101, Pismo Beach Camping & hiking among sandy beaches & dunes.	76	B5
DOCKWEILER STATE BEACH, Venice Swimming, picnicking, fishing.	187	A4	POINT DUME BEACH, Hwy 1 Good beach for picnicking, hiking or fishing.	96	E2
DOHENY STATE BEACH, Puerto & Del Obispo Sts Surfing, camping, fire rings & picnic areas.	202	B4	POINT REYES NATIONAL SEASHORE, near Olema Sandy beach, tide pools; picnic, camp, hike.	37	D5
EAST BEACH, E Cabrillo Blvd, Santa Barbara BBQ & picnic facilities, volleyball courts.	174	E4	POINT SAL STATE BEACH, Sal Point Rd Many varieties of marine life.	86	A1
EL CAPITAN STATE BEACH, Avenida del Capitan Surfing, hiking, camping, boat rentals.	87	A4	POMPONIO STATE BEACH, Hwy 1 S of Half Moon Bay Lovely beach for picnicking and fishing.	N	B3
EL DORADO BEACH, off Hwy 50, South Lake Tahoe On the south shore of lovely Lake Tahoe.	129	A3	PORT HUENEME BEACH, off Hueneme Rd Fishing pier, playground, bike paths.	96	B1
EMMA WOOD STATE BEACH, Hwy 101 & Hwy 33 Camping, fishing and swimming.	88	A5	REDONDO BEACH, Redondo Beach Adjacent to King Harbor Marina; swim, fish.	S	A2
GAZO CREEK ANGLING ACCESS, Gazo Creek Rd Beach access for fishing.	N	C4	REFUGIO STATE BEACH, Refugio Rd Tidepools; camping, fishing.	86	E4
GOLETA BEACH COUNTY PARK, 5990 Sandspit Rd Fishing pier, swimming, boat hoist.	87	B4	RIO DEL MAR STATE BCH, Rio Del Mar Blvd, Aptos Clean sandy beach, jetty; nearby shopping.	54	B2
GRAYWHALE COVE STATE BEACH, N of Half Moon Bay Good beach for fishing.	N	A1	ROBERT H MEYER MEM STATE BEACH, Hwy 1 W of Malibu Swimming, picnicking facilities, fishing.	96	E2
GREENWOOD STATE BEACH, Hwy 1 near Elk. Fishing, picnicking and exhibits.	30	C2	ROBERT W. CROWN MEMORIAL STATE BEACH, Alameda Day use only; youth programs offered.	L	D5
HALF MOON BAY STATE BEACH, near Half Moon Bay Camp on bluffs above beaches, hike, picnic.	N	B2	ROYAL PALMS BEACH, Paseo dl Mar, Ls Angeles Good beach to swim, picnic, or fish.	S	C3
HERMOSA BEACH, btwn Redondo & Manhattan Beaches Public fishing pier, swimming, surfing.	S	A1	SALINAS RIVER STATE BEACH, Potrero Rd Wide sandy beach & dunes; clamming & fishing.	54	B3
HUNTINGTON BEACH STATE PARK, Huntington Beach Sandy beach, good surfing, picnicking.	T	B4	SAN BUENAVENTURA STATE BEACH, Harbor Bl, Ventura Good swimming, beach equipment rentals.	175	C3
ISLA VISTA COUNTY BEACH PARK, Camino Del Sur Sandy beach, tidepools.	87	B4	SAN CLEMENTE STATE BEACH, San Clemente Surfing, camping; BBQ & picnic facilities.	105	D1
J D PHELAN BEACH, El Camino del Mar, Sn Francisco Swimming cove protected from the wind.	141	A2	SAN ELIJO STATE BEACH, Cardiff Good beach for camping, fishing and swimming.	106	B4
LAS TUNAS BEACH, near Jct Hwy 1 & Hwy 27 Swimming in the surf, fishing, and picnicking.	Q	A4	SAN GREGORIO STATE BCH, Hwy 1 S of Half Moon Bay Good fishing beach; picnicking.	N	B3
LEADBETTER BEACH, Shoreline Dr, Santa Barbara Very wide, sandy beach; picnic facilities.	174	C5	SAN ONOFRE STATE BEACH, San Onofre Surf fishing, clamming; surfing & camping.	105	E2
LEO CARRILLO STATE BEACH, S of Hwy 101 Good surfing, diving and swimming.	96	D2	SAN SIMEON STATE BEACH, Hwy 1 Camping, hiking; dunes to explore.	75	B1
LEUCADIA STATE BEACH, Leucadia Scenic beach for fishing and swimming.	106	B4	SANTA CRUZ BEACH, Beach St Swimming, surfing, surf fishing.	169	D4
LITTLE RIVER STATE BEACH, South of Trinidad Beautiful beaches, delta, nature trails.	9	E4	SANTA MONICA STATE BEACH, Palisades Beach Rd Most popular beach in the Los Angeles area.	Q	B4
MALIBU LAGOON STATE BEACH, near Malibu Site of famous surfrider beach, swimming.	97	B2	SCHOONER GULCH STATE BEACH, Hwy 1 S of Pt. Arena Picnicking, beach & a scenic overlook.	30	C4
MANCHESTER STATE BEACH, near Point Arena Beaches, sand dunes, Point Arena Lighthouse.	30	B3	SEACLIFF STATE BEACH, 5 mi S of Hwy 1 Swimming; marine museum - open in summer.	54	B2
MANHATTAN BEACH, Manhattan Beach Public fishing pier, swimming, surfing.	S	A1	SILVER STRAND STATE BEACH, 5000 Hwy 75, Coronado Beautiful beach to swim, picnic, or fish.	V	B4
MANRESA STATE BEACH, off San Andreas Rd Sandy beach, tide pools.	54	B2	SONOMA COAST STATE BEACH, N of Bodega Bay Camp, hike, picnic; scenic beaches.	37	B2
MARINA STATE BEACH, 10 mi N of Monterey Good fishing area.	54	B4	SOUTH CARLSBAD STATE BEACH, S of Carlsbad Camping, fishing and swimming.	106	B3

NAME & ADDRESS	PAGE	GRID	NAME & ADDRESS	PAGE	GRID
STILLWATER COVE, Hwy 1 S of Walsh Landing	37	A1	DEL NORTE COAST REDWOODS ST PK, S of Crescnt City	1	E4
Good swimming and fishing.			Camping, picnicking, hiking, fishing&exhibits.		
SUNSET STATE BEACH, W of Watsonville	54	B2	D. L. BLISS STATE PARK, N of Emerald Bay	35	E3
Scenic bluffs; camp, fish, clam dig, picnic.			Camping, beach, trails, dense forest.		
THORNTON STATE BEACH, off Hwy 35 E of Daly City	L	B5	DOHENY STATE BEACH, 25300 Harbor Dr, Dana Point	202	B4
Good fishing; hiking trails.			115+ sites, fire rings, beach, swim, fish.		
TOPANGA STATE BEACH, Topanga Canyon Blvd	Q	A4	DONNER MEMORIAL STATE PARK, 2 mi W of Truckee	35	D1
Swimming in the surf, picnicking.			Open mid-May to mid-Sept., Memorial Museum.		
TORREY PINES STATE BEACH, S of Del Mar	V	A1	EAGLE LAKE, 20 mi N of Susanville	20	E2
Scenic beach for hiking, swimming, exploring.			300+ dev sites; boat, waterski, fish, hike.		
TRINIDAD STATE BEACH, off Hwy 101, Trinidad	9	E4	EL CAPITAN STATE BEACH, Avenida del Capitan	87	A4
Beaches, bluffs, nature trails, picnicking.			Surfing, hiking, camping & boat rentals.		
TWIN LAKES STATE BEACH, Santa Cruz	54	A2	EMERALD BAY STATE PARK, Hwy 89 near Emerald Bay	35	E3
Swimming, fire pits; day use only-no camping.			Scenic; camping, picnicking and swimming.		
WEST BEACH, Cabrillo Bl, Santa Barbara	174	D4	EMMA WOOD STATE BEACH, Jct Hwy 101 & Hwy 33	88	A5
Sandy beach; restaurants & specialty shops.			Camping, swimming and fishing.		
WESTPORT-UNION LANDING STATE BEACH, N of Westport	22	B3	FALLEN LEAF LAKE, Southwest of Lake Tahoe	35	E3
Fishing and camping.			200+ dev sites; boat, fish, swim, horses.		
Wm. RANDOLPH HEARST STATE BEACH, Hwy 1, Sn Simeon	75	B1	FOLSOM LAKE STATE REC AREA, 1 mile N of Folsom	34	B5
Picnic facilities; boating, fishing, swimming.			Camping, boating, fishing, waterskiing;horses.		
WILL ROGERS STATE BEACH, N of Santa Monica	Q	B4	FOREST OF NISENE MARKS, 4 miles N of Aptos	P	B5
Wide sandy beach; surfing, picnicking.			Camping, picnicking, hiking trails.		
WINDANSEA BEACH, foot of Palomar St	V	A2	FREMONT PEAK STATE PARK, S of San Juan Bautista	54	D3
Surfboarding & spectator beach; no swimming.			Camping, hiking trails, picnicking.		
WIPEOUT BEACH, Coast Blvd, La Jolla	105	A3	FURNACE CREEK CAMPGROUND, Furnace Creek Ranch	62	A5
Sandy beach, swimming and fishing.			Camping facilities in the heart of Death Vly.		
ZMUDOWSKI STATE BEACH, 1 mi N of Moss Landing	54	B3	GAVIOTA STATE PARK, Gaviota Beach Rd	86	D4
Fishing and horseback riding.			Camping, fishing, boat launch, picnic areas.		
			GEORGE HATFIELD STATE REC AREA, 28 mi W of Merced	47	D4
			Camping, hiking, fishing, and picnicking.		
CAMPGROUNDS			GOLD HILL CAMPGROUND, SW of Gorman	88	D2
			Primitive camping near Hungry Valley SVRA		
ANDREW MOLERA STATE PARK, W of Hwy 1, Big Sur	64	B2	GRIZZLY CREEK REDWOODS STATE PARK, E of Fortuna	16	B3
Camping, hiking, sandy beaches and meadows.			Scenic; camp, fish, nature trails, creeks.		
ANTELOPE LAKE, 45 miles NE of Quincy	21	A4	GROVER HOT SPRINGS STATE PARK, W of Markleeville	36	B5
200+ dev sites; boat, waterski, fish, hike.			Camping; fishing and swimming in hot creeks.		
ANZA BORREGO DESERT STATE PARK, San Diego County	108	A4	HALF MOON STATE BCH Near Half Moon Bay	N	B2
Beautiful wildflowers in spring; camp & hike.			51 dev sites; no swimming, fish, picnic.		
ATASCADERO STATE BEACH, Jct of Hwy 1 & Hwy 41	75	D3	HARRIS BEACH STATE PARK, N of Crescent City	1	C2
Camping and picnicking facilities.			Camping, lodging, dining.		
AUSTIN CREEK STATE RECREATION AREA, E of Ft Ross	37	C1	HENDY WOODS STATE PARK, near Philo on Hwy 128	30	D3
Primitive camping; picnicking area.			Camp, picnic, fish, hike, swim.		
BASS LAKE, E of Oakhurst	49	E4	HENRY COE STATE PARK, 14 mi NE of Morgan Hill	P	E4
220+ dev sites; boat, waterski, fish, hike.			Picturesque camping and picnic grounds.		
BENBOW LAKE STATE REC AREA, 2 mi S of Garberville	22	B1	HENRY COWELL REDWOODS STATE PARK, N of Santa Cruz	N	E5
Camp, fish, horse trails, swim, & picnic.			Equestrian trails, camping, hiking, fishing.		
BIG BASIN REDWOODS STATE PARK, on Hwy 236	N	D4	HIDDEN VIEW, 17 miles N of Madera	49	B5
Camping alongside the historic redwoods.			Scenic area to camp, swim and fish.		
BIG PINE CANYON, 10 miles W of Big Pine	51	C5	HOLLISTER HILLS VEHICULAR REC AREA, Cienega Rd	54	E3
Campgrounds, picnic areas, hiking.			Camping, motorcycling & 4-wheel drive trails.		
BOLSA CHICA STATE BEACH, N of Huntington Beach	T	A3	HUMBOLDT REDWOODS STATE PARK, Redwood Highway	16	A4
Camping, body surfing, picnicking & swimming.			Tallest redwoods; camp, fish, hike, picnic.		
BOTHE-NAPA VALLEY STATE PARK, on Hwy 29	38	A1	HUNGRY VALLEY STATE VEHICULAR REC AREA, Gorman	88	E2
Camping, swimming, picnicking & hiking.			Primitive camping; off-road vehicle use.		
BRANNAN ISLAND STATE REC AREA, S of Rio Vista	M	D2	HUNTINGTON LAKE, North of Camp Sierra	50	B5
Camping, fishing, swimming, boating; Vis Ctr.			300+ dev sites; boat, waterski, fish, horses.		
BUTANO STATE PARK, E of Hwy 1 at Gazos Creek Rd	N	C4	INDIAN GRINDING ROCK STATE HIST PK, S of Volcano	41	A2
Camping and recreational facilities.			Restored Miwok Indian Vlg; camping facilities.		
CALAVERAS BIG TREES STATE PARK, E of Arnold	41	D3	JENKINSON LAKE, 18 miles E of Placerville	35	B5
Camping among the redwood groves.			290+ dev sites; boat, fish, swim, hike.		
CAMANCHE RESERVOIR, W of San Andreas	40	C3	J SMITH REDWOODS STATE PARK, NE of Crescent City	1	E4
1150+ dev sites; boat, fish, hike, swim.			Camping, picnicking, hiking, fishing&exhibits.		
CARPINTERIA STATE BEACH, Linden Av	87	D4	JUNE LAKE LOOP, 18 miles North of Mammoth Lakes	50	A1
Camping, picnicking, fishing pier, boat ramp.			280+ dev sites; boat, fish, backpack, horses.		
CASTLE CRAG STATE PARK, S of Dunsmuir	12	D3	LAKE ELSINORE STATE REC AREA, near I-15 & Hwy 74	99	B4
Camping, fishing, hiking, swimming.			Camping, swimming, fishing and boating.		
CASTLE ROCK STATE PARK, near Jct Hwy 9 & Hwy 35	N	E4	LAKE HENSHAW, off Hwy 76, Santa Ysabel	107	B3
Scenic park for camping, picnicking, & hiking.			400+ dev sites; fish, boat, hike.		
CASWELL MEMORIAL STATE PARK, Hwy 99 S of Manteca	47	B2	LAKE MCCLURE, S of Coulterville	48	D2
Camping, fishing, swimming, and hiking.			550+ dev sites; housebt, fish, swim, picnic.		
CHINA CAMP STATE PARK, N of San Rafael	L	B3	LAKE MENDOCINO, N of Ukiah	31	B2
Camping and recreation facilities.			300+ dev sites; boat, waterski, fish, hike.		
CLEAR LAKE STATE PARK, near Lakeport	31	D3	LAKE NACIEMENTO, 40 mi NW of Paso Robles	65	D5
Camping, hiking, picnicking and boating.			350+ dev sites; swim, hike, boat, waterski.		
COL. ALLENSWORTH STATE HIS PK, 20 mi N of Wasco	68	B4	LAKE OROVILLE STATE REC AREA, NE of Oroville	25	D4
Camping, historical exhibits.			Camp, fish, boat, waterski, horseback ride.		
COLUSA-SACRAMENTO RIVER STATE REC AREA, Colusa	33	A1	LAKE PERRIS STATE REC AREA, off Ramona Expwy	99	C3
Camping, boating and waterskiing.			Camping, bicycle trails, boat rentals.		
CUYAMACA RANCHO STATE PARK, on Hwy 79, Julian	107	C4	LAKE SAN ANTONIO RECREATION AREA, W of Bradley	65	D4
In old Indian territory; camp, hike; horses.			650+ dev sites; boat, fish, swim, horses, hike		

POINTS OF INTEREST INDEX

NAME & ADDRESS	PAGE	GRID	NAME & ADDRESS	PAGE	GRID
LEO CARRILLO STATE BEACH, S of Hwy 101 Good surfing, diving and swimming.	96	D2	SAN CLEMENTE STATE BEACH, San Clemente Surfing, camping; barbeque, picnic facilities.	105	D1
LITTLE GRASS VALLEY LAKE, W of Gibsonville Camping and recreational facilities.	26	C3	SAN ELIJO STATE BEACH, Cardiff Camping & picnicking on the beach; swimming.	106	B4
LOPEZ LAKE, 23 miles N of Santa Maria 300+ sites, boat, fish, waterski, picnic area.	76	C4	SAN LUIS RES STATE REC AREA, 16 mi W of Los Banos Lovely area to camp, waterski, fish & hike.	55	C1
MacKERRICHER STATE PARK, N of Fort Bragg Rocky beaches, sand dunes, nature trails.	22	B5	SAN ONOFRE STATE BEACH, San Onofre Surf fishing, clamming, surfing and camping.	105	E2
MALAKOFF DIGGINS STATE HIST PK, NE of Nevada City Camping along colorful slopes.	26	D5	SAN SIMEON STATE BEACH, Hwy 1, Morro Bay Camping and hiking; sand dunes to explore.	75	B1
MANCHESTER STATE BEACH, near Point Arena Camping on sandy beaches among sand dunes.	30	B3	SEACLIFF STATE BEACH, 5 mi S of Hwy, Aptos Camp, swimming.	54	B2
McARTHUR-BURNEY FALLS MEM STATE PK, NE of Burney Well developed park with camping and fishing.	13	C4	SHASTA LAKE, off I-5 N of Redding 400+ sites, fishing, boating & waterskiing.	18	B1
McCONNELL STATE RECREATION AREA, 5 mi SE of Delhi Camping, picnicking, fishing and swimming.	48	A3	SILVER STRAND STATE BEACH, 5000 Hwy 75, Coronado RV camping, picnic, fish, boating, swim.	V	B4
MCGRATH STATE BEACH, Off Hwy 101, Oxnard 174 sites, visitor ctr, hike, fishing.	96	A1	SILVERWOOD LAKE STATE RECREATION AREA, Hwy 138 Camping, swimming, boating and fishing.	91	B5
MILLERTON LAKE REC AREA, 22 miles E of Madera Camping, boating, fishing & horseback riding.	57	D1	SINKYONE WILDERNESS ST PK, Humboldt & Mendocno Co Tent camping, picnicking, hiking and fishing.	22	A1
MONTANA DE ORO STATE PARK, Pecho Valley Rd Barbeque facilities; camping, riding & hiking.	75	E3	SMITH RIVER NATIONAL RECREATION AREA, Hwy 199 Camping, rafting, fishing, hiking, hunting.	2	B3
MORRO BAY STATE PARK, on Morro Bay Camping, fishing, clam digging, boating.	75	D3	SONOMA COAST STATE BEACH, N of Bodega Bay Camp, hike, picnic; scenic beaches.	37	B2
MT DIABLO STATE PARK, Diablo Rd Camp on the Peak, hiking trails.	M	B4	SOUTH CARLSBAD STATE BEACH, S of Carlsbad Scenic beach for camping, fishing or swimming.	106	B3
MT SAN JACINTO STATE PARK, Hwy 111 near Palm Spgs Hiking, picnicking and limited camping.	100	B3	STAMPEDE RESERVOIR 250+ dev sites, boat, waterski, fish, hike.	27	D4
MOUNT TAMALPAIS STATE PARK, 6 mi N of Hwy 1 Camping, hiking, equestrian trails.	L	A3	STANDISH HICKEY STATE REC AREA, 1 mi N of Leggett Camping, fishing, hiking trails, swimming.	22	C2
NEW BRIGHTON STATE BEACH, off Hwy 1 Scenic camping; fishing and swimming.	54	A2	STOVEPIPE WELLS CAMPGROUND, Death Valley Natl Park 200 campsites (RV & tents) in the valley.	61	C4
OAKWOOD LAKE RESORT, off I-5 S of Manteca Camping, watersports and shopping.	47	A1	SUGARLOAF RIDGE STATE PARK, Adobe Canyon Rd Camping, fishing and riding.	38	A2
OCOTILLO WELLS STATE VEHICULAR REC AREA, Hwy 78 Off-road 4-wheel drive vehicle trails.	108	B3	SUGAR PINE POINT STATE PARK, N of Meeks Bay Camping, swimming, fishing and hiking.	35	E2
PALOMAR MOUNTAIN STATE PARK, Birch Hill Rd Beautiful area to camp or enjoy a picnic.	107	A2	SUNSET CAMPGROUND, Furnace Creek Ranch, Death Vly Campsites near the heart of Death Valley.	62	A5
PATRICKS POINT STATE PARK, N of Trinidad Camping, hiking, biking, picnicking.	9	D3	SUNSET STATE BEACH, W of Watsonville Scenic beach to camp, fish, dig for clams.	54	B2
PAUL M. DIMMICK WAYSIDE CAMPGROUND, W of Navarro Primitive campgrounds; swim, fish, picnic.	30	C2	TAHOE STATE RECREATION AREA, N of Tahoe City Camp, swim, fish, boat, picnic.	35	E2
PFEIFFER BIG SUR STATE PARK, E of Hwy 1, Big Sur Hiking, camping, swimming and fishing.	64	B2	TEXAS SPRINGS CAMPGROUND, Furnace Creek Ranch RV and tent campsites in scenic Death Valley.	62	A5
PICACHO STATE RECREATION AREA, W of Picacho Camping, fishing, hiking and sailing.	110	C4	TOPAZ LAKE, east of Markleeville 200+ dev sites, boat, waterski, fish, swim.	36	E5
PISMO DUNES STATE VEHICULAR REC AREA, Pismo Beach Off-road, 4-wheel drive trails; camp & picnic.	76	B5	TRINITY LAKE, 44 miles NW of Redding 400+ sites, sail, wtrski, fish, hrseback riding	12	A4
PISMO STATE BEACH, off Hwy 101, Pismo Beach Camping & hiking along sandy beaches & dunes.	76	B5	TUOLUMNE MEADOWS, Tioga Pass Rd Camp, fish, backpack, mtn climb, horses.	43	A5
PLUMAS EUREKA STATE PARK, Hwy A14 at Johnsville Camping, scenic creeks, trails, lakes & mtns.	26	E2	TURLOCK LAKE STATE REC AREA, SW of La Grande Waterski, fish, boat, hike and camp.	48	B2
POINT MUGU STATE PARK, Hwy 1 Camp near the ocean; hiking, swimming&fishing.	96	C2	UNION VALLEY RESERVOIR, 17 mi N of Riverton 270+ dev sites; boat, fish, swim, hike.	35	C4
PORTOLA STATE PARK, W of Hwy 35 Camping, recreational facilities.	N	D4	VAN DAMME STATE PK, S of Fort Bragg 73 sites, hike, nearby swimming.	30	C1
PRAIRIE CREEK REDWOODS STATE PARK, N of Orick Camping, fishing, picnic areas, hiking.	10	A1	WESTPORT UNION LANDING STATE BCH, N of Westport Camping and fishing.	22	B3
PROVIDENCE MTNS STATE REC AREA, Essex Rd Camping facilities in scenic surroundings.	94	B1	WOODSON BRIDGE STATE REC AREA, SE of Corning Camping, fishing, swimming, nature trail.	24	D2
RED ROCK CANYON STATE PARK, Hwy 14 at Ricardo Camping, picnicking, hiking and exhibits.	80	B3	COLLEGES & UNIVERSITIES		
REFUGIO STATE BEACH, Refugio Rd Tidepools; camping and fishing.	86	E4			
RICHARDSON GROVE STATE PARK, S of Garberville Scenic camping area; fish, swim, hike.	22	B1	CAL STATE COLLEGE, BAKERSFIELD, 9001 Stockdale Hy Small campus; good student-professor ratio.	78	C3
ROCK CREEK LAKE, SW of Toms Place 220+ dev sites, fish, hike, backpack, boat.	51	A3	CALIF STATE POLYTECH UNIV, POMONA, 3801 W Temple Outstanding programs in architecture.	U	B2
ROLLINS RESERVOIR, N of Colfax 240+ dev sites, hike, fish, boat, waterski.	34	D2	CAL STATE POLYTECH UNIV, SAN LUIS OBISPO Noted for studies in agriculture & business.	172	B1
RUSSIAN GULCH STATE PARK, S of Fort Bragg Camp, hike to waterfall, rocky headlands.	30	A1	CAIFORNIA STATE UNIVERSITY, CHICO, W 1st St Offers a variety of quality academic programs.	124	B4
SADDLEBACK BUTTE STATE PARK, E of Lancaster Camping, picnicking, and hiking trails.	90	C3	CALIF STATE UNIV, DOMINGUEZ HLLS, 1000 E Victoria Noted as a leader in innovative programs.	S	D1
SALTON SEA STATE RECREATION AREA, off Hwy 111 Good area to camp, boat, waterski, or hike.	108	E2	CALIF STATE UNIV, FRESNO, Shaw & Cedar Av Noted for agriculture, business, engineering.	57	C3
SALT POINT STATE PARK, N of Fort Ross off Hwy 1 Camping, beaches, underwater preserve, trails.	37	A1	CAL STATE UNIV, FULLERTON, 800 N State College Bl Good academic opportunities in many subjects.	T	D1
SAMUEL P. TAYLOR STATE PARK, off Hwy 1 near Olema Camping, fishing, winter sports, riding.	37	E4	CAL STATE UNIV, HAYWARD, 25800 Carlos Bee Bl Strong programs in sciences & liberal arts.	M	A5

NAME & ADDRESS	PAGE	GRID
CALIF STATE UNIV, LONG BEACH, 1250 Bellflower Bl	T	A2
One of largest universities in CSUC system.		
CALIF STATE UNIV, LOS ANGELES, 5151 State Coll Dr	R	B4
Wide spectrum of programs with an urban focus.		
CALIF STATE UNIV, MONTEREY BAY, 100 Campus Center	54	B4
Added to the CSU system in 1995.		
CAL STATE UNIV, NORTHRIDGE, 18111 Nordhoff St	Q	B2
A broad range of educational opportunities.		
CALIF STATE UNIV, SACRAMENTO, 6000 J St	39	E1
Situated halfway between S F & the Sierras.		
CAL STATE UNIV, SAN BERNARDINO, 5000 University	99	B1
On a 3-3 system: 3 quarters, 3 classes.		
CAL STATE UNIV, STANISLAUS, 801 W Monte Vista Av	47	D3
Small, intimate campus in San Joaquin Valley.		
CAL TECH-CALIF INSTITUTE OF TECH, 1201 E Calif Bl	190	D4
Largest private technical college in Calif.		
CLAREMONT COLLEGES, College Av & Foothill Blvd	203	A1
Distinguished group of six schools & colleges.		
CLAREMONT GRADUATE SCHOOL, Claremont Colleges	203	A1
Studies in educatn, business, history, Englsh.		
CLAREMONT McKENNA COLLEGE, Claremont Colleges	203	B2
Studies in political science & economics.		
HARVEY MUDD COLLEGE, Claremont Colleges	203	A1
Studies in sciences, engineering, mathematics.		
HUMBOLDT STATE UNIV, Arcata	10	A5
Beautiful campus in a redwood forest.		
LOYOLA-MARYMOUNT UNIV, LA, Loyola Bl & W 80th St	188	A4
Fine academic Catholic university.		
PEPPERDINE UNIV, 24255 W Pacific Coast Hy, Malibu	97	A2
Private univ; noted for studies in business.		
PITZER COLLEGE, Scott Hall, Claremont Colleges	203	B1
Studies in liberal arts and humanities.		
POMONA COLLEGE, Sumner Hall, Claremont Colleges	203	B2
Studies in history, social & natural sciences.		
ST MARYS COLLEGE, St Marys Rd, Moraga	L	E4
Studies in liberal arts & economics.		
SAN DIEGO STATE UNIV, 5300 Campanile Dr	V	C3
Largest in the CSUC system.		
SAN FRANCISCO STATE UNIV, 1600 Holloway Av	L	A5
Many interdisciplinary programs.		
SAN JOSE STATE UNIVERSITY, 125 S 7th St	152	C4
Campus of 27,000 students in Santa Clara Vly.		
SCRIPPS COLLEGE, Balch Hall, Claremont Colleges	203	B1
Studies in social sci, literature, fine arts.		
SCRIPPS INST OF OCEANOGRAPHY, San Diego	211	A1
Branch of UCSD, oceanographic research.		
SCRIPPS INST SUBMERGED LAND AREA, San Diego	211	A1
Part of Scripps Institute of Oceanography.		
SONOMA STATE UNIV, 1801 E Cotati Av	38	A3
Offers programs in sciences and liberal arts.		
STANFORD UNIVERSITY, Junipero Serra Blvd	147	A3
Distinguished univ; beautifl church on campus.		
UNIV OF CALIF, BERKELEY, 2200 University Av	156	B2
Oldest & largest of the Univ Of Cal campuses.		
UNIV OF CALIF, DAVIS, Russell Bl & La Rue	136	B3
Studies in law, medicine, agricultre, science.		
UNIV OF CALIF, IRVINE, Campus Dr	200	D2
Good programs in sciences & medicine.		
UNIV OF CALIF, LOS ANGELES, 405 Hilgard Av	180	C1
Outstanding liberal arts & medical schools.		
UNIV OF CALIF, RIVERSIDE, 900 University Av	205	E3
Desert campus lies at base of foothills.		
UNIV OF CALIF, SAN DIEGO, La Jolla Village Dr	V	A2
Specializes in physicl & naturl sci, medicine.		
UNIV OF CALIF, SAN FRANCISCO, 3rd & Parnassus Avs	141	E5
Small campus, tours available.		
UNIV OF CALIF, SANTA BARBARA, Ward Memorial Bl	87	A4
Beautiful campus beside the ocean.		
UNIV OF CALIF, SANTA CRUZ, Hill St	169	A1
Overlooks bay, excellent marine research dept.		
UNIVERSITY OF NEVADA, LAS VEGAS, Flamingo Rd	210	E3
Noted for music & theater; concert hall.		
UNIVERSITY OF NEVADA, RENO, N Virginia & 9th Sts	130	B1
Beautiful site overlooking Truckee Meadows.		
UNIVERSITY OF THE PACIFIC, Stadium Dr, Stockton	160	B2
Noted for Liberal Arts & Sciences.		
UNIVERSITY OF SAN DIEGO, Alcala Park	213	B4
Fine academic programs, small campus.		
UNIVERSITY OF SAN FRANCISCO, 2130 Fulton St	141	E3
Fine academic programs on a small campus		

NAME & ADDRESS	PAGE	GRID
UNIVERSITY OF SANTA CLARA, The Alameda	151	C3
Mission Santa Clara is on this campus.		
UNIV OF SOUTHERN CALIF, 3551 University Av, L A	185	C5
Largest private university in California.		

GOLF COURSES

NAME & ADDRESS	PAGE	GRID
ALMADEN GOLF & COUNTRY CLUB, San Jose	P	B4
BERMUDA DUNES COUNTRY CLUB, 42360 Adams St	101	A4
CYPRESS POINT COUNTRY CLUB, 17 Mile Dr	53	A4
DESERT INN & COUNTRY CLUB, Las Vegas	210	C1
ELDORADO COUNTRY CLUB, Indian Wells	100	E4
FAIRBANKS RANCH COUNTRY CLUB, San Diego	106	C4
GRAEAGLE MEADOWS, Graeagle	27	A3
INDIAN WELLS COUNTRY CLUB, 4600 Club Dr, Riversde	100	E4
LA COSTA COUNTRY CLUB, Carlsbad	106	C3
LA QUINTA COUNTRY CLUB, Eisenhower Dr & 50th Av	101	A4
LOS ANGELES CNTRY CLUB, 10101 Wilshire Bl, Westwd	183	A1
MISSION HILLS COUNTRY CLUB, Rancho Mirage	100	D4
OAKMONT COUNTRY CLUB, Glendale	Q	E2
PEBBLE BEACH GOLF LINKS, off 2nd Av	168	B3
PLUMAS PINES COUNTRY CLUB, Blairsden	27	A2
RIVIERA COUNTRY CLUB, Pacific Palisades	Q	B4
SPYGLASS HILL G C, Spyglass Hill & Stevenson	53	B4
TAMARISK C C, 70240 F Sinatra Dr, Rancho Mirage	100	D4
THE MIRAGE GOLF CLUB, 3650 S Las Vegas Bl, LV	210	A3
TORREY PINES GOLF COURSE, La Jolla	V	A1

HARBORS

NAME & ADDRESS	PAGE	GRID
ALAMEDA HARBOR, Embarcadero & 9th Av	158	B4
Major shipping center of northern California.		
BODEGA HARBOR, Hwy 1 at Bodega Bay	37	C3
Small but busy harbor; parks nr harbor & bay.		
INNER HARBOR, between Oakland & Alameda	157	D4
Busy commercial section of SF Bay.		
LONG BEACH HARBOR, Ocean Blvd	192	A5
Shares largest man-made harbr with Ls Angeles.		
LOS ANGELES HARBOR, Seaside Av	191	C5
Busy commercial port of state's largest city.		
PORT HUENEME HARBOR, end of Hueneme Rd	96	B1
Dominated by US Naval installation.		
PORT OF SACRAMENTO, off Lake Washington	39	D1
Furthest inland port of Sac deep-watr channel.		
PORT OF STOCKTON, off Hwy 5 in Stockton	160	A5
Busy inland agricultural seaport.		
RICHMOND INNER HARBOR, Richmond	155	B5
Commercial port in San Francisco Bay.		
SAN DIEGO BAY, W of I-5	V	C4
Busy deepwater port, home of USN 11th Fleet.		
SAN FRANCISCO HARBOR, Fisherman's Wharf	L	B4
Major commercial port; 1st in W Coast shippng.		
SANTA CRUZ HARBOR	169	E4
Small commercial harbor in Monterey Bay.		

HISTORICAL SITES

NAME & ADDRESS	PAGE	GRID
ALPINE COUNTY HIST COMPLEX, Hwy 89, Markleeville	36	C5
Historic museum and restored buildings.		
ANDERSON MARSH STATE HIST PARK, near Clear Lake	32	A3
Buildings from Anderson Ranch & Indian site.		
ANGELS HOTEL, Angels Camp	41	B4
Hotel in Twains The Jumpng Frog of Calv Co'.		
ARROYO DE CANTUA, off Hwy 5	66	D1
Headqrtrs of notorious bandit Jquin Murieta.		
ASTRONOMICAL OBSERVATORY, off Shake Ridge Rd	41	A2
1st observ in Cal - discvrd Great Comet 1861.		
AVERY HOTEL, Moran Rd, Avery	41	C3
Wooden hotel built in 1853.		
BALE GRIST MILL ST HISTORIC PARK, on Hwy 29	38	B1
Restored mill was built in 1846.		
BANNING PARK, 401 E M St, Wilmington	S	C2
House built in 1850s by Gen Phineas Banning.		
BARNSDALL PARK, 4800 Hollywood Bl	182	B4
Site of Frank Lloyd Wright's Hollyhock House.		

POINTS OF INTEREST INDEX

NAME & ADDRESS	PAGE	GRID
BENICIA CAPITOL STATE HISTORIC PARK, H & 1st Sts	153	B4
Capitol of California in 1853.		
BIDWELL MANSION ST HIST PK, 525 Esplanade, Chico	124	B4
Restored Victorian home of Chico founder.		
BODIE STATE HISTORICAL PARK, Bodie, off Hwy 395	43	C3
Gold boom town, now a restored ghost town.		
BOK KAI TEMPLE (CHINESE JOSS HOUSE), Marysville	33	D2
Only temple in USA for worship of River God.		
BORAX MUSEUM, Furnace Creek Ranch, Death Valley	62	A5
Memorabilia from the old borax mine.		
BOWERS MANSION, Washoe Valley	36	B1
Granite home built 1864 wth rewards of mining.		
BRAND PARK, SF Mission Blvd, Los Angeles	Q	C1
Picturesque atmosphere of early Cal missions.		
BRIDGEPORT COVERED BRIDGE, Bridgeport	34	B1
Longest single-span wood-covered bridge in US.		
BURBANK MEMORIAL GARDENS, Santa Rosa Av	131	D4
A living memorial dedicated to the naturalist.		
CALICO GHOST TOWN, 10.5 miles NE of Barstow	92	A1
Restored mining town - tour of mine & museum.		
CALIFORNIA CITRUS ST HIST PK, Van Buren Blvd	99	B3
Visitor center, grove with 80 varieties.		
CALIFORNIA STANDARD OIL WELL, McKittrick Field	77	E3
Discovery well started new oil field in 1899.		
CALIF STATE MINING & MINERAL MUSEUM, Mariposa	49	B3
Displays of Calif gold, diamonds and fossils.		
CAMP CURTIS, 1 mi N of Arcata.	9	E5
Estab for the protection of white settlers.		
CAMP SALVATION, Calexico	112	B4
Refugee ctr for emigrants in search of gold.		
CAMRON STANFORD HOUSE, 14418 Lakeside Dr	158	A3
Built in 1876 it serves as the Oakland Museum.		
THE CASTLE, 70 S B St, Virginia City	36	D1
Built 1868 - restored; antique furnishings.		
CATALINA ISLAND MUSEUM, Casino Building	97	B4
Features displays on the island's history.		
CHARCOAL KILNS, near Wildrose, Death Vly Natl Park	71	D2
Large old kilns used during the mining days.		
CHILDREN'S PARK, S Morton Bl, Modesto	162	D4
Childrens playground wth old train & airplane.		
CHINESE TEMPLE, E of Oroville	25	D4
A temple of worship for over 10,000 Chinese.		
CHUMASH PAINTED CAVE ST HIST PK, Painted Cave Rd	87	C4
Chumash cave painted with native artwork		
COL THOMAS BAKER MEMORIAL, City Hall, Bakersfield	166	C3
Civic Center commemorates friend of travelers.		
COLUMBIA CITY HOTEL, Main St, Columbia	41	C4
Hotel built in 1856 which is still in use.		
COLUMBIA STATE HISTORIC PARK, N of Columbia	41	C4
Gold boom town in 1850s, now preserved.		
CONCANNON VINEYARD, S of Livermore	P	D1
Estab Livermore Vly as a select wine district.		
CONGREGATIONAL CHURCH, Jesus Maria Rd	41	A3
Built 1853 - oldest Congregtnl Church in Ca.		
COTTONWOOD CHARCOAL KILNS, N of Cartago	70	B1
Blt 1870s to char wood for mines at Owens Lk.		
DEATH VALLEY GATEWAY, mouth of Furnace Creek	72	B1
Natural entrance to Death Vly used by settlrs.		
DE LA GUERRA PLAZA, 15 E De La Guerra St	174	C4
Shopping arcade in historic adobes.		
DEL NORTE COUNTY HISTORICAL MUSEUM, Crescent City	1	D4
Largest museum in Northern California.		
DIEGO SEPULVEDA ADOBE, 1900 Adams Av, Costa Mesa	197	A5
Old ranch adobe now houses a museum.		
DRYTOWN, N of Amador	40	E2
1st town in Ama, in which gold was discvrd.		
D STEWART COUNTY STORE, in Ione	40	C2
The 1st brick bldg, built in Lone Vly, 1856.		
DUNSMUIR HOME & GARDENS, 2960 Peralta Oaks Ct	L	E5
Blt 1899, Greek revival mansion, 48 acre grdn.		
EL PRESIDIO DE SANTA BARBARA, 210 E Canon Perdido	174	C3
One of four presidios built in Calif, 1782.		
EL PUEBLO DE LOS ANGELES, Main & Arcadia Sts	186	B3
State historic pk with many historic landmrks.		
EMPIRE MINE STATE HIST PK, Colfax Rd	127	D4
Oldst quartz mine in operatn for over 100 yrs.		
ESTUDILLO HOME, S of San Leandro	L	E5
Home of the family which founded San Leandro.		
EUGENE O'NEILL NATIONAL HIS SITE, NW of Danville	M	A4
Rangr-guided tour of ONeills 1937 Tao House.		

NAME & ADDRESS	PAGE	GRID
FELTON COVERED BRIDGE, off Graham Hill Rd, Felton	P	A5
1 of 3 remaining coverd bridgs in Sta Cruz Co.		
FERNANDO PACHECO ADOBE, Concord	M	B3
Restored adobe house originally built in 1843.		
FORT HUMBOLDT STATE HISTORIC PARK, Eureka	121	A3
Exhibits of logging & military life.		
FORT JANESVILLE, near Janesville	21	B4
Fort built for protection from Indian attacks.		
FORT MASON, Golden Gate National Recreation Area	143	A1
Former army hdqurtrs houses mus; cultural ctr.		
FORT POINT NATL HISTORIC PARK, Golden Gate Park	141	C1
Built in 1861 to control access to SF Bay.		
FT ROSS STATE HIST PARK, at Fort Ross	37	A1
Restored Russian outpost; museum and beach.		
FORT TEJON STATE HISTORIC PARK, Ft Tejon Rd, Lebec	88	D1
Former military center; summer programs.		
FRESNO FLATS HISTORIC PARK, Rd 427, Oakhurst	49	D4
Historic buildings and artifacts of Madera Co.		
GASLAMP QUARTER, Downtown San Diego	215	E4
Victorian bldgs, shops, nightclubs, theaters.		
GIANT DESERT FIGURES, 18 miles north of Blythe	103	C3
3 giant figures - 2 animals, 1 coiled serpent.		
GOLD BUG MINE, off Bedford Rd, Placerville	138	E1
Exposed gold veins in old mine shaft; tours.		
GOLD COUNTRY, HIGHWAY 49, from Mariposa to Vinton	41	A3
300 mi drive through the historic Mother Lode.		
GRANVILLE P SWIFT ADOBE, N of Orland	24	D3
Rodeos were held annually at this site.		
GRASS VALLEY MUSEUM, Chapel St, Grass Valley	127	B4
Built in 1855; artifacts from early Grass Vly.		
HARMONY BORAX WORKS, Furnace Creek, Death Valley	62	A5
Preserved processing plant nr borax discovery.		
HAROLD LLOYD ESTATE, 1740 Greenacres, Beverly Hls	Q	C3
Once home to the silent screen actor.		
HEARST SAN SIMEON STATE HIST MONUMENT, off Hwy 1	75	B1
Tours of fabulous estate of William R Hearst.		
HERITAGE HILL, Lk Forest Dr & Serrano, Lk Forest	98	D4
Restored historicl bldgs of central Orange Co.		
HOTEL LEGER, Main St, Mokelumne Hill	41	A3
Victorian style hotel, garden pool & theatre.		
INDIAN GRINDING ROCK STATE HIST PK, S of Volcano	41	A2
Restored Miwok Indian village, museum.		
IOOF HALL, Mokelumne Hill	41	A3
1st 3-story bldg in the interior of the state.		
JACK LONDON STATE HISTORIC PARK, Glen Ellen	38	B2
Museum is in House of Happy Walls.		
JACOBY BUILDING, 8th & H, Arcata	10	A5
Princpl supply store for Klmth-Trnty miners.		
J. J. JACKSON MUSEUM, Highway 299, Weaverville	17	D1
Trinity Co. history; Indian & mining displays.		
JOHN MUIR NATIONAL HISTORIC SITE, 4204 Alhambra	154	B4
House built 1882; visitor's center & tours.		
JOSE E BORONDA ADOBE, 333 Boronda Rd, Salinas	171	A2
Restored adobe, artifacts, historic photos.		
KEANE WONDER MINE & MILL, off Daylight Pass Ctoff	61	E4
Well-preserved historic remains of silvr mine.		
KENTUCKY MINE HISTORIC PARK, NE of Sierra City	27	A4
Restored stamp mill & old gold mine buildngs.		
KERN CO MUSEUM & PIONEER VILLAGE, 3801 Chester	166	C2
Exhibits of pioneer and Indian history.		
KEYESVILLE, 4 miles W of Isabella	79	C1
Center of placer & quartz gold mining,1853-70.		
KIT CARSON MARKER, Kit Carson	35	D5
Replica of orig instriptn cut from Kit's tree.		
LAKE COUNTY MUSEUM, 255 N Forbes St, Lakeport	31	D3
In old courthouse, Indian & pioneer displays.		
LAKEPORT HISTORICAL MUSEUM, 175 3rd St, Lakeport	31	C3
Displays of indian baskets & other artifacts.		
LA PURISIMA MSSN STATE HIST PK, 3 mi NE of Lompoc	86	C2
Restored mission, exhibits. Open 9-4:30 daily.		
LARKIN HOUSE, Jefferson St & Calle Principal	167	E4
Served as American Consulate 1843 to 1846.		
LAWS RAILROAD MUSEUM & HIST SITE, NE of Bishop	51	D3
Restored 1880's RR depot, locomotive, equip.		
LELAND STANFORD WINERY, off Hwy 680	P	B2
Founder of Stanfrd Uni, operated here in 1869.		
LIVERMORE MEMORIAL MONUMENT, Livermore	P	C1
Remembrance of the 1st settler of Livermore.		
L A CO MUSEUM OF NATURAL HIST, 900 Exposition Bl	185	C5
Exhibits include Indian artfcts, gems & mummy.		

NAME & ADDRESS	PAGE	GRID
LOS ENCINOS STATE HIST PK, 16756 Moorpark St	Q	B3
This historic park features 1849 Osa Adobe.		
LOS ROBLES ADOBE, 3 mi N of Lemoore	67	C1
Restored adobe house, built in 1849.		
LOTT HOME, 1735 Montgomery St, Oroville	25	C4
Restored; furnished 1856 home of Judse C Lott.		
LOWER LAKE STONE JAIL, Lower Lake	32	A3
Claimed to be smallest jail in US, built 1876.		
LUMMIS HOME STATE HISTORIC MNT, 200 E Av 43, LA	R	B3
Built 1895 by Charles F Lummis.		
MALAKOFF DIGGINS STATE HIST PK, NE of Nevada City	26	D5
Colorful slopes exposed by hydraulic mining.		
MARIPOSA COUNTY COURTHOUSE, Mariposa	49	B3
Built 1854 after Mariposa became the Co seat.		
MARIPOSA CO HIST CTR & MUS, 12th St & Jessie St	49	B3
Early Gold Rush equip, stamp mill, buildngs.		
MARSHALL'S BLACKSMITH SHOP, Gold Trail Pk	34	E4
Marshall was a smithy & qualified carpenter.		
MARSHALL GOLD DISCOVERY STATE HIST PARK, Hwy 49	34	D4
Marshalls discov in 1848 started Gold Rush'.		
MARY AARON MUSEUM, 704 D St, Marysville	33	D2
Restored home - gold rush tools, pictures.		
MARY AUSTIN'S HOUSE, Independence	59	E3
Wrote books depicting beauty of Owens Valley.		
McKITTRICK BREA PIT, 1/2 mi W of McKittrick	77	E3
Animals were trapped in ancient asphalt pit.		
MENDOCINO PRESBYTERIAN CHURCH, Main St, Mendocino	30	C1
Blt 1868 of redwood, 1 of oldest still in use.		
METHODIST CHURCH, S of Ione	40	C3
Dedicatd Lone City Centenary Church in 1866.		
MINERS FOUNDRY, 325Spring St, Nevada City	128	C3
Manufactured machinery for gold miners.		
MONO COUNTY HISTORICAL MUSEUM, Bridgeport City Pk	43	B3
Restored ele sch, houses many histrcl artfcts.		
MONTEREY STATE HIST PARK, 210 Olivier St	167	E3
Includes many buildings of historic interest.		
MORMON STATION STATE HIST MON, N of Gardnerville	36	B3
Museum has pioneer items & displays; old fort.		
MORMON STOCKADE, Court St, San Bernardino	207	D2
Site of 1851 stockade built for protection.		
MORRO ROCK, off the coast of Morro Bay	75	D3
Important navigational landmark for 300+ yrs.		
MOTHER COLONY HOUSE, 400 N West St, Anaheim	193	B2
First house built in Anaheim.		
MURPHYS, 9 mi NE of Angels Camp	41	C4
Victorian houses, old jail, hotels, church.		
MURPHY'S HOTEL, off Hwy 4 in Murphys	41	C4
Early guests included Mark Twain & Gen Grant.		
MUSEUM OF NATURAL HIST, State Pk Rd, Sta Barbara	174	B2
Displays, films & lectures.		
NAPA COUNTY HISTORICAL MUSEUM, in Calistoga	38	A1
County history of the late 1800s.		
NAPA VALLEY RAILROAD DEPOT, Calistoga	38	B1
Built 1868, is now the Southern Pacfic depot.		
NATIONAL HISTORIC SHIPS, Hyde St Pier, Aquatic Pk	143	B1
Museum of 5 ships; includes the Balclutha.		
NATIONAL HOTEL, 2 Water St, Jackson	40	E2
Built in 1849, survived the 1862 fire.		
NEVADA STATE HIST MUS, 1650 N Virginia St, Reno	28	B4
Indian, pioneer, mineral, gambling exhibits.		
OCTAGON HOUSE, 2645 Gough St, San Francisco	143	A2
Eary San Francisco home built in 1861.		
ODD FELLOWS MEMORIAL, Kirkwood	36	A5
Here rests the Unknown Pioneer, 1849.		
OLD CUSTOM HOUSE, Fisherman's Wharf	167	E3
Oldest government building in California.		
OLDEST HOUSE NORTH OF SF BAY, N of Novato	L	A2
Built 1776 by an Indian chief.		
OLD FIREHOUSE No 1, 214 Main St, Nevada City	128	C2
Indian baskets, pioneer and Donner Party itms.		
OLD FOLSOM POWERHOUSE, Folsom	34	B5
Long distance generating plant built in 1890s.		
OLD HOMESTEAD, Crockett	L	D3
Built in 1867 - 1st American home in Crockett.		
OLD SACRAMENTO STATE HISTORIC PARK, 2nd & I Sts	137	A2
Business district during Gold Rush; restored.		
OLD SPANISH LIGHTHOUSE, Point Loma	V	A4
Lighthouse constructed 1854 - 1855.		
OLD STOVEPIPE WELL, off Hwy 190, Death Valley	61	D4
Site of underground well marked by stovepipe.		

NAME & ADDRESS	PAGE	GRID
OLD TOWN SAN DIEGO STATE HISTORIC PARK	213	A5
Restored Spanish-style bldgs; museums, shops.		
OLVERA STREET, 130 Paseo de la Plaza	186	B2
Shopping & dining in birthplace of Ls Angeles.		
PEPPARD CABIN, off Hwy 70 in Quincy	26	C2
Cabin built in 1888; made of hand hewn logs.		
PERALTA HOME, W of Castro Valley	L	E5
The first brick home built in Alameda County.		
PETALUMA ADOBE ST HISTORIC PARK, 3325 Adobe Rd	L	A1
Relics displayed in 1836 adobe house.		
PETER LASSEN GRAVE, 5 mi E of Susanville	21	A4
In memory of a pioneer killed by Indians.		
PIGEON PT LIGHTHOUSE, Pigeon Pt Rd, San Mateo Co.	N	C4
Constructed in 1872 and still in use.		
PIONEER YOSEMITE HISTORY CENTER, Wawona	49	C3
Historical buildings, covered bridge, cabins.		
PIONEER SCHOOLHOUSE, 2 mi E of Quincy	26	C1
1st schoolhouse in Plumas Co, built in 1857.		
PLUMAS COUNTY MUSEUM, 500 Jackson Street, Quincy	26	C2
Artifacts of early Plumas County		
PLYMOUTH TRADING POST, Plymouth	40	E2
Office & commissary of the many small mines.		
POINT FERMIN HISTORIC LIGHTHOUSE, Paseo Del Mar	S	C3
Located in Angels Gate Park.		
POINT SUR STATE HISTORIC PARK, Monterey County	64	A1
Ranger-guided tours of lighthouse & Moro Rock.		
PONY EXPRESS REMOUNT STATION, off Hwy 88	36	B4
An important remount station in the 1860s.		
PRESIDIO OF MONTEREY, Pacific St	167	E3
Now House Defense Language Institute.		
PRESIDIO OF SAN FRANCISCO, NW end Lombrd	141	C2
Active Army Post fr 1776; 1450 Acres, hikng.		
RAILTOWN 1897 STATE HISTORIC PARK, Jamestown	41	B5
26 acre park with trains on exhibit.		
RANCHO OLOMPALI ST HIST PK, US 101 N of Novato	38	A4
Historic Miwok village and exhibits.		
RANDSBURG GHOST TOWN, Hwy 395 S of Ridgecrest	80	D3
Residents live in restored 19th Century bldgs.		
RED BRICK GRAMMAR SCHOOL, Altaville	41	A4
Built 1848 - it is one of the oldest in Ca.		
RENEGADE CANYON NATURL HIST LNDMRK, nr China Lake	70	D5
Remarkable prehistoric rockpile collection.		
RHYOLITE, off Hwy 374, Nevada	62	A2
Once a booming silver town, now in ruins.		
RICHARDSON ADOBE, 2.5 mi S of Soledad	65	B1
Built 1843, later used as stage station & PO.		
ROCKVILLE STONE CHAPEL, Rockville	L	D1
Volunteer pioneers built chapel in 1856.		
ROOP'S FORT, Weatherlow St, Susanville	20	E3
Built in 1854 - Emigrant trains stopped here.		
ST JAMES EPISCOPAL CHURCH, Sonora	163	B3
Oldest Episcopal Church in California.		
SAINT TERESA'S CHURCH, Bodega	37	C3
Built of redwood in 1859; still in use.		
SAINT VINCENT'S SCHOOL, north of San Rafael	L	B3
Founded in 1855.		
SALVIO PACHECO ADOBE, Concord	M	B3
Two-story home was the 1st built in the vly.		
SAN DIEGO PLAZA, Old Town, San Diego	213	A5
Center of Mexican Pueblo, blt 1830s; restored.		
SAN FRANCISCO MARITIME NAT'L HIST PK, end Hyde Av	143	B1
Historic ships, guided & self-guided tours.		
SAN JUAN BAUTISTA STATE HIST PARK, 2nd St, SJB	54	D3
Incl mission, Plaza Hotel, & house built 1841.		
SAN PASQUAL BATTLEFIELD STATE HIST PARK, Hwy 78	106	E3
Battle site between Dragoons & Californios.		
SAN RAFAEL ADOBE, 1330 Dorothy Dr, Glendale	Q	E2
Adobe and hacienda built in 1865.		
SANTA BARBARA HISTORICAL MUS, 136 E De La Guerra	174	C3
Exhibits of state & local history.		
SANTA CRUZ CITY MUSEUM, 1305 E Cliff Dr	169	E3
Natural history of Santa Cruz County.		
SANTA CRUZ COUNTY HIST MUS, Cooper & Front Sts	169	D3
Artifacts & history of early Santa Cruz Co.		
SANTA MARIA VALLEY HIST MUSEUM, 616 S Broadway	173	C3
Pioneer Indian & Spanish historical exhibits.		
SCOTT MUSEUM, off Hwy 3 in Trinity Center	11	E4
Features Indian artifacts and antiques.		
SISSON MUSEUM, off Hwy 5 north of Dunsmuir	12	C2
Features the geology & history of gold mining.		

NAME & ADDRESS	PAGE	GRID
SKIDOO, off Skidoo Rd in Death Valley	61	D5
Ruins of mining town that once flourished.		
SNELLING COURTHOUSE, Snelling	48	C3
1st courthouse in Merced County, built 1857.		
SONOMA HISTORIC PARK, W Spain St & 3rd St W	132	D3
Home of General Vallejo built in 1850.		
SONORA OPERA HALL, 250 S Washington St, Sonora	163	C4
Historic opera house built in 1886.		
STEVENSON HOUSE, 530 Houston St, Monterey	167	E4
Living quarters of Robert Louis Stevenson.		
STONE HOUSE, 6 mi N of Middleton	32	A4
Oldest building in Lake County, 1st blt 1854.		
SUSPENSION BRIDGE, S of Chico	25	B3
Bidwell Bar Bridge was the 1st in Calif, 1856.		
SUTTER'S FORT STATE HIST PARK, 28th & L Sts, Sact	137	D3
Features relics of Gold Rush Era.		
TEMPLE OF KUAN TI, Albion St, Mendocino	30	B1
Chinese house of worship.		
TUMCO MINES, 4 mi NE of Ogilby	110	C5
Largest stamp mill in US was located here.		
VALLECITO BELL MONUMENT, Vallecito	41	B4
Used to call the town together until 1939.		
VIRGINIA CITY, NE of Carson City, Nevada	36	D1
Old mining town - churches, hotels, homes.		
VOLCANO, 12 mi NE of Jackson	41	A2
Gold rush bldgs - hotel, jail, brewery, PO.		
WATTS TOWER STATE HISTORIC PARK, 1765 E 107th St	R	A5
Unusual tower studded with glass & shell.		
WEAVERVILLE JOSS HOUSE STATE HIST PK, Weaverville	17	C1
Chinese worship house built in 1874.		
WILL ROGERS STATE HISTORIC PARK, Sunset Blvd	Q	B4
Will Rogers' home located in 186 acre park.		
WOODLAND OPERA HOUSE STATE HIST PARK, Woodland	33	C5
Built in 1895 to serve Sacramento Valley.		
YORBA-SLAUGHTER ADOBE, 5.5 miles south of Chino	U	D3
Early American architecture, built in 1850s.		
YUCAIPA ADOBE, Yucaipa	99	D2
Oldest house in San Bernardino Co, built in 1842.		

H HOTELS

NAME & ADDRESS	PAGE	GRID
* Indicates information obtained from AAA.		
*ADOBE INN-CARMEL, Dolores St & 8th Av	168	B3
19 units; fireplaces, pool, sauna; restaurant.		
*AHWAHNEE HOTEL, E end of Yosemite Valley	63	D1
123 rooms; an elegant hotel built in the 1920's.		
*AIRPORTER GARDEN HOTEL, 18700 MacArthur Blvd, Irvine	198	C5
212 rooms; pool, sauna, dining, across from John Wayne Airport.		
AIRPORT MARINA HOTEL, 8601 Lincoln Blvd, LA	188	A5
770 rooms; pool, dining room, LAX transportation		
*ALADDIN, 3667 Las Vegas Bl, Las Vegas	210	B2
Casino, restaurants, entertainment, shops.		
*ALEXIS PARK RESORT, 375 E Harmon Av, Las Vegas	210	D3
500 rooms; pools, putting green, tennis.		
*AMERICANA CANTON HOTEL, S Palm Canyon	100	C4
460 rooms; golf, tennis, health spa, 3 pools.		
*ANAHEIM INN AT THE PARK, 1855 S Harbor Blvd, Anaheim	193	C4
500 rooms; pool, restaurant & coffee shop.		
*ANAHEIM HILTON & TOWERS, 777 W Convention Wy	193	C5
1576 rooms; restaurants, entertainment.		
*ANAHEIM MARRIOTT HOTEL, 700 W Convention Wy	193	C5
1033 units; pools, whirlpool, 4 restaurants, shops		
ANAHEIM PZ RESORT HOTEL, 1700 S Harbor Bl, Anaheim	193	C4
301 rooms; pool, dining room.		
*ANA HOTEL SF, 50 3rd St, San Francisco	143	D3
667 rooms; restaurant, lounge, downtown.		
*BALLY'S CASINO RESORT, 3645 Las Vegas Bl, Las Vegas	210	B2
2818 rooms; casino, restaurants, entertainment.		
*BALLYS HOTEL - RENO, 2500 E 2nd St, Reno	28	C4
Casino, restaurants, theatres, shows, shops.		
*BARBARY COAST HOTEL, 3595 Las Vegas Blvd S	210	B2
200 rooms; casino, restaurant, entertainment.		
*BARSTOW HOLIDAY INN, 1511 E Main St, Barstow	208	D#
148 rooms; pool, whirlpool, restaurant.		
*BERKELEY MARINA MARRIOTT, 200 Marina Bl, Berkeley	L	C4
373 rooms; indoor pool, sauna, restaurant.		
*BEST WESTERN BONANZA INN, 1001 Clark Av, Yuba Cty	125	C2
125 rooms; convention center, restaurant.		
*BEST WESTERN CAMERON PARK INN, 3361 Coach Ln	34	C5

NAME & ADDRESS	PAGE	GRID
61 rooms; pool. Restaurant adjacent.		
*BEST WESTERN HANALEI HOTEL, 2270 Hotel Cir, San Diego	213	B4
412 rooms; pool & whirlpool, entertainment.		
BST WSTRN JAMAICA BAY INN, 4175 Admiralty Wy, LA	187	B3
42 units; htd pool, whirlpl, bike rentals.		
*BEST WESTERN OCEANSIDE INN, 1680 Oceanside Blvd	106	B3
80 rooms; pool & sauna, movies, dining room.		
*BEST WESTERN PONDEROSA MOTOR INN, 1100 H St	137	C2
98 units; pool & sauna, 3 blocks from capitol.		
*BEST WESTERN ROYAL LAS VEGAS, 99 Convention Ctr	209	D5
237 units; pool, restaurant and casino.		
*BEST WESTERN STATION HOUSE INN, 901 Park Av, S Lake Tahoe	36	A3
100 rooms; near beach, casinos and skiing.		
BEVERLY HERITAGE HOTEL, 3350 Av of the Arts, CM	198	A3
238 rooms; near the Performing Arts Center		
*BEVERLY HILLS HOTEL, 9641 Sunset Blvd	183	A1
194 rooms; pool, 2 restaurants.		
*BEVERLY HILTON HOTEL, 9876 Wilshire Blvd	183	A2
Large hotel offers exceptional facilities.		
BILL'S, Hwy 50 in South Lake Tahoe	129	E1
Casino, shows and restaurant.		
*BILTMORE HOTEL, 506 S Grand Av, Los Angeles	186	A3
Lovely long established hotel of the 1920's.		
BINION'S HORSESHOE HOTEL, 128 Fremont, Las Vegas	209	C2
367 rooms; casino, pool, cafe.		
BOURBON STREET HOTEL, 120 E Flamingo St, Ls Vegas	210	B3
Casino, restaurant, shows.		
*BREAKERS MOTEL, Morro Bay Bl & Market, Morro Bay	75	E3
25 rooms; ocean view, pool, restaurant.		
*BUFFALO BILLS RESORT & CASINO, I - 15 & State Line, Jean	84	C1
1246 rooms; home of the world's tallest roller coaster		
*BURBANK AIRPORT HILTON & CONV CTR, 2500 Hollywood Wy	179	B2
495 rooms; pool, sauna, whirlpool.		
*CAESAR'S PALACE, 3570 Las Vegas Bl, Las Vegas	210	B2
1509 rooms; casino, restaurants, entertainment, shops.		
*CAESAR'S TAHOE, 1 blk N of US 50, Stateline, Nevada	129	E1
Cafe, convention facilities, golf, hlth club.		
*CALIFORNIA HOTEL, 1st & Ogden, Las Vegas	209	C2
635 rooms; dining room & coffee shop, casino.		
*CARRIAGE HOUSE INN, Junipero Av nr 8th Av, Carml	168	C3
13 units; fireplaces, bay windows; early Amer.		
*CARMEL VLY RANCH RES, 1 Old Ranch Rd, Carmel Vly	54	B5
100 rooms; tennis courts, 2 pools, golf.		
*CATAMARAN RESORT HOTEL, 3999 Mission Bl, San Diego	212	A2
312 rooms; on Mission Bay, restaurant, recreation.		
*CENTURY PLAZA HOTEL, 2025 Avenue of the Stars	183	A2
Near Shubert Theater & ABC Entertainment Ctr.		
*CIRCUS-CIRCUS, 2880 Las Vegas Blvd, Las Vegas	209	B5
2793 rooms; casino, game room, circus acts.		
*CIRCUS-CIRCUS, 500 N Sierra St, Reno	130	B2
Hotel, casino, restaurant, entertainment.		
*CLAREMONT RESORT, Ashby & Domingo Avs, Oakland	156	C3
Lovely hotel & tennis club with vw of S F Bay.		
CLARION HOTEL, 20200 Sherman Wy, Los Angeles	177	A2
100 room suites, pool.		
*CLARION HOTEL, 401 E Millbrae Av, Millbrae	144	E5
435 rooms; dining room & coffee shop, pool.		
*CLARION HOTEL, 700 16th St, Sacramento	137	C2
239 rooms; near State Capitol, airport transportation.		
CLARION HOTEL BAY VIEW, 660 K st, San Diego	215	E4
312 rooms; sauna, exercise room, restaurant.		
*COLONIAL INN, 910 Prospect St, La Jolla	105	B2
75 rooms; swimming pool, dining room.		
*COLONY HARBORTOWN MARINA RESRT, 1050 Schoonr Dr, Ventura	175	E5
154 rooms; pool & restaurant.		
COLORADO BELLE HOTEL & CASINO, 2100 S Casino Dr, Laughlin	85	D5
1280 rms; casino, restrnts, pool&spa, fish, wtrski		
*CONCORD HILTON, 1970 Diamond Blvd, Concord	38	E5
328 rooms; pool & whirlpool, exercise room, restaurant.		
*CONESTOGA INN, 1240 S Walnut St, Anaheim	193	B4
254 units; pool, whirlpool, restaurant.		
*COTO DE CAZA, 14 mi E of I-5 via El Toro Rd	98	E5
100 rooms; pools & saunas, fishing, tennis.		
*CROWN STERLING SUITES, 3100 E Frontera, Anaheim	194	C1
224 suites; pool, whirlpool, sauna, steam room, dining.		
*CRWN STERLING SUITES - LAX, 1440 E Imperial Av, El Segundo	189	C2
350 rooms; near Los Angeles Internatl Airport.		
*CROWN STERLING SUITES, 901 Calaveras Bl, Milpitas	P	B2
266 suites; pool, whirlpool & sauna, restaurant.		
CROWN STLG SUITES, 250 Gateway Bl, S Sn Francisco	144	C1

NAME & ADDRESS	PAGE	GRID
Bay views; indoor pool, restaurant.		
*CROWN STERLING SUITES, 1325 E Dyer Rd, Santa Ana	198	C2
303 suites; indoor pool, sauna, dining room.		
*DANA POINT HILTON, 34402 Pacific Coast Hwy, Dana Pt	202	B4
200 suites; ocean views, pool, sauna, restaurant.		
*DANISH COUNTRY INN, 1455 Mission Dr, Solvang	86	E3
81 rooms; pool, whirlpool, meeting rooms.		
DEBBIE REYNOLDS HOTEL, 305 Conv Ctr Dr, Las Vegas	209	C5
200 rooms; restaurants, shows, movie museum.		
*DEL MAR HILTON, 15575 Jimmy Durante Bl, Del Mar	106	B4
245 room; pool, spas, tennis, near beach.		
*DEL WEBB'S HIGH SIERRA, 255 N Sierra St	129	E1
Casino, restaurant, entertainment, shops.		
*DISNEYLAND HOTEL, 1150 W Cerritos Av, Anaheim	193	B4
1131 rooms; served by Disneyland Monorail.		
*DOUBLETREE CLUB HOTEL, 1985 E Grand Av, ELS	189	C3
215 rooms; pool, exercise room, Lax shuttle.		
*DOUBLETREE CLUB HOTEL, 7 Hutton Centre Dr, Santa Ana	198	B3
168 rooms; pool, exercise room, near John Wayne airport.		
*DOUBLETREE HOTEL, 191 N Los Robles Av, Pasadena	190	C3
350 rooms; pool, sauna, whirlpool, steamroom, health club.		
*DOUBLETREE HOTEL, 3555 Round Barn Bl, Sta Rosa	37	E2
247 rooms; pool, golf and tennis.		
*DOUBLETREE HOTEL, 2055 Harbor Bl, Ventura	175	D3
284 rooms; pool, health club, spa.		
*DOUBLETREE HOTEL AT THE CITY, 100 The City Dr, Orange	195	E1
451 rooms; pool, whirlpool, tennis, dining.		
DOUBLETREE HOTEL - LAX, 5400 Century Blvd, Los Angeles	189	E1
731 rooms; pool, sauna, dining & entertainment.		
*DOUBLETREE MARINA DEL REY, 4100 Admirality Wy, LA	187	B3
300 rooms; pool, dining room, entertainment.		
*DREAM INN, 175 W Cliff Dr,Sta Cruz	169	D4
164 rooms; entertainment, pool, whirlpool, resort on beach.		
DUNFEY HOTEL, 1770 S Amphlett Blvd, San Mateo	145	B2
266 rms; pool, 2 restaurants, pets allowed.		
EDGEWATER HOTEL & CASINO, 2020 Casino Dr,Laughlin	85	D5
1450 rms; casino, restrnt, bowl, wtrski, fish.		
EL CORTEZ HOTEL, 600 E Fremont St, Las Vegas	209	E1
316 room with a convenient downtown location.		
*ELDORADO HOTEL, 345 N Virginia St, Reno	130	B2
Casino, restaurant and entertainment.		
*EMBASSY SUITES, 211 E Huntington Dr, Arcadia	R	D3
194 suites, pool and sauna.		
*EMBASSY SUITES, 900 E Birch St, Brea	T	D1
229 suites, restaurant, laundry, pool. sauna.		
*EMBASSY SUITES, 7762 Beach Blvd, Buena Park	T	B2
203 rooms; whirlpool & pool, dining.		
*EMBASSY SUITES, 1211 Garvey, Covina	98	C2
264 rooms; restaurant, attractive grounds.		
*EMBASSY SUITES, 8425 Firestone Blvd, Downey	R	B5
220 rooms; sauna, whirlpool & swimming pool.		
*EMBASSY SUITES, 2120 Main St, Irvine	198	D4
293 suites; pool, whirlpool, restaurant.		
*EMBASSY SUITES, 4130 Lake Tahoe Blvd, Lake Tahoe	129	E4
400 units; pool, fitness room.		
*EMBASSY SUITES, 1117 N H St, Lompoc	86	B3
156 suites; pool, whirlpool, fitness ctr.		
*EMBASSY SUITES, 9801 Airport Bl, Los Angeles	189	D1
215 suites; near LAX, pool, sauna, exercise rm		
*EMBASSY SUITES, 74-700 Hwy 111, Palm Desert	100	D4
196 rooms; rstrnt, pool, sundeck, sauna.		
*EMBASSY SUITES, 101 McInnis Pkwy, San Rafael	139	C1
236 suites; indoor pool, exercise rm, laundry.		
*EMBASSY SUITES, 2885 Lakeside Dr, Santa Clara	P	B3
257 rooms; cafe, gift shop, pool, sauna.		
*EMBASSY SUITES, 29345 Rancho Calif Rd, Temecula	106	D1
136 suites; restaurant, exercise room.		
*EMBASSY SUITES HOTEL, 1345 Treat Blvd, Walnut Creek	M	A3
249 units; indoor pool,exercise rm,restaurant.		
*EMBASSY SUITES SAN DIEGO BAY, 601 Pacific Hwy,	215	D4
337 suites; pool, whirlpl, sauna, dining.		
*EMBASSY STES, SD/LA JOLLA, 4550 La Jolla Vlg Dr	V	B2
Near beaches, freeways and unique shopping.		
*EMERALD SPGS HOLIDAY INN, 325 E Flamingo Rd, Las Vegas	210	D2
150 rooms; pool, restaurant, entertainment.		
*ENCINA LODGE, 2220 Bath St, Santa Barbara	174	A3
122 units; lovely grounds, pool, sauna.		
ESSEX HSE HTL&RACQUET CLB,44916 N 10th St,Lncstr	90	A2
151 rooms, pool, tennis, restaurant & lounge.		
*EUREKA INN, 518 7th St, Eureka	113	D1

NAME & ADDRESS	PAGE	GRID
Historic hotel, pool, restaurant.		
*EXCALIBUR HOTEL & CASINO, 3850 Las Vegas Blvd S, LV	210	B4
4032 rooms; casino, 7 theme restaurants,entertainment.		
*FAIRMONT HOTEL, 170 S Market St, San Jose	152	B4
541 rms;sauna,steamrm,hlth club,restaurant.		
*FAIRMONT HOTEL & TOWER, 950 Mason St, Sn Francso	143	C3
Atop Nob Hill, offers excellent vw; roof grdn.		
*FESS PARKERS RED LION RESORT, Santa Barbara	174	E4
360 units; pool, sauna, tennis, exercise room.		
FITZGERALDS HOTEL, 301 E Fremont St, Las Vegas	209	C2
650 units, casino, restaurant, buffet.		
*FITZGERALDS HOTEL, 255 Virginia St, Reno	130	B2
345 units; casino and restaurant.		
*FLAMINGO HILTON, 3555 Las Vegas Bl, Las Vegas	210	B2
3600 rooms; casino, restaurant, entertainment, shops.		
FLAMINGO HILTON, 1900 Casino Dr, Laughlin	85	D5
2000 rooms, restaurants, tennis, pool.		
*FLAMINGO HILTON RENO, 255 N Sierra St, Reno	130	B3
Lovely hotel with pool, casino & restaurants.		
*FOREST INN SUITES, 1101 Park Av, South Lake Tahoe	129	E2
125 units; lovely grounds, 2 pools, saunas.		
*FOUR QUEENS, 202 E Fremont St, Las Vegas	209	C1
709 rooms; casino, restaurant, entertainment.		
*FOUR SEASONS BILTMORE HTL, 1260 Channel Dr, Sta Barb	87	D4
236 rooms; overlooks ocean; pool, restaurant.		
*FOUR SEASONS CLIFT HOUSE, 495 Geary St, SF	143	C3
329 units; newly renovated rooms, restaurant.		
*FOUR SEASONS HOTEL, 300 S. Doheny Dr, Ls Angeles	183	D1
285 rooms; pool, whirlpool, exercise room, dining room.		
*FOUR SEASONS HOTEL, 690 Newport Ctr Dr, Newport Bch	200	A4
285 rooms; tennis, pool, 3 dining rooms.		
FREMONT HOTEL, 200 Fremont St, Las Vegas	209	E1
Casino, restaurant, game room.		
*FRESNO HILTON INN, 1055 Van Ness Av, Fresno	165	D4
192 units; pool, dining room.		
*FURNACE CREEK INN, off Hwy 190 in Death Valley	62	A5
Tennis, golf, lawn games; airport transport.		
*GOLDEN NUGGET HOTEL, 129 E Fremont St, Las Vegas	209	E1
1907 rooms; casino, restaurant, video arcade.		
GOLD STRIKE HOTEL / CASINO, 1 Main St , Jean	74	C5
800 rooms; 5 restaurants, pool, 5 cent arcade		
GOLD RIVER, Casino Dr, Laughlin	85	C4
1000 rms; casino, restrnts, pool,conventn ctr.		
GRAND HOTEL, 1 Hotel Wy, Anaheim	193	C4
243 rooms; entertainment, dinner theater.		
*GRAND HYATT SN FRANCISCO, 345 Stockton St, SF	143	C3
693 units; 3 restaurants, entertainment.		
GRISWOLDS CLAREMONT CTR, 555 W Foothill Bl, Clmnt	203	A1
276 rooms; steambath, pool, whirlpool.		
GROVELAND HOTEL, 18767 Main St, Groveland	48	D1
Historic 17 room hotel established in 1850.		
*HACIENDA, 3950 Las Vegas Bl, Las Vegas	210	B4
Casino, restaurants, entertainment, shops.		
*HACIENDA HOTEL - LAX, 525 N Sepulveda Blvd, El Segundo	189	C3
636 rooms; pool, whirlpool, exercise room, airport transportation		
*HARRAH'S, on US 50, Stateline, Nevada	129	E1
Casino, cafe, theater, restaurants, sauna.		
HARRAH'S DEL RIO, 2900 S Casino Dr, Laughlin	85	D5
1658 rms; casino, rstrnts,shows,pool,spa,beach.		
*HARRAHS - LAS VEGAS, 3475 Las Vegas Bl S, Las Vegas	210	B2
1711 rooms; 5 restaurants, casino, pool.		
*HARRAH'S RENO, 3131 S Virginia St	130	B2
Name entertainment & recreational facilities.		
*HARVEY'S, on US 50, Stateline, Nevada	129	E1
Casino, pool, cafes, restaurants.		
*HERITAGE INN, 204 Harding Blvd, Roseville	34	A4
101 large rooms; spacious grounds, restaurant.		
*HILL HOUSE INN, 10701 Pallette Dr, Mendocino	30	B1
44 rooms; Victorian decor, near ocean.		
*HILTON GARDEN, 27710 The Old Rd, Santa Clarita	89	B4
152 rooms; pool, health club, business center.		
*HILTON HOTEL, 39900 Balentine, Newark	P	A2
318 rooms; pool, sauna, whirlpool, dining.		
*HILTON SUITES - ORANGE, 400 N State College Bl	193	E5
230 suites; pools, sauna, fitness center, cafe & lounge		
HILTON-WATERFRONT, 21100 Pac Cst Hy, Huntntn Bch	T	B4
296 rooms; pool,tennis,spa,health club,restrnt.		
*HOLIDAY HOTEL, Mill & Center St, Reno	130	B2
195 units; casino, restaurant, entertainment.		
*HOLIDAY INN, 1511 E Main St, Barstow	208	D3

POINTS OF INTEREST INDEX

NAME & ADDRESS	PAGE	GRID
148 rooms; pool, whirlpool, Garden Court Cafe.		
*HOLIDAY INN, 7000 Beach Blvd, Buena Park	T	B2
245 units; whirlpool, swimming pool.		
*HOLIDAY INN, 1755 N Highland Av, Hollywood	181	C4
470 units, pool, laundry, rooftop dining.		
*HOLIDAY INN, 3475 Las Vegas Bl, Las Vegas	210	B2
Casino, entertainment, shops.		
*HOLIDAY INN, 1000 E 6th St, Reno	130	C2
286 units; casino, pool, dining room.		
HOLIDAY INN, 1200 University Av, Riverside	205	E3
207 units; sauna, whirlpool, dining room.		
*HOLIDAY INN, 300 J St, Sacramento	137	B2
Pool, dining room, movies.		
*HOLIDAY INN, 1010 Northgate Dr, San Rafael	139	B1
224 rooms; restaurant, suites, entertainment.		
*HOLIDAY INN ANAHEIM AT THE PARK, 1221 S Harbor Bl	193	B3
254 rooms; pool, whirlpool, restaurant.		
*HOLIDAY INN BAY BRIDGE, 1800 Powell St, Emeryville	L	C4
279 rooms; luxury rooms, dining and entertainment.		
HOLIDAY INN BAYVIEW, 530 W Pico Bl, Santa Monica	Q	B4
309 rooms, cafe, lounge, salon, laundry.		
*HOLIDAY INN BEACH RESORT, 450 E Harbor Bl, Ventura	175	B3
260 rooms; near San Buenaventura State Beach.		
HOLIDAY INN BRENTWOOD, 170 N Church Ln, LA	180	A1
211 rooms, rooftop restaurant, suites, pool.		
*HOLIDAY INN BURBANK, 150 E Angeleno Av, Burbank	Q	E2
490 rooms; suites, sauna.		
*HOLIDAY INN CENTRE PLAZA, 2233 Ventura St, Fresno	165	E4
320 rooms; near the convention center.		
*HOLIDAY INN CHICO, 685 Manzanita Ct, Chico	124	B2
174 rooms; lounge, restrnt, convention ctr.		
*HOLIDAY INN CITY CENTER, 1020 S Figueroa St, LA	185	E3
195 rooms; pool, restaurant, gift shop.		
*HOLIDAY INN CONV CENTER, 500 E 1st St, Long Beach	192	E3
216 rooms; pool, exercise room, restaurant & lounge.		
*HOLIDAY INN COSTA MESA, 3131 Bristol St	197	E4
230 rooms; restaurant, pool, sauna, exercise room.		
*HOLIDAY INN CROWNE PLAZA, 600 Airport Bl, Burlingame	N	C1
405 rooms; lounge, gift shop, jogging trail.		
*HOLIDAY INN CROWNE PZ, 5985 W Century Bl, L. A.	189	D1
615 rooms; pool, sauna, whirlpl, exercise rm.		
*HOLIDAY INN CROWN PZ, 300 N Harbor Dr, Redondo Bch	S	B2
339 rms; lounge, entertainment, tennis, pool.		
*HOLIDAY INN DOWNTOWN LA, 750 Garland Av, LA	185	E3
205 rooms, cafe and lounge, pool.		
*HOLIDAY INN FAIRFIELD, 1350 Holiday Ln, Fairfield	135	A3
142 rooms; lounge, restaurant.		
*HOLIDAY INN FINANCIAL DISTRICT, 750 Kearny St, SF	143	D2
566 rooms, rooftop pool, panoramic views.		
*HOLIDAY INN FISHERMANS WHARF, 1300 Columbus Av, SF	143	B1
580 rooms, restaurant, lounge, cafe, suites.		
*HOLIDAY INN FRESNO AIRPORT, 5090 E Clinton Av, Fresno	57	D3
210 rooms, near the airport.		
*HOLIDAY INN GOLDEN GATEWAY, 1500 Van Ness Av, SF	143	B3
500 rooms; cafe, club, rooftop pool.		
HOLIDAY INN HARBOR VIEW, 1617 1st Av, San Diego	215	D3
203 rooms, rooftop restaurant, pool.		
HOLIDAY INN HOTEL CIRCLE, 595 Hotel Cir S, San Diego	213	D4
318 rooms; pool, whirlpool, exercise room, restaurant.		
HOLIDAY INN HUNTINGTON BEACH, 7667 Center Av	T	B3
224 rooms, lounge, gift shop, indoor pool.		
HOLIDAY INN IRVINE, 17941 Von Karman Av, Irvine	198	D4
340 rooms; pool, sauna, whirlpool, dining room.		
HOLIDAY INN LA MIRADA, 14299 Firestone Blvd	T	B1
300 rooms, restaurant, lounge, pool, giftshop.		
HOLIDAY INN - LAX, 9901 S La Cienega Bl, Los Angeles	189	E1
403 rooms; pool, exercise room, dining room, LAX transportation.		
HOLIDAY INN MAINGATE, 1850 Harbor Blvd, Anaheim	193	C4
312 rooms; pool, wading pool, dining room.		
HOLIDAY INN MISSION DE ORO, 13070 S Hwy 33, Santa Nella	55	C1
159 rooms;pool, restaurant, conference center.		
HOLIDAY INN MISSION VALLEY/STADIUM, 3805 Mrphy Cyn Rd, SD	214	D1
Pool, whirlpool, exercise room, dining & entertainment.		
HOLIDAY INN NORTH EAST, 5321 Date Av, Sacramento	34	A5
230 rooms; pool, whirlpool, exercise room, dining		
HOLIDAY INN OAKLAND, 500 Hegenberger Rd, Oakland	159	E3
290 rooms, lounge, fitness room.		
HOLIDAY INN ON THE BAY,1355 N Harbor Dr, Sn Diego	215	C3
600 rooms; pool, dining room, lounges.		
HOLIDAY INN PALO ALTO, 625 El Camino Real	147	B2

NAME & ADDRESS	PAGE	GRID
334 rooms; cafe, club, fitness rm, whirlpool.		
HOLIDAY INN - PK CTR PZ, 282 Almaden Bl, San Jose	152	B4
230 rooms; downtown, close to airport.		
HOLIDAY INN PASADENA, 303 E Cordova St, Pasadena	190	C4
318 rooms; pool, tennis courts, dining room, laundry		
HOLIDAY INN PLEASANTON, 11950 Dublin Cyn Rd	M	B5
248 rooms; lounge, pool, exercise room.		
HOLIDAY INN RESORT, 1000 Aguajito Rd, Monterey	54	B4
203 units; pool, sauna, tennis, putting green.		
HOLIDAY INN RIVERSIDE, 3400 Market St, Riverside	205	B2
286 rooms; pool, dining room & entertainment.		
*HOLIDAY INN SD BAYSIDE, 4875 N Harbor Dr, San Diego	V	A3
237 rooms; pool, whirlpool, exercise room, dining.		
HOLIDAY INN SAN FRANCISCO CIVIC CENTER, 50 8th St	143	C4
389 rooms; restaurant, lounge, gift shop.		
HOLIDAY INN SF AIRPORT, 275 S Airport Bl, S SF	144	C1
275 rooms; cafe, sports lounge, gift shop.		
HOLIDAY INN SAN JOSE N, 777 Belew Dr, Milpitas	P	B2
305 rooms; Italian restaurant, live entertainment.		
HOLIDAY INN SANTA CRUZ, 611 Ocean St, Santa Cruz	169	D3
167 rooms; restaurant, lounge, pool, spa.		
*HOLIDAY INN SELECT, 1221 Chess Dr, Foster City	145	D1
238 rooms; restaurants, lounge, swimming.		
HOLIDAY INN THOUSAND OAKS, 495 N Ventu Park Rd	96	D1
154 rooms, restaurant, pool, exercise room.		
HOLIDAY INN TORRANCE, 21333 Hawthorne Bl,Torrance	S	B2
386 rooms, restaurant, lounges, giftshop.		
HOLIDAY INN TORRANCE, 19800 S Vermont Av,Torrance	S	C2
336 rooms, restaurant, pool, sundeck.		
*HOLIDAY INN-UNION SQUARE, 480 Sutter St, SF	143	C3
401 units; restaurant & coffee shop.		
HOLIDAY INN VALLEJO, 1000 Fairgrounds Dr, Vallejo	134	E1
165 rooms, restaurant, lounge, pool, spa.		
HOLIDAY INN VICTORVILLE, 15494 Palmdale Rd	91	B3
161 rms, rstrnt, lounge/live entertain, pool.		
HOLIDAY INN VISALIA, 9000 W Airport Dr, Visalia	68	A1
258 rms; entertainment lounge, indoor pool.		
HORIZON, on US 50, Stateline, Nevada	129	D1
539 deluxe rms; restaurants, pool, conv. ctr.		
*HOTEL DEL CORONADO, on Coronado Peninsula	V	B4
Elegant beachfront hotel built in the 1880's.		
HOWARD JOHNSON, 1380 S Harbor Blvd, Anaheim	193	C5
320 rooms; 2 htd pools, whirlpool, restaurant.		
HYATT FISHERMANS WHARF,555 N Point St,Sn Francsco	143	B1
313 units; pool, exercise room.		
HYATT GRND CHAMPINS RSRT, 44-600 Indian Wells Ln	100	E4
336 rooms; rstrnts, tennis, golf, pools.		
HYATT ISLANDIA, 1441 Quivira Rd, San Diego	212	B4
422 rooms; pool & whirlpool, dining room & lounge.		
*HYATT LAKE TAHOE RESORT HOTEL, Country Club Dr	36	B1
460 rooms; pool, beach, sauna, tennis.		
*HYATT AT LOS ANGELES AIRPORT, 6225 W Century	189	C1
594 rooms; pool, sauna, dining and entertainment.		
HYATT NEWPORTER , 1107 Jamboree Rd, Newport Beach	199	E4
410 rooms; tennis, pools, golf, restaurant.		
HYATT-OAKLAND INT'L AIRPORT, Hegenberger, Oakland	159	D3
335 rooms; pool & wading pool, dining room.		
HYATT PALO ALTO, 4290 El Camino Real	147	E5
200 units; pool, putting green, restaurant.		
HYATT REGENCY, 3777 La Jolla Vlg Dr, La Jolla	V	A2
400 rms; tennis, pool, hlth club, restaurant.		
*HYATT REGENCY, 1 Old Golf Course Rd, Monterey	54	B4
579 rooms; pools & whirlpool, golf, tennis.		
HYATT REGENCY, 1001 Broadway, Oakland	157	E3
488 rooms; pool, restaurant and lounge.		
*HYATT REGENCY, 5 Embarcadero Ctr, San Francisco	143	E3
Striking arch, glss elvatr, revolvng rftp bar.		
HYATT REGENCY ALICANTE, 100 Pz Alicante, Grdn Grv	195	C1
396 rooms; pool, whirlpool, tennis, dining room.		
HYATT REGENCY IRVINE, 17900 Jamboree Rd, Irvine	198	E4
536 rooms; close to John Wayne Airport.		
HYATT REGENCY LONG BEACH, 200 S Pine Av, Long Beach	192	D3
521 rooms; pool & whirlpool, exercise room.		
HYATT REGENCY LOS ANGELES, 711 S Hope St, LA	186	A3
487 units; at Broadway Plaza; LAX transport.		
HYATT REGENCY SACRAMENTO, 1209 L St	137	C3
502+ rooms; restaurants, pool & jacuzzi.		
HYATT REGENCY SAN DIEGO, 1 Market Pl, San Diego	215	D4
875 waterview rooms; rooftop lounge, fitness room.		
HYATT REGENCY SF AIRPORT, 1333 Bayshore Hwy	45	C3

NAME & ADDRESS	PAGE	GRID
791 rooms; swimming pool, beautiful grounds.		
HYATT REGENCY SUITES PALM SPRINGS, 285 N Palm Cyn	206	A3
192 rooms; pool, sauna, whirlpool, restaurants, health club.		
HYATT RICKEYS, 4219 El Camino Real, Palo Alto	147	E5
350 units; health club, pool, putting green.		
*HYATT SAN JOSE, 1740 N 1st St	151	E1
475 rooms; putting green, dining room.		
HYATT-WESTLAKE, 880 S Westlake Bl, Westlake Village	96	E1
258 rooms; pool, whirlpool, dining room.		
IMPERIAL PALACE, 3535 Las Vegas Blvd, Las Vegas	210	B2
1500 rooms; pools, entertainment, casino.		
*INN AT NAPA VLY-A CROWN STLG STE, 1075 California Bl	133	B4
205 suites; located in the heart of wine country.		
INN AT SPANISH BAY, 2700 17 Mile Dr, Pebble Beach	167	A3
270 units; golf, putting green, tennis, pool & sauna		
JACKIE GAUGHANS PLAZA HOTEL, 1 Main St, Las Vegas	209	C1
1037 rooms; casino, restaurant, entertainment.		
JW MARRIOTT HOTEL, 2151 Av of Satrs, Century City	183	B3
367 rooms; 2 pools, sauna, whirlppol, health club, dining.		
LA CASA DEL ZORRO, CR S-3, Borrego Springs	107	E2
Studios, suites and casitas.		
*LA COSTA RESORT & SPA, Costa Del Mar Rd, Carlsbad	106	C3
547 rooms & houses; golf, tennis, health spa.		
LA JOLLA MARRIOTT. 4240 La Jolla Village Dr	V	B2
360 rooms; pool, whirlppol, dining room.		
LAKE ARROWHEAD RESORT, Lake Arrowhead Village	91	C5
257 rooms; pool, whirlpool, boat dock.		
*LA QUINTA, 2180 Hilltop Dr, Redding	18	C2
148 rooms; pool, whirlpool, restaurant.		
*LA QUINTA HTL GOLF & TENNIS RSRT, Eisenhower Dr	100	E4
269 rooms; lovely grounds, pool, tennis, golf.		
LA SIESTA VILLAS, Hwy 111, Palm Springs	100	C3
18 luxurious villas, swimming pool.		
*LAS VEGAS HILTON, 3000 Paradise Rd, Las Vegas	209	D5
3174 rooms; casino, restaurants, star entertainment.		
*LE BARON HOTEL, 1350 N First St, San Jose	151	E1
327 rooms; pool, steamroom, entertainment.		
LE MERIDIEN SAN DIEGO, 2000 2nd St, Coronado	215	D5
300 rooms; 3 pools, sauna & whirlpool, dock, waterski, bike.		
*L'ERMITAGE, 9291 Burton Wy, Beverly Hills	183	C1
Elegant suites in the European tradition.		
LOEWS CORONADO BAY RES,4000 Crndo Bay Rd,Coronado	V	C4
450 rooms; tennis, exercise room.		
LOEWS SANTA MONICA BEACH HOTEL, 1700 Ocean Av	Q	B4
352 rooms; ocean views, pool.		
LONG BEACH AIRPORT MARRIOTT, 4700 Airport Pz Dr	S	E2
311 rooms; 2 pools, restaurant, exercise room.		
LONG BEACH HILTON, 2 World Trade Ctr, Long Beach	192	D3
393 rooms; pool, exercise room, dining & entertainment.		
LA AIRPORT HILTON & TOWERS, 5711 W Century Bl, LA	189	D1
1236 rooms; pool, dining room, entertainment.		
*LOS ANGELES AIRPORT MARRIOTT, 5855 W Century Blvd	189	D1
1010 rooms; pool, sauna, dining & entertainment.		
*LOS ANGELES HILTON HTL, 930 Wilshire Blvd, LA	185	E3
900 units; pool, shopping; public facilities.		
*LUXOR LAS VEGAS, 3900 Las Vegas Blvd S	210	B4
2526 rooms; casino, restaurants, oval arena.		
*MADONNA INN, 100 Madonna Rd, Sn Luis Obspo	172	B4
109 unusually decorated rooms; restaurnt,cafe.		
MANDARIN ORIENTAL, 222 Sansome St, SF	143	D3
View of bay, restaurant.		
MARINA DEL REY HOTEL, 13534 Bali Wy,Marina Dl Rey	187	C3
159 rooms; pool, dining room & lounge.		
MARINA DEL REY MARRIOTT, 13480 Maxella Av	187	D3
281 rooms; pool & whirlppol, dining room.		
*MARINA INTERNATIONAL HOTEL, 4200 Admiralty Wy	187	C3
135 units; pool, whirlpool, LAX transportation.		
*MARINERS INN, 6180 Moonstone Dr, Cambria	75	C2
26 rooms; whirlpool. Across from the beach.		
*MARK HOPKINS HOTEL, 1 Nob Hill, San Francisco	143	C3
Elegnt lndmrk htl, panoramic vw Top of Mark.		
MARRIOTTS DESERT SPRINGS RESORT, Palm Desert	100	E3
891 rooms; pool, tennis, golf, restaurant.		
MARRIOTT HOTEL, 2355 N Main St, Walnut Creek	M	A3
337 rooms; pool, exercise room, restaurant.		
MARRIOTT HOTEL IRVINE, 18000 Von Karman Av, Irvine	198	D4
489 rooms; pool, sauna, tennis, exercise room.		
MARRIOTT FISHERMAN'S WHARF, 1250 Columbus Av, S F	143	B1
257 rooms, restaurant and lounge.		
MARRIOTT- LAGUNA CLFS RESRT AT DANA PT, 25135 Pk Lantern	202	B4

NAME & ADDRESS	PAGE	GRID
350 rooms; 2 pools, whirlpool & sauna, tennis, restaurant.		
*MARRIOTT'S RANCHO LAS PALMAS RESORT, Bob Hope Dr	100	E4
456 rooms; pools, golf, tennis, bicycles.		
MARRIOTT SAN DIEGO MARINA, 333 W Harbor Dr	215	D4
1355 rooms; pools, sauna, tennis, dining.		
MARRIOTT SAN RAMON, 2600 Bishop Dr, San Ramon	M	B5
372 rooms; pool & whirlpool, sauna, restaurants.		
MARRIOTT SUITES COSTA MESA, 500 Anton Bl	198	A3
253 suites; near Performing Arts Center & shopping.		
MARRIOTT'S TENAYA LODGE, 1122 Hwy 41, Fish Camp	49	D3
242 rooms; restrnts, swimming, horseback riding.		
MARRIOTT TORRANCE, 3635 Fashion Wy, Torrance	S	B2
487 rooms; 2 pools, sauna, whirlpool.		
*MAXIM, 160 E Flamingo, Las Vegas	210	B3
Casino, restaurant, entertainment, shops.		
MENDOCINO HOTEL, 45080 Main St, Mendocino	30	B1
Restored 1878 Victorian hotel.		
MGM GRAND, 3799 Las Vegas Bl S, Las Vegas	210	B3
5005 rooms, restaurants, 4 casinos, theme park.		
MIRAGE, 3400 Las Vegas Bl, Las Vegas	210	B2
3044 rooms, unique hotel, waterfalls, volcano, tigers.		
MIRAMAR SHERATON, 101 Wilshire Bl, Santa Monica	Q	B4
300 rooms, near Santa Monica Beach.		
MONTE CARLO RESORT & CASINO, 3770 S Lake Vegas Bl,Las Vegas	210	B3
3,014 rooms and suites,shopping, dinning, 90,000 sq ft casino.		
MONTECITO INN, 1295 Coast Vlg Rd, Montecito	87	D4
60 rooms & suites; restored historic inn.		
MONTEREY PLAZA, 400 Cannery Row, Monterey	167	E3
291 rooms; pool, restaurant and lounge.		
MONTFIELD PARK HOTEL, 8110 Aero Dr, San Diego	214	A1
225 rooms; pool, sauna, whirlpool, exercise room, restaurant.		
*MOONSTONE INN, 5860 Moonstone Beach Dr, Cambria	75	B2
9 rooms with an ocean view from each.		
MURPHY'S HOTEL, 457 Main St, Murphys	41	C4
Historical monument still in full operation.		
*NAPA VALLEY LODGE BEST WSTRN, 2230 Madison St,Yountville	38	C2
55 rooms; lovely view, pool & whirlpool		
NEVADA LANDING, I - 15 exit 12, Jean	74	C5
303 rooms; 90,000 sq. foot casino		
NEW OTANI HOTEL, 120 S Los Angeles St, Los Angeles	186	B3
435 rooms; beautiful garden, pool & sauna.		
NEWPORT BEACH MARRIOTT HOTEL, 900 Newport Ctr Dr	200	A4
570 rooms; 2 pools, tennis, dining & entertainment.		
NEWPORT BEACH MARRIOTT SUITES, 500 Bayview Cir	200	B1
250 rooms; pool, sauna, whirlpool, dining.		
OAKLAND AIRPORT HILTON, 1 Hegenberger Rd, Oakland	159	D4
367 rooms; pool, restaurant, entertainment.		
OJAI VALLEY INN, Off Hwy 150, Ojai	88	B4
218 rms; pools, golf, tennis, dining room.		
ONTARIO AIRPORT HILTON, 700 N Haven Av, Ontario	U	E2
309 rooms; dining, whirlpool & swimming pool.		
OXNARD HILTON, 600 Esplanade, Oxnard	176	C1
160rms;pool&whirlpl,tennis,jogging track,VCRs.		
PACIFIC SUITES HOTEL, 333 Madonna Rd, SLO	172	B4
195 rooms; pool, at Central Coast Plaza Mall.		
PALA MESA RESORT, 2001 Old Hwy 395, Fallbrook	106	C2
135 rooms; pool, whirlpool, golf, tennis.		
PALM SPRINGS HILTON RESORT, 400 E Tahquitz Wy	206	B4
260 rooms; pool, sauna, whirlpool, tennis, health club, dining.		
PALM SPRINGS RIVIERA RESORT, 1600 N Indian Cyn Dr	206	B2
480 rooms; 2 pools, wading pool, tennis & golf.		
PAN PACIFIC HOTEL, 1717 S West St, Anaheim	193	B4
502 rooms; pool, whirlpool, across from Disneyland		
PAN PACIFIC HOTEL, 500 Post St, San Francisco	143	C3
331 units; a preferred hotel, restaurant.		
PARC FIFTY FIVE, 55 Cyril Magnin St, S F	143	C3
1015 rooms, downtown, restaurant and lounge.		
PARK HYATT HOTEL, 333 Battery St, San Francisco	143	D2
360 rooms, bay views, restaurant.		
PASADENA HILTON, 150 S Los Robles Av, Pasadena	190	C4
291 rooms; entertainment, dining room, pool.		
PENINSULA BEVERLY HILLS, 9882 Sta Monica Bl, B H	183	B2
200 rooms, pool, sauna, steamroom, exercise room.		
*PEPPER TREE INN, 3850 State St, Santa Barbara	87	C4
150 rooms; patios, 2 pools & sauna, whirlpool.		
*PICADILLY INN AIRPORT, 5115 E McKinley, Fresno	57	D3
185 rooms; pool, whirlpool, restaurant.		
*PICADILLY INN-SHAW, 2305 W Shaw Av, Fresno	57	C3
203 rooms; pool, airport trans, restaurant.		
PINE INN, Ocean Av, Carmel	168	B3

POINTS OF INTEREST INDEX

NAME & ADDRESS	PAGE	GRID
49 rooms; Victorian decor, beautiful view.		
PLAZA INN, 111 E March Ln, Stockton	160	B1
195 rooms; restaurant, lounge, dancing, live entertainment.		
PLEASANTON HILTON, 7050 Johnson Dr, Pleasanton	M	B5
298 rooms; racquetball, tennis, swimming pool.		
PRIMADONNA RESORT, I-15 & State Line, Jean	84	C1
660 rooms, casino, restaurants, pool.		
*QUAIL LODGE, 8205 Valley Greens Dr, Carmel Vly	54	B5
100 rooms; scenic grounds, golf, tennis.		
QUALITY HOTEL-MAINGATE, 616 Convention Wy, Anaheim	193	C5
284 rooms; pool, dining room & coffee shop.		
QUEEN MARY, 1126 Queens Hwy, Long Beach	192	E4
Historic British luxury liner, rstrd rooms.		
RADISSON BEL-AIR SUMMIT,11461 Sunst Bl,Ls Angeles	180	A1
162 rms; pool, tennis, VCR in rooms.		
RADISSON HOLLYWOOD ROOSEVELT HOTEL, 7000 Hollywood Bl	181	C4
380 rooms; swimming, restaurants, lounge.		
RADISSON HOTEL, 500 Leisure Ln, Sacramento	137	E1
309 rms; pvt lake,paddleboats,pool,par course.		
RADISSON HOTEL, 300 S Court St, Visalia	68	B1
201 rooms; pool, exercise room, restaurant.		
RADISSON HOTEL HARBOR VIEW, 1646 Front St, San Diego	215	D2
333 rooms; pool, restaurant, sauna.		
RADISSON HOTEL SAN DIEGO,1433 Cm del Rio S,San Diego	214	A4
260 rooms; pool, sauna, dining & entertainment.		
RADISSON HOTEL SF AIRPORT, 1177 Airport Bl, Burlingame	N	D1
305 rooms; dining room & coffee shop.		
*RADISSON HOTEL SANTA BARBARA, 1111 E Cabrillo	87	D4
174 rooms; ocean view, pool, dining room.		
RADISSON INN, 700 National City Bl, National City	V	C4
180 units, harbor views, pool, exercise room.		
RADISSON PLAZA HOTEL, 18800 MacArthur Bl, Irvine	198	C5
289 rooms; pool, tennis, exercise room, restaurant.		
RADISSON PLAZA HOTEL, 1400 Parkview Av,Manhattan Bch	189	D5
380 rooms; golf, pool &whirlpool, sauna, dining room.		
RADISSON PLAZA HOTEL, 1471 N 4th St, San Jose	152	A1
184 rooms; pool, whirlpool, coffee shop.		
RAMADA EXPRESS, 2121 Casino Dr, Laughlin	85	D5
1501 rms, restaurants, pool, mini train ride.		
*RAMADA HOTEL, 6th & Lake St, Reno	130	B2
250 units; casino and restaurant.		
RAMADA HOTEL, 2726 Grand Av, Santa Ana	198	D2
183 rooms; exercise room, pool & whirlpool.		
*RAMADA INN, 114 E Highway 246, Buellton	86	D3
98 rooms; pool, convention & conference facil.		
RAMADA INN, 5865 Katella Av, Cypress	T	B2
180 units, dining room, pool.		
RAMADA INN AIRPORT N,6333 Bristol Pky,Culver City	188	C3
268 rooms; pool, whirlpool, exercise room.		
RAMADA SUITES, 2050 N Preisker Ln, Santa Maria	173	C1
210 suites, pool, restaurant.		
*RANCHO BERNARDO INN, 17550 Bernardo Oaks Dr	106	D4
236 rooms; 2 pools, golf, bicycling, tennis.		
RED LION HOTEL, 3050 Bristol St, Costa Mesa	198	A4
484 rooms; pool, sauna, near Performing Arts Center.		
RED LION HOTEL, 100 W Glenoaks Bl, Glendale	R	A2
350 rooms, pool, spa, sauna, exercise room.		
RED LION HOTEL, 1150 Ninth St, Modesto	162	A3
265 rooms; restaurants, pools, exercise room.		
RED LION HOTEL, 222 N Vineyard, Ontario	U	E2
340 rooms, pool, spa, exercise room, lounge.		
*RED LION HOTEL, 1830 Hilltop Dr, Redding	18	C2
194 rooms; pool, putting green, dining room.		
RED LION HOTEL, 1 Red Lion Dr, Rohnert Park	38	A3
245 rooms; pool, spa, tennis, exercise room.		
RED LION HOTEL, 7450 Hazard Center Dr, San Diego	213	E4
300 rooms; fountain cafe, pools, tennis courts.		
RED LION HOTEL, 2050 Gateway Pl, San Jose	151	D1
507rms;exercise room,jogging track,pool,dining		
RED LION HOTEL - LAX, 6161 Centinela Av, Culver City	188	C3
368 rooms, pool, whirlpool, restaurant.		
RED LION INN, 3100 Cm del Rio Ct, Bakersfield	166	A2
262 units; pool, whirlpool.		
RED LION INN, 1929 4th St, Eureka	121	E1
180 Rooms, pool, dining room.		
RED LION INN, 2001 Point West Wy, Sacramento	39	E1
448 rooms; pools, airport trans, dining room.		
REGENT BEVERLY WILSHIRE, 9500 Wilshire Blvd	183	C2
Long established with excellent accomodations.		
RENO HILTON, 2500 E 2nd St, Reno, Nevada	28	B4

NAME & ADDRESS	PAGE	GRID
2001 rms, casino, fitness ctr, pool, tennis.		
RESIDENCE INN, 1700 S Clementine St, Anaheim	193	C4
200 rooms; near Disneyland & convention center.		
RESIDENCE INN, 201 N State College Bl, Orange	196	A1
105 rooms & suites; pool, whirlpool, sports court.		
*RIO BRAVO RESORT, 11200 Lake Ming Rd, Rio Bravo	78	E2
112 rooms; tennis, golf, pools, airstrip.		
RIO SUITE HOTEL, 3700 W Flamingo Rd, Las Vegas	210	A2
1410 rooms; casino, sand-bottom pools, restaurants.		
RITZ CARLTON, 33533 Ritz Carlton Dr, Dana Point	105	D1
393 rooms; golf, tennis, pools, ocean view.		
RITZ CARLTON, 600 Stockton St, San Francisco	143	C3
336 rooms, indoor pool, health club.		
RITZ CARLTON MARINA DEL REY, 4375 Admiralty Wy	187	C3
306 rooms & suites, pool, sauna, tennis, dining.		
RIVERSIDE RESORT, 1650 Casino Dr, Laughlin	85	D5
1403 rooms, casino, restaurants, 750 RV spaces.		
*RIVIERA, 2901 Las Vegas Bl, Las Vegas	209	C5
Casino, restaurants, entertainment, shops.		
SACRAMENTO HILTON, 2200 Harvard St, Sacramento	39	A3
336 rooms, pool, restaurant and lounge.		
*SACRAMENTO INN, 1401 Arden Wy, Sacramento	39	E1
387 rooms; pools, putting green, dining room.		
*SAHARA (DEL WEBB'S), 2535 Las Vegas Bl, Las Vegas	209	C4
Casino, restaurants, entertainment, shops.		
SAN BERNARDINO HILTON, 285 E Hospitality Ln	207	D5
247 rooms; dining room, pool & whirlpool.		
*SAN DIEGO HILTON, 1775 E Mission Bay Dr	212	E3
357 rooms; pools, beach, rental boats & bikes.		
SAN DIEGO MISSION VLY HILTON, 901 Camino Del Rio S	213	E4
350 rooms; pool, sauna, exercise room.		
SAN DIEGO MARRIOTT-MISSION VLY, 8757 Rio San Diego	214	B3
350 rooms; pool, sauna, health club, tennis, restaurant.		
SAN DIEGO PRINCESS RESORT, 1404 W Vacation Rd	212	B3
462 rooms; 5 pools, tennis, golf , dining.		
*SANDS, 3355 Las Vegas Bl, Las Vegas	210	B2
Casino, restaurants, star entertainment.		
*SANDS REGENCY, Arlington & 3rd Sts, Reno	130	A2
Casino, cafe, and shops.		
SAN FRANCISCO AIRPORT HILTON, SF INTERNATL AIRPRT	144	D4
Restaurant, entertainment, swimming pool.		
SAN FRAN AIRPORT MARRIOTT, Bayshore Hy,Burlingame	N	C1
689 rooms; dining, health club, pool.		
SF HILTON & TOWERS, 333 O'Farrell, San Francisco	143	C3
Shops, sundeck & pool; air, RR & bus transprt.		
SAN FRANCISCO MARRIOTT, 55 4th St, San Francisco	143	D3
Indoor pool, health club, restaurant.		
SAN JOSE HILTON & TOWERS, 300 Almaden Bl, San Jose	152	B4
355 rooms, business ctr, health club, pool.		
SAN TROPEZ SUITE HOTEL, 455 E Hamon Av, Las Vegas	210	D3
150 rooms; pool, whirlpool, exercise room.		
*SANTA CLARA MARRIOTT, 2700 Great America Parkway	P	B3
764 rooms; near Great America Theme Park.		
SANTA MARIA AIRPRT HILTON, 3455 Skyway Dr	86	B1
190 rooms, business services, pool.		
SANTA MARIA INN, 801 S Broadway, Santa Maria	173	B4
166 rms; pool, sauna, whirlpool, exercise rm.		
SHERATON, 12111 Point East Dr, Rancho Cordova	40	B1
265 rooms; dining room, swimming pool.		
SHERATON-ANAHEIM, 1015 W Ball Rd, Anaheim	193	B3
491 rooms; entertainment, dining, pool.		
*SHERATON AT FISHERMAN'S WHARF, 2500 Mason St, SF	143	B1
525 units; pool, restaurant and coffee shop.		
SHERATON CERRITOS, 12725 Ctr Court Dr, Cerritos	T	A1
203 rooms, dining room, pool.		
*SHERATON DESERT INN, 3145 Las Vegas Bl, Las Vegas	209	B5
821 rooms; casion, restaurants, entertainment.		
SHERATON GRANDE, 333 S Figueroa St, Los Angeles	186	A3
470 rooms, near Music Center & downtown.		
SHERATON GRANDE TORREY PINES, 10950 N Torrey Pines	V	A1
400 rooms; golf, tennis, health club.		
SHERATON HARBOR ISLAND, 1590 Harbor Island Dr	215	A2
350 rooms, near San Diego Internat'l Airport.		
SHERATON HARBOR ISLAND HOTEL, 1380 Harbor Island Dr	215	B2
1050 rooms, tennis courts, swimming pool, dining.		
SHERATON HOTEL & CONF CTR, 45 John Glenn Dr, Concord	M	A3
331 rooms; conference center , entertainment.		
SHERATON INN, 5101 California Av, Bakersfield	78	C3
200 rooms; pool and restaurant.		
*SHERATON INN SUNNYVALE, 1100 N Mathilda Av	148	E4

NAME & ADDRESS	PAGE	GRID
174 rooms; pool, restaurant, cocktail lounge.		
SHERATON LONG BEACH, 333 E Ocean Bl, Long Beach	192	E3
460 rooms, dining room, entertainment, pool.		
SHERATON L A AIRPORT, 6101 W Century Blvd	189	C1
807 rooms; pool, whirlpool, dining & entertainment.		
SHERATON L A HARBOR, 601 S Palos Verdes St, San Pedro	191	B4
244 rooms; fitness center, pool, sauna, dining.		
SHERATON MONTEREY, 350 Calle Principal, Monterey	167	E3
338 rooms, 2 restaurants, pool, jacuzzi.		
*SHERATON NEWPORT BEACH, 4545 MacArthur Blvd	198	B5
338 rooms; pool, whirlpool, tennis, basketball.		
SHERATON NORWALK HOTEL, 13111 Sycamore Dr,Norwalk	T	B1
175 rooms; pool, health club, restrnt, lounge.		
SHERATON-PALACE HTL, 2 New Montgomery St, SF	143	D3
551 rooms, lounge and restaurant, historical.		
SHERATON PLEASANTON, 5115 Hopyard Rd	M	B5
214 rooms, rstrnt, lounge, pool, weight room.		
SHERATON PREMIERE, off Lankershim, Universal City	181	A1
450 rooms; exercise room, pool & whirlpool.		
SHERATON RESORT INDUSTRY HILLS, 1 Industry Hls Pky	R	E4
298 rooms; 2 swimming pools, tennis, golf.		
SHERATON RIVERSIDE, 3400 Market, Riverside	205	B2
296 units; dining room and entertainment.		
SHERATON ROSEMEAD HOTEL, 888 Montebello Rd	R	C4
150 rooms; restrnt, pool, health club, lounge.		
SHERATON SF AIRPORT, 1177 Airport Bl, Burlingame	N	D1
305 rooms; dining room & coffee shop; pools.		
SHERATON SMUGGLERS INN, 3737 N Blackstone, Fresno	57	C3
210 rooms; beautiful landscape, pool, restrnt.		
SHERATON SUITES FAIRPLEX, 600 W McKinley Av	U	B2
247 suites, rstrnt, lounge, pool & spa.		
SHERATON TOWNHOUSE, 2961 Wilshire Bl, Los Angeles	185	C2
300 rooms, pool, sauna, tennis, dining room.		
SHERATON UNIVERSAL, 333 Universal Ter Pkwy	181	A1
475 rooms; entertainment, pool & sauna.		
*SHORE CLIFF LODGE, 2555 Price St, Pismo Beach	76	B4
99 rooms; ocean view, heated pool, restaurant.		
*SILVERADO COUNTRY CLUB RESORT, 1600 Atlas Peak	38	D2
260 rooms; 8 pools, golf, tennis, bicycles.		
SOFITEL MA MAISON, 8555 Beverly Bl, Los Angeles	183	E1
311 rooms; pool, sauna, exercise, dining room & restaurant.		
SPA HOTEL & MINERAL SPGS, 100 N Indian Cyn Dr, Palm Springs	206	B3
230 rooms; pool, hot mineral pool, health spa.		
*STANFORD COURT, 905 California St, Nob Hill	143	C3
Gracious 1900s decor in Old Stanford House.		
*STOCKTON HILTON, 2323 Grand Canal Blvd, Stockton	40	A5
202 rooms; 3 pools, dining room & coffee shop.		
STRATOSPHERE, 2000 South Las Vegas Bl, Las Vegas	209	C4
1,500 rooms & suites, Tallest free standing observation tower in the USA		
SUNDANCE HOTEL, 301 E Fremont St, Las Vegas	209	C2
650 units; restaurant, buffet and casino.		
*SUNNYVALE HILTON , 1250 Lakeside Dr	P	A3
372 rooms; pool, restaurant, airport trans.		
SURF AND SAND HOTEL, 1555 S Coast Hwy, Laguna Bch	201	C3
157 rms; oceanfrnt rms with view, pool, beach.		
SUTTON PLACE HOTEL, 4500 MacArthur Blvd, Newport Beach	198	C5
435 rooms; pool, whirlpool, sauna, tennis.		
*TAHOE SEASONS RESORT, Saddle & Keller, Lk Tahoe	129	E3
160 units; tennis courts and restaurant.		
*THE AUTRY HOTEL, 4200 E Palm Cyn Dr,Palm Springs	100	D3
180 rooms; 3 pools, tennis, entertainment.		
THE CHATEAU, 4195 Solano Av, Napa	38	C2
115 rooms; Country-French atmosphere, pool.		
THE EMPRESS HTL OF LA JOLLA, 7766 Fay Av, La Jlla	105	B3
72 rooms; pools, exercise room, dining room.		
*THE INN AT RANCHO SANTA FE, Linea del Cielo	106	C4
80 rooms and cottages on tree-shaded grounds.		
THE LODGE AT PEBBLE BEACH, on the 17 Mile Drive	53	B5
159 units; pool, sauna, golf course.		
THE PARK HOTEL, 300 N Main St, Las Vegas	209	E1
435 rooms, entertainment, casino.		
*THE TREE HOUSE BEST WESTERN, off I-5, Mt Shasta	12	C2
94 rooms; indoor pool, bicycles, dining room.		
*THE WESTGATE, 1055 2nd Av, San Diego	215	D3
223 units; elegant decor, restaurant.		
*TICKLE PINK MOTOR INN, 155 Highland Dr, Carmel	54	A5
35 rooms; beautiful view and lovely location.		
TOWN & COUNTRY HOTEL, 500 Hotel Circle N, San Diego	213	D4
955 rooms; 4 pools, whirlpool, dining & entertainment.		
TRAVELODGE RSRT HTL &MARINA, 700 Queensway Dr, Lng Beach	192	D4

NAME & ADDRESS	PAGE	GRID
Located on the waterfront next to Queen Mary.		
TREASURE ISLAND - MIRAGE, 3300 Las Vegas Bl, LV	210	B1
2900 rooms, casino, restaurants, shops, shows.		
*TROPICANA, 3801 Las Vegas Bl S, Las Vegas	210	B4
1910 rooms, casino, entertainment, theater, pools.		
UNIVERSAL CITY HILTON, 555 Universal Terrace Pkwy	181	B1
456 rooms, 2 dining rooms, pool.		
*UNIVERSITY HILTON, 3540 E Figueroa St, LA	185	C5
241 units; next to USC campus; pool.		
U S GRANT HOTEL, 326 Broadway, San Diego	215	D3
280 rooms, 1900's decor, restaurant, lounge.		
VEGAS WORLD HOTEL, 2000 Las Vegas Bl S, Las Vegas	209	C4
529 rooms, casino, entertainment.		
VILLA HOTEL, 4000 S El Camino Real, San Mateo	145	B4
286 rms; pool, restaurant & coffeeshop.		
*VISCOUNT HOTEL, 9750 Airport Blvd,LA	189	D1
575 rooms, near Los Angeles Intl Airport.		
WARNER CTR HILTON & TOWERS, 6360 Canoga Av, Woodland Hills	177	C3
329 rooms; restrnt, health club, 2 pools,tennis.		
WARNER CENTER MARRIOTT, 21850 Oxnard St, Woodland Hills	177	C3
473 rooms; 2 dining rms, pools, exercise rm, sauna.		
WAWONA HOTEL, S entrance to Yosemite Valley	49	D3
A grand mountain resort built in the 1800's.		
*WELK RESORT CENTER, 8860 Lawrence Welk Dr, Escondido	106	D3
132 rooms; pool, golf, tennis, entertainment.		
*WEST BEACH INN, 306 W Cabrillo Blvd	174	C4
45 units; across from yacht harbor & beach.		
WESTIN HOTEL, 1 Old Bayshore Hwy, Millbrae	144	E5
388 rms; pool, hlth club, sauna, restrnt&grill		
WESTIN HOTEL, 5101 Great Amer Pkwy, Santa Clara	P	A3
500 rooms, hlth fitness ctr, restrnts, pool.		
*WESTIN BONAVENTURE, 404 S Figueroa, Los Angeles	186	A3
Rooftop restaurant & revolving cocktail lounge.		
WESTIN RESORT, 71-333 Dinah Shore Dr, Rancho Mirage	100	D3
512 rooms, 3 pools, 2 golf courses, tennis.		
*WESTIN ST FRANCIS, Union Square, San Francisco	143	C3
Fashionable shops, skyline view from elevator.		
*WESTIN SOUTH COAST PLAZA, 666 Anton Bl,Costa Msa	198	A3
390 rooms; pool, exercise room, near Performing Arts Center		
*WESTWOOD MARQUIS HTL & GRDNS,930 Hilgard Av,Westwood	180	D2
250 elegant suites; pool, sauna, whirlpool.		
WHISKEY PETES, I-15 & Stateline, Jean	84	B1
777 rooms; restaurants, casino, pool.		
WILSHIRE PLAZA HOTEL, 3515 Wilshire Blvd, LA	185	B2
400 rooms; entertainment, diningroom, pool.		
WYNDHAM PALM SPRINGS, 888 E Tahquitz Wy, Palm Springs	206	C4
410 rooms; health club, pool, sauna, 2 dining rooms.		

⛪ MISSIONS

NAME & ADDRESS	PAGE	GRID
MSN BASILICA SAN DIEGO DE ALCALA, 10818 SD Msn Rd	214	E3
1769, 1st missn estblshd along El Camino Real.		
MISSION LA PURISIMA CONCEPCION, 4 mi NE of Lompoc	86	B2
1787, 11th missn, rebuilt by original methods.		
MISSION NUESTRA SENORA DE LA SOLEDAD, off US 101	65	A1
1791, 13th missn, stood in ruins for 100 yrs.		
MISSION SAN ANTONIO DE PADUA, off U S 101	65	B3
1771, 3rd msn, one of largest restored missns.		
MISSION SAN ANTONIO DE PALA, off Hwy 76	106	E2
Built in 1816 to help the Sn Luis Rey Mission.		
MISSION SAN BUENAVENTURA, Main & Figueroa Sts	175	B2
1782, 9th missn, last founded by Father Serra.		
MISSION SAN CARLOS BORROMEO, 3080 Rio Dr, Carmel	168	B4
1770, 2nd missn, burial place of Father Serra.		
MSN SAN FERNANDO REY DE ESPANA, 15151 SF Msn Bl	Q	C1
1797, 17th msn, destroyed by '71 quake; rstrd.		
MISSION SAN FRANCISCO DE ASIS, Dolores & 16th Sts	142	C4
1776, 6th missn, chapel unchanged for 175 yrs.		
MISSION SAN FRANCISCO SOLANO, Spain & 1st Sts	132	D3
1823, 21st missn, northernmost & last of msns.		
MISSION SAN GABRIEL ARCANGEL, 537 W mission Dr	R	C3
1771, 4th missn, at crossroads in early Calif.		
MISSION SAN JOSE, 43300 Mission Blvd	P	B2
1777, 14th missn, noted for outstanding music.		
MISSION SAN JUAN BAUTISTA, off US 101	54	D3
1797, 15th msn, near othr buildngs of msn era.		
MISSION SAN JUAN CAPISTRANO, off I-5 at Ortega	202	E1
1776, 7th mission, swallows return annually.		
MISSION SAN LUIS OBISPO, Chorro & Monterey Sts	172	C3

NAME & ADDRESS	PAGE	GRID
1772, 5th mission, 1st misn to use tile tools.		
MISSION SAN LUIS REY DE FRANCIA, on Hwy 76	106	B3
1798, 18th missn, most successful of all msns.		
MISSION SAN MIGUEL ARCANGEL, 801 Mission St	66	A5
1797, 16th missn, last msn secularized - 1834.		
MISSION SAN RAFAEL ARCANGEL, A St & 5th Av	139	D3
1817, 20th missn, founded to aid sick Indians.		
MISSION SANTA BARBARA, Laguna & Los Olivos Sts	174	B2
1786, 10th missn, famed as most beautiful msn.		
MISSION SANTA CLARA DE ASIS, 820 Alviso St	151	B2
1777, 8th missn, bell dated 1798 still clangs.		
MISSION SANTA CRUZ, School & Emmet Sts	169	D2
1791, 12th msn, destroyed, replica built 1931.		
MISSION SANTA INES, 1760 Mission Dr	86	E3
1804, 19th mission, favorite mission of many.		
MISSION SANTA YSABEL, Hwy 79 near Julian	107	C3
Blt 1818, contains mus & Indian burial grnds.		

🌲 PARKS (STATE & FEDERAL) & NATIONAL FORESTS

NAME & ADDRESS	PAGE	GRID
ADM WILLIAM STANDLEY STATE REC AREA, Laytonville	22	C3
Beautiful scenery; no camping facilities.		
AHJUMAWI LAVA SPRINGS STATE PARK, Island Rd	13	E3
Accessible by boat only.		
ALAMEDA PARK, Micheltorea & Anacapa Sts	174	C3
Displays 280 species of plants and shrubs.		
AMERICAN RIVER PARKWAY, from Nimbus Dam	137	B1
23 mi long greenbelt along banks of Sacto Riv.		
ANCIENT BRISTLECONE PINE FOREST, White Mountn Rd	52	A3
4600 yr old pine forest, nature trails.		
ANDREW MOLERA STATE PARK, W of Hwy 1, Big Sur	64	B2
50 campsites, sandy beach, hiking, meadows.		
ANGELES NATIONAL FOREST, N of Los Angeles	Q	D1
In rugged mtns of LA, hiking & winter sports.		
ANGEL ISLAND STATE PARK, E San Francisco Bay	L	B4
Isl pk has hiking, bike rentl, picnc, day use.		
ANNADEL STATE PARK, Channel Dr	38	A2
Riding & hiking.		
ANTELOPE VALLEY CAL POPPY RESERVE, W of Lancaster	89	D2
Scenic area for picnicking.		
ANZA BORREGO DESERT STATE PARK, San Diego County	108	A4
Beautiful wildflowers in spring; camp, hike.		
ARMSTRONG REDWOODS STATE RESERVE, E of Fort Ross	37	C1
Giant redwoods, picnicking, hiking trails.		
AUBURN STATE REC AREA, 1 mile South of Auburn	34	D3
Camp; riding & hiking trails on American River.		
AUSTIN CREEK STATE RECREATION AREA, E of Ft Ross	37	C1
Camp, horseback ride, meadows, vlys, forests.		
AZALEA STATE RESERVE, off Hwy 101, Arcata	10	A4
Beautiful azaleas bloom late May - early June.		
BENBOW LAKE STATE REC AREA, 2 mi S of Garberville	22	B1
Horse trails, fish, hike, swim, picnic.		
BENICIA STATE RECREATION AREA, W of Benicia	L	D2
Good fishing; picnicking facilities.		
BIDWELL-SACRAMENTO RIVER STATE PARK, W of Chico	25	A3
River access. picnicking and fishing.		
BIG BASIN REDWOODS STATE PARK, on Hwy 236	N	D4
First state park to preserve redwoods.		
BOGGS MOUNTAIN STATE FOREST, N of Hwy 175	32	A4
Picnicking; hiking trails.		
BONELLI REGIONAL COUNTY PARK, Park Rd, San Dimas	U	B2
Picnicking facilities and hiking trails.		
BORDER FIELD STATE PK, Monument Rd 15 mi S of SD	V	B5
Good area to picnic, fish, swim, or hike.		
BOTHE-NAPA VALLEY STATE PARK, on Hwy 29	38	A1
Hiking, picnic & camping areas, swimming pool.		
BRANNAN ISLAND, South of Rio Vista	M	D2
Boat, fish, camp, hike; visitors center.		
BROOKSIDE PARK, Rosemont Av, Pasadena	190	A3
Site of Rosebowl; swimming, hiking, golfing.		
BUCKSKIN MOUNTAIN STATE PARK, Hwy 95, Arizona	104	C1
Scenic area to hike and picnic.		
BURTON CREEK STATE PARK, E of Tahoe State Park	35	E1
Camping and picnicking.		
BUTANO STATE PARK, E of Hwy 1 at Gazos Creek Rd	N	C4
Camping, recreational facilities.		
CABRILLO NATIONAL MONUMENT, Point Loma, San Diego	V	A4
Visitors ctr with historic progrms & displays.		
CALAVERAS BIG TREES STATE PARK, E of Arnold	41	D3

NAME & ADDRESS	PAGE	GRID
2 giant Redwood groves - self-guided tours.		
CANDLESTICK POINT RECREATION AREA, US 101	L	C5
Scenic hiking trails; picnicking & fishing.		
CASTLE CRAG STATE PARK, S of Dunsmuir	12	D3
Pinnacles, crags, cliffs, green pines, rec.		
CASTLE ROCK STATE PARK, near Jct Hwy 9 and Hwy 35	N	E4
Nature & hiking trails; picnicking & camping.		
CASWELL MEMORIAL STATE PARK, Hwy 99 S of Manteca	47	B2
Camp, fish, swim, hike, picnic.		
CHABOT REGIONAL PARK, Lake Chabot	L	E5
5000 acre park; fish, picnic, moto-X, boat.		
CHANNEL ISLANDS NATIONAL PARK, off Santa Barbara	87	C5
Consists of 5 islands, 20 to 60 mi offshore.		
CHINA CAMP STATE PARK, N of San Rafael	L	B3
Recreational facilities and camping.		
CHINO HILLS STATE PK, off Hy 71, Sn Bernardino Co	U	C4
Hiking trails, picnic areas.		
CLEAR LAKE STATE PARK, near Lakeport	31	D3
Camp, boat, wtrski, hike, fish, swim, picnic.		
CLEVELAND NATL FOREST, San Diego & Orange Co's	107	B4
Hiking, boating, riding, fishing, camping.		
COL. ALLENWORTH STATE HIST PARK, 20 mi N of Wasco	68	B4
Historical exhibits; picnicking facilities.		
CRYSTAL COVE STATE PARK, N of Laguna Beach	T	D5
3 miles of beaches for swimming & picnicking.		
CUYAMACA RANCHO STATE PARK, on Hwy 79, Julian	107	C4
In old Indian territory; camp, hike; horses.		
DAYTON STATE PARK, Hwy 50 near Dayton	36	D1
Hiking and picnicking facilities.		
DEATH VALLEY NATIONAL PARK, Hwy 190	61	B3
Vast & colorful desert; record summer temps.		
DEL NORTE COAST REDWOODS ST PK, S of Crescent Cty	1	E4
Dense forests, giant redwoods, good camping.		
DESOLATION WILDERNESS AREA, SW shore of Lake Tahoe	35	D4
Camping, boating, swimming, fishing and hiking.		
DEVIL'S POSTPILE NATL MONUMNT, Mammoth Lakes Area	50	C2
Spectacular mass of hexagonal basalt columns.		
D. L. BLISS STATE PARK, North of Emerald Bay	35	E3
Dense forest, trails, camping, beach area.		
DONNER MEMORIAL STATE PARK, 2 mi W of Truckee	35	D1
Rec at Donner Lake, Donner Prty memorial, mus.		
EL DORADO NATIONAL FOREST, north of Hwy 88	36	A4
Rugged mtns, dense foliage, scattered lakes.		
EMERALD BAY STATE PARK, Emerald Bay	35	E3
Scenic; camping, swimming, picnicking.		
FLOYD LAMB STATE PK, 9209 Tule Spgs Rd, Las Vegas	74	D1
Fishing and picnicking.		
FOREST OF NISENE MARKS, 4 mi N of Aptos	P	B5
Picnicking, hiking trails, and camping.		
FREMONT FORD STATE REC AREA, 5 mi E of Gustine	47	D4
Good area for fishing.		
FREMONT NATIONAL FOREST, SE Oregon	7	D2
Good fishing, camping & rock climbing.		
FREMONT PEAK STATE PARK, S of San Juan Bautista	54	D3
Picnicking, hiking trails and camping.		
GARRAPATA STATE PARK, Hwy 1, Carmel	54	A5
Good fishing and hiking trails.		
GAVIOTA STATE PARK, Gaviota Beach Rd	86	D4
Camping, fishing, boat launch, picnic areas.		
GEORGE HATFIELD STATE REC AREA, 28 mi W of Merced	47	D4
Picnicking, fishing, hiking and camping.		
GOLDEN GATE NATL REC AREA, San Francisco & Marin	141	A2
Gardens, historic sites, rec facilities.		
GOLDEN GATE PARK, between Lincoln Wy & Fulton St	141	B4
Vast city park, walk, equestrn trails, skate.		
GRIZZLY CREEK REDWOODS STATE PARK, E of Fortuna	16	B3
Scenic; camp, fish, nature trails, creeks.		
GROVER HOT SPRINGS STATE PARK, W of Markleeville	36	B5
Camping, swim at hot springs, fish in creeks.		
HARRIS BEACH STATE PARK, N of Crescent City	1	C2
Camping, lodging, dining.		
HARRY A MERLO STATE RECREATION AREA, N of Eureka	9	E3
Boating and fishing.		
HENDY WOODS STATE PARK, near Philo on Hwy 128	30	D3
Picnic, camp, fish, hike and swim.		
HENRY COE STATE PARK, 14 mi NE of Morgan Hill	P	E4
Picturesque; camp & picnic grnds, day use fee.		
HENRY COWELL REDWOODS STATE PK, 5 mi N on Hwy 9	N	E5
Equestrn trails, hiking, fishing, picnic grds.		
HOLLISTER HILLS VEHICULAR REC AREA, S of Hollistr	54	E3
Motorcycle trails; hiking, camping, picnickng.		

NAME & ADDRESS	PAGE	GRID	NAME & ADDRESS	PAGE	GRID
HUMBOLDT LAGOON STATE PARK, Hwy 101 N of Eureka Visitors Center; camping and hiking.	9	E3	MT DIABLO STATE PARK, Diablo Rd Hiking trails, campsites on peak.	M	B4
HUMBOLDT REDWOODS STATE PARK, Redwood Hwy Tallest redwoods, camp, fish, picnic, hike.	16	A4	MT SAN JACINTO STATE PARK, Hwy 111 near Palm Spgs Hiking, picnicking, some camping.	100	B4
HUNGRY VALLEY STATE VEHICULAR REC AREA, Gorman Camping, off-road trails.	88	E2	MT TAMALPAIS STATE PARK, 6 mi N Hwy 1, Marin Co Hiking, equestrian trails, camping.	L	A3
INYO NATIONAL FOREST, near Calif-Nevada border Winter sports, boat facilities, camping.	51	D3	MUIR WOODS NATL MONUMENT, Mt Tamalpais State Park Named for naturalist John Muir; day hikes.	L	A4
JACKSON STATE FOREST, Hwy 20 near Dunlap Scenic area for hiking and picnicking.	30	C1	NEVADA STATE PARK, N of Carson City, Nevada Rec at Washoe Lake-camp, boat, nature trails.	36	C1
JOAQUIN MILLER PARK, Skyline Bl Named for Poet of the Sierras.	L	D4	NOJOQUI FALLS COUNTY PARK, S of Solvang Picnic facilities with a view of the falls.	86	E3
JOSHUA TREE NATIONAL PARK, S of Hwy 62 Camp, hike, climb rocks in desert environment.	101	A2	OCOTILLO WELLS STATE VEHICULAR REC AREA, Hwy 78 Trails for off-road vehicle use; camping.	108	B3
J SMITH REDWOODS STATE PARK, NE of Crescent City Giant redwoods, camping, Smith River fishing.	1	E4	OLD PERPETUAL GEYSER, Hwy 395, Lakeview Geyser erupts every 90 seconds 60 feet high.	7	C1
JUG HANDLE STATE RESERVE, near Noyo Self-guided nature trails; picnicking.	22	C5	OREGON CAVES NATIONAL MONUMENT, off Hwy 46 Spectacular formations of mineral deposits.	2	E2
JULIA PFEIFFER BURNS STATE PARK, E & W of Hwy 1 Picnic areas, hike to view McWay Waterfall.	64	C2	PALOMAR MOUNTAIN STATE PARK, Birch Hill Rd Sierra-like country, many camps, picnic sites.	107	A2
KERN NAT'L WILDLIFE REFUGE, 19 mi West of Delano Refuge for migrating & winter waterfowl.	67	D5	PARK MOABI, off I-40 Boat rentals & ramp, camping, fishing.	95	D2
KING RANGE NATL CONSERVATION AREA, Cape Mendocino Camp, picnic, hike, backpack, scenic shores.	15	E5	PATRICKS POINT STATE PARK, N of Trinidad Camping, hiking, biking, picnicking.	9	D3
KINGS BEACH STATE REC AREA, NE of Tahoe City Picnicking, swimming, fishing & boating.	36	A1	PAUL M. DIMMICK WAYSIDE CAMPGROUND, W of Navarro Primitive campground with swimming & fishing.	30	C2
KINGS CANYON NATIONAL PARK, Hwy 180 Trails, backpacking, horses, camping, fishing.	59	B2	PETRIFIED FOREST, on Petrified Forest Hwy Ancient redwoods preserved in volcanic ash.	38	A1
KLAMATH NATIONAL FOREST, Siskiyou County Camping, boating, fishing, riding.	3	D3	PFEIFFER BIG SUR STATE PARK, E of Hwy 1, Big Sur 215+ dev sites - hiking, store, swim , fish.	64	B2
KRUSE RHODODENDRON STATE RESERVE, N of Ft Ross Colorful rhododendrons bloom April thru June.	37	A1	PINNACLES NATIONAL MONUMENT, on Hwy 146 Remnant of volcanic mtn; hike & explore caves.	55	B5
LAKE EARL STATE PARK, 8 miles N of Crescent City Fishing; primitive camping sites.	1	D3	PIO PICO STATE HIST PARK, Whittier Blvd, Whittier Second adobe home of last Mexican governor.	R	D4
LAKE HAVASU STATE PARK, S of Interstate 40 Resorts, camping, boat rentals, hunting.	96	B4	PISMO DUNES STATE VEHICULAR REC AREA, Pismo Beach Sand dunes, off-road trails; swim, camp, fish.	76	B5
LAKE TAHOE NEVADA STATE PARK, E Lake Tahoe Boating, swimming, fishing, hiking, picnicking.	36	B1	PLACERITA CYN STATE PARK, Hwy 14 N of Sn Fernando Scenic area for picnicking and hiking.	89	C5
LAKES BASIN RECREATION AREA, Blairsden Old glacial area,X-country ski, lodging, boats	27	A2	PLUMAS EUREKA STATE PARK, Hwy A14 at Johnsville Scenic creeks, mountains, lakes and trails.	26	E2
LASSEN NATIONAL FOREST, S of Hwy 299 Dense foliage throughout this lake rec area.	13	D5	PLUMAS NATIONAL FOREST, south of Hwy 36 Waterfall, lakes, grassy valleys, woodlands.	20	B5
LASSEN PEAK, Lassen Volcanic National Park. Only active volcano in Cal, last erupted 1921.	19	D3	POINT LOBOS STATE RESERVE, W of Hwy 1 Spectacular view of coast; swim in China Cove.	54	A5
LASSEN VOLCANIC NATIONAL PARK, S of Hwy 44 Volcanoes, lava flows, hot springs, lakes.	19	E2	POINT MUGU STATE PARK, Hwy 1 Scenic campsite; fish, swim, picnic, hike.	96	C2
LAVA BEDS NATIONAL MONUMENT, 30 mi S of Tulelake Cooled lava forming cones, canyons & caves.	5	D4	PORTOLA STATE PARK, W of Hwy 35 Camping, recreational facilities.	N	D4
LOS OSOS OAKS STATE RESERVE, Los Osos Valley Rd Hiking trails through beautiful scenery.	75	E3	PRAIRIE CREEK REDWOODS STATE PARK, N of Orick Good camping, scenic trails thru lush forest.	10	A1
LOS PADRES NATIONAL FOREST, near Santa Barbara Camping, riding, fishing, hiking, hunting.	76	D4	PROVIDENCE MTNS STATE REC AREA, Essex Rd Scenic area for camping; exhibits.	94	B1
MacKERRICHER STATE PARK, Hwy 1 N of Fort Bragg Camping, hiking and fishing.	22	B5	RANCHO SIERRA VISTA, Ventura County Native American Cultural Center.	96	C1
MAILLIARD REDWOODS STATE RES, NW of Cloverdale Scenic area for picnicking.	31	A4	RED ROCK CANYON STATE PARK, Hwy 14 at Ricardo Picnicking, hiking trails, camping facilities.	80	B3
MALIBU CREEK STATE PARK, Malibu Canyon Rd Picnicking, fishing, hiking trails.	97	A2	REDWOOD NATIONAL PARK, Crescent City, Orick Giant redwoods, picturesque coast & rivers.	2	A4
McARTHUR-BURNEY FALLS MEM STATE PK, NE of Burney Well developed, scenic park.	13	C4	RICHARDSON GROVE STATE PARK, south of Garberville Scenic, camp, fish, swim, hiking trails.	22	B1
McCONNELL STATE RECREATION AREA, 5 mi SE of Delhi Picnicking, fishing, swimming and camping.	48	A3	ROBERT LOUIS STEVENSON STATE PK, off Hwy 29 Scenic area for picnicking and hiking.	32	A5
MENDOCINO HEADLANDS STATE PARK, S of Fort Bragg Rocky bluffs, hiking, wave carved tunnels.	30	A1	ROEDING PARK, north of Belmont Av, Fresno Picnic areas, boat rides, children's zoo.	165	B2
MENDOCINO NATIONAL FOREST, E of Hwy 101 Scenic wilderness, horseback riding, hiking.	24	A4	ROGUE RIVER NATIONAL FOREST, South Central Oregon Fishing & white-water rafting on Rogue River.	3	C2
MITCHELL CAVERNS NAT'L PRESRV, NW I-40 near Essex Caverns with interesting limestone formations.	94	B1	RUSSIAN GULCH STATE PARK, S of Fort Bragg Rocky headlands, camping, hike to waterfall.	30	A1
MODOC NATIONAL FOREST, south of Cal-Oregon border Good fishing and hunting; volcanic features.	13	E1	SADDLEBACK BUTTE STATE PARK, E of Lancaster Scenic area for picnicking, hiking & camping.	90	C3
MONO BASIN NAT'L FOREST SCENIC AREA, Hwy 120 S Dedicated by Congress to protect Mono Lake.	43	D5	SALTON SEA STATE RECREATION AREA, off Hwy 111 Camp, hike, picnic, boat, waterski.	108	E2
MONTANA DE ORO STATE PARK, Pecho Valley Rd Barbeque, camping, riding & hiking.	75	E3	SALT POINT STATE PARK, N of Fort Ross off Hwy 1 Underwater presrve, beachs, tidepools, trails.	37	A1
MONTGOMERY WOODS STATE RESERVE, Orr Springs Nature trails, picnicking.	31	A2	SAMUEL P TAYLOR STATE PARK, off Hwy 1 Camping, fishing, riding, winter sports.	37	E4
MORRO BAY STATE PARK, on Morro Bay Camping, fishing, clam digging, boating.	75	D3	SAN BERNARDINO NATIONAL FOREST, Hwy 18 Camping, picnicking; year-round sports.	U	D1
MOUNTAIN HOME TRACT STATE FOREST, N of Hwy 90 Beautiful streams, mountains, forests.	69	B2	SAN BRUNO MOUNTAIN STATE PARK, S of Daly City Enjoy a picnic amid the beautiful scenery.	L	B5

POINTS OF INTEREST INDEX

NAME & ADDRESS	PAGE	GRID
SAN FRANCISCO BAY WILDLIFE REFUGE, south S F Bay	N	E2
Preservation of nature at its best.		
SAN FRANCISCO FISH & GAME REFUGE, off Hwy 280	N	B1
Lovely area for hiking and picnicking.		
SAN GABRIEL WILDERNESS AREA, off Hwy 2	R	E1
Preserve of natural & rugged mountain country.		
SAN ONOFRE STATE PARK, off I-5, San Onofre	105	E1
Scenic area for hiking and picnicking.		
SANTA MONICA MTNS NAT'L REC AREA, Los Angeles Co	96	E2
Nature trails to hike and ranger programs.		
SEQUOIA NATIONAL FOREST, Hwy 198	69	D2
Fishing, camping, boating, winter sports.		
SEQUOIA NATIONAL PARK, Hwy 198	59	B5
With Kings Canyon, museum, logging, rec area.		
SHADOW CLIFFS REGIONL RECREATION AREA, Pleasanton	P	C1
Swim, fish, boat, picnic, bike & waterslide.		
SHASTA NATIONAL FOREST, off I-5	13	D2
Large lakes, steep mountains, rec facilities.		
SHASTA STATE HISTORIC PARK, 6 miles W of Redding	18	B2
Restored buildings were blt in Gold Rush days.		
SIERRA NATIONAL FOREST, S of Yosemite Natl Park	49	C3
Grand sequoias; wtrsports at lakes, hunting.		
SINKYONE WILDERNESS ST PK, Humboldt & Mendocno Co	22	A2
Tent camping, picnicking, hiking & fishing.		
SISKIYOU NATIONAL FOREST, SW Oregon	1	E2
Rugged mtns, winding creeks, old mining towns.		
SIX RIVERS NATIONAL FOREST, NW corner of CA	10	D3
Many rivers, good fishing, forest-coverd mtns.		
SMITHE REDWOODS STATE RESERVE, E of Hwy 101	22	C2
Trails to waterfall, Eel River, picnicking.		
SMITH RIVER NATIONAL RECREATION AREA, Hwy 199	2	B3
Rafting, fishing, hiking, hunting, camping.		
SPRING MTN RANCH, Blue Diamond Rd, Blue Diamond	74	B3
Tours, picnicking, hiking.		
STANDISH HICKEY STATE REC AREA, 1 mi N of Leggett	22	C2
Picnicking, hiking, biking, camping.		
STANISLAUS NATIONAL FOREST, SE of Hwy 4	41	D4
Deep, stream-cut canyons, meadows, evergreens.		
SUGARLOAF RIDGE STATE PARK, Adobe Canyon Rd	38	B2
Fishing, riding & camping.		
SUGAR PINE POINT STATE PARK, north of Meeks Bay	35	E2
Grove of sugar pines; camp, cross-country ski.		
TAHOE NATIONAL FOREST, W of Lake Tahoe	26	E3
Good fishing, camping, snow skiing, scenic.		
TAHOE STATE RECREATION AREA, N of Tahoe City	35	E2
Good camping, boating, beach, nature trails.		
TECOLOTE CYN NATURAL PK, Linda Vista Rd, Sn Diego	213	B2
Large natural park in the city of San Diego.		
TOIYABE NATIONAL FOREST, E Sierra Nev into Nevada	73	D1
Camp, fish, hunt; forest, grass, sagebrush.		
TOMALES BAY STATE PARK, Tomales Bay	37	D4
Hike to scenic beaches; rocky, wave-cut coves.		
TOPANGA STATE PARK, Hwy 27, in Santa Monica Mtns	Q	A4
Picnicking, hiking, horseback riding.		
TORREY PINES STATE RESERVE, S of Del Mar	V	A1
Beautiful hiking area; nature trail, exhibits.		
TRINITY NATIONAL FOREST, along Hwy 299	17	B3
Good hunting and fishing; rivers & lakes.		
TULE ELK RESERVE STATE PARK, Tupman Rd	78	B3
Several acres grazed by native valley elk.		
TURLOCK STATE REC AREA, Hwy 132 East of Modesto	48	B2
Camp; hiking, swimming and fishing available.		
VAN DAMME STATE PARK, south of Fort Bragg	30	C1
Camp near beach, hiking trails, Pygmy Forest.		
W. IDE ADOBE STATE HIS PARK, 2 mi NE of Red Bluff	18	D4
Home of the California Pioneer. Picnic & swim.		
WILDER RANCH STATE PARK, Hwy 1 N of Santa Cruz	53	E2
Nature trails, beach and historical exhibits.		
WILL ROGERS STATE HISTORIC PARK, Sunset Bl	Q	B4
Will Roger's home locatd within 186 acre park.		
WOODSON BRIDGE STATE REC AREA, SE of Corning	24	D2
Camping, fishing, swimming, nature trail.		
YOSEMITE NATIONAL PARK, off Hwy 120	49	D1
Beautiful waterfalls, lakes, canyons, streams, moutains.		

POINTS OF INTEREST

NAME & ADDRESS	PAGE	GRID
ABC ENTERTAIN CTR, 2040 Av of Stars, Centry Cty	183	B2
Galleries, restaurants, boutiques, theaters.		

NAME & ADDRESS	PAGE	GRID
A B C STUDIOS, 4151 Prospect Av, L. A.	182	C4
Tour sets & watch filming of TV programs.		
ACADEMY OF SCIENCES, Golden Gate Park	141	D4
Renowned science museum including Morrison Planetarium.		
AEROSPACE MUSEUM, Balboa Park, San Diego	215	E2
Aeronautical displays of the past and present.		
ALABAMA HILLS, Off Hwy 136, near Lone Pine	60	A4
Backdrop for motion picture & TV westerns.		
ALCATRAZ ISLAND, San Francisco Bay	L	B4
Former maximum security prison; 1/2 day tours.		
AMADOR COUNTY MUSEUM, 225 Church St, Jackson	40	E2
Working models of old gold mines.		
AMER CAROUSEL MUSEUM, 633 Beach St, San Francisco	143	B1
Carousel art from New York and Philadelphia.		
AMERICAN FOREST PRODUCTION MILL, North Fork	49	E5
Tours of the lumber mill are conducted daily.		
AMERICAN VICTORIAN MUSEUM, 325 Spring St	128	B2
Collection of Victorian artifacts.		
AMTRAK STATION, Kettner & D St, San Diego	215	C3
Train station with access to zoo & othr sites.		
ANAHEIM CONVENTION CENTER, Katella & Harbor	193	B5
Concerts, sports events, shows.		
ANAHEIM STADIUM, 2000 State College Bl, Anaheim	194	A5
Home of Angels baseball.		
ANGEL'S CAMP MUSEUM, Main St, Angels Camp	41	B4
History museum; also known for Frog Jumping.		
ANO NUEVO STATE RESERVE, off Hwy 1, San Mateo Co.	N	C5
Reserve for seals, sea lions & elephant seals.		
ANSEL ADAMS CENTER, 250 Fourth St, San Francisco.	143	D4
Five exhibit galleries, library, bookstore.		
ANTELOPE VALLEY INDIAN MUSEUM, 15701 E Avenue M	90	C3
Exhibits of Indian artifacts.		
ANZA-BORREGO VISITOR CENTER, State Park Headqtrs	107	D2
Information and Ranger Station.		
APPLEGATE ZOO, 25th St, Merced	170	C2
Wild animals, birds, picnic, rose grdn, rides.		
ARCO PLAZA, 505 S Flower St, Los Angeles	186	A3
Subterranean shopping center.		
ARMAND HAMMER MUS, 10899 Wilshire Bl, Los Angeles	180	C2
250 million dollar art collection.		
ARROWHEAD POND OF ANAHEIM, Katella & Douglas Rd	194	A4
Center for entertainment and sporting events.		
ARTIST'S DRIVE, Death Valley National Park	72	A1
Rainbow-colored canyon of geological interest.		
ASIAN ART MUS, near Japanese Tea Grdn, Gld Gate Pk	141	C4
Outstanding Oriental collection; jade display.		
ATMOSPHERIUM & PLANETARIUM, University of Nevada	130	A1
Space & star programs shown on dome ceilings.		
AUDUBON CANYON RANCH, N on Hwy 1, Stinson Beach	38	A5
Former dairy ranch now a wildlife sanctuary.		
AVENUE OF THE GIANTS, N of Garberville	16	C4
Scenic route thru groves of majestic redwoods.		
BADWATER, in Death Valley, south of Hwy 190	72	A1
Lowest pt in N America, 282' below sea level.		
BALBOA PARK, off Hwy 163 in San Diego	216	A2
Large central park; gardens, zoo, museums.		
BALBOA PAVILION, Balboa Bl, Newport Beach	199	D5
Beautiful landmark of Newport Bay; cruises.		
BATTERY POINT LIGHTHOUSE, Crescent City	1	D4
Tours & museum include history of lighthouse.		
BAY MEADOWS RACETRACK, S Delaware, San Mateo	145	B3
Thoroughbred, harness & quarter horse racing.		
BERKELEY AQUATIC PARK, Polk St, San Francisco	L	C4
Curved fishing pier creates cold swim lagoon.		
BERKELEY ROSE GARDENS, Euclid Av & Bayview	156	A1
1000's of different varieties of roses.		
BIDWELL PARK, E 4th St, Chico	124	D4
Swimming pool, picnic, golf, nature trails.		
BIG PINE CANYON, 10 miles W of Big Pine	51	C5
Campgrounds, picnic areas, hiking.		
BIRD ROCK, Bird Rock Av, La Jolla	105	B5
Birdwatching in a natural coastal setting.		
BISHOP CREEK CANYON, SW of Bishop on Hwy 168	51	B4
Steep canyon walls with waterfalls, trails.		
BOWERS MUSEUM, 2002 N Main St, Santa Ana	196	B3
Historical pioneer, Indian & Spanish displays.		
BRADBURY BUILDING, 304 Broadway, Los Angeles	186	B3
Distinguished 19th Century structure.		
BREN EVENTS CENTER, UC Irvine Campus, Irvine	200	D2
Concerts; campus & community events.		
BRIDALVEIL FALL, Yosemite National Park	63	A2

NAME & ADDRESS	PAGE	GRID
View millions of salmon & steelhead.		
FEATHER RIVER RAILROAD MUSEUM, Portola	27	B2
Over 50 trains; summer train rides.		
FERRY BUILDING EMBARCADERO, foot of Market St	143	E2
Bay trafic hist, world trade ctr, mineral mus.		
FISHERMANS VILLAGE, 13755 Fiji Wy, Marine Del Rey	187	C4
New England themed shopping/dining complex.		
FISHERMAN'S WHARF, off Foam St, Monterey	167	E3
Art gallery, shopping & theater.		
FISHERMAN'S WHARF, ft of Taylor at Jefferson, S F	143	B1
Open air markets, restaurants, vw fshng fleet.		
FLEET SPACE THEATER & SCIENCE CENTER, Balboa Park	216	A2
Exquisite celestial displays and films.		
FLYING LADY MUS, 15060 Foothill Rd, Morgan Hill	P	E5
Features vintage airplanes and cars.		
FOREST LAWN MEMORIAL PARK, 1712 S Glendale Av	179	D5
Large collection of stained glass & statuary.		
THE FORUM, Manchester & Prairie Sts	Q	D5
Popular center for sports & entertainment.		
FOSSIL FALLS, Cinder Rd	70	C3
Ancient Indian site and petroglyphs.		
FRESNO ART MUSEUM, 2223 N 1st St, Fresno	165	E1
8 galleries, Amer sculpt, Ca art, Mexican art.		
FRESNO CONVENTION CENTER, Tulare & M Sts	165	E4
Various shows, conventions, exhib & displays.		
FRESNO CO FAIRGRNDS, Kings Cyn Rd & Maple Av	57	C3
FRESNO METROPOLITAN MUSEUM, Van Ness Av, Fresno	165	D3
Natural and historical exhibits.		
FROST AMPHITHEATER, Stanford University	147	A3
Outdoor theater which seats 9,500.		
FURNACE CREEK VISITOR CENTER, Death Valley	62	A5
Ranger talks, museum, information & gift shop.		
GAMBLE HOUSE, 4 Westmoreland Pl, Pasadena	190	B3
Great architectural work, originl furnishings.		
GENE AUTRY WESTERN HERITAGE MUS, Griffith Pk, LA	182	C1
Old West exhibits; firearms, paintings.		
GENERAL GRANT GROVE, Redwd Mtn Kings Cyn Nat'l Pk	58	E4
Seasonal festivities, horse & foot trails.		
GEN PATTON MEM MUSEUM, Chiriaco Summit	101	E4
WWII dsrt training ctr, exhibits,natrl science		
GEORGE G HOBERG VISTA POINT, 875 Lakeport Bl	31	D3
Picnic, old Indian prayer hill, wildflowers.		
GHIRARDELLI SQUARE, N Point, Beach & Larkin Sts	143	A1
Shops, outdoor cafes by old chocolate factory.		
GIANT FOREST, Sequoia National Forest	59	A4
One of largest & finest Sequoia groves.		
GILROY HISTORICAL MUSEUM, 195 Fifth St, Gilroy	54	D2
Gilroy pioneer families' historical items.		
GLACIER POINT, S of Curry Village	63	D2
3200' abve the vly, vw vly & snow-covrd peaks.		
GOLDEN CANYON, S of Hwy 190, Death Valley	62	A5
Hike through dramatically colored, scenic cyn.		
GOLDEN GATE BRIDGE, on Hwy 101	141	C1
Famous bridge offers spectacular view.		
GOLD COUNTRY, HIGHWAY 49, Mariposa to Vinton	27	D3
Historic 300 mi drive through the Mother Lode.		
GOLD COUNTRY MUSEUM, 1273 High St, Auburn	126	C4
Displays of early mining equipment.		
GOLDEN GATE PROMENADE, along SF Bay shoreline	141	D1
Walkway along marina green.		
GRACE HUDSON MUSEUM, 431 S Main St, Ukiah	123	D3
Art, Indian baskets, historic photos.		
GRAND CANYON OF THE TUOLUMNE, N of White Wolf	42	C5
Trails to deep-cut canyons, waterfalls, mdws.		
GRAND CENTRAL MARKET, Hill & 4th Sts	186	A3
Food bazaar specializing in foods of Mexico.		
GREAT PETALUMA MILL, 6 Petaluma Bl N	L	A1
Shops & restaurants in restored grain mill.		
GREAT VLY MUS NATURL HIST, 1100 Stoddard, Modesto	162	A3
Plants & animals indigenous to Central Valley.		
GREYSTONE MANSION, 501 N Doheny Rd, Beverly Hills	Q	C3
Historic mansion and surrounding park.		
GRIFFITH OBSERVATORY, 2800 Observatory Rd	182	B3
Features displys, planetarium, laserium shows.		
GRIFFITH PARK, Los Feliz Bl & Riverside Dr	182	B2
One of nation's largest municipal parks.		
GUINNESS WORLD OF RECORDS MUS, 2780 Ls Vegas Blvd	209	B5
Displays, films and exhibits; open daily.		
HAGGIN MUSEUM, Rose St & Pershing Av, Stockton	160	B4
Historical displays, paintings & art objects.		

NAME & ADDRESS	PAGE	GRID
HAKONE GARDENS, 21000 Big Basin Wy, Saratoga	P	A4
Picturesque Japanese gardens.		
HANCOCK PARK, 5801 Wilshire Bl, Los Angeles	184	A2
La Brea Tar Pits, LA County Museum of Art.		
HAPPY ISLES NATURE CENTER, Yosemite Valley	63	D2
Mus, ranger explains vly featres & Indn caves.		
HASTINGS BUILDING, 2nd & J Sts	137	A2
Museum featuring the history of Sacramento.		
HAVASU NATIONAL WILDLIFE REFUGE, Lake Havasu	96	A3
Good fishing, many beaches along river.		
HAYWARD AREA HISTORICAL SOCIETY MUS, 22701 Main	146	E2
California & local historical exhibits.		
HERSHEY CHOCOLATE CO, 120 S Sierra Av, Oakdale	47	E1
Visitors center, tours of chocolate factory.		
HI-DESERT NATURE MUS, 57117 29 Palms Hwy, Yuc Vly	100	D1
Open Wed-Sun 1 to 5 PM, live desert reptiles.		
HISTORIC GOVERNOR'S MANSION, 16th & Sts, Sacramento	137	C3
Victorian gothic mansion built in 1877; tours,		
HOLLYWOOD BOULEVARD, Los Angeles	181	D4
Possibly the best known street in L A.		
HOLLYWOOD PARK RACE TRACK, 1050 Prairie St	Q	D5
Features thoroughbred & harness racing.		
HOLLYWOOD WAX MUSEUM, 6767 Hollywood Bl	181	C4
Life-sized figures of many famous moviestars.		
HOMESTAKE GOLD MINE, Jct of Napa, Lake, Yolo Co's	32	B4
Tours May-October, gold discovered in 1978.		
HONEY LAKE, SE of Susanville	21	C4
Sierra Ordnance Depot - military facility.		
HOOPA TRIBAL MUSEUM, on Hwy 96, Hoopa	10	C4
Baskets, weapons & art;tours of local villages		
HOT CREEK, 3 miles off US 395 on Owens River Rd	50	E2
Boiling hot springs, paved hiking trails.		
HUNTINGTON LIBRARY, 1151 Oxford Rd	R	C3
Includes an art gallery & botanical gardens.		
HURD CANDLE FACTORY, 3020 St Helena Hwy North	38	B1
Distinctive hand-made candles.		
INDIAN CULTURAL CENTER, Yosemite Village	63	D1
Indian history in the area, displays, relics.		
INDIAN VALLEY MUSEUM, Taylorsville	20	D5
Located near an original Maidu settlement.		
IRVINE BOWL PARK, off Laguna Canyon Rd	201	B2
Natural amphitheater-Pageant of the Masters.		
INYO VISITOR CTR Off Hwy 395 1-1/2 mi S Lone Pine	60	B4
Information, exhibits, maps of S Inyo County.		
JACK LONDON SQUARE, foot of Broadway	157	E4
Site of the 1st & Last Chance Saloon.		
JACK MURPHY STADIUM, Inland Fwy (805) @ Friars Rd	214	C3
Home of the Padres and the Chargers.		
JACKSON SQUARE, Jackson & Montgomery Sts	143	D2
Former Barbary Coast; now shopping plaza.		
JAPAN CENTER, Post & Geary Sts, Japantown	143	A3
Hub of growing Japantown; traditional culture.		
JAPANESE TEA GARDEN, Golden Gate Park	141	C4
Creatd 1894; oriental landscape, cherry trees.		
JOHNSON VALLEY OHV AREA, Bessemer Mine Rd, SBCO	92	C3
154,700 acre off-highway vehicle area		
J PAUL GETTY MUS, 17985 Pacific Coast Hwy, Malibu	Q	A4
Roman and Greek antiquities; art collection.		
JUNIPERO SERRA MUSEUM, 2727 Presidio Dr,San Diego	213	A4
Artifacts, documents about early California.		
KELLY GRIGGS MUSEUM, 311 Washington, Red Bluff	18	D5
Restored Victorian home; furnshd wth antiques.		
KINGS RIVER, Kings Canyon National Park	59	B2
Middle fork runs thru natl pk; exclnt fishing.		
KLAMATH COUNTY MUS, 1451 Main St, Klamath Falls	5	B1
History of the area.		
KLAMATH NATL FST INTERPRTVE MUS, 1312 Fairlane Rd	4	B4
Displays, exhibits from wildlife to botany.		
KNIGHT MARITIME MUS, 550 Cl Principal, Monterey	167	E4
Exhibits feature history of whaling industry.		
LA BREA TAR PITS, 5801 Wilshire Bl, Los Angeles	184	B2
Displys of prehistoric animals found in pits.		
LADY BIRD JOHNSON REDWOOD GROVE, US 101, Orick	10	A2
One mile trail through redwoods.		
LAGUNA ART MUSEUM, 307 Cliff Dr, Laguna Beach	201	A3
Features continually changing collections.		
LAGUNA SECA RECREATION AREA, Hwy 88, Monterey	54	C4
Laguna Seca Raceway; camping and picnicking.		
LA JOLLA CAVES, 1325 Coast Blvd, La Jolla	105	C2
Formed by wave action; curio shop.		

COPYRIGHT 1997 Thomas Bros. Maps®

POINTS OF INTEREST INDEX

NAME & ADDRESS	PAGE	GRID
OAKLAND ZOO, Knowland Dr & 98th Av	L	E5
Picinic area, amusmt pk, aerial trm, baby zoo.		
OAKWOOD LAKE RESORT, off I-5 S of Manteca	47	A1
Water theme park with camping facilities.		
OIL MUSEUM, Hwy 33, Taft	78	A5
History of oil industry & processing methods.		
OLD EAGLE THEATER, J & Front Sts	137	B2
First theater in California, opened in 1849.		
OLD FAITHFUL GEYSER OF CALIFORNIA, on Tubbs Rd	38	A1
Eruptions occur every 50 minutes.		
OLD TIMERS MUSEUM, Highway 4, Murphys	41	C3
Built 1865; Indian display, historic items.		
OLD TOWN ART GUILD, G & 2nd Sts, Eureka	121	C1
Galleries, gift shops, art supplies.		
ONE LOG HOUSE, Phillipsville	16	C4
2000 year old log home hewn from 40 ton tree.		
ORANGE EMPIRE RAILWAY MUSEUM, Perris	99	B4
An extensive collection of early trains.		
PAGE MUSEUM, 5801 Wilshire Blvd	184	B2
Exhibits of prehistoric animals from tar pits.		
PAINTED GORGE, off Hwy 195, N of Salton Sea	101	C5
Bluffs of colorfully layered rock.		
PALM SPRINGS AERIAL TRAMWAY, Tramway Dr	100	C3
Spectacular view of desert floor below.		
PALM SPRINGS DESERT MUS, 101 Museum Dr, Palm Spgs	206	A3
Fine art displays, desert exhibits.		
PALOMAR OBSERVATORY, Hwy 56, Mt Palomar	107	A2
Operated by Cal Tech; tours; 200" telescope.		
PARDEE HOME MUSEUM, 672 11th St, Oakland	157	E3
Oakland lndmk, living history of 3 generations		
PAULEY PAVILION, U C L A Campus	180	C1
Features many sports events.		
PEACH TREE RANCH, 26500 Stockdale Hwy, Kern Co	78	B3
Open daily, peaches, apples, plums.		
PIER 39, northern waterfront, San Francisco	143	C1
Recreates old SF street scene; shops, rstrnts.		
PLACER COUNTY VISITORS INFORMATION CTR, Newcastle	34	B4
Historical & informational displays 24 hours.		
PLANES OF FAME MUSEUM, Chino Airport	U	D3
World War II memorabilia & plane collection.		
PT ARENA LIGHTHOUSE & MUS, off Hwy 101, Pt Arena	30	B3
Daily tours; maritime artifacts.		
POINT HUENEME, end of Hueneme Rd	96	B1
Marks entrance to Port Hueneme Harbor.		
POINT LOMA, 10 miles W on Catalina Bl	V	A4
Site Cabrillo Nat Monmt, lighthse, scenic vw.		
POINT PINOS LIGHTHOUSE, Monterey Harbor	167	A1
Oldest lighthouse still in use on West Coast.		
PONDEROSA RANCH, Tahoe Blvd, Incline Village	36	B1
Westrn town amusmnt pk, Bonanza TV shw site.		
PORTS O'CALL VILLAGE, on Harbor Blvd, San Pedro	191	B4
Nautical shopping village with harbor tours.		
QUEEN MARY, Pier J, Long Beach	192	E4
Tours, restaurants & hotel on famous liner.		
RACETRACK, Death Valley National Park	60	E3
Clay playa, rocks tilt during high winds.		
RAINBOW BASIN NAT'L NATRL LNDMK, 10 mi N Barstow	81	D5
Natural landmark of color sediment layers.		
RAINBOW FALLS, within Devils Postpile Monument	50	C3
San Joaquin River plunges 101 feet.		
RAMONA BOWL & MUSEUM, 2 mi SE of Hemet	99	E4
Home of the annual Ramona Pageant.		
RANCHO SANTA ANA BOTANIC GARDENS, Foothill Blvd	203	A1
Exclusively native plants of California.		
RASOR OFF HIGHWAY VEHICLE AREA, Hwy 15 & Rasor Rd	83	A5
Off road trails.		
REDDING CONV & VISITORS BUREAU, 777 Auditorium Dr	122	C1
Local information and event schedule.		
REDDING MUSEUM & ART CENTER, 1911 Rio, Redding	18	B2
Interesting Indian relics & art coll displayed.		
RICE VLY DUNES OFF HWY VEH AREA, Hwy 62	103	C2
Sand dunes, off road trails.		
RICHMOND ART CENTER, Barrett Av, Richmond	155	B3
Displays of painting & other art objects.		
RIM OF THE WORLD HIGHWAY	99	E1
Scenic route leads to mountain resort areas.		
RIVERSIDE ART MUSEUM, 3425 Seventh St, Riverside	205	C2
On register of historic places; art exhibits.		
RIVERSIDE MUNICIPAL MUSEUM, 3720 Orange,Riverside	205	B2
Indian artifacts, citrus industry exhibits.		
R M NIXON PRES LIBRARY & BIRTHPLACE, Yorba Linda	T	E1

NAME & ADDRESS	PAGE	GRID
Memorabilia; exhibits & photographs; farmhouse		
ROARING CAMP/BIG TREES NARROW GAUGE RAILRD,Felton	P	A5
Restored 1880's steam locomotives featured.		
ROBERT RIPLEY MEMORIAL MUSEUM, in Juilliard Park	131	D4
Museum is in the Church of One Tree.		
RED ROCK CYN REC LANDS, Hwy 160, Clark Co, Nevada	74	B2
Scenic loop, visitors center, hiking.		
ROSE BOWL, in Brookside Park	190	A3
Famous stadium of New Year's Football game.		
ROSICRUCIAN EGYPTIAN MUS & PLANETARIUM, San Jose	151	D4
Largest Egyptian collection on the West Coast.		
ROY ROGERS MUSEUM, I-15, Victorville	91	B3
Memorabilia of Roy Rogers and Dale Evans.		
R REAGAN PRES LIB, 40 Presidential Dr, Simi Vly	88	E5
Life of 40th U.S. President.		
SACRAMENTO HIST MUS, 101 I St, Old Sacramento	137	A2
17th century maps and gold nugget collections.		
SACRAMENTO NATIONAL WILDLIFE REFUGE, S of Willows	24	D5
Nesting area for migratory waterfowl.		
SACRAMENTO SCIENCE CTR & JR MUSEUM, 3615 Auburn	33	D5
Nature trails and animals to touch.		
SACRAMENTO ZOO, 3930 W Land Park Dr, Sacramento	137	B5
Over 400 animals in simulated environment.		
SALTON SEA NATIONAL WILDLIFE REFUGE, E of Hwy 111	109	A3
Scenic view of nesting birds at Salton Sea.		
SAN BERNARDINO COUNTY MUSEUM, Redlands	99	C2
Artifacts and history of the early settlers.		
SAND DUNES, E of Stovepipe Wells, Death Valley	62	D4
Shifting sand creates scenic area for a walk.		
SAN DIEGO-LA JOLLA UNDERWATER PK, Torrey Pines Rd	V	A1
Protected marine life area open to public vw.		
SAN DIEGO MUSEUM OF ART, Balboa Park, San Diego	216	A2
Contains American and European art.		
SN DIEGO RAILROAD MUSEUM, Highway 94, Campo	112	D2
Exhibits of the Pacific SW Railway.		
SAN DIEGO WILD ANIMAL PARK, 5 mi W Esconddo CA 78	106	D3
Tour through preserve for endangered species.		
SAN DIEGO ZOO, Balboa Park, San Diego	215	E1
One of the largest and lovliest in the world.		
SAN FRANCISCO ART INSTITUTE, 800 Chestnut, SF	143	B2
Three galleries; tours available.		
S.F. MUSEUM MODERN ART, Van Ness & McAllister	143	B4
20th century art, changing exhibits.		
SAN FRANCISCO-OAKLAND BAY BRIDGE, I-80	L	C4
Main link to East Bay.		
SAN FRANCISCO ZOO, Sloat Bl & 45th Av	L	B5
Rated among the top six zoos in the world.		
SAN LUIS OBISPO CO HIST MUSEUM, 696 Monterey	172	B3
Displays of early Californian & Indian relics.		
SAN ONOFRE VISITOR'S CENTER, off I-5	105	E1
Nuclear power generating plant with displays.		
SANTA ANA ZOO, 1801 E Chestnut, Santa Ana	196	D4
Primates, birds, large mammals, petting zoo.		
SANTA ANITA PARK, 285 W Huntington Dr	R	D3
One of the nation's famous horseracing tracks.		
STA BARBARA BOTANICAL GARDEN, 1212 Mission Cyn Rd	174	B1
65 acres of native Calif trees, plants, cacti.		
SANTA BARBARA CO COURTHOUSE, downtown Sta Barbara	174	C3
One of the most beautiful buildings in West.		
SANTA BARBARA MUSEUM OF ART, State & Anapamu Sts	174	B3
Orientl & American art glasswares, scultpres.		
SANTA BARBARA ZOO, 500 Ninos Dr, Santa Barbara	87	C4
Exotic animals in natural habitat; picnic area		
STA CRUZ BIG TREES & PACIFIC RR, 6 mi from S Cruz	53	E1
Historic RR from Roaring Camp to Santa Cruz.		
SANTA CRUZ BOARDWALK, near Municipal Pier	169	D4
Shopping, restaurants, outdoor shows, rides.		
SANTA CRUZ LIGHTHOUSE, West Cliff Dr, Santa Cruz	169	D5
Historic lighthouse.		
SANTA CRUZ MUNICIPAL PIER, off West Cliff Dr	169	E5
Shops and arcades over the ocean.		
SAUSALITO FERRY TERMINAL, Anchor St	L	B4
Commuter service to San Francisco.		
SAWDUST FESTIVAL, Laguna Cyn Rd, Laguna Beach	201	B2
Annually July-Aug; Arts&crafts festival, tour.		
SCOTIA LUMBER MILL, Main St, Scotia	16	A3
Tour mill, debarking, sawing, shipping logs.		
SCOTTY'S CASTLE, Death Valley National Park	61	B1
Tour unique mansion built by Death Vly Scotty.		
SCRIPPS AQUARIUM MUSEUM, 8602 La Jolla Shores	211	A1
Sea exhibits & tidepools.		

NAME & ADDRESS	PAGE	GRID
SEAL ROCKS, Golden Gate National Recreation Area	L	A5
View of seal and bird habitats.		
SESPE WILDLIFE AREA, E of I-5 off Hwy 126.	88	C4
Established to preserve near-extinct condors.		
SEVENTEEN MILE DRIVE, Monterey Peninsula	53	B2
Magnificent drive between Carmel & Monterey		
SHASTA CAVERNS, off O'Brien, 20 mi N of Redding.	18	C1
Variety of crystal formations, tours, gift shop.		
SHASTA DAM & POWER PLANT, 15 miles NW of Redding	18	B1
2nd largest dam in the US; excellent view of Mt Shasta		
SHRINE DRIVE-THRU TREE, Myers Flat	16	B4
Drive through living tree; logging display.		
SIERRA BUTTES, N of Sierra City	27	A4
Giant rugged granite outcrops, scenic.		
SIERRA MONO INDIAN MUSEUM, St 274 & St 225, North Fork	49	E5
Artifacts of Native Indian tribes.		
SIERRA NEVADA MUSEUM OF ART, 549 Court St, Reno	130	A3
Collections of art from all over the world.		
SIERRA VALLEY MUSEUM, Loyalton	27	D3
19th Century & Depression era exhibits.		
SILVERADO MUSEUM, 1490 Library Ln, Napa	38	B1
Memorabilia of Robert Louis Stevenson.		
SISKIYOU COUNTY MUSEUM, 910 S Main St, Yreka	4	A4
Indian objects, displays of old & new industry.		
SOLVANG, Hwy 246	86	E3
Authentic Danish village.		
SONY STUDIOS, Culver City	188	B1
Major motion picture studio.		
SOUTH COAST BOTANICAL GARDENS, 26300 Crenshaw Bl	S	B2
Calif native plants & trees; man-made lake.		
SOUTH COW MTN OHV REC AREA, 5 mi W of Lakeport	31	C2
Off Hwy trails, camp, picnic.		
SOUTHWEST MUSEUM, 234 Museum Dr, Los Angeles	R	A3
American Indian artifacts, library, store.		
SPORTS ARENA, Exposition Park, Los Angeles	185	C5
Hosts sporting events for college and professional athletes.		
STATE CAPITOL, Capitol Mall, Sacramento	137	B3
Daily guided tours through capitol building.		
STATE INDIAN MUSEUM, 2618 K St, Sacramento	137	D3
features various California Indian cultures.		
STATE LIBRARY, 914 Capitol Mall, Sacramento	137	B3
Founded in 1850, Public Library.		
STEARNS WHARF, lower State St. Santa Barbara	174	E4
The main pier extends beyond State Street.		
STEINBECK HOUSE, 132 Central Av, Salinas	171	B3
Birthplace of author, restaurant & gift shop.		
STEINHART AQUARIUM, Golden Gate Park	141	D4
In Acadmy of Sci; features circular fish tank.		
STEWART INDIAN MUS, 5366 Snyder Av, Carson City	36	C2
Indian artifacts, open daily.		
STODDARD VALLEY OHV AREA, I-15 & Sidewinder Rd	91	D2
33,500 acre off-highway vehicle area.		
STRYBING ARBORETUM, South Dr, Golden Gate Park	141	C4
More than 5000 plant species displayed.		
SUPERSTITION MTN OHV AREA, Wheeler Rd, Imp Co	108	D4
Off highway vehicle trails.		
SUTTER BUTTES, Near West Butte	33	B1
Listed as world's smallest mountain range.		
TECOPA HOT SPRINGS, west of Hwy 127	72	E4
Old Indian healing pl, baths open to public.		
TELEGRAPH HILL, at Lombard & Kearny Sts	143	C2
Park, Coit Tower at top with view; tours.		
TELEVISION CITY - CBS, 7800 Beverly Blvd	184	A1
Actual site of many telecasts.		
THOMAS BROS. MAPS RETAIL STORE, 17731 Cowan, Irvine	198	C3
Corporate office and showroom.		
THOMAS BROS. MAPS AND BOOKS, 521 W 6th St, Los Angeles	186	A3
Retail store		
THOMAS BROS. MAPS AND BOOKS, 550 Jackson St, San Francisco	142	E2
Retail store		
TITUS CANYON, E of Hwy 374, Death Valley Natl Park	62	D3
Colorful, exciting drive thru a narrow canyon.		
TOWE FORD MUSEUM, 2200 Front St, Sacramento	137	A3
Most complete collection of antique Fords.		
TRAVIS AIR FORCE MUSEUM, 3rd & E St, Fairfield	39	B3
Displays of various aircraft.		
TREES OF MYSTERY, 16 miles S of Crescent City	1	E5
Unusual&handcarved redwood trees; Indian Mus.		
TRITON MUSEUM, 1505 Warburton Av, Santa Clara	151	A2
Home of national & international art exhibits.		
TRONA PINNACLES, S of Trona near Pinnacle	81	B1

NAME & ADDRESS	PAGE	GRID
Tall pinnacles formed by algae of a sea.		
TUCKER WILDLIFE SANCTUARY, 28322 Modjeska Canyon	98	E4
Features a variety of hummingbirds.		
TULARE COUNTY MUSEUM, 27000 S Mooney, Mooney Grv	68	B2
Restored buildings; Indian & Pioneer artifcts.		
TULE LAKE NATL WILDLIFE REFUGE, S of Tulelake	5	D3
Great stopping point for migrating waterfowl.		
TUOLUMNE COUNTY MUSEUM, 158 W Bradford, Sonora	163	B3
Located in the old jail; gold rush objects.		
TUOLUMNE COUNTY VISITORS BUREAU, 55 Stockton Rd	163	C3
Local information and event schedule.		
20TH CENTURY FOX STUDIO, Pico Blvd	183	B3
One of the oldest studios in Hollywood.		
UBEHEBE CRATER, Death Valley National Park	61	A2
Crater created by volcanic steam explosion.		
UNDERSEA WORLD, Hwy 101 S of Crescent City	1	D4
View sea plants & animals, scuba diving show.		
UNION SQUARE, Geary, Powell, Post & Stockton Sts	143	C3
Fashionable shopping center; park, fountain.		
UNION STATION, 800 N Alameda St, Los Angeles	186	C2
One of the landmarks of Los Angeles.		
UNOCAL OIL MUSEUM, 1003 Main St, Santa Paula	88	B5
History of discovery & drilling of oil in Cal.		
VICTORIAN TOUR HOUSE, 401 Pine St, Nevada City	128	C2
Privately owned restored home-tours by appt.		
VIKINGSHOLM, at Emerald Bay	35	E3
Large Scandanavian castle with furnishings.		
VISITOR CENTER YOSEMITE VILLAGE, Yosemite Lodge	63	C1
Displays, photos of Yosemite, films.		
WARM SPGS DAM & FISH HATCHERY, 11 mi NW Healdsbrg	31	C5
Visitor ctr & camping; dam created Lk Sonoma.		
WARNER BROS STUDIOS, 4000 Warner Blvd, Burbank	179	C5
Offers tours of day's activity on the lot.		
WARREN FIRE MUSEUM, Curry St, Carson City	36	B2
Old firefighting trucks, equipment & pictures.		
WASSAMA ROUND HOUSE STATE HIST, 55 mi N of Fresno	49	C4
Picturesque picnic area.		
WAYFARER'S CHAPEL, 5755 Palos Verde Dr	S	B3
Striking glass church sits atop hill by sea.		
WESTERN RAILWAY MUSEUM, Highway 12 E of Fairfield	M	B1
Restored rail cars, rides, exhibits & museum.		
WHISKEYTOWN-SHASTA-TRINITY REC, NW of Redding	18	A1
Camp, backpack, picnic, boat, water sports.		
WHITNEY PORTAL, W from Lone Pine	59	E4
Starting point for Mt Whitney trail.		
WILLIAM S HART PARK, Newhall Av at Sn Fernando Rd	89	B5
Tour the silent screen actor's beautiful home.		
WINCHESTER MYSTERY HOUSE, Winchester Bl, San Jose	151	B5
Fascinating house and museum.		
WINNERS CIRCLE RCH, 59911 Lakeview Hy, Petaluma	L	B1
Miniature horses bred and trained; sales.		
WOODMINSTER AMPHITHEATER, S of Orinda	L	E4
Centerpiece of pk, sumr concerts, light opera.		
WRIGLEY MEMORIAL & BOTANICAL GARDN, Avalon Cyn Rd	97	A5
Beautiful cactus, flowers & trees at monument.		
YOSEMITE FALLS, Yosemite National Park	63	D1
Two beautiful waterfalls fall over 2,400 feet.		
YOSEMITE MTN SUGAR PINE RR, Hwy 41 N of Sugr Pine	49	D3
4 miles trip on a steam-powered railroad.		
YOSEMITE VALLEY, Mariposa County	63	A1
Picturesque, campng, domes, wtrflls, meadow.		
YOSEMITE WILDLIFE MUS, 2040 Yosemite Pky, Merced	48	C4
M-Sat, 10-5; North American wildlife displays.		
YREKA WESTERN RR, off I-5 & Central Eureka Exit	4	B4
Blue Goose shortline RR through Shasta Vly.		
YUMA TERRITORIAL PRISON ST HIST PK, off I-8, Yuma	112	D5
Blt 1876, operated until 1909; museum & tour.		
ZABRISKIE POINT, off Hwy 190 in Death Valley	62	B5
Overlooks Death Vly from badland of Black Mtn.		
ZALUD HOUSE MUSEUM, 393 N Hocket, Porterville	68	D3
1891 home with period furniture.		

⛵ **RECREATION LAKES, RIVERS & MARINAS**

NAME & ADDRESS	PAGE	GRID
ALPINE LAKE, 51 mi NE of Angels Camp	42	A1
100+ dev sites - boat, backpack, fish, swim.		
ANDERSON RESERVOIR, Hwy 101, S of San Jose	P	D5
Fishing and boating facilities.		
ANTELOPE LAKE, 45 miles NE of Quincy	21	A4
200+ dev sites - boat, waterski, fish, hike.		

POINTS OF INTEREST INDEX

POINTS OF INTEREST INDEX

SKI AREAS

THEATERS

COPYRIGHT 1997 *Thomas Bros. Maps*®

INDEXES

POINTS OF INTEREST INDEX

NAME & ADDRESS	PAGE	GRID
TERRACE THEATER, Ocean Blvd, Long Beach	192	E3
Features drama, opera, dance & symphony.		
THE MUSIC CENTER, 135 N Grand Av, Los Angeles	186	A2
3 theatre complex for drama, music & opera.		
TOWER THEATER, 1201 N Wishon Av, Fresno	165	C2
30's movie house is now performing arts center		
WARNORS CTR FOR PERFORM ARTS, 1400 Fulton, Fresno	165	D3
Landmrk bldg home for community events&theater		
WILSHIRE THEATER, 8440 Wilshire Blvd, Los Angeles	183	E2
Classic theater - features plays & musicals.		

WINERIES

NAME & ADDRESS	PAGE	GRID
Many of the wineries located in the Napa Valley are shown on Page 29 in this Driver's Guide.		
ADELAIDA CELLARS, 5805 Adelaida Rd, Paso Robles	75	E1
Winery and tasting room are open daily.		
ALDERBROOK WINERY, 2306 Magnolia Dr, Healdsburg	37	D1
Tasting room open daily; tours by appointment.		
ALEXANDER VLY VINEYARDS, 8644 Hwy 128, Healdsburg	31	E5
Wine tasting; tours by appointment.		
ALTAMURA WINERY, 4240 Silverado Tr, Napa	29	E4
Tasting room open daily; appointmnt suggested.		
AMADOR CITY WINERY, Hwy 49 & Water St, Amador	40	D2
Winery and tasting room are open daily.		
A. NONINI WINERY, 2640 N Dickenson, Fresno	57	B3
Winery tours, tasting and retail sales.		
ARCIERO WINERY, Hwy 46 & Jardine Rd, Paso Robles	76	B1
Winery and tasting room are open daily.		
ARROWHEAD WINERY, 14347 Sonoma Hwy, Glen Ellen	29	B5
Tasting room open daily.		
AUSTIN CELLARS, 2923 Grand Av, Los Olivos	86	E3
Tasting room and retail sales; picnic area.		
BABCOCK VINEYARDS, 5175 Hwy 246, Lompoc	86	C3
Open Saturdays & Sundays, 10 am - 4:30 pm.		
BALLARD CYN WINERY, 1825 Ballard Cyn Rd, Solvang	86	E3
Tours by appointment only; tasting room.		
BANDIERA WINERY, 555 S. Cloverdale Bl, Cloverdale	31	C4
Tasting & sales open Tuesday through Sunday.		
BARGETTO WINERY, 700 Cannery Row, Monterey	167	E2
Tasting room and gift shop.		
BARGETTOS STA CRUZ WNRY, 3535 N Main St, Soquel	54	A2
Tasting room and tours.		
BARON VINEYARDS, 1981 Penman Spgs Rd, Paso Robles	76	B1
Tasting room open daily.		
BEAULIEU VINEYARD, 1960 St Helena Hwy, Rutherford	29	C3
Open daily for tasting and guided tours.		
BEAUCANÓN, 1695 St Helena Hwy, St Helena	29	C3
Open daily for tasting and guided tours.		
BELLA ROSA WINERY, Hwy 99 & Pond Rd, McFarland	68	B5
Winery and tasting room are open daily.		
BELLEROSE VINEYARD, 435 W Dry Ck Rd, Healdsburg	37	A1
Hours Tues-Fri 1-5, Sat-Sun 11-4:30.		
BELVEDERE WINERY, 4035 Westside Rd, Healdsburg	37	D1
Tasting room open daily; group tours by appt.		
BERGFELD 1885 WINE CELLARS, 401 St Helena Hwy	29	C3
Open daily for tasting and tours.		
BERINGER VINEYARDS, 2000 Main St, St Helena	29	B3
Tours of Rhine House, Beringer caves; tasting.		
BERNARDO WINERY, 13330 Pas Di Verano N, Escondido	106	D4
Wine tasting, sales & gift shop; picnic area.		
BIANCHI VINEYARDS, 5806 N Modoc Av, Kerman	57	A3
Winery and tasting room are open daily.		
BOEGER WINERY, 1709 Carson, Placerville	35	A4
Wine tasting; self guided tours.		
BONNY DOON VINEYARD, 10 Pine Flat Rd, Santa Cruz	N	E5
Open for tours and tasting.		
BRANDER VINEYARD, Hwy 154 & Refugio, Los Olivos	86	E3
Open Monday-Saturday for wine tasting & tours.		
BRITTON CELLARS, 40620 Calle Contento, Temecula	99	D5
Daily tasting & sales; picnic area.		
BUENA VISTA WINERY, 1800 Old Winery Rd, Sonoma	L	C1
Historic landmark of Cal's first wine cellars.		
BYINGTON WINERY, 21850 Bear Creek Rd, Los Gatos	P	A4
Tasting room open daily; picnic area.		
BYRON WINERY, 5230 Tepusquet Rd, Santa Maria	86	D1
Daily tours, wine tasting and retail sales.		
CACHE CELLARS, Pedrick Rd, Davis	39	B2
Tasting room open daily; groups by appointmnt.		
CACHE CREEK WINERY, Route 21, Woodland	33	B5

NAME & ADDRESS	PAGE	GRID
Tours and tasting offered daily.		
CADENASSO WINERY, 1955 W Texas St, Fairfield	135	A4
Winery and tasting room are open daily.		
CAKEBREAD CELLARS, 8300 St Helena Hy, Rutherford	29	D3
Tasting tours by appointment.		
CALIFORNIA CELLAR MASTERS, 212 W Pine St, Lodi	40	A4
Winery and tasting room are open daily.		
CALLAWAY WINERY, 32720 Ro California Rd, Temecula	99	D5
Tours and tasting room; picnic facilities.		
CAPARONE WINERY, San Marcos Rd, Paso Robles	66	A5
Tasting and sales available daily.		
CAREY CELLARS, 1711 Alamo Pintado Rd, Solvang	86	E3
Daily tours&tasting; picnic area available.		
CARMENET VINEYARD, 1700 Moon Mtn Dr, Sonoma	38	B3
Open by appointment only.		
CARNEROS CREEK WINERY, 1285 Dealy Ln, Napa	38	C3
Tasting and tours; open Wednesday - Sunday.		
CASA DE FRUTA, 6680 Pacheco Pass Hy, Hollister	54	E2
Open daily; gourmet deli.		
CASWELL VINEYARDS, 8860 Hwy 12, Kenwood	38	A2
Open for tours and tasting Wednesday - Monday.		
CAYMUS VINEYARDS, 8700 Conn Creek Rd, Rutherford	29	D3
Guided tours and tasting by appointment.		
CHALK HILL, 10300 Chalk Hill Rd, Healdsburg	37	E1
Tours and tasting by appointment.		
CHAMISAL VINEYARD, 7525 Orcutt Rd, Sn Luis Obispo	76	B4
Wine tasting & retail sales; picnic area.		
CHARLES KRUG WINERY, 2800 Main St, St Helena	29	C2
Guided tours and wine tasting daily.		
CHATEAU DE LEU, 1635 W Mason Rd, Suisun	L	E1
Wine tasting & sales; picnic facilities.		
CHATEAU JULIEN WINERY, 8940 Carmel Vly Rd, Carmel	54	B5
Tasting room open daily; groups by appointmnt.		
CHATEAU MONTELENA, 1429 Tubbs Ln, Calistoga	29	A1
Tours by appointment; store open daily.		
CHATEAU POTELLE WINERY, 3875 Mt Veeder Rd, Napa	29	C4
Tasting room is open daily.		
CHATEAU ST JEAN, 8555 Sonoma Hwy, Kenwood	38	A2
Tasting, self-guided tours.		
CHATEAU SOUVERAIN, 400 Souverain Rd, Geyserville	31	D5
Open daily for tours and tasting.		
CHATOM VINEYARDS, 1969 Highway 4, Murphys	41	C4
Winery & tasting room open daily.		
CHIMNEY ROCK WINERY, 5350 Silverado Trail, Napa	29	E4
Hours 10-5 daily.		
CHRISTIAN BROTHERS, 2555 Main St, St Helena	29	B2
Open daily for tasting and tours.		
CILURZO VINEYARD, 41220 Calle Contento, Temecula	99	D5
Informal tours and wine tasting; picnic area.		
CLINE CELLARS, Cypress Rd & Sellars Av, Oakley	M	D3
Daily tasting & sales; picnic area.		
CLOS DU BOIS, 5 Fitch St, Healdsburg	37	E1
Tasting room and sales; tours by appointment.		
CLOS DU VAL VINEYARDS, 5330 Silverado Tr, Napa	29	E4
Tasting & tours by appointment; retail sales.		
CLOS PEGASE, 1060 Dunaweal Ln, Calistoga	29	A1
Open daily for tasting and tours.		
CONCANNON VINEYARD, 4590 Telsa Rd, Livermore	P	D1
Wine tasting room; tours by appointment.		
CONN CREEK WINERY, 8711 Silverado Tr, Napa	29	D3
Open daily for tasting and tours.		
CONROTTO WINERY, 1690 Hecker Pass Hwy, Gilroy	54	D2
Tasting room and retail sales open daily.		
CORBETT CANYON, 353 Shell Beach Rd, Sn Luis Obspo	76	B4
Wine tasting & sales; picnic facilities.		
COSENTINO, St Helena Hwy, Yountville	29	D4
Hours 10-5 daily.		
CRESTON MANOR VINEYARDS & WINERY, Hwy 58, Creston	76	D2
Tours, wine tasting & sales; picnic area.		
CULBERTSON WINERY, 32575 Ro Calif Rd, Temecula	99	D5
Open daily for tours and tasting.		
CUVAISON WINERY, 4550 Silverado Tr, Calistoga	29	A1
Tasting room; picnic area, tours by appt.		
DAVID BRUCE WINERY, 21439 Bear Creek Rd, Ls Gatos	P	A4
Tasting room open daily; tours by appointment.		
DAVIS BYNUM WINERY, 8075 Westside Rd, Healdsburg	37	D1
Tasting rm open daily 10AM-5PM; tours by appt.		
DEER PARK, 29103 Champagne Blvd, Escondido	106	D3
Tasting & self-guided tours 10-5 daily.		
DEER PARK WINERY, 1000 Deer Park Rd, Deer Park	29	C2
Retail sales; tours by appointment.		

POINTS OF INTEREST INDEX

NAME & ADDRESS	PAGE	GRID
LOST HILLS WINERY, 3125 E Orange Av, Acampo	40	A4
Open daily 9-5 for tasting & sales.		
LOUIS M MARTINI, 254 St Helena Hwy, St Helena	29	C3
Guided tours and wine tasting room open daily.		
LYETH VNYRD&WINERY, 24625 Chianti Rd, Geyserville	31	C4
Tasting room; appointment required.		
LYTTON SPGS WINERY, 650 Lytton Spgs Rd, Healdsbrg	31	D5
Tasting room open daily; tours by appointment.		
MAISON DUETZ WINERY, 453 Deutz Dr, Arroyo Grande	76	C4
Winery, tasting room open daily;appt suggestd.		
MARIANA VINEYARDS, 23600 Cngrss Spgs Rd, Saratoga	N	E4
Open daily for tasting tours, by appt.		
MARKHAM WINERY, 2812 St Helena Hwy, St Helena	29	B2
Tasting room open daily; tours by appointment.		
MARK WEST VNYDS 7000 Trenton-Healdsbrg Rd Frstvle	37	D2
Tasting room open daily.		
MARTIN BROS. WINERY, Hwy 46, Paso Robles	76	B1
Tasting room and sales; picnic area.		
MARTINELLI VINEYARDS, 3362 River Rd, Windsor	37	D1
Hours 10-5 daily.		
MARTINI & PRATI WINERY, 2191 Laguna Rd, Sta Rosa	37	D2
Open daily for tasting and tours.		
MASTANTUONO, Hwy 46 & Vineyard Dr, Templeton	76	A1
Tasting room open daily.		
MATANZAS CK WNRY, 6097 Bennett Vly Rd, Sta Rosa	38	A2
Hours M-Sat 10-4, Sun 12-4.		
MAURICE CARRIE WINERY, 34255 Ro Calif Rd,Temecula	99	D5
Winery and tasting room are open daily.		
MAYACAMAS VINEYARDS, 1155 Lokoya Rd, Napa	29	C4
No tasting; tours by appointment.		
MAZZOCCO VNYRDS, 1400 Lytton Spgs Rd, Healdsburg	31	D5
Tasting room open daily 10AM to 4PM.		
McDOWELL VLY VINEYARDS, 3811 SR 175, Hopland	31	C3
Tasting room, retail sales; tours by appt.		
MENDOCINO VINEYARDS, 2399 N State St, Ukiah	31	B2
Tasting room open daily; tours by appointment.		
MENGHINI WINERY, 1150 Julian Orchards Dr, Julien	107	C3
Hours 10-4 Fri-Mon.		
MERLION WINERY, 1224 Adams St, St Helena	29	B3
Open daily; appointment required for tasting.		
MERRYVALE WINERY, 1000 Main St, St Helena	29	C3
Hours 10-5:30 daily.		
MILANO WINERY, 14594 S Hwy 101, Hopland	31	B3
Tasting room, retail sales; tours by appt.		
MILAT VINEYARDS, 1091 St Helena Hwy, St Helena	29	C3
Hours 10-6 daily.		
MILL CREEK VINEYARDS, 1401 Westside Rd, Healdsbrg	37	D1
Open daily; tasting room and picnic area.		
MILLIAIRE WINERY, 276 Main St, Murphys	41	C4
Winery & tasting room open daily.		
MIRASSOU VINEYARDS, 3000 Aborn Rd, San Jose	P	C4
Tasting room and tours available.		
MISSION VW VINEYARDS, 3360 N River Rd, San Miguel	66	A5
Winery & tasting open daily; groups by appt.		
MONTALI WINERY, 600 Addison St, Berkeley	45	C1
Tasting room and sales; picnic area.		
MONTEREY PENINSULA WNRY, 786 Wave St, Monterey	167	D2
Tasting room, open daily 10AM-5PM; no tours.		
MONTEREY VINEYARDS, 800 S Alta St, Gonzales	54	E5
Tours and tasting available.		
MONTEVINA WINERY 20680 Shenandoah Sch Rd Plymouth	40	E1
Tasting room open daily.		
MONTICELLO CELLARS, 4242 Big Ranch Rd, Napa	29	E5
Tasting available for fee; tours.		
MONT ST JOHN CELLARS, 5400 Old Sonoma Rd, Napa	38	C3
Wine tasting & sales; picnic facilities.		
MOSBY WINERY, 9496 Santa Rosa Rd, Buellton	86	D3
Tours and tasting available daily by appt.		
MT PALOMAR, 33820 Rancho California Rd, Temecula	99	D5
Guided tours, tasting, sales & deli; picnic.		
MUMM NAPA VALLEY, 8445 Silverado Tr, Rutherford	29	D3
Open daily for tours, tasting & retail sales.		
MURPHY GOODE, 4001 Highway 128, Geyserville	31	D5
Open for tasting; tours require appointment.		
NAPA BEAUCANNON, 1695 St Helena Hwy	29	C3
Open daily for tours and tasting.		
NAPA CREEK WINERY, 1001 Silverado Tr, St Helena	29	C3
Tasting room open daily.		
NAVARRO WINERY, 5801 Hwy 128, Philo	30	E2
Tasting room open daily; tours by appointment.		

NAME & ADDRESS	PAGE	GRID
NERVO WINERY, 19550 Geyserville Av, Geyserville	31	D5
Open daily for tasting; no tours.		
NEVADA CITY WINERY, 321 Spring St, Nevada City	128	B2
Tours and tasting daily; picnic area.		
NICHELINI VINEYARD, 2950 Sage Cyn Rd, St Helena	29	E3
Tasting room; no tours.		
OAK RIDGE VINEYARDS, 6100 E Hwy 12, Lodi	40	B4
Tasting room open daily; Fall tours.		
OBESTER WINERY, 12341 San Mateo, Half Moon Bay	N	C2
Tasting room and retail sales; picnic area.		
OLSON VINEYARDS, 3620 Road B, Redwood Valley	31	B1
Tasting room open daily; tours by appointment.		
OPICI WINERY, 10150 Highland Av, Alta Loma	U	E1
Open daily; by apppointmnt for groups,tasting.		
PARADISE VINTNERS, 1656 Nunneley Rd, Paradise	25	D3
Winery and tasting room are open daily.		
PARDUCCI WINE CELLARS, 501 Parducci Rd, Ukiah	31	A2
Tasting room, tours hourly.		
PASTORI, 23189 Geyserville Av, Cloverdale	31	D5
Open daily for tasting; no tours.		
PAT PAULSEN VINEYARDS, Asti Rd, Asti	31	D5
Tasting room.		
PAUL MASSON VINEYARD, 13150 Saratoga Av, Saratoga	46	A5
By appointment tours.		
PEDRIZZETTI WINERY, 1645 San Pedro Av, Morgan Hll	P	D4
Tasting room open daily; tours by appointment.		
PEDRONCELLI, 1220 Canyon Rd, Geyserville	31	C5
Open all week for tasting; tours by appointmt.		
PEJU PROVINCE WINERY, 8466 St Helena Hy, Rutherfd	29	C3
Tasting room and retail sales.		
PESENTI WINERY, 2900 Vineyard Dr, Templeton	76	A2
Informal winery tours; wine tasting & sales.		
PHILLIPS FARMS WINERY&VNYRDS, 4580 W Hwy 12, Lodi	40	A4
Open daily 8-6, for tasting & retail sales.		
PINA CELLARS, 8060 Silverado Tr, Rutherford	29	D3
Open Mon-Fri for wine tasting,weekends by appt		
PINE RIDGE WINERY, 5901 Silverado Trail, Napa	29	E4
Wine tasting & picnic area; tours by appt.		
PIPER SONOMA CELLARS, 11457 Old Redwood Hwy	37	D1
Guided tours and tasting room.		
PRESTIGE VINEYARDS, 6115 Paseo dl Norte, Carlsbad	106	C3
Winery and tasting room are open daily.		
PRESTON VINEYARDS, 9282 W Dry Ck Rd, Healdsburg	31	C5
Tasting & tours; open Mon - Fri, 11AM to 3 PM.		
QUADY WINERY, 13181 Road 24, Madera	57	A2
Tours and tasting offered Monday - Friday.		
RANCHO SISQUOC WINERY, Foxen Cyn Rd SE of Sisquoc	86	D1
Tours and sales; tasting room.		
R & J COOK WINERY, Netherlands Rd, Clarksburg	39	D2
Tasting & sales daily; picnic area.		
RAPAZZINI WINERY, 4350 Monterey Hwy, Gilroy	54	D2
Tours and wine tasting daily.		
RAYMOND VINEYARD & CELLAR, 849 Zinfandel Ln, St Helena	29	C3
Tours by appointment only.		
RETZLAFF VINEYARDS, 1356 S Livermore Av	M	C5
Open for tasting and tours.		
R H PHILLIPS VINEYARDS, Routes 12A & 87, Esparto	33	A5
Open daily for tasting and tours.		
RIDGE VINEYARDS, 17100 Montebello Rd, Cupertino	N	E3
Open for tasting&retail sales; tours by appt.		
RIVER OAKS VINEYARDS, Lytton Statn Rd, Healdsburg	31	D5
Tasting room open daily; tours by appointment.		
ROBERT KEENAN WINERY, 3660 Spring Mtn, St Helena	29	A2
Open Mon-Sat; appointment suggested.		
ROBERT MONDAVI WINERY, 7801 St Helena Hwy, Oakville	29	A2
Tasting & tours; musical events & art exhibit.		
ROBERT PEPI WINERY, 7585 St Helena Hwy, Oakville	29	D4
Winery tours and tasting by appointment.		
ROBERT SINSKEY VINEYARDS, 6320 Silverado Tr, Napa	29	E4
Tasting rm open daily; tours by appointment.		
ROBERT STEMMLER, 3805 Lambert Bridge Rd, Healdsbg	31	D5
Wine tasting and retail sales; picnicking.		
RODNEY STRONG, 11455 Old Redwood Hwy, Healdsburg	37	D1
Tasting & sales; concerts & cultural events.		
ROSS-KELLER, 985 Orchard Av, Nipomo	76	C5
Open daily Apr-Nov; Wed-Sun, Dec-Mar.		
ROSS-KELLER WINERY, 900 McMurray Rd, Buellton	86	D3
Tours and tasting daily.		
ROUDON-SMITH TSTG RM, 2364 Bean Ck Rd, Scotts Vly	P	A5
Tasting room and sales Wed-Sun; no tours.		

POINTS OF INTEREST INDEX

Introducing...

The Thomas Guide ® CD-ROM

The Thomas Guide on a PC!

32 BIT APPLICATION

The Thomas Guide CD-ROM, our new easy-to-use desktop mapping software, is an ideal business or personal tool for quickly getting where you want to go. Based on the same data used to produce the Thomas Guides, the Thomas Guide CD-ROM provides the assurance of the most up-to-date and accurate map data anywhere. Now, on your own computer, you can:

❖ View actual Thomas Guide pages on-screen. Crisp detail and full color make it easy to see destinations and surrounding areas

    ❖ Look up locations by street address, city, point of interest, or Thomas Bros. page

    ❖ Zoom in to see an area close-up, and zoom out to see the big picture

    ❖ Select and save up to 10 addresses or points of interest for future use

    ❖ Copy maps to other software programs for presentations and other projects

<u>**System Requirements:**</u>
CD-ROM Drive
Minimum 486 DX2 IBM or compatible
SVGA Monitor (256 Color)
8 MB RAM
Microsoft Windows® V3.1, 95 or NT
10-20 MB Hard Disk Space (depending on map area)

<u>**Printer Requirements:**</u>
Printers (M/S compatible)
Inkjets, bubble jets, and laserjets with 4MB RAM

Available for selected counties.
Call for pricing and availability today!

1-800-899-6277

e-mail: comments@thomas.com
World Wide Web: http://www.thomas.com

WHAT IS THOMAS BROS. MAPS®

EDUCATIONAL FOUNDATION?

SPECIAL PROGRAMS

"GEOGRAPHY IS EVERYWHERE"

Available to schools, libraries and other groups on request, "Geography Is Everywhere" is a curriculum driven newsletter for teachers. Regular features include geography ideas, lessons plans, reviews of geography products, a theme bibliography and hands-on geography activities.

Thomas Bros. Maps Educational Foundation was established in 1989 to bring geography awareness to students during the early years of their education. We find that even the youngest child can discover a helpful connection with the community by using local maps as a geography tool.

Schools, libraries, museums and community service groups all have access to Thomas Bros. Maps Educational Foundation. Here a wealth of resources -- ranging from ideas and instructional materials to detailed lesson plans -- are available to enhance learning by making geography come alive for children. Workshops, sponsored by the Foundation staff, instruct teachers how to integrate geography with other disciplines such as history, science, language arts, and math to create a positive classroom experience. Outside the school setting, the Foundation works with organizations and community service groups to organize innovative hands-on geography activities for children.

COMMUNITY MAP KITS

A child gazing at a globe, asks "Where do I live?" To help students understand their community, we created the "Community Map Kit". Each kit includes one large wall map, 35 smaller laminated maps and two copies of Thomas Bros. Maps Street Guides. The wall map and laminated maps are selected by the teacher to best fit classroom needs.

GEOGRAPHY RESOURCE CENTER

The Center, located at Thomas Bros. Maps headquarters in Irvine, CA, houses resource books, children's literature, geography games, educational toys, globes, maps and software. Come in and share ideas with the Foundation staff!! All products are available for review and may be borrowed.

THE FOUNDATION'S MISSION

❧ *The Thomas Bros. Maps Educational Foundation is a public non-profit organization dedicated to expanding students' horizons through the study of geography, ethnic, cultural, social and human values.*

The Foundation provides geography programs, assistance and education through:

❧ *Researching, designing and producing resource materials for teaching geography.*

❧ *Showing the value of integrating geographic concepts into various aspects of teaching curricula.*

❧ *Facilitating the exchange of ideas and resources among teachers and education administrators by providing networking opportunities and sponsoring seminars and workshops.*

❧ *Establishing and administering scholarships to study cartography and other geography-related disciplines.*

*"Our Children:
   Their World
Our Challenge:
   Their Future"*

**THOMAS BROS. MAPS®
EDUCATIONAL FOUNDATION**
17731 COWAN, IRVINE, CA 92714
714-863-1984 • FAX 714-757-1564 • 800-899-6277

The **Thomas Guide**® for Windows®...
comprehensive coverage for all of California on one CD-ROM!

- Utilizes the Thomas Bros. Maps Page & Grid ™
- Manage data points and territories geographically
- Customize & print presentation-quality maps
- Copy & paste to other Windows applications
- Interface with Global Positioning Systems (GPS)
- Annual updates available!

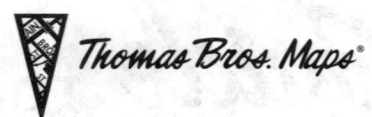

Thomas Bros. Maps®

PRODUCT INFORMATION LIST

Classic Thomas Guides®

California

ITEM #	DESCRIPTION
3028	Alameda County
4028	Alameda / Contra Costa Counties
4037	Alameda / Santa Clara Counties
3065	Central Valley Cities (All urban areas from Stockton to Bakersfield)
3027	Contra Costa County
4025	Golden Gate Counties (Marin, San Francisco, San Mateo, Santa Clara)
3054	Los Angeles County
4054	Los Angeles / Orange Counties
4053	Los Angeles / Ventura Counties
3025	Marin County
3042	Monterey County - '95 Edition
3055	Orange County
4055	Orange / Los Angeles Counties
3056	Riverside County
4056	Riverside / Orange Counties
4058	Riverside / San Diego Counties
3023	Sacramento County including portions of Placer & El Dorado Counties
4024	Sacramento / Solano Counties
3051	San Bernardino County
4051	San Bernardino / Riverside Counties
3057	San Diego County including Imperial County
4057	San Diego / Orange Counties
3035	San Francisco County
4030	San Francisco / Alameda / Contra Costa Counties
4026	San Francisco / San Mateo Counties
3036	San Mateo County
3052	Santa Barbara and San Luis Obispo Counties
4052	Santa Barbara and San Luis Obispo / Ventura Counties
3037	Santa Clara County
4036	Santa Clara / San Mateo Counties
3022	Solano County including portions of Napa & Yolo Counties
3020	Sonoma County - '95 Edition
3053	Ventura County

Arizona - Oregon - Washington

3072	Phoenix Metro Area
3099	Portland Metro Area including Vancouver, WA; Multnomah and Clackamas, OR
3090	King County
4090	King / Pierce Counties
4091	King / Pierce / Snohomish Counties
4092	King / Snohomish Counties
3091	Pierce County
3092	Snohomish County

NEW Metropolitan Bay Area Thomas Guide®

3002	Metropolitan Bay Area (Alameda, Contra Costa, Marin, San Francisco, San Mateo, Santa Clara)

California Road Atlas

3001	California Road Atlas & Driver's Guide

ZIP Code Edition Thomas Guides®

California

4328	Alameda / Contra Costa Counties
3365	Central Valley Cities (All urban areas from Stockton to Bakersfield)
4325	Golden Gate Counties (Marin, San Francisco, San Mateo, Santa Clara)
3354	Los Angeles County
4354	Los Angeles / Orange Counties
4353	Los Angeles / Ventura Counties
3355	Orange County
3323	Sacramento County including portions of Placer & El Dorado Counties
4351	San Bernardino / Riverside Counties
3357	San Diego County including Imperial County
4352	Santa Barbara & San Luis Obispo / Ventura Counties
3337	Santa Clara County

Oregon - Washington

3399	Portland Metro Area including Vancouver, WA; Multnomah and Clackamas, OR
4391	King / Pierce / Snohomish Counties

NEW Thomas Guide CD-ROM®

California

53067	Los Angeles / Orange Counties
53057	Bay Area - 6 Bay Area Counties (Alameda, Contra Costa, Marin, San Francisco, San Mateo, Santa Clara)

Census Tract Edition Thomas Guides®

California - Oregon - Washington

ITEM #	DESCRIPTION
4128	Alameda / Contra Costa Counties
4125	Golden Gate Counties (Marin, San Francisco, San Mateo, Santa Clara)
4154	Los Angeles / Orange Counties - '96 Ed.
3123	Sacramento County including portions of Placer & El Dorado Counties - '94 Ed.
4151	San Bernardino / Riverside Counties - '96 Ed.
3157	San Diego County including Imperial County - '94 Ed.
4152	Santa Barbara and San Luis Obispo / Ventura Counties - '92 Ed.
3199	Portland Metro Area including Vancouver, WA; Multnomah and Clackamas, OR - '93 Ed.
4191	King / Pierce / Snohomish Counties - '95 Ed.

Commercial and Assessor's Edition Thomas Guides®

California

1454	Los Angeles County Commercial Filler - '96 Ed.
1554	Los Angeles County Commercial Assessor's Filler - '96 Ed.
1455	Orange County Commercial Filler - '96 Ed.
1555	Orange County Commercial Assessor's Filler - '96 Ed.

Large Print Edition Thomas Guides®

California - Washington

4854	Los Angeles / Orange Counties - '96 Ed.
3823	Sacramento County including portions of Placer & El Dorado Counties - '96 Ed.
3857	San Diego County including Imperial County - '96 Ed.
4891	King / Pierce / Snohomish Counties - '96 Ed.

Wall Maps

California

8055	Bay Area Arterial (not available with oak sticks) - 28" x 40"
8001	Bay Area Freeway & Artery
5001	California Folding Map (includes 12 regional tours and tour maps)
8091	California Wall Map
8056	State of California (not available with oak sticks) - 28" x 40"
8094	Central California Sectional
6011	East Bay (Alameda/Contra Costa Counties) (with ZIP Codes)
6071	Los Angeles County - Central
6072	Los Angeles County - South
7068	Los Angeles / Orange Counties
7268	Los Angeles / Orange Counties (with ZIP Codes)
7072	Northern California 6 Bay Area Counties
7272	Northern California 6 Bay Area Counties (with ZIP Codes)
7054	Northern Los Angeles County (Antelope Valley to Downtown)
7254	Northern Los Angeles County (with ZIP Codes)
6074	Orange County
6205	Sacramento County including Placerville (with ZIP Codes)
6075	San Bernardino / Riverside Counties (Inland Empire)
7076	San Bernardino / Riverside Counties (expanded coverage)
7276	San Bernardino / Riverside Counties (with ZIP Codes)
8157	San Diego Arterial (with ZIP Codes) (not available with oak sticks)
7080	San Diego County
7280	San Diego County (with ZIP Codes)
6048	San Diego County - North
6049	San Diego County - South
6070	San Fernando Valley
6073	San Gabriel Valley
7266	Santa Barbara / Ventura Counties (with ZIP Codes)
6208	South Bay (with ZIP Codes)
8054	Southern California Arterial (not available with oak sticks) - 40" x28"
8145	Southern California Freeway & Artery
8045	Southern California Freeway & Artery (with page overlay)
8095	Southern California Sectional

Arizona - Oregon - Washington

6085	Phoenix and Vicinity
6299	Portland Metropolitan Area (with ZIP Codes)
6081	King County
6084	Pierce County
6083	Snohomish County
7290	King / Pierce / Snohomish Counties (with ZIP Codes)

GeoFinder® Pro For Windows®

California

Available coverage for the Bay Area, Los Angeles / Orange / Ventura, Sacramento, San Bernardino / Riverside, and San Diego Counties

Oregon - Washington

Available Metro coverage for Portland, Oregon and Seattle, Washington

* For more information, or to order, please contact Customer Service at 1-800-899-6277 or email us at cust_serv@thomas.com or visit us at our web site at http://www.thomas.com